Lecture Notes in Computer Science   **11619**

Commenced Publication in 1973
Founding and Former Series Editors:
Gerhard Goos, Juris Hartmanis, and Jan van Leeuwen

More information about this series at http://www.springer.com/series/7407

Sanjay Misra · Osvaldo Gervasi ·
Beniamino Murgante · Elena Stankova ·
Vladimir Korkhov · Carmelo Torre ·
Ana Maria A. C. Rocha ·
David Taniar · Bernady O. Apduhan ·
Eufemia Tarantino (Eds.)

Computational Science and Its Applications – ICCSA 2019

19th International Conference
Saint Petersburg, Russia, July 1–4, 2019
Proceedings, Part I

 Springer

Editors
Sanjay Misra ⓘ
Covenant University
Ota, Nigeria

Beniamino Murgante ⓘ
University of Basilicata
Potenza, Italy

Vladimir Korkhov ⓘ
Saint Petersburg State University
Saint Petersburg, Russia

Ana Maria A. C. Rocha ⓘ
University of Minho
Braga, Portugal

Bernady O. Apduhan
Kyushu Sangyo University
Fukuoka, Japan

Osvaldo Gervasi ⓘ
University of Perugia
Perugia, Italy

Elena Stankova ⓘ
Saint Petersburg State University
Saint Petersburg, Russia

Carmelo Torre ⓘ
Polytechnic University of Bari
Bari, Italy

David Taniar ⓘ
Monash University
Clayton, VIC, Australia

Eufemia Tarantino ⓘ
Polytechnic University of Bari
Bari, Italy

ISSN 0302-9743 ISSN 1611-3349 (electronic)
Lecture Notes in Computer Science
ISBN 978-3-030-24288-6 ISBN 978-3-030-24289-3 (eBook)
https://doi.org/10.1007/978-3-030-24289-3

LNCS Sublibrary: SL1 – Theoretical Computer Science and General Issues

This Springer imprint is published by the registered company Springer Nature Switzerland AG
The registered company address is: Gewerbestrasse 11, 6330 Cham, Switzerland

Preface

These six volumes (LNCS volumes 11619–11624) consist of the peer-reviewed papers from the 2019 International Conference on Computational Science and Its Applications (ICCSA 2019) held in St. Petersburg, Russia during July 1–4, 2019, in collaboration with the St. Petersburg University, St. Petersburg, Russia.

ICCSA 2019 was a successful event in the International Conferences on Computational Science and Its Applications (ICCSA) series, previously held in Melbourne, Australia (2018), Trieste, Italy (2017), Beijing, China (2016), Banff, Canada (2015), Guimaraes, Portugal (2014), Ho Chi Minh City, Vietnam (2013), Salvador, Brazil (2012), Santander, Spain (2011), Fukuoka, Japan (2010), Suwon, South Korea (2009), Perugia, Italy (2008), Kuala Lumpur, Malaysia (2007), Glasgow, UK (2006), Singapore (2005), Assisi, Italy (2004), Montreal, Canada (2003), and (as ICCS) Amsterdam, The Netherlands (2002) and San Francisco, USA (2001).

Computational science is a main pillar of most of the current research, industrial and commercial activities, and plays a unique role in exploiting ICT innovative technologies. The ICCSA conference series have been providing a venue to researchers and industry practitioners to discuss new ideas, to share complex problems and their solutions, and to shape new trends in computational science.

Apart from the general track, ICCSA 2019 also included 33 workshops, in various areas of computational sciences, ranging from computational science technologies, to specific areas of computational sciences, such as software engineering, security, artificial intelligence, and blockchain technologies. We accepted 64 papers distributed in the five general tracks, 259 in workshops and ten short papers. We would like to show our appreciations to the workshop chairs and co-chairs.

The success of the ICCSA conference series, in general, and ICCSA 2019, in particular, is due to the support of many people: authors, presenters, participants, keynote speakers, workshop chairs, Organizing Committee members, student volunteers, Program Committee members, Advisory Committee members, international liaison chairs, reviewers and people in other various roles. We would like to thank them all.

We also thank our publisher, Springer, for accepting to publish the proceedings, for sponsoring part of the best papers awards and for their kind assistance and cooperation during the editing process.

We cordially invite you to visit the ICCSA website http://www.iccsa.org where you can find all relevant information about this interesting and exciting event.

July 2019

Osvaldo Gervasi
Beniamino Murgante
Sanjay Misra

Welcome to St. Petersburg

Welcome to St. Petersburg, the Venice of the North, the city of three revolutions, creation of czar Peter the Great, the most European city in Russia. ICCSA 2019 was hosted by St. Petersburg State University, during July 1–4, 2019.

St. Petersburg is the second largest city in Russia after Moscow. It is the former capital of Russia and has a lot of attractions related to this role in the past: imperial palaces and parks both in the city center and suburbs, respectable buildings of nobles and state institutions, multitude of rivers and canals with more than 300 bridges of various forms and sizes. Extraordinary history and rich cultural traditions of both imperial Russia and the Soviet Union attracted and inspired many examples of world's greatest architecture, literature, music, and visual art, some of which can be found in the famous Hermitage and State Russian Museum located in the heart of the city. Late June and early July is the season of white nights where the sun sets only for a few hours, and the nighttime is covered with mysterious twilight.

What to do in the city:

- Enjoy the white nights, see the open bridges during the night and cargo ships passing by from Ladoga Lake to the Gulf of Finland and back. Dvortsovy bridge is open at about 1am. Be sure to stay on the correct side of the river when the bridges open!
- Visit Hermitage (Winter palace) and State Russian Museum to see great examples of international and Russian art, and the Kunstkammer, the oldest museum of St. Petersburg founded by Peter the Great.
- Travel to St. Petersburg suburbs Peterhof and Tsarskoe Selo to see imperial palaces and splendid parks, famous Peterhof fountains.
- Eat Russian food: borsch (beetroot soup), pelmeni and vareniki (meat and sweet dumplings), bliny (pancakes), vinegret (beetroot salad), drink kvas and maybe some vodka.
- Walk around and inside the Peter and Paul Fortress, the place where the city began in 1703.
- Visit the Mariinsky Theater for famous Russian ballet and opera.
- Have a boat tour along the Neva River and canals to look at the city from the water.
- Walk along Nevsky Prospect, the main street of the city.
- Climb St. Isaac's Cathedral colonnade to enjoy great city views.
- Go down to the Metro, the city's underground train network with some Soviet-style museum-like stations.
- Pay a visit to the recently renovated Summer Garden, the oldest park of St. Petersburg.
- Visit a new modern open space on the New Holland Island to see modern art exhibitions, performances and just to relax and enjoy sitting on the grass with an ice cream or lemonade during a hot summer day.

St. Petersburg State University is the oldest university in Russia, an actively developing, world-class center of research and education. The university dates back to 1724, when Peter the Great founded the Academy of Sciences and Arts as well as the first Academic University and the university preparatory school in Russia. At present there are over 5,000 academic staff members and more than 30,000 students, receiving education in more than 400 educational programs at 25 faculties and institutes.

The venue of ICCSA is the Faculty of Economics located on Tavricheskaya Street, other faculties and university buildings are distributed all over the city with the main campus located on Vasilievsky Island and the natural science faculties (Mathematics and Mechanics, Applied Mathematics and Control Processes, Physics, Chemistry) located on the campus about 40 kilometers away from the city center in Peterhof.

Elena Stankova
Vladimir Korkhov
Nataliia Kulabukhova

Organization

ICCSA 2019 was organized by St. Petersburg University (Russia), University of Perugia (Italy), University of Basilicata (Italy), Monash University (Australia), Kyushu Sangyo University (Japan), University of Minho, (Portugal).

Honorary General Chairs

Antonio Laganà	University of Perugia, Italy
Norio Shiratori	Tohoku University, Japan
Kenneth C. J. Tan	Sardina Systems, Estonia

General Chairs

Osvaldo Gervasi	University of Perugia, Italy
Elena Stankova	St. Petersburg University, Russia
Bernady O. Apduhan	Kyushu Sangyo University, Japan

Program Committee Chairs

Beniamino Murgante	University of Basilicata, Italy
David Taniar	Monash University, Australia
Vladimir Korkov	St. Petersburg University, Russia
Ana Maria A. C. Rocha	University of Minho, Portugal

International Advisory Committee

Jemal Abawajy	Deakin University, Australia
Dharma P. Agarwal	University of Cincinnati, USA
Rajkumar Buyya	Melbourne University, Australia
Claudia Bauzer Medeiros	University of Campinas, Brazil
Manfred M. Fisher	Vienna University of Economics and Business, Austria
Marina L. Gavrilova	University of Calgary, Canada
Yee Leung	Chinese University of Hong Kong, SAR China

International Liaison Chairs

Ana Carla P. Bitencourt	Universidade Federal do Reconcavo da Bahia, Brazil
Giuseppe Borruso	University of Trieste, Italy
Alfredo Cuzzocrea	ICAR-CNR and University of Calabria, Italy
Maria Irene Falcão	University of Minho, Portugal
Robert C. H. Hsu	Chung Hua University, Taiwan
Tai-Hoon Kim	Hannam University, South Korea
Sanjay Misra	Covenant University, Nigeria

Takashi Naka   Kyushu Sangyo University, Japan
Rafael D. C. Santos   National Institute for Space Research, Brazil
Maribel Yasmina Santos   University of Minho, Portugal

Workshop and Session Organizing Chairs

Beniamino Murgante   University of Basilicata, Italy
Sanjay Misra   Covenant University, Nigeria
Jorge Gustavo Rocha   University of Minho, Portugal

Award Chair

Wenny Rahayu   La Trobe University, Australia

Publicity Committee Chairs

Elmer Dadios   De La Salle University, Philippines
Hong Quang Nguyen   International University (VNU-HCM), Vietnam
Daisuke Takahashi   Tsukuba University, Japan
Shangwang Wang   Beijing University of Posts and Telecommunications,
                                China

Workshop Organizers

Advanced Transport Tools and Methods (A2TM 2019)

Massimiliano Petri   University of Pisa, Italy
Antonio Pratelli   University of Pisa, Italy

Advanced Computational Approaches in Fractals, Wavelet, Entropy and Data Mining Applications (AAFTWTETDT 2019)

Yeliz Karaca   University of Massachusetts Medical School, USA
Yu-Dong Zhang   University of Leicester, UK
Majaz Moonis   University of Massachusettes Medical School, USA

Advances in Artificial Intelligence Learning Technologies: Blended Learning, STEM, Computational Thinking and Coding (AAILT 2019)

Alfredo Milani   University of Perugia, Italy
Sergio Tasso   University of Perugia, Italy
Valentina Poggioni   University of Perugia, Italy

Affective Computing and Emotion Recognition (ACER-EMORE 2019)

Alfredo Milani   University of Perugia, Italy
Valentina Franzoni   University of Perugia, Italy
Giulio Biondi   University of Florence, Itay

Advances in Information Systems and Technologies for Emergency Management, Risk Assessment and Mitigation Based on the Resilience Concepts (ASTER 2019)

Maurizio Pollino	ENEA, Italy
Marco Vona	University of Basilicata, Italy
Beniamino Murgante	University of Basilicata, Italy

Blockchain and Distributed Ledgers: Technologies and Application (BDLTA 2019)

Vladimir Korkhov	St. Petersburg State University, Russia
Elena Stankova	St. Petersburg State University, Russia

Bio and Neuro-inspired Computing and Applications (BIONCA 2019)

Nadia Nedjah	State University of Rio de Janeiro, Brazil
Luiza de Macedo Mourell	State University of Rio de Janeiro, Brazil

Computer Aided Modeling, Simulation, and Analysis (CAMSA 2018)

Jie Shen	University of Michigan, USA
Hao Chen	Shanghai University of Engineering Science, China
Youguo He	Jiangsu University, China

Computational and Applied Statistics (CAS 2019)

Ana Cristina Braga	University of Minho, Portugal

Computational Mathematics, Statistics, and Information Management (CMSIM 2019)

M. Filomena Teodoro	Portuguese Naval Academy and Lisbon University, Portugal

Computational Optimization and Applications (COA 2019)

Ana Maria Rocha	University of Minho, Portugal
Humberto Rocha	University of Coimbra, Portugal

Computational Astrochemistry (CompAstro 2019)

Marzio Rosi	University of Perugia, Italy
Dimitrios Skouteris	Master-up, Perugia, Italy
Fanny Vazart	Université Grenoble Alpes, France
Albert Rimola	Universitat Autònoma de Barcelona, Spain

Cities, Technologies, and Planning (CTP 2019)

Beniamino Murgante	University of Basilicata, Italy
Giuseppe Borruso	University of Trieste, Italy

Econometrics and Multidimensional Evaluation in the Urban Environment (EMEUE 2019)

Carmelo M. Torre	Polytechnic of Bari, Italy
Pierluigi Morano	Polytechnic of Bari, Italy
Maria Cerreta	University of Naples Federico II, Italy
Paola Perchinunno	University of Bari, Italy
Francesco Tajani	University of Rome La Sapienza, Italy

Future Computing System Technologies and Applications (FISTA 2019)

Bernady O. Apduhan	Kyushu Sangyo University, Japan
Rafael Santos	National Institute for Space Research, Brazil

Geographical Analysis, Urban Modeling, Spatial Statistics (GEO-AND-MOD 2019)

Beniamino Murgante	University of Basilicata, Italy
Giuseppe Borruso	University of Trieste, Italy
Hartmut Asche	University of Potsdam, Germany

Geomatics for Resource Monitoring and Control (GRMC 2019)

Eufemia Tarantino	Polytechnic of Bari, Italy
Rosa Lasaponara	Italian Research Council, IMAA-CNR, Italy
Benedetto Figorito	ARPA Puglia, Italy
Umberto Fratino	Polytechnic of Bari, Italy

International Symposium on Software Quality (ISSQ 2019)

Sanjay Misra	Covenant University, Nigeria

Land Use Monitoring for Sustainability (LUMS 2019)

Carmelo M. Torre	Polytechnic of Bari, Italy
Alessandro Bonifazi	Polytechnic of Bari, Italy
Pasquale Balena	Polytechnic of Bari, Italy
Beniamino Murgante	University of Basilicata, Italy
Eric Gielen	Polytechnic University of Valencia, Spain

Machine Learning for Space and Earth Observation Data (ML-SEOD 2019)

Rafael Santos	Brazilian National Institute for Space Research, Brazil
Karine Reis Ferreira	National Institute for Space Research, Brazil

Mobile-Computing, Sensing, and Actuation in Cyber Physical Systems (MSA4CPS 2019)

Saad Qaisar	National University of Sciences and Technology, Pakistan
Moonseong Kim	Seoul Theological University, South Korea

Quantum Chemical Modeling of Solids with Computers: From Plane Waves to Local Structures (QuaCheSol 2019)

Andrei Tchougréeff	Russia Academy of Sciences, Russia
Richard Dronskowski	RWTH Aachen University, Germany
Taku Onishi	Mie University and Tromsoe University, Japan

Scientific Computing Infrastructure (SCI 2019)

Vladimir Korkhov	St. Petersburg State University, Russia
Elena Stankova	St. Petersburg State University, Russia
Nataliia Kulabukhova	St. Petersburg State University, Russia

Computational Studies for Energy and Comfort in Building (SECoB 2019)

Senhorinha Teixeira	University of Minho, Portugal
Angela Silva	Viana do Castelo Polytechnic Institute, Portugal
Ana Maria Rocha	University of Minho, Portugal

Software Engineering Processes and Applications (SEPA 2019)

Sanjay Misra	Covenant University, Nigeria

Smart Factory Convergence (SFC 2019)

Jongpil Jeong	Sungkyunkwan University, South Korea

Smart City and Water. Resource and Risk (Smart_Water 2019)

Giuseppe Borruso	University of Trieste, Italy
Ginevra Balletto	University of Cagliari, Italy
Gianfranco Becciu	Polytechnic University of Milan, Italy
Chiara Garau	University of Cagliari, Italy
Beniamino Murgante	University of Basilicata, Italy
Francesco Viola	University of Cagliari, Italy

Sustainability Performance Assessment: Models, Approaches, and Applications Toward Interdisciplinary and Integrated Solutions (SPA 2019)

Francesco Scorza	University of Basilicata, Italy
Valentin Grecu	Lucia Blaga University on Sibiu, Romania
Jolanta Dvarioniene	Kaunas University, Lithuania
Sabrina Lai	University of Cagliari, Italy

Theoretical and Computational Chemistry and Its Applications (TCCMA 2019)

Noelia Faginas Lago	University of Perugia, Italy
Andrea Lombardi	University of Perugia, Italy

Tools and Techniques in Software Development Processes (TTSDP 2019)

Sanjay Misra	Covenant University, Nigeria

Virtual Reality and Applications (VRA 2019)

Osvaldo Gervasi	University of Perugia, Italy
Sergio Tasso	University of Perugia, Italy

Collective, Massive and Evolutionary Systems (WCES 2019)

Alfredo Milani	University of Perugia, Italy
Valentina Franzoni	University of Rome La Sapienza, Italy
Rajdeep Niyogi	Indian Institute of Technology at Roorkee, India
Stefano Marcugini	University of Perugia, Italy

Parallel and Distributed Data Mining (WPDM 2019)

Massimo Cafaro	University of Salento, Italy
Italo Epicoco	University of Salento, Italy
Marco Pulimeno	University of Salento, Italy
Giovanni Aloisio	University of Salento, Italy

Program Committee

Kenneth Adamson	University of Ulster, UK
Vera Afreixo	University of Aveiro, Portugal
Filipe Alvelos	University of Minho, Portugal
Remadevi Arjun	National Institute of Technology Karnataka, India
Hartmut Asche	University of Potsdam, Germany
Ginevra Balletto	University of Cagliari, Italy
Michela Bertolotto	University College Dublin, Ireland
Sandro Bimonte	CEMAGREF, TSCF, France
Rod Blais	University of Calgary, Canada
Ivan Blečić	University of Sassari, Italy
Giuseppe Borruso	University of Trieste, Italy
Ana Cristina Braga	University of Minho, Portugal
Massimo Cafaro	University of Salento, Italy
Yves Caniou	Lyon University, France
José A. Cardoso e Cunha	Universidade Nova de Lisboa, Portugal
Leocadio G. Casado	University of Almeria, Spain
Carlo Cattani	University of Salerno, Italy
Mete Celik	Erciyes University, Turkey
Hyunseung Choo	Sungkyunkwan University, South Korea
Min Young Chung	Sungkyunkwan University, South Korea
Florbela Maria da Cruz Domingues Correia	Polytechnic Institute of Viana do Castelo, Portugal
Gilberto Corso Pereira	Federal University of Bahia, Brazil
Alessandro Costantini	INFN, Italy
Carla Dal Sasso Freitas	Universidade Federal do Rio Grande do Sul, Brazil
Pradesh Debba	The Council for Scientific and Industrial Research (CSIR), South Africa
Hendrik Decker	Instituto Tecnológico de Informática, Spain

Frank Devai	London South Bank University, UK
Rodolphe Devillers	Memorial University of Newfoundland, Canada
Joana Matos Dias	University of Coimbra, Portugal
Paolino Di Felice	University of L'Aquila, Italy
Prabu Dorairaj	NetApp, India/USA
M. Irene Falcao	University of Minho, Portugal
Cherry Liu Fang	U.S. DOE Ames Laboratory, USA
Florbela P. Fernandes	Polytechnic Institute of Bragança, Portugal
Jose-Jesus Fernandez	National Centre for Biotechnology, CSIS, Spain
Paula Odete Fernandes	Polytechnic Institute of Bragança, Portugal
Adelaide de Fátima Baptista Valente Freitas	University of Aveiro, Portugal
Manuel Carlos Figueiredo	University of Minho, Portugal
Valentina Franzoni	University of Rome La Sapienza, Italy
Maria Celia Furtado Rocha	PRODEB–PósCultura/UFBA, Brazil
Chiara Garau	University of Cagliari, Italy
Paulino Jose Garcia Nieto	University of Oviedo, Spain
Jerome Gensel	LSR-IMAG, France
Maria Giaoutzi	National Technical University, Athens, Greece
Arminda Manuela Andrade Pereira Gonçalves	University of Minho, Portugal
Andrzej M. Goscinski	Deakin University, Australia
Sevin Gümgüm	Izmir University of Economics, Turkey
Alex Hagen-Zanker	University of Cambridge, UK
Shanmugasundaram Hariharan	B.S. Abdur Rahman University, India
Eligius M. T. Hendrix	University of Malaga/Wageningen University, Spain/The Netherlands
Hisamoto Hiyoshi	Gunma University, Japan
Mustafa Inceoglu	EGE University, Turkey
Jongpil Jeong	Sungkyunkwan University, South Korea
Peter Jimack	University of Leeds, UK
Qun Jin	Waseda University, Japan
A. S. M. Kayes	La Trobe University, Australia
Farid Karimipour	Vienna University of Technology, Austria
Baris Kazar	Oracle Corp., USA
Maulana Adhinugraha Kiki	Telkom University, Indonesia
DongSeong Kim	University of Canterbury, New Zealand
Taihoon Kim	Hannam University, South Korea
Ivana Kolingerova	University of West Bohemia, Czech Republic
Nataliia Kulabukhova	St. Petersburg University, Russia
Vladimir Korkhov	St. Petersburg University, Russia
Rosa Lasaponara	National Research Council, Italy
Maurizio Lazzari	National Research Council, Italy
Cheng Siong Lee	Monash University, Australia
Sangyoun Lee	Yonsei University, South Korea

Jongchan Lee	Kunsan National University, South Korea
Chendong Li	University of Connecticut, USA
Gang Li	Deakin University, Australia
Fang Liu	AMES Laboratories, USA
Xin Liu	University of Calgary, Canada
Andrea Lombardi	University of Perugia, Italy
Savino Longo	University of Bari, Italy
Tinghuai Ma	NanJing University of Information Science and Technology, China
Ernesto Marcheggiani	Katholieke Universiteit Leuven, Belgium
Antonino Marvuglia	Research Centre Henri Tudor, Luxembourg
Nicola Masini	National Research Council, Italy
Eric Medvet	University of Trieste, Italy
Nirvana Meratnia	University of Twente, The Netherlands
Noelia Faginas Lago	University of Perugia, Italy
Giuseppe Modica	University of Reggio Calabria, Italy
Josè Luis Montaña	University of Cantabria, Spain
Maria Filipa Mourão	IP from Viana do Castelo, Portugal
Louiza de Macedo Mourelle	State University of Rio de Janeiro, Brazil
Nadia Nedjah	State University of Rio de Janeiro, Brazil
Laszlo Neumann	University of Girona, Spain
Kok-Leong Ong	Deakin University, Australia
Belen Palop	Universidad de Valladolid, Spain
Marcin Paprzycki	Polish Academy of Sciences, Poland
Eric Pardede	La Trobe University, Australia
Kwangjin Park	Wonkwang University, South Korea
Ana Isabel Pereira	Polytechnic Institute of Bragança, Portugal
Massimiliano Petri	University of Pisa, Italy
Maurizio Pollino	Italian National Agency for New Technologies, Energy and Sustainable Economic Development, Italy
Alenka Poplin	University of Hamburg, Germany
Vidyasagar Potdar	Curtin University of Technology, Australia
David C. Prosperi	Florida Atlantic University, USA
Wenny Rahayu	La Trobe University, Australia
Jerzy Respondek	Silesian University of Technology Poland
Humberto Rocha	INESC-Coimbra, Portugal
Jon Rokne	University of Calgary, Canada
Octavio Roncero	CSIC, Spain
Maytham Safar	Kuwait University, Kuwait
Chiara Saracino	A.O. Ospedale Niguarda Ca' Granda - Milano, Italy
Haiduke Sarafian	The Pennsylvania State University, USA
Francesco Scorza	University of Basilicata, Italy
Marco Paulo Seabra dos Reis	University of Coimbra, Portugal
Jie Shen	University of Michigan, USA

Qi Shi	Liverpool John Moores University, UK
Dale Shires	U.S. Army Research Laboratory, USA
Inês Soares	University of Coimbra, Portugal
Elena Stankova	St. Petersburg University, Russia
Takuo Suganuma	Tohoku University, Japan
Eufemia Tarantino	Polytechnic of Bari, Italy
Sergio Tasso	University of Perugia, Italy
Ana Paula Teixeira	University of Trás-os-Montes and Alto Douro, Portugal
Senhorinha Teixeira	University of Minho, Portugal
M. Filomena Teodoro	Portuguese Naval Academy and University of Lisbon, Portugal
Parimala Thulasiraman	University of Manitoba, Canada
Carmelo Torre	Polytechnic of Bari, Italy
Javier Martinez Torres	Centro Universitario de la Defensa Zaragoza, Spain
Giuseppe A. Trunfio	University of Sassari, Italy
Pablo Vanegas	University of Cuenca, Equador
Marco Vizzari	University of Perugia, Italy
Varun Vohra	Merck Inc., USA
Koichi Wada	University of Tsukuba, Japan
Krzysztof Walkowiak	Wroclaw University of Technology, Poland
Zequn Wang	Intelligent Automation Inc., USA
Robert Weibel	University of Zurich, Switzerland
Frank Westad	Norwegian University of Science and Technology, Norway
Roland Wismüller	Universität Siegen, Germany
Mudasser Wyne	SOET National University, USA
Chung-Huang Yang	National Kaohsiung Normal University, Taiwan
Xin-She Yang	National Physical Laboratory, UK
Salim Zabir	France Telecom Japan Co., Japan
Haifeng Zhao	University of California, Davis, USA
Fabiana Zollo	University of Venice Cà Foscari, Italy
Albert Y. Zomaya	University of Sydney, Australia

Additional Reviewers

Adewumi Oluwasegun	Covenant University, Nigeria
Afreixo Vera	University of Aveiro, Portugal
Agrawal Akshat	International Institute of Information Technology Bangalore, India
Aguilar Antonio	University of Barcelona, Spain
Ahmad Rashid	Microwave and Antenna Lab, School of Engineering, South Korea
Ahmed Waseem	Federal University of Technology, Nigeria
Alamri Sultan	Taibah University, Medina, Saudi Arabia
Alfa Abraham	Kogi State College of Education, Nigeria
Alvelos Filipe	University of Minho, Portugal

Amato Federico	University of Basilicata, Italy
Amin Benatia Mohamed	Groupe Cesi, Francia
Andrianov Serge	Institute for Informatics of Tatarstan Academy of Sciences, Russia
Apduhan Bernady	Kyushu Sangyo University, Japan
Aquilanti Vincenzo	University of Perugia, Italy
Arjun Remadevi	National Institute of Technology Karnataka, India
Arogundade Oluwasefunmi	Federal University of Agriculture, Nigeria
Ascenzi Daniela	University of Trento, Italy
Ayeni Foluso	Southern University and A&M College, USA
Azubuike Ezenwoke	Covenant University, Nigeria
Balacco Gabriella	Polytechnic of Bari, Italy
Balena Pasquale	Polytechnic of Bari, Italy
Balletto Ginevra	University of Cagliari, Italy
Barrile Vincenzo	Mediterranean University of Reggio Calabria, Italy
Bartolomei Massimiliano	Spanish National Research Council, Spain
Behera Ranjan Kumar	Indian Institute of Technology Patna, India
Biondi Giulio	University of Florence, Italy
Bist Ankur Singh	KIET Ghaziabad, India
Blecic Ivan	University of Cagliari, Italy
Bogdanov Alexander	St. Petersburg State University, Russia
Borgogno Mondino Enrico Corrado	University of Turin, Italy
Borruso Giuseppe	University of Trieste, Italy
Bostenaru Maria	Ion Mincu University of Architecture and Urbanism, Romania
Braga Ana Cristina	University of Minho, Portugal
Cafaro Massimo	University of Salento, Italy
Capolupo Alessandra	University of Naples Federico II, Italy
Carvalho-Silva Valter	Universidade Estadual de Goiás, Brazil
Cerreta Maria	University Federico II of Naples, Italy
Chan Sheung Wai	Hong Kong Baptist Hospital, SAR China
Cho Chulhee	Seoul Guarantee Insurance Company Ltd., South Korea
Choi Jae-Young	Sungkyunkwan University, South Korea
Correia Anacleto	Base Naval de Lisboa, Portugal
Correia Elisete	University of Trás-Os-Montes e Alto Douro, Portugal
Correia Florbela Maria da Cruz Domingues	Instituto Politécnico de Viana do Castelo, Portugal
Costa e Silva Eliana	Polytechnic of Porto, Portugal
Costa Lino	Universidade do Minho, Portugal
Costantini Alessandro	Istituto Nazionale di Fisica Nucleare, Italy
Crawford Broderick	Pontificia Universidad Católica de Valparaíso, Chile
Cutini Valerio	University of Pisa, Italy
D'Acierno Luca	University of Naples Federico II, Italy
Danese Maria	Italian National Research Council, Italy
Dantas Coutinho Nayara	University of Perugia, Italy
Degtyarev Alexander	St. Petersburg State University, Russia

Dereli Dursun Ahu	UNSW Sydney, Australia
Devai Frank	London South Bank University, UK
Di Bari Gabriele	University of Florence, Italy
Dias Joana	University of Coimbra, Portugal
Diaz Diana	National University of Colombia, Colombia
Elfadaly Abdelaziz	University of Basilicata, Italy
Enriquez Palma Pedro Alberto	Universidad de la Rioja, Spain
Epicoco Italo	University of Salento, Italy
Esposito Giuseppina	Sapienza University of Rome, Italy
Faginas-Lago M. Noelia	University of Perugia, Italy
Fajardo Jorge	Universidad Politécnica Salesiana (UPS), Ecuador
Falcinelli Stefano	University of Perugia, Italy
Farina Alessandro	University of Pisa, Italy
Fattoruso Grazia	ENEA, Italy
Fernandes Florbela	Escola Superior de Tecnologia e Gestão de Bragancca, Portugal
Fernandes Paula	Escola Superior de Tecnologia e Gestão, Portugal
Fernández Ledesma Javier Darío	Universidad Pontificia Bolivariana, Bolivia
Ferreira Ana C.	University of Lisbon, Portugal
Ferrão Maria	Universidade da Beira Interior, Portugal
Figueiredo Manuel Carlos	Universidade do Minho, Portugal
Florez Hector	Universidad Distrital Francisco Jose de Caldas, Colombia
Franzoni Valentina	University of Perugia, Italy
Freitau Adelaide de Fátima Baptista Valente	University of Aveiro, Portugal
Friday Agbo	University of Eastern Finland, Finland
Frunzete Madalin	Polytechnic University of Bucharest, Romania
Fusco Giovanni	Laboratoire ESPACE, CNRS, France
Gabrani Goldie	Bml Munjal University, India
Gankevich Ivan	St. Petersburg State University, Russia
Garau Chiara	University of Cagliari, Italy
Garcia Ernesto	University of the Basque Country, Spain
Gavrilova Marina	University of Calgary, Canada
Gervasi Osvaldo	University of Perugia, Italy
Gilner Ewa	Silesian University of Technology, Poland
Gioia Andrea	University of Bari, Italy
Giorgi Giacomo	University of Perugia, Italy
Gonçalves Arminda Manuela	University of Minho, Portugal
Gorbachev Yuriy	Geolink Technologies, Russia
Gotoh Yusuke	Kyoto University, Japan
Goyal Rinkaj	Guru Gobind Singh Indraprastha University, India
Gümgüm Sevin	Izmir Economy University, Turkey

Gülen Kemal Güven	Istanbul Ticaret University, Turkey
Hegedus Peter	University of Szeged, Hungary
Hendrix Eligius M. T.	University of Malaga, Spain
Iacobellis Vito	Polytechnic of Bari, Italy
Iakushkin Oleg	St. Petersburg State University, Russia
Kadry Seifedine	Beirut Arab University, Lebanon
Kim JeongAh	George Fox University, USA
Kim Moonseong	Korean Intellectual Property Office, South Korea
Kolingerova Ivana	University of West Bohemia, Czech Republic
Koo Jahwan	Sungkyunkwan University, South Korea
Korkhov Vladimir	St. Petersburg State University, Russia
Kulabukhova Nataliia	St. Peterburg State University, Russia
Ladu Mara	University of Cagliari, Italy
Laganà Antonio	Master-up srl, Italy
Leon Marcelo	Universidad Estatal Peninsula de Santa Elena – UPSE, Ecuador
Lima Rui	University of Minho, Portugal
Lombardi Andrea	University of Perugia, Italy
Longo Savino	University of Bari, Italy
Maciel de Castro Jessica	Universidade Federal da Paraíba, Brazil
Magni Riccardo	Pragma Engineering S.r.L., Italy
Mandanici Emanuele	University of Bologna, Italy
Mangiameli Michele	University of Catania, Italy
Marcellini Moreno	Ecole normale supérieure de Lyon, France
Marghany Maged	Universiti Teknologi Malaysia, Malaysia
Marques Jorge	Universidade de Coimbra, Portugal
Martellozzo Federico	University of Florence, Italy
Mengoni Paolo	University of Florence, Italy
Migliore Marco	University of Cassino e del Lazio Meridionale, Italy
Milani Alfredo	University of Perugia, Italy
Milesi Alessandra	Istituto Auxologico Italiano, Italy
Mishra Biswajeeban	University of Szeged, Hungary
Molaei Qelichi Mohamad	University of Tehran, Iran
Monteiro Vitor	University of Minho, Portugal
Moraes João Luís Cardoso	University of Porto, Portugal
Moura Ricardo	Universidade Nova de Lisboa, Portugal
Mourao Maria	Universidade do Minho, Portugal
Murgante Beniamino	University of Basilicata, Italy
Natário Isabel Cristina Maciel	Universidade Nova de Lisboa, Portugal
Nedjah Nadia	Rio de Janeiro State University, Brazil
Nocera Silvio	University of Naples Federico II, Italy
Odun-Ayo Isaac	Covenant University, Nigeria
Okewu Emmanuel	University of Lagos, Nigeria
Oliveira Irene	University of Trás-Os-Montes e Alto Douro, Portugal
Oluranti Jonathan	Covenant University, Nigeria

Osho Oluwafemi	Federal University of Technology Minna, Nigeria
Ozturk Savas	The Scientific and Technological Research Council of Turkey, Turkey
Panetta J. B.	University of Georgia, USA
Pardede Eric	La Trobe University, Australia
Perchinunno Paola	University of Bari, Italy
Pereira Ana	Instituto Politécnico de Bragança, Portugal
Peschechera Giuseppe	University of Bari, Italy
Petri Massimiliano	University of Pisa, Italy
Petrovic Marjana	University of Zagreb, Croatia
Pham Quoc Trung	Ho Chi Minh City University of Technology, Vietnam
Pinto Telmo	University of Minho, Portugal
Plekhanov Evgeny	Russian Academy of Economics, Russia
Poggioni Valentina	University of Perugia, Italy
Polidoro Maria João	University of Lisbon, Portugal
Pollino Maurizio	ENEA, Italy
Popoola Segun	Covenant University, Nigeria
Pratelli Antonio	University of Pisa, Italy
Pulimeno Marco	University of Salento, Italy
Rasool Hamid	National University of Sciences and Technology, Pakistan
Reis Marco	Universidade de Coimbra, Portugal
Respondek Jerzy	Silesian University of Technology, Poland
Riaz Nida	National University of Sciences and Technology, Pakistan
Rimola Albert	Autonomous University of Barcelona, Spain
Rocha Ana Maria	University of Minho, Portugal
Rocha Humberto	University of Coimbra, Portugal
Rosi Marzio	University of Perugia, Italy
Santos Rafael	National Institute for Space Research, Brazil
Santucci Valentino	University Stranieri of Perugia, Italy
Saponaro Mirko	Polytechnic of Bari, Italy
Sarafian Haiduke	Pennsylvania State University, USA
Scorza Francesco	University of Basilicata, Italy
Sedova Olya	St. Petersburg State University, Russia
Semanjski Ivana	Ghent University, Belgium
Sharma Jeetu	Mody University of Science and Technology, India
Sharma Purnima	University of Lucknow, India
Shchegoleva Nadezhda	Petersburg State Electrotechnical University, Russia
Shen Jie	University of Michigan, USA
Shoaib Muhammad	Sungkyunkwan University, South Korea
Shou Huahao	Zhejiang University of Technology, China
Silva-Fortes Carina	ESTeSL-IPL, Portugal
Silva Ângela Maria	Escola Superior de Ciências Empresariais, Portugal
Singh Upasana	The University of Manchester, UK
Singh V. B.	University of Delhi, India

Skouteris Dimitrios	Master-up, Perugia, Italy
Soares Inês	INESCC and IPATIMUP, Portugal
Soares Michel	Universidade Federal de Sergipe, Brazil
Sosnin Petr	Ulyanovsk State Technical University, Russia
Sousa Ines	University of Minho, Portugal
Stankova Elena	St. Petersburg State University, Russia
Stritih Uros	University of Ljubljana, Slovenia
Tanaka Kazuaki	Kyushu Institute of Technology, Japan
Tarantino Eufemia	Polytechnic of Bari, Italy
Tasso Sergio	University of Perugia, Italy
Teixeira Senhorinha	University of Minho, Portugal
Tengku Adil	La Trobe University, Australia
Teodoro M. Filomena	Lisbon University, Portugal
Torre Carmelo Maria	Polytechnic of Bari, Italy
Totaro Vincenzo	Polytechnic of Bari, Italy
Tripathi Aprna	GLA University, India
Vancsics Béla	University of Szeged, Hungary
Vasyunin Dmitry	University of Amsterdam, The Netherlands
Vig Rekha	The Northcap University, India
Walkowiak Krzysztof	Wroclaw University of Technology, Poland
Wanderley Fernando	New University of Lisbon, Portugal
Wang Chao	University of Science and Technology of China, China
Westad Frank	CAMO Software AS, USA
Yamazaki Takeshi	University of Tokyo, Japan
Zahra Noore	University of Guilan, India
Zollo Fabiana	University of Venice Ca' Foscari, Italy
Zullo Francesco	University of L'Aquila, Italy
Žemlička Michal	Charles University in Prague, Czech Republic
Živković Ljiljana	Republic Agency for Spatial Planning, Serbia

Sponsoring Organizations

ICCSA 2019 would not have been possible without tremendous support of many organizations and institutions, for which all organizers and participants of ICCSA 2019 express their sincere gratitude:

Springer Nature Switzerland AG, Germany
(http://www.springer.com)

St. Petersburg University, Russia
(http://english.spbu.ru/)

University of Perugia, Italy
(http://www.unipg.it)

University of Basilicata, Italy
(http://www.unibas.it)

Monash University, Australia
(http://monash.edu)

Kyushu Sangyo University, Japan
(www.kyusan-u.ac.jp)

Universidade do Minho, Portugal
(http://www.uminho.pt)

Contents – Part I

High Performance Computing and Networks

Geometric Modeling, Graphics and Visualization

Advanced and Emerging Applications

Information Systems and Technologies

Computational Methods, Algorithms and Scientific Applications

A Variant of the George-Liu Algorithm

S. L. Gonzaga de Oliveira[1(✉)], A. A. A. M. Abreu[2], C. Osthoff[3],
and L. N. Henderson Guedes de Oliveira[4]

[1] Universidade Federal de Lavras, Lavras, MG, Brazil
sanderson@ufla.br
[2] Instituto Federal de Educação, Ciência e Tecnologia de Santa Catarina,
Canoinhas, SC, Brazil
alexandre.abreu@ifsc.edu.br
[3] Laboratório Nacional de Computação Científica (LNCC), Petrópolis, RJ, Brazil
osthoff@lncc.br
[4] Universidade do Estado do Rio de Janeiro, Nova Friburgo, RJ, Brazil
nelio@iprj.uerj.br

Abstract. This paper evaluates a variant of the George-Liu algorithm
for finding a pseudoperipheral vertex in a graph aiming at returning
a vertex having a larger eccentricity than the original algorithm. The
experiments show that the Reverse Cuthill-McKee method with ordering
started with vertices given by the new variant of the George-Liu algorithm yields promising results when applied to small symmetric matrices.

Keywords: Pseudoperipheral vertices ·
Reverse Cuthill-McKee method · Bandwidth reduction ·
Profile reduction · Reordering algorithms · Graph labeling ·
Sparse matrices · Orderings

1 Introduction

Heuristics for bandwidth and profile reductions are used to achieve low computational and storage costs for solving sparse linear systems. Thus, there has
been given much attention to heuristics for bandwidth and profile reductions
(see [1–8] and references therein). The bandwidth and minimization problems
are of great interest because they are related to a large number of real-world
problems in science and engineering [4,5]. As a consequence, the importance of
matrix bandwidth and profile reductions has made these challenging problems
subject to numerous research efforts (see [3–6] and references therein).

Let $G = (V, E)$ be a graph where V and E are sets of vertices and edges, respectively. The bandwidth of G for a vertex labeling
$S = \{s(v_1), s(v_2), \cdots, s(v_{|V|})\}$ (i.e., a bijective mapping from V to the set
$\{1, 2, \cdots, |V|\}$) is defined as $\beta(G) = \max\limits_{\{v,u\} \in E} [|s(v) - s(u)|]$ where $s(v)$ and
$s(u)$ are labels of vertices v and u, respectively. The profile is defined as
$profile(G) = \sum\limits_{v \in V} \max\limits_{\{v,u\} \in E} [|s(v) - s(u)|]$. Let A be an $n \times n$ symmetric matrix

© Springer Nature Switzerland AG 2019
S. Misra et al. (Eds.): ICCSA 2019, LNCS 11619, pp. 3–12, 2019.
https://doi.org/10.1007/978-3-030-24289-3_1

associated with a connected undirected graph $G = (V, E)$. Equivalently, the bandwidth of row i of matrix A is given by $\beta_i(A) = i - \min_{1 \leq j < i} [j : a_{ij} \neq 0]$ and the bandwidth of a matrix A is defined as $\beta(A) = \max_{1 \leq i \leq n} [\beta_i(A)]$. The profile of a matrix A is defined as $profile(A) = \sum_{i=1}^{n} \beta_i(A)$.

The Reverse Cuthill-McKee (RCM) method [9] starting with a pseudoperipheral vertex given by the George-Liu (GL) algorithm [10], termed RCM-GL [11], is one of the best-known and widely used heuristics for bandwidth and profile reductions of matrices [1,4–6,12]. Previous publications [4,5] report the RCM-GL method [11] as potentially being one of the most promising low-cost heuristics for bandwidth reductions.

Few algorithms can compete with the RCM-GL method [11] in bandwidth results when considering execution times [4,5]. The reason is that the RCM-GL method [11] yields reasonable bandwidth results at low cost. This may be the reason why this method is available on the MATLAB [11,13,14] and GNU Octave [11,15] mathematical softwares as the function $symrcm$[1], and on Boost C++ Library [16][2]. Thus, the Reverse Cuthill-McKee method [9] is a well-known and successful heuristic for reducing bandwidth and profile of matrices. The method is identified as one of the most important and amply used bandwidth reduction methods [1,4–6,12,13] because the method yields accurate approximations to the solution at low execution times. Although the Reverse Cuthill-McKee method [9] remains in common use, it is well-known that the method is not trouble-free [1]. The choice of the initial pseudoperipheral vertex influences the quality of the results given by this method.

The Reverse Cuthill-McKee method [9] is a kind of heuristic known as level set reorderings, where the vertices in a graph are labeled considering that level sets subdivide the vertices, i.e., each level set contains a group of vertices considering the distance from a given starting vertex. Thus, the quality of the bandwidth results will be strongly influenced by the selection of the starting vertex and by the ordering of the vertices within level sets. In general, the Reverse Cuthill-McKee method yields better results when the width of a level structure rooted at the starting vertex is small, and its eccentricity is very close to the diameter of the graph. Additionally, the computing times of an algorithm for the identification of an appropriate starting vertex for the Reverse Cuthill-McKee method can be even higher than the running times of the Reverse Cuthill-McKee method itself. Thus, the bandwidth results of the Reverse Cuthill-McKee method executed after an algorithm for the selection of a starting vertex must be substantially better than the bandwidth results reached by the Reverse Cuthill-McKee method without the use of such a kind of algorithm.

The purpose of this paper is to evaluate a variant of the George-Liu algorithm. Specifically, this paper applies an alternative algorithm for finding

---

[1] https://www.mathworks.com/help/matlab/ref/symrcm.html?requestedDomain= www.mathworks.com, https://octave.sourceforge.io/octave/function/symrcm.html.
[2] http://www.boost.org/doc/libs/1_38_0/libs/graph/doc/cuthill_mckee_ordering. html.

pseudoperipheral vertices along with the Reverse Cuthill-McKee method [9] for bandwidth and profile reductions of matrices. We compare its results with the results of the original George-Liu [10] and Reid-Scott [17] algorithms for determining the starting vertex for the Reverse Cuthill-McKee method. We refer to these three algorithms together with the Reverse Cuthill-McKee method as RCM-GL(k), RCM-GL [11], and RCM-RS, respectively.

Section 2 briefly describes the Reverse Cuthill-McKee [9] and George-Liu [10] algorithms. This section also introduces a variant of the George-Liu algorithm. Section 3 describes how we conducted the simulations in this study. Section 4 shows the results. Specifically, we experimentally analyze the effectiveness of the proposed algorithm for finding pseudoperipheral vertices for the Reverse Cuthill-McKee method [9]. Finally, Sect. 5 addresses the conclusions.

2 A Variant of the George-Liu Algorithm for Finding Pseudoperipheral Vertices

The Reverse Cuthill-McKee method [9] is based on graph-theoretical concepts. It labels the vertices of a graph $G(V, E)$ in order of increasing distance from a given pseudoperipheral vertex v. Specifically, the method labels vertices with the same distance from the vertex v in order of increasing degree. Finally, the ordering is reversed. Therefore, the final label of vertex v is $|V|$. Ordering the vertices in such manner partitions them into *level sets* according to the distance from the pseudoperipheral vertex v. Given a vertex $v \in V$, the level structure $\mathscr{L}(v)$ rooted at vertex v, with depth $\ell(v)$, is the partitioning $\mathscr{L}(v) = \{L_0(v), L_1(v), \ldots, L_{\ell(v)}(v)\}$ where $L_0(v) = \{v\}$ and $L_i(v) = Adj(L_{i-1}(v)) - \bigcup_{j=0}^{i-1} L_j(v)$, for $i = 1, 2, 3, \ldots, \ell(v)$, $\ell(v)$ is the *eccentricity* of vertex v, and $Adj(U) = \{w \in V : (u \in U \subseteq V)\ \{u, w\} \in E\}$. In particular, the *width* of a rooted level set is defined as $b(\mathscr{L}(v)) = \max_{0 \le i \le \ell(v)} |L_i(v)|$. It is therefore desirable to find v with large $\ell(v)$ and a rooted level set $\mathscr{L}(v)$ with small width.

Algorithm 1 shows a pseudocode of the Reverse Cuthill-McKee method [9]. The method receives a graph $G = (V, E)$ and a pseudoperipheral vertex $v \in V$. The method labels the vertices of a graph (see line 8) with the same distance from the pseudoperipheral vertex v in order of increasing degree (see line 6). The method reverses the final ordering. Therefore, the final label of vertex v is $|V|$ at line 2. Thus, Algorithm 1 begins the numbering with the label $s(|V|)$ (see lines 2–4 in Algorithm 1). Algorithm 1 returns the new labeling at line 10.

Algorithm 2 shows the George-Liu algorithm [10]. The George-Liu algorithm begins with an arbitrary vertex v (see line 2 in Algorithm 2) and builds its rooted level structure $\mathscr{L}(v)$ (see line 3). Then, the algorithm builds the rooted level structure $\mathscr{L}(u)$ of the vertex $u \in L_{\ell(v)}(v)$ with minimum degree (see lines 5 and 6). If $\ell(u) > \ell(v)$ (see line 7), then u is attributed to v (i.e., $v \leftarrow u$) as well as $\mathscr{L}(v) \leftarrow \mathscr{L}(u)$ is computed (see line 8), and the process is repeated; otherwise, the process stops and v is the pseudoperipheral vertex found (see line 10 in Algorithm 2).

Input: a connected graph $G = (V, E)$; a vertex $v \in V$;
Output: a labeling $S = \{s(1), s(2), ..., s(|V|)\}$;
1 **begin**
2   $s(|V|) \leftarrow v$;
3   $i \leftarrow |V|$;
4   $j \leftarrow |V|$;
5   **while** $(i > 0)$ **do**
6   **foreach** $(vertex\ w \in Adj(s(j)) - \{s(|V|), \ldots, s(i)\}$, *in order of increasing degree*) **do**
7     $i \leftarrow i - 1$;
8     $s(i) \leftarrow w$;
9    $j \leftarrow j - 1$;
10   **return** S;

Algorithm 1. The Reverse Cuthill-McKee method [9].

Input: graph $G = (V, E)$;
Output: pseudo-peripheral vertex $v \in V$;
1 **begin**
2   $v \leftarrow ArbitraryVertex(V)$;
3   $\mathscr{L}(v) \leftarrow BuscaEmLargura(v)$; // build a rooted level structure
4   **repeat**
5    $u \leftarrow MinimumDegreeVertex(L_{\ell(v)}(v))$;
6    $\mathscr{L}(u) \leftarrow BuscaEmLargura(u)$; // build a rooted level structure
7   **if** $\ell(u) > \ell(v)$ **then**
8     $v \leftarrow u$; $\mathscr{L}(v) \leftarrow \mathscr{L}(u)$;
9   **until** $(u \neq v)$;
10   **return** v;

Algorithm 2. The George-Liu algorithm [10].

Algorithm 3 shows a pseudocode of a variant of the George-Liu algorithm [10]. This variant of the George-Liu [10] algorithm verifies k vertices in $L_{\ell(w)}(w)$ (note that v is attributed to w at line 6 of Algorithm 3) where k is a parameter of the algorithm, instead of verifying only one vertex with minimum degree in $L_{\ell(w)}(w)$, as the George-Liu algorithm [10] performs. If $|L_{\ell(w)}(w)| < k$, then the other $k - |L_{\ell(w)}(w)|$ vertices are verified in the previous levels of $L_{\ell(w)}(w)$, that is, in $L_{\ell(w)-1}(w), L_{\ell(w)-2}(w)$, and so on. In particular, the GL(k) algorithm is reduced to the original George-Liu algorithm [10] for $k = 1$.

Reid and Scott [17] proposed another pseudoperipheral vertex finder based on the George-Liu algorithm [10]. The Reid-Scott algorithm [17] relies on finding a pseudoperipheral vertex with a large eccentricity and small $b(\mathscr{L}(v))$. It sorts vertices in $L_{\ell(v)}(v)$ in order of ascending degree and limits the search to one representative of each degree. Additionally, the Reid-Scott algorithm [17] considers up to five vertices in $L_{\ell(v)}(v)$, omitting any that is a neighbor of a vertex already considered.

Input: connected undirected graph $G = (V, E)$; unsigned integer k;
Output: pseudoperipheral vertex $v \in V$;

```
1  begin
2  │  if (k > |V| − 1) then k ← |V| − 1;
3  │  v ← ArbitraryVertex(V); // initial vertex
4  │  ℒ(v) ← Breadth-First-Search(v); // build the rooted level structure
5  │  repeat
6  │  │  k ← 0; j ← 0; w ← v;
   │  │  // k vertices are verified in the last level(s) of ℒ(w)
7  │  │  while (j < k) do
   │  │  │  // sort vertices in L_{ℓ(w)−k}(w) in order of ascending degree
8  │  │  │  F ← SortVertices(L_{ℓ(w)−k}(w)); // F is a priority queue
9  │  │  │  while (F ≠ ∅ ∧ j < k) do
10 │  │  │  │  u ← Remove(F);
   │  │  │  │  // build the rooted level structure
11 │  │  │  │  ℒ(u) ← Breadth-First-Search(u);
12 │  │  │  │  if (ℓ(u) > ℓ(v)) then
13 │  │  │  │  └  v ← u; ℒ(v) ← ℒ(u);
14 │  │  │  └  j ← j + 1;
   │  │  │  // if |L_{ℓ(w)}(w)| < n, then the other n − |L_{ℓ(w)}(w)| vertices
   │  │  │  are verified in L_{ℓ(w)−1}(w), L_{ℓ(w)−2}(w), ⋯,
15 │  │  └  k ← k + 1; // until k vertices are observed
16 │  until (v = w);
17 └  return (v);
```

Algorithm 3. A variant of the George-Liu algorithm [10].

3   Description of the Tests

The bandwidth results obtained by the Reverse Cuthill-McKee method [9] is proportional to the eccentricity of the starting vertex v and the width $b(\mathscr{L}(v))$ [9,11,18]. Thus, we evaluate the bandwidth and profile results provided by the Reverse Cuthill-McKee method [9] along with three pseudoperipheral vertex finders. To appraise the bandwidth and profile reductions provided by the Reverse Cuthill-McKee method [9] started with a pseudoperipheral vertex given by the George-Liu [10] and Reid-Scott [17] algorithms, and the new variant of the George-Liu algorithm described in Algorithm 3, this paper uses 50 symmetric matrices contained in the SuiteSparse sparse matrix collection [19].

The Reverse Cuthill-McKee method [9] and the algorithms for finding pseudoperipheral vertices were implemented using the C++ programming language. We used the g++ version 4.8.2 compiler.

The workstation used in the execution of the simulations featured an Intel® Core™ i5-3570 (6144 KB Cache, CPU 3.40 GHz, 12 GB of main memory DDR3 1333 MHz) (Intel; Santa Clara, CA, United States). This machine used a Slackware 14.1 64-bit operating system with Linux kernel-version 3.10.17.

4   Results and Analysis

This section presents the bandwidth and profile results obtained by the RCM-GL [11], RCM-RS, and RCM-GL(k) methods applied to 50 symmetric matrices contained in the SuiteSparse sparse matrix collection [19]. The tables below show the characteristics of the matrix (name, size (k), original bandwidth (β_0), and profile (profile$_0$)).

Tables 1 and 2 contain the results of the RCM-GL(k), RCM-RS, and RCM-GL [11] methods applied to reduce the bandwidth and profile of 15 and 35 symmetric matrices, respectively. The tables show the smallest k such that the RCM-GL(k) algorithm returns better results than the George-Liu [10] and Reid-Scott [17] algorithms do. Specifically, Table 1 shows the results of the methods applied to a set composed of 15 symmetric matrices. The table reveals that the three methods find the same number of best bandwidth and profile results when applied to this set composed of 15 symmetric matrices. On the other hand, Table 2 shows that the RCM-GL(k) method delivered the best bandwidth and profile results in the other dataset used in this study. Figure 1 shows the number of best bandwidth and profile results yielded by the three methods evaluated here when applied to 50 symmetric matrices.

Table 1. Results of the Reverse Cuthill-McKee method [9] along with three algorithms for finding pseudoperipheral vertices when applied to reduce bandwidth and profile of a set composed of 15 symmetric matrices.

Matrix	n	Bandwidth				Profile			
		β_0	GL(2)	RS	GL	profile$_0$	GL(2)	RS	GL
ash85	85	39	10	10	10	1153	589	589	589
bcspwr01	39	38	7	7	7	292	122	122	122
bcspwr02	49	34	13	13	13	377	234	234	234
bcspwr03	118	115	21	21	21	1288	804	804	804
bcsstk01	48	35	26	26	26	851	683	683	683
bcsstk04	132	47	54	54	54	3631	3717	3717	3717
bcsstk05	153	28	26	26	26	2449	2313	2313	2313
bcsstk22	138	111	14	14	14	2124	863	863	863
can_144	144	142	18	18	18	7355	1074	1074	1074
can_161	161	79	30	30	30	3378	3079	3079	3079
dwt_234	234	48	19	19	19	1765	1363	1363	1363
lund_A	147	23	23	23	23	2870	2303	2303	2303
lund_B	147	23	23	23	23	2870	2303	2303	2303
nos1	237	4	4	4	4	780	467	467	467
nos4	100	13	12	12	12	766	755	755	755
Number of best results		4	14	14	14	1	14	14	14

Table 2. Results of the Reverse Cuthill-McKee method [9] along with three algorithms for finding pseudoperipheral vertices when applied to reduce bandwidth and profile of a set composed of 35 symmetric matrices.

Matrix	n	Bandwidth				Profile			
		β_0	GL(23)	RS	GL	profile$_0$	GL(77)	RS	GL
494_bus	494	428	62	62	62	40975	10566	10566	10566
662_bus	662	335	85	135	135	45165	20664	32903	32903
685_bus	685	550	72	72	79	28621	17551	17551	17457
ash292	292	24	34	34	34	4224	4659	4659	4659
bcspwr04	274	265	49	65	65	21015	4331	4825	4825
bcspwr05	443	435	59	59	59	36248	8825	8825	8825
bcsstk06	420	47	50	50	50	14691	13241	13241	13241
bcsstk19	817	567	21	21	21	74051	9457	9457	9457
bcsstk20	485	20	19	19	19	4309	4416	4416	4416
bcsstm07	420	47	50	50	50	14691	13310	13310	13310
can_292	292	282	75	75	65	23170	8977	8977	9706
can_445	445	403	92	92	92	22321	23808	23808	23808
can_715	715	611	157	157	157	72423	41231	41293	41293
can_838	838	837	137	137	155	207200	34254	39198	40835
dwt_209	209	184	35	35	35	9503	3914	3914	3914
dwt_221	221	187	16	16	16	9910	2011	2011	2011
dwt_245	245	115	45	45	45	3934	4177	4177	4177
dwt_310	310	28	13	13	13	2696	2695	2695	2695
dwt_361	361	50	25	25	25	5084	5139	5139	5139
dwt_419	419	356	34	34	34	39726	8230	8232	8232
dwt_503	503	452	58	58	58	35914	14816	15544	15544
dwt_592	592	259	42	42	42	28805	10983	10983	10983
dwt_878	878	519	37	37	37	26055	21034	21034	21034
dwt_918	918	839	72	72	72	108355	24347	24347	24347
dwt_992	992	513	63	63	63	262306	36296	36296	36296
gr_30_30	900	31	59	59	59	26970	33872	33872	33872
jagmesh1	936	778	27	27	27	37240	21817	21817	21817
nos2	957	4	4	4	4	3180	1907	1907	1907
nos3	960	43	79	79	79	39101	46168	46168	46168
nos5	468	178	88	88	88	27286	25381	25381	25381
nos6	675	30	16	16	16	16229	9305	9305	9305
nos7	729	81	65	65	65	53144	34110	34110	34110
plat362	362	249	56	56	56	45261	11018	11018	11018
plskz362	362	248	24	24	24	43090	4635	4635	4635
sherman1	1000	100	57	57	57	34740	26109	26109	26109
Number of best results		5	**30**	28	27	6	**29**	23	23

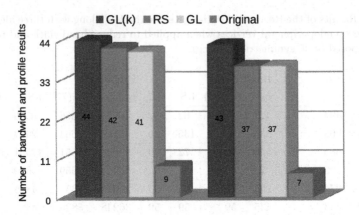

Fig. 1. The number of best bandwidth and profile results obtained using three pseudoperipheral vertex finders along with the Reverse Cuthill-McKee method [9] applied to 50 symmetric matrices when considering the results presented in Tables 1 and 2.

The execution times of the RCM-GL(k) method are proportional to the parameter used. Figure 2 (as line charts for clarity) shows the running times of the three methods when applied to the 50 symmetric matrices. The execution times of the RCM-GL(k) method were competitive with the RCM-GL method [11] when applied to the 50 symmetric matrices used in this study. Additionally, the execution times of the RCM-GL(k) algorithm was lower (or similar) than the processing times or the RCM-RS method.

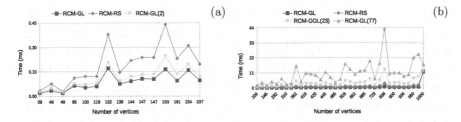

Fig. 2. Execution costs, in milliseconds, of the RCM-GL [11], RCM-RS, and RCM-GL(k) methods applied to sets composed of (a) 15 and (b) 35 symmetric matrices.

5   Conclusions

This paper evaluated a new variant of the George-Liu algorithm [10]. Specifically, this paper compared the results of the new algorithm with the results of the original George-Liu [10] and Reid-Scott [17] algorithms for finding initial vertices for the Reverse Cuthill-McKee method [9] when applied to 50 small symmetric matrices.

The results obtained by the new variant of the George-Liu algorithm applied to a set of standard benchmark matrices taken from the SuiteSparse sparse matrix collection [19] show that the proposed method compared favorably with the two others algorithms for finding pseudoperipheral vertices evaluated here when executed along with the Reverse Cuthill-McKee method [9]. Specifically, the simulations presented in this paper show that the Reverse Cuthill-McKee method [9] with ordering started with a pseudoperipheral vertex given by the new variant of the George-Liu algorithm obtains better results for reducing bandwidth and profile of small symmetric matrices than using the original George-Liu [10] or Reid-Scott [17] algorithms. Parallel approaches of these algorithms are the future steps of this investigation.

References

1. Benzi, M., Szyld, D.B., Van Duin, A.: Orderings for incomplete factorization preconditioning of nonsymmetric problems. SIAM J. Sci. Comput. **20**(5), 1652–1670 (1999)
2. Camata, J.J., Rossa, A.L., Valli, A.M.P., Catabriga, L., Carey, G.F., Coutinho, A.L.G.A.: Reordering and incomplete preconditioning in serial and parallel adaptive mesh refinement and coarsening flow solutions. Int. J. Numer. Meth. Fluids **69**(4), 802–823 (2012)
3. Chagas, G.O., Gonzaga de Oliveira, S.L.: Metaheuristic-based heuristics for symmetric-matrix bandwidth reduction: a systematic review. Procedia Comput. Sci. **51**, 211–220 (2015). https://doi.org/10.1016/j.procs.2015.05.229
4. Gonzaga de Oliveira, S.L., Bernardes, J.A.B., Chagas, G.O.: An evaluation of reordering algorithms to reduce the computational cost of the incomplete Cholesky-conjugate gradient method. Comput. Appl. Math. **37**(3), 2965–3004 (2018)
5. Gonzaga de Oliveira, S.L., Bernardes, J.A.B., Chagas, G.O.: An evaluation of low-cost heuristics for matrix bandwidth and profile reductions. Comput. Appl. Math. **37**, 1412–1471 (2018)
6. Bernardes, J.A.B., Gonzaga de Oliveira, S.L.: A systematic review of heuristics for profile reduction of symmetric matrices. Procedia Comput. Sci. **51**, 221–230 (2015)
7. Kaveh, A., Bijari, S.: Bandwidth, profile and wavefront optimization using PSO, CBO, ECBO and TWO algorithms. Iran. J. Sci. Technol. Trans. Civ. Eng. **41**(1), 1–12 (2017)
8. Kaveh, A.: Bandwidth, profile, and wavefront optimization using CBO, ECBO, and TWO algorithms. Applications of Metaheuristic Optimization Algorithms in Civil Engineering, pp. 235–256. Springer, Cham (2017). https://doi.org/10.1007/978-3-319-48012-1_13
9. George, A.: Computer implementation of the finite element method. Ph.D. thesis, Stanford University, Stanford (1971)
10. George, A., Liu, J.W.H.: An implementation of a pseudoperipheral node finder. ACM Trans. Math. Softw. **5**(3), 284–295 (1979)
11. George, A., Liu, J.W.: Computer Solution of Large Sparse Positive Definite Systems. Prentice-Hall, Englewood Cliffs (1981)
12. Gonzaga de Oliveira, S.L., Abreu, A.A.A.M., Robaina, D.T., Kischnhevsky, M.: An evaluation of four reordering algorithms to reduce the computational cost of the Jacobi-preconditioned conjugate gradient method using high-precision arithmetic. Int. J. Bus. Intell. Data Min. **12**(2), 190–209 (2017)

13. Gilbert, J.R., Moler, C., Schreiber, R.: Sparse matrices in MATLAB: design and implementation. SIAM J. Matrix Anal. **3**(1), 333–356 (1992)
14. The MathWorks, Inc.: MATLAB (1994–2018). http://www.mathworks.com/products/matlab/
15. Eaton, J.W., Bateman, D., Hauberg, S., Wehbring, R.: GNU Octave version 4.0.0 manual: a high-level interactive language for numerical computations (2015)
16. Boost: Boost C++ libraries (2017). http://www.boost.org/. Accessed 28 June 2017
17. Reid, J.K., Scott, J.A.: Ordering symmetric sparse matrices for small profile and wavefront. Int. J. Numer. Meth. Eng. **45**(12), 1737–1755 (1999)
18. Cuthill, E., McKee, J.: Reducing the bandwidth of sparse symmetric matrices. In: ACM Proceedings of the 1969 24th International Conference, pp. 157–172. ACM, New York (1969)
19. Davis, T.A., Hu, Y.: The University of Florida sparse matrix collection. ACM Trans. Math. Softw. **38**(1), 1–25 (2011)

Numerical Solution of Nonlinear Cross Diffusion Problems

Günter Bärwolff[✉] and Julia Baumbach

Institute of Mathematics, Technische Universität Berlin, Straße des 17. Juni 136,
10623 Berlin, Germany
baerwolf@math.tu-berlin.de

Abstract. This paper considered cross-diffusion equations. With those equations the concentration development in a certain region during an interesting time-interval can be described.

Cross-diffusion means the diffusion of some species which influence each other. The population dynamics of different species is a famous example of cross-diffusion.

The implicit time-integration of such parabolic equations leads to nonlinear equation systems which requires a huge computational amount.

To avoid this amount we discuss a linear scheme proposed by Murakawa [2] and investigate his properties.

Keywords: Cross diffusion problems, Linear time integration scheme ·
Finite volume method

1 Introduction

This paper deals with the so called cross-diffusion equations. These are nonlinear parabolic partial differential equations and there components influence each other. This means that every component of the solution we are looking for was influencing the other ones and vice versa. Compared to classic diffusion equations it is necessary to solve nonlinear equation system in the case of implicit time integration schemes (Euler backward). But we will discuss special linear schemes which are easy to implement. These schemes are very sensitive but they are a good alternative to the huge amount in the case of the solution nonlinear equation system with a certain kind Newtons method.

1.1 Some Necessary Terms and Definitions

In this paper Ω describes a 1d or 2d bounded region with a smooth boundary $\partial\Omega$. On this region we investigate the concentration during the time in the interval $[0, T]$ where $T > 0$. Our cross diffusion system lives on the space-time cylinder $Q = \Omega \times (0, T]$. $M \in \mathbb{N}$ is the number of considered species which influence each other. For vector valued functions (for example $z : \mathbb{R}^M \to R^M$) we denote the i-th component by z_i $(i = 1, \ldots, m)$. With Z^n we denote the approximation of a function z at the n-th time step. With a bold sub-index, for instance z_0 or Z_0 we denote the given initial conditions.

© Springer Nature Switzerland AG 2019
S. Misra et al. (Eds.): ICCSA 2019, LNCS 11619, pp. 13–24, 2019.
https://doi.org/10.1007/978-3-030-24289-3_2

1.2   The Cross-Diffusion Equations

With the above discussed preparations we will now formulate the cross-diffusion equations. We are looking for a function $z = (z_1, \ldots, z_M) : \bar{\Omega} \times (0, T] \to \mathbb{R}^M$, $M \in \mathbb{N}$ with

$$\frac{\partial \mathbf{z}}{\partial t} = \Delta\beta(\mathbf{z}) + f(\mathbf{z}) \quad \text{in } Q$$
$$\beta(z) = \mathbf{0} \quad \text{on } \partial\Omega \times (0, T],$$
$$\mathbf{z}(\cdot, 0) = \mathbf{z_0} \quad \text{in } \Omega. \tag{1}$$

The functions $\beta = (\beta_1, \ldots, \beta_M)$ and $f = (f_1, \ldots, f_M)$ are defined as functions

$$\beta, f : \mathbb{R}^M \to \mathbb{R}^M.$$

$\mathbf{z_0} = (z_{01}, \ldots, z_{0M}) : \Omega \to \mathbb{R}^M$ are the given initial conditions. To illustrate the nonlinearity of the cross-diffusion problems we write down an example of Shigesada, Kawasaki and Teramoto [1] for two different components

$$\frac{\partial z_1}{\partial t} = \Delta[(a_1 + b_1 z_1 + c_1 z_2)z_1] + (g_{10} - g_{11} z_1 - g_{12} z_2)z_1,$$
$$\frac{\partial z_2}{\partial t} = \Delta[(a_2 + b_2 z_2 + c_2 z_1)z_2] + (g_{20} - g_{21} z_1 - g_{12} z_2)z_2, \tag{2}$$

This model describes the competition of two different populations which influence each other. a_i, b_i, c_i and g_{ij} are non-negative constants ($i = 1, 2, j = 0, 1, 2$). z_1, z_2 describe the population density of the species. g_{i0} is the growth-rate of the i-th species while g_{ii} stands for an intra-specific concurrence value and $g_{ij}, i \neq j$ stands for the inter-specific concurrence value.

The obvious time integration scheme, for example used by Chen and Jüngel [4], is

$$\frac{\mathbf{Z}^n - \mathbf{Z}^{n-1}}{\tau} = \Delta\beta(\mathbf{Z}^n) + f(\mathbf{Z}^n) \quad \text{in } \Omega,$$
$$\beta(\mathbf{Z}^n) = \mathbf{0} \quad \text{on } \partial\Omega, \tag{3}$$

where τ is the used time-step. But the time-discretisation (3) means the solution of a nonlinear equations system

$$\mathbf{Z}^n - \tau\Delta\beta(\mathbf{Z}^n) - \tau f(\mathbf{Z}^n) = \mathbf{Z}^{n-1}$$

in every time-step.

The scheme (3) is applicable but there some disadvantages like very huge non-symmetric matrices because of the necessary spatial discretisation which will discussed a bit later. To overcome the named problems Murakawa [2] developed an approximative time integration scheme for the solution of cross-diffusion problems of type (1). This algorithm should be discussed in the next sections.

2   Murakawas Method

We consider the discretisation of the time interval $[0, T]$ with the time-step $\tau = T/N_T$, $N_T \in \mathbb{N}$. Instead of a straight-forward Euler-backward method Murakawa proposed the following linear scheme

$$
\begin{aligned}
\mathbf{U}^n - \frac{\tau}{\mu}\Delta \mathbf{U}^n &= \beta(\mathbf{Z}^{n-1}) + \frac{\tau}{\mu}f(\mathbf{Z}^{n-1}) \quad \text{in } \Omega, \\
\mathbf{U}^n &= \mathbf{0} \quad \text{on } \partial\Omega, \\
\mathbf{Z}^n &:= \mathbf{Z}^{n-1} + \mu(\mathbf{U}^n - \beta(\mathbf{Z}^{n-1})) \quad \text{in } \Omega.
\end{aligned}
\tag{4}
$$

μ is a free parameter which can be used to optimise the method. $\mathbf{U}$ is an approximation of $\beta(\mathbf{Z})$. $\mathbf{Z}^n$ is an approximation of $z(\cdot, n\tau)$.

There are also other boundary conditions than the second line of (4) possible, for example homogeneous or inhomogeneous Neumann boundary conditions. The advantage of the scheme (4) consists in the very friendly equation for the solution of $\mathbf{U}^n$ which is elliptic and leads after the spatial discretisation to a linear equation system with a positiv-definite coefficient matrix.

3   Some Mathematical Properties of the Scheme (4)

With the choice of appropriate Hilbert-spaces it is possible to formulate (4) in a weak form. Murakawa proved the existence of weak solutions $\mathbf{U}$ and $\mathbf{Z}$ and if we interpret these solutions as piece-wise constant interpolations during the time the following proposition holds. The main assumptions on the initial value and the functions β and f are

(1) β is Lipschitz-continuous with $\beta(\mathbf{0}) = \mathbf{0}$
(2) f is Lipschitz-continuous
(3) There is a constant $a > 0$ with

$$
\sum_{i=1}^{M}((\beta_i(\xi) - \beta_i(\eta))(\xi_i - \eta_i) \geq a|\xi - \eta|^2
$$

  for a.e. $\xi, \eta \in \mathbb{R}^M$
(4) It should be $\mathbf{z}_0 \in L^2(\Omega)^M$

With (1) to (4) the main assumptions of the propositions of convergence and stability of the discussed methods are valid. The conditions (1) and (3) guarantee the parabolicity of the above noted cross-diffusion system. In the following should only mentioned some basic results of the method.

Theorem 1. *We have for the weak solution* $\mathbf{z} \in L^2(\Omega)^M$ *the global error*

$$
E := \|\beta(\mathbf{z}) - \mathbf{U}\|_{L^2(\Omega)^M} + \|\int_0^t (\beta(\mathbf{z}) - \mathbf{U})dt\|_{L^\infty(0,T;H^{-1}(\Omega))^M}
$$

$$
+ \|\mathbf{z} - \mathbf{Z}\|_{L^\infty(0,T;H^{-1}(\Omega))^M}
$$

and the estimation

$$\mathbf{z} \in L^2(\Omega)^M \longrightarrow E + ||\mathbf{z} - \mathbf{Z}||_{L^2(Q)^M} = O(\sqrt{\tau})$$

$$\mathbf{z} \in L^2(\Omega)^M \longrightarrow E + ||\mathbf{z} - \mathbf{Z}||_{L^2(Q)^M} = O(\tau)$$

This means convergence and stability.

To prove this theorem one need several lemmata and theorems of the theory of Hilbert- and Sobolev-spaces (compactness and imbedding theorems) which can found in the papers of Murakawa [2,3].

To get an idee of finding a good choice of the parameter μ we consider the equivalent formulations of (1) and (4)

$$\frac{1}{\beta'(\mathbf{z})} \frac{\partial \beta(\mathbf{z})}{\partial t} = \Delta\beta(\mathbf{z}) + f(\mathbf{z})$$

$$\frac{\partial \mathbf{z}}{\partial t} = \frac{1}{\beta'(\mathbf{z})} \frac{\partial \beta(\mathbf{z})}{\partial t}$$

and

$$\mu \frac{\mathbf{U}^n - \beta(\mathbf{Z}^{n-1})}{\tau} = \Delta\mathbf{U}^n + f(\mathbf{Z}^{n-1}),$$

$$\frac{\mathbf{Z}^n - \mathbf{Z}^{n-1}}{\tau} = \mu \frac{\mathbf{U}^n - \beta(\mathbf{Z}^{n-1})}{\tau}$$

If we compare the continuous and the time-discrete system we find that

$$\mu \approx \frac{1}{\beta'(\mathbf{z})}$$

is a good choice. But the choice of μ can and should also be supported by numerical experiments.

4   Discretisation of (3) and (4) in Space

We use a finite-volume method for the spatial discretisation. This means we consider the balance of the fluxes on the boundary of finite volumes, in a number K 1d finite intervals and in 2d finite cells. Therefore we discretise Ω by a union of finite cells ω_j

$$\Omega = \cup_{j=1}\omega_j, \ \omega_j \cap \omega_i = N, \text{ measure of } N \text{ equals zero.}$$

For example by balancing the equations (4) over ω_j we get a system of K equations of type

$$\mathbf{U}_j^n - \frac{\tau}{\mu}\Delta_h\mathbf{U}_j^n = \beta(\mathbf{Z}_j^{n-1}) + \frac{\tau}{\mu}f(\mathbf{Z}_j^{n-1}) \quad j = 1,\ldots,K,$$

$$\mathbf{Z}_j^n := \mathbf{Z}_j^{n-1} + \mu(\mathbf{U}_j^n - \beta(\mathbf{Z}_j^{n-1})) \quad j = 1,\ldots,K, \tag{5}$$

where we closed the system by including the boundary conditions.

Δ_h is a finite approximation of the Laplacian Δ. In the finite volume discretisation method the discretisation of a diffusion term Δu is done as follows. We start with the integral balance

$$\int_\Omega \Delta u \, dv$$

and

$$\int_\Omega \Delta u \, dv = \sum_{j=1}^K \int_{\omega_j} \Delta u \, dv$$

is obvious. Now we use the theorem of Gauß-Ostrogradski (divergence-theorem) to move to flux integrals

$$\int_{\omega_j} \Delta u \, dv = \sum_{s=1}^{j_s} \int_{\gamma_{js}} \nabla u \cdot \mathbf{n}_{\gamma_{js}} \, d\partial\gamma_{js} \tag{6}$$

where j_s is the number of boundary pieces γ_{js} of the finite-volume/cell ω_j. The fluxes or directional derivatives $\nabla u \cdot \mathbf{n}_{\gamma_{js}}$ are now approximated by finite differences of values of the u-values in the cell-centers. In the case of simple structured grids the cells are rectangles and the number of boundary parts of all cells are equal to 4. The sum of the right side of (6) together with the approximated fluxes is the finite approximation of Δu.

For the Euler-backward time integration method we get, starting from (3)

$$\frac{\mathbf{Z}_j^n - \mathbf{Z}_j^{n-1}}{\tau} = \Delta_h \beta(\mathbf{Z}_j^n) + f(\mathbf{Z}_j^n) \quad j = 1, \cdots, K, \tag{7}$$

(also by closing the system by using the boundary information). The term $\Delta_h \beta(\mathbf{Z}_j^n)$ is more complicated as the corresponding term $\Delta_u \mathbf{U}_j^n$.

We have to mention that in the 1d case or in the case of structured equidistant grids in 2d problems the finite-volume method is very close to finite-difference methods.

5 Solution Methods for the Linear Equations (5) and the Non-linear Systems (7)

The linear systems (5) are solved by iterative Krylov-space methods or by direct methods (Gauß). For the nonlinear systems (7) we use the Trust-Region-Dogleg-, the Trust-Region- and the Levenberg-Marquard-Algorithm. We took these algorithms given by Matlab or Octave. The non-linear algorithms are realised by the fsolve-command und the linear solution one get by the backslash-command.

But during our numerical experiments we observed, that the ressources of Matlab or Octave are not good enough to solve problems with very fine spatial discretisations.

6 Numerical Experiments - 1d

The following 1d- and 2d-examples are part of the master-thesis [5], where one can find a lot of other instructive numerical examples.

First we considered a 1d examples with 2 species ($M = 2$). To recognise the functions β and f we state the relevant equation system

$$\frac{\partial z_1}{\partial t} = \Delta[(a_1 + b_1 z_1 + c_1 z_2)z_1] + (g_{10} - g_{11}z_1 - g_{12}z_2)z_1,$$

$$\frac{\partial z_2}{\partial t} = \Delta[(a_2 + b_2 z_2 + c_2 z_1)z_2] + (g_{20} - g_{21}z_1 - g_{12}z_2)z_2,$$

Based on this system we define 3 test-examples. The first one reads as

$$\frac{\partial z_1}{\partial t} = \Delta[(0,04 + 0,04\alpha z_2)z_1] + (2,8 - 1,1z_1 - z_2)z_1,$$

$$\frac{\partial z_2}{\partial t} = \Delta[(0,04 + 2\alpha z_1)z_2] + (3,0 - z_1 - 1,1z_2)z_2, \tag{8}$$

We work with $\alpha = 1$. For $\alpha = 0$ the initial value $(z_1, z_2) = (\frac{8}{21}, \frac{50}{21})$ gives a stable steady state solution. Therefore we use the initial value

$$z_1(x,0) = \frac{8}{11} + \frac{8}{11}R/100$$
$$z_2(x,0) = \frac{50}{11} + \frac{50}{11}R/100$$

where $R \in \mathbb{R}$ is an equally distributed random number of the interval $(0, 1)$. As Ω we use in this 1d example the unit interval. For all species we use homogeneous Neumann boundary conditions.

Space grid size h	$\tau = 2^{-5}$ (linear)	$\tau = 2^{-5}$ (nonlinear)	$\tau = 2^{-7}$ (linear)	$\tau = 2^{-7}$ (nonlinear)
1/8	0,14	7,57	4,28	21,15
1/16	0,25	11,77	8,00	36,44
1/32	0,49	16,48	15,44	66,37
1/64	0,95	63,27	30,47	249,51
1/128	1,90	241,09	60,61	958,09
1/265	3,83	970,58	121,92	3913,63

This table shows the computational times to reach a steady state solution (on a quad core personal computer, the times can be proportional scaled to computers with higher performance). For the solution with the linear algorithm we got a linear growth of the times with respect to the used grid refinement. On the other hand the growth of the computational times of the nonlinear algorithm is exponential. The influence of μ in this example was not significant. We used for all species $\mu = 1$.

As a second 1d example we consider the cross-diffusion system

$$\frac{\partial z_1}{\partial t} = \Delta[(10^{-5} + 10^{-2}z_1 + 10^{-1}z_2)z_1] + (2, 8 - 1, 1z_1 - z_2)z_1,$$

$$\frac{\partial z_2}{\partial t} = \Delta[(10^{-5} + 10^2 z_1 + 10^{-2}z_2)z_2] + (3, 0 - z_1 - 1, 1z_2)z_2, \tag{9}$$

As initial conditions we use

$$z_1(x, 0) = \frac{8}{11}(1 - 0, 1\exp(-x^2))$$

$$z_2(x, 0) = \frac{50}{11}(1 + 0, 1\exp(-x^2))$$

for $x \in (0, 1)$. Homogeneous Neumann boundary conditions are used. For the first species we use $\mu = 7$ and or the second one $\mu = 0.03$.

The computational times for the solution of the second 1d example are similar to those of the first example.

As a third 1d example we consider the equation system

$$\frac{\partial z_i}{\partial t} = \Delta\beta_i(\mathbf{z}) + d_i \text{div}(z_i \nabla p) \quad \text{in} \quad \Omega$$

$$\frac{\partial \beta_i(\mathbf{z})}{\partial \nu} + d_i z_i \frac{\partial p}{\partial \nu} = 0 \quad \text{on} \quad \partial\Omega \times (0, T),$$

$$z_i(\cdot, 0) = z_{0i} \quad \text{in} \quad \Omega \tag{10}$$

with $\beta_i(\mathbf{z}) = (a_i + b_i z_i + c_i z_j)z_i$ for $(i, j) \in \{(1, 2), (2, 1)\}$, $p(x) = 1.5(x - 0.5)^2$, $z_{10} = 10$, $z_{20} = 20$. In this example we use $\Omega =]0, L[=]0, 3[$ and $]0, T] =]0, 10]$.

As a discretisation of the system (10) we use the finite difference or finite volume method resp. The coefficients $a_i = c_i = d_i = 1$ are fixed. For the coefficients b_i we use the values 0 and 0.1. The spatial discretisation parameter is $h = L/N_X$ where $N_X + 1 = 301$ is the number of mesh points. The time-step parameter is $\tau = 10^{-3}$ and $N_T = T/\tau$ is the number of time-levels. For μ we used the value 10^{-3}.

Let $Z_i^{j,n}$ be the numerical approximation of $z_i(jh, n\tau)$. For the numerical solution $\{Z_i^{j,n-1}\}_{i=1,2,j=0,\dots,N}$, $(n = 1, \dots, N_T)$, is to solve

$$U_i^{j,n} - \frac{\tau}{\mu h^2}(U_i^{j+1,n} - 2U_i^{j,n} + U_i^{j-1,n})$$

$$-\frac{d_i \tau}{2h}(U_i^{j+1,n} - U_i^{j-1,n})p_x(jh) - d_i \tau U_i^{j,n} p_{xx}(jh)$$

$$= \beta_i(\mathbf{Z}^{j,n-1}) + \frac{d_i \tau}{2\mu h}(\mathbf{Z}^{j+1,n-1} - \mathbf{Z}^{j-1,n-1} - \mu\beta_i(\mathbf{Z}^{j-1,n-1}))p_x(jh)$$

$$+\frac{d_i \tau}{\mu}(\mathbf{Z}^{j,n-1} - \mu\beta_i(\mathbf{Z}^{j,n-1}))p_{xx}(jh),$$

$$\frac{U_i^{-1,n} - U_i^{1,n}}{2h} - d_i(\mathbf{Z}^{0,n-1} - \mu(U_i^{0,n} - \beta_i(\mathbf{Z}^{0,n-1})))p_x(0) = 0,$$

$$\frac{U_i^{Nx+1,n} - U_i^{Nx-1,n}}{2h} + d_i(\mathbf{Z}^{Nx,n-1} - \mu(U_i^{Nx,n} - \beta_i(\mathbf{Z}^{Nx,n-1})))p_x(L) = 0,$$

to get with $\{U_i^{j,n}\}_{i=1,\dots,M,\,j=0,\dots,N_X}$ the U-values at the new time-level n. After that we compute with

$$Z_i^{j,n} = Z_i^{j,n-1} + \mu(U_i^{j,n} + \beta_i(\mathbf{Z}^{j,n-1}))$$

the values $\{Z_i^{j,n}\}_{i=1,2,\,j=-1,\dots,N_X+1}$ at the new time-level.

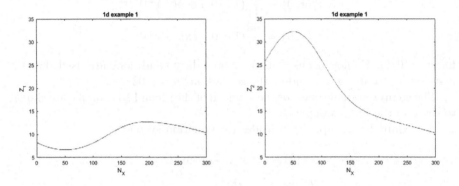

Fig. 1. 1d solution, 3rd example, first (left) and second (right) species, with $b_i = 0$

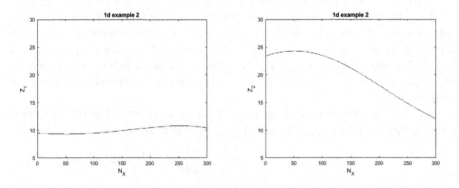

Fig. 2. 1d solution, 3rd example, first (left) and second (right) species, with $b_i = 0, 1$

The results showed in Figs. 1 and 2 represent the steady states. The computations were finished when the condition

$$\max_{0<j<N_X} \frac{|Z^{j,n} - Z^{j,n-1}|}{|Z^{j,n-1}|} < 10^{-5} \tag{11}$$

was fulfilled.

In the 4th example we considered the same model (9) as in the 3rd one. We consider large diffusion coefficients a_i compared to b_i. The coefficients $b_i = 0,001$, $c_i = d_i = 1$ are fixed. The Figs. 3 and 4 show the results for $a_i = 10$ and $a_i = 100$.

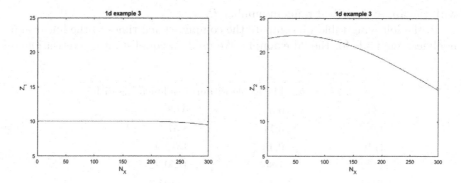

Fig. 3. 1d solution, 4th example, first (left) and second (right) species, with $a_i = 10$

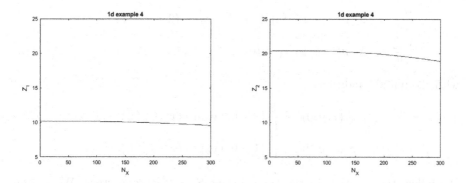

Fig. 4. 1d solution, 3rd example, first (left) and second (right) species, with $a_i = 100$

The steady states are reached if the condition (11) was fulfilled.

7 Numerical Experiments - 2d

For the 2d experiments we consider

$$\frac{\partial z_1}{\partial t} = \Delta[(0,04 + 0,04z_2)z_1] + (2,8 - 1,1z_1 - z_2)z_1,$$
$$\frac{\partial z_2}{\partial t} = \Delta[(0,04 + 2z_1)z_2] + (3,0 - z_1 - 1,1z_2)z_2, \tag{12}$$

on $\Omega = (0,1)^2$. As initial conditions we use

$$z_1(x,y,0) = \frac{8}{11} + \frac{8}{11}R/100$$

$$z_2(x,y,0) = \frac{50}{11} + \frac{50}{11}R/100$$

with the above described random number R.

In the following table we compare the computational times of the linear and nonlinear methods for the 2d example. We used an equidistant discretisation.

Grid size $h_x = h_y$	Linear algorithm	Nonlinear algorithm
1/4	0,03	0,63
1/8	0,14	8,57
1/16	0,45	151,99
1/32	1,80	1850,22
1/64	7,45	29405,92

As a second 2d example we consider the cross diffusion system

$$\frac{\partial z_1}{\partial t} = \Delta[(10^{-5} + 10^{-2}z_1 + 10^{-1}z_2)z_1] + (2,8 - 1,1z_1 - z_2)z_1,$$

$$\frac{\partial z_2}{\partial t} = \Delta[(10^{-5} + 10^2 z_1 + 10^{-2}z_2)z_2] + (3,0 - z_1 - 1,1z_2)z_2, \qquad (13)$$

with the initial conditions

$$z_1(x,y,0) = \frac{8}{11}(1 - 0,1\exp(-(x^2 + y^2)))$$

$$z_2(x,y,0) = \frac{50}{11}(1 + 0,1\exp(-(x^2 + y^2))).$$

We follow the solution in the time during $S = [\frac{3}{\tau}]^1$ time steps. We use an equidistant discretisation $h_x = h_y = \frac{1}{64}$ and $\tau = 2^{-6}$. The solution of this problem faults with the use of the μ-values of the second 1d example ($\mu_1 = 7$ for the first species and $\mu_2 = 0,03$ for the second one).

Here we investigate the behaviour of the nonlinear method for different values of μ_1, namely $\mu_1 \in \{0,03, 0,5, 1, 2,5\}$.

The following Figs. 5, 6, 7 and 8 show that there will be a influence of μ to the time position of the solution. The figures show that small values of μ show results, which are closer to the wanted steady state.

---

[1] The function $[q]$ gives the largest integer back, which is less than q.

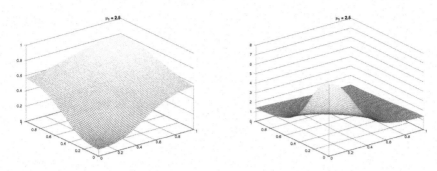

Fig. 5. 2d solution, first and second species, with $\mu = 2, 5$

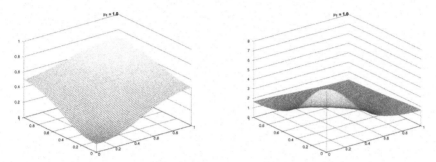

Fig. 6. 2d solution, first and second species, with $\mu = 1, 0$

8 Resumee

First of all we have to note, that it is very useful to have linear time-integration schemes to approximate cross-diffusion systems. Thus we can save a lot of computational time compared to nonlinear systems coming from implicit Euler-backward discretisation. Especially the growth of the computational time with respect to the spatial grid refinement of the linear scheme is significantly slower then the time growth of the nonlinear scheme.

The analysis of the test examples in which occur convergence and stability problems during the numerical solution shows that this is the case if we have a very strong cross-diffusion, which results in weakening the parabolicity of the system.

The choice of the parameter μ is also a crucial point with respect to time-truth of the numerical solution. The choice of appropriate time and space discretisation parameters, τ and h, must be further investigated. Especially the space grid resolution must be fine enough to resolve fine-scale properties of the solution in case of complicated initial distributions of the species.

If we are only interested in steady state solutions the choice of μ has no influence. Certain choices of different μ values falsify the time of the modeled process on the other hand, i.e. for different values of μ the solutions after a

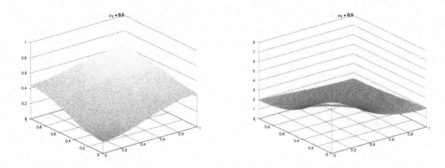

Fig. 7. 2d solution, first and second species, with $\mu = 0,5$

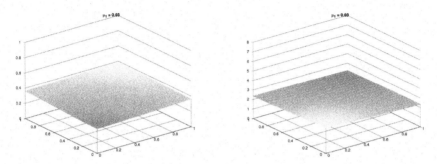

Fig. 8. 2d solution, first and second species, with $\mu = 0,03$

certain time-step n (that is $t = n\tau$) differ. The use of different μ values faster the modeled process or slowed down the process.

At the end our experiences with linear time discretisation scheme are very promising. But there must still investigate applicable rules for the choice of the time and space discretisation parameters and the choice of the free parameter μ.

References

1. Shigesada, N., Kawasaki, K., Teramoto, E.: Spatial segregation of interacting species. J. Theor. Biol. **79**, 83–99 (1979)
2. Murakawa, H.: A linear scheme to approximate nonlinear cross-diffusion systems. ESAIM: M"AN **45**, 1141–1161 (2011)
3. Murakawa, H.: Error estimates for discrete-time approximation of nonlinear cross-diffusion systems. SIAM J. Numer. Anal. **52**(2), 955–974 (2014)
4. Chen, L., Jüngel, A.: Analysis of a multidimensional parabolic population model with strong cross-diffusion. SIAM J. Math. Anal. **36**, 301–322 (2006)
5. Baumbach, J.: Numerische Untersuchungen eines linearen Zeitintegrationsschemas für nichtlineare Kreuz-Diffusionsprobleme. Master-thesis, TU Berlin (2018)

An Experimental Analysis of Heuristics for Profile Reduction

S. L. Gonzaga de Oliveira[1]([✉]), C. Osthoff[2],
and L. N. Henderson Guedes de Oliveira[3]

[1] Universidade Federal de Lavras, Lavras, MG, Brazil
sanderson@ufla.br
[2] Laboratório Nacional de Computação Científica (LNCC), Petrópolis, RJ, Brazil
osthoff@lncc.br
[3] Universidade do Estado do Rio de Janeiro, Nova Friburgo, RJ, Brazil
nelio@iprj.uerj.br

Abstract. This paper concentrates on low-cost heuristics for profile reduction. Low-cost methods for profile reduction are mainly heuristic in nature and based on graph-theoretic concepts. The contribution of this paper is twofold. Firstly, the paper includes a section involving a numerical examination of the current state-of-art metaheuristic and graph-theoretic methods for matrix profile reduction. With the support of extensive experiments, this paper shows that the metaheuristic-based algorithm is capable of reducing the profile of some matrices where the other algorithms do not perform well, but on average, the profile reduction obtained is similar for these algorithms, whereas the metaheuristic-based algorithm takes seven orders of magnitude more running time. These high execution times make the metaheuristic-based algorithm a noncontender for sparse matrix factorization and related problems. Secondly, this paper experimentally evaluates a hybrid algorithm based on the MPG and NSloan heuristics. This paper also evaluates the new hybrid heuristic for profile reduction when applied to matrices arising from two application areas against the most promising low-cost heuristics for solving the problem. The results obtained on a set of standard benchmark matrices show that the new hybrid heuristic method does not compare favorably with existing low-cost heuristics for profile reduction when applied to large-scale matrices.

Keywords: Profile reduction · Sparse matrices · Graph labelling · Combinatorial optimization · Graph theory · Search methods · Reordering algorithms · Renumbering · Ordering · Graph algorithm · Permutation of sparse matrices

1 Introduction

The solution of linear systems composed of large-scale sparse matrices is one of the most relevant computational kernels in scientific computing. Specifically,

© Springer Nature Switzerland AG 2019
S. Misra et al. (Eds.): ICCSA 2019, LNCS 11619, pp. 25–36, 2019.
https://doi.org/10.1007/978-3-030-24289-3_3

the solution of many real-world and applied problems in science and engineering (e.g., thermal and model reduction problems) reduces to solving large-scale sparse linear systems. The solution of large-scale sparse linear systems is usually a part of the numerical simulation that demands a high computational cost in execution times and memory requirements. Thus, the study to reduce the computational cost of solving linear systems composed of large-scale sparse matrices is a significant topic in numerical mathematics because of its importance in many numerical simulations.

Iterative linear system solvers that handle large-scale sparse matrices tend to suffer from poor memory performance because of the inefficient use of cache if they do not consider the order of how to process the matrix rows and columns. Simulations can generally gain substantial improvements in execution costs by accessing data with an appropriate order (e.g., [2,4,6,9,10]). Thus, the simulation should adequately label the vertices (of the sparse graph corresponding to a sparse matrix) so that data associated with adjacent vertices tend to be stored in nearby memory locations to improve cache hit rates. Therefore, spatial locality (a cache block brings in variables that the near future computation will use) should be considered an essential aspect when designing a new algorithm.

An appropriate vertex numbering is desirable to guarantee that the associated coefficient matrix will have a small profile for the low-cost solution of large and sparse linear systems, and to reduce the memory requirements of a linear system, depending on the data structure used. Thereby, the use of heuristics for profile reduction is a way of designing an application to return a sequence of graph vertices with spatial locality. The matrix profile reduction also favors direct methods for solving linear systems. Reordering rows and columns of sparse matrices also contributes to improving the arithmetic intensity of the sparse matrix-vector multiplication [21], which is the most critical aspect in the kernel of the conjugate gradient method [11,14]. As a consequence, the resulting linear system is much easier to compute than the original linear system, even when the linear system is composed of multiple right-hand side vectors [9]. Thus, heuristics for profile reduction are used to obtain low processing and small storage costs for solving large sparse linear systems.

The profile reduction is also crucial for increasing the effectiveness of data structures to represent large-scale matrices, such as applications that use the skyline data structure [7]. Another area where reordering rows and columns of sparse matrices is of fundamental importance is in serial and parallel adaptive mesh refinement. As the mesh is adapted, sparsity changes dynamically and reordering should be employed [3].

Heuristics for profile reduction belong to a family of renumbering algorithms that place nonzero coefficients of a sparse matrix close to the main diagonal. Let $A = [a_{ij}]$ be an $n \times n$ symmetric matrix associated with a connected undirected graph $G = (V, E)$ where V and E are sets of vertices and edges, respectively. The profile of a matrix A is defined as $profile(A) = \sum_{i=1}^{n} [\beta_i]$ where $\beta_i = i - \min_{1 \le j \le i} [j \mid a_{ij} \neq 0]$ and $a_{ii} \neq 0$.

The profile minimization problem is a well known $\mathcal{NP}$-hard [15] computational search problem studied for over a half-century. The reason is that it is related to a vast range of scientific and engineering application areas. Thus, practitioners have proposed a wide variety of heuristic methods for reordering the rows and columns of a sparse matrix to reduce its profile (see [1,10] and references therein). Since this is an intense field of research, practitioners continue to devote efforts to developing heuristics for profile reductions that are capable of reducing the profile of the instances to a considerable extent (e.g., see [17]).

Metaheuristic approaches are common alternatives to graph-theoretical optimization techniques in several fields. Specifically, metaheuristic-based heuristics for profile optimization have been proposed recently (see [17] and references therein). Palubeckis [17] provides a list of applications that require the solution of the profile reduction problem where runtime is not a critical issue. Thus, these applications may apply a metaheuristic algorithm for profile optimization. In the case of a heuristic for profile reduction applied as a preprocessing step while solving linear systems, however, there has been a limited exploration of such techniques mainly because the heuristics for this problem must reach low computational costs. In general, computational costs (time and space) of metaheuristic-based heuristics for profile optimization are impractical when the objective is to accelerate a linear system solver [1,8–10].

This paper focuses on the group of applications based on sparse matrix factorization and related problems so that the experiments conducted here evaluate low-cost (time and space) heuristics for profile reductions against the state-of-the-art metaheuristic-based algorithm for this problem [17]. Apart from substantially reducing the profile, a heuristic must also achieve low computational costs, i.e., it can neither be slow nor show large memory requirements. To provide more specific details, an adequate vertex labeling of a graph corresponding to a matrix contained in a linear system may reduce the computational times of a (possibly preconditioned) linear system solver, such as the conjugate gradient method [6] (as previously mentioned, by improving cache hit rates [2,4]). Additionally, the profile reductions obtained by a reordering algorithm are not directly proportional to the computational time reduction of solving linear systems. Moreover, the objective is to minimize the total computing time of the simulation including the preprocessing time required by the reordering heuristic, at least when only a single linear system is to be solved [10]. Therefore, a vertex labeling algorithm must perform at low-cost [9].

This paper evaluates a modified heuristic against the Sloan's [19], MPG [16], NSloan [13], Sloan-MGPS [18], and Hu-Scott [12] heuristics. The new heuristic for profile reduction is a hybrid algorithm of the MPG [16] and NSloan [13] heuristics. This paper also compares the profile results obtained by these low-cost heuristics with the state-of-the-art metaheuristic-based algorithm for profile reduction [17].

Section 2 describes the heuristics evaluated in this computational experiment and states a modified heuristic for profile reduction. Section 3 describes how this paper conducted the tests in this computational experiment. Section 4 shows the experimental results. Finally, Sect. 5 addresses the conclusions.

2   Related Work

Sloan [19] proposed one of the most important heuristics in this field. His heuristic is still one of the most widely used reordering algorithm for reducing the profile size of sparse matrices (e.g., [1,9,10,13,16,18]). The reason is that it is inexpensive (in terms of execution times and storage costs) and generates quality solutions. Sloan's heuristic [19] employs two weights in its priority scheme in order to label the vertices of the instance: w_1, associated with the distance $d(v,e)$ from the vertex v to a pseudo-peripheral (target end) vertex e that belongs to the last level of the level structure rooted at a starting vertex s, and w_2, associated with the degree of each vertex. The priority function $p(v) = w_1 \cdot d(v,e) - w_2 \cdot (deg(v) + 1)$ employed in Sloan's heuristic [19] presents different scales for both criteria. The value of $deg(v) + 1$ ranges from 1 to $m + 1$ (where $m = \max\limits_{v \in V}[deg(v)]$ is the maximum degree found in the graph $G = (V, E)$), and $d(v,e)$ ranges from 0 (when $v = e$) to the eccentricity $\ell(e)$ (of the target end vertex e).

The MPG [16], NSloan [13], and Sloan-MGPS [18] heuristics are based on Sloan's heuristic [19]. Specifically, the Sloan-MGPS heuristic [18] is essentially the Sloan's heuristic [19] with the starting and target end vertices given by an algorithm named modified GPS [18] instead of using the original Sloan's algorithm for finding these two pseudo-peripheral vertices.

The MPG heuristic [16] employs two max-priority queues: t contains vertices that are candidate vertices to be labeled, and q contains vertices belonging to t and also vertices that can be inserted to t. Similarly to Sloan's heuristic [19] (and its variations), the current degree of a vertex is the number of adjacencies to vertices that neither have been labeled nor belong to q. A main loop performs three steps. First, a vertex v is inserted into q in order to maximize a specific priority function. Second, the current degree $cdeg(v)$ of each vertex $v \in t$ is observed: the algorithm labels a vertex v if $cdeg(v) = 0$, and the algorithm removes from t a vertex v (i.e., $t \leftarrow t - \{v\}$) if $cdeg(v) > 1$. Third, if t is empty, the algorithm inserts into t each vertex $u \in q$ with priority $p_u \geq p_{max}(q) - 1$ where $p_{max}(q)$ returns the maximum priority among the vertices in q. The priority function in the MPG heuristic is $p(v) = d(v,e) - 2 \cdot cdeg(v)$.

Kumfert and Pothen [13] normalized the two criteria used in Sloan's algorithm with the objective of proposing the Normalized Sloan (NSloan) heuristic [13]. These authors used the priority function $p(v) = w_1 \cdot d(v,e) - w_2 \cdot \lfloor d(s,e)/m \rfloor \cdot (deg(v) + 1)$.

Regarding Sloan's [19], NSloan [13], and Sloan-MGPS [18] heuristics, this paper established the two weights as described in the original papers. When the authors suggested more than one pair of values in the original papers, exploratory investigations were performed to determine the pair of values that obtains the best profile results [10]. Thus, the two weights are assigned as $w_1 = 1$ and $w_2 = 2$ for Sloan's and Sloan-MGPS [18] heuristics, and as $w_1 = 2$ and $w_2 = 1$ for the NSloan heuristic [13].

In addition to the four low-cost heuristics for profile reductions selected from reviews of the literature [9,10], this paper evaluates a modified MPG heuristic in this paper. The new heuristic for profile reduction is essentially a hybrid of the MPG [16] and NSloan [13] heuristics. Specifically, the new heuristic is based on the MPG heuristic [16] in conjunction with the normalized scheme proposed by Kumfert and Pothen [13]. This heuristic uses the priority function $p(v) = d(v, e) - 2 \cdot d(s, e) / \max_{v \in V}[deg(v)] \cdot (cdeg(v))$. This paper refer to this new heuristic as the NMPG heuristic.

The Hu-Scott heuristic [12] is a multilevel algorithm that uses a maximal independent vertex set for coarsening the adjacency graph of the matrix and Sloan-MGPS heuristic [18] on the coarsest graph. This paper also analyzes the results yielded by the state-of-the-art metaheuristic algorithm for profile reduction [17] against five low-cost heuristics. The MSA-VNS heuristic is a hybrid algorithm based on the multi-start simulated annealing (MSA) algorithm along with the Variable Neighborhood Search (VNS) metaheuristic [17].

3   Description of the Tests

This paper divides the experiments into two main parts. The first part of the experiments compares the results of five low-cost heuristics for profile reductions with the results obtained by the MSA-VNS heuristic [17]. Palubeckis [17] compared the results of his heuristic with the results of the previous state-of-the-art metaheuristic algorithms for profile reduction when applied to two groups of matrices: 38 (ranging from 24 to 292 vertices) and 39 matrices (ranging from 307 to 2,680 vertices). The SuiteSparse matrix collection [5] contains these matrices. Since the matrices of the first group are too small for today's standards, this paper uses the 39 matrices of the second group to compare the six heuristics evaluated in this computational experiment.

Palubeckis [17] implemented his heuristic in the C++ programming language, and performed his experiments on a workstation containing an Intel® Core™ 2 Duo CPU running at 3.0 GHz. To provide a reasonable comparison of the running times, we performed the executions of the five low-cost heuristics for profile reductions evaluated here on a workstation containing an Intel Core™ 2 Duo CPU running at 2.3 GHz (Intel; Santa Clara, CA, United States). Although the profile reduction heuristics evaluated here are deterministic algorithms, 10 serial runs for each matrix were carried out to obtain average results to mitigate possible interferences in the execution costs.

This appraisal also employs the C++ programming language to implement five low-cost heuristics for profile reduction (Sloan's, MPG, NSloan, Sloan-MGPS, and NMPG heuristics). The implementations of these five heuristics for profile reductions appraised here employ binary heaps to code the priority queues (although the original Sloan's algorithm [19] used a linked list to code it). A previous publication [10] shows the testing and calibration performed to compare the implementations with the ones used by the original proposers of the four low-cost heuristics (Sloan's [19], MPG [16], NSloan [13], and Sloan-MGPS [18]) to ensure that the codes employed here were comparable to the formerly proposed algorithms.

A second part of the experiments uses 15 real symmetric matrices contained in the SuiteSparse matrix collection [5]. We also used the Hu-Scott heuristic [12], namely the MC73 routine, contained in the HSL [20], in this experiment. We employed the Fortran programming language to use this routine. The workstations used in the execution of the simulations with these 15 matrices contained an Intel® Core™ i7-4770 (CPU 3.40 GHz, 8 MB Cache, 8 GB of main memory DDR3 1.333 GHz) (Intel; Santa Clara, CA, United States). We performed three sequential runs for each large-scale matrix. The profile reduction depends on the choice of the initial ordering, and this paper considers the original ordering given in the instance contained in the SuiteSparse matrix collection [5].

4   Results and Analysis

The first part of the experiments (in Sect. 4.1) compares the profile results of five low-cost heuristics (Sloan's, MPG, NSloan, Sloan-MGPS, and NMPG) with the results of the state-of-the-art metaheuristic algorithm for profile reduction (i.e., the MSA-VNS heuristic [17]) when applied to instances ranging from 307 to 2,680 vertices. These experiments show that the MSA-VNS heuristic yields better profile results than the five other heuristics evaluated do, at much higher execution costs. Thus, the second part of the experiments (in Sect. 4.2) shows the results of six low-cost heuristics for profile reductions (i.e., including the Hu-Scott heuristic) when applied to 15 instances ranging from 19,994 to 1,228,045 vertices [up to 47,851,783 edges (or nonzero coefficients)].

4.1   Comparison of the Results Obtained Using State-of-the-Art Metaheuristic Algorithm Against Five Low-Cost Heuristics

Tables 1 and 2 show the characteristics of the instance (name, size, original profile ($profile_0$)) and the average values of profile obtained when using six heuristics applied to reduce the profile of 39 small matrices. Figure 1 shows that the MSA-VNS heuristic [17] obtains better profile reductions than the five other heuristics evaluated do in this computational experiment. The figure shows that the MSA-VNS heuristic achieves much higher profile rate reduction than the five other heuristics included in this appraisal when applied to some instances (e.g., can445, bcsstk20, can634, dwt869). Additionally, the MSA-VNS heuristic [17] reduced the profile of the gr_30_30 and instances nos3, whereas, in general, the five other low-cost heuristics increased the profiles of these two instances. On the other hand, Fig. 1 shows that in general the profile rate reduction obtained by the six heuristics evaluated are similar.

Figure 2 (in line charts for clarity) shows that the executions costs of the MSA-VNS heuristic is much higher than the five other heuristics for profile reduction evaluated here. The experiments conducted here reveal that the MSA-VNS heuristic [17] achieved its results with a higher processing cost of at least seven magnitudes in relation to the five other heuristics evaluated. For example, Sloan's [19], NSloan [13], Sloan-MGPS [18], MPG [16], and NMPG heuristics computed

Table 1. Results of six heuristics applied to reduce the profile of 26 instances contained in the SuiteSparse matrix collection [5]. Palubeckis [17] obtained the results of the MSA-VNS heuristic (times in seconds) in simulations performed on an Intel® Core™ 2 Duo running at 3.0 GHz [17]. The five other heuristics (times in milliseconds) were executed on a machine containing an Intel® Core™ 2 Duo running at 2.3 GHz. (Continued on Table 2.)

Matrix	Result	profile$_0$ /size	MSA-VNS (s)	SLOAN-MGPS (ms)	MPG (ms)	SLOAN (ms)	NSLOAN (ms)	NMPG (ms)
dwt307	profile	7825	6172	6842	6883	6813	6842	6883
	time (s)	307	266.2	0.017	0.042	0.004	0.011	0.044
dwt310	profile	2696	2630	2661	2657	2658	2641	2666
	time (s)	310	42.5	0.009	0.037	0.004	0.006	0.039
dwt346	profile	8708	5788	6214	6189	6191	6214	6189
	time (s)	346	272.5	0.019	0.056	0.006	0.012	0.059
dwt361	profile	5084	4631	4706	4755	4699	4706	4758
	time (s)	361	181.3	0.012	0.038	0.004	0.008	0.040
plat362	profile	45261	8206	8517	8517	8511	8517	8517
	time (s)	362	276.8	0.019	0.071	0.006	0.012	0.076
lshp406	profile	13224	5955	6282	6203.2	6260	6194	6191
	time (s)	406	114.7	0.017	0.055	0.005	0.011	0.058
dwt419	profile	39726	6073	6794	6714	6836	6794	6714
	time (s)	408	268.3	0.044	0.096	0.008	0.028	0.102
bcsstk06	profile	14691	12829	13771	13870	13691	13771	13870
	time (s)	419	270.6	0.019	0.068	0.006	0.012	0.071
bcspwr05	profile	36248	2608	3849	4414	4095	3862	4803
	time (s)	420	272.4	0.024	0.090	0.007	0.015	0.098
can445	profile	22321	14199	18035	16511	17295	18035	16511
	time (s)	443	276.5	0.016	0.052	0.006	0.011	0.051
nos5	profile	27286	19896	20447	20494	20549	20447	20494
	time (s)	445	275.7	0.050	0.083	0.009	0.031	0.087
bcsstk20	profile	4309	2602	3242	3124	3248	3177	3123
	time (s)	485	291.1	0.013	0.066	0.007	0.008	0.067
dwt492	profile	33790	2805	2866	2958	2856	2861	2938
	time (s)	492	269.1	0.014	0.067	0.007	0.009	0.067
494bus	profile	40975	2592	4327	4738	4486	3882	4667
	time (s)	494	287.5	0.017	0.046	0.005	0.010	0.045
dwt503	profile	35914	11428	14259	14164	13608	14259	14164
	time (s)	503	753.7	0.035	0.081	0.008	0.022	0.087
dwt512	profile	6018	3820	4150	4167	4322	4150	4169
	time (s)	512	696	0.022	0.085	0.011	0.013	0.088
lshp577	profile	22816	10035	10625	10499	10607	10488	10469
	time (s)	577	457.8	0.028	0.078	0.007	0.018	0.082
dwt592	profile	28805	8816	9697	9580	9871	9177	9437
	time (s)	592	576.7	0.027	0.074	0.008	0.017	0.078
dwt607	profile	30008	12431	13856	14470	13825	13856	14470
	time (s)	607	739.9	0.042	0.114	0.012	0.026	0.119
can634	profile	68586	25170	38033	33896	34609	38033	33896
	time (s)	634	767.1	0.099	0.122	0.014	0.062	0.129
662bus	profile	45165	5994	9180	10023	9701	8587.1	10339
	time (s)	662	762.4	0.032	0.075	0.006	0.021	0.071
nos6	profile	16229	9095	9095.000	9095.000	9095.000	9095.000	9095
	time (s)	675	600.2	0.024	0.060	0.006	0.015	0.063
685bus	profile	28621	5993	8547.700	9674.000	8560.000	8912.000	8716
	time (s)	685	769.9	0.028	0.078	0.008	0.020	0.076
can715	profile	72423	20280	30423.000	29810.000	30695.000	30423.000	29810
	time (s)	715	1697.1	0.078	0.122	0.011	0.049	0.122
nos7	profile	53144	34110	34698.000	35202.000	34473.000	34690.000	35321
	time (s)	729	1380.7	0.084	0.127	0.011	0.052	0.132
dwt758	profile	23113	6364	6967.000	6534.000	6983.000	6490.000	6535
	time (s)	758	1528.1	0.023	0.090	0.010	0.015	0.095

Table 2. Results of six heuristics applied to reduce the profile of 13 instances contained in the SuiteSparse matrix collection. Palubeckis [17] obtained the results of the MSA-VNS heuristic (times in seconds) in simulations performed on an Intel® Core™ 2 Duo running at 3.0 GHz [17]. The five other heuristics (times in milliseconds) were executed on a machine containing an Intel® Core™ 2 Duo running at 2.3 GHz. (Continued from Table 1.)

Matrix	Result	$profile_0$ /size	MSA-VNS (s)	SLOAN-MGPS (ms)	MPG (ms)	SLOAN (ms)	NSLOAN (ms)	NMPG (ms)
lshp778	profile	36284	15652	16630.000	16424.000	16592.000	16399.000	16373
	time (s)	778	1364.3	0.046	0.118	0.009	0.027	0.123
bcsstk19	profile	74051	7240	8613.000	8450.000	9250.000	20837.000	22146
	time (s)	817	1651.8	0.024	0.126	0.011	0.042	0.122
dwt869	profile	19528	11806	14672.000	14493.000	14918.000	14916.000	15521
	time (s)	869	1609	0.040	0.100	0.011	0.027	0.106
dwt878	profile	26055	16903	18967.000	18227.000	18783.000	19522.000	18237
	time (s)	878	1606.3	0.047	0.095	0.011	0.032	0.100
gr_30_30	profile	26970	23836	28764.000	26970.000	28664.000	26538.000	26970
	time (s)	900	1616.5	0.070	0.098	0.012	0.041	0.104
dwt918	profile	108355	15007	16332.000	15768.000	16852.000	17754.000	19199
	time (s)	918	1734.3	0.046	0.144	0.015	0.032	0.147
nos2	profile	3180	1907	1907.000	1910.000	1907.000	1907.000	1910
	time (s)	957	1783.7	0.017	0.095	0.011	0.011	0.099
nos3	profile	39101	35916	39673.000	40195.000	39457.000	39673.000	40195
	time (s)	960	1739.4	0.067	0.216	0.021	0.042	0.231
dwt992	profile	262306	31620	33013.200	33376.000	32960.000	33012.000	33376
	time (s)	992	1678.4	0.053	0.193	0.017	0.034	0.208
dwt1005	profile	121070	29631	33980.000	33413.000	33737.000	33980.000	33413
	time (s)	1005	1694.4	0.094	0.162	0.016	0.058	0.171
dwt1007	profile	25786	18880	22852.000	21321.900	22882.000	20184.000	21424
	time (s)	1007	1613.5	0.060	0.114	0.015	0.034	0.121
dwt1242	profile	110188	31756	35611.000	36102.000	36377.000	33937.000	39951
	time (s)	1242	1727.9	0.090	0.167	0.016	0.056	0.166
dwt2680	profile	587863	82575	87621.000	88130.000	87242.000	90123.000	91656
	time (s)	2680	3221.4	0.230	0.389	0.041	0.164	0.406

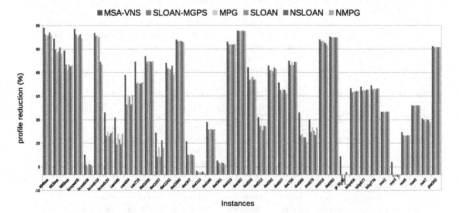

Fig. 1. Results of six heuristics applied to reduce the profile of 39 instances contained in the SuiteSparse matrix collection [5].

the instance dwt2680 (i.e., the largest instance contained in this dataset) in 0.04, 0.16, 0.23, 0.39, and 0.41 ms (in simulations performed on an Intel® Core™ 2 Duo running at 2.3 GHz), respectively, whereas the MSA-VNS heuristic computed this instance in more than 3221 s (in simulations performed on an Intel® Core™ 2 Duo running at 3.0 GHz). As an example, Sloan's heuristic [19] computes an instance composed of 1,228,045 vertices in two seconds.

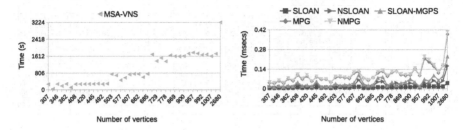

Fig. 2. Execution times of six heuristics applied to reduce the profile of 39 instances contained in the SuiteSparse matrix collection. Palubeckis [17] obtained the results of the MSA-VNS heuristic (times in seconds (s)) in simulations performed on an Intel® Core™ 2 Duo running at 3.0 GHz [17]. The simulations with the five other heuristics (times in milliseconds (msecs)) were performed on an Intel® Core™ 2 Duo running at 2.3 GHz.

On 34 of the 39 matrices contained in the dataset used here, the MSA-VNS heuristic [17] delivers smaller profiles than any other previously known profile reduction algorithm does. While this result is impressive, the MSA-VNS heuristic is very slow, taking approximately $2n^2$ milliseconds for a matrix of order n. It is not practical for larger instances.

The quality and time of the MSA-VNS algorithm may depend on the setting of its parameters. However, we considered the results provided by its original publication [17], which are expected to have the best parameters. Since low-cost heuristics for profile reductions [10] yield in general reasonable profile results at much lower costs than the state-of-the-art metaheuristic algorithm for profile reduction [17], Sect. 4.2 concentrates on evaluating six low-cost heuristics for profile reductions when applied to larger matrices (up to 1,228,045 vertices).

4.2 Results of Six Low-Cost Heuristics for Profile Reductions

This section describes the results of six low-cost heuristics for profile reductions applied to a dataset comprised of 15 symmetric matrices contained in the SuiteSparse matrix collection. Table 3 shows the matrix's name and size, the value of the initial profile of the instance (profile$_0$), and the average values of profile obtained when using each heuristic. The same table also highlights the best profile results.

Table 3 shows that the Hu-Scott heuristic yielded the highest number of best profile results when applied to symmetric instances originating from thermal (in

Table 3. Results of six heuristics applied to reduce the profile of 15 symmetric matrices contained in the SuiteSparse matrix collection [5] originating from thermal (four matrices) and model reduction (11 matrices) problems.

matrix	size	profile$_0$	Hu-Scott	NMPG	MPG	NSloan	Sloan-MGPS	Sloan
thermal2	1,228,045	53,657,335,080	587,662,601	586,063,633	584,643,264	587,246,981	609,179,419	593,981,740
thermo mech_dM	204,316	10,671,293,780	28,549,159	30,796,587	30,825,327	30,939,618	32,276,780	31,984,980
thermo mech_TC	102,158	2,667,823,445	13,477,995	15,346,513	15,412,663	15,446,340	16,109,532	16,021,130
thermo mech_TK	102,158	2,667,823,445	13,372,590	15,398,294	15,504,258	15,493,278	16,109,532	15,906,569
Nr. best results	0		3	0	1	0	0	0
bone010	986,703	8,846,266,758	187,539,359	1,471,105,979	2,231,282,192	1,282,743,704	1,687,120,778	1,571,237,233
boneS10	914,898	6,345,023,025	2,147,483,647	3,742,417,527	3,742,417,527	3,823,790,163	3,952,972,833	3,890,992,689
boneS01	127,224	331,330,356	245,645,928	320,120,227	302,253,322	330,301,515	320,695,596	308,162,745
filter3D	106,437	260,719,523	68,760,290	86,376,100	87,199,353	95,192,166	98,931,960	97,975,438
rail79841	79,841	551,148,483	11,968,229	8,910,916	12,851,179	9,830,923	14,398,928	13,732,868
t3dh	79,171	250,243,367	154,218,807	160,795,113	158,470,211	160,944,302	164,226,809	160,693,484
gas_sensor	66,917	69,391,231	63,046,780	65,044,792	72,856,073	68,858,703	69,736,475	71,821,911
t3dl	20,360	14,726,265	14,392,289	14,146,144	14,081,961	44,263,732	14,754,577	14,654,390
rail20209	20,209	60,032,258	1,295,632	1,172,744	1,744,663	1,214,743	1,562,130	1,632,981
LF10000	19,998	49,990	69,988	49,990	49,990	49,990	49,990	49,990
LFAT5000	19,994	84,958	54,978	34,984	34,984	34,984	34,984	34,984
Nr. best results	1		6	4	3	2	2	2

three instances) and model reduction (in six instances) problems. On the other hand, the same table shows that the MPG heuristic delivered the best profile result when applied to the highest matrix (*thermal2*) used in this study.

Figure 3 (in line charts for clarity) shows the execution times of the six low-cost heuristics for profile reductions evaluated. The Sloan and NSloan heuristics obtained lower execution times than the four other heuristics evaluated. On average, the Hu-Scott, NMPG, and MPG heuristics obtained similar execution times.

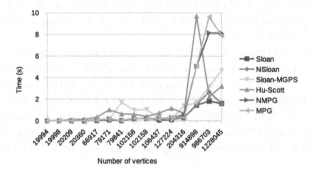

Fig. 3. Execution times (in seconds) of six heuristics for profile reductions in simulations using 15 symmetric instances contained in the SuiteSparse matrix collection.

5   Conclusions

This computational experiment evaluated five existing low-cost heuristics for profile reduction (variants of Sloan's algorithm [19]) along with a new hybrid heuristic based on the MPG [16] and NSloan [13] heuristics, termed NMPG heuristic. This computational experiment also compared the results provided by a metaheuristic algorithm based on simulated annealing and variable neighborhood search metaheuristics [17] with low-cost heuristics for profile reduction. As expected, the simulations conducted in this paper show that the state-of-the-art metaheuristic algorithm for profile reduction [17] reaches better profile results than low-cost heuristics do at much higher execution costs. Currently, no metaheuristic-based heuristic for profile reduction exists in the literature that can successfully reduce the profile of large-scale matrices at a reasonable amount of time. In this field, scientific and engineering applications apply low-cost heuristics for profile reductions when the computational time is a critical subject. Consequently, in the case of instances of rather large dimensions, a practical option is to use low-cost heuristics for obtaining satisfactory-quality solutions for problem instances defined by such matrices. The experiments conducted here were carried out on several matrices arising from different application domains. The results show that the metaheuristic algorithm provides better profile results, but takes a lot more time than graph-theoretic heuristics for profile reduction.

This paper also applied six low-cost heuristics to 15 matrices arising from thermal and model reduction problems. Numerical experiments show that the NMPG heuristic provides, in general, further worthwhile gains when compared with classical heuristics in this field (Sloan's [19], MPG [16], NSloan [13], Sloan-MGPS [18]). However, the NMPG heuristic for profile reduction did not perform better than Hu-Scott heuristic did when applied to matrices arising from the application domains used here.

The next step in this work is to evaluate low-cost heuristics for profile reductions implemented using parallel libraries (e.g., OpenMP, Galois, and Message Passing Interface systems) and in GPU-accelerated computing. Similarly, regarding massively parallel computing, an evaluation of these heuristics implemented within the Intel® Math Kernel Library running on Intel® Xeon® Many Integrated Core Architecture and Scalable processors is another future step of this investigation.

References

1. Bernardes, J.A.B., Gonzaga de Oliveira, S.L.: A systematic review of heuristics for profile reduction of symmetric matrices. Procedia Comput. Sci. **51**, 221–230 (2015). https://doi.org/10.1016/j.procs.2015.05.231
2. Burgess, D.A., Giles, M.: Renumbering unstructured grids to improve the performance of codes on hierarchial memory machines. Adv. Eng. Softw. **28**(3), 189–201 (1997)
3. Camata, J.J., Rossa, A.L., Valli, A.M.P., Catabriga, L., Carey, G.F., Coutinho, A.L.G.A.: Reordering and incomplete preconditioning in serial and parallel adaptive mesh refinement and coarsening flow solutions. Int. J. Numer. Meth. Fluids **69**(4), 802–823 (2012)
4. Das, R., Mavriplis, D.J., Saltz, J.H., Gupta, S.K., Ponnusamy, R.: The design and implementation of a parallel unstructured Euler solver using software primitives. AIAA J. **32**(3), 489–496 (1994)

5. Davis, T.A., Hu, Y.: The University of Florida sparse matrix collection. ACM Trans. Math. Softw. **38**(1), 1–25 (2011)
6. Duff, I.S., Meurant, G.A.: The effect of ordering on preconditioned conjugate gradients. BIT Numer. Math. **29**(4), 635–657 (1989)
7. Felippa, C.A.: Solution of linear equations with skyline-stored symmetric matrix. Comput. Struct. **5**(1), 13–29 (1975)
8. Gonzaga de Oliveira, S.L., Abreu, A.A.A.M., Robaina, D.T., Kischnhevsky, M.: An evaluation of four reordering algorithms to reduce the computational cost of the Jacobi-preconditioned conjugate gradient method using high-precision arithmetic. Int. J. Bus. Intell. Data Min. **12**(2), 190–209 (2017)
9. Gonzaga de Oliveira, S.L., Bernardes, J.A.B., Chagas, G.O.: An evaluation of reordering algorithms to reduce the computational cost of the incomplete Cholesky-conjugate gradient method. Comput. Appl. Math. **37**(3), 2965–3004 (2018)
10. Gonzaga de Oliveira, S.L., Bernardes, J.A.B., Chagas, G.O.: An evaluation of low-cost heuristics for matrix bandwidth and profile reductions. Computat. Appl. Math. **37**(1), 641–674 (2018). (First Online: 5 July 2016)
11. Hestenes, M.R., Stiefel, E.: Methods of conjugate gradients for solving linear systems. J. Res. Natl. Bur. Stan. **49**(36), 409–436 (1952)
12. Hu, Y., Scott, J.A.: A multilevel algorithm for wavefront reduction. SIAM J. Sci. Comput. **23**(4), 1352–1375 (2001)
13. Kumfert, G., Pothen, A.: Two improved algorithms for envelope and wavefront reduction. BIT Numer. Math. **37**(3), 559–590 (1997)
14. Lanczos, C.: Solutions of systems of linear equations by minimized iterations. J. Res. Natl. Bur. Stan. **49**(1), 33–53 (1952)
15. Lin, Y.X., Yuan, J.J.: Profile minimization problem for matrices and graphs. Acta Mathematicae Applicatae Sinica **10**(1), 107–122 (1994)
16. Medeiros, S.R.P., Pimenta, P.M., Goldenberg, P.: Algorithm for profile and wavefront reduction of sparse matrices with a symmetric structure. Eng. Comput. **10**(3), 257–266 (1993)
17. Palubeckis, G.: A variable neighborhood search and simulated annealing hybrid for the profile minimization problem. Comput. Oper. Res. **87**, 83–97 (2017)
18. Reid, J.K., Scott, J.A.: Ordering symmetric sparse matrices for small profile and wavefront. Int. J. Numer. Meth. Eng. **45**(12), 1737–1755 (1999)
19. Sloan, S.W.: A Fortran program for profile and wavefront reduction. Int. J. Numer. Meth. Eng. **28**(11), 2651–2679 (1989)
20. STFC. The Science and Technology Facilities Council. HSL. A collection of Fortran codes for large scale scientific computation. http://www.hsl.rl.ac.uk. Accessed Dec 2015
21. Williams, S., Waterman, A., Patterson, D.: Roofline: an insightful visual performance model for multicore architectures. Commun. ACM **52**(4), 65–76 (2009)

Computational Peculiarities
of the Method of Initial Functions

Alexander V. Matrosov$^{(\boxtimes)}$ (iD)

Saint Petersburg State University, Saint Petersburg, Russia
a.matrosov@spbu.ru

Abstract. The paper investigates the computational features of the method of initial functions. Its idea is to express the components of the stress and strain state of an elastic body through initial functions defined on the initial line (a 2D problem) or surface (a 3D problem). A solution by the method of initial functions for a linear-elastic orthotropic rectangle under plane deformation is constructed. Its implementation when initial functions are represented by trigonometric functions is given. The influence of the value of a load harmonic on stable computations is studied on the example of bending of a free-supported rectangle of average thickness under the normal load specified on its upper boundary face. The causes of computational instability of the algorithm of the method of initial functions are found out. A modified algorithm is presented to increase twice the limit value of the "stable" harmonic. It is noted that calculations with a long mantissa should be cardinally performed to solve the problem of unstable computations. The results of computational experiments to determine the maximum harmonics for stable calculations of orthotropic rectangle depending on its relative thickness and mantissa length are presented. Implementation of the algorithm of the initial function method and calculations are performed using the system of analytical calculations Maple.

Keywords: Computational instability · Method of initial functions · Orthotropic solid

1 Introduction

Currently, computational methods of mechanics are the main tool for modeling the behavior of a complex mechanical system. Analytical approaches make it possible to obtain solutions as the expansion in series of functions most often for constructions of a simple configuration: a rectangle, a circle, a parallelepiped, a sphere, etc. For verification of numerical solutions to have such analytical solutions even for bodies of simple configuration, but made of materials with complex physicomechanical properties, is a good deal. Finding such solutions requires not only a high mathematical culture, but sometimes even a simple guess about the type of solution. However, for some types of configurations,

© Springer Nature Switzerland AG 2019
S. Misra et al. (Eds.): ICCSA 2019, LNCS 11619, pp. 37–51, 2019.
https://doi.org/10.1007/978-3-030-24289-3_4

there is a universal algorithm for constructing an analytical solution in the form of trigonometric series – a method of initial functions (MIF).

The history of this method begins with the work of Lur'e [1], in which he proposed a symbolic way of recording the solution of a system of partial differential equations in displacements of the elasticity theory. The essence of his approach was that the system of partial differential equations was considered as a system of ordinary differential equations with respect to one of the variables, and the differentiation operators with respect to other variables were simply considered as some symbolic parameters. The solution of this system was obtained as a linear combination of the unknown functions and their derivatives, defined on the initial plane $z = 0$, using singular operators in other variables. In his next works [2,3], using the solution obtained, he solves the problem of an infinite isotropic layer loaded on the two bounding surfaces $z = const$, connecting the unknown displacements and their derivatives on the initial plane with the loads specified on these surfaces.

This approach to constructing a solution was not yet the method of initial functions. The latter was born in the work of Vlasov [4], in which he, using the symbolic method of recording the solution of A.I. Lur'e, proposed a method for constructing the solution of the mixed equations of elasticity theory directly through the components of the stress-strain state defined on the initial plane: displacements u_0, v_0, w_0 and stresses σ_z^0, τ_{yz}^0, τ_{xz}^0. In the matrix-operator form, this solution can be written as:

$$\mathbf{U} = \mathbf{L}\mathbf{U}^0.$$

Here $\mathbf{U} = \{u, v, w, \sigma_z, \tau_{yz}, \tau_{xz}, \sigma_x, \sigma_y, \tau_{xy}\}$ is a vector of the stress-strain state components of the layer, $\mathbf{U}^0 = \{u_0, v_0, w_0, \sigma_z^0, \tau_{yz}^0, \tau_{xz}^0\}$ is a vector of initial functions defined on the initial plane $z = 0$ and $\mathbf{L}$ is a matrix of operators of the method of initial functions. In the literature it is called the basic relation of the method of initial functions.

After the works of Vlasov [5,6] the method of initial functions becomes very popular among a large community of scientists. The basic relations of the method of initial functions was obtained for the plane problem of elasticity theory in a rectangular orthogonal coordinate system [7–10], for the axisymmetric problem of elasticity theory in a cylindrical orthogonal coordinate system for both an isotropic continuum and an orthotropic one [11–14]. The problems of bending multilayer and layered systems with isotropic and orthotropic layers was solved [15–19]. The method of initial functions was useful in the construction of refined theories of bending of high beams and thick plates [20,21].

The method of initial functions is a universal method for constructing a solution in any canonical region of the corresponding coordinate system. The implementation of the method by trigonometric series can be carried out only in the form of a computer program. However, in this connection, it should be noted that one feature of the solutions obtained by the method of initial functions is their computational instability. To achieve satisfactory accuracy for practice, it is sometimes necessary to keep members with large harmonics in rows. But the calculations by the initial function method at the same time can be performed with a large error. It depends on the geometric parameters of the calculated area, for example, the ratio of the sides of the rectangle or parallelepiped, and physicomechanical characteristics of the material. The natural way to eliminate the computational instability of an algorithm is to perform calculations with long mantissa. The then level of development of both computer technology and programming environments did not allow to overcome this drawback of the initial method functions, which did not allow it to establish itself widely in computational practice. But attempts to develop stable algorithms were made [22].

Modern computer technology with its high performance and new programming systems, which make it easy to go to calculations with different mantissa lengths (Maple, Python, Mathematica), makes it possible to implement computational stable algorithm of the initial function method. In this paper the results of the study of computational stability of the initial functions method based on the implementation of the algorithm of the method of initial functions in the system of analytical calculations Maple are presented. All computational experiments were performed on the example of the analysis of an orthotropic free-supported rectangle.

2   Theoretical Model

Let's consider a linearly elastic orthotropic rectangle in Cartesian orthogonal coordinate system Oxy under plane deformation (see Fig. 1). On the initial line $(x = 0)$ the loads $\sigma_x^p = q\sin(py)$, $\tau_{xy}^p = 0$, $p = \dfrac{m\pi}{A}$ (m is an integer, a harmonic of the load) are specified.

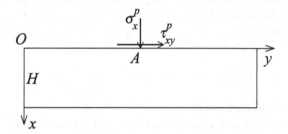

Fig. 1. A design scheme of an orthotropic rectangle.

In the case of plane deformation the equilibrium equations in displacements for an orthotropic body in a Cartesian orthogonal coordinate system Oxy in the absence of mass forces in the operator form can be written as

$$
\begin{aligned}
\left(A_{1,1}\partial_x^2 + A_{6,6}\partial_y^2\right) u\left(x, y\right) + \left(A_{1,2} + A_{6,6}\right)\partial_x\partial_y v\left(x, y\right) = 0, \\
\left(A_{1,2} + A_{6,6}\right)\partial_x\partial_y u\left(x, y\right) + \left(A_{6,6}\partial_x^2 + A_{2,2}\partial_y^2\right) v\left(x, y\right) = 0.
\end{aligned}
\tag{1}
$$

Here $u\,(x,y)$, $v\,(x,y)$ are the displacements along the axis Ox and Oy respectively, $A_{i,j}$ are elastic constants of the material and symbols ∂_x and ∂_y are differential operators with respect to the variables x and y.

According to the algorithm of the MIF the Eq. (1) are considered as ordinary differential equations with respect to the variable x while the differential operator ∂_y is assumed to be a symbolic parameter. The solution of the system of these equations is searched in the form of linear combinations of the displacements and the normal and tangential stresses defined on the initial line $x = 0$ (so called initial functions)

$$
\begin{aligned}
u(x,y) &= L_{1,1}(\partial_y, x)\,u^0\,(y) + L_{1,2}(\partial_y, x)\,v^0\,(y) + \\
&\quad + L_{1,3}(\partial_y, x)\,\sigma^0\,(y) + L_{1,4}(\partial_y, x)\,\tau_{xy}^0\,(y)\,, \\
v(x,y) &= L_{2,1}(\partial_y, x)\,u^0\,(y) + L_{2,2}(\partial_y, x)\,v^0\,(y) + \\
&\quad + L_{2,3}(\partial_y, x)\,\sigma^0\,(y) + L_{2,4}(\partial_y, x)\,\tau_{xy}^0\,(y)\,.
\end{aligned}
\tag{2}
$$

Here $L_{ij}(\partial_y, x)$ $(i = 1, 2, j = 1, \ldots, 4)$ are unknown operator-functions (the MIF operators) and $u^0\,(y)$, $v^0\,(y)$, $\sigma_x^0\,(y)$, $\tau_{xy}^0\,(y)$ are independent and arbitrary initial functions.

Substitution (2) to (1) makes it possible to obtain the four systems of two ordinary differential equations for determining the unknown operator-functions $L_{ij}(\partial_y, x)$

$$
\begin{aligned}
\left(A_{1,1}\frac{d^2}{dx^2} + A_{6,6}\partial_y^2\right) L_{1,j} + (A_{1,2} + A_{6,6})\,\partial_y\frac{d}{dx}L_{2j} &= 0, \\
(A_{1,2} + A_{6,6})\,\partial_y\frac{d}{dx}L_{1,j} + \left(A_{2,2}\partial_y^2 + A_{6,6}\frac{d^2}{dx^2}\right) L_{2,j} &= 0, \quad j = 1, \ldots, 4.
\end{aligned}
\tag{3}
$$

To solve the systems (3) requires to know the initial values of the MIF operators: their values and the values of their first derivatives at the point $x = 0$. Assuming in the representation (2) $x = 0$ the values of the operators on the initial line are easily obtained

$$
L_{i,j}(0) = \delta_i^j \quad (i = 1, 2, j = 1, \ldots, 4).
\tag{4}
$$

In (4) δ_i^j is the Kronecker delta.

To get the values for derivatives with respect to the variable x we use the Hooke's generalized law

$$
\begin{aligned}
\sigma_x &= A_{1,1}\varepsilon_x + A_{1,2}\varepsilon_y, \\
\tau_{xy} &= A_{6,6}\varepsilon_{xy}, \\
\sigma_y &= A_{1,2}\varepsilon_x + A_{2,2}\varepsilon_y
\end{aligned}
\tag{5}
$$

and the Cauchy relations

$$
\begin{aligned}
\varepsilon_x &= \frac{d}{dx}u, \\
\varepsilon_x &= \partial_y v, \\
\varepsilon_{xy} &= \frac{d}{dx}v + \partial_y u.
\end{aligned}
\tag{6}
$$

Substitution (6) into (5) gives the representation of the stress components through the displacements

$$\sigma_x = A_{1,1}\frac{d}{dx}u + A_{1,2}\partial_y v,$$
$$\tau_{xy} = A_{6,6}\frac{d}{dx}v + A_{6,6}\partial_y u, \tag{7}$$
$$\sigma_y = A_{1,2}\frac{d}{dx}u + A_{2,2}\partial_y v.$$

Evaluating first two equations in (7) at $x = 0$ and taking into account the representations (2) the required values of derivatives of the MIF operators are obtained as

$$\left.\frac{dL_{1,1}}{dx}\right|_{x=0} = 0, \quad \left.\frac{dL_{1,2}}{dx}\right|_{x=0} = -\frac{A_{1,2}}{A_{1,1}}\partial_y, \quad \left.\frac{dL_{1,3}}{dx}\right|_{x=0} = \frac{1}{A_{1,1}}, \quad \left.\frac{dL_{1,4}}{dx}\right|_{x=0} = 0,$$
$$\left.\frac{dL_{2,1}}{dx}\right|_{x=0} = -\partial_y, \quad \left.\frac{dL_{2,2}}{dx}\right|_{x=0} = 0, \quad \left.\frac{dL_{2,3}}{dx}\right|_{x=0} = 0, \quad \left.\frac{dL_{2,4}}{dx}\right|_{x=0} = \frac{1}{A_{6,6}}. \tag{8}$$

The solution of the systems (3) with initial values (4) and (8) gives the following values of the MIF operator-functions $L_{i,j}$ $(i = 1, 2, j = 1, \ldots .4)$

$$L_{1,1} = \left[\left(-A_{1,1}A_{2,2} + A_{1,2}^2 + A_{1,2}A_{6,6} + A_{1,1}A_{6,6}\alpha_1^2\right)\cos\left(\alpha_1\partial_y x\right)\right.$$
$$\left. + \left(A_{1,1}A_{2,2} - A_{1,2}^2 - A_{1,2}A_{6,6} - A_{1,1}A_{6,6}\alpha_2^2\right)\cos\left(\alpha_2\partial_y x\right)\right]/d,$$
$$L_{1,2} = A_{6,6}\left[\alpha_2\left(-A_{2,2} - A_{1,2}\alpha_1^2\right)\sin\left(\alpha_1\partial_y x\right)\right.$$
$$\left. +\alpha_1\left(A_{2,2} + A_{1,2}\alpha_2^2\right)\sin\left(\alpha_2\partial_y x\right)\right]/d,$$
$$L_{1,3} = \left[\alpha_2\left(-A_{2,2} + A_{6,6}\alpha_1^2\right)\sin\left(\alpha_1\partial_y x\right)\right.$$
$$\left. +\alpha_1\left(A_{2,2} - A_{6,6}\alpha_2^2\right)\sin\left(\alpha_2\partial_y x\right)\right]/(\partial_y\alpha_1\alpha_2 d),$$
$$L_{1,4} = (A_{1,2} + A_{6,6})\left[\cos\left(\alpha_1\partial_y x\right) - \cos\left(\alpha_2\partial_y x\right)\right]/(\partial_y d), \tag{9}$$
$$L_{2,1} = A_{6,6}\left[\alpha_2\left(-A_{1,2} - A_{1,1}\alpha_1^2\right)\sin\left(\alpha_1\partial_y x\right)\right.$$
$$\left. +\alpha_1\left(A_{1,2} + A_{1,1}\alpha_2^2\right)\sin\left(\alpha_2\partial_y x\right)\right]/(\alpha_1\alpha_2 d),$$
$$L_{2,2} = A_{6,6}\left[\left(A_{1,2} + A_{1,1}\alpha_1^2\right)\cos\left(\alpha_1\partial_y x\right) + \left(-A_{1,2} - A_{1,1}\alpha_2^2\right)\cos\left(\alpha_2\partial_y x\right)\right]/d,$$
$$L_{2,3} = (A_{1,2} + A_{6,6})\left[\cos\left(\alpha_1\partial_y x\right) - \cos\left(\alpha_2\partial_y x\right)\right]/(\partial_y d),$$
$$L_{2,4} = \left[\alpha_2\left(-A_{6,6} + A_{1,1}\alpha_1^2\right)\sin\left(\alpha_1\partial_y x\right)\right.$$
$$\left. +\alpha_1\left(A_{6,6} - A_{1,1}\alpha_2^2\right)\sin\left(\alpha_2\partial_y x\right)\right]/(\partial_y\alpha_1\alpha_2 d).$$

Here $\alpha_1 = \sqrt{\dfrac{2d_4}{d_2 - d}}$, $\alpha_2 = \sqrt{\dfrac{2d_4}{d_2 + d}}$, $d = \sqrt{d_2^2 - 4d_0 d_4}$, $d_0 = A_{2,2}A_{6,6}$, $d_2 = A_{1,1}A_{2,2} - 2A_{1,2}A_{6,6} - A_{1,2}{}^2$, $d_4 = A_{1,1}A_{6,6}$.

Now the operator representations (2) of the displacements with the operators (9) are fully defined. To use them for analysing elastic structures the type of initial functions should be specified and then the results of the impact of the MIF operator-functions on them should be calculated.

Let the initial functions are chosen as trigonometric functions $u^0 = \overline{u}^0 \sin{(py)}$, $v^0 = \overline{v}^0 \cos{(py)}$, $\sigma_x^0 = \overline{\sigma}_x^0 \sin{(py)}$, $\tau_{xy}^0 = \overline{\tau}_{xy}^0 \cos{(py)}$, $p = m\pi/A$ and the overlined coefficients are real constants. It should define how the MIF operator-functions impact on the corresponding trigonometric functions:

$$(L_{i,1}\left(\partial y, x\right))\sin{(py)}, \, (L_{i,2}\left(\partial y, x\right))\cos{(py)}, \, (L_{i,3}\left(\partial y, x\right))\sin{(py)},$$

$$(L_{i,4}\left(\partial y, x\right))\cos{(py)}, \quad i = 1, 2.$$

To determine the result of impacting of the MIF operator on any function this operator should be expanded in the power series. Each member of these series will contain integer power of the symbol ∂_y. Then it should perform a differentiation operation on the variable y of the function so many times what is the degree of the symbol ∂_y. Let's show how an operator $\sin{(\alpha\partial_y x)}$ impacts the function $\sin{(py)}$:

$$(\sin{(\alpha\partial_y x)})\sin{(py)} = \left(\sum_{i=0}^{\infty}\frac{(-1)^i(\alpha\partial_y x)^{2i+1}}{(2i+1)!}\right)\sin{(py)}$$

$$= \sum_{i=0}^{\infty}\frac{(-1)^i(\alpha x)^{2i+1}}{(2i+1)!}\frac{d^{2i+1}\sin{(py)}}{dy^{2i+1}}$$

$$= \sum_{i=0}^{\infty}\frac{(-1)^i(\alpha x)^{2i+1}}{(2i+1)!}(-1)^i(p)^{2i+1}\cos{(py)}$$

$$= \sum_{i=0}^{\infty}\frac{(-1)^{2i}(\alpha p x)^{2i+1}}{(2i+1)!}\cos{(py)} = \sinh{(\alpha p x)}\cos{(py)}.$$

Using this technique, the results of the impact of all transcendental operators on the trigonometric functions that compose the MIF operators are presented below

$$\sin{(\alpha\partial_y x)}\left(\sin(py)\right) = \sinh{(\alpha py)}\cos(py),$$

$$\sin{(\alpha\partial_y x)}\left(\cos(py)\right) = -\sinh{(\alpha py)}\sin(py),$$

$$\partial_y \sin{(\alpha\partial_y x)}\left(\sin(py)\right) = -p\sinh{(\alpha p x)}\sin(py),$$

$$\partial_y \sin{(\alpha\partial_y x)}\left(\cos(py)\right) = -p\sinh{(\alpha p x)}\cos(py),$$

$$\frac{\sin{(\alpha\partial_y x)}}{\partial_x}\left(\sin(py)\right) = \frac{\sinh{(\alpha p x)}}{p}\sin(py),$$

$$\frac{\sin{(\alpha\partial_y x)}}{\partial_x}\left(\cos(py)\right) = \frac{\sinh{(\alpha p x)}}{p}\cos(py),$$

$$\cos{(\alpha\partial_y x)}\left(\sin(py)\right) = \cosh{(\alpha p x)}\sin(py),$$

$$\cos{(\alpha\partial_y x)}\left(\cos(py)\right) = \cosh{(\alpha p x)}\cos(py),$$

$$\partial_y \cos(\alpha \partial_y x)(\sin(py)) = p \cosh(\alpha px) \cos(py),$$
$$\partial_y \cos(\alpha \partial_y x)(\cos(py)) = -p \cosh(\alpha px) \sin(py).$$

After evaluating the impact of the MIF operators on the corresponding trigonometric functions the displacements u and v will be obtained as expressions depending on hyperbolic functions. Using the Cauchy relations (6), the stress components will be also expressed through initial functions. Finally the MIF solution can be written in the matrix form as

$$\mathbf{U} = \mathbf{TL}\overline{\mathbf{U}}^0. \tag{10}$$

In (10) $\mathbf{U} = \{u, v, \sigma_x, \sigma_y, \tau_{xy}\}$ is the vector of the stress-strain state (SSS) components, $\overline{\mathbf{U}}^0 = \{\overline{u}^0, \overline{v}^0, \overline{\sigma}_x^0, \overline{\tau}_{xy}^0\}$ is the vector of the coefficients of the initial functions, $\mathbf{T} = \lceil \sin(py), \cos(py), \sin(py), \sin(py), \cos(py) \rfloor$ is a diagonal matrix of dimensions (5×5) and $\mathbf{L}$ is a matrix of dimensions (5×4) with following elements:

$$L_{1,1} = L_{3,3} = \big[(A_{1,1}A_{6,6}\alpha_1^2 - A_{1,1}A_{2,2} + A_{1,2}^2 + A_{1,2}A_{6,6}) \cosh(\alpha_1 px)$$
$$+ (-A_{1,1}A_{6,6}\alpha_2^2 + A_{1,1}A_{2,2} - A_{1,2}^2 - A_{1,2}A_{6,6}) \cosh(\alpha_2 px) \big] / d,$$

$$L_{1,2} = -L_{4,3} = -A_{6,6} \big[\alpha_2 (-A_{1,2}\alpha_1^2 - A_{2,2}) \sinh(\alpha_1 px)$$
$$+ \alpha_1 (A_{1,2}\alpha_2^2 + A_{2,2}) \sinh(\alpha_2 px) \big] / (\alpha_1 \alpha_2 d),$$

$$L_{1,3} = \big[\alpha_2 (A_{6,6}\alpha_1^2 - A_{2,2}) \sinh(\alpha_1 px)$$
$$+ \alpha_1 (-A_{6,6}\alpha_2^2 + A_{2,2}) \sinh(\alpha_2 px) \big] / (\alpha_1 \alpha_2 d),$$

$$L_{1,4} = -L_{2,3} = \big[(A_{1,2} + A_{6,6}) (\cosh(\alpha_1 px) - \cosh(\alpha_2 px)) \big] / (pd),$$

$$L_{2,1} = -L_{3,4} = A_{6,6} \big[\alpha_2 (-A_{1,1}\alpha_1^2 - A_{1,2}) \sinh(\alpha_1 px)$$
$$+ \alpha_1 (A_{1,1}\alpha_2^2 + A_{1,2}) \sinh(\alpha_2 px) \big] / (\alpha_1 \alpha_2 d),$$

$$L_{2,2} = L_{4,4} = A_{6,6} \big[(A_{1,1}\alpha_1^2 + A_{1,2}) \cosh(\alpha_1 px)$$
$$+ (-A_{1,1}\alpha_2^2 - A_{1,2}) \cosh(\alpha_2 px) \big] / d,$$

$$L_{2,4} = \big[\alpha_2 (A_{1,1}\alpha_1^2 - A_{6,6}) \sinh(\alpha_1 px)$$
$$+ \alpha_1 (-A_{1,1}\alpha_2^2 + A_{6,6}) \sinh(\alpha_2 px) \big] / (\alpha_1 \alpha_2 d),$$

$$L_{3,1} = -p \left\{ \alpha_2 \left[-A_{1,2}^2 A_{6,6} + \alpha_1^2 \left(A_{1,1}^2 A_{2,2} - A_{1,1} A_{1,2}^2 - 2 A_{1,1} A_{1,2} A_{6,6} \right) - \right. \right.$$
$$\left. + \alpha_1^4 A_{1,1}^2 A_{6,6} \right] \sinh (\alpha_1 px)$$
$$+ \alpha_1 \left[A_{1,2}^2 A_{6,6} + \alpha_2^2 \left(-A_{1,1}^2 A_{2,2} + A_{1,1} A_{1,2}^2 + 2 A_{1,1} A_{1,2} A_{6,6} \right) \right.$$
$$\left. \left. + \alpha_2^4 A_{1,1}^2 A_{6,6} \right] \sinh (\alpha_2 px) \right\} / (\alpha_1 \alpha_2 d) ,$$

$$L_{3,2} = -L_{4,1} = -p A_{6,6} \left(-A_{1,1} A_{2,2} + A_{1,2}^2 \right) \left(\cosh (\alpha_1 px) - \cosh (\alpha_2 px) \right) / d,$$

$$L_{4,2} = -p A_{6,6}^2 \left[\alpha_2 \left(-A_{1,1} \alpha_1^4 - 2 A_{1,2} \alpha_1^2 - A_{2,2} \right) \sinh (\alpha_1 px) \right.$$
$$\left. + \alpha_1 \left(A_{1,1} \alpha_2^4 + 2 A_{1,2} \alpha_2^2 + A_{2,2} \right) \sinh (\alpha_2 px) \right] / (\alpha_1 \alpha_2 d) ,$$

$$L_{5,1} = -p \left\{ \alpha_2 \left[-A_{1,2} A_{2,2} A_{6,6} \right. \right.$$
$$+ \alpha_1^2 \left(A_{1,1} A_{1,2} A_{2,2} - A_{1,1} A_{2,2} A_{6,6} - A_{1,2}^3 - A_{1,2}^2 A_{6,6} \right)$$
$$\left. - A_{1,1} A_{1,2} A_{6,6} \alpha_1^4 \right] \sinh (\alpha_1 px)$$
$$+ \alpha_1 \left[A_{1,2} A_{2,2} A_{6,6} + \alpha_2^2 \left(-A_{1,1} A_{1,2} A_{2,2} + A_{1,1} A_{2,2} A_{6,6} + A_{1,2}^3 + A_{1,2}^2 A_{6,6} \right) \right.$$
$$\left. \left. + A_{1,1} A_{1,2} A_{6,6} \alpha_2^4 \right] \sinh (\alpha_2 px) \right\} / (\alpha_1 \alpha_2 d) ,$$

$$L_{5,2} = -p A_{6,6} \left(A_{1,1} A_{2,2} - A_{1,2}^2 \right) \left(\alpha_1^2 \cosh (\alpha_1 px) - \alpha_2^2 \cosh (\alpha_2 px) \right) / d,$$

$$L_{5,3} = A_{6,6} \left(\left(A_{1,2} \alpha_1^2 + A_{2,2} \right) \cosh (\alpha_1 px) + \left(-A_{1,2} \alpha_2^2 - A_{2,2} \right) \cosh (\alpha_2 px) \right) / d,$$

$$L_{5,4} = - \left[\alpha_2 \left(-A_{2,2} A_{6,6} + \left(A_{1,1} A_{2,2} - A_{1,2}^2 - A_{1,2} A_{6,6} \right) \alpha_1^2 \right) \sinh (\alpha_1 px) \right.$$
$$\left. + \alpha_1 \left(A_{2,2} A_{6,6} + \left(-A_{1,1} A_{2,2} + A_{1,2}^2 + A_{1,2} A_{6,6} \right) \alpha_2^2 \right) \sinh (\alpha_2 px) \right] / (\alpha_1 \alpha_2 d) .$$

How to analyse the mechanical problem with the MIF solution (10)? Usually the initial line is associated with one of the boundary line of a solid (see Fig. 1). In this case two of the initial functions become equal specified boundary conditions. Two unknown initial functions can be found by satisfying boundary conditions on the boundary line $x = H$. For this with the solution (10) the corresponding SSS components are evaluated on this boundary and equate to the boundary condition to get a system to find unknown initial functions. We will call this technique the first MIF algorithm. In our problem two initial functions σ_x^0, τ_{xy}^0 are known. Two unknown initial functions can be found from the system

$$L_{3,1}(H)\bar{u}^0 + L_{3,2}(H)\bar{v}^0 = - \left(L_{3,3}(H)\bar{\sigma}_x^0 + L_{3,4}(H)\bar{\tau}_{xy}^0 \right),$$
$$L_{5,1}(H)\bar{u}^0 + L_{5,2}(H)\bar{v}^0 = - \left(L_{5,3}(H)\bar{\sigma}_x^0 + L_{5,4}(H)\bar{\tau}_{xy}^0 \right). \tag{11}$$

Note that on the vertical lines $y = 0, A$ of the rectangle the free support boundary conditions are satisfied: $u = 0$, $\sigma_y = 0$.

3   Investigation of the Solution and Discussion

Consider the behavior of the MIF solution (10) with increasing harmonic m of normal load $\overline{\sigma}_x^0 = q \sin (m\pi y/A)$ on the upper boundary of the rectangle with no load on the bottom boundary. Let the technical constants of the orthotropic material are $E_x = 10^6$, $E_y = 25\,10^6$, $\nu_{yx} = 0.25$, $\nu_{xy} = (E_x/E_y)\,\nu_{yx}$, $G_{xy} = 5\,10^5$ and the ratio of the width of the rectangle to its height is equal $A/H = 4$. The elastic constants $A_{i,j}$ are expressed through the technical modules of elasticity

as $A_{1,1} = \dfrac{E_x}{1 - \nu_{xy}\nu_{yx}}$, $A_{2,2} = \dfrac{E_y}{1 - \nu_{xy}\nu_{yx}}$, $A_{1,2} = \dfrac{E_x\nu_{yx}}{1 - \nu_{xy}\nu_{yx}} = \dfrac{E_y\nu_{xy}}{1 - \nu_{xy}\nu_{yx}}$,

$A_{6,6} = G_{xy}$.

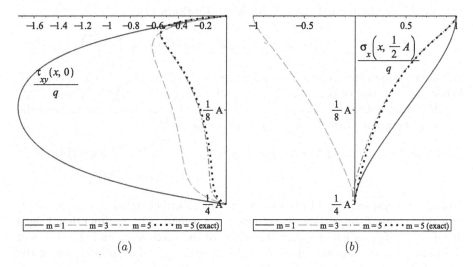

Fig. 2. Dimensionless shear stresses τ_{xy}/q (a) in the cross section $y = 0$ and normal stresses σ_x/q (b) in the cross section $y = A/2$ across the plate thickness when calculating by the first MIF algorithm. (Color figure online)

The dimensionless shear stresses τ_{xy}/q (the cross section $y = 0$) and normal stresses σ_x/q (b) (the cross section $y = A/2$) under three loads with harmonics $m = 1, 3, 5$ are presented on the Fig. 2. Calculations have been performed with double precision (16 decimal digits in the mantissa). The stresses under load with a harmonic of $m = 5$ in the neighbourhood of the bottom boundary are calculated with an error. This is evident for normal stress σ_x (the red dashdotted line in the Fig. 2b) which becomes negative in the lower part of the plate. For shear stresses, this fact is not so obvious (see the red dashdotted line in the Fig. 2a). To verify this, the Fig. 2 also presents a graph of the exact calculation of the shear stress (see the black dotted line). Minor differences start at the middle of the plate and reach the highest values at the lower boundary. With a further increase in harmonics, the region of unstable calculation expands, starting ever closer to the upper boundary of the plate. In this case, the errors can reach enormous values, reaching up to orders of tens.

What is the reason for such a behavior of our analytical solution (10)? The answer lies in the structure of the solution. It is necessary to do the calculation of the difference between two large quantities. The normal stress $\sigma_x(x, y)$ is calculated according to the MIF solution by the formula

$$\sigma_x(x, y) = \left[L_{3,1}(x)\, \overline{u}^0 + L_{3,2}(x)\, \overline{v}^0 + L_{3,3}(x)\, \overline{\sigma}_x^0 + L_{4,4}(x)\, \overline{\tau}_{xy}^0 \right] \sin\left(\frac{m\pi y}{A}\right).$$

From the boundary conditions on the upper face of the rectangle, it is determined that $\overline{\sigma}_x^0 = q$ and $\overline{\tau}_{xy}^0 = 0$ and the values of the initial displacements $\overline{u}^0$ and $\overline{v}^0$ can be found when solving the linear algebraic system (11). Thus, the formula for calculating the normal stress $\sigma_x(x, y)$ is transformed as

$$\sigma_x(x, y) = \left[L_{3,1}(x)\, \overline{u}^0 + L_{3,2}(x)\, \overline{v}^0 + L_{3,3}(x)\, q \right] \sin\left(\frac{m\pi y}{A}\right). \tag{12}$$

Consider computing with a mantissa length equal to 16 (double precision). When $m = 1$ the displacements $\overline{u}^0 = -1.333821951997764\,10^{-6}q$ and $\overline{v}^0 = -1.790251182\overline{184309}\,10^{-6}q$, thus the formula (12) for evaluating the value of the stress in the point $(49H/50, A/2)$ gives following result

$$\sigma_x(49H/50, A/2) = -1.51435897383\overline{9687}\,10^7\,\overline{u}^0 + 1.12569414523283\overline{43}\,10^8\,\overline{v}^0$$
$$- 0.1103210932\overline{2631}\,q.$$

Overlined digits in decimal notation represent incorrect digits that were determined by comparison with the exact calculations made with the mantissa length equal to 20. Taking into account the errors of the coefficients and the values of the initial functions in the given formula, the theoretical absolute error of the normal stress is expressed as

$$\Delta = \left[10^{-5}10^{-6} + 10^7 10^{-16} \right] + \left[10^{-5}10^{-6} + 10^8 10^{-16} \right] + \left[10^{-10} \right] = 10^{-9}.$$

Here in square brackets are the absolute errors of three members of the sum in (12). Substituting numerical values for $\overline{u}^0$ and $\overline{v}^0 q$ into the formula for σ_x, we get that the value of the normal stress is calculated as the difference

$$\sigma_x(49H/50, A/2) = \left(32.0861851 8\overline{321481} - 32.0845713 90\overline{48015} \right) q$$
$$= 0.0016137927 3\overline{4682} q. \tag{13}$$

It should be seen that the absolute error is two orders of magnitude less than theoretical one. This is a great result. But with increasing harmonics, the coefficients in the formula and the initial functions themselves are calculated with a large error, which leads to a catastrophic loss of accuracy. For $m = 5$ we have the following results:

Table 1. Limit values of harmonics for stable calculations depending on the geometric dimensions of the orthotropic rectangle and the mantissa length for the first MIF algorithm.

A/H	Mantissa length				
	16	24	32	40	48
10	14	22	30	39	47
6	8	13	18	23	28
4	5	9	12	15	18
2	2	4	6	7	9

$$\sigma_x\,(49H/50, A/2) = -2.9152639749\overline{48411}\,10^{17}\,\overline{u}^0$$
$$+2.041089167\overline{896948}\,10^{18}\,\overline{v}^0 - 4.109354721633\overline{858}\,10^9\,q,$$

$$\overline{u}^0 = -9.6\overline{48117714642594}\,10^{-8}q, \overline{v}^0 = -1.1\overline{76697993193913}\,10^{-8}q,$$

$$\Delta = \left[10^6 10^{-8} + 10^{17} 10^{-10}\right] + \left[10^7 10^{-8} + 10^{18} 10^{-11}\right] + \left[10^{-3}\right] = 10^7,$$

$$\sigma_x\,(49H/50, A/2) = \left(2.8\overline{12680999955915}\,10^{10} - 2.8\overline{12680999957558}\,10^{10}\right)q$$
$$= -0.\overline{16440418280285}\,10^{-1}q.$$

We see that there are no true digits in the obtained numerical value. Moreover, even the sign is negative, which can not be from a physical point of view. Such a behavior of the constructed solution is due to the fact that as the harmonic increases, the values of the matrix components and the vector of the right-hand side of the ill-conditioned linear system (11) begin to grow. The length of the mantissa is not enough to accurately represent the integer part of a number of large order. Increasing the length of the mantissa, the MIF solution allows to obtain exact numerical values. The value of the "stable" mantissa depends on material characteristics and the ratio of geometrical dimensions of the rectangle. Table 1 shows the "stable" mantissa values for the considered orthotropic material.

A way to increase the harmonic of stable calculations with a given mantissa can be offered. It is necessary to change the coordinate system by shifting the axis Oy to a point located in the middle of the height of the rectangle. In this case, the initial functions will no longer be equal to the given boundary conditions. Four equations will be required to find all four unknown initial functions

$$L_{3,1}(-H/2)\overline{u}^0 + L_{3,2}(-H/2)\overline{v}^0 + L_{3,3}(-H/2)\overline{\sigma}_x^0 + L_{3,4}(-H/2)\overline{\tau}_{xy}^0 = \sigma_x^-,$$
$$L_{4,1}(-H/2)\overline{u}^0 + L_{4,2}(-H/2)\overline{v}^0 + L_{4,3}(-H/2)\overline{\sigma}_x^0 + L_{4,4}(-H/2)\overline{\tau}_{xy}^0 = \tau_{xy}^-,$$
$$L_{3,1}(H/2)\overline{u}^0 + L_{3,2}(H/2)\overline{v}^0 + L_{3,3}(H/2)\overline{\sigma}_x^0 + L_{3,4}(H/2)\overline{\tau}_{xy}^0 = \sigma_x^+,$$
$$L_{4,1}(H/2)\overline{u}^0 + L_{4,2}(H/2)\overline{v}^0 + L_{4,3}(H/2)\overline{\sigma}_x^0 + L_{4,4}(H/2)\overline{\tau}_{xy}^0 = \tau_{xy}^+.$$

Table 2. Limit values of harmonics for stable calculations depending on the geometric dimensions of the orthotropic rectangle and the mantissa length for the second MIF algorithm.

A/H	Mantissa length				
	16	**24**	**32**	**40**	**48**
10	25	45	61	81	91
6	15	27	37	49	59
4	9	17	23	31	39
2	5	9	12	16	19

Here σ_x^+, τ_x^+ are boundary conditions on the upper rectangle's face and σ_x^-, τ_x^- are ones on the lower rectangle's face. We will call this algorithm the second MIF algorithm. Figure 2 shows stable calculations up to the eleventh harmonic (exclusively). We can also observe the difference in the calculated stresses ($m = 11$) with double precision (red dashdotted graphs) and exact results (black dotted graphs).

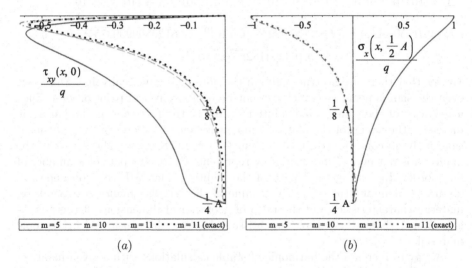

$$\begin{array}{cccc} \text{—— } m=5 & \text{—— } m=10 & \text{——·— } m=11 & \text{····· } m=11 \text{ (exact)} \end{array}$$

(a)   (b)

Fig. 3. Dimensionless shear stresses τ_{xy}/q (a) in the cross section $y = 0$ and normal stresses σ_x/q (b) in the cross section $y = A/2$ across the plate thickness when calculating by the second MIF algorithm.

This technique increases the limit value of the harmonic for the mantissa length because the maximum value of the coordinate x is equal $\pm H/2$ (see Table 2).

4   Conclusion

We have seen that MIF solutions of bending problems of linear-elastic orthotropic rectangular plates under boundary conditions in the form of trigonometric functions have computational instability that does not allow them to be used directly for loads represented by trigonometric series.

Computational experiments have shown that with the increase of the load harmonic the computational instability of the algorithm of the method of initial function begins to manifest itself. Starting with a certain harmonic number, calculations of the stress-strain state components in the neighbourhood of the lower face of the plate begin to be performed with a large error. This error forms from errors in the determination of unknown initial functions solving an ill-conditioned system of linear equations and errors in the representation of the coefficients of this system and its right parts having an order greater than the number of significant digits in the mantissa of the representation of real numbers.

This disadvantage of the method can be partially overcome by combining the initial line with the median line of the rectangle. The limiting values of "stable" harmonics are doubled, which is associated with a decrease in two times the coordinate values of the boundary lines of the rectangle.

But this approach does not definitively solve the problem of instability of computations. Radical results can be achieved by increasing the length of the mantissa in the representation of real numbers. Of course, this is due both to time costs and to the increase in the amount of RAM used. However, with the presence of high-speed modern computers, as well as analytical computing systems (for example, Maple) and programming languages (for example, Python) with the possibility of a simple transition to calculations with a mantissa of arbitrary length, these shortcomings do not seem to be so significant.

In conclusion, we note that the presented investigation of the stability of the method of initial functions were used in computational algorithms based on a common solution for an isotropic/orthotropic rectangle. This solution was obtained by the superposition method as the sum of two (for the plane problem) and three (for the spatial problem) solutions obtained by the method of initial functions in each of the independent coordinates. With its help, the problems of bending a grillage [23] and an isotropic/orthotropic rectangle [24] with arbitrary boundary conditions on all their faces were investigated. For the plane problem of the theory of elasticity, a method of analytical decomposition has been developed on the basis of the general solution for analysing complex inhomogeneous elastic systems [25].

References

1. Lur'e, A.I.: On the problem of equilibrium of a plate of variable thickness. Proc. Leningrad Ind. Inst. **5**, 57–80 (1936)
2. Lur'e, A.I.: On the problem of equilibrium of a plate of variable thickness. J. Appl. Math. Mech. **6**(2/3), 151–160 (1942)

3. Lur'e, A.I.: Three Dimensional Problems of Theory of Elasticity. Willey, New York (1964)
4. Vlasov, V.Z.: Method of initial functions in problems of the theory of elasticity. Bull. USSR Acad. Sci. **7**, 49–69 (1955)
5. Vlasov, V.Z.: Method of initial functions in problems of theory of thick plates and shells. In: Proceedings of 9th International Conference of Applied Mechanics, vol. 6, pp. 321–330. University of Brussels, Belgium (1957)
6. Vlasov, V.Z., Leontev, N.N.: Beams, plates and shells on elastic foundations. NASA-TTF-357 TT65-50135 (1966)
7. Das, Y.C., Setlur, A.V.: Method of initial functions in two-dimensional elastodynamic problems. J. Appl. Mech. Trans. ASME **37**(1), 137–140 (1970)
8. Iyengar, K.K.T.S., Chandrashekhara, K., Sebastian, V.K.: Thick rectangular beams. J. Eng. Mech. Div. ASCE **100**(6), 1277–1282 (1974)
9. Kameswara Rao, N.S.V., Das, Y.C.: A mixed method in elasticity. J. Appl. Mech. Trans. ASME **44**(1), 51–56 (1977)
10. Sundara Raja Iyengar, K.T., Raman, P.V.: Free vibration of rectangular beams of arbitrary depth. Acta Mech. **32**(4), 249–259 (1979)
11. Volkov, A.N.: Theory of thick shells on the basis of the method of initial functions. Soviet Appl. Mech. **7**(10), 1093–1097 (1974)
12. Sundara Raja Iyengar, K.T., Chandrashekhara, K., Sebastian, V.K.: Thick circular cylindrical shells under axisymmetric loading. Acta Mech. **23**(1–2), 137–144 (1975)
13. Celep, Z.: On the axially symmetric vibration of thick circular plates. Ing. Arch. **47**(6), 411–420 (1978)
14. Faraji, S., Archer, R.R.: Method of initial functions for thick shells. Int. J. Solids Struct. **21**(8), 851–863 (1985)
15. Iyengar, K.T.S., Pandya, S.K.: Application of the method of initial functions for the analysis of composite laminated plates. Ing. Arch. **56**(6), 407–416 (1986)
16. Galileev, S.M., Matrosov, A.V., Verizhenko, V.E.: Method of initial functions for layered and continuously inhomogeneous plates and shells. Mech. Compos. Mater. **30**(4), 386–392 (1995)
17. Galileev, S.M., Matrosov, A.V.: Method of initial functions in the computation of sandwich plates. Int. Appl. Mech. **31**(6), 469–476 (1996)
18. Dubey, S.K.: Analysis of homogeneous orthotropic deep beams. J. Struct. Eng. (Madras) **32**(2), 109–116 (2005)
19. Matrosov, A.V., Shirunov, G.N.: Analyzing thick layered plates under their own weight by the method of initial functions. Mater. Phys. Mech. **31**(1–2), 36–39 (2017)
20. Gao, Y., Wang, M.: Refined theory of deep rectangular beams based on general solutions of elasticity. Sci. China Ser. G-Phys. Astron. **49**(3), 291–303 (2006)
21. Ghugal, Y.M., Sharma, R.: A refined shear deformation theory for exure of thick beams. Latin Am. J. Solids Struct. **8**(2), 183–195 (2011)
22. Galileev, S.M., Matrosov, A.V.: Method of initial functions: stable algorithms in the analysis of thick laminated composite structures. Compos. Struct. **39**(3–4), 255–262 (1997)
23. Goloskokov, D.P., Matrosov, A.V.: Comparison of two analytical approaches to the analysis of grillages. In: Proceedings of the International Conference on "Stability and Control Processes" in Memory of V.I. Zubov, SCP 2015, Art. No. 7342169, pp. 382–385. Institute of Electrical and Electronics Engineers Inc. (2015)

24. Matrosov, A.V.: A superposition method in analysis of plane construction. In: Proceedings of the International Conference on "Stability and Control Processes" in Memory of V.I. Zubov, SCP 2015, Art. No. 7342156, pp. 414–416. Institute of Electrical and Electronics Engineers Inc. (2015)
25. Goloskokov, D.P., Matrosov, A.V.: Approximate analytical solutions in the analysis of elastic structures of complex geometry. In: AIP Conference Proceedings of 8th Polyakhov's Reading, vol. 1959, Art. No. 070013. American Institute of Physics Inc. (2018)

Clustering Data Streams: A Complex Network Approach

Sandy Porto[1] and Marcos G. Quiles[2]([✉])

[1] National Institute for Space Research (INPE), São José dos Campos, SP, Brazil
`sandyporto@gmail.com`
[2] Institute of Science and Technology, Federal University of São Paulo (UNIFESP),
São José dos Campos, SP, Brazil
`quiles@unifesp.br`

Abstract. Clustering data streams is an interesting and challenging problem. Although several solutions have been proposed in the literature, some drawbacks remain. For instance, how to deal effectively with the offline process for partitioning the micro-clusters into macro-clusters is still an open problem. Typically, the k-means algorithm is considered in this phase, which despite precise results, require a mandatory user-defined parameter k, that defines the number of expected clusters. In this paper, we propose a new clustering method for data stream, named Prototype Networks. This method takes the complex network structure to represent the set of micro-clusters. This approach has proven to be advantageous mainly because these networks have an inherent community structure. As a consequence, the offline phase might be easily handled by a community detection algorithm, such as Infomap. The communities detected represents the cluster structure of the data assuming that the network construction was designed for this purpose. Computer experiments demonstrated the feasibility of the proposed approach. Moreover, the proposed method can detect automatically the number of clusters in evolving scenarios, which is a useful feature when dealing with data streams with concept drift.

Keywords: Data streams · Clustering · Complex network

1 Introduction

Data streams are a concept of data in which elements are streamed live [2,6,13, 14,21,22]. Due to its live nature, the volume of data might overcome the computational resources making it difficult to apply traditional machine learning techniques. Moreover, data patterns, such as clusters, can evolve through time, imposing an additional challenge when dealing with data streams [15,18,19,24,27].

Similarly to traditional machine learning scenarios, several tasks can be performed with data streams, such as data classification and data clustering [2,6]. Here we will focus on the data clustering problem, which might be roughly defined as the problem of partitioning the samples into groups of similar objects.

© Springer Nature Switzerland AG 2019
S. Misra et al. (Eds.): ICCSA 2019, LNCS 11619, pp. 52–65, 2019.
https://doi.org/10.1007/978-3-030-24289-3_5

Several approaches have been proposed to deal with data clustering of data streams [14, 21]. A critical restriction imposed on data stream algorithms is the one-pass constraint. It states that each sample must be analyzed only once by the algorithm. To overcome this limitation, algorithms have employed the strategy of dividing the task into two phases, named online and offline [1, 4]. The online phase, which is conditioned to the one-pass constraint, is responsible for summarizing the incoming data. On the other hand, the offline one is accountable for analyzing the summary provided by the online phase to extract the partitions and detecting the changes into the data trend [2, 3, 6, 29].

Considering the importance of the summary structure generated by the online phase and taken into account by the second, here, we investigate an alternative data representation via a complex network framework [11, 12, 20]. Explicitly, data prototypes are modeled as nodes and their similarities encoded into the links of the network. As a consequence, the generated network highlights the structure of the micro-clusters and their relations encoded in a powerful relational structure, a complex network.

A Complex Network posses many features that can be extracted from its structure; among them, there is a topological feature known as community structure that divides the vertices into groups according to their links density. Thus, these communities, once revealed by a community detection algorithm, might be interpreted as a clusters partition if the creation and maintenance of the network are designed for this purpose. In summary, we propose a clustering algorithm in which the online phase is responsible for generating the network of prototypes, or the summary of the samples, while the offline phase carries out the community detection process, or the clustering partition.

Three experiments were performed. The first two evaluate the clustering accuracy achieved by our approach, and the third one verifies whether the community structure of the network evolves revealing the natural cluster evolution existent in the data flow. Results showed that the communities in the network indeed follows the changes in the cluster pattern, demonstrating the capacity of the method for detecting changes in the data flow, such as drifts. Although revealing the evolution of the cluster structure on evolving data, our method delivers a slightly lower accuracy in comparison to benchmark approaches, such as the CluStream algorithm, which is still one of the drawbacks of our approach.

This paper is organized as follows. Section 2 presents the related work. Our proposed algorithm, named Prototype Network, is presented in Sect. 3. Section 4 presents our experiments and results. Finally, in Sect. 5, some conclusions are discussed.

2   Related Work

Nowadays, data have been generated in large quantities and the significant technological advance of the last two decades is directly related to this phenomenon [2, 19, 29, 30]. Advances in hardware and software have allowed anyone to have access to some sort of data flow even on a large scale [7,29]. To cite a few examples: social networks data, such as Facebook, Twitter, Waze, Uber, Google Maps; time series related to finance, actions and exchange, or associated with the processing of earth observation images can be used for almost anyone with some knowledge on how to manipulate it.

These data flows are known in the literature as a data stream, that is, a sequence of objects generated and made available automatically at high frequency through the most varied type of sources. Data streams have received much attention in recent years because manipulating, observing, mining, grouping, classifying and seizing this type of data is being demanded by a variety of organizations [3–5,31].

However, this availability of data has no practical value if it cannot be intelligently transformed into meaningful information [7]. These flows need to be stored and analyzed in some way, even though they have a different kind of restrictions, for instance, a finite set of resources, particularly processing time and memory usage [2,7,29,31]. Beyond difficulties discussed above, data streams have yet even more challenges, for example, the clustering of evolving data, i.e., how to cluster data that is fluid? In the next section, these challenges behind this task are highlighted.

2.1   Challenges of Clustering Data Streams

Firstly, from a computational point of view, a data stream F can be represented as a sequence of objects $x^1, x^2, \cdots, x^N$, such that $F = \left\{x^i\right\}_{i=1}^{N}$, and $N \to \infty$ because that sequence is potentially unlimited. Secondly, each object x^i has intrinsic to itself a time stamp i, which can be assumed as a primary key. Thirdly, the object x^i is a vector of attributes of dimension n, such that $x^i = \left[x_j^i\right]_{j=1}^{n}$. Fourthly and finally, the value of each attribute x_j^i can be continuous, categorical or mixed [8,15,29,31].

Therefore, due to time constraints, it is necessary that the objects from the data streams can be processed, analyzed and the model possibly updated as fast as the arrival rate of the data [5,19]. In addition, space constraints make it unworkable or impractical to store a copy of each received object. In this way, an abstraction step can be used as a way of cutting the data into relevant attributes [7,31].

After the abstraction data phase, the result needs to be processed, analyzed and compared, so the model can decide what to do with the sample. The object can be discarded or incorporated into the model, either way, the decision, and possibly update should perform faster than the arrival of new data. For comparison, in traditional data analysis, a representative or decision model is usually created after analyzing the data in its entirety more than once [4,8,19]. In the context of data streams, it is also likely that the model has to keep at least some meta-data (timestamp, for example) in this process, as these can contribute to the detection of concept drifts.

In short, the large amount of data flowing into the system cannot be stored in its entirety. Thus, their contribution to the model construction and update is minimal. However, in some cases, if the tools mentioned above, the collection of meta-data and the abstraction steps, combined with an adequate structure to keep an information summary of data, it is possible to create a framework which can lead to near-optimal results. The structure used in this work is inspired by Micro-Clustering approach used by Aggarwal *et al.* in CluStream Algorithm [1,2,4] which are detailed in the next sections.

2.2   Micro-clustering Approach

The summary structure has to be concise enough for updating model be efficient and, at the same time, to contain temporal and space data enough to ensure an accurate cluster partition through time. Those constraints are difficult to achieve and raise the following questions: (a) the structure has to save all data ever received or will erase information identified as imprecise or old? If it decides to delete information, in which moments in time? and (b) how that same structure can be the model that will provide cluster partition and detect concept drift through time?

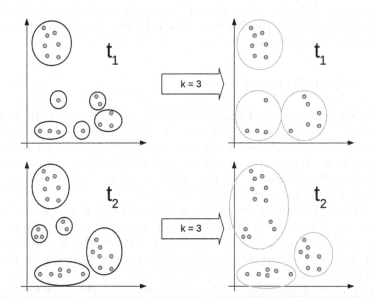

Fig. 1. Macro-cluster creation setting parameter k to 3 on CluStream.

CluStream uses a concept known as *micro-clusters* that are efficient to collect data from a data stream. The micro-clusters maintain statistical information about nearby samples in data space. CluStream process the data twice, first the online phase is responsible for processing the arriving data and to alter the micro-clusters if necessary, and the offline component is responsible for analyzing the summary in order to obtain current cluster partition and to maintain an index which will tracking changes in relevant aspects to detect concept drift. In this scenario, the micro-clusters set composes the *summary structure*.

Comparison of the results when applying k-means on micro-cluster's state is also useful to detect major changes in data. In Fig. 1, the macro-clusters, which are the result of applying k-means ($k = 3$) on micro-clusters at time t_1 and time t_2, could give insights on how data changes.

One problem of using k-means is the mandatory user-defined parameter k. After all, if the k value could be discovered alongside the clusters themselves, thus the clustering would become parameter-free. This paper proposes a summary structure that besides keep micro-clusters information, also keeps information about how much these micro-clusters get together or split out trough time. That extra information provides inputs for clustering process that makes unnecessary to predetermine parameter k's value, even though costs accuracy and effectiveness. Nevertheless, that could be used in some context.

The algorithm proposes in this paper stores the summary in a structure inspired by Complex Networks. These networks have a property known as *community structure*, that could be interpreted as a representation of data partition in clusters. For that, one has to perform some community detection algorithm in the network, for example, Infomap, which do not need to predetermine the value of parameter k [25,26].

3   Prototype Network

This paper proposes a novel method based on a complex network structure. The method, named Prototype Network, or PN, considers two sets: vertices $V = \{v_1, v_2, \cdots, v_n\}$, and a set of edges $E = \{(v_i, v_j) \mid v_i \text{ and } v_j \text{ are neighbors}\}$, which jointly are represented as $PN = \{(V, E)\}$. Each vertex and edge are represented as list structures. Vertices are indexed by its integer primary key i and a tuple (i, j) is assigned to each edge.

The Prototype Network structure considered in this work contains a function that adds a new vertex that contains the object x^i to the network $PN = newVertex(PN, x^i)$. In this function the object x^i is loaded to a vertex v_i, added to the network and the network is updated if necessary, following the flowchart contained in the Fig. 2.

In the context of this paper, the Prototype Network will be used for clustering a Data Stream, so there are some restrictions on time and memory. The time constraint says that the update of the structure must be as fast as the arrival rate of new objects and the memory constraint says that the structure can not grow at the same pace as the data stream because this would lead to an unlimited structure.

Thus, when a new vertex is added to the network, the structure invokes the function that chooses the neighbors for it. The *chooseNeighborhood*() function

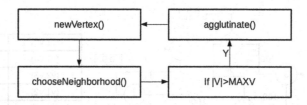

Fig. 2. The following steps after calling the *newVertex*() function. First, the *chooseNeighborhood*() function is invoked that choose which vertices already in the network will make pair with the new one, after that, it is verified if the size of the network, that is, the number of vertices becomes higher than parameter *MAXV*. If yes, the algorithm calls the *agglutinate*() function, which decreases the number of vertices by merging two of them into one and adding the newly merged vertex using the *newVertex*() function itself.

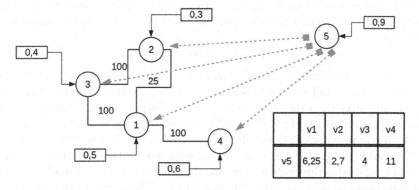

Fig. 3. Prototype Network before choose the neighborhood for vertex v_5. The network to the left possess four vertices and four edges, the vertices v_1, v_2, v_3, v_4, and the edges (v_1, v_3), (v_2, v_3), (v_1, v_2), (v_1, v_4), the value of object x for each vertex is represented in rectangles attached to the circles and the value of similarity of each edge is represented by numbers attached to the line. The red arrows show which pair of vertices have their similarity calculated. Finally, in bottom right, a table resuming the results of similarities. (Color figure online)

choose some existing vertices that will link to the new one. For each selected vertex, a new edge is created. Additionally, a user-defined parameter, called *MAXV*, tells the maximum number of vertices allowed in the network structure.

The function *newVertex*() is continually invoked until the number of vertices exceeds *MAXV*. When this occurs, the Prototype Network runs the agglutination method, which involves merging pairs of network's vertices in order to reestablish $|V| = MAXV$.

It can be seen that there are two crucial steps to prototype network algorithm: neighborhood choice (Figs. 3 and 4) and agglutination (Figs. 4 and 5). The choice of the neighborhood occurs when a new vertex is added, the data sample loaded into the vertex will be compared to the data stored in the other vertices of the

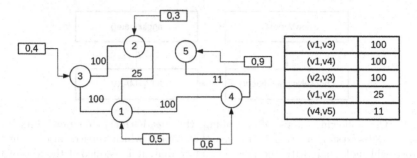

Fig. 4. Resulting Prototype Network after choosing neighborhood for vertex v_5 and showing all current edges on the network.

network, one by one, as shown in Fig. 3. Here, the comparison between patterns is performed via a similarity measurement based on the Euclidean Distance, as in Eq. 1.

$$sim(v_i \rightarrow x, v_j \rightarrow x) = 1/dist(v_i \rightarrow x, v_j \rightarrow x) \tag{1}$$

After this calculation, a cut-off strategy is used to define the neighbors of the new vertex, the cutoff is established by choosing only those vertices that have greater similarity than the mean plus standard deviation of all computed similarities. For example, in Fig. 3, the similarities obtained are 6.25, 2.7, 4 and 11, so the mean is approximately 6 and the standard deviation is approximately 3.6, so the threshold value is $6 + 3.6 = 9.6$, all possible connections in which the similarity are below this threshold are discarded. Therefore, in this example, only the v_4 will be assumed as a neighbor of new vertex v_5. The weight of that edge is set accordingly to the similarity between these nodes, that in this example is 11.

The other crucial step, the *agglutinate()* function, examines the set of edges and verifies those that have greater weight. Assuming that *MAXV* parameter value for the network in Fig. 4 is 4, some edge, and therefore a pair of nodes will be agglutinate (merged). As explained previously, this weight is proportional to the similarity between the objects stored in the vertices. In the network presented in Fig. 4, the possible values are shown in the table depicted in this figure.

Assuming, that edge (v_2, v_3) is selected, the two vertices v_2 and v_3 are submitted to the following process: it saves the objects information and delete the two vertices of the network, merges the information of the two objects (i.e. compute the centroid) and adds a new vertex with the resulting object represented by the new centroid. This process is presented in Fig. 5.

The addition of the agglutinated vertex follows the same process of adding a new object, so it calls the function *newVertex()* that determine the neighbors using the function *chooseNeighborhood()*, and, if necessary, performs the agglutination method again, as reproduced in Fig. 5. The final result of vertex v_5 addition can be seen in Fig. 5.

Finally, to perform the partition of the network and reveal the clusters, a community detection method is applied, which divides the vertices into groups according to the edge's densities. It is worth noting that each vertex represents

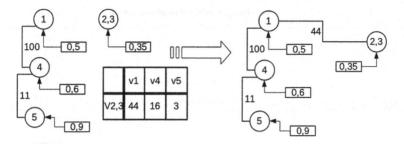

Fig. 5. Final Result Network after choose the neighbourhood for vertex v_5 and performed the *agglutinate*() function.

a prototype of the sample, or a micro-cluster, thus, more than one object is assigned to it. Thus, if vertex v_i is determined as part of community C^i, all objects represented by v_i will be considered belonging to the same group of all other objects of vertices of C^i. Although any community detection method could be taken into account, here, we adopted the Infomap algorithm [25,26], due to is higher efficiency and absence of parameters.

4 Experiments

Three experiments were performed to evaluate the Prototype Network. The first two evaluates the accuracy of the clustering process and compares its outcome with the results provided by the CluStream algorithm. The third experiment checks if the number of communities in the structure follows the change in the number of clusters of the data as the data stream evolves. Eventually, the data stream experiences a change in the number of groups, which might increases or decreases. However, detecting the emergence of a new community is especially difficult as time is needed to rule out the hypothesis that arriving new data are not just noises.

It should be stated that the CluStream algorithm was adopted as a competitor in our experiments due to the following reasons: (1) The CluStream is considered a benchmark algorithm in the literature; (2) it is on of the most cited methods for clustering data streams; and (3) both CluStream and Prototype Network use the micro-clustering approach.

All the experiments treated in this work were carried out on a PC with an Intel i3-6100 3.70 GHz processor with 4 cores and 8 Gb of RAM running Ubuntu 16.04.5 LTS 64-bit Operating System. The entire development of the algorithm was performed in R [23] in RStudio version 1.1.456. The packages *igraph* [9] and *stream* [16,17] were used, respectively, for the treatment of complex network-like structures, and for the generation of synthetic data and implementation and execution of the CluStream algorithm used in the experiments.

The CluStream algorithm had its parameter M set to 200, that is, the structure consists of 200 micro-clusters, and its parameter h set to 1000, although

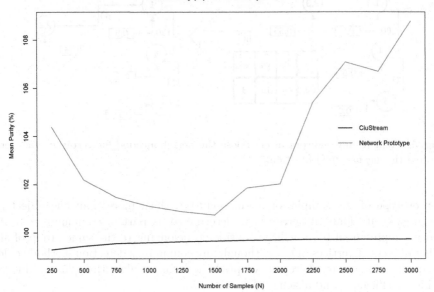

Fig. 6. First experiment result when $k = 3$. Mean Purity (%) value for the first N samples being N equal to 250 until 3000. (Color figure online)

these values do not influence results in this experiment. In the prototype network, the $MAXV$ parameter was also set to 200, that is, the network will consist of a vertex set of at most 200 vertices.

In order to execute the k-means for CluStream algorithm, the parameter k must be adjusted to be equal to the number of true classes. In the Infomap algorithm, the network itself is the only input parameter. The return result of each is compared to the true class and the purity of the partition in clusters is measured.

The value of the accuracy is calculated using the purity measure that verifies what percentage of the elements in each cluster belong to the dominant class. The dominant class of a cluster is the true class to which the majority cluster's elements belong. The purity measure is a positive value and best value is 100%, but results could be lower or higher than that, if the number of clusters n_C is equal or lower than k, than the purity will assume a value between 0 and 100, in the other case, if number of clusters n_C is higher than k, but two or more of clusters actually belongs to the same true classes, than purity will be higher than 100%.

Considering that $|C_i|$ is the size of cluster C_i, and $|C_i^d|$ is quantity of elements which belong to dominant class d, than purity could be calculated according to Eq. 2.

$$purity = \frac{\sum_{i=1}^{n_c} \frac{|C_i^d|}{|C_i|}}{k} \times 100\% \qquad (2)$$

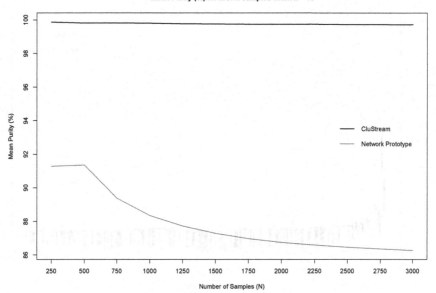

Fig. 7. First experiment result when $k = 10$. Mean Purity (%) value for the first N samples being N equal to 250 until 3000. (Color figure online)

The first experiment uses a ten-dimensional data stream with $N = 3000$ samples generated by the package *stream*. Each arriving object is analyzed and inserted into the structure, either the structure of the micro-clusters or the prototype network. After that, the k-means is applied to the micro-clusters and the Infomap community detection algorithm to the prototype network. Two versions of this experiment were analyzed: (1) when the data generated were divided into three clusters, thus $k = 3$, and (2) with ten clusters, $k = 10$.

The results can be seen in Figs. 6 and 7, both shows the evolution of purity mean measured every time the data stream received 250 samples, that is, the graph shows the mean value of purity for the first N results for clusters partition for each algorithm when the number of samples N was equal to 250, 500, 750 and so on until reach 3000 samples.

Because the CluStream has parameter k fixed, purity measured will always be between 0 and 100, and the algorithm achieves 100% most of the time in both versions of the experiment, $k = 3$ and $k = 10$. Prototype Network, on the other hand, might achieve mean values higher than 100% when $k = 3$, which indicates that, occasionally, $n_C > k$, i.e. two or more clusters belongs to the same correct class. When $k = 10$, Prototype Network mean purity value decay over time reaching 85%.

The second experiment uses a database available in the UCI repository [10], called Vehicle Silhouettes [28]. The eighteen attributes of this data set are numbers extracted from the processing of 846 different images that have silhouettes of four different types of vehicles. Therefore, the database has 846 instances,

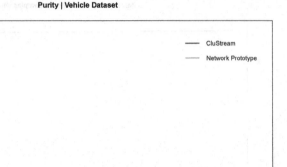

Fig. 8. First experiment result for Vehicle Data set. The graph shows purity value for CluStream and Prototype Network after arrival of each new sample. (Color figure online)

$N = 846$, 18 dimensions, and four classes. Although the database is normally interpreted in its entirety in traditional algorithms, in this experiment it was adapted to imitate the behavior of a data stream, that is, each instance is presented separately to the model.

The results of this experiment show the evolution of the purity value with each introduction of a new object for both CluStream and Prototype Network, and can be seen in Fig. 8. The graph shows that, in this case, the Prototype Network algorithm obtained even better results than CluStream. In addition, it is possible to observe in this experiment that Prototype Network algorithm had better results in the discovery of the number of clusters, since it has a purity value less than or equal to 100% most of the time.

Next, the third experiment evaluates whether the number of communities follows automatically the number of clusters in data stream. In special, when new clusters are introduced to the algorithm. This experiment also considered data generated by package *stream*. However, the data is reorganized so that groups of classes are put together in batches that will be presented to the algorithm. The goal is to simulate the arrival of several new clusters in the data stream at certain moments in time and, without disregarding the old data, verify if the community structure also increases the number of communities, following the movement of the clusters.

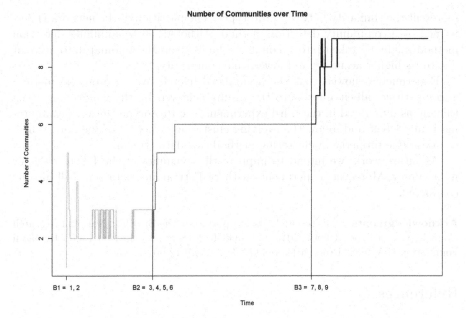

Fig. 9. Second experiment results. Shows how number of communities changes as new samples of each batch are introduced to the Prototype Network Structure. (Color figure online)

This experiment assume a ten-dimensional data stream with $N = 3000$ samples. The data is divided into nine true classes and three batches $B_1 = \{1, 2\}$, $B_2 = \{3, 4, 5, 6\}$ and $B_3 = \{7, 8, 9\}$, in total batch B_1 has 717 elements, batch B_2 has 1313 elements, batch B_3, 970, summing up the 3000 samples. The order of the elements is as follow, at first, only elements of batch 1 appear in the data stream but at random order within the batch, followed by the elements of batch 2, and then batch 3, also at random order within each other.

Figure 9 shows the number of communities in the network structure at each processing of a new object. Initially, the structure still are in construction phase, but eventually stable in 2 or 3 communities, although the number of true classes was just 2 for batch B_1, than when batch B_2 is introduced, rapidly the network adjust itself and stable in six communities which is the number of true classes too. Finally, batch B_3 is introduced, and after a transient, it reaches the same number of true classes correctly.

5   Conclusions

Developing methods able to deal with evolving data stream is still a big challenge. Here, we have proposed a novel method, named Prototype Network (PN). The PN provides a new manner to summarize the data into micro-clusters, prototypes, represented as vertices in a network structure. The edges between vertices represent the similarity between prototypes. The partition of the network is performed by a community detection method. Although any community detection method might be taken into account, we have taken the Infomap into account due to its higher accuracy and lower time complexity.

Experiments showed that the accuracy delivered by the proposed method is competitive, albeit inferior to the results achieved by the CluStream. Even though, as illustrated in the third experiment, the Prototype Network can automatically detect and follow the evolving clustering structure of the data, which is a desirable property in clustering methods for data stream.

As future work, we intend to improve the dynamics of the PN to enhance its accuracy. Moreover, experiments with real streaming data sets will also be conducted.

Acknowledgments. This research was supported by the Brazilian National Research Council (CNPq Proc. 310908/2015-9 & 434886/2018-1) and the São Paulo Research Foundation (FAPESP Proc. 2011/18496-7 & 2015/50122-0).

References

1. Aggarwal, C.C.: A framework for diagnosing changes in evolving data streams. In: Proceedings of the 2003 ACM SIGMOD International Conference on Management of Data, SIGMOD 2003, pp. 575–586. ACM, New York (2003)
2. Aggarwal, C.C.: Data Streams: Models and Algorithms. Advances in Database Systems. Springer, Heidelberg (2006). https://doi.org/10.1007/978-0-387-47534-9
3. Aggarwal, C.C.: An Introduction to Data Streams. In: Aggarwal, C.C. (ed.) Data Streams. Advances in Database Systems, vol. 31, pp. 1–8. Springer, Boston (2007). https://doi.org/10.1007/978-0-387-47534-9_1
4. Aggarwal, C.C., Han, J., Wang, J., Yu, P.S.: A framework for clustering evolving data streams. In: Proceedings of the 29th International Conference on Very Large Data Bases, VLDB 2003, vol. 29, pp. 81–92. VLDB Endowment (2003). http://dl.acm.org/citation.cfm?id=1315451.1315460
5. Aggarwal, C.C., Yu, P.S.: On clustering massive text and categorical data streams. Knowl. Inf. Syst. **24**(2), 171–196 (2010)
6. Amini, A., Wah, T.Y., Saboohi, H.: On density-based data streams clustering algorithms: a survey. J. Comput. Sci. Technol. **29**(1), 116–141 (2014)
7. de Andrade Silva, J., Hruschka, E.R., Gama, J.: An evolutionary algorithm for clustering data streams with a variable number of clusters. Expert Syst. Appl. **67**, 228–238 (2017)
8. Barddal, J.P., Gomes, H.M., Enembreck, F.: SNCStream: a social network-based data stream clustering algorithm. In: Proceedings of the 30th Annual ACM Symposium on Applied Computing, SAC 2015, pp. 935–940. ACM, New York (2015)
9. Csardi, G., Nepusz, T.: The igraph software package for complex network research. InterJournal Complex Syst. **1695**, 1–9 (2006). http://igraph.org
10. Dua, D., Graff, C.: UCI machine learning repository (2019). http://archive.ics.uci.edu/ml
11. Estrada, E.: The Structure of Complex Networks: Theory and Applications. Oxford University Press, Oxford (2011)

12. Costa, L.F., Rodrigues, F.A., Travieso, G., Boas, P.R.V.: Characterization of complex networks: a survey of measurements. Adv. Phys. **56**, 167–242 (2007)
13. Gaber, M.M., Zaslavsky, A., Krishnaswamy, S.: A survey of classification methods in data streams. In: Aggarwal, C.C. (ed.) Data Streams. Advances in Database Systems, vol. 31, pp. 39–59. Springer, Boston (2007). https://doi.org/10.1007/978-0-387-47534-9_3
14. Gama, J.: A survey on learning from data streams: current and future trends. Progress Artif. Intell. **1**(1), 45–55 (2012)
15. Guha, S., Mishra, N., Motwani, R., O'Callaghan, L.: Clustering data streams. In: Proceedings of the 41st Annual Symposium on Foundations of Computer Science, FOCS 2000, p. 359. IEEE Computer Society, Washington, DC (2000). http://dl.acm.org/citation.cfm?id=795666.796588
16. Hahsler, M., Bolaños, M., Forrest, J.: Introduction to stream: an extensible framework for data stream clustering research with R. J. Stat. Softw. **76**(14), 1–50 (2017)
17. Hahsler, M., Bolanos, M., Forrest, J.: Stream: infrastructure for data stream mining (2018), R package version 1.3-0. https://CRAN.R-project.org/package=stream
18. Haidar, D., Gaber, M.M.: Data stream clustering for real-time anomaly detection: an application to insider threats. In: Nasraoui, O., Ben N'Cir, C.-E. (eds.) Clustering Methods for Big Data Analytics. USL, pp. 115–144. Springer, Cham (2019). https://doi.org/10.1007/978-3-319-97864-2_6
19. Hyde, R., Angelov, P., MacKenzie, A.: Fully online clustering of evolving data streams into arbitrarily shaped clusters. Inf. Sci. **382–383**, 96–114 (2017)
20. Newman, M.: Networks: An Introduction. Oxford University Press, Oxford (2010)
21. Nguyen, H.L., Woon, Y.K., Ng, W.K.: A survey on data stream clustering and classification. Knowl. Inf. Syst. **45**(3), 535–569 (2015)
22. Qin, Y., Sheng, Q.Z., Falkner, N.J., Dustdar, S., Wang, H., Vasilakos, A.V.: When things matter: a survey on data-centric Internet of Things. J. Netw. Comput. Appl. **64**, 137–153 (2016)
23. R Core Team: R: A Language and Environment for Statistical Computing. R Foundation for Statistical Computing, Vienna (2018). https://www.R-project.org/
24. Rodrigues, P.P., Araújo, J., Gama, J., Lopes, L.: A local algorithm to approximate the global clustering of streams generated in ubiquitous sensor networks. Int. J. Distrib. Sens. Netw. **14**(10) (2018). https://doi.org/10.1177/1550147718808239
25. Rosvall, M., Axelsson, D., Bergstrom, C.T.: The map equation. Eur. Phys. J. Spec. Top. **178**(1), 13–23 (2009)
26. Rosvall, M., Bergstrom, C.T.: Maps of random walks on complex networks reveal community structure. Proc. Nat. Acad. Sci. **105**(4), 1118–1123 (2008)
27. Shao, J., Tan, Y., Gao, L., Yang, Q., Plant, C., Assent, I.: Synchronization-based clustering on evolving data stream. Inf. Sci. (2018)
28. Siebert, J.P.: Vehicle Recognition using rule based methods. TRM, 87-018, Turing Institute (1987)
29. Silva, J.A., Faria, E.R., Barros, R.C., Hruschka, E.R., Carvalho, A.C.P.L.F., Gama, J.: Data stream clustering: a survey. ACM Comput. Surv. **46**(1), 13:1–13:31 (2013)
30. Xu, J., Wang, G., Li, T., Deng, W., Gou, G.: Fat node leading tree for data stream clustering with density peaks. Know. Based Syst. **120**(C), 99–117 (2017)
31. Zhou, A., Cao, F., Qian, W., Jin, C.: Tracking clusters in evolving data streams over sliding windows. Knowl. Inf. Syst. **15**(2), 181–214 (2008)

Normalized Gain and Least Squares to Measure of the Effectiveness of a Physics Course

C. A. Collazos[1(✉)], Alejandra Rojas[1], Hermes Castellanos[1],
Diego Beltrán[2], César A. Collazos[2], Darío Melo[3], Iván Ruiz[1],
Iván Ostos[1], Carlos A. Sánchez[1], Emiro De-la-Hoz-Franco[4],
Farid Meléndez-Pertuz[4], and César Mora[5]

[1] Universidad Manuela Beltrán, Vicerrectoría de Investigaciones,
Bogotá D.C., Colombia
cacollazos@gmail.com
[2] Escuela Colombiana de Ingeniería, Facultad de Ingeniería,
Bogotá D.C., Colombia
[3] Departamento de Tecnología e Informática, Universidad EAN,
Bogotá D.C., Colombia
[4] Departamento de Ciencias de la Computación y Electrónica,
Universidad de la Costa, Barranquilla, Colombia
[5] Centro de Investigación en Ciencia Aplicada y Tecnología Avanzada
del Instituto Politécnico Nacional, México DF, México

Abstract. We present a quantitative analysis using the concepts of Normalized Gain and Least Squares in a process of Physics Teaching. This paper presents the results of the strategy based in The Construction of Prototypes (TCP) and Project Based Learning (PrBL) which was applied in a course of Mechanics in Bogotá-Colombia. The strategy focuses on three topics of Rotational Dynamics Teaching (RDT) specifically at centripetal force, Inertia moment and theorem de parallel axes and angular momentum conservation. We present results and analysis of employed method.

Keywords: Normalized Gain · Least squares · Projects-based learning

1 Introduction

This paper takes some aspects of constructivism and more particularly uses the project-based learning and active learning. The project-based learning proposes interdisciplinary teaching activities in long or medium term and focuses on the student, instead of short and isolated educational processes. The instructional strategies based on projects are rooted in the constructivist approach that evolved from the work of psychologists and educators such as Lev Vygotsky, Jerome Bruner, Jean Piaget and John Dewey [1, 2]. Active learning for its part according to the approach that gives Sokoloff states that teaching physics can be undertaken using current technologies such as data acquisition systems and sensors. There are introductory laboratory modules defined

© Springer Nature Switzerland AG 2019
S. Misra et al. (Eds.): ICCSA 2019, LNCS 11619, pp. 66–77, 2019.
https://doi.org/10.1007/978-3-030-24289-3_6

using data acquisition tools with the computer to help students develop important physics concepts while they acquire skills in the laboratory, as in [3–6].

Data acquisition systems such as those presented in [3–6], allow the use of computers for mathematical and physical modeling, based on observations of real experiments. Besides, it also allows the cycle experimental of prediction, observation and validation that is fundamental in the research of the physics education. There are situations in which computation technologies are used to increase the efficiency of teaching physics and other sciences [7–11].

Despite the advantages of the use of data acquisition systems and computers, it is important to note that such costs are quite high, therefore we made a low-cost timer which is presented in [12]. This timer allows students to experiment properly with rotational dynamics projects as a complement to data acquisition systems and computers.

This research presents the results obtained in the design and construction of prototypes for centripetal force (P1), Moment of Inertia and Parallel Axis Theorem (P2) and Conservation of Angular Momentum based on our experience in 2018-1with student's projects belonging to Faculties of Engineering in the Manuela Beltrán University (MBU) and Colombian School of engineering (CSE) in Bogotá, Colombia. The paper is structured as follows: Sect. 2 we present the Methodology. Section 2.5 we present the results. Section 3 we present the conclusions of the strategy employed.

2 Methodology

2.1 Evaluation

Strategy (PrBL) and (TCP) to the (RDT) have two types of evaluation, one is the evaluation of projects ((Eva-1), (Eva-2), (Eva-3)) in subgroups of 3 students and the other is the conceptual multiple-choice test that is individual, (Si) and (Sf). Conceptual test for its part consists of 15 questions that were excerpted and translated the question bank of Mark Riley [13], is available in [14]. The questionnaire has 5 questions for each of the thematic of the projects (P1), (P2), (P3), (Annex 1). The conceptual evaluation is applied in the first week of classes (Si) and last week.

2.2 Population

The pedagogical strategy (PrBL) and (TCP) in the (RDT) was applied to eight groups (experimental group) where four groups (156 students) belonged to the (MBU) and four groups (144 students) belonged to the (CSE). Each group was made up of approximately 40 students. Subgroups were formed later with three students and exceptionally four students. In the case of (MBU) 52 subgroups were consolidated, in the case of (CSE) were formed 48 subgroups. Additionally, there were eight groups to which were applied traditional instructions (TI) (Control Group). The Fig. 1 illustrates the population.

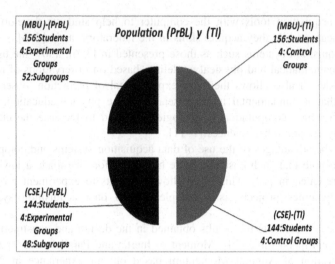

Fig. 1. Population

2.3   Theoretical Fundaments (Gain and Least Squares)

Using the concept of gain of Hovland (1947) used by Hake in [15], is defined the gain g by Eq. (1).

$$g = \frac{S_f - S_i}{100 - S_i} \tag{1}$$

Where $g = 0$ if $(S_i) = 100$; (S_f) (Post-Test) corresponds to the conceptual test applied after applying the strategy (PrBL) and (TCP) to the (RDT) and (TI). S_i (Pre-Test) corresponds to the entrance test without applying any strategy or traditional instruction. We proceeded to determine the average gain of each of the 4 experimental groups and 4 control groups before and after applying the strategy and traditional instruction in (CSE) and (MBU). Ordering the Eq. (1) we have the Eq. (2).

$$(Sf - Si) = (g) - \left(\frac{g}{100}\right)(Si) \tag{2}$$

Thus for a data set in [16], the best curve that fits is one for which the sum of the squares of the deviations is a minimum, then: $J^2 = \sum(y_i - \hat{y}_i)^2 = $ minimun, y_i is the experimental value and corresponds to the measured values $(Sf - Si)$ and $\hat{y}_i$ is the theoretical value of $(Sf - Si)$.

For Eq. (2) is given the first-degree polynomial: $\hat{y} = a + bx$. In this case $a = (g)$, $b = \left(\frac{g}{100}\right)$ and $x = (Si)$. For N pairs of data, the regression parameters a and b are obtained from the following Eqs. (3) and (4) respectively:

$$a = \frac{\sum_{i=1}^{N} x_i^2 \sum_{i=1}^{N} y_i - \sum_{i=1}^{N} x_i \sum_{i=1}^{N} (x_i y_i)}{N \sum_{i=1}^{N} x_i^2 - \left(\sum_{i=1}^{N} x_i\right)^2} \tag{3}$$

$$b = \frac{N \sum_{i=1}^{N} (x_i y_i) - \sum_{i=1}^{N} x_i \sum_{i=1}^{N} y_i}{N \sum_{i=1}^{N} x_i^2 - \left(\sum_{i=1}^{N} x_i\right)^2} \tag{4}$$

Considering that the line is calculated to approximate the experimental data obtained in the process of learning, it is convenient to measure the degree of linear association between two variables $(Sf - Si)$ and (Si).

There is a quantitative measure of the data that follows the straight line obtained by the least squares fit. It is given by the values called correlation coefficient r which is calculated using Eq. (5).

$$r = \frac{N \sum_{i=1}^{N} x_i y_i - \sum_{i=1}^{N} x_i \sum_{i=1}^{N} y_i}{\sqrt{\left[N \sum_{i=1}^{N} x_i^2 - \left(\sum_{i=1}^{N} x_i\right)^2\right]\left[N \sum_{i=1}^{N} y_i^2 - \left(\sum_{i=1}^{N} y_i\right)^2\right]}} \tag{5}$$

For the analysis of the data are considered a good correlation, $|r| > 0.9$. In the case of the regressions is possible to determine the standard error a (σ_a) and b (σ_b). In the linear regression method, we assume that the real values a and b (a* and b*, respectively) should be in a certain range so that the regression line is acceptable. The ranges for a* and b*, are:

Range of a*: $(a - \sigma a < a < a + \sigma a)$
Range of b*: $(b - \sigma b < b < b + \sigma b)$

The values of σa and σb, known as standard errors of a and b respectively, are calculated using Eqs. (6) and (7).

$$\sigma_a = \sigma_y \sqrt{\frac{\sum_{i=1}^{N} x_i^2}{N \sum_{i=1}^{N} x_i^2 - \left(\sum_{i=1}^{N} x_i\right)^2}} \tag{6}$$

$$\sigma_b = \sigma_y \sqrt{\frac{N}{N \sum_{i=1}^{N} x_i^2 - \left(\sum_{i=1}^{N} x_i\right)^2}} \tag{7}$$

Where:

$$\sigma_y = \sqrt{\frac{\sum_{i=1}^{N} (\delta y_i)^2}{N - 2}} \text{y } \delta y_i = y_i - (a + b x_i)$$

Therefore, the range of experimental error of the regression obtained is between the graphs of the following Eq. (8).

$$Y_{max} = (a + \sigma_a) + (b + \sigma_b)x$$
$$Y_{min} = (a - \sigma_a) + (b - \sigma_b)x$$
(8)

In the case of gain, the Eq. (8) are represented by Eq. (9):

$$(Sf - Si)g\left(\frac{g + \sigma_g}{100}\right)_{max}$$
$$(Sf - Si)g\left(\frac{g - \sigma_g}{100}\right)_{min}$$
(9)

Equation (9) are valid only when we work with experimental samples (experimental or control groups) belonging to the same population (University). In the case of working with a different population is recommended to use standard deviation instead of standard error. This produces more dispersion models and thus greater reliability.

2.4 Experimental Data (Conceptual Test)

To calculate the average gain score we use a histogram obtained for an experimental group of 40 students (MBU) before and after the strategy was applied. Figure 2 show the average obtained before the test (S_i, Pre-test) that is 21.98 points and the average obtained after the test (S_f, Post-test) that is 45.96 points over 100 points. After implementing the strategy using the Eq. 1 we determined the average gain $\bar{g} = 30.74$ of one experimental group (MBU) using (PrBL). The average gain of each of the 4 control groups and 4 experimental groups (CSE) and (MBU) are presented in Tables 1 and 2 respectively.

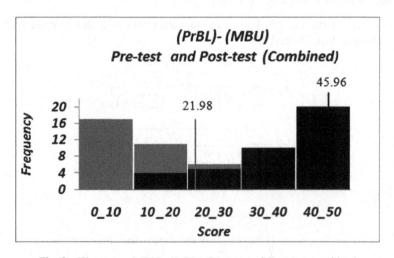

Fig. 2. Histogram (MBU), (PrBL), Pre-test and Post-test combined

Table 1. Average gains for (MBU)

(S_i)	(S_f)	$(S_f - S_i)$	$\bar{g}$
22.07	42.08	20.01	25.68
19.94	43.98	24.04	30.03
21.98	45.96	23.98	30.74
20.06	48.04	27.98	35.00
25.94	35.96	10.02	13.53
23.90	31.90	8.00	10.51
22.04	34.03	11.99	15.38
17.96	27.98	10.02	12.21

Table 2. Average gains for (CSE)

(S_i)	(S_f)	$(S_f - S_i)$	$\bar{g}$
23.98	56.99	33.01	43.42
22.12	56.07	33.95	43.59
19.91	57.95	38.04	47.50
21.16	61.08	39.92	50.63
26.08	40.05	13.97	18.90
21.96	32.94	10.98	14.07
20.13	34.11	13.98	17.50
15.96	31.97	16.01	19.05

The blank area in Tables 1 and 2 corresponds to the experimental groups and the gray area corresponds to the control groups. Based on the gain equation is a linear model and due to the dispersion of the data we apply the method of least squares as in Sect. 2.3.

Figures 3, 4, 5 and 6 show the maximum and minimum models of experimental and control groups in (MBU) and (CSE), based on Eq. (10). This methodology allows to look at the dispersion σ_g of the gain g with the (PrBL) and (TI) using least squares.

Figures 7 and 8 show simultaneously the experimental groups and control (MBU) and (CSE) with the models calculated by the method of least squares and the correlation coefficient r.

2.5   Quantitative Analysis Results

Based on theoretical Fundaments of Sect. 2.3, the mathematical models were obtained for each educational process. Figure 9 shows all groups (control and experimental) in (MBU) and (CSE), indicating the gain and the classification provided by Hake in [10].

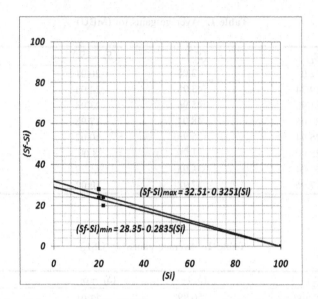

Fig. 3. Experimental groups (MBU), (PrBL), maximum model (top), minimal model (bottom), $g = 30.43$; $\sigma_g = 2.08$

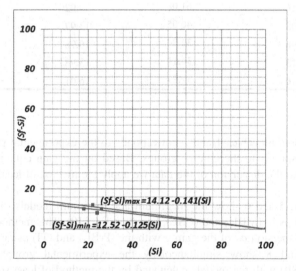

Fig. 4. Control groups (MBU), (TI), maximum model (top), minimal model (bottom), $g = 13.04$; $\sigma_g = 1.14$

Figure 9 also shows that the gain for the (MBU) with (PrBL) is (30.43 ± 2.08) and is located in medium gain, but with (TI) is (13.04 ± 1.14) and is located in low gain. For (CSE) with (PrBL) is (46.52 ± 1.88) and is located in medium gain, but with (TI) is (17.48 ± 1.23) and is located in low gain. The results show the efficiency of (PrBL) in contrast to the (TI) at both universities.

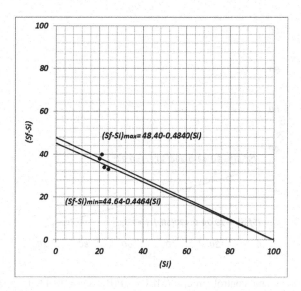

Fig. 5. Experimental groups (CSE), (PrBL), maximum model (top), minimal model (bottom), $g = 46.52$; $\sigma_g = 1.88$

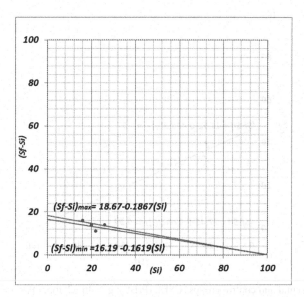

Fig. 6. Experimental groups (CSE), (TI), maximum model (top), minimal model (bottom), $g = 17.48$; $\sigma_g = 1.23$

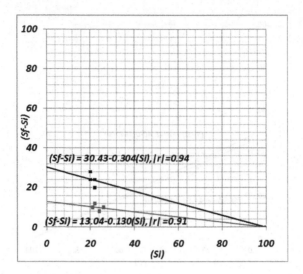

Fig. 7. Experimental and control groups (MBU), (PrBL): $g = 30.43$, top; (TI): $g = 13.04$, bottom.

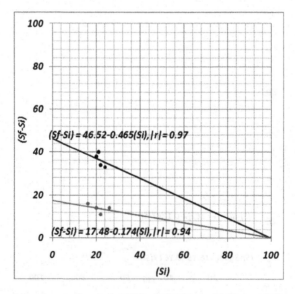

Fig. 8. Experimental and control groups (CSE), (PrBL): g = 46.52, top; (TI): $g = 17.48$, bottom

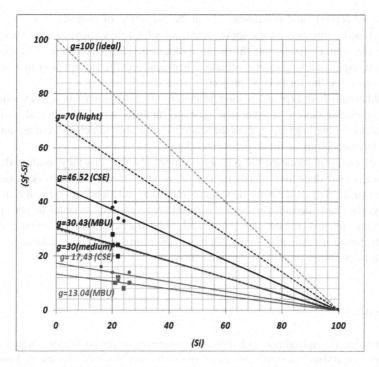

Fig. 9. Experimental (black) and control (gray) groups (CSE, MBU), red (ideal: $g = 100$), blue (hight: $g \geq 70$), green (medium: $70 > g \geq 30$), low ($g < 30$) (Color figure online)

3 Conclusions

The method used in this work is part of the current curriculum of both universities (MBU) and (SCE). Moreover, this research can be applied in various areas of physics, such as optics, electromagnetism, Physics of Sound, Biophysics, Thermodynamics, Fluid Mechanics and Modern Physics, among others. The prototypes for Mechanics (Rotational Dynamics) are show in [17–21], for Electromagnetism (Electrostatic) in [22, 23] and Fluid Mechanics in [24].

Based on the results (Sect. 2.4), the strategy allows for gains in the medium range. Results obtained a gain to (MBU) of (30.43 ± 2.08) and to (SCE) of (46.52 ± 1.88). The methodology used in this paper presents a gain compared to traditional instruction (TI), which had a lower gain range than for the (MBU) that was of (13.04 ± 2.08) and to (SCE) that was of (17.43 ± 1.24).

General speaking, the results analysis scheme allows quantitative measurement and qualitatively evaluate the strategy used. It was possible to establish that the students:

- Built prototypes that allowed them to properly conceptualize the topics of rotational cinema.
- Identified and corrected some mistaken concepts related to the fundamental principles of rotational dynamics.

- Engaged actively and collaboratively in the execution of projects.
- Developed a question on the topic raised, for which they carried out the review of different sources (pages on the web, books, journals of scientific dissemination, sought expert advice, among others). Then selected the information that allowed them to solve the formulated project.
- Could establish an experimentation process (prediction, observation and validation). Although the theory of error and graphic analysis was difficult and generated confusion at the beginning, then the students were able to perform correct analyses and interpretations of the experimental data.
- Constructed and modeled the prototype physically. For this they used methods of inductive and deductive reasoning that allowed to identify the physical variables involved as well as defining dependent variables, independent and constant. Similarly, they obtained measures of the mentioned variables in order to perform the analysis. In this regard the theoretical and practical solution of the project strengthened investigative skills, such as: observing, analyzing, deducing, conjecturing, designing, producing, among others.

References

1. Hernández, C.: Aprendizaje de la Física en estudiantes de diseño Industrial dentro de una innovación pedagógica consistente en el constructivismo, Tesis de Maestria en Educación, Uniandes (2004)
2. Vygotsky, L.: Pensamiento y lenguaje. Alfa y Omega, México (1985)
3. Thornton, R.K., Sokoloff, D.R.: Learning motion concepts using real-time microcomputer-based laboratory tools. Am. J. Phys. **58**, 858–867 (1990)
4. Mokros, J.R., Tinker, R.F.: The impact of MicroComputer Based Labs on children's ability to interpret graphs. J. Res. Sci. Teach. **24**, 369–383 (1987)
5. McDermott, L.C., Rosenquist, M.L., van Zee, E.H.: Student difficulties in connecting graphs and physics: examples from kinematics. Am. J. Phys. **55**, 503–513 (1987)
6. Redish, E.F., Saul, J.M., Steinberg, R.N.: On the effectiveness of active-engagement microcomputer-based laboratories. Am. J. Phys. **65**, 45–54 (1997)
7. Stankova, E.N., Barmasov, A.V., Dyachenko, N.V., Bukina, M.N., Barmasova, A.M., Yakovleva, T.Yu.: The use of computer technology as a way to increase efficiency of teaching physics and other natural sciences. In: Gervasi, O., et al. (eds.) ICCSA 2016. LNCS, vol. 9789, pp. 581–594. Springer, Cham (2016). https://doi.org/10.1007/978-3-319-42089-9_41
8. Lisachenko, D.A., Barmasov, A.V., Bukina, M.N., Stankova, E.N., Vysotskaya, S.O., Zarochentseva, E.P.: Best practices combining traditional and digital technologies in education. In: Gervasi, O., et al. (eds.) ICCSA 2017. LNCS, vol. 10408, pp. 483–494. Springer, Cham (2017). https://doi.org/10.1007/978-3-319-62404-4_36
9. Dyachenko, N.V., Barmasov, A.V., Stankova, E.N., Struts, A.V., Barmasova, A.M., Yakovleva, T.Yu.: Prototype of informational infrastructure of a program instrumentation complex for carrying out a laboratory practicum on physics in a university. In: Gervasi, O., et al. (eds.) ICCSA 2017. LNCS, vol. 10408, pp. 412–427. Springer, Cham (2017). https://doi.org/10.1007/978-3-319-62404-4_30

10. Comas, Z., Echeverri, I., Zamora, R., Vélez, J., Sarmiento, R., Orellana, M.: Tendencias recientes de la Educación Virtual y su fuerte conexión con los Entornos Inmersivos. Revista Espacios **38**, 4–10 (2017)
11. Stankova, E.N., Dyachenko, N.V., Tibilova, G.S.: Virtual laboratories: prospects for the development of techniques and methods of work. In: Gervasi, O., et al. (eds.) ICCSA 2018. LNCS, vol. 10963, pp. 3–11. Springer, Cham (2018). https://doi.org/10.1007/978-3-319-95171-3_1
12. Collazos, C.A.: Construcción de un prototipo para experimentos de Mécanica. Lat. Am. J. Phys. Educ. **4**(Suppl. 1), 840–843 (2010)
13. http://www.fisicacollazos.260mb.com. Accessed 15 Jan 2019
14. Riley, M.: Test Bank. W. H. Freeman and Company, New York (2003)
15. Hake, R.R.: Interactive-engagement vs traditional methods: a six-thousand-student survey of mechanics test data for introductory physics courses. Am. J. Phys. **66**, 64–74 (1997)
16. Spiegel, M.: Estadística. McGraw-Hill, Madrid (1991)
17. Collazos, C.A.: Prototipo para la Enseñanza de la dinámica rotacional (conservación del momento angular). Lat. Am. J. Phys. Educ. **3**, 446–448 (2009)
18. Collazos, C.A.: Enseñanza de la conservación del momento angular por medio de la construcción de prototipos y el aprendizaje basado en proyectos. Lat. Am. J. Phys. Educ. **3**, 428–432 (2009)
19. Collazos, C.A.: Prototipo para la Enseñanza de la dinámica rotacional (Momento de Inercia y teorema de ejes paralelos). Lat. Am. J. Phys. Educ. **3**, 619–624 (2009)
20. Collazos, C.A., Mora, C.E.: Prototipo para medir Fuerza Centrípeta en función de masa, radio y periodo. Lat. Am. J. Phys. Educ. **5**, 520–525 (2011)
21. Collazos, C.A., Mora, C.E.: Experimentos de mecánica con temporizador de bajo costo. Revista Brasileira de Ensino de Física **34**, 4311 (2012)
22. Collazos, C.A., Otero, H.R., Isaza, J., Mora, C.: Enseñanza de la Electrostática por Medio de la Construcción de Prototipos de Bajo Costo y el Aprendizaje Basado en Proyectos. Formación universitaria **9**, 115–122 (2016)
23. Collazos, C.A., Otero, H.R., Isaza, J.J., Mora, C.: Diseño y Construcción de una Máquina de Wimshurst para La Enseñanza de la Electrostática. Formación universitaria **9**, 107–116 (2016)
24. Castellanos, H.E., Collazos, C.A., Farfan, J.C., Meléndez-Pertuz, F.: Diseño y Construcción de un Canal Hidráulico de Pendiente Variable. Información tecnológica **28**, 103–114 (2017)

A Model to Study the Strange Quark
$s - \bar{s}$ Asymmetry in Nucleon Sea

I. A. Monroy[1]([✉]), J. C. Sanabria[2], and C. A. Collazos[3]

[1] Universidad Distrital Francisco José de Caldas, Bogotá, Colombia
ignacioalbertom@gmail.com
[2] Universidad de los Andes, Bogotá, Colombia
jcsanabria@uniandes.edu.co
[3] Universidad Manuela Beltrán, Bogotá, Colombia
cacollazos@gmail.com

Abstract. We study the strange quark $s - \bar{s}$ asymmetry in the nucleon sea using a model in which the proton wave function includes a Kaon meson-Hyperon Fock state. Parameters of the model are fixed by fitting the $s - \bar{s}$ asymmetry obtained from global fits to Deep Inelastic Scattering data. We discuss possible effects of the $s - \bar{s}$ asymmetry on the measurement of the Weinberg angle by the NuTeV Collaboration.

Keywords: Strange sea · Asymmetry

1 Introduction

Nucleons are one of the most important particles in the nature, they compose majority of all matter in the universe. A nucleon is either a proton or a neutron, the component of an atomic nucleus. In the standard model of elementary particles proton and neutron are classified into family of particles known as hadrons, which are composed of more elementary particles named *quarks*. Proton is composed by three quarks: 2 quarks *up*(u) and one quark *down*(d). Particles with two quarks also exist and they are named mesons. Quarks into hadrons interact each other by gluons(g), particles mediator of the strong interaction. At the present there are six quarks with different mass values, associate to them their corresponding antiparticles, or in general antimatter. Currently the precise study of the quark physics into hadrons is a main challenge in the high energy of physics made by experiments as CERN in order to understand the nature and origin of the universe.

Quarks model was confirmed with the study of nucleons structure in process of deep inelastic scattering (DIS) in the 1960s by colliding leptons as electrons, muons and neutrinos with nucleon targets in a similar way as Rutherford's scattering, whose study determined the existence of the nucleons into atomos. In DIS leptons have a high energies to break up the nucleons and collide with the quarks, producing after of collision new particles, mainly hadrons. Additionally,

S. Misra et al. (Eds.): ICCSA 2019, LNCS 11619, pp. 78–88, 2019.
https://doi.org/10.1007/978-3-030-24289-3_7

in the scale of DIS energy values, gluon splitting process related with matter anti matter production of quarks q anti quarks $\bar{q}$ inside nuclons -known as *sea quarks*- was a astonishing result that scientificts in that epoc could not expected. Parton model making by Feynman could explain in a better way the structure of nucleons: valence quarks, gluons process and sea quarks are inside nucleons with a momentum fraction given by a probability density function $q(x)$, known as *parton density functions*. In general quarks sea densities for quarks up u and down d inside nucleons are not symetrical, but in the case of heavier quarks as the strange s, charm c, bottom b and top t is expected that quarks sea densities would be symmetric.

The first studies about a possible asymmetry in the strange sea of the nucleon dates from 1987, when Signal and Thomas [1] discussed the possibility of a $K^+\Lambda$ pair component in the proton wavefunction. Since then on, several models have been proposed for the nucleon structure, allowing for an asymmetric $s - \bar{s}$ [2,3]. However, no experimental evidence was presented on this subject until the global fit of DIS data by Barone *et al.* [5] in 2000. Most recently, the $s - \bar{s}$ asymmetry in the nucleon sea was called for as a possible explanation.

From a theoretical point of view, it is interesting to note that although sea quarks in the nucleon originating in gluon splitting necessarily have symmetric momentum distributions, after interacting with the valence quarks and the remaining partons in the sea, their momentum distributions do not have to be equal. This can be interpreted as the formation of a virtual $K^+\Lambda$ pair in the nucleon structure. Being this the case, it is easy to see that, since the s and the $\bar{s}$ quarks are part of the Λ and K^+ respectively, then their momentum distributions would be different. This difference, which is merely a consequence of the interaction of sea quarks with the remaining partons in the nucleon, has to be understood as part of the non-perturbative dynamics responsible for the formation of the nucleon as a bound state of quarks and gluons. Recall also the $\bar{u} - \bar{d}$ asymmetry and the Gottfried Sum Rule violation, known since the New Muon Collaboration results [6,7], which can also been explained in terms of a $n\pi^+$ and $\Delta^{++}\pi^-$ components in the proton wave function [10].

In this work, we shall consider a model for the strange sea of the proton which can describe the form of the $s - \bar{s}$ asymmetry extracted from global fits to DIS data. After fixing the parameters of the model, in Sect. 2.3, we shall study the effect of this asymmetry, together with possible effects coming from the non isoscalarity of the target, in the determination of $\sin^2 \theta_W$ by the NuTeV Collaboration [8]. Section 4 will be devoted to discussion and conclusions.

2 A Model for the $s - \bar{s}$ Asymmetry

Different models [1–4] have attempted to predict the $s - \bar{s}$ asymmetry. Among them, the most promising approach seems to be the Meson Cloud Model (MCM). In the MCM fluctuations of the proton to kaon-hyperon virtual states are responsible for the $s - \bar{s}$ asymmetry. Since the s quark belong to the hyperon particle state and the $\bar{s}$ quark to the Kaon particle state, the asymmetry arises naturally due to the different momentum carried by the kaon and the hyperon in the fluctuation. A squeme view of these process are shown as a Feynman diagram in the Fig. 1. Here hyperon state is given Λ particle state which is compose uds quarks and Kaon particle state compose by $u\bar{s}$ quarks. Two different approaches exist within the MCM. The first is based in a description of the form factor of the extended proton-kaon-hyperon vertex [1,3] and, the second one, in terms of parton degrees of freedom [4]. In the first approach, the knowledge of the form factors is crucial to get a reasonable description of the $s - \bar{s}$ asymmetry (see e.g. Ref. [3]). In the second one, fluctuations are generated through gluon emission from the constituent valence and its subsequent splitting to a $s - \bar{s}$ pair [4]. This $s - \bar{s}$ pair then recombines with constituent quarks to form a kaon-hyperon bound state. In what follows, we will adopt the second approach.

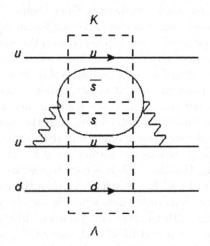

Fig. 1. Scheme view of Feynman diagram process: gluon emission from the constituent valence and its subsequent splitting process produces a $s\bar{s}$ pair which interact with valence quarks u and d generating K^+ and Λ^0 virtual states (shown with dashed boxes). After that virtual states, the $s\bar{s}$ pair recombines into a gluon which is reabsorbed by a valence quark

2.1   The Model

We start by considering a simple picture of the nucleon in the infinite momentum frame as being formed by three dressed valence quarks - valons, $v(x)$ - which carry all of its momentum [11]. In the framework of the MCM, the nucleon can fluctuate to a meson-baryon bound state carrying zero net strangeness, that is

$$\int_0^1 [s(x) - \bar{s}(x)]dx = 0 \tag{1}$$

where x is the momentum fraction. As a first step in such a process, we may consider that each valon can emit a gluon which, before interacting, decays perturbatively into a $s\bar{s}$ pair The probability of having such a perturbative $q\bar{q}$ pair can then be computed in terms of Altarelli-Parisi splitting functions [12]

$$P_{gq}(z) = \frac{4}{3}\frac{1 + (1 + z^2)}{z},$$

$$P_{qg}(z) = \frac{1}{2}(z^2 + (1 + z)^2). \tag{2}$$

These functions have a physical interpretation as the probability of gluon emission and $q\bar{q}$ creation with momentum fraction z from a parent quark or gluon respectively. Hence,

$$q(x, Q^2) = \bar{q}(x, Q^2)\frac{\alpha_{st}^2(Q^2)}{(2\pi)^2}\int_1^x \frac{dy}{y}P_{qg}\left(\frac{x}{y}\right)\int_1^y \frac{dz}{z}P_{gq}\left(\frac{y}{z}\right)v(z) \tag{3}$$

is the joint probability density of obtaining a quark or anti-quark coming from subsequent decays $v \to v + g$ and $g \to q + \bar{q}$ at some fixed low Q^2. As the valon distribution does not depend on Q^2 [11], the scale dependence in Eq. 3 only exhibits through the strong coupling constant $\alpha_{st}(Q^2)$. The range of values of Q^2 at which the process of virtual pair creation occurs in this approach is typically below 1 GeV^2, as dictated by the valon model of the nucleon. For definiteness, we will use $Q = 0.7$ GeV as in Ref. [11], for which $\alpha_{st}(Q^2) \approx 0.3$, is still sufficiently small to allow for a perturbative evaluation of the $q\bar{q}$ pair production. Since the scale must be consistent with the valon picture, the value of Q^2 is not really free and cannot be used to control the flavor produced at the $gq\bar{q}$ vertex. Instead, this role can be ascribed to the normalization constant N, which must be such that to a heavier quark corresponds a lower value of N.

Once a $s\bar{s}$ pair is produced, it can rearrange itself with the remaining valons so as to form a most energetically favored meson-baryon bound state. When the nucleon fluctuates into a meson-baryon bound state, the meson and baryon probability densities $P_M(x)$, and $P_B(x)$ inside the nucleon are not independent. Actually, to ensure the zero net strangeness of the nucleon and momentum conservation, the in-nucleon meson and baryon distributions must fulfill two basic constraints,

$$\int_0^1 [P_B(x) - P_M(x)]dx = 0 \tag{4}$$

$$\int_0^1 [xP_B(x) + xP_M(x)]dx = 1 \tag{5}$$

for all momentum fractions x. The meson, $P_M(x)$, and baryon, $P_B(x)$, probability density functions have to be calculated by means of effective techniques in order to deal with the non-perturbative quatum cromodynamics (QCD) processes inherent to the dressing of quarks into hadrons. In Ref. [4], these probability densities have been related to the cross section for meson production by recombination, and the model by Das and Hwa [13] was used to obtain them. In this work, since the aim is to compare the model to experimental data by means of a fit, we will follow a different approach. Let us note that, for reasonable valon distributions in the nucleon and sea quark distributions of the form given by Eq. (3), the result of using the recombination model gives for the meson probability density a function of the form $x^a(1-x)^b$. Then we will assume

$$P_M(x) = \frac{1}{\beta(a_{KN}+1, b_{KN}+1)} x^{a_{KN}}(1-x)^{b_{KN}} \qquad (6)$$

which is properly normalized to one. If for the in-nucleon baryon probability we use the same functional form as for the meson,

$$P_B(x) = \frac{1}{\beta(a_{HN}+1, b_{HN}+1)} x^{a_{HN}}(1-x)^{b_{HN}} \qquad (7)$$

it is automatically satisfied the requirement of zero net strangenes. In addition, interpreting a_{KN}, b_{KN}, a_{HN} and b_{HN} as parameters of the model, and recognizing that Eq. (4) fix one of them as a function of the remaining three by means of

$$\frac{\Gamma(a_{KN}+b_{KN}+2)\Gamma(a_{KN}+2)}{\Gamma(a_{KN}+1)\Gamma(a_{KN}+b_{KN}+3)} + \frac{\Gamma(a_{HN}+b_{HN}+2)\Gamma(a_{HN}+2)}{\Gamma(a_{HN}+1)\Gamma(a_{HN}+b_{HN}+3)} = 1 \qquad (8)$$

then the momentum conservation sum rule is also fulfilled. The non-perturbative strange and anti-strange sea distributions in the nucleon can be now computed by means of the two-level convolution formulas

$$s_B(x) = \int_1^x \frac{dy}{y} P_B(y) s\left(\frac{y}{z}\right), \qquad (9)$$

$$\bar{s}_M(x) = \int_1^x \frac{dy}{y} P_H(y) \bar{s}\left(\frac{y}{z}\right), \qquad (10)$$

where the sources $s_B(x)$ and $\bar{s}_M(x)$ are primarily the probability densities of the strange valence quark and anti-quark in the baryon and meson respectively, evaluated at the hadronic scale Q^2 [1]. In principle, to obtain the non-perturbative distributions given by Eqs. (9) and (11), one should sum over all the strange meson-baryon fluctuations of the nucleon but, since such hadronic Fock states are necessarilly off-shell, the most likely configurations are those closest to the nucleon energy-shell, namely $\Lambda^0 K^+$, $\Sigma^0 K^+$ and $\Sigma^+ K^0$, for a proton state.

2.2   Fit to $x(s(x) - \bar{s}(x))$ Data

In order to fit to experimental data on the $s - \bar{s}$ asymmetry and to extract the parameters of the model, we will use

$$\bar{s}_K(x) = \frac{1}{\beta(a_K+1, b_K+1)} x^{a_K}(1-x)^{b_K} \qquad (11)$$

$$s_H(x) = \frac{1}{\beta(a_H+1, b_H+1)} x^{a_H}(1-x)^{b_H} \qquad (12)$$

which are consistent with the hypothesis that the in meson and baryon are formed by valons. Then the $s - \bar{s}$ asymmetry of the nucleon is given by

$$xs(x) - \bar{s}(x) = N^2(xs^{NP}(x) - \bar{s}^{NP}(x)) \tag{13}$$

at the valon scale $Q^2 = 0.49$ GeV^2, and where N^2 is the probability of the $|HK\rangle$ Fock state in the proton wave function, which is related to the probability of having a $s(x) - \bar{s}$ pair out of Eq. (3). The model has then a total of 8 parameters to be fixed by fits to experimental data. Results of the fit to experimental data from Ref. [14] are shown in Fig. 2 and Table 1. For the experimental data, we extracted 27 segments from the allowed band in Fig. 2 of Ref. [14] and assumed that the midpoint of each segment is the most probable value which we interpreted as the value for the asymmetry, while the half lenght of the segment was interpreted as the error bar. Notice however that this procedure has to be taken only as a way to fit our model inside the allowed region for the $s(x) - \bar{s}$ asymmetry. The fit was performed by minimizing the χ^2 using MINUIT. In the fitting procedure, since the allowed bars for the $s - \bar{s}$ asymmetry are given at $Q^2 = 20$ GeV^2, the parameters where chosen, then the asymmetry was evolved from $Q^2 = 0.49$ GeV^2 to $Q^2 = 20$ GeV^2, the $\chi^2$was evaluated and the procedure was repeated until a minimum was reached.

Table 1. Fit results. Parameters a_{KN}, b_{KN} are for the Kaon probability density in the nucleon, a_{HN}, b_{HN} for the Hyperon probability density, a_K, b_K for the anti-strange valon proba bility density in the Kaon and a_H, b_H for the strange valon density in the Hyperon. The χ^2/d.o.f. $= 0.15$ and $b_{HN} = 1.11$ is the result of the constraint due to the momentum sum rule of Eq. (7)

Parameter	Value
a_{KN}	$2.06 \pm 2.62 \times 10^{-7}$
b_{KN}	2.14 ± 0.11
a_K	5.14 ± 1.93
b_K	0.90 ± 0.34
a_{HN}	1.17 ± 0.35
a_H	9.47 ± 0.61
b_H	2.51 ± 0.61
N^2	0.04 ± 0.02

2.3 Discusion of Effects of $s(x) - \bar{s}(x)$

The effect of the asymmetry in the strange sea in the nucleon has a surprised result in the DIS. In general the size of this asymmetry depends of the scale value energy of Q^2. As it mentioned before analysis of results of $x[s(x) - \bar{s}(x)]$

asymmetry by Barone *et al.* [5] is given to a scale $Q^2 = 20$ GeV^2. Most recently, the $x[s(x) - \bar{s}(x)]$ asymmetry in the nucleon sea was called for as a possible explanation [6] for the almost 3σ difference between the NuTeV $\sin^2\theta_W$ result [8] and global fits [9]. The evolution has been done at next-to-leading order (NLO) with the Eq. (3) and a value of

$$S^- = \int_0^1 x[s(x) - \bar{s}(x)]dx = 0.87 \times 10^{-4} \tag{14}$$

at $Q^2 = 20$ GeV^2 has been obtained, which is also the average Q^2 reported by NuTeV. Although this value of S^- is small to account for the anomalous result for reported by NuTeV, it is positive. It is also conceivable that, by performing a next-to-next-leading-orden (NNLO) evolution, the negative contribution of the perturbative asymmetry in $s(x) - \bar{s}(x)$ be compensated by a bigger positive non-perturbative asymmetry. In Fig. 3, the xs and $x\bar{s}$ distributions are displayed at the Q^2 scale where the evolution starts, namely, $Q^2 = 0.49$ GeV^2.

3   The Effect of $s(x) - \bar{s}(x)$ on the Determination of $\sin^2\theta_W$

The weak mixing angle is one of the basic parameters of the standard model of electroweak interactions. An experimental value for $\sin^2\theta_W$ has been obtained, using the *on-shell* renormalization scheme, from a global fit to the precise electroweak measurements performed by the LEP experiments at CERN and the SLD experiment at SLC, together with data from several other experiments at Fermilab [9]. This global analysis lends a value of

$$\sin^2\theta_W = 0.2227 \pm 0.004 \tag{15}$$

excluding the data from CCFR and NuTeV experiments. The NuTeV collaboration reported a value of $\sin^2\theta_W$ extracted from the analysis of neutrino ν and anti-neutrino $\bar{\nu}$ charged current (CC) and neutral current (NC) scattering data [8]. The *on shell* value obtained by this experiment is

$$\sin^2\theta_W = 0.22773 \pm 0.00135_{stat} \pm 0.00093_{sys} \tag{16}$$

which is $\sim 3\sigma$ away from the electroweak global fit value. Due to an inevitable contamination of the muon and anti-muon neutrinos $\nu_\mu(\bar{\nu}_\mu)$ beams with electron muons $\nu_e(\nu_e)$, and the impossibility of separating CC $\nu_e(\nu_e)$ induced interactions from the NC $\nu_\mu(\nu_\mu)$ induced ones on an event by event bases, the NuTeV result was obtained by performing a full simulation of the whole experiment, in which the value of the weak mixing angle was adjusted so that the Monte Carlo yield the best de scription of the experimental data. The NuTeV Monte Carlo included, among may other things, a detailed simulation of the neutrino(antineutrino) beam, a detailed model of the N cross section, QED radiative corrections, charm-production-threshold effects, strange and charm sea scattering, quasi-elastic scattering, neutrino-electron scattering, non-isoscalar-target

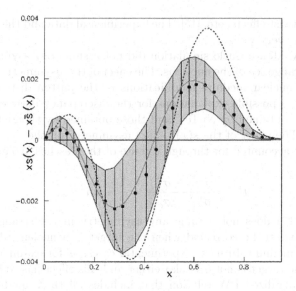

Fig. 2. The model compared to experimental data at $Q^2 = 20$ GeV^2 (full line). The curve is the result of the fit, data points were extracted to fit in the shadowed region as given in Ref. [14] (see the text). The dashed line is the model at $Q^2 = 20$ GeV^2

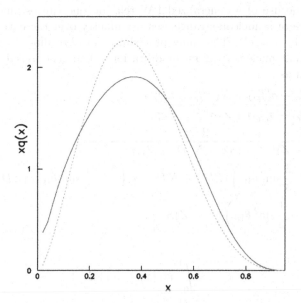

Fig. 3. The $xs(x)$ (full line) and $x\bar{s}$ (dashed line) at $Q^2 = 0.49$ GeV^2 as given by the model.

effects, higher twist effects, etc. [15]. The experimental data and the Monte Carlo results compare very well.

The NuTeV Monte Carlo simulation did not assume any asymmetry in the strange-antistrange sea of the nucleons. The effect of this asymmetry and possible effects due to nuclear medium modifications to the parton distributions have been explored as possible explanations for the discrepancy between the results for the $\sin^2 \theta_W$ obtained by NuTeV and those obtained by the global fit to the DIS data [9]. The effect of the $s(x) - \bar{s}(x)$ asymmetry on the determination of $\sin^2 \theta_W$ can be accounted for through the use of the Paschos-Wolfenstein (PW) relation [16]

$$R^- = \frac{\sigma_{NC}^{\nu N} - \sigma_{NC}^{\bar{\nu} N}}{\sigma_{CC}^{\nu N} - \sigma_{CC}^{\bar{\nu} N}} = \frac{1}{2} - \sin^2 \theta_W. \tag{17}$$

Equation (17) does not assume any asymmetry in the strange sea of the nucleon, and has to be corrected when the target is a nucleus, due to effects of the nuclear medium. In most experimental cases, as for example the NuTeV experiment, the target is not isoscalar either and this effect has to be taken into account. A generalized PW relation that includes all these modifications can easily be obtained. The extraction of the $\sin^2 \theta_W$ by NuTeV did not resort to any PW relation because of the impossibility to separate effectively the charged current form the neutral current signals.

Through the use of a generalized PW relation one can estimate the effect of the presence of a nucleon-strange- sea asymmetry over the extraction of the $\sin^2 \theta_W$ done by NuTeV. The same procedure can also allow to estimate the effect of different nuclear medium modifications. The generalized PW relation can be written as:

$$
\begin{aligned}
R^- &= \frac{Z(\sigma_{NC}^{\nu p} - \sigma_{NC}^{\bar{\nu} p}) + N(\sigma_{NC}^{\nu n} - \sigma_{NC}^{\bar{\nu} n})}{Z(\sigma_{CC}^{\nu p} - \sigma_{CC}^{\bar{\nu} p}) + Z(\sigma_{CC}^{\nu n} - \sigma_{NC}^{\bar{\nu} n})} \\
&= \frac{2}{[(3N - Z)U^- + (3Z - N)D^- + 3(N + Z)S^-]} \times \\
&\quad \left[\left(\frac{1}{4} - \frac{2}{3} \sin^2 \theta_W \right) (ZU^- + ND^-) + \left(\frac{1}{4} - \frac{1}{3} \sin^2 \theta_W \right) (ZD^- + NU^-) \right. \\
&\quad \left. + \left(\frac{1}{4} - \frac{1}{3} \sin^2 \theta_W \right) (N + Z)S^- \right],
\end{aligned}
\tag{18}
$$

where

$$U^- = \int_0^1 x[u(x) - \bar{u}(x)]dx, \tag{19}$$

$$D^- = \int_0^1 x[d(x) - \bar{d}(x)]dx, \tag{20}$$

$$S^- = \int_0^1 x[u(x) - \bar{u}(x)]dx, \tag{21}$$

and Z and N are the proton and neutron numbers of the target nucleus. The NuTeV Collaboration extracted $\sin^2 \theta_W$ from a full simulation of the experiment in which a symmetric strange sea was assumed ($S^- = 0$). From this, and the use of the generalized PW relation, one could determine the value of R^- consistent with the results of NuTeV, by evaluating

$$R^-_{\text{NuTeV}} = R^- [S^- = 0, Z, N, \sin^2 \theta_W^{\text{NuTeV}}], \qquad (22)$$

where N and Z correspond to the iron target used, and $\sin^2 \theta_W^{\text{NuTeV}}$ to the value reported by the experiment. Assuming R^-_{NuTeV}, the value of $\sin^2 \theta_W$ from the global analysis of the DIS data ($\sin^2 \theta^{\text{Global}}$), and the parametrizations of Gluck, Reya and Vogt for the parton distributions of $u(x)$ and $d(x)$ [17], one can evaluate the level of asymmetry in the strange sea of the nucleon that could explain the NuTeV result,

$$S^- = \frac{1}{[(\frac{3}{2} R^-_{\text{NuTeV}} - (\frac{1}{4} - \frac{1}{3} \sin^2 \theta_W)]} \left[(ZU^- + ND^-) \left(\frac{1}{4} - \frac{2}{3} \sin^2 \theta_W^{\text{Global}} \right) + \right.$$
$$\left. (ZD^- + NU^-) \left(\frac{1}{4} - \frac{1}{3} \sin^2 \theta_W^{\text{Global}} \right) - \frac{R^-_{\text{NuTeV}}}{2} [(3N - Z)U^- + (3Z - N)D^-] \right]$$
$$= 0.004013. \qquad (23)$$

The strange asymmetries predicted by our model is, again, given by

$$S^- = \int_0^1 x[s(x) - \bar{s}(x)]dx = 0.87 \times 10^{-4}, \qquad (24)$$

which are two orders of magnitude smaller. Since our parametrizations for $x[s(x) - \bar{s}(x)]$ are in agreement with the experimental data from [14], one can conclude that the anomalous value for $\sin^2 \theta_W$ reported by NuTeV cannot be explained in terms of a possible asymmetry in the strange sea of the nucleon.

4   Conclusions

We have presented a model, based in fluctuations of the proton wavefunction to a generic Hyperon-Kaon Fock state, that closely reproduces experimental data on the extrange sea asymmetry of the nucleon. The model has a total of 8 parameters which have been fixed by fits to experimental data. No NNLO effects in the evolution of the xs and $x\bar{s}$ have been considered, however the negative asymmetry introduced by NNLO evolution effects should be compensated by a large and positive asymmetry coming from the non-perturbative dynamics associated to the confining phase of QCD.

We investigated also the effect of such an asymmetry on the result presented by the NuTeV experiment on the measurement of $\sin^2 \theta_W$. In the study we considered, in addition, effects coming from the non isoscalarity of the NuTeV target. Considering all together, we found that the effect of the $x[s(x) - \bar{s}(x)]$ asymmetry in the nucleon sea is too small to account for the almost 3σ difference among the $\sin^2 \theta_W$ result by NuTeV and the world average.

References

1. Signal, A.I., Thomas, A.W.: Phys. Lett. B **191**, 205 (1987)
2. Brodsky, S.J., Ma, B.Q.: Phys. Lett. B **381**, 317 (1996)
3. Burkard, M., Warr, B.J.: Phys. Rev. D **45**, 958 (1992)
4. Christiansen, H.R., Magnin, J.: Phys. Lett. B **445**, 8 (1998)
5. Barone, V., Pascaud, C., Zomer, F.: Eur. Phys. J. C-Part. Fields **12**, 243 (2000)
6. Amaudruz, P., et al. (New Muon Collaboration): Phys. Rev. Lett. **66**, 2712 (1991)
7. Arneodo, M., et al. (New Muon Collaboration): Phys. Rev. D **50**, 1 (1994)
8. Zeller, G.P., et al. (NuTeV Collaboration): Phys. Rev. Lett. **88**, 091802 (2002). [Erratum Phys. Rev. Lett. **90**, 239902 (2003)]
9. Report No. CERN-EP/2001-98; hep-ex/0112021. and reference [21] quoted in reference [7]
10. Magnin, J., Christiansen, H.R.: Phys. Rev. D **61**, 054006 (2000)
11. Hwa, R.C.: Phys. Rev. D **22**, 759 (1980); Phys. Rev. D **22**, 1593 (1980)
12. Altarelli, G., Parisi, G.: Nucl. Phys. B **126**, 298 (1977)
13. Das, K.P., Hwa, R.C.: Phys. Lett. B **68**, 459 (1977)
14. Portheault, B.: 11th International Workshop On Deep In- elastic Scattering (DIS 2003) (2003). hep-ph/0406226
15. Zeller, G.P.: Ph.D. thesis, Northwestern University (2002)
16. Paschos, E.A., Wolfenstein, L.: Phys. Rev. D **7**, 91 (1973)
17. Gluck, M., Reya, E., Vogt, A.: Eur. Phys. J. C **5**, 461 (1998)

Economical Sixth Order Runge–Kutta Method for Systems of Ordinary Differential Equations

Alexey S. Eremin[(✉)], Nikolai A. Kovrizhnykh, and Igor V. Olemskoy

Saint-Petersburg State University, Saint-Petersburg, Russia
{a.eremin,i.olemskoj}@spbu.ru, sagoyewatha@mail.ru

Abstract. Structural partitioning of systems of ordinary differential equations is made on base of right-hand side dependencies on the unknown variables. It is used to construct fully explicit Runge–Kutta methods with several computational schemes applied to different parts of the system. The constructed structural methods require fewer right-hand side evaluations (stages) per step for some parts of the system than classic explicit Runge–Kutta methods of the same order. The full structural form of the system is presented, which after permutation of variables can be applied to any system of ordinary differential equation. For such structure a multischeme method is formulated and conditions of the sixth order are written down. We present simplifying conditions and reduce the system to a solvable smaller system. A particular computational scheme, that requires seven stages for a group without special structure and only six stages for other equations, is presented. Its sixth order is confirmed by a numerical convergence test.

Keywords: explicit Runge–Kutta · Partitioned methods ·
Structural partitioning · Order conditions · Multischeme methods

1 Introduction

Nowadays Runge–Kutta type methods (RKs) are one of the most widely used class of numerical methods for solving ordinary differential equations (ODEs). They have been intensively studied for more than a century and each new challenge in numerical treatment of ODEs like stiffness or geometrical properties preservation gave new inspiration to researchers for constructing and modifying Runge–Kutta methods. There is a lot of literature on the topic. One can find basics in classical textbooks on general numerical analysis, like [12,22], as well as read special monographs on ODE solution as [3,8].

New methods are proposed every year. Obviously they are not new kinds of "classical" explicit methods, but usually are designed to have one or few special properties or are intended for some peculiar classes of ODE systems.

© Springer Nature Switzerland AG 2019
S. Misra et al. (Eds.): ICCSA 2019, LNCS 11619, pp. 89–102, 2019.
https://doi.org/10.1007/978-3-030-24289-3_8

It is well known that partitioning of variables in ODE systems helps to simplify or reduce the system analytically. However even without analytical simplification it might be useful to separate the system into two or more parts and treat them numerically in different ways, i.e. to apply different (though interconnected) numerical schemes. Often this partitioning can be done in some natural way, say different parts of the system correspond to the unknowns of different physical nature. In other cases the partitioning is made on base of the system structure, stiffness or characteristic speeds of the processes.

Pioneer papers dealing with partitioning proposed methods for stiff problems of ODEs which were split up into "stiff" and "non-stiff" subsystems. Those methods were named implicit-explicit, since the "non-stiff" part was solve by fast explicit scheme and only the "stiff" part was solved by an implicit one (e.g. [9, 23]). In many recent paper such methods are called multischeme. Multischeme methods are studied to obtain simplectic integrators [13,14,29], to treat partial differential equations with parts of different physical nature [10,11], to solve fast and slow processes in large systems with different step sizes [27,28].

Here we consider the partitioning based on the right-hand side functions dependence on the unknowns. The structure of such dependencies can be used to construct fully explicit multischeme Runge–Kutta methods with fewer total right-hand side evaluations than *classic* explicit RKs require per step (the constraints known as *Butcher barriers* [3,8]).

We have presented several types of structural partitioning in [5]. Using the same denotations as there we present a *full structurally partitioned* system. It contains the *general group* of unknown functions — all those that don't have structural properties — and two *structural groups*.

$$
\begin{cases}
y_0'(t) = f_0(t, y_0, y_{11}, ..., y_{1,n_1}, y_{21}, ..., y_{2n_2}), \\
y_{1r}'(t) = f_{1r}(t, y_0, y_{11}, ..., y_{1,r-1}, y_{21}, ..., y_{2n_2}), & r = 1, ..., n_1, \\
y_{2r}'(t) = f_{2r}(t, y_0, y_{11}, ..., y_{1,n_1}, y_{21}, ..., y_{2,r-1}), & r = 1, ..., n_2.
\end{cases}
\tag{1}
$$

We distinguish between every unknown function in the first $(y_{11}, ..., y_{1,n_1})$ and the second $(y_{21}, ..., y_{2,n_2})$ structural groups since the numerical method is implemented differently to each of them. At the same time all the unknowns and equations in the general group are treated in the same way and the denotation y_0 can be formally considered as a vector of arbitrary length.

Any system of ODEs can be rewritten to have the structure (1). The general algorithm of finding the permutation of unknowns to obtain the structure (1) can be found in [17]. It is designed to maximize the size of structural groups, since the advantage over classic RKs is provided for the right-hand sides within them. In the worst case when for every possible r the derivative y_r' depends on y_r, no structural group can be formed and all the equations are included into the vector y_0. In this case the method studied in the present paper reduces to a classic Runge–Kutta method. However many problems of celestial mechanics, high-energy physics or some schemes of partial differential equations spatial discretization allow reformulation with a suitable structure (1) (see e.g. [24–26]).

Remark 1. In some systems all equations are included into the first or second structural group. In this case the advantage over the classic RKs is more considerable. The fifth order method can be constructed with four stages for every equation [15,18] (along with six for classic RKs). The sixth order method for the system with two structural groups requires six stages [1,6,20,21], while classic RKs require seven. The similar advantage can be obtained for continuous Runge–Kutta methods as well [5,7].

In the present paper we construct an explicit partitioned Runge–Kutta type method of order six for the system (1). It uses seven stages for the equations of general group (the mentioned Butcher's barrier) and only six stages for every equation of the first and second structural groups.

In the next section we present the general form of structurally partitioned system and the explicit Runge–Kutta type method for it.

The third section deals with sixth order conditions of the considered method and describes the simplifying assumptions on the methods parameters.

The algorithm of solving the system and one possible solution are given in Sect. 4 and the convergence test for a simple test problem in the last section.

2 Structural Numerical Method

Considering the initial point t_0 we write down the computational scheme for the Runge–Kutta type one-step method for obtaining the approximate solution in the point $t_0 + h$, where h is the step size.

$$y_0(t_0 + h) \approx y_0(t_0) + h \sum_{i=1}^{s_0} b_{0i} K_{0i},$$

$$y_{1r}(t_0 + h) \approx y_{1r}(t_0) + h \sum_{i=1}^{s_1} b_{1i} K_{1ri}, \quad r = 1, ..., n_1, \qquad (2)$$

$$y_{2r}(t_0 + h) \approx y_{2r}(t_0) + h \sum_{i=1}^{s_2} b_{2i} K_{2ri}, \quad r = 1, ..., n_2.$$

The difference from the formal expansion of classic Runge–Kutta methods to the systems of ODEs is that the right-hand side functions are evaluated one by one in strict order $K_{01}, K_{111}, K_{121}, ..., K_{1n_11}, K_{211}, ..., K_{2n_21}, K_{02}, K_{112}, ..., K_{1n_12}, K_{212}$, etc. according to

$$K_{0i} = f_0 \Big(t_0 + c_{0i}h, y_0(t_0) + h \sum_{j=1}^{i-1} a_{00ij} K_{0j},$$

$$y_{11}(t_0) + h \sum_{j=1}^{i} a_{01ij} K_{11j}, \ ..., \ y_{1,n_1}(t_0) + h \sum_{j=1}^{i} a_{01ij} K_{1,n_1,j},$$

$$y_{21}(t_0) + h \sum_{j=1}^{i-1} a_{02ij} K_{21j}, \ ..., \ y_{2n_2}(t_0) + h \sum_{j=1}^{i-1} a_{02ij} K_{2n_2j} \Big),$$

$$K_{1ri} = f_{1r}\Big(t_0 + c_{1i}h, y_0(t_0) + h\sum_{j=1}^{i} a_{10ij}K_{0j}, \qquad\qquad r = 1, ..., n_1,$$

$$y_{11}(t_0) + h\sum_{j=1}^{i} a_{11ij}K_{11j}, \; ..., \; y_{1,r-1}(t_0) + h\sum_{j=1}^{i} a_{11ij}K_{1,r-1,j},$$

$$y_{21}(t_0) + h\sum_{j=1}^{i-1} a_{12ij}K_{21j}, \; ..., \; y_{2n_2}(t_0) + h\sum_{j=1}^{i-1} a_{12ij}K_{2n_2j}\Big),$$

$$(3)$$

$$K_{2ri} = f_{2r}\Big(t_0 + c_{2i}h, y_0(t_0) + h\sum_{j=1}^{i} a_{20ij}K_{0j}, \qquad\qquad r = 1, ..., n_2,$$

$$y_{11}(t_0) + h\sum_{j=1}^{i} a_{21ij}K_{11j}, \; ..., \; y_{1n_1}(t_0) + h\sum_{j=1}^{i} a_{21ij}K_{1n_1j},$$

$$y_{21}(t_0) + h\sum_{j=1}^{i} a_{22ij}K_{21j}, \; ..., \; y_{2,r-1}(t_0) + h\sum_{j=1}^{i} a_{22ij}K_{2,r-1,j}\Big).$$

In each formula i varies in the corresponding range from 1 to s_0, s_1 or s_2. Notice that in general the algorithms demands that either $s_0 = s_1 = s_2$, or $s_0 = s_1 = s_2 + 1$, or $s_1 = s_2 = s_0 - 1$. The last case is the best for efficiency.

After the paper [2] it's being conventional to collect coefficients of Runge–Kutta type methods into so-called Butcher tables. Here we use an extended Butcher table for structural methods of the form

c_0	A_{00}	A_{01}	A_{02}	b_0
c_1	A_{10}	A_{11}	A_{12}	b_1
c_2	A_{20}	A_{21}	A_{22}	b_2

Here $b_v = (b_{v1}, ..., b_{vs_v})^T$ and $c_v = (c_{v1}, ..., c_{vs_v})^T$ are vectors and $A_{uv} = \{a_{uvij}\}$ are $[s_u \times s_v]$-matrices for $u, v = 0, 1, 2$.

Each group (general or structural) is referred to three blocks of parameters A_{uv}. The table form of the method corresponds to its structural properties and their algorithmic use. The matrices A_{00}, A_{01}, A_{02} and A_{12} are strictly lower-triangular (as is the case with classic explicit Runge–Kutta methods), but A_{10}, A_{20}, A_{11}, A_{21} and A_{22} are lower-triangular, i.e. can have non-zero diagonal elements.

Remark 2. As mentioned above, if a system (1) has no structural properties and no structural groups can be formed ($n_1 = n_2 = 0$) then the method reduces to classic Runge–Kutta method using only c_{0i}, b_{0i} and a_{00ij} coefficients. As a result of this we cannot construct a structural method of order p with s_0 smaller than a minimal number of stages required for a classic explicit Runge–Kutta method, i.e. s_0 respects usual Butcher barriers [8]. A structural methods is more efficient when $s_1 = s_2 = s_0 - 1$, and the efficiency grows as the size of the structural groups grows over the size of the general group.

In the following section we present the conditions of the sixth order, which form quite large system of algebraic equations. We apply additional relations between the method's coefficients, named simplifying conditions, and reduce the original large system to a much smaller one.

3   Conditions for the Sixth Order

The method (2), (3) is a one-step explicit method, so the convergence theorems can be applied, i.e. its convergence order equals its local order for smooth enough problems (e.g. [8]). In order to construct a method of order six we should find the coefficients such that the Taylor expansions in respect of h of the exact and numerical solutions are the same up to the h^6 terms, for each component. This means that for any problem smooth enough and some vector norm $\| \cdot \|$ there exist such positive numbers $C_0, C_{11}, ..., C_{1n_1}, C_{21}, ..., C_{2n_2}$ that for any h small enough

$$\|y_0(t_0 + h) - y_0(t_0) - h \sum_{i=1}^{s_0} b_{0i} K_{0i}\| < C_0 h^7,$$

$$|y_{1r}(t_0 + h) - y_{1r}(t_0) - h \sum_{i=1}^{s_1} b_{1i} K_{1ri}| < C_{1r} h^7, \quad r = 1, ..., n_1, \quad (4)$$

$$|y_{2r}(t_0 + h) - y_{2r}(t_0) - h \sum_{i=1}^{s_2} b_{2i} K_{2ri}| < C_{2r} h^7, \quad r = 1, ..., n_2.$$

Remark 3. Instead of considering the order componentwise in (4) we could use a vector norm over all unknown functions $y_0(t), y_{11}(t), ..., y_{1n_1}(t), y_{21}(t), ..., y_{2n_2}(t)$ simultaneously, but this doesn't change the order conditions, which follow.

It is well known [8] that a classic sixth order Runge–Kutta method requires at least seven stages and for such method the order conditions form a system of 37 nonlinear algebraic equations with 28 unknown parameters b_{0i} and a_{00ij} (in terms of Remark 2). The parameters c_{0i} are linearly dependent on a_{00ij}, so we don't count them in this consideration.

In [1,20] sixth order methods for systems without general group with only six stages for each unknown were constructed. In case of $n_1 = n_2 = 1$ the number of order conditions is 74 and number of parameters is 48. However if $n_1 > 1$ and $n_2 > 1$ the parameters a_{11ij} and a_{22ij} are used as well and in this case we obtain a system of 292 order conditions for 90 parameters [21].

In case of full system (1) we construct a sixth order method with $(s_0, s_1, s_2) = (7, 6, 6)$ stages. Besides of so-called *basic simplifying conditions* which connect c-parameters to a-parameters

$$\sum_{j=1}^{i-1} a_{00ij} = \sum_{j=1}^{i-1} a_{01ij} = \sum_{j=1}^{i-1} a_{02ij} = c_{0i}, \quad i = 1, ..., 7,$$

$$\sum_{j=1}^{i} a_{10ij} = \sum_{j=1}^{i} a_{11ij} = \sum_{j=1}^{i-1} a_{12ij} = c_{1i}, \quad i = 1, ..., 6, \quad (5)$$

$$\sum_{j=1}^{i} a_{20ij} = \sum_{j=1}^{i} a_{21ij} = \sum_{j=1}^{i} a_{22ij} = c_{2i}, \quad i = 1, ..., 6,$$

we have a system of 1224 order conditions obtained with the extension of labeled-trees theory for classic Runge–Kutta methods [3, 4]. In the following system the indices u, v, w, α and β can be 0, 1 or 2 in any combination. The summation is made over all possible (and meaningful) values of the summation indices.

$$\sum_i b_{ui} c_{ui}^q = \frac{1}{q+1}, \quad q = 0, 1, ..., 5,$$

$$\sum_i b_{ui} c_{ui}^q \sum_j a_{uvij} c_{vj} = \frac{1}{2 \cdot (q+3)}, \quad q = 0, 1, 2, 3,$$

$$\sum_i b_{ui} c_{ui}^q \sum_j a_{uvij} c_{vj}^2 = \frac{1}{3 \cdot (q+4)}, \quad q = 0, 1, 2,$$

$$\sum_i b_{ui} c_{ui}^q \sum_j a_{uvij} \sum_k a_{vwjk} c_{wk} = \frac{1}{6 \cdot (q+4)}, \quad q = 0, 1, 2,$$

$$\sum_i b_{ui} c_{ui}^q \left(\sum_j a_{uvij} c_{vj} \right) \left(\sum_k a_{uwik} c_{wk} \right) = \frac{1}{4 \cdot (q+5)}, \quad q = 0, 1,$$

$$\sum_i b_{ui} c_{ui}^q \sum_j a_{uvij} c_{vj}^3 = \frac{1}{4 \cdot (q+5)}, \quad q = 0, 1,$$

$$\sum_i b_{ui} \sum_j a_{uvij} c_{vj}^q \sum_k a_{vwjk} c_{wk}^d = \frac{1}{10(q+d)(1+d)},$$

$$(q, d) \in \{(0, 2), (0, 3), (1, 1), (1, 2), (2, 1)\},$$

$$\sum_i b_{ui} \sum_j a_{uvij} c_{vj}^q \sum_k a_{vwjk} c_{wk}^d \sum_l a_{waklj} c_{\alpha l}^\rho = \frac{1}{60(s + 2d + 2\rho)},$$

$$(q, d, \rho) \in \{(0, 0, 1), (1, 0, 1), (0, 1, 1)\},$$

$$\sum_i b_{ui} \left(\sum_j a_{uvij} c_{vj} \right) \left(\sum_j a_{uwik} c_{wk}^2 \right) = \frac{1}{36}, \tag{6}$$

$$\sum_i b_{ui} \sum_j a_{uvij} c_{vj}^4 = \frac{1}{30},$$

$$\sum_i b_{ui} \left(\sum_j a_{uvij} \sum_k a_{vwjk} c_{wk} \right) \left(\sum_l a_{u\alpha il} c_{\alpha l} \right) = \frac{1}{72},$$

$$\sum_i b_{ui} c_{ui} \sum_j a_{uvij} c_{vj} \sum_k a_{vwjk} c_{r,\xi} = \frac{1}{48},$$

$$\sum_i b_{ui} c_{ui} \sum_j a_{uvij} \sum_k a_{vwjk} c_{r,\xi}^2 = \frac{1}{72},$$

$$\sum_i b_{ui} \sum_j a_{uvij} \left(\sum_k a_{vwjk} c_{wk} \right) \left(\sum_l a_{v\alpha jl} c_{\alpha l} \right) = \frac{1}{120},$$

$$\sum_i b_{ui}c_{ui} \sum_j a_{uvij} \sum_k a_{vwjk} \sum_l a_{w\alpha kl}c_{\alpha l} = \frac{1}{144},$$

$$\sum_i b_{ui} \sum_j a_{uvij} \sum_k a_{vwjk} \sum_l a_{w\alpha kl}c_{\alpha l}^2 = \frac{1}{360},$$

$$\sum_i b_{ui}c_{ui} \sum_j a_{uvij} \sum_k a_{vwjk} \sum_l a_{w\alpha kl} \sum_m a_{\alpha\beta lm}c_{\beta m} = \frac{1}{720}.$$

The total number of parameters to be defined (including c-parameters) for (7,6,6) stages is 221.

Every classic sixth order Runge–Kutta method constructed by now has its b_2 parameter equal to zero. We make the same assumption for all three groups and additionally we assume that for all three groups the first right-hand side computation is done in the initial point of the step, i.e.

$$b_{02} = b_{12} = b_{22} = c_{01} = c_{11} = c_{21} = 0. \tag{7}$$

Next step to simplify the system is to introduce special assumptions known in the literature as *simplifying conditions* [3]. For different high-order Runge–Kutta methods different simplifying conditions can be used, each combination resulting into a separate family of solutions. We tried to apply various simplifying conditions and ended up with using different simplifying conditions of classic Runge–Kutta methods for different groups of parameters in system (6). These simplifying conditions are gathered blockwise and presented in the Table 1.

Table 1. Simplifying conditions for the system (6)

$q = 0, 1, 2; \ d = 0, 1; \ i = 3, ..., 7; \ k = 2, ..., 6; \ \kappa = 1, ...5; \ l = 1, ..., 6; \ m = 3, ..., 6$

$\sum_{j=1}^{i-1} a_{00ij}c_{0j}^q = \frac{c_{0i}^{q+1}}{q+1}$	$\sum_{j=1}^{i-1} a_{01ij}c_{1j}^d = \frac{c_{0i}^{d+1}}{d+1}$	$\sum_{j=1}^{i-1} a_{02ij}c_{2j}^d = \frac{c_{0i}^{d+1}}{d+1}$
$\sum_{j=3}^{7} b_{0j}c_{0j}^{d+1}a_{00j2} = 0$	$\sum_{j=3}^{7} b_{0j}c_{0j}^2 a_{01j2} = 0$	$\sum_{j=3}^{7} b_{0j}c_{0j}^2 a_{02j2} = 0$
$\sum_{j=l+1}^{7} b_{0j}a_{00jl} = b_{0l}(1 - c_{0l})$	$\sum_{j=l+1}^{7} b_{0j}c_{0j}^d a_{01jl} = \frac{b_{1l}(1-c_{1l}^{d+1})}{d+1}$	$\sum_{j=l+1}^{7} b_{0j}c_{0j}^d a_{02jl} = \frac{b_{2l}(1-c_{2l}^{d+1})}{d+1}$
$\sum_{j=1}^{k} a_{10kj}c_{0j}^q = \frac{c_{1k}^{q+1}}{q+1}$	$\sum_{j=1}^{k} a_{11kj}c_{1j}^d = \frac{c_{1k}^{d+1}}{d+1}$	$\sum_{j=1}^{m-1} a_{12mj}c_{2j}^d = \frac{c_{1m}^{d+1}}{d+1}$
$\sum_{j=2}^{6} b_{1j}c_{1j}^{d+1}a_{10j2} = 0$	$\sum_{j=2}^{6} b_{1j}c_{1j}^2 a_{11j2} = 0$	
$\sum_{j=l}^{6} b_{1j}a_{10jl} = b_{0l}(1 - c_{0l})$	$\sum_{j=l}^{6} b_{1j}c_{1j}^d a_{11jl} = \frac{b_{1l}(1-c_{1l}^{d+1})}{d+1}$	$\sum_{j=\kappa+1}^{6} b_{1j}a_{12j\kappa} = b_{2\kappa}(1 - c_{2\kappa})$
$\sum_{j=1}^{k} a_{20kj}c_{0j}^q = \frac{c_{2k}^{q+1}}{q+1}$	$\sum_{j=1}^{k} a_{21kj}c_{1j}^d = \frac{c_{2k}^{d+1}}{d+1}$	$\sum_{j=1}^{k} a_{22kj}c_{2j}^d = \frac{c_{2k}^{d+1}}{d+1}$
$\sum_{j=2}^{6} b_{2j}c_{2j}^{d+1}a_{20j2} = 0$	$\sum_{j=2}^{6} b_{2j}c_{2j}^2 a_{21j2} = 0$	
$\sum_{j=l}^{6} b_{2j}a_{20jl} = b_{0l}(1 - c_{0l})$	$\sum_{j=l}^{6} b_{2j}c_{2j}^d a_{21jl} = \frac{b_{1l}(1-c_{1l}^{d+1})}{d+1}$	$\sum_{j=l}^{6} b_{2j}c_{2j}^d a_{22jl} = \frac{b_{2l}(1-c_{2l}^{d+1})}{d+1}$

The reducing of the original system with use of simplifying conditions can be found in details in [16,21]. Here we present only the reduced system consisting of 47 equations (obtained from 1224 equations of (6)):

$$\sum_{i=1}^{s_u} b_{ui} c_{ui}^q = \frac{1}{q+1}, \quad u = 0,1,2, \quad q = 0,1,...,5,$$

$$\sum_{i=5}^{7} b_{0i} c_{0i} \sum_{j=4}^{i-1} a_{00ij} \sum_{k=3}^{j-1} a_{0wjk} c_{wk}^2 = \frac{1}{72}, \quad w = 0,1,$$

$$\sum_{i=4}^{7} b_{0i} c_{0i} \sum_{j=3}^{i-1} a_{00ij} \sum_{k=2}^{j-1} a_{0wjk} c_{wk}^2 = \frac{1}{72}, \quad w = 1,2,$$

$$\sum_{i=4}^{7} b_{0i} c_{0i} \sum_{j=3}^{i-1} a_{00ij} c_{0j}^3 = \frac{1}{24},$$

$$\sum_{i=4}^{7} b_{0i} c_{0i}^2 \sum_{j=3}^{i-1} a_{01ij} c_{1j}^2 = \frac{1}{18}, \qquad \sum_{i=3}^{7} b_{0i} c_{0i}^2 \sum_{j=2}^{i-1} a_{02ij} c_{2j}^2 = \frac{1}{18},$$

$$\sum_{i=4}^{6} b_{1i} c_{1i} \sum_{j=3}^{i} a_{10ij} \sum_{k=3}^{j-1} a_{00jk} c_{0k}^2 = \frac{1}{72},$$

$$\sum_{i=3}^{6} b_{ui} c_{ui} \sum_{j=3}^{i} a_{u0ij} c_{0j}^3 = \frac{1}{24}, \quad u = 1,2,$$

$$\sum_{i=3}^{6} b_{1i} c_{1i} \sum_{j=3}^{i} a_{10ij} \sum_{k=2}^{j-1} a_{0wjk} c_{wk}^2 = \frac{1}{72}, \quad w = 1,2,$$

$$\sum_{i=4}^{6} b_{1i} c_{1i} \sum_{j=4}^{i} a_{10ij} \sum_{k=3}^{j-1} a_{01jk} c_{1k}^2 = \frac{1}{72}, \tag{8}$$

$$\sum_{i=3}^{6} b_{1i} c_{1i}^2 \sum_{j=3}^{i} a_{10ij} c_{0j}^2 = \frac{1}{18},$$

$$\sum_{i=4}^{6} b_{1i} c_{1i} \sum_{j=3}^{i-1} a_{12ij} \sum_{k=3}^{j} a_{20jk} c_{0k}^2 = \frac{1}{72},$$

$$\sum_{i=4}^{6} b_{2i} c_{2i} \sum_{j=4}^{i} a_{20ij} \sum_{k=3}^{j-1} a_{0wjk} c_{wk}^2 = \frac{1}{72}, \quad w = 0,1,$$

$$\sum_{i=3}^{6} b_{2i} c_{2i} \sum_{j=3}^{i} a_{20ij} \sum_{k=2}^{j-1} a_{0wjk} c_{wk}^2 = \frac{1}{72}, \quad w = 1,2,$$

$$\sum_{i=3}^{6} b_{1i} c_{1i}^2 \sum_{j=2}^{i} a_{11ij} c_{1j}^2 = \frac{1}{18}, \qquad \sum_{i=3}^{6} b_{1i} c_{1i}^2 \sum_{j=2}^{i-1} a_{12ij} c_{2j}^2 = \frac{1}{18},$$

$$\sum_{i=3}^{6} b_{1i}c_{1i} \sum_{j=2}^{i-1} a_{12ij}c_{2j}^q = \frac{1}{(1+q)(3+q)}, \quad q = 1,2,3;$$

$$\sum_{i=3}^{6} b_{1i}c_{1i} \sum_{j=2}^{i-1} a_{12ij} \sum_{k=2}^{j} a_{2wjk}c_{wk}^2 = \frac{1}{72}, \quad w = 1,2,$$

$$\sum_{i=4}^{6} b_{1i}c_{1i} \sum_{j=3}^{i-1} a_{12ij} \sum_{k=3}^{j} a_{21jk}c_{1k}^2 = \frac{1}{72},$$

$$\sum_{i=3}^{6} b_{2i}c_{2i}^2 \sum_{j=2}^{i} a_{2vij}c_{vj}^2 = \frac{1}{18}, \quad v = 1,2.$$

Together with 198 simplifying conditions from Table 1 the total number of equations is 245, i.e. five times fewer than the original system (6). The number of unknown parameters (considering conditions (5)) is 202 now.

The reduced system (8) keeps the peculiarities of the original system: visible block structure and nonlinear relations between parameters within and between the blocks.

4   Particular Computational Scheme

Here we make certain special assumptions to find a particular solution of the reduced system:

$$c_{02} = a_{0021} = a_{0121} = a_{0221} = \frac{2}{15}, \quad c_{12} = c_{22} = c_{03} = c_{13} = \frac{1}{5},$$

$$c_{23} = c_{0,4} = \frac{1}{3}, \quad c_{05} = \frac{2}{3}, \quad c_{06} = \frac{4}{5}, \quad c_{07} = c_{16} = c_{26} = 1. \tag{9}$$

We leave $c_{24} = \alpha$ to be a free parameter. The remaining node parameters c_{14}, c_{15} and c_{25} can be found from the reduced system:

$$c_{14} = \frac{5\alpha - 2}{5(2\alpha - 1)}, \quad c_{15} = c_{25} = \frac{4\alpha - 3}{5\alpha - 4}.$$

Now the b-parameters (weights) are determined from the first equations of the reduced (or original) system, i.e. from the pure quadrature order conditions:

$$b_{01} = \frac{7}{96}, \quad b_{03} = \frac{125}{672}, \quad b_{04} = \frac{27}{112}, \quad b_{05} = \frac{27}{112}, \quad b_{06} = \frac{125}{672}, \quad b_{07} = \frac{7}{96},$$

$$b_{11} = \frac{15\alpha^2 - 18\alpha + 5}{12(5\alpha - 2)(4\alpha - 3)}, \quad b_{13} = \frac{125(5\alpha^2 - 5\alpha + 1)}{48(3\alpha - 1)(15\alpha - 11)},$$

$$b_{14} = \frac{125(2\alpha - 1)^5}{12(3\alpha - 1)(15\alpha^2 - 20\alpha + 7)(5\alpha - 2)(5\alpha - 3)},$$

$$b_{15} = \frac{(5\alpha - 4)^5}{12(15\alpha^2 - 20\alpha + 7)(15\alpha - 11)(\alpha - 1)(4\alpha - 3)},$$

$$b_{16} = \frac{15\alpha^2 - 27\alpha + 11}{48(5\alpha - 3)(\alpha - 1)}, \quad b_{21} = \frac{25\alpha^2 - 20\alpha + 1}{60\alpha(4\alpha - 3)},$$

$$b_{24} = \frac{1}{60(3\alpha - 1)(5\alpha^2 - 8\alpha + 3)\alpha(\alpha - 1)},$$

$$b_{25} = \frac{(5\alpha - 4)^5}{60(5\alpha^2 - 8\alpha + 3)(7\alpha - 5)(\alpha - 1)(4\alpha - 3)},$$

$$b_{23} = \frac{81(5\alpha^2 - 5\alpha + 1)}{40(3\alpha - 1)(7\alpha - 5)}, \quad b_{26} = \frac{5\alpha^2 - 15\alpha + 9}{120(\alpha - 1)^2}.$$

It is natural to demand that all c-parameters lie in $[0,1]$ and that all weights b are positive, i.e. lie in $[0,1]$ as well. This is provided when α satisfies

$$\alpha \in \left\{ \left(\frac{2 - \sqrt{3}}{5}, \frac{1}{5} \right) \cup \left(\frac{1}{5}, \frac{5 - \sqrt{5}}{10} \right) \right\}.$$

We choose $\alpha = \frac{1}{10}$ and solve the rest of the system as a sequence of linear subsystems. We omit the details and present only the computed values of the parameters.

$$A_{00} = \begin{pmatrix} 0 & & & & & \\ \frac{2}{15} & & & & & \\ \frac{1}{20} & \frac{3}{20} & & & & \\ \frac{11}{108} & \frac{-5}{36} & \frac{10}{27} & & & \\ \frac{23}{54} & \frac{-5}{18} & \frac{-35}{54} & \frac{7}{6} & & \\ \frac{-83}{125} & \frac{3}{5} & \frac{9}{5} & \frac{-189}{125} & \frac{72}{125} & \\ \frac{23}{28} & \frac{-15}{28} & \frac{-80}{49} & \frac{108}{49} & \frac{-18}{49} & \frac{25}{49} \end{pmatrix}, \quad A_{01} = \begin{pmatrix} 0 & & & & & \\ \frac{2}{15} & & & & & \\ \frac{1}{10} & \frac{1}{10} & & & & \\ \frac{1}{18} & \frac{-5}{54} & \frac{10}{27} & & & \\ \frac{20}{81} & \frac{-5}{27} & \frac{-5}{27} & \frac{64}{81} & & \\ \frac{-206}{975} & \frac{2}{5} & \frac{62}{95} & \frac{-2944}{7725} & \frac{43218}{127205} & \\ \frac{145}{546} & \frac{-5}{14} & \frac{80}{931} & \frac{7936}{15141} & \frac{12250}{25441} & 0 \end{pmatrix},$$

$$A_{02} = \begin{pmatrix} 0 & & & & \\ \frac{2}{15} & & & & \\ \frac{1}{10} & \frac{1}{10} & & & \\ \frac{1}{18} & \frac{5}{18} & 0 & & \\ \frac{-4}{9} & \frac{-25}{9} & \frac{5}{3} & \frac{20}{9} & \\ \frac{314}{325} & \frac{22}{5} & \frac{-1494}{1075} & \frac{-88}{25} & \frac{4802}{13975} \\ \frac{-141}{182} & \frac{-45}{14} & \frac{2988}{2107} & \frac{1360}{441} & \frac{2450}{5031} & 0 \end{pmatrix},$$

$$C_0 = \begin{pmatrix} 0 \\ \frac{2}{15} \\ \frac{1}{5} \\ \frac{1}{3} \\ \frac{2}{3} \\ \frac{4}{5} \\ 1 \end{pmatrix}, \quad A_{10} = \begin{pmatrix} 0 & & & & \\ \frac{1}{20} & \frac{3}{20} & & & \\ \frac{1}{20} & \frac{3}{20} & & & \\ \frac{255}{2048} & -\frac{495}{2048} & \frac{945}{2048} & \frac{63}{2048} & \\ \frac{30953}{600250} & \frac{429}{3430} & \frac{2717}{168070} & \frac{199329}{600250} & \frac{457938}{2100875} \\ \frac{95}{676} & -\frac{165}{676} & \frac{395}{1183} & \frac{393}{1183} & -\frac{45}{1183} & \frac{1125}{2366} \end{pmatrix},$$

$$C_1 = \begin{pmatrix} 0 \\ \frac{1}{5} \\ \frac{1}{5} \\ \frac{3}{8} \\ \frac{26}{35} \\ 1 \end{pmatrix}, \quad A_{11} = \begin{pmatrix} 0 & & & & \\ \frac{1}{10} & \frac{1}{10} & & & \\ \frac{1}{10} & 0 & \frac{1}{10} & & \\ \frac{1}{24} & 0 & \frac{5}{16} & \frac{1}{48} & \\ \frac{18817}{154350} & 0 & \frac{871}{36015} & \frac{252928}{540225} & \frac{9}{70} \\ -\frac{3581}{39546} & 0 & \frac{107935}{134862} & \frac{370688}{1096641} & \frac{2701125}{4299529} & 0 \end{pmatrix}, \quad (10)$$

$$C_2 = \begin{pmatrix} 0 \\ \frac{1}{5} \\ \frac{1}{5} \\ \frac{1}{3} \\ \frac{1}{10} \\ \frac{26}{35} \\ 1 \end{pmatrix}, \qquad A_{12} = \begin{pmatrix} 0 \\[2pt] \frac{1}{5} \\[2pt] \frac{1}{10} & \frac{1}{10} \\[2pt] \frac{45}{1024} & \frac{615}{2048} & \frac{63}{2048} \\[2pt] -\frac{167401}{60025} & \frac{244751}{24010} & \frac{3393039}{840350} & \frac{814112}{84035} \\[2pt] \frac{60745}{4394} & \frac{16415}{338} & -\frac{848271}{50869} & -\frac{54400}{1183} & \frac{120050}{94471} \end{pmatrix},$$

$$A_{20} = \begin{pmatrix} 0 \\[2pt] \frac{1}{20} & \frac{3}{20} \\[2pt] \frac{11}{108} & -\frac{5}{36} & \frac{10}{27} \\[2pt] \frac{19}{800} & \frac{33}{160} & -\frac{5}{32} & \frac{21}{800} \\[2pt] \frac{6877}{120050} & \frac{429}{3430} & -\frac{143}{33614} & \frac{1677}{4802} & \frac{90558}{420175} \\[2pt] \frac{20}{151} & -\frac{165}{604} & \frac{865}{2114} & \frac{615}{2114} & -\frac{81}{2114} & \frac{2025}{4228} \end{pmatrix}, \qquad B_0 = \begin{pmatrix} \frac{7}{96} \\ 0 \\ \frac{125}{672} \\ \frac{27}{112} \\ \frac{27}{112} \\ \frac{125}{672} \\ \frac{7}{96} \end{pmatrix},$$

$$A_{21} = \begin{pmatrix} 0 \\[2pt] \frac{1}{10} & \frac{1}{10} \\[2pt] \frac{1}{18} & -\frac{5}{54} & \frac{10}{27} \\[2pt] \frac{163}{1800} & \frac{11}{80} & -\frac{7}{48} & \frac{4}{225} \\[2pt] \frac{2773}{22050} & \frac{143}{1715} & \frac{1378}{19551} & \frac{3792256}{7949025} & \frac{3483}{27398} \\[2pt] -\frac{1876}{17667} & \frac{55}{302} & \frac{61790}{60249} & -\frac{362624}{979839} & \frac{4862025}{7683182} & 0 \end{pmatrix}, \qquad B_1 = \begin{pmatrix} \frac{67}{936} \\ 0 \\ \frac{1375}{6384} \\ \frac{8192}{32445} \\ \frac{2100875}{5495256} \\ \frac{169}{2160} \end{pmatrix},$$

$$A_{22} = \begin{pmatrix} 0 \\[2pt] \frac{1}{10} & \frac{1}{10} \\[2pt] \frac{1}{18} & \frac{5}{18} & 0 \\[2pt] \frac{2}{15} & \frac{1}{12} & 0 & -\frac{7}{60} \\[2pt] -\frac{547}{14406} & \frac{5603}{7203} & \frac{69498}{84035} & \frac{152048}{252105} & \frac{9}{70} & 0 \\[2pt] \frac{2011}{5889} & \frac{2195}{906} & -\frac{42768}{45451} & \frac{4640}{3171} & \frac{108045}{168818} & 0 \end{pmatrix}, \qquad B_2 = \begin{pmatrix} \frac{5}{104} \\ 0 \\ \frac{891}{2408} \\ \frac{200}{1701} \\ \frac{420175}{1086696} \\ \frac{151}{1944} \end{pmatrix}.$$

5 Numerical Convergence Test

Since we don't have an error estimator embedded into the presented scheme, we make only the convergence test to confirm the declared sixth order of the method.

The system of four equations

$$\begin{aligned}
y_1' &= 2xy_1y_3 & &= f_1(x, y_1, y_3), \\
y_2' &= 2xy_3 & &= f_2(x, y_3), \\
y_3' &= -2x(y_2 - 1) & &= f_3(x, y_2), \\
y_4' &= 10xy_3y_1^5 & &= f_4(x, y_1, y_3),
\end{aligned} \tag{11}$$

with the initial conditions $y_1(0) = y_2(0) = y_3(0) = y_4(0) = 1$ has the exact solution

$$y_1 = \exp(\sin x^2), \quad y_2 = \sin x^2 + 1, \quad y_3 = \cos x^2, \quad y_2 = \exp(5\sin x^2).$$

Here we have 1 unknown in the general group (y_1), one in the first structural group (y_2) and two in the second structural group (y_3, y_4).

We solve it at the interval $[0,5]$ with constant step size h and compute the maximal norm of the exact error in every step Err. We change the step size as $h = \frac{1}{3} \cdot \left(\frac{3}{2}\right)^k$ for $k = 1, ..., 11$. The results are presented at Fig. 1a and in the Table 2 as Test 1. The average slope of the segmented line for h small enough shows the rate of convergence in double logarithmic scale. The test confirms the sixth order of the method.

In order to check the case of several equations in the first structural group, we make the change of variables $u_1 = y_1$, $u_2 = y_3$, $u_3 = y_4$, $u_4 = y_2$. In this case two equation are in the first group and one is in the second group. The results of the same test for this system are presented at Fig. 1b and in the Table 2 as Test 2.

Table 2. Results of the numerical tests of convergence

k	Test 1		Test 2	
	Err	Order	Err	Order
1	14.6832		5.00611	
2	1.11106	6.15	1.95241	2.24
3	$2.58338 \cdot 10^{-1}$	3.52	$2.41613 \cdot 10^{-1}$	5.04
4	$8.90772 \cdot 10^{-3}$	8.18	$6.31942 \cdot 10^{-3}$	8.85
5	$3.24414 \cdot 10^{-4}$	8.17	$3.66468 \cdot 10^{-4}$	7.02
6	$3.35677 \cdot 10^{-5}$	5.59	$4.19328 \cdot 10^{-5}$	5.35
7	$2.64534 \cdot 10^{-6}$	6.27	$3.36406 \cdot 10^{-6}$	6.22
8	$2.46517 \cdot 10^{-7}$	5.85	$3.02240 \cdot 10^{-7}$	5.94
9	$2.11060 \cdot 10^{-8}$	6.05	$2.70710 \cdot 10^{-8}$	5.94
10	$1.79768 \cdot 10^{-9}$	6.07	$2.28522 \cdot 10^{-9}$	6.09
11	$2.09015 \cdot 10^{-10}$	5.31	$2.29279 \cdot 10^{-10}$	5.67

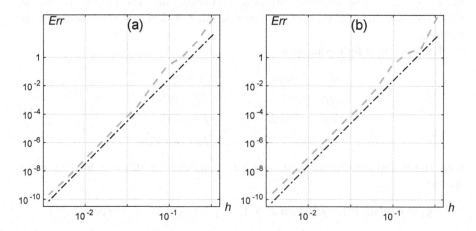

Fig. 1. The global error to step size ratio in the double logarithmic scale. The reference lines have slope 6.

6   Conclusion

The presented sixth order method for many systems transformable to the structure (1) provides better per step performance than formal application of classic Runge–Kutta methods to such systems. However, practical use of RKs nowadays require an automatic time step size control which is usually based on local error estimation. For RKs it is most often made with use of embedded scheme of lower order, and it can also be done within the structural partitioning approach [18,19]. This requires solution of even more complicated system of order conditions.

References

1. Bubnov, V.P., Eremin, A.S., Kovrizhnykh, N.A., Olemskoy, I.V.: Comparative study of the advantages of structural numerical integration methods for ordinary differential equations. SPIIRAS Proc. **4**(53), 51–72 (2017)
2. Butcher, J.C.: On Runge-Kutta processes of high order. J. Australian Math. Soc. **4**(2), 179–194 (1964)
3. Butcher, J.C.: Numerical Methods for Ordinary Differential Equations, 2nd edn. Wiley, Chichester (2008)
4. Butcher, J.C., Chan, T.M.H.: The tree and forest spaces with applications to initial-value problem methods. BIT Numer. Math. **50**, 713–728 (2010)
5. Eremin, A.S., Kovrizhnykh, N.A.: Continuous extensions for structural Runge–Kutta methods. In: Gervasi, O., et al. (eds.) ICCSA 2017. LNCS, vol. 10405, pp. 363–378. Springer, Cham (2017). https://doi.org/10.1007/978-3-319-62395-5_25
6. Eremin, A.S., Kovrizhnykh, N.A., Olemskoy, I.V.: An explicit one-step multischeme sixth order method for systems of special structure. Appl. Math. Comput. **347**, 853–864 (2019)
7. Eremin, A.S., Olemskoy, I.V.: Functional continuous Runge-Kutta methods for special systems. In: Proceedings of the International Conference on Numerical Analysis and Applied Mathematics 2015 (ICNAAM-2015)/AIP Conference Proceedings, vol. 1738, p. 100003 (2016)
8. Hairer, E., Nørsett, S.P., Wanner, G.: Solving Ordinary Differential Equations I: Nonstiff Problems. Springer Series in Computational Mathematics, 3rd edn. Springer, Heidelberg (2008). https://doi.org/10.1007/978-3-540-78862-1
9. Hofer, E.: A partially implicit method for large stiff systems of ODEs with only few equations introducing small time-constants. SIAM J. Numer. Anal. **13**(5), 645–663 (1976)
10. Huang, D., Persson, P.O., Zahr, M.: High-order, linearly stable, partitioned solvers for general multiphysics problems based on implicit-explicit Runge-Kutta schemes. Comput. Methods Appl. Mech. Eng. **346**, 674–706 (2019)
11. Ketcheson, D.I., MacDonald, C., Ruuth, S.J.: Spatially partitioned embedded Runge-Kutta methods. SIAM J. Numer. Anal. **51**(5), 2887–2910 (2013)
12. Kincaid, D., Cheney, W.: Numerical Analysis: Mathematics of Scientific Computing, Pure and Applied Undergraduate Texts, vol. 2, 3rd edn. AMS, Providence (2002)
13. McLachlan, R., Ryland, B., Sun, Y.: High order multisymplectic Runge-Kutta methods. SIAM J. Sci. Comput. **36**(5), A2199–A2226 (2014)

14. Monovasilis, T., Kalogiratou, Z., Simos, T.E.: A family of trigonometrically fitted partitioned Runge-Kutta symplectic methods. Appl. Math. Comput. **209**(1), 91–96 (2009)

15. Olemskoy, I.V.: Fifth-order four-stage method for numerical integration of special systems. Comput. Math. Math. Phys. **42**(8), 1135–1145 (2002)

16. Olemskoy, I.V.: Structural approach to the design of explicit one-stage methods. Comput. Math. Math. Phys. **43**(7), 918–931 (2003)

17. Olemskoy, I.V.: Modifikatsiya algoritma vydeleniya strukturnykh osobennostei [modification of structural properties detection algorithm]. Vestn. St-Petersburg Uni. Appl. Math. Comp. Sci. Contr. Proc. **2**, 55–64 (2006). [In Russian]

18. Olemskoy, I.V., Eremin, A.S.: An embedded method for integrating systems of structurally separated ordinary differential equations. Comput Math. Math. Phys. **50**(3), 414–427 (2010)

19. Olemskoy, I.V., Eremin, A.S.: An embedded fourth order method for solving structurally partitioned systems of ordinary differential equations. Appl. Math. Sci. **9**(97–100), 4843–4852 (2015)

20. Olemskoy, I.V., Eremin, A.S., Ivanov, A.P.: Sixth order method with six stages for integrating special systems of ordinary differential equations. In: 2015 International Conference "Stability and Control Processes" in Memory of V.I. Zubov (SCP), pp. 110–113 (2015)

21. Olemskoy, I.V., Kovrizhnykh, N.A.: A family of sixth-order methods with six stages. Vestn. St-Petersburg Uni. Appl. Math. Comp. Sci. Contr. Proc. **14**(3), 215–229 (2018)

22. Ralston, A., Rabinowitz, P.: A First Course in Numerical Analysis. Dover Books on Mathematics, 2nd edn. Dover Publications, New York (2001)

23. Rentrop, P.: Partitioned Runge-Kutta methods with stiffness detection and stepsize control. Numer. Math. **47**, 545–564 (1985)

24. Respondek, J.S.: Controllability of dynamical systems with constraints. Syst. Control Lett. **54**(4), 293–314 (2005)

25. Respondek, J.S.: Numerical simulation in the partial differential equation controllability analysis with physically meaningful constraints. Math. Comput. Simul. **81**(1), 120–132 (2010)

26. Respondek, J.S.: Incremental numerical recipes for the high efficient inversion of the confluent Vandermonde matrices. Comput. Math. Appl. **71**(2), 489–502 (2016)

27. Sandu, A., Günther, M.: A generalized-structure approach to additive Runge-Kutta methods. SIAM J. Numer. Anal. **53**(1), 17–42 (2015)

28. Sandu, A., Günther, M.: Multirate generalized additive Runge-Kutta methods. Numer. Math. **133**(3), 497–524 (2016)

29. Wang, D., Xiao, A., Li, X.: Parametric symplectic partitioned Runge-Kutta methods with energy-preserving properties for Hamiltonian systems. Comput. Phys. Commun. **184**(2), 303–310 (2013)

Dynamic Public Transit Labeling

Mattia D'Emidio[1](✉) [iD] and Imran Khan[2](✉)

[1] Department of Information Engineering, Computer Science and Mathematics,
University of L'Aquila, L'Aquila, Italy
`mattia.demidio@univaq.it`
[2] Gran Sasso Science Institute (GSSI), L'Aquila, Italy
`imran.khan@gssi.it`

Abstract. We study the journey planning problem in transit networks which, given the timetable of a *schedule-based transit system*, asks to answer to queries such as, e.g., "seek a journey that arrives at a given destination as early as possible". The state-of-the-art solution to such problem, in terms of query time, is *Public Transit Labeling* (PTL), proposed in [Delling et al., SEA 2015], that consists of three main ingredients: (i) a graph data structure for storing transit networks; (ii) a compact labeling-based representation of the transitive closure of such graph, computed via a time-consuming preprocessing routine; (iii) an efficient query algorithm exploiting both graph and precomputed data to answer quickly to queries of interest at runtime.

The major drawback of PTL is not being practical in *dynamic scenarios*, when the network's timetable can undergo updates (e.g. *delays*). In fact, even after a single change, precomputed data become outdated and queries can return incorrect results. Recomputing the labeling-based representation from scratch, after a modification, is not a viable option as it yields unsustainable time overheads. Since transit networks are inherently dynamic, the above represents a major limitation of PTL.

In this paper, we overcome such limit by introducing a *dynamic algorithm*, called D-PTL, able to update the preprocessed data whenever a delay affects the network, without recomputing it from scratch. We demonstrate the effectiveness of D-PTL through a rigorous experimental evaluation showing that its update times are orders of magnitude smaller than the time for recomputing the preprocessed data from scratch.

Keywords: Journey planning · Dynamic graph algorithms ·
2-Hop-Cover labeling · Algorithm engineering · Massive datasets ·
Networks

This work has been partially supported by the Italian National Group for Scientific Computation GNCS-INdAM – Program "Finanziamento GNCS Giovani Ricercatori 2018/2019" – Project "Efficient Mining of Distances in Fully Dynamic Massive Graphs".

© Springer Nature Switzerland AG 2019
S. Misra et al. (Eds.): ICCSA 2019, LNCS 11619, pp. 103–117, 2019.
https://doi.org/10.1007/978-3-030-24289-3_9

1   Introduction

Computing best journeys in *schedule-based transit systems* (consisting, e.g., of trains, buses, etc.) is a problem that has been faced at least once by everybody who ever traveled [2]. In particular, the *journey planning problem* asks, given an *input timetable* (i.e. the description, in terms of departure and arrival times, of transits of vehicles between stops within the system) to answer to natural queries such as, e.g., "What is the best journey from some stop A to some other stop B if I want to depart at time t?".

Despite its simple formulation, the problem is much more challenging w.r.t., for instance, to the route planning problem in road networks which has been the subject of many recent studies (see, e.g., [2,9,12]). This is due to the fact that schedule-based transit systems exhibit an inherent time-dependent component that requires more complex modeling assumptions to obtain meaningful results. For this reason, recently, transit companies have invested a lot of resources to develop software systems, called *journey planners* (see, e.g., *Google Transit*[1] or *bahn.de*[2]), to be able to answer efficiently to such kind of queries and to provide best journeys w.r.t. to some metric of interest. Depending on the considered metric and modeling assumptions, the problem can be specialized into a plethora of optimization problems [2].

The most common type of query is the *earliest arrival query*, which asks for computing a journey that minimizes the total traveling time from a given departure stop to a given arrival stop, if one departs at a distinguished departure time. Another prominent type of query is the *profile query*, which instead asks to retrieve a set of journeys from a given departure stop to a given arrival stop if departure time can lie within a given range. Further types of queries can be obtained by considering multiple optimization criteria simultaneously or according to the abstraction at which the problem has to be solved. If, for instance, one wants to optimize the time required by a passenger for moving from one vehicle to another one within a stop (i.e., *transfer time*), then the problem is called *realistic* while it is referred to as *ideal* otherwise [6]. In this paper, we focus on the realistic scenario. To solve the mentioned variants, a great variety of models and techniques have been proposed in the literature [5,11,13–15]. We refer to the very recent survey of Bast et al. [2] for a comprehensive overview.

The state-of-the-art method, achieving the smallest query times on large sets of real-world inputs, is *Public Transit Labeling* (PTL, for short) a preprocessing-based approach that has been experimentally shown to outperform all other solutions, achieving order of milliseconds query times on average even in continental-sized networks [4,7,11,17]. Such approach essentially consists of three main ingredients: (i) a well-known graph data structure for storing transit networks, i.e. the *time–expanded graph*; (ii) a compact labeling-based representation of the transitive closure of the said graph, computed via a (time-consuming) preprocessing step; (iii) an efficient query algorithm exploiting both the graph

---

[1] https://maps.google.com/landing/transit/index.html.
[2] https://www.bahn.de.

and the precomputed data to answer quickly to queries of interest at runtime. Unfortunately, PTL has the major drawback of not being practical in *dynamic scenarios*, that is when the network can undergo to unpredictable updates (e.g. due to *delays* affecting the route traversed by a given vehicle). In particular, even after a single change to the network, queries can return incorrect results since the preprocessed data can become easily outdated and do not reflect properly the transitive closure. Recomputing the labeling-based data from scratch, after an update occurs, is not a viable option as it yields unsustainable time overheads, up to tens of hours [11]. Since transit networks are inherently dynamic (delays can be very frequent), the above represents a major limitation of PTL.

Dynamic approaches to update graphs and corresponding labeling-based representations of transitive closures have been investigated in the past, in other application domains, due to the effectiveness of such structures [1,8,10,16]. However, none of these can be directly employed in the PTL case, where time constraints imposed by the time-expanded graph add a further level of complexity to the involved data structures.

Our Contribution. In this paper, we overcome the above mentioned limit by presenting a new *dynamic algorithm*, named *Dynamic Public Transit Labeling* (D-PTL, for short), that is able to update the information precomputed by PTL whenever a delay occurs in the transit network, without performing a recomputation it from scratch. Notice that, decreases in departure times are typically not allowed in transit networks, since, to preserve the integrity of pre-planned connections, if a vehicle arrives early at a given stop, it just waits [2]. Hence updating the information in such case is not necessary. However, our solution can be easily extended to manage such scenario.

We discuss the correctness of D-PTL and analyze its computational complexity in the worst case. Asymptotically speaking, the proposed solution is worse than the recomputation from scratch. However, we present an extensive algorithm-engineering based experimental study, conducted on real-world networks of large size, that shows that D-PTL always outperforms the from scratch computation in practice. In particular, our results show that D-PTL is able to update both the graph and the labeling structure orders of magnitude faster than the recomputation from scratch. Our data also highlight that the updated graph and labeling structure induce both query time performance and space overhead that are equivalent to those that are obtained by the recomputation from scratch, thus making D-PTL an effective approach to handle the journey planning problem in dynamic transit networks.

Structure of the Paper. The paper is organized as follows. Section 2 gives the notation, describe the basics of PTL and of the labeling technique [11]. In Sect. 3 we present our new dynamic algorithm and discuss its correctness and complexity. Section 4 describe our experimental study while Sect. 5 concludes paper and outlines possible future research directions.

2   Background

We are given an *input timetable*, consisting of data concerning: stops, vehicles (e.g. trains, buses or any means of transportation) connecting stops, and departure and arrival times of vehicles at stops. More formally, a timetable T is defined by a triple $T = (Z, S, C)$, where Z is a set of *vehicles*, S is a set of *stops* (often in the literature also referred to as *stations*), and C is a set of *elementary connections* whose elements are 5-tuples of the form $c = (Z, s_i, s_j, t_d, t_a)$. Such a tuple is interpreted as vehicle $Z \in Z$ leaves *departure stop* $s_i \in$ S at *departure time* t_d, and the immediately next stop of vehicle Z is stop $s_j \in$ S at time t_a (i.e. t_a is the *arrival time* of Z at *arrival stop* $s_j \in$ S). Departure and arrival times are integers in $\{0, 1, \ldots, t_{max}\}$ representing time in minutes after midnight, where t_{max} is the largest time allowed within the timetable (typically $t_{max} = (n \cdot 1440 - 1)$, where n is the number of days that are represented by the timetable). We assume $|C| \geq \max\{|S|, |Z|\}$, that is we do not consider vehicles and stops that do not take part to any connection. Moreover, we consider the realistic scenario, that is each stop $s_i \in$ S has an associated *minimum transfer time*, denoted by MTTP_i, which is the time, in minutes, required for moving from one vehicle to another inside stop s_i.

A *trip* $\text{TRIP}_i = (c_1, c_2, \ldots, c_k)$ is a sequence of k connections that: (i) are operated by a same vehicle; (ii) share pairwisely departure and arrival stop, i.e., formally, we have $c_{i-1} = (Z, s_i, s_j, t_d, t_a)$ and $c_i = (Z, s_j, s_k, t'_d, t'_a)$ with $t'_d > t_d$ for any $i \in [2, k]$. Clearly, connections in a trip are ordered in terms of the associated departure times, hence we say connection c_j *follows* connection c_{j-1} in a trip TRIP_i whenever the departure time of the former is larger than that of the latter. Similarly, we say connection c_j *precedes* connection c_{j+1} in TRIP_i.

An *earliest arrival query* $\text{EA}(s_i, s_j, \tau)$ asks, given a triple s_i, s_j, τ of *source stop* s_i, *target stop* s_j and departure time $\tau \geq 0$, to compute a *quickest journey*, i.e. a *journey* that starts at any $t \geq \tau$, connects s_i to s_j, and minimizes traveling time. A *journey* $J = (c_1, c_2, \ldots c_n)$ connecting two stops s_i to s_j is a sequence of n connections that: (i) can be serviced by different vehicles; (ii) allow to reach a given *target stop* starting from a distinguished *source stop* at a given departure time $\tau \geq 0$, i.e. the departure stop of c_1 is s_i, the arrival stop of c_n is s_j and the departure time of c_1 is larger than or equal to τ; (iii) is formed by connections that satisfy the time constraints imposed by the timetable, namely that if the vehicle of connection c_i is different w.r.t. that of c_{i+1} at a stop s_h, then the departure time of c_{i+1} must be larger than the arrival time of c_i plus MTTP_h. As well as trips, journeys are implicitly ordered by time according departure times of the connections. The *traveling time* of a journey is given by the difference between arrival time of its last connection and τ. A *profile query* $\text{PQ}(s_i, s_j, \tau, \tau')$ asks for the *set of non-dominated journeys* between stops s_i and s_j in the time range $\langle \tau, \tau' \rangle$, subject to $\tau < \tau'$, i.e. the set of journeys connecting stops s_i and s_j that start at any time in $[\tau, \tau']$ and are non-dominated journeys. A journey is non-dominated if and only if the departure time (arrival time, respectively) of its first connection is smaller than that of any other in the set.

Public Transit Labeling. The state-of-the art approach to answer the above queries is based on a graph representation of the transit network [11], and it is discussed in the following.

In particular, the input timetable $\mathcal{T} = (\mathcal{Z}, \mathrm{S}, \mathcal{C})$ associated to the transit network is modeled via a *reduced time–expanded graph* (RED-TE, for short) [6], that is a directed acyclic graph $G(V, A)$. Note that aperiodic timetables can be effectively represented as directed acyclic graphs [11]. Starting from initially empty sets V and A, the graph is built as follows. For each elementary connection $c = (Z, s_i, s_j, t_d, t_a)$ we add two vertices to V, namely a *departure vertex* v_d^c and *arrival vertex* v_a^c, respectively, each having an associated time $time(v_d^c)$ and $time(v_a^c)$, respectively, that is equal to the departure and arrival times of the connection, i.e. $time(v_d^c) = t_d$ and $time(v_a^c) = t_a$. Departure and arrival vertices are logically stored within the corresponding stop, that is each vertex v_d^c (v_a^c, respectively) belongs to the *set of departure* (*arrival*, respectively) *vertices* DV^i (AV^j, respectively) of stop s_i (s_j, respectively). In addition, for each connection we also insert a directed *connection arc* (v_d^c, v_a^c) to A, connecting the corresponding two departure and arrival vertices. Moreover, for each trip $\mathrm{TRIP}_i = (c_0, c_1, \ldots, c_k)$ we add to A a *bypass arc* $(v_a^{c_i}, v_a^{c_{i+1}})$ connecting the two arrival vertices. Furthermore, for any pair of vertices $u, v \in \mathrm{DV}^i$, we add to A a *waiting arc* (u, v) if $time(v) \geq time(u)$ and there is no w in DV^i such that $time(v) \geq time(w) \geq time(u)$. Finally, for each $u \in \mathrm{AV}^i$ and for each $v \in \mathrm{DV}^i$, we add to A a *transfer arc* (u, v) if $time(v) \geq time(u) + \mathrm{MTTP}_i$ and there is no $w \in \mathrm{DV}^i$ such that $time(w) < time(v)$ and $time(w) \geq time(u) + \mathrm{MTTP}_i$.

Given a RED-TE graph $G = (V, A)$, we say a vertex u *is reachable from* (*reaches*, respectively) another vertex v if and only if there exists a path from v to u (from u to v, respectively) in G, i.e. a sequence of arcs $((v, v_1), (v_1, v_2), \ldots, (v_k, u))$. The *cost* of a path is the sum of weights of the arcs in the path, where the *weight* of an arc (i, j) is given by the positive (by construction) difference $time(j) - time(i)$ between the times of its endpoint vertices. It is easy to see how, in a RED-TE graph built as described above, all paths from a vertex u to a vertex v in G have the same cost [6,11], which is given by $time(v) - time(u)$ (again positive by construction). Given a graph G, any approach for computing a so–called 2-Hop-Cover *reachability labeling* L (2HCR labeling, for short) of G associates two labels to each vertex $v \in V$, namely a *backward label* $\mathrm{L}_{in}(v)$ and a *forward label* $\mathrm{L}_{out}(v)$ [7], where a label is a set of vertices of G. In particular, for any two vertices $u, v \in V$, $\mathrm{L}_{out}(u) \cap \mathrm{L}_{in}(v) \neq \emptyset$ if and only if there exists a path from u to v in G [7]. Vertices $\{h : h \in \mathrm{L}_{out}(u) \cap \mathrm{L}_{in}(v)\}$ are called *hub vertices* for pair u, v, and each element in said set is a vertex lying on a path from u to v in G. The size of a 2HCR labeling is given by the sum of the sizes of the label entries and it is known that computing a 2HCR labeling of minimum size is NP-Hard [7]. However, numerous approaches have been presented to heuristically improve both the time to compute the labeling and its size [3,18,19]. Among them, the one in [19], called BUTTERFLY, has been shown to exhibit superior performance for directed acyclic graphs. Moreover, the solution is suited for *dynamic graphs*, i.e. the authors also provide a dynamic algorithm that is able to update the 2HCR labeling L of a graph G to reflect changes occurring on G itself. In particular, given a graph G, a 2HCR labeling L of G, and an update operation occurring on G, the algorithm is able to compute another labeling L' that is a 2HCR labeling for G', where G' is the graph obtained by applying the update on G. Note that, in this scenario, updates can be *incremental* (*decremental*, respectively), if they are additions (removals, respectively) of a vertex/arc. Throughout the paper, we denote by INC-BU(G, L, v) (DEC-BU(G, L, v), respectively) the result of the application of the dynamic algorithm of [19] to the labeling L of a graph G to handle an incremental (decremental, respectively) operation occurring on vertex/arc v (we refer the reader to [19] for more details on the above dynamic algorithms).

It is known that any 2HCR labeling, along with the above described RED-TE graph model, can be used to answer to queries of interest on timetable (we refer the reader to [11] for more details). However, in order to obtain very fast query time, compatible with modern applications, in [11] a customization of the general approach, tailored for RED-TE graphs, has been proposed under the name of *Public Transit Labeling* (PTL, for short).

The main idea underlying PTL is to compact labels, and to associate them to stops, rather than to vertices. In particular, PTL computes a RED-TE graph G, a 2HCR labeling L of G, and a set of *stop labels* SL of L [11]. For the sake of clarity we remark that the approach in [11] relies on a classic time–expanded graph. However, there is a one-to-one correspondence between RED-TE graphs and classic time–expanded graphs [6].

In details, we have a *forward stop label* $\text{SL}_{out}(i)$ and a *backward stop label* $\text{SL}_{in}(i)$ for each stop $s_i \in$ S. A forward (backward, respectively) stop label is a list of pairs of the form $(v, stoptime_i(v))$ where v is a *hub vertex* reachable (that reaches, respectively) from at least one vertex in DV^i (AV^i, respectively) and $stoptime_i(v)$ encodes the latest departure (earliest arrival, respectively) time from s_i to reach hub vertex v (from the stop, say s_v, of vertex v to reach s_i, respectively) For efficiency purposes, entries in $\text{SL}_{out}(i)$ ($\text{SL}_{in}(i)$, respectively) are stored as sorted arrays, in increasing order of hub vertices (according to distinct ids are assigned to vertices). The set of stop labels is usually referred to as *stop labeling* of G (or of L). Similarly to the general 2HCR labeling case, queries on the timetable can be answered via stop labels by scanning the entries associated to source and target stops. Query algorithms exploit the information in the stop labeling to discard dominated journeys to the stored hubs and to achieve query times of the order of milliseconds [11].

3   Dynamic Public Transit Labeling

In this section, we introduce *Dynamic Public Transit Labeling* (D-PTL, for short), a new dynamic algorithm able to update a RED-TE graph $G = (V, A)$, the corresponding 2HCR labeling L and stop labeling SL, as a consequence of a delay affecting a connection of the transit network. Formally, a *delay* is an increase in the departure time of an elementary connection of a finite quantity $\delta > 0$. It is easy to see how a delay can induce an arbitrary number of changes to both the graph and labelings [6,11], depending on the structure of the trip the connection belongs to, thus in turn inducing arbitrarily wrong answers to queries.

A general dynamic strategy to achieve the purpose of updating both G, the 2HCR labeling L and the stop labeling SL, after a delay, while preserving the correctness of the queries, is to first update the graph representing the timetable (via, e.g., the solutions in [5,6,15]) and then reflect all these changes on both L and SL by: (i) detecting and removing obsolete label entries; and (ii) adding new updated label entries induced by the new graph, as done in other works on the subject [10,19]. However, this results in a quite high computational effort, as shown by preliminary experimentation we conducted. Thus, in order to minimize the number of changes to both L and SL, we exploit the specific structure of the RED-TE graph and propose a dynamic algorithm that interleaves phases of update of the graph with phases of update of the labeling L via the dynamic algorithms of [19]. At the end of such phases, changes to L are reflected onto its compact representation SL through a dedicated routine. In particular, our algorithm is based on the following observation: a delay affecting a connection of a trip might be propagated to all subsequent connections in the same trip, if any. Hence, the impact of a given delay on both the graph and the labelings strongly depends on δ, on the structure of the trip and, in particular, on the departure times of subsequent connections. Therefore, D-PTL processes connections of a trip incrementally, and in order w.r.t. departure time, by executing two subroutines, called, respectively, *removal phase* (Algorithm REM-D-PTL for short) and *insertion phase* (Algorithm INS-D-PTL for short) that update L along with the graph. The former, described in Algorithm 1, takes care of removing from G vertices and arcs, associated with the delayed connection, that *violate* the RED-TE constraints.

We say a vertex (arc, respectively) *violates* the RED-TE constraints whenever the associated time (the difference of the times of the endpoints, respectively) does not satisfy at least one of the inequalities imposed by the RED-TE model discussed in Sect. 2. Note that, vertex and arcs of the above kind can be: (a) departure and arrival vertices of the delayed connection; (b) departure and arrival vertices following the delayed connection in the same trip; (c) arcs adjacent to vertices in (a) and (b).

The latter, instead, described in Algorithm 2, adds to G vertices and arcs, according to the delayed connection, in such a way G is a RED-TE graph properly representing the updated timetable. Then, it also updates accordingly L.

The behavior of algorithm is customized depending on the effect of the delay on the original G. In particular, we have a different update path by Algorithm 2 depending on whether the vertices associated to the connection are removed or not from the graph by Algorithm 1. We distinguish four cases:

Algorithm 1. Algorithm REM-D-PTL.

Input: RED-TE graph G, delay $\delta > 0$, delayed connection c_m, trip
$\qquad$ TRIP$_i = (c_0, c_1, \ldots, c_m, \ldots, c_k)$
Output: RED-TE graph G not including vertices of connections violating
$\qquad$ RED-TE constraints, 2HCR labeling L of G

```
1  foreach cj, j = m to k do
2  │   Let ss and st be departure and arrival, respectively, stops of cj;
3  │   PRED ← ∞; SUCC ← ∞;
4  │   time(v_d^{cj}) ← time(v_d^{cj}) + δ;
5  │   time(v_a^{cj}) ← time(v_a^{cj}) + δ;
6  │   foreach v ∈ Nout(v_d^{cj}) do                 // Outgoing arcs (if any)
7  │   │   if v ∈ DV^s then                          // Waiting arc in the graph
8  │   │   │   SUCC ← v;
9  │   if time(v_d^{cj}) > time(SUCC) then
10 │   │   foreach v ∈ Nin(v_d^{cj}) do              // Incoming arcs (if any)
11 │   │   │   if v ∈ DV^s then                      // Waiting arc in the graph
12 │   │   │   │   PRED ← v;
13 │   │   │   if v ∈ AV^s then                      // Transfer arc in stop ss
14 │   │   │   │   Ā ← Ā ∪ {v};
15 │   │   V ← V \ {v_d^{cj}};
16 │   │   L ← DEC-BU(G, L, v_d^{cj});
17 │   │   if PRED ≠ ∞ and SUCC ≠ ∞ then
18 │   │   │   A ← A ∪ {(PRED, SUCC)};               // Add waiting arc
19 │   │   foreach w ∈ Ā do
20 │   │   │   A ← A ∪ {(w, SUCC)};                  // Add transfer arcs
21 │   │   L ← INC-BU(G, L, SUCC);
22 │   foreach v ∈ Nout(v_a^{cj}) do                 // Outgoing arcs (if any)
23 │   │   if v ∈ DV^t and time(v) < time(v_a^{cj}) + MTTPt then
24 │   │   │   V ← V \ {v_a^{cj}};
25 │   │   │   L ← DEC-BU(G, L, v_a^{cj});
26 │   if G has not changed then break;
```

(a) $v_d^{c_j} \in V$ and $v_a^{c_j} \in V$;
(b) $v_d^{c_j} \notin V$ and $v_a^{c_j} \in V$;
(c) $v_d^{c_j} \in V$ and $v_a^{c_j} \notin V$;
(d) $v_d^{c_j} \notin V$ and $v_a^{c_j} \notin V$.

In more details Algorithm 2 incorporates specific sub-routines, described in Algorithms 3, 4 and 5, whose purpose is to update of specific parts of the graph and to handle the mentioned different topological cases.

Finally, the two above phases are then followed by a bundle update of SL by a suitable procedure, described in Sect. 3.1.

Algorithm 2. Algorithm INS-D-PTL.

Input: Graph G, delay $\delta > 0$, delayed connection c_m, trip
$\qquad$ TRIP$_i = (c_0, c_1, \ldots, c_m, \ldots, c_k)$
Output: RED-TE graph G including vertices of connections affected by the
$\qquad$ delay, 2HCR labeling L of G

---

1   **foreach** c_j, $j = m$ **to** k **do**
2   Let s_s and s_t be departure and arrival, respectively, stops of c_j;
3   PRED $\leftarrow \infty$; SUCC $\leftarrow \infty$;
4   **foreach** $v \in N_{out}(v_d^{c_j})$ **do**   // Outgoing arcs (if any)
5   **if** $v \in$ DV^s **then**   // Waiting arc in the graph
6   SUCC $\leftarrow v$;
7   **foreach** $v \in N_{in}(v_d^{c_j})$ **do**   // Incoming arcs (if any)
8   **if** $v \in$ DV^s **then**   // Waiting arc in the graph
9   PRED $\leftarrow v$;
10   **if** $v_d^{c_j} \in V$ **and** $v_a^{c_j} \in V$ **then**   // Case a) - Both not removed
11   Call REWIRETRANSFERDEP$(G, v_d^{c_j}, \text{SUCC}, s_s)$;
12   **if** G has changed **then**
13   L $\leftarrow$ INC-BU$(G, L, v_d^{c_j})$;
14   **else if** $v_d^{c_j} \notin V$ **and** $v_a^{c_j} \notin V$ **then**   // Case b) - Both Removed
15      $V \leftarrow V \cup \{v_d^{c_j}\}$;   // Add $v_d^{c_j}$ to G
16   Call REWIREWAITINGDEP$(G, v_d^{c_j}, s_s)$;
17   Call REWIRETRANSFERDEP$(G, v_d^{c_j}, \text{SUCC}, s_s)$;
18   L $\leftarrow$ INC-BU$(G, L, v_d^{c_j})$;
19      $V \leftarrow V \cup \{v_a^{c_j}\}$; $A \leftarrow A \cup \{(v_d^{c_j}, v_a^{c_j})\}$; // Add $v_a^{c_j}$ and connection arc
       to G
20   Call REWIREARR$(G, v_a^{c_j}, \text{TRIP}_i, s_t)$;
21   L $\leftarrow$ INC-BU$(G, L, v_a^{c_j})$;
22   **else if** $v_d^{c_j} \notin V$ **and** $v_a^{c_j} \in V$ **then**   // Case c) - Only $v_d^{c_j}$ removed
23      $V \leftarrow V \cup \{v_d^{c_j}\}$;
24      $A \leftarrow A \cup \{(v_d^{c_j}, v_a^{c_j})\}$;   // Add $v_d^{c_j}$ and connection arc to G
25   Call REWIREWAITINGDEP$(G, v_d^{c_j}, s_s)$;
26   Call REWIRETRANSFERDEP$(G, v_d^{c_j}, \text{SUCC}, s_s)$;
27   L $\leftarrow$ INC-BU$(G, L, v_d^{c_j})$;
28   **else**   // Case d) - Only $v_a^{c_j}$ removed
29      $V \leftarrow V \cup \{v_a^{c_j}\}$;
30      $A \leftarrow A \cup \{(v_d^{c_j}, v_a^{c_j})\}$;   // Add $v_a^{c_j}$ and connection arc to G
31   Call REWIREARR$(G, v_a^{c_j}, \text{TRIP}_i, s_t)$;
32   L $\leftarrow$ INC-BU$(G, L, v_a^{c_j})$;

3.1 Updating the Stop Labeling

Once both the graph and the 2HCR labeling have been updated, if a corresponding compressed stop labeling SL is available and one wants to reflect the
mentioned updates on said compressed structure, a straightforward way would
be that of recomputing the stop labeling from the scratch, via e.g. the routine

---

Algorithm 3. Algorithm REWIRETRANSFERDEP.

Input: RED-TE graph G, vertices $v_d^{c_j}$ and SUCC, stop s_s
Output: (Partially updated) RED-TE graph G

```
 1  if SUCC = ∞ then                                        // Case a.1)
 2  |   CANDIDATES ← ∅;
 3  |   foreach v ∈ AV^s do
 4  |   |   TO_ADD ← true;
 5  |   |   foreach u ∈ N_out(v) do        // Outgoing transfer arcs (if any)
 6  |   |   |   if u ∈ DV^s then                       // Has transfer arc
 7  |   |   |   |   TO_ADD ← false;
 8  |   |   |   |   break;
 9  |   |   if TO_ADD and time(v_d^{c_j}) ≥ time(v) + MTTP_s then
    |   |   |   CANDIDATES ← CANDIDATES ∪ {v} ;
10  |   foreach v ∈ CANDIDATES do  A ← A ∪ {(v, v_d^{c_j})};
11  else                                                    // Case a.2)
12  |   T ← ∅;
13  |   foreach v ∈ AV^s do
14  |   |   foreach u ∈ N_out(v) do        // Outgoing transfer arcs (if any)
15  |   |   |   if u = SUCC and time(v_d^{c_j}) ≥ time(v) + MTTP_s then
    |   |   |   |   T ← T ∪ {(v, u)};
16  |   foreach (v, u) ∈ T do
17  |   |   A ← A \ {(v, u)};
18  |   |   A ← A ∪ {(v, v_d^{c_j})};
```

Algorithm 4. Algorithm REWIREWAITINGDEP.

Input: (Partially updated) RED-TE graph G, vertex $v_d^{c_j}$, stop s_s
Output: (Partially updated) RED-TE graph G

```
 1  if DV^s \ {v_d^{c_j}} ≠ ∅ then
 2  |   m ← argmax_{v ∈ DV^s} time(v);
 3  |   if time(v_d^{c_j}) ≥ time(m) then                   // Add waiting arc
 4  |   |   A ← A ∪ {(m, v_d^{c_j})};
 5  else
 6  |   Let m_1, m_2 ∈ DV^s be such that time(m_1) ≤ time(v_d^{c_j}) ≤ time(m_2);
 7  |   A ← A \ {(m_1, m_2)};                        // Remove outdated waiting arc
 8  |   A ← A ∪ {(m_1, v_d^{c_j}), (v_d^{c_j}, m_2)};      // Add new waiting arcs
```

---

in [11]. This computational effort is not large as that required for recomputing the 2HCR labeling. However, we propose a dynamic routine that is incorporated in D-PTL and avoids (and it is faster than) the recomputation from scratch of the stop labeling as well, described in what follows. Our routine requires, during the execution of Algorithms 1, 2, to compute two sets of so–called *updated stops*, denoted, respectively, by US_{out} and US_{in}. These are defined as the stops $s_i \in S$ such that vertices in DV^i (AV^i, respectively) had their time value or forward label (backward label, respectively) changed during Algorithm REM-D-PTL or during

---

Algorithm 5. Algorithm REWIREARR.

Input: (Partially updated) RED-TE graph G, vertex $v_a^{c_j}$, trip
　　TRIP$_i = (c_0, c_1, \ldots, c_m, \ldots, c_k)$, stop s_t.
Output: (Partially updated) RED-TE graph G

1　TEMP_NODE $\leftarrow \infty$;
2　TEMP_TIME $\leftarrow \infty$;
3　**foreach** $v \in \mathrm{DV}^t$ **do**
4　　**if** $time(v) \geq time(v_a^{c_j}) + \mathrm{MTTP}_t$ **then**　　　// Search for minimum
5　　　**if** $time(v) \leq$ TEMP_TIME **then**
6　　　　TEMP_TIME $\leftarrow time(v)$;
7　　　　TEMP_NODE $\leftarrow v$;
8　$A \leftarrow A \cup \{(v_a^{c_j}, \text{TEMP\_NODE})\}$;　　　// Add proper transfer arc
9　**if** $j > 0$ **then**　　　　　　// Not first connection of the trip
10　　$A \leftarrow A \cup \{(v_a^{c_{j-1}}, v_a^{c_j})\}$;　　　　　// Add bypass arc
11　**if** $j < k$ **then**　　　　　// Not last connection of the trip
12　　$A \leftarrow A \cup \{(v_a^{c_j}, v_a^{c_{j+1}})\}$;　　　　// Add bypass arc

---

Algorithm INS-D-PTL. Sets US$_{out}$ and US$_{in}$ can be easily determined by inserting stops satisfying the property in said sets during the execution of Algorithms 1, 2, after each update to time or labels.

Once this is done we update the stop labeling SL by recomputing only the entries of SL$_{out}(i)$ (SL$_{in}(i)$, respectively) for each $s_i \in$ US$_{out}$ (for each $s_i \in$ US$_{in}$, respectively). To this aim, for each stop $s_i \in$ US$_{out}$ ($s_i \in$ US$_{in}$, respectively) we first reset SL$_{out}(i)$ (SL$_{in}(i)$, respectively) to the emptyset. Then, we scan departure (arrival, respectively) vertices in decreasing (increasing, respectively) order w.r.t. time and add entries to SL$_{out}(i)$ (SL$_{in}(i)$, respectively) accordingly. In particular, for all departure (arrival, respectively) vertices v of s_i in the above mentioned order, we add a pair $(u, stoptime_i(v))$ for each u in SL$_{out}(i)$ (SL$_{in}(i)$, respectively) only if there is no pair SL$_{out}(i)$ (SL$_{in}(i)$, respectively) having u as hub vertex. This guarantees that each pair contains latest departure (earliest arrival, respectively) times. After updating the stop labels, we sort both SL$_{out}(i)$ and SL$_{in}(i)$ to restore the ordering according to the hub vertices [11]. Details on how to update the stop labeling by executing the procedure are given in Algorithm 6. We are now ready to give the following results, whose proof, due to space limitations, is deferred to the full version of the paper.

Theorem 1 (Correctness). *Given an input timetable and a corresponding* RED-TE *graph G. Let L be a corresponding* 2HCR *labeling and let $\delta > 0$ be a delay occurring on a connection, i.e. an increase of δ on its departure time. Let SL be a stop labeling associated to L. Moreover, let G', L', and SL' be the output of* D-PTL *when applied to both G, L and SL. Then: (i) G' is a* RED-TE *graph for the updated timetable; (ii) L' is a* 2HCR *labeling for G'; (iii) SL' is a stop labeling for L'.*

Algorithm 6. Algorithm for updating the stop labeling.

Input: Outdated stop labeling SL, 2HCR labeling L of G, sets US_{out}, US_{in}
Output: Stop labeling SL of L

1 **foreach** $s_i \in \text{US}_{out}$ **do**
2 $\quad Q \leftarrow \emptyset$;
3 $\quad \text{SL}_{out}(i) \leftarrow \emptyset$;
4 $\quad$ **while** $\{\text{DV}^s \setminus Q\} \neq \emptyset$ **do**
5 $\qquad m \leftarrow argmax_{v \in \text{DV}^s}\, time(v)$;
6 $\qquad$ **foreach** $u \in \text{L}_{out}(m)$ **do**
7 $\qquad\quad$ **if** $u \notin \text{SL}_{out}(i)$ **then**
8 $\qquad\qquad$ $|\;$ Add $(u, time(m))$ to $\text{SL}_{out}(i)$;
9 $\qquad\quad Q \leftarrow Q \cup \{m\}$;
10 Sort $\text{SL}_{out}(i)$ w.r.t. hub vertices;
11 **foreach** $s_i \in \text{US}_{in}$ **do**
12 $\quad Q \leftarrow \emptyset$;
13 $\quad \text{SL}_{in}(i) \leftarrow \emptyset$;
14 $\quad$ **while** $\{\text{AV}^s \setminus Q\} \neq \emptyset$ **do**
15 $\qquad m \leftarrow argmin_{v \in \text{DV}^s}\, time(v)$;
16 $\qquad$ **foreach** $u \in \text{L}_{in}(m)$ **do**
17 $\qquad\quad$ **if** $u \notin \text{SL}_{in}(i)$ **then**
18 $\qquad\qquad$ $|\;$ Add $(u, time(m))$ to $\text{SL}_{in}(i)$;
19 $\qquad\quad Q \leftarrow Q \cup \{m\}$;
20 Sort $\text{SL}_{in}(i)$ w.r.t. hub vertices;

Theorem 2 (Complexity). *Algorithm* D-PTL *takes* $\mathcal{O}(|\mathcal{C}|^3 \log |\mathcal{C}|)$ *computational time in the worst case.*

Notice that, Theorem 2 implies that D-PTL is slower than the recomputation from scratch via PTL in the worst case. However, our experimental study shows D-PTL always outperforms PTL in practice.

4 Experimental Study

In this section, we present our experimental study to assess the performance of D-PTL. In particular, we implemented, in C++, both PTL and D-PTL, and developed a simulation environment to test the two algorithms on given input transit networks. We conducted experiments as follows.

For each input, we build the RED-TE graph G and execute PTL to compute both the 2HCR labeling L and the stop labeling SL. Then, we select a connection c_j of the timetable uniformly at random and delay it by δ minutes, where δ is randomly chosen within $[5, time(m) - time(v_d^{c_j}) + 10]$ and $m = argmax_{v \in \text{DV}^s}\, time(v)$. Finally, we run D-PTL to update both the graph and the labelings. In parallel, we run PTL to recompute graph and labelings from scratch. We repeat the above for 50 connections After each execution, we measure both the update time of D-PTL and the running time of PTL. Moreover, we also measure the *average size of the labelings* and the *average query time*. The former is the average space occupancy in megabytes of the labelings while the latter is obtained by computing the average time to answer to 100 000 queries, of both earliest arrival and profile type via the query algorithms of [11]. This is done to evaluate the quality of the obtained data structures w.r.t. relevant factors like size and query time. For each query, for the sake of validity, we compare the result by comparing the two outputs with the result of an exhaustive Dijkstra's-like visit on the graph [15].

As inputs to our experiments, we considered real-world transit networks whose data is publicly available [3], as done in other studies of this kind [5,6,11,14]. Details of the considered inputs are given in Table 1 where we report, for each network, the number of stops, the size of the corresponding RED-TE graph $G = (V, A)$, the time for preprocessing the network to compute the 2HCR labeling L and the stop labeling SL, resp., and the size of both L and SL, in megabytes. All our code has been compiled with GNU g++ v.5 (O3 opt. level) under Linux (Kernel 4.4.0-47). All tests have been executed on a workstation equipped with an Intel Xeon© CPU and 128 GB of main memory.

Table 1. Details of input datasets: preprocessing time is expressed in seconds, sizes in megabytes.

Network	# stops	Graph		Preprocessing time		Labeling size	
		$|V|$	$|A|$	L	SL	L	SL
London	5 221	3 066 852	5 957 246	4 494.00	5.19	5 856	529
Madrid	4 698	3 971 870	7 859 375	10 559.10	13.66	12 295	2 653
Rome	9 273	5 502 796	10 893 752	17 081.05	30.18	18 531	5 262
Melbourne	27 237	9 757 352	18 389 454	3 774.00	12.79	8 293	1 136

Analysis. The results of our experiments are summarized in Table 2, where we report the average time taken by D-PTL to update L and SL ì, resp. (cf 2nd and 3rd columns), the average time taken by PTL for recomputing from scratch L and SL, resp., (cf 4th and 5th columns) and the average speed-up obtained by using D-PTL instead of PTL (cf 6th column), that is the ratio of average total time taken by PTL to the average total update time of D-PTL.

In Table 2 we can observe that D-PTL is able to update L and SL in a time that is orders of magnitude smaller than that taken by the recomputation (up to more than 600 times smaller). Moreover, the speed-up seem to increase as the network size increases, thus suggesting that D-PTL scales well against input size. Furthermore, our experiments show that graphs and labelings updated via D-PTL and those recomputed from scratch are equivalent in terms of both query times and space overhead, thus confirming that the use of D-PTL does not induce any degradation in the performance of the data structures. Results supporting these claims are postponed to the full version of the paper due to space constraints.

---

[3] Public Transit Feeds Archive – https://transitfeeds.com/.

All above observations are a strong evidence of the fact that D-PTL is a very effective and practical option for journey planning when dynamic, delay-prone networks have to be handled, especially when they are of very large size and yet require fast query answering.

Table 2. Comparison between D-PTL and PTL in terms of computational time, in seconds, to update and recompute from scratch, resp., the data structures.

Network	D-PTL		PTL		Speed-up
	L	SL	L	SL	
London	8.64	2.48	4417.65	5.50	397.77
Madrid	17.47	7.76	10495.40	14.20	416.55
Rome	12.36	14.49	16847.00	29.50	628.55
Melbourne	4.08	7.25	3807.00	11.50	337.03

5   Conclusion

We have studied the journey planning problem and have presented D-PTL, the first dynamic algorithm that enables the use of the state-of-the-art solution (PTL) in dynamic scenarios. We have shown, through extensive experimentation, that D-PTL is orders of magnitude faster than the recomputation from scratch, while at the same time preserving the performance in terms of query time and space overhead. Several research directions deserve further investigation. Perhaps the most relevant one is to adapt D-PTL to support multi-criteria queries. In [11] such queries are handled by encoding transfers as arc costs, by computing shortest path labels based on these costs, and by adjusting the query algorithm to compute Pareto optimal solutions. Unfortunately updating shortest path labels is a challenging task, computationally speaking [1,8,10] and it would be interesting to adapt one known technique to the scenario considered in this paper. Another worth future work could be to extend the experimentation to larger and more diverse inputs, to strengthen the obtained conclusions.

References

1. Akiba, T., Iwata, Y., Yoshida, Y.: Dynamic and historical shortest-path distance queries on large evolving networks by pruned landmark labeling. In: Proceedings of 23rd International World Wide Web Conference (WWW 14), pp. 237–248. ACM (2014)
2. Bast, H., et al.: Route planning in transportation networks. In: Kliemann, L., Sanders, P. (eds.) Algorithm Engineering. LNCS, vol. 9220, pp. 19–80. Springer, Cham (2016). https://doi.org/10.1007/978-3-319-49487-6_2
3. Cheng, J., Huang, S., Wu, H., Fu, A.W.C.: Tf-label: a topological-folding labeling scheme for reachability querying in a large graph. In: Proceedings of 2013 ACM SIGMOD International Conference on Management of Data (SIGMOD 2013), pp. 193–204. ACM (2013)

4. Cicerone, S., D'Emidio, M., Frigioni, D.: On mining distances in large-scale dynamic graphs. In: Aldini, A., Bernardo, M., (eds.) Proceedings of the 19th Italian Conference on Theoretical Computer Science, Urbino, Italy. CEUR Workshop Proceedings, vol. 2243, pp. 77–81. CEUR-WS.org, 18–20 September 2018. http://ceur-ws.org/Vol-2243/paper6.pdf
5. Cionini, A., D'Angelo, G., D'Emidio, M., Frigioni, D., Giannakopoulou, K., Paraskevopoulos, A., Zaroliagis, C.D.: Engineering graph-based models for dynamic timetable information systems. In: Proceedings of 14th Workshop on Algorithmic Approaches for Transportation Modelling, Optimization, and Systems (ATMOS14) (2014)
6. Cionini, A., D'Angelo, G., D'Emidio, M., Frigioni, D., Giannakopoulou, K., Paraskevopoulos, A., Zaroliagis, C.D.: Engineering graph-based models for dynamic timetable information systems. J. Discrete Algorithms **46–47**, 40–58 (2017)
7. Cohen, E., Halperin, E., Kaplan, H., Zwick, U.: Reachability and distance queries via 2-hop labels. SIAM J. Comput. **32**(5), 1338–1355 (2003)
8. D'Angelo, G., D'Emidio, M., Frigioni, D.: Distance queries in large-scale fully dynamic complex networks. In: Mäkinen, V., Puglisi, S.J., Salmela, L. (eds.) IWOCA 2016. LNCS, vol. 9843, pp. 109–121. Springer, Cham (2016). https://doi.org/10.1007/978-3-319-44543-4_9
9. D'Angelo, G., D'Emidio, M., Frigioni, D.: Fully dynamic update of arc-flags. Networks **63**(3), 243–259 (2014). https://doi.org/10.1002/net.21542
10. D'Angelo, G., D'Emidio, M., Frigioni, D.: Fully dynamic 2-hop cover labeling. ACM J. Exp. Algorithmics **24**(1), 1.6:1–1.6:36 (2019). https://doi.org/10.1145/3299901
11. Delling, D., Dibbelt, J., Pajor, T., Werneck, R.F.: Public transit labeling. In: Bampis, E. (ed.) SEA 2015. LNCS, vol. 9125, pp. 273–285. Springer, Cham (2015). https://doi.org/10.1007/978-3-319-20086-6_21
12. Delling, D., Goldberg, A.V., Pajor, T., Werneck, R.F.: Customizable route planning in road networks. Transp. Sci. **51**(2), 566–591 (2017). https://doi.org/10.1287/trsc.2014.0579
13. Delling, D., Pajor, T., Werneck, R.F.: Round-based public transit routing. Transp. Sci. **49**(3), 591–604 (2015)
14. Dibbelt, J., Pajor, T., Strasser, B., Wagner, D.: Connection scan algorithm. ACM J. Exp. Algorithmics **23**, 1.7:1–1.7:56 (2018)
15. Pyrga, E., Schulz, F., Wagner, D., Zaroliagis, C.: Efficient models for timetable information in public transportation systems. ACM J. Exp. Algorithmics **12**(2.4), 1–39 (2008)
16. Qin, Y., Sheng, Q.Z., Falkner, N.J.G., Yao, L., Parkinson, S.: Efficient computation of distance labeling for decremental updates in large dynamic graphs. World Wide Web **20**(5), 915–937 (2017)
17. Wang, S., Lin, W., Yang, Y., Xiao, X., Zhou, S.: Efficient route planning on public transportation networks: a labelling approach. In: Proceedings of 2015 ACM International Conference on Management of Data (SIGMOD 2015), pp. 967–982. ACM (2015)
18. Yano, Y., Akiba, T., Iwata, Y., Yoshida, Y.: Fast and scalable reachability queries on graphs by pruned labeling with landmarks and paths. In: Proceedings of 22nd ACM International Conference on Information & Knowledge Management (CIKM 2013), pp. 1601–1606. ACM (2013)
19. Zhu, A.D., Lin, W., Wang, S., Xiao, X.: Reachability queries on large dynamic graphs: a total order approach. In: Proceedings of 2014 ACM SIGMOD International Conference on Management of Data (SIGMOD 2014), pp. 1323–1334. ACM (2014)

Mobile Localization Techniques Oriented to Tangible Web

Osvaldo Gervasi[1]([📧])(iD), Martina Fortunelli[2], Riccardo Magni[2],
Damiano Perri[1](iD), and Marco Simonetti[3]

[1] Department of Mathematics and Computer Science,
University of Perugia, Perugia, Italy
`osvaldo.gervasi@unipg.it, osvaldo.gervasi@gmail.com`
[2] Pragma Engineering SrL, Perugia, Italy
[3] Liceo Scientifico e Artistico "G. Marconi", Foligno, Italy

Abstract. We implemented a system able to locate people indoor, with the purpose of providing assistive services. Such approach is particularly important for the Art, for providing information on exhibitions, art galleries and museums, and to allow the access to the cultural heritage patrimony to people with disabilities.

The system may provide also very important information and input to elderly people, helping them to perceive more deeply the reality and the beauty of art.

The system is based on Beacons, very small and low power consumption devices, and Human Body Communication protocols. The Beacons, Bluetooth Low Energy devices, allow to obtain a position information related to predetermined reference points, and through proximity algorithms, locate a person or an object of interest.

The position obtained has an error that depends from the interferences present in the area. The union of Beacons with Human Body Communication, a recent wireless technology that exploits the human body as a transmission channel, makes it possible to increase the accuracy of localization.

The basic idea is to exploit the localization derived from Beacons to start a search for an electrical signal transmitted by the human body and to distinguish the position according to the information contained in the signal. The signal is transmitted by capacitance to the human body and revealed by a special resonant circuit (antenna) adapted to the microphone input of the mobile device.

1 Introduction

The proliferation of wireless devices in the last years has resulted in a wide range of services including indoor localization [2]. Indoor localization is the process of obtaining a device or user location in an indoor setting or environment. Indoor device localization has been extensively investigated over the last few decades, mainly in industrial settings and for wireless sensor networks and robotics. However, it is only less than a decade ago since the wide-scale proliferation of smart

© Springer Nature Switzerland AG 2019
S. Misra et al. (Eds.): ICCSA 2019, LNCS 11619, pp. 118–128, 2019.
https://doi.org/10.1007/978-3-030-24289-3_10

phones and wearable devices with wireless communication capabilities have made the localization and tracking of such devices synonym to the localization and tracking of the corresponding users and enabled a wide range of related applications and services.

User and device localization have wide-scale applications in health sector, industry, disaster management [18], building management, surveillance, and other innovative areas as Internet of Things (IoT) [16], smart cities [14] and smart environments.

In most devices there is a GPS receiver that allows to easily locate, by satellite signal, a terminal in an open space; unfortunately, for indoor clients most services become unavailable due to the lack of (or a weak) communication signal. It is important to emphasize that, depending on the information we want to obtain, there are two methods for identifying the position of a client: localization and proximity.

Localization is a method used mainly in navigation in open space (outdoor) using the GPS signal: this technology allows obtaining precise information on the user's position. The satellite signal cannot be transmitted inside buildings, and is therefore unusable indoor: this has led to the development of alternative technologies, such as radio, infrared, ultrasound or magnetic fields.

The results obtained with these techniques does not provide an absolute position data, but relative position information is provided, that has then to be interpreted to provide a reliable position. Therefore, these technologies are identified with the term *proximity techniques*. In this context it is necessary to calculate the distance from the various points of interest that will lead to determining, after the execution of certain algorithms, the position sought [13].

The state of the art on the subject of indoor positioning and tracking is such that there is not a single technology that appears to dominate, but several technologies are adopted, each characterized by advantages and disadvantages. The main technologies for indoor localization are described in the Table 1.

Various indoor navigation technologies have been tested in order to identify the best one for locating a person indoor, inside a museum or a room, and then being able to trace her/his movements. We selected the Bluetooth Low Energy (BLE) technology, a new protocol designed for reducing the battery consumption and for optimizing the communications among Internet of Things (IoT) devices.

We use Beacons for localizing and then tracing people in indoor areas, transmitting the data to a mobile device, using BLE and the Human Body Communication protocols. The data transmitted by a BLE Beacon is contained in packets formatted according to the Bluetooth Core Specification.

Applications interact with Beacons in two different ways:

Monitoring: action activated when entering and leaving the region of Beacon monitoring, works whether the application is running, paused or stopped;
Ranging: action activated based on the proximity of the Beacon, it works only when the application is running.

Therefore the monitoring allows to identify the Beacon regions, while the ranging is used to interact with a specific Beacon. The standardized Beacon

Table 1. Overview of indoor technologies

Technology	Advantages	Disadvantages
Infrared	Low cost	Short range and need to maintain visual contact
Bluetooth	Infrastructure availability	Channel saturation in the case of a large number of users per unit area
Ultrasounds	Limited battery consumption and poor maintenance	Reflection of sound waves in the presence of obstacles
RFID active	Reading from great distances	Fairly high costs, need for power supply, large size
RFID passive	Infinite average life, reduced cost, small dimensions and resistant to external shocks and stresses	Radius and reduced reading range
Dead-reckoning	Low cost	High energy consumption and low range
Wifi	Infrastructure availability	Low accuracy, channel saturation, poor information security
Ultra-wide band	Accuracy of the order of 1 m, robust to multi-path phenomena, does not require visual contact	Very high costs
Zigbee	Low cost, long battery life and accuracy of the order of 1 m	Limited penetration of the walls
Bluetooth Low Energy	Low energy consumption, reduced costs, large-scale distributed network	Unidirectional

protocols are IBeacon and Eddystone; in our work we adopted the Eddystone protocol, developed by Google Inc. and released under the open source Apache License 2.0 [10].

The implemented system is relevant to provide assistive services to people, in particular for elderly people, who can take advantage of the system in case they feel lost or disoriented. The system may be also used for general purpose services, in particular to provide specific informations on artifacts in a museum or in an art gallery, art, history and tourism information nearby relevant monuments or popular meeting points in a city or a suburb.

The present work is addressing also the theme of so called *tangible web* [11, 12] interactions, which are completing the sensory engagement with audio and video of multimedia interfaces. The idea to associate a value of haptic exploration in retrieving information (i.e. from web sources) humanises the learning experience offering a contextual feedback which is related to forms and textures sensed by touch. The chance to detect such interaction, identifying the specific user's device, allows the access to specific information which is related to the experience that the user is making in a certain moment, adding contextual or related information or feelings (i.e. sounds and music).

The basis of such developments could be recognised in both afferent and efferent stimulations: in terms of afferent stimula, the current work is making use of recent applications of HBC - Human Body Communication solutions - which are proposing a "natural" paradigm in the relationship between the artifact and the device weared by the user.

The development of such technology will offer the chance to produce emotionally enriched explorations of artifacts also for those who are deprived of vision (low vision-blind persons), as mentioned in the reported use case.

2 The Human Body Communication

Human Body Communication (HBC) is a recent wireless technology which is part of the Body Area Network (BAN), able to interconnect wearable devices at distances lower than 1 m. The human body becomes the communication medium defined as "Body-wire channel" that can propagate frequencies in the range from 10 KHz to 100 MHz.

The human body is made up of ions and can suffer harmful effects depending on the frequency, the intensity of the current, the path followed by the current, and the duration of the interaction [3]. Generally high frequencies are less dangerous because they are accompanied by a skin effect, in fact the possibility of fibrillation decreases, as the current passes outward without affecting the heart, although at the same time there is a reduction of the impedance on the human body, which determines a current increase at the same voltage.

There are directives, issued by the ICNIRP, the International Commission on Non-Ionizing Radiation Protection, and IEEE, Standard for Safety Levels, that limit the time of exposure to electric, magnetic and electromagnetic fields. It has been proven that the pain threshold varies between 100 kHz and 1 MHz. Below 100 kHz one can feel a slight stimulation of muscles and nerves, from 100 kHz to 10 MHz one feels a sensation of heat, while for over 10 MHz one is beyond the percentage of energy that the human body is able to absorb when it is exposed to the action of a radio-frequency electromagnetic field (RF).

In literature, there are two approaches of HBC: galvanic coupling and capacitive coupling. Both methods use body as transmission medium, but they differ in the coupling between signal and human body. In the present work we have analyzed only the capacitive coupling.

2.1 Capacitive Coupling

In the 1990s, Zimmerman [4] explained that electrical signals with a frequency lower than 100 kHz interacts with the human body. When a very high frequency comes in touch with the body, the electrical energy does not remain confined but propagates around it as if to simulate an antenna.

Figure 1 shows the model of a conventional circuit and the near-field coupling mechanism around the human body is described. The signal is transmitted between the body channel transceivers by making a current loop, which is composed of the transmitter electrode, the body channel, the receiver electrode, and the capacitive return path through the external ground. As the communication frequency increases for a high data rate, the coupling capacitances of the return path have less effect and the body impedance cannot be ignored. As the transmission length of the body channel increases, both the resistance of the body and the coupling capacitance to the external ground increase. These elements cause signal loss at the receiver, and its amount depends on the channel length.

The Zimmerman's theses is the base reference for further studies, that are different for the amplitude of the coupling, the frequency range, the signal modulation method and the speed of data transmission.

Capacitive coupling has several weaknesses:

- The return path of the signal must be managed. The ground conduction is the base for the transmission.
- The transmission channel of the dominant signal is on the surface of the arm, because the signal is distributed like a wave.
- The same contacts can emit dispersal fields.
- Higher the carrier frequency is, more the transmission by irradiation through the air becomes relevant.

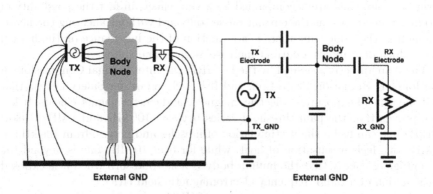

Fig. 1. Model of a circuit based on human body communication.

In a recent study Namjun Cho and co-workers [1] provided two empirical formulas that express the characteristic of the communication channel and of the minimal area of contact as a function of several parameters.

3   Signal Analysis on Mobile Environments

Signal analysis is a process of different check that where apply in many different environments including the Mobile one. Signal Analysis allows to get only the significant part of the signal that represent the data using a device called filter.

A filter removes some unwanted components from a signal, this means removing some frequencies to suppress interfering signals and reduce background noise. There are many different types of filters, classified according to their properties: passive or active, analog or digital, discrete-time or continuous-time etc. In order to apply a digital filter in Mobile environments it is necessary to obtain a digital signal. The original analog signal has to be sampled, reading the signal at regular time intervals, quantize the signal, and encode it with discrete values. The types of digital filters analyzed are: Finite Impulse Response (FIR) and Infinite Impulse Response (IIR). We selected the FIR filter, whose impulse response is of finite duration because it settles to zero in finite time.

The filtered signal is transformed with a digital technique, in a impulse train of 0, when no signal is resent, and 1, when the signal is present, that represents the data after the On-Off keying (OOK). On-Off keying is the simplest form of amplitude-shift keying modulation, which variations is in amplitude of a carrier wave. Modulation is the process of varying one or more properties, as amplitude, frequency, phase etc., of a periodic waveform, called the carrier signal, with a modulating signal that contains the information that have to be transmitted.

The last part of signal analysis is the check of correctness of the transmitted data. Error revelation is an important technique to auto detect errors between information's data without correct them. The cyclic redundancy check (CRC) is an error-detecting code with checksum where the reminder of a polynomial division of the contents data follows some data blocks.

The described setup is summarized in Fig. 2. The components that appear in the Figure are described in Table 2.

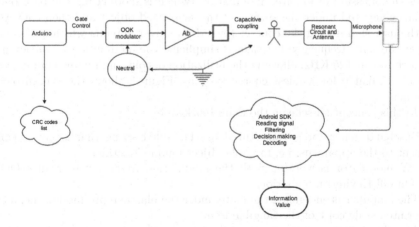

Fig. 2. The setup of the experimental apparatus.

Table 2. Description of the setup elements

Element	Description
Arduino	Board Arduino Uno with microcontroller ATmega328, velocity 16 MHz, flash memory 32 KB, SRAM 2 KB and EEPROM memory 1 KB. The program generates on the exit pin a bit sequence at 100 bps, modulated to 1 KHz.
Modulator OOK	Wave shapes generator HM130 from 0 to 10 MHz. The square wave generated at 155 kHz with 50 Ω input and exit gate
Ab	HF (High Frequency) frequency amplifier with resonant circuit on exit
Neutral	Ground reference
Resonant Circuit Antenna	Weared unit connected to the microphone of the mobile phone (dimensions: 50 × 30 × 4 mm)
Mobile Device	Smartphone Android 4.4 (KitKat)

Philip Koopman proposed the guidelines for identifying the best polynomial function related to 8 bits payload. In particular he compared 3 different polynomial: DARC-8, CRC-8 and C2. C-2 show the best performance with a frame length of 119 and a payload greater than 10 bits, while DARC-8 showed the best performance with 8 bits payload. So the polynomial function selected was DARC-8.

4 The Electronic Apparatus

The electronic apparatus developed for data communication implements the interfaces for inductive human body transmission of signals. The scheme provides the emission of low-freq modulation (which is modulating the base band signal) generated under the surface of the sensorized object and then conveyed by the user skin during the contact toward a receiver antenna which is resonating at the same frequency. For sake of simplicity, the modulation frequency has been chosen at 125 KHz, allowing the utilization of coils and related components already available for wireless charge systems. Figure 3 shows the overall block scheme.

In this conceptual scheme the main blocks are:

- Baseband generator is constituted by the coded string that is periodically sent to the apparatus. i.e. tangible object unique identifier
- SW modulator is working with the modulation frequency to realize OOK (On-Off Keying) modulation
- The amplifier is energizing the plate under the plastic reproduction (i.e. a 3D printed scale copy of the tangible item)
- The skin interface conveys the energy coming from the capacitive coupling toward a wrist-placed detection system

- The resonant demodulator is trimmed around the central modulation frequency producing a demodulated input at low level (2–5 mV)
- The microphone input of the mobile device is detecting the modulation allowing a the receiver process to recognize data string

5   The Implemented Libraries in Android

The present part is focused on the libraries implemented in Android. The code implemented can be divided in four different parts in which we consider the signal acquisition, the signal filtering, the decisioning and finally the encoding.

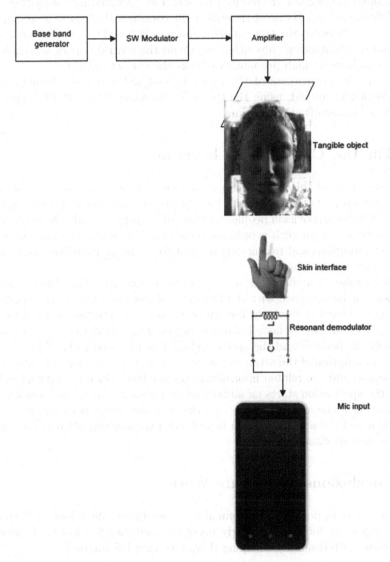

Fig. 3. Electronic apparatus

The signal is acquired in realtime through the microphone in PCM (Pulse Code Modulation) for n seconds. After the recording the signal is filtered with a FIR filter with 20 TAP, that was compared to the one obtain with LabVIEW library. Results of many tests underline that the use of filter is not necessary because rumor doesn't hold the signal's presence or absence.

The third part check if in an instant t the signal is present or not. After bringing all the samples positive, it is applied an average function based on a window that take k samples with some overlays in order to obtain a greater precision. The window dimension can be determined only through experiments. The results are then "decimated" with a technique in which the samples occurring in the same millisecond are reduced to one. The "decimating" algorithm reads tree different values, if one of these is '1', it considers that there is signal. Also the distance between the tree different samples is based on experimental tests. The aim of "decimating" algorithm is to read the central part of a millisecond, in order to have an high probability of take the correct measure.

Finally the correctness of the result is analysed and the reliability of the transmission is verified, using the Cyclic Redundancy Check (CRC), detecting the frames transmitted with errors.

6 The Use Case: Art for Everyone

Many use cases of this project can be identified in everyday life, in particular the implemented system may help elderly people and people with disabilities, such as blind or hypovision people, who are for example excluded from the visual art. The only way for such people to access visual art is through the tactile and auditory sensations and taking into account this type of disabilities we took the cue to carry out this project.

Let us take an archaeological museum as an example, the visitor with disabilities may be equipped with the headset and sensors necessary to capture the signal transmitted through the human body connection to the microphone jack. The application may be installed in the personal mobile device of the visitor so that only the headset and the antenna should be provided to her/him.

The description of the artifacts may start as soon as the visitor is intercepted by a beacon and the related information transmitted. Once the artifact is identified, the application starts an audio that describes it, and if more sensors have been installed, the audio may describe the area the visitor is touching.

The use of the application can be extended to painting, photography, architecture, and all visual arts.

7 Conclusions and Future Work

The present work describes a system able to localize people indoor and is particularly important for helping elderly people in case they feel lost or disoriented, and people with disabilities helping them receiving information.

This work is another pillar on the way we started several years ago, helping people with disabilities to recover in part the limitations originated by their health status [5–9,15,17].

The system may be improved optimizing the number of beacons required to cover indoor areas and to improve its precision adopting triangulation methods.

References

1. Cho, N., Yoo, J., Song, S., Lee, J., Jeon, S., Yoo, H.: The human body characteristics as a signal transmission medium for intrabody communication. IEEE Trans. Microw. Theory Tech. **55**(5), 1080–1086 (2007)
2. Gkelias, A., Zafari. F., Leung, K.: A survey of indoor localization systems and technologies, September 2017
3. Fish, R.M., Geddes, L.A.: Conduction of electrical current to and through the human body: a review. Eplasty **9**, e44 (2009)
4. Gersheneld, N., Zimmerman, T., Allport, D.: Non-contact system for sensing and signalling by externally induced intra-body currents. US Patent 5,914,701 (1999)
5. Gervasi, O., Franzoni, V., Riganelli, M., Tasso, S.: Automating facial emotion recognition. Web Intell. **17**(1), 17–27 (2019)
6. Gervasi, O., Magni, R., Ferri, M.: A method for predicting words by interpreting labial movements. In: Gervasi, O., et al. (eds.) ICCSA 2016. LNCS, vol. 9787, pp. 450–464. Springer, Cham (2016). https://doi.org/10.1007/978-3-319-42108-7_34
7. Gervasi, O., Magni, R., Macellari, S.: A brain computer interface for enhancing the communication of people with severe impairment. In: Murgante, B., et al. (eds.) ICCSA 2014. LNCS, vol. 8584, pp. 709–721. Springer, Cham (2014). https://doi.org/10.1007/978-3-319-09153-2_53
8. Gervasi, O., Magni, R., Riganelli, M.: Mixed reality for improving tele-rehabilitation practices. In: Gervasi, O., et al. (eds.) ICCSA 2015. LNCS, vol. 9155, pp. 569–580. Springer, Cham (2015). https://doi.org/10.1007/978-3-319-21404-7_42
9. Gervasi, O., Magni, R., Zampolini, M.: Nu!rehavr: virtual reality in neuro tele-rehabilitation of patients with traumatic brain injury and stroke. Virtual Reality **14**(2), 131–141 (2010)
10. Google Inc., Eddystone-eid (ephemeral id), May 2016
11. Ishii, H.: Tangible bits: beyond pixels. In: Proceedings of the 2nd International Conference on Tangible and Embedded Interaction, TEI 2008, pp. xv–xxv. ACM, New York (2008)
12. Ishii, H.: SIGCHI lifetime research award talk: Making digital tangible (2019)
13. Moghtadaiee, V., Dempster, A.G., Lim, S.: Indoor localization using fm radio signals: a fingerprinting approach. In: 2011 International Conference on Indoor Positioning and Indoor Navigation, pp. 1–7, September 2011
14. Ansari, I.S., Granelli, F., Usman, M., Asghar, M.R., Qaraqe, K.A.: Technologies and solutions for location-based services in smart cities: past, present, and future. IEEE Access **6**, 22248–22248 (2018)
15. Riganelli, M., Franzoni, V., Gervasi, O., Tasso, S.: EmEx, a tool for automated emotive face recognition using convolutional neural networks. In: Gervasi, O., et al. (eds.) ICCSA 2017. LNCS, vol. 10406, pp. 692–704. Springer, Cham (2017). https://doi.org/10.1007/978-3-319-62398-6_49

16. Shit, R.C., Sharma, S., Puthal, D., Zomaya, A.Y.: Location of things (lot): a review and taxonomy of sensors localization in IOT infrastructure. IEEE Commun. Surv. Tutorials **20**(3), 2028–2061 (2018)
17. Zampolini, M., Magni, R., Gervasi, O.: An X3D approach to neuro-rehabilitation. In: Gervasi, O., Murgante, B., Laganà, A., Taniar, D., Mun, Y., Gavrilova, M.L. (eds.) ICCSA 2008. LNCS, vol. 5073, pp. 78–90. Springer, Heidelberg (2008). https://doi.org/10.1007/978-3-540-69848-7_8
18. Zelenkauskaite, A., Bessis, N., Sotiriadis, S., Asimakopoulou, E.: Interconnectedness of complex systems of internet of things through social network analysis for disaster management. In: 2012 Fourth International Conference on Intelligent Networking and Collaborative Systems, pp. 503–508, September 2012

Influence of Drivers' Behavior on Traffic Flow at Two Roads Intersection

Ivan Miranda de Almeida[1], Regina Celia P. Leal-Toledo[1], Elson M. Toledo[3]([⊠]),
Diego Carrico Cacau[1], Rene Constâncio Nunes de Lima[1], and Sandra Malta[2]

[1] Fluminense Federal University, Av. Gal. Milton Tavares de Souza s/n,
São Domingos, Niteroi, Brazil
ivanmiranda600@hotmail.com, leal@ic.uff.br, {dc_cacau,renelima}@id.uff.br
[2] National Laboratory of Scientific Computing - LNCC, Av. Getulio Vargas 333,
Petropolis, Brazil
smcm@lncc.br
[3] Juiz de Fora Federal University, Rua Jose Kelmer s/n, Juiz de Fora, Brazil
emtc@lncc.br

Abstract. This paper presents a model to evaluate how heterogeneities in road traffic caused by different driver's profiles affect the dynamics of traffic on a road with an unsigned intersection. These driver's profiles, defined by the use of different acceleration policies, are not observed in usual measurements and can only be evaluated through computational simulations. A modified Nagel-Schreckenberg (NaSch) cellular automata model with a Probability Density Function (PDF) Beta is used to model these distinct behaviors, where each driver profile is represented by a Beta PDF. The analysis of space-time diagrams herein obtained and traditional traffic diagrams corroborate the importance of taking into account different profiles of drivers on the road.

Keywords: Traffic flow · Cellular automata · Road intersection ·
Driver's behavior · Computational simulations

1 Introduction

Traffic flow directly affects the quality of life of citizens in modern cities. Traffic jams and their psychological effects, besides the pollution associated with heavy traffic are some of the reasons why a better understanding of traffic flow has received so much attention in the last decades. Several solutions have been proposed to try to mitigate the effects of the increasing amount of vehicles in big centers, whether by the use of electric vehicles to minimize air pollution, or autonomous cars, in order to reduce traffic jams and reduce the number of traffic accidents. However in any situation it becomes important to know traffic dynamics and the understanding of its behavior in different situations. In order to study and to analyze traffic flow's characteristics, many mathematical models, both macroscopic and microscopic, have been employed. In the microscopic

© Springer Nature Switzerland AG 2019
S. Misra et al. (Eds.): ICCSA 2019, LNCS 11619, pp. 129–141, 2019.
https://doi.org/10.1007/978-3-030-24289-3_11

modeling Cellular Automata (CA) methods have been applied with good results, since the dynamics of the CA tries to closely mimic the movement of all vehicles and their interactions. Some of the main advantages of CA models are that they are easily implemented, lead to moderate computational cost and keep the basic features of the phenomenon [1–3]. As an example we can mention that there is already, in North Rhine-Westphalia [4], a CA model presenting on-line information about the freeway to guide drivers passing trough it. Recently, in all types of modeling, it has been tried to evaluate how the different drivers profiles affect the dynamics of the road traffic, in particular, the aggressive and the cautious or timid direction [5–14]. In this context, in particular, the CA models can be of great interest because it allows to describe the behavior of each driver profile that one wants to represent. Zamith et al. [12] proposes a CA model where the driver profiles, defined by the use of different acceleration policies are modeled using a non-uniform Probability Density Function (PDF), the PDF Beta. Thus, different parameters of PDF Beta will define different acceleration policies, where each driver "tries" to accelerate more aggressively or cautiously. In recent published works Leal-Toledo et al. [13] and Almeida et al. [14] used the same proposal to modify the traditional probabilistic NaSch model [15] in order to evaluate the effects of different acceleration profiles and their influence in the occurrence of dangerous situations that can lead to road accidents.

Considering the importance of the understanding of traffic flow in modeling signed or not, urban and highways crossings [16–18], in the present work we intend to show how important are the above considerations evaluating the influence of different acceleration profiles when there are a unsigned intersection in the road. For this purpose we model a intersection with a closed circuit, as proposed in Marzoug et al. [18], where two perpendicular roads cross in the middle. Marzoug et al. [18] showed that the fundamental diagram depends strongly on the probability of priority P and it exhibits four phases: free flow, the plateau, the jamming phases and a new phase occurring for any value of $P \neq 0.5$. These phases disappear gradually as one increases the probability P, and disappear completely for $P = 0.5$. In this work, we present how the different acceleration policies alter these results, as well as we evaluate the influence of braking probability on them. Different values of maximal velocities are also computed and for the purpose of comparing the influence of the acceleration policies on the results, in each analysis the same V_{max} is considered for all profiles.

The paper is structured as follows: Sect. 2 presents the modified NaSch model, with heterogeneity in acceleration and deceleration policies. In Sect. 3 we describe the intersection model used in our simulations. Next, in Sect. 4, we show some results to illustrate how different acceleration policies affect the flow traffic at two roads with an interception. Discussions and conclusions are presented in Sect. 5.

2   Nagel-Schreckenberg Model with Driver's Behavior

Despite being a simple model, the automata cellular NaSch model [15] is able to represent traffics main characteristics such as the spontaneous occurrence of traffic jams and the relation between traffic flow and density, representing the free and congested flow [16]. It's a one-dimensional probabilistic cellular automata (CA) traffic model where space and time are discretized resulting that the lane is described by a lattice of cells that are occupied or not by vehicles and in its traditional form a vehicle occupies only one cell.

In CA models, at any instant of time t, a vehicle occupies the cell $x(i,t)$ and has the velocity $v(i,t)$, which tells how many cells it will move at that instant of time. The number of unoccupied cells in front of each vehicle, generally called as gap, is denoted by $d(i,t) = x(i+1,t) - x(i,t-1) - L$, where $L = 1$ is the vehicles' length, and the vehicle $i+1$ is considered to be in front of the vehicle i. As usual, periodic boundary condition can be considered and traditional NaSch model can be described by four simple rules applied simultaneously to all vehicles (Algorithm 1):

Table 1. Algorithm 1.

Acceleration:	$v(i,t+1) = min[v(i,t) + A, V_{max}]$
Deceleration:	$v(i,t+1) = min[v(i,t+1), d(i,t)]$
Random deceleration:	$v(i,t+1) = max[v(i,t+1) - A, 0]$, with a probability p_b
Movement:	$x(i,t+1) = x(i,t) + v(i,t+1)$

In Table 1 we have the following parameters: V_{max}, the maximum velocity that a vehicle can reach; A, the acceleration rate of the vehicles and $A = 1\,cell/s^2$ in traditional NaSch model; p_b, a stochastic parameter, modeling the uncertainty in driver behavior and representing the probability that a vehicle, randomly, do not accelerate to reach the maximum velocity or even slows down. In NaSch model typical cell length is 7.5 m and each time step corresponds to one second, resulting vehicles' speed multiples of 1 cell/s, which is equivalent to 27 km/h. In order to take into account traffic influence of driver's behavior in a modified NaSch model we considered the evaluation of how different acceleration policies influence the traffic dynamics. It was proposed that the acceleration A, which in the NaSch model is a constant, can assume different values. To do this, a more refined network discretization is used to allow the representation of these different policies. Each vehicle may then occupy more than one cell, as can be seen in Fig. 1, and each driver profile tends to accelerate in a characteristic way: abruptly (aggressive profile) or more smoothly (non-aggressive profile). A non-uniform Probability Density Function (PDF) is used to describe trends in the drivers' acceleration policy. The new acceleration parameter is stochastic and is calculated as:

$$A = int[(1 - \alpha)A_{max}] \tag{1}$$

where α is a random value between 0 and 1 and int returns the nearest integer of its argument. Therefore, the probability p models the drivers' intention to

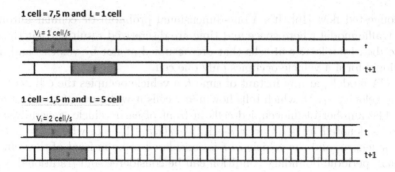

Fig. 1. Discretization scheme

accelerate while α models how they will accelerate and α is modeled by a continuous Beta Function (PDF), defined by:

$$B(a,b) = \frac{\Gamma(a+b)}{\Gamma(a)\Gamma(b)} x^{a-1}(1-x)^{b-1} \tag{2}$$

where $0 \leq x \leq 1$ and $\Gamma(n+1) = n!$, being n a positive integer. Depending on the values of the parameters a and b, the majority of α values will tend to different values between 0 and 1 and those closer to 0 will produce accelerations A closer to A_{max}, while those closer to 1 will produce accelerations A closer to 0. In fact, the α values float around the Beta mean value, which are given by $\mu = \frac{a}{a+b}$. Thus, it is possible to predict each profile acceleration trend based on the average of the Beta function used to model it. Therefore, each profile is given by a different pair (a, b) of parameters, defining one PDF Beta function, and the different mean values of these distributions model the desired acceleration tendencies as shown in Fig. 2.

3   Intersection Model

For the purpose of the present work, where we intend to evaluate the influence of different acceleration profiles at an unsigned intersection of two roads, we consider a closed circuit, as proposed in Marzoug et al. [18], where two perpendicular roads cross in the middle. In this configuration we will consider that the crossing consists of the intersection of two stretches of roads: R1 and R2. In R1 the vehicles move from top to bottom and in R2 vehicles move from left to right. In this closed circuit, the exit of R1 is the entrance of R2 and the exit of R2 is the entrance of R1, as shown in Fig. 3.

In the traditional Nasch model the road intersection is composed by one cell. Thus in our modification, the crossing is composed by the number of cells that the vehicle occupies. As in Marzoug et al. [18], we denote G1 and G2 as the distances of the vehicle to the intersection cell. When two vehicles can cross at the same time-step, the priority is given to the vehicle in R1 with probability P, and to the vehicle in R2 with probability $1 - P$. Near to the intersection the vehicle that has priority moves with its normal velocity and the vehicle that does not have priority decelerates, as described in Algorithm 1, where $d_i = G_i$ is the distance to the intersection.

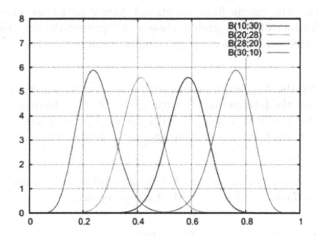

Fig. 2. PDF Beta functions

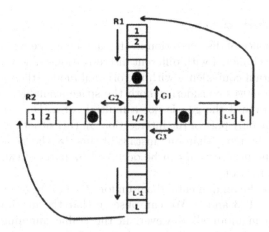

Fig. 3. Crossing scheme

4   Numerical Results and Discussion

For all results here presented the total length of the circuit is 30 km, and the results are obtained after 20,000 time steps. The first 17,000 steps were discarded since transient effects were not the target here and the density ρ is the percentage of cells occupied on the road.

To maintain analogy with the traditional NaSch model, a vehicle occupies 7.5 m, divided in n cells, where the length of cells l_c are given by $l_c = (7.5/n)\,m$, and $A_{max} = n\,cell/s^2$. For results presented here we took $n = 5$ and we called p_b the probability of braking and P the priority probability of the vehicle in $R1$ (Fig. 3). Besides the results from traditional NaSch model, we present results when $n = 5$ for four different profiles chosen to represent the different acceleration policies, with distinct averages and similar variance [14]. So, we consider in this work:

$B(10, 30)$ for the Aggressive profile, with $\mu = 4\,cell/s^2 = 6\,m/s^2$;
$B(20, 28)$, for the Intermediary I, with $\mu = 3\,cell/s^2 = 4.5\,m/s^2$;
$B(28, 20)$, for the Intermediary II, with $\mu = 2\,cell/s^2 = 3\,m/s^2$
$B(30, 10)$, for the Cautious or Non-Aggressive profile, with $\mu = 1\,cells/s^2 = 1.5\,m/s^2$.

Here μ is the average of all values of A, in Algorithm 1. In traditional NaSch model, $\mu = 1\,cells/s^2 = 7.5\,m/s^2$, with A always equal n.

4.1 The Deterministic Case ($p_b = 0$)

To compare with results obtained by Marzoug et al. [18], we consider the case where $p_b = 0$ in NaSch model.

(i) *Influence of discretization*

To show the influence of discretization in this modeling, we will initially present results of the NaSch model with different discretizations. The vehicle occupies n cells and to maintain equivalence with the original model, the intersection has n cells. The vehicle moves considering both the space available for its movement and its velocity, even if the gap is not a multiple of n. Due to these factors a vehicle can occupy only part of the intersection. In this situation the intersection may be occupied by more than one instant of time by the same vehicle even if it moves. Also, the intersection can be occupied by parts of two vehicles which are in the same direction.

Figure 4 shows the fundamental diagram for $P = 0.5$, $V_{max} = (5 \times n)\,cell/s = 135\,km/h$ for $n = 1$, 3 and 5. We can observe that the maximum flow in the plateau region is maintained. However, in the traffic jamming region, a new phase arises where there is no flow of vehicles. This is caused by vehicles that remain more than one instant of time at the intersection and by the priority that is given only to vehicles that can pass through the intersection at that instant of time. These situations can not be represented by the traditional NaSch model. It should be remembered that this configuration was generated in a closed circuit, and this is the reason which allows zero flow to occur, since there is no possibility of movement when parts of the road are occupied by vehicles as can be illustrated in Fig. 5.

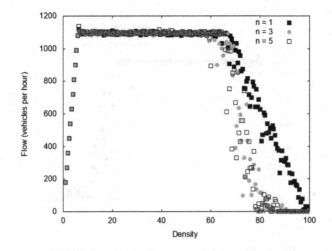

Fig. 4. Flow-density diagram ($P = 0.5$ $V_{max} = 135$ km/h)

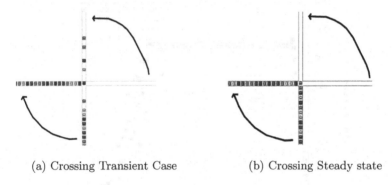

(a) Crossing Transient Case   (b) Crossing Steady state

Fig. 5. Crossing at different timesteps

(ii) *Proposed model*

It is worth noting that in the modified NaSch model $p_b = 0$ has the same meaning as in the traditional model: the probability of not accelerating or braking. This means that $p_b = 0$ makes all vehicles accelerate whenever possible. However, in our model, unlike the NaSch model, the acceleration is not constant, and is modeled by the Beta Function, making possible the definition of driver profiles based on the mean of the distribution.

To illustrate, we present in Figs. 6 and 7 comparisons for flow-density diagrams, with discretization $n = 5$, for the NaSch and NaSch modified model, for extreme behaviors which are aggressive and cautious profiles with, respectively, maximum velocities $Vmax = 15\,cell/s$ and $V_{max} = 25\,cell/s$ and priority $P = 0.5$. It can be noticed that the cautious profile presents the same flow in the region of low density, where the flow is free. However, the flow drops quickly when there is interaction between vehicles. In this phase, the flow remains practically constant, but the flow in cautious profile is much lower than the NaSch

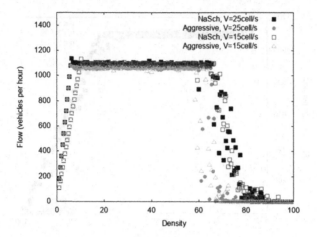

Fig. 6. Flow-density diagram: agressive drivers

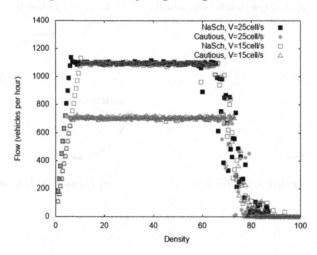

Fig. 7. Flow-density diagram: cautious drivers

model and the aggressive profile. This is because the cautious driver takes longer to resume his velocity when he needs to brake due to the approach of another vehicle. Thereafter, in a fourth step, the velocity becomes close to zero, for the reasons described in the previous example.

4.2 Probabilistic Cases ($P_b \neq 0$)

(i) *Comparing all profiles*

Figures 8 and 9 present respectively results for the flow-density and velocity-density diagrams for the NaSch model compared with the four profiles defined at the beginning of the session: aggressive, intermediate I, intermediate II and

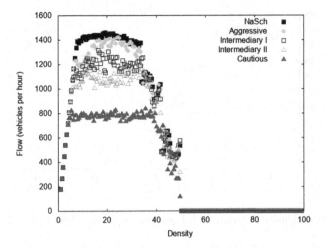

Fig. 8. Flow-density diagram: drivers' behavior comparison ($P = 1$, $p_b = 0.01$)

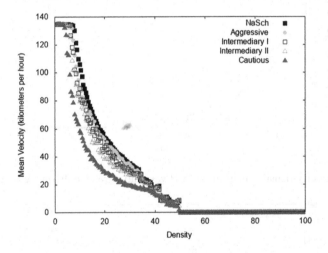

Fig. 9. Velocity-density diagram: drivers' behavior comparison ($P = 1$, $p_b = 0.01$)

cautious, for $n = 5$, $P = 1$ and $p_b = 0.01$. We can observe the existence of four phases defined by Marzoug et al. [18]. We can also observe that both, the second phase (plateau region) (Fig. 8) and the mean velocities (Fig. 9) decrease with the average acceleration of each profile, with a more pronounced difference in the cautious profile.

(ii) *Results for several priorities at the intersection*(P)

Next, Figs. 10 and 11 present flow-density and velocity-density results for the aggressive profile of the modified NaSch model with $p_b = 0.3$, for $V_{max} = 25\,cell/s$ and in Figs. 12 and 13 for $V_{max} = 15\,cell/s$, respectively, for different values of P.

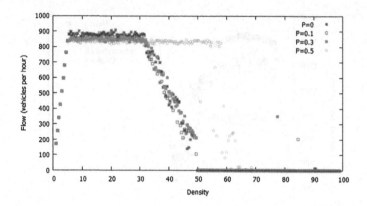

Fig. 10. Flow-density diagram with P varying: agressive driver (V = 135 km/h)

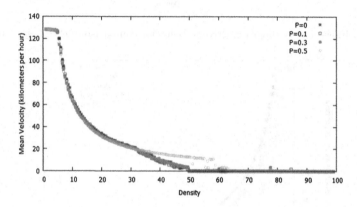

Fig. 11. Velocity-density diagram with P varying: agressive driver (V = 135 km/h)

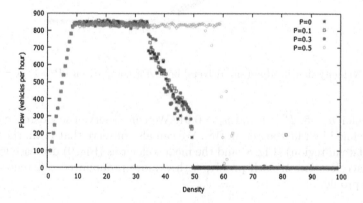

Fig. 12. Flow-density diagram with P varying: agressive driver (V = 81 km/h)

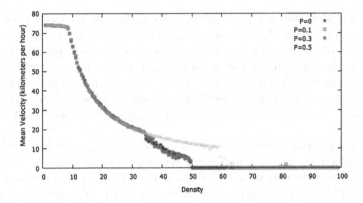

Fig. 13. Velocity-density diagram with P varying: agressive driver (V= 81 km/h)

We can observe that the results show the same discontinuity between the third and fourth phase described by Marzoug et al. [18] when the density $\rho = 50$, except when $P = 0.5$ where this discontinuity occurs when $\rho = 60$. In this case, in the results presented in Marzoug et al. [18], diagrams present only three phases, since the discretization used in the traditional NaSch model does not allow the representation of the situations described in Sect. 4.1 (i).

5   Conclusions

In this work we presented a model to evaluate how driver's behavior, defined by different accelerations policies, can affect the traffic flow on a road with an unsigned intersection. We looked for whether the way drivers speed up to reach the same maximum speed, influences the dynamics of traffic and how it influences if there is an unsigned intersection on that road. This is usually an unobservable behavior and that is why modeling the problem and performing computational simulations becomes fundamental for the understanding of traffic dynamics. To this end we modeled an intersection with a closed circuit, as proposed for Marzoug et al. [18], where we have two transversal roads crossing in their middle, leading to an eight shape (Fig. 3).

We used a modified version of the NaSch model that includes heterogeneities due to different acceleration policies for vehicles under the same velocity limit, using a continuous probability density function, the Beta function, to model it. The usage of functions with different mean values made possible the consideration of drivers with different steering behaviours, given by their acceleration profile.

From the results we conclude that the proposed model represents the four phases of the flow, as described by Marzoug et al. [18] for the same configuration of the road: free flow, the plateau, the jamming phase and the intermediate phase, where flow decreases. However, we have verified that the most refined discretization allows the representation of situations not representable by the traditional model, with a vehicle partially occupying the intersection or having parts of two vehicles in the same direction, occupying the intersection. It is also noticed that the representation of the different acceleration profiles decisively interfere in the modeling of the problem, since more cautious profiles significantly alter the flow-density and velocity-density diagrams. These factors lead us to conclude that this type of modeling is necessary when analyzing more complex topologies, with the existence of more crossings, roundabout, traffic signals among others.

With the approach here considered, driver's behaviors besides being able to be described by different maximum velocity, can also estimate if the way these drivers reaches this velocity influences the dynamics of traffic and how it influences. This is an unobservable behavior in usual measurements and thus usually disregarded in traffic flow analysis.

Acknowledgement. Authors thank CNPq/PIBIC/PIBIT (UFF, LNCC) scholarship.

References

1. Larraga, M.E., del Ro, J.A., Schadschneider, A.: New kind of phase separation in a CA traffic model with anticipation. J. Phys. A: Math. Gen. **37**(12), 3769 (2004)
2. Knospe, W., Santen, L., Schadschneider, A., Schreckenberg, M.: Towards a realistic microscopic description of highway traffic. J. Phys. A: Math. Gen. **33**(48), L477 (2000)
3. Hafstein, S.F., Chrobok, R., Pottmeier, A., Schreckenberg, M.: A high-resolution cellular automata traffic simulation model with application in a freeway traffic information system. Comput. Aided Civ. Infrastruct. Eng. **19**(5), 338–350 (2004)
4. Precht, L., Keinath, A., Krems, J.F.: Efects of driving anger on driver behavior - results from naturalistic driving data. Transp. Res. Part F: Traffic Psychol. Behav. **45**, 75–92 (2017)
5. Cheng, R.: An extended continuum model accounting for the driver's timid and aggressive attributions. Phys. Lett. A **381**(15), 1302–1312 (2017)
6. Wen, H.: The effect of driver's characteristics on the stability of traffic flow under honk environment. Nonlinear Dyn. **84**(3), 1517–1528 (2016)
7. Peng, G., He, H., Lu, W.-Z.: A new car-following model with the consideration of incorporating timid and aggressive driving behaviors.ÿPhysica A: Stat. Mech. Appl. **442**, 197–202 (2016)
8. Bette, H.M., Habel, L., Emig, T., Schreckenberg, M.: Mechanisms of jamming in the Nagel-Schreckenberg model for traffic flow. Phys. Rev. E **95**(1), 012311 (2017)
9. Qu, X., Yang, M., Yang, F., Ran, B., Li, L.: An improved single-lane cellular automaton model considering driver's radical feature. J. Adv. Transp. **2018**, 10 (2018). ID 3791820
10. Malecki, K.: A computer simulation of traffic flow with on-street parking and drivers' behaviour based on cellular automata and a multi-agent system. J. Comput. Sci. **28**, 32–42 (2018)
11. Zamith, M., Leal-Toledo, R.C.P., Toledo, E.M., MagalhÆes, G.V.P.: A new stochastic cellular automata model for traffic flow simulation with drivers' behavior predicition. J. Comput. Sci. **9**, 51–57 (2015)

12. Leal-Toledo, R.C.P., Magalhães, G.V.P., Almeida, I.M., Toledo, E.M.: Traffic flow simulation under the influence of different acceleration policies. In: Proceedings of the International Conference on Scientific Computing, pp. 90–93. CSREA Press, Las Vegas (2017)
13. Almeida, I.M., Leal-Toledo, R.C.P., Toledo, E.M., Cacau, D.C., Magalhães, G.V.P.: Drivers' behavior effects in the occurrence of dangerous situations which may lead to accidents. In: Mauri, G., El Yacoubi, S., Dennunzio, A., Nishinari, K., Manzoni, L. (eds.) ACRI 2018. LNCS, vol. 11115, pp. 441–450. Springer, Cham (2018). https://doi.org/10.1007/978-3-319-99813-8_40
14. Nagel, K., Schreckenberg, M.: A cellular automaton model for freeway traffic. J. de Phys. I(2), 2221–2229 (1992)
15. Qi-Lang, L., Jiang, R., Min, J., Xie, J.-R., Wang, B.H.: Phase diagrams of heterogeneous traffic flow at a single intersection in a deterministic Fukui-Ishibashi cellular automata traffic model. Europhys. Lett. 108(2), 28001–28008 (2014)
16. Brockfeld, E., Barlovic, R., Schadschneider, A., Schreckenberg, M.: Optimizing traffic lights in a cellular automaton model for city traffic. Phys. Rev. E 64(5), 10 (2001)
17. Nagatani, T.: Traffic states and fundamental diagram in cellular automaton model of vehicular traffic controlled by signals. Phys. A: Stat. Mech. Appl. 388(8), 1673–1681 (2009)
18. Marzoug, R., Ez-Zahraouy, H., Benyoussef, A.: Cellular automata traffic flow behavior at the intersection of two roads. Phys. Scr. 89(6), 1–7 (2014)

Quantify Physiologic Interactions Using Network Analysis

Thuy T. Pham$^{(\boxtimes)}$ and Eryk Dutkiewicz

Faculty of Engineering and IT, University of Technology Sydney,
Sydney, NSW 2006, Australia
thuy.pham@uts.edu.au

Abstract. To better understand the neural interactions amongst human organ systems, this work provides a framework of data analysis to quantify forms of neural signalling. We explore network interactions among the human brain and motor controlling. The main objective of this work is to provoke unique challenges in the emerging Network Physiology field. The proposed method applies network analysis techniques including power coherence for connectivity discovering and correlation measurement for profiling relationships. We used a well-designed dataset of 50 subjects over 14 different scenarios for each individual. We found network models for these interactions and observed informative network behaviours. The information can be used to study impaired communications that can lead to dysfunction of organs or the entire system such as sepsis.

Keywords: Physiology network · Data analysis · Brain ·
Network interactions

1 Introduction

The human body consists of diverse physiological organ systems of which each has its own structural and functional complexity, causing transient and nonlinear output information from each system [1]. Furthermore, complex signalling between these organ systems and sub-systems has been found among distinct physiologic states, e.g., wake and sleep; light and deep sleep; dreams; consciousness and unconsciousness (i.e., a person fails to respond normally to painful stimuli, light, or sound) [2,3]. Therefore, at the system level, the human organism can be considered as an integrated network with its own regulatory mechanism among physiological organ systems. Each organ system, referred to as a node continuously interacts with each other to maintain their functions. Recent works [4,5] showed that impaired communications can lead to dysfunction of organs or the entire system such as sepsis. However, the mechanisms of interactions over space and time scales are not well-understood and in need of a suitable analysing tool or theory-based framework [6].

© Springer Nature Switzerland AG 2019
S. Misra et al. (Eds.): ICCSA 2019, LNCS 11619, pp. 142–151, 2019.
https://doi.org/10.1007/978-3-030-24289-3_12

The main challenge to study these interactions is the network complexity [3]. Each node of the network represents an individual physiological system and thus has different characteristics and outputs against others, therefore it is hard to identify and quantify their signalling. For example, each organ can be characterized by unsteady, periodic and non-linear output signals [7]. Furthermore, physiological organ systems operate in a wide range of time scales (ms to hours) and can be chaotic oscillators [8]. In contrast to traditional complex network theory, edges (i.e., links) in this field are non-deterministic, i.e., they do not constitute static connection graphs. In fact, changes in physiologic state can lead to collective network behaviours [3].

As a result, approaches in this area often span from statistical physics, applied mathematics to biomedical signals processing, human physiology and clinical medicine [3]. Recently, interdisciplinary methods have been found to address the aforementioned challenges. Biomedical engineers, data scientists, physiologists and medical specialists have worked as a team to shape a new field of Network Physiology [6]. Latest achievement examples are discoveries of differences in nonlinear heart dynamics during rest and exercise [9], a network-analysis tool to localize the epileptogenic zone [10], synchronous behaviour in network model based on human cortico-cortical connections [11], network structure of the human musculoskeletal system shapes neural interactions on multiple time scales [12].

Earlier nonlinear methods were used to tackle the complexity in non-linearity including phase synchronization, coherence in heart and brain [13], mutual information [14], and the Granger causal analysis [15]. Lately, the time delay stability [16] has been a new concept to identify physiologic interactions across distinct physiologic states (e.g., brain-organ communications as a signature of neuroautonomic control [16]). Specifically, if the time delay between systems is more consistent, the interaction is more stable and longer periods of the delay stability indicate stronger coupling [16]. These methods quantified the strength and directionality of links in the network.

From a data science perspective, information calculating has been applied to find the network of interaction. For example, entropy was measured between the brain and the heart [14]. Time-variant coherence analysis was introduced to study the control network of the cardiovascular and cardiorespiratory systems in patients with epilepsy [13]. Temporal interactions were investigated with bursts of activity in neural networks [17] to show whether bursting arise from inherent nodes or as a result of network interaction. Coherence measurement over time scale were found in latest works [10–12].

Above approaches have not been targeted to data mining for a diverse recording system at a large scale. More appropriate techniques should be deeply based on advances in complex network theory. Several pioneers proposed in near similar fields such as human symptoms-disease network [18]. The typical approach often involves weighted correlation analysis for module detection, variable selection, topological information extraction. Nevertheless, these methods adopted *temporal network* forms (i.e., modelling as graphs of vertices coupled by edges) [19]. Though the *static* network topologies were developed to time-dependent

models [19], the complex activities of individual nodes and the time-variant
links were missed [6]. Hence, merging of those techniques could help alleviate
aforementioned unique challenges in the network physiology.

We propose network analysis techniques such as power coherence to model
the connectivity of network and correlation measures for profiling relationships.
The main contribution of this work: propose a new framework of using network
analysis techniques for physiology interactions within a human body.

2   Methods

From graph theory perspective, we consider each data channel (i.e., one of 64
recording location on the scalp) as a node of a network. The relationship between
two electrophysiological signals recorded at two nodes is the *link* (or edge) of
two nodes. The strength of the relationship is called *weight* of the link. In this
work, to compute the weight, we first computed pairwise spectral coherence C_{xy}
between the two data windows of nodes x and y. C_{xy} is calculated by the Fourier
transform (the Welch method [20] Eq. 1) between two EEG channels across time
windows (size of 2.5s sliding each second) in the frequency range of 30–90 Hz
(so-called *gamma* band).

$$C_{xy}(\omega) = \frac{P_{xy}(\omega)}{\sqrt{P_{xx}(\omega).P_{yy}(\omega)}} \tag{1}$$

where ω is frequency, $P_{xx}(\omega)$ is the power spectrum of signal x, $P_{yy}(\omega)$ is the
power spectrum of signal y, and $P_{xy}(\omega)$ is the cross-power spectrum for signals x
and y. When $P_{xx}(\omega) = 0$ or $P_{yy}(\omega) = 0$, then also $P_{xy}(\omega) = 0$ and we assume that
$C_{xy}(\omega)$ is zero. The power and cross spectra are estimated by the Fourier trans-
form. In the continuous domain, let $\mathfrak{F}_x(\omega)$ and $\overline{\mathfrak{F}_x(\omega)}$, denote the Fourier transform and its conjugate of signal x, respectively, i.e. $\mathfrak{F}_x(\omega) = \int\limits_{-\infty}^{+\infty} x(t).e^{-j\omega t}dt$.

Then, the neural interactions are represented by a three-dimension matrix
of which one dimension is for time windows and the others are for a connectivity matrix, C. The centrality of a node at a time point is measured by the
strength and number of connections a node makes with others. In this work, the
centrality is computed from the singular vector decomposition of C. The leading
eigenvector is extracted to represent for each node (further details of *eigenvector
centrality* was analysed in the earlier works [10]).

To analyse properties of the constructed network, we propose to depict the
strength of relationship between two nodes across time windows (i.e., the entire
experiment task) using the Pearson correlation coefficient definition [21]. Because
we are looking for the strength of relationships, the direction of the coefficients
is ignored (i.e., coefficients $=|r|$ and is from $0 \to 1$). When $|r|$ is closer to 1, the
more closely two nodes are related. In order to investigate leading interactions,
we applied a threshold p $(0 < p < 1)$ to filter out minor links (i.e., links with
small weights, thus, represent weak relationships). Specifically, we preserved a

proportion p of the links with largest weights; all other links including self-node connections were assigned with weight of 0. We can vary this p to better visualise the network models. The proposed method was implemented using MATLAB scripts R2018b (The MathWorks Inc., Natick, MA, 2000).

3 Datasets

We used a well-designed dataset of 50 subjects across 14 different scenarios for each individual. This data set is a portion of a larger collection [22] originally contributed to PhysioBank [23] by Gerwin Schalk and his colleagues using their BCI2000 system [24] (www.bci2000.org) at Wadsworth Center, New York State Department of Health, Albany, NY. W.A.

The dataset consists of 700 electroencephalogram (EEG) recordings. This measurement technique depicts electrical activity of the brain as wave patterns. Electrodes (i.e., small metal discs with thin wires) were placed on the scalp, and then send signals to a computer for further processes. The system was used in this dataset is a 64-channel type (Fig. 1) that covers the scalp from frontal left /right, central left/right, to occipital left/ right. The electrode map is as per the

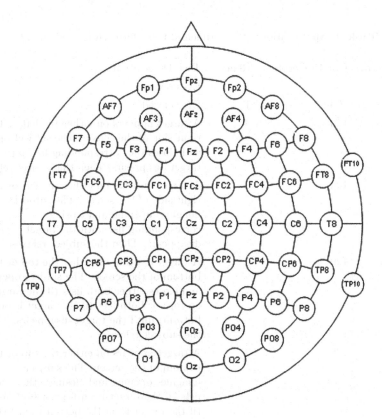

Fig. 1. The electrode map of 64 channels from BCI2000 [22].

international 10-10 system (excluding electrodes Nz, F9, F10, FT9, FT10, A1, A2, TP9, TP10, P9, and P10). The numbers below each electrode name indicate the order in which they appear in the records.

There are 14 experimental runs for each individual as in Table 1. Each recording measures for one or two minutes. Sampling rate was set at 160 samples per second. Raw EEG data were filtered by a Butterworth notch filter of order 4 (built-in MATLAB function) for the range of 59.5–60.5 Hz. We eliminated correlated noise across channels by taking an average signal from all recordings of the same subject and subtract this from each channel. We also discarded channels which were labelled as *artefacts contaminated*. Each network is calculated for each subject then we investigate neural interactions by looking at the average network for each scenario (i.e., averaging weights of the same link during a same task description across 50 subjects).

4 Results

We varied parameter p from only $1 \rightarrow 100\%$ for the proportion of links with largest weights to be preserved. Figure 2 (a, b, c) illustrates examples of different p in the same Baseline 1 task (i.e., when the subject only open eyes Table 1).

Table 1. Specifications of experimental tasks for each individual [22].

Task Name	Length (seconds)	Repeats	Task Description
Baseline 1	60	1	Eyes open
Baseline 2	60	1	Eyes closed
Task 1	120	3	A target appears on either the left or the right side of the screen. The subject opens and closes the corresponding fist until the target disappears. Then the subject relaxes
Task 2	120	3	A target appears on either the left or the right side of the screen. The subject imagines opening and closing the corresponding fist until the target disappears. Then the subject relaxes
Task 3	120	3	A target appears on either the top or the bottom of the screen. The subject opens and closes either both fists (if the target is on top) or both feet (if the target is on the bottom) until the target disappears. Then the subject relaxes
Task 4	120	3	A target appears on either the top or the bottom of the screen. The subject imagines opening and closing either both fists (if the target is on top) or both feet (if the target is on the bottom) until the target disappears. Then the subject relaxes

We found that at level of 30% preserved links the network constructed still has a high level of complication for analysis by visualisation method. In the scope of this work, we suggest to further analyse the model with 5% preserved links.

According to the top 5% of all possible relationships, we can clearly observe major interactions by the colour and size of each node which are upon the number of connections associated with the node. The links are also illustrated in a similar way in the grayscale. For example, Fig. 2(c, d) compares two networks between baselines (i.e., open and close eyes). In the *open eyes* action, the main active areas are at electrodes FT7, T7, then TP1, FC1, FCz. In the *close eyes* action, most active electrodes shifted to electrode POz, PO4, PO8 (Fig. 2c, d).

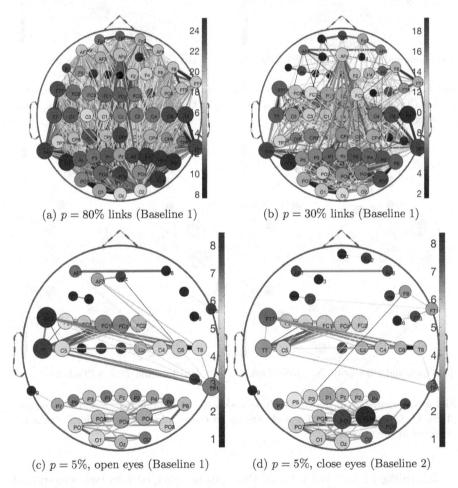

(a) $p = 80\%$ links (Baseline 1) (b) $p = 30\%$ links (Baseline 1)

(c) $p = 5\%$, open eyes (Baseline 1) (d) $p = 5\%$, close eyes (Baseline 2)

Fig. 2. Varying the proportion parameter p for preserved links with largest weights. (a, b, c) are for different p in the same Baseline 1 (Table 1). (c, d) are between open and close eyes when $p = 5\%$. Colour and size of each node are up to the number of connections. Links are weighted in the grayscale.

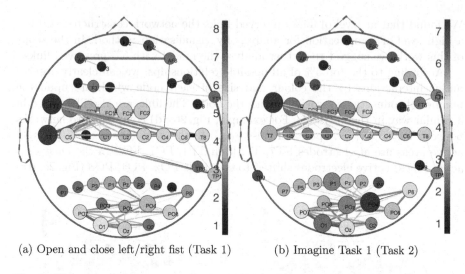

(a) Open and close left/right fist (Task 1)   (b) Imagine Task 1 (Task 2)

Fig. 3. Comparisons of networks across tasks. (a, b) are for Task 1 and its *imagine* version (Table 1). Colour and size of a node are up to the number of connections. Links are weighted in the grayscale.

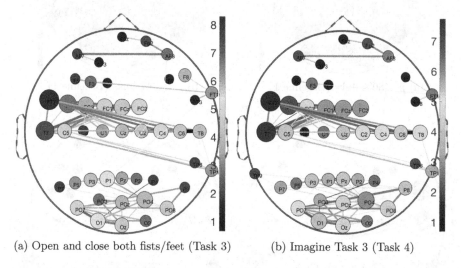

(a) Open and close both fists/feet (Task 3)   (b) Imagine Task 3 (Task 4)

Fig. 4. Comparisons of networks across tasks. (a, b) are for Task 3 and the *imagine* (Table 1). Colour and size of a node are up to the number of connections. Links are weighted in the grayscale.

Regarding to four other tasks, they can be grouped into two scenarios of controlling movements (open and close) of one or both hands/feet. In both scenarios, each subject was asked to do and imagine doing the action. Figures 3 and 4 shows four networks construct through these four tasks. We noted that state of the network only changed slightly between acting on one to both hands

(Figs. 3a and 4a). However, the changes of network appeared clearly between doing the action and imagine doing so (Fig. 3a, b). Specifically, more connections appeared in the back area of the scalp (e.g., electrode PO4, POz, and O1) than in the task of *in action*.

5   Conclusion

In this work, we attempt to analyse physiologic networks. We propose a framework to construct relationships between nodes using power spectral coherence and singular decomposition. Then we use correlation measurements to represent major interactions through largest link weights and node attributes. We demonstrated the method with a real dataset of 64 EEG channels across different experimental tasks such as open and close one hand or both hands or imagine doing each of these actions.

We found changes in network properties between these different tasks. At level of more than 5% preserved links, the network is highly complicated to analyse by visualisation method. Major interactions are depicted by the number of connections associated with the node. During *open eye* tasks, electrodes of FT7, T7, then TP1, FC1, FCz are main active areas. During *close eye* tasks, the participating area shifted to electrode POz, PO4, PO8.

In other tasks (i.e., two scenarios of controlling movements (open and close) of one or both hands/feet), state of the network only changed slightly between acting on one to both hands. However, more connections appeared in the back area of the scalp (e.g., electrode PO4, POz, and O1) when imagining the task than doing so in action.

6   Discussion

These informative network behaviours can be used to study impaired communications that can lead to dysfunction of organs or the entire system such as sepsis. For example, in the next steps of this works, we will intensively investigate changes in network topologies and other characteristics to find associations of neural interactions between different controlling scheme of the brain and other body parts. This may require new data collections and more specific experimental designs of trials. Nevertheless, the framework of this work will continue to be applied to the aforementioned extension or even a new clinical application such as network analysis for freezing of gait monitoring in patients with Parkinson's disease [25, 26]. The underlying mechanism of the freezing is not well-understood while sensory information channels have been successfully demonstrated in our earlier works [25–27]. Therefore, this network-based framework would open a new way to investigate freezing of gait occurrences.

References

1. Karasik, R., et al.: Correlation differences in heartbeat fluctuations during rest and exercise. Phys. Rev. E **66**(6), 062902 (2002)
2. Bartsch, R.P., Liu, K.K., Bashan, A., Ivanov, P.C.: Network physiology: how organ systems dynamically interact. PloS One **10**(11), e0142143 (2015)
3. Ivanov, P.C., Liu, K.K.L., Lin, A., Bartsch, R.P.: Network physiology: from neural plasticity to organ network interactions. In: Mantica, G., Stoop, R., Stramaglia, S. (eds.) Emergent Complexity from Nonlinearity, in Physics, Engineering and the Life Sciences. SPP, vol. 191, pp. 145–165. Springer, Cham (2017). https://doi.org/10.1007/978-3-319-47810-4_12
4. Deisboeck, T., Kresh, J.Y.: Complex Systems Science in Biomedicine. Springer, New York (2007). https://doi.org/10.1007/978-0-387-33532-2
5. Moorman, J.R., Lake, D.E., Ivanov, P.C.: Early detection of sepsis–a role for network physiology? Crit. Care Med. **44**(5), e312–e313 (2016)
6. Ivanov, P.C., Liu, K.K., Bartsch, R.P.: Focus on the emerging new fields of network physiology and network medicine. New J. Phys. **18**(10), 100201 (2016)
7. Ivanov, P.C., Amaral, L.N., Goldberger, A.L., Stanley, H.E.: Stochastic feedback and the regulation of biological rhythms. EPL (Europhys. Lett.) **43**(4), 363 (1998)
8. Xu, L., Chen, Z., Hu, K., Stanley, H.E., Ivanov, P.C.: Spurious detection of phase synchronization in coupled nonlinear oscillators. Phys. Rev. E **73**(6), 065201 (2006)
9. Gómez-Extremera, M., Bernaola-Galván, P.A., Vargas, S., Benítez-Porres, J., Carpena, P., Romance, A.R.: Differences in nonlinear heart dynamics during rest and exercise and for different training. Physiol. Meas. **39**(8), 084008 (2018)
10. Li, A., et al.: Using network analysis to localize the epileptogenic zone from invasive EEG recordings in intractable focal epilepsy. Netw. Neurosci. **2**(02), 218–240 (2018)
11. Protachevicz, P.R., et al.: Synchronous behaviour in network model based on human cortico-cortical connections. Physiol. Meas. **39**(7), 074006 (2018)
12. Kerkman, J.N., Daffertshofer, A., Gollo, L.L., Breakspear, M., Boonstra, T.W.: Network structure of the human musculoskeletal system shapes neural interactions on multiple time scales. Sci. Adv. **4**(6), eaat0497 (2018)
13. Piper, D., Schiecke, K., Pester, B., Benninger, F., Feucht, M., Witte, H.: Time-variant coherence between heart rate variability and EEG activity in epileptic patients: an advanced coupling analysis between physiological networks. New J. Phys. **16**(11), 115012 (2014)
14. Faes, L., Nollo, G., Jurysta, F., Marinazzo, D.: Information dynamics of brain-heart physiological networks during sleep. New J. Phys. **16**(10), 105005 (2014)
15. Stramaglia, S., Cortes, J.M., Marinazzo, D.: Synergy and redundancy in the granger causal analysis of dynamical networks. New J. Phys. **16**(10), 105003 (2014)
16. Bashan, A., Bartsch, R.P., Kantelhardt, J.W., Havlin, S., Ivanov, P.C.: Network physiology reveals relations between network topology and physiological function. Nat. Commun. **3**, 702 (2012)
17. Ferrari, F.A., Viana, R.L., Gomez, F., Lorimer, T., Stoop, R.: Macroscopic bursting in physiological networks: node or network property? New J. Phys. **17**(5), 055024 (2015)
18. Zhou, X., Menche, J., Barabási, A.L., Sharma, A.: Human symptoms-disease network. Nat. Commun. **5**, 4212 (2014)
19. Holme, P., Saramäki, J.: Temporal networks. Phys. Rep. **519**(3), 97–125 (2012)
20. Challis, R., Kitney, R.: Biomedical signal processing (part 3 of 4): the power spectrum and coherence function. Med. Biol. Eng. Comput. **28**(6), 509–524 (1990)

21. Pearson, K.: Vii. mathematical contributions to the theory of evolution.–iii. regression, heredity, and panmixia. Philos. Trans. R. Soc. Lond. A, **187**, 253–318 (1896). containing papers of a mathematical or physical character
22. Schalk, G., McFarland, D.J., Hinterberger, T., Birbaumer, N., Wolpaw, J.R.: EEG motor movement/imagery dataset (2009)
23. Goldberger, A.L., et al.: Physiobank, physiotoolkit, and physionet. Circulation **101**(23), e215–e220 (2000)
24. Schalk, G., McFarland, D.J., Hinterberger, T., Birbaumer, N., Wolpaw, J.R.: BCI 2000: a general-purpose brain-computer interface (BCI) system. IEEE Trans. Biomed. Eng. **51**(6), 1034–1043 (2004)
25. Pham, T.T., et al.: Freezing of gait detection in Parkinson's disease: a subject-independent detector using anomaly scores. IEEE Trans. Biomed. Eng. **64**(11), 2719–2728 (2017)
26. Pham, T.: Applying Machine Learning for Automated Classification of Biomedical Data in Subject-Independent Settings. Springer theses. Springer, Switzerland (2018). https://doi.org/10.1007/978-3-319-98675-3
27. Pham, T.T., Nguyen, D.N., Dutkiewicz, E., McEwan, A.L., Leong, P.H.: Wearable healthcare systems: a single channel accelerometer based anomaly detector for studies of gait freezing in Parkinson's disease. In: 2017 IEEE International Conference on Communications (ICC), pp. 1–5. IEEE (2017)

Effects in the Algorithm Performance from Problem Structure, Searching Behavior and Temperature: A Causal Study Case for Threshold Accepting and Bin-Packing

V. Landero[1($\boxtimes$)], Joaquín Pérez[2], L. Cruz[3], Tania Turrubiates[4],
and David Ríos[1]

[1] Universidad Politécnica de Apodaca (UPAP), Apodaca, Nuevo León, Mexico
vanesa.landero.najera@gmail.com, drios@upapnl.edu.mx
[2] Departamento de Ciencias Computacionales, Centro Nacional de Investigación
y Desarrollo Tecnológico (CENIDET), AP 5-164, 62490 Cuernavaca, Mexico
jperez@hotmail.com
[3] División de Estudios de Posgrado e Investigación,
Instituto Tecnológico de Ciudad Madero (ITCM), Cd. Madero, Mexico
lcruzreyes@prodigy.net.mx
[4] Instituto Tecnológico Superior de Álamo Temapache, Veracruz, Mexico

Abstract. A review of state of art reveals that the characterization and analysis of the relation between problem-algorithm has been focused only on problem features or on algorithm features; or in some situations on both, but the algorithm logical is not considered in the analysis. The above for selecting an algorithm will give the best solution. However there is more knowledge for discovering from this relation. In this paper, significant features are proposed for describing problem structure and algorithm searching fluctuation; other known metrics were considered (Autocorrelation Coefficient and Length) but were not significant. A causal study case is performed for analyzing causes and effects from: Bin-Packing problem structure, Temperature, searching behavior of Threshold Accepting algorithm and final performance to solving problem instances. The proposed features permitted in the causal study to find relations cause-effect; which gave guidelines for designing a Threshold Accepting self-adaptive algorithm. Its performance outperforms to original algorithm in 74% out of 324 problem cases. The causal analysis on relevant information from problem, algorithm (both) and algorithm logical could be an important guideline to discover rules or principles over several problem domains, which permit the design of self-adaptive algorithms to give the best solution to complex problems.

1 Introduction

The majority of reviewed related works from some disciplines as combinatorial optimization, machine learning, artificial intelligence have characterized the relation between problem and algorithm focusing only on problem information, some examples [1–4]; or algorithm, some examples [5–7]; other only one problem and algorithm information [8–12]. This relation has been analyzed in the majority cases to select the

© Springer Nature Switzerland AG 2019
S. Misra et al. (Eds.): ICCSA 2019, LNCS 11619, pp. 152–166, 2019.
https://doi.org/10.1007/978-3-030-24289-3_13

most indicated algorithm [2, 11, 13–15]; or predict the problems hardness [16, 17]; or built hyper-heuristics [18]; or adjust control parameter [6, 9, 12, 19–23]. The objective principal is to give the best solution to some problem.

However, these not include both information about: problem (problem structure) and algorithm (behavior in its search trajectory); the algorithm logical design; for analyzing deeply causes and effects between problem-algorithm; it is to say, why this relation becomes successful in some problem instances and why not in other, what problem feature are related to algorithm feature, which is the algorithm logical design; and how they relate in some way for obtaining the best solution on instances set. These causal relations found over several problems domains could give guidelines for discovering theories that permit to self-adapt the algorithm logical, depending on problem structure, searching behavior and give the best solution to any problem.

In order to be able to give small, but relevant steps according to above, firstly, starting for a specific domain; in this paper, firstly, a reviewing of state of art from disciplines combinatorial optimization, machine learning, artificial intelligence about information type and approaches for characterizing and analyzing the relation between problem-algorithm is presented in Sect. 2, and a reflection about this long trajectory of these related works is performed. In Sect. 3, a framework is proposed for characterizing the One Dimension Bin-Packing problem and Tabu Search algorithm. In Sect. 4, a causal study case is presented, where the relation between One-Dimension Bin-Packing problem and Tabu Search algorithm is analyzed, the found causes and effects between proposed features from problem and algorithm, considering the algorithm logical design, gave knowledge that permitted design a Threshold Accepting self-adaptive algorithm. In Sect. 5, an analysis of performance results of original and self-adaptive algorithms is performed; where a statistical test was applied. Finally, in Sect. 6, conclusions about the performed work are presented, as well as research future works.

2   Reviewing State of Art: Information and Analysis Approaches

This section emphasizes two main issues, information type and the approaches considered to analyze the relation between problem and algorithm. Table 1 presents some investigations of both. The column 2 indicates if the analysis was based on problem features (F). The column 3 indicates if the analysis was based on algorithm features (A) and column 4 indicates if the analysis considered some algorithm logical area. The last column indicates the analysis approach performed. The analysis approach in this paper is referred to procedure for discovering knowledge from experimentation data, which permits the analysis of the relation between problem and algorithm. Some of these: Unsupervised Learning (UL), Supervised Learning (SL), Regression Analysis (RA), Functions of Probability Distribution (FD), Exploratory Analysis (EA), Causal Analysis (CA).

Some related works considered problem features for building models, using machine learning, specifically supervised learning (SL), to learn patterns identified from data, model and use it to make predictions about who would be the most appropriate algorithm to solve better a new problem instance. Several algorithms have

Table 1. Relevant causes

Work	Problem	Algorithm searching	Algorithm logical	Analysis approach
[2]	✓			UL
[13]	✓			SL
[24]	✓			SL
[25]	✓			FD
[26]		✓		EA
[27]			✓	EA
[28]			✓	EA
[29]		✓	✓	EA
[7]	✓		✓	SL
[3]	✓			UL-SL
[9]	✓		✓	RA
[19]	✓		✓	SL
[10]	✓	✓		EA
[6]			✓	SL
[21]	✓		✓	SL
[11]	✓	✓	✓	SL
[30]	✓	✓		SL
[12]	✓		✓	SL
[22]			✓	RA
[23]			✓	EA
This paper	✓	✓	✓	CA

been utilized by some related works: Case-base reasoning [1], decision trees [2, 3, 24], Support Vector Machine (SVM) [13].

Other related works in the context of model-based algorithm portfolio considered only the algorithm performance as information for analyzing. It is to say, the performance of all algorithms is measured by means some function, so too, this performance is characterized and adjusted to a model, either by a regression model [16] or a probability distribution model [14]. Other related works in the context of feature-based portfolio, considered some problem features for building a model, applying supervised learning [25]. The model can be utilized in an off-line way or an on-line way [31], where model is updated and system changes to another algorithm to give the best solution to new problem instance.

Other related works analyze relations between problem features and algorithm performance by means an unsupervised learning model, and identify key problem features. Some methods from this approach have been utilized by some related works, which are K-means clustering [2], Self-organizing maps [3].

Some other related works obtain knowledge by means exploratory analysis [7, 28], supervised learning [6], which permits to configure the algorithm in a way that it can produce the better results. There is no clearly reasons for what kind of problem instances, a algorithm configuration will produce better results. It is to say, what is the problem structure that permits to one configured algorithm to give the best results. Montero considers this information very relevant to adjust the algorithm logical [32]. There exists some related works that included problem features for analyzing the parameter control and algorithm performance by means supervised learning [12, 19, 21], as well as, this approach in the context of algorithm portfolio [9]. The searching methodology of algorithm is also analyzed with problem features and algorithm performance [29] by supervised learning, using the method k-nearest neighbor.

There exists related works that considered problem and algorithm features in their work by supervised learning [30], Exploratory Analysis [10]. However, the algorithm logical area could have given relevant knowledge for understanding more deeply the relationship that exists between problem and algorithm.

As it can be observed in Table 1, the majority of related works not includes in their works features from problem, from algorithm and the logical design. A model is built by means method Random Forest in [11], where features from problem and algorithm are considered, as well as, information of algorithm logical area. However, due nature of built model structure, which it is used for predicting the best algorithm to solve a problem instance, it is difficult to interpret the learned knowledge. It is to say, to identify the principal causes and effects about the algorithm performance, and understand better the relation between problem and algorithm; why an algorithm is best for a certain set of instances of a problem and why not in another.

3 Proposed Framework: Causal Analysis and Proposed Features

In this paper, a causal study case is presented for analyzing causes and effects that there exists between problem features, algorithm features, algorithm logical and algorithm performance; having as framework the One Dimension Bin-Packing problem and Threshold Accepting algorithm. Past works [33–35] have suggested that causal analysis is important for obtaining relevant knowledge, structured as causes and effects, from relationship problem-algorithm. As an extension from these related works, we proposed significant features for obtaining a new characterization from problem structure and algorithm searching fluctuation; which also permit to discover latent knowledge structured as a formal causal model. So too, such discovering gives rules for designing a new self-adaptive Threshold Accepting algorithm that outperforms to original algorithm for solving instances of One Dimension Bin-Packing problem.

In this section, a brief description of causal analysis is presented; where the literature nomenclature will be used for describing proposed features and causal study case.

3.1 Causal Analysis

This approach consists, in general terms, of identifying the principal causes of the behavior of some phenomenon, representing them in the form of relations cause-effect in a causal model. A causal model consists of a Directed Acyclic Graph (DAG) over a set $V = \{V_1, \ldots, V_n\}$ of vertices, representing features of interest, and a set E of directed edges, or arrows, that connect these vertices.

These graphs can be causally interpreted if they have the features: Causal Markov condition, Minimality condition, Faithfulness condition. These features make the connection between causality and probability [36]. Causal modeling has four phases. The first phase is structure learning, where its objective is to find the principal structure of causal relations between several relevant features and a data set; it is to say, a causal graph G is found that represents the causal structure $G = (V, E)$; there exist several algorithms of structure learning, one of them is PC algorithm (Peter&Clark). The set E is described as:

$E = \{C_1, C_2, ..., C_n\}$, where each $C_i \in E$ is a set of ordered pairs,
$C_i = \{(v_i, y_1), (v_i, y_2), ..., (v_i, y_n)\}$, it is
$C_i = \{(v_i \in V; y_k \in V) \mid v_i \neq y_k, y_k$ is a direct cause of v_i relative to V and there is a directed edge from y_k to v_i in $G\}$

The second phase is estimation of the found causal relations; one of algorithms that perform it is Counting algorithm [37]. The third phase is the interpretation of causal model; the causal relations with higher magnitudes are analyzed and interpreted. The fourth phase is the causal model validation.

3.2   Characterizing One Dimension Bin-Packing Problem

The problem One Dimension Bin-Packing (BPP) is considered as combinatorial optimization problem NP-hard [38]. It consists to pack k items into minimum number of bins or containers mb; subjects to, all items packed in one bin or container does not exceeds the container capacity c (it is for all bins). The fitness function $f(x_i)$ for one solution x_i of One Dimension Bin-Packing problem is described in [39].

In this paper propose characterize the problem structure by means new feature vc. It is the coefficient of normalized pearson variation, from object sizes that are not multiple of container size; it considers the information obtained by feature f, proposed by [2]. The feature vc is described by expressions 1 and 2, where fr_i is the frequency of size s_i, dv is standard deviation of frequencies set Fre and me is the mean.

So too, in this experimentation, the features b and os are considered, which were significant in past experimentations [33–35]. The feature b describes the use of container; the proportion of total size that can be assigned to a container with capacity c. The feature os measures the variability of a sample of solutions generated randomly.

$$Fre = \{fr_i \mid s_i \bmod c \neq 0\} \tag{1}$$

$$vc = \frac{dv}{me}.(1 - f) \tag{2}$$

The set V begins to be built with the values of these features for each problem instance (see Expression 3). For set V, the rows represent the problem instances and columns are the values of these variables; where m is the total of problem instances.

$$V = \{\{b_1, vc_1, os_1\}, \{b_2, vc_2, os_2\}, ..., \{b_m, vc_m, os_m\}\} \tag{3}$$

3.3   Characterizing the Threshold Accepting Algorithm: Searching Fluctuation

The Threshold Accepting algorithm is described in [40]. In general terms, it starts generating a feasible initial solution. An iterative process is performed until freezing is reached. During this process, a neighborhood solution y is generated from one actual solution x; if the difference between fitness function values for these solutions $f(y) - f(x)$ is less than temperature value T, then solution y is the new actual solution. The temperature value T is decremented by freezing factor μ.

The term of searching fluctuation or behavior, in past experimentations and this work, refers to above algorithm iterative process. It is to say, all generated solutions are seen as the path traced by algorithm in axis "x" and the fitness function value of each from these solutions is represented in axis "y". The algorithm searching fluctuation has been characterized by feature tm in past works [33–35]. The feature tm is the average of valley sizes identified for all algorithm runs; it has been significant in past experimentations for characterizing behavior of algorithms Tabu Search and Threshold Accepting.

In this paper, the algorithm searching fluctuation is also characterized by new features pp, pn and dv; where pp is the positive slope and pn is the negative slope from one valley identified during the iterative process. Figure 1 shows one identified valley; axis "y" is the value of fitness function $f(x_i)$ for each generated solution x_i (axis "x"), during algorithm iterative process. Also the positive (pp - left side) and negative (pn - right side) slopping of an identified valley are shown.

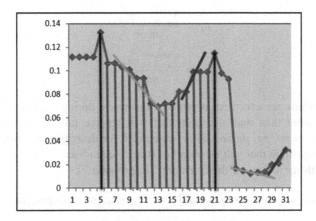

Fig. 1. Positive and negative slopes

The new features pp and pn are calculated by means of the approximation to tangent of a curve in one point; it is obtained by means of the secant defined by two points (one is where the tangent crosses and another is closed to curve). Figure 2 shows the slope of a curve in a point A, which is defined by the straight T. Also is shown how can be approximated this slope by means the secant; it is defined by points A and B.

When B is going to A, k and h going to 0, but its quotient is going to a determinate value; which is the slope of AT. Expression 4 defines the calculating of the slope of a curve in two points very closed ($x_0 + h$, x_0). Features pp and pn (Expressions 5 and 6) describe the average of the negative and positive slopping of the found valleys in all algorithm runs ($nrun$). The feature vd measures the dispersion of found valleys.

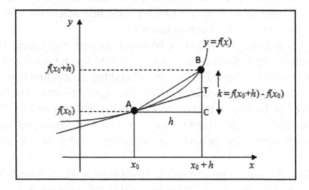

Fig. 2. Calculating a slope

$$slope = \frac{f(x_0 + h) - f(x_0)}{h} \quad (4)$$

$$pp = \frac{\sum_{run=1}^{nrun} pp_{run}}{ncor} \quad (5)$$

$$pn = \frac{\sum_{run=1}^{nrun} pn_{run}}{nrun} \quad (6)$$

The algorithms are executed in problem instances, during execution (considering that there is more than one algorithm that will resolve problem instances). These proposed features tm, pp, pn and dv are calculated for describing the behavior during searching of algorithm that will be object of study (see in Sect. 4). The set V continues to be built with the values of these features (Expression 7).

$$V = \{\{b_1, vc_1, os_1, tm_1, pp_1, pn_1, vd_1\}, \ldots, \{b_m, vc_m, os_m, tm_m, pp_m, pn_m, vd_m\}\} \quad (7)$$

3.4   Characterizing Algorithm Performance

After execution of each problem instance (1, 2, ..., m), the algorithm performance is measured by features *time* and *quality*, described in expressions 8 and 9. The evaluations number of fitness function for feasible and infeasible solutions is considerate for *time*. The quality is the ratio between the best solution found by algorithm Q_f (final number of containers) and theoretical solution Q_t (sum of object sizes divided by container capacity c), described by expression 10.

$$time = feasibles + infeasibles \tag{8}$$

$$quality = \frac{Q_f}{Q_t} \tag{9}$$

$$Q_t = \frac{\sum_{i=1}^{k} s_i}{c} \tag{10}$$

A set D is being built, mapping these performance features to each algorithm with the specific order as Expression 11; where n is the total of algorithms executed. The values of $quality_{11}$, $time_{11}$ meaning the performance of algorithm 1 for problem instance 1; the values of $quality_{12}$, $time_{12}$ meaning the performance of algorithm 2 for problem instance 1; the values of $quality_{m1}$, $time_{m1}$ meaning the performance of algorithm 1 for problem instance m; the values of $quality_{m2}$, $time_{m2}$ meaning the performance of algorithm 2 for problem instance m, and so on.

$$D = \left\{ \begin{array}{l} \{\{quality_{11}, time_{11}\}, \{quality_{12}, time_{12}\}, \ldots, \{quality_{1n}, time_{1n}\}\} \\ \{\{quality_{m1}, time_{m1}\}, \{quality_{m2}, time_{m2}\}, \ldots, \{quality_{mn}, time_{mn}\}\} \end{array} \right\} \tag{11}$$

The function r considers information of algorithm a_t from set D for one problem instance i (consider a_t as algorithm that will be object of study). Expression 12 describes the function r_i. This function returns the performance scope of algorithm a_t compared to other algorithms for problem instance i. The set R contains the values for all problem instances (see Expression 13). The set V is finally described by the values of set R in the last column; with specific order described by Expression 14; rows represent problem instances and columns represent information from proposed features for describing problem structure, algorithm searching fluctuation, algorithm performance scope.

$$r_i(a_t, i) = \left\{ \begin{array}{l} 1, \; if \; (D(quality_{it}) = D(quality_{i\alpha}) \; and \; D(time_{it}) > D(time_{i\alpha})) \\ \qquad\qquad\qquad or \\ D(quality_{it}) > D(quality_{i\alpha}), \forall \, \alpha \neq t; \; quality_{it} \in D; \; quality_{i\alpha} \in D; \\ \qquad\qquad 0, \, otherwise. \end{array} \right. \tag{12}$$

$$R = \{r_1(a_t, 1), r_2(a_t, 2), \ldots, r_m(a_t, m)\} \tag{13}$$

$$V = \left\{ \begin{array}{l} \{b_1, vc_1, os_1, tm_1, pp_1, pn_1, vd_1, r_1\}, \\ \{b_2, vc_2, os_2, tm_2, pp_2, pn_2, vd_2, r_2\}, \ldots, \\ \{b_m, vc_m, os_m, tm_m, pp_m, pn_m, vd_m, r_m\} \end{array} \right\} \tag{14}$$

4   Causal Study Case of Relation Between Bin-Packing Problem and Threshold Accepting

The latent relation between One Dimension Bin-Packing problem (BPP) and Threshold Accepting Algorithm is analyzed by means causal analysis; considering the proposed problem and algorithm features. For considering the logical design of algorithm in the analysis, understanding the relation of this with the problem structure, algorithm behavior, algorithm performance; we considered in our analysis to study the important logical area of initializing temperature control parameter T. Two algorithms a_1 and a_2 were considered, which they are different only in this logical area (initializing temperature control parameter T). The procedure of algorithm a_1 is to fix T to 1. For algorithm a_2, a sampling method without replacement is performed over problem solutions space to fix the initial temperature T. The set of algorithms $\{a_1, a_2\}$ is applied to 324 instances of problem BPP, where each algorithm is executed 16 times in each instance (runs number $nrun$); it was observed a very small variance between best solutions found of these runs. The algorithm that will object of study was selected randomly, it is a_2. These 324 problem instances is considered as training set (*instances* 1) and were selected randomly from Beasley, Scholl and Klein repositories [41, 42]. So too, other different 324 problem instances were selected randomly from these repositories, which are considered as test set (*instances* 2).

4.1   Discovering Causal Structure

The values of set V, representing proposed features b, vc, os, tm, pp, pn, dv, are normalized by means of method min-max; after that, these values are discretized using the method MDL [43]. So too, with the objective of considering metrics known by scientific community, autocorrelation coefficient (ac) and autocorrelation length (al), described in [44], were calculated and discretized. A set V_2 is built almost the same as set V, with the only difference that it contains the ac, al metrics instead of features tm, pp, pn, dv proposed for characterizing the algorithm searching behavior. The set V_2 has b, vc, os, ac, al and set R as last column.

The method PC [36] was performed, using as input the sets V and V_2, for discovering causal structures E and E_2; where causal inference software Hugin [45] with a confidence level 95% was used. Expressions 15, 16 and Fig. 3(a, b) show the learned structures. E with tm, pp, pn describes better the direct causes of algorithm performance scope (in terms of algorithm searching behavior) than E_2 with known metrics ac, al. Therefore, E will be considered for continuing with study case.

$$E = \left\{ \begin{array}{c} \{(R,pn),(R,pp),(R,tm),(R,vc)\},\{(os,b),(os,pp)\}, \\ \{(pn,vc),(pn,vd)\},\{(pp,pn)\},\{(b,vc)\} \end{array} \right\} \tag{15}$$

$$E_2 = \left\{ \begin{array}{c} \{(R,vc)\},\{(b,R),(b,vc),(b,ac)\}, \\ \{(al,os),(al,ac)\},\{(os,b)\} \end{array} \right\} \tag{16}$$

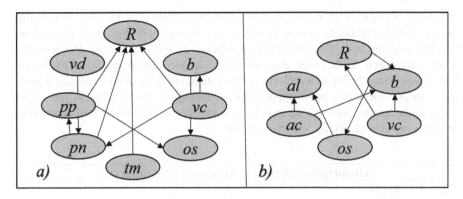

Fig. 3. Causal structures

The method Counting [36] was performed to estimate the causal relations from structure E. The function cR (Expression 17) is used to identify the direct causes of algorithm performance scope, in terms of set R. Table 2 shows the intervals of each feature and the major estimations for whose causal relations identified by function cR.

$$cR(E) = \{e_i = (v_i, y_k) \mid v_i = "R", \forall\, e_i \in C_i,\ C_i \in E\} \qquad (17)$$

Table 2. Relevant causes

	%
$P(R = 1 \mid vc = 2, pn = 3, pp = 2, tm = 2)$	100
$P(R = 1 \mid vc = 2, pn = 2, pp = 2, tm = 2)$	100
$P(R = 0 \mid vc = 1, pn = 1, pp = 1, tm = 1)$	60

4.2 Understanding Discovered Knowledge: Design of Self-adaptive Algorithm

The interest algorithm a_2 corresponded better to problem instances where their structure had a variability of object size frequencies in the second interval; there are more possibilities for generating neighbor solutions, which can be accepted. The logical design forces the algorithm to begin with an initial temperature smaller than 1; it is taken of value of the objective function (values are between 0 and 1, being the optimal 1) of one solution from a sample of solutions generating randomly; being its searching very restrictive for accepting neighbor solutions. The algorithm behavior during its searching found valleys with sizes in the second interval, positive and negative slopping in the second and third interval; meaning that algorithm could enter and leave from these valleys, and does not stagnate in local optimal. The algorithm a_2 wins in time in the majority of instances; it found the best solution faster than algorithm a_1. However, a_2 had disadvantage with problem instances, where their structure had a variability of object size frequencies in the first interval; there is not many possibilities for generating neighbor solutions, its behavior is almost flat (valley sizes, positive and negative slopping in the first interval); its condition of small temperature does not allow it to move much, ends faster than algorithm a_1 and lost in quality. The learned knowledge permit to design a self-adaptive threshold accepting algorithm (sa). It adjust automatically the temperature initial value; if feature vc has a value in the second interval, the temperature will be initialized from one solution taken from a solutions sample generated randomly; otherwise it will 1.

Self-Adaptive Threshold Accepting Algorithm (sa)
1   **Begin**
2        $S = 100$; size of neighborhood; $\mu = 0.85$; freezing factor;
3        $x = x^*$; initial feasible solution;
4   Calculate vc from parameters of problem instance
5   If (vc=2) Then
6   T = a solution chosen randomly from solutions space.
7   Else $T = 1$
8   Repeat
9   Repeat
10   For $i = 1$ to S
11   y = neighbor solution $\in$ N(x)
12   If $f(y) - f(x) < T$ Then $x = y$
13   Else solution y is rejected
14                   $i = i + 1$
15   Until termal equilibrium is reached
16               $T = \mu T$
17   Until freezing is reached
18   **End**

5   Results Verification

Algorithm a_2 was executed in problem instances set *instances* 2; where sets D', R' were obtained. The set V', for algorithm a_2 also was obtained with proposed features and set R'. The set V' is normalized and discretized. The causal structure E is used with set V' for predicting values and to form the set R_p (predicted R values). The sets R' and R_p were compared. The causal model obtained an accuracy percentage of 84.88%, using the causal inference software NETICA [46]. The model validation indicates that knowledge learned and structured as E can be used to predict which algorithm will give the best solution to one new problem instance.

On the other hand, the self-adaptive Threshold Accepting algorithm was executed on set *instances* 1. Then, the experimentation results on algorithms (a_2, sa) were analyzed. The algorithm sa corresponded better to 239 problem instances from 324, representing the 74% percentage. In the instances with same *quality* for algorithms a_2

and *sa*, the time of algorithm *sa* is much less than a_2. It is to say, the differences are very big. Due the above, there is not necessity to verify significance on these differences. Then, the *quality* for both algorithms only is analyzed more deeply. The values of *quality* does not assume a normal distribution, therefore, we applied a non-parametric statistical test Wilcoxon of two dependent samples, using a confidence level of 95%. The null and alternative hypothesis H_0 and H_a were formulated, expressions 18 and 19; where μ_1 is the mean of quality performance results of algorithm a_2 and μ_2 is the mean of self-adaptive algorithm *sa*. The statistical software Dataplot [47] was used.

$$H_0 : \mu_1 - \mu_2 = 0 \tag{18}$$

$$H_a : \mu_1 - \mu_2 \neq 0 \tag{19}$$

The results of application of statistical test were: a calculated statistical value of 2.4802 and a theoretical statistical value of 1.96. Therefore, the null hypothesis H_0 is rejected and the alternative hypothesis H_a is accepted. There is a significant difference between means. The self-adaptive algorithm *sa* improves the performance of analyzed algorithm a_2.

6   Conclusions

In this paper, new features for characterizing problem structure and algorithm searching fluctuation were proposed. A causal study case could have performed with these proposed features; in the framework of Bin-Packing problem and Threshold Accepting algorithm, considering also information about algorithm logical area. These features were relevant, significant and permitted in the causal analysis to discover relations cause-effect from relationship between problem and algorithm. The causal structure obtained an accuracy percentage of 84.88% over another problem instances set (test data). The causal relations learned represent knowledge between problem structure, algorithm searching behavior, logical design (specifically in the logical area of initializing the temperature) and its performance. A self-adaptive Threshold Accepting algorithm was designed from the above discovered knowledge; it considers the problem structure to initialize the temperature. The performance results of original algorithm and self-adaptive algorithm were analyzed. The self-adaptive algorithm solved 74% of 324 problem instances better than analyzed algorithm. An application of the Wilcoxon statistical test, using a 95% of confidence level, over these results, indicates a significant difference. The proposed framework could be a methodological guideline for discovering knowledge and designing self-adaptive algorithms that adjust better to real problems. As next task, is interesting to analyze more about the knowledge discovered from relation problem-algorithm. It is to say, considering also the information of relations cause-effect; from proposed features *tm*, *pp*, *pn* (direct causes) and algorithm performance scope (effect); for constantly adjusting the algorithm logical during execution, depending searching behavior. As future work is to study the relation between problem BPP and other algorithms Genetic, Ant Colony Optimization; and so on for other optimization problems.

References

1. Soares, C., Pinto, J.: Ranking learning algorithms: using IBL and Meta-learning on accuracy and time results. J. Mach. Learn. **50**(3), 251–277 (2003)
2. Pérez, J., Pazos, R.A., Frausto, J., Rodríguez, G., Romero, D., Cruz, L.: A statistical approach for algorithm selection. In: Ribeiro, C.C., Martins, S.L. (eds.) WEA 2004. LNCS, vol. 3059, pp. 417–431. Springer, Heidelberg (2004). https://doi.org/10.1007/978-3-540-24838-5_31
3. Smith-Miles, K., van Hemert, J., Lim, X.Y.: Understanding TSP difficulty by learning from evolved instances. In: Blum, C., Battiti, R. (eds.) LION 2010. LNCS, vol. 6073, pp. 266–280. Springer, Heidelberg (2010). https://doi.org/10.1007/978-3-642-13800-3_29
4. Vanchipura, R., Sridharan, R.: Development and analysis of constructive heuristic algorithms for flow shop scheduling problems with sequence-dependent setup times. Int. J. Adv. Manuf. Technol. **67**, 1337–1353 (2013)
5. Le, M.N., Ong, Y.S., Jin, Y., Sendhoff, B.: Lamarckian memetic algorithms: local optimum and connectivity structure analysis. Memetic Comput. **1**(3), 175–190 (2009)
6. Cayci, A., Menasalvas, E., Saygin, Y., Eibe, S.: Self-configuring data mining for ubiquitous computing. Inf. Sci. **246**, 83–99 (2013)
7. Tavares, J.: Multidimensional knapsack problem: a fitness landscape analysis. IEEE Trans. Syst. Man Cybern. Part B **38**(3), 604–616 (2008)
8. Pérez, J., Cruz, L., Landero, V.: Explaining performance of the threshold accepting algorithm for the bin packing problem: a causal approach. Polish J. Environ. Stud. **16**(5B), 72–76 (2007)
9. Xu, L., Hoos, H., Leyton-Brown, K.: Hydra: automatically configuring algorithms for portfolio-based selection. In: AAAI, vol. 10, pp. 210–216 (2010)
10. Quiroz, M., Cruz, L., Torrez, J., Gómez, C.: Improving the performance of heuristic algorithms based on exploratory data analysis. In: Castillo, O., Melin, P., Kacprzyk, J. (eds.) Recent Advances on Hybrid Intelligent Systems, Studies in Computational Intelligence. SCI, vol. 452, pp. 361–375. Springer, Heidelberg (2013). https://doi.org/10.1007/978-3-642-33021-6_29
11. Hutter, F., Xu, L., Hoos, H., Leyton-Brown, K.: Algorithm runtime prediction: methods & evaluation. Artif. Intell. **206**, 79–111 (2014)
12. Ries, J., Beullens, P.: A semi-automated design of instance-based fuzzy parameter tuning for metaheuristics based on decision tree induction. J. Oper. Res. Soc. **66**(5), 782–793 (2015)
13. Yong, X., Feng, D., Rongchun, Z.: Optimal selection of image segmentation algorithms based on performance prediction. In: Proceedings of the Pan-Sydney Area Workshop on Visual Information Processing, pp. 105–108. Australian Computer Society, Inc. (2004)
14. Yuen, S., Zhang, X.: Multiobjective evolutionary algorithm portfolio: choosing suitable algorithm for multiobjective optimization problem. In: IEEE Congress on Evolutionary Computation (CEC), Beijing, China, pp. 1967–1973 (2014)
15. Wagner, M., Lindauer, M., Misir, M., et. al.: A case of study of algorithm selection for the travelling thief problem. J. Heuristics 1–26 (2017)
16. Leyton-Brown, K., Hoos, H., Hutter, F., Xu, L.: Understanding the empirical hardness of NP-complete problems. Mag. Commun. ACM **57**(5), 98–107 (2014)

17. Mull, N., Fremont, D.J., Seshia, S.A.: On the hardness of SAT with community structure. In: Creignou, N., Le Berre, D. (eds.) SAT 2016. LNCS, vol. 9710, pp. 141–159. Springer, Cham (2016). https://doi.org/10.1007/978-3-319-40970-2_10

18. Cruz, L., Gómez, C., Pérez, J., Landero, V., Quiroz, M., Ochoa, A.: Algorithm Selection: From Meta-learning to Hyper-heuristics. INTECH Open Access Publisher (2012)

19. Pavón, R., Díaz, F., Laza, R., Luzón, M.V.: Experimental evaluation of an automatic parameter setting system. Expert Syst. Appl. 37(7), 5224–5238 (2010)

20. Hoos, H.H.: Automated algorithm configuration and parameter tuning. In: Hamadi, Y., Monfroy, E., Saubion, F. (eds.) Autonomous Search, pp. 37–71. Springer, Heidelberg (2011). https://doi.org/10.1007/978-3-642-21434-9_3

21. Yeguas, E., Luzón, M.V., Pavón, R., Laza, R., Arroyo, G., Díaz, F.: Automatic parameter tuning for evolutionary algorithms using a Bayesian case-based reasoning system. Appl. Soft Comput. 18, 185–195 (2014)

22. Biedenkapp, A., Lindauer, M.T., Eggensperger, K., Hutter, F., Fawcett, C., Hoos, H.H.: Efficient parameter importance analysis via ablation with surrogates. In: AAAI, pp. 773–779 (2017)

23. Blot, A., Pernet, A., Jourdan, L., Kessaci-Marmion, M.-É., Hoos, H.H.: Automatically configuring multi-objective local search using multi-objective optimisation. In: Trautmann, H., et al. (eds.) EMO 2017. LNCS, vol. 10173, pp. 61–76. Springer, Cham (2017). https://doi.org/10.1007/978-3-319-54157-0_5

24. Guo, H., Hsu, W.H.: A learning-based algorithm selection meta-reasoner for the real-time MPE problem. In: Webb, G.I., Yu, X. (eds.) AI 2004. LNCS (LNAI), vol. 3339, pp. 307–318. Springer, Heidelberg (2004). https://doi.org/10.1007/978-3-540-30549-1_28

25. Guerri, A., Milano, M.: Learning techniques for automatic algorithm portfolio selection. In: Burke, V.A. (ed.) Proceedings of the 16th Biennial European Conference on Artificial Intelligence, pp. 475–479. IOS Press, Valencia (2004)

26. Hoos, H.H., Smyth, K., Stützle, T.: Search space features underlying the performance of stochastic local search algorithms for MAX-SAT. In: Yao, X., et al. (eds.) PPSN 2004. LNCS, vol. 3242, pp. 51–60. Springer, Heidelberg (2004). https://doi.org/10.1007/978-3-540-30217-9_6

27. Konak, A.: Simulation optimization using tabu search: an empirical study. In: Kuhl, M.E., Steiger, N.M., Armstrong, F.B., Joines, J.A. (eds.) Proceedings of Winter simulation Conference, pp. 2686–2692 (2005)

28. Chevalier, R.: Balancing the effects of parameter settings on a genetic algorithm for multiple fault diagnosis. In: Artificial Intelligence. University of Georgia (2006)

29. Nikolić, M., Marić, F., Janičić, P.: Instance-based selection of policies for SAT solvers. In: Kullmann, O. (ed.) SAT 2009. LNCS, vol. 5584, pp. 326–340. Springer, Heidelberg (2009). https://doi.org/10.1007/978-3-642-02777-2_31

30. Munoz, M., Kirley, M., Halgamuge, S.: Exploratory landscape analysis of continuous space optimization problems using information content. IEEE Trans. Evol. Comput. 19(1), 74–87 (2015)

31. Gagliolo, M., Schmidhuber, J.: Learning dynamic algorithm portfolios. Ann. Math. Artif. Intell. 47(3–4), 295–328 (2006)

32. Montero, E., Riff, M.-C.: On-the-fly calibrating strategies for evolutionary algorithms. Inf. Sci. 181, 552–566 (2011)

33. Pérez, J., et al.: An application of causality for representing and providing formal explanations about the behavior of the threshold accepting algorithm. In: Rutkowski, L., Tadeusiewicz, R., Zadeh, L.A., Zurada, Jacek M. (eds.) ICAISC 2008. LNCS (LNAI), vol. 5097, pp. 1087–1098. Springer, Heidelberg (2008). https://doi.org/10.1007/978-3-540-69731-2_102

34. Pérez, J., et al.: A causal approach for explaining why a heuristic algorithm outperforms another in solving an instance set of the bin packing problem. In: An, A., Matwin, S., Raś, Z. W., Ślęzak, D. (eds.) ISMIS 2008. LNCS (LNAI), vol. 4994, pp. 591–598. Springer, Heidelberg (2008). https://doi.org/10.1007/978-3-540-68123-6_64

35. Pérez, J., Cruz, L., Pazos, R., Landero, V., Pérez, V.: Application of causal models for the selection and redesign of heuristic algorithms for solving the bin-packing problem. Polish J. Environ. Stud. 17(4C), 25–30 (2008). (ACS-AISBIS 2008)

36. Spirtes, P., Glymour, C., Scheines, R.: Causation, Prediction, and Search, 2nd edn. The MIT Press, Cambridge (2001)

37. Korb, K.: Bayesian Artificial Intelligence. Chapman and Hall, London (2004)

38. McGeoch, C.C.: Experimental analysis of algorithms. In: Pardalos, P.M., Romeijn, H.E. (eds.) Handbook of Global Optimization. Nonconvex Optimization and Its Applications, vol. 62, pp. 489–513. Springer, Boston (2002). https://doi.org/10.1007/978-1-4757-5362-2_14

39. Khuri, S., Schütz, M., Heitkötter, J.: Evolutionary heuristics for the bin packing problem. In: Artificial Neural Nets and Genetic Algorithms, pp. 285–288. Springer, Vienna (1995). https://doi.org/10.1007/978-3-7091-7535-4_75

40. Dueck, G., Scheuer, T.: Threshold accepting: a general purpose optimization algorithm appearing superior to simulated annealing. J. Comput. Phys. 90(1), 161–175 (1990)

41. Beasley, J.E.: OR-Library. Brunel University (2006). http://people.brunel.ac.uk/~mastjjb/jeb/orlib/binpackinfo.html

42. Scholl, A., Klein, R. (2003). http://www.wiwi.uni-jena.de/Entscheidung/binpp/

43. Fayyad, U., Irani, K.: Multi-Interval Discretization of Continuous-Valued Attributes for Classification Learning. IJCAI 1022–1029 (1993)

44. Merz, P., Freisleben, B., et al.: Fitness landscapes and memetic algorithm design. New Ideas Optim. 245–260 (1999)

45. Hugin Expert. www.hugin.com

46. Norsys Corporation. www.norsys.com

47. Dataplot. www.itl.nist.gov/div898/software/dataplot/homepage.htm

Towards the Adaptation of an Active Measurement Protocol for Delay/Disruption-Tolerant Networking

Carlos H. Lamb[1], Bruno L. Dalmazo[2]($\boxtimes$) (ID), and Jeferson C. Nobre[2] (ID)

[1] University of Vale do Rio dos Sinos, São Leopoldo, Brazil
carloslamb@gmail.com
[2] Federal University of Rio Grande do Sul, Porto Alegre, Brazil
{bldalmazo,jcnobre}@inf.ufrgs.br

Abstract. Delay/Disruption-Tolerant Networking (DTN) can be characterized by high delays and disconnections between the participating nodes. Despite these characteristics, DTN needs network management features similar to those found in conventional networks such as, for example, latency monitoring in message exchanges. One of the approaches commonly used for such monitoring is the use of standardized protocols for active measurements, such as, for example, the Two-Way Active Measurement Protocol (TWAMP). However, protocols like TWAMP are not prepared for DTN because they consider conventional network environments, such as the Internet. This paper describes the Delay/Disruption-Tolerant Two-Way Active Measurement Protocol (DTWAMP), a proposed extension for TWAMP which enables the execution of active measurements in DTN. In addition, experiments were performed to evaluate the proposed solution. The results demonstrate that DTWAMP has desirable properties to perform monitoring tasks in DTN.

Keywords: Delay/Disruption-Tolerant Networking ·
Active measurements · Two-Way Active Measurement Protocol

1 Introduction

Computer networks employ different architectures to perform communication between the participating nodes. These architectures consider some assumptions about the exchange of messages. For example, the TCP/IP architecture, used in the Internet, was developed for environments with low latency and small packet loss [4]. However, this architecture does not perform well for all types of communication networks. There are network environments, considered challenging, that have the difficulty of maintaining end-to-end communication with low latency and small packet loss (e.g., TCP needs a convergence layer to operate in such environments [11]). One of the most commonly used architectures for these environments is called Delay/Disruption Tolerant Networking (DTN) [4], which

© Springer Nature Switzerland AG 2019
S. Misra et al. (Eds.): ICCSA 2019, LNCS 11619, pp. 167–178, 2019.
https://doi.org/10.1007/978-3-030-24289-3_14

is standardized by the Internet Engineering Task Force (IETF). The protocol implied in such standard is the Bundle Protocol (BP) [2,10].

The DTN communication particularities impact on the tasks execution, among them management ones. In any case, a DTN has network management needs as well as traditional computer networks [1]. In this context, active measurement mechanisms are an important tool to monitor and the health of a network as a whole. Such mechanisms inject synthetic traffic into specific network paths to measure the network performance in terms of, for example, delay, jitter, and packet/frame loss. Due to DTN characteristics like high latency and frequent disconnections, the TCP/IP network management tools tend not to perform in an adequate way. Such tools usually need closed loops that depends on the timeliness of management messages among management entities (e.g, manager and agent). Besides that, TCP/IP network management produces "chatty" interactions, which are feasible only in low delay environments.

The use of standardized two-way measurement protocols, such as the Two-Way Active Measurement Protocol (TWAMP) [6], can provide detailed information about round-trip metrics in an interoperable fashion. The evaluation of these metrics is performed using the results obtained during the exchange of test messages between two nodes. However, these protocols were designed to operate on a TCP/IP network and their direct use in a DTN would hardly present the expected results. In this context, there are some measurement *ad hoc* tools, such as *DTNperf* [3], that can perform two-way measurements. Unfortunately, such tools does not follow measurement standards either in the employed architecture or in the format of test messages. This can hamper the interoperability of measurement mechanisms among heterogeneous DTN nodes and even the comparison of different measurement results.

The present work presents the Delay/Disruption-Tolerant Measurement Protocol (DTWAMP), an extension for TWAMP to provide two-way measurements in DTN. Such extension allows the use of a standardized protocol in a DTN environment to deliver different round-trip metrics between two DTN nodes. The main contribution is to support interoperable monitoring tasks in DTN. The performed evaluation highlighted the feasibility and the performance of the proposed protocol. Furthermore, the experiments were conducted using a proof of concept implementation, developed using a well-established DTN framework.

This paper is organized as follows. In Sect. 2, the background on Active Measurements and DTN is presented. The DTWAMP is described in Sect. 3. In Sect. 4, the evaluation of the proposed solution is depicted. The Sect. 5 presents the related work. Finally, the concluding remarks are described in Sect. 6.

2   Background

This section presents the main background concepts for the proposed solution depicted in the present work. These concepts are divided into two subsections. In the first subsection, active measurement mechanisms are highlighted, specially regarding TWAMP. This section closes with a discussion about network management properties and challenges in DTN.

2.1   Active Measurement Mechanisms

Active measurement mechanisms can be employed in different contexts, such as pre-deployment service validation and live network-wide SLA monitoring. A well-defined injection of measurement traffic (i.e., test messages) in the networking infrastructure is usually called a measurement session [9]. In this context, active measurements are performed either one-way or two-way (i.e., round-trip). Two-way measurements, which are common in TCP/IP networks, employ time stamps applied at the echo destination to achieve better accuracy. Thus, they do not require synchronization between local and remote clocks. However, it is difficult to isolate the direction in which performance issues are experienced using two-way measurements.

The IETF's TWAMP [6] supports round-trip measurement through the exchange of timestamps between two hosts. In general, TWAMP architecture is usually composed of two hosts having specific functions, the client node (the controller) and the server node (responder). TWAMP consists of two protocols, the TWAMP-Control and the TWAMP-Test. In TWAMP-Control, there are at least eight exchanges of messages between the controller and responder to establish a test session. After such establishment, the test session is started and TWAMP-Test is responsible for transmitting test messages of the same size between the nodes in both directions. The results obtained during this exchange of messages is used to evaluate the network performance between the controller and the responder [6].

TWAMP also has a reduced version, called TWAMP Light, in which it is not necessary to exchange control messages to establish the measurement session [6]. TWAMP Light does not specify how the establishment of such session between the controller and the responder is performed, thus it assumes that a previous relation exists, for example, through a configuration file. In a TWAMP Light measurement session, there is only the exchange of test message (i.e., there is no TWAMP-Control). Since TWAMP-Control requires several messages to configure the measurement session, the use of TWAMP Light provides quicker measurement results and less measurement overhead.

2.2   Delay/Disruption-Tolerant Management

The IETF DTN architecture is described in RFC 4838 [4]. Such architecture combines the use of a message switching technique and the persistent data storage, defining an overlay layer called the Bundle Layer, located between the transport layer and the application layer. Devices that use the bundle layer are considered as DTN nodes, and the messages carried by such nodes are called bundles [4]. The Bundle layer has an aggregation protocol, the Bundle Protocol (BP) [10], which defines the format of bundles as well as their use. The format of the bundles is defined by a mandatory primary block, an optional payload block, and a set of optional extension blocks [4].

DTN management is required to assure an adequate operation in DTN. Traditional management solutions, such as Simple Network Management Protocol

(SNMP) and Network Configuration Protocol (NETCONF), are examples of management protocols that can not be used in DTN environments due to the high delay/disruption-tolerant end-to-end communications. Although there are works which present solutions for the management of DTNs based on these protocols (e.g., SNMP [7]), they were either developed for specific DTN scenarios or still need implementation.

DTN management cannot employ protocols that need to establish control loops across the network infrastructure. Thus, it is not possible for the management application to be fully aware of the local network conditions at the remote device to be managed. This is a critical constraint in defining how management tools should define, transmit, and receive their data. In this context, the Asynchronous Management Architecture (AMA) and the Asynchronous Management Protocol (AMP) [1] relax this constraint for management tasks. Despite the development of AMP, there are no standards for active measurement protocols to be deployed in DTN. In this context, even with less interactions, TWAMP Light still is not tailored for DTN.

3   Delay/Disruption-Tolerant Measurement Protocol (DTWAMP)

The present paper proposes DTWAMP, an extension of TWAMP to provide two-way measurements in DTN. In these networks, the delivery of a message to its destination can take a significant amount of time (e.g., hours). This ends up influencing how DTN nodes communicate with each other, as well as services such as network management. The DTWAMP can be useful for calculating performance metrics, such as delay, jitter, and bundle loss within the DTN infrastructure. For example, with the measurement results of the bi-directional delay between two DTN nodes, DTN applications can configure the required life time that an application message must have. In this context, DTWAMP is an adaptation of TWAMP Light for DTN environments. DTWAMP has a simple logical (depicted in Fig. 1, composed by the *controller*, which initiates the emission of test messages, and the responder, which replies test messages.

Test messages

CONTROLLER   RESPONDER

Fig. 1. DTWAMP logical model

The following assumptions are considered for the proposed solution. The DTWAMP works with TWAMP non-authentication mode test messages, thus it is not applied any security controls to test messages exchanged between nodes.

This is because TWAMP Light does not have TWAMP-Control, which is necessary to provide authentication and encryption [6]. In addition, DTWAMP controller assumes that the responder is reachable and start replying test messages as soon as it receives them. Also, to perform the exchange of TWAMP-Test messages in a DTN, such messages must be adapted to the BP format. In this context, we assume that is possible to transport TWAMP-test messages using the BP in most DTN infrastructures. Finally, we modeled "collaborative" intermediate DTN nodes in the sense that they may carry all test messages that are exchanged between the controller and the responder.

This section is organized as follows. First, the messages format employed by DTWAMP is presented. After that, the proof of concept implementation of DTWAMP is described.

3.1 Messages Format

The TWAMP establishes that test messages exchanged between the controller and the responder during the TWAMP-Test use fields with fixed sizes [6]. This is done to ensure that the test messages transmitted during the test session have equal size in both directions. Therefore, DTWAMP employs fixed sizes in the controller and responder data that will be transmitted by the block text data of the payload block of the bundle. In this context, the BP does not specify the size of the *block body date* field of the payload block of the bundle since it is defined as a variable size [10]. Thus, since the responder has a larger amount of information to provide, we defined a specific *packet padding* field in the controller message to match the responder message.

DTWAMP messages are transported through bundles in the same sense as test messages used by TWAMP Light are transmitted using TCP/IP. The test messages specified in Fig. 2 are the payload block of the bundles forwarded by the controller and the responder. *Block Type, Proc. Flags* and *Block Lenght* are the original fields of the *payload* block of a bundle (represented in green background in Fig. 2) [10]. In terms of the controller, the DTWAMP transmits the *Sequence Number, Timestamp* and *Packet Padding* fields (represented in gray background in Fig. 2(a)) as payload data of the bundle. The *Sequence Number* field is an integer beginning with 1 that is incremented by the number of bundles sent. The field *Timestamp* has the time registered before sending the bundle to the responder node. The packet padding field has the fixed value of 20 bytes to be able to match the *payload* size of controller bundles to the responder ones.

The responder employs the *Sequence Number, Timestamp, Receive Timestamp, Sender Sequence Number,* and *Sender Timestamp* fields (represented in gray background in Fig. 2(b)). The *Sequence Number* field uses the same *Sequence Number* provided by the controller. The *timestamp* field employs the time recorded before sending the bundle to the controller node. The *Receive Timestamp* field uses the time recorded when the *controller* bundle is received. The *Sender Sequence Number* and *Sender Timestamp* fields have the values reported by the controller.

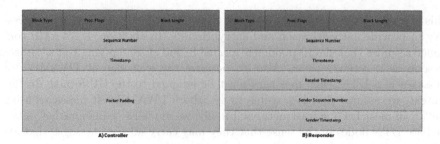

Fig. 2. DTWAMP test messages format

The IETF DTN architecture uses *timestamps* since it depends on the synchronization between DTN nodes to perform activities such as routing between nodes and the deletion of bundles according to their expiration time [4]. Although TWAMP defines *timestamps* as the number of seconds from the beginning of the year 1900 [6], DTWAMP, as a DTN application, uses the *timestamp* defined by RFC 5050 [10] which employs the number of seconds from the beginning of year 2000.

The fields used by the DTWAMP controller and responder as bundle payload data are based on the TWAMP non-authentication test messages. In this context, not all fields of TWAMP-test messages are relevant for the DTN environments. The *error estimate*, *TTL* (Time To Live), and *MBZ* fields are not used by the DTWAMP. The *error estimate* field is not used because this field is a calculation that shows the error and synchronization estimate between the test messages. As in a DTN environment there may be constant oscillations during communication between nodes, such as high latency and disconnections, DTWAMP does not use this field.

The *TTL* field, which is used by the responder in TWAMP, is another field that was not used in the DTWAMP. This field is defined according to the TTL from the IP header of the packet received by the TWAMP node [6]. Since the primary block of each bundle has a *lifetime* field that determines the payload lifetime of the bundle [10], the *TTL* field was not adapted for the DTWAMP.

3.2 Implementation

We implemented DTWAMP as a proof of concept using the C programming language. The *dtnperf* application, which is an open source application made available through the DTN2 reference implementation, was used as the starting code. The DTWAMP controller is based on the *dtnperf-server* and the DTWAMP responder is based on the *dtnperf-client*.

The DTWAMP implementation defines the controller as responsible to initiate message exchange, to calculate the *round-trip* metrics, and to display the measurement results. The responder just acts as a reflector. The controller computes the raw time and number of transmitted bundles and the round-trip results as well as summary information (e.g., average round-trip delay for each direction).

The DTWAMP controller application provides two modes of operations for reporting the round-trip delay between two DTN nodes. The first option, *time mode*, defines the duration of the measurement session (in seconds). In this mode, if specified duration ends during the transmission of a bundle, the controller still wait for this bundle. The second mode of operation, *bundle mode*, defines the number of bundles to be exchanged during a measurement session between two DTN nodes.

4 Evaluation

The objective of the evaluation presented in this section is to demonstrate the feasibility of the DTWAMP in different scenarios when performing the round-trip delay between two DTN nodes. First, the environment used for the evaluation is described. Then, the performed experiments are depicted. Finally, the experimental results are discussed.

4.1 Experimental Environment

The DTN environment used in the evaluation is the DTN2 reference implementation[1]. The DTN2 implements the BP as defined on the RFC 5050 [10]. The BP agent and its support code is implemented as a unix daemon (dtnd). The DTN applications interact with *dtnd* through Remote Procedure Calls (RPCs). The employed operation system is Ubuntu Linux.

The network delay was configured individually on the DTN nodes using the *netem*[2]. The delay was configured as specified in the experiments. The DTN nodes use Network Time Protocol (NTP) to ensure synchronization. The experiments were repeated ten times and the variance of the obtained results was minimal.

4.2 Experiments

The first experiment was performed using DTWAMP *time mode* (configuration - 600 s) and its results can be visualized in Fig. 3. Initially, the experiment was executed without any additional delay in the environment to provide a baseline (in the bars indicated as "0"). Then, the delay was initially set with 500 milliseconds (ms). After that, the delay was incremented in each subsequent experiment in 500 ms steps, until the last experiment (3500 ms). During this experiment, there was no other network traffic between the DTN hosts.

Figure 3 shows the results obtained from the first experiment. In this figure, "C-R" represents the delay in the controller node - responder node direction; R-C represents the delay in the responder node - controller node direction; and C-C represents the round-trip delay. In this experiment, it is possible to verify that the delays collected by DTWAMP are similar to the delay values configured on the netem.

---

[1] DTN2 source code - https://sourceforge.net/projects/dtn/.

[2] netem - https://wiki.linuxfoundation.org/networking/netem.

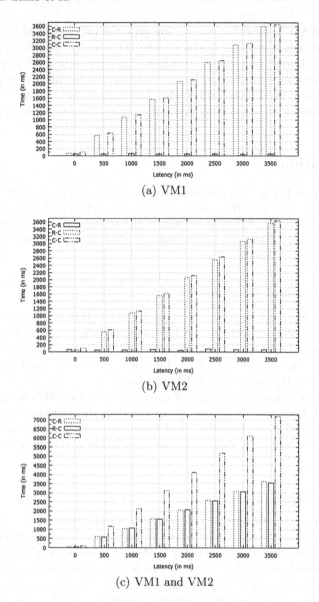

(a) VM1

(b) VM2

(c) VM1 and VM2

Fig. 3. DTWAMP measurement results obtained with delays configured in the VMs

The largest difference between the configured and the measured delay considering VM1-VM2 is found on the execution with 2500 ms. However, even in this experiment, the times obtained in VM1 (2594 ms) have a small difference, being only 1.21 % greater than those found in VM2 (2563 ms). Regarding the VM2-VM1, the biggest difference is found in the experiment with 500 ms latency.

In this experiment, the dealays collected in VM1 (630 ms) are only 3.45 % higher than those found in VM2 (609 ms).

If we compare the bundle output times of the controller to the response of Fig. 4 with the experiment from VM1, the difference is minimal between them. The biggest difference is found in the experiment with 3,500 ms latency. In this experiment, the times obtained in Fig. 4 (3628 ms) are only 1.09 % greater than those found in the VM1 latency experiment only (3589 ms). With respect to the output times of the texting respond to the controller of the experiment from VM2, the major difference compared to Fig. 4 is found in the experiment with 500 ms latency. In this experiment, the times obtained in Fig. 4 (577 ms) are 4.15 % greater than those found in the VM2-only latency experiment (554 ms). In these comparisons, the biggest difference found is with respect to the experiment with 500 ms latency of Fig. 4 (1182 ms) and 1,000 ms latency of the experiment with latency only in VM2 (1135 ms). In this comparison, the *round-trip* time of the controller in Fig. 4 is 4.14 % greater than that found in the VM2 experiment.

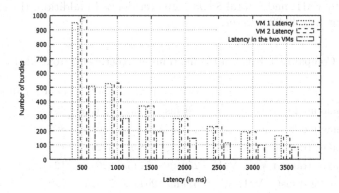

Fig. 4. DTWAMP results obtained with delays specified on both VMs and the number of bundles sent in latency experiments

The number of bundles sent during the delayed experiments decreased due to increased delay. Figure 4 shows the number of bundles sent during the DTWAMP operation in each experiment with latency performed. In Fig. 4 it can be seen that the number of bundles sent during the experiments of Fig. 3 are equivalent. Only in the experiment with 500 ms latency, VM2 sent 32 bundles more (3.36%) than VM1. However, if we compare with the experiments in Fig. 4 (delays in the two VMs), the number of sent bundles decreased by 48.37% (476 bundles less). This number is expected since delay is configured in both directions.

The initial experiments were performed under no background traffic.Then, additional experiments were executed to demonstrate the operation of the DTWAMP when there is traffic in the DTN infrastructure. The network traffic considered for this experiments was the transfer of an 1 GB file between two DTN nodes. Before the experiments were carried out, the average transfer time of such file was calculated in two situations: transfer of the file through the *dukto*[3] application over TCP/IP and the transfer of the file using bundles, through the *dtncp* application (from the DTN2 implementation). The average file transfer time by *dukto* was 40 s, while *dtncp* was 70 s.

The first two experiments were performed with the DTWAMP in the *time mode* configured with 40 and 70 s respectively, under normal conditions, and their results can be visualized in Table 1. The following experiments were performed as follows: In VM1, the file was transferred from the same to VM2 through *dukto* and the DTWAMP was executed with 40 s of time. Then the file was transferred through *dtncp* and executed the DTWAMP with *time mode* of 70 s. In both experiments, the DTWAMP was executed in parallel with the transfer of the file between the nodes. Subsequently, the same experiments were performed from VM2. The results obtained can be visualized in Table 1. In the experiments performed both from VM1 and from VM2, it can be observed that the average times presented have differences according to the transfer mode used in each experiment. In addition, it can be noted that the bundle transfer from VM2, as compared to VM1, had a total 86.93% greater delay. In addition, the amount of bundles sent was 40.22% lower.

Table 1. Comparation between the file transfer experiments from VM1 and VM2

	C-R	R-C	C-C	Sent bundles
Time mode 40 ms	46 ms	35 ms	83 ms	487
Time mode 70 ms	47 ms	33 ms	80 ms	867
Dukto transfer VM1-VM2	93 ms	258 ms	352 ms	115
Dukto transfer VM2-VM1	253 ms	71 ms	325 ms	124
Bundle transfer VM1-VM2	511 ms	261 ms	773 ms	92
Bundle transfer VM2-VM1	472 ms	972 ms	1445 ms	55

4.3 Discussion

The results demonstrated in Fig. 4 and Table 1, in summary, prove that the DTWAMP can be executed in latency environments, as long as they are supported by the DTN2 standard configuration. For larger latencies, you need to check for additional DTN2 settings. In addition, with the knowledge of the estimated time of sending and receiving a message between two DTN nodes, the other DTN applications can define the lifetime of this message. If you can not change the lifetime of the message, DTN applications can also analyze whether the message can be sent and/or received within the estimated time, thus avoiding unnecessary traffic.

Experiments performed during file transfer as a bundle demonstrate that the node that is sending the file has its most affected time than the one receiving the

---

[3] Dukto R6 - http://www.msec.it/dukto.

file as a bundle. While in the transfer by the textit dukto, through the TCP/IP network, the opposite happens, the node that is receiving the file has its time more affected than the one that is sending the file. This experiment can also be considered as an experiment in which there was an increase of processing by the nodes, since the file was not transferred by the DTN network.

5   Related Work

This section presents briefly some measurement tools which use the DTN2 implementation. These tools can be characterized by the execution of active measurements to deliver their metrics [8].

Davis and Doria [5] proposed *dtnping*, which is a DTN version of TCP/IP ping. Comparing with DTAMP, dtnping is also a active measurement mechanism that exchanges bundles between DTN nodes. However, dtnping does not follow a standard to define neither its architecture or its messages. This hampers fair performance evaluations on different DTN infrastructures. Besides that, it also impacts the use of comparable measurement tools.

Caini *et al.* [3] proposed *dtnperf*, which is a DTN application similar to TCP/IP iperf. The main dtnperf feature is to provide the throughput between two DTN nodes. The architecture of this application is similar to the DTWAMP one, composed by two entities: the *dtnperf-client*, which computes the performance metrics and the configuration options, and the *dtnperf-server*, which only reflects test messages. However, *dtnperf* uses the bundle receiving flag, while DTWAMP employs specific *timestamps* during the communication of two DTN nodes. In addition, *dtnperf* does not respect any measurement standard (in the same sense as dtnping).

6   Final Remarks

One of the major challenges in DTN management is the lack of an end-to-end connection between DTN nodes. This is one of the main reasons why traditional management tools are not directly employed in DTN. In the context of measurement mechanisms, there is neither a standardized measurement protocol or one based on Internet standards. This hampers the execution of measurement tasks in different DTN infrastructures and measurement tools.

The present paper describe DTWAMP, an extension for TWAMP to provide two-way measurements in DTN. Such extension adapts a special TWAMP mode, TWAMP Light, to delay/disruption-tolerant infrastructures. In order to demonstrate the feasibility of the proposed solution, experiments were performed to show the DTWAMP operation considering configured delay as ground truth. In addition, synthetic bundle traffic was added to verify how DTWAMP would react when there were other types of bundles being carried by DTN nodes. DTWAMP can be used by DTN applications to produce the estimated delay for an application bundle, which can be used to predict the Quality of Service perceived for this application.

Although the DTWAMP presented positive results in the performed evaluation, new features can improve the protocol. For example, the DTWAMP messages could be adapted to use TWAMP-Test authenticated and encrypted mode in order to improve their security features. Besides that, regarding the transport of test messages, the DTWAMP sends them through a exclusive bundle which incurs in a significant overhead. Thus, in future work, we aim at adapted the DTWAMP messages to be transmitted along with other bundles either as an opportunistic send or piggybacking. Finally, DTWAMP was not evaluated in environments that have frequent disconnects. Therefore, it is necessary to include such environments in future evaluations to highlight the properties of the protocol in DTN scenarios with pose disconnections.

References

1. Birrane, E.: Asynchronous management architecture. Work in progress as an internet-draft, draft-birrane-dtn-ama-06 (2017)
2. Burleigh, S., Fall, K., Birrane, E.: Bundle protocol version 7. Work in progress as an internet-draft, draft-ietf-dtn-bpbis-10 (2017)
3. Caini, C., d'Amico, A., Rodolfi, M.: Dtnperf_3: a further enhanced tool for delay-/disruption-tolerant networking performance evaluation. In: 2013 IEEE Global Communications Conference (GLOBECOM), pp. 3009–3015. IEEE (2013)
4. Cerf, V., et al.: Delay-tolerant networking architecture. RFC 4838 (informational) (2007)
5. Davies, E., Doria, A.: Functional specification for DTN infrastructure software comprising RFC 5050 bundle agent and associated components. version 1.2 (2010)
6. Hedayat, K., Krzanowski, R., Morton, A., Yum, K., Babiarz, J.A.: Two-way active measurement protocol (TWAMP). RFC 5357 (request for comments) (2008)
7. Isento, J.N., Dias, J.A., Canelo, F., Rodrigues, J.J., Proenca, M.: Moni4VDTN: a monitoring system for vehicular delay-tolerant networks. In: 2012 IEEE International Conference on Communications (ICC), pp. 1188–1192. IEEE (2012)
8. Nobre, J.C., Mozzaquatro, B.A., Granville, L.Z.: Network-wide initiatives to control measurement mechanisms: a survey. IEEE Commun. Surv. Tutor. **20**(2), 1475–1491 (2018). https://doi.org/10.1109/COMST.2018.2797170
9. Roy, A., Acharya, T., DasBit, S.: Quality of service in delay tolerant networks: a survey. Comput. Netw. **130**, 121–133 (2018). https://doi.org/10.1016/j.comnet.2017.11.010. http://www.sciencedirect.com/science/article/pii/S1389128617304188
10. Scott, K., Burleigh, S.: Bundle protocol specification. RFC 5050 (request for comments) (2007)
11. Sipos, B., Demmer, M., Ott, J., Perreault, S.: Delay-tolerant networking TCP convergence layer protocol version 4. Work in progress as an internet-draft, draft-ietf-dtn-tcpclv4-06 (2018)

A Proposal for IP Spoofing Mitigation at Origin in Homenet Using Software-Defined Networking

Manoel F. Ramos[1], Bruno L. Dalmazo[2]($\boxtimes$) (iD), and Jeferson C. Nobre[2] (iD)

[1] University of Vale do Rio dos Sinos, São Leopoldo, Brazil
manoel@dropreal.com
[2] Federal University of Rio Grande do Sul, Porto Alegre, Brazil
{bldalmazo,jcnobre}@inf.ufrgs.br

Abstract. Computer networks are continually evolving, making the execution of security tasks increasingly complex. Also, the development of new networking environments, such as the Internet Engineering Task Force (IETF) Home Networking (Homenet), usually is not followed by advances in security mechanisms for these environments. In this context, IP Spoofing, the obfuscation of the actual network address of the attacker either or amplify or redirect communications responses to a given target, is an example of network attack that can be employed in several infrastructures. Considering Homenet, the utilization of IPv6 does not avoid such attacks since the Neighbor Discovery Protocol (NDP), which is responsible for neighborhood discovery in IPv6, does not have mechanisms of validation of network and link addresses in its packet header (i.e., source-address validation). The present work proposes a solution to mitigate the use of IP Spoofing attacks originated in a Homenet using Software-Defined Networking (SDN) features. The results from the experimental evaluation demonstrate that the proposed method has desirable properties to avoid such attacks without increasing the complexity of the Homenet architecture.

Keywords: IP Spoofing · Homenet · SDN

1 Introduction

Computer networks are constantly evolving, making their configurations increasingly complex. This provides a significant increase on the security challenges related to supported services [1]. In home networking (i.e., domestic networking), this complexity becomes an even more important challenge, since there are no network administrators to implement security policies and to ensure an adequate operational state of the networking infrastructure [7].

The Internet Engineering Task Force (IETF) *Home Networking* (Homenet) Working Group (WG) proposed a solution to allow self-management in home networks, including self-configuration, which can avoid human intervention and,

S. Misra et al. (Eds.): ICCSA 2019, LNCS 11619, pp. 179–192, 2019.
https://doi.org/10.1007/978-3-030-24289-3_15

consequently, the need of technical knowledge from the home user [3]. In this context, it is also necessary to address security features. Homenet has vulnerabilities analogous to those found on traditional networks. Considering self-* properties, self-protection will be need to perform security tasks in an autonomic manner. However, this is not present in current Homenet specification.

Homenet is known to be vulnerable to several network attacks. One of this attacks is IP address spoofing [8]. Such attacks falsify source addresses contained in the headers of network packets, either to amplify/redirect communication responses to a particular target or to ensure the anonymity of the attacker. Also, IP spoofing is usually an initial step for various types of attacks. Fortunately, as the deployed IP addresses in a Homenet are controlled, network programmability can be used to validate source IP addresses.

Software-Defined Networking (SDN) has become a significant network programmability alternative to enhance the security of computer networks by providing the separation of data and control plane, and centralizing decision making over network traffic through the network controller [4]. In this context, SDN can help facing IP Spoofing at origin in home networks (such as IETF Homenet), avoiding that external targets are compromised by attacks originated in the home hosts.

The present paper presents a method for IP Spoofing mitigation in origin at a Homenet using SDN. The main contribution is the support of a solution based on the Homenet standards for the validation of source addresses. This solution employs to use control data in a programmatic fashion. We developed a proof of concept implementation to investigate the properties of the proposed solution.

This paper is organized as follows. In Sect. 2, the background is presented. In Sect. 3, it is described the proposed solution. Section 4 details the evaluation and the experiments performed, followed by the related work described in Sect. 5. Finally, Sect. 6 presents the conclusion about this study and future work.

2   Background

This section presents the central theoretical concepts needed to develop this work. We describe these concepts in two subsections. First, the IETF Homenet and its composing protocols are introduced. Then, this section closes with the presentation of fundamental concepts on SDN.

2.1   Homenet

Homenet is an IETF WG that aims to focus on the evolution of home networks by developing and providing a simple, self-configuring architecture to address IPv6 prefix configuration requirements for routers, network management, name resolution (Domain Name System - DNS) and network discovery services [3]. This architecture can be employed in several contexts, such as Internet of Things (IoT) [5]. Homenet employs two main protocols for its operation: the DNCP (Distributed Node Consensus Protocol) and the Home Networking Control Protocol (HNCP).

Homenet uses the DNCP to receive information from routers through discovery services, negotiations, and autonomous bootstrapping services. In addition, Homenet uses the HNCP with a DNCP profile for sharing information about the state of routers in Homenet. This use allows automatic discovery of gateways and receiving/delegating the prefixes for hosts and routers that have (or not) support from HNCP [3].

For IPv6 prefix assignment, Homenet uses the Distributed Prefix Assignment Algorithm that uses a flooding mechanism, which allows each node to advertise its directly connected prefixes. Also, the algorithm randomly creates an IPv6 /64 prefix and assigns the addresses to the hosts. Devices connected to Homenet will receive the IP addresses through the HNCP protocol. For non-HNCP hosts, the task is made through DHCPv6-PD or SLAAC [3].

2.2 Software-Defined Networking (SDN)

Some traits of SDN can be highlighted in the context of the present work. We will describe two of such traits. The first is the separation of the control plane from the data plane. The control plan decides how to handle network traffic and the data plane forwards traffic as the control plan decides. The second feature is that SDN consolidates the control plane; thus the programmable interface supports direct control over the state of the elements contained in the data plane, such as switches and routers.

SDN integrates the physical and virtual elements, allowing the controller to manage the network in an automated and centralized way. All traffic can be analyzed by the controller, which can decide what action to take on the passing flows. When the switches receive specific network packets, they will analyze their flow tables and, if the origin and destination are not known, the switches will forward the data to the controller [4].

3   Proposal for Mitigation IP Spoofing in Homenet at Origin Using SDN

The proposed solution is the use of an SDN application which uses the controller API to allow a global view of all network traffic through flow analysis. This application, called *SPOOFING_SRC_CONTROL*, is responsible for analyzing and handling the IPv6 addresses of each packet that comes out of Homenet. This verification is done by consulting the addresses provided by the HNCP protocol to the Homenet internal hosts. This section describes the proposed solution. First, the rationale of the solution is presented. Then, the algorithms of the proposed solution are depicted.

The proposed solution runs as an application on the Homenet router, and it can control the entire home network topology. SDN controller may be located on the edge router itself, where it analyses all network traffic and decides if packets can be added to the switch's flow table. In this context, decision making is done by comparing the MAC and IPv6 addresses entered in the switch flow table. If the IPv6 addresses of a respective packet are not inserted in this table or the IPv6 address is already assigned to another MAC address, the switch forwards the packet to the SDN controller, which then decides what action to take.

The proposed solution can be abstracted in some steps as follows. First, this starts when a switch is unaware of the source and destination IPv6 address of an incoming packet to be forwarded to a particular destination. This packet is sent to the controller (step 1), which will then verify that the destination and source addresses are different from internal Homenet addresses. Then, the controller will query the database containing the IPv6 and MAC addresses of the Homenet hosts generated by the HNCP protocol. After this, the controller processes the address and sends the necessary action on the respective packet for the implied switch. The switch updates its flow table with the action defined by the controller.

Algorithm 1. MOD_CONTROL()

Input: IP_SRC, MAC_SRC, IP_DST, LOCAL_NETWORK_ADDRESS.
Output: SDN_STATUS.
if *IP_DST == LOCAL_NETWORK_ADDRESS* **then**
   if *IP_SRC != LOCAL_NETWORK_ADDRESS* **then**
    | SDN_STATUS = ALLOWED
   end
   else
     SDN_STATUS = VERIFICATION
     ANL_IP_SRC = IP_SRC
     ANL_MAC_SRC = MAC_SRC
     MOD_VERIFY_IP-MAC()
     if *SPOOFING_STATUS == NO* **then**
     | SDN_STATUS = ALLOWED
     end
     if *SPOOFING_STATUS == YES* **then**
     | SDN_STATUS = BLOCKED
     end
     if *SPOOFING_STATUS == FAIL* **then**
     | SDN_STATUS = BLOCKED
     end
   end
end

Three algorithms compose the proposed solution. In this context, SPOOF-ING_SRC_CONTROL consists of MOD_CONTROL(), MOD_VERIFY_IP-MAC(), and MOD_IPMAC_SEARCH() submodules. The MOD_CONTROL() module is responsible for deciding on the correct action to be taken on the previously analyzed network packet. It needs the MOD_VERIFY_IP-MAC() and MOD_IPMAC_SEARCH() submodules for its operation. The Algorithm 1 describes storing the packet source IP address information (in the IP_SRC variable), the source MAC address (in the MAC_SRC variable), and the destination IP address of the packet (in the IP_DST variable). In addition, MOD_CONTROL() has the variable LOCAL_NETWORK_ADDRESS, which has the value corresponding to the IPv6 address of the Homenet local network.

LOCAL_NETWORK_ADDRESS is extracted from the database of the addresses assigned by HNCP to Homenet. The first action of MOD_CONTROL() is to analyze whether the value contained in the IP_DST variable corresponds to the same prefix of the value of the LOCAL_NETWORK_ADDRESS variable and if the source address (IP_SRC) is different from the local network. This process is done to verify if the packet destination is the local network or an external network (Internet), in addition to verifying if it is Homenet internal traffic. If the packet is destined for some internal Homenet host, it is released by the system through the SDN_STATUS function and no further verification is performed by closing the module.

The SDN_STATUS function is responsible for executing the system actions internally and, before the SDN controller, its values are: VERIFICATION that has the internal action of the proposed system to initiate the verification process of the source IPv6 address analyzed; ALLOWED that has the action to be taken by the SDN controller in which to release the flow in the switch; and BLOCKED, which has an action to be taken by the SDN controller in which it will block the flow in the switch.

Algorithm 2. MOD_VERIFY_IP-MAC()

Input: ANL_IP_SRC, ANL_MAC_SRC.
Output: SPOOFING_STATUS.
MOD_IP-MAC_SEARCH()
if $DB\_SERVER\_STATUS\ !=\ OK$ **then**
| SPOOFING_STATUS = FAIL
end
else
   if $SEARCH\_MAC\ ==\ XX\_XX\_XX\_XX\_XX\_XX$ **then**
   | SPOOFING_STATUS = YES
   end
   else
      VERIFY_IP = SEARCH_IP
      if $VERIFY\_IP\ ==\ ANL\_IP\_SRC$ **then**
      | SPOOFING_STATUS = NO
      end
      else
      | SPOOFING_STATUS = YES
      end
   end
end

The first value to be generated by the SDN_STATUS function is VERIFICATION, in which the system initiates the verification process by storing the IP_SRC values in the ANL_IP_SRC variable and the MAC_SRC variable in the ANL_MAC_SRC variable. After this, the MOD_VERIFY_IP-MAC() submodule is executed, feeding the value of the SPOOFING_STATUS variable into MOD_CONTROL(). SPOOFING_STATUS has three types of values, **FAIL** that is generated when the MOD_VERIFY_IP-MAC() submodule did not obtain complete results that prove the existence of IP Spoofing, **NO** that is generated when the MOD_VERIFY_IP-MAC() submodule validated MAC and IPv6 addresses and did not identify the use of the IP Spoofing technique in the packet and **YES** that is generated when the MOD_VERIFY_IP-MAC() submodule validated the MAC and IPv6 addresses and identified the use of the IP Spoofing technique in the packet.

If the value of SPOOFING_STATUS is equal to FAIL, the proposed system could not analyze the addresses and prove the existence of the IP Spoofing technique. This incident may occur in cases of unavailability in the consultation process or in an attack on the database of the addresses assigned to Homenet. In this case, the system can enter two different types of values in the variable SDN_STATUS according to the security policy established by the administrator of the Homenet environment at the moment of configuring the solution. These values are: ALLOWED to release the packet stream; and BLOCKED to block packet flow. If the value of SPOOFING_STATUS is equal to NO, the variable SDN_STATUS receives the ALLOWED value, which indicates to the system that the packet must be released through the SDN controller because it was able to verify the addresses and did not identify the existence of the IP technique Spoofing. Finally, when the SPOOFING_STATUS value is equal to YES, the SDN_STATUS variable receives the value BLOCKED, which tells the system that the SDN controller should discard the packet because it has identified the use of the IP Spoofing technique.

The submodule MOD_VERIFY_IP-MAC(), described in Algorithm 2, works in conjunction with the MOD_IP-MAC_SEARCH() submodule and generates results for the completion of the MOD_CONTROL() module. MOD_VERIFY_IP-MAC() receives the values of ANL_IP_SRC and ANL_MAC_SRC generated by the MOD_CONTROL(). Your first action is to start the MOD module IP-MAC_SEARCH(). After this, the value of DB_SERVER_STATUS generated by the submodule MOD_IP-MAC_SEARCH() is analyzed.

DB_SERVER_STATUS may contain two distinct values, being they FAIL when the MOD_IP-MAC_SEARCH() submodule was not able to execute the address localization process and OK when the MOD_IP-MAC_SEARCH() submodule successfully executed the address localization process. If the value of DB_SERVER_STATUS is other than OK, SPOOFING_STATUS receives the FAIL value. If the value of DB_SERVER_STATUS is equal to OK, the verification process starts.

It is first checked whether the SEARCH_MAC value received by executing the MOD_IP-MAC_SEARCH() submodule is equal to XX_XX_XX_XX_XX_XX. If so, this indicates that the MAC address contained in ANL_MAC_SRC is not in

---

Algorithm 3. MOD_IP-MAC_SEARCH()

Input: DB_SERVER, ANL_IP_SRC, ANL_MAC_SRC.
Output: SEARCH_MAC, SEARCH_IP, DB_SERVER_STATUS.
Connection with DB_SERVER
if *DB_SERVER is not accessible* **then**
  | DB_SERVER_STATUS = FAIL
end
else
    DB_SERVER_STATUS = OK
    Search ANL_MAC_SRC em DB_SERVER
    if *ANL_MAC_SRC is not found* **then**
      | SEARCH_MAC = XX_XX_XX_XX_XX_XX
    end
    else
      | SEARCH_MAC = ANL_MAC_SRC
      | SEARCH_IP = *IPv6 assigned to the MAC located in DB_SERVER;*
    end
end

---

the database of the list of assigned IP addresses. Thus, the SPOOFING_STATUS value is defined as YES. If not, VERIFY_IP receives the SEARCH_IP value extracted from the module IP-MAC_SEARCH(). If the value of VERIFY_IP is equal to the value of ANL_IP_SRC, the source addresses are in compliance and SPOOFING_STATUS is given the value NO. Finally, if the value of VERIFY_IP is different from ANL_IP_SRC, the use of the IP Spoofing technique is identified and SPOOFING_STATUS receives the value YES, ending the execution of the submodule, giving sequence in the analysis process.

The submodule MOD_IP-MAC_SEARCH(), described in Algorithm 3, has the responsibility of locating the values of ANL_IP_SRC and ANL_MAC_SRC in the database of the list of IPv6 addresses assigned to Homenet. It is started through submodule MOD_VERIFY_IP-MAC().

4 Evaluation

In this section, the experiments carried out to evaluate the solution proposed in a Homenet are presented. First, the topology employed on the simulation (Experimental Scenario) is explained. Then, the implementation of the proposed solution is depicted. Finally, the performed experiments and their results are presented.

4.1 Experimental Scenario

The test infrastructure and its topology were implemented using a virtual environment in which it was possible to evaluate the proposed solution. Figure 1 shows the complete implementation topology. Routers A, B, and C (ISP) communicate through the OSPFv3 protocol and the automatic distribution of IPv6 addressing was used by the DHCPv6-PD service. Hosts B and C are ISP customers as well as Client A, the gateway of Homenet. Each of the hosts has a network interface connected to their respective gateways.

4.2   Development and Implementation of the Proposed Solution

SPOOFING_SRC_CONTROL was developed and implemented on the RYU controller. RYU was developed in the Python programming language, so SPOOF-ING_SRC_CONTROL was also developed in Python. The RYU driver has been compiled to support the proposed solution. The system is started by the controller when the switch does not know the source and destination (IPv6 or MAC) of the incoming packet because in its flow table there is no such information. With this, the switch sends the packet to the RYU controller which executes SPOOFING_CONTROL through its "_packet_in_handler" function before executing the add_flow function.

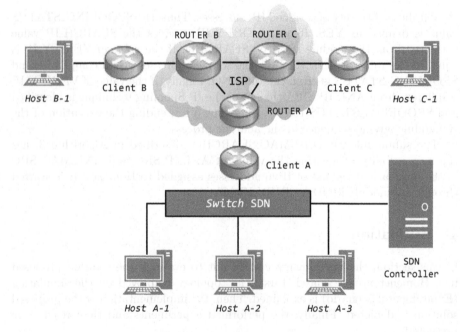

Fig. 1. Simulation infrastructure.

SPOOFING_SRC_CONTROL checks the Homenet source address according to the submodule MOD_VERIFY_IP-MAC(). SPOOFING_SRC_CONTROL has a function, developed according to the submodule MOD_IP-MAC_SEARCH(), which is responsible for querying the prefixes and IPv6 addresses assigned to Homenet via HNCP. such queries check the source address in each packet. If the source IPv6 address is different from the Homenet or the source MAC address is different from that contained in the assigned address base and the destination address is also different from the Homenet, the use of the IP Spoofing technique is identified and the packet is discarded by the controller.

4.3   Experiments

As shown in Fig. 1, the communication for this experiment was made between Homenet hosts (Hosts A-1, A-2 and A-3) and the other external hosts, ISP clients (Host B-1 and Host C-1). The HNCP protocol assigned two IPv6 prefixes to the Homenet interface on its router and the internal Hosts A-1, A-2, and A-3). For these experiments, the Homenet environment with multihoming support was not implemented. For the use of the IP Spoofing and MAC Spoofing technique in IPv6 networks, the NMAP[1] software was used. The experiments were carried out 10 (ten) times to validate their results, and the observed variance was low.

Three experiments using the IP Spoofing technique were performed in the environment shown in Fig. 1. The experiment 1 validates the use of IP Spoofing at the source through the communication of Homenet hosts with external hosts (Host B-1 and Host C-1), comparing IPv6 addresses and MAC addresses; experiment 2 validates the source communication between Homenet's internal hosts (Hosts A-1, A-2 and A3), also comparing IPv6 addresses and MAC addresses; and experiment 3 validates the communication between the internal hosts in Homenet with the external communication, however, using only the validation of the Homenet source addresses through the assigned IPv6 prefix, not validating the MAC addresses of the Homenet hosts.

Results. The Fig. 2 shows the communication results between Hosts A-1, A-2, and A-3 with Host B-1 (Fig. 1) in a Homenet (experiment 1) without enabling the In the time period of 60 s, the NMAP was run, with IP Spoofing and MAC Spoofing enabled, and Ping6 on all Homenet hosts, successively, to Host B-1. found that Homenet is vulnerable to using the techniques of IP Spoofing and MAC Spoofing. The consumption of network traffic was measured by capturing the results from the output interface of the Homenet eth1 router through the use of the IFTOP software. NMAP totaled the average consumption of 5055 bytes/s (average of 1685 bytes/s per Homenet host) and Ping6 totaled the average consumption of 2412 bytes/s (average of 804 bytes/s per Homenet host) of the traffic generated by Homenet's internal hosts.

The Fig. 3 shows the result of the same communication of hosts A-1, A-2 and A-3 with host B-1 in a Homenet (experiment 1), however, with SPOOF-ING_SRC_CONTROL enabled on the SDN controller. In the first 20 s of execution, SPOOFING_SRC_CONTROL was executed to validate the host A-1

---

[1] NMAP - https://nmap.org/.

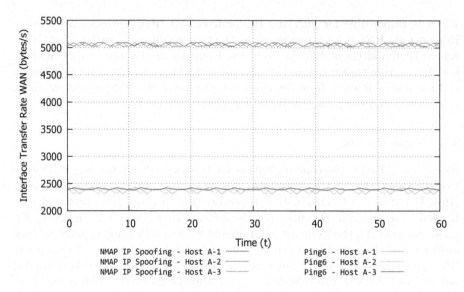

Fig. 2. Applicability of IP Spoofing and MAC Spoofing WITHOUT the proposed solution.

address, where communication of the same was terminated at IP Spoofing detection. In the next 10 and 20 s (30 and 40), the same process was executed on host A-2 and host A-3, terminating their communication after the detection of IP Spoofing. This same test procedure was performed for the validation of source MAC addresses, in which it obtained the same result and proving that the solution is also efficient to counter the use of the MAC Spoofing technique at the origin.

In experiment 2, the proposed solution was efficient in mitigating and blocking the use of the IP Spoofing and MAC Spoofing techniques at the origin. The results were captured at the interface of Mininet via the IFTOP software.

In experiment 3, only IP Spoofing was detected and blocked in communication with Homenet's external hosts, because in this experiment, it is not possible to compare the MAC addresses because the HNCP query base is related only to the IPv6 prefix assigned to the Homenet. This also impacted on the process of verifying the IP Spoofing internally generated in Homenet between its hosts.

Performance Analyzes. Performance analyzes were performed to identify the processing power and memory of the solution in the SDN controller. For this, HTOP software was used, installed directly in RYU controller.

The Fig. 4 shows the result of the processing and memory consumption of the RYU controller without the use of the proposed solution. Within the 60-s period, when the controller did not manipulate the switch's flow table, it had a variation between 0.3% and 0.7% in processing consumption and 1.3% in memory consumption. In seconds 11, 12, 13, 33, 34 and 35 the switch, which was unknown

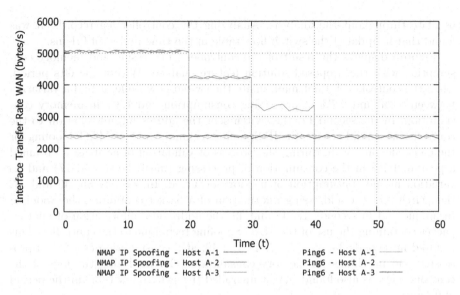

Fig. 3. Applicability of IP Spoofing and MAC Spoofing WITH the proposed solution.

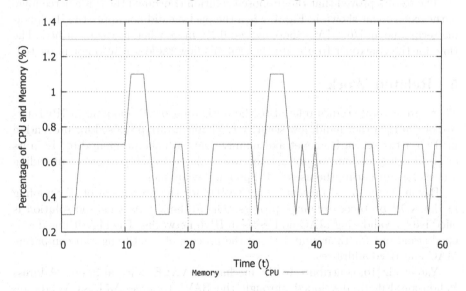

Fig. 4. Computational consumption WITHOUT use of proposed solution.

to the source and destination information of two network packets, forwarded them to the check by the RYU controller, in which it validated the network addresses of the packets and has added the information in the switch flow table. These checks generated a peak of 1.1% in each processing consumption. The RAM consumption was not changed and the same 1.3% consumption did not oscillate throughout the analysis. Analyzing the controller log records, it was found that it updated the switch flow table in the time period of 0.1 ms.

Figure 5 displays the result of the controller's processing and memory consumption with the proposed solution feature enabled. Within the 60 s period, when the controller did not manipulate the switch flow table, it had a variation between 0.3% and 0.7% in processing consumption and 1.3% in memory consumption. In the second 17, the switch sent the addressing information to the controller which did not use the IP Spoofing technique and/or MAC Spoofing for the controller in which, during the process of validation of addresses, obtained a peak of 1.1% in the consumption of processing (until the second 17) and no variation in the consumption of memory occurred. In seconds 35, 36 and 37, the switch sent the addressing information of a packet containing the Spoofing technique and in seconds 47, 48 and 49, the addressing information of another packet containing the use of the MAC Spoofing technique to the controller. This resulted in seconds 35, 36, 37, 47, 48 and 49, at a consumption of 1.2% of processing and no change in memory consumption. By analyzing the logs of the controller, it was also found that it upgraded the switch flow table in the period of 0.1 ms.

The results proved that the proposed solution consumed the same percentage of the experiment shown in Fig. 4, when the package did not apply the IP Spoofing technique and/or MAC Spoofing and 0.1% more when it was identified. The time for the controller to update the switch's flow table was also not impacted.

5   Related Work

There are several studies related to the mitigation of IP Spoofing in IPv4 networks. On the other hand, few security mechanisms are proposed for prevention in IPv6 networks, in Homenet and mainly deal with the problem directly in its origin. In this section, we present the work related to the purpose of providing a basis for mitigating the use of IP Spoofing techniques.

Barbhuiya et al. [2] present an active IDS for the prevention of IP Spoofing in the NDP protocol exchange process. The authors state that the solution is effective for validating MAC addresses in IPv6 networks. The algorithms developed stand out for their simplicity in the process of identifying and comparing MAC and IPv6 addresses.

Yao et al. [10] contribute to the mechanism VAVE (Virtual Source Address Validation Edge), developed through the SAVI (Source Address Validation Improvement) framework, which uses the Openflow protocol to mitigate IP Spoofing in incoming traffic on a local network. One of the negative factors of this solution is that the SAVI protocol requires adaptations to the current protocols of the Internet, a negative factor to make it a standard protocol before the IETF.

Yan et al. [9] have developed an experiment to implement the SAVI protocol on a local network. In this contribution, the positive factor is that the authors consult DHCPv6 servers to carry out the validation process through NDP messages issued by SAVI.

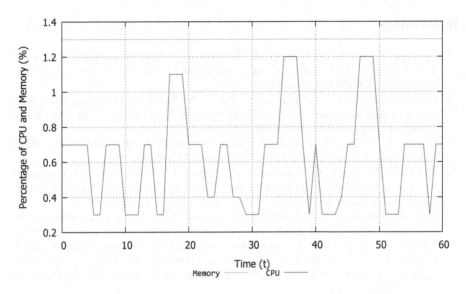

Fig. 5. Computational consumption WITH use of proposed solution.

Finally, Mowla et al. [6] propose a defense mechanism to IP Spoofing in the traffic of received data, validating the legitimate traffic and blocking the Spoofing. The solution is composed of SDN based on Content Distribution Network Interconnection (CDNi) technology, along with ALTO (Application Layer Traffic Optimization) technology. The purpose is to use SDN to detect IP Spoofing, following a mechanism to feed rules into SDN switches through the controller using the markup maps provided by the ALTO server.

6   Conclusions and Future Work

IPv6 networks are vulnerable regarding IP Spoofing techniques which consequently affects any network that uses IPv6, such as IETF Homenet. In the present paper, an efficient mechanism was proposed for the validation of IPv6 addresses at the origin in a Homenet. The results obtained highlighted the efficiency in the mitigation of IP and MAC Spoofing process when the packets are coming out from a Homenet. Besides that, the results also presented the low consumption of the computational resources consumed by the solution. Such consumption is constrained in the SDN controller.

Despite the encouraging results, there is also room for improvements. As future work, we intend to investigate the process of feeding the base of the network addresses assigned to Homenet should be a priority, extending the evaluation of the proposed solution in a Homenet environment using the multihoming feature in an ISP with MSP support and in conventional IPv6 networks.

References

1. Bannour, F., Souihi, S., Mellouk, A.: Distributed SDN control: survey, taxonomy, and challenges. IEEE Commun. Surv. Tutor. **20**(1), 333–354 (2018). https://doi.org/10.1109/COMST.2017.2782482
2. Barbhuiya, F., Bansal, G., Kumar, N., Biswas, S., Nandi, S.: Detection of neighbor discovery protocol based attacks in IPv6 network. Netw. Sci. **2**(4), 91–113 (2013). https://doi.org/10.1007/s13119.013.0018.2
3. Chown, T., Arkko, J., Brandt, A., Troan, O., Weil, J.: IPv6 home networking architecture principles. RFC 7368 (Informational), October 2014
4. da Costa Cordeiro, W.L., Marques, J.A., Gaspary, L.P.: Data plane programmability beyond OpenFlow: opportunities and challenges for network and service operations and management. J. Netw. Syst. Manag. **25**(4), 784–818 (2017)
5. Mars, D., Gammar, S.M., Lahmadi, A., Saidane, L.A.: Using information centric networking in internet of things: a survey. Wirel. Pers. Commun. **105**, 1–17 (2019)
6. Mowla, N., Doh, I., Chae, K.: An efficient defense mechanism for spoofed IP attack in SDN based CDNi. In: Proceedings of the International Conference on Information Networking (ICOIN), pp. 92–97, January 2015. https://doi.org/10.1109/ICOIN.2015.7057863
7. Sivaraman, V., Gharakheili, H.H., Vishwanath, A., Boreli, R., Mehani, O.: Network-level security and privacy control for smart-home IoT devices. In: 2015 IEEE 11th International Conference on Wireless and Mobile Computing, Networking and Communications (WiMob), pp. 163–167, October 2015. https://doi.org/10.1109/WiMOB.2015.7347956
8. Xu, K., Wang, F., Egli, R., Fives, A., Howell, R., Mcintyre, O.: Object-oriented big data security analytics: a case study on home network traffic. In: Cai, Z., Wang, C., Cheng, S., Wang, H., Gao, H. (eds.) WASA 2014. LNCS, vol. 8491, pp. 313–323. Springer, Cham (2014). https://doi.org/10.1007/978-3-319-07782-6_29
9. Yan, Z., Deng, G., Wu, J.: SAVI-based IPv6 source address validation implementation of the access network. In: 2011 International Conference on Proceedings of Computer Science and Service System (CSSS), pp. 2530–2533, June 2011. https://doi.org/10.1109/CSSS.2011.5974125
10. Yao, G., Bi, J., Xiao, P.: Source address validation solution with OpenFlow/NOX architecture. In: 2011 19th IEEE International Conference on Proceedings of Network Protocols (ICNP), pp. 7–12, October 2011. https://doi.org/10.1109/ICNP.2011.6089085

Parallel OpenMP and CUDA Implementations of the N-Body Problem

Tushaar Gangavarapu$^{(\boxtimes)}$ (iD), Himadri Pal, Pratyush Prakash, Suraj Hegde, and V. Geetha (iD)

Department of Information Technology, National Institute of Technology Karnataka, Surathkal, Mangaluru, India
tushaargvsg45@gmail.com, himadripal37@gmail.com, pratyushprakash@gmail.com, suraj1997pisces@gmail.com, geethav@nitk.edu.in

Abstract. The N-body problem, in the field of astrophysics, predicts the movements of the planets and their gravitational interactions. This paper aims at developing efficient and high-performance implementations of two versions of the N-body problem. Adaptive tree structures are widely used in N-body simulations. Building and storing the tree and the need for work-load balancing pose significant challenges in high-performance implementations. Our implementations use various cores in CPU and GPU via efficient work-load balancing with data and task parallelization. The contributions include OpenMP and Nvidia CUDA implementations to parallelize force computation and mass distribution, and achieve competitive performance in terms of speedup and running time which is empirically justified and graphed. This research not only aids as an alternative to complex simulations but also to other big data applications requiring work-load distribution and computationally expensive procedures.

Keywords: All-Pairs algorithm · Barnes-Hut algorithm · CUDA · N-body simulations · OpenMP · Parallel processing · Performance

1 Introduction

The N-body problem in astrophysics is the problem of predicting the individual motions of a group of celestial bodies, interacting gravitationally [3]. Scientific and engineering applications of such simulations to anticipate certain behaviors include biology, molecular and fluid dynamics, semiconductor device simulation, feature engineering, and others [14,15,18]. The gravitational N-body problem [23] aims at computing the states of N bodies at a time T, given their initial states (velocities and positions). The naive implementation of the N-body problem has a complexity of $O(N^2)$ which is inefficient in terms of both power consumption and performance, leaving much room to improve the effectiveness of the execution of these simulations using data and task parallelism, aided with utilities such as OpenMP (distribution among processors) [9,16] and Nvidia CUDA (distribution among Graphical Processing Units (GPUs)) [2].

© Springer Nature Switzerland AG 2019
S. Misra et al. (Eds.): ICCSA 2019, LNCS 11619, pp. 193–208, 2019.
https://doi.org/10.1007/978-3-030-24289-3_16

With Appel [7] and Barnes-Hut [8] algorithms, the N-body simulation is significantly faster, with the time complexity of $O(N)$ for Appel and $O(NlogN)$ for the Barnes-Hut algorithm. Even with such adaptive tree optimizations, significant improvement in the performance can be seen when implemented in parallel. In this paper, we review existing All-Pairs and Barnes-Hut algorithms to solve the N-body problem, and then propose our method of parallelization to achieve work-load balancing using data and task parallel approaches effectively. We then draw conclusions from the presented results to assess the potential of parallelization in terms of running time and speedup. The key contributions of this paper are mainly three-fold:

- Design of OpenMP and CUDA implementations of the All-Pairs algorithm, to parallelize force computation.
- Design of OpenMP implementation of the Barnes-Hut algorithm, to parallelize both force computation and mass distribution.
- We present a detailed evaluation of the performance of the parallel algorithms in terms of speedup and running time on galactic datasets [1] with bodies ranging from 5 to 30,002.

The rest of this paper is structured as follows: Sect. 2 gives a detailed overview of the All-Pairs and Barnes-Hut algorithms to solve the N-body problem. Section 3 reviews relevant existing works in the field of parallel N-body simulations. Section 4 explains our proposed approaches to parallelize the All-Pairs and Barnes-Hut simulations and presents their implementations using OpenMP and CUDA. Section 5 presents the evaluation of the proposed approaches and Sect. 6 reviews the significant implications of such parallelization and concludes with future enhancements.

2   The Gravitational N-Body Problem

The gravitational N-body problem [23] is concerned with interactions between N bodies (stars or galaxies in astrophysics), where each body in a given system of bodies, affects every other body. The creation of galaxies, effects of black holes, and even the search for dark matter are associated with the N-body problem [17], thus making it one of the most widely experimented problem.

The Problem: Given the initial states (velocities and positions) of N bodies, compute the states of those bodies at time T using the instantaneous acceleration on every body at regular time steps.

In this section, we present two commonly used algorithms: (1) *All-Pairs*, which is best suited for a smaller number of bodies and (2) *Barnes-Hut*, which scales efficiently to a large number of bodies (e.g., molecular dynamics); to solve the N-body problem.

2.1   The All-Pairs Algorithm

The traditional All-Pairs algorithm is an exhaustive brute-force that computes instantaneous pair-wise acceleration between each body and every other body.

Any two bodies (B_i, B_j) in the system of N bodies are attracted to each other with force $(\overrightarrow{F_{ij}})$ that is inversely proportional to the square of the distance (r_{ij}) between them (see Eq. 1, G is the universal gravitational constant).

$$\overrightarrow{F_{ij}} = \frac{Gm_i m_j}{r_{ij}^2} \hat{r}_{ij} \tag{1}$$

Also, a body (B_i) of mass (m_i) experiences acceleration $(\overrightarrow{a_i})$ due to the net force acting on it $(F_i = \sum_{j \neq i} \overrightarrow{F_{ij}})$ from $N - 1$ bodies (see Eq. 2).

$$\overrightarrow{F_i} = \overrightarrow{a_i} m_i \tag{2}$$

From Eqs. 1 and 2, the instantaneous pair-wise acceleration $(\overrightarrow{a_i})$ acting on a body (B_i) due to another body (B_j) can be given by Eq. 3 (G is the universal gravitational constant).

$$\overrightarrow{a_i} = \frac{Gm_j}{r_{ij}^2} \hat{r}_{ij} \tag{3}$$

The All-Pairs method given by Algorithm 1 essentially computes pair-wise accelerations and updates the forces acting on all bodies, thus updating their state. Such an update can be programmatically achieved by using an in-place update of a double nested loop, thus resulting in a time complexity of $O(N^2)$. Usually, the All-Pairs method is not used on its own, but as a kernel to compute forces in close-range interactions [27]. Since the All-Pairs algorithm takes substantial time to compute accelerations, it serves as an interesting target for parallelization.

Algorithm 1. Sequential All-Pairs Algorithm (2 Dimensions)

```
1:  Function calculate_force() is
2:      foreach i: body do
3:          find_force(i, particles)

4:  Function find_force(i: body, particles) is
5:      foreach j in particles do
6:          if j ≠ i then
7:              d_sq = distance(i, j)
8:              force[i].x += d_x * mass(i) / d_sq^3
9:              force[i].y += d_y * mass(i) / d_sq^3
```

2.2   The Barnes-Hut Algorithm

The Barnes-Hut algorithm [4,5,8,33] is one of the most widely used approximations of the N-body problem, primarily by clustering groups of distant close bodies together into a "pseudo-body." Empirical evidence proves that the Barnes-Hut heuristic method requires far fewer operations than the All-Pairs method, thus useful in cases of a large number of bodies where an approximate but efficient solution is more feasible.

Each pseudo-body has an overall mass and center of mass depending on the individual bodies it contains (its children). The Barnes-Hut algorithm uses an adaptive tree structure (quad-tree for 2D or oct-tree for 3D)[1]. A tree structure is created with each node bearing four children (see Fig. 1).

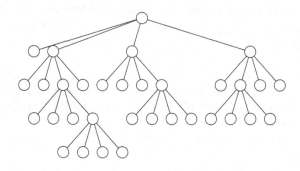

Fig. 1. Example of a quad-tree used in the Barnes-Hut algorithm.

Once built, the tree describes the whole system, with internal nodes representing pseudo-bodies and leaf nodes representing the N bodies [13]. The tree is then used in computation and updating of a body's state. The Barnes-Hut method given by Algorithm 2 implements the following steps to achieve the realization of a spatial system into a quad-tree:

– Division of the whole domain into four square regions (quads).
– If any of these quads contain more than one body, recursively divide that region into four square regions until each square holds a maximum of one body.
– Once the tree is built, perform a recursive walk to calculate the center of mass ($\vec{c}$) at every node as $\sum_i \vec{c_i} m_i / \sum m_i$ (i is a child of the node).

Each body uses the constructed tree to compute the acceleration it experiences due to every other body. The Barnes-Hut algorithm approximates bodies that are too far away using a fixed accuracy parameter (threshold (θ)), and the approximation is called the opening condition. Based on the center of mass, the opening condition is given by $l/D < \theta$ (see Fig. 2, blue body represents the body under consideration) where l is the width of the current internal node and D is the distance of the body from the center of mass of the pseudo-body. Threshold determines the number of bodies to be grouped together and thus determines the accuracy of computations. Heuristics show that Barnes-Hut method can approximate the N-body problem in $O(NlogN)$ time. Depending on the dispersion of bodies in the system an adaptive tree is constructed (usually unbalanced) which poses challenges of building, storing, and work-load balancing.

---

[1] In this paper, we have considered quad-tree to implement the Barnes-Hut algorithm.

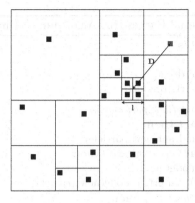

Fig. 2. An example of the pseudo-bodies used in the Barnes-Hut algorithm.

3   Related Work

In 1994, the Virgo Consortium was founded to perform cosmological simulations such as universe formation, tracking the creation of galaxies and black holes on supercomputers; and the most significant problem worked on by them till date is the "Millennium Run" [6]. Their simulations traced around 10 billion particles (each particle represented 20 million galaxies) using code called GAlaxies with Dark matter intEracT (GADGET) [31] along with MPI-HYDRA and FLASH, initially written sequentially but has since been developed to run in parallel to model a broad range of astronomical problems. MPI-HYDRA simulates galaxy and star formations while FLASH simulates thermonuclear flashes seen on the surface of compact stars.

There exist several works in the literature to optimize the N-body problem. Starting with Appel [7], and Barnes and Hut [8] who optimized the N-body problem using adaptive tree structures from $O(N^2)$ to $O(N)$ and $O(NlogN)$ time complexities respectively. An $O(N)$ fast multipole method was developed by Greengard and Rokhlin [21,22], and they showed the fast multipole approach (FMM) to be accurate to any precision. This was further extended by Sundaram [32] to allow updating of different bodies at different rates which further reduced the time complexity. However, adaptive multipole method in 3 dimensions is complex and has an issue of large overheads.

Various approaches to parallelize the algorithms mentioned above have been developed over the years. Salmon [29] used multipole approximations to implement the Barnes-Hut algorithm on NCUBE and Intel iPSC, message passing architectures. An impressive performance was reported from extensive runs on the 512 node Intel Touchstone Delta by Warren and Salmon [36]. Singh [30] implemented the Barnes-Hut algorithm for the DASH, an experimental prototype. Bhatt *et al.* [10,19] implemented the filament fluid dynamic problem using the Barnes-Hut method. 16 Intel Pentium Pro processors were used by Warren *et al.* [35] to obtain a sustained performance. Blelloch and Narlikar [11]

Algorithm 2. Sequential Barnes-Hut Algorithm (2 Dimensions)

1: **Function** *build_tree()* **is**
2:     Reset Tree
3:     **foreach** *i: particle* **do**
4:         root_node→insert_to_node(i)

5: **Function** *insert_to_node(new_particle)* **is**
6:     **if** *num_particles > 1* **then**
7:         quad = get_quadrant(new_particle)
8:         **if** *subnode(quad) does not exist* **then**
9:             create subnode(quad)
10:        subnode(quad)→insert_to_node(new_particle)
11:    **else if** *num_particles == 1* **then**
12:        quad = get_quadrant(new_particle)
13:        **if** *subnode(quad) does not exist* **then**
14:            create subnode(quad)
15:        subnode(quad)→insert_to_node(existing_particle)
16:        quad = get_quadrant(new_particle)
17:        **if** *subnode(quad) ≠ NULL* **then**
18:            create subnode(quad)
19:        subnode(quad)→insert_to_node(new_particle)
20:    **else**
21:        existing_particle ← new_particle
22:    num_particles++

23: **Function** *compute_mass_distribution()* **is**
24:    **if** *new_particles == 1* **then**
25:        center_of_mass = particle.position
26:        mass = particle.mass
27:    **else**
28:        **forall the** *child quadrants with particles* **do**
29:            quadrant.compute_mass_distribution
30:            mass += quadrant.mass
31:            center_of_mass = quadrant.mass * quadrant.center_of_mass
32:        center_of_mass /= mass

33: **Function** *calculate_force(target)* **is**
34:    Initialize force ← 0
35:    **if** *num_particles == 1* **then**
36:        force = gravitational_force(target, node)
37:    **else**
38:        **if** *l/D < θ* **then**
39:            force = gravitational_force(target, node)
40:        **else**
41:            **forall the** *node : child nodes* **do**
42:                force += node.calculate_force(node)

43: **Function** *compute_force()* **is**
44:    **forall the** *particles* **do**
45:        force = root_node.calculate_force(particle)

---

both implemented and compared in NESL (parallel programming language) the Barnes-Hut algorithm, FMM, and the parallel multipole tree algorithm.

Board *et al.* [12] implemented an adaptive FMM method in three dimensions on shared memory machines. Zhao and Johnsson [38] described a non-adaptive version of Greengard and Rokhlin's method in three dimensions on the Connection Machine CM-2. Mills *et al.* [25] prototyped the FMM in Proteus (an architecture-independent language) using data parallelization, which was then implemented by Nyland *et al.* [26]. Pringle [28] implemented the FMM both in two and three dimensions on the Meiko Computer Surface CS-1 which is a parallel computer with distributed memory and explicit message passing interface.

Liu and Bhatt [24] explained their experiences with parallel implementation of the Barnes-Hut algorithm on the Connection Machine CM-5. A highly efficient, high performance and scalable implementation of the N-body simulation on FPGA was demonstrated by Sozzo *et al.* [18]. Totoo and Loidl [34] compared the parallel implementation of the All-Pairs and Barnes-Hut algorithms in Haskell, a functional programming language. The Tree-Code Particle-Mesh method developed by Xue [37] combines the particle-mesh algorithm with multiple tree-code to achieve better solutions with low computational costs. Nylons [27] accelerated the All-Pairs algorithm using CUDA and presented a sustained performance. Burtscher and Pingali [13] implemented the Barnes-Hut algorithm with irregular trees and complex traversals in CUDA.

4   Proposed Methodology

There are many considerations such as storage, load-balancing, and others in parallelizing the algorithms to solve the N-body problem. Following subsections elucidate on the challenges in parallelization and relevant parallel considerations to overcome those challenges.

Algorithm 3. OpenMP Implementation of the All-Pairs Algorithm

---

1: **Function** *calculate_force()* **is**
2:      *#pragma omp parallel for*
3:      **foreach** *i: body* **do**
4:          find_force(i, particles)

5: **Function** *find_force(i: body, particles)* **is**
6:      *#pragma omp parallel for reduction (+ : force[i].x, force[i].y)*
7:      **foreach** *j in particles* **do**
8:          **if** $j \neq i$ **then**
9:              d_sq = distance(i, j)
10:             force[i].x += d_x * mass(i) / d_sq^3
11:             force[i].y += d_y * mass(i) / d_sq^3

4.1 Parallel All-Pairs Algorithm in OpenMP and CUDA

The traditional brute-force All-Pairs algorithm, with $O(N^2)$ time complexity serves as an interesting target for parallelization. This approach can be easily parallelized, as it is known in advance, precisely how much work-load balancing is to be done. The work can be partitioned using a simple block partition strategy since the number of bodies is known and updating each body takes the same amount of calculation. Algorithm 3 provides pseudo-code of the All-Pairs algorithm in parallel using OpenMP. We assign each process a block of bodies each $numPlanets/numProcessors$ in size, to compute forces acting on those bodies (all processes perform the same number of computations). Thus, the work-load is equally and efficiently partitioned among processes. Algorithm 4 reports the pseudo-code of the All-Pairs algorithm in CUDA.

Algorithm 4. CUDA Implementation of the All-Pairs Algorithm

1: **Function** *calculate_force()* **is**
2:     **foreach** *i: body* **do**
3:         *find_force* $<<< BLOCKS, THREADS\_PER\_BLOCK >>>$
         (index, particles, force, size)

4: **Function** *find_force(i: body, particles, force, size)* **is**
5:     $j = particles[treadIdx.x + blockIdx.x * blockDim.x]$
6:     **if** $j \neq i$ **then**
7:         d_sq = distance(i, j)
8:         force[i].x += d_x * mass(i) / d_sq^3
9:         force[i].y += d_y * mass(i) / d_sq^3

4.2 Parallel Barnes-Hut Algorithm in OpenMP

The Barnes-Hut algorithm poses several challenges in the parallel implementation of which, decomposition and communication have a severe impact. To begin with, the cost of building and traversing a quad-tree can increase significantly when divided among processes. The irregularly structured and adaptive nature of the algorithm makes the data access patterns dynamic and irregular, and the nodes essential to a body cannot be computed without traversing the quad-tree. Decomposition is associated with work-load balancing while communication bottleneck is a severe issue that requires the need for minimization of communication volume.

Building a quad-tree needs synchronization. Since the computation of the center of mass of a pseudo-body depends on the center of masses of corresponding sub-bodies, data dependencies are predominant and thus implying tree level-wise parallelization. For force computation, we need other particles' center of mass, but we do not modify the information and thus can be parallelized. The value of the fixed accuracy parameter (θ) plays a prominent role and must be

---

Algorithm 5. Force Computation Parallelization of Barnes-Hut Algorithm

---

```
1:  Function compute_force() is
2:      #pragma omp parallel for
3:      forall the particles do
4:          force = root_node.calculate_force(particle)

5:  Function calculate_force(target_body) is
6:      force = 0
7:      if num_particles == 1 then
8:          force = gravitational_force(target_body, node)
9:      else
10:         if l/D < θ then
11:             force = gravitational_force(target_body, node)
12:         else
13:             #pragma omp parallel for
14:             forall the node : child nodes do
15:                 #pragma omp critical
16:                     force += node.calculate_force(node)
```

---

optimized. Higher values of θ imply that fewer nodes are considered in the force computation thus increasing the window for error; while lower values of θ will bring the Barnes-Hut approximation time complexity closer to that of the All-Pairs algorithm. Algorithm 5 presents pseudo-code of force parallelization (as explained above) of the Barnes-Hut algorithm.

In computing the center of mass of the nodes, some level of parallelization can be achieved in-spite of data dependencies as the computation for each quad in the tree is independent of the other which speeds up the process significantly. Algorithm 6 depicts the parallelization of the center of mass computation.

Algorithm 6. Mass Distribution Parallelization of Barnes-Hut Algorithm

---

```
1:  Function compute_mass_distribution() is
2:      if new_particles == 1 then
3:          center_of_mass = particle.position
4:          mass = particle.mass
5:      else
6:          #pragma omp parallel for
7:          forall the child quadrants with particles do
8:              quadrant.compute_mass_distribution
9:              #pragma omp critical
10:             mass += quadrant.mass
11:             center_of_mass = quadrant.mass * quadrant.center_of_mass
12:         center_of_mass /= mass
```

Parallelization of the Barnes-Hut algorithm has many issues, the significant issue being the lack of prescience on the number of computations per process; which make it a complex parallelization problem. It can be observed that, with the increase in the quad-tree traversal depth, the number of force calculations increases significantly and the exact depth is dependent on the position of the current body.

5   Evaluation, Results, and Analysis

The sequential All-Pairs algorithm was implemented in C++, with parallelization in OpenMP and CUDA. OpenMP's multi-threading [9] fork-join model was used to fork a number of slave threads and separate the errand among them. The separated tasks are then performed simultaneously, with run-time environment assigning threads to distinct tasks. The segment of code intended to run in parallel is stamped likewise with a preprocessor order that is used to join the outputs of the processes in order after they finish execution of their corresponding task. Each thread can be identified with an ID, which can be acquired using OpenMP's `omp_get_thread_num()` method. CUDA allows the programmer to take advantage of the massive parallel computing power of an Nvidia graphics card to perform any general-purpose computation [2,20]. To run efficiently on CUDA, we used hundreds of threads (the more the number of threads, the faster the computation). Since the All-Pairs algorithm can be broken down into hundreds of threads, CUDA proves to be the best solution. GPUs use massive parallel interfaces to connect with their memory and are approximately ten times faster than a typical CPU-to-memory interface.

This section focuses on running the algorithms described in the above section, in serial and in parallel. All the algorithms were tested using data with a number of bodies ranging from 5 to 30,002 in the galactic datasets [1]. All tests for sequential and OpenMP implementations were performed on nearly identical machines with the following specifications:

- *Processor*: i5 7200U @ 4 × 3.1 GHz
- *Memory*: 8 GB DDR3 @ 1333 MHz
- *Network*: 10/100/1000 Gigabit Local Area Network (LAN) Connection

All tests for CUDA implementations were performed on a server with the following specifications:

- *Processor*: Intel Xeon Processor @ 2 × 2.40 GHz
- *Memory*: 8 GB RAM
- *Tesla GPU*: 1 × TESLA C-2050 (3 GB Memory)

Speedup (S) is a measure of the relative performance of any two systems, here parallel implementations over sequential implementations. Speed up can be estimated using Eq. 4.

$$S = \frac{\text{Time}_{\text{sequential}}}{\text{Time}_{\text{parallel}}} \tag{4}$$

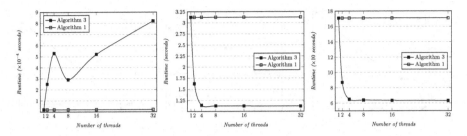

Fig. 3. Parallel vs. sequential running time for (left) 5 bodies in *Planets* [1], (center) 4,000 bodies in *galaxymerge2* [1], and (right) 30,002 bodies in *galaxy30k* [1] using Algorithm 3.

Note that the execution times collected to measure the performance and impact of parallelization is collected five times to overrule bias caused by any other system processes that are not under the control of the experimenter. In every run for time measurement, the order of experimentation for a given dataset is shuffled. The individual measurements are then averaged to represent the running time taken by the parallel algorithm accurately.

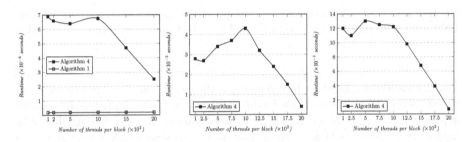

Fig. 4. Parallel vs. sequential running time for (left) 5 bodies in *Planets* [1], (center) 4,000 bodies in *galaxymerge2* [1], and (right) 30,002 bodies in *galaxy30k* [1] using Algorithm 4. (Serial execution takes more than 100 times the parallel execution time and hence is not graphed).

In this paper, we graphed (see Figs. 3, 4, 5 and 6) the parallel implementations against their respective sequential implementations to visualize the effect of speedup. We also present the results of the performance of the Barnes-Hut algorithm when both force computation and mass distribution are parallelized (see Table 1). Also, we present the effect of the fixed accuracy parameter (θ) on the Barnes-Hut algorithm (see Fig. 7).

For inputs with a smaller number of celestial bodies, we observe that the sequential execution is faster than parallelized OpenMP code in case of both All-Pairs and Barnes-Hut algorithms (see Figs. 3 (left), 5 (left), and 6 (left)). Such behavior can be attributed to the high cost of initialization of threads and their

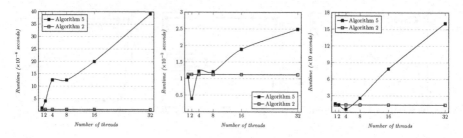

Fig. 5. Parallel vs. sequential running time for (left) 5 bodies in *Planets* [1], (center) 4,000 bodies in *galaxymerge2* [1], and (right) 30,002 bodies in *galaxy30k* [1] using Algorithm 5.

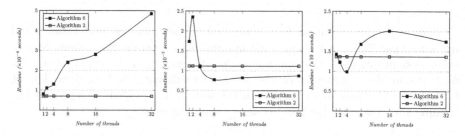

Fig. 6. Parallel vs. sequential running time for (left) 5 bodies in *Planets* [1], (center) 4,000 bodies in *galaxymerge2* [1], and (right) 30,002 bodies in *galaxy30k* [1] using Algorithm 6.

communication overheads, which outweighs the execution time for a lesser number of bodies. With the increase in the number of bodies, the OpenMP parallel implementation runs faster than its sequential counterpart which is attributed to the fact that execution time is larger than the thread spawn overheads (see Figs. 3 (center) and (right), 5 (center) and (right), 6 (center) and (right)). However, it can also be noticed from the graphs that increasing the threads beyond four, either does not change (see Figs. 3 (center), (right) and 6 (center)) or increases (see Figs. 5 (center), (right), and 6 (right)) the running time. This is because the CPU on the testing machine does not support more than four cores. Greater speedups are observed with the increase in the number of bodies. Also, it is interesting to note that with better hardware that supports a greater number of cores, the results can be bettered further.

While the OpenMP implementations have a bottleneck over the number of cores on the test machine, parallelization with CUDA outperforms any such limitations (see Fig. 4 (left), (center) and (right)). It can be observed that CUDA implementation provides an exponential decrease in the running time, which is because GPUs has an exponentially larger thread pool as compared to CPUs. It can be seen from Fig. 4 (left) that, for a smaller number of bodies, the parallel running time gradually decreases with the increase in the number of threads per block due to the communication overhead over the peripheral component

Table 1. Performance of the OpenMP parallelization with force computation and mass distribution of the Barnes-Hut algorithm on various galactic datasets [1].

Dataset	Size	Serial time (s)	Parallel time per thread count (s)					
			1	2	4	8	16	32
asteroids1000	1,000	0.023097	0.020348	0.021905	0.030464	0.063325	0.121116	0.221256
cluster2582	2,582	0.004927	0.005837	0.005042	0.011231	0.008328	0.011733	0.014243
collision1	2,000	0.004917	0.004829	0.004447	0.006030	0.005751	0.009468	0.012608
collision2	2,002	0.006227	0.006008	0.006098	0.006309	0.006821	0.009951	0.013182
galaxy1	802	0.015414	0.015616	0.015217	0.020928	0.045315	0.072090	0.110689
galaxy2	652	0.012274	0.012615	0.014664	0.023931	0.028826	0.040485	0.072064
galaxy3	2,001	0.091639	0.087738	0.084466	0.141264	0.264529	0.488200	0.975077
galaxy4	502	0.012875	0.013325	0.010431	0.012065	0.027304	0.037397	0.051786
galaxy10k	10,001	0.032405	0.032411	0.031647	0.027545	0.050811	0.075314	0.171779
galaxy20k	20,001	2.325312	2.357691	1.422882	0.557520	3.697054	7.312913	17.061886
galaxy30k	30,002	13.663441	14.492622	8.259973	3.813991	22.588013	48.301931	90.741782
galaxyform2500	2,500	0.007052	0.005922	0.006162	0.006707	0.008641	0.011501	0.016563
galaxymerge1	2,000	0.004920	0.005160	0.004812	0.006784	0.006742	0.008701	0.018789
galaxymerge2	4,000	0.011205	0.010364	0.003930	0.012193	0.011976	0.018860	0.024891
galaxymerge3	2,901	0.009433	0.009095	0.009045	0.015460	0.011692	0.012852	0.019202
planets	5	0.000070	0.000160	0.000526	0.002250	0.002246	0.002997	0.004918
saturnrings	11,987	0.024471	0.024749	0.020095	0.025863	0.032043	0.038763	0.064468
spiralgalaxy	843	0.017879	0.017627	0.023605	0.024740	0.052584	0.091534	0.166260

interconnect lanes. For $4,000$ bodies (see Fig. 4 (center)), the speedup of parallel implementation was observed to be 100 and for $30,002$ bodies (see Fig. 4 (right)), the speedup was approximately 250. These results establish the potential of CUDA in parallel programming and multi-processing support over traditional CPUs.

Table 1 presents the results of the OpenMP Barnes-Hut implementation with both force parallelization and mass distribution. The results show that for a large number of bodies (e.g., *galaxy30k* with $30,002$ bodies), the method proved to be superior as compared to Algorithms 5 and 6. However, for a smaller number of bodies (e.g., *planets* with 5 bodies), the method had a massive bottleneck of communication overheads and thread spawn initialization.

The effect of the fixed accuracy parameter used for approximation in the Barnes-Hut algorithm on running time is shown in Fig. 7. The value of θ determines the depth of traversal of the quad-tree. Smaller values of θ mean deeper traversals, implying larger running times while larger values of θ imply lower accuracy and lower running time. It was observed that the number of computations increased as $\theta \approx 0.0$. We experimentally found that with $\theta = 0.4$, an efficient trade-off between the running time and accuracy can be achieved (all results presented above use $\theta = 0.4$).

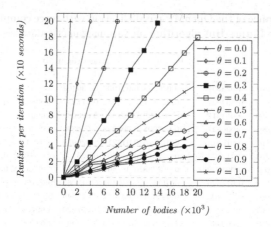

Number of bodies (×10³)

Fig. 7. Effect of the fixed accuracy parameter on the Barnes-Hut algorithm.

6   Conclusions

In this paper, we analyzed two prominent approaches to solve the gravitational N-body problem: the naive All-Pairs approach and an adaptive quad-tree based Barnes-Hut approach. We presented data and task parallel implementations of the algorithms considered, using OpenMP and CUDA. We evaluated the challenges in the parallelization of the Barnes-Hut algorithm and two significant parallel considerations. It was observed that until a certain level of parallelization the running time decreases and then increases afterward. The performance analysis of these methods establishes the potential of parallel programming in big data applications. We achieved a maximum speedup of approximately 3.6 with OpenMP implementations and about 250 with CUDA implementation. The OpenMP implementations experienced a massive bottleneck of the number of cores on the testing machine. Also, we experimentally determined the optimal value of the fixed accuracy parameter for an efficient trade-off between the running time and accuracy.

In the future, we aim at extending the Barnes-Hut implementation and FMM approach to CUDA and message-passing clusters over the LAN, each node parallelized using OpenMP; and also evaluate their performance in terms of speedup and running time. We also aim at considering even larger samples of bodies to evaluate our proposed parallel implementations effectively.

References

1. COS 126 Programming Assignment: N-Body Simulation, September 2004. http://www.cs.princeton.edu/courses/archive/fall04/cos126/assignments/nbody.html. Accessed 07 May 2018
2. CUDA C Programming Guide, October 2018. https://docs.nvidia.com/cuda/cuda-c-programming-guide/index.html#cuda-general-purpose-parallel-computing-architecture. Accessed 07 May 2018

3. n-body problem - Wikipedia, October 2018. https://en.wikipedia.org/wiki/N-body_problem. Accessed 7 May 2018
4. The Barnes-Hut Algorithm: 15–418 Spring 2013, October 2018. http://15418.courses.cs.cmu.edu/spring2013/article/18. Accessed 7 May 2018
5. The Barnes-Hut Galaxy Simulator, October 2018. http://beltoforion.de/article.php?a=barnes-hut-galaxy-simulator. Accessed 7 May 2018
6. World's Largest Supercomputer Simulation Explains Growth of Galaxies, October 2018. https://phys.org/news/2005-06-world-largest-supercomputer-simulation-growth.html. Accessed 7 May 2018
7. Appel, A.W.: An efficient program for many-body simulation. SIAM J. Sci. Stat. Comput. **6**(1), 85–103 (1985)
8. Barnes, J., Hut, P.: A hierarchical O (N log N) force-calculation algorithm. Nature **324**(6096), 446 (1986)
9. Barney, B.: OpenMP, Jun 2018. https://computing.llnl.gov/tutorials/openMP. Accessed 07 May 2018
10. Bhatt, S., Liu, P., Fernandez, V., Zabusky, N.: Tree codes for vortex dynamics: application of a programming framework. In: International Parallel Processing Symposium. Citeseer (1995)
11. Blelloch, G., Narlikar, G.: A practical comparison of TV-body algorithms. In: Parallel Algorithms: Third DIMACS Implementation Challenge, 17–19 October 1994, vol. 30, p. 81 (1997)
12. Board Jr., J.A., Hakura, Z.S., Elliott, W.D., Rankin, W.T.: Scalable variants of multipole-accelerated algorithms for molecular dynamics applications. Technical report. Citeseer (1994)
13. Burtscher, M., Pingali, K.: An efficient CUDA implementation of the tree-based barnes hut N-body algorithm. In: GPU computing Gems Emerald edition, pp. 75–92. Elsevier (2011)
14. Carugati, N.J.: The parallelization and optimization of the N-body problem using OpenMP and OpenMPI (2016)
15. Chanduka, B., Gangavarapu, T., Jaidhar, C.D.: A single program multiple data algorithm for feature selection. In: Abraham, A., Cherukuri, A.K., Melin, P., Gandhi, N. (eds.) ISDA 2018 2018. AISC, vol. 940, pp. 662–672. Springer, Cham (2020). https://doi.org/10.1007/978-3-030-16657-1_62
16. Dagum, L., Menon, R.: OpenMP: an industry standard api for shared-memory programming. IEEE Comput. Sci. Eng. **5**(1), 46–55 (1998)
17. Damgov, V., Gotchev, D., Spedicato, E., Del Popolo, A.: N-body gravitational interactions: a general view and some heuristic problems. arXiv preprint astro-ph/0208373 (2002)
18. Del Sozzo, E., Di Tucci, L., Santambrogio, M.D.: A highly scalable and efficient parallel design of N-body simulation on FPGA. In: 2017 IEEE International Parallel and Distributed Processing Symposium Workshops (IPDPSW), pp. 241–246. IEEE (2017)
19. Fernandez, V.M., Zabusky, N.J., Liu, P., Bhatt, S., Gerasoulis, A.: Filament surgery and temporal grid adaptivity extensions to a parallel tree code for simulation and diagnosis in 3D vortex dynamics. In: ESAIM: Proceedings. vol. 1, pp. 197–211. EDP Sciences (1996)
20. Garland, M., et al.: Parallel computing experiences with CUDA. IEEE Micro **4**, 13–27 (2008)
21. Greengard, L., Rokhlin, V.: A fast algorithm for particle simulations. J. comput. Phys. **73**(2), 325–348 (1987)

22. Greengard, L., Rokhlin, V.: A new version of the fast multipole method for the laplace equation in three dimensions. Acta Numer. **6**, 229–269 (1997)
23. Heggie, D., Hut, P.: The gravitational million-body problem: a multidisciplinary approach to star cluster dynamics (2003)
24. Liu, P., Bhatt, S.N.: Experiences with parallel N-body simulation. IEEE Trans. Parallel Distrib. Syst. **11**(12), 1306–1323 (2000)
25. Mills, P.H., Nyland, L.S., Prins, J.F., Reif, J.H.: Prototyping N-body simulation in Proteus. In: Proceedings of the Sixth International Parallel Processing Symposium, pp. 476–482. IEEE (1992)
26. Nyland, L.S., Prins, J.F., Reif, J.H.: A data-parallel implementation of the adaptive fast multipole algorithm. In: Proceedings of the DAGS 1993 Symposium (1993)
27. Nylons, L.: Fast N-body simulation with CUDA (2007)
28. Pringle, G.J.: Numerical study of three-dimensional flow using fast parallel particle algorithms. Ph.D. thesis, Napier University of Edinburgh (1994)
29. Salmon, J.K.: Parallel hierarchical N-body methods. Ph.D. thesis, California Institute of Technology (1991)
30. Singh, J.P.: Parallel hierarchical N-body methods and their implications for multiprocessors (1993)
31. Springel, V., Yoshida, N., White, S.D.: GADGET: a code for collisionless and gasdynamical cosmological simulations. New Astron. **6**(2), 79–117 (2001)
32. Sundaram, S.: Fast algorithms for N-body simulation. Technical report, Cornell University (1993)
33. Swinehart, C.: The Barnes-Hut Algorithm, January 2011. http://arborjs.org/docs/barnes-hut. Accessed 07 May 2018]
34. Totoo, P., Loidl, H.W.: Parallel Haskell implementations of the N-body problem. Concurr. Comput.: Pract. Exp. **26**(4), 987–1019 (2014)
35. Warren, M.S., Becker, D.J., Goda, M.P., Salmon, J.K., Sterling, T.L.: Parallel supercomputing with commodity components. In: PDPTA, pp. 1372–1381 (1997)
36. Warren, M.S., Salmon, J.K.: A parallel hashed oct-tree N-body algorithm. In: Proceedings of the 1993 ACM/IEEE conference on Supercomputing, pp. 12–21. ACM (1993)
37. Xue, G.: An o(n) time hierarchical tree algorithm for computing force field in N-body simulations. Theor. Comput. Sci. **197**(1–2), 157–169 (1998)
38. Zhao, F., Johnsson, S.L.: The parallel multipole method on the connection machine. SIAM J. Sci. Stat. Comput. **12**(6), 1420–1437 (1991)

Minimizing the Energy of a Quad Rotor in Free Final Time Using Bocop Software

Lounis Abbes[1], Kahina Louadj[1,2($\boxtimes$)], Philippe Marthon[2], Abdelkrim Nemra[3], and Mohamed Aidene[1]

[1] Laboratoire de Conception et Conduites Systèmes de Production (L2CSP), Tizi-Ouzou, Algeria
lounis.bes85@yahoo.fr, aidene@mail.ummto.dz
[2] IRIT-ENSEEIHT, Toulouse, France
louadj_kahina@yahoo.fr, Philippe.marthon@enseeiht.fr
[3] Laboratoire Robotique et Productique, Ecole Militaire Polytechnique, Bordj El Bahri, Algiers, Algeria
karim_nemra@yahoo.fr

Abstract. An unmanned aerial vehicle (UAV) become increasingly present in military and commercial applications, the flight path efficiency and integration with current manned aircraft become important research topics to address in the coming years. In this paper, the optimal control problem for the quad-rotor to minimize energy is considered. For this, formulate this problem to an optimal control problem which minimizes energy of quad-rotor in free final time. The Solution for this, used a discretization method, and simulation results are given by Bocop software.

Keywords: Final time · Bocop · Optimal control

1 Introduction

An Unmanned Aerial Vehicle is an aircraft with no pilot on board [1–3]. UAVs can be remote controlled aircraft (e.g. flown by a pilot at a ground control station) or can fly autonomously based on pre-programmed flight plans or more complex dynamic automation systems. UAVs are currently used for a number of missions, including reconnaissance and attack roles. For the purposes of this article, and to distinguish UAVs from missiles, a UAV is defined as being capable of controlled, sustained level flight and powered by a jet or reciprocating engine. In addition, a cruise missile can be considered to be a UAV, but is treated separately on the basis that the vehicle is the weapon. The acronym UAV has been expanded in some cases to UAVS (Unmanned Aircraft Vehicle System). The FAA has adopted the acronym UAS (Unmanned Aircraft System) to reflect the fact that these complex systems include ground stations and other elements besides the actual air vehicles [6].

Some early UAVs are called drones because they are no more sophisticated than a simple radio controlled aircraft being controlled by a human pilot (sometimes called the operator) at all times. More sophisticated versions may have

© Springer Nature Switzerland AG 2019
S. Misra et al. (Eds.): ICCSA 2019, LNCS 11619, pp. 209–221, 2019.
https://doi.org/10.1007/978-3-030-24289-3_17

built-in control and/or guidance systems to perform low level human pilot duties such as speed and flight path stabilization, and simple prescripted navigation functions such as waypoint following.

From this perspective, most early UAVs are not autonomous at all. In fact, the field of air vehicle autonomy is a recently emerging field, whose economics is largely driven by the military to develop battle ready technology for the warfighter. Compared to the manufacturing of UAV flight hardware, the market for autonomy technology is fairly immature and undeveloped. Because of this, autonomy has been and may continue to be the bottleneck for future UAV developments, and the overall value and rate of expansion of the future UAV market could be largely driven by advances to be made in the field of autonomy.

Autonomy is commonly defined as the ability to make decisions without human intervention. To that end, the goal of autonomy is to teach machines to be "smart" and act more like humans. The keen observer may associate this with the development in the field of artificial intelligence made popular in the 1980s and 1990s such as expert systems, neural networks, machine learning, natural language processing, and vision. However, the mode of technological development in the field of autonomy has mostly followed a bottom-up approach, and recent advances have been largely driven by the practitioners in the field of control science, not computer science. Similarly, autonomy has been and probably will continue to be considered an extension of the controls field. In the foreseeable future, however, the two fields will merge to a much greater degree, and practitioners and researchers from both disciplines will work together to spawn rapid technological development in the area [4, 5].

To some extent, the ultimate goal in the development of autonomy technology is to replace the human pilot. It remains to be seen whether future developments of autonomy technology, the perception of the technology, and most importantly, the political climate surrounding the use of such technology, will limit the development and utility of autonomy for UAV applications [26, 29].

In our case, We choose quad-rotors drone which is handy, allow vertical take-off and landing, as well as flying in hard to - Reach areas. The disadvantages are its mass and the consumption of energy caused by motors. The drone can perform three flight modes; hover, vertical flight and translation flight. In our work, we are interested in a translation flight that corresponds to the navigation on a horizontal plane, it is ensured by basing itself on pitch and roll tilting movements [25].

In the present study, our aim is to minimize energy for quadrotor in free final time. To solve this problem, let's build an optimal control problem in free final time. Using Bocop Software [28], we solve this problem with discretization method as Midpoint method in small step to insure convergence [24, 27]. The work presented in this paper is organized as follows: In Sect. 1, a dynamic model of the quad-rotor is considered. In Sect. 2, discussion, simulation results given by Bocop software and conclusion are provided in Sect. 3.

2   Quad-Rotor Mathematical Model

A quad-rotor is an aerial vehicle which rotates by producing differentials in thrust between it's for motors. The following section presents the mathematical model of the quad-rotor.

The motion of the quad-rotor can be divided into two subsystems, rotational subsystem (roll, pitch and yaw) and translation subsystem (altitude and x and y position).

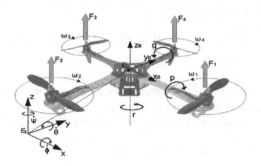

Fig. 1. Quad-rotor

2.1   Rotational Equations of Motion

The rotational equations of motion are derived in the body frame using the Newton-Euler method with the following general formalism,

$$J\dot{w} + w \times Jw \times M_G = M_B \tag{1}$$

where

- J: Quad-rotor's diagonal inertia Matrix.
- w: Angular body rates.
- M_B: Gyroscopic moments due to rotor's inertia.
- M_G: Moments acting on the quad-rotor in the body frame.
- $J\dot{w}$ and $w \times Jw$ represent the rate of change of angular momentum in the body frame.
- M_G: represent the gyroscopic moments due to the rotor's inertia J_r. The Gyroscopic moments are defined to be $w \times \begin{bmatrix} 0 & 0 & J_r w_r \end{bmatrix}^T$, thus the rotational equation of the quad-rotor's motion can be written as

$$J\dot{w} + w \times Jw + w \times \begin{bmatrix} 0 & 0 & J_r w_r \end{bmatrix}^T = M_B \tag{2}$$

where
- J_r: rotor's inertia.
- Ω : rotor's relative speed $\Omega_r = -w_1 + w_2 - w_3 + w_4$.

The inertia matrix for the quad-rotor is a diagonal matrix, the off-diagonal elements, which are the product of inertia, are zero due to the symmetry of the quad-rotor:

$$J = \begin{bmatrix} I_x & 0 & 0 \\ 0 & I_y & 0 \\ 0 & 0 & I_z \end{bmatrix} \tag{3}$$

where I_x, I_y and I_z are the area moments of inertia about the principle axes in the body frame.

Equations (4), (5) show the aerodynamique force F_i and moment M_i produced by the ith rotor $i = \overline{1,4}$

$$F_i = K_f w_i^2$$
$$M_i = K_m w_i^2 \tag{4}$$

where K_f and K_M are the aerodynamic force and moment constants respectively and w_i is the angular velocity of the rotor i.

Thus, the total moment about the $x-$ axis can be expressed as

$$\begin{aligned} M_x &= -F_2 l + F_4 l \\ &= -(K_f w_2^2) l + (K_f w_4^2) l \\ &= l K_f (-w_2^2 + w_4^2) \end{aligned} \tag{5}$$

the moment about $y-$ axis

$$\begin{aligned} M_y &= -F_1 l - F_3 l \\ &= (K_f w_1^2) l - (K_f w_3^2) l \\ &= l K_f (-w_1^2 - w_3^2) \end{aligned} \tag{6}$$

the moment about $z-$axis

$$\begin{aligned} M_z &= M_1 - M_2 + M_3 - M_4 \\ &= (K_m w_1^2) - (K_m w_2^2) + (K_m w_3^2) - (K_m w_4^2) \\ &= K_m (-w_1^2 - w_2^2 + w_3^2 - w_4^2) \end{aligned} \tag{7}$$

Combining Eqs. (5), (6) and (7) in vector form, we get,

$$M_B = \begin{bmatrix} l K_f (-w_2^2 + w_4^2) \\ l K_f (w_1^2 - w_4^2) \\ K_m (w_1^2 - w_2^2 + w_3^2 - w_4^2) \end{bmatrix} \tag{8}$$

where l is the moment arm, which is the distance between them axis of rotation each rotor to the engine for the body reference frame which should coincide with the center of the quad-rotor.

3   Translation Equations of Motion

The translation equations of the equations of the quad-rotor are based on Newton's second law and they are derived in the earth inertial frame

$$m\ddot{r} = \begin{bmatrix} 0 \\ 0 \\ mg \end{bmatrix} + RF_B \tag{9}$$

- $r = [x, y, z]^T$: Quad-rotor's distance from the inertial frame.
- m: Quad-rotor's mass.
- g: gravitationnal acceleration $g = 9,81m/s^2$.
- F_B: non gravitational forces acting on the quad-rotor in the body frame

$$F_B = \begin{bmatrix} 0 \\ 0 \\ K_f(w_1^2 + w_2^2 + w_3^2 + w_4^2) \end{bmatrix} \tag{10}$$

The first two rows of the force vector are zeros as there is no forces in the X and Y directions, the last row is the thrust forces produced by the propellers.

The drag forces F_a can be given as:

$$F_a = K_t\dot{r} \tag{11}$$

where K_t is a matrix called the aerodynamic translation coefficient matrix and $\dot{r}$ is the time derivative of the position vector r.

$$m\ddot{r} = \begin{bmatrix} 0 \\ 0 \\ mg \end{bmatrix} + RF_B - F_a \tag{12}$$

And Drag moment is defined as follows:

$$M_a = K_r\dot{\eta} \tag{13}$$

where K_r is a constant matrix called the aerodynamic rotation coefficient matrix and $\dot{\eta}$ is the Euler rates.

$$J\dot{w} + w \times Jw + w \times \begin{bmatrix} 0 & 0 & J_rw_r \end{bmatrix}^T = M_B - M_a \tag{14}$$

Let be defined the state vector of the quad-rotor as

$$X = [x_1, x_2, x_3, x_4, x_5, x_6, x_7, x_9, x_{10}, x_{11}, x_{12}]^T \tag{15}$$

which is mapped to the degrees of freedom of the quad-rotor in the following manner.

$$X = [\phi, \dot{\phi}, \theta; \dot{\theta}, \psi, \dot{\psi}, x, \dot{x}, y, \dot{y}, z, \dot{z}]^T \tag{16}$$

The state vector defines the position of the quad-rotor in space and its angular and linear velocities.

3.1   Control Input Vector u

A control input vector u, considering of four inputs, is defined as:

$$u = \begin{bmatrix} u_1 \ u_2 \ u_3 \ u_4 \end{bmatrix} \tag{17}$$

$$u_1 = K_f(w_1^2 + w_2^2 + w_3^2 + w_4^2) \tag{18}$$

$$u_2 = K_f(w_1^2 + w_4^2) \tag{19}$$

$$u_3 = K_f(w_1^2 - w_3^2) \tag{20}$$

$$u_4 = K_m(w_1^2 - w_2^2 + w_3^2 - w_4^2) \tag{21}$$

$$\begin{bmatrix} u_1 \\ u_2 \\ u_3 \\ u_4 \end{bmatrix} = \begin{bmatrix} K_f & K_f & K_f & K_f \\ 0 & -K_f & 0 & K_f \\ K_f & 0 & -K_f & 0 \\ K_m & -K_m & K_m & -K_m \end{bmatrix} \begin{bmatrix} w_1^2 \\ w_2^2 \\ w_3^2 \\ w_4^2 \end{bmatrix} \tag{22}$$

where:

- u_1: lift force.
- u_2, u_3, u_4: aerodynamical moments developed by the system.

Substituting (16)–(19) in Eq. (8), the equation of the total moments acting on the quad-rotor becomes:

$$M_B = \begin{bmatrix} lu_2 \\ lu_3 \\ u_4 \end{bmatrix} \tag{23}$$

Substituting (21) into the rotational equation of motion (4), can be derived,

$$\begin{bmatrix} I_x & 0 & 0 \\ 0 & I_y & 0 \\ 0 & 0 & I_z \end{bmatrix} \begin{bmatrix} \ddot{\varphi} \\ \ddot{\theta} \\ \ddot{\psi} \end{bmatrix} + \begin{bmatrix} \dot{\varphi} \\ \dot{\theta} \\ \dot{\psi} \end{bmatrix} \times \begin{bmatrix} I_x & 0 & 0 \\ 0 & I_y & 0 \\ 0 & 0 & I_z \end{bmatrix}$$
$$\begin{bmatrix} \dot{\varphi} \\ \dot{\theta} \\ \dot{\psi} \end{bmatrix} + \begin{bmatrix} \dot{\varphi} \\ \dot{\theta} \\ \dot{\psi} \end{bmatrix} \times \begin{bmatrix} 0 \\ 0 \\ J_r w_r \end{bmatrix} = \begin{bmatrix} lu_2 \\ lu_3 \\ u_4 \end{bmatrix} \tag{24}$$

Expanding that, leads to:

$$\begin{bmatrix} I_x\ddot{\varphi} \\ I_y\ddot{\theta} \\ I_y\ddot{\psi} \end{bmatrix} \begin{bmatrix} \dot{\theta}I_z\dot{\psi} - \dot{\psi}I_y\dot{\theta} \\ \dot{\psi}I_x\dot{\varphi} - \dot{\varphi}I_z\dot{\psi} \\ \dot{\theta}I_y\dot{\theta} - \dot{\theta}I_x\dot{\varphi} \end{bmatrix} + \begin{bmatrix} \dot{\theta}J_r w_r \\ -\dot{\varphi}J_r w_r \\ 0 \end{bmatrix} = \begin{bmatrix} lu_2 \\ lu_3 \\ u_4 \end{bmatrix} \tag{25}$$

Rewriting the last equation to have the angular acceleration in terms of the other variables:

$$\ddot{\varphi} = \frac{l}{I_x}u_2 - \frac{J_r}{I_x}\dot{\theta}w_r + \frac{I_y}{I_z}\dot{\psi}\dot{\theta} - \frac{I_z}{I_x}\dot{\theta}\dot{\psi} \tag{26}$$

$$\ddot{\theta} = \frac{l}{I_y}u_3 - \frac{J_r}{I_y}\dot{\varphi}w_r + \frac{I_z}{I_y}\dot{\varphi}\dot{\psi} - \frac{I_x}{I_y}\dot{\psi}\dot{\varphi} \tag{27}$$

$$\ddot{\psi} = \frac{1}{I_z}u_4 + \frac{I_x}{I_z}\dot{\theta}\dot{\psi} - \frac{I_y}{I_z}\dot{\varphi}\dot{\theta} \tag{28}$$

to simplify, define

$$a_1 = \frac{I_y - I_z}{I_x}, a_2 = \frac{J_r}{I_x}, a_3 = \frac{I_z - I_x}{I_y}, a_4 = \frac{J_r}{I_y},$$

$$a_5 = \frac{I_x - I_y}{I_z}, b_1 = \frac{l}{I_x}, b_2 = \frac{l}{I_y}, b_3 = \frac{1}{I_x}$$

Using the above notation of $a_1 \rightarrow a_5$ and $b_1 \rightarrow b_3$, Eqs. (24)–(26) can then be rewritten in a simpler form in terms of the system states

$$\ddot{\varphi} = b_1 u_2 - a_2 x_4 w_r + a_1 x_4 x_6 \tag{29}$$

$$\ddot{\theta} = b_2 u_3 + a_4 x_2 w_r + a_3 x_2 x_6 \tag{30}$$

$$\ddot{\psi} = b_3 u_4 + a_5 x_2 x_4 \tag{31}$$

Substituting equation (16)–(19) in Eq. 10, the equation of the total moments acting on the quad-rotor becomes:

$$F_B = \begin{bmatrix} 0 \\ 0 \\ -u_1 \end{bmatrix} \tag{32}$$

Embedding that into the translational equation of motion (9) and expanding the term, we get

$$m\begin{bmatrix} \ddot{x} \\ \ddot{y} \\ \ddot{z} \end{bmatrix} = \begin{bmatrix} 0 \\ 0 \\ mg \end{bmatrix}$$
$$+ \begin{bmatrix} c\psi c\theta & c\psi s\varphi s\theta & s\theta s\psi + c\varphi c\psi s\theta \\ c\theta s\psi & c\theta c\psi + s\varphi s\psi s\theta & c\varphi s\psi s\theta - c\psi s\theta \\ -s\theta & c\theta s\varphi & c\varphi c\theta \end{bmatrix}\begin{bmatrix} 0 \\ 0 \\ -u_1 \end{bmatrix} \tag{33}$$

$$m\begin{bmatrix} \ddot{x} \\ \ddot{y} \\ \ddot{z} \end{bmatrix} = \begin{bmatrix} 0 \\ 0 \\ mg \end{bmatrix}$$
$$+ \begin{bmatrix} (c\varphi s\psi + c\varphi c\psi s\theta)(-u_1) \; (c\theta s\psi s\theta - c\psi s\varphi)(-u_1) \\ -(c\varphi c\theta)(-u_1) \end{bmatrix} \tag{34}$$

Rewriting Eq. (32) to have acceleration in term of the other variables, we get

$$\ddot{x} = \frac{-u_1}{m}(sin\varphi sin\psi + cos\varphi cos\psi sin\theta) \tag{35}$$

$$\ddot{y} = \frac{-u_1}{m}(cos\varphi sin\psi sin\theta - cos\psi sin\varphi) \tag{36}$$

$$\ddot{z} = g - \frac{-u_1}{m}(cos\varphi cos\theta) \tag{37}$$

Rewriting in terms of the state variable X

$$\ddot{x} = \frac{-u_1}{m}(sinx_1 sinx_5 + cosx_1 cosx_5 sinx_3) \tag{38}$$

$$\ddot{y} = \frac{-u_1}{m}(cosx_1 sinx_5 sinx_3 - cosx_5 sinx_1) \tag{39}$$

$$\ddot{z} = g - \frac{-u_1}{m}(cosx_1 cosx_3) \tag{40}$$

Using the equation of the rational angular acceleration. Equations (27)–(29), and those of translation, Eqs. (35)–(37), the mathematical model of the quad-rotor can be written in a state space representation as follows

$$\begin{cases}
\dot{x}_1 = \dot{\varphi} = x_2, \\
\dot{x}_2 = \ddot{\varphi} = a_1 x_4 x_6 + a_2 x_4 \Omega + b_1 u_1, \\
\dot{x}_3 = \dot{\theta} = x_4, \\
\dot{x}_4 = \ddot{\theta} = a_3 x_2 x_6 + a_4 x_2 \Omega + b_2 u_2, \\
\dot{x}_5 = \dot{\psi} = x_6, \\
\dot{x}_6 = \ddot{\psi} = a_5 x_2 x_4 + b_3 u_3, \\
\dot{x}_7 = \dot{z} = x_8, \\
\dot{x}_8 = \ddot{z} = \frac{u_4}{m}(cosx_1 sinx_3 cosx_5 + sinx_1 sinx_5), \\
\dot{x}_9 = \dot{x} = x_{10}, \\
\dot{x}_{10} = \ddot{x} = \frac{u_4}{m}(cosx_1 sinx_3 sinx_5 - sinx_1 cosx_5), \\
\dot{x}_{11} = \dot{y} = x_{12}, \\
\dot{x}_{12} = \ddot{y} = \frac{cosx_1 cosx_3}{m} u_4 - g, \\
-\pi/2 \leq x_1 \leq \pi/2, -\pi/2 \leq x_3 \leq \pi/2, \\
-\pi \leq x_5 \leq \pi, x_i(0) = 0, i = \overline{1,12}, \\
-20 \leq u_j \leq 20, j = \overline{1,3}, 0 \leq u_4 \leq 20.
\end{cases} \tag{41}$$

where $g(m/s^2)$: gravity acceleration; $I_x, I_y, I_z(kg/m^2)$:roll, pitch and yaw inertia moments respectively, $J_r(kg/m^2)$: the rotor inertia; $m(kg)$: mass; $x, y, z(m)$: longitudinal, lateral and vertical motions respectively; $\phi, \theta, \psi(rad)$: roll, pitch and yaw angles, respectively; $w_k(rad/s)$: rotor angular velocity, where, k equal to 1, 2, 3 and 4; $d(m)$: the distance between the quad-rotor center of mass and the propeller rotation axis; $u_1, u_2, u_3(N.m)$: aerodynamical roll, pitch and yaw moments respectively; $u_4(N)$: lift force.

With $\Omega = w_1 - w_2 + w_3 - w_4$, $a_1 = \frac{I_y - I_z}{I_x}$, $a_2 = \frac{-J_r}{I_x}$, $a_3 = \frac{I_z - I_x}{I_y}$, $a_4 = \frac{J_r}{I_y}$, $a_5 = \frac{I_x - I_y}{I_z}$, $b_1 = \frac{d}{I_x}$, $b_2 = \frac{d}{I_y}$, $b_3 = \frac{d}{I_z}$.

Then, the criterion is formulate as follows:

$$J = \rho \int_0^{t_f} (u_1^2 + u_2^2 + u_3^2 + u_4^2)dt \qquad (42)$$

where $t_f(second)$: free final time.

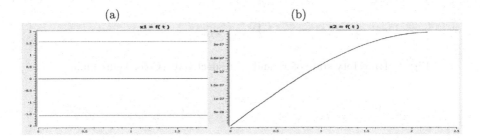

Fig. 2. Trajectory state of x_1 and x_2 respectively. (Color figure online)

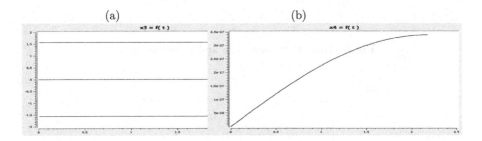

Fig. 3. Trajectory state of x_3 and x_4 respectively. (Color figure online)

4   Simulation and Discussion

$\omega = 340; d = 0.23;\ m = 0.6;\ I_x = I_y = 7.5e - 3,\ I_z = 1.3e - 2;\ J_r = 6e - 5;\ g = 9.8.$

The red line is the delimiter of x_1, x_3, x_5 respectively. And the blue line is the trajectories.

The results given by Bocop software are presented in Figs. 1, 2, 3, 4, 5, 6, 7 and 8. And Figs. 9 and 10, is the criterion for different values of ρ. When $10^{-5} < \rho < 1$ and, $10^{-2} < \rho < 1$, the minimum is not reached. Else, the optimal solution is ensured in 7 iterations with 1.41 s, and final time $t_f = 2.17214$ s (Fig. 11).

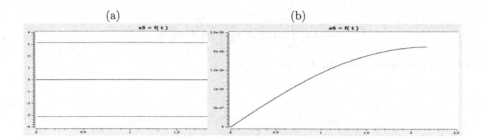

Fig. 4. Trajectory state of x_5 and x_6 respectively. (Color figure online)

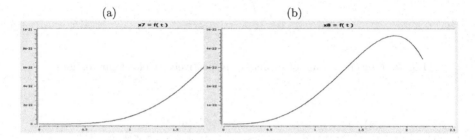

Fig. 5. Trajectory state of x_7 and x_8 respectively.

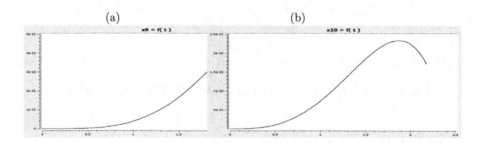

Fig. 6. Trajectory state of x_9 and x_{10} respectively.

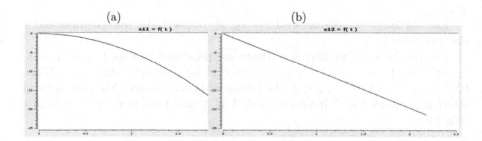

Fig. 7. Trajectory state of x_{11} and x_{12} respectively.

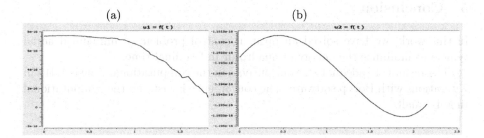

Fig. 8. Control u_1 and u_2 respectively.

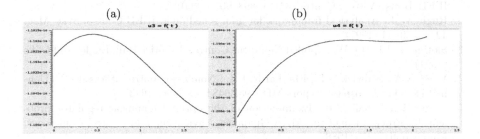

Fig. 9. Control of u_3 and u_4 respectively.

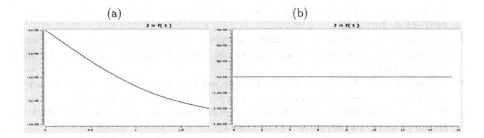

Fig. 10. The criterion J of $\rho = 0.0002$ and $\rho = 0.002$ respectively.

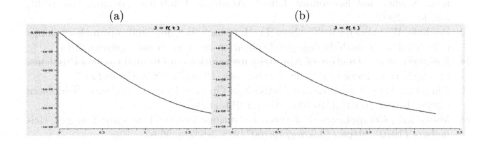

Fig. 11. The criterion J of $\rho = 0.0004$ and $\rho = 0.0005$ respectively.

5   Conclusion

In this work, we have solved an optimal control problem of unmanned aerial vehicle to minimize the energy of quadrotor in free final time.

The results are adequate for our purpose in the computational time is 1.41 s in 7 iterations with Bocop software. The convergence is fast and the computational time is small.

References

1. Shamma, J.F., Athans, M.: Analysis of gain scheduled control for nonlinear plants. IEEE Trans. Autom. Control **35**(8), 898–907 (1990)
2. Rugh, W.J.: Analytical framework for gain scheduling. IEEE Control Syst. Mag. **11**(1), 79–84 (1991)
3. Slotine, J.-J.E., Li, W.: Applied Nonlinear Control. Prentice Hall, Englewood Cliffs (1991)
4. Wise, K.A., Sedwick, J.L., Eberhardt, R.L.: Nonlinear control of missiles McDonnell Douglas Aerospace Report MDC 93B0484, October 1993
5. Ehrler, D., Vadali, S.R.: Examination of the optimal nonlinear regulator problem. In: Proceedings of the AIAA Guidance, Navigation, and Control Conference, Minneapolis, MN (1988)
6. Beard, R., et al.: Autonomous vehicle technologies for small fixed-wing UAVs. AIAA J. Aerosp. Comput. Inform. Commun. **2**, 92–108 (2005)
7. Guo, W., Gao, X., Xiao, Q.: Multiple UAV cooperative path planning based on dynamic Bayesian network. In: Control and Decision Conference (CCDC), pp. 2401–2405, July 2008
8. Mechirgui, M.: Commande Optimale minimisant la consommation d'énergie d'un Drone;Relai de communication, Maîtrise en Génie Eléctrique, Montréal, Le 15 Octobre 2014
9. Boudjellal, A.A., Boudjema, F.: Commande par Backstepping basée sur un Observateur Mode Glissant pour un Drone de type Quadri-rotor. ICEE (2013)
10. Hull, D.G.: Optimal Control Theory for Applications. Springer, New York (2003). https://doi.org/10.1007/978-1-4757-4180-3
11. Trelat, E.: Contrôle optimal: théorie et applications. Vuibert, collection Mathématiques Concrètes (2005)
12. Sethi, S.P., Thompson, G.L.: Optimal Control Theory: Applications to Management Science and Economics. Kluwer Academic Publishers, Boston, Dordrecht, London (2000)
13. Bouhafs, W., Abdellatif, N. , Jean, F., Harmand, J.: Commande optimale en temps minimal d'un procédé biologique d'épuration de l'eau. Arima, Janvier 2013
14. Zaslavski, A.J.: Structure of Approximate Solutions of Optimal Control Problems. Springer, Heidelberg (2013). https://doi.org/10.1007/978-3-319-01240-7
15. Akulenko, L.D.: Problems and Methods of Optimal Control. Springer, Heidelberg (1994). https://doi.org/10.1007/978-94-011-1194-2
16. Mufti, I.H.: Computational Methods in Optimal Control Problems. Springer, Heidelberg (1970). https://doi.org/10.1007/978-3-642-85960-1
17. Pytlak, R.: Numerical Methods for Optimal Control Problems With State Constraints. Spinger, Heidelberg (1999). https://doi.org/10.1007/BFb0097244

18. Athans, M., Falb, P.: Optimal Control: An Introduction to the Theory and Its Applications. Dover Publications Inc., Mineola (2007)
19. Demim, F., Louadj, K., Aidene, M., Nemra, A.: Solution of an optimal control problem with vector control using relaxation method. Autom. Control Syst. Eng. J. **16**(2) (2016). ISSN 1687–4811
20. Louadj, K., Aidene, M.: Optimization of a problem of optimal control with free initial state. Appl. Math. Sci. **4**(5), 201–216 (2010)
21. Kahina, L., Mohamed, A.: Adaptive method for solving optimal control problem with state and control variables. Math. Probl. Eng. **2012**, 15 p. (2012)
22. Kahina, L., Mohamed, A.: Direct method for resolution of optimal control problem with free initial condition. Int. J. Differ. Eqn. **2012**, 8 p. (2012). Article ID 173634
23. Kahina L., Mohamed A.: A problem of optimal control with free initial state. In: Proceedings du Congres National de Mathematiques Appliquees et Industrielles, SMAI 2011, Orleans du 23rd May to au 27th, pp 184–190 (2011)
24. Titouche, S., Spiteri, P., Messine, F., Mohamed, A.: Optimal control of a large thermic. J. Control Syst. **25**, 50–58 (2015)
25. Geisert, M., Mansard, N.: Trajectory generation for quadrotor based systems using numerical optimal control. In: IEEE International Conferenceon Robotics and Automation (ICRA) Stockholm, Sweden, 16–21 May 2016
26. Demim, F., Nemra, A., Louadj, K., Hamerlain, M.: Simultaneous localization, mapping, and path planning for unmanned vehicle using optimal control. Adv. Mech. Eng. **10**(1), 1–25 (2018)
27. Ortega, J.M., Rheinboldt, W.C.: Iterative Solution of Nonlinear Equations in Several Variables. Academic Press, New York (1970)
28. Bonnans, F., Martinon, P., Grélard, V.: Bocop - A collection of examples. [Research Report] RR-8053, INRIA (2012)
29. Louadj, K., Demim, F., Nemra, A., Marthon, P.: An optimal control problem of unmanned aerial vehicle. In: International An Conference on Control, Decision and Information Technologies (CoDIT 2018), 10 April 2018–13 April 2018, Thessaloniki (2018)

High Performance Computing and Networks

Modeling Energy Consumption
Based on Resource Utilization

Lucas Venezian Povoa[1,2]([✉]), Cesar Marcondes[2], and Hermes Senger[3]

[1] Federal Institute of São Paulo (IFSP), Caraguatatuba, Brazil
`venezian@ifsp.edu.br`
[2] Aeronautics Institute of Technology (ITA), São José dos Campos, Brazil
`hermes@ufscar.br`
[3] Federal University of São Carlos (UFSCar), São Carlos, Brazil
`marcondes@ita.br`

Abstract. Power management is an expensive and important issue for large computational infrastructures such as datacenters, large clusters, and computational grids. However, measuring energy consumption of scalable systems may be impractical due to both cost and complexity for deploying power metering devices on a large number of machines. In this paper, we propose the use of information about resource utilization (e.g. processor, memory, disk operations, and network traffic) as proxies for estimating power consumption. We employ machine learning techniques to estimate power consumption using such information which are provided by common operating systems. Experiments with linear regression, regression tree, and multilayer perceptron on data from different hardware resulted into a model with 99.94% of accuracy and 6.32 watts of error in the best case.

Keywords: Computer architecture · Energy consumption modeling

1 Introduction

Over the years, managing energy efficiency of Information and Communication Technologies (ICT) has increasingly emerged as one of the most critical environmental challenges. Due to ever increasing demand for computing resources, emissions footprint, increased energy price and tougher regulations, improving energy efficient became priority for datacenters, especially to the massive ones. This concern is pervasive in ICT, from development of more energy efficient devices to greener virtualization, resource consolidation, and, finally, definition of new architectures, services, and best practices.

In 2007, a Gartner's Report showed that ICT industry generated 2% of global CO2 [1] emissions. From which, 23% came from datacenters. A Greenpeace's report [2] stated that "datacenters are the factories of the 21st century in the Information Age", however, they can consume as much electricity as 180,000 homes.

© Springer Nature Switzerland AG 2019
S. Misra et al. (Eds.): ICCSA 2019, LNCS 11619, pp. 225–240, 2019.
https://doi.org/10.1007/978-3-030-24289-3_18

Constant reduction in computation resources prices, accompanied with popularization of on-line businesses, and wide spread of Internet and wireless networks, lead to the rapid growth of massive datacenters, consuming large amounts of energy. Indeed, nowadays, datacenters that execute Internet applications consume around 1.3% of the energy produced in the world [3]. It is expected in 2020 that this amount will rise to near 8% [4]. In such scenario, improving power efficiency on ICT installations and datacenters is mandatory. To overcome this challenge, several strategies have been proposed, such as resource consolidation [5–7], and improving resources utilization [8].

In general, better energy efficiency can be achieved by means of actuation strategies which need the continuous power consumption measurement. The deployment of power meters may be prohibitive in terms of cost in datacenters with many thousands of computers. Furthermore, external metering instruments require physical system access or invasive probing [9], which can be not available. On the other hand, software estimators for power consumption can be easily deployed at almost negligible cost.

An usual approach is to use internal performance counters provided by the hardware [10] and by the operating system to derive models that estimate power consumption [11–14]. Such models can be used by on-the-fly power saving strategies which need continuous power consumption estimation. Other possible applications include simulators that evaluate the power consumption of workloads based on performance and resource usage counters (e.g., register file usage, number of page faults, number of I/O operations per second).

In a previous work [15], we studied the correlation between a set of resource utilization counters provided by an operating system and the power consumption on a typical server machine. In this paper, we propose three novel models that use counter of both performance and resource utilization as proxies for power consumption, overtaking state-of-the-art accuracy. Besides that, differently from most of the related work, our models are not limited to predict power consumption of specific components, but of whole machine. We assume a good model should include all performance counters which significantly influence the power consumption. However, the excess of parameters and non-linear relations between these variables and power consumption can produce complex and inaccurate models. Having this on mind, we also investigate which operating system counters can be used to build robust and accurate models. Now, we further elaborate on correlation analysis and estimation of power consumption from resource utilization variables (i.e., counters) provided by operating systems. With this purpose, we apply nine models based on (*i*) Multiple Linear Regression (MLR), (*ii*) Regression Tree (RET), and (*iii*) Multilayer Perceptron (MLP), an Artificial Neural Network (ANN) which are experimentally evaluated on two different hardware[1].

---

[1] Models were implemented in R (using RSNNS) and source code are available under the GNU General Public License version 3 at https://github.com/lucasvenez/ecm along with the employed dataset.

Remainder of this paper is organized as follows. Section 2 describes the modeling approach, the workload, and the testbed used for experiments. Section 3 shows our variable analysis and selection approach. Section 4 describes proposed power consumption models based on the MLR, RET, and MLP methods. Section 5 presents the analysis of each proposed model. Section 6 describes some related work and compare some of them with our results. Finally, Sect. 7 points out our final remarks.

2   Modeling Energy Consumption from Resource Consumption Data

This paper aims to provide a characterization of the power consumption for a wide variety of machines. We propose new models which provide accurate estimations for the power consumption. Our models are based on resource utilization measurements commonly supported by the operating system used from commodity computers to datacenter servers.

2.1   Modelling Approach

In order to model power consumption for different computers, we employed a six-steps method.

1. *Data Collection:* comprehends a synthetic workload execution while an agent is used to collect data about resource utilization from the operating system [16,17]. The agent captures forty seven variables from the directory */proc.*
2. *Feature Engineering:* this step aims to calculate new variables from the raw ones in order to improve generalization and accuracy of models.
3. *Variables Selection:* in this step variables that are influential to power consumption are selected. We employed a correlation method called Maximal Information Coefficient (MIC) [18] that evaluates the correlation of a pair variables regardless of the distribution.
4. *Model Construction:* aims to fed models with resource utilization samples and reads of the actual energy consumption measured in the testbed.
5. *Model Analysis:* focus on evaluating models accuracy through a set of different metrics with a special attention to avoid overfitting.

The final step is called *Model Selection*, where the best model for power consumption is selected.

2.2   Data Collection

We built a synthetic workload instead of using real applications or benchmarks aiming to conceive energy consumption models which are suitable for any application, while avoiding collinearity problems which may compromise regression models [14,19].

Our workload was designed to avoid cross dependency among the variables fed to the model and produce as much as possible power consumption states for all system components such as memory, hard disk, processor, network interfaces and I/O operations [20]. It was implemented by using three open source tools: (*i*) *stress* [21] was used to produce utilization of resources such as processor, memory, hard disk and I/O operations; (*ii*) *cpulimit* [22] was utilized to generate random periods of idleness to produce several levels of processor utilization; and (*iii*) *iperf* [23] was employed to generate network traffic.

Workload was produced with the following characteristics. CPU utilization varied between 0% and 100% in several cycles, being increased in steps of 5% each. Each experiment was composed by $P_i = 2i - 1$ processes with $1 \leq i \leq N_{cpu}$, where N_{cpu} is the number of processors in the machine for the ith test. Memory utilization ranged from 512 MB to the physical memory size. For the ith experiment, one application process allocates $M_i = 256(i + 1)$ MB of memory, such that $1 \leq i \leq M_{size}/256 - 1$. Hard disk utilization varied from 1 GB to 64 GB, being produced by one process. For each experiment, the amount of disk space allocated is $C_i = 2i - 1 \mod 17$ GB, where i is the experiment number.

I/O workload was expressed by the number of processes that performed the message exchanges between main memory and hard disks. The amount of processors exchanging messages was given by $P_i = 10i \mod 10^2$, where i is the experiment number.

At first, only one parameter was selected to vary for each experiment, in order to capture its influence on power consumption. Then, parameters were varied to test every all-to-all combinations of several parameter levels, in order to capture their influence on power consumption as well as parameter interactions. For each combination of parameters and level, the workload is executed for two minutes. The overall experiment took about thirty hours to be carried out, producing about 51,000 entries for each dataset, each entry containing measures from 47 variables of resources utilization and the power consumption.

2.3   Testbed Used for Experiments

Testbed used for experiments is depicted in Fig. 1. Some nodes were instrumented to measure power consumption while running workloads. We employed two nodes with different architectures in the experiments, which have their hardware configuration summarized in Table 1.

Table 1. Hardware configurations with one 1 Gbps network interface running Ubuntu 11.10 kernel 3.0.0-12.

Hardware	A1	A2
Processor model	Intel Core i5-2400	AMD Opteron 246
Cores	4	2
Frequency	3.10 GHz	2.00 GHz
Memory	4GB SDRAN	8GB SDRAN
Disk	1 × 500 GB	4 × 240 GB

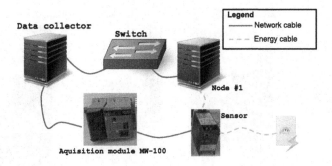

Fig. 1. Experiment environment with a node, an energy consumption meter, a module and a data storage.

In order to obtain precise power consumption measures, we used a power sensor Yokogawa model 2375A10 [24]. This device works connected to the power supply, and provides data to one data acquisition module model MW-100-E-1D [25]. The acquisition module probes and saves measures on power consumption in watts every 100 ms. Our agent collected data from the acquisition module via a network interface using the telnet protocol every second along with the resource utilization variables.

3 Variables Analysis and Selection

Designing accurate models depend upon a good selection of resource utilization counters with appropriate transformations that present significant influence on power consumption and do not produce noise.

3.1 Feature Engineering

We transformed each independent variable v_j with cumulative values using equation $v_{i,j} - v_{i-1,j}$, where i is the sample index of the jth variable. Because the number of processing cores of different architectures can vary, we summarized their values into a unique variable $ct = \sum_{j=1}^{m} c_{i,j}$, where m is the number of cores, i is the sample index, and $c_{i,j}$ is the data related to the ith sample of the jth core. This approach was also applied for multiple hard disks. These simple transformations help to improve accuracy and generalization, enabling a unique model to be applied for different hardware architectures.

3.2 Variable Selection

For the sake of clearness and understandability, a model for estimating energy consumption should be simple, i.e., to consider only a subset composed of the most influential variables on energy consumption. With this purpose we identified from the set of observed variables the subset with the highest correlation with the dependent one (i.e., the energy consumption).

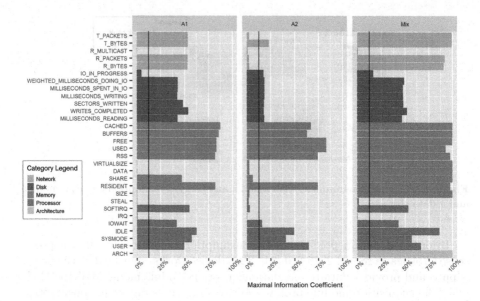

Fig. 2. Maximal information coefficient for the dataset of each architecture and for the mixture thereof.

In order to evaluate the correlation among variables, two main criteria should be considered. The *generality* refers to the capacity of identifying any relation type, not limited to specific types of correlation functions such as linear, exponential and periodic correlations. Later, the *equitability* is the ability to provide a unique index to express relation with the same noise level, even for functions of different types. With these two criteria on mind, we chose a method named MIC, which is part of a set of tools named Maximal Information-based Nonparametric Exploration (MINE) [18], to identify and select the most impacting variables for power consumption. MIC produces values between 0 and 1, where zero means absence of correlation between the pair of variables and 1 means full correlation.

For each architecture we generated a dataset containing the variables previously described. A third dataset (Mix) containing merged data from the two previous datasets plus one variable that describes whether the sample is related to the architecture A1 (value -1) or architecture A2 (value 1). Figure 2 shows results of the MIC between each independent variable, i.e., operating system's variables, and the dependent variable. In the chart the vertical black line represents the threshold of 10%, which was applied with the purpose of finding a reduced set of the most impacting coefficients and produce a model with good understandability.

3.3   Dependent Variable Analysis

Dependent variable distribution defines the method that can be used for modeling its behavior. The Kolmogorov-Smirnov test [26] resulted in *p-values* less

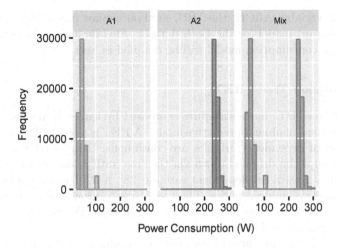

Fig. 3. Energy consumption histogram.

than $2.2e - 16$, which confirm that the dependent variable has no Gaussian distribution considering a significance level of 5%. This is evidenced in Fig. 3. Datasets A1, A2, and Mix present an average energy consumption (watts) of 46.08, 249.23, and 142.62, respectively. Their standard deviation are 15.26, 7.74, and 102.19. It is noteworthy that the architectures A1 and A2 have an stable energy consumption but in different ranges.

4 Modeling Power Consumption

In this section we describe several models using different techniques for estimating power consumption based on the most influential variables described in the previous Section.

4.1 Multiple Linear Regression

A MLR is a type of regression analysis that maps a set of input values X to a response value y, requiring that $y \sim N(\mu, \sigma^2)$. Because the datasets do not follow a normal distribution, we consider the Central Limit Theorem (CLT), which states that when the size of a given sample increases, the sampling distribution of its average or sum tends to a normal distribution [27]. CLT justifies modelling the energy consumption with the MLR defined as $\hat{y} = \alpha + \beta x + \epsilon$, where $\hat{y}$ is the estimated value of the energy consumption, α is the intersection point of the line of adjustment with the ordinate, β is the regression coefficients vector, x is the vector of independent variables, and ϵ is the average random error.

This method employs the least-squares method for estimating the coefficients vector β. Despite of the high correlation between the dependent variable and the independent variable ARCH, the MRL method cannot incorporate the former into the resultant model for the Both dataset. This limitation for generating a global energy consumption model will be detailed in Sect. 5.2.

4.2 Regression Tree - RET

A Decision Tree (DT) has a structure composed by leaves, branches and nodes aiming to define a nonlinear predictive model. A RET is a particular case of a DT, where values of dependent variables are continuous. Using a RET as predictor requires a sample be dropped down via the tree until a leaf, which returns the average of its values of the dependent variable [28]. A RET is created by splitting a node p into two children nodes. The tree stops to grow when the complexity index β_p of a node p is less or equals to a threshold α. For the experiments the threshold α was set as 1%.

RET models are easy interpreted, but our results show that important variables are excluded for the model, which evidence a limitation of this method for modeling energy consumption. The resulting model for the Mix dataset represents our worst model, which considers only one independent variable for defining itself. Some variation in RET's hyper-parameters was performed without improvements in final results described in Sect. 5.2.

4.3 Multilayer Perceptron

A MLP is an Artificial Neural Network model that maps a set of input values into a set of output values [29] after a learning process. It can be successfully applied in different areas, e.g., Biometrics [30], Thermal Engineering [31], Ocean Engineering [32], Climatology [33].

The MLP is composed by an input layer with n sensory units, h hidden layers with n_h neurons each, and an output layer with t neurons. A MLP has L layers, excluding the input layer, and its input values are propagated layer-by-layer. Its learning process can be supervised or unsupervised. Once we collected both the input and output variables, this research applied the supervised learning process. The supervised learning process was performed with the backpropagation algorithm with chunk update (also know as mini-batch), which has the following steps: *(i)* forward step, where a set of input values is provided to the sensory units, and its effect is propagated layer-by-layer; and *(ii)* backward step, where the weights are adjusted in accordance with an error-correction rule respecting the Mini-Batch Stochastic Gradient Descent method [34] after p (chunk size) executions of the forward step for different samples. Before starting the MLP training, all variable v_j had its values normalized, where $v_{ij} = (v_{ij} - min(v_j))/(max(v_j) - min(v_j))$.

The backward step starts by computing the error $e = \frac{1}{n}\sum_p^i(\hat{y} - y)^2$. Mean Squared Error was employed once it incorporates both the bias and the variance of a model [35]. After that, local gradient δ_j^L related to neuron j at output layer L was computed according to $\delta_j^L = e_j^L \times \varphi'(v^L)$. When one neuron j is located at a hidden layer $0 < l < L$, the local gradient δ_j^l related to neuron j at hidden layer l was computed by $\delta_j^l = \varphi'(v_j^l) \sum_{k=1}^{g}[\delta_k^{l+1} w_{kj}^{l+1}]$, where φ' is the derivative of activation function φ, and g is the number of neurons at layer $l+1$. New values for weight w_{ij}^l at layer l is defined according to $w_{ij}^l(n+1) = w_{ij}^l(n) - \eta/p \sum_m^n [\delta_j^l(m) y_i(m)]$, where n is the iteration number, p is the chunk size, and η is the learning-rate.

For setting the MLP's configuration for each architecture, we applied an empirical method consisting of *(i)* selecting a random and non-sequential subset of registers from our sample, 15% of all registers for train and 5% for test; *(ii)* starting the model weights with a random Gaussian distribution with values between 0 and 1; *(iii)* ranging the number of hidden layers from 1 until a descendant precision of the model; *(iv)* ranging the number of neurons at each layer from $\lceil \frac{v}{10} \rceil$ to $2v$, where v is the number of independent variables at the model; *(v)* ranging the learning-rate from 0.000 to 1.000 by 0.005; and *(vi)* calculating the model accuracy with test subset using the Coefficient of Determination R^2 metric.

In our study, the better configuration (i.e., with greatest R^2) for the MLP consists of 3 hidden layers, where each one has the number of nodes equals to double of the number of input variables, an output neuron representing the energy consumption value, a learning rate $\eta = 5$, and a chunk size $p = 50$. We employed the *tahn* function, as activation function φ, which yields larger partial derivatives with small changes in inputs [36].

5   Evaluating the Proposed Models

In this section, the power consumption models proposed are evaluated. For this purpose, different metrics and the 10-fold cross-validation (CV) method were employed.

5.1   Employed Accuracy Metrics

Four different classes of metrics were applied to evluate the proposed models: scale-dependent, percentage error, relative error, and scale-free error metrics [37]. *Scale-dependent* metrics are simple to understand and calculate, but cannot be applied to compared models of series with different scales. *Percentage error* metrics are scale independent, overcoming the limitations of scale dependent metrics. However, such metrics return infinite or undefined values when zeroes exist within the series. *Relative error* metrics are also scale independent metrics but they are restricted to some statistic methods when errors are small. Finally, *scale-free error* metrics never provide infinite or undefined values, and they can be applied to compare different estimate methods either over a single or multiple series.

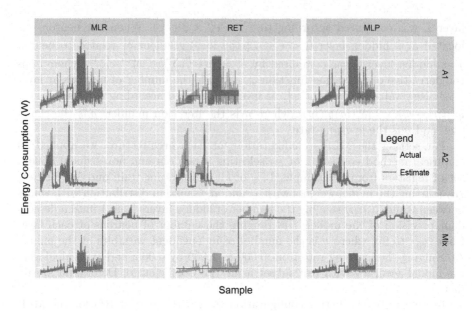

Fig. 4. Comparison between actual and estimated values.

For the sake of comparison to other models proposed in the literature, six metrics were used to evaluate the proposed models:

1. Squared Error (SE): is defined as $SE_i = (y_i - \hat{y}_i)^2$, where y_i is the ith observed value, and $\hat{y}_i$ is the ith estimate value.
2. Absolute Error (AE): defined as $AE_i = |y_i - \hat{y}_i|$. Although these two early metrics are scale-dependent, they are widely used in related literature (e.g., [15,38]).
3. Percentage Error (PE): is a metric given by the ratio between the difference and defined as $PE_i = (y_i - \hat{y}_i)/y_i$ [37]. In this metric, positive and negative values can cancel each other, leading the average to approach to zero.
4. Absolute Percentage Error (APE): like PE, this is also a percentage error metric, except by using the absolute value $APE_i = |(y_i - \hat{y})/y_i|$ [37].
5. Absolute Scaled Error (ASE): this is a scale-free error metric, which is frequently used to measure accuracy [39]. ASE avoids the common problems in conventional accuracy metrics described previously. It is defined as $ASE_i = |y_i - \hat{y}_i|(\frac{1}{(n-1)} \sum_{j=2}^{n} |y_j - y_{j-1}|)^{-1}$, where n is the sample size. All the above mentioned metrics (1–5) metrics provide values closer to zero for better models and far from zero for worse ones. The PE metric can provide either negative and positive values, while the remainder metrics result only in positive values.
6. Last employed metric is $R^2 = 1 - \sum_{i}^{n}(y_i - \hat{y}_i)^2(\sum_{i}^{n}(y_i - \bar{y})^2)^{-1}$, which shows how well the estimated values produced by a model fit the actual ones. Results lie between 0 and 1, where 0 means a model does not provide any explanation about the data, and 1 refers to a perfect adjust.

5.2   Models Accuracy

Accuracy of each proposed model is evaluated applying the 10-fold cross valida-tion method [40]. For each test, the estimated value for the power consumption is compared to the actual measured value. Table 2 presents the average and standard deviation for the six metrics. All models presented $R^2 > 91\%$. In par-ticular, MLR models have low average errors for all metrics considering A1 and A2 architectures. However, when MLR is applied to fit the mix of architectures into a unique model, the error increases significantly. A similar effect occurs with RET models, whose accuracy is even worse than MLR models for the mix of architectures.

MLP models presented the best accuracy from the experiments. However, MLR are simpler and less costly models whose accuracy approach the MLP's accuracy. It suggests non-linear relations with low significance between the inde-pendent variables and the dependent one. This evidence is supported by the average and standard deviation, which are close but not equal.

Noticeably, RET models present the worst accuracy from the three models. This can be explained as RET clusters data before estimating the power con-sumption. Indeed, power consumption cannot be explained for a small subset of dependent variables. However, all of the variables provide enough information for estimating power consumption, which hinders the clustering.

Figure 4 shows actual values compared to estimated ones generated with test set in each fold. Considering the results, we can conclude the MLP models pro-vide better estimations for power consumption, while MLR are simpler models which present similar performance in terms of accuracy. Furthermore, experi-mental results also show that RET models do not provide accurate estimations for power consumption when compared to MLP and MLR models, mainly when dealing with mixed architectures in the same estimator.

6   Related Work

A large number of papers has been published on modeling computers power consumption, including some surveys [41–43]. Several models have been pro-posed to estimate the energy consumption of processors [11,12,14,44]. Most of

Table 2. Average and the standard deviation of the Squared Error (SE), Absolute Error (AE), Percentage Error (PE), Absolute Percentage Error (APE), Absolute Scaled Error (ASE), and R^2 metrics obtained by the 10-fold cross-validation.

Arch.	Method	Average					Standard Deviation					R^2
		SE	AE	PE	APE	ASE	SE	AE	PE	APE	ASE	
A1	*MLR*	7.2878	1.6858	-0.4008%	3.8598%	1.2426	56.1252	2.1064	5.6912%	4.1994%	1.5532	96.8650%
	RET	14.8066	2.8970	-0.7901%	6.8144%	2.1249	54.7590	2.5281	8.9543%	5.8610%	1.8534	93.6364%
	MLP	6.1053	1.4895	0.0332%	3.3382%	1.1040	56.3053	1.9594	5.1738%	3.9961%	1.4517	97.3777%
A2	*MLR*	4.9962	1.3446	-0.0078%	0.5332%	2.2536	21.4396	1.7845	0.8705%	0.6880%	2.9887	91.6575%
	RET	4.8958	1.3094	-0.0067%	0.5164%	2.2015	20.3679	1.7828	0.8573%	0.6844%	2.9973	91.8226%
	MLP	3.7707	1.1169	-0.0115%	0.4424%	1.8725	18.0375	1.5873	0.7533%	0.6115%	2.6572	93.7082%
Mix	*MLR*	14.0595	2.6209	-0.4336%	3.7864%	2.5888	53.7892	2.6807	5.9828%	4.6517%	2.6474	99.8654%
	RET	150.7207	7.7339	-4.1102%	11.7914%	7.6287	533.8658	9.5315	19.3902%	15.9341%	9.4011	98.5565%
	MLP	6.3264	1.5471	-0.3946%	2.3506%	1.5232	48.7559	1.9796	4.3027%	3.6313%	1.9479	99.9394%

them consist of linear regression-based models which are fed with hardware performance counters. In [13], a model was proposed combining real total power measurement with hardware counters measurement to estimate per-component energy consumption. Our approach is different from those works because our goal is to estimate energy consumption for the entire machine, not limited to the processor.

Other papers address the modeling of the entire computer (e.g., from commodity computers to datacenter servers) proposing linear models composed by the summation of the energy consumed by its subcomponents [45–48]. For instance, Lewis et al. [45] propose an aggregated model which considers CPU, memory, electromechanical components, peripherals, and hard disk consumption. The models have coefficients for each component that are adjusted using linear regression. The energy consumed by virtual machines is also modeled in [47]. Other non linear models are also proposed for modeling the entire computer energy consumption [49,50]. Our work is different as our objective is not to model energy consumption of the computer as an explicit summation of the consumption of its subcomponents. Instead, our models are fed with system variables carefully selected (by their ability to explain the model) in order to estimate energy consumption with high accuracy. Also, our work propose and compare models based on three different techniques.

As mentioned, regression models are numerous for modeling energy consumption. For instance, Piga [38] defined a global center-level approach to power and performance optimization for Web Server Datacenters. Their model is based on linear and non-linear regression techniques, while using the k-means to identify non-linear correlation and the Correlation-based Feature Selection (CFS) for removing independents variables that do not provide significant explanation for the power consumption. Our focus, instead is to model individual computers based on observable operating system measures.

Da Costa et al. [20] modeled computer energy consumption based on performance counters provided by two tools (Linux `pidstat` and `collectd`). The paper describes the methodology for reducing from a set of 165 explanatory variables to a small number of variables which can explain the model with high accuracy. The model is intended to estimate energy consumption at process level. Our work is different regarding the variety of techniques used, and modeling the whole machine energy consumption.

Comparing our models with the best related work results, considering the absolute percentage error, our best MLP specific and global models presented an error rate of 2.35%, and 0.44%, correspondingly, while [20,38,45,51] have an error rate of ~4.0%, ~4.4%, ~10.0%, and ~6.0%, respectively.

By the best of our knowledge, our work provides the following novel contributions: (i) it proposes and compares three different models to estimate the power consumption for more than one hardware configuration; (ii) it employs the MIC method to analysis correlation between independent variables and the power consumption; (iii) the proposed models are fed with commodity system variables commonly provided by Linux, for better portability; (iv) it analysis accuracy using several metrics along with cross-validation in order to verify precision and overfitting issues; and (v) it overtakes accuracy of the state-of-the-art energy consumption models for datacenter nodes.

7 Conclusion

The management of power consumption of individual machines is a relevant feature in several environments, from small devices with limited resources to large datacenters with thousands of nodes. In this we present a characterization of energy consumption of entire machines based on resources utilization variables. Experiments were carried out using synthetic workloads in order to discover what resources and modeling methods present higher correlation to energy consumption. We show that it is possible to estimate energy consumption by sampling variables provided by common operating systems and employing MLR, RET, or MLP methods. We proposed nine models that provide accurate estimation on energy consumption with an accuracy of 99.9%, and average squared error of 6.32 watts with standard deviation of 48.76.

All models evaluated can be fully implemented in software, providing a cost-effective mechanism for estimating energy consumption. Such models can be deployed in a wide range of devices, from single small devices with limited resources to thousands of machines in a large datacenter at no additional cost and negligible overhead. Our proposal can be useful for several aims, e.g., to provide instant information on energy consumption in a per machine basis.

List of Abbreviations

ANN: Artificial Neural Network; CFS: Correlation-based Feature Selection; ICT: Information and Communication Technologies; MIC: Maximal Information Coefficient; MLP: Multilayer Perceptron; MLR: Multiple Linear Regression; RET: Regression Tree.

Acknowledgement. Authors thank CAPES and RNP for partially supporting this research. Hermes Senger thanks CNPq (Contract Number 305032/2015-1) and FAPESP (Process numbers 2018/00452-2, and 2018/22979-2) for their support.

References

1. Gartner: Gartner energy & utilities it summit 2007: an invitation only event. Technical report, Gartner, Dallas, EUA, September 2007
2. Cook, G.: How clear is your cloud? Catalysing an energy revolution. Technical report, Greenpeace International, Amsterdam, The Netherlands, April 2012. http://goo.gl/yd1FAS
3. Gao, P.X., Curtis, A.R., Wong, B., Keshav, S.: It's not easy being green. In: Proceedings of the ACM SIGCOMM 2012 Conference on Applications, Technologies, Architectures, and Protocols for Computer Communication, SIGCOMM 2012, pp. 211–222. ACM, New York (2012)

4. Koomey, J.: Growth in data center electricity use 2005 to 2010, vol. 1, p. 2010. Analytics Press, Oakland (2011)
5. Orgerie, A.-C., Assunção, M., Lefèvre, L.: Energy aware clouds. In: Cafaro, M., Aloisio, G. (eds.) Grids, Clouds and Virtualization. Computer Communications and Networks, pp. 143–166. Springer, Heidelberg (2011). https://doi.org/10.1007/978-0-85729-049-6_7
6. Lee, Y., Zomaya, A.: Energy efficient utilization of resources in cloud computing systems. J. Supercomput. **60**, 268–280 (2012)
7. Song, Y., Wang, H., Li, Y., Feng, B., Sun, Y.: Multi-tiered on-demand resource scheduling for VM-based data center. In: CCGRID 2009, pp. 148–155 (2009)
8. Barroso, L.A., Hölzle, U.: The case for energy-proportional computing. Computer **40**(12), 33–37 (2007)
9. Song, S., Su, C., Rountree, B., Cameron, K.W.: A simplified and accurate model of power-performance efficiency on emergent GPU architectures. In: 2013 IEEE 27th International Symposium On Parallel and Distributed Processing (IPDPS), pp. 673–686. IEEE (2013)
10. Naveh, A., Rajwan, D., Ananthakrishnan, A., Weissmann, E.: Power management architecture of the 2nd generation intel®core™microarchitecture, formerly code-named sandy bridge. In: Hot Chips (2011)
11. Contreras, G., Martonosi, M.: Power prediction for intel xscale® processors using performance monitoring unit events. In: Proceedings of the 2005 International Symposium on Low Power Electronics and Design, ISLPED 2005, pp. 221–226. IEEE (2005)
12. Joseph, R., Martonosi, M.: Run-time power estimation in high performance micro-processors. In: Proceedings of the 2001 International Symposium on Low Power Electronics and Design, pp. 135–140. ACM (2001)
13. Isci, C., Martonosi, M.: Runtime power monitoring in high-end processors: methodology and empirical data. In: Proceedings of the 36th Annual IEEE/ACM International Symposium on Microarchitecture, p. 93. IEEE Computer Society (2003)
14. Bertran, R., Gonzalez, M., Martorell, X., Navarro, N., Ayguade, E.: Decomposable and responsive power models for multicore processors using performance counters. In: Proceedings of the 24th ACM International Conference on Supercomputing, pp. 147–158. ACM (2010)
15. Povoa, L.V., Bignatto Jr, P.W., Monteiro, C.E., Mueller, D., Marcondes, C.A.C., Senger, H.: A model for estimating energy consumption based on resources utilization. In: IEEE Symposium on Computers and Communications (ISCC), pp. 1–6. IEEE Computer Society (2013)
16. Dusso, P.M.: A monitoring system for WattDB: an energy-proportional database cluster. Graduation thesis, Informatics Institute, Federal University of Rio Grande do Sul, Porto Alegre, Brazil, July 2012. http://goo.gl/8gheFW
17. Dusso, P.M.: Energyagent (2012). https://github.com/pmdusso/energyagent
18. Reshef, D.N., et al.: Detecting novel associations in large data sets. Science **334**(6062), 1518–1524 (2011)
19. Pazzani, M.J., Bay, S.D.: The independent sign bias: gaining insight from multiple linear regression. In: Proceedings of the Twenty-First Annual Meeting of the Cognitive Science Society, pp. 525–530 (1999)
20. Da Costa, G., Hlavacs, H.: Methodology of measurement for energy consumption of applications. In: 2010 11th IEEE/ACM International Conference on Grid Computing, pp. 290–297. IEEE (2010)
21. Waterland, A.: Stress (2014). http://people.seas.harvard.edu/texttildelowapw/stress/

22. Marletta, A.: cpulimit (2012). https://github.com/opsengine/cpulimit
23. NLANR/DAST: Iperf - The TCP/UDP Bandwidth Measurement Tool (2011). https://iperf.fr/
24. Yokogawa Electric Corporation: 0.5 Class Transducer for Power Application (2009). http://goo.gl/f43ZwV
25. Yokogawa Electric Corporation: Data Acquisition Unit MW100 (2013). http://goo.gl/7mcNV8
26. Marsaglia, G., Tsang, W.W., Wang, J.: Evaluating Kolmogorov's distribution. J. Stat. Softw. **8**(18), 1–4 (2003)
27. Rice, J.R.: Mathematical Statistics and Data Analysis, 3rd edn. Thomson Books/Cole, USA (2007)
28. Breiman, L., Friedman, J., Stone, C.J., Olshen, R.A.: Classification and Regression Trees. Chapman and Hall, New York (1984)
29. Haykin, S.: Neural Networks: A Comprehensive Foundation, 2nd edn. Prentice Hall, Upper Saddle River (1998)
30. Semwal, V.B., Raj, M., Nandi, G.: Biometric gait identification based on a multilayer perceptron. Robot. Auton. Syst. **65**, 65–75 (2015). https://doi.org/10.1016/j.robot.2014.11.010
31. De Lozzo, M., Klotz, P., Laurent, B.: Multilayer perceptron for the learning of spatio-temporal dynamics–application in thermal engineering. Eng. Appl. Artif. Intell. **26**(10), 2270–2286 (2013). https://doi.org/10.1016/j.engappai.2013.07.001
32. Altunkaynak, A.: Prediction of significant wave height using geno-multilayer perceptron. Ocean Eng. **58**, 144–153 (2013). https://doi.org/10.1016/j.oceaneng.2012.08.005
33. Velo, R., López, P., Maseda, F.: Wind speed estimation using multilayer perceptron. Energy Convers. Manag. **81**, 1–9 (2014). https://doi.org/10.1016/j.enconman.2014.02.017
34. Li, M., Zhang, T., Chen, Y., Smola, A.J.: Efficient mini-batch training for stochastic optimization. In: Proceedings of the 20th ACM SIGKDD International Conference on Knowledge Discovery and Data Mining, KDD 2014, pp. 661–670. ACM, New York (2014). https://doi.org/10.1145/2623330.2623612
35. Goodfellow, I., Bengio, Y., Courville, A.: Deep Learning. MIT Press, Cambridge (2016). http://www.deeplearningbook.org
36. Ng, W.W.Y., Zeng, G., Zhang, J., Yeung, D.S., Pedrycz, W.: Dual autoencoders features for imbalance classification problem. Pattern Recogn. **60**, 875–889 (2016). https://doi.org/10.1016/j.patcog.2016.06.013
37. Hyndman, R.J., Koehler, A.B.: Another look at measures of forecast accuracy. Int. J. Forecast. **22**, 679–688 (2006)
38. de Paula Rosa Piga, L.: Modeling, characterization, and optimization of web server power in data centers. Ph.D. thesis, Institute of Computing (IC), University of Campinas (UNICAMP), Campinas, Brazil, November 2013
39. Hyndman, R.J.: Another look at forecast accuracy metrics for intermittent demand. Foresight: Int. J. Appl. Forecast. **4**, 43–46 (2006)
40. Kohavi, R.: A study of cross-validation and bootstrap for accuracy estimation and model selection. In: Proceedings of the 14th International Joint Conference on Artificial Intelligence - Volume 2. IJCAI 1995, pp. 1137–1143. Morgan Kaufmann Publishers Inc., San Francisco (1995)
41. Reda, S., Nowroz, A.N.: Power modeling and characterization of computing devices: a survey. Found. Trends Electron. Design Autom. **6**(2), 121–216 (2012)

42. Orgerie, A.-C., de Assuncao, M.D., Lefevre, L.: A survey on techniques for improving the energy efficiency of large-scale distributed systems. ACM Comput. Surv. (CSUR) **46**(4), 47 (2014)

43. Dayarathna, M., Wen, Y., Fan, R.: Data center energy consumption modeling: a survey. IEEE Commun. Surv. Tutor. **18**(1), 732–794 (2016). https://doi.org/10.1109/COMST.2015.2481183

44. Bertran, R., Gonzalez, M., Martorell, X., Navarro, N., Ayguade, E.: A systematic methodology to generate decomposable and responsive power models for CMPs. IEEE Trans. Comput. **62**(7), 1289–1302 (2013)

45. Lewis, A.W., Ghosh, S., Tzeng, N.-F.: Run-time energy consumption estimation based on workload in server systems. HotPower **8**, 17–21 (2008)

46. Orgerie, A.-C., Lefèvre, L., Guérin-Lassous, I.: Energy-efficient bandwidth reservation for bulk data transfers in dedicated wired networks. J. Supercomput. **62**(3), 1139–1166 (2012)

47. Xiao, P., Hu, Z., Liu, D., Yan, G., Qu, X.: Virtual machine power measuring technique with bounded error in cloud environments. J. Netw. Comput. Appl. **36**(2), 818–828 (2013)

48. Lent, R.: A model for network server performance and power consumption. Sustain. Comput.: Inf. Syst. **3**(2), 80–93 (2013)

49. Fan, X., Weber, W.-D., Barroso, L.A.: Power provisioning for a warehouse-sized computer. In: ACM SIGARCH Computer Architecture News, pp. 13–23. ACM (2007)

50. Tang, C.-J., Dai, M.-R.: Dynamic computing resource adjustment for enhancing energy efficiency of cloud service data centers. In: 2011 IEEE/SICE International Symposium on System Integration (SII), pp. 1159–1164. IEEE (2011)

51. Dhiman, G., Mihic, K., Rosing, T.: A system for online power prediction in virtualized environments using Gaussian mixture models. In: 2010 47th ACM/IEEE Design Automation Conference (DAC), pp. 807–812 (2010). https://doi.org/10.1145/1837274.1837478

Silent Consensus: Probabilistic Packet Sampling for Lightweight Network Monitoring

Marcel Wallschläger[✉], Alexander Acker[✉], and Odej Kao[✉]

Complex and Distributed Systems, Technische Universität Berlin,
Ernst-Reuter-Platz 7, 10587 Berlin, Germany
{marcel.wallschlaeger,alexander.acker,odej.kao}@tu-berlin.de

Abstract. Artificial intelligence based methods for operations of IT-systems (AIOps) support the process of maintaining and operating large IT infrastructures on different levels, e.g. anomaly detection, root cause analysis, or initiation of self-stabilizing activities. The foundation for the deployment of such methods are extensive and reliable metric data on the current state of the overall system. In particular, network information expressing the core parameters latency, throughput, and bandwidth have crucial impact on modern IoT and edge computing environments. Collecting the data is a challenging problem, as the communication is limited to existent network protocols, and adding new features requires a major infrastructure adaptation. The usage of additional monitoring protocols increases the CPU/network overhead and should be avoided as well. Therefore, we propose a two step approach for measuring latency between adjacent hops without manipulating or generating any network traffic. Inspired by audio and image compression algorithms, we developed a probabilistic method named *silent consensus*, where we keep the precision within a desired interval while reducing the overhead significantly. This method identifies the same packets on a sequence of network hops solely by observing the regular traffic. A linear regression helps to predict packets that are likely to appear after a fixed temporal offset based on a constrained set of historic observations. A correction of the predicted entity increases the probability for consensus between the involved hops. An extensive experimental evaluation proves that the approach delivers the expected foundation for further analysis of the network streams and the overall system.

Keywords: Network monitoring · Packet sampling · Measurement · Traffic engineering

1 Introduction

The cloud and virtualization trend, the increasing number of IoT applications with dynamically linked devices, and the embedding in real-world (smart) environments drive the creation of large multi-layered systems. These are typically

© Springer Nature Switzerland AG 2019
S. Misra et al. (Eds.): ICCSA 2019, LNCS 11619, pp. 241–256, 2019.
https://doi.org/10.1007/978-3-030-24289-3_19

characterized by a high number of attached devices with varying processing power, by a heterogeneous network traffic ranging from several bytes generated by IoT devices up to 4K video streams, and finally by increasingly important QoS requirements. In particular, the latency matters in case of many modern applications such as industry automation or self-driving cars. A significant support for this optimization across highly interconnected systems is provided by the software defined networking trend, as the traffic priorities, sending rates, and other parameters of the involved devices can be influenced dynamically and during the run-time. The adaptation requires however a precise picture of the current topology and traffic situation. Therefore, network monitoring solutions gained a significant importance during the last decades and enter currently a new phase of development driven by the increasing network complexity, heterogeneous nature of IoT networks, and the rising traffic volume. In this paper we focus on a novel approach for lightweight network monitoring, which is targeting video streaming applications as one of the major driver for the high-volume network traffic.

The sum of all forms of IP video including streaming, video on demand (VoD), file sharing, gaming, and video conferencing are in the range of 80% to 90% of the internet traffic today and expected to keep this share until 2022 [6]. However, this type of applications is not uniform, as they differ regarding the QoS requirements. While streaming applications demand a high bandwidth and can use buffering to mask delays, gaming applications are designed for synchronous communication between many actors and thus rely on low latency. The next development steps such as virtual reality even increase the latency requirements.

The network providers are aware of the QoS challenges and already reacted by introducing additional intelligence into maintenance, for examples as NREs (network reliability engineers) or as artificial intelligence based methods for IT operations (AIOps). They rely on precise measurements to recognize, localize, and remediate any upcoming anomalies threatening the guaranteed QoS demands. Traditional active latency measurement strategies such as ping or traceroute are not suitable for this type of maintenance, as they can only detect a limited number of latency anomalies since they are not treated the same as the user traffic. Further approaches implement active measurement, where additional traffic is generated to observe the network quality. For example, an in-band-telemetry provides latency information on top of the user traffic by appending arrival and departure times at each network hop onto a traversing user packet. Such an additive information requires space in a packet. Encapsulation protocols like VXLAN or Geneve solve this problem, but also expose the risk of packet growth beyond the original MTU size, resulting in fragmentation and additional network packets [13,16,22].

This paper aims at an alternative approach by introducing a lightweight solution for passive monitoring to observe routes, inter hop latencies, and throughput for packet streams. It utilizes a probabilistic packet sampling in both TCP directions on each network device in order to follow the same packet along the network path. A time stamp ordered sequence of the packets along with the sequence number and host:port pairs shows the route and allows a latency approximation between each hop pair along the route. The sequence number comparison of successive packets contributes to the throughput estimation, which is then up-scaled to an entire switch and used to detect bottlenecks. As related to other probabilistic packet sampling methods (e.g. [25,27]), our approach does not introduce any traffic overhead besides the monitoring data itself. The networks hops require neither additional coordination messages nor a manipulation of existent packets is needed to synchronize their probing policies. The quality of the developed solution is proven by experimental measurements in a simulated environment.

The remainder of the paper is organized as follows. Section 2 provides an introduction into the related work on monitoring, probabilistic packet sampling, and P4 network monitoring. The silent consensus approach is then explained in Sect. 3. Section 4 presents an evaluation based on a video-streaming use-case. Finally, Sect. 5 concludes the paper with an outlook of open questions.

2   Related Work

Software defined networking (SDN) and the rising trend of programmable data planes make networks more dynamically at cost of increased complexity. The idea of self-optimizing and self-driving networks require trustworthy monitoring information for their operations [10].

The traditional network traffic monitoring falls into two categories: packet level sampling and flow level sampling. Packet level sampling is based on *libpcap* or on running a dedicated network traffic capturing system. Packet level sampling deploys filtering methods to capture solely a relevant subset of all packets. However, a packet sampling cannot be applied to the entire network traffic due to its sheer volume. A flow level sampling collects information for each individual connection, where advanced techniques are designed on top of programmable data-planes [9,29] or on dynamic query based approaches [14,15,18,28]. These query interfaces are integrated into a data analysis framework like Apache Flink [1] designed for streaming analytic. Further references explicitly covered the resource overhead of packet sampling [7,26]. In opposite to these query-based approaches, the approach of probabilistic packet sampling aims at reducing the overhead by minimizing the number of packets to be examined and thus resulting into fast control loops. OpenSample for example exploits the TCP sequence numbers and time stamps to produce such high-speed control loops [25]. Compared to the approach of the presented paper, OpenSample analyzes sampled packets per network node in a high frequency to obtain the throughput information. However, it does not provide latency and path information for ongoing TCP-connections.

The dynamic nature of today's networks with frequently changing routes exposes additional challenges to the monitoring tools. SDN-enabled flexibility allows the integration of new network devices automatically as well as a fast reaction to hardware faults or overload situations. However, this flexibility is limited by the necessity to support existing, often vendor-specific protocols over long period of time. Therefore, add-on solution such as encapsulation protocols are developed to work around this problem. A prominent example is VXLAN, which was implemented in software-switches for cloud applications [21]. Nevertheless, the adoption takes time as well, as the vendors must design new products and bring these to the market.

The idea of programmable networking is followed by several vendors. Thereby, programmable processor are build into network devices, which provides the capability to customize them for specific requirements. Barefoot networks promotes customizable network devices [2], which allows a protocol implementation in software. To provide standardization among different vendors, P4 (Programming Protocol-Independent Packet Processors) is widely considered a de facto standard programming language for network devices [3,5]. Building uppon that, Shahbaz et al. published *Pisces* a software switch based on Open vSwitch (OVS) that is P4-programmable. The performance evaluation showed that P4 programmable software switches can process packets as fast as the original Open vSwitch [24]. The currently promoted hardware switches provide dynamically programmable packet handling without any additional overhead [4]. Since the P4 release in 2014, several publications showed its importance in network research, namely p4guard (firewall implemented in P4) or the network monitoring technique in-band-telemetry (INT) [8,17,19].

3   Silent Consensus

In this section we present an approach for a latency measurement without altering existing or introducing additional network traffic, solely utilizing TCP sequence numbers. The concept of the incremental calculation of those numbers based on the packet payload size is depicted in Fig. 1. The TCP sequence number is a 32-bit integer field in the header, separately maintained for both directions of each connection. The number of bytes in the packet payload is used to calculate its growth.

In order to enable a fine-grained diagnosis during anomaly situations, e.g. deterioration of QoS for clients, an identification of all possibly affected network hops is required. Information about the packet delay between each hop allows the pair-wise identification of the network devices that are responsible for an increased latency. Furthermore, recent information about the throughput of each hop represent a valuable metric for determining the faulty network devices. Utilizing the sequence number, we propose a hop-to-hop latency measurement by determining the arrival time of the same packet at each network component. Assuming the ability to determine the arrival times $t^{(h1)}$ and $t^{(h2)}$ of a packet p_y with the same sequence number y at two successive network hops $h1$ and $h2$, the hop-to-hop delay is defined as

$$\Delta t^{(h1,h2)}(p_y) = t^{(h2)}(p_y) - t^{(h1)}(p_y). \tag{1}$$

The main challenge is to identify the same packet in a successive chain of network hops without altering the existing or adding new packets. In case of successful

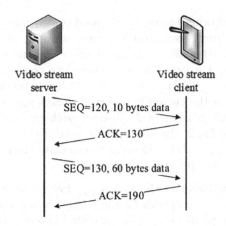

Fig. 1. Concept of the incremental TCP sequence number update during a TCP connection between a server and client. The TCP sequence number increases in dependence of the size of the TCP packet payload.

identification, we can compute many attributes, e.g. latency and throughput. For a successful identification, we rely on a probabilistic packet sampling and aim at maximizing the probability of sampling the same packet at every network device.

A straightforward solution for identifying the same packet on every network hop is to use predefined sequence numbers or packet counts, i.e. every nth packet. However, such static solutions have major drawbacks in case of a volatile throughput or packet losses. Throughput variations may range between Bytes/s and GBytes/s which result in alternating monitoring intervals. An initial constant guess on n combined with an increasing throughput might end up as an unnecessarily high monitoring traffic overhead due to a large number of sampled packets. Therefore, a fixed packet sampling frequency independent from the network traffic volume is a key requirement. This would necessitate an adjustment of n depending on the current throughput. Furthermore, as different TCP connections within a network have different purposes, they differ in terms of throughput, which demands the synchronization to be done for each ongoing connection. However, the additional overhead of synchronizing n between hops violates the requirement of not adding additional traffic.

To overcome the described problems, we introduce a hop-specific adjustment method to sample packets from an ongoing directed TCP connection. A network administrator configures a fixed sampling frequency f, at which monitoring metrics from every network hop should be reported. Considering t_i with $i = 1, 2, \ldots$ as a set of monitoring time stamps, the interval between two consecutive observations is

$$\Delta t_S = t_{i+1} - t_i = \frac{1}{f}. \tag{2}$$

Due to the fixed monitoring frequency, we need to determine a packet that will likely appear around each given sampling time stamp t_i at every network hop h_m, where $1 \leq m \leq M$ with M as the number of hops between source and destination. However, it exists a delay between two consecutive network hops, means that $t^{(h1)}(p_y) > t^{(h2)}(p_y) > \cdots > t^{(hM)}(p_y)$. Based on this, if every network device reports the currently observed packet p_{y_j}, where $j = 1, \ldots, M$ at a time t_i, the result is a set of M distinct packets, i.e. $\{y_j | 1 < j < M\}_{\neq}$. However, as stated in Eq. 2, the same packet is required to be observed across every hop, i.e. $\{y_j | 1 < j < M\}_{=}$, in order to calculate the latencies. We resolve this issue with a two step predictive approach:

1. Each network node forecasts the packet p_{y_+} for the next observation timestamp t_{i+1}, where $y_+ > y$ applies for the packet sequence numbers.
2. A correction of the prediction p_{y_+} is calculated in order to increase the probability of $\{y_j | 1 < j < M\}_{=}$, i.e. each network device predicts a packet with the same sequence number.

3.1 Next Packet Prediction

The packet arrival time depends on the throughput, so a reliable TCP throughput forecasting is necessary. Related approaches apply forecasting based on machine learning methods [11,12,20,23]. However, all approaches have the common goal of predicting the long-term throughput for a collection of different protocols and thus, focus on training models with data on hourly or daily basis. As shown in Fig. 2(a), the raw throughput value usually underlies strong variations, which poses a challenge for accurate predictions and demands complex models. On the other hand, the TCP sequence number, as an additive representation of the throughput, shows an approximately linear progress (see Fig. 2(b)). We state that the approximately linear progress of TCP sequence numbers together with the connection-based prediction allows a utilization of linear regressive forecasting models trained on data points from the recent past. Having a window of

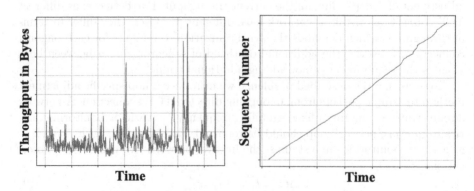

Fig. 2. (a) Throughput of a 480p video stream (b) TCP sequence number of a 480p video stream.

recently observed TCP sequence numbers $t_{i-w}(p_{y_1}), t_{i-(w-1)}(p_{y_2}), \ldots, t_i(p_{y_w})$, with w as window size, the goal is to predict a future packet p_{y_+} at time t_{i+1}. As we use the TCP sequence number to identify packets, these are defined as the dependent variable that needs to be predicted based on the time of its observation, described as

$$y_+ = \omega_1 \cdot t_{i+1} + \omega_0. \tag{3}$$

Utilizing the recent history of TCP sequence numbers together with the observation time stamps, we determine the parameters ω_1 and ω_0 by solving Eq. 3 for the least L-2 norm

$$\underset{\omega_1, \omega_0}{\mathrm{argmin}} \|y - (\omega_1 \cdot t + \omega_0)\|_2^2. \tag{4}$$

Using the recent history window allows the adjustment of the model to a temporally changing throughput but requires its retraining at each monitoring interval t_i. The retraining rate depends on the user defined sampling frequency f. Given the model fitting duration Δt_{fit}, the time to predict the next sequence number $\Delta t_{predict}$ and the monitoring interval Δt_S defined in Eq. 2, it must be assured that $\Delta t_S - (\Delta t_{fit} + \Delta t_{predict}) > 0$. The quantity of both Δt_{fit} and $\Delta t_{predict}$ depends on the number of model parameters in Eq. 3 while Δt_{fit} additionally depends on the historic window size w. Thus, we restrict our model to two parameters ω_0 and ω_1 while advising to keep the window size w as low as possible in order to support high frequent monitoring rates. Another limitation rises from the natural delay between the first and last network hop and entails the definition $\Delta t^{(h1, hM)} > \Delta t_S$, i.e. the defined packet sampling interval Δt_S cannot exceed the delay between the first and last network hop. For our approach, a packet that is transmitted through the network must have a realistic chance to be observed by each network device before a monitoring time interval Δt_S expires.

3.2 Prediction Synchronization

To determine the delay between every adjacent pair of network nodes, each node has to predict an identical sequence number. However, there exist two inherent sources of uncertainty. First, we must guess the future TCP connection throughput based on recent history in order to predict the next sequence number. As network traffic usually exposes non-deterministic behavior combined with the intended simplicity of our forecasting model, the predicted value will usually deviate from the actual observed value. Furthermore, due to a natural delay between each network hop, they observe distinct sequence numbers at every monitoring timestamp t_i. As our method is applied on packets from directed TCP connections, this aspect can be rendered more precisely as network nodes located closer to the source are observing a more recent extract of the packet stream than nodes located closer to the destination. Therefore, different packet sequence numbers are used to train the models at each network device, which results in heterogeneous model parameter values. Thus, the predicted sequence numbers will differ for every network hop. This delay-induced model parameter divergence is the second source of uncertainty.

Based on this, we propose to adjust the predicted TCP sequence number in a way that increases the probability of being identical at each network hop. The aspect of determining identical TCP sequence numbers across several network devices without exchanging any messages except the regular TCP packets is referred to as *silent consensus*. For this, the TCP number metric space is divided into bins of fixed size k. After that, the predicted future value y_+ is adjusted by applying

$$y'_+ = \lfloor \frac{y_+}{k} \rfloor \cdot k. \tag{5}$$

This relaxes the requirement for the linear regressive forecasting of predicting the same TCP sequence number across each network device towards the requirement of predicting a sequence number that lies in the same bin. The defined adjustment from Eq. 5 is subject to two problematic cases (note that a mixture of both is also possible). First, due to the floor operation, the corrected sequence number y'_+ can end up being smaller than the last observed value y. This case can be detected individually on each network device. As the method operates on directed TCP sessions, it is impossible to observe packets from the past. Thus, this case is trivially corrected by selecting the next bin, i.e. $y'_+ + k$. Second, the predictions are not guaranteed to lie in identical bins. This results in a subset of nodes or no nodes at all to reach silent consensus. To further increase the probability of making identical predictions, we propose to use a number l of ascending bins y'_+, $y'_+ + k$, $y'_+ + 2k$, $\ldots$, $y'_+ + lk$. This poses a trade-off between increasing the chance of having identical predictions across the nodes and the amount of monitoring data that has to be transmitted to the monitoring data sink.

4   Evaluation

The target system for the silent consensus algorithm evaluation consists of two VMs which are connected via a network path containing three switches. The scenario is visualized in Fig. 3. The mean latency between the two VMs is 3 ms, whereby the latency between switch1 and switch2 is higher than the latency between switch2 and switch3.

The traffic between the VMs is generated by an Nginx-based video streaming server running on one of the VMs. The other VMs hosts an ffmpeg-client which requests video streams through the RTMP protocol. An exemplary video can be requested in three different resolutions: 4k (530 MB), high definition (290 MB) and 480p (50 MB). During the video transmission, the traffic on the three switches is recorded with the tcpdump tool. Therefore, the conducted experiments result in nine PCAP files, i.e. one for each combination of switch and video resolution. These files form the evaluation basis for our prototypical implementation of the proposed silent consensus algorithm[1].

The following Sect. 4.1 shows the evaluation results of using linear regression for forecasting future sequence numbers. After that, Sect. 4.2 describes the evaluation of the silent consensus approach based on the forecasting results.

---

[1] https://github.com/mwallschlaeger/silent_consensus_packet_sampling.

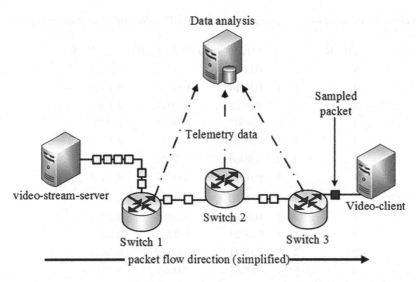

Fig. 3. Evaluation setup consisting of two virtual machines (video stream server and video client) connected by three network hops (switches). The server VMs are able to stream videos at different resolutions. Network traffic can be monitored with tcpdump individually on each switch.

4.1 Forecasting TCP Sequence Numbers

We define three major run time parameters for the TCP forecasting. Parameter $\Delta t_S = \frac{1}{f}$ is the interval, in which our system will predict a future sequence number, i.e. the time difference between the moment of prediction and the sequence number to be predicted. The other two parameters are the amount of historic TCP sequence number values w considered for the prediction and si as the number of history values considered within each interval Δt_S. We evaluate the linear regression forecasting with interval values $\Delta t_S = \{1, 2, 5, 10\}\, s$ in combination with $w = \{2, 3, 5\}$. Further we run the evaluation with two different values of $si = \{1, 2\}$.

Table 1 shows the mean absolute percentage error $(MAPE)$ for each combination of the above defined system parameters. The results of each switch are averaged for every configuration.

The $MAPE$ results show a value below 2% for the lowest resolution 480p. The best configuration predicts the sequence number one second into the future using the two historical values resulting into $MAPE$ of 0.06%. For the HD resolution, where the average throughput is more than twice as much as for the 480p resolution, the $MAPE$ is below 5%. Considering smaller than five second forecast, the $MAPE$ is below 3%. Analogously, the best configuration here is a short-term forecasting using $w = 2$ historical sequence numbers from the last second to forecast the sequence number of the next second. The forecasting for

Table 1. Mean absolute percentage error (MAPE) for different configurations.

Δt_S in [s]	w	si	MAPE 480p	MAPE HD	MAPE 4K
1	2	2	0,0006	0,0015	0,0620
1	2	1	0,0014	0,0033	0,1343
1	3	1	0,0012	0,0033	0,1268
1	3	2	0,0007	0,0017	0,0658
1	5	1	0,0015	0,0043	0,1511
1	5	2	0,0008	0,0020	0,2723
1	*	*	0.0011	0.0027	0.1354
2	2	2	0,0049	0,0110	0,3754
2	2	1	0,0022	0,0063	0,2355
2	3	1	0,0023	0,0072	0,2423
2	3	2	0,0021	0,0050	0,1928
2	5	1	0,0031	0,0095	0,2947
2	5	2	0,0027	0,0060	0,1971
2	*	*	0.0028	0.0076	0.2563
5	2	2	0,0197	0,0452	1,5018
5	2	1	0,0060	0,0181	0,5845
5	3	1	0,0062	0,0199	0,5610
5	3	2	0,0076	0,0191	0,5684
5	5	1	0,0081	0,0284	0,7304
5	5	2	0,0070	0,0200	0,5402
5	*	*	0.0092	0.0251	0.7477
10	2	2	0,0439	0,1009	3,0760
10	2	1	0,0104	0,0356	0,9640
10	3	1	0,0124	0,0441	1,0869
10	3	2	0,0165	0,0437	1,1829
10	5	1	0,0149	0,0473	1,2771
10	5	2	0,0159	0,0463	1,1205
10	*	*	0.0190	0.0547	1.4512

the 4k video stream has a minimum $MAPE$ of 6.2%. However for some configurations, the $MAPE$ of the 4k stream goes up to 150% or even 307%. This high error results from using only one second of historical data to forecast 5 or 10 s into the future.

4.2 Silent Consensus

The evaluation of the silent consensus function is based on the forecasting results of the previous section. The results are summarized in Table 2.

To enable the observation of a packet p_y on each network hop (switch) $\{h1, h2, h3\}$, we conduct a number of sequence number predictions $pred$. The total number of predictions is defined by $\lfloor \frac{T}{\Delta t_S} \rfloor - 1$, where T is the total experiment duration. The subtraction by one results from the fact that the first Δt_S must be used as offset to aggregate initial training data. A prediction $pred$ can be either correct (denoted as $true$) or incorrect (denoted as $false$).

Table 2. Silent consensus accuracy for different configurations and video stream resolutions.

Δt_S in [s]	w	si	ACC 480p	ACC HD	ACC 4K
1	2	2	0.8065	0.7291	0.8266
1	2	1	0.7941	0.7167	0.8188
1	3	1	0.7639	0.6878	0.7888
1	3	2	0.7872	0.7096	0.8012
1	5	1	0.7031	0.6296	0.7234
1	5	2	0.7562	0.6812	0.7671
1	*	*	0.7685	0.6924	0.7876
2	2	2	0.8037	0.7414	0.8193
2	2	1	0.7663	0.6915	0.8006
2	3	1	0.7053	0.6332	0.7398
2	3	2	0.7648	0.6959	0.7742
2	5	1	0.5841	0.5174	0.6158
2	5	2	0.7015	0.6380	0.7111
2	*	*	0.7210	0.6529	0.7435
5	2	2	0.8174	0.7380	0.8253
5	2	1	0.6666	0.6031	0.7063
5	3	1	0.5161	0.4516	0.5645
5	3	2	0.6854	0.5887	0.6935
5	5	1	0.225	0.15	0.2916
5	5	2	0.5416	0.45	0.55
5	*	*	0.5754	0.4969	0.6052
10	2	2	0.8360	0.7377	0.8196
10	2	1	0.6721	0.4918	0.7049
10	3	1	0.5084	0.2711	0.5593
10	3	2	0.6949	0.5423	0.6440
10	5	1	0.3272	0.1272	0.3818
10	5	2	0.5636	0.2545	0.4909
10	*	*	0.6004	0.4041	0.6001

$$pred_i = \begin{cases} true, & \text{if } p_y^{h1} = p_y^{h2} = p_y^{h3} \\ false, & \text{otherwise} \end{cases}. \tag{6}$$

Equation 6 states that a prediction result is regarded as *true* if the same packet, identified by its TCP sequence number, was observed on each network hop. Otherwise the prediction result is set to *false*. Based on this, the accuracy is defined as the ratio of *true* to the total number of predictions, formally defined as follows.

$$ACC = \frac{|pred^{true}|}{|pred|}. \tag{7}$$

For this evaluation k was set to 10. We used $l = 2$ ascending grids, thus having y'_+ and $y'_+ + k$.

The parameter value $\Delta t_S = 1\,$s shows the best results. Further, it is revealed that an increasing value of w, results in an accuracy decrease of the silent consensus (Table 2).

Furthermore, considering the results of the forecasting evaluation, the consensus function shows acceptable accuracy values even for parameter configurations where the forecasting $MAPE$ values were high, e.g. for $\Delta t_S = 5\,$s, $w = 2$, $si = 2$ or $\Delta t_S = 10\,$s, $w = 2$ and $si = 2$. This contra-intuitive aspect is explained by the fact that the consensus function requires a consistent forecasting on each network hop, and not on an accurate one. As long all hops achieve similar forecasting results, i.e. the forecast sequence number is similar for each hop, the silent consensus has a high probability of selecting the same packet.

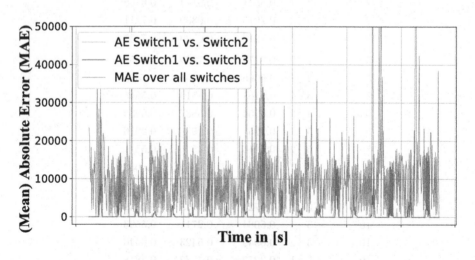

Fig. 4. Comparison of absolute error (AE) over time between the forecasting values of switch1 and switch2 and the forecasting values switch1 and switch3 in comparison to the MAE over all individual forecasting results. Based on the configuration $\Delta t_S = 5\,$s, $w = 2$, $si = 1$ of the 480p video stream. (Color figure online)

Figure 4 shows the absolute error (AE) between the sequence number forecast of switch1 and switch2 (blue line), and switch1 and switch3 (orange line). The grey line presents the mean absolute error (MAE) for each interval step Δt_S, whereby the mean of all three error values is calculated. The AE is 0 when the switches predict the same sequence number, independent of the correctness of the predictions. We observe that the error between switches spikes several times during the experiment. These spikes could be related to network congestion or application specific behavior like buffering in the video client, or processing on the server side. Further, this would interfere with the communication and invalidate the recent history entries w, resulting in a lower forecasting accuracy. Compared to the error between the switches, the forecasting precision behaves independent.

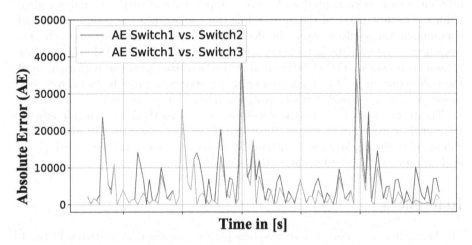

Fig. 5. Comparison of AE over time between the forecasting values of switch1 and switch2 and the forecasting values switch1 and switch3 in comparison to the MAE over all individual forecasting results. Based on the configuration $\Delta t_S = 5$ s, $w = 2$, $si = 2$ of the high definition video stream.

As shown, the accuracy of the silent consensus depends on the similarity of the predicted sequence numbers among the network hops. Therefore, the predictions results are better for reliable hop-to-hop connections. Variations in latency or frequent network congestion between network node pairs will reduce the prediction accuracy. Also, once such fluctuations occurred, the time span where they are considered for the training of the prediction model should be as low as possible. This explains the better accuracy results for lower value of parameter w. As an example for comparison, Fig. 5 shows the sequence number forecast errors for the evaluation configuration $\Delta t_S = 5$ s, $w = 2$, $si = 2$ of the high definition video stream. Compared to Fig. 4, which shows several spikes, the configuration for the HD stream shows a high number of small errors, which are caused by a large difference between the forecasted sequence numbers of the different switches. That leads to a small number of identical predicted sequence numbers between the switches.

5   Conclusion

The presented approach shows a novel mechanism for network packet sampling to obtain latency, path and throughput information for each communication flow as foundation for anomaly detection and remediation. The approach analyses a minimal number of packets within a limited time window (1 to 10 s) and tracks the path of those packets from one network hop to the next. Based on the recorded timestamps between the hops, a number of the relevant traffic attributes can be computed and used as input into subsequent analysis algorithms. The advantage of the approach is the low overhead in computation and communication resulting from the decentralized decision making, as each network device individually determines which packet is to be sampled using a silent consensus function. The experimental evaluation examined the performance of the two major steps. The measured accuracy showed a probability of over 80% to sample the same packet when using an interval of one second.

The future work includes the development of a method for dynamic adjustment of the core parameter k, i.e. the width of the considered time window, which will simplify the deployment significantly. Moreover, we extend the experimental evaluation to IoT and edge computing scenarios.

References

1. Alexandrov, A., et al.: The stratosphere platform for big data analytics. VLDB J. Int. J. Very Large Data Bases **23**(6), 939–964 (2014)
2. Arista Networks, Inc.: arista.comwhite paperarista 7170 multi-function programmable networking. Technical report, Arista (2018). https://www.arista.com/assets/data/pdf/Whitepapers/7170_White_Paper.pdf
3. Bosshart, P., et al.: P4: Programming protocol-independent packet processors. ACM SIGCOMM Comput. Commun. Rev. **44**(3), 87–95 (2014)
4. Bosshart, P., et al.: Forwarding metamorphosis: fast programmable match-action processing in hardware for sdn. In: ACM SIGCOMM Computer Communication Review, vol. 43, pp. 99–110. ACM (2013)
5. Brebner, G.: P4 for an FPGA target. In: P4 Workshop (2015)
6. Cisco: Cisco visual networking index: forecast and trends, 2017–2022. Technical report, Cisco (2018). https://www.cisco.com/c/en/us/solutions/collateral/service-provider/visual-networking-index-vni/white-paper-c11-741490.pdf
7. Curtis, A.R., Mogul, J.C., Tourrilhes, J., Yalagandula, P., Sharma, P., Banerjee, S.: DevoFlow: scaling flow management for high-performance networks. In: ACM SIGCOMM Computer Communication Review, vol. 41, pp. 254–265. ACM (2011)
8. Datta, R., Choi, S., Chowdhary, A., Park, Y.: P4Guard: designing P4 based firewall. In: MILCOM 2018–2018 IEEE Military Communications Conference (MILCOM), pp. 1–6. IEEE (2018)

9. Duffield, N.G., Grossglauser, M.: Trajectory sampling for direct traffic observation. IEEE/ACM Trans. Netw. (ToN) **9**(3), 280–292 (2001)
10. Feamster, N., Rexford, J.: Why (and how) networks should run themselves. CoRR abs/1710.11583 (2017). http://arxiv.org/abs/1710.11583
11. Feng, Y., Wu, X., Hu, Y.: Forecasting research on the wireless mesh network throughput based on the support vector machine. Wirel. Pers. Commun. **99**(1), 581–593 (2018)
12. Goyal, M., Guerin, R., Rajan, R.: Predicting TCP throughput from non-invasive network sampling. In: INFOCOM 2002. Proceedings of the IEEE Twenty-First Annual Joint Conference of the IEEE Computer and Communications Societies, vol. 1, pp. 180–189. IEEE (2002)
13. Gulenko, A., Wallschläger, M., Kao, O.: A practical implementation of in-band network telemetry in Open vSwitch. In: 2018 IEEE 7th International Conference on Cloud Networking (CloudNet), pp. 1–4. IEEE (2018)
14. Gupta, A., Birkner, R., Canini, M., Feamster, N., Mac-Stoker, C., Willinger, W.: Network monitoring as a streaming analytics problem. In: Proceedings of the 15th ACM Workshop on Hot Topics in Networks, pp. 106–112. ACM (2016)
15. Gupta, A., et al.: Sonata: query-driven network telemetry. arXiv preprint arXiv:1705.01049 (2017)
16. Kim, C., et al.: In-band network telemetry (INT). Technical report, The P4 Language Consortium (2016). https://p4.org/assets/INT-current-spec.pdf. Accessed 01 June 2018
17. Kim, C., Sivaraman, A., Katta, N., Bas, A., Dixit, A., Wobker, L.J.: In-band network telemetry via programmable dataplanes. In: ACM SIGCOMM Symposium on SDN Research (SOSR) (2015)
18. Liu, Z., Vorsanger, G., Braverman, V., Sekar, V.: Enabling a RISC approach for software-defined monitoring using universal streaming. In: Proceedings of the 14th ACM Workshop on Hot Topics in Networks, p. 21. ACM (2015)
19. Liu, Z., Bi, J., Zhou, Y., Wang, Y., Lin, Y.: NetVision: towards network telemetry as a service. In: 2018 IEEE 26th International Conference on Network Protocols (ICNP), pp. 247–248. IEEE (2018)
20. Lu, D., Qiao, Y., Dinda, P.A., Bustamante, F.E.: Characterizing and predicting TCP throughput on the wide area network. In: Proceedings of the 25th IEEE International Conference on Distributed Computing Systems, ICDCS 2005, pp. 414–424. IEEE (2005)
21. Mahalingam, M., Dutt, D.G., Duda, K., Agarwal, P.: Virtual eXtensible Local Area Network (VXLAN): a framework for overlaying virtualized layer 2 networks over layer 3 networks. RFC 7348, RFC Editor, August 2014. https://www.rfc-editor. org/rfc/rfc7348.txt
22. Mestre, P.: In-band OAM for IPv6. Technical report, Cisco, June 2016. https:// www.cisco.com/c/en/us/td/docs/ios-xml/ios/ipv6_nman/configuration/15-mt/ ip6n-15-mt-book/ioam-ipv6.pdf
23. Mirza, M., Sommers, J., Barford, P., Zhu, X.: A machine learning approach to TCP throughput prediction. SIGMETRICS Perform. Eval. Rev. **35**(1), 97–108 (2007). https://doi.org/10.1145/1269899.1254894
24. Shahbaz, M., et al.: PISCES: a programmable, protocol-independent software switch. In: SIGCOMM Conference, pp. 525–538. ACM (2016)
25. Suh, J., Kwon, T.T., Dixon, C., Felter, W., Carter, J.: OpenSample: a low-latency, sampling-based measurement platform for commodity SDN. In: 2014 IEEE 34th International Conference on Distributed Computing Systems (ICDCS), pp. 228–237. IEEE (2014)

26. Tammana, P., Agarwal, R., Lee, M.: Simplifying datacenter network debugging with pathdump. In: OSDI, pp. 233–248 (2016)
27. Yoon, S., Ha, T., Kim, S., Lim, H.: Scalable traffic sampling using centrality measure on software-defined networks. IEEE Commun. Mag. **55**(7), 43–49 (2017)
28. Yu, M., Jose, L., Miao, R.: Software defined traffic measurement with opensketch. In: NSDI, vol. 13, pp. 29–42 (2013)
29. Zhu, Y., et al.: Packet-level telemetry in large datacenter networks. In: ACM SIGCOMM Computer Communication Review, vol. 45, pp. 479–491. ACM (2015)

A Knowledge-Based Computational Environment for Real-World Data Processing

Man Tianxing[1] , Nataly Zhukova[1,2] , Vasily Meltsov[3] ,
and Yulia Shichkina[4(✉)]

[1] ITMO University, St. Petersburg, Russia
mantx626@gmail.com, nazhukova@mail.ru
[2] St. Petersburg Institute for Informatics and Automation of the Russian
Academy of Sciences, St. Petersburg, Russia
[3] Vyatka State University, Kirov, Russia
meltsov69@mail.ru
[4] St. Petersburg State Electrotechnical University "LETI", St. Petersburg, Russia
strange.y@mail.ru

Abstract. The data contains knowledge. Researchers working in various fields are struggling to extract information from specific data sets. But data processing is a complex process. Real-world data must be converted multiple times to become useful knowledge. This process is very unfriendly to non-computer professional researchers. The lack of knowledge related to data processing makes their work unsatisfactory. The main purpose of this paper is to build a computational environment based on ontology technology, which provides selection and description of data processing algorithms to help the users extract information from the real-world data. This article provides a real case to indicate the rationality of this computational environment. The authors extracted significant conclusions from a data set of the acid-base state at patients.

Keywords: Data processing · Ontology · Computational environment

1 Instruction

With the rapid development of information technology, researchers in various fields are paying more and more attention to real-world data contained the knowledge. Extracting significant knowledge from the data generated in daily life is a fantasy work. But data processing is a quite complex process so that many non-computer professional researchers are confused about the construction of the entire data processing process. In fact, most researchers who are trying to extract information from data are not working in the Internet industry, such as market analysis, medical, financial investment and so on.

The main purpose of this paper is to create a knowledge-based computational environment (KBCE) for real-world data processing based on ontology technology. Based on the KBCE users can select appropriate data processing algorithms and build the entire data processing process according to the characteristics of the data set and the requirements of the task step by step.

© Springer Nature Switzerland AG 2019
S. Misra et al. (Eds.): ICCSA 2019, LNCS 11619, pp. 257–269, 2019.
https://doi.org/10.1007/978-3-030-24289-3_20

KBCE is an ontology that contains the knowledge about data processing and its logical relationships. The authors create the classes of algorithms, mathematics, input features, output features, and process, and define object property that expresses their inner relationships and data property that describes the specific parameter settings of the classes. Because it is based on ontology technology, KBCE expresses more logical relationships more explicitly than traditional taxonomies. The advantages of KBCE are as follows:

- KBCE is different from other reviews about data processing. It describes the entire data processing process including data preprocessing, classification, clustering, and even evaluation modules to provide a complete workflow for the user. A large number of facts prove that in data mining systems, data preprocessing accounts for 60% to 80% of the total workload [1]. A complete description of data preprocessing is significant to real-world data processing.
- KBCE is built based on the ontology technology, so it can be easily expanded according to the requirements of users. Even users can customize the specialized computing environment by linking knowledge in the field.
- In addition to the description of the algorithmic process, KBCE also summarizes the performance and application of data processing algorithms based on a large number of experiments and articles. The user could input the characteristics of the data set and the task requirements to get the appropriate solution. With KBCE users can make decisions based on the true performance of the algorithm rather than their intuition.
- The expression of ontology is user-friendly. Although users may have no experience in the computer industry, as an ontology KBCE presents clear logical definition and relationships like a mind may so that they can understand their selection and the entire data processing process.

The structure of this paper is as follows: Sect. 2 introduces background knowledge and related work. Section 3 presents the structure and the main components of KBCE. Section 4 describes the workflow of KBCE. In Sect. 5 the authors apply KBCE on a real-world data set about the acid-base state (ABS) of the patients to achieve some medical conclusions to indicate the rationality of KBCE. In Sect. 6 the authors present the conclusions of KBCE and future work.

2 Background

2.1 Data Processing

With the rapid development of the information industry, people have accumulated more and more data. The real-world data contains a lot of important information. So how to analyze data at a higher level to make it significant becomes essential. Data processing has become a very active frontier in computer science. In fact, most of the researchers, who are trying to extract information from data, work in non-computer fields, such as market analysis, medical, climate analysis [2–4] and so on.

Many studies are applying the methods and models on ideal data rather than the intricate real-world data sets. In general, it is inevitable that there are redundant data, missing data, uncertain data and inconsistent data [5–7]. According to the principle of "garbage in, garbage out" [8], inappropriate data formats can result in expensive operating costs and long response time and affect the correctness of the patterns extracted from the data set and the accuracy of the output models. So the real-world data processing process is a complex process form multiple conversions and the final information extraction as the Fig. 1 shows.

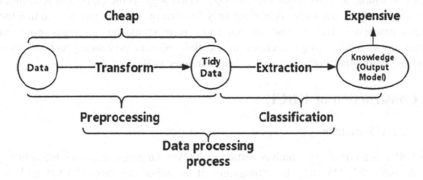

Fig. 1. General data processing process

2.2 Reviews of Recommendation Systems of Data Processing

Fernández-Delgado did a series of interesting experiments about applying more than one hundred classification algorithms on different data sets to present "There is no best classifier, only the most suitable classifier" [9]. This situation is also existing in data processing. The size, quality and type of data sets and users' requirements all affect the performance of the algorithm. The algorithm which is suitable for all the situations doesn't exist.

Researchers have provided some solutions to provide data processing users with advice on algorithmic choices. Scikit-learn is the most commonly used machine learning (ML) python package for python users. Its developers also provide a classic ML algorithm selection scheme [10]. Some computer science researchers have proposed various automatic selection methods for supervised machine learning problem [11]. The practical application effects of clustering algorithms are also summarized [12]. Some studies focus on the processing of specific data forms. Bagnall [13] and Fawaz [14] present great reviews of time series classification algorithms. Although these reviews provide excellent content. But too much professional knowledge is confusing the researchers who don't work in computer science. The purpose of this article is to present a user-friendly and complete computational environment of data processing.

2.3   Ontology Technology

Ontology is a formal specification for communication and knowledge sharing between different subjects in the domain by defining the relationships among the concepts that are commonly recognized in the field by describing and capturing domain knowledge [15]. It is an explicit, formal, shared conceptualization. So it can be regarded as a formal knowledge, even a knowledge of management knowledge which can satisfy the academic research community to share the expression of knowledge. The conceptual model is ideal for building recommendation and interpretation systems. Some researchers have tried to apply the ontology technology to the algorithm recommendation system [16], but such systems are only focused on specific purposes so that they are not extensive. The purpose of this paper is to create an ontology about data processing as a knowledge interface in the field of data processing and an understandable computing environment for non-computer professionals.

3   Construction of KBCE

3.1   Basic Structure

The KBCE is an ontology which is written with OWL language and available at https://github.com/529492252/KBCE-ontology.git. It is edited in Protégé-5.5.0 and was checked by HermiT 1.3.8.413 reasoner to make sure it is consistent.

KBCE has two main parts: the creation of class and the definition of property which are shown in Fig. 2. They are used to describe the logic relationships about the process and performance of data processing. The basic structure is in Fig. 3.

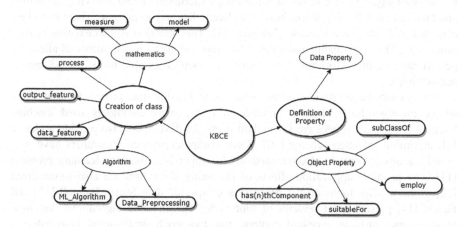

Fig. 2. The main components of KBCE

In KBCE most of the classes are concrete operations, but the authors also define some abstract concepts to make the logic clearer. And object property is used to describe the logic as Fig. 3 shown. In ontology the other kind property "data property" is still important to provide the parameter settings of algorithms.

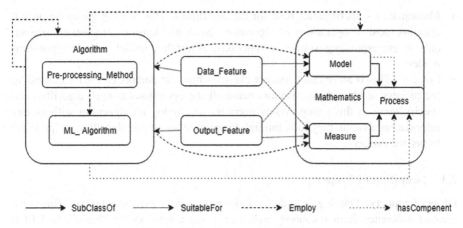

Fig. 3. The basic structure of KBCE

3.2 Creation of Classes

Knowledge is the foundation of KBCE. It is difficult to sort out the knowledge related to data processing because there are too many different angles of taxonomies. In the conceptual model of ontology, class means thing with certain attributes. Such a statement is precisely suitable for describing complex data processing knowledge. The authors mainly create such classes:

- Algorithm - algorithms for data processing that can be common ML algorithms and special methods oriented on data preprocessing. Figure 4 present part of the class "Algorithm".
- Data_Feature - characteristics of input datasets, including size, length etc.
- Output_feature - features of the output such as the number of classes of classification task. And the users' requirements are classified to this group like speed, accuracy, interpretability etc.

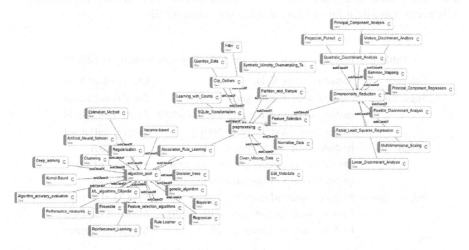

Fig. 4. Part of class "Algorithm" (main dimensionality reduction methods are shown)

- Mathematics - mathematics base for the algorithms. This is a big group because it contains most of operations of algorithms. Such as Measure – measures between data in corresponding similarity functions; Algorithm model – basic algorithms models.
- Process - This is an abstract concept classes which the authors create for describing the process of algorithms. Authors name all the operations in each algorithm and specify them in this group. When users try to employ an algorithm without any information about it, they look through the content about this algorithm in "process" to get the process.

3.3   Definition of Property

Object Property. Ontology can define more properties to present relations. This is the greatest difference from taxonomy which only has a relationship "has-a". In KBCE some main object properties are defined:

- subclassOf - basic property to link father class to subclass.
- employ - links the algorithm and their core content. Such as measures and models that can affect the performance of algorithms.
- has(n)thComponent - Links the algorithms and their components to describe the processes of the algorithms. The authors define the steps of the algorithm by assigning a value to n present the sequence of the operations.
- suitableFor - links input data characteristics and users' requirements to the algorithms, defining suitable algorithms for processing data with known characteristics.

Data Property. Since KBCE is oriented to non-computer professional researchers, the parameters setting is usually a problem for them. Data property is used to define the value or range of the operations. And when users want to input a data characteristic, the data property can guide users to translate it into a class in KBCE.

As the Table 1 shown the data characteristics are defined by data property "hasSize", if user input a value of the size of train data set, Length or No. of classes, the reasoner of KBCE can translate it into a class in ontology automatically.

Table 1. The data characteristics are defined by data property "hasSize"

Category	Range of Class Value	Class in KBCE
Train size	hasSize some xsd:integer[< 100]	SmallTrainDataset
	hasSize some xsd:integer[>= 100, <=500]	SmallTrainDataset
	hasSize some xsd:integer[> 500]	LargeTrainDataset
Length	hasSize some xsd:integer[< 300]	ShortDataset
	hasSize some xsd:integer[>= 300, <=700]	MediumDataset
	hasSize some xsd:integer[> 700]	LongDataset
No. of classes	hasSize some xsd:integer[< 10]	FewClassDataset
	hasSize some xsd:integer[>= 10, <=30]	MediumClassDataset
	hasSize some xsd:integer[> 30]	ManyClassDataset

4   Generation of Data Processing Process Based on KBCE

KBCE is primarily for non-computer professionals. Its purpose is to clearly present the logical structure of data processing knowledge so that users can perform fewer steps to get better results. The generation of the KBCE data processing process is to sequentially input the task conditions to obtain a suitable set of algorithms. Finally choose the most suitable algorithm. Specific steps are as follows:

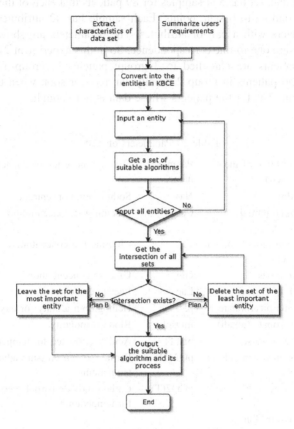

Fig. 5. The workflow of KBCE

1. Acquire user requirements and extract the characteristics of the data set.
2. Enter the task conditions and convert them to entries in KBCE.
3. Get the appropriate set of algorithms in turn.
4. Extract the intersection of the set of suitable algorithms.
5. If the intersection does not exist, Plan A deletes the least important entry and then performs step 3; Plan B is directly selected in all current suitable algorithms (shown in Fig. 5).
6. Output the selected algorithm.
7. (Optional) Describe the selected algorithm based on the outward links.

5 Case Study

To indicate the feasibility of KBCE, the authors analysis a real-world data set about acid-base state (ABS) of patients to extract information based on KBCE. The dynamics of the ABS in cavernous sinus (CS) was studied for 89 patients with cardiac surgical pathology during the postoperative period in the operating room and in the cardio-resuscitation unit. Doctors want to make a systematic analysis on it.

The original data set has 534 samples for 89 patients that each of them has up to 6 samples corresponding to 6 state points. Each sample has 42 attributes which come from 21 parameters with a pair of attributes. The parameters are shown in Table 2. Paired attributes are one-to-one correspondence. So in this experiment 21 attributes are selected. The patients are classified to 3 group: patients in group 1 have healthy physical state and patients in group 2 usually can recover soon when the parameters change, and group 3 is for the patients whose data is not enough.

Table 2. Parameters of ABS

Parameter name	Description of the parameter	Parameter name	Description of the parameter
pH	Acidity	Na+	Sodium ion concentration
pO2	Oxygen partial pressure	Ca ++	Calcium ion concentration
pCO2	Carbon dioxide partial pressure	Cl-	Chlorine Ion concentration
ABE	Excess base	Glu	Glucose concentration
SBE	Lack of reason	Lac	Lactate content
cHCO3	Plasma bicarbonate	p50	Hemoglobin affinity for oxygen
cHCO3-st	Bicarbonate (alkali)	mOsm	Blood osmolarity
sO2	Oxygen boost	pH(T)	Acidity corrected for temperature
ctHb	Reference hemoglobin level	pO2(T)	Partial oxygen pressure adjusted for temperature
Htc	Hematocrit	pCO2(T)	Carbon dioxide partial pressure adjusted for temperature
K+	Potassium ion concentration		

The doctor hopes to extract intrinsic characteristics of parameters change for the patients in different groups. It should be important to distinguish patients in group 1 and group 2. General classification algorithms can classify the patients precisely. So this experiment is used to figure out the coherent consistency of the parameters in this data set.

The average dynamics of ABS is given in Fig. 6. Authors hope to extract more information from this data set. With the intuition they applied some cluster algorithms on the data set and compared with the existing labels. But the results are unsatisfactory. So they tried to analysis this data set based on KBCE for extracting deep knowledge.

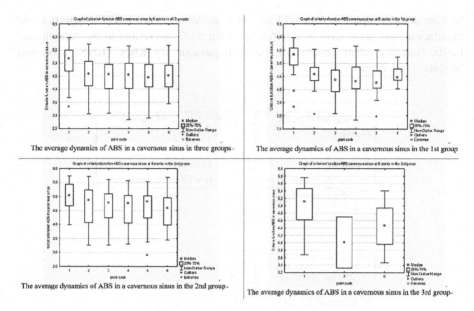

Fig. 6. The average dynamics of ABS in a cavernous sinus in all groups and in each group [17]

The original data set is not tidy enough, several preprocessing operations are provided by KBCE as Figs. 7 and 8 shown. There are too many missing values, which is missing at random (MAR), in the original data set. KBCE classifies them into two groups: MAR more than 50% means more than 50% values are missing in each row or column or both of them; MAR less than 50% means less than 50% values are missing in each row or column. KBCE suggests to "Delete_Rows" for MAR more than 50%

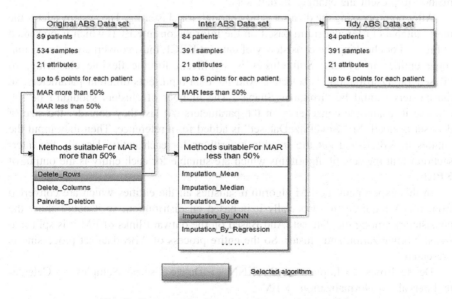

Fig. 7. Preprocessing based on data set characteristics

because some samples in data set lose too many values. And KBCE suggests using imputation methods to deal with MAR less than 50%. According to the data characteristic "interdependent" the system selects "Imputation_By_KNN" (KNN - k-Nearest Neighbor Algorithm).

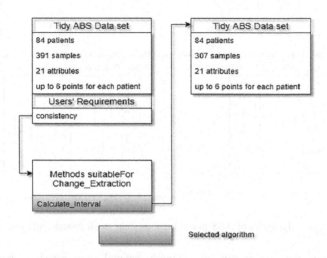

Fig. 8. Preprocessing based on user's requirements

As the Fig. 8 shown consistency of the parameters is user's requirement, and KBCE converts the requirement to the analysis of the variations between different points in different groups. KBCE suggests that to analysis the intervals is the best method to present the changes in data sets.

After preprocessing the data set is tidy enough for clustering. The system selects the most suitable cluster algorithm based on the information in KBCE which is presented in Fig. 9. For checking the consistency of data set KBCE must convert consistency into some entities in system. Soft cluster is significant for the flexible clustering, so "Based_on_Distribution" is selected. And the data represents different parameters, so the clusters should be "Irregular_Shape". The number of clusters shouldn't be set, because it means the consistency of the parameters. At last they consider the size of data set is small. So "SmallSizeDataset" is added for a reference. Then they input the entities in KBCE and get the suitable algorithms for each entity. Usually the intersection of all the sets of algorithms which are suitable for each entity is the output of KBCE.

In this experiment the EM algorithm satisfies all the entities which are converted from user's requirement, especially it is based on distribution, so it could show the consistency among the data set. And Based on the outward links of EM it is split into steps: Normalization and cluster. So the entire process of ABS data set processing is presented:

Delete_Rows -> Imputation_By_KNN -> Delete_Useless_Samples -> Calculate_Intervals -> Normalization -> EM

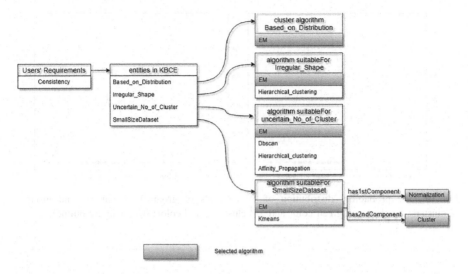

Fig. 9. Select the most suitable cluster algorithm in KBCE (EM- Expectation Maximization)

Based on EM algorithm the authors consider the changes among all the points in different groups. They present interesting results. The comparison of the intervals between 1st point and 2nd point in group 1 and group 2 is a typical example which is presented in Table 3.

Table 3. The results of clustering intervals between 1st point and 2nd point in group 1 and group 2 with EM algorithm

Dataset	No. of samples	No. of cluster	Likelihood
group1_diff12_norm	29	1 {29}	89.23071
group2_diff12_norm	31	2 {8,23}	92.30114

According to the table content, the intervals in group 1 are clustered into 1 cluster. That means the data is compact and respectively changes of parameters are consistent in group 1. On the other hand, the distribution in group 2 is blurred. This conclusion is significant for doctor's work. In Figs. 10 and 11 the probability distribution of the 1st and 33th intervals in group 1 and group are separately shown.

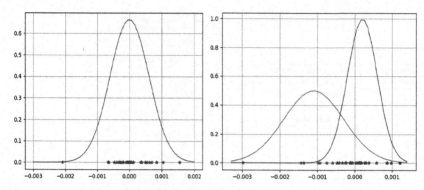

Fig. 10. The probability distribution of 1st intervals of group 1 (1 cluster) and group 2 (2 clusters: 1st cluster in green color and 2nd cluster in red color) (Color figure online)

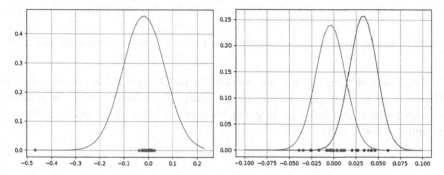

Fig. 11. The probability distribution of 33th intervals of group 1 (1 cluster) and group 2 (2 clusters: 1st cluster in green color and 2nd cluster in red color) (Color figure online)

6   Conclusion

This paper presents a knowledge-based computational environment for real-world data processing. It is built based on ontology so that it is flexible and understandable for non-computer professional researchers. Users can get reasonable advice about selecting the suitable data processing algorithm and understand these algorithms very easily according to the logical description in KBCE. The case indicates that KBCE usually provides a complete and reasonable data processing solution.

The research was funded by RFBR and CITMA according to the research project no. 18-57-34001.

References

1. Romano, D.: Data mining leading edge: insurance & banking. In: Proceedings of Knowledge Discovery and Data Mining (1997)
2. Stankova, E.N., Balakshiy, A.V., Petrov, D.A., Shorov, A.V., Korkhov, V.V.: Using technologies of OLAP and machine learning for validation of the numerical models of convective clouds. In: Gervasi, O., et al. (eds.) ICCSA 2016. LNCS, vol. 9788, pp. 463–472. Springer, Cham (2016). https://doi.org/10.1007/978-3-319-42111-7_36
3. Stankova, E.N., Ismailova, E.T., Grechko, I.A.: Algorithm for processing the results of cloud convection simulation using the methods of machine learning. In: Gervasi, O., et al. (eds.) ICCSA 2018. LNCS, vol. 10963, pp. 149–159. Springer, Cham (2018). https://doi.org/10.1007/978-3-319-95171-3_13
4. Stankova, E.N., et al.: OLAP technology and machine learning as the tools for validation of the numerical models of convective clouds. Int. J. Bus. Intell. Data Min. **14**(1–2), 254–266 (2019)
5. Düntsch, I., Gediga, G.: Rough set data analysis. In: Encyclopedia of Computer Science and Technology (2000)
6. Pawlak, Z.: Why rough sets? In: Proceedings of IEEE 5th International Fuzzy Systems, vol. 2. IEEE (1996)
7. Shichkina, Y.A., Degtyarev, A.B., Koblov, A.A.: Technology of cleaning and transforming data using the knowledge discovery in databases (KDD) technology for fast application of data mining methods. CEUR Workshop Proceedings, vol. 1787, pp. 428–434 (2016)
8. Chapman, A.D.: Principles of data quality. GBIF (2005)
9. Fernández-Delgado, M., et al.: Do we need hundreds of classifiers to solve real world classification problems? J. Mach. Learn. Res. **15**(1), 3133–3181 (2014)
10. Pedregosa, F., et al.: Scikit-learn: machine learning in Python. J. Mach. Learn. Res. **12**, 2825–2830 (2011)
11. Luo, G.: A review of automatic selection methods for machine learning algorithms and hyper-parameter values. Netw. Model. Anal. Health Inform. Bioinform. **5**(1), 18 (2016)
12. Xu, R., Wunsch, D.: Survey of clustering algorithms. IEEE Trans. Neural Networks **16**(3), 645–678 (2005)
13. Bagnall, A., et al.: The great time series classification bake off: an experimental evaluation of recently proposed algorithms (2016). Extended version. arXiv preprint arXiv:1602.01711
14. Fawaz, H.I., et al.: Deep learning for time series classification: a review (2018). arXiv preprint arXiv:1809.04356
15. Studer, R., Benjamins, V.R., Fensel, D.: Knowledge engineering: principles and methods. Data Knowl. Eng. **25**(1), 161–198 (1998)
16. Bernstein, A., Provost, F., Hill, S.: Toward intelligent assistance for a data mining process: an ontology-based approach for cost-sensitive classification. IEEE Trans. Knowl. Data Eng. **17**(4), 503–518 (2005)
17. Synthesis of integral models of system dynamics of an acid-base state of patients at operative measures. http://www.actascientific.com/ASMS-3-2.php
18. Tianxing, M., Zhukova, N.: An ontology of machine learning algorithms for human activity data processing. Learning **10**, 12 (2018)

Geometric Modeling, Graphics and Visualization

Adaptive Hierarchical Mesh Detail Mapping and Deformation

Bruno José Dembogurski[1]([⊠]) and Anselmo Antunes Montenegro[2]

[1] Universidade Federal Rural do Rio de Janeiro, Rio de Janeiro, Brazil
brunodembogurski@ufrrj.br
[2] Universidade Federal Fluminense, Rio de Janeiro, Brazil
anselmo@ice.ufjf.br

Abstract. In this work, we present a new method for controlled deformation and detail addition to 3d shapes represented as variable resolution meshes. The input data is a surface with arbitrary genus, represented by a polygonal mesh, and a set of parameters for edition control: positional information, the level of resolution, mesh features and direction of propagation of the deformation. An adaptive hierarchical mesh structure is constructed using an iterative feature-sensitive simplification method that concomitantly generates the parameterization of the mesh. The coarsest level of the representation defines the base domain which stores the original geometry via a local parameterization process. We apply local modifications to the base domain according to predefined functions; a noise function for details or any geometric deformation. In the sequel, the deformation of the base mesh is propagated to the original mesh. Our main contribution is a method that relies on the power of adaptive hierarchical structures to generate details with a greater degree of control by using a set of operators that explore the data structure properties as well as the information extracted and computed from the mesh.

Keywords: Detail mapping on meshes · Mesh editing ·
Hierarchical meshes · Feature-sensitive decimation · Mesh processing

1 Introduction

An important problem in the area of geometry processing is mesh geometry editing, which can be burdensome when a large amount of vertices must be manipulated to make a meaningful change [7]. To deal with such a problem, it is usually necessary to build new representations on top of the raw input data. This representation can be obtained, for example, by fitting spline models or computing sophisticated computational manifold structures. Frequently, a parameterization processes has to be computed in order to construct an appropriate representation, what might become a complex task in the case of surfaces with genuses that are different from zero.

© Springer Nature Switzerland AG 2019
S. Misra et al. (Eds.): ICCSA 2019, LNCS 11619, pp. 273–288, 2019.
https://doi.org/10.1007/978-3-030-24289-3_21

In this work, we investigate the problem of detail addition and mesh deformation with special emphasis in controlling the mapping of procedurally generated details onto shapes described by meshes. There are many works in the literature that tackle issues related to mesh editing. Nevertheless, as far as we are concerned, very few works deal with the problem of controlling procedurally generated details using geometrical and topological information to achieve a better control of the procedural detail mapping process. We propose the use of a variable resolution parameterized mesh representation and a set of deformation operators that take for granted the adjacency information, hierarchical structure and adaptability of the mesh representation to guide the deformation. We demonstrate by experiments that the proposed representation and the designed operators can offer sufficient level of control and expressiveness power to produce many different deformations and detail addition effects. An example of our method steps can be seen in Fig. 4.

The main contributions of this work are:

- A new method for deforming and adding details to meshes with arbitrary genus in an adaptive and controlled way, based on a combination of variable resolution mesh representations, operators for procedural noise generation and mesh subdivision.
- The proposal of a *general deformation handle* that generalizes the idea of *deformation handle* [2] in mesh editing. General deformation handles consider mesh features, the level of resolution and direction of propagation of the deformation.
- An improvement in the process of base domain generation for variable resolution mesh representations by using feature-preserving decimation. This makes features available for controlled edition even in the coarsest levels of the mesh representation differently from multiresolution mesh editing based on fairing.

2   Related Work

According to [4], it is possible to group mesh deformation techniques into two categories: *surface-based deformations* and *space-based deformations*. Surface-based deformations offer a higher degree of control as vertices can be manipulated and constrained individually whereas space-based deformations define deformation implicitly by deforming space. Deformation methods can also be classified as *linear* or *non-linear* depending on the type of energy minimization required for computing the solution based on optimization strategies. Our work can be classified as a topological variable resolution surface-based deformation controlled by the mesh vertices' position, features detected, the levels of resolution of its vertices and the direction of deformation. This section presents a brief description of works related to surface-based multiresolution and feature-aware approaches. For a more general review of shape editing and deformation we refer the reader to [4,17].

Multiresolution Deformation. Multiresolution deformation techniques decompose the original surface into a low-pass filtered coarse approximation and high-frequency details. Modifications are applied to the coarse version of the surface, e.g., by *transformation propagation* [2] or any arbitrary editing technique. Finally, the stored high-frequency details are added to the edited version of the coarse approximation. In the literature we can find two main approaches for building multiresolution mesh representations: *subdivision-based* [3,21,24] and *simplification-based* [9]. In [24], Zorin et al. propose a multiresolution representation that is constructed using a combination of the Loop subdivision scheme with Taubin's faring technique [18] in which details are encoded in local frames. Velho et al. in [21] also propose a similar multiresolution representation but differs by using the Catmull-Clark subdivision scheme. Smoothing is done through a quasi-interpolation and the mesh is represented as an atlas. One important characteristic of [21] is that they also deal with the problem of procedural detail creation. Subdivision-based representations require meshes with subdivision connectivity and also have the drawback that the features that are supposed to be edited do not necessarily match the topology in the coarser levels.

Progressive Mesh Editing. In [6], Derzapf et al. present a method for parallel editing of *Progressive Meshes* [8], a data structure for representing meshes as a coarse mesh associated with a set of edge collapse operations and their local and global attributes. Derzapf et al. propose a CUDA GPU implementation of a new simplification algorithm that enables edition of progressive meshes in real time. In their method, they propose the storage of all operations based on the labeling of vertices after computing edge collapses in their data structure. Modifications are automatically propagated to finer resolutions using an encoding of the split operations based on local coordinate systems. The way they propagate modifications is similar to ours since the geometrical information of each vertex is also stored in a local coordinate system. The main difference is the usage of the *edge-weld* operation instead of *vertex split* and we do not store any operation. Furthermore, differently from our method, the approach presented by Derzapf et al. cannot change the connectivity of the mesh.

Adaptive Multiresolution Meshes. Maximo et al. [13] present an adaptive multiresolution mesh representation exploring the computational differences between the CPU and the GPU. They consider a dense mesh as input and simplify it to a base domain in a similar fashion to the work presented in [11], however, using an atlas structure. Its main objective is to show the adaptive control of the mesh resolution in CPU-GPU coupled applications. Differently from Maximo, we use an A4-k mesh representation instead of an A4-8 because the feature sensitive decimation used in our representation construction produces meshes with vertices that have valency different from four and eight.

Semantic Mesh Editing. In [23], Yumer et al. deal with the problem of controlled mesh editing in a very different and innovative way. They propose a method for creating deformations based on semantic attributes rather than using detailed geometric manipulations. For this, they formulate deformations as a problem of constrained path traversal in a geometric space of shapes where models in the shape set are seen as regression points. Thus, a database of shapes can be seen as a continuous deformation space. They argue and show via use cases that a non-expert user can produce semantically guided shape variations by using their exploration and design interface in a way that would be quite difficult using other approaches.

Feature-Aware Shape Edition. Dekkers et al. proposed in [5] a new mesh editing scheme that supports both elastic deformation, via a modification of a conventional Laplacian editing method, and plastic deformation by adding and removing triangles in low salience regions that absorb most of the deformation energy.

3   Problem Definition

Given a mesh M and a *general deformation handler* GDH represented by a set of 3-ples (R, L, VF) where $R \subset M$ defines a region of interest, L represents the levels of detail of the vertices in R, and VF is a vector field, compute a new mesh M' by defining as transform $T : M \to M'$ where T is a composition of deformation operators D_i.

4   Methodology

Mesh edition based on multiresolution analysis and synthesis requires mesh fairing which eventually removes important features that may be used for controlled edition. In this work, we propose a different approach that tries to overcome this problem. It is based on the representation of the surface as a parameterized variable resolution mesh coupled with a set of extensible deformation operators. Our reasoning behind this choice takes in consideration that variable resolution meshes are able to express adapted mesh hierarchies with an overall better preservation of important features, making it possible to achieve a more precise control of the deformation even when applied at coarse resolutions. Since the representation is a completely parameterized adaptive hierarchical topological structure, it is possible to navigate through the mesh's levels of resolution and spatial adjacency to perform any sort of geometry deformation and detail addition, which can be smoothly propagated across the regions of the mesh. The result of such process can be propagated to the most refined levels of the shape representation in a simple way.

5   Proposed Method

Our method is composed of three main steps: (a) representation construction (by concomitant decimation and parameterization), (b) refinement and (c) deformation/detail generation which are described below.

5.1   Construction of the Mesh's Representation

Our mesh representation is based on the variable resolution a4-k structure introduced by Velho in [20]. This is a powerful structure for the representation of objects at multiple levels of detail. The hierarchical structure of the variable resolution a4-k mesh is built using a simplification process that uses a set of local modifications defined on clusters of two triangle faces. These modifications are made through the *Stellar Operators edge flip*, *edge split* and *edge weld* and cause minimum changes in a local neighborhood. The refinement and deformation/detail addition can be performed at any level or region of the mesh. As new vertices are inserted or modified, they are reparameterized producing a very powerful representation.

Mesh Simplification. Our mesh simplification algorithm is a feature-sensitive extension of the *Four-face Cluster Technique* presented in [19].

Feature lines are one of the most prominent characteristics of a surface where sharp details usually appear. These are extremely important to this work, because the preservation of important features in the hierarchy, especially in the base mesh, allows a greater level of positional and directional control in the deformation and detail generation process. This is even more evident for meshes representing man-made artifacts. In our approach, we use the *Tensor-feature Analysis* as proposed by [14] couple with a *Voting Scheme* and the *Neighboring Vertex Coincidence* (NVC) criterion, introduced by Wang in [22], that separates weak-edge vertices from noise ones.

In order to guarantee that the main features are preserved in the base domain mesh through the simplification procedure, we mark all features we want to be preserved as *unremovable*. After this process, an independent set of clusters that covers most of the mesh is selected. During this step, every vertex that is related to an important feature of the surface is marked as unremovable and is not included in the cluster list, thus maintaining feature lines and corners untouched. The cluster simplification creates a geometric modification in the 1-ring neighborhood of faces of the vertex being removed, meaning that both boundary vertices and edges remain unchanged.

The feature preservation scheme creates a less uniform distribution of valencies across the mesh. This is one of the reasons for using an a4-k mesh since the maintenance of an a4-8 structure under this circumstance would be a hard task, requiring frequent reparameterizations.

Mesh Parameterization Guided by Simplification. Our method uses a parameterization approach based on the MAPS [11] parameterization. Although other global parameterization methods could be used, the MAPS scheme is compatible with our idea of concomitant parameterization and hierarchical construction, and is able to deal with arbitrary genus surface without the need for cutting the mesh to generate a structure with the topology of a disk. Moreover, it is very simple to include our feature-preservation scheme in the MAPS-based paremetertization.

After the simplification process, the resulting structure is a hierarchical parameterized mesh with initial levels $M^0, M^1, M^2, \ldots M^{l_{max}}$, where l_{max} is the level of the coarsest mesh. As the deformation process is performed, such mesh levels of resolution can be modified in a adaptive way relying on the nice properties of the a4-k mesh structure.

5.2 Deformation

In our approach deformation operators are used to deform the mesh. A discrete deformation operator is defined as a map $D : M \times (R, L, VF) \rightarrow M'$ where R is a region of interest defined by a subset of the vertices V of the mesh together with its adjacency relationships, L is the level of detail of the vertices in R and VF is a vector field defined on R, that guides the direction of displacement.

One of the fundamental properties of the proposed operators is their capability to use the level of detail of the vertices in a given region to modulate the intensity of the deformation. It also may take vector fields to define directional constraints on the deformation enabling greater control as well as the adjacency information of the vertices $v \in R$.

Parameterization Update After Deformation. After applying any combination of deformation operators to the mesh, we must update the coordinates of the vertices or define the parameterization of newly inserted vertices. This update is performed once, immediately after the completion of the detail addition process. First we perform a simple check, verifying whether a vertex v in a given triangle is supposed to be deformed or not. The coordinates of a deformed vertex v are updated using the barycentric coordinates $\alpha(v), \beta(v), \gamma(v)$, defined by the parametrization, in conjunction with its detail represented by its height value $h(v)$ in the local frame. The height value $h(v)$ is also used to retrieve the 3D coordinates of a vertex in the mesh's global refinement step which reconstructs the finest levels of representation of the mesh from the base mesh.

5.3 Adaptive Refinement

In order to reconstruct a mesh level K^{l-1} from the current mesh in level K^l we must walk across the triangles of K^l checking which vertices in the parametrized structure needs to be re-inserted. Each triangle is associated to a multimap data structure containing its parameterized vertices grouped by their levels of detail defined just before they are removed in the simplification step. Each group of vertices with the same level l can be retrieved using the access key given by l. Thus, to obtain the vertices that must be re-inserted at each level l, we only need to recover the entries with that key value. These vertices are then stored in a temporary queue ordered by their removal order. This guarantees that the insertion order respects the order of vertex removal, by *edge weld*, in the simplification process.

An *edge split* operation is used to re-insert a vertex. To decide which edge must be split when a vertex is inserted, we compute its Euclidean distance to the triangles candidate edges and select the one that is closer.

During parameterization, the vertices of a given triangle may be parameterized onto different triangles on the base domain [11]. These singular cases generate overlapping edges during the refinement process and must be dealt with to properly rebuild the original geometry. A common approach is to subdivide such triangles until all vertices that belong to the same triangle are re-parameterized to the same triangle in the base domain [13].

In our approach, we used a heuristic solution in which we do not fix overlaps in the parameterization, doing so in the insertion operation. During the insertion step, we check if the distance from the current vertex position p to the center of the edge e to be split is greater than the length of any of the edges $(e_{t_1}, e_{t_2}, e_{t_3})$ of the new triangle t. If this is true, we search for the right insertion edge e_{n_t}, which, usually, is in one of the neighboring triangles n_t.

There are also challenges regarding the reconstruction of the original surface that must be tackled. A particularly tough one is how to restore the original mesh state when operations of vertex valence correction (edge flips) were needed. Intuitively, while refining, we want the vertex degree to be the same as before it was when removed. To achieve that, a vertex degree check must be performed, verifying if the inserted vertex has its original degree. If this is not true, we must perform *edge flip* operations to correct the vertex degree. After correcting a vertex degree in the mesh refinement step, we approximate the geometry of the original input mesh. The experiments have shown that only very few triangles have different geometry when compared with the original mesh and their aspect ratios are similar to the original ones.

6   Operators

We present a set of operators that are used to compute the deformation of the mesh geared by the regions of interest, the level of detail of its elements and a directional vector field. These operators can be divided into three groups: *auxiliary operators*, *deformation operators* and *composite operators*. Auxiliary operators do not perform deformations on the geometry of the mesh but carry on actions that aid the deformation process. There are two auxiliary operators: one responsible for a local refinement of the mesh, the *subdivision operator*, and a second one, the *feature-based query operator* which is used to select regions of interest satisfying some criterion. The deformation operators are used to modify the geometry of the mesh. We defined here three basic deformation operators: the *smoothing operator*, the *procedural detail operator* and the *geometric operator*. *Composite operators* combine two or more auxiliary and/or deformation operators to compute more complex effects.

6.1 Subdivision

The proposed subdivision operator explores the local adaptivity properties of the a4-k structure to deal with cases where the region of interest in not sufficiently refined for the creation of a specific deformation effect. It generates new samples by creating a concentric subdivision pattern around a valency four vertex from its link towards the center of the subdivided region where the vertex lies in. Figure 1 shows that this process only modifies the region restricted to the original 1-ring of the selected vertex. The use of such operator in a specific region of interest R requires that the vertices $v \in R$ define an independent vertex set. We denote the subdivision operator by $sub\ (R)$ where R is a region of interest composed of a set of independent vertices. Whenever a vertex has valency different from four it must have its connectivity changed by using the *edge flip* operator so that subdivision can be performed.

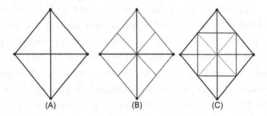

Fig. 1. (a) Input example of a degree four neighborhood. (b) One step of subdivision, where all link edges (green) are split. (c) Second step, where all even edges (red) are split. Every step following this one, switches between even (red) and odd edges (blue) for splitting. (Color figure online)

6.2 Smoothing

When combined with other operators the subdivision is usually followed by the use of a smoothing mask for smoother results. We based our smoothing operator on the smoothing component of the Loop subdivision scheme presented in [12]. The smoothing operator is represented by $smt\ (v)$ and takes as an input a vertex v. We decided to separate the smoothing operator from the subdivision as their use in combination is not mandatory.

6.3 Feature-Based Query Operator

This operator is used to retrieve feature-based filtered regions of interest FR which can be used as an input by other operators that require regions of interest as an argument. It is possible to return a set of vertices that satisfy any kind of property that characterizes a feature, for instance, features computed using the *Voting Tensor* algorithm. Such operator can also select a buffer zone around feature vertices by selecting a set of vertices that are not considered feature vertices on their own but are close enough to a minimum number of feature vertices.

We defined two versions of the feature-based filter operator: $fbqo$ (R, d, k) which returns a region of interest composed of vertices that are features themselves or that contains within its neighborhood, defined by a distance d, at least k feature vertices; the $cfbqo(R, d, k)$ which returns the complementary region to a feature-based filtered region. In our implementation, we used a topological distance instead of a geodesic distance but this would be easy to modify by using, for example, the Fast Marching Algorithm [16]. The resulting region must be pre-processed into an independent set if it is to be used as an input to the *subdivision operator*. We can define very powerful operators that rely on feature-based filtered regions because we can leverage feature information to modulate the desired deformations. Moreover, feature information can be propagated and attenuated when buffer zones are specified accordingly.

6.4   Geometric Operators

The geometric operators are usually used to produce deformations in medium to large scale. We define here a general geometric operator as $geom$ (R) that takes as an input ta region of interest R given by a connected set of vertices. For the experiments, we implemented two specific instances of the geometric operator: the tapper operator tpr (R,r), where r is a non-uniform scaling and the twist operator, twt (R,θ) where θ is the twisting angle. In both operators, r and θ, respectively, are piecewise linear non-decreasing functions of one of the coordinates of the 3d embedding space [1].

Procedural Detail Operators. Consider a noise function $nf(x) : \mathbb{R}^3 \rightarrow \mathbb{R}$. The basic idea is to compute the value of a noise function at the coordinates $p(v)$ of a vertex $v \in V$ and use it as the intensity of the displacement of v in some direction $\boldsymbol{d}(v) : V \rightarrow \mathbb{R}^3$. Aiming to leverage the level of detail information, we modulate the local intensity of the deformation caused by the noise value $nf(p(v))$ via a function $I(lv, F) : \{0, \dots, l_{max}\} \times \mathbb{R} \rightarrow \mathbb{R}^+$ where $lv(v) : V \rightarrow \{0, \dots, l_{max}\}$ associates v to its level of detail and $F : V \rightarrow \mathbb{R}$ defines some measure computed on v, for instance, its Gaussian curvature $\kappa(v)$. Usually, $I(lv, F)$ is an attenuation function defined by a monotonic decreasing function of $lv(v)$. We define a general procedural detail operator as:

$$pdo(v, \boldsymbol{d}) = p(v) + I(lv(v), F(p(v))nf(p(v))\boldsymbol{d}(v) \tag{1}$$

A simple effect can be produced by considering $\boldsymbol{d}(v) = \boldsymbol{n}(v)$ where $\boldsymbol{n}(v)$ is the discrete estimate of the normal of v at M and $I = \frac{1}{lv(v)+1}$. This configuration produces stronger displacements at the finer components of the mesh. We mark a vertex as *noised* to avoid accumulating local deformations through the levels, but it is also possible to combine noise values generated in different levels to produce different effects.

We propose two instances of the procedural detail operator. In the first one, the noise function is based on the *Turbulence Function* proposed by Perlin [15] and the second one is based on the *Gabor Noise* [10] proposed by Lagae et al. The turbulence noise function, presented in Eq. 2, is a weighted sum of band pass noises. It can be controlled via four parameters: amplitude a, frequency fr, gain g and lacunarity lc. Lacunarity and gain define, respectively, the rate of change of the frequency and amplitude of the noise per octave and regulate the fractal behavior of the noise.

$$TN(v, a, lc, fr, g) = \sum_i a \left| \frac{(lc^i) * fr * p(v)}{g^i * a} \right| \qquad (2)$$

Lacunarity usually takes values in $[1, 3]$ for a fractal behavior, whereas the gain is usually set to be the inverse of the lacunarity. Typical values are $fr = 2$, $lc = f$, $g = 0.5$ and $a = g$. The use of the previous values as arguments produces details where features align across scales so we must carefully modulate such parameters through the different levels of detail of the mesh. In our experiments, we defined the lacunarity and the gain in terms of the level of detail l respectively as $lc(l) = 1.1 + l * 0.1$ and $g(l) = 0.8/(l + 1)$. This configuration produced noise details that are smooth on large scales and rough on small scales. Our turbulence detail operator is represented as $tnpdo(v, a, lc, fr, g)$ defined by a generalization of Eq. 2 with the parameters a, lc and g depending on $lv(v)$.

Gabor noise [10] is a sparse convolution anisotropic noise based on a Gabor Kernel with accurate spectral control, which is able to provide a setup-free surface texturing. A band-pass Gabor noise presented in [10] is defined as:

$$GN(p, \dots) = \sum_i w_i g(K_i, a_i, F_{0,i}, \omega_{0,i}; p - p_i), \qquad (3)$$

where w_i are the random weights, K represents the amplitude, a_i is the bandwidth, F_0 is the frequency and ω_0 is the orientation of the cosine in the kernel $g(p)$ as presented in Eq. 4:

$$g(p) = K e^{-\pi a^2 |p|^2} \cos \left[2\pi F_0 \left(p_x \cos \omega_0 + p_y \sin \omega_0 \right) \right], \qquad (4)$$

We can configure the parameters of the Gabor noise in a way similar to the setup of the Perlin noise. Also, the random positions p_i are distributed according to a Poisson process with mean λ.

The anisotropic feature of the Gabor Noise is paramount to the generation of detail aligned or guided by the features of a mesh as will be shown in the results section. To define a detail operator based on the Gabor Noise we can either modify the noise function directly or change the phase-augmented Gabor kernel. Perturbing the Gabor kernel can be done by regulating the K, a, ω variables, all at once or individually, according to the resolution level, which is similar to what is proposed for the turbulence and other functions. We can also modify the number of impulses per kernel according to this method, moving this value always as a power of two.

The idea is to find a nice relation between the many levels of resolution. Intuitively, for a better distribution, a higher number of impulses is preferred while manipulating the coarser levels, since the higher frequencies will be a dominant force. Also, this is a valuable tool for controlling which frequencies we want at each scale.

We define the Gabor Noise operator as gno (v, l, $\mathbf{K}$, $\mathbf{a}$, $\mathbf{F_0}$, Ω, $\mathbf{p}$) where $\mathbf{K}$, $\mathbf{a}$, $\mathbf{F_0}$, Ω, $\mathbf{p}$ are vectorial versions of the parameters in Eq. 3 that also depend on the level of detail of v.

6.5   Composite Operators

Composite operators produce more complex effects through the combination of two or more operators or by computing a procedure with such operators. We present two composite operators: *Variation Operator* and the *Organic Operator*.

The main purpose of the *variation operator* is to create detail variation across the surface of the object and through its many levels of resolution. This is achieved by modulating the frequency and the amplitude of the noise function, through each resolution level, in order to obtain the desired texture effect. It is basically an application of the procedural detail operator that relies on the 4-k mesh structure to use neighborhood relationships to propagate the noise from a vertex v to a neighbor vertex v' and increase or decrease its influence according to a topological distance $td(v, v')$ or geodesic distance $gd(v, v')$. To define the variation operator we use a variation of the procedural noise in Eq. 1 where the noise function nf is given by Perlin's *Turbulence Function* whose parameters are modulated by $lv(v)$, $I = \frac{1}{lv(v)+1}$ and α is the distance attenuation factor.

$$varo(v, v', \boldsymbol{d}, td, \alpha) = p(v) + \frac{I}{\alpha td(p(v), p'(v))}(\boldsymbol{d}(p(v))nf \qquad (5)$$

The *organic operator* aims at creating organic looking structures. It relies on the *subdivision* and *smoothing operators* to create different shapes, but, for more general purposes, can be used without them.

This operator is composed of two steps, a global one, and a local one. The global step generates a deformation that produces an overall mesh detail texture, i.e. the patterns obtained through the noise functions presented before. The local step performs local manipulations creating more complex detail structures as a function of the level of detail.

Algorithm 1 describes the organic operator, which is used to create some of the images in the results section.

Algorithm 1 applies a deformation at a vertex v and propagates its effect to the vertex k-ring. Next, it performs a refinement on this new deformed region executing n steps of the subdivision operator. Finally, it deforms the refined area by choosing a random vertex v' within it and uses its normal to apply the procedural noise operator in v'. This will generate a wide area with an organic look because the vertices on the k-ring will be pushed outwards. We denote the *organic operator* as $orgo(R,l,k)$.

Data: Input region R, $k - ring$ defines the propagation neighborhood, and
attenuation factor α

Result: Deformation of the refined region around vertices in R

for *Each* $v \in R$ **do**
   pdo($v, \boldsymbol{n}(v)$);
   for *Each* $v' \in$ *the k-ring of* v **do**
      | varo($v, v', \boldsymbol{n}, td, \alpha$)
   end
   apply n **passes of:** sub(v);
   find random vertex v' in the refined area around v
   $\boldsymbol{d} \leftarrow \boldsymbol{n}(v')$;
   pdo($v, \boldsymbol{d}$);
end

Algorithm 1. Creating extensions with the organic operator.

7   Results

Tests were performed in an Asus GT50vt notebook with an Intel Core 2 Duo
CPU with 4 GB of RAM and a nVidia 9800M GTS GPU with 512 MB.

In Fig. 2, we present two ways to perform feature-based deformation. In the
left figure, the deformation is restricted to the line feature area, whereas on the
right we see it applied to a fan-disk centered at each vertex of the line features.

Fig. 2. Example of a deformation restricted to the feature line's area. In the bottom
left we see an erosion on the fandisk across feature lines and, at the bottom right, a
deformation to create a kneaded effect.

Figure 3 (left) illustrates an application of the organic operator. There are
some steps necessary to generate this effect. First, we must select the region

of interest R disturb it with noise and then propagate the deformation across the 2-ring neighborhood area of each $v \in R$. We used the *variation operator* for this where the propagation is done in the following way: after moving the vertex in the direction of its normal we propagate the displacement value to the neighboring area with attenuation weight $\alpha = 1.5$ for the 1-ring and $\alpha = 2.0$ for the 2-ring vertices. The objective of this displacement is to create bumps with a smooth appearance. The next deformation is used to move the vertices in opposite directions creating a wide area at the top of the bump as shown in Fig. 3 (right). After this stage, the operator *tpndo*$(v, l, fr, a, lc = 6.0, g = 0.3)$ with default values of frequency and amplitude is used to create the idea of trees, bumpy ground and/or organic extensions.

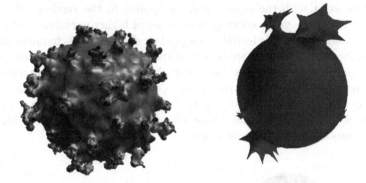

Fig. 3. (left) Example of an alien planet or virus cell using guided positioning. (right) Creating bumps with wide areas using variation operator.

In order to present a full view of our techniques pipeline, in Fig. 4 we show various steps of the same model being simplified, modified and refined. From left to right, starting with an original mesh (with roughly 40k vertices), we proceed to create a base mesh, through the mentioned simplification process, with approximately 1k vertices. The middle skull shows how the removed vertices are mapped over each face (triangle) the model. Next, a deformation is performed, in this specific case a twist operator, and a reparameterization step is executed to guarantee the consistency of the mesh needed during the refinement process. Finally, the last skull presents the model after all possible refinement steps, and how the deformation is correctly propagated from the base mesh to the higher levels of detail.

Figure 5 (right) illustrates a complete example where several operators are combined for a final modeling effect. We use as an input a skull mesh Fig. 5 (left) with its mean curvature calculated. It is easy to spot the high curvature areas around the eyes, nose, and teeth. In this particular example, we want to create a beard effect, without deforming the area of the teeth, and also to give a hair appearance to this bald model.

Fig. 4. Steps of our method from left to right: input mesh (~40k vertices), base mesh (~1k vertices) created through the simplification process, parameterization mapping, deformation and remapping, and, finally, the result of the refinement proces

We first start with the *tnpdo* operator applied to the vertices v in a ROI filtered by curvature value selecting only those of higher curvature and y value below the nose region. This introduces a random displacement characterizing the beard. In the second step, we apply only at the coarsest level, the *tapper operator* (tpr) in the x and y coordinates while maintaining z untouched. After a few steps of refinement and deformation propagation, we apply the *twist operator tst* in the region of higher z coordinate to create a curl effect followed by a *gaussian noise operator gdo* in the same region that creates details aligned with the z direction, producing the hair movement.

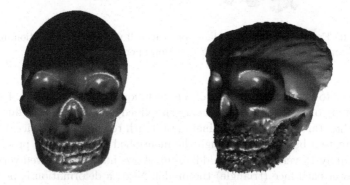

Fig. 5. (left) Original mesh. (right) Deformation of hair and beard.

8   Conclusion

This work proposes a new framework for adaptive multiresolution mesh detail addition and deformation. These are performed on a 3D shape represented by an adaptive parameterized variable resolution mesh representation together with a set of deformation and auxiliary operators. Our modeling pipeline enables deformation and detail addition at any level of the representation. Also, it does not build a geometrical multiresolution representation. Instead, it uses a topological multiresolution representation based on feature-sensitive simplification.

In such representation, features such as strong edges, weak edges and corners, when present in the original shape, are kept even at the coarsest levels enabling the use of such elements as control elements and input to deformation or detail addition. We argue that features are important elements for mesh edition operation and must be made available for manipulation whenever possible.

Operators are devised to work with a generalized deformation handle which includes regions of interest, its corresponding levels of detail and a directional vector field that characterizes the direction of propagation of the deformation. Differently from other similar works we do not rely on remeshing of the original mesh and also do not store sequences of operation performed at the adaptive representation.

Different experimental results have shown that our method is able to produce quite promising results especially considering controlled procedural detail addition. The possibility of adding detail aligned with features and specific directions on the mesh is one of the most powerful effects we presented. As a result, there are many possibilities for future research.

In this work, the focus is on the representation, operator definition and control specification. Hence, implementation of the method up to now is still not optimized to enable interactive manipulation. We intend to pursue, in the future, interactive rates as well as ways of converting friendly user-interactive mechanisms into sequences of deformation operators that take as input automatically specified general deformation handles.

In the presented method, controlling the procedural detail scale according to the level of detail of the mesh requires an artificial discretization of the signals scale as our representation does not build a continuum of mesh representations. Also, looking for ways of describing a continuous version of our representation as in geometrical multiresolution, but keeping the most important features of the mesh at coarser levels is a major goal. This would make possible to leverage all the possibilities of our method and at the same time achieve a better syntonization of the levels of detail with the scales of procedural signals.

References

1. Barr, A.H.: Global and local deformations of solid primitives. In: Proceedings of the 11th Annual Conference on Computer Graphics and Interactive Techniques, SIGGRAPH 1984, pp. 21–30. ACM, New York (1984)
2. Bendels, G.H., Klein, R., Schilling, A.: Image and 3d-object editing with precisely specified editing regions. In: Ertl, T., et al. (eds.) Vision, Modeling and Visualisation 2003, pp. 451–460. Akademische Verlagsgesellschaft Aka GmbH, Heidelberg (2003)
3. Biermann, H., Martin, I.M., Zorin, D., Bernardini, F.: Sharp features on multiresolution subdivision surfaces. Graph. Models **64**(2), 61–77 (2002)
4. Botsch, M., Pauly, M., Rossl, C., Bischoff, S., Kobbelt, L.: Geometric modeling based on triangle meshes. In: ACM SIGGRAPH 2006 Courses, SIGGRAPH 2006. ACM, New York (2006). https://doi.org/10.1145/1185657.1185839
5. Dekkers, E., Kobbelt, L.: Geometry seam carving. Comput. Aided Des. **46**, 120–128 (2014)

6. Derzapf, E., Grund, N., Guthe, M.: Parallel progressive mesh editing. In: Eurographics Symposium on Parallel Graphics and Visualization, Swansea, Wales, UK, 2014, Proceedings, pp. 33–40 (2014). https://doi.org/10.2312/pgv.20141082
7. Eck, M., DeRose, T., Duchamp, T., Hoppe, H., Lounsbery, M., Stuetzle, W.: Multiresolution analysis of arbitrary meshes. In: Proceedings of the 22nd Annual Conference on Computer Graphics and Interactive Techniques, SIGGRAPH 1995, pp. 173–182. ACM, New York (1995)
8. Hoppe, H.: Progressive meshes. In: Proceedings of the 23rd Annual Conference on Computer Graphics and Interactive Techniques, SIGGRAPH 1996, pp. 99–108. ACM, New York (1996). https://doi.org/10.1145/237170.237216
9. Kobbelt, L., Stamminger, M., Seidel, H.P.: Using subdivision on hierarchical data to reconstruct radiosity distribution 16(3), C347–C355 (1997). https://doi.org/10.1111/1467-8659.16.3conferenceissue.36, Proceedings Eurographics 1997
10. Lagae, A., Lefebvre, S., Drettakis, G., Dutré, P.: Procedural noise using sparse gabor convolution. In: ACM SIGGRAPH 2009 Papers, SIGGRAPH 2009, pp. 54:1–54:10. ACM, New York (2009)
11. Lee, A.W.F., Sweldens, W., Schröder, P., Cowsar, L., Dobkin, D.: Maps: multiresolution adaptive parameterization of surfaces. In: Proceedings of the 25th Annual Conference on Computer Graphics and Interactive Techniques, SIGGRAPH 1998, pp. 95–104. ACM, New York (1998). https://doi.org/10.1145/280814.280828
12. Loop, C.: Smooth Subdivision Surfaces Based on Triangles. Department of Mathematics, University of Utah (1987)
13. Maximo, A., Velho, L., Siqueira, M.: Adaptive multi-chart and multiresolution mesh representation. Comput. Graph. 38, 332–340 (2014). https://doi.org/10.1016/j.cag.2013.11.013
14. Medioni, G., Tang, C.K., Lee, M.S.: Tensor voting: theory and applications. In: Proceedings of RFIA (2000)
15. Perlin, K.: An image synthesizer. In: Proceedings of the 12th Annual Conference on Computer Graphics and Interactive Techniques, SIGGRAPH 1985, pp. 287–296. ACM, New York (1985)
16. Sethian, J.A.: A fast marching level set method for monotonically advancing fronts. In: Proceedings National Academy of Sciences, pp. 1591–1595 (1995)
17. Sorkine, O., Botsch, M.: Tutorial: interactive shape modeling and deformation. In: EUROGRAPHICS (2009)
18. Taubin, G.: A signal processing approach to fair surface design. In: Proceedings of the 22nd Annual Conference on Computer Graphics and Interactive Techniques, SIGGRAPH 1995, pp. 351–358. ACM, New York (1995). https://doi.org/10.1145/218380.218473
19. Velho, L.: Mesh simplification using four-face clusters. In: Shape Modeling International, pp. 200–208. IEEE Computer Society (2001)
20. Velho, L., Gomes, J.: Variable resolution 4-k meshes: concepts and applications. Comput. Graph. Forum 19(4), 195–212 (2000)
21. Velho, L., Perlin, K., Biermann, H., Ying, L.: Algorithmic shape modeling with subdivision surfaces. Comput. Graph. 26(6), 865–875 (2002)
22. Wang, S., Hou, T., Su, Z., Qin, H.: Diffusion tensor weighted harmonic fields for feature classification, pp. 93–98 (2011)
23. Yümer, M.E., Chaudhuri, S., Hodgins, J.K., Kara, L.B.: Semantic shape editing using deformation handles. ACM Trans. Graph. 34(4), 86 (2015)
24. Zorin, D., Schröder, P.: Subdivision for Modeling and Animation. Technical report, SIGGRAPH 2000 (2000). Course Notes

Multithreading in Laser Scanning Data Processing

Vladimir Badenko[1]([⊠]) [iD], Serafim Tammsaar[1] [iD],
Kirill Beliaevskii[1] [iD], Alexander Fedotov[1] [iD],
and Konstantin Vinogradov[2] [iD]

[1] Peter the Great St. Petersburg Polytechnic University,
Polytechnicheskaya 29, 195251 St. Petersburg, Russia
vbadenko@gmail.com, {serafim.tammsaar,
kirill.beliaevskii}@spbpu.com, afedotov@spbstu.ru
[2] Saint-Petersburg State University,
Universitetskaya Emb. 13B, 199034 St. Petersburg, Russia
kostyal495@mail.ru

Abstract. Laser scanning is one of the modern and actively-developing remote sensing techniques, resulting in a point cloud, containing a set of different attributes for each point. One of the positive features of laser scanning is the high accuracy of the results; this is achieved by obtaining a large number of points describing the scanned object. In some circumstances, point clouds may contain billions of points, which require hundreds of gigabytes to be stored. Loading and processing of such huge data require large time and computational resources. The first problem is such massive point clouds initial downloading and pre-processing. The standard approach is the sequential processing of laser scanning results, which requires a significant amount of time. In this paper, we have conducted research and testing of various approaches for loading and processing of point clouds, one of the proposed approaches is the use of multithreading to significantly reduce time. The guideline for improvement of processing of laser scanning point clouds with use of multithreading is presented.

Keywords: Algorithm · Laser scanning data · Point cloud ·
Parallel processing · Multithreading

1 Introduction

Laser scanning is a common method for 3D data capture, which allows obtaining information about the shape (three-dimensional coordinates) and appearance (color and intensity of reflection beams) of objects in the real world [1, 2], the results are presented in the form of a point cloud, then these data can be used to build spatial digital models of measured objects [3, 4]. The use of laser scanning point cloud is common in many spheres, for example, land surveying, architecture, geologic exploration activities, industrial enterprises, civil engineering, and more [5, 6]. Specific examples of the tasks to be solved are forest management [7], 3D city modeling [8], road inventory [9],

© Springer Nature Switzerland AG 2019
S. Misra et al. (Eds.): ICCSA 2019, LNCS 11619, pp. 289–305, 2019.
https://doi.org/10.1007/978-3-030-24289-3_22

ground surface reconstruction [10], pipeline detection [11], and wire detection [12]. Moreover, this is only a small part of the issues solved using laser scanning data, for example, the fastest growing branch is as-built BIM [13–17].

One of the key issues when working with point clouds is a large amount of information that needs to be processed [18–21]. Any work with laser scanning data can be divided into two stages: loading and pre-processing of data; data processing (specific algorithm) [15, 22]. Most of the research is focused on optimizing the processing stage [1, 2, 4, 23]. However, there are tasks that do not require a lot of time for the data processing stage, for example, a preview of a point cloud [15, 22]. In such tasks, the loading and pre-processing stage takes most of the time [24]. The most common approach to increasing load speed is to increase the bandwidth of the data bus, which can be achieved by using a faster solid state drive (SSD) or RAID [25]. But in order to increase the speed of loading even more, multithreading can be used.

The results of research and testing of various approaches in the loading and pre-processing stage is discussed in this paper. A sequential reading of a point cloud from a file with subsequent processing can be considered the standard approach. We hypothesized that in some situations the use of multithreading can help significantly speed up the loading of a point cloud. To test this hypothesis in this paper, experiments have been conducted using various approaches to loading laser scanning data. In addition, some standard libraries will be tested and compared. In conclusion, we will provide recommendations and describe further plans.

2 Materials and Methods

2.1 Point Cloud Loading and Pre-processing

The main problem of loading laser scanning data is too large volume, the size of point clouds can amount to hundreds of gigabytes. Thus, it will not be possible to load all data into RAM at once. There are many solutions to this problem, the two simplest are: (1) splitting the original point cloud into separate sections; (2) loading the point cloud with part by part.

The first approach is that each section is a small point cloud, so that each section can be loaded and processed separately. In the second approach, the cloud is sequentially loaded in parts, the loaded part is processed, and then the next part of the file is loaded.

These approaches are not suitable for all algorithms since there are algorithms that need neighboring points for all points to work, and when processing only a section of the cloud, there are no neighbor points for endpoints. In the first approach, this problem is easily solved by modifying the partitioning algorithm; it's enough to break up a point cloud into sections with small intersecting indents, the size of which depends on the algorithm used. In the second approach, you will have to use a spatial data structure, for example, an octree [26], but for this, you first need to build a spatial data structure for the entire point cloud. In further tests, the second approach is used, since to implement the first one, it is still necessary to load the initial point cloud.

2.2   Existing Approaches

Many different formats are used to store point clouds, such as OBJ, PLY, XYZ, PCD, LAS and many others [27]. During the tests, we used LAS VERSION 1.4 file format, since this is common and public format [28].

In this paper the existing approaches are considered on the example of LAStools [29] and PDAL [30] libraries, as they are the most widely used at the moment [31].

These libraries also use the approach of block loading of the source point cloud, which was described above. Thus, the point cloud sections are loaded and pre-processed sequentially in a single thread. Thus, the next point cloud section will be loaded only after the completion of the previous one, which may slow down the loading process.

We propose to load and pre-process point cloud data in parallel manner to increase algorithm throughput. This can be achieved on modern multi-core systems using multithreading. Thus, our approach is to separate the loading process into two phases executed in a distinct thread.

2.3   Background

Several tests have been developed and implemented to study various methods of laser scanning data loading (Table 1). The tests were written in the C++ programming language, as this language allows you to perform low-level work with memory, which is necessary for working with large amounts of data.

Table 1. List of tests

Title	Description
Test 1	Loading a file using a temporary buffer. Buffer creation time is not measured
Test 2	Loading a file using the temporary buffer. The buffer creation time is measured
Test 3	Loading a file using the temporary buffer. The buffer creation time is measured. All loaded data are copied to the internal data structure
Test 4	Loading a file using the temporary buffer. The buffer creation time is measured. Only the coordinates of the loaded points are copied to the internal data structure
Test 5	Loading a file using several temporary buffers. The buffer creation time is measured. All loaded data is copied to the internal data structure. Using two threads: the first one loads the data into one of the free buffers, the second one copies the data
Test 6	Loading a file using several temporary buffers. The buffer creation time is measured. A part of the data will be preprocessed. All loaded data is copied to the internal data structure. Using two threads: the first one loads the data into one of the free buffers, the second one copies the data
Test 7	Loading a file using several temporary buffers. The buffer creation time is measured. A part of the data will be preprocessed. All loaded data is copied to the internal data structure. Using three threads: the first one loads the data into one of the free buffers, the second one and third one copies the data
Test 8	Loading a file using PDAL
Test 9	Loading a file using LAStools

Test 1 and Test 2 are standard sequential readings of a file in parts, these tests are necessary to determine the dependence of the file loading time on the size of the temporary buffer. Test 3 and Test 4 based on Test 2. These tests allow to estimate the effect of delays between loading parts of a file on the total loading time. Test 8 and Test 9 are tests of existing libraries.

One of the features of the LAS format is various point formats. Depending on the point format specified in the file header (point format ID), each point has its own set of attributes described in the file format specification, so the size of one point can vary from 20 bytes to 67 bytes. Parameters of laser scanning point clouds for tests are presented in Table 2.

Test bench configuration:

CPU: Intel® Core™ i7-7820HQ CPU @ 2.90 GHz
RAM: 2 x SODIMM DDR4 2400 MHz
SSD: Samsung SSD 850 PRO 1 TB
OS: Ubuntu 18.04
File system: Ext4

Table 2. Clouds for testing

Title	Number of point records	Point format ID	Point size, bytes	Point cloud size, GB
Cloud 1	42'211'048	3	24	1.4
Cloud 2	150'000'000	5	63	9.5
Cloud 3	300'000'000	10	67	20.1

3   Results and Discussion

3.1   Loading with Temporary Buffer

To begin with, it is necessary to investigate the dependence between the file read speed and the size of the temporary buffer. Test 1 and Test 2 were developed for this.

Pseudocode for Test 1:

```
Reader r(filepath);        // Point Cloud reader
Buffer b(bufferSize);      // Temporary buffer
/* Time measurement starts here */
while(r.readChunk(b, b.size())) {}     // Read all points
/* Time measurement ends here */
```

The results of the first test, the dependence between the file read speed and the size of the temporary buffer are shown in Fig. 1.

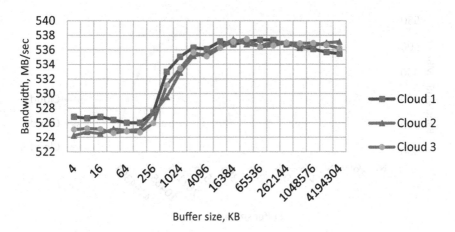

Fig. 1. The results of the first test, the dependence between the file read speed and the size of the temporary buffer.

From the observed data (Fig. 1), we can conclude that for clouds of different sizes the dependence of the load time on the buffer size is the same, it is also worth noting that using too small buffer slows down the loading speed by about 2–3%. In Fig. 1 you can see that in most cases the loading speed is close to the maximum for the SSD [12] used in the test bench.

Pseudocode for Test 2 are following:

```
Reader r(filepath);        // Point Cloud reader
/* Time measurement starts here */
Buffer b(bufferSize);      // Temporary buffer
while(r.readChunk(b, b.size())) {}    // Read all points
/* Time measurement ends here */
```

The results of the second test, the dependence between the file read speed and the size of the temporary buffer are shown in Fig. 2.

Based on the observed results (Fig. 2), it can be concluded that after exceeding a certain size, the creation time of the temporary buffer can greatly affect the total file load time. The smaller the difference between the file size and the buffer size, the stronger the influence. In the case where the buffer size exceeds the size of the point cloud itself more than three times, the file load speed drops by almost 60%. From the above data, we can conclude that the optimal buffer size for loading is somewhere between 2 and 32 MB. In Fig. 2, you can see that the load speed depends on the data bus bandwidth.

Possible approaches to accelerate the load of the point cloud: (1) multithreaded reading from a file; (2) reading part of the data from a file. Using multithreaded reading from the file does not make sense, since the maximum bandwidth of the data bus has been reached, therefore, using this approach will not improve the load speed.

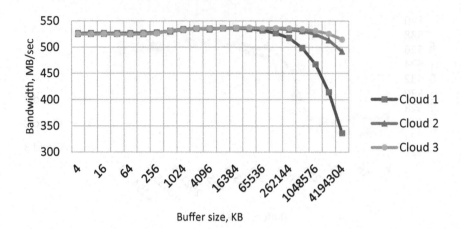

Fig. 2. The results of the second test, the dependence between the file read speed and the size of the temporary buffer.

Since many algorithms need only the coordinates of the points to work, then it would be possible to read only the coordinates, ignoring the other attributes. For example, for a format of point 10, it would be possible to save 55 bytes since the coordinates occupy only 12 bytes, this would allow downloading 82% less data. Unfortunately, in LAS format, the data of each point is stored sequentially, which means that it will be necessary to read small pieces of a file many times. But the operating system reads from the file in large blocks (the minimum block size for Ubuntu is 4 KB), so you will still have to read the entire file. This approach is suitable for storage formats where point attributes are stored sequentially, but not the points themselves.

Due to the first two tests, we found out the optimal buffer size for a simple file load, but no one loads a point cloud without a reason. The following tests will simulate a common situation where data downloaded from a file need to be copied into internal data structures. For this, Test 3 and Test 4 were developed.

Pseudocode for Test 3 are following:

```
Reader r(filepath);       // Point Cloud reader
Container c(r.getPointCnt()); // Point Cloud container

/* Time measurement starts here */
Buffer b(bufferSize);
while(r.readChunk(b, b.size())) // For all chunks
  c.pushAllData(b);// Push all ready data to end of con-
tainer
/* Time measurement ends here */
```

The results of the third test, the dependence between the file read speed and the size of the temporary buffer are shown in Fig. 3.

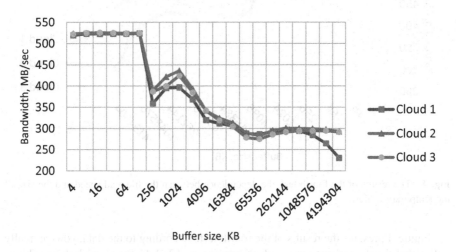

Fig. 3. The results of the third test, the dependence between the file read speed and the size of the temporary buffer.

Figure 3 presents the results of the third test; according to the data, it is clear that the load time dependence on the buffer size is the same for point clouds of different sizes. An interesting fact is that at a certain point the load time greatly increases by about 35–45% for different clouds, this happens because the delays caused by copying the loaded data interrupt the file system cache. To solve this problem, you can try to apply a slightly upgraded approach, described above, not to copy all the data, but to copy only the necessary data. In the fourth test, only the coordinates of the point are copied, which theoretically should reduce the delays between reading from the file.

Pseudocode for Test 4 is following:

```
Reader r(filepath);     // Point Cloud reader
Container c(r.getPointCnt()); // Point Cloud container
/* Time measurement starts here */
Buffer b(bufferSize);
while(r.readChunk(b, b.size())) // For all chunks
    c.pushOnlyXYZData(b);  // Push only xyz coordinates to
end of container
/* Time measurement ends here */
```

The results of the fourth test, the dependence between the file read speed and the size of the temporary buffer are shown in Fig. 4.

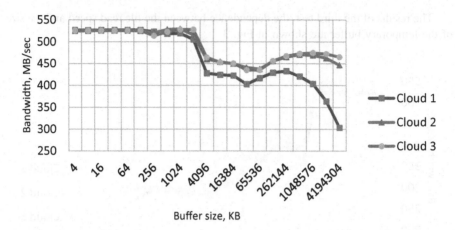

Fig. 4. The results of the fourth test, the dependence between the file read speed and the size of the temporary buffer.

Figure 4 presents the results of the fourth test. According to the data, you can really notice that the throughput increased on average by 12–23% for larger buffers. This is due to the reduction of delays between reading from the file. In addition, you may notice that the increase in load time comes earlier for Cloud 1 and is higher, this is due to the fact that copying only the coordinates of the point reduced the amount of copy data for Cloud 1 to only 8 bytes (per point), whereas for Cloud 2–51 bytes, for Cloud 3–55 bytes. Thus, the optimal buffer size for loading and copying of data is 16–128 KB, in addition, reducing the amount of copied data also improves the overall situation with the file load time.

3.2   Parallel Loading and Preprocessing

The next step is to use multithreading to eliminate delays between reading from a file, for this we developed Test 5. The main idea of this test is the use of several temporary buffers and two lock-free queues, one queue contains free buffers, the second one contains the occupied ones. In this test, two threads are used: the first thread loads data from the file into the free buffer, the second thread copies the data from the occupied buffer to the internal data structure. In the test, we used five temporary buffers.

Pseudocode for Test 5 is following:

```
Reader r(filepath);        // Point Cloud reader
Container c(r.getPointCnt());   // Point Cloud container

/* Time measurement starts here */

// Queue for freed buffers (Lock-free)
Queue<Buffer> freeQ(queueLength);
/* Push free buffers to freeQ */
// Queue for loaded buffers (Lock-free)
Queue<Buffer> loadedQ(queueLength);

auto t1 = std::thread([&]
{
  while(/* not all points reaed from file */) {
    Buffer b = freeQ.pop();    // Pop free buffer from
queue
    r.readChunk(b, b.size());    // Read file chunk to
buffer
    loadedQ.push(buffer);    // Push points to queue
  }
});
auto t2 = std::thread([&]
{
  while(/* not received stop signal */) {
    if(Buffer b = loadedQ.pop()){ // Pop points from
queue
      c.pushAllData(b);  // Push all readed data to end of
container
      freeQ.push(buffer);  // Push used buffer to queue
    }
  }
});
// Wait for threads ends
t1.join();
t2.join();
/* Time measurement ends here */
```

The results of the fifth test, the dependence between the file read speed and the size of the temporary buffer are shown in Fig. 5.

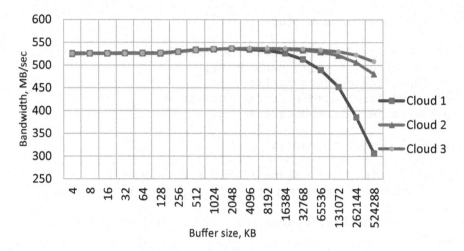

Fig. 5. The results of the fifth test, the dependence between the file read speed and the size of the temporary buffer.

Figure 5 presents the results of the fifth test. According to the data, the use of multithreading has reduced the delay between reading parts of the file. With the correct choice of the number of temporary buffers and their size, you can achieve such a file load time as in Test 2, taking into account that in Test 5, in addition to reading the file, all the data is also copied. Unfortunately, due to the use of several temporary buffers, an increase in load time occurs much earlier than in Test 2.

Test 6 simulates the usual situation for processing laser scanning data when some of the loaded data needs to be pre-processed. The simplest example of such a situation is the application of displacement and scaling to the coordinates of a point. Pseudocode for Test 6 is following:

```
Reader r(filepath);        // Point Cloud reader
Container c(r.getPointCnt());    // Point Cloud container

/* Time measurement starts here */

// Queue for freed buffers (Lock-free)
Queue<Buffer> freeQ(queueLength);
/* Push free buffers to freeQ */
// Queue for loaded buffers (Lock-free)
Queue<Buffer> loadedQ(queueLength);

auto t1 = std::thread([&]
{
  while(/* not all points readed from file */) {
    Buffer b = freeQ.pop();    // Pop free buffer from
queue
    r.readChunk(b, b.size());    // Read file chunk to
buffer
    loadedQ.push(buffer);    // Push points to queue
  }
});
auto t2 = std::thread([&]
{
  while(/* not received stop signal */) {
    if(Buffer b = loadedQ.pop()){ // Pop points from
queue
      preprocess (b);  // Preprocess XYZRGBData
      c.pushAllData(b);  // Push all readed data to end of
container
      freeQ.push(buffer);  // Push used buffer to queue
    }
  }
});
// Wait for threads ends
t1.join();
t2.join();
/* Time measurement ends here */
```

The results of the sixth test, the dependence between the file read speed and the size of the temporary buffer are shown in Fig. 6.

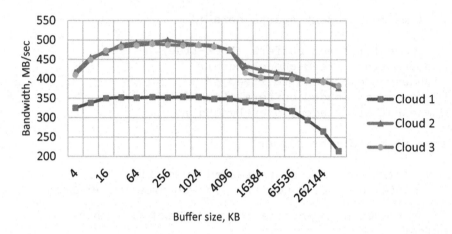

Fig. 6. The results of the sixth test, the dependence between the file read speed and the size of the temporary buffer.

Figure 6 presents the results of the sixth test, the data show an increase in file load time, for the best cases, up to almost 54% for Cloud 1 and about 11% for Cloud 2 and Cloud 3. This is due to the fact that the thread responsible for pre-processing and copying is no longer up to its tasks, as a result of which there are delays in reading the file. In Fig. 6, you can see a big difference in the load speed of Cloud 1, this is because the pre-processing function affects 90% of Cloud 1 data, and only 28.6% of Cloud 2 data and 26.9% of Cloud 3 data.

To solve the problem in Test 6, we developed Test 7. The main idea is the use of three threads, the third thread, like the second one, is used for pre-processing and copying of the loaded data.

Pseudocode for Test 7 is following:

```
Reader r(filepath);        // Point Cloud reader
Container c(r.getPointCnt());    // Point Cloud container

/* Time measurement starts here */

// Queue for freed buffers (Lock-free)
Queue<Buffer> freeQ(queueLength);
/* Push free buffers to freeQ */
// Queue for loaded buffers (Lock-free)
Queue<Buffer> loadedQ(queueLength);

auto t1 = std::thread([&]
{
  while(/* not all points readed from file */) {
    Buffer b = freeQ.pop();    // Pop free buffer from
queue
    r.readChunk(b, b.size());    // Read file chunk to
buffer
    loadedQ.push(buffer);    // Push points to queue
  }
});
auto f = [&]()
{
  while(/* not received stop signal */) {
    if(Buffer b = loadedQ.pop()){ // Pop points from
queue
      c.pushAllData(b);// Push all readed data to end of
container
      freeQ.push(buffer);  // Push used buffer to queue
    }
  }
};

auto t2 = std::thread(f);
auto t3 = std::thread(f);
// Wait for threads ends
t1.join();
t2.join();
t3.join();
/* Time measurement ends here */
```

The results of the seventh test, the dependence between the file read speed and the size of the temporary buffer are shown in Fig. 7.

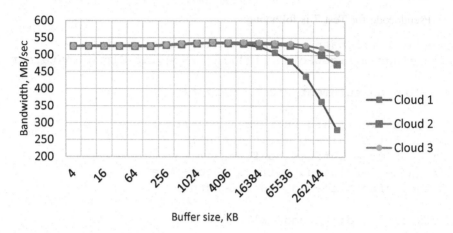

Fig. 7. The results of the seventh test, the dependence between the file read speed and the size of the temporary buffer.

Figure 7 presents the results of the seventh test, the data almost coincides with the results of Test 5, this was achieved by introducing an additional thread for pre-processing and copying, which made it possible to eliminate delays in reading the file by the first thread. Due to this, almost the maximum load speed was achieved, taking into account that in parallel with the loading, all data are pre-processed and copied.

At this point, we can conclude when correctly setting parameters such as the number of temporary buffers, the size of temporary buffers and the number of processing threads, you can achieve optimal results when loading and processing a point cloud.

3.3   Third-Party Libraries

Test 8 and Test 9 were developed for testing third-party libraries. We chose two most common libraries for loading LAS files in C++: PDAL and LAStools.

PDAL is an open source library for working with point cloud data, one of the possibilities provided by this library is load files in LAS format. Unfortunately, this library does not support loading of Cloud 2 and Cloud 3 because of the point format, so testing was performed only on Cloud 1.

LAStools is one of the most common open source laser scanning data processing tools. This set of tools allows you to load LAS files using the LASlib library. Unfortunately, this library supports reading the file only by one point, so there is no possibility to adjust the size of the temporary buffer.

The test results are presented in the Table 3.

Table 3. Results for Test 8 and Test 9

Test cloud	PDAL (Test 8) load time, ms	LAStools (Test 9) load time, ms	Our approach load time, ms
Cloud 1	10552	5089	2552
Cloud 2	–	23895	16791
Cloud 3	–	44057	35698

4 Conclusions

As a result of a survey of various approaches for loading a point cloud, we identified problems with the standard data loading method. The problem is the increase in file load time when an intermediate pre-processing of loaded data occurs. Pre-processing makes delays between reading parts of a file because of what bandwidth drops.

To solve this problem, it was proposed to separate the loading of the raw section of the file and its pre-processing. For this, multithreading was used, and this decision eliminated the delays between reading. Proper configuration of parameters such as the size of the temporary buffer, the number of temporary buffers and the number of preprocessing threads can allow you to achieve the maximum file load speed. The study showed that for all cases the optimal buffer size is in the range of 32–128 KB, the number of temporary buffers and the number of pre-processing threads is very dependent on the pre-processing algorithm, the more complex the algorithm, the more pre-processing threads are necessary to maintain a balance between loading and pre-processing. As a result, it was possible to reach the maximum file load speed limited by the data bus bandwidth.

This study was conducted using the Ubuntu operating system with the Ext4 (Fourth Extended File System). The next step is to run these tests using a Windows operating system with the NTFS (New Technology File System) to confirm the results of our tests.

Acknowledgements. The research was supported by Ministry of Education and Science of Russia within the framework of the Federal Program "Research and Development in Priority Areas for the Development of the Russian the Science and Technology Complex for 2014–2020" (project ID RFMEFI58417X0025).

References

1. Puente, I., González-Jorge, H., Martínez-Sánchez, J., Arias, P.: Review of mobile mapping and surveying technologies. Measurement **46**(7), 2127–2145 (2013)
2. Guan, H., Li, J., Cao, S., Yu, Y.: Use of mobile LiDAR in road information inventory: a review. Int. J. Image Data Fusion **7**(3), 219–242 (2016)
3. Badenko, V., Zotov, D., Fedotov, A.: Hybrid processing of laser scanning data. In: E3S Web of Conferences – EDP Sciences, vol. 33, article number 01047 (2018)
4. Dore, C., Murphy, M.: Current state of the art historic building information modelling. Int. Arch. Photogramm. Remote Sens. Spat. Inf. Sci. **42**, 185–192 (2017)

5. Vosselman, G., Coenen, M., Rottensteiner, F.: Contextual segment-based classification of airborne laser scanner data. ISPRS J. Photogramm. Remote Sens. **128**, 354–371 (2017)
6. Tomljenovic, I., Höfle, B., Tiede, D., Blaschke, T.: Building extraction from airborne laser scanning data: an analysis of the state of the art. Remote Sens. **7**(4), 3826–3862 (2015)
7. Penner, M., Woods, M., Pitt, D.: A comparison of airborne laser scanning and image point cloud derived tree size class distribution models in boreal Ontario. Forests **6**(11), 4034–4054 (2015)
8. Heo, J., Jeong, S., Park, H.-K., Jung, J., Han, S., Hong, S., Sohn, H.-G.: Productive high-complexity 3D city modeling with point clouds collected from terrestrial LiDAR. Comput. Environ. Urban Syst. **41**, 26–38 (2013)
9. Pu, S., Rutzinger, M., Vosselman, G., Elberink, S.O.: Recognizing basic structures from mobile laser scanning data for road inventory studies. ISPRS J. Photogramm. Remote Sens. **66**(6), S28–S39 (2011)
10. Badenko, V., Fedotov, A., Vinogradov, K.: Algorithms of laser scanner data processing for ground surface reconstruction. In: Gervasi, O., et al. (eds.) ICCSA 2018. LNCS, vol. 10961, pp. 397–411. Springer, Cham (2018). https://doi.org/10.1007/978-3-319-95165-2_28
11. Son, H., Kim, C., Kim, C.: Fully automated as-built 3D pipeline extraction method from laser-scanned data based on curvature computation. J. Comput. Civ. Eng. **29**(4), B4014003 (2014)
12. Guo, B., Li, Q., Huang, X., Wang, C.: An improved method for power-line reconstruction from point cloud data. Remote Sens. **8**(1), 36 (2016)
13. Hichri, N., Stefani, C., De Luca, L., Veron, P., Hamon, G.: From point cloud to BIM: a survey of existing approaches. Int. Arch. Photogramm. Remote Sens. Spat. Inf. Sci. ISPRS Arch. **40**(5W2), 343–348 (2013)
14. Barazzetti, L.: Parametric as-built model generation of complex shapes from point clouds. Adv. Eng. Inform. **30**(3), 298–311 (2016)
15. Volk, R., Stengel, J., Schultmann, F.: Building Information Modeling (BIM) for existing buildings—literature review and future needs. Autom. Constr. **38**, 109–127 (2014)
16. Badenko, V., Fedotov, A., Zotov, D.: Extracting features from laser scanning point cloud. In: SHS Web of Conferences, vol. 44, article number 00013 (2018)
17. Badenko, V., Volgin, D., Lytkin, S.: Deformation monitoring using laser scanned point clouds and BIM. In: MATEC Web of Conferences, vol. 245, article number 01002 (2018)
18. Liu, X., Meng, W., Guo, J., Zhang, X.: A survey on processing of large-scale 3D point cloud. In: El Rhalibi, A., Tian, F., Pan, Z., Liu, B. (eds.) Edutainment 2016. LNCS, vol. 9654, pp. 267–279. Springer, Cham (2016). https://doi.org/10.1007/978-3-319-40259-8_24
19. Kukko, A., Kaartinen, H., Hyyppä, J., Chen, Y.: Multiplatform mobile laser scanning: usability and performance. Sensors **12**(9), 11712–11733 (2012)
20. Murphy, M., McGovern, E., Pavia, S.: Historic building information modelling-adding intelligence to laser and image based surveys of European classical architecture. ISPRS J. Photogramm. Remote Sens. **76**, 89–102 (2013)
21. Axelsson, P.: Processing of laser scanner data - algorithms and applications. ISPRS J. Photogramm. Remote Sens. **54**(2–3), 138–147 (1999)
22. Tang, P., Huber, D., Akinci, B., Lipman, R., Lytle, A.: Automatic reconstruction of as-built building information models from laser-scanned point clouds: a review of related techniques. Autom. Constr. **19**(7), 829–843 (2010)
23. Zhang, J., Lin, X.: Advances in fusion of optical imagery and LiDAR point cloud applied to photogrammetry and remote sensing. Int. J. Image Data Fusion **8**(1), 1–31 (2017)
24. Pfeifer, N., Mandlburger, G., Otepka, J., Karel, W.: OPALS - a framework for airborne laser scanning data analysis. Comput. Environ. Urban Syst. **45**, 125–136 (2014)

25. Patterson, D.A., Gibson, G., Katz, R.H.: A case for redundant arrays of inexpensive disks (RAID). SIGMOD Rec. **17**(3), 109–116 (1988)
26. Han, S.: Towards efficient implementation of an octree for a large 3D point cloud. Sensors **18**(12), 4398 (2018)
27. Vo, A.V., Laefer, D.F., Bertolotto, M.: Airborne laser scanning data storage and indexing: state-of-the-art review. Int. J. Remote Sens. **37**(24), 6187–6204 (2016)
28. LAS Specification, Version 1.4, Revision 13, 15 July 2013. http://www.asprs.org/a/society/committees/standards/LAS_1_4_r13.pdf. Accessed 15 Mar 2019
29. rapidlasso GmbH Homepage. https://rapidlasso.com/lastools/. Accessed 15 Mar 2019
30. PDAL - Point Data Abstraction Library Homepage. https://pdal.io/. Accessed 15 Mar 2019
31. Van Natijne, A.L., Lindenbergh, R.C., Hanssen, R.F., Lindenbergh, R.C., Hanssen, R.F.: Massive linking of PS-InSAR deformations to a national airborne laser point cloud. Int. Arch. Photogramm. Remote Sens. Spat. Inf. Sci. **42**(2), 1137–1144 (2018)

Airborne Object Detection Using Hyperspectral Imaging: Deep Learning Review

T. T. Pham[1,4]([envelope]), M. A. Takalkar[1,4], M. Xu[1,4], D. T. Hoang[2], H. A. Truong[3], E. Dutkiewicz[1], and S. Perry[1,4]

[1] Faculty of Engineering and IT, University of Technology Sydney, Ultimo, Australia
`thuy.pham@uts.edu.au`
[2] Hanoi University of Science and Technology, Hanoi, Vietnam
[3] Vietnam National University, Hanoi, Vietnam
[4] DMTC, Hawthorn, Australia

Abstract. Hyperspectral images have been increasingly important in object detection applications especially in remote sensing scenarios. Machine learning algorithms have become emerging tools for hyperspectral image analysis. The high dimensionality of hyperspectral images and the availability of simulated spectral sample libraries make deep learning an appealing approach. This report reviews recent data processing and object detection methods in the area including hand-crafted and automated feature extraction based on deep learning neural networks. The accuracy performances were compared according to existing reports as well as our own experiments (i.e., re-implementing and testing on new datasets). CNN models provided reliable performance of over 97% detection accuracy across a large set of HSI collections. A wide range of data were used: a rural area (Indian Pines data), an urban area (Pavia University), a wetland region (Botswana), an industrial field (Kennedy Space Center), to a farm site (Salinas). Note that, the Botswana set was not reviewed in recent works, thus high accuracy selected methods were newly compared in this work. A *plain* CNN model was also found to be able to perform comparably to its more complex variants in target detection applications.

Keywords: Hyperspectral imaging · Classification · Remote sensing · Deep learning

1 Introduction

Hyperspectral imaging (HSI) techniques gathers and processes data from across the electromagnetic spectrum. Each pixel in a hyperspectral image is obtained with several spectral bands that can be used for object/material detection. The spatial and spectral properties of specific objects show similarities or differences from one another, thereby allowing the discrimination of different objects in the same perspective based on the image data analysis.

© Springer Nature Switzerland AG 2019
S. Misra et al. (Eds.): ICCSA 2019, LNCS 11619, pp. 306–321, 2019.
https://doi.org/10.1007/978-3-030-24289-3_23

Developing efficient methods to process hyperspectral images with hundreds of channels is often a challenging task due to several factors such as high dimensionality, the lack of training samples, mixed pixels, light-scattering mechanisms during acquisition, nonlinear and complex data due to different atmospheric and geometric distortions [22]. One example, the "Hughes phenomenon" [25] showed the overall mean accuracy is a function of three parameters: measurement complexity, data set size, and the prior probability of the pattern classes. Thus, high dimensionality can influence the accuracy performance. Furthermore, [32], the position of the sun, imaging angle and direction may cause intra-class differences [1,21,45]. Therefore, besides appropriate classification techniques, data reduction and feature extraction have been found crucial to the accuracy performance of object detection [21,22]. For example, among attempts using support vector machine (SVM) [2,32,46], a more recent work [36] was based on independent component analysis and morphological features. Meanwhile, sparsity-based algorithms [15,16,20] showed that the sparse representation of a pixel can predict the class label of the test sample better than classical SVMs. Recently, deep-learning approaches [14,17,28,35,39–41,43,47,49–52] make use of hierarchically extracted deep features. The framework of [14] was a combination of principle component analysis (PCA), stacked autoencoders architecture, and logistic regression. While most works used convolutional neural networks (CNN) excessively increasing network depth, the more recent learning [43] used a deep feature fusion network that utilised the correlated information among different hierarchical layers, thus more discriminative features.

Existing surveys focussed on challenges of HSI processing as a comprehensive tutorial/overview (e.g., [10,22]). While the recent review [22] covered broad topics including classification, unmixing, dimensionality reduction, resolution enhancement, denoising, change detection, and fast computing, this work analyses the latest methods (since 2014) from the object detection application point of view. The main contributions of this work are:

- We review methods that relate to data pre-processing and object detection algorithms using HSI data.
- We systemically summarise the accuracy performance according to existing individual comparisons.
- We implemented and re-evaluated deep-learning methods using a larger set of popular HSI images while existing comparisons only used one or two datasets in common with each other. Thus, this review includes new test trials for several compared methods.
- Our observations suggest important directions in applying deep-learning approaches to target detection scenarios with HSI data.

2   Data Pre-processing Methods

2.1   Hyperspectral Data Representations

Spectral and spatial information are two fundamental representation types for HSI [27]. When performing spatial and spectral sampling, the information is sampled at the sensor's spatial and spectral resolution; i.e., a 3D "hypercube" $X \in R^{n_1 \times n_2 \times n_b}$ is obtained, containing $n = n_1 \times n_2$ and n_b bands [10]. In the spectral representation, each pixel is defined in the spectral space $x \in R^{n_b}$. In the spatial representation, each image band is a matrix $X_i \in R^{n_1 \times n_2}$. Because of the high spatial correlation within bands, neighbouring pixels likely represent similar material. Spatial (or *contextual*) information can provide the adjoining pixel relationships and thus may improve the classification accuracy [27].

A combined representation of these two types was called spatial-spectral feature. There are two common strategies to combine: extracting spectral and spatial features separately or directly from sample cubes of the HSI. In spatial-spectral representation, spectral information processing incorporates adjacent relationships of pixels, while spatial information analysis for a single band considers the relationships with other bands [26,41,49].

2.2   Challenges and Pre-processing Techniques

Redundancy Reduction: Because the dimension of HSI data is often large (tens of thousands), this causes a high computational cost in object detection applications, especially in deep learning approaches [14]. On the other hand, the sparseness of HSI data has been demonstrated in earlier works [15,16,20]. Therefore, selecting an appropriate subset of bands was considered an efficient process. Band selection can be done using the highest class-separability criterion [2,19] or information theory-based methods [23]. Other techniques include a kernel method for the selection based on nonlinear dependence between spectral bands and class labels [13] and minimized the error probability using a Bayes classifier [11].

Limited Annotated Training Samples: Collecting HSI data and annotating each pixel are labour-consuming tasks thus the training sets found in existing works were often in limited size. Recently, Li et al. [28] used *pixel pair features* (PPF) to mitigate the problem of training label shortage. PPF was based on *combined pairs* of pixels in a training set. Specifically, two pixels are randomly chosen from a labelled training set, and a subtle rule deduces the label of each *PPF pair* based on the labels of both pixels. If two pixels have same labels, the pair is assigned the same label. If the pixels do not have the same labels, the pair is labelled as "extra", a newly added auxiliary class. The random combination of pixels significantly increases the number of labelled training instances.

3   Object Detection Methods

Detection approaches can be grouped into two directions: "two-step" that consists of a hand-crafted feature extraction step with classification afterwards, and "one-step" (i.e., feature extraction is integrated within the classification model). The former group include conventional methods (e.g., SVMs [2,32,46], sparsity-based [15,16,20]) while the latter was recently introduced in deep learning (DL) models (e.g., [28,35,39,41,43,49–51]).

3.1   Two-Step Approaches

Most traditional feature extraction methods for HSI have been using statistical theory, fuzzy theory, and machine learning [10,22]. For example, linear extraction techniques include PCA [42], minimum noise fraction (MNF) [38], independent component analysis (ICA) [8], and linear discriminant analysis (LDA) [6]. In the spatial domain, existing works used Gabor filter banks [33]. Meanwhile, several approaches used nonlinear transformations such as morphological analysis [9,42], kernel methods [12], and manifold regularisation [3–5,29].

Then, hand-crafted features were used as inputs of conventional classifiers such as the K-nearest neighbour classifier (KNN) [29] and SVM [2,26,37,46]. For instance, Ma et al. [29] deployed a manifold structure from the pixel values then utilised a weighted KNN classifier. In another work, Tuia and Camp-Valls [37] employed SVM with a kernel to train directly from images. Meanwhile, Ji et al. [26] addressed both the pixel spectral and spatial constraints then formulated the relationships among pixels in a hypergraph structure. Their hyperedge is generated by using distance among pixels, where each pixel is connected with its K-nearest neighbours in the feature space.

Recently, deep learning approaches were used for automated feature extraction step from internal layers of a neural network; then these *features* were used as inputs of conventional classifiers. Auto-encoders and deep belief networks were typical examples of this direction [14,24,40]. Auto-encoder (AE) is an unsupervised learning method to learn fewer representations from high dimensional data space and not require annotated training sets [40]. The approach reduced the reconstruction error between the input data at the encoding layer and its reconstruction at the decoding layer [40]. Stacked Auto-encoder (SAE) is a model comprising a number of AE layers with a greedy layer-wise training scheme and a logistic regression layer for classification [14]. Deep belief network (DBN) [24] is a another DL model in which nonlinear description of objects can be analysed. DBN combines the advantages of unsupervised and supervised learning. It is also an automated feature extraction process. DBN was introduced to apply for HSI data using a back-propagation network and a SVM classifier as the final step of classification [48].

3.2   One-Step Approaches

In another approach, DL has also been suggested in one-step solutions (i.e., automatically extract *deep* information from pre-processed HSI data and blindly feed this information into the classification layer of the network). These *deep* features were considered high-level and abstract representations, thus, could be more robust and efficient than lower-level hand-crafted features. Existing works followed this direction include CNN variants [41,50,51], auto-encoders [14,40]. CNN structures were typically designed to process data that come in the form of multiple arrays, e.g., a multispectral image composed of many 2-D arrays containing pixel intensities in the multiple band channels. Due to the properties of natural signals, namely, local connections, shared weights, pooling, and the use of multiple layers, CNN has been suggested for the HSI classification applications as a *one-step* strategy [17,39,41,43,50,51]. The architecture of a typical CNN is integrated as a series of layers for different assignments including input, convolution, pooling, normalization, *drop-out* and output. Convolutional layers were considered the most important layers that extract features. Specifically, a few first layers provided low-level information such as edges, lines and corners while the latter ones described more abstract features such as structures, objects, and shapes. Typically, after each convolutional layer, there exist pooling layers that are created by computing some local non-linear operation of a particular feature over a region of the image. The process guarantees that the similar outcome can be obtained, even when image features have small translations or rotations, which is essential for scene classification and detection. Then, normalization layers aim to improve generalisation inspired by inhibition schemes presented in the real neurons of the brain. In the last few layers of the network. A *dropout* training method [44] has been recently suggested to reduce over-fitting effects [39,41,43].

4   HSI Datasets

Due to the application-oriented purpose of this survey, we categorised scenarios of target detection scene as follows: rural area, urban, industrial field, and natural reserves. We selected popular public datasets for each scene type as in Table 1. Indian Pines data [7] (DS1) represents a rural area. Pavia University campus site [31] (DS2) represents an urban area. Botswana image [18] (DS3) illustrates a swarm and delta region. Kennedy Space Center HSI [34] (DS4) is an example for an industrial field. Other datasets in Table 1 including Salinas Valley, Houston, and Pavia City share a near similar scene and settings, thus, are briefly compared according to previous results (Table 2). Specific details of datasets tested in this work are depicted as follows.

Rural Area (Dataset 1): This scene shot was taken in 1992 at a 2 × 2-mile area at 20 m spatial resolution of Northwest Tippecanoe County, Indiana (USA) by AVIRIS sensor (224 spectral reflectance bands ranging 0.4–2.5 µm). This is so-called *Indian Pines data* and are provided by Purdue University [7] as a subset of the original capture. The public part consists of 145 × 145 pixels and covers agriculture land, forest, and other natural perennial vegetation. In the human living area, the scene contains roads, major dual lane highways, a rail line, low density housing, and other built structures. In the farm field, as in June, the field is in early stages of growth. The manual labels mark 16 object classes (Fig. 1). The image was removed the portion with water absorption, specifically in bands of 104–108, 150–163, and 220 [7]. Thus, there are 200 bands used out of 224 in total of the raw shot.

Table 1. Specifications of publicly available datasets.

Name	Scene type	Location	Size (Pixels)	Spatial resolution (m/pixel)	Spectral band (used/total)
DS1	Rural	Northwestern Indiana, USA. 1992	145 × 145	20	200/224
DS2	Urban	Pavia University Campus, Pavia, Italy	610 × 340	1.3	103/116
DS3	Wetlands	Okavango Delta, Botswana (Africa)	1476 × 256	30	145/242
DS4	Industrial field	Kennedy Space Center, FL, USA	512 × 614	18	176/224
DS5	Farm	Salinas Valley, California, USA	512 × 217	3.7	204/224
Other	Urban	University of Houston campus	–	2.5	114
Other	Urban	Pavia, Italy	1096 × 1096	1.3	102/114

Urban Area (Dataset 2): The Pavia University scene was captured at the University of Pavia campus, Pavia, Italy, from a reflective optics system imaging spectrometer (airborne by the German Aerospace Agency, sponsored by the European Union). The spectrometer has 115 band channels ranging 0.43–0.86 μm. The spatial resolution is 1.3 m per pixel. The publicly portion of the dataset has the size of 640 × 340 pixels provided by Pavia University (Italy) [31]. There are 9 classes of objects in the image: asphalt, meadow, gravel, trees, painted metal sheet, bare soil, bitumen, self-blocking bricks, and shadows (Details of number samples for each object are listed in Fig. 2). Due to noise, only 103 channels were further processed. The image was corrected atmospherically, but not geometrically [31].

Wetland Area (Dataset 3): In 2001–2004, National Aeronautics and Space Administration (NASA) collected from the Earth Observer-1 satellite a sequence of HSI images over the Okavango Delta, Botswana. This scene is one of the world's largest freshwater wetlands (approximately 15,000 km^2). The Hyperion sensor on the satellite has 30 m pixel resolution and 242 bands covering the 400–2500 nm (10 nm windows) [18]. The public data portion was a 7.7 km strip

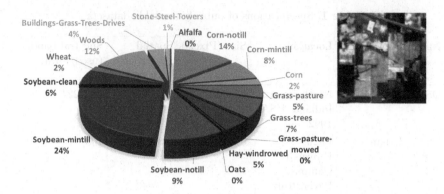

Fig. 1. Objects distribution of the scene and RGB image for Indian Pines.

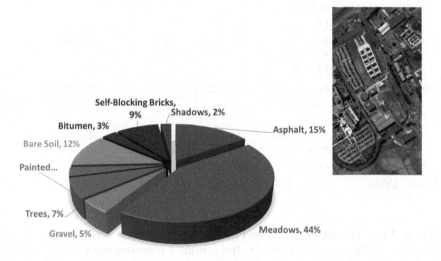

Fig. 2. Objects distribution of the scene and RGB image for Pavia University Campus.

acquired on May 31, 2001 (Fig. 3). The set includes seasonal swamps, and woodlands of the Delta. The data was pre-processed by the provider to reduce the effects of miscalibration, and intermittent anomalies [18]. Noisy bands (due to water absorption) were removed, and the remaining 145 bands were: [10–55, 82–97, 102–119, 134–164, 187–220].

Industrial Field (Dataset 4): Kennedy Space Center (KSC) located on Merritt Island, Florida is one of ten field centres of NASA. The AVIRIS instrument (Airborne Visible/Infrared Imaging Spectrometer) was used to capture KSC site on March 23, 1996. The specifications of the sensor were: 224 bands of 10 nm width; wavelengths from 400–2500 nm [34]. The KSC data, collected from an altitude of approximately 20 km, have a spatial resolution of 18 m (Fig. 4). After

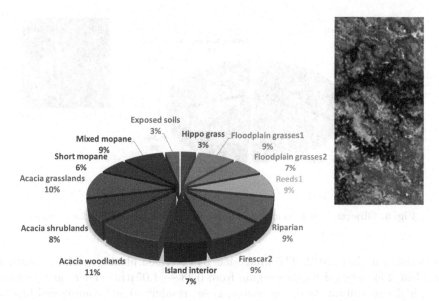

Fig. 3. Objects distribution of the scene and a section of RGB for Botswana delta.

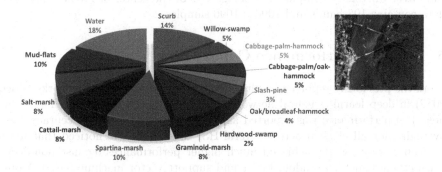

Fig. 4. Objects distribution of the scene and a section of RGB for KSC.

being pre-processed (e.g., water absorption and low SNR bands removed), 176 bands were used further. Class labels of pixels were derived by KSC personnel using colour infrared photography and Landsat Thematic Mapper (TM) imagery.

Farm (Dataset 5): Salinas Valley HSI data was captured by the 224-band AVIRIS sensor over Salinas Valley, California. The spatial resolution was 3.7 m. The data comprises 512 × 217 samples. Noisy bands with water absorption were [108–112], [154–167], 224. There are 16 objects labelled in this data set including vegetable matter, bare soils, and vineyard fields (Fig. 5).

Other Datasets: There are other popular HSI collections that were used in existing comparisons. Houston campus site image was provided by the University

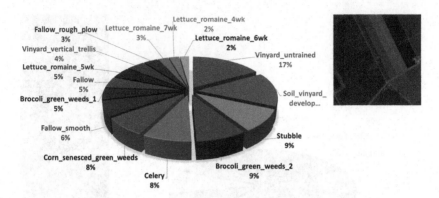

Fig. 5. Objects distribution of the scene and a section of RGB for Salinas.

of Houston in June 2012. The image has 349 × 1,905 pixels (spatial resolution of 2.5 m, 144 spectral bands ranging from 0.38 → 1.05 μm). There are parking lots, highway, railway, tree, soil, water, grass, residential and commercial blocks in the scene. Pavia city data set was collected by the similar instrument with the Pavia University campus. The image was of the center of Pavia, Italy. The data contains 103 bands and 1096 × 1096 samples.

5   Existing Performance Comparisons

From the previously reported results, Table 2 lists latest noticeable works (since 2017) in deep learning neural network approaches and a few of baseline methods. The performance was reported as percentage % for overall accuracy (i.e., averaging for all classes) across several HSI collections. We noticed that most of deep learning works achieved much higher performances against non-deep-learning ones such as random forest and support vector machine based. Moreover, among recent deep learning methods, most of CNN variants performed comparably. However, not all of works used the same experiment datasets.

6   Experiments

6.1   Settings

In response to the aforementioned reviews of literature reports, we carried out our own experiments to re-evaluate a selected groups of works with a broader set of HSI. First, we implemented the method of FDSSC [47] as it was the latest and had the highest accuracy (over 99%). As FDSSC is a CNN variant, we also implemented a plain CNN model as a baseline. We selected a simple CNN in [50] as it was well described and recently reported but was missed in state-of-art comparisons. Then we deployed the SAE-LR [14] approach because it is an unsupervised learning type of detection while CNNs are supervised ones.

Table 2. Comparisons of accuracy performance across public HSI images as reported in existing works. Overall accuracy performance is calculated for all classes (%) in each dataset used or '-' if not used. IndianP: DS1. PaviaU: DS2. KSC: DS3. PaviaC: Pavia City data. Houston: Houston University campus (Sect. 4).

Methods	IndianP	PaviaU	PaviaC	KSC	Salinas	Houston	Reported work (reference, year)
SAE-LR [14]	-	-	98.52	98.76	-	-	Proposed vs. RBF-SVM, EMP RBF-SVM ([14], 2014)
DC-CNNaug [51]	98.76	99.68	-	-	-	-	Proposed vs. DC-CNN, CNN, SSDL ([51], 2017)
CNN [50]	64.19	67.85	-	-	85.24	-	Proposed vs. SVM, KNN ([50], 2017)
RNN-GRU-PRetanh [35]	88.63	88.85	-	-	-	89.85	Proposed vs. RNN-LSTM, RNN GRU-tanh, CNN, SVM-RBF, RF 200 trees ([35], 2017)
RNN-GRU-tanh [35]	85.71	80.70	-	-	-	85.73	Baseline ([35], 2017)
RNN LSTM [35]	80.52	77.99	-	-	-	85.41	Baseline ([35], 2017)
CNN [35]	84.18	80.51	-	-	-	85.42	Baseline ([35], 2017)
SVM-RBF [35]	72.78	78.82	-	-	-	77.09	Baseline ([35], 2017)
RF-200 trees [35]	69.79	71.37	-	-	-	72.93	Baseline ([35], 2017)
FDSSC [47]	99.75	99.97	-	99.96	-	-	Proposed vs. CNN, SAE-LR, 3D-CNN-LR, SSRN ([47], 2018)
CNN [30]	95.96	99.38	-	99.31	-	-	Baseline ([47], 2018)
SAE-LR [14]	96.53	98.46	-	92.99	-	-	Baseline ([47], 2018)
DFFN [43]	98.52	98.73	-	-	98.87	-	Proposed vs. DRNN, DCNN, RVCANet, SVM ([43], 2018)
DRN [43]	98.36	98.52	-	-	98.48	-	baseline ([43], 2018)
DCNN [43]	97.93	97.19	-	-	95.05	-	baseline ([43], 2018)

SAE-LR: Stacked Autoencoder with Logistic Regression. RF: Random Forest. SVM-RBF: Support Vector Machines - Radial Basis Function. EMP: Extended Morphological Profiles CNN: Convolutional Neural Network. DC-CNNaug: Dual Channel CNN + Augmentation. FDSSC: Fast Dense Spectral–Spatial CNN DFFN: Deep feature fusion network RNN: Recurrent Neural Network. DRN: Deep residual CNN. DCNN: Deep plain CNN.

From Table 2, the SAE-LR was reported to have high accuracy but did not perform consistently in later works as a baseline (e.g., in the report of [47]).

These three methods were re-evaluated on Indian Pines data [7] for a rural area; Pavia University campus site [31] for an urban area; Botswana image [18] for a wetland region; Kennedy Space Center [34] for an industrial field; and Salinas data for farming areas (Sect. 4). Note that, the Botswana data was not reported recently (Table 2) thus it is newly tested for all of three implemented methods. For each dataset, we repeated and recorded the accuracy performance metric 10 times. Therefore, the experiment results were listed as mean and standard deviation format in Table 3.

Our experiments were executed on two separate computing systems: a server of Ubuntu (16.04 LTS, Intel Core i5-5200U processor, 4 cores of 2.20 GHz, Nvidia GeForce 940M GPU) and a Windows 10 (Home 64-bit; Intel(R) Core(TM) i7 NVIDIA GeForce GTX 1070 GPU). Algorithms were implemented in Python 3.6.6; Tensorflow (GPU version) 1.12.0 Keras 2.2.4. We used PyTorch environment to more quickly run models for various HSI inputs. We utilised a newer optimizer to optimize the loss function than the ones in earlier works. Specifically, we used the Adam optimizer with 1000 epochs. The optimization is stopped when the loss value does not decrease any more.

We split the training, validation, and test sets as the ratio of 3 : 1 : 6 consistently across five datasets for the experiments with the first two works: SAE-LR [14] and CNN [50]. Note that this splitting might be different from the original settings of the CNN work [50]. They suggested 15 training samples per classes after varying the size in a range from 3 to 15. For the work of FDSSC [47], we kept the same settings as it was reported for the sake of reproducibility (i.e., 2 : 1 : 7 for Indian Pines and KSC; 10 : 5 : 85 for Pavia University; and 2 : 1 : 7 for new tests).

6.2   Experimental Results

Table 3 summarises our experimental results for deep learning methods across public HSI images. Overall accuracy performance is calculated for all classes (% mean ± standard deviation). Three of methods achieved very high accuracy levels for all classes. The auto-encoder approach performed dramatically up on each individual dataset. For instance, the model reached 98% of accuracy for the Pavia University, Salinas, and Botswana data but yielded only 58% for the KSC collection. Meanwhile, the two CNN variants performed consistently over 97% of overall accuracy.

Table 3. Our test results of emerging models across public HSI images. Accuracy performance is calculated for all classes (% mean ± standard deviation).

Methods (reference, year)	IndianP	PaviaU	Salinas	KSC	Botswana
SAE-LR [14] 2014	84.65 ± 2.70^a	98.32 ± 0.09^a	97.79 ± 0.11^a	57.29 ± 1.23^a	97.40 ± 0.18
CNN [50] 2017	99.14 ± 0.23	97.86 ± 0.19	96.50 ± 0.21	97.02 ± 0.30^a	99.85 ± 0.15^a
FDSSC [47] 2018	99.77 ± 0.11	99.98 ± 0.01	99.95 ± 0.03^a	99.96 ± 0.07	99.78 ± 0.24^a

[a]: Newly tested datasets comparing with earlier works.
IndianP: DS1. PaviaU: DS2. KSC: DS3. Botswana: DS4. Salinas (Sect. 4).
SAE-LR: Stacked Autoencoder with Logistic Regression [14]. CNN: Convolutional Neural Network. FDSSC: Fast Dense Spectral–Spatial CNN [47].

7   Conclusion

In this report, hyperspectral image analysis was reviewed particularly for object detection applications. Several HSI data representations were summarised from spectral/spatial characteristics to hand-crafted or automated feature extraction using deep-learning methods.

In terms of data sources, we reported publicly available datasets commonly used for HSI analysis. We found limited research on off-nadir data for our target detection focus but some available in other areas of HSI applications such as material discrimination [45], atmospheric compensation [1,2]. We recommend that future works should investigate this scenario of data collection to expand further and more efficient HSI-based target detection applications.

Regarding to technical approaches for HSI object detection, we described both hand-crafted feature extraction in-cooperated conventional methods (e.g., support vector machine or decision trees) and automated feature extraction using deep learning neural networks. According to existing comparisons (summarised in Table 2), deep learning neural networks performed much better than the conventional ones. Unsupervised features (e.g., intermediate information from auto-encoders (SAE-LR [14])) may act as mid-level representations and hence provide more semantic features and more robust detection accuracy than the low-level ones (i.e., hand-crafted).

8   Discussion

Based on our observations for a selected group of works, we found CNN models provided comparatively reliable performance of over 97% detection accuracy across a large set of HSI collections. We included data for a rural area (Indian Pines data [7]), an urban area (Pavia University campus site [31]), a wetland region (Botswana image [18]) an industrial field (Kennedy Space Center [34]), and a farm site (Salinas data, Sect. 4). Note that, the Botswana data was not reported recently (Table 2) thus it is newly tested for all of three implemented methods.

According to our experimental experience, we confirmed the non-consistent performance of SAE-LR [14] found in earlier comparisons (Tables 2 and 3). This is probably due to the fact that the algorithm depends heavily on the reconstruction error between the input data at the encoding layer and its reconstruction at the decoding layer which in turns relates much on the quality of each dataset. We hypothesize that with a robust pre-processing procedure, the SAE-LR can work well for unsupervised HSI data. It should be noted that we used the Adam optimizer when deploying the work of SAE-LR [14] that used a basic optimizer of stochastic gradient descent thus it took the original experiments four to six hours to complete a trial. Furthermore, we observed CNN models detected objects comparably despite of a *plain* design (i.e., without using residual learning and feature fusion) or a more complex architecture in recent reports except for one report of a simple CNN [50]. The authors of [50] only yielded less than 67% for

Indian Pines and Pavia University sets (Table 2). Therefore, we re-evaluated this design in our experiments and found it actually worked well (above 97% across all five datasets). Hence, we suggest that a simple CNN model can perform well for target detection rather than complex variants.

Acknowledgment. This paper includes research that was supported by DMTC Limited (Australia). The authors have prepared this paper in accordance with the intellectual property rights granted to partners from the original DMTC project.

References

1. Adler-Golden, S.M., Bernstein, L.S., Matthew, M.W., Sundberg, R.L., Ratkowski, A.J.: Atmospheric compensation of extreme off-nadir hyperspectral imagery from hyperion. In: Algorithms and Technologies for Multispectral, Hyperspectral, and Ultraspectral Imagery XIII, vol. 6565, p. 65651P. International Society for Optics and Photonics (2007)
2. Archibald, R., Fann, G.: Feature selection and classification of hyperspectral images with support vector machines. IEEE Geosci. Remote Sens. Lett. **4**(4), 674–677 (2007)
3. Bachmann, C.M., Ainsworth, T.L., Fusina, R.A.: Exploiting manifold geometry in hyperspectral imagery. IEEE Trans. Geosci. Remote Sens. **43**(3), 441–454 (2005)
4. Bachmann, C.M., et al.: Bathymetric retrieval from hyperspectral imagery using manifold coordinate representations. IEEE Trans. Geosci. Remote Sens. **47**(3), 884 (2009)
5. Bachmann, C.M., Ainsworth, T.L., Fusina, R.A., Topping, R., Gates, T.: Manifold coordinate representations of hyperspectral imagery: improvements in algorithm performance and computational efficiency. In: 2010 IEEE International Geoscience and Remote Sensing Symposium (IGARSS), pp. 4244–4247. IEEE (2010)
6. Bandos, T.V., Bruzzone, L., Camps-Valls, G.: Classification of hyperspectral images with regularized linear discriminant analysis. IEEE Trans. Geosci. Remote Sens. **47**(3), 862–873 (2009)
7. Baumgardner, M.F., Biehl, L.L., Landgrebe, D.A.: 220 band aviris hyperspectral image data set: June 12, 1992 indian pine test site 3, September 2015. https://doi.org/10.4231/R7RX991C, https://purr.purdue.edu/publications/1947/1
8. Bayliss, J.D., Gualtieri, J.A., Cromp, R.F.: Analyzing hyperspectral data with independent component analysis. In: 26th AIPR Workshop: Exploiting New Image Sources and Sensors, vol. 3240, pp. 133–144. International Society for Optics and Photonics (1998)
9. Benediktsson, J.A., Palmason, J.A., Sveinsson, J.R.: Classification of hyperspectral data from urban areas based on extended morphological profiles. IEEE Trans. Geosci. Remote Sens. **43**(3), 480–491 (2005)
10. Bioucas-Dias, J.M., Plaza, A., Camps-Valls, G., Scheunders, P., Nasrabadi, N., Chanussot, J.: Hyperspectral remote sensing data analysis and future challenges. IEEE Geosci. Remote Sens. Mag. **1**(2), 6–36 (2013)
11. Bruzzone, L., Serpico, S.B.: A technique for feature selection in multiclass problems. Int. J. Remote Sens. **21**(3), 549–563 (2000)
12. Camps-Valls, G., Bruzzone, L.: Kernel-based methods for hyperspectral image classification. IEEE Trans. Geosci. Remote Sens. **43**(6), 1351–1362 (2005)

13. Camps-Valls, G., Mooij, J., Scholkopf, B.: Remote sensing feature selection by kernel dependence measures. IEEE Trans. Geosci. Remote Sens. **7**(3), 587–591 (2010)
14. Chen, Y., Lin, Z., Zhao, X., Wang, G., Gu, Y.: Deep learning-based classification of hyperspectral data. IEEE J. Sel. Top. Appl. Earth Obs. Remote Sens. **7**(6), 2094–2107 (2014)
15. Chen, Y., Nasrabadi, N.M., Tran, T.D.: Hyperspectral image classification using dictionary-based sparse representation. IEEE Trans. Geosci. Remote Sens. **49**, 3973–3985 (2011)
16. Chen, Y., Nasrabadi, N.M., Tran, T.D.: Hyperspectral image classification via kernel sparse representation. IEEE Trans. Geosci. Remote Sens. **51**(1), 217–231 (2013)
17. Chen, Y., Jiang, H., Li, C., Jia, X., Ghamisi, P.: Deep feature extraction and classification of hyperspectral images based on convolutional neural networks. IEEE Trans. Geosci. Remote Sens. **54**(10), 6232–6251 (2016)
18. Crawford, M.M., Ghosh, J.: Random forests of binary hierarchical classifiers for analysis of hyperspectral data. In: IEEE Workshop on Advances in Techniques for Analysis of Remotely Sensed Data 2003, pp. 337–345 (2003)
19. De Backer, S., Kempeneers, P., Debruyn, W., Scheunders, P.: A band selection technique for spectral classification. IEEE Geosci. Remote Sens. Lett. **2**(3), 319–323 (2005)
20. Fotiadou, K., Tsagkatakis, G., Tsakalides, P.: Spectral super-resolution for hyperspectral images via sparse representations. In: Living Planet Symposium, vol. 740, p. 417 (2016)
21. Gewali, U.B., Monteiro, S.T., Saber, E.: Machine learning based hyperspectral image analysis: a survey. arXiv preprint arXiv:1802.08701 (2018)
22. Ghamisi, P., et al.: Advances in hyperspectral image and signal processing: a comprehensive overview of the state of the art. IEEE Geosci. Remote Sens. Mag. **5**(4), 37–78 (2017)
23. Guo, B., Gunn, S.R., Damper, R.I., Nelson, J.D.: Band selection for hyperspectral image classification using mutual information. IEEE Geosci. Remote Sens. Lett. **3**(4), 522–526 (2006)
24. Hinton, G.E., Osindero, S., Teh, Y.W.: A fast learning algorithm for deep belief nets. Neural Comput. **18**(7), 1527–1554 (2006)
25. Hughes, G.: On the mean accuracy of statistical pattern recognizers. IEEE Trans. Inf. Theor. **14**(1), 55–63 (1968)
26. Ji, R., Gao, Y., Hong, R., Liu, Q., Tao, D., Li, X.: Spectral-spatial constraint hyperspectral image classification. IEEE Trans. Geosci. Remote Sens. **52**(3), 1811–1824 (2014)
27. Landgrebe, D.A.: Signal theory methods in multispectral remote sensing, vol. 29. Wiley, Hoboken (2005)
28. Li, W., Wu, G., Zhang, F., Du, Q.: Hyperspectral image classification using deep pixel-pair features. IEEE Trans. Geosci. Remote Sens. **55**(2), 844–853 (2017)
29. Ma, L., Crawford, M.M., Tian, J.: Local manifold learning-based k-nearest-neighbor for hyperspectral image classification. IEEE Trans. Geosci. Remote Sens. **48**(11), 4099–4109 (2010)
30. Makantasis, K., Karantzalos, K., Doulamis, A., Doulamis, N.: Deep supervised learning for hyperspectral data classification through convolutional neural networks. In: 2015 IEEE International Geoscience and Remote Sensing Symposium (IGARSS), pp. 4959–4962, July 2015. https://doi.org/10.1109/IGARSS.2015.7326945

31. Marinoni, A., Gamba, P.: A novel approach for efficient p-linear hyperspectral unmixing. IEEE J. Sel. Top. Signal Process. **9**(6), 1156–1168 (2015)
32. Melgani, F., Bruzzone, L.: Classification of hyperspectral remote sensing images with support vector machines. IEEE Trans. Geosci. Remote Sens. **42**(8), 1778–1790 (2004)
33. Mirzapour, F., Ghassemian, H.: Improving hyperspectral image classification by combining spectral, texture, and shape features. Int. J. Remote Sens. **36**(4), 1070–1096 (2015)
34. Morgan, J.: Adaptive hierarchical classifier with limited training data. Ph.D. thesis, Department of Mechanical Engineering, University of Texas at Austin (2002)
35. Mou, L., Ghamisi, P., Zhu, X.X.: Deep recurrent neural networks for hyperspectral image classification. IEEE Trans. Geosci. Remote Sens. **55**(7), 3639–3655 (2017)
36. Mura, M.D., Villa, A., Benediktsson, J.A., Chanussot, J., Bruzzone, L.: Classification of hyperspectral images by using extended morphological attribute profiles and independent component analysis. IEEE Geosci. Remote Sens. Lett. **8**, 542–546 (2011)
37. Na, L., Wunian, Y.: Hyperspectral remote sensing image feature extraction based on kernel minimum noise fraction transformation. Remote Sens. Technol. Appl. **2**, 013 (2013)
38. Nielsen, A.A.: Kernel maximum autocorrelation factor and minimum noise fraction transformations. IEEE Trans. Image Process. **20**(3), 612–624 (2011)
39. Nogueira, K., Penatti, O.A., dos Santos, J.A.: Towards better exploiting convolutional neural networks for remote sensing scene classification. Pattern Recogn. **61**, 539–556 (2017)
40. Özdemir, A.O.B., Gedik, B.E., Çetin, C.Y.Y.: Hyperspectral classification using stacked autoencoders with deep learning. In: 2014 6th Workshop on Hyperspectral Image and Signal Processing: Evolution in Remote Sensing (WHISPERS), pp. 1–4. IEEE (2014)
41. Paoletti, M., Haut, J., Plaza, J., Plaza, A.: A new deep convolutional neural network for fast hyperspectral image classification. ISPRS J. Photogrammetry Remote Sens. (2017)
42. Plaza, A., Martinez, P., Plaza, J., Perez, R.: Dimensionality reduction and classification of hyperspectral image data using sequences of extended morphological transformations. IEEE Trans. Geosci. Remote Sens. **43**(3), 466–479 (2005)
43. Song, W., Li, S., Fang, L., Lu, T.: Hyperspectral image classification with deep feature fusion network. IEEE Trans. Geosci. Remote Sens. **56**(6), 3173–3184 (2018)
44. Srivastava, N., Hinton, G., Krizhevsky, A., Sutskever, I., Salakhutdinov, R.: Dropout: a simple way to prevent neural networks from overfitting. J. Mach. Learn. Res. **15**(1), 1929–1958 (2014)
45. Suen, P.H., Healey, G., Slater, D.: The impact of viewing geometry on material discriminability in hyperspectral images. IEEE Trans. Geosci. Remote Sens. **39**(7), 1352–1359 (2001)
46. Tarabalka, Y., Fauvel, M., Chanussot, J., Benediktsson, J.A.: SVM- and MRF-based method for accurate classification of hyperspectral images. IEEE Geosci. Remote Sens. Lett. **7**, 736–740 (2010)
47. Wang, W., Dou, S., Jiang, Z., Sun, L.: A fast dense spectral-spatial convolution network framework for hyperspectral images classification. Remote Sens. **10**(7), 1068 (2018)
48. Xinhua, J., Heru, X., Lina, Z., Yanqing, Z.: Hyperspectral data feature extraction using deep belief network. Int. J. Smart Sens. Intell. Syst. **9**(4) (2016)

49. Yang, X., Ye, Y., Li, X., Lau, R.Y., Zhang, X., Huang, X.: Hyperspectral image classification with deep learning models. IEEE Trans. Geosci. Remote Sens. (2018)
50. Yu, S., Jia, S., Xu, C.: Convolutional neural networks for hyperspectral image classification. Neurocomputing **219**, 88–98 (2017)
51. Zhang, H., Li, Y., Zhang, Y., Shen, Q.: Spectral-spatial classification of hyperspectral imagery using a dual-channel convolutional neural network. Remote Sens. Lett. **8**(5), 438–447 (2017)
52. Zhong, P., Gong, Z., Schnlieb, C.: A diversified deep belief network for hyperspectral image classification. In: ISPRS-International Archives of the Photogrammetry, Remote Sensing and Spatial Information Sciences, XLI-B7, pp. 443–449 (2016)

A New Strategy for Scattered Data Approximation Using Radial Basis Functions Respecting Points of Inflection

Martin Cervenka, Michal Smolik$^{(\boxtimes)}$, and Vaclav Skala

Faculty of Applied Sciences, University of West Bohemia, Plzen, Czech Republic
{cervemar,smolik,skala}@kiv.zcu.cz

Abstract. The approximation of scattered data is known technique in computer science. We propose a new strategy for the placement of radial basis functions respecting points of inflection. The placement of radial basis functions has a great impact on the approximation quality. Due to this fact we propose a new strategy for the placement of radial basis functions with respect to the properties of approximated function, including the extreme and the inflection points. Our experimental results proved high quality of the proposed approach and high quality of the final approximation.

Keywords: Radial basis functions · Approximation · Stationary points

1 Introduction

The Radial basis functions (RBF) are well known technique for scattered data approximation in d-dimensional space in general. A significant advantage of the RBF application is its computational complexity, which is nearly independent of the problem dimensionality. The formulation is leading to a solution of a linear system of equations $\boldsymbol{Ax} = \boldsymbol{b}$. There exists several modifications and specifications of the RBF use for approximation. The method of RBF was originally introduced by Hardy in a highly influential paper in 1971 [8,9]. The paper [8] presented an analytical method for representation of scattered data surfaces. The method computes the sum of quadric surfaces. The paper also stated the importance of the location of radial basis functions. This issue is solved by several papers. Some solutions are proposed by the papers [3,15,16], which use the regularization in the forward selection of radial basis function centers. The paper [31] presents an improvement for the problem with the behavior of RBF interpolants near boundaries. The paper [13] compares RBF approximations with different radial basis functions and different placement of those radial basis functions. However, all the radial basis functions are placed with some random or uniform distribution. A bit more sophisticated placement is presented in [14].

The research was supported by projects Czech Science Foundation (GACR) No. 17-05534S and partially by SGS 2019-016.

© Springer Nature Switzerland AG 2019
S. Misra et al. (Eds.): ICCSA 2019, LNCS 11619, pp. 322–336, 2019.
https://doi.org/10.1007/978-3-030-24289-3_24

The selection of a shape parameter is another problem. Wrong selection of this parameter can lead to an ill-conditioned problem or to an inaccurate approximation. The selection of the best shape parameter is thus very important. Fornberg and Wright [5] presents an algorithm which avoids this difficulty, and which allows numerically stable computations of Multi-Quadric RBF interpolants for all shape parameter values. The paper [29] derives a range of suitable shape parameters using the analysis of the condition number of the system matrix, error of energy and irregularity of node distribution. A lot of approaches for selection of a good value of the shape parameter use some kind of random generator. Examples of this approaches are [2, 20]. The paper [1] proposes a genetic algorithm to determine a good variable shape parameter, however the algorithm is very slow.

2   Radial Basis Functions

The Radial basis function (RBF) is a technique for scattered data interpolation [17] and approximation [4, 27]. The RBF interpolation and approximation is computationally more expensive compared to interpolation and approximation methods that use an information about mesh connectivity, because input data are not ordered and there is no known relation between them, i.e. tessellation is not made. Although RBF has a higher computational cost, it can be used for d-dimensional problem solution in many applications, e.g. solution of partial differential equations [11, 33], image reconstruction [28], neural networks [7, 10, 32], vector fields [24, 26], GIS systems [12, 18], optics [19] etc. It should be noted that it does not require any triangulation or tessellation mesh in general. There is no need to know any connectivity of interpolation points, all points are tied up only with distances of each other. Using all these distances we can form the interpolation or approximation matrix, which will be shown later.

The RBF is a function whose value depends only on the distance from its center point. Due to the use of distance functions, the RBFs can be easily implemented to reconstruct the surface using scattered data in 2D, 3D or higher dimensional spaces. It should be noted that the RBF interpolation and approximation is not separable by dimension. For the readers reference a compressed description of the RBF is given in the following paragraphs, for details consider [25, 26].

Radial function interpolants have a helpful property of being invariant under all Euclidean transformations, i.e. translations, rotations and reflections. It does not matter whether we first compute the RBF interpolation function and then apply a Euclidean transformation, or if we first transform all the data and then compute the radial function interpolants. This is a result of the fact that Euclidean transformations are characterized by orthonormal transformation matrices and are therefore two-norm invariant. Radial basis functions can be divided into two groups according to their influence. The first group are "global" RBFs [21]. Application of global RBFs usually leads to ill-conditioned system, especially in the case of large data sets with a large span [13, 23]. An example of "global" RBF is the Gauss radial basis function.

$$\varphi(r) = e^{-\epsilon r^2}, \tag{1}$$

where r is the distance of two points and ϵ is a shape parameter.

The "local" RBFs were introduced in [30] as compactly supported RBF (CSRBF) and satisfy the following condition:

$$\varphi(r) = (1 - r)_+^q P(r)$$
$$= \begin{cases} (1 - r)^q P(r) & 0 \le r \le 1 \\ 0 & r > 1 \end{cases} \tag{2}$$

where $P(r)$ is a polynomial function, r is the distance of two points and q is a parameter.

2.1   Radial Basis Function Approximation

RBF interpolation was originally introduced by [8] and is based on computing the distance of two points in any k-dimensional space. The interpolated value, and approximated value as well, is determined as (see [22]):

$$h(\boldsymbol{x}) = \sum_{j=1}^{M} \lambda_j \varphi(\|\boldsymbol{x} - \boldsymbol{\xi}_j\|) \tag{3}$$

where λ_j are weights of the RBFs, M is the number of the radial basis functions, φ is the radial basis function and $\boldsymbol{\xi}_j$ are centers of radial basis functions. For a given dataset of points with associated values, i.e. in the case of scalar values $\{\boldsymbol{x}_i, h_i\}_1^N$, where $N \gg M$, the following overdetermined linear system of equations is obtained:

$$h_i = h(\boldsymbol{x}_i) = \sum_{j=1}^{M} \lambda_j \varphi(\|\boldsymbol{x}_i - \boldsymbol{\xi}_j\|) \tag{4}$$
$$\text{for } \forall i \in \{1, \dots, N\}$$

where λ_j are weights to be computed; see Fig. 1 for a visual interpretation of (3) or (4) for a $2\frac{1}{2}D$ function. Point in $2\frac{1}{2}D$ is a $2D$ point associated with a scalar value.

Equation (4) can be rewritten in a matrix form as

$$A\boldsymbol{\lambda} = \boldsymbol{h}, \tag{5}$$

where $A_{ij} = \varphi(\|\boldsymbol{x}_i - \boldsymbol{\xi}_j\|)$ is the entry of the matrix in the i-th row and j-th column, the number of rows $N \gg M$, M is the number of unknown weights $\boldsymbol{\lambda} = [\lambda_1, \dots, \lambda_M]^T$, i.e. a number of reference points, and $\boldsymbol{h} = [h_1, \dots, h_N]^T$ is a vector of values in the given points. The presented system is overdetermined, i.e. the number of equations N is higher than the number of variables M. This linear system of equations can be solved by the least squares method (LSE) as

$$A^T A \boldsymbol{\lambda} = A^T \boldsymbol{h}, \tag{6}$$

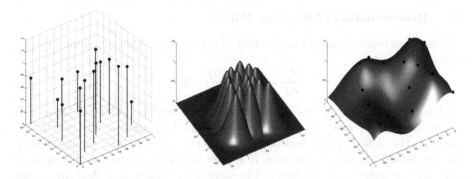

Fig. 1. Data values, the RBF collocation functions, the resulting interpolant (from [26]).

where the matrix $A^T A$ is symmetrical. Another possibility to solve the overdetermined system of linear equations $A\lambda = h$ is using the QR decomposition.

The RBF approximation can be done using "global" or "local" functions. When using "global" radial basis functions, the matrix A will be full and ill conditioned in general. When using "local" radial basis functions, the matrix A might be sparse, which can be beneficial when solving the overdetermined system of linear equations $A\lambda = h$.

3 Proposed Approach

We propose a new approach for scattered data approximation of $2\frac{1}{2}D$ functions using Radial basis functions with respecting inflection points of the function. Inflection points are computed from the discrete mesh and from curves given by implicit points. For a simplicity, the proposed approach is demonstrated on sampled regular grid.

The input $2\frac{1}{2}D$ function $f(x, y)$ is for the sake of simplicity of evaluation sampled on a regular grid. For a general case neighbours have to be determined, e.g. by using a kd-tree. One important feature when computing the RBF approximation is the location of radial basis functions. We will show two main groups of locations, where the radial basis functions should be placed.

The first group are extreme points of the input data set. Most of the radial basis functions have the property of having its maximum at its center (we will use only those) and thus it is very suitable to place the radial basis functions at the locations of extreme points.

The second group are inflection points of the input data set. The inflection points are important as the surface crosses its tangent plane, i.e. the surface changes from being concave to being convex, or vice versa. The surface at those locations should be approximated as accurately as possible in order to maintain the main features of the surface.

3.1 Determination of Extreme Points

The local extreme points of the function $f(x,y)$ can be either minimum or maximum, i.e.

$$\frac{\partial f}{\partial x} = 0 \quad \& \quad \frac{\partial f}{\partial y} = 0. \tag{7}$$

The decision if a point is a local extreme point can be done using only surrounding points. In our case, i.e. regular grid, we use four surrounding points, i.e. point on the right, left, up and down. In general case, neighbor points need to be determined, e.g. using a kd-tree. If a point is a local maximum, then all four surrounding points must be lower. The same also applies to a local minimum, i.e all four surrounding points must be higher (Fig. 2).

4	6	8	6	5	4	3	4	5
5	7	6	5	5	2	1	3	5
6	8	7	7		3	2	2	4
9	4	4	5	5	4	4	3	5

Fig. 2. Location of local extreme points. The values 1 and 8 (green) are local extremes, i.e. local minimum and local maximum. The value 4 (red) is not a local extreme as the four surrounding values are higher and smaller as well. (Color figure online)

The situation on the border of the input data set is a little bit different as we cannot use all four surrounding points, there will always be at least one missing. One solution is to skip the border of the input data set, however in this way we could omit some important extremes. Therefore, we determine the extremes from only three or two surrounding points.

3.2 Determination of Inflection Points

The second group of important locations for radial basis functions placement are inflection points, which forms actually curves of implicit points. The inflection points are located where the Gaussian curvature is equal zero. The Gaussian curvature for $2\frac{1}{2}D$ function $f(x,y)$ is computed as

$$k_{gauss} = \frac{\dfrac{\partial^2 f}{\partial x^2}\dfrac{\partial^2 f}{\partial y^2} - \left(\dfrac{\partial^2 f}{\partial x \partial y}\right)^2}{\left(\left(\dfrac{\partial f}{\partial x}\right)^2 + \left(\dfrac{\partial f}{\partial y}\right)^2 + 1\right)^2}. \tag{8}$$

The Gaussian curvature is equal zero when

$$\frac{\partial^2 f}{\partial x^2}\frac{\partial^2 f}{\partial y^2} - \left(\frac{\partial^2 f}{\partial x \partial y}\right)^2 = 0. \tag{9}$$

This formula is equivalent to the calculation using the Hessian matrix, i.e.

$$\begin{vmatrix} \dfrac{\partial^2 f}{\partial x^2} & \dfrac{\partial^2 f}{\partial x \partial y} \\ \dfrac{\partial^2 f}{\partial y \partial x} & \dfrac{\partial^2 f}{\partial y^2} \end{vmatrix} = 0. \tag{10}$$

To find out the locations, where the Gaussian curvature, i.e. the determinant of Hessian matrix, is equal zero, we can sample the following function from the input discrete data set.

$$I(x,y) = \frac{\partial^2 f}{\partial x^2} \frac{\partial^2 f}{\partial y^2} - \left(\frac{\partial^2 f}{\partial x \partial y} \right)^2. \tag{11}$$

An application example of (11) can be seen in Fig. 3.

Now, we need to find out the locations, where this sampled function is equal zero. We again use the four surrounding points. If at least one is positive and at least one is negative, then there must be a zero value in between them. For the simplicity and to speed-up the calculation we consider the center point as the inflection point (see Figs. 3 and 4 for illustration).

4	6	8	6	5	4	-2	-3	-4
5	2	6	5	5	2	1	-1	-5
2	1	3	7		3	2	2	4
-2	-1	0	5	5	4	4	3	5

Fig. 3. Location of inflection points. The green positions with values 1 are considered as inflection points. The red position with value 4 is not an inflection point as all four surrounding values from (11) are positive. (Color figure online)

The resulting inflection points form a curve of implicit points. It is quite densely sampled. However, for the purpose of the RBF approximation, we can reduce the inflection points to obtain a specific number of inflection points or reduce them as the distance between the closest two is larger than some threshold value.

3.3   RBF Approximation with Respecting Inflection Points

In the previous chapters, we presented the location of radial basis functions for $2\frac{1}{2}D$ function approximation. These locations are well placed to capture the main shape of the function $f(x,y)$. However we should add some more additional points to cover the whole approximation space. One set of additional radial basis functions is placed on the border and in the corners. The last additional radial basis functions are placed at locations with Halton distribution [4]

$$Halton(p)_k = \sum_{i=0}^{\lfloor \log_p k \rfloor} \frac{1}{p^{i+1}} \left(\left\lfloor \frac{k}{p^i} \right\rfloor \bmod p \right), \tag{12}$$

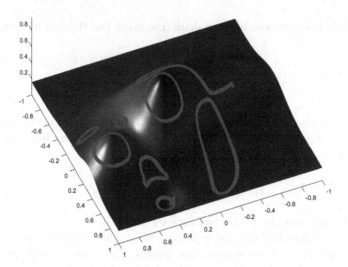

Fig. 4. An example of $2\frac{1}{2}D$ function with the curves of inflection points. The red curve represents the location of inflection points calculated using (11). (Color figure online)

where p is the prime number and k is the index of the calculated element, see Fig. 5 for an example of denerated points distribution. It is recommended to use different primes for x and y coordinate.

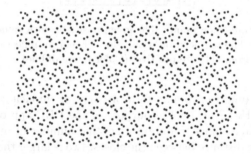

Fig. 5. The example of 10^3 Halton points. The Halton sequence was generated using two prime numbers $[2,3]$, i.e. for x coordinates a Halton sequence with the prime number 2 and for y coordinates a Halton sequence with the prime number 3.

Knowing all the positions of radial basis functions, we can compute the RBF approximation of the $2\frac{1}{2}D$ function. For the calculation we use the approach described in Sect. 2.1.

4   Experimental Results

In this section, we test the proposed approach for Radial basis function approximation. We tested the approach on all standard testing functions from [6]. In this paper we present the experimental results on only three testing functions, while the results for other testing functions are similar. The selected testing functions are the following

$$f_1(x,y) = \frac{2}{11}\left(\sin\left(4x^2 + 4y^2\right) - (x+y) + \frac{5}{2}\right) \tag{13}$$

$$f_2(x,y) = \frac{3}{4}e^{-\frac{1}{4}((9x-2)^2+(9y-2)^2)} + \frac{3}{4}e^{-\frac{1}{49}(9x+1)^2-\frac{1}{10}(9y+1)^2}$$
$$+ \frac{1}{2}e^{-\frac{1}{4}(9x-7)^2-\frac{1}{4}(9y-3)^2} - \frac{1}{5}e^{-(9x-4)^2-(9y-7)^2} \tag{14}$$

$$f_3(x,y) = \frac{1}{9}\tanh\left(9y - 9x\right) + 1 \tag{15}$$

All testing functions $z = f(x,y)$ were "normalized" to the interval $x,y \in \langle-1,1\rangle$ and the "height" z to $\langle0,1\rangle$ in order to easily compare the proposed approximation properties and approximation error for all testing functions and we used Gaussian radial basis function in all experiments.

$$\varphi(r) = e^{-\epsilon r^2}. \tag{16}$$

Only some representative results are presented in this chapter. The visualization of (13) is in Fig. 6, the visualization of (14) is in Fig. 9 and the visualization of (15) is in Fig. 12.

The first function (13) is an inclined sine wave. This function contains inflection points formed in the elliptical shapes as can be seen in Fig. 8b. In the experiments we used the Gaussian radial basis function with a shape parameter $\epsilon = 1$. The visualization of original function together with the RBF approximation is in Fig. 6. The approximation consists of 246 radial basis functions (78 are at locations of inflection points and extremes, 24 are at the borders and 144 are Halton points). It can be seen that the RBF approximation is visually identical to the original one. Also precision of approximation is very high, see Fig. 8a

To have a more closer look at the quality of RBF approximation, we computed the isocontours of the both original and approximated functions, see Fig. 7. Those isocontours are again visualy identical and cannot be seen any difference.

To compare the original and RBF approximated functions, we can compute the approximation error using the following formula for each point of evaluation.

$$Err = |f(x,y) - f_{RBF}(x,y)|, \tag{17}$$

where $f(x,y)$ is the value from input data set and $f_{RBF}(x,y)$ is the approximated value. Absolute error is used for evaluations data are normalized to $\langle-1,1\rangle \times \langle-1,1\rangle \times \langle0,1\rangle$ as described recently. If we compute the approximation error for all input sample points, then we can calculate the average approximation error, which is $2.37 \cdot 10^{-4}$, and also the histogram of approximation error, see Fig. 8a. It can be seen that the most common approximation errors are quite low values below 0.4%. The higher approximation errors appear only few times. This proves a good properties of the approximation method.

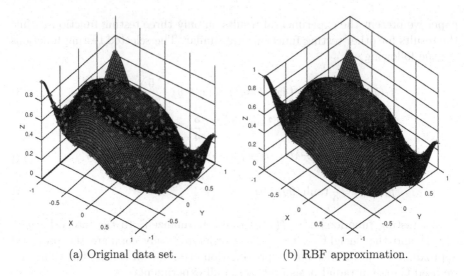

(a) Original data set.   (b) RBF approximation.

Fig. 6. The RBF approximation of $2\frac{1}{2}D$ function (13). The total number of RBF centers is 246 (red marks). (Color figure online)

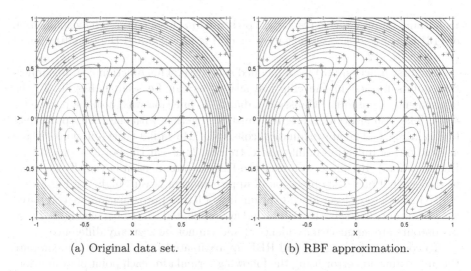

(a) Original data set.   (b) RBF approximation.

Fig. 7. The comparison of function isocontours.

The next testing function (14) is visualized together with the RBF approximation in Fig. 9. This function consists of four hills and the RBF approximation preserves the main shape. The only small difference is at the borders, which can be seen in more details in Fig. 10. The Gauss function with the shape parameter $\epsilon = 26$ was used as radial basis function.

The average approximation error is $2.75 \cdot 10^{-3}$ and the distribution of the approximation error can be seen in the histogram in Fig. 11.

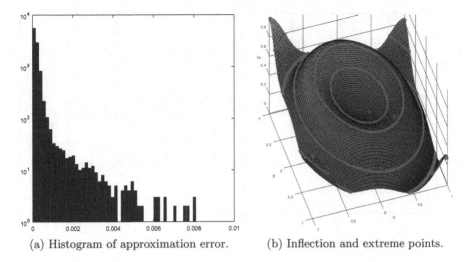

(a) Histogram of approximation error.   (b) Inflection and extreme points.

Fig. 8. The histogram (a) of approximation error for the function (13). The horizontal axis represents the absolute approximation error computed as (17). It should be noted, that the vertical axis is in logarithmic scale. The visualization (b) of all located inflection and extreme points.

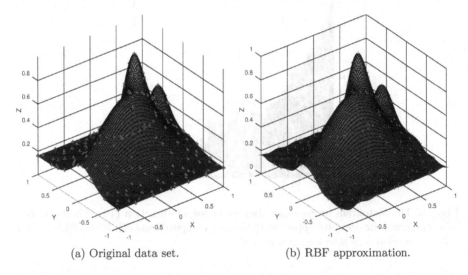

(a) Original data set.   (b) RBF approximation.

Fig. 9. The RBF approximation of $2\frac{1}{2}D$ function (14). The total number of RBF centers is 244 (red marks). (Color figure online)

The last function (15) for testing the proposed RBF approximation is visualized in Fig. 12a. This function is quite exceptional, because it has a sharp cliff on $x = y$. Such sharp cliffs are always very hard to approximate using the RBF. However using the proposed distribution of the radial basis functions, we are

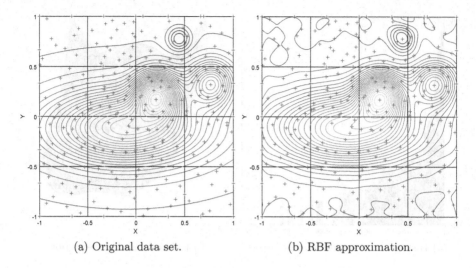

(a) Original data set.   (b) RBF approximation.

Fig. 10. The comparison of function isocontours.

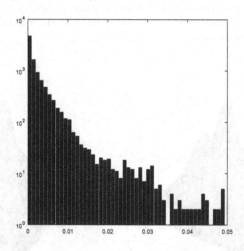

Fig. 11. The histogram of approximation error for the function (14). The horizontal axis represents the absolute approximation error computed as (17). It should be noted, that the vertical axis is in logarithmic scale.

able to approximate the sharp cliff quite well, see Fig. 12b. The problem, that comes up, is the wavy surface for $y > x$, see more details in Fig. 13. The Gauss function with the shape parameter $\epsilon = 25$ was used as the radial basis function.

The average approximation error for this specific function is $1.22 \cdot 10^{-2}$. This result is quite positive as the function is very hard to approximate using the RBF approximation technique. The histogram of the approximation error is visualized in Fig. 14.

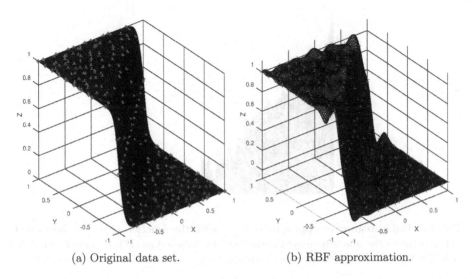

(a) Original data set.   (b) RBF approximation.

Fig. 12. The RBF approximation of $2\frac{1}{2}D$ function (15). The total number of RBF centers is 244 (red marks). (Color figure online)

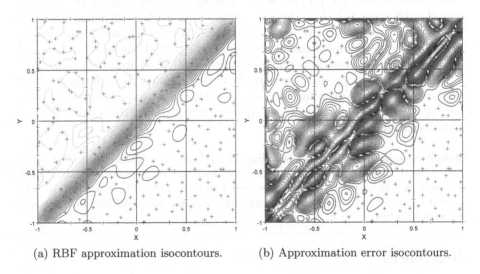

(a) RBF approximation isocontours.   (b) Approximation error isocontours.

Fig. 13. The visualization of approximated function isocontours (a). The visualization of approximation error as isocontours plot (b), please note that the average approximation error is $1.22 \cdot 10^{-2}$.

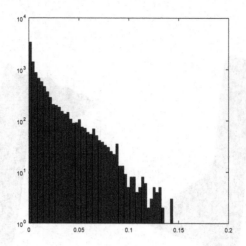

Fig. 14. The histogram of approximation error for the function (15). The horizontal axis represents the absolute approximation error computed as (17). It should be noted, that the vertical axis is in logarithmic scale.

5   Conclusion

We presented a new approach for approximation of $2\frac{1}{2}D$ scattered data using Radial basis functions respecting inflection points in the given data set. The RBF approximation uses the properties of the input data set, namely the extreme and the inflection points to determine the location of radial basis functions. This sophisticated placement of radial basis functions significantly improves the quality of the RBF approximation. It reduces the needed number of radial basis functions and thus creates even more compressed RBF approximation, too.

In future, the proposed approach is to be extended to approximate $3\frac{1}{2}D$ scattered data, while utilizing the properties of the input data set for the optimal placement of radial basis functions. Also efficient finding a shape parameters is to be explored.

Acknowledgments. The authors would like to thank their colleagues at the University of West Bohemia, Plzen, for their discussions and suggestions, and anonymous reviewers for their valuable comments and hints provided. The research was supported by projects Czech Science Foundation (GACR) No. 17-05534S and partially by SGS 2019-016.

References

1. Afiatdoust, F., Esmaeilbeigi, M.: Optimal variable shape parameters using genetic algorithm for radial basis function approximation. Ain Shams Engineering J. **6**(2), 639–647 (2015)

2. Biazar, J., Hosami, M.: Selection of an interval for variable shape parameter in approximation by radial basis functions. In: Advances in Numerical Analysis 2016 (2016)

3. Chen, S., Chng, E., Alkadhimi, K.: Regularized orthogonal least squares algorithm for constructing radial basis function networks. Int. J. Control **64**(5), 829–837 (1996)

4. Fasshauer, G.E.: Meshfree Approximation Methods with MATLAB, vol. 6. World Scientific (2007)

5. Fornberg, B., Wright, G.: Stable computation of multiquadric interpolants for all values of the shape parameter. Comput. Math. Appl. **48**(5–6), 853–867 (2004)

6. Franke, R.: A critical comparison of some methods for interpolation of scattered data. Technical report, Naval Postgraduate School Monterey CA (1979)

7. Ghosh-Dastidar, S., Adeli, H., Dadmehr, N.: Principal component analysis-enhanced cosine radial basis function neural network for robust epilepsy and seizure detection. IEEE Trans. Biomed. Eng. **55**(2), 512–518 (2008)

8. Hardy, R.L.: Multiquadric equations of topography and other irregular surfaces. J. Geophys. Res. **76**(8), 1905–1915 (1971)

9. Hardy, R.L.: Theory and applications of the multiquadric-biharmonic method 20 years of discovery 1968–1988. Comput. Mathe. Appl. **19**(8–9), 163–208 (1990)

10. Karim, A., Adeli, H.: Radial basis function neural network for work zone capacity and queue estimation. J. Transp. Eng. **129**(5), 494–503 (2003)

11. Larsson, E., Fornberg, B.: A numerical study of some radial basis function based solution methods for elliptic PDEs. Comput. Math. Appl. **46**(5), 891–902 (2003)

12. Majdisova, Z., Skala, V.: Big geo data surface approximation using radial basis functions: a comparative study. Comput. Geosci. **109**, 51–58 (2017)

13. Majdisova, Z., Skala, V.: Radial basis function approximations: comparison and applications. Appl. Math. Model. **51**, 728–743 (2017)

14. Majdisova, Z., Skala, V., Smolik, M.: Determination of stationary points and their bindings in dataset using RBF methods. In: Silhavy, R., Silhavy, P., Prokopova, Z. (eds.) CoMeSySo 2018. AISC, vol. 859, pp. 213–224. Springer, Cham (2019). https://doi.org/10.1007/978-3-030-00211-4_20

15. Orr, M.J.: Regularised centre recruitment in radial basis function networks. Centre for Cognitive Science, Edinburgh University. Citeseer (1993)

16. Orr, M.J.: Regularization in the selection of radial basis function centers. Neural Comput. **7**(3), 606–623 (1995)

17. Pan, R., Skala, V.: A two-level approach to implicit surface modeling with compactly supported radial basis functions. Eng. Comput. **27**(3), 299–307 (2011)

18. Pan, R., Skala, V.: Surface reconstruction with higher-order smoothness. Vis. Comput. **28**(2), 155–162 (2012)

19. Prakash, G., Kulkarni, M., Sripati, U.: Using RBF neural networks and Kullback-Leibler distance to classify channel models in free space optics. In: 2012 International Conference on Optical Engineering (ICOE), pp. 1–6. IEEE (2012)

20. Sarra, S.A., Sturgill, D.: A random variable shape parameter strategy for radial basis function approximation methods. Eng. Anal. Bound. Elem. **33**(11), 1239–1245 (2009)

21. Schagen, I.P.: Interpolation in two dimensions - a new technique. IMA J. Appl. Math. **23**(1), 53–59 (1979)

22. Skala, V.: Fast interpolation and approximation of scattered multidimensional and dynamic data using radial basis functions. WSEAS Trans. Math. **12**(5), 501–511 (2013)

23. Skala, V.: RBF interpolation with CSRBF of large data sets. Procedia Comput. Sci. **108**, 2433–2437 (2017)
24. Smolik, M., Skala, V.: Spherical RBF vector field interpolation: experimental study. In: 2017 IEEE 15th International Symposium on Applied Machine Intelligence and Informatics (SAMI), pp. 000431–000434. IEEE (2017)
25. Smolik, M., Skala, V.: Large scattered data interpolation with radial basis functions and space subdivision. Integr. Comput.-Aided Eng. **25**(1), 49–62 (2018)
26. Smolik, M., Skala, V., Majdisova, Z.: Vector field radial basis function approximation. Adv. Eng. Softw. **123**(1), 117–129 (2018)
27. Smolik, M., Skala, V., Nedved, O.: A comparative study of LOWESS and RBF approximations for visualization. In: Gervasi, O., et al. (eds.) ICCSA 2016. LNCS, vol. 9787, pp. 405–419. Springer, Cham (2016). https://doi.org/10.1007/978-3-319-42108-7_31
28. Uhlir, K., Skala, V.: Reconstruction of damaged images using radial basis functions. In: 2005 13th European Signal Processing Conference, pp. 1–4. IEEE (2005)
29. Wang, J., Liu, G.: On the optimal shape parameters of radial basis functions used for 2-D meshless methods. Comput. Methods Appl. Mech. Eng. **191**(23–24), 2611–2630 (2002)
30. Wendland, H.: Computational aspects of radial basis function approximation. Stud. Comput. Math. **12**, 231–256 (2006)
31. Wright, G.B.: Radial basis function interpolation: numerical and analytical developments (2003)
32. Yingwei, L., Sundararajan, N., Saratchandran, P.: Performance evaluation of a sequential minimal radial basis function (RBF) neural network learning algorithm. IEEE Trans. Neural Netw. **9**(2), 308–318 (1998)
33. Zhang, X., Song, K.Z., Lu, M.W., Liu, X.: Meshless methods based on collocation with radial basis functions. Comput. Mech. **26**(4), 333–343 (2000)

Efficient Simple Large Scattered 3D Vector Fields Radial Basis Functions Approximation Using Space Subdivision

Michal Smolik[(✉)] and Vaclav Skala

Faculty of Applied Sciences, University of West Bohemia, Plzen, Czech Republic
{smolik,skala}@kiv.zcu.cz

Abstract. The Radial basis function (RBF) approximation is an efficient method for scattered scalar and vector data fields. However its application is very difficult in the case of large scattered data. This paper presents RBF approximation together with space subdivision technique for large vector fields.

For large scattered data sets a space subdivision technique with overlapping $3D$ cells is used. Blending of overlapped $3D$ cells is used to obtain continuity and smoothness. The proposed method is applicable for scalar and vector data sets as well. Experiments proved applicability of this approach and results with the tornado large vector field data set are presented.

Keywords: Vector field · Radial Basis Functions · Critical point · Tornado · Simplification · Approximation · Space subdivision · Data compression · Visualization

1 Introduction

Interpolation or approximation methods of scattered $3D$ vector field data mostly use tessellation of the given domain, i.e. triangulation or tetrahedralization, etc. Space subdivision techniques are often used to increase speed-up and decrease memory requirements in combination of adaptive hierarchical methods, i.e. quadtree, octree etc. However, the Radial Basis Functions (RBF) is not a separable (by dimension) approximation. In general, the meshless methods mostly based on RBF.

Data are split into subdomains, processed and blended together with partition of unity in [28]. The contribution [28] is an extension of well-known method [16], which construct surface model from large data sets using multi-level partition of unity. Downsampling [17] leads to a coarse-fine hierarchy, where points in each hierarchy level are used incrementally for better approximation. Parallel

The research was supported by projects Czech Science Foundation (GACR) No. GA17-05534S and partially by SGS 2019-016.

S. Misra et al. (Eds.): ICCSA 2019, LNCS 11619, pp. 337–350, 2019.
https://doi.org/10.1007/978-3-030-24289-3_25

version of this approach [29] claims $O(N)$ computational complexity using generalized minimal residual method (GMRE) with the Schwartz iterative method [3]. Optimization of centers and weights of RBF methods was explored in [25] with combination of hierarchical decomposition. There are many other related modifications of RBF approximation with a specific focus available, e.g. parallelism of [7] for mesh deformation, incremental RBF interpolation [1], computation of RBF with Least square error [12] with preconditioning aspects and domain decomposition.

The method for topological information visualization for vector fields is well known [11]. The vector fields are very complex data sets and the topological skeleton represents a compact visualization. The vector field topology can be simplified using [26]. This approach computes clusters of critical points, where the distance is represented by the weight of merging critical points. The critical points in one cluster are merged together and can create a higher order critical point or cancel each other. The method generates the piece-wise linear representation after building clusters containing singularities. The paper [27] presents an approach for simplified visualization of vector fields. The authors prove that the $3D$ vector field inside some closed region can be represented by the $2D$ vector field on the surface over this region. The vector filed that uses the Delaunay triangulation is described in [4]. It removes vertices from the Delaunay triangulation close to critical points and prevents topological changes using local metric while removing some vertices. Numerical comparison between global and local RBF methods was explored in [2] to find out the advantages and disadvantages of local RBF methods use for $3D$ vector field approximation. The classification of critical points using Hessian matrix is presented in [21]. Vector field approximation for the $2D$ case preserving topology and memory reduction was presented in [10]. It is based on segmentation and flow in a separate region is approximated by a linear function. The paper [23,24] proposes an approach for RBF approximation of vector field and selection of important critical points. Robust detection of critical points is described in [20].

We propose a new simple and robust approach for large scattered $3D$ vector fields data approximation using space subdivision. Usually, the whole data set needs to be processed at once [13,14]. Other relevant methods are not easy to implement. Using the space subdivision methods with respecting the continuity of the resulting approximation, the proposed approach enables to process large data vector fields.

2   Proposed Approach

The $3D$ vector field data sets come usually from numerical simulations and are very large. Such vector fields can be approximated for the visualization purposes or to minimize the data set size. In our proposed approach for approximation of $3D$ vector fields we use modified algorithm described in [22], which computes $2D$ interpolation of height data sets.

In the following part we introduce a new approach for large $3D$ vector field data approximation using RBF and space subdivision respecting continuity of the final approximation result. Space subdivision application leads to significant computational speed-up, decrease of memory requirements and better robustness of computation, too.

There are three main steps of the algorithm: space subdivision, data approximation of each cell and blending, i.e. joining approximations over overlapping cells. The Algorithms 1 and 2 present relevant pseudocodes.

Algorithm 1. Pseudocode of the proposed approach for RBF approximation.

1: **procedure** RBF(*Points P*)   ▷ $P_i = \{\boldsymbol{x}_i, \boldsymbol{v}_i\}$
2:     **for all** cells in grid **do**
3:         Enlarge cell for approximation by $\varPsi$
4:         $p \leftarrow$ Points in enlarged cell
5:         $\xi \leftarrow$ RBF centers in enlarged cell
6:         Compute RBF approximation of p

Algorithm 2. Pseudocode of approximated value calculation using the proposed RBF approximation method.

1: **procedure** RBF(*Point p*)   ▷ $p = \{x, y, z\}$
2:     Find neighboring cells
3:     Determine distances to cells
4:     Compute approximated RBF values for all cells
5:     Blend RBF approximated values together   ▷ using distances to cells

---

2.1   Space Subdivision

The divide and conquer (D&C) strategy is used in the proposed algorithm. The input data set is divided into several domains. In this paper for simplicity of explanation, we use a rectangular grid for divide and conquer strategy, where the grid size for $3D$ data set is $n \times m \times l$. We can use any kind of space division, however the proposed approach is easy to explain sung the regular orthogonal grid and thus it was used in the presented experiments for its simplicity.

The given data need to be splitted into overlapping cells respecting the created grid for application of the space subdivision. Each domain of the grid is enlarged to a cell which includes some neighboring points from the neighborhood domains (it will be explained latter on), see Fig. 1.

2.2   Cells RBF Approximation

In the proposed approach, we use the "global" Thin Plate Spline (TPS) radial basis function, which is shape parameter free and minimizes the tension of the final approximation [5]. The TPS has the following formula

$$\varphi(r) = r^2 \log r = \frac{1}{2} r^2 \log r^2 \tag{1}$$

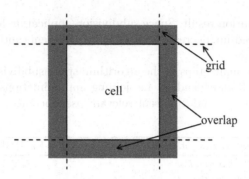

Fig. 1. $3D$ regular orthogonal grid ($2D$ analogy) of one cell. Each cell has points that are inside the domain plus pints from the overlapping parts (grey color).

Now, the given points are splited into overlapping $3D$ cells. The RBF approximation needs the centers of radial basis functions. The RBF centers have the Halton distribution [8] and are placed inside the enlarged cell. The number of centers for RBF approximation of each cell can be selected according to the required quality of approximation.

Points inside of a cell are approximated using the RBF approximation with the TPS function. This approximation uses the standard solution of the linear system of equations (2). Each cell is approximated independently and therefore the computation can be done totally in parallel, which increases the performance and speed-up, too. However, the memory requirements would be higher as multiple RBF matrices need to be stored simultaneously. This should be considered when determining the size of a grid for space subdivision.

$$v_i = v(x_i) = \sum_{j=1}^{M} \lambda_j \varphi(\|x_i - \xi_j\|),$$

$$\text{for } \forall i \in \{1, \ldots, N\} \tag{2}$$

where $v_i = [v_i^{(x)}, v_i^{(y)}, v_i^{(z)}]$, M is the number of the RBF centers. Solution of the linear system of equations is a vector $\lambda = [\lambda_1, \lambda_2, \ldots, \lambda_M]^T$, where $\lambda_i = [\lambda_i^x, \lambda_i^y, \lambda_i^z]^T$. These values will be used later. However, the matrix for the RBF computation can be discarded as it will not be needed any more.

2.3 Reconstruction Function and Cells Blending

The already computed approximated cells overlap. To get the final continuous representation of the $3D$ vector field, we need to join the RBF approximations of cells.

The RBF approximation usually has problems with a precision on a border [15,19] and thus we cannot use the whole enlarged cell for blending. The overlapping part of each border is Ψ. For the blending phase we will use only half of the overlapping part, see the blue part in Fig. 2, Therefore the size of this overlapping part is ψ, i.e. $(2\psi = \Psi)$.

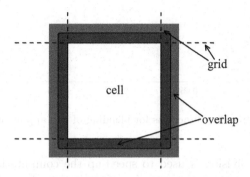

Fig. 2. Visualization of the overlap part used for blending (blue color). (Color figure online)

To blend all the neighborhood cell together, we use modified trilinear interpolation ("blending") of those neighborhood cells. The computed value obtained for each cell is to be weighted by a coefficient α. The coefficients α are determined as

$$\alpha' = \left[1 - min\left(1, \frac{distance\ from\ the\ border}{\psi}\right)\right]^2, \qquad (3)$$

where *distance from the border* is the shortest distance from the location to the border using the Euclidean metric. The final blending coefficients α_i are computed using Eq. (3) as

$$\alpha_i = \frac{\alpha_i'}{\sum\limits_{j=1}^{2^k} \alpha_j'}, \qquad (4)$$

where $i = \{1, \ldots, 2^k\}$ and k is the dimension, i.e. $k = 3$ for $3D$ vector field data set. The visualization of blending functions for blending of two approximations can be seen in Fig. 3. The initial and the final phase of blending function is more attracted to value 0, resp. 1, thus the final approximation is more smooth.

After computing the proposed RBF approximation with space subdivision and blending, we end up with an analytical form of the approximated vector field. This vector field is the simplified representation of the original data set. Moreover the analytical formula of the vector field can be used for further processing and visualization.

2.4   Speed-Up of the Proposed Approach (Approximation)

The RBF approximation has actually two parts. First, the RBF coefficients computation. And second, computation of the function value for the given position x.

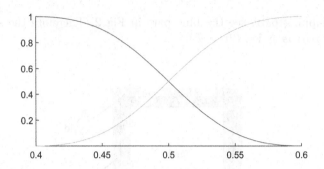

Fig. 3. Blending functions for blending of two approximations.

The space subdivision is used to speed-up the computation of vector field radial basis function approximation, i.e. computation of λ values, and reduces memory requirements, too.

The asymptotic time complexity of solving overdetermined system of linear equations with QR decomposition [6] and Householder matrix transformation [9] is

$$O\left(2NM^2 - \frac{2}{3}M^3\right),\tag{5}$$

where N is the total number of input points, M is the number of centers for RBF and $N > M$.

Let us assume that the input vector field data set has an uniform distribution of points and the input vector field is divided into G cells. The best size of overlapping part was experimentally selected as $\Psi = 30\%$, i.e. $\psi = 15\%$. The smaller overlapping part can result in non-smooth blending and larger overlapping part will result in higher computation costs while the approximation quality will not increase much more.

The number of points inside the enlarged cell is different depending on the location of the cell. In Fig. 4 are visualized 3 different type of cells, when the

Fig. 4. Visualization of different type of cells according to the number of points inside the enlarged cell.

cells with the same color have the same number of points inside the enlarged cell. There is one more group of cells, that has the same number of points inside the enlarged cell. This group of cells is inside the cube visualized in Fig. 4. In our computations of time complexity, we will assume, that the number of points inside each enlarged cell is the same and is equal to

$$n = (1 + 2\Psi)^3 \frac{N}{G}, \tag{6}$$

where G is the total number of cells and n is the number of points inside the enlarged cell. The constant Ψ is the size of overlapping parts.

The proposed RBF approximation method time complexity can be estimated as:

$$O\left(G\left(2nm^2 - \frac{2}{3}m^3\right)\right), \tag{7}$$

where m is the number of centers for RBF approximation. The value of m is calculated as

$$m = n\frac{M}{N}. \tag{8}$$

The speed-up of the proposed algorithm for vector field RBF approximation compared to the standard RBF approximation is

$$\nu = \frac{O\left(2NM^2 - \frac{2}{3}M^3\right)}{O\left(G\left(2nm^2 - \frac{2}{3}m^3\right)\right)} = \frac{G^3(1 - 3N)}{(1 + 2\Psi)^9\left(G - 3N\left(1 + 2\Psi\right)^3\right)}, \tag{9}$$

where Ψ is the size of overlapping parts. For large values of N, i.e. $N > 10^6$, the expected speed-up is given as Eq. (10) and the visualization of speed-up is in Fig. 5.

$$\nu \approx \frac{G^3}{(1 + 2\Psi)^{12}}. \tag{10}$$

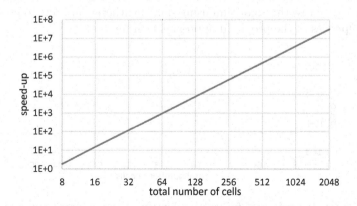

Fig. 5. Expected speed-up of the proposed approach of vector field RBF approximation compared to the standard one (note that the axes are logarithmic).

An example of the speed-up for the size of overlapping 30% is as the following

$$\nu \approx \frac{G^3}{(1 + 2 \cdot 0.3)^{12}} = \frac{G^3}{1.6^{12}} \approx \frac{G^3}{281}. \tag{11}$$

2.5 Speed-Up of the Function Evaluation

In this part we present how the function evaluation speed-up the vector field RBF approximation computation. Moreover, it also speed-up the evaluation of the approximation function as well. For the standard RBF function evaluation, the time complexity can be estimated as:

$$O(M). \tag{12}$$

In the case of the proposed algorithm, the time of RBF evaluation can be estimated as:

$$O\left(2^3 m\right), \tag{13}$$

where the maximum number of blended approximations is 2^3, i.e. 8. Using Eqs. (12) and (13), we can determine the theoretical speed-up of the proposed method for evaluation of one function value of the vector field RBF approximation:

$$\eta = \frac{O(M)}{O(2^3 m)} = O\left(\frac{G}{2^3 (1 + 2\Psi)^3}\right), \tag{14}$$

where Ψ is the size of overlapping parts. For most grid resolutions, i.e. number of cells, the speed-up $\eta \gg 1$, is shown in Fig. 6. Note that the η axis, i.e. speed-up, is in logarithmic scaling.

3 Experimental Results

In this part we present experimental results. The proposed $3D$ vector field RBF approximation is especially convenient for large vector field data set approximation. Firstly we test the algorithm using small synthetic data sets to present and prove properties of the proposed approximation method.

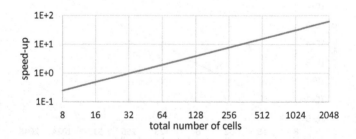

Fig. 6. Expected speed-up of function evaluation of the proposed approach for vector field RBF approximation compared to the standard one (note that the axes are logarithmic).

Secondly, the experimental results with real data sets containing $5.5 \cdot 10^8$ points are presented. Experiments proved that the proposed method is capable to process significantly larger data on a desktop computer.

3.1 Synthetic Data Set

Firstly, we tested the blending of two $1\frac{1}{2}D$ simple functions together to verify expected properties of the proposed approach. We used two blending functions from Fig. 3 and performed the blending on two functions that are visualized in Fig. 7. The two functions are blended in interval [0.4; 0.6] and the result is visualized in Fig. 7.

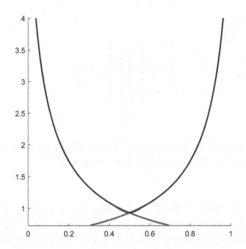

Fig. 7. Blending of two functions (red) and the result after blending (black). (Color figure online)

Secondly, we tested the blending of two $2\frac{1}{2}D$ functions together. The result of blending two $2\frac{1}{2}D$ functions together at different locations is visualized at Fig. 8. It can be seen that the blending result is continuous and smooth, as expected.

3.2 Real Data Set

In these experiments, we used the EF5 tornado data set (from [18])[1], see Fig. 9a. The data set contains $5.5 \cdot 10^8$ $3D$ points with associated $3D$ vector.

---

[1] Data set of EF5 tornado courtesy of Leigh Orf from Cooperative Institute for Meteorological Satellite Studies, University of Wisconsin, Madison, WI, USA.

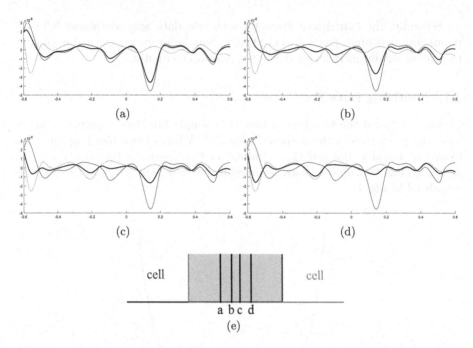

Fig. 8. Blending of two $2\frac{1}{2}D$ functions together. Visualization of blending for different "cut" of $2\frac{1}{2}D$ function (a–d), see (e) for "cut" location.

We computed the vector field approximation using the proposed approach with different number of centers for radial basis functions. The vector field RBF approximation when using only 0.1% of the number of input points as the number of RBF centers is visualized in Fig. 9b. It means, that the vector field approximation is visually almost identical with the original vector field data set even thought a high compression ratio $(1 : 10^3)$ is achieved. Visualization of $2D$ slices is visualized in Fig. 10. Again, the approximated vector field is almost identical with the original vector field.

The approximation error for different number of centers for radial basis functions is visualized in Fig. 11. The approximation error is computed using the formula

$$Err = \frac{\sum_{i=1}^{N} \|v_i - \bar{v}_i\|}{\sum_{i=1}^{N} \|\bar{v}_i\|}, \tag{15}$$

where $\bar{v}_i$ is the original vector, v_i is the approximated vector and N is the number of vectors.

This experiments also proved expected precision depending on the number of centers of the RBF approximation.

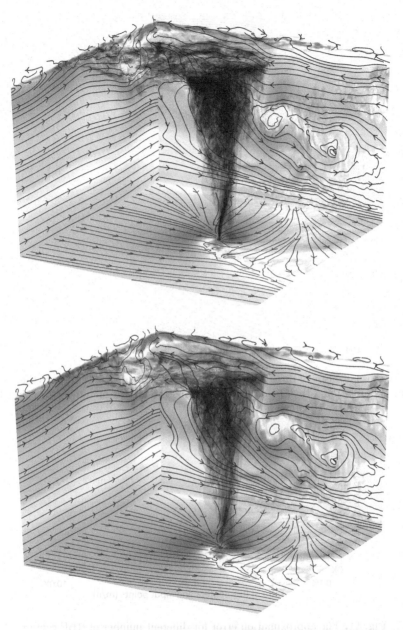

Fig. 9. Visualization of the $3D$ tornado vector field data set. Red central part represents the shape of tornado vortex and the yellow color on faces represents the speed of vector field. The original vector field (top) and the RBF approximated vector field (bottom). (Color figure online)

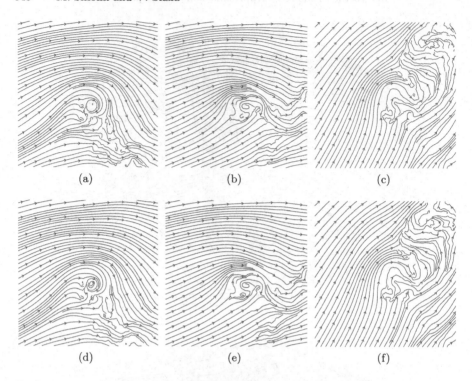

Fig. 10. Visualization of three $2D$ vector field slices. The top row represents the original vector field (a–c) and the bottom row represents the approximated vector field (d–f).

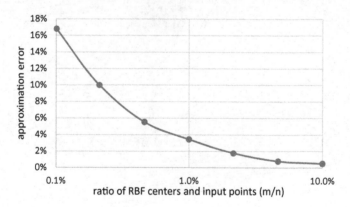

Fig. 11. The approximation error for different number of RBF centers.

4   Conclusion

We presented a new approach for large scale $3D$ vector field meshless approximation using RBF. The method significantly speeds-up the RBF parameters calculation, i.e. λ values, and the final RBF evaluation as well.

The proposed approximation method is based on partially overlapping cells. These overlapping cells are continuously blended together in order to obtain approximation of the whole large data set. Due to the space subdivision, the approach decreases memory and computational requirements. The proposed algorithm can be parallelized easily as well.

Experiments made on synthetic and real data proved high performance and computational robustness. The result of the proposed is an analytical description of simplified 3D vector field. This is very useful in further processing of the vector field and visualization as well.

Acknowledgments. The authors would like to thank their colleagues at the University of West Bohemia, Plzen, for their discussions and suggestions. The research was supported by projects Czech Science Foundation (GACR) No. GA17-05534S and partially by SGS 2019-016.

References

1. Beatson, R.K., Light, W.A., Billings, S.D.: Fast solution of the radial basis function interpolation equations: domain decomposition methods. SIAM J. Sci. Comput. **22**(5), 1717–1740 (2001)
2. Cabrera, D.A.C., Gonzalez-Casanova, P., Gout, C., Juárez, L.H., Reséndiz, L.R.: Vector field approximation using radial basis functions. J. Comput. Appl. Math. **240**, 163–173 (2013)
3. Cai, X.-C., Sarkis, M.: A restricted additive Schwarz preconditioner for general sparse linear systems. SIAM J. Sci. Comput. **21**(2), 792–797 (1999)
4. Dey, T.K., Levine, J.A., Wenger, R.: A Delaunay simplification algorithm for vector fields. In: 15th Pacific Conference on Computer Graphics and Applications, PG 2007, pp. 281–290. IEEE (2007)
5. Duchon, J.: Splines minimizing rotation-invariant semi-norms in Sobolev spaces. In: Schempp, W., Zeller, K. (eds.) Constructive Theory of Functions of Several Variables, pp. 85–100. Springer, Heidelberg (1977). https://doi.org/10.1007/BFb0086566
6. Golub, G.H., Van Loan, C.F.: Matrix computations, vol. 3. JHU Press (2012)
7. Haase, G., Martin, D., Offner, G.: Towards RBF interpolation on heterogeneous HPC systems. In: Lirkov, I., Margenov, S.D., Waśniewski, J. (eds.) LSSC 2015. LNCS, vol. 9374, pp. 182–190. Springer, Cham (2015). https://doi.org/10.1007/978-3-319-26520-9_19
8. Halton, J.H.: Algorithm 247: radical-inverse quasi-random point sequence. Commun. ACM **7**(12), 701–702 (1964)
9. Householder, A.S.: Unitary triangularization of a nonsymmetric matrix. J. ACM (JACM) **5**(4), 339–342 (1958)
10. Koch, S., Kasten, J., Wiebel, A., Scheuermann, G., Hlawitschka, M.: 2D vector field approximation using linear neighborhoods. Vis. Comput. **32**(12), 1563–1578 (2016)
11. Laramee, R.S., Hauser, H., Zhao, L., Post, F.H.: Topology-based flow visualization, the state of the art. In: Hauser, H., Hagen, H., Theisel, H. (eds.) Topology-Based Methods in Visualization, pp. 1–19. Springer, Heidelberg (2007). https://doi.org/10.1007/978-3-540-70823-0_1

12. Ling, L., Kansa, E.J.: Preconditioning for radial basis functions with domain decomposition methods. Math. Comput. Model. **40**(13), 1413–1427 (2004)
13. Majdisova, Z., Skala, V.: A radial basis function approximation for large datasets. Proc. SIGRAD **2016**(127), 9–14 (2016)
14. Majdisova, Z., Skala, V.: Big geo data surface approximation using radial basis functions: a comparative study. Comput. Geosci. **109**, 51–58 (2017)
15. Majdisova, Z., Skala, V.: Radial basis function approximations: comparison and applications. Appl. Math. Model. **51**, 728–743 (2017)
16. Ohtake, Y., Belyaev, A., Alexa, M., Turk, G., Seidel, H.-P.: Multi-level partition of unity implicits. In: ACM Siggraph 2005 Courses, pp. 463–470. ACM (2005)
17. Ohtake, Y., Belyaev, A.G., Seidel, H.: A multi-scale approach to 3D scattered data interpolation with compactly supported basis function. In: 2003 International Conference on Shape Modeling and Applications (SMI 2003), pp. 153–164, 292 (2003)
18. Orf, L., Wilhelmson, R., Wicker, L.: Visualization of a simulated long-track ef5 tornado embedded within a supercell thunderstorm. Parallel Comput. **55**, 28–34 (2016)
19. Skala, V.: Fast interpolation and approximation of scattered multidimensional and dynamic data using radial basis functions. WSEAS Trans. Math. **12**(5), 501–511 (2013)
20. Skala, V., Smolik, M.: A new approach to vector field interpolation, classification and robust critical points detection using radial basis functions. In: Silhavy, R. (ed.) CSOC2018 2018. AISC, vol. 765, pp. 109–115. Springer, Cham (2019). https://doi.org/10.1007/978-3-319-91192-2_12
21. Smolik, M., Skala, V.: Classification of critical points using a second order derivative. Procedia Comput. Sci. **108**, 2373–2377 (2017)
22. Smolik, M., Skala, V.: Large scattered data interpolation with radial basis functions and space subdivision. Integr. Comput.-Aided Eng. **25**(1), 49–62 (2018)
23. Smolik, M., Skala, V., Majdisova, Z.: 3D vector field approximation and critical points reduction using radial basis functions. In: International Conference on Applied Physics, System Science and Computers. Springer (2018)
24. Smolik, M., Skala, V., Majdisova, Z.: Vector field radial basis function approximation. Adv. Eng. Softw. **123**(1), 117–129 (2018)
25. Süßmuth, J., Meyer, Q., Greiner, G.: Surface reconstruction based on hierarchical floating radial basis functions. Comput. Graph. Forum **29**(6), 1854–1864 (2010)
26. Tricoche, X., Scheuermann, G., Hagen, H.: A topology simplification method for 2D vector fields. In: Visualization 2000, Proceedings, pp. 359–366. IEEE (2000)
27. Weinkauf, T., Theisel, H., Shi, K., Hege, H.-C., Seidel, H.-P.: Extracting higher order critical points and topological simplification of 3D vector fields. In: Visualization, 2005, VIS 2005, pp. 559–566. IEEE (2005)
28. Yang, J., Wang, Z., Zhu, C., Peng, Q.: Implicit surface reconstruction with radial basis functions. In: Braz, J., Ranchordas, A., Araújo, H.J., Pereira, J.M. (eds.) VISIGRAPP 2007. CCIS, vol. 21, pp. 5–12. Springer, Heidelberg (2008). https://doi.org/10.1007/978-3-540-89682-1_1
29. Yokota, R., Barba, L.A., Knepley, M.G.: PetRBF-a parallel O(N) algorithm for radial basis function interpolation with gaussians. Comput. Methods Appl. Mech. Eng. **199**(25), 1793–1804 (2010)

Human Action Recognition Using Convolutional Neural Networks with Symmetric Time Extension of Visual Rhythms

Hemerson Tacon[1], André S. Brito[1], Hugo L. Chaves[1],
Marcelo Bernardes Vieira[1(✉)], Saulo Moraes Villela[1],
Helena de Almeida Maia[2], Darwin Ttito Concha[2], and Helio Pedrini[2]

[1] Department of Computer Science, Universidade Federal de Juiz de Fora,
Juiz de Fora, Brazil
{hemerson,andre.brito,hugo.chaves}@ice.ufjf.br,
{marcelo.bernardes,saulo.moraes}@ufjf.edu.br
[2] Institute of Computing, University of Campinas, Campinas, Brazil
{helena.maia,darwin.ttito}@liv.ic.unicamp.br, helio@ic.unicamp.br

Abstract. Despite the expressive progress of deep learning models on the image classification task, they still need enhancement for efficient human action recognition. One way to achieve such gain is to augment the existing datasets. With this goal, we propose the usage of multiple Visual Rhythm crops, symmetrically extended in time and separated by a fixed stride. The symmetric extension preserves the video frame rate, which is crucial to not distort actions. The crops provide a 2D representation of the video volume matching the fixed input size of the 2D Convolutional Neural Network (CNN) employed. In addition, multiple crops with stride guarantee coverage of the entire video. Aiming to evaluate our method, a multi-stream strategy combining RGB and Optical Flow information is extended to include the Visual Rhythm. Accuracy rates fairly close to the state-of-the-art were obtained from the experiments with our method on the challenging UCF101 and HMDB51 datasets.

Keywords: Deep learning · Action recognition · Data augmentation · Video analysis · Visual rhythm

1 Introduction

In the last years, much progress has been made in the field of image classification. This success is the result of the combination of large image datasets, such as ImageNet [1], and the creation of new CNN approaches [2,3]. A natural

All authors thank CAPES, FAPEMIG (grant CEX-APQ-01744-15), FAPESP (grants #2017/09160-1 and #2017/12646-3), CNPq (grant #305169/2015-7) for the financial support, and NVIDIA for the grant of two GPUs (GPU Grant Program).

© Springer Nature Switzerland AG 2019
S. Misra et al. (Eds.): ICCSA 2019, LNCS 11619, pp. 351–366, 2019.
https://doi.org/10.1007/978-3-030-24289-3_26

consequence of this success was the exploitation of these advances in the field of video classification. In this domain, one problem consists in recognizing the main action executed by a person along a video. A solution to this problem is crucial to automate many tasks and it has outstanding applications: video retrieval, intelligent surveillance and autonomous driving [4–6]. This specific problem is called human action recognition and it is the subject of this paper.

The time dimension that is presented in videos produces a significant data increase if compared to images. Although some works have used 3D CNNs [5,7], the additional data of time dimension makes it prohibitive to use them without any previous polling step [8,9]. Most of recent works have used 2D CNNs for action recognition and this choice requires a video volume representation in a 2D space [9–11]. Such representation also needs to match the input size of the employed neural network which is commonly fixed. Another problem related to the data is the lack of massive labeled datasets. The existing ones [12,13] tend to be poorly annotated [6]. A workaround is to augment some well established datasets [14,15]. However, once their video lengths vary between samples, the time dimension manipulation is not simple and special cautions are required when performing the augmentation. For instance, keeping the original video frame rate is critical for the action recognition problem. Any variation in the frame rate could alter the action speed and distort it. When classifying a video with "walking" action, for example, this could be easily confused with the "running" action if a video with the first action had its frame rate increased compared to a video containing the second action.

In previous works, the usage of Visual Rhythms (VRs) [16–19] was proposed to address the issues imposed by time dimension handling. The VR is a 2D video representation with combined 1D RGB information varying in time. In this work, we propose a data augmentation for the VR by extending it symmetrically in time. This augmentation is an improvement of our previous work [19]. It is assumed that most actions presented from back to front in time can be properly classified. Furthermore, abrupt brightness changes are not introduced such as the periodic extension used in [19]. The symmetric extension in time also allows the extraction of multiple VR crops without deformations in frame rate. In addition, the crop dimensions can also be set to match any required input size of the employed neural network. All of these characteristics together make the symmetric extension a proper method to augment video datasets.

Our experiments are performed on two well-known challenging datasets, HMDB51 [15] and UCF101 [14]. A modified version of the widely known InceptionV3 network [2] is used. When combined with other features in a multi-stream architecture, the VR provides complementary information, which is crucial to achieve accuracy rates close to state-of-the-art methods. It is used the multi-stream architecture presented in [19]. This architecture takes RGB, Optical Flow and symmetrically extended VR images as input. It is empirically showed that symmetrically extended VRs can improve the final classification accuracy.

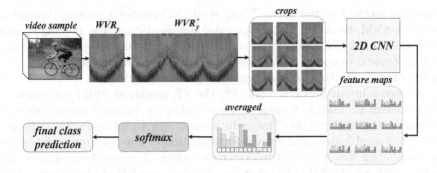

Fig. 1. Overview of the Visual Rhythm stream. After symmetric extension, n_w crops apart from each other by a stride s are extracted in the center (yellow). Depending on the dataset, extra crops aligned with the image top (magenta) and bottom (cyan) are extracted. All crops are applied to the CNN. The resulting features are averaged and the final class is predicted through a softmax layer. (Color figure online)

2   Related Work

The VR is a spatio-temporal slice of a video, i.e., a predefined set of pixels forming an arbitrary 2D surface embedded in a 3D volume of a video. Despite it has been first employed to detect camera transitions (cut, wipe and dissolve) in videos [16,17], the term VR was just mentioned a couple of years later by Kim et al. [20]. The first employment of VRs in the human action recognition problem was accomplished by Torres and Pedrini [21]. They utilized high-pass filters to obtain regions of interest (ROI) in VRs of videos. It is argued that the action patterns are present in only some parts of the VR.

By extracting the VR from videos, we attempt to reduce the human action recognition problem to image classification. There are highly successful convolutional neural networks [2,3] for this problem. Aiming to take advantage of such CNNs, many works have proposed to combine distinct 2D representations of the videos. The RGB information is a basic feature for this purpose. But even multiple image frames are not able to capture movement correlations along time and fail to distinguish similar actions [22]. In order to complement RGB based CNNs, many works have employed Optical Flow sequences as temporal features to supply the correlations along time [23–25]. Thus, a two-stream model was proposed to exploit and merge these two features [26,27]. This method showed to be successful and other extensions emerged combining more than two streams [9–11].

Despite the success of multi-stream methods, they do not allow communication between streams [23,25–27]. This lack of interaction hinders the models from learning spatio-temporal features [6]. An attempt to address this problem was proposed by Feichtenhofer et al. [10] with an architecture that provided a multiplicative interaction between spatial and temporal features. Another way to address this issue is to merge the spatial and temporal information into a single feature. To represent such spatio-temporal features, it is necessary to apply a pooling method to the video. Wang et al. [9] propose a pooling descriptor, based on SVM, to obtain a compact video representation. The pooling scheme is coupled into a CNN model and trained end-to-end. Similarly, the VR is also a kind of spatio-temporal feature. In the VR, a spatial dimension (X or Y axis) and the temporal dimension are aggregated into a 2D feature.

As shown in our previous work [19], the VR combined with a multi-stream model makes it possible to explore time and space interactions in videos to improve action recognition. The main interest was to introduce the VR as a spatio-temporal feature and show its contribution to a well-known architecture. A contribution was a method to detect the better direction (horizontal or vertical) to extract the VR. The criterion was to use the VR of the direction with more movement. Typical data augmentation techniques were also applied to the VRs. Such techniques significantly increased the classification accuracy. Motivated by this, we propose the use of multiple VR crops, symmetrically extended and separated by a fixed stride. This method consists of a proper data augmentation for the VR. Furthermore, some parameters related to the VR are explored aiming to extract more relevant information from video sequences.

3   Proposed Method

An overview of the VR stream is depicted in Fig. 1. It consists of a classification protocol using a version of the InceptionV3 network with VRs. A VR is computed for each video and its data augmentation is driven by symmetric extension. Multiple crops with fixed stride are extracted from the symmetric extension. The final class prediction is the averaged prediction of all crops.

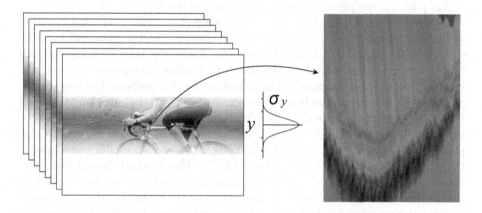

Fig. 2. Horizontal weighted rhythm: y is the middle row in this example.

3.1   Visual Rhythm

In most cases, the trajectory that is formed by the points in P is compact and thus the VR represents a 2D subspace embedded in video volume XYT. For instance, if P is the set of points of a single frame row, the resulting VR is a plane parallel to XT. Analogously, setting P as a single frame column results in a plane that is parallel to YT.

The proposal of [18,19], that takes the mean VR formed by all rows, was adapted. The reason is that the underlying moving object in a video is more likely to be observed far from the frame borders. By weighting the VRs far to the main object's location as the closest ones, one might hinder the motion representation. Instead, we propose to weight less as the VRs get farther from a reference row or column. Let $P_r = \{(r, 1), (r, 2), \cdots, (r, w)\}$ be the set of points forming the row r. We define the horizontal weighted VR as:

$$\mathrm{WVR}_y = \sum_{r=1}^{h} VR_{P_r} \cdot g(r - y, \sigma_y) \cdot \left[\sum_{r=1}^{h} g(r - y, \sigma_y) \right]^{-1} \tag{1}$$

where y is the reference row of the horizontal VR, and $g(s, \sigma) = e^{-\frac{s^2}{\sigma^2}}$ is the weighting function that decays as the other VRs get farther from the reference y. Thus, the horizontal VR used in this work is defined by two parameters: the reference row y and standard-deviation σ_y. Figure 2 depicts a video of the *Biking* class of UCF101 (240 frames with 320×240 pixels), forming a VR of 320×240 elements. In practice, an interval $y \pm d_y$, is defined from σ_y such that outer rows have zero weight. In practice, to make the parameter y invariant to video height h, we define a factor f_y such that $y = \alpha_y \cdot h$.

3.2   Symmetric Extension with Fixed Stride Crops

The symmetric extension of a VR, named WVR_y, is

$$\mathrm{WVR}_y^+(i, k) = \begin{cases} \mathrm{WVR}_y(i, f - m), & \text{for} \lfloor k/f \rfloor \text{odd} \\ \mathrm{WVR}_y(i, m + 1), & \text{otherwise} \end{cases} \tag{2}$$

where $1 \leq i \leq w$, m is the remainder of the integer division of k by f and $k \in \mathbb{Z}$. Thus, the WVR is composed of several copies of the VR concatenated several times along the temporal dimension with the even occurrences being horizontally flipped. Figure 3 shows a video of the *Biking* class of UCF101 (Fig. 2) extended three times. The premise is as follows: the action performed backwards in time also represents the class and can be used to reinforce the NN training.

The VR is extracted from each video in the dataset. Our proposal is to use multiple crops from each extended VR as a data augmentation process. Each crop is formed by the image constrained in a $w_{CNN} \times h_{CNN}$ window (matching the CNN's input). A crop with lower left coordinates x and t is defined as:

$$\mathrm{C}_{xt}^+(a, b) = \mathrm{WVR}_y^+(x + a, t + b), \tag{3}$$

with $x \leq a < x+h_{CNN}$ and $t \leq b < t+w_{CNN}$. The VR is extended symmetrically until n_w crops are extracted using a stride s, i.e., the first crop is taken at $t = 0$ and all subsequent $n_w - 1$ crops are taken s frames ahead the previous one. The resulting set of crops for a fixed row x is $\{C_{xt}^+ \mid t = js\}$, for $j \in \{0, 1, ..., n_w - 1\}$.

If h_{CNN} is smaller than w, i.e., the video frame width is greater than the corresponding dimension of the CNN, the crops are centered in X as depicted in Fig. 3. This approach assumes that the main action motion is mostly performed in this region. Notice that the top and bottom sides are not reached by the crops. In order to include these regions, extra n_w crops keeping the stride s from each other are obtained, aligned with the top and bottom borders. Thus, up to $3 \cdot n_w$ crops can be obtained depending on the application. This is useful to get all information in X and for most videos reinforce the central information. The mean and standard-deviation are computed to normalize each RGB channel of all crops.

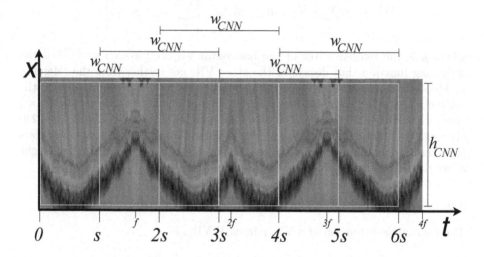

Fig. 3. Symmetric extension of a VR covering five squared crops: the frame width is $w = 320$ pixels, the corresponding video length is $f = 240$ frames, the stride between crops is $s = 150$ pixels and the crop dimensions are $w_{CNN} = h_{CNN} = 299$. The central area in X is selected in this example.

3.3   Video Classification Protocol

At inference time and for video classification, all the augmented crops are applied to the CNN and their last layer feature maps are extracted (just before softmax activation) and averaged. The softmax activation is applied to this average feature maps and then used to predict the sample class. We argue that this process might yield better class predictions based on the assumption that multiple crops taken at different time positions are representative of distinct portion of the underlying action in the video. The whole process is depicted in Fig. 1. In training stage, however, each crop is processed as a distinct sample and separately classified, i.e. the average is not taken into account.

4   Experimental Results

Datasets. The proposed method was evaluated through experiments performed on two challenging video action datasets: UCF101 [14] and HMDB51 [15]. The UCF101 dataset contains 13320 videos. All videos have fixed frame rate and resolution of 25 FPS and 320×240 pixels, respectively. This dataset covers a broad scope of actions from the simplest to the most complex ones. An example of the latter is playing some sport or playing some instrument. These videos were collected from Youtube and divided into 101 classes. Since they were uploaded by multiple users, there is a great diversity in terms of variations in camera motion, object appearance and pose, object scale and viewpoint. This diversity is essential to replicate the variety of actions that a more realistic scenario could have. HMDB51 is an action recognition dataset containing 6766 videos from 51 different action classes. The HMDB51 includes a wide variety of samples collected from various sources, including blurred videos, or with lower quality, and actions performed in distinct viewpoints. The evaluation protocol used for both datasets is the same. The average accuracy of the three training/testing splits available for both datasets is reported as the final result.

Implementation Details. The Keras framework [28] was used for all experiments. A slightly modified version of the InceptionV3 network [2] initialized with ImageNet [1] weights was used in the experiments of the Visual Rhythm Parameterization section. The InceptionV3 was modified to have an additional fully connected layer with 1024 neurons and 60% of dropout. The softmax classifier was adapted to match the number of classes in each dataset. It was used in the experiments that explored the variation of VR parameters.

All training parameters were kept the same for both datasets. Some Keras random data augmentation approaches (horizontal flip, vertical flip and zoom in the range of 0.8 to 1.2) were applied to the VRs. The network was trained with the following parameters: learning rate of $1e^{-3}$, batch size of 16, Stochastic Gradient Descent (SGD) optimizer with momentum of 0.9 and categorical cross entropy loss function. The early stopping training strategy is adopted with patience of 6 epochs. The learning rate was also scaled down by a factor of 10 after 3 epochs without any improvement in the loss function. The learning rate decrease was limited to $1e^{-6}$.

The representation of the video through the weighted VR depends on the choice of two parameters: a reference row (or column) α_y and the standard-deviation σ_y. The impacts of these parameters are explored in the first two experiments. The results show that the right choice of these parameters can help to improve the accuracy in both datasets. These results also provide evidence that the main action of the videos tends to focus around a certain region of the frames. We also perform experiments varying the symmetrical extension parameters aiming to achieve the better settings for it. The results corroborate the assumption that a data augmentation method is essential for increasing the accuracy rates.

4.1   Visual Rhythm Parameterization

A sequence of experiments was performed to discover the best set of parameters for WVR$^+$. The WVR approach is used as baseline comparison method in order to assess the performance gain along these experiments. The mean accuracy reached with WVR is 64.84% and 34.34% in UCF101 and HMDB51 datasets, respectively. All the evaluations used horizontal VRs. This is justified by its superior accuracy in contrast to the vertical one [19]. Throughout the experiments, the best parameters are employed in the subsequent executions. Initially, the parameters used for VR and the symmetric extension are: $\alpha_y = 0.5$ (middle row), $n_w = 1$ and only the central crop in X is extracted. Since InceptionV3 expects input images of 299 × 299 pixels, w_{CNN} and h_{CNN} are both set to 299. The method depicted in Fig. 1 is employed in all experiments.

In the first experiment, we compare the impact of the variation of the σ_y parameter. The following values for σ_y were tested: 7, 15, 33, 49 and 65. These values were chosen with the purpose of verifying if the region in which the action is performed is concentrated in a small area or it is more vertically spread. The results are shown in Table 1. The better standard-deviation for UCF101 was 33 and for HMDB51 it was 15. This indicates that actions on UFC101 tend to occur in a more spread region compared to HMDB51, since a smaller standard-deviation means more concentrated Gaussian weighting around the middle row.

Table 1. Comparison of accuracy rates (%) for UCF101 and HDMB51 varying the σ_y parameter

σ_y	UCF101 (%)	HMDB51 (%)
7	63.29	33.66
15	63.85	**33.99**
33	**65.26**	33.40
49	64.62	32.24
65	63.00	31.46

In the second experiment, we show the influence of the reference row on the accuracy rate. As mentioned earlier, a factor α_y is used instead the parameter y. The values chosen for the factor were: 0.40, 0.45, 0.50, 0.55 and 0.60. Values above 0.5 indicate the lower part of the image. Because the samples in both datasets come from multiple sources, the main action in each video may not happen exactly in the center of the video. This is the case of the UCF101. It was empirically observed that the better results were obtained when the reference row is located just below the center of the video. The mean action position in this dataset tends to be shifted around 5% below the middle of the video (Table 2).

Table 2. Comparison of mean accuracy rates (%) of UCF101 and HMDB51 varying the α_y factor

α_y	UCF101 (%)	HMDB51 (%)
0.40	62.82	30.06
0.45	64.83	31.00
0.50	65.26	**33.99**
0.55	**65.32**	33.35
0.60	65.24	33.48

In the next experiment, the number of windows n_w is increased in order to check if the accuracy rate also increases. The premise is that with more windows it is possible to cover the entire temporal extension of the video present in WVR$^+$. It is expected that the additional windows incorporates more discriminant aspects of the video. The n_w values used are: 1, 2, 3 and 4. In this experiment the stride s between the windows is fixed to 299 matching the w_{CNN} size. Thus, consecutive and non-overlapping crops are obtained. Table 3 show the results of this experiment. The expected correlation between n_w and the accuracy rate can be endorsed by the results.

Table 3. Comparison of accuracy rates (%) of UCF101 and HMDB51 datasets varying n_w parameter

n_w	UCF101 (%)	HMDB51 (%)
1	65.32	33.99
2	65.64	34.42
3	66.19	34.03
4	**67.70**	**34.99**

The fourth experiment consists of using windows that overlaps each other along the time dimension. When the extended VR completes a cycle it begins to repeat its temporal patterns as shown in Fig. 3. Crops can be extracted along the extended time with or without direct overlapping, consecutively or not. Consecutive and non-overlapping neighbor crops are obtained with $s = w_{CNN}$. Gaps between the crops are obtained by using stride $s > w_{CNN}$. Overlaps between consecutive crops occur when using $s < w_{CNN}$. In this work, we investigate the cases having $0 < s \leq w_{CNN}$. Notice that multiple parts of the VR, forward or backward in time, will be repeated unless $w_{CNN} + (n_w - 1) \cdot s < f$.

We used the strides 13, 25, 274, 286 and 299 that have a direct relation with video frame rate. Since all videos have 25 FPS, each 25 columns of the VR represents one second of the video. With a stride of 25, for instance, two consecutive crops overlap each other along their entire length except for the first second of the current crop and the last second of the next crop. On the other hand, with a stride of 274 the overlap occurs only between the last second of a crop and the first second of the following crop. Table 4 shows the results of this experiment. Notice that $s = 299$ provided the best accuracy for both datasets. This is exactly the same width of the CNN input. Further experiments are necessary to check if there is some relation between the stride s and the architecture input size.

Table 4. Comparison of accuracy rates (%) for UCF101 and HMDB51 varying the stride s parameter

s	UCF101 (%)	HMDB51 (%)
13	66.26	34.10
25	65.60	33.75
274	66.56	33.86
286	66.18	34.09
299	**67.70**	**34.99**

We also used the top and bottom regions in X direction. Therefore, each video is covered by 12 windows. The results are presented in Table 5, using the best parameters found in previous experiments: $n_w = 4$ and $s = 299$ for both datasets, $\alpha_y = 0.55$ and $\sigma_y = 0.33$ for UCF101 and $\alpha_y = 0.5$ and $\sigma_y = 0.15$ for HMDB51. The extra 8 crops helped to increase the accuracy rate in both datasets. Similar to the previous experiment, the use of the extra regions produced an overlap between the crops along the spatial dimension. However, more experiments need to be performed to assess how the overlap in X can be explored for data augmentation.

Table 5. Comparison of accuracy rates (%) for UCF101 and HMDB51 when extra crops are used

Regions	UCF101 (%)	HMDB51 (%)
Central	67.70	34.99
Central + Top + Bottom	**68.01**	**35.29**

Figures 4 and 5 show the accuracy difference between the best result of WVR$^+$ (Table 5) and the baseline method WVR for UCF101 and HMDB51 datasets, respectively. Only differences for the split 1 of both datasets are shown. Blue bars mean the WVR$^+$ were better by the given amount. Conversely, red bars favor the WVR. For the UCF101, WVR$^+$ performs better in 62 classes, worse in 31 classes, with even results in 8 classes. For the HMDB51, WVR$^+$ performs better in 24 classes, worse in 18 classes, with even results in 9 classes. The classes which demonstrated improvement for the proposed method seem to share some characteristics among each other. They often present actions with certain cyclic movements (e.g., *Brushing Teeth, Playing Violin, Typing*). This kind of action takes full advantage of the symmetrical extension of VR. Since the reverse movement generates patterns very similar to the one generated by the original movement, the multiple crops reinforce this kind of action and increase accuracy of them.

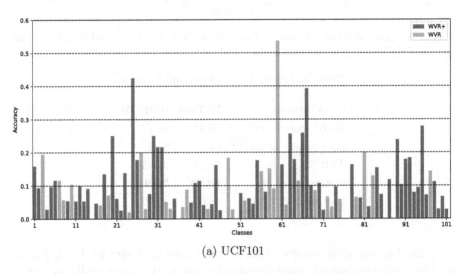

(a) UCF101

Fig. 4. Accuracy difference for each class between WVR$^+$ (blue) and WVR (red) for split 1 of UCF101. (Color figure online)

4.2   Multi-stream Classification Using Visual Rhythms

Our goal in this section is to show that our method can complement multi-stream architectures to get more competitive accuracy rates. The results of individual streams are shown in Table 6. The first three approaches, RGB*, Horizontal-mean and Adaptive Visual Rhythm (AVR), are contributions of our previous work [19]. Similar to other multi-stream networks [26,29], the Optical Flow performs better in both datasets. So, the other streams are crucial to complement the Optical Flow and to improve accuracy when combined. In order to achieve competitive results, experiments were performed merging the three streams: our best WVR$^+$ setup, the RGB* and the Optical Flow. The multi-stream approach of our previous work [19] was adopted to accomplish this purpose.

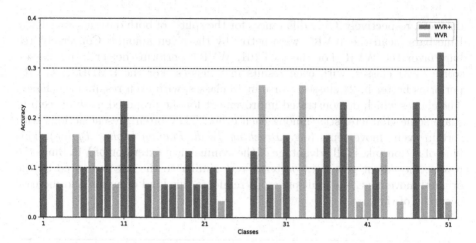

Fig. 5. Accuracy difference for each class between WVR$^+$ (blue) and WVR (red) for split 1 of HMDB51. (Color figure online)

Table 6. Results for single-stream features.

Single-Stream	UCF101	HMDB51
RGB* images [19]	86.61	51.77
Horizontal - mean [19]	62.37	35.57
AVR [19]	64.74	39.63
Optical flow [19]	**86.95**	**59.91**
Our method WVR$^+$	68.01	35.29

Table 7 presents the results of our method combined with RGB* and Optical Flow features through multi-stream late fusion. More specifically, at testing stage, three weights were evaluated through a grid search strategy. For each weight, we tested every value from 0 to 10 with a 0.5 step. It was observed that a higher accuracy is reached when the combination is done with the feature maps before the softmax normalization. The best combination found for UCF101 was 7.5, 6.0 and 1.0, respectively for Optical Flow, RGB* and WVR$^+$. And the best combination found for HMDB51 was 3.5, 1.5 and 0.5, respectively for Optical Flow, RGB* and WVR$^+$. We obtained 93.8% for UCF101 and 65.7% for HMDB51. Although WVR$^+$ by itself is not able to achieve accuracy rates comparable to the state-of-the-art (Table 7), our multi-stream method achieve fairly competitive accuracy rates. It is overcame only by the state-of-the-art work presented in [7] and the others that were also pre-trained with the Kinetics [30] dataset. Considering the UCF101, our method outperforms the proposal of [19], using the InceptionV3. Our approach is not better than the ResNet152 result for the UCF101. Due to the differences between InceptionV3 and ResNet152, further investigation is needed. The HMDB51 accuracy rate is lower than previous methods due to the lack of vertical VR information. The possible fusion with vertical VRs, however, makes our method promising.

Table 7. Comparison of accuracy rates (%) for UCF101 and HMDB51 datasets

Method	UCF101 (%)	HMDB51 (%)
iDT + HSV [31]	87.9	61.1
Two-Stream [26]	88.0	59.4
Two-Stream TSN [25]	94.0	68.5
Three-Stream TSN [25]	94.2	69.4
Three-Stream [32]	94.1	70.4
Two-Stream I3D [7]	98.0	80.7
I3D + PoTion [11]	**98.2**	80.9
SVMP+I3D [9]	-	81.3
DTPP (Kinetics pre-training) [22]	98.0	**82.1**
TDD+iDT [33]	91.5	65.9
LTC+iDT [34]	91.7	64.8
KVMDF [24]	93.1	63.3
STP [35]	94.6	68.9
L²STM [36]	93.6	66.2
Multi-Stream + ResNet152 [19]	94.3	68.3
Multi-Stream + InceptionV3 [19]	93.7	69.9
Our method	93.8	67.1

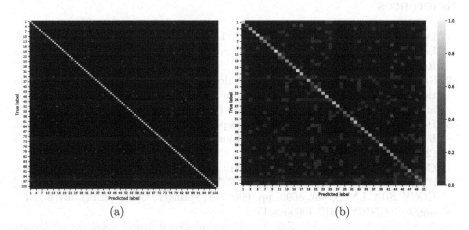

(a)   (b)

Fig. 6. Confusion matrix of the final multi-stream method for split 3: (a) UCF101. (b) HMDB51.

The confusion matrices of our multi-stream method applied for UCF101 and HMDB51, respectively, are shown on Figs. 6a and b. On UCF101 is possible to notice a reasonable misclassification between *Body Weight Squats* and *Lunges* classes (indexes 15 and 52 respectively) because their similar motion aspect.

5 Conclusions and Future Work

In this work, we proposed an approach to deal with video classification using a 2D representation of videos. The method consists of symmetrically extending the temporal dimension of the VR and taking crops apart by a stride. This method maintains the video frame rate and allows multiple samples of the underlying motion pattern to be obtained. It also provides data augmentation which is valuable for training 2D CNNs with small datasets. Furthermore, we explore the parameters of our method and verified that each dataset requires different settings to achieve better performance. Experimental results show that our method improves accuracy rates if compared to the resized horizontal VR. Results for HMDB51, which is more challenging, show that the information of the vertical rhythm can be valuable to improve the method efficiency. We also showed that our method achieves fairly competitive results compared to state-of-the-art approaches when combined with other features in a multi-stream architecture. As future work, it is worthy to investigate how multiple directions of VRs can be used for a single video. Vertical VRs, for instance, may improve recognition rates. More experiments are needed to check the relationship between the stride s and the network input size. It is also important to test our method with other 2D CNNs, such as ResNet152.

References

1. Deng, J., Dong, W., Socher, R., Li, L.-J., Li, K., Fei-Fei, L.: ImageNet: a large-scale hierarchical image database. In IEEE Conference on Computer Vision and Pattern Recognition (2009)
2. Szegedy, C., Vanhoucke, V., Ioffe, S., Shlens, J., Wojna, Z.: Rethinking the inception architecture for computer vision. In: IEEE Conference on Computer Vision and Pattern Recognition, pp. 2818–2826 (2016)
3. He, K., Zhang, X., Ren, S., Sun, J.: Deep residual learning for image recognition. In: IEEE Conference on Computer Vision and Pattern Recognition, pp. 770–778 (2016)
4. Ciptadi, A., Goodwin, M.S., Rehg, J.M.: Movement pattern histogram for action recognition and retrieval. In: Fleet, D., Pajdla, T., Schiele, B., Tuytelaars, T. (eds.) ECCV 2014. LNCS, vol. 8690, pp. 695–710. Springer, Cham (2014). https://doi.org/10.1007/978-3-319-10605-2_45
5. Ji, S., Wei, X., Yang, M., Kai, Y.: 3D convolutional neural networks for human action recognition. IEEE Trans. Pattern Anal. Mach. Intell. **35**(1), 221–231 (2013)
6. Kong, Y., Fu, Y.: Human action recognition and prediction: a survey. arXiv preprint arXiv:1806.11230 (2018)

7. Carreira, J., Zisserman, A., Vadis, Q.: Action recognition? A new model and the kinetics dataset. In: IEEE Conference on Computer Vision and Pattern Recognition, pp. 4724–4733. IEEE (2017)
8. Bilen, H., Fernando, B., Gavves, E., Vedaldi, A., Gould, S.: Dynamic image networks for action recognition. In: IEEE Conference on Computer Vision and Pattern Recognition, pp. 3034–3042 (2016)
9. Wang, J., Cherian, A., Porikli, F., Gould, S.: Video representation learning using discriminative pooling. In: IEEE Conference on Computer Vision and Pattern Recognition, pp. 1149–1158 (2018)
10. Feichtenhofer, C., Pinz, A., Wildes, R.P.: Spatiotemporal multiplier networks for video action recognition. In: IEEE Conference on Computer Vision and Pattern Recognition, pp. 7445–7454. IEEE (2017)
11. Choutas, V., Weinzaepfel, P., Revaud, J., Schmid, C.: PoTion: pose motion representation for action recognition. In: IEEE Conference on Computer Vision and Pattern Recognition (2018)
12. Abu-El-Haija, S., et al.: Youtube-8M: a large-scale video classification benchmark. arXiv preprint arXiv:1609.08675 (2016)
13. Karpathy, A., Toderici, G., Shetty, S., Leung, T., Sukthankar, R., Fei-Fei, L.: Large-scale video classification with convolutional neural networks. In: IEEE Conference on Computer Vision and Pattern Recognition, pp. 1725–1732 (2014)
14. Soomro, K., Zamir, A.R., Shah, M.: UCF101: a dataset of 101 human actions classes from videos in the wild. arXiv preprint arXiv:1212.0402 (2012)
15. Kuehne, H., Jhuang, H., Stiefelhagen, R., Serre, T.: HMDB51 a large video database for human motion recognition. In: Nagel, W., Kröner, D., Resch, M. (eds.) High Performance Computing in Science and Engineering, pp. 571–582. Springer, Heidelberg (2013). https://doi.org/10.1007/978-3-642-33374-3_41
16. Ngo, C.-W., Pong, T.-C., Chin, R.T.: Camera break detection by partitioning of 2D spatio-temporal images in MPEG domain. In: IEEE International Conference on Multimedia Computing and Systems, vol. 1, pp. 750–755. IEEE (1999)
17. Ngo, C.-W., Pong, T.-C., Chin, R.T.: Detection of gradual transitions through temporal slice analysis. In: IEEE Computer Society Conference on Computer Vision and Pattern Recognition, vol. 1, pp. 36–41. IEEE (1999)
18. Souza, M.R.: Digital video stabilization: algorithms and evaluation. Master's thesis, Institute of Computing, University of Campinas, Campinas, Brazil (2018)
19. Concha, D.T., Maia, H.A., Pedrini, H., Tacon, H., Brito, A.S., Chaves, H.L., Vieira, M.B.: Multi-stream convolutional neural networks for action recognition in video sequences based on adaptive visual rhythms. In: IEEE International Conference on Machine Learning and Applications. IEEE (2018)
20. Kim, H., Lee, J., Yang, J.-H., Sull, S., Kim, W.M., Moon-Ho Song, S.: Visual rhythm and shot verification. Multimedia Tools Appl. **15**(3), 227–245 (2001)
21. Torres, B.S., Pedrini, H.: Detection of complex video events through visual rhythm. Vis. Comput., 1–21 (2016)
22. Zhu, J., Zhu, Z., Zou, W.: End-to-end video-level representation learning for action recognition. In: 2018 24th International Conference on Pattern Recognition (ICPR), pp. 645–650. IEEE (2018)
23. Ng, J.Y.-H., Hauknecht, M., Vijayanarasimhan, S., Vinyals, O., Monga, R., Toderici, G.: Beyond short snippets: deep networks for video classification. In: IEEE Conference on Computer Vision and Pattern Recognition, pp. 4694–4702 (2015)

24. Zhu, W., Hu, J., Sun, G., Cao, X., Qiao, Y.: A key volume mining deep framework for action recognition. In: IEEE Conference on Computer Vision and Pattern Recognition, pp. 1991–1999. IEEE (2016)
25. Wang, L., Xiong, Y., Wang, Z., Qiao, Y., Lin, D., Tang, X., Gool, L.V.: Temporal segment networks: towards good practices for deep action recognition. In: Leibe, B., Matas, J., Sebe, N., Welling, M. (eds.) ECCV 2016. LNCS, vol. 9912, pp. 20–36. Springer, Cham (2016). https://doi.org/10.1007/978-3-319-46484-8_2
26. Simonyan, K., Zisserman, A.: Two-stream convolutional networks for action recognition in videos. In: Advances in Neural Information Processing Systems, pp. 568–576 (2014)
27. Simonyan, K., Zisserman, A.: Very deep convolutional networks for large-scale image recognition. arXiv preprint arXiv:1409.1556 (2014)
28. Chollet, F., et al.: Keras (2015). https://keras.io
29. Wang, L., Xiong, Y., Wang, Z., Qiao, Y.: Towards good practices for very deep two-stream convnets. arXiv preprint arXiv:1507.02159 (2015)
30. Kay, W., Carreira, J., Simonyan, K., Zhang, B., Hillier, C., Vijayanarasimhan, S., Viola, F., Green, T., Back, T., Natsev, R., Suleyman, M., Zisserman, A.: The kinetics human action video dataset. arXiv preprint arXiv:1705.06950 (2017)
31. Peng, X., Wang, L., Wang, X., Qiao, Y.: Bag of visual words and fusion methods for action recognition: comprehensive study and good practice. Comput. Vis. Image Underst. **150**, 109–125 (2016)
32. Wang, H., Yang, Y., Yang, E., Deng, C.: Exploring hybrid spatio-temporal convolutional networks for human action recognition. Multimedia Tools Appl. **76**(13), 15065–15081 (2017)
33. Wang, L., Qiao, Y., Tang, X.: Action recognition with trajectory-pooled deep-convolutional descriptors. In: IEEE Conference on Computer Vision and Pattern Recognition, pp. 4305–4314 (2015)
34. Varol, G., Laptev, I., Schmid, C.: Long-term temporal convolutions for action recognition. arXiv preprint arXiv:1604.04494 (2016)
35. Wang, Y., Long, M., Wang, J., Yu, P.S.: Spatiotemporal pyramid network for video action recognition. In: IEEE Conference on Computer Vision and Pattern Recognition, pp. 2097–2106. IEEE (2017)
36. Sun, L., Jia, K., Chen, K., Yeung, D.Y., Shi, B.E., Savarese, S.: Lattice long short-term memory for human action recognition. arXiv preprint arXiv:1708.03958 (2017)

Simple and Fast $O_{exp}(N)$ Algorithm for Finding an Exact Maximum Distance in E^2 Instead of $O(N^2)$ or $O(N \lg N)$

Vaclav Skala and Michal Smolik[✉]

Faculty of Applied Sciences,
University of West Bohemia, Univerzitni 8, CZ 30614 Plzen, Czech Republic
skala@kiv.zcu.cz
http://www.VaclavSkala.eu

Abstract. Finding a maximum distance of points in E^2 or in E^3 is one of those. It is a frequent task required in many applications. In spite of the fact that it is an extremely simple task, the known "Brute force" algorithm is of $O(N^2)$ complexity. Due to this complexity the run-time is very long and unacceptable especially if medium or larger data sets are to be processed. An alternative approach is convex hull computation with complexity higher than $O(N)$ followed by diameter computation with $O(M^2)$ complexity. The situation is similar to sorting, where the bubble sort algorithm has $O(N^2)$ complexity that cannot be used in practice even for medium data sets.

This paper describes a novel and fast, simple and robust algorithm with $O(N)$ expected complexity which enables to decrease run-time needed to find the maximum distance of two points in E^2. It can be easily modified for the E^k case in general. The proposed algorithm has been evaluated experimentally on larger different datasets in order to verify it and prove expected properties of it.

Experiments proved the advantages of the proposed algorithm over the standard algorithms based on the "Brute force", convex hull or convex hull diameters approaches. The proposed algorithm gives a significant speed-up to applications, when medium and large data sets are processed. It is over 10 000 times faster than the standard "Brute force" algorithm for 10^6 points randomly distributed points in E^2 and over 4 times faster than convex hull diameter computation. The speed-up of the proposed algorithm grows with the number of points processed.

Keywords: Maximum distance · Algorithm complexity

1 Introduction

A maximum distance of two points in the given data set is needed in many applications. A standard "Brute Force" algorithm with $O(N^2)$ complexity is usually used, where N is a number of points in the given data set. Such algorithm leads to very high run-time if larger data sets are to be processed. As the computer memory capacity increases, larger data sets are to be processed. Typical data sets in computer graphics contain usually 10^5–10^7 and even more of points. In spite of the CPU speed increases, the run-time even for such a simple task leads to unacceptable processing time for today's applications.

© Springer Nature Switzerland AG 2019
S. Misra et al. (Eds.): ICCSA 2019, LNCS 11619, pp. 367–380, 2019.
https://doi.org/10.1007/978-3-030-24289-3_27

Of course, there is a very special case when points are distributed on a circle only. This requires the $O(N^2)$ algorithm if we want to find **all the couples** of points as there is $N(N - 1)/2$ couples. In all other cases "output sensitive" algorithms should be faster.

However, our task is just to find the maximum distance, not all the pairs having a maximum distance. So the complexity of this algorithm should be lower. Also due to the numerical precision points do not lie exactly on a circle if data have this very specific property.

The new proposed algorithm with $O(N)$ expected complexity is based on the following assumptions:

- Any pre-processing with a lower complexity than the optimal run-time one should speed-up processing of the given data set. In our case the optimal algorithm covering all the special cases is of $O(N^2)$ complexity and therefore preprocessing with complexities $O(lgN), O(N), O(N lgN)$ etc. should speed up the run-time.
- General properties, including geometrical ones, of input data should be carefully analyzed in order to find all useful information that can lead to faster pre-processing and the final run-time.
- If data are not organized in a very special way, e.g. points are on the Axis Aligned Bounding Box (AABB) boundary only or points are on a circle etc., we can use an algorithm with "output sensitive" complexity and we should get additional speed-up.

In general, algorithms should not depend on very specific presumptions or technological issues unless the algorithm is targeted to very specific technological platform or applications. Any algorithm must be stable and robust to input data properties, in general.

2   Brute Force Algorithm

The standard "Brute Force" algorithm uses two nested loops in order to find a maximum distance. Algorithms with such approach can be found in many text-books dealing with fundamental algorithms and data structures, e.g. Hilyard and Theilet (2007), Mehta and Sahni (2005), Sahni (1998), Sedgwick (2002), Wirth (1976). Such algorithms can be represented by Algorithm 1 in general as:

```
function distance_2 (A , B: point);
{   distance_2:=(A.x-B.x)*(A.x-B.x) + (A.y-B.y)*(A.y-B.y)};
# Square of the distance ‖ A - B ‖ is actually computed #

d := 0;
for i := 1 to N-1 do
 for j := i+1 to N do
  {
    d0 := distance_2(Xᵢ , Xⱼ);
    if d < d0 then d := d0
  };
d := SQRT (d) # if needed #
```

Standard "Brute Force" algorithm
Algorithm 1

The Algorithm 1 is clearly of $O(N^2)$ complexity and processing time increases significantly with number of points processed, see Table 2.

In practice, it can be expected that points are not organized in a very specific manner, e.g. points on a circle etc., and points are uniformly distributed more or less. In this case "output sensitive" algorithms usually lead to efficient solutions.

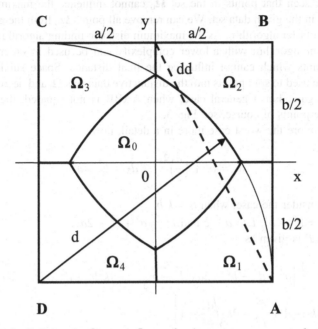

Fig. 1. Splitting the Ω_0 set to Ω_i sets for the worst case – squared area

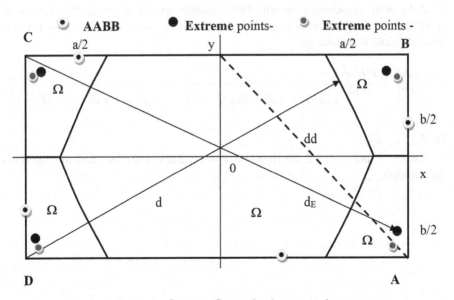

Fig. 2. Splitting the Ω_0 set to Ω_i sets for the rectangular area case

Let points are inside of an Axis Aligned Bounding Box (AABB) defined as $<-a/2, a/2> \times <-b/2, b/2>$. Then Fig. 1 presents a typical situation for the worst case when AABB is a square ($a = b$), while the Fig. 2 presents general AABB situation for the case $a > b$. In the following we will explore the worst case, i.e. situation at the Fig. 1, and the first maximum distance estimation d is $d = a$.

It can be seen that points in the set Ω_0 cannot influence the maximum distance computation in the given data set. We can remove all points Ω_0 from the given data set Ω and obtain faster algorithm. As the maximum distance finding algorithm is of $O(N^2)$ complexity an algorithm with a lower complexity can be used in order to find and eliminate points which cannot influence the final distance. Space subdivision techniques can be used to split points into the disjunctive data sets Ω_i and decrease run-time complexity again. For a general case, when AABB is not squared, the Ω_0 set will contain more points of course, see Fig. 3.

Let us explore the worst case more in a detail, now.

$$d_1 = b^2 + \left(\frac{a}{2}\right)^2 \qquad d_2 = b^2 + a^2$$

Let us consider the case, when $a = k\,b$.

Then $\xi^2 = d^2 - b^2$, $L = a - \xi$ and $L^2 = a^2 + \xi^2 - 2a\xi$.

The area P is given as

$$P = \frac{1}{2}L^2 = \frac{1}{2}\left[a^2 + d^2 - b^2 - 2a\sqrt{d^2 - b^2}\right] = \frac{1}{2}\left[k^2b^2 + d^2 - b^2 - 2kb\sqrt{d^2 - b}\right]$$

$$= \frac{1}{2}b^2\left[k^2 - 1 + \frac{d^2}{b^2} - 2k\sqrt{\frac{d^2}{b^2} - 1}\right]$$

If the most consuming parts with $O(N^2)$ complexity is considered, then the speed-up of the proposed algorithm over the "Brute Force" algorithm for uniformly distributed points is defined as:

$$v = \left[\frac{ab}{4P}\right]^2 = \frac{k^2b^2b^2}{b^2b^2}\frac{k^2}{4\left[k^2 - 1 + d^2 - 2k\sqrt{d^2 - 1}\right]^2} = \frac{k^2}{4\left[k^2 - 1 + d^2 - 2k\sqrt{d^2 - 1}\right]^2}$$

for $d_1 \leq d \leq d_2$.

For $k = 1$ and $d \to \sqrt{2}$ the speed-up $v \to \infty$ that is expected from the algorithm specification.

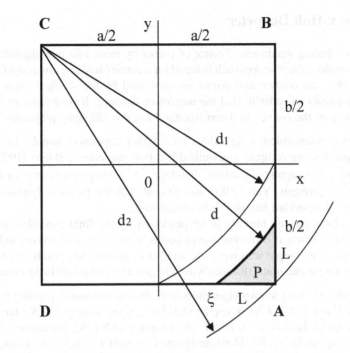

Fig. 3. Distances definitions for a general AABB

It can be seen that for a non-squared AABB distances are defined as

Table 1. Distances determination

E^2	$d_1^2 = [\max\{a, b\}]^2 + \frac{1}{2}[\min\{a, b\}]^2$	$d_2 = a^2 + b^2$
E^3	$d_1^2 = [\max\{a, b, c\}]^2 + \frac{1}{2}[\min\{a, b, c\}]^2$	$d_2 = a^2 + b^2 + c^2$

a, b are sizes of the AABB in E^2, resp. a, b, c are sizes of the AABB in E^3

For the E^3 case, some minor changes have to be made as we have 6 points defining the AABB and $6 + 6$ extreme points in the AABB, i.e. points having the longest distance and the shortest distance from the relevant AABB corner and the Ω_0 set is to be split to sets $\Omega_0, ..., \Omega_6$. However, the computational time is more or less the same as the same number of points is processed and the preprocessing is of $O(N)$ complexity. It can be seen that the extension to E^k is straightforward and simple to implement.

3   Convex Hull Diameter

The idea of finding maximum distance of points by more effective algorithms is not new. Reasonably effective approach is based on a convex hull construction of the given data set. Then the convex hull points are processed by the standard algorithm with $O(N^2)$ complexity in order to find the maximum distance. It is obvious that all techniques based on the convex hull construction have the following properties:

- Convex hull construction algorithms for a higher dimension than E^2, i.e. for E^3 or E^k in general, are complex and quite difficult to implement. Skiena (1997) proved that the "gift wrapping algorithm" has $O\left(n^{k/2+1}\right)$ complexity in the case of k dimensional problem. Yao (1981) has proved that for the two dimensional case specialized algorithm has $O(N \, lgN)$ complexity.
- Points of the convex hull are to be processed by the **final** algorithm with $O(h^2)$ complexity, where h is the number of points of the computed convex hull, i.e. the technique is an output sensitive. The number of convex hull points might be quite high, while the maximum distance is usually given by two points in the given data set.

Generally, the well known algorithms have the computational complexities as follow: Brute Force $O(N^4)$, Gift Wrapping $O(N \, h)$, Graham Scan $O(N \, lgN)$, Jarvis March $O(N \, lgN)$, Quick Hull $O(h \, N)$, Divide-and-Conquer $O(N \, lgN)$, Monotone Chain $O(N \, lgN)$, Incremental $O(N \, lgN)$, Marriage-before-Conquest $O(n \, lgh)$, see Barber (1996), O'Rourke (1998), Yao (1981), Kirkpatrik (1986), Chan (1996), Avis (1997), WEB[1].

Some algorithms directed to the diameter of a convex hull computation can be found in Snyder (1980), Dobkin (1979), Shamos (1978), other convection algorithm can be found in Skala (2016a, b). It should be noted that if the number h of the resulted convex hull is close to N, than algorithms with the complexity $O(h \, N)$ are becoming algorithms with $O(N^2)$ complexity etc.

The extension to a higher dimension is not easy and some algorithms cannot be extended even for E^3, e.g. Graham Scan etc. or the complexity of the actual implementation is prohibitive for practical use.

4   Proposed Algorithm

The new proposed algorithm was developed for larger data sets and it is based on "in-core" technique, i.e. all data are stored in a computer memory. The fundamental requirements for the algorithm development were: simplicity, robustness and simple extensibility to E^3. The proposed algorithm is based on two main principles:

---

[1] WEB   ref's   http://softsurfer.com/Archive/algorithm_0109/algorithm_0109.htm#Convex_Hull_ Algorithms (retrieved 2012-08-21).

- Remove as many non-relevant points as possible
- Divide and conqueror technique in order to decrease algorithm complexity

The Fig. 1 shows five regions Ω_i, where the given points are located. The algorithm is described for the E^2 case and its extension to E^3 is straightforward. It should be noted that the worst case is presented, i.e. when AABB is a square. Let us assume that the points that cannot contribute to the final maximum distance are located in the region Ω_0, which contains points closer to all corners of the AABB than the *minimal* edge length of the AABB or known distance estimation. Then the given data set Ω can be reduced to $\Omega = \Omega - \Omega_0$. In order to decrease expected number of points to be processed, we need to process this data set Ω to get more information on those points. As the standard algorithm for maximum distance is of $O(N^2)$ complexity, we can use any pre-processing of $O(N)$ or $O(N \lg N)$ complexity to decrease number of points to be left for the final processing with the algorithm of $O(N^2)$ complexity.

It can be seen that the following principal steps have to be made:

1. Pre-processing: can be performed with $O(N)$ complexity:
   a. Find the bounding AABB and extreme points, i.e. two extreme points for each axis (max. 4 points).
   b. Find the most distant "extreme" points [max] for each corner of the AABB (max. 4 points).
   c. Find the minimum distant "extreme" points [min] for each corner of the AABB (max. 4 points).
   d. Determine the longest mutual distance d between those found points (max.12 points).
      It should be noted that the worst case is a squared AABB and found distance $d \geq a$.
      For a rectangular window found distance $d \geq max\{a, b\}$.
   e. Determine points of Ω_0 that cannot contribute to the maximum distance, i.e. points having a smaller distance than the found distance d from all corners of the AABB and extreme points. Remove the Ω_0 points from the original data set Ω.
   f. Split remaining points to new sets Ω_i, $i = 1,..,4$, see the Fig. 1.

The number $S_{\Omega 0}$ of points in the Ω_0 set can be estimated as:

$$S_{\Omega 0} = \int_{a/2}^{a\sqrt{3}/2} \sqrt{a^2 - x^2}\,dx = a^2(\frac{\pi}{3} - \sqrt{3} + 1)$$

For the uniform distribution of points the Ω set, the number of points to be processed, i.e. number of points outside of the Ω_0 set, is $qN = 0{,}684\ N$, where:

$$q = \frac{S_\Omega - S_{\Omega 0}}{S_\Omega} = \frac{a^2 - a^2(\frac{\pi}{3} - \sqrt{3} + 1)}{a^2} = \frac{\pi}{3} - \sqrt{3} \cong 0.684$$

As the "Brute Force" algorithm is of the $O(N^2)$, the speed up expected is approx.:

$$v = 1/(0.684)^2 = 2.13$$

It should be noted that the distance $d \gg a$ in practical data sets and the Ω_0 set contains much more points which can be removed from the final processing, see Table 1 actually compared points, i.e. last column.

It can be seen that if found distance $d \geq dd$, see Fig. 1, then the comparison of points from the neighbor data sets is not needed, where:

$$dd = \sqrt{\left(a^2 + (b/2)^2\right)} \leq \sqrt{a^2 + a^2/4} = \frac{\sqrt{5}}{2}\,a \quad \text{for} \quad a \leq b$$

2. Run-time steps of the proposed algorithm:
   a. Taking an advantage of space subdivision, find the maximum distance d between points of $[\Omega_1, \Omega_3]$, i.e. one point from Ω_1 and the second point is from Ω_3 as there can be expected the longest distance between the given points - this step is $O(N^2)$ complexity.
   b. Remove points from the Ω_2 and Ω_4 datasets closer to the related corner of the AABB than already found distance d - this step is $O(N)$ complexity.
   c. Find a new maximum distance d between points of $[\Omega_2, \Omega_4]$ - this step is $O(N^2)$ complexity.
   d. If already found distance $d \leq dd$ then
      i. Reduce $\Omega_1, \Omega_2, \Omega_3, \Omega_4$ - steps are $O(N^2)$ complexity
      ii. find a new maximum distance d between points of $[\Omega_1, \Omega_2]$, $[\Omega_2, \Omega_3]$, $[\Omega_3, \Omega_4]$ and $[\Omega_4, \Omega_1]$. It is necessary to note that if $d > dd$, then the Ω_0 boundary crosses the AABB and points in the neighbors regions cannot contribute to the maximum distance.

As can be seen the algorithm is very simple and easy to implement.

function distance_2 (**A** , **B**: point);
{ distance_2:=(A.x-B.x)*(A.x-B.x) + (A.y-B.y)*(A.y-B.y)};
Square of the distance $\|\mathbf{A} - \mathbf{B}\|$ is actually computed

function S_Dist (Ω_A , Ω_B : set)
{ d := 0; d0 := 0;
   for each point **X** from Ω_A **do**
      for each point **Y** from Ω_B **do**
      { d0 := distance_2 (**X** , **Y**); **if** d0 > d **then** d := d0
      };
      S_Dist := d
}

1. **Q** := points forming the AABB for the given set Ω and extreme points [max and min] **XX** for each corner of the AABB.
   # 8 points found at maximum, complexity $O(N)$ #
2. d_M=max { $\mathbf{Q}_i$, $\mathbf{Q}_j$ }
   # Determine the maximum distance d_M of the points in **Q** #
   # by the "Brute Force" algorithm with $O(M^2)$ complexity#
   # only max. 8 points are to be processed #
3. # the set Ω is to be split into Ω_i sets#
   for all points **X** from the set Ω
   { i := index of the region Ω_i for the point **X**
      d = distance of the point **X** and of the opposite AABB corner for the set Ω_i.
      # do not store points having higher distance from a AABB corner than d_M #
      if $d \geq d_M$ **then**
      { STORE (**X** , Ω_i); # store a point **X** in the Ω_i set #
         d_M := d ; # update the maximum distance d_i for the region i#
         $\mathbf{XX}_i$:= **X** # update $\mathbf{XX}_i$ – one extreme point for each region Ω_i #
      }
   }
4. # new maximum distance estimation based on extreme points of sets Ω_i found in step 3#
   d_q = max { $\mathbf{XX}_i$, $\mathbf{XX}_j$ },   i, j =1,…,4
   d_M = max { d_M , d_q }
5. # The "diagonal" regions are to be tested with $O(N^2)$ algorithm #
   # REDUCE (Ω_i , d_M) remove points from the Ω_i set with smaller distance from the opposite AABB corner #
   REDUCE (Ω_1 , d_M);   REDUCE (Ω_3 , d_M);
   d_M := max { d_M , S_Dist(Ω_1 , Ω_3) };
   REDUCE (Ω_2 , d_M);   REDUCE (Ω_4 , d_M);
   d_M := max { d_M , S_Dist(Ω_2 , Ω_4) }
6. # neighbor regions should be tested if necessary #
   if $d_M \leq dd$ **then**
   { REDUCE (Ω_1 , d_M); REDUCE (Ω_2 , d_M);
      REDUCE (Ω_3 , d_M); REDUCE (Ω_4 , d_M);
      d_M := max { d_M , S_Dist(Ω_1 , Ω_2) }; d_M := max { d_M , S_Dist(Ω_2 , Ω_3)
   };
      d_M := max { d_M , S_Dist(Ω_3 , Ω_4) }; d_M := max { d_M , S_Dist(Ω_4 , Ω_1) }
   }
7. d := SQRT (d_M)   # compute the final distance as a square root of d #

Fast maximum distance algorithm
Algorithm 2

Implementation Notes
There are several possibilities how to further improve the proposed algorithm especially in the context of the specific programming language and data structures used. Nevertheless, the influence of this is small as experiments proved and for the expected data sizes do not have any significant influence.

Generally, it is recommended:

- The "array list" construction should be used for storing Ω_i sets; this construction enables to increase an array size without reallocation and data copying,
- Two or higher dimensional arrays for storing x, y values should not be used, as for each array element one addition and one multiplication operations are needed (computational cost is hidden in the index evaluation). Data should be stored in two arrays **X** and **Y**, or as pairs (x, y) in one-dimensional structure array **XY** etc.
- Square of a distance should be used in order to save multiple square root evaluations. It is possible as the square function is monotonically growing and can be used for comparison operations.
- Store data in a linked list as only a sequential pass is required and remove, resp. insert operation is simple and no data overwriting is required.

It should be noted that the Ω_i sets are determined by an arc of a circle, i.e. the separation function is quadratic. Experiments proved that if a half-space separation function is used, the proposed algorithm is faster as only a linear function is evaluated.

5   Experimental Results

The standard "Brute Force", convex hull (Quick Hull) and proposed algorithms were implemented in C# and Pascal/Delphi, verified and extensively tested for different sizes of the given data sets and different data set types (random, uniform, clustered etc.) as well. Standard PC with 2,8 GHz Intel Pentium 4, 1 GB RAM with MS Windows XP was used.

Cumulative results obtained during experiments are presented in Table 2. Experiments made proved that a significant speed-up has been reached. It is necessary to note that the speed-up 100 means that the computation is *100 times faster*. It can be seen that for 10^6 points the speed-up is 10 000, i.e. computation is 10^4 **times faster** and grows with the number of points nearly exponentially, see Fig. 5 - note that axes scale is logarithmic.

Table 2. Experimental results for uniformly distributed points [* values obtained by extrapolation]

| Points $10^3 *$ N | Computational time [ms] | | | Speed-up | | | Compared | |
	Brute Force (BF)	Quick Hull (QH)	New	BF/QH	BF/New	QH/New	QH	New
100	137 760	108	15	1 281	9 462	7,38	405,1	16,1
160	353 920	178	25	1 987	14 364	7,23	454,0	23,7
250	865 760	260	56	3 332	15 460	4,64	486,0	26,9
400	2 216 480	451	84	4 911	26 387	5,37	583,1	26,1
630	5 498 080	720	167	7 635	32 946	4,32	661,2	32,7
1 000	13 783 840	1 130	259	12 197	53 277	4,37	707,1	25,3

(continued)

Table 2. (*continued*)

Points 10^{3*} N	Computational time [ms]			Speed-up			Compared	
	Brute Force (BF)	Quick Hull (QH)	New	BF/QH	BF/New	QH/New	QH	New
1 600	35 467 040	1 721	364	20 603	97 437	4,73	735,9	30,8
2 500	86 591 680	3 069	664	28 217	130 378	4,62	761,9	22,3
4 000	221 673 760*	5 523	1 231	40 139	180 094	4,49	751,2	23,1
6 300	507 556 000*	9 544	1 708	53 183	297 164	5,59	750,0	23,5
10 000	1 106 173 600*	15 064	2 470	73 432	447 916	6,10	750,0	23,2

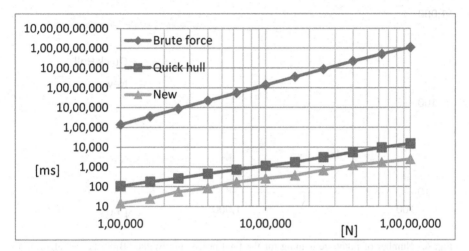

Fig. 4. Computational time of the "Brute force", Quick hull and the proposed algorithm

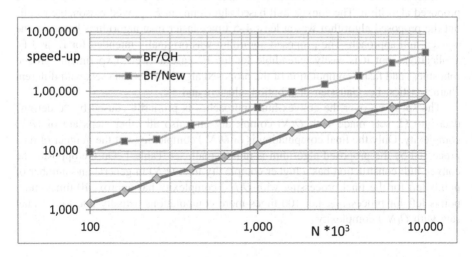

Fig. 5. Speed up of the Quick hull and the proposed algorithm over the Brute force algorithm.

The experiments proved that the speed-up grows significantly with the number of points processed, see Figs. 4 and 5. The final step of the proposed algorithm of $O(N^2)$ complexity has a low influence and that the preprocessing steps significantly decrease number of points processed in the final step. This is due to the very low number of points remaining for the final evaluation for maximum distance, see Table 2, where "QH" presents number of points finally processed after construction by the Quick Hull method, while "New" presents number of points finally processed by the proposed algorithm (Fig. 6).

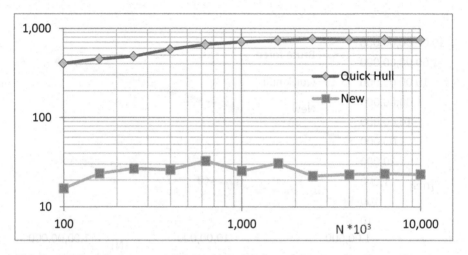

Fig. 6. Number of points remaining for the final processing by the "Brute Force" algorithm

Several convex hulls algorithms were used in order to compare efficiency of the proposed algorithm. The convex hull based algorithms in E^2 proved reasonable results but the proposed algorithm was at least 4–5 times faster than algorithms based on the convex hull approach. The proposed algorithm was originally intended for E^2 and E^3 applications, but it is easily extendible for the E^k case as well. Experiments proved robustness and faster computation of the proposed algorithm for data sets with different characteristics, i.e. Gaussian distribution, clusters and etc.

The speed-up over the convex-hull approaches is primarily caused by "ordering" data into Ω_i sets made with $O(N)$ complexity and also all other steps are of $O(N)$ complexity. Only the final computation is of $O(N^2)$ complexity, but the number of data processed by the proposed algorithm is rather small, see Table 1. On the opposite the convex hull construction has a higher complexity than $O(N)$ in general and number of points left for the final processing with $O(N^2)$ complexity has approx. 10 times more points left for processing, i.e. 100 times more computations actually due to the final step with $O(N^2)$ complexity.

6 Conclusion

A new simple, easy to implement, robust and effective algorithm for finding a maximum distance of points in E^2 was developed. The experimental results clearly proved that the proposed algorithm is convenient for medium and large data sets. Algorithm speed-up grows significantly with the number of points processed. The proposed algorithm can be easily extended to E^3 by a simple modification. In the E^3 case, we have to process $\Omega_1, ..., \Omega_8$ data subsets. For the E^k case the original data must be split to data sets Ω_i, where $i = 1,...,2^k$. Nevertheless the memory requirements and preprocessing time remain the same as we have to only split data from the Ω set to the to Ω_i datasets which are smaller.

The experiments also proved that the algorithm offers higher speed-up than algorithms based on convex-hull in E^2 and it is easy to implement it as well. The experimental tests were made on a squared interval that is considered to be the worst case for testing of algorithm properties as far as the computational time is concerned. For oblong intervals, the proposed algorithm runs even faster. Another nice property is its extensibility to the E^k case on the contrary to algorithms based on convex hull.

It is necessary to note that the presented algorithm is "output sensitive" type, so it is not convenient for an extremely special cases, when all points are points of a circle as $N (N - 1)/2$ points have the same distance etc. However, even in this case the algorithm is faster than the "Brute Force" and algorithms based on a convex hull construction. It can be seen that the presented algorithm can be extended for the E^3 data sets as well.

Acknowledgments. The authors would like to thank their colleagues at the University of West Bohemia, Plzen, for their discussions and suggestions, and anonymous reviewers for their valuable comments and hints provided. The research was supported by projects Czech Science Foundation (GACR) No. GA17-05534S and partially by SGS 2019-016.

References

Barber, C.B., Dobkin, D.P., Huhdanpaa, H.: The quickhull algorithm for covex hulls. ACM Trans. Math. Softw. **22**(4), 469–483 (1996)

Dobkin, D.P., Snyder, L.: On a general method of maximizing and minimizing among certain geometric problems. In: Proceedings of the 20th Annual Symposium on the Foundations of Computer Science, pp. 9–17 (1979)

Hilyard, J., Teilhet, S.: C# Coockbook. OReilly, Newton (2007)

Mehta, D.P., Sahni, S.: Handbook of Data Structures and Applications. CRC Press, Boca Raton (2005)

O'Rourke, J.: Computational Geometry in C. Cambridge University Press, Cambridge (1998)

Sahni, S.: Data Structures and Applications in C++. McGraw-Hill, New York (1998)

Sedgwick, R.: Algorithms in Java. Addison Wesley Professional, Boston (2002)

Shamos, M.I.: Computational geometry. Ph.D. thesis, Yale University (1978)

Skala,V., Majdisova, Z., Smolik, M.: Space subdivision to speed-up convex hull construction in E3. Adv, Softw. Eng. **91**, 12–22 (2016a). ISSN 0965-9978

Skala, V., Smolik, M., Majdisova, Z.: Reducing the number of points on the convex hull calculation using the polar space subdivision in E2. In: SIBGRAPI 2016, pp. 40–47. IEEE (2016b). ISBN 978-1-5090-3568-7, ISSN 2377-5416

Skiena, S.S.: "Convex Hull." §8.6.2 in The Algorithm Design Manual, pp. 351–354. Springer, New York (1997)

Snyder, W.E., Tang, D.A.: Finding the extrema of a region. IEEE Trans. Pattern Anal. Mach. Intell. **PAMI-2**, 266–269 (1980)

Wirth, N.: Algorithms + Data Structures = Program. Prentice Hall, Upper Saddle River (1976)

Yao, A.C.-C.: A lower bound to finding convex hulls. J. ACM **28**, 780–787 (1981)

Kirkpatrick, D.K., Seidel, R.: Ultimate planar convex hull algorithm? SIAM J. Comput. **15**, 287–299 (1986)

Chan, T.: Optimal output-sensitive convex hull algorithms in two and three dimensions. Discrete Comput. Geom. **16**(3), 361–368 (1996)

Avis, D., Bremner, D., Seidel, R.: How good are convex hull algorithms? Comput. Geom.: Theory Appl. **7**(5-6), 265–301 (1997)

Advanced and Emerging Applications

A Machine Learning Approach to the Early Diagnosis of Alzheimer's Disease Based on an Ensemble of Classifiers

Sonia Valladares-Rodríguez[1], Luis Anido-Rifón[1]([✉]),
Manuel J. Fernández-Iglesias[1], and David Facal-Mayo[2]

[1] Department of Telematics Engineering, University of Vigo, Vigo, Spain
lanido@gist.uvigo.es
[2] Unit of Psychogerontology, University of Santiago de Compostela,
Santiago de Compostela, Spain

Abstract. The present article discusses the ability of an ensemble of machine learning models to implement classification strategies to discriminate among mild cognitive impairment (MCI), Alzheimer's disease (AD) and Cognitive Unimpaired (CU). For this, a battery of games that assesses the most relevant markers for the early diagnosis of cognitive impairment (i.e., memory, executive functions, attention and gnosias) was implemented, and a pilot study was carried out with 64 individuals (28 CU, 16 MCI and 20 AD). Participants were administered a collection of classical pen-and-paper tests, and then interacted with all games in the battery. A set of four ensembles of classifiers were applied and relevant metrics were computed to assess the classification power of this approach. According to the classification metrics computed, best classification results are obtained using the Random Forest Classifier algorithm, with average F1 score = 0.99, accuracy = 1.00, and Cohen's kappa = 0.98. The experiments performed indicate that artificial intelligence techniques and serious games can be used to automate some aspects of the clinical diagnosis of individuals with cognitive impairment. However, more research is needed to obtain the required normative data for clinical validity.

Keywords: Machine learning · Ensemble methods · Alzheimer's disease · Early detection · Cognitive impairment · Serious games

1 Introduction

There were an estimated 46.8 million people worldwide living with dementia in 2015, and this number was close to 50 million in 2017. This figure will almost double every 20 years, reaching 75 million in 2030 and 131.5 million in 2050 [1]. Particularly, Alzheimer's disease is the most common cause of dementia, as it accounts for 60% to 80% of all cases. It is considered a slowly progressive brain disease that begins well before clinical symptoms emerge. Alzheimer (AD) is one of the most prevalent diseases and one of the most relevant health threats worldwide [2].

Diagnosing AD requires a careful and comprehensive medical evaluation, including an examination of the person's physical and mental status. Focusing in cognitive

© Springer Nature Switzerland AG 2019
S. Misra et al. (Eds.): ICCSA 2019, LNCS 11619, pp. 383–396, 2019.
https://doi.org/10.1007/978-3-030-24289-3_28

markers, state-of-the-art diagnostic procedures for AD are based on neuropsychological paper-and-pencil tests [3, 4]. These tests have some relevant limitations, as they are perceived as intrusive [5] and influenced by the white-coat effect (WCE) [6]; they provide a late diagnosis [7]; they lack ecological validity [8]; and they are strongly dependent on confounding factors (e.g., age, educational level [9], practice effect [3]), and prone to processing errors due to their manual processing.

Due to the need of alternative mechanisms supporting an early diagnosis, we can find in the scientific literature several proposals such as the digitalization of classical tests, the introduction of game-inspired elements (e.g., rewards, challenges, simulated environments) and the implementation of technology-based solutions such as immersive 3D environments or online interactive software applications, among others.

The proposal discussed in this paper relies on the use of gamification techniques and machine learning, and the introduction of digital touch devices. More specifically, this paper discusses the ability of a digital battery composed of 7 games to assess the cognitive status in a non-intrusive and ecological way [10–12]. Cognitive areas tackled are episodic memory, executive functions, attention, semantic memory, working memory, procedural memory and gnosias. These cognitive areas, and specially the three first ones, are early markers of cognitive alterations with a relevant diagnostic value for mild cognitive impairment (MCI) and AD [13, 14].

To support the diagnosis of cognitive impairment, traditional analysis procedures rely on survival analysis [15], polynomial regression analysis [16], multinomial logistic regression analysis [17] and Markov models [13]. These techniques' performance could be improved thorough machine learning (ML), a scientific discipline that focuses on how computers learn from data [18] to build classifiers by automatically learning the inherent structure of a data set. In this study, we focused on supervised learning ML, whose initial goal is the prediction of a known output or target. This innovative technique has a great potential for supporting diagnosis prediction, risk estimation, response prediction and classification learning for diagnosis [19–22]. These techniques, and more specifically ensemble methods such as Random Forest (RF), Extra Trees classifier (ET) or boosting classifiers, are used for the automated classification of medical datasets (e.g., MRI scans, PET images, biomarkers, etc.) as either Alzheimer's disease or healthy controls [23]. Such techniques do not rely on a single cognitive area of interest, which may result in low specificity and sensitivity due to higher inter-subject variability of the aforementioned disease. On the contrary, these techniques analyse different biomarkers or cognitive constructs, resulting in higher discriminative power. They are discussed in this paper as a means to automate some aspects of the clinical diagnosis of individuals with cognitive impairment.

Section 2 introduces the dataset used and the experiment performed, while Sect. 3 presents the results obtained and Sect. 4 discusses these results and their impact in the early diagnosis of MCI and AD. Finally, the conclusions of this research work and possible future directions are proposed.

2 Materials and Methods

2.1 Data and Instruments

Participants

This study was carried out from a cross-sectional sample of 64 senior adults over 55 years old (range = 57–95; average = 77.03; SD = 7.23, cf. Table 1). All participants were recruited in the Pontevedra province of Galicia, Spain, with the support of the associations of relatives of Alzheimer's patients in the area. The basic inclusion criterion was being 55+ years old, and exclusion criteria included an advanced cognitive impairment, severe motor, hearing or visual disability, and technophobia. Participants should attend a socio-cognitive workshop in any of the collaborating associations, and no previous educational level or technological skills were required. Among the 64 participants, 20 subjects were previously diagnosed with AD, 16 participants had MCI, and 28 non-cognitively-impaired subjects served as controls. This latter group is referred as the CU group in the rest of this paper.

Table 1. Participants' characteristics and their distribution according to the Galician population

Variable		Sample n (%)	Galician population[a] n (%)
Gender	Female	42 (65.63)	571277 (55.4)
	Male	22 (34.38)	459914 (44.6)
		Mean (SD)	
Age (55 + years)	n = 64	77.01 (7.23)	n > 62, confidence level = 95%, error = 7.5% according Galician population[a] and stratified proportional sampling [24]
Educational level		1.84 (1.2)	–
Exercise level		3.64 (0.99)	–
Socialize level		3.28 (1.05)	–
Chronic treatment		0.84 (0.36)	–

Note: Sociodemographic characteristics: gender, age, educational level (i.e., 0 = illiterate; 1 = ability to read and write; 2 = primary school; 3 = secondary school; 4 = high school; 5: vocational training; 6 = university), exercise level and socialization level, all of them based on a 5-point Likert scale: 1(never) to 5 (always); and finally, chronic treatment (i.e., 0 = no; 1 = yes).
[a]Galician population of people aged 55 years and over, according to a study by the Galician Institute of Statistics (2017).

The study design was approved by the Galician institutional ethics committee (registration code 2016/477)) and was conducted in accordance with the provisions of the Declaration of Helsinki, as revised in Seoul 2008. Before their involvement in the pilot project, all subjects read and understood patient information sheets and gave their written informed consent to use the anonymized data gathered.

Neuropsychological Assessment

Participants underwent a demographic and health interview to gain some insight on their quality of life and cognition levels [25] prior to the experiment. They also completed an extensive neuropsychological and cognitive assessment, including the MMSE – Mini-metal Examination State test [26], the Spanish version of CVLT - California Verbal Learning Test [27], AD8 - Adapted Dementia Screening Interview, ADL - Barthel scale of activities of daily living, and a questionnaire about memory complaints. Data gathered using these tests were used as golden standard data and also to initially discriminate subjects suffering MCI from healthy controls. According to standard diagnostic criteria, MCI would likely be present in participants that would present normal cognitive functions and their capabilities to carry out everyday activities were not compromised, they would refer memory complaints, they would obtain a low score in the Spanish version of CVLT according to subject's age and educational, and a level equal or greater than 2 in the AD8 test. Participants who suffered AD—facilitated by participating organizations with a prior medical diagnosis—were not asked to take the Spanish version of CVLT to avoid frustration.

Game Assessment

Data acquisition in order to detect MCI or AD was carried out through specifically designed digital games running in touch devices. All games are based on the gamification of existing neurophysiological tests [28–30], and were designed according to a methodology based on participatory design focused on the end user. In other words, the vision of senior adults captured in participatory design workshops and focus groups [31, 32] drove the design process from a technical and aesthetical perspective. Besides, experts in neurology, neuropsychology and geriatrics, and participating patients' associations provided the expertise required to ensure the validity of the new tool for cognitive assessment. The collaboration with health professionals [33] from an early design stage was deemed necessary to guarantee both content and clinical validity.

The battery of games, named Panoramix [10–12], is composed of seven serious games targeting seven different cognitive areas: (1) Episodix is based on the gamification of the California Verbal Test (CLVT), which is widely used to assess episodic memory; (2) Attentix evaluates attention capabilities of player; (3) Executix addresses executive functions and it is based on the gamification of the Tower of Hanoi (TOT) game [34]; (4) Workix, which is based on the Corsi Cubes Test [30], evaluates working memory; (5) Semantix is based on the gamification of the Pyramids and Palm-trees test [35] to evaluate semantic memory; (6) Prospectix addresses prospective memory through the Pursuit Rotor Task test [36]; and finally (7) Gnosix focuses on visual gnosias, that is, the ability to visually recognize different elements and assigning meaning to them (Fig. 1).

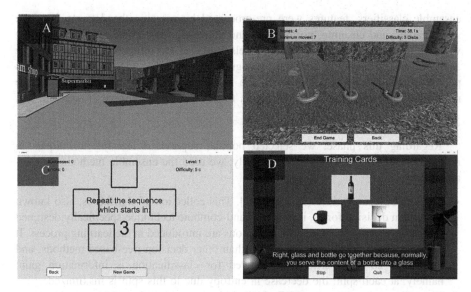

Fig. 1. Some captures of Panoramix: A: Episodix; B: Executix; C: Attentix and D: Semantix

2.2 Organisation of the Experiment

The proposed approach consisted of three phases, namely data collection, pre-processing, and classification.

1. Data Collection

The procedure to gather data from participants, based on game assessment, consisted on three consecutive stages:

1. Firstly, subjects would play the first part of Episodix, which targets immediate and short-term memory.
2. Secondly, they would play two additional games in the battery (i.e., Executix, Attentix, Procedurix, Semantix, Workix or Gnosix).
3. Finally, participants would play the second part of Episodix to assess long-term memory and their recognition capabilities.

Note that game playing for data collection [10] emulates the administration of CVLT, only that using serious games instead of pen-and-paper tests, and breaks being used to evaluate other cognitive markers. Moreover, data collection was carried out at the same time and location as the compulsory socio-cognitive workshops to guarantee the ecological validity of neuropsychological evaluation by integrating the latter in participants' daily routines. This was particularly relevant for patients with cognitive impairment due to the high prevalence of the white-coat effect [6].

2. Pre-processing

Data analytics was performance under a Python ecosystem and using the Scikit-Learn machine learning library [37]. Before training and testing data with the ML ensemble classifiers, features were pre-processed by merging the datasets from the seven games, and cleaning, normalizing and preparing the complete dataset. Missing values due to the different difficulty levels achieved by different participants were addressed by means of substitution by cognitive group (i.e., AD, MCI or HC). This popular interpolation method replaces the missing data for a given attribute by the mean of all known values of that attribute, for the different cognitive groups [38, 39].

3. Classification

Regarding this phase, we selected popular supervised learning techniques in medical research [19–21]. More specifically, we used the ensemble methods enumerated below:

- Random Forest classifier (i.e., RF) [40]. This collection of algorithms, also known as random decision forest, is a perturb-and-combine technique specifically designed for decision trees where random alterations are introduced in the learning process. It provides better prediction capabilities than other decision tree-based methods, and thee most common criterion employed for classification is information gain; namely, at each split, the decrease in entropy due to this split is maximized.
- Extra Trees classifier (i.e., ET) [41]. This ensemble of classifiers is based on unpruned top-down decision trees and also on the perturb-and-combine strategy. They are typically used to enhance precision in predictions provided by traditional decision trees. The ET algorithm builds an ensemble of unpruned decision or regression trees according to the classical top-down procedure.
- Gradient Boosting classifier (i.e., GB) [42]. A classification technique based on decision trees, which produces a prediction solution in the form of an ensemble of weak prediction models. It optimizes a cost function by iteratively choosing a function—weak hypothesis—that points towards the negative gradient direction.
- Ada Boost (i.e., AB) [43]. This machine learning meta-algorithm, is adaptive in the sense that subsequent weak learners are tweaked in favour of those instances misclassified by previous classifiers. AB maintains a set of weights over the original training set and adjusts these weights after each classifier is learned by the base learning algorithm. This algorithm is sensitive to noisy data and outliers, and also, it tends not to over-fit.

For each of the previous algorithms, metrics were computed based on the four possible results of the classification of participants according to their cognitive status, that is, True Positive (TP), True Negative (TN), False Positive (FP), and False Negative (FN). "Positive" means that the subject was classified in that cognitive category, while "Negative" means that the subject was not classified in that category. "True" means that the classification was correct, and "False" means that it was erroneous. From these results, the following values are defined:

- F1-score, which represents a weighted harmonic average of precision and recall.

$$F1(F1\ score) = 2 * \frac{P * R}{P + R}$$

- Accuracy, a combined value of precision and specificity.

$$Accuracy = \frac{TP + TN}{(TP + FP + TN + FN)}$$

- The Cohen's kappa coefficient (K) [44] was included as a robust measure of the concordance of the observed participants' classification for each algorithm along the experiments performed. In other words, it provides a measure of the validity of the classification when confronted with a random classification. K value ranges are interpreted according to an existing consensus [45]: 0-0.20 Insignificant (i.e., ML-based classification would not be distinguishable from random classification); 0.21–0.40 Median; 0.41–0.60 Moderate; 0.61–0.80 Substantial; and 0.81-1.00 Almost perfect.
- Sensitivity or true positive rate:

$$Sensitivity\ (TPR) = \frac{TP}{(TP + FN)}$$

- Specificity or true negative rate:

$$Specificity\ (TNR) = \frac{TN}{(TN + FP)}$$

For the above ML algorithms, we plotted the Receiver Operating Characteristic (ROC) curve, which represents sensitivity as a function of fall-out, and is widely used in the diagnostic field.

Finally, the normalized confusion matrix, will be also plotted, as useful graphs in diagnosis-related fields [46].

Metrics above are utilized as macro values, as they are the best metrics to show the performance of classifiers on non-uniformly distributed datasets with respect to the categories considered. Furthermore, a 10-fold cross-validation strategy [47] was adopted to train and evaluate the proposed classifiers in order to prevent overfitting due to the use of the same data for the training and testing of classifiers. Data analytics in all cases was carried out in a Jupyter Notebook/Python ecosystem under the machine learning library Scikit-Learn [37].

3 Results

All participants played all the games in the Panoramix battery twice. Obtained datasets were merged and processed with the machine learning algorithms above, that is, Random forest (RF); Extra Trees classifier (ET); Gradient Boosting classifier (GB); and Ada Boost classifier (AB). Then, with regard to predicted validity, the metrics in the previous section were computed to estimate the classification abilities by cognitive group (cf. Table 2):

Table 2. Metrics about predicted validity of Panoramix (dataset = 7-games).

Ensemble methods	Metrics		
	F1-score	Accuracy	Cohen's kappa ↓
Random Forest (RF)	0.99	1.00	0.98
Extra Tree (ET)	0.97	1.00	0.97
Gradient Boosting (GB)	0.97	1.00	0.97
Ada Boost (AB)	0.96	0.99	0.96

- F1 score: average values obtained were 0.99 for RF; 0.97 for ET; 0.97 for GB; and 0.96 for AB.
- Accuracy: the average value obtained for correctly classified subjects was the maximum value (i.e., Accuracy = 1) for RF, ET and BG; and slightly lower, 0.99 for AB.
- Cohen's kappa: the average value obtained for the concordance of the observed participants' classification for each algorithm was 0.98 for RF; 0.97 for ET and GB; and finally, 0.96 for GB.

Experiments were performances with a 10-fold cross validation.

3.1 Specificity or True Negative Rate

In relation to the ability of Panoramix to correctly reject cognitively-unimpaired subjects, that is, the specificity of Panoramix, was also computed for each ML algorithm and cognitive group (cf. Table 3). On the one hand, specificity value for CU controls and also for AD group, is the maximum value, 1.00, for all classifiers. On the other hand, in the case of participants affected by MCI, the specificity score is lower, 0.7 for the four ML algorithms.

Table 3. Specificity or true negative rate of Panoramix (detailed by cognitive group)

Specificity (TNR)	CU	MCI	AD
Random Forest (RF)	1.00	0.7	1.00
Extra Tree (ET)	1.00	0.7	1.00
Gradient Boosting (GB)	1.00	0.7	1.00
Ada Boost (AB)	1.00	0.7	1.00

3.2 Sensitivity or True Positive Rate

In relation to the capabilities of Panoramix to correctly detect subjects with cognitive impairment (i.e., MCI or AD subjects), namely, the true positive rate, the following results were obtained (cf. Table 4). Firstly, in the case to detect participants with AD, the sensitivity score is above 0.92 for the all ML classifiers, achieving the best performance for RF (i.e., 1.00). On the other hand, the best sensitivity performance of Panoramix tool is for RF classifier (i.e., 1.00) for all participants, regardless of their cognitive group. In the case of subject with MCI, the sensitivity score achieved the unit for all ML ensemble algoritms.

Table 4. Sensitivity or true positive rate of Panoramix (detailed by cognitive group)

Sensitivity (TPR)	CU	MCI	AD
Random Forest (RF)	1.00	1.00	1.00
Extra Tree (ET)	0.98	1.00	0.97
Gradient Boosting (GB)	0.98	1.00	0.95
Ada Boost (AB)	0.98	1.00	0.92

3.3 ROC Curve

The ROC curve was computed to assess the classifier's performance, detailed by cognitive class, as depicted in the Fig. 2. Particularly, it shows a high average AUC for each cognitive class and for all Ml algorithms, above 0.95. Best performance is for subjects with AD, (i.e., AUC = 0.98–0.99) for all participants. In the case of CU or controls subjects the value of AUC = 0.98, again regardless for each algorithm. Finally, in the case of MCI group, the AUC score slightly slow, 0.96 for RF, ET and GB, while 0.96 for AB.

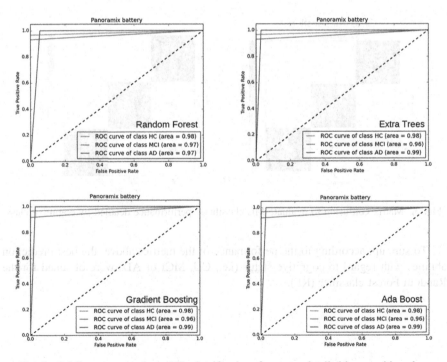

Fig. 2. ROC curve to evaluate ML classifiers' performance detailed by cognitive class

3.4   Confusion Matrix

In the same line as the ROC, the normalized confusion matrix shows scores very close to 1 for all cognitive classes (cf. Fig. 3). Particularly, the ratio between true and predicted labels is 1 for the AD group and for all ML classifiers. In the case of controls or CU group, this rate achieves a value of 0.97. Finally, this score is lower for the participants with MCI: 0.95 for RF; 0.93 for ET; 0.92 for GB; and slightly worse for AB, 0.89.

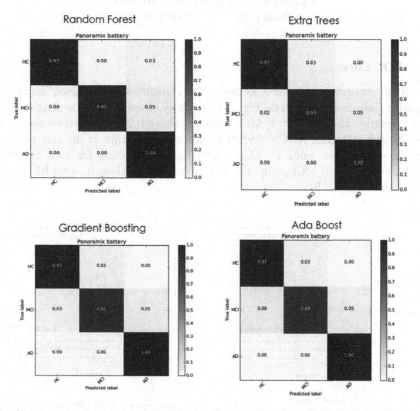

Fig. 3. Matrix confusion to evaluate ML classifiers' performance detailed by cognitive class

To sum up, according to the performance of the metrics above, the best prediction abilities with regard to cognitive status (i.e., CU, MCI or AD) were obtained for the Random Forest classifier (RF).

4 Discussion and Conclusion

The purpose of this study was to evaluate four ensemble machine learning models (i.e., RF, ET, GB, and AB), to construct classification models to discriminate among cognitively healthy individuals (i.e., CU group), participants with MCI and people affected by AD. For this, we used the seven cognitive games in the Panoramix battery [10–12] by means of a pilot experiment with statistical significance for the target population considered. In this study, we applied the classifiers discussed to the complete dataset, to gather more information about the predictive validity of the games and to obtain the best ML configuration to prepare a prototype to be eventually introduced in clinical settings.

Based on the results, the classification performance of four ensembles of classifiers was analysed using a 10-fold stratified cross validation procedure [44]. Best results were obtained for the Random Forest method, in line with previous supervised classification studies targeting the detection of cancer [46] and dementia [47]. In our case, accuracy is the index parameter, with average values Accuracy = 1.00, F1-score = 0.99 and Cohen's kappa = 0.98. These results indicate that Panoramix is a high-quality tool to predict cognitive impairment, both according to the rate of correctly classified subjects (i.e., Accuracy), as well as from the point of view of (the harmonic average of) precision and sensitivity (i.e., F1 score). Moreover, findings are robust when compared to a random prediction, as the values of Cohen's kappa obtained are almost perfect [41] for all classifiers, above 0.96.

Regarding the ability of the game battery to correctly reject cognitively-unimpaired subjects, namely, the specificity of Panoramix, excellent results were obtained with all the algorithms (i.e., true negative rate above 0.97 for all cognitive classes). A sensitivity study was also carried out to assess the ability of Panoramix to correctly detect subjects with cognitive impairment, MCI or AD. In this case, the RF classifier performs with practically full sensitivity for all cognitive groups (i.e., 1.00 regardless cognitive class).

In relation to the limitations of this study, it is worth mentioning that for the results to be soundly considered as highly representative for the Western European population and to guarantee clinical normative validity, a larger trial, including subjects adequately distributed according to age and gender groups, and involving at least two countries to consider cultural or linguistic factors, would be necessary. However, the results discussed in this paper are highly promising and already have statistical significance for Galicia. Moreover, despite of applying mean imputation to handle missing data, which may contribute to underrepresent the variability in the data, the impact in actual data sets is limited because this value was computed by cognitive group and not for all subjects.

As it was demonstrated in this paper, ensemble ML methods support the construction of classification models for the discrimination among CU, MCI and AD. Besides, these classifiers' performance is clearly better in comparison to other popular approaches (e.g., Support Vector Machines), without affecting output metrics.

Thus, the experiments reported indicate that artificial intelligence techniques can be used to automate aspects of clinical diagnosis, using the data obtained from a battery of serious games. Furthermore, discrimination was performed in a nonintrusive, non-frustrating way, which is especially relevant when targeting elder adults that may suffer cognitive impairments.

Acknowledgment. This work has been partially supported by 'Rede Galega de Investigación en Demencias' (IN607C-2017/02) funded by Axencia Galega de Innovación GAIN – Xunta de Galicia and 'Agrupación Estratéxica Consolidada de Galicia accreditation 2016-2019) funded by Xunta de Galicia and the European Regional Development Fund – ERDF.

References

1. Prince, M.J.: World Alzheimer Report 2015: the global impact of dementia: an analysis of prevalence, incidence, cost and trends. Alzheimer's Disease International (2015)
2. WHO: First WHO ministerial conference on global action against dementia: meeting report, WHO Headquarters, Geneva, Switzerland, 16–17 March 2015
3. Lezak, M.D.: Neuropsychological Assessment. Oxford University Press, Oxford (2004)
4. Howieson, D.B., Lezak, M.D.: The neuropsychological evaluation. In: Essentials of Neuropsychiatry and Behavioral Neurosciences, pp 29–46. American Psychiatric Pub (2010)
5. Chaytor, N., Schmitter-Edgecombe, M.: The ecological validity of neuropsychological tests: a review of the literature on everyday cognitive skills. Neuropsychol. Rev. **13**, 181–197 (2003)
6. Mario, B., Massimiliano, M., Chiara, M., et al.: White-coat effect among older patients with suspected cognitive impairment: prevalence and clinical implications. Int. J. Geriatr. Psychiatry **24**, 509–517 (2009)
7. Holtzman, D.M., Morris, J.C., Goate, A.M.: Alzheimer's disease: the challenge of the second century. Sci. Transl. Med. **3**, 77sr1 (2011)
8. Knight, R.G., Titov, N.: Use of virtual reality tasks to assess prospective memory: applicability and evidence. Brain Impair. **10**, 3–13 (2009)
9. Cordell, C.B., Borson, S., Boustani, M., et al.: Alzheimer's association recommendations for operationalizing the detection of cognitive impairment during the medicare annual wellness visit in a primary care setting. Alzheimer's Dement **9**, 141–150 (2013)
10. Valladares-Rodriguez, S., Perez-Rodriguez, R., Facal, D., et al.: Design process and preliminary psychometric study of a video game to detect cognitive impairment in senior adults. PeerJ **5**, e3508 (2017). https://doi.org/10.7717/peerj.3508
11. Valladares-Rodriguez, S., Pérez-Rodriguez, R., Fernandez-Iglesias, J.M., et al.: Learning to detect cognitive impairment through digital games and machine learning techniques. Methods Inf. Med. **57**, 197 (2018)
12. Valladares-Rodriguez, S., Fernández-Iglesias, M.J., Anido-Rifón, L., et al.: Episodix: a serious game to detect cognitive impairment in senior adults. A psychometric study. PeerJ **6**, e5478 (2018). https://doi.org/10.7717/peerj.5478
13. Facal, D., Guàrdia-Olmos, J., Juncos-Rabadán, O.: Diagnostic transitions in mild cognitive impairment by use of simple Markov models. Int. J. Geriatr. Psychiatry **30**, 669–676 (2015). https://doi.org/10.1002/gps.4197
14. Juncos-Rabadán, O., Pereiro, A.X., Facal, D., et al.: Prevalence and correlates of cognitive impairment in adults with subjective memory complaints in primary care centres. Dement. Geriatr. Cogn. Disord. **33**, 226–232 (2012)
15. Ding, D., Zhao, Q., Guo, Q., et al.: Progression and predictors of mild cognitive impairment in Chinese elderly: a prospective follow-up in the Shanghai Aging Study. Alzheimer's Dement. Diagn. Assess Dis. Monit. **4**, 28–36 (2016)
16. Cloutier, S., Chertkow, H., Kergoat, M.-J., et al.: Patterns of cognitive decline prior to dementia in persons with mild cognitive impairment. J Alzheimer's Dis. **47**, 901–913 (2015)

17. Han, J.W., Kim, T.H., Lee, S.B., et al.: Predictive validity and diagnostic stability of mild cognitive impairment subtypes. Alzheimer's Dement. **8**, 553–559 (2012)
18. Abu-Mostafa, Y.S., Magdon-Ismail, M., Lin, H.-T.: Learning from Data. AMLBook, New York (2012)
19. Lehmann, C., Koenig, T., Jelic, V., et al.: Application and comparison of classification algorithms for recognition of Alzheimer's disease in electrical brain activity (EEG). J. Neurosci. Methods **161**, 342–350 (2007). https://doi.org/10.1016/j.jneumeth.2006.10.023
20. Tripoliti, E.E., Fotiadis, D.I., Argyropoulou, M., Manis, G.: A six stage approach for the diagnosis of the Alzheimer's disease based on fMRI data. J. Biomed. Inform. **43**, 307–320 (2010)
21. Maroco, J., Silva, D., Rodrigues, A., et al.: Data mining methods in the prediction of dementia: a real-data comparison of the accuracy, sensitivity and specificity of linear discriminant analysis, logistic regression, neural networks, support vector machines, classification trees and random forests. BMC Res. Notes **4**, 299 (2011)
22. Patel, M.J., Andreescu, C., Price, J.C., et al.: Machine learning approaches for integrating clinical and imaging features in late-life depression classification and response prediction. Int. J. Geriatr. Psychiatry **30**, 1056–1067 (2015)
23. Williams, J.A., Weakley, A., Cook, D.J., Schmitter-Edgecombe, M.: Machine learning techniques for diagnostic differentiation of mild cognitive impairment and dementia. In: Workshops at the Twenty-Seventh AAAI Conference on Artificial Intelligence (2013)
24. Barlett, J.E., Kotrlik, J.W., Higgins, C.C.: Organizational research: determining appropriate sample size in survey research. Inf. Technol. Learn. Perform. J. **19**, 43 (2001)
25. Banerjee, S., Smith, S.C., Lamping, D.L., et al.: Quality of life in dementia: more than just cognition. An analysis of associations with quality of life in dementia. J. Neurol. Neurosurg. Psychiatry **77**, 146–148 (2006)
26. Cockrell, J.R., Folstein, M.F.: Mini-mental state examination (MMSE). Psychopharmacol. Bull. **24**, 689–692 (1987)
27. Delis D.C., Kramer, J.H., Kaplan, E., Ober, B.A.: California Verbal Learning Test: Adult version, Psychologi. San Antonio, Texas (1987)
28. Selnes, O.A.: A Compendium of Neuropsychological Tests: Administration, Norms, and Commentary, Ilustrada. Oxford University Press, Oxford (1991)
29. Howard, D., Patterson, K.: The Pyramid and Palm Trees Test: A Test of Semantic Access from Words and Pictures. Thames Val Test Company, Bury St Edmunds (1992)
30. Kaplan, E., Fein, D., Morris, R., Delis, D.: WAIS-R NI manual. Psychological Corporation, San Antonio (1991)
31. Liamputtong, P.: Focus Group Methodology: Principle and Practice. Sage Publications, Thousand Oaks (2011)
32. Diaz-Orueta, U., Facal, D., Nap, H.H., Ranga, M.-M.: What is the key for older people to show interest in playing digital learning games? Initial qualitative findings from the LEAGE project on a multicultural european sample. GAMES Health Res. Dev. Clin. Appl. **1**, 115–123 (2012)
33. Brox, E., Fernandez-Luque, L., Tøllefsen, T., et al.: Healthy gaming–video game design to promote health. Appl. Clin. Inform. **2**, 128–142 (2011)
34. Ahonniska, J., Ahonen, T., Aro, T., Lyytinen, H.: Suggestions for revised scoring of the tower of hanoi test. Assessment **7**, 311–319 (2000)
35. Howard, D., Patterson, K.E.: The Pyramids and Palm Trees Test: A Test of Semantic Access from Words and Pictures. Thames Valley Test Company, Suffolk (1992)
36. Rami, L., Bosch, B., Sanchez-Valle, R., Molinuevo, J.L.: The memory alteration test (M@T) discriminates between subjective memory complaints, mild cognitive impairment and Alzheimer's disease. Arch. Gerontol. Geriatr. **50**, 171–174 (2010)

37. Pedregosa, F., Varoquaux, G., Gramfort, A., et al.: Scikit-learn: machine learning in Python. J. Mach. Learn. Res. **12**, 2825–2830 (2011)
38. Batista, G.E., Monard, M.C.: An analysis of four missing data treatment methods for supervised learning. Appl. Artif. Intell. **17**, 519–533 (2003)
39. García-Laencina, P.J., Sancho-Gómez, J.L., Figueiras-Vidal, A.R.: Pattern classification with missing data: a review. Neural Comput. Appl. **19**, 263–282 (2010)
40. Breiman, L.: Random forests. Mach. Learn. **45**, 5–32 (2001)
41. Geurts, P., Ernst, D., Wehenkel, L.: Extremely randomized trees. Mach. Learn. **63**, 3–42 (2006)
42. Payan, A., Montana, G.: Predicting Alzheimer's disease: a neuroimaging study with 3D convolutional neural networks. arXiv Prepr arXiv:150202506 (2015)
43. Freund, Y., Schapire, R.E.: A decision-theoretic generalization of on-line learning and an application to boosting. J. Comput. Syst. Sci. **55**, 119–139 (1997)
44. Cohen, J.: A coefficient of agreement for nominal scales. Educ. Psychol. Meas. **20**, 37–46 (1960)
45. Landis, J.R., Koch, G.G.: The measurement of observer agreement for categorical data. Biometrics **33**, 159–174 (1977)
46. Bradley, A.P.: The use of the area under the ROC curve in the evaluation of machine learning algorithms. Pattern Recogn. **30**, 1145–1159 (1997)
47. Witten, I.H., Frank, E., Hall, M.A., Pal, C.J.: Data Mining: Practical machine learning tools and techniques. Morgan Kaufmann, Burlington (2016)

Low Bit Rate 2D Seismic Image Compression with Deep Autoencoders

Ana Paula Schiavon[1]([✉]), João Paulo Navarro[2], Marcelo Bernardes Vieira[1], and Pedro Mário Cruz e Silva[2]

[1] Universidade Federal de Juiz de Fora, Juiz de Fora, Brazil
apschiavon@ice.ufjf.br, marcelo.bernardes@ufjf.edu.br
[2] NVIDIA, São Paulo, Brazil
{jpnavarro,pcruzesilva}@nvidia.com

Abstract. In this paper, we present a deep learning approach for very low bit rate seismic data compression. Our goal is to preserve perceptual and numerical aspects of the seismic signal whilst achieving high compression rates. The trade-off between bit rate and distortion is controlled by adjusting the loss function. 2D slices extracted from seismic 3D amplitude volumes feed the network for training two simultaneous networks, an autoencoder for latent space representation, and a probabilistic model for entropy estimation. The method benefits from the intrinsic characteristic of deep learning methods and automatically captures the most relevant features of seismic data. An approach for training different seismic surveys is also presented. To validate the method, we performed experiments in real seismic datasets, showing that the autoencoders can successfully yield compression rates up to 68:1 with an average PSNR around 40 dB.

Keywords: Seismic data compression · Deep autoencoders · Geophysical image processing · High bit-depth compression

1 Introduction

The quality of acquisition sensors has been evolved significantly in the past years. This fact implies on higher resolution signals to process, to storage, and to transmit. The use of effective compressing algorithms plays an important role in seismic processing, aiming to deal with the substantial increase in data resolution. Generally speaking, reliance on compression algorithms in terms of signal reconstruction is a concern in the field due to the dilemma of choosing *loss-less* methods, with perfect reconstruction, or *lossy* compression, with a greater reduction on storage with allowed reconstruction distortions.

Typical compression methods benefit from the extensive oscillatory nature of the seismic data to model the algorithms. This leads to approaches involving

Authors thank CAPES, FAPEMIG (grant CEX-APQ-01744-15) for the financial support, and NVIDIA for the donation of one GPU as part of the GPU Grant Program.

© Springer Nature Switzerland AG 2019
S. Misra et al. (Eds.): ICCSA 2019, LNCS 11619, pp. 397–407, 2019.
https://doi.org/10.1007/978-3-030-24289-3_29

transformations to wavelets and cosine domains [1]. The so-called transform-based methods consider the representation of the volume in these domains, storing and processing only on a small subset of the total coefficients. A wavelet-transform based compression algorithm was proposed in [2], allowing extremely high compression ratios with considerably small errors. Other techniques such as low-rank methods are focused in working directly on lower dimensional matrices sampled from the higher dimensional wavefield [3].

Recently, some methods explored standard video and image compression techniques. With similar performance to a licensed commercial wavelet-based scheme used by the industry, experiments performed in [4] indicated that the JPEG-XR can be used to fast compress seismic images allowing to control the quality or bit rate target. Motivated by the performance of video codecs, a codec under the HEVC [5] intra coding framework is presented in [6] to compress seismic images, outperforming the previously published compression schemes. Considering the similarity between 3D seismic data and videos, an extension of this method was proposed in [7] aiming to explore the temporal redundancy in three-dimensional data. This method surpasses the previous method and it is less time-consuming.

However, one may notice that most of these approaches are exposed to any sort of dataset bias. The challenge in working with compression for seismic domain relies on the difficulty of detaching parts of the signal that represent physical properties from those who do not. We argue that capturing all variances and inconsistencies that may be present in seismic signals such as noise, interferences, and processing inaccuracies in a deterministic fashion is not practical. Machine Learning techniques is a viable way to face this problem. In this sense, these techniques were employed in [8] to compress seismic signals directly from the field. They trained a shallow autoencoder to compress the data while a Restricted Boltzmann Machine was used to optimize its parameters. In addition to achieving interesting preliminary results (10:1 and a PSNR of 30 dB), this approach can capture the most representative features using only a portion of the dataset.

The popularity of Deep Learning (DL) algorithms has considerably increased in recent years due to consistent advances in solving complex computer science tasks such as image classification, speech to text, and translation. Recently, deep neural network approaches are taking momentum in solving low-level problems in image processing, such as super-resolution and image compression, leading to impressive state-of-the-art results. Complementing the autoencoder with an adversarial training, the proposal of [9] to image compression outperforms all previous codecs producing visually agreeable reconstructions for very low bit rates. With competitive performance to the previous work, [10] proposed an image compression system based in two networks trained concurrently. A probabilistic model is used to learn the dependencies between symbols in the autoencoder latent representation, and another autoencoder uses it for entropy estimation, in order to control the rate-distortion trade-off.

The main contribution of this work is the extension of the method proposed by [10] for low bit rate compression of seismic volumes. More specifically, we propose a training and inference schemes tuned for seismic compression of multiple volumes. Our method is trained using a collection of seismic 2D-slices to feed the network. A DL method based on conditional probabilistic deep autoencoder is tuned to exploit the inherent features of seismic data.

2   Proposed Method

We extend the end-to-end pipeline proposed by [10]. Our goal is to compress an amplitude seismic volume training simultaneously two deep networks: a compressing autoencoder and a probabilistic model. The first deals with the rate-distortion trade-off between a small number of bits and small distortions. The second is a 3D-CNN that learns the dependencies between the symbols of the autoencoder latent representation. Both models were trained to balance the trade-off. We provide training and inference schemes for 2D-slice based seismic volume compression.

2.1   Probabilistic Autoencoder

By definition, an autoencoder is an unsupervised learning algorithm that is trained to adjust its weights aiming to set the target values to be equal to the inputs. The compressive autoencoder is a model composed of an encoder, a decoder, and a quantizer [11]. The encoder $E : \mathcal{R}^d \to \mathcal{R}^m$ maps the input $\mathbf{x}$ to a lower dimension latent space. The quantizer $Q : \mathcal{R} \to C$ discretizes the latent representation $\mathbf{z}$, obtaining $\hat{\mathbf{z}} = Q(\mathbf{z})$, and allowing it to be losslessly encoded into a bitstream through arithmetic coding strategy. The decoder D reconstructs the image $\hat{\mathbf{x}} = D(\hat{\mathbf{z}})$ from its quantized representation through the losslessly decoded bitstream. The goal is to minimize the rate-distortion trade-off $d(\mathbf{x}, \hat{\mathbf{x}}) + \beta H(\hat{\mathbf{z}})$, where d is a function that measures the distortion between the original image and its reconstruction, H is the entropy of the quantized latent representation and β controls the trade-off.

The quantization combines the works of [12,13]. The authors used a clustering based quantization, where each entry of the latent representation is changed by the index of the nearest centroid. The encoder and the decoder are 2D-CNNs with the particularity that the last layer of the encoder has an additional feature map, named importance map. This map is used to generate a binary 3D mask $\lceil \mathbf{m} \rceil$ that is applied to the feature maps volume. It allows different regions of the image to be represented by a different number of bits, according to the detail level. Since the mask binarization is not a differentiable operation, a soft approximation in the backward pass of the back propagation is used.

The probabilistic model $P(\hat{\mathbf{z}})$ is a 3D-CNN that models the conditional probability of a symbol belonging to a centroid given the previous symbols to it, learning their dependencies in the latent representation of the autoencoder [14].

Considering the distribution

$$p(\hat{\mathbf{z}}) = \prod_{i}^{m} (\hat{\mathbf{z}}_i | \hat{\mathbf{z}}_{i-1}, \dots, \hat{\mathbf{z}}_1), \qquad (1)$$

this network is used to estimate each term $(\hat{\mathbf{z}}_i | \hat{\mathbf{z}}_{i-1}, \dots, \hat{\mathbf{z}}_1)$:

$$P_{i,l}(\hat{\mathbf{z}}) \approx p(\hat{\mathbf{z}}_i = C_l | \hat{\mathbf{z}}_{i-1}, \dots, \hat{\mathbf{z}}_1), \qquad (2)$$

where $l = \{1, \dots, L\}$ and L is the size of the centroids set C.

The losses of both models are based on the rate-distortion trade-off. Given the set of training seismic images $\mathbf{X}$, we train over minibatches $\mathbf{X}_B = \{\mathbf{x}^{(1)}, \cdots, \mathbf{x}^{(B)}\}$ of crops from $\mathbf{X}$.

Since the models are trained simultaneously, the entropy term H is calculated using two approaches: first, instead of encoding the entire masked symbol volume, the 3D binarized mask $\lceil \mathbf{m} \rceil$ is encoded and subsequently the symbols of the volume that are not zero. This is used by the autoencoder, since it allows the encoder to easily control the spatial allocation of bits [15]. The second, uses the distribution $p(\hat{\mathbf{z}})$, since it does not have direct access to the mask and needs to learn the dependencies on the entire masked symbol volume [14]. The loss function for the probabilistic model P is defined as:

$$\mathcal{L}_P := \frac{1}{B} \sum_{j=1}^{B} d(\mathbf{x}^{(j)}, \hat{\mathbf{x}}^{(j)}) + \beta \sum_{i=1}^{m} - \log P_{i,I(\hat{z}_i^{(j)})}, \qquad (3)$$

where $P_{i,I(\hat{z}_i^{(j)})}$ specifies for each voxel i in the entire masked symbol volume the probabilities of belonging to each index $I(\hat{z}_i)$ of the centroids set. The loss function for the autoencoder is given by:

$$\mathcal{L}_{E,D,Q} = \frac{1}{B} \sum_{j=1}^{B} d(\mathbf{x}^{(j)}, \hat{\mathbf{x}}^{(j)}) + \beta \sum_{i=1}^{m} - \lceil \mathbf{m}_i \rceil \log P_{i,I(\hat{z}_i^{(j)})}. \qquad (4)$$

Notice that this loss incorporates the probabilistic model as the entropy term of the autoencoder with the benefit of being weighted by $\lceil \mathbf{m} \rceil$. In next sections, we propose training and inference schemes, based on this compression model, taking into account the characteristics of seismic 2D-slices.

2.2 Training Scheme

Figure 1 presents our training pipeline. Initially, we perform a preprocessing step, aiming to adapt the volumes to the network input. Seismic sections are numerically represented as one channel 32-bit floating-point. But the model proposed by [10] was designed for general purpose image compression with 3-channels of 8-bit unsigned integers. We have verified that pre-trained models based on ImageNet did not fit our specific data domain. The fine-tuning approach using initial

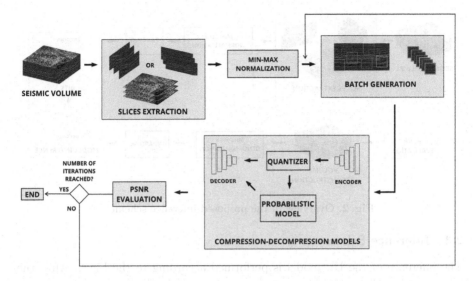

Fig. 1. Overview of the proposed training scheme.

weights from 8-bit images for network optimization led to higher iterations until convergence. For this reason, we adapted the network and all metrics to work with seismic data and trained all models from scratch for a collection of volumes.

The encoder-decoder performs 2D convolutions and thus the training dataset was formed by extracting slices of the inline, crossline or time-depth directions. Then, the slices are normalized using min-max strategy. This is important because the original network was designed to work in the [0,1] interval quantized with 8-bits for low-dynamic range images. Since seismic data are quantized with 32-bits, its range values are wider and the min-max is arbitrary across different volumes. In order to train multiple volumes at the same time, the min-max from all volumes are used.

The batch generation is performed extracting random crops from the slices and randomly flipping them. In the case of a training set composed by various datasets, the batch is built with crops from all of them at the same quantity. In this way, we are preventing the model from being biased by one dataset. Since the number of slices of a dataset can vary, smaller datasets will provide crops of repeated slices. In general, given the random nature of the cropping, the chance of an exactly repeated crop is negligible.

The batch is then used to feed the encoder. The output of the encoder is quantized and it is used by the probabilistic model to estimate the entropy and to calculate the centroids. These centroids and the quantizer output are used by the decoder to reconstruct the batch images. We perform a PSNR evaluation between the initial and reconstructed batches. This metric was chosen to be maximized by the training step instead the original Multi-Scale Structural Similarity (MS-SSIM) for images. The PSNR is simpler to compute and yielded better overall results. The training step is repeated until the maximum number of iterations is reached.

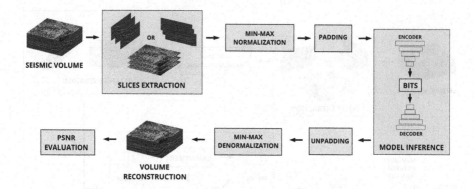

Fig. 2. Overview of the proposed inference scheme.

2.3   Inference Scheme

The inference of the DL model is performed according to the Fig. 2. After the training step, the network is tuned for compression of seismic slices normalized in [0,1] range. Given a seismic volume, the slices are extracted in one of the directions and then normalized with its min-max values. If their shapes are not divisible by the network subsampling factor, they are padded with a border extension. We propose the symmetric border extension since it better preserves the frequencies of the seismic volume. The encode/decode are then performed for model inference. Both input and output are unpadded to guarantee coherence of the metric evaluation. The slices are denormalized to reconstruct the compressed seismic volume. Finally, we evaluate the error between the original and reconstructed volumes.

3   Experimental Results

To validate the proposed method, we perform experiments in different 3D stacked seismic volumes available on SEG Open Data repository [16]. Our method was implemented using the TensorFlow framework, and all runs performed on a single GPU NVIDIA Tesla V100. We verified that the following hyper-parameter space was suitable for all datasets: Adam optimizer, batch-size of 32, initial learning rate of $8 \cdot 10^{-5}$ for the autoencoder and $1 \cdot 10^{-4}$ for the probabilistic model, both with step decay of 0.1 every 10 epochs, and crop size of 128×128. Reconstruction quality is reported as PSNR and SNR in decibels (dB) due to its sensibility to small error variations, and compression rate as bits-per-voxel (bpv), expressing the average number of bits necessary to represent the 32-bits amplitude values.

3.1   Training Protocol

From SEG Open Data repository [16] we selected five seismic surveys: Kahu3D, Parihaka3D, Netherlands F3-Block, Penobscot3D and Waihapa3D volumes.

Netherlands F3-Block, Penobscot3D and Waihapa3D were used only for test-ing. We also reserved 10% of training volume slices for validation (randomly chosen), so we could define appropriate hyper-parameters such as number of epochs. Normalizing by standardization leads to impressive reduction in epochs, with initial average PSNR of 25 dB in contrast with 10 dB.

The details of the seismic surveys, such as size and grid dimension are shown in Table 1. Slices were extracted from volumes in (x, z) (inline), (y, z) (crossline) and (x, y) (time-depth) planes.

Table 1. Uncompressed dataset properties.

Dataset	Size (GB)	Grid dimension
Kahu3D	6.17	$(584 \times 1695 \times 1498)$
Parihaka3D	3.86	$(920 \times 1124 \times 874)$
Netherlands F3-Block	1.25	$(631 \times 951 \times 463)$
Penobscot3D	0.60	$(401 \times 301 \times 1251)$
Waihapa3D	0.29	$(201 \times 291 \times 1238)$

3.2 Results and Discussion

Due its similarity, we use the inline and crossline directions alongside to train a single model with good performance in both directions. Since the time-depth direction is too different from the previous, its results were obtained training another model using only this direction.

Table 2 shows the comparison between the three possible planes used in the inference step. Notice that the crossline direction has similar results compared to the inline. This is expected since the volume in both directions have similar characteristics. The results of the model trained and inferred with the time-depth plane is clearly worse than the others. The data in the time-depth directions seems noisy if compared to the other planes. The compression model is less efficient, requiring an extra tuning of its hyper-parameters.

We trained the model using only slices from Kahu and Parihaka datasets. Netherlands F3-Block is known to be a noisy survey, thus naturally harder to compress. But even under this condition, it took only four epochs for the model to reach an interesting PSNR of 35.56. This result highlights the generalization capabilities of the method. With a SNR = 29.56, however, one may not consider that the relevant original information was preserved. A deeper qualitative anal-ysis is needed to correlate the minimum bit rate and PSNR that do not result in relevant losses. We also need to train with more seismic surveys to further increase generality power. Since the software and the data used by the state-of-the-art results are private, we are not able to report the performance of our method on them.

Table 2. Results for testing sets. Overall average compression ratio is 68:1.

Dataset	Direction	bpv	PSNR	SNR
Netherlands F3_Block	Inline	0.45	35.56	29.56
	Crossline	0.46	35.07	29.08
	Time-depth	0.40	33.45	27.46
Penobscot3D	Inline	0.39	40.48	34.47
	Crossline	0.37	42.00	35.99
	Time-depth	0.36	37.11	31.10
Waihapa3D	Inline	0.65	34.81	29.30
	Crossline	0.66	34.55	29.04
	Time-depth	0.47	35.21	29.70

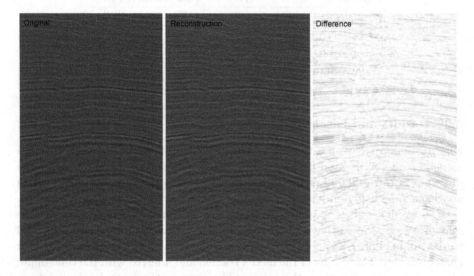

Fig. 3. Section reconstruction from an image in Penobscot test set. Despite the minor differences (right), overall reconstruction preserves most relevant seismic features, important for geological interpretations. Compression ratio = 86:1 and PSNR = 42 dB.

Figure 3 depicts a complete slice compression and decompression result for the Penobscot dataset. Even with a 86:1 compression, the details are fairly preserved with PSNR = 42 dB. Figure 4 shows a crop from a slice of the Waihapa volume (Fig. 4a) compressed in different bit rates. The extreme compression in Fig. 4b and c introduced high frequencies in the original slice (Fig. 4a). One may notice a less effective PSNR gain as we move to higher compression ratios when compared to HVEC-based methods [6,7]. Considering the Figs. 3, 4d and e, along with our observations, bit rates resulting in at least PSNR = 36 dB tend to better preserve details.

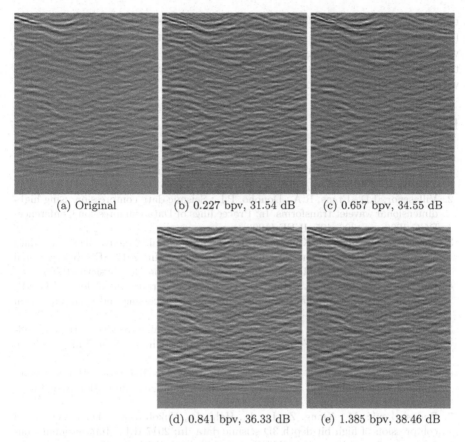

(a) Original   (b) 0.227 bpv, 31.54 dB   (c) 0.657 bpv, 34.55 dB

(d) 0.841 bpv, 36.33 dB   (e) 1.385 bpv, 38.46 dB

Fig. 4. Two dimensional crops extracted from Waihapa volume. The method maximizes PSNR during optimization while achieving low bit rates.

As aforementioned, we performed the standardization operation on both first and last layers, leading to a drastically reduced convergence time. Using a single NVIDIA Tesla V100 we were able to train a model within the interval of 1 hour. We expect to explore parallel approaches such as Horovod [17] to distribute training between multi-GPU as we increase total amount of training data.

4 Conclusions

In this paper, we presented a deep learning approach for 3D seismic data compression. The network is fed with two-dimensional 32-bits sections from the original volume, training at the same time two networks, one for latent space representation, and other for entropy estimation. The bit rate of the compressed volume is controlled by hyper-parameter tuning. The method benefits from the intrinsic characteristic of deep learning approaches and automatically captures the most relevant features of the data. It presents promising results in data reconstruction with high PSNR values at low bit rates. High compression rates (up to 68:1 and PSNR = 40 dB in average) are obtained by training models with multiple seismic surveys on a single procedure. As future work, we intend to improve our workflow so more volumes are aggregated to the training dataset without introducing biases.

References

1. Averbuch, A.Z., Meyer, F., Stromberg, J., Coifman, R., Vassiliou, A.: Low bit-rate efficient compression for seismic data. IEEE Trans. Image Process. **10**(12), 1801–1814 (2001). https://doi.org/10.1109/83.974565
2. Villasenor, J.D., Ergas, R.A., Donoho, P.L.: Seismic data compression using high-dimensional wavelet transforms. In: Proceedings of Data Compression Conference-DCC 1996, pp. 396–405. IEEE (1996)
3. Zhang, Y., Da Silva, C., Kumar, R., Herrmann, F., et al.: Massive 3D seismic data compression and inversion with hierarchical tucker. In: 2017 SEG International Exposition and Annual Meeting. Society of Exploration Geophysicists (2017)
4. Liu, Y., Xiong, Z., Lu, L., Hohl, D.: Fast SNR and rate control for JPEG XR. In: 2016 10th International Conference on Signal Processing and Communication Systems (ICSPCS), pp. 1–7. IEEE (2016)
5. Sullivan, G.J., Ohm, J.R., Han, W.J., Wiegand, T., et al.: Overview of the high efficiency video coding (HEVC) standard. IEEE Trans. Circuits Syst. Video Technol. **22**(12), 1649–1668 (2012)
6. Radosavljević, M., Xiong, Z., Lu, L., Vukobratović, D.: High bit-depth image compression with application to seismic data. In: Visual Communications and Image Processing (VCIP), pp. 1–4. IEEE (2016)
7. Radosavljević, M., Xiong, Z., Lu, L., Hohl, D., Vukobratović, D.: HEVC-based compression of high bit-depth 3D seismic data. In: 2017 IEEE International Conference on Image Processing (ICIP), pp. 4028–4032. IEEE (2017)
8. Nuha, H., Mohandes, M., Liu, B.: Seismic-data compression using autoassociative neural network and restricted boltzmann machine. SEG Tech. Program Expanded Abs. **2018**, 186–190 (2018)
9. Rippel, O., Bourdev, L.: Real-time adaptive image compression. In: International Conference on Machine Learning, pp. 2922–2930 (2017)
10. Mentzer, F., Agustsson, E., Tschannen, M., Timofte, R., Van Gool, L.: Conditional probability models for deep image compression. In: IEEE Conference on Computer Vision and Pattern Recognition (CVPR) (2018)
11. Theis, L., Shi, W., Cunningham, A., Huszár, F.: Lossy image compression with compressive autoencoders. CoRR abs/1703.00395 (2017)
12. Agustsson, E., et al.: Soft-to-hard vector quantization for end-to-end learning compressible representations. In: Advances in Neural Information Processing Systems, pp. 1141–1151 (2017)
13. Theis, L., Shi, W., Cunningham, A., Huszár, F.: Lossy image compression with compressive autoencoders. In: International Conference on Learning Representations (2017). https://openreview.net/pdf?id=rJiNwv9gg
14. Van Oord, A., Kalchbrenner, N., Kavukcuoglu, K.: Pixel recurrent neural networks. In: International Conference on Machine Learning, pp. 1747–1756 (2016)
15. Li, M., Zuo, W., Gu, S., Zhao, D., Zhang, D.: Learning convolutional networks for content-weighted image compression. arXiv preprint arXiv:1703.10553 (2017)

16. SEG: Open data (2019). http://wiki.seg.org/wiki/Open_data. Accessed 10 Jan 2019
17. Sergeev, A., Balso, M.D.: Horovod: fast and easy distributed deep learning in TensorFlow. CoRR abs/1802.05799 (2018). http://arxiv.org/abs/1802.05799

Application of Artificial Intelligence Methods in Sustainable Building Design

Ewa Gilner[1,2](✉) , Adam Galuszka[1] ,
and Tomasz Grychowski[1]

[1] Institute of Automatic Control, Silesian University of Technology,
Akademicka 16, 44-100 Gliwice, Poland
{ewa.gilner,adam.galuszka,tomasz.grychowski}@polsl.pl
[2] Rolfe Judd Sp. z o.o., Podchorążych 1, 40-043 Katowice, Poland
ewag@rolfe-judd.co.uk

Abstract. The need to reduce energy consumption, resources, the introduction of new and ecological materials, the multiplicity of modern technologies available, and the complexity and multi-branch nature of architectural and construction projects means that designers must make complex and difficult decisions. This work presents the subject of currently available and used in the AEC industry project tools and provides an overview of the possibilities of using artificial intelligence methods and tools, such as Knowledge Based Engineering (KBE), fuzzy logic, neural networks, genetic algorithms, Monte-Carlo simulation. These methods can be used in the early design stage to improve decision making process and to optimize both the design process and the project itself.

Keywords: Architectural design · Pareto genetic algorithms ·
Knowledge Based Engineering · AEC managing tools · Decision making

1 Introduction - New Challenges in the Architectural and Construction Design Process

Sustainable building design is a comprehensive process that involves many parties that need to cooperate but cannot operate independently. Due to the need to reduce energy consumption and raw materials use, the multitude of modern technologies available, and the less available and expensive lands in the desired areas, there are countless of difficult decisions to be made during the building design and construction process [1].

The need to meet the legislative requirements, the pressure from the Investors to limit the budget and minimize project completion time maintaining high standards at the same time, puts the project teams ahead of a huge challenge: creating an individual concept and implementing multi-disciplinary, comprehensive and compatible project documentation that meets all the criteria given. The success of the project depends on a successful exchange of information, coordination and the ability to select the most favorable solutions and compromises. Unlike serial products, each architectural project is an individual solution that is not subject to validation and correctness tests on living models. Due to the individuality of every project the only chance to detect and eliminate imperfections before starting the production is design stage.

This paper contains a comparison analysis of the traditional approach to the AEC (architecture, engineering, construction) design process and novel design methods. In the last one participants use platforms and tools to help them design, communicate, evaluate solutions, determine budget and coordinate multi-branch design. In addition, it will present a review of the literature on the possibilities and limitations of the use of artificial intelligence methods in improving the design process.

2 Comparison of Traditional Design Methods and Advanced Tools and Platforms to Improve the AEC Project Process

In the architectural and construction industry today, the most widely used systems are: cad drawing software's used to develop 2D drawings and 3D modeling softwares to complement the design. Any change made to the project needs to be implemented separately in all drawings the change applies. At the same time, you can observe a slow transformation of the way the project is developed due to the introduction of BIM (Building Information Modeling) system as a work tool. This technology allows developing comprehensive, multi-branch 3d model of the designed object that helps to detect project defects, facilitate inter-branch coordination and saves costs related to adjustments in the execution phase. According to researches it can save about 20% of time spent checking and correcting cad drawings [2] and 30% of the time needed to prepare the documentation [3].

According to the report published in 2017, 12% of respondents using BIM on daily basic at work, 21% of organizations use it at various levels and 78% plan to introduce this technology [4]. Another research stays that using BIM is more common in larger enterprises and its users are usually younger industry representatives. The biggest barrier for introducing BIM is competency shortages and low rates for projects [5].

However, BIM system has its limitations. Possible checks of collisions, codes and rules can be applied to the completed model, after carrying out the majority of design works and after the phase covering the majority of design decisions. Then the phase of corrections and changes takes place. In some cases the corrections needed may be small but sometimes drastic and requiring a huge amount of work, time and costs.

Recently the new possibilities of using BIM in AEC has been developed. In 2018 the research was published [6] combining BIM platform possibilities to create environment for managing adaptive smart façade shading system to reduce energy consumption and improve indoor microclimate. Also the possibilities od transferring data from BIM into Game environment were taken and using the game engine to create evacuation strategy was proposed [7, 8]. The similar approach for using game engine on exported BIM 3d data has been taken to allow for late stage design review of healthcare buildings [9].

3   Application of Artificial Intelligence Methods in the Design Process

Due to the limitations of currently widely used design methods in the architectural and construction industry, attempts are made to improve the design process using the methods of artificial intelligence (AI - Artificial Intelligence) [10]. Attempts to use AI tools in design began in the 1980s [11]. Tools using Knowledge Based Engineering KBE, fuzzy logic, neural networks, and genetic algorithms find a wide application in the design of AEC [1, 12]. The following is an overview of publications about using AI modeling in architectural design.

3.1   Possibilities of Using KBE in the AEC Project Process

One of the most characteristic features of a knowledge-based organization (KBO) is the use of knowledge, experience and the ability to assess the problem by the staff employed. This distinguishes them from other organizations that have physical assets (e.g., airplanes, hotels, commercial goods) and organizations that are rather an inter-mediary and interpreter of information without producing a specific product [13, 14]. According to this definition, the organizations of the AEC industry are an example of KBO organization.

Architectural, constructional and mechanical & electrical (M&E) design offices are evaluated primarily due to their experience and potential to provide the specific project. These organizations are employed based on their ability to deliver the project, as the product itself is not yet created at the stage of selecting the designer [1].

For this reason, the greatest value for this type of organization is the knowledge and experience of staff that can easily be lost if employees change the organization. In addition, the sharing of acquired knowledge depends on the skill and willingness to provide it, which does not guarantee that all of organization projects will benefit from the knowledge of the staff that is at the disposal of the organization at a specific moment. The use of knowledge engineering tools - KBE (knowledge based engi-neering) can help in the effectiveness of gathering and sharing knowledge.

KBE is a field of research aimed at increasing the efficiency of the design process through the use of experience and knowledge of completed project processes and their already known effects. Knowledge Engineering Systems allow you to use the experi-ence and knowledge gathered both by experienced and untrained designers, shortening the time to complete the task and reducing the risk of mistakes. Diagrams of knowledge engineering systems help in particular in the acceleration of routine tasks (which according to Calkin and Stokes constitute about 80% of all activities) allowing the designer - a specialist - to concentrate on creative and innovatory work [15, 16], which will affect the quality of the target product. Unlike BIM technology, which enables validation of the created model, the KBE task would enable Rule and Code compliance auto checking during the design phase [16].

KBE since the 1980s was mainly developed in the automotive, space and ship-building industries while in the AEC industry only to a small extent. In 2011, Hay-maker presented a system scheme proposal for AEC design process based on the use of comprehensive knowledge for a given branch that would lead designers step by step, learning and improving on the basis of received corrections and guidelines. The proposed system would consist of requirements specific to the project and broad knowledge consistent with the subject of the project. To make design decisions, the project team undergoes a 6-step process including: selection of the project team, goal definition, goal hierarchy definition, analysis of alternatives, impact analysis (each of the alternatives for each objective) and value estimation (based on a specific impact and hierarchy of values). According to Haymaker, each of the six main steps, indirect actions and dependencies between them can be properly described and automated. Similar approach have been taken by using Process Integration and Design Optimization software to carry multiple alternative for the design of classroom building instead of very few possible using traditional methods [17].

In 2015, in his publication, Singer and Bormann present an innovative approach to the KBE tools in civil engineering, which allowed the team to generate a bridge model based on given parameters: type and data concerning the bridge structure and the area. His team declared further research into the use of KBE tools in the architectural and construction industry.

3.2 Possibilities and Limitations of Using the Fuzzy Logic Method in Architectural Design

Architecture is a broad concept, considered to be one of the most important fields of art [18] and at the same time an Engineering discipline called Land Engineering according to the classification of fields and disciplines of the OECD (Organization for Economic Cooperation and development). Therefore, the quality of architecture can be assessed in many aspects: aesthetic, cultural, social, as well as economic, energy-efficient, and in the aspect of using innovative technologies. Similarly, each of its components is difficult to assess unequivocally, that is, mathematically speaking, binary (truth or false). Fuzzy logic, which is used as a problem solving tool, gives a set of indirect results - similar to human conclusions that may be used in the analysis of architectural problems. The result of the analysis cannot be unambiguously assessed as good or bad as the following examples show.

The fuzzy logic modeling method was already used in the spatial planning analysis to assess the location of individual houses of the existing housing estate [19]. The assessment was made in terms of distance from the desired places (beach and store), privacy of the location, the distance from the neighbour and view values. The analysis was performed using the Takagi-Sugeno fuzzy modeling method. The result of the analysis correctly indicated the assessment of the houses location attractiveness.

Fuzzy logic was also used to evaluate the coefficient of average daylight based on the set geometry, openness of the facade, reflectance [20]. In 2001 & 2003 Ciftcioglu and Durmisevic used Takagi-Sugeno method to determine the level of safety and comfort in the underground subway station [21, 22] based on a number of factors, including lighting, visual attractiveness, human presence, legibility of visual information, noise, temperature, etc.

3.3 The Use of Pareto Front and Genetic Algorithm in the Architectural Design

Genetic algorithms are supposed to imitate evolution. The offspring inherits the best traits selected from the group of "parents" during the evolution of many generations. Finding the best-developed offspring can also find application in the project design process [11, 12]. Due to the previously mentioned tightening of energy consumption regulations and limiting access to the resources, the growing need to reduce energy as much as possible is observed. In her work on the design of energy-saving buildings, Professor Luisa Caldas conducts research on the use of the Generative System GENE_ARCH in the early and intermediate design phase [23–25]. The system uses the Genetic Algorithm, Pareto optimization and DOE2 software. DOE2 software is available for free and is used to perform a building energy analysis allowing estimating energy consumption and usage costs based on the description of the building layout, construction, M&E systems designed, weather data and utility rates.

The system has been tested for various geographical locations and for selected tasks: finding the optimal location of windows in relation to the optimal amount of daylight and the minimum energy costs per annum; selection of optimal materials in terms of insulation requirements, costs and CO2 emissions; evolution of the desired shape of the building optimal in terms of the amount of daylight and the amount of heat supplied.

The use of the Pareto genetic algorithm allowed obtaining a group of possible solutions. The solutions are optimal in terms of energy use, material costs and the amount of daylight, leaving the final decision in the selection and implementation of the chosen solution to the designer.

In the research carried by Flager at All in 2009 [17] the optimization results of structural cost versus energy cost have been demonstrated by Pareto Front as in previous examples allowing for best solution evaluation.

3.4 Possibilities of Using Monte Carlo Simulation in the Early Stage of Designing Energy-Saving Construction

Another method tested to facilitate and improve the efficiency of design decisions at the early stage of the architectural design is a simulation developed and presented in the Torben Østergård dissertation in cooperation with the Danish office MOE [26].

The tools used are based on Monte Carlo simulations and sensitivity and uncertainty analysis as well as variability of design parameters using probability distributions. Their usefulness was presented in order to determine optimal design solutions affecting the energy efficiency of the building (energy demand, optimal amount of daylight, thermal comfort for residential buildings). The results allowed for recognition of the most desirable components of the considered building (window spans, overhangs over windows, insulating properties of windows, blinds, wall thickness, insulation thickness, etc.).

4   Proposed Development of the Research

4.1   Application of Artificial Intelligence Methods in the Implementation Stage of Design Process

While the above case studies show the attempt to apply AI modelling methods in early design stage the amount of routine tasks is performed during the tender and construction phase of design process. The implementation stage consists of value engineering application, detailed design, choice of materials, detailed specification and scheduling. Decisions made during this phase have a huge impact on project budget and final result.

To ensure that materials choices are made objectively and are not driven by lack of knowledge or benefits offered by providers and contractors interests, automation of selection process might be best solution. In the Fig. 1. we propose the concept of architectural design steps automation using AI.

The first step would be creating products database and systematize products relevant information and certifications. Next step would allow for initial verification and automatically performed rejection of products not meeting the criteria from the set of solution based by simply False or True Logic. During the next step AI set of optimization methods would be applied to indicate the best solution in terms of specified major criteria and determining the impact on those criteria by choosing the specific product. In the next step the most optimal solution would be chosen from the best solutions accessed in previous step. The last step would allow the team to accept automatically chosen solution or to choose different solution based by graphically presented set of best possibly solutions. AI methods such as Genetic algorithm, Pareto optimization and Fuzzy Logic would be proposed and tested as AI optimization methods for objective materials choice [27].

4.2   Application of Artificial Intelligence Methods to Assume Required Daily Light Provision for Representative Room

Usually energy performance and daylight analysis are performed after the design is complete and then the recommendations are given and the energy demand is established. Only for some technologically advanced buildings complex and complicated design process is performed to find best solutions in terms of energy performance.

In the future research we would try to find soft computing methodology that would allow specifying the optimum window sizes for representative rooms in specific location for main exposure directions. The aim would be to find best window sizes to achieve best energy performance for the room. The idea of the proposed methodology would be to create simply and easily accessible tool that could be applied on early stage of the design. That would help to design sustainable buildings not only by using the best performed materials but also by using the tool recommendation and might help sustainable design become more common and accessible.

The process would consists of using DOE software to perform energy use analysis on 3d model of typical office rooms and open space generated either by CAD or 3D BIM model. The representative rooms dimensions and windows size would match the

Creating products database and
systematize products relevant
information and certification

Initial veryfication and
automatically perform rejection of
products not meeting the criteria
from the set of soluton based by
simply False or True Logic

Results of other selection
processes performed
independently

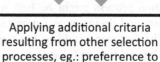

Application of AI set of
optimization methods to indicate
the best set of solution in terms of
specified major criteria and
determining the impact on that
criteria by choosing the specific
product

Applying additional critaria
resulting from other selection
processes, eg.: preferrence to
choose the same provider

Automatically performed selection
of the most optimal solution,
based on the highest score
obtained in previous step by using
different AI methods

Application of AI set of
optimization methods to indicate
the best set of solution in terms of
specified major criteria and
determining the impact on that
criteria by choosing the specific
product

Team accept automatically chosen
solution or can choose different
solution based by graphicly
presented set of best possibly
solutions.

Automatically performed selection
of the most optimal solution,
based on the highest score
obtained in previous step by using
different AI methods

Team accept automatically chosen
solution or can choose different
solution based by graphicly
presented set of best possibly
solutions.

Fig. 1. The proposed concept of architectural design steps automation using AI.

office structural and façade grid according to Modern Office Standards Poland (MOSP) 2016 for cellular plan and open space plan as shown in Fig. 2 [28]. The room would have North, East, South and West exposure direction in central location in Poland. Then optimization by Pareto genetic algorithm would be perform to visualize best and worst possible solutions in terms of energy consumption and daily light provision based on windows size, type of glazing and type of blinds used.

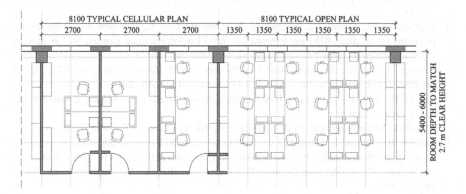

Fig. 2. Representative office grid based on modern office standards Poland 2016

5 Conclusions

AEC's design offices, consisting mainly of small and medium-sized enterprises, have less power to develop technology that helps them deliver the product than large enterprises operating on a broad international mass production market. Therefore the process of incorporating novel design tools is slow comparing to other industries.

The development of BIM technology is driven by the fact that these tools are used not only by designers, but also by investors, developers and contractors, and throughout the life of the building (Building Lifecycle Management) setting the new path of the AEC design process.

The application of artificial intelligence in the early project phases, which is possible in accordance with the above examples, would have a huge impact on improving, accelerating and rationalizing the decisions making in the early design phase. It would also make it possible to improve the energy efficiency of buildings, enabling it to meet stringent regulations and the increasing pressure to reduce the cost of building operations. The purpose of using new tools would not be to replace the designer, but to minimize routine tasks, indicate the best possible solutions, leaving decisions and creative design tasks in the hands of architects and AEC consultants.

Acknowledgment. This work was supported by the following Projects: Ministry of Science and Higher Education funds 10/DW/2017/01/1 for the first (Ewa Gilner) author. Institute of Automatic Control BK Grant 02/010/BK18/0102 (BK/200/Rau1/2018) in the year 2019 for the second (Adam Galuszka) and third (Tomasz Grychowski) author. The analysis has been performed with the use of IT infrastructure of GeCONiI Upper Silesian Centre for Computational Science and Engineering (NCBiR grant no POIG.02.03.01-24-099/13).

References

1. Haymaker, J.R.: Opportunities for AI to improve sustainable building design processes. In: AAAI 2011 Spring Symposium on Artificial Intelligence and Sustainable Design (SS-11-02) (2011)
2. Migilinskas, D., Popov, V., Juocevicius, V., Ustinovichius, L.: The benefits, obstacles and problems of practical BIM implementation. In: 11th International Conference on Modern Building Materials, Structures and Techniques, MBMST (2013)
3. Czmoch, I., Pękała, A.: Traditional Design versus BIM Based Design. In: XXIII R-S-P seminar, Theoretical Foundation of Civil Engineering (23RSP) (2014)
4. Pietras, F., Wójcik, A.: Rozwój Building Information Modeling w Polsce. Badanie Antal. (2017). www.antal.pl
5. Autodesk, MillwardBrown: BIM – Polska Perspektywa. Raport z Badania (2015, in polish)
6. Ceranic, B., Nguyen T., Callaghan C.: Shape grammar and kinetic façade shading systems: a novel approach to climate adaptive building design with a real time performance evaluation. In: International Conference Geomapplica Geomatics, Remote Sensing and Earth Observation (2018)
7. Atila, U., Karas, I.R., Turan, M.K., Rahmand, A.A.: Design of an intelligent individual evacuation model for high rise building fires based on neural network within the scope Of 3d GIS. In: ISPRS Annals of the Photogrammetry, Remote Sensing and Spatial Information Sciences, Volume II-2/W1, ISPRS 8th 3DGeoInfo Conference and WG II/2 Workshop, Istanbul, Turkey (2013)
8. Rüppel, U., Schatz, K.: Designing a BIM-based serious game for fire safety evacuation simulations. Adv. Eng. Inform. **25**, 600–611 (2011)
9. Kumar, S.: Developing an experienced-based design review application for healthcare facilities using a 3D game engine. J. Inform. Technol. Constr. (ITcon). **16** 85–104 (2011). http://www.itcon.org/2011/6
10. Gilner, E.: Wykorzystanie sztucznej inteligencji w zrównoważonym projektowaniu budynków. In: Strategie 2019 (accepted book chapter in polish). Wydawnictwo Politechniki Śląskiej (2019)
11. Brown, D.: Artificial intelligence for design process improvement. In: Clarkson, W.J., Eckert, C. (eds.) Design Process Improvement A Review of Current Practice, pp. 158–173. Springer, Cambridge (2004). https://doi.org/10.1007/978-1-84628-061-0_7
12. Gałuszka, A., Pacholczyk, M., Bereska, D., Skrzypczyk, K.: Planning as artificial intelligence problem – short introduction and overview. In: Nawrat, A., Simek, K., Świerniak, A. (eds.) Advanced Technologies for Intelligent Systems of National Border Security, vol. 440, pp. 95–103. Springer, Heidelberg (2012). https://doi.org/10.1007/978-3-642-31665-4_8. ISBN 978-3-642-31664-7
13. Winch, G., Schneider, E.: The strategic management of architectural practice. Constr. Manag. Econ. **11**(6), 467–473 (1993). https://doi.org/10.1080/01446199300000052
14. Winch, G., Schneider, E.: Managing the knowledge-based organization: the case of architectural practice. J. Manage. Stud. **30**(06), 0022–2380 (1993)
15. Reddy, E.J., Shridhar, C., Rangadu, V.P.: Knowledge based engineering: notion, approaches and future trends. Am. J. Intell. Syst. **5**(1), 1–17 (2015). https://doi.org/10.5923/j.ajis.20150501.01

16. Singer, D., Bormann, A.: A novel knowledge-based engineering approach for infrastructure design. In: The Fourth International Conference on Soft Computing Technology in Civil, Structural and Environmental Engineering, Prague, Czech Republic (2015)

17. Flager F., Welle, B., Bansal, P., Soremekun, G., Haymaker, J.: Multidisciplinary process integration and design optimization of a classroom building. J. Inform. Technol. Constr. (ITcon) **14**, 595–612 (2009). http://www.itcon.org/2009/38

18. Estreicher, K. (młodszy): Historia sztuki w zarysie, Warszawa 1986. Państwowe Wydawnictwo Naukowe (1973)

19. Çekmis, A.: Fuzzy logic in architectural site planning design. In: 12th International Conference on Application of Fuzzy Systems and Soft Computing, ICAFS 2016, Vienna, Austria (2016)

20. Zemmouri, N., Schiller, M.E.: Application of fuzzy logic in interior daylight estimation. Rev. Energ. Ren. **8**, 55–62 (2005)

21. Ciftcioglu, O.: Design enhancement by fuzzy logic in architecture. In: The IEEE International Conference on Fuzzy Systems, 0-7803-7810-5/03/$17.00200 03. IEEE (2003)

22. Ciftcioglu, O., Durmisevic, S.: Fuzzy logic in architectural design. In: 2nd International Conference in Fuzzy Logic and Technology, Leicester, United Kingdom (2001)

23. Caldas, L.: GENE_ARCH: an evolution-based generative design system for sustainable architecture. In: Smith, I.F.C. (ed.) EG-ICE 2006. LNCS (LNAI), vol. 4200, pp. 109–118. Springer, Heidelberg (2006). https://doi.org/10.1007/11888598_12

24. Caldas, L.: Generation of energy-efficient patio houses: combining GENE_ARCH and a marrakesh medina shape grammar. In: Spring Symposium on Artificial Intelligence and Sustainable Design, AAAI 2011 (SS-11-02) (2011)

25. Caldas, L., Norford, L.K., Rocha, J.M.: An evolutionary model for sustainable design. In: AAAI 2011 Spring Symposium on Artificial Intelligence and Sustainable Design (SS-11-02) 2003). https://doi.org/10.1108/14777830310479450

26. Østergård, T.: Proactive building simulations for early design support: multi-actor decision-making basedon Monte Carlo simulations and global sensitivity analysis. Aalborg Universitetsforlag. Ph.D.-serien for Det Ingeniør- og Naturvidenskabelige Fakultet, Aalborg Universitet (2017). https://doi.org/10.5278/vbn.phd.eng.00017

27. Gałuszka, A., Krystek, J., Swierniak, A., Lungoci, C., Grzejszczak, T.: Information management in passenger traffic supporting system design as a multi-criteria discrete optimization task. Arch. Control Sci. **2017**(2), 229–238 (2017)

28. Rolfe Judd Architecture, CBRE: Modern Office Standard Polska (2016). www.mosp.pl

Information Systems and Technologies

Method of Comprehensive Estimation
of Natural and Anthropogenic Territory Safety
in the Case of Krasnoyarsk Region

Tatiana Penkova[1,2(✉)] and Anna Metus[1]

[1] Institute of Computational Modelling of the Siberian Branch of the Russian
Academy of Sciences, 50/44 Akademgorodok, Krasnoyarsk 660036, Russia
{penkova_t,metus}@icm.krasn.ru
[2] Siberian Federal University, 79 Svobodny pr., Krasnoyarsk 660041, Russia

Abstract. This paper presents a new technique of comprehensive analytical estimation of natural and anthropogenic territory safety based on the creation of a geographically-oriented safety standard and integral assessment of the state of environment and technosphere objects. The standard presents a normative model that provides a correct estimation of territory safety taking into account its individual characteristics. The basic elements and principles of territory safety standard creation are suggested in this paper. In order to estimate territory safety, the authors propose an algorithm to calculate the estimate of territory safety as an integral estimate of the comprehensive indicator based on the multidimensional estimates of the basic indicators using the results of on-line analytical processing of monitoring data. In contrast to existing methods, the proposed algorithm uses the ranges of the normative values and assesses the significance of indicators change relative to standard ranges, it allows us to regulate the velocity of estimates change when the actual values of the indicators deviate from the normative ranges. Also, the author's technique is oriented at forming the multidimensional estimates in the context of several observation points. Proposed solutions are described through their application to the territories of the Krasnoyarsk region.

Keywords: Prevention of emergencies ·
Estimation of natural and anthropogenic safety ·
Geographically-oriented standard · Territorial management

1 Introduction

Early prevention of natural and anthropogenic emergencies is a major factor for effective territory safety management [1–5]. To decrease the risk of emergencies one has to provide comprehensive monitoring of the current processes, adequate assessment of the state of territory safety and reasonable decision-making process. A lot of studies show that the management of territory safety should be carried out in two basic directions: operational and strategic control [6, 7]. The operational control provides permanent monitoring of parameters of the state of environment and technosphere objects, detection of preconditions for occurrence of emergencies; it is aimed at

© Springer Nature Switzerland AG 2019
S. Misra et al. (Eds.): ICCSA 2019, LNCS 11619, pp. 421–433, 2019.
https://doi.org/10.1007/978-3-030-24289-3_31

organising preventive measures to exclude some possible accidents or mitigate their consequences. In contrast, the strategic control is focused on reducing the overall risk in the territory; it provides collection, storage and comprehensive analysis of safety indicators; it is aimed at planning activities and developing management recommendations for risk reduction, improving the organisational structure of the subdivisions responsible for elimination of emergencies. To deal with the problems of increasing the safety of vital activity of the population and territories, the operational control systems are being actively introduced [8–10]. At present, online observation networks for potential sources of emergencies are created, weather and seismic stations are unfolded within the territory, different control sensors and video monitoring systems are being introduced at various facilities. Apart from the on-line monitoring tools, the theoretical research in the field of strategic control of the territory safety is also developed actively. In Russia as well as in the world, there are a large number of studies related to methods of risk analysis, current state assessment and emergency prediction. However, as usual, natural and technogenic processes are considered independently that makes it difficult to assess the situation comprehensively taking into account the influence of many factors [11]. Generally, three principal approaches are used to assess the state of territory safety. The first one, a probabilistic approach, makes it possible to calculate an estimate of the emergency risk by applying the mathematical models that link the presuppositions with a probability of event's occurrence. Methods of this type are used to calculate individual, collective and social risks and, as a rule, they are oriented to specific technical objects. Application of these methods to the territories requires the improvement of the regulatory base and significant adaptation of computational models. The second one, a statistical approach, allows for forming quantitative estimates based on data analysis for certain period of observation. Advantages of methods of this type include their objectivity, ability to investigate the dynamic of changes of the observed parameters and form the summary indicators. However, these methods cannot be used for rarely observed events, they do not allow to obtain the operational estimates of the current state and, moreover, do not give the possibility to interpret the quantitative estimates. The third one, a heuristic approach, allows for forming the qualitative assessments when the formal methods are too complicated and the initial database is insufficient to obtain a univocal analytical solution. In addition, application of methods of this type without analytical support leads to some errors of a subjective nature. Thus, the above considered confirms the topicality and necessity of the hybrid approach that makes it possible to have the comprehensive assessments of natural and technogenic territory safety taking into account the specific influence of risk factors on each other and their temporal development for the particular territory.

The outline of this paper is as follows: Sect. 1 contains the introduction. Section 2 describes the author's method of comprehensive analytical estimation of natural and anthropogenic territory safety. Creation of the safety standard is described here in detail using particular examples for Krasnoyarsk territories. Section 3 presents a new algorithm for calculation of integral estimation of the territory safety. Section 4 demonstrates some results of algorithm application. Conclusion comprises the basic outcomes and tasks for future research.

2 Comprehensive Estimation of Natural and Anthropogenic Territory Safety

2.1 The Object of Study

The Krasnoyarsk region is the second largest federal subject of Russia and the third largest subnational governing body by area in the world. The Krasnoyarsk region lies in the middle of Siberia and occupies an area of 2.4 million square kilometres, which is 13% of the country's total territory. This territory is characterised by a heightened level of natural and technogenic emergencies which is determined by social-economic aspects, large resource potential, geographical location and climatic conditions. According to the annual report of the Krasnoyarsk Ministry of Emergency [12, 13], in the territory there are many accident prone technosphere objects: 2 radiation-related objects; 45 chemically-dangerous objects; 89 fire-hazardous and dangerously explosive objects; almost 500 hydraulic facilities that have been in operation for more than 30 years; 9 critically important objects, a lot of survival objects including boiler plants, power plants, pipelines and networks. Moreover, the territory is located in seven climatic zones. A number of large-scale natural emergencies are recorded each year, namely: flood, forest fire, gale-strength wind, anomalously low temperature and snow avalanche.

Therefore, operational and strategic monitoring, as well as the estimation of the state of environment and technosphere objects, are extremely actual problems for Krasnoyarsk region. The solution of these issues should be based on a comprehensive consideration of risk factors taking into account the singularity of the territories and formation of an integral estimate of the state which can be detailed to identify abnormal situations.

2.2 The Technique of Comprehensive Estimation of Natural and Anthropogenic Territory Safety

The new technique of comprehensive estimation of natural and anthropogenic territory safety is based on creation of a geographically-oriented safety standard and integral assessment of the state of environment and technosphere objects [14].

Creation of the natural and anthropogenic territory safety standard – is a process of developing a geographically-oriented normative model that is required for correct estimation of the actual state of territory safety and presents the safety target level based on the individual characteristics of the territory and the real possibilities of its achievement [15]. The standard is developed by experts using federal, regional normative specifications and data analysis results [16]. Figure 1 presents the IDEF0 diagram of the standard creation process. IDEF0 model describes the functions (e.g. activities, actions, processes or operations); inputs and outputs as the data needed to perform the function and the data that is produced as a result of the function respectively; controls which constrain or govern the function and mechanisms which can be thought of as a person or device which performs the function.

Integral estimation of the state of natural and anthropogenic territory safety – is a process of calculating the integral estimate of the comprehensive indicator based on the

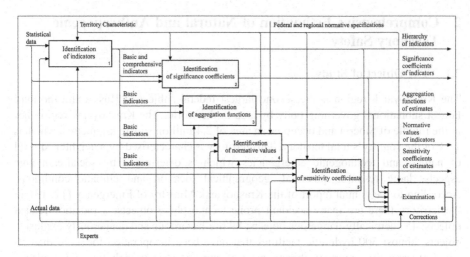

Fig. 1. IDEF0 diagram of creation of the natural and anthropogenic territory safety standard.

hierarchy of estimates of basic indicators using the results of on-line analytical processing of monitoring data. This process is performed by OLAP-system in accordance with the created standard and author's algorithm. Figure 2 presents the IDEF0 diagram of the territory safety estimation process.

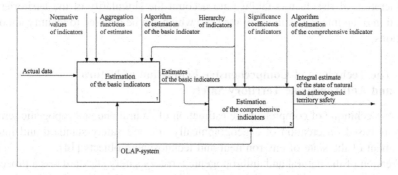

Fig. 2. IDEF0 diagram of integral estimation of the state of territory safety.

Creation of the Natural and Anthropogenic Territory Safety Standard. This process consists of the following basic stages:

- Identification of indicators
- Identification of significance coefficients
- Identification of aggregation function
- Identification of normative values
- Identification of sensitivity coefficients

Identification of indicators – is a process of forming the hierarchy of indicators that characterise the natural and anthropogenic risk factors for emergencies [17]. The hierarchy contains two types of indicators: the basic indicators – a set of primary statistical indicators that are formed by OLAP-models and present the lowest level of hierarchy, and the comprehensive indicators – a set of aggregation levels of basic indicators in accordance with monitoring fields that present the intermediate and upper levels of the hierarchy. Figure 3 shows an example of comprehensive indicators for territory safety control.

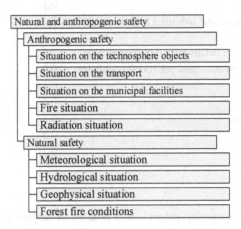

Fig. 3. An example of comprehensive indicators for territory safety control.

Identification of significance coefficients – is a process of calculating the relative weights (u_k) that characterise the contribution of the lower-level indicators of the hierarchy to the upper-level indicators $(u_k > 0, \sum u_k = 1)$. Significance coefficients are determined for each territory taking into account its physical, geographical and socio-economic characteristics. Table 1 presents an example of significance coefficients for two territories: for the municipal area in the central part of the region as a metropolis (Krasnoyarsk area) and for the municipal area with intensive mining of minerals in the northern part of the region (Turukhansky area).

Identification of aggregation function – is a process of determining the functions (f_{agr}^k) that provide a transition from multidimensional estimates (i.e. in the context of several observation points) to one-dimensional estimates (i.e. in the context of territory as a whole). The aggregation function (e.g. minimum, maximum, average) is determined by the trend (i.e. the level of safety increases the increase of decrease in the values of the indicators) and the qualitative features of indicators (i.e. the worst recorded value of indicator has a greater or lesser impact on the estimate of indicator). For example, the "average" aggregation function is signed for indicators of radiation and geophysical situations and the "maximum" aggregation function is signed for indicators of the meteorological and hydrological situations.

Table 1. An example of significance coefficients.

Indicator	Significance coefficients	
	Krasnoyarsk area	Turukhansky area
Anthropogenic safety	0.8	0.4
Situation on the technosphere objects	0.35	0.2
Situation on the transport	0.3	0.2
Situation on the municipal facilities	0.1	0.3
Fire situation	0.1	0.2
The number of household and industrial fires per 10,000 population	0.4	0.3
The number of fires with deaths per 10,000 population	0.3	0.3
The number of fires with casualties per 10000 population	0.3	0.4
Radiation situation	0.15	0.1
Natural safety	0.2	0.7
Meteorological situation	0.3	0.2
Hydrological situation	0.2	0.3
Geophysical situation	0.3	0.05
Forest fire conditions	0.2	0.45

Identification of normative values – is a process of determining the range of normative values of indicators taking into account their multidimensionality $\left(\left[N_j^k; Z_j^k \right] \right)$ The normative values of indicators characterise the normal state of safety using statistical data analysis results. The range of normative values is identified by statistical characteristics such as median (P_{jMe}^k) and standard deviation (σ_j^k) as follows [18]:

$$
\left[N_j^k; Z_j^k \right] = \begin{cases} \left[0; P_{jMe}^k + \sigma_j^k \right], & \text{if } P_{jMe}^k - \sigma_j^k < 0 \\ \left[P_{jMe}^k - \sigma_j^k; P_{jMe}^k + \sigma_j^k \right], & \text{if } P_{jMe}^k - \sigma_j^k > 0 \end{cases} \tag{1}
$$

For example, for Turukhansky area the normative rages of "Number of events Abnormally cold weather" indicator are the following: [0;4] for such points of observation as Bor, Vorogovo and Igarka; [1, 3] for such points of observation as Vereshchagino, Kureika and Turukhansk; [1, 2] for such points of observation as Svetlogorsk and Yanov Stan; [0;5] for Soviet Rechka; [0;3] for Verkhneimbatsk; [0;2] for Kellog.

Identification of sensitivity coefficients – is a process of determining the coefficients (q_k) that regulate the velocity of estimate change when the actual value of the indicator deviates from the normative value. The sensitivity coefficient takes the following values: $0 < q < 1$ when the velocity of estimate change should increase with the increase in the deviation of the actual indicator value from the normative; $q > 1$ when the velocity of estimate change should decrease with the increase in the deviation of the actual indicator value from the normative and $q = 1$ when the velocity of estimate change outside the normative should remain constant.

For example, for basic indicators of the fire situation there are the following values of sensitivity coefficients: $q = 0.3$ for "The number of fires with deaths per 10,000 population" indicator; $q = 0.8$ for "The number of fires with casualties per 10,000 population" indicator and $q = 1$ for "The number of household and industrial fires per 10,000 population" indicator.

The process of creating the safety standard is completed by an examination where experts can check the normative model by applying it to actual data and making the necessary corrections. The detailed technique of safety standard development, its principles, rules and normative values for the Krasnoyarsk region territories are presented in the work [15].

Integral Estimation of the State of Natural and Anthropogenic Territory Safety. This process consists of the following basic stages:

- Estimation of the basic indicators
- Estimation of the comprehensive indicators

Estimation of the basic indicators – is a process of calculating the multidimensional estimates of the basic indicators in the context of several observation points and aggregating these estimates across the territory in accordance with the set function. Estimates of the basic indicators characterise the correspondence of the actual values to the normative and allow for estimating the significance of indicators change relative to the standard range taking into account the indicators multidimensionality and estimates sensitivity. The calculation of multidimensional estimates is performed in the form of OLAP-models.

Estimation of the comprehensive indicators – is a process of calculating the integral estimates of the comprehensive indicators using estimates of the basic indicators and their significance coefficients.

Estimation of the basic and comprehensive indicators is performed by applying the safety standard in accordance with the proposed algorithm.

3 Algorithm of the Integral Estimation of the State of Natural and Anthropogenic Territory Safety

The algorithm of the integral estimation of the state of natural and anthropogenic territory safety presents the development of the author's method of wellbeing estimation [19, 20] with the addition of OLAP-models to the hierarchy of formation of the comprehensive indicator: the integral estimates are calculated on the basis of multidimensional estimates of indicators using the multidimensional normative values. In addition, the proposed algorithm takes into account the velocity of estimate change when the actual value of the indicator deviates from the normative value.

The integral estimate of the comprehensive indicator is calculated using the estimates of the basic indicators and their significance coefficients as follows:

$$\sum_I = \sum_{k=1}^{n} u_k I_K \tag{2}$$

where $I_\sum$ – is an integral estimate of the comprehensive indicator; I_k – is an estimate of k-th basic indicator; u_k – is a significance coefficient of k-th indicator set in the standard; n – is a number of indicators at the same level of the hierarchy.

The estimate of the basic indicator is calculated as an aggregation of the multidimensional estimates of the indicator as follows:

$$I_k = f_{agr}^k \left(i_1^k, \ldots, i_m^k \right) \tag{3}$$

where $i_j^k, j \in \{1 \ldots m\}$ – is a multidimensional estimate k-th basic indicator calculated in j-th observation point; f_{agr}^k – is an aggregation function for k-th basic indicator set in the standard.

The multidimensional estimates of the basic indicator are calculated in the form of OLAP-model and characterise the compliance of the actual values to the normative in the context of individual observation points. The multidimensional estimates are calculated as follows:

$$i_j^k = 1 + \Delta P_j^k S_j^k \tag{4}$$

where $S_j^k = \pm 1$ – is a coefficient which reflects the trend of k-th indicator, $S_j^k = 1$ when the safety state is improving with an increase in the value of the indicator, $S_j^k = -1$ when the safety state is improving with a decrease in the value of the indicator; ΔP_j^k – is a compliance coefficient of actual values of k-th indicator with normative in j-th observation point.

Compliance coefficient is calculated by:

$$\Delta P_j^k = \begin{cases} 0, & \text{if } P_j^k \in \left[N_j^k; Z_j^k \right] \\ \left(\dfrac{P_j^k - Z_j^k}{Z_j^k - N_j^k} \right)^{qk}, & \text{if } P_j^k > Z_j^k \\ -\left(\dfrac{N_j^k - P_j^k}{Z_j^k - N_j^k} \right)^{qk}, & \text{if } P_j^k < N_j^k \end{cases} \tag{5}$$

where q_k – is a sensitivity coefficient of estimate for k-th indicator set in the standard; $\left[N_j^k; Z_j^k \right]$ – is a range of normative values for k-th indicator in j-th observation point set in the standard; N_j^k – is a lower limit of the range; Z_j^k – is an upper limit of the range; P_j^k – is an actual value of k-th indicator in j-th observation point.

In the case when the actual value of indicator falls within the range, the compliance coefficient $\Delta P_j^k = 0$; In the case when the actual value of indicator is above the upper limit of the range, the compliance coefficient has a positive value $\Delta P_j^k > 0$; In case when the actual value of indicator is below the lower limit of the range, the compliance coefficient has a negative value $\Delta P_j^k < 0$. The value of the coefficient ΔP_j^k in combination with the value of the coefficient S_j^k makes it possible to obtain a quantitative estimate of the indicator. As a result, the value of estimate can be identified as $i_j^k > 1$ that demonstrates a significant improvement of indicator.

Thus, the generated hierarchy of estimates allows for obtaining comprehensive quantitative characteristics of the state of territory safety, performing a comparative analysis with other territories and, if necessary, detailing the estimates for particular monitoring fields and indicators that give us the opportunity to identify the underlying causes of the current state. In contrast to the existing approaches, the proposed solution allows for calculating geographically-oriented estimates. The algorithm calculates integral estimates based on multi-dimensional estimates of indicators using the multidimensional normative values and takes into account the velocity of estimate change when the actual value of the indicator deviates from the normative value.

4 Application of the Algorithm for Integral Estimation of the State of Natural and Anthropogenic Territory Safety

Let us consider the example of integral estimation of "Fire situation" comprehensive indicator for the Krasnoyarsk area that consists of two subareas (i.e. two points of observation): Krasnoyarsk city and Peschanka village (Table 2).

At the first stage, we calculate the estimates of the basic indicators, namely, the multidimensional estimates in the context of the two observation points (i.e. Krasnoyarsk city and Peschanka village), and then we aggregate them for the Krasnoyarsk area as a whole. Previously, we calculated the compliance coefficient according to Formula 5. As can be seen from Table 2, the actual values of indicators in Krasnoyarsk city are above the upper limits of the normative ranges, therefore, the compliance coefficient is calculated according to the second condition; the actual values of indicators in Peschanka village are below the lower limits of the ranges, therefore, the compliance coefficient is calculated according to the third condition. Thus, for "The number of household and industrial fires per 10,000 population" indicator in Krasnoyarsk city the compliance coefficient is identified as: $\Delta P_{11} = ((3.721 - 2.52)/(2.52)^1 = 0.48$; in Peschanka village the compliance coefficient is identified as: $\Delta P_{12} = ((1.882 - 1.346)/(7.54 - 1.880)^1 = -0.09$. Taking into account the indicators trends, the estimate in Krasnoyarsk city is identified as: $i_{11} = 1 + 1.48 \cdot (-1) = 0.52$; the estimate in Peschanka village is identified as: $i_{12} = 1 + (-0.09)(-1) = 1.09$. Analogically, we calculate the estimates for other indicators as follows: $i_{21} = 0.44$; $i_{22} = 2.38$; $i_{31} = 0.43$ and $i_{32} = 1.84$. The aggregation of the multidimensional estimates for considered indicators is defined by the "minimum" function (i.e. by the worst value recorded in observation points). Thus, the estimate of "The number of household and industrial fires per 10,000 population" indicator is $i_1 = \min(0.52; 1.09) = 0.52$. The estimates of "The number of fires with casualties per 10000 population" and "The number of fires with deaths per 10,000 population" indicators are $i_2 = 0.44$ and $i_3 = 0.43$ respectively.

Table 2. Example of integral estimation of "Fire situation" comprehensive indicator for Krasnoyarsk area.

Indicators/Observation points	Significance coefficient, u_k	Sensitivity coefficient, q_k	Lower limit of normative range, N_j^k	Upper limit of normative range, Z_j^k	Actual value, P_j^k	Estimate, $I_{\sum}, I_k, i_j^k$
Fire situation	0.12	–	–	–	–	0.47
1. The number of household and industrial fires per 10,000 population	0.4	–	–	–	–	0.52
1.1 Krasnoyarsk city	–	1.0	0	2.520	3.721	0.52
1.2 Peschanka village	–	1.0	1.882	7.540	1.346	1.09
2. The number of fires with deaths per 10,000 population	0.3	–	–	–	–	0.44
2.1 Krasnoyarsk city	–	0.8	0.005	0.041	0.058	0.44
2.2 Peschanka village	–	0.8	1.103	1.839	0	2.38
3. The number of fires with casualties per 10000 population	0.3	–	–	–	–	0.43
3.1 Krasnoyarsk city	–	0.3	0.012	0.036	0.039	0.43
3.2 Peschanka village	–	0.3	0.755	2.115	0	1.84

At the second stage, we calculate the integral estimate of the "Fire situation" comprehensive indicator for the Krasnoyarsk area based on significance coefficients of basic indicators as follows: $I_{Fire} = 0.4 \cdot 0.52 + 0.3 \cdot 0.44 + 0.3 \cdot 0.43 = 0.47$.

In accordance with the described algorithm, the integral estimates of all comprehensive indicators for the Krasnoyarsk area have been calculated. For anthropogenic safety indicators we have the following estimates: $I_{TechObj} = 1.23$, $I_{Transp} = 1.0$, $I_{MunFacil} = 0.43$, $I_{Rad} = 1.0$. For natural safety indicators we have the following estimates: $I_{Meteo} = 1.17, I_{Hydro} = 1.0, I_{GeoPhys} = 1.0, I_{ForestFire} = 1.05$. Integral estimates of the comprehensive indicators of higher level are calculated on the basis of significance coefficients of the comprehensive indicators of lower level as follows: $I_{Anthr} = 0.97$, $I_{Natur} = 1.06$, $I_{NaturAnthr} = 0.99$. Estimation results show that the worst situation in Krasnoyarsk municipal area is observed for such indicators as "Fire situation" with $I_{Fire} = 0.47$ and "Situation on the municipal facilities" with $I_{MunFacil} = 0.43$, that require more careful study, special actions and measures aimed at improving the state of safety for this territory. However, the remaining indicators demonstrate the very good level of anthropogenic and natural safety. Moreover, some of them, such as "Situation on the technosphere objects" with $I_{TechObj} = 1.23$, "Meteorological situation" with $I_{Meteo} = 1.17$ and "Forest fire conditions" with $I_{ForestFire} = 1.05$ show the significant improvement of safety according to normative values. As a result, we can see high values of estimates for comprehensive indicators and high level of safety state in general Krasnoyarsk municipal area.

The integral estimates of comprehensive indicators for all territories of the Krasnoyarsk region have been calculated similarly. Figure 4 represents the visualization of the integral estimation results on the geographic map. On this map, the green colour

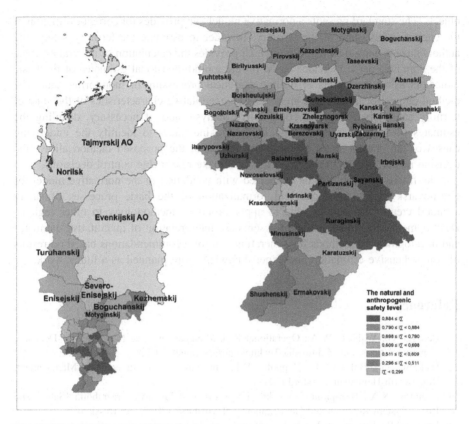

Fig. 4. Visualization of the integral estimation of the state of natural and antropogenic safety for territories of Krasnoyarsk region. (Color figure online)

corresponds to the high values of the integral estimate, the yellow colour corresponds to the mean values of integral estimate and the red colour corresponds to the low values of integral estimates.

As can be seen, the best state of natural and anthropogenic safety is observed in central and northern groups of areas, including such cities as Yeniseisk, Lesosibirsk, Krasnoyarsk, as well as areas of Balakhta, Sukhobuzimsky and Kazachinsky. The worst state of the territory safety is observed in Nizhneingashsky area and Minusinsk city. The implementation of the proposed method gives the authority to control the state of safety of the territories, to detect the risk factors of the municipal areas and to form the basis for reasonable decision making.

5   Conclusion

This paper presents the method of comprehensive estimation of natural and anthropogenic territory safety that includes creation of the geographically-oriented safety standard and integral assessment of the state of the environment and technosphere objects. The standard presents a normative model that provides for correct estimation of the current safety state of the territory. In order to estimate the territory safety, the authors have proposed an algorithm which provides the calculation of integral estimate of the comprehensive indicator based on the multidimensional estimates of the basic indicators using the results of on-line analytical processing of monitoring data. The method allows for obtaining comprehensive quantitative characteristics of the state of territory safety, performing a comparative analysis and, if necessary, detailing the estimates for particular monitoring fields and indicators to identify the underlying causes of the current state. The implementation of the proposed method allows the decision maker to detect the risk factors and make reasonable control decisions.

The future research will be connected with validation of the normative model for Krasnoyarsk region territories and formalization of the basic processes of safety standard creation to will be able to apply proposed methodology to other regions. Development of estimation scale for semantic interpretation of quantitative estimates and development of methods for generating control recommendations based on results of comprehensive estimation and expert knowledge are planned as a future work.

References

1. Beroggi. G., Wallace, W.A.: Operational Risk Management: The Integration of Decision, Communications and Multimedia Technologies. Springer (2012)
2. Haddow, G., Bullock, J., Coppola, D.P.: Introduction to Emergency Management. Butterworth-Heinemann, Oxford (2017)
3. Mahutov, N.A.: Bezopasnost' i riski: sistemnyye issledovaniya i razrabotki [Safety and Risks: System Research and Development], Novosibirsk (2017). (in Russian)
4. Bolov, V.R., Bogotyrev, E.Ya., Bykov, A.A., et al.: Sovremennyye sistemy monitoringa i prognozirovaniya chrezvychaynykh situatsiy [Modern monitoring and forecasting system of emergencies], Moscow (2013). (in Russian)
5. Osipov, V.I., Larionov, V.I., Burova, V.N., Frolova, N.I., Sushchev, S.P.: Methodology of natural risk assessment in Russia. Nat. Hazards **88**, 17–41 (2017). https://doi.org/10.1007/s11069-017-2780-z
6. Yamalov, I.U.: Modelirovaniye protsessov upravleniya i prinyatiya resheniy v usloviyakh chrezvychaynykh situatsiy [Modeling of management and decision-making processes in emergency situations], Moscow (2013). (in Russian)
7. Moskvichev, V.V., Bychkov, I.V., Potapov, V.P., Taseiko, O.V., Shokin, Yu.I.: Informatsionnaya sistema territorial'nogo upravleniya riskami razvitiya i bezopasnost'yu [Information system for territorial risk and safety management development]. Vestnik RAN [Herald of the Russian Academy of Sciences], N 8, vol. 87, pp. 696–705 (2017). (in Russian)
8. Faleev, M.I., Malyshev V.P., Makiev Yu.D., et al.: Ranneye preduprezhdeniye o chrezvychaynykh situatsiyakh [Early prevention of emergencies] (2015). (in Russian)
9. Penkova, T., Nicheporchuk, V., Metus, A.: Comprehensive operational control of the natural and anthropogenic territory safety based on analytical indicators. In: Polkowski, L., Yao, Y., Artiemjew, P., Ciucci, D., Liu, D., Ślęzak, D., Zielosko, B. (eds.) IJCRS 2017, Part I. LNCS (LNAI), vol. 10313, pp. 263–270. Springer, Cham (2017). https://doi.org/10.1007/978-3-319-60837-2_22

10. Penkova, T.G., Korobko, A.V., Nicheporchuk, V.V., Nozhenkova, L.F.: On-line modelling and assessment of the state of technosphere and environment objects based on monitoring data. Procedia Comput. Sci. **35**, 156–165 (2014). https://doi.org/10.1016/j.procs.2014.08. 095. 18th Annual Conference on Knowledge-Based and Intelligent Information & Engineering Systems
11. Metus, A.M.: Aktual'nyye zadachi kompleksnogo otsenivaniya prirodno-tekhnogennoy bezopasnosti territorii [Actual issues for comprehensive estimation of natural and technogenic safety of the territory]. Molodoy uchenyy [Young scientist] **11**, 89–92 (2015). (in Russian)
12. Gosudarstvennyy doklad o sostoyanii zashchity naseleniya i territoriy Krasnoyarskogo kraya ot chrezvychaynykh situatsiy prirodnogo i tekhnogennogo kharaktera: Glavnoye upravleniye MCHS Rossii po Krasnoyarskomu krayu [The State of Natural and Anthropogenic Emergencies Protection of Territory and Population in the Krasnoyarsk Region. Annual Report of Ministry of Emergency], Krasnoyarsk (2018). (in Russian)
13. Moskvichev, V.V., Shokin, Yu.I.: Antropogennyye i prirodnyye riski na territorii Sibiri [Anthropogenic and natural risks on the territory of Siberia]. Vestnik RAN [Herald of the Russian Academy of Sciences], N 2, vol. 82, pp. 131–140 (2012). (in Russian)
14. Penkova T.G., Metus A.M.: Kontseptual'naya model' integral'nogo analiticheskogo otsenivaniya prirodno-tekhnogennoy bezopasnosti territorii [Conceptual model of integral analytical estimation of natural and technogenic territory safety]. Informatizatsiya i svyaz' [Informatization and communication], N 2, pp. 65–71 (2016). (in Russian)
15. Nicheporchuk, V., Penkova, T., Metus, A.: Formirovaniye standarta prirodno-tekhnogennoy bezopasnosti territoriy Krasnoyarskogo kraya [Formation of the standard of natural and technogenic safety of the Krasnoyarsk territory]. Problemy bezopasnosti i chrezvychaynykh situatsiy [Safety and emergencies problems], N 2, pp. 41–52 (2018). (in Russian)
16. Penkova, T.: Analysis of natural and technogenic safety of the Krasnoyarsk region based on data mining techniques. In: Link, S., Trujillo, J.C. (eds.) ER 2016. LNCS, vol. 9975, pp. 102–112. Springer, Cham (2016). https://doi.org/10.1007/978-3-319-47717-6_9
17. Nicheporchuk, V., Penkova, T.: Sistema analiticheskikh pokazateley dlya strategicheskogo kontrolya prirodno-tekhnogennoy bezopasnosti territoriy [The system of analytical indicators for strategic control of the natural and technogenic territory safety]. Problemy analiza riska [Issues of risk analysis], N 1, vol. 15. pp. 70–77 (2018). (in Russian)
18. Glantz S.A. Primer of Biostatistics (1999)
19. Penkova, T.: Decision making support technique based on territory wellbeing estimation. In: Neves-Silva, R., Jain, L.C., Howlett, R.J. (eds.) Intelligent Decision Technologies. SIST, vol. 39, pp. 513–523. Springer, Cham (2015). https://doi.org/10.1007/978-3-319-19857-6_44
20. Penkova, T.: Method of wellbeing estimation in territory management. In: Murgante, B., et al. (eds.) ICCSA 2014, Part IV. LNCS, vol. 8582, pp. 57–68. Springer, Cham (2014). https://doi.org/10.1007/978-3-319-09147-1_5

Investigation of the Hydraulic Unit Operation Features Based on Vibration System Data Mining

Tatiana Penkova[1,2(✉)] and Anna Korobko[1]

[1] Institute of Computational Modelling, Siberian Branch of the Russian Academy of Sciences, 50/44 Akademgorodok, Krasnoyarsk 660036, Russia
Penkova_t@icm.krasn.ru
[2] Siberian Federal University, 79 Svobodny pr., 660041 Krasnoyarsk, Russia

Abstract. The software and hardware level used for on-line monitoring of the hydropower equipment functioning parameters as well as the large amounts of stored data create the necessary conditions for application of innovative methods and technologies of data analysis in the tasks of analytical assessment of equipment condition. This paper presents the results of detecting the operational patterns of the hydraulic unit in various modes and functioning conditions based on the data mining techniques – principal component analysis and cluster analysis – applied to the monitoring data of the vibration control system. In multidimensional data space, two principal components have been selected and interpreted taking into account the contribution of the data attributes to the principal components. On the plane of the first two principal components, a five-cluster structure has been constructed to define the moments of time when the system demonstrates a characteristic behaviour. In addition, the monitored parameters have been analysed in terms of time series at characteristic moments of time. As a result, the comprehensive multidimensional analysis of monitoring data has allowed us to discover the hydraulic unit operation patterns and dependencies, determine the character of the influence induced by its constructive elements and work out the ratio between the ranges of key parameters in various modes of equipment operation.

Keywords: Multi-dimensional data analysis · Principal component analysis · Cluster analysis · Vibration control system · Hydropower equipment · Estimation of technical condition

1 Introduction

Modern requirements for cost-effective maintenance of equipment dictate the need to shift from scheduled preventive maintenance to maintenance and repair of equipment based on its technical condition [1–4]. At present, the guidelines in the field of hydroelectric power plants establish monitoring requirements for the state of hydropower equipment during operation and determine the rules and procedure for forming an integral assessment of the technical condition of the main equipment [5, 6]. The level of software and hardware used for on-line monitoring of the functioning parameters of

© Springer Nature Switzerland AG 2019
S. Misra et al. (Eds.): ICCSA 2019, LNCS 11619, pp. 434–446, 2019.
https://doi.org/10.1007/978-3-030-24289-3_32

hydropower equipment, as well as the large amounts of accumulated data, create the necessary conditions for application of innovative methods and technologies of data analysis in the tasks of the analytical assessment of equipment condition without interruptions in its operation [7]. This work is aimed at detecting and studying the operational patterns of the hydraulic unit in various modes and conditions by considering the mutual influence of functional elements based on the application of principal component analysis and cluster analysis to the monitoring data of the vibration control system. Principal component analysis (PCA) is one of the most common techniques used to describe variation patterns in multidimensional data and one of the simplest and most robust ways of doing dimensionality reduction. PCA is a mathematical procedure that uses an orthogonal transformation to convert a set of observations of possibly correlated variables into a set of values of linearly uncorrelated variables called principal components [8]. Cluster analysis is a tool for discovering and identifying associations and structure within the data. Cluster analysis provides insight into the data by dividing the dataset of objects into groups (i.e. clusters) of objects, so that objects in a cluster are more similar to each other than to objects in other clusters [9]. Data mining techniques provide an effective tool for discovering previously unknown, nontrivial, practically useful and interpreted knowledge needed to make decisions [10].

This paper presents a comprehensive multi-dimensional analysis of monitoring data of the vibration control system for one of the hydraulic units of the Hydroelectric Power Station for the period from 25 June 2015 to 15 September 2015. In multidimensional data space, two principal components were selected and interpreted taking into account the contribution of the data attributes to the principal components. On the plane of the first two principal components, a five-cluster structure was constructed to define the moments of time when the system demonstrates a characteristic behaviour. In addition, the monitored parameters were analysed in terms of time series at characteristic moments of time. As a result, the comprehensive analysis of monitoring data allowed us to discover patterns and dependencies in the hydraulic unit operation, determine the character of the influence induced by its constructive elements and work out the ratio between the ranges of key parameters in various modes of equipment operation. Within this research, the analysis and visualisation of multidimensional data were conducted using the ViDaExpert tools [11].

The outline of this paper is as follows: Sect. 1 contains the introduction. Section 2 describes the original monitoring data. Section 3 presents the results of the multidimensional analysis of vibration monitoring data. Subsection 3.1 presents the results of the principal component analysis: identification and interpretation of principal components. Subsection 3.2 presents the results of cluster analysis: construction of the five-cluster structure and detailed analysis of data distribution on the clusters considering the values of key parameters. Section 4 contains the conclusions..

2 Monitoring Data Description

According to the theory of multi-dimensional data analysis, the original data are represented as a set of objects and a set of attributes. The set of objects contains the moments of time in the hydraulic unit operation throughout three months (i.e. from

07:00 am 25 June 2015 to 11:00 pm 15 September 2015) aggregated by hour. The set of attributes contains the parameters registered by Automated Control System of Technological Processes and Vibration Control System. Controlled parameters are measured by sensors located on the equipment on the left bank and on the downstream side. Data attributes are listed in Table 1.

Table 1. List of the data attributes.

No	Attribute	Description
1	A_POWER	Active power, MW
2	R_POWER	Reactive power, MW
3	RV_GB_DS	Relative vibration of the generator bearing (downstream, radially), μm
4	RV_GB_LB	Relative vibration of the generator bearing (left bank, radially), μm
5	RV_HB_DS	Relative vibration of the heel of the thrust bearing (downstream, vertically), μm
6	RV_HB_LB	Relative vibration of the heel of the thrust bearing (left bank, vertically), μm
7	RV_TB_DS	Relative vibration of the turbine bearing (downstream, radially), μm
8	RV_TB_LB	Relative vibration of the turbine bearing (left bank, radially), μm
9	AV_GB_DS	Absolute vibration of the generator bearing (downstream, radially), μm
10	AV_GB_LB	Absolute vibration of the generator bearing (left bank, radially), μm
11	AV_FH_DS	Absolute vibration of the heel of the thrust bearing (downstream, vertically), μm
12	AV_FH_LB	Absolute vibration of the heel of the thrust bearing (left bank, vertically), μm
13	AV_TB_DS	Absolute vibration of the turbine bearing (downstream, radially), μm
14	AV_TB_LB	Absolute vibration of the turbine bearing (left bank, radially), μm

Original dataset was analysed to identify preliminary correlation. The correlation coefficients between attributes are shown in Table 2. The results of correlation analysis demonstrated a strong linear relationship between the paired parameters (i.e. parameters measured by sensors on the same functional element on different sides). Since it is impractical to consider both parameters in the pair, the analysis is performed for parameters registered by sensors on the left bank. Within the analysed attributes, active power is a regulated parameter that is determined by the power generation plan.

The results of correlation analysis allow us to detect the following dependencies. Active power significantly affects the relative vibration of the heel of the thrust bearing (A_POWER ~ RV_HB_LB) and relative vibration of the turbine bearing (A_POWER ~ RV_TB_LB). At the same time, the values of relative vibration of the heel of the thrust bearing and the turbine bearing are strongly related to each other (RV_HB_LB ~ RV_TB_LB). An inverse relationship is observed between active power and both relative and absolute vibration of the generator bearing (A_POWER ~ -RV_GB_LB, A_POWER ~ -AV_GB_LB). The values of relative and absolute vibration of the generator bearing are also strongly interconnected

Table 2. Correlation coefficients between attributes.

No	2	3	4	5	6	7	8	9	10	11	12	13	14
1	**-0.72**	**-0.72**	**-0.79**	**0.80**	**0.76**	**0.80**	**0.79**	**-0.92**	**-0.88**	-0.01	-0.03	-0.50	0.15
2		0.71	**0.78**	-0.55	-0.46	-0.56	-0.57	0.71	0.65	0.10	0.14	0.51	0.26
3			**0.97**	-0.27	-0.22	-0.35	-0.34	**0.86**	**0.86**	0.26	0.32	0.33	0.06
4				-0.40	0.33	-0.47	-0.47	**0.89**	**0.87**	0.21	0.26	0.46	0.11
5					**0.99**	**0.95**	**0.95**	-0.54	-0.48	0.09	0.11	-0.48	0.11
6						**0.93**	**0.93**	-0.49	-0.44	0,05	0.08	-0.42	0.19
7							**0.99**	-0.55	-0.48	-0.08	-0.04	-0.59	-0.10
8								-0.54	-0.47	-0.07	-0.03	-0.62	-0.12
9									**0.99**	0.15	0.20	0.23	0.35
10										0.17	0.23	0.18	0.31
11											**0.99**	0.39	-0.18
12												0.32	-0.23
13													0.47

(RV_GB_LB ~ AV_GB_LB). Moreover, a strong inverse relationship is observed between active and reactive power (A_POWER ~ -R_POWER). Correlation analysis of the initial data has allowed us to establish the presence of relations between key parameters, determine the strength of their influence on each other and figure out the general characteristic patterns of the system.

3 Multi-dimensional Analysis of Vibration Monitoring Data

3.1 Principal Component Analysis

In order to apply the multi-dimensional data analysis, we formed a dataset which contains 1229 objects and 8 attributes. The principal component analysis was implemented to reduce the dimension of multi-dimensional space and identify patterns in the structure of multi-dimensional data. In general, the method allows identifying k components based on k initial attributes. Table 3 shows the results of calculating the eigenvectors of the covariance matrix arranged in order of descending eigenvalues.

The combination of Kaiser's rule and the Broken-stick model [12] helped to identify four principal components (PC1, PC2, PC3 and PC4). Figure 1 illustrates the eigenvalues of components. As Fig. 1 shows, Kaiser's rule determines one principal component – eigenvalue of the first component is significantly greater than the average value; the Broken-stick model gives four principal components – the line of Broken-stick model cuts off the eigenvalues of first four components.

The nature of the principal components is described by the weights of the attributes (i.e. eigenvalues) presented in Table 3. We can see that the first principal component (PC1) is characterised by a significant positive contribution of active power, relative vibration of the heel of the thrust bearing and the turbine bearing and a significant negative contribution of absolute and relative vibration of the generator bearing and reactive power. Obviously, the first component demonstrates all strong relations identified at the stage of correlation analysis. The second principal component (PC2) is

Table 3. Results of principal component calculation.

Components	1	2	3	4	5	6	7	8
Eigenvalues	0.543	0.192	0.137	0.091	0.027	0.008	0.002	0.001
Accumulated dispersion	0.543	0.734	0.871	0.962	0.989	0.997	0.999	1.000
1　A_POWER	**0.466**	0.128	0.072	0.007	0.219	0.294	0.755	0.238
2　R_POWER	**−0.394**	0.225	0.061	−0.388	0.788	−0.058	−0.041	0.121
3　RV_GB_LB	**−0.406**	0.254	−0.287	−0.237	−0.296	0.727	0.073	−0.103
4　RV_HB_LB	**0.362**	**0.359**	**−0.373**	**−0.307**	−0.160	−0.118	−0.341	0.592
5　RV_TB_LB	**0.393**	0.148	**−0.482**	−0.194	0.197	−0.105	−0.014	−0.710
6　AV_GB_LB	**−0.413**	0.038	**−0.453**	0.015	−0.202	−0.540	0.530	0.096
7　AV_FH_LB	**−0.413**	**0.585**	−0.123	**0.768**	0.180	0.041	−0.117	0.001
8　AV_TB_LB	−0.074	**0.612**	**0.563**	−0.269	−0.325	−0.253	0.109	−0.234

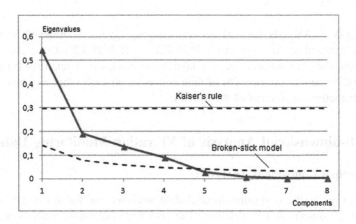

Fig. 1. Eigenvalues of components.

characterised by a significant positive contribution of absolute vibration of the heel of the thrust bearing and the turbine bearing as well as a positive contribution of relative vibration of the heel of the thrust bearing. The third principal component (PC3) is characterised by a significant positive contribution of absolute vibration of the turbine bearing, a significant negative contribution of relative vibration of the turbine bearing, absolute vibration of the generator bearing and negative contribution of relative vibration of the heel of the thrust bearing. The fourth principal component is charac-terised by a significant positive contribution of absolute vibration of the heel of the thrust bearing and negative contribution of reactive power. Taking into account the high information content of the first and second main components in the data structure (73% of accumulated dispersion), the further multi-dimensional analysis and interpretation of its results are performed in the context of the first two principal components.

3.2   Cluster Analysis

In order to identify the structure and discover patterns within the data, the cluster analysis was performed using the common centroid-based clustering method k-means. The k-means clustering is done by minimizing the sum of squares of distances between data and the corresponding cluster centroid. For k-means method, the most important and difficult question is the identification of the number of clusters that should be considered. In this study, the number of clusters was determined through the PCA technique: the number of clusters that depend on the number of principal components. Thus, referring back to the previous section, four principal components form the five-cluster structure (k = 5). The results of the clustering of the studied multi-dimensional dataset on the PCA plot are presented in Fig. 2.

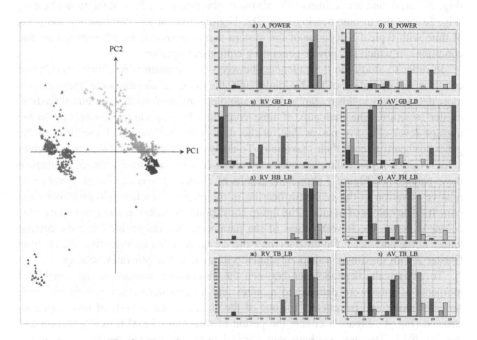

Fig. 2. Five-cluster data structure. (Color figure online)

The analysed objects are divided into three large groups that are characterised by low, medium and high values of active power. In the largest group, where high values of active power are observed, additional three clusters stand out by the values of vibrations. Thus, the five-cluster data structure includes: Cluster 1 (blue) – 24 objects, Cluster 2 (green) – 349 objects, Cluster 3 (light blue) – 114 objects, Cluster 4 (yellow) – 415 objects and Cluster 5 (red) – 327 objects.

The data distribution as per the clusters in terms of parameters is presented in Fig. 2 as a set of histograms. Cluster 1 (blue) (2% of data) differs from other clusters, it is characterised by low values of active power (appr. 120 MW, Fig. 2a) and all other parameters that correspond to the moments when the hydraulic unit is stopped or started. Cluster 2 (green) (28% of data) is characterised by average values of power activity (appr. 215 MW, Fig. 2a) and rather high values of other parameters including maximum values of absolute and relative vibration of the generator bearing (Fig. 2c and d). Cluster 3 (light blue) (9% of data) is characterised by maximum values of active power (appr. 430 MW, Fig. 2a) and maximum values of absolute vibration of the heel of the thrust bearing support and the turbine bearing (Fig. 2e and h). Cluster 4 (yellow) (34% of data) is characterised by close to maximum values of active power (appr. 415 MW, Fig. 2a), maximum values of relative vibration of the turbine bearing (Fig. 2g) and close to minimum values of absolute and relative vibration of the generator bearing (Fig. 2c and d). Cluster 5 (red) (27% of data) is characterized by high values of active power (appr. 400 MW, Fig. 2a), minimum values of reactive power (Fig. 2b), minimum values of absolute and relative vibration of the generator bearing (Fig. 2c and d) and low values of the absolute vibration of the heel of the thrust bearing (Fig. 2e) and the turbine bearing (Fig. 2h). Highlighted clusters combine the moments of time with typical behaviour of the system that corresponds to different modes and conditions in which the power generating equipment operates.

In order to study the dependencies between the parameters in certain modes and conditions of operation of the hydraulic unit, the obtained clusters were analysed in a more detailed way in this research. As an example, consider Cluster 2 (green) of the five-cluster structure. The moments of time combined by this cluster correspond to the average level of active power, but, at the same time, the values of vibration of the generator bearing reach their maximum. To analyse the nature of the system behaviour at high values of particular parameters the data were clustered over a range of values of these parameters. Figure 3 shows the results of clustering over the range of values of relative vibration of the generator bearing in the plane of the first two principal components. The colour of points in the figure corresponds to a certain range of values: blue colour indicates the lowest values of the parameter, red colour indicates the highest values of the parameter. On the data map, there is an area that includes five objects from Cluster 2 with maximum values of relative vibration of the generator bearing.

To analyse the dependencies between the monitoring parameters, the considered moments of time were detailed to minutes and a comparative diagram for the time series of monitored parameters for one of the characteristic periods of time was constructed (Fig. 4). Figure 4 covers the period of time from 19:00 h to 22:00 h on 21st August 2015. The area marked with vertical lines depicts one of the characteristic periods of time from 20:00 h to 21:00 h when the values of relative vibration of the generator bearing (RV_GB_LB) are at their maximum. As Fig. 4 shows, a change in active power at the upper limit of average values and an increase in reactive power lead to an increase in relative vibration of the generator bearing (RV_GB_LB) (appr. 60%) and a significant increase in absolute vibration of the heel of the thrust bearing (AV_FH_LB) (appr. 45%) and absolute vibration of the turbine bearing (AV_TB_LB) (appr. 17%), however the values of absolute vibration of the generator bearing (AV_GB_LB) remain unchanged. Apart from this, in the considered period, there is an increase in the relative vibration of the heel of the thrust bearing (RV_HB_LB) and the turbine bearing (RV_TB_LB). This behaviour was observed mainly in the evening from 19:00 h to 22:00 h with the duration of not more than one hour per day in the second half of August.

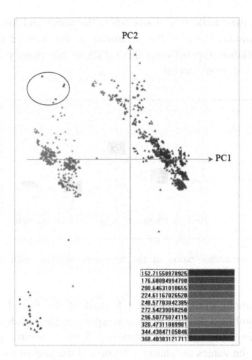

Fig. 3. Results of clustering over the range of values of relative vibration of the generator bearing (RV_GB_LB) on the PCA plot. (Color figure online)

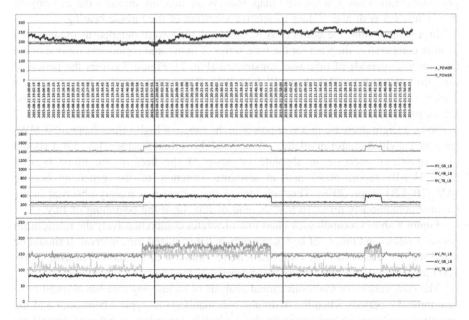

Fig. 4. Diagram of comparing the time series of monitored parameters at the moments with high values of RV_GB_LB.

Figure 5 shows the candlestick charts where the upper and lower shadows set the minimum and maximum value of the parameter in the original dataset. This graph demonstrates the relationship between the values of the main parameters and their ranges in the analyzed time interval.

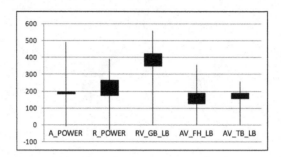

Fig. 5. Diagram of parameter ratios in the moments of time with maximum values of RV_GB_LB.

As another example, consider Cluster 5 (red) of the five-cluster structure. The moments of time combined by this cluster correspond to the high level of active power, but, at the same time, the values of vibration of the generator bearing reach their minimum, whereas the values of relative vibration of the heel of the thrust bearing and the turbine bearing are quite high. Figure 6 shows the results of clustering over the range of values of relative vibration of the turbine bearing in the plane of the first two principal components. On the data map, there is an area that includes the 215 objects from Cluster 5 with high values of relative vibration of the turbine bearing.

In a similar vein, the considered moments of time were detailed to minutes and another comparative diagram for the time series of monitored parameters for one of the characteristic periods of time was constructed (Fig. 7). Figure 7 covers the period of time from 02:00 h to 09:00 h on 1st July 2015. The area marked with vertical lines depicts one of the characteristic periods of time from 05:00 h to 06:00 h when the values of relative vibration of the turbine bearing (RV_TB_LB) are high. As Fig. 7 suggests, a slight decrease in active power in the range of high values (appr. 450 MW) leads to a slight decrease in relative vibration of the turbine bearing (RV_TB_LB) and to a significant increase in absolute vibration of the heel of the thrust bearing (AV_FH_LB) (appr. 50%) and in absolute vibration of the generator bearing (AV_GB_LB) (appr. 30%). This behavior of the system was mainly observed in the daytime continuously up to 16 h at the end of June or at the beginning of July.

Figure 8 shows a candlestick chart that illustrates comprehensively the relationship between values and ranges of key parameters in the analyzed time interval. It should be noted that the observed high values of relative vibration of the turbine bearing (appr. 1600 μm) are a distinctive feature and property of the researched hydraulic unit.

The comprehensive multi-directional analysis of monitoring data has allowed us to determine the periods when the hydraulic unit manifests its typical behaviour and the operating conditions characteristic for them, identify dependencies between parameters and their influence on each other and on the behavior of the system as a whole

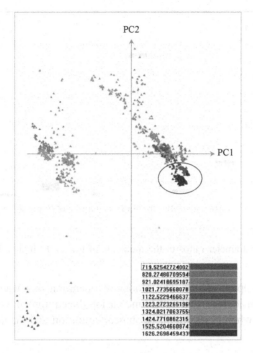

Fig. 6. Results of clustering over the range of values of relative vibration of the turbine bearing (RV_TB_LB) on the PCA plot.

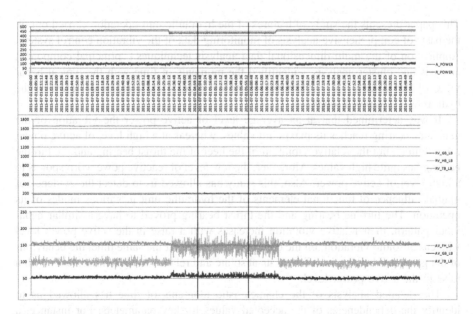

Fig. 7. Diagram of comparing the time series of monitored parameters at the moments with high values of RV_TB_LB.

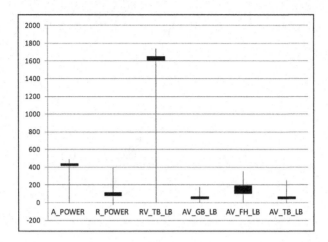

Fig. 8. Diagram of parameter ratios in the moments of time with high values of RV_TB_LB.

considering the accepted values. The modes of operation that lead to high values of vibration can be considered as adversely increasing the equipment wear, which must be taken into account when assessing the technical condition and managing the hydraulic unit life.

4   Conclusion

This paper presents the study of features of the hydraulic unit operation carried out on the basis of comprehensive analysis of monitoring data of the vibration control system. Application of the multi-dimensional data analysis techniques – principal component analysis and cluster analysis – identified the moments of time with the typical behaviour of the system that correspond to various modes and conditions in which the hydropower equipment operates.

It was determined that at an average level of active power the vibration of the generator bearing reaches its maximum values, whereas at a high level of active power it is minimal, but the relative vibration of the heel of the thrust bearing and the turbine bearing has quite high values. Moreover, the low level of reactive power corresponds to a high level of active power. Also, this study has allowed us to detect the evidence of mutual influence of functional elements of the hydraulic unit in various modes of its operation. The turbine bearing and the thrust bearing proved to have a similar behaviour pattern, their relative vibration increases with a raise in the active power level whereas absolute vibration, on the contrary, decreases. At the same time, the behaviour of the generator bearing is different, its absolute and relative vibration decreases with a raise in the active power level.

The detailed analysis of the characteristic moments of time has allowed us to identify the dependencies of the accepted values for key parameters. For instance, a slight change in the amplitude of active power at the upper limit of average values (appr. 200 MW) leads to a significant increase in the relative vibration of the generator bearing (appr. 60%), absolute vibration of the heel of the thrust bearing (appr. 45%) and absolute vibration of the turbine bearing (appr. 60%); a slight decrease in active power in the range of high values (appr. 450 MW) leads to a slight decrease in the relative vibration of the turbine bearing (in the range of its maximum values, appr. 1600 µm) and to a significant increase in the absolute vibration of the thrust bearing support (appr. 50%) and in the absolute vibration of the generator bearing (appr. 30%).

The revealed dependencies between parameters, ranges and ratios of their values in various operating modes present the unique characteristics and distinctive properties of the particular hydraulic unit and jointly form the so-called "analytical portrait" of the hydraulic unit. A change in the technical condition of the hydraulic unit over time may manifest itself in a change in the detected dependencies between parameters, and therefore by comparing the "analytical portraits" it will be possible to identify the dynamics of equipment wear. Formalisation and verification of statistical reliability of the identified dependencies and characteristic ratios of the parameter values will help form a knowledge base with the acceptable and unacceptable modes of the hydraulic unit operation and the features of its behaviour in various conditions. The technological basis that is being developed will provide a new solution for analytical assessment of the state of equipment without putting it out of operation and resource management of the energy system.

References

1. Gurinovich, V.D., Savelev, V.A., Yanchenko, Yu.A.: Metodologicheskie aspekty perekhoda na tekhnicheskoe obsluzhivanie i remont s uchetom tekhnicheskogo sostoyaniya oborudovaniya [Methodological aspects of the transition to maintenance and repair taking into account the technical condition of the equipment]. Metodicheskie voprosy issledovaniya nadezhnosti bolshikh sistem energetiki: sbornik statey. [Methodical issues of the study of the reliability of large energy systems: a collection of articles], no. 66, pp. 448–454 (2015). (in Russian)
2. Gurinovich, V.D., Yanchenko, Yu.A., Savelev, V.A.: Zadachi, problemy i usloviya perekhoda na tekhnicheskoe obsluzhivanie i remont energeticheskogo oborudovaniya po tekhnicheskomu sostoyaniyu. [Tasks, problems and conditions of transition to the maintenance and repair of power equipment based on the technical condition]. Metodicheskie voprosy issledovaniya nadezhnosti bolshikh sistem energetiki: sbornik statey. [Methodical issues of the study of the reliability of large energy systems: a collection of articles], no. 68, pp. 634–642 (2017). (in Russian)
3. Kovalev, A.V., Trushin, N.N., Salnikov, V.S.: Prognozirovanie tekhnicheskogo sostoyaniya tekhnologicheskogo oborudovaniya. [Forecasting the technical condition of technological equipment]. Izvestiya TulGU. Tekhnicheskie nauki. [News of Tula State University. Technical science], no. 11. Part. 2, pp. 554–559 (2014). (in Russian)
4. Akhmetkhanov, R.S., Dubinin, Ye.F., Kuksova, V.I.: Metod klasterizatsii diagnosticheskikh dannykh pri vibrodiagnostike tekhnicheskikh system. [The clustering method of diagnostic data for vibration diagnostics of technical systems]. Vestnik nauchno-tekhnicheskogo razvitiya. [Bulletin of scientific and technological development], no. 5(117), pp. 3–6 (2017). (in Russian)

5. Standart organizatsii: Gidroelektrostantsii. Metodiki otsenki tekhnicheskogo sostoyaniya osnovnogo oborudovaniya [Organization standard: Hydroelectric power stations. Methods for assessing the technical condition of the main equipment], STO 70238424.27.140.001-2011. Order of NP "INVEL" of 01.04.2011 No. 25 (2011). (in Russian)

6. Metodika otsenki tekhnicheskogo sostoyaniya osnovnogo tekhnologicheskogo oborudovaniya i liniy elektroperedachi elektricheskikh stantsiy i elektricheskikh setey [Methods of assessing the technical condition of the main technological equipment and power lines of power plants and electrical networks]. Prikaz Ministerstva energetiki Rossiyskoy Federatsii ot 26.07.2017 № 676. [Order of the Ministry of Energy of the Russian Federation of 26.07.2017 No. 676] (2017) (in Russian)

7. Penkova, T., Korobko, A., Valov, Yu.: Issledovaniye osobennostey funktsionirovaniya gidroagregata na osnove kompleksnogo analiza dannykh vibratsionnogo kontrolya [The study of features of hydraulic unit functioning based on the comprehensive analysis of vibration control system data]. Pribory i sistemy. Upravleniye, kontrol', diagnostika. [Instruments and systems. Management, monitoring, diagnostics], no. 12, pp. 36–45 (2018). https://doi.org/10.25791/pribor.12.2018.000. (in Russian)

8. Abdi, H., Williams, L.: Principal components analysis. Wiley Interdisc. Rev. Comput. Stat. 2(4), 439–459 (2010)

9. Jain, A., Dubes, R.: Algorithms for Clustering Data. Michigan State University. Prentice Hall (1988)

10. Williams, G.J., Simoff, S.J.: Data Mining: Theory, Methodology, Techniques, and Applications. Springer, Heidelberg (2006). https://doi.org/10.1007/11677437

11. Gorban, A., Pitenko, A., Zinovyev, A.: ViDaExpert: user-friendly tool for nonlinear visualization and analysis of multidimensional vectorial data. Cornell University Library (2014). http://arxiv.org/abs/1406.5550

12. Peres-Neto, P., Jackson, D., Somers, K.: How many principal components? stopping rules for determining the number of non-trivial axes revisited. Comput. Stat. Data Anal. 49(4), 974–997 (2005)

The Use of Spaceborne and Oceanic Sensors to Model Dengue Incidence in the Outbreak Surveillance System

Kittisak Kerdprasop[1,2] (iD), Nittaya Kerdprasop[1,2(✉)] (iD),
Kacha Chansilp[2] (iD), and Paradee Chuaybamroong[3] (iD)

[1] Data and Knowledge Engineering Research Unit,
Suranaree University of Technology, Nakhon Ratchasima, Thailand
{kerdpras,nittaya}@sut.ac.th
[2] School of Computer Engineering,
Suranaree University of Technology, Nakhon Ratchasima, Thailand
kacha@sut.ac.th
[3] Department of Environmental Science, Thammasat University,
Pathumthani, Thailand
paradee@tu.ac.th

Abstract. This research focuses on the development of a computational data-driven modeling method to be used in the dengue outbreak surveillance system. The outbreak-level forecasting is based on the estimation of dengue fever cases in Thailand using both statistical and data mining techniques. Major statistical techniques used in this research are linear regression and generalized linear model. The data mining algorithms used in our study are chi-squared automatic interaction detection (CHAID), classification and regression tree, artificial neural network, and support vector machine. The input data are from four sources, which are remotely sensed indices from the NOAA satellite to represent vegetation health and other related weather conditions, rainfall, the oceanic Niño index (ONI) for justifying climate variability affecting amount of rainfall, and historical dengue cases in Thailand to be used as the modeling target. In the modeling process, these data are lagged from 1 up to 24 months to observe time-series effect. On comparing performances of models built from different algorithms, we found that CHAID is the best one yielding the least error on estimating dengue cases. From the CHAID models to forecast dengue cases in Bangkok metropolitan and Nakhon Ratchasima in the northeast of Thailand, the high level of ONI is the most important factor. The large amount of rainfall is significant factor contributing to dengue outbreak in Chiang Mai in the north and Songkhla in the south.

Keywords: Dengue outbreak surveillance system · Incidence modeling · Remote sensing · Oceanic index · Chi-squared automatic interaction detection · CHAID

© Springer Nature Switzerland AG 2019
S. Misra et al. (Eds.): ICCSA 2019, LNCS 11619, pp. 447–460, 2019.
https://doi.org/10.1007/978-3-030-24289-3_33

1 Introduction

Dengue is the viral infectious disease that does not spread directly from people to people, but it transmits to people through the female mosquito in the *Aedes* species. The sign of dengue infection is like the flu illness. The common symptoms are mild fever, severe headache, muscle ache, and join pain [1, 2]. Patients with mild dengue fever can recover within a week under appropriate treatment. For some patients, the infection can develop into a fatal severe dengue, called dengue haemorrhagic fever, that causes severe complications such as plasma leakage, internal bleeding, and organ impairment leading to deadly internal bleeding.

Dengue outbreak is a serious public health problem occurring every year in many tropical countries such as Thailand, Malaysia [3], Singapore [4, 5], Vietnam, and Philippines [6]. Recently, some other areas including Australia [7], Saudi Arabia [8], Central Mexico [9], and southern part of China [10] also reported the dengue epidemic. In Thailand, during the past decade there are almost hundred deadly cases from dengue infection each year [2]. A large number of researchers in public health community have tried to study the epidemic patterns of dengue fever in several regions of Thailand using either ground-based [11, 12] or satellite-based data [13–16].

The dengue outbreak situation in Thailand is in the peak period during the rainy season. Rainfall and some other related factors such as temperature and humidity are thus expected to be the important causes for dengue transmission. But the reported correlation of temperature and humidity to the dengue incidence in Thailand is quite low. On the contrary, rainfall has been concluded as a determinant factor for dengue transmission. The reports from other countries also show the common observation that rainfall is significantly correlated with dengue incidence.

In our previous work [17], we found that some satellite based indices such as vegetation health index can be used to infer the recent rainfall and subsequently employed to estimate the possibility of dengue outbreak. In this research, we thus adopt the satellite indices with other data sources such as climate variability to build a model for estimating the dengue cases across Thailand. The modeling module is to serve as the incidence predictor in our surveillance system to monitor the dengue outbreak event. The input from satellite and oceanic sensors incorporating with historical dengue cases are used to build a predictive model for estimating the number of dengue cases in the outbreak surveillance system.

The intuitive idea of designing a dengue outbreak surveillance system is according to the concern of the World Health Organization (WHO) that currently dengue has become a major intensified epidemic that expands rapidly across more than hundred countries and threatening more than three billion people worldwide [1]. The control and prevention of dengue epidemic is important for countries in tropical region such as Thailand and other ASEAN countries. Prevention through immunization is not an effective strategy because the dengue vaccine is still in an early stage and it needs careful pre-vaccination screening [1]. The main strategy to control the dengue virus transmission is the efficient prevention of adult mosquitoes to lay eggs. For disease control, active monitoring and surveillance of dengue case incidence should also be carried out.

We thus propose the outbreak surveillance system with the modeling process as a core module of the system. Detail of modeling process as well as the data sources of spaceborne and oceanic sensors are explained in Sect. 2. The built model and the model assessment results are shown in Sect. 3. We finally conclude this work in Sect. 4.

2   A Dengue Incidence Modeling Method

2.1   Study Area

In this research, we consider dengue cases across Thailand in the four regions: central, north, northeast, and south. The representative areas for each region are that Bangkok metropolitan in the central part of the country, Chiang Mai province in the north, Nakhon Ratchasima province in the northeast, and Songkhla province in the south. The locations of the four provinces are shown in Fig. 1.

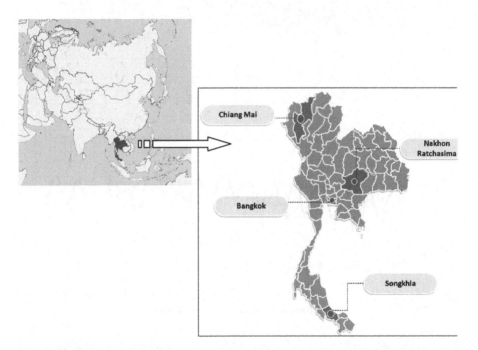

Fig. 1. Areas of study: Chiang Mai in the north, Nakhon Ratchasima in the northeast, Bangkok metropolitan at the central, and Songkhla in the south of Thailand.

Upon visually investigate the coincidence of dengue infection incidence and amount of rainfall in each of the four provinces, we found that the co-occurrence of the two events are subtle as shown by the plots of dengue cases (with dashed line) and rainfall amount (solid line) in Fig. 2. From this preliminary observation, we thus consider adopting other factors to build an accurate model to capture dengue outbreak events. The information used for model building is mainly the indices from remote sensing and the oceanic Nino index computed from the equatorial Pacific sea surface temperature anomaly to capture climate variability.

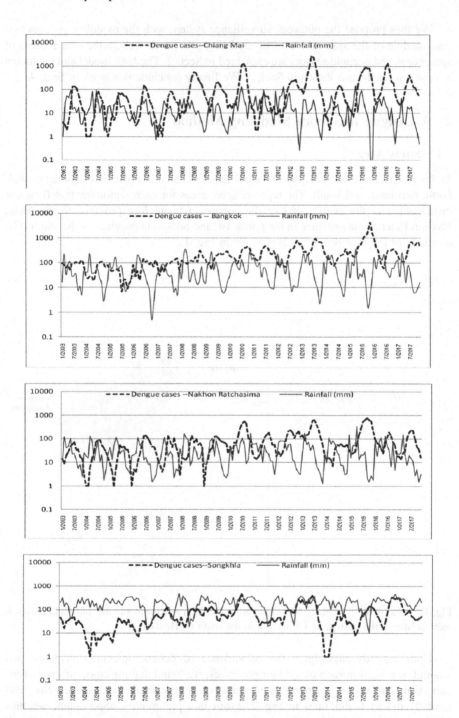

Fig. 2. The plots showing subtle co-occurrence of dengue incidence and amount of rainfall in the four provinces: Chiang Mai, Bangkok, Nakhon Ratchasima, and Songkhla.

2.2   Remote Sensing and Oceanic Nino Index Data

From the preliminary observations that predicting dengue incidences based on rainfall [18] as a sole factor is not accurate enough for planning an efficient outbreak control, we thus consider adopting other factors to build a model for an early warning for the dengue outbreak events. In this work, we use five remote sensing indices that can be a proxy to characterize vegetation greenness [19–21]. These indices are vegetation health index (VHI), smoothed and normalized difference vegetation index (SMN), smoothed brightness temperature index (SMT), vegetation condition index (VCI), and temperature condition index (TCI). These remotely sensed data are made available by the National Oceanic and Atmospheric Administration (NOAA) of the United States [22]. The NOAA satellites are equipped with the advanced very high resolution radiometer (AVHRR) to detect moisture and heat that are radiated from the Earth surface [23, 24]. Several visible and infrared radiated channels are detect from the 4 km spatial resolution and used to compute the indices that are helpful for crop monitoring. The SMN index is used for estimating the greenness of vegetation. SMT is the index to estimate the thermal condition in vegetation. High SMT refers to the dry condition of vegetation. VCI captures the anomaly in vegetation greenness. TCI represents the thermal condition required by plants; the higher TCI, the more favorable condition. VHI is the combined estimation of moisture and thermal conditions appropriate for vegetation; the higher is the better.

Besides the remote sensing indices to reflect rainfall impacts and subsequently the dengue incidences, we also consider the influence of climate variability on the anomaly of rainfall in each region of the country by incorporating Oceanic Nino index (OCI) as another important factor for our model creation process. The ONI is computed [25] from the anomaly of sea surface temperature (SST) at the region called Niño3.4 in the Pacific Ocean at the equator line (5°N–5°S and 170°–120°W), as shown in Fig. 3. The SST is collected each month to compute ONI by averaging from the 3-month periods: the current one, the previous, and the following month. This 3-month average value is then compared to a thirty-year average [26] to check temperature deviation. For instance, to compute ONI of April, the SST anomalies in March, April, and May are to be averaged.

If the ONI values observed in five consecutive months are +0.5 °C or higher than the normal value averaging from the thirty-year period, then the phenomenon called El Niño (the warm event) is announced. On the contrary, if the ONI values in five consecutive periods are –0.5 °C or lower than the normal value, the opposite phenomenon called La Niña (the cold event) is announced. Examples of ONI values are shown in Table 1 with the cold period in bold italic font and the warm in bold.

The El Niño and La Niña are the opposite events of the Pacific climate pattern known as the El Niño-Southern Oscillation, or ENSO. The major side effect of El Niño to the Southeast Asian area is higher temperature and less precipitation than normal, whereas the occurrence of La Niña causes excessive rainfall than usual. Temperature and rain are important factors to the rapid spread of mosquito that causes dengue fever. We thus include ONI as the representative of the ENSO events in our modeling process.

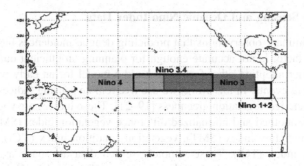

Fig. 3. Location of the Niño3.4 region for measuring sea surface temperature. (source: https://www.ncdc.noaa.gov/teleconnections/enso/indicators/sst/)

Table 1. ONI values during the past five years (2014 to 2018).

	2014	2015	2016	2017	2018
January	−0.4	0.6	2.5	−0.3	−0.9
February	−0.4	0.6	2.2	−0.1	−0.8
March	−0.2	0.6	1.7	0.1	−0.6
April	0.1	0.8	1.0	0.3	−0.4
May	0.3	1.0	0.5	0.4	−0.1
June	0.2	1.2	0.0	0.4	0.1
July	0.1	1.5	−0.3	0.2	0.1
August	0.0	1.8	−0.6	−0.1	0.2
September	0.2	2.1	−0.7	−0.4	0.4
October	0.4	2.4	−0.7	−0.7	0.7
November	0.6	2.5	−0.7	−0.9	0.9
December	0.7	2.6	−0.6	−1.0	0.8

2.3   Modeling Process

The proposed dengue outbreak surveillance system (as shown in Fig. 4) is composed of four main modules: data entry, data exploration, model building, and visualization modules. The focus of this paper is the dengue incidence modeling, which is a core module of our outbreak surveillance system. The steps in data access, extraction, preparation, model induction and evaluation, which are the parts from data entry to model building modules, are graphically illustrated in Fig. 5.

Operational details in model building can be explained as follows. The first step is for data access and extraction. In this work, we use data from four main sources. Three of them are remote sensing indices, rainfall measures, and SST anomaly (or ONI) are from the NOAA websites [18, 22, 25]. The fourth source is from the Bureau of Epidemiology, Thailand [27] that reports dengue cases from all provinces. We collect cases during the years 2003–2017 from the four targeted provinces. These data sources

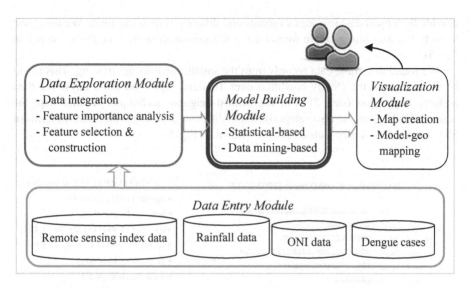

Fig. 4. A framework of dengue outbreak surveillance system.

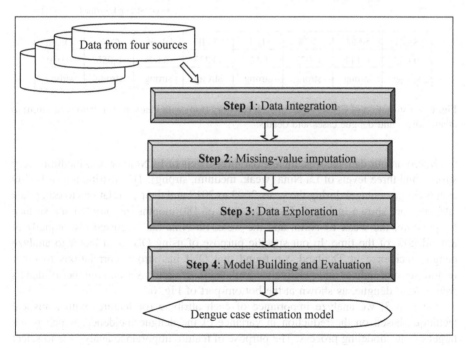

Fig. 5. Proposed model building method to estimate dengue incidences.

provide their open data in various formats and different time-frame units. We thus have to unify the data into a single format using the unique monthly time-frame (step 1 in Fig. 5).

We found that some data records from the satellite sensors are missing. This might be the case from the cloudy condition over Thailand region on those days. We then perform imputation (step 2) with the nearest-neighbor technique. At this step, the numeric ONI values are also categorized into different degrees of intensities in terms of SST anomaly in degree Celsius [28] as shown in Fig. 6.

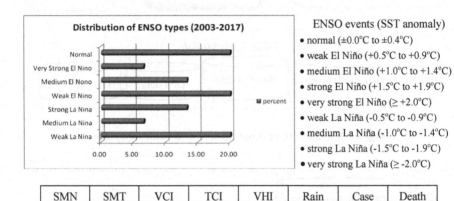

SMN	SMT	VCI	TCI	VHI	Rain	Case	Death
0.035	0.144	0.077	-0376	-0.233	-0.096	0.056	0.030
strong	strong	strong	strong	strong	strong	strong	strong

Fig. 6. Distribution of ENSO types in each category (top) with Pearson correlations (bottom) to other indices and dengue cases and deaths.

Based on our data records, there exist three levels of El Niño (weak, medium, very strong) and three levels of La Niña (weak, medium, strong). The distribution of ENSO events (in percentage) during the years 2003 to 2017 and their correlations to other data attributes are shown in Fig. 6. From the total of 180 months, the normal sea surface temperature, the weak El Niño, and the weak La Niña had occurred also equally at around 20% of the time. In our specific purpose of using ONI as a factor to analyze dengue incidence in Thailand, we found that ONI has strong correlations to other remote sensing indices and positively correlated to dengue cases and number of deaths from severe dengue, as shown at the bottom part of Fig. 6.

On step 3, we analyze importance of each attribute (or feature) with statistical technique based on the reduction in variance of the dengue incidence, which is the target of our modeling process. The purpose of feature importance analysis is to select only attributes contributing the most to the accurate prediction of dengue incidences. At this step, we also perform data lagging from 1 month up to 24 months. This is for the observation of the impact from historical data on estimating the future dengue cases.

We then build different kinds of predictive models and evaluate forecasting performances of those models. The algorithms used in model building are linear regression (LR), generalized linear model (GLM), support vector machine (SVM), artificial neural network (ANN), classification and regression tree (CART), and chi-squared automatic interaction detection (CHAID).

In our experimentation, we apply around 50 percents of data for training the algorithm to build model. On tuning algorithm parameters to achieve the best predictive performance, we use another validation set of data (approximately 20%). To assess the model performance, we employ the remaining 30% of data as a test set.

3   Model Evaluation and Results

On the preparation of training data sets, we prepare two kinds of training data: the data set with lagging periods from 1 up to 24 months, and the data set with no lagging. This is the preliminary step prior to building the final models. The main purpose of this step is for observing the impact of time series events on predicting the dengue incidences.

The measurements that we used for selecting the best scheme on data preparation are mean absolute error (MAE) and correlation. The MAE is the error of the model on predicting dengue cases. Correlation measures the association between predictive features and the target attribute. Therefore, we are looking for the training data set that yields lower MAE but higher correlation (Table 2).

Table 2.   Comparative results of models built from the lagged and non-lagged data.

Province/Region	24-month lagged data		Non-lagging data	
	MAE	Correlation	MAE	Correlation
Bangkok/Central	156.064	0.510	146.406	0.474
Chiang Mai/North	135.555	0.815	165.679	0.621
Nakhon Ratchasima/Northeast	62.368	0.565	79.741	0.091
Songkla/South	49.001	0.823	57.119	0.623
Average	**100.747**	**0.678**	**112.236**	**0.452**

The output we observed from the experimental results is that the 24-month lagging data set yields the predictive model with lower MAE and higher correlation to the target attribute than the data set with no lagging. We thus choose the data set with attribute lagging to build the model. The six classification algorithms are then applied with the 24-month lagging data set and the results are summarized in Table 3.

It turns out that CHAID is the best forecasting model for all four provinces. Compared to other modeling algorithm, CHAID uses less predictive features and produces the most correlated model with less error. The CHAID algorithm generates a tree-based model with conditional events on the left-hand-side of the tree, and other additional conditions to be co-considered are displayed with indentation on the

Table 3. Performance of the models built from the 24-month lagged data.

Province	Algorithm	No. variables	Correlation	Relative error
Chiang Mai	**CHAID**	12	**0.881**	**0.223**
	GLM	30	0.640	0.590
	LR	29	0.611	0.627
	ANN	30	0.532	0.718
	CART	30	0.000	1.001
	SVM	30	0.412	1.115
Bangkok	**CHAID**	8	**0.852**	**0.275**
	LR	30	0.634	0.598
	SVM	30	0.432	1.034
	CART	17	0.731	0.491
	GLM	30	0.634	0.598
	ANN	30	0.364	0.901
Nakhon Ratchasima	**CHAID**	11	**0.856**	**0.268**
	GLM	30	0.717	0.487
	LR	29	0.635	0.597
	CART	9	0.557	0.692
	ANN	30	0.489	0.762
	SVM	30	0.532	1.065
Songkhla	**CHAID**	7	**0.856**	**0.268**
	GLM	30	0.643	0.587
	LR	29	0.642	0.587
	ANN	30	0.454	0.800
	CART	30	0.000	1.002
	SVM	30	0.453	1.015

following lines. Forecasting target is the estimated number of dengue patients displayed as number in red bold fonts. The highest three cases are stressed with underlines. We show the CHAID models built from the 24-month lagging data of Bangkok metropolitan area in Fig. 7.

The three most serious cases of dengue outbreak in each province are illustrated in Table 4 with the predictive factors at each outbreak level displayed on the right hand side. For instance, the number of dengue infected patients in Chiang Mai province can reach 1,748 if all of the following three factors occur:

- amount of rainfall in the past eighth month is more than 0.1 inches
- amount of rainfall in the past seventh month is less than 0.1 inches
- amount of rainfall in the past fifteenth month is more than 1.98 inches

In Bangkok, the predictive factors are different. The number of dengue patients in Bangkok can be as high as 3,084 if the following two factors occur:

- the ONI is higher than 1
- amount of rainfall in the current month is less than 0.3 inches

```
ONI ≤ 1
        rain_Lag7 ≤ 2.430
                rain_Lag6 ≤ 2.520
                        TCI ≤ 28.976
                                rain_Lag18 ≤ 0.880  ➔ 207.857
                                rain_Lag18 > 0.880  ➔ 91.167
                        TCI > 28.976 and TCI ≤ 35.960  ➔ 79.727
                        TCI > 35.960 and TCI ≤ 44.303
                                ONI ≤ -0.400  ➔ 118.25
                                ONI > -0.400 and ONI ≤ -0.300  ➔ 314.0
                                ONI > -0.300  ➔ 121.75
                        TCI > 44.303
                                rain_Lag6 ≤ 0.920  ➔ 69.933
                                rain_Lag6 > 0.920  ➔ 116.8
                rain_Lag6 > 2.520
                        TCI ≤ 60.333
                                rain_Lag9 ≤ 4.270]  ➔ 184.0
                                rain_Lag9 > 4.270  ➔ 544.5
                        TCI > 60.333  ➔ 594.0
        rain_Lag7 > 2.430]
                VCI ≤ 34.525  ➔ 412.649
                VCI > 34.525  ➔ 147.944
ONI > 1
        rain ≤ 0.300  ➔ 3084.0
        rain > 0.300  ➔ 662.0
```

Fig. 7. The CHAID model to estimate dengue incidences in Bangkok. (Color figure online)

The oceanic Nino index (ONI) is also the most important factor to be considered for dengue outbreak estimation in Nkahon Ratchasima province. But in Songkhla area, the amount of rainfall in the current month is the best predictor for dengue cases.

4   Conclusion

This research work presents the application of sensor data obtained from the NOAA-AVHRR that had been used to compute indices such as VHI, VCI, TCI, SMN, SMT to reflect greenness of vegetation on the global surface. Besides these spaceborne indices, we also apply the index computed from the sea surface temperature (SST) anomaly in the equatorial Pacific region Niño3.4. The SST anomaly is the temperature deviation measurement to identify either the normal, warm, or cold events occurred in the Pacific ocean climate.

The warm events are those months that the SST are +0.5 °C or higher than the normal long-term temperature. The cold events occur when the SST anomaly are –0.5 °C or lower than the norm. The warm episodes are called El Niño, whilst the cold ones are

458   K. Kerdprasop et al.

Table 4. The top-3 cases of CHAID model to estimate dengue outbreak in each province.

Province	Outbreak Estimation	Predictive Factors
Chiang Mai	Dengue cases ≈ 1748	rain_Lag8 > 0.1 inch & rain_Lag7 ≤ 0.1 inch & rain_Lag15 > 1.98 inch
	Dengue cases ≈ 1653	rain_Lag8 ≤ 0.1 inch & rain_Lag16 > 1.98 inch
	Dengue cases ≈ 1195	rain_Lag8 ≤ 0.1 inch & rain_Lag16 ≤ 1.98 inch & TCI is in the range (19.63, 30.425]
Bangkok	Dengue cases ≈ 3084	ONI > 1 & rain in current month ≤ 0.3 inch
	Dengue cases ≈ 662	ONI > 1 & rain in current month > 0.3 inch
	Dengue cases ≈ 594	ONI ≤ 1 & rain_Lag7 ≤ 2.43 inch & rain_Lag6 > 2.52 inch & TCI > 60.33
Nakhon Ratchasima	Dengue cases ≈ 653	ONI > 1 & rain_Lag18 > 2.03 inch
	Dengue cases ≈ 421	ONI > 1 & rain_Lag18 ≤ 2.03 inch & rain_Lag22 ≤ 0.28 inch
	Dengue cases ≈ 416	ONI ≤ 1 & rain_Lag16 > 2.49 inch & rain_Lag17 is in the range (2.49, 3.60] inch
Songkhla	Dengue cases ≈ 351	rain in current month ≤ 10.55 inch & VHI > 54.053 & rain_Lag21 ≤ 1.68 inch
	Dengue cases ≈ 349	rain in current month > 10.55 inch & rain_Lag11 ≤ 4.2 inch
	Dengue cases ≈ 233	rain in current month > 10.55 inch & rain_Lag11 > 4.2 inch & rain_Lag21 is in the range (7.57, 10.01] inch

called La Niña. Both cold and warm episodes are the natural phenomena called the El Niño-Southern Oscillation, or ENSO.

The scientists and climatologists from the NOAA, U.S.A., devise the measurement based on the SST anomaly and call the metric as the Oceanic Nino Index (ONI) to capture variability of sea surface temperature in the Pacific Ocean. On the first week of each month, the updated ONI values are announced. We employ this ONI value together with the NOAA-AVHRR indices as important oceanic and remote-sensing factors to predict number of infected dengue patients in Thailand.

From the experimental results, we found that ONI is the most important factor and it is the first condition that the CHAID algorithm considers for building tree models for Bangkok and Nakhon Ratchasima provincial areas. Other important factors appeared in the models of these two provinces are TCI, VCI, and amount of rainfall in the current month and in the past up to 18 months. In Chiang Mai, ONI has no role in the dengue incidence forecasting. Amount of rain in the past, TCI, and SMN are predictive factors appeared in the model. To predict dengue cases in Songkhla, rain in current month, VHI, VCI, and ONI are important factors.

Acknowledgment. This work was financially supported by grants from the Thailand Toray Science Foundation, the National Research Council of Thailand, and Suranaree University of Technology through the funding of the Data and Knowledge Engineering Research Unit.

References

1. Cogan, J.E.: Dengue and severe dengue. Fact sheets, World Health Organization (2018). http://www.who.int/news-room/fact-sheets/detail/dengue-and-severe-dengue
2. Department of Disease Control, Ministry of Public Health: Dengue Surveillance Report (2018). http://www.thaivbd.org/n/home
3. Dom, N.C., Ahmad, A.H., Latif, Z.A., Ismail, R., Pradhan, B.: Coupling of remote sensing data and environmental related parameters for dengue transmission risk assessment in Subang Jaya, Malaysia. Geocarto Int. **28**(3), 258–272 (2013)
4. Hii, Y., Rocklov, J., Ng, N., Tang, C., Pang, F., Sauerborn, R.: Climate variability and increase in intensity and magnitude of dengue incidence in Singapore. Glob. Health Action **2**, 124–132 (2009)
5. Loh, B., Song, R.J.: Modeling dengue cluster size as a function of Aedes aegypti population and climate in Singapore. Dengue Bull. **25**, 74–78 (2001)
6. Su, G.L.S.: Correlation of climatic factors and dengue incidence in Metro Manila, Philippines. AMBIO: J. Hum. Environ. **37**(4), 292–294 (2008)
7. Hasan, T., Bambrick, H.: The effects of climate variables on the outbreak of dengue in Queensland 2008–2009. Southeast Asian J. Trop. Med. Public Health **44**(4), 613–622 (2013)
8. Khormi, H.M., Kumar, L.: Modeling dengue fever risk based on socioeconomic parameters, nationality and age groups: GIS and remote sensing based case study. Sci. Total Environ. **409**, 4713–4719 (2011)
9. Moreno-Madrinan, M.J., et al.: Correlating remote sensing data with the abundance of pupae of the dengue virus mosquito vector, Aedes aegypti, in Central Mexico. ISPRS Int. J. Geo-Inf. **3**, 732–749 (2014)
10. Qi, X., et al.: The effects of socioeconomic and environmental factors on the incidence of dengue fever in the pearl river delta, China 2013. PLoS Neglected Trop. Dis. **9**(10), e0004159 (2015)

11. Chaikoolvatana, A., Singhasivanon, P., Haddawy, P.: Utilization of a geographical information system for surveillance of Aedes aegypti and dengue haemorrhagic fever in north-eastern Thailand. Dengue Bull. **31**, 75–82 (2007)

12. Tipayamongkholgul, M., Fang, C., Klinchan, S., Liu, C., King, C.: Effects of the El Nino-Southern oscillation and dengue epidemics in Thailand, 1996–2005. BMC Publ. Health **9**, 1–15 (2009). article 422

13. Kiang, R.K., Soebiyanto, R.P.: Mapping the risks of malaria, dengue and influenza using satellite data. In: International Archives of the Photogrammetry, Remote Sensing and Spatial Information Sciences, vol. XXXIX-BB, pp. 83–86 (2012)

14. Nakhapakorn, K., Tripathi, N.K.: An information value based analysis of physical and climatic factors affecting dengue fever and dengue haemorrhagic fever incidence. Int. J. Health Geographics **4**, 1–13 (2005)

15. Nitatpattana, N., et al.: Potential association of dengue haemorrhagic fever incidence and remote senses land surface temperature, Thailand, 1998. Southeast Asian J. Trop. Med. Public Health **38**(3), 427–433 (2007)

16. Sithiprasasna, R., Linthicum, K.L., Lerdthusnee, K., Brewer, T.G.: Use of geographical information system to study the epidemiology of dengue haemorrhagic fever in Thailand. Dengue Bull. **21**, 68–73 (1997)

17. Kerdprasop, K., Kerdprasop, N.: Rainfall estimation models induced from ground station and satellite data. In: 24th International MultiConference of Engineers and Computer Scientists, pp. 297–302 (2016)

18. NOAA: Climate Data Online. National Centers for Environmental Information, NOAA, U.S.A. (2018). https://www.ncdc.noaa.gov/cdo-web/

19. Kogan, F.: Operational space technology for global vegetation assessment. Bull. Am. Meteorol. Soc. **82**(9), 1949–1964 (2001)

20. Kogan, F.: 30-year land surface trend from AVHRR-based global vegetation health data. In: Kogan, F. et al. (eds.) Use of Satellite and In-situ Data to Improve Sustainability, pp. 119–123. Springer, Dordrecht (2011). https://doi.org/10.1007/978-90-481-9618-0_14

21. Kogan, F., Guo, W.: Early detection and monitoring droughts from NOAA environmental satellites. In: Kogan, F. et al. (eds.) Use of Satellite and In-situ Data to Improve Sustainability, pp. 11–18. Springer, Dordrecht (2011). https://doi.org/10.1007/978-90-481-9618-0_2

22. NOAA STAR: Global Vegetation Health Products. Center for Satellite Applications and Research, NOAA, U.S.A. (2018). https://www.star.nesdis.noaa.gov/smcd/emb/vci/VH/vh_browseByCountry_province.php

23. Kageyama, Y., Sato, I., Nishida, M.: Automatic classification algorithm for NOAA-AVHRR data using mixels. In: 2007 IEEE International Geoscience and Remote Sensing Symposium, pp. 2040–2043 (2007)

24. Li, C., et al.: Post calibration of channels 1 and 2 of long-term AVHRR data record based on SeaWiFS data and pseudo-invariant targets. Remote Sens. Environ. **150**, 104–119 (2014)

25. NOAA National Weather Service: Cold & Warm Episodes by Season. Climate Prediction Center, NOAA, U.S.A. (2018). http://origin.cpc.ncep.noaa.gov/products/analysis_monitoring/ensostuff/ONI_v5.php

26. Huang, B., et al.: Extended reconstructed sea surface temperature, version 5 (ERSSTv5): upgraded, validations, and intercomparisons. J. Clim. **30**(20), 8179–8205 (2017)

27. Bureau of Epidemiology: Dengue Fever. Department of Disease Control, Ministry of Public Health, Thailand (2018). http://www.boe.moph.go.th/boedb/surdata/disease.php?ds=66

28. Null, J.: El Niño and La Niña Years and Intensities Based on Oceanic Niño Index (ONI). Golden Gate Weather Services (2018). https://ggweather.com/enso/oni.htm/

Anomaly Detection with Machine Learning Technique to Support Smart Logistics

Nittaya Kerdprasop[1,2(✉)] ⓘ, Kacha Chansilp[2] ⓘ,
Kittisak Kerdprasop[1,2] ⓘ, and Paradee Chuaybamroong[3] ⓘ

[1] Data and Knowledge Engineering Research Unit, Nakhon Ratchasima,
Thailand
[2] School of Computer Engineering, Suranaree University of Technology,
Nakhon Ratchasima, Thailand
{nittaya,kacha,kerdpras}@sut.ac.th
[3] Department of Environmental Science, Thammasat University,
Pathumthani, Thailand
paradee@tu.ac.th

Abstract. Accurate planning and cost-effective management on product delivery are among key factors leading to the success of most manufacturing sectors in the current era of the fourth industrial revolution, or Industry 4.0. In this work, we focus our study on the development of a model based on machine learning technique to support smart logistics by detecting anomaly events on the big stream of electronic orders obtained from ubiquitous customers. We use the data-driven approach to build the order-anomaly model and present the built model as the classification and regression tree. Our model in a tree formalism is to be used as an automatic detector for unusual events inherent in the customers' order stream. The anomaly events should invoke special care in the smart logistics environment that delivery tasks are performed in an automatic manner. Early detection of anomaly ordering events is expected to improve accuracy on delivery planning.

Keywords: Anomaly detection · Order anomaly model · Smart logistics · Classification and regression tree · Machine learning

1 Introduction

Traditional logistics process deals with the delivery of products to the right place at the right time. The main processes in logistics include the three main steps [1] of order processing and transport planning, order shipping, and order billing. For smart logistics, digital data from ubiquitous sources and state-of-the-art technologies play their crucial roles on turning the regular shipping process into the intelligent transport system (ITS) by means of the radio frequency identification (RFID) tagging with goods to be delivered. The current capability of ITS has been argued [2] to be extended to fulfill the need of being an efficient linkage between the smart city, the customer side, and the smart industry, the producer side.

© Springer Nature Switzerland AG 2019
S. Misra et al. (Eds.): ICCSA 2019, LNCS 11619, pp. 461–472, 2019.
https://doi.org/10.1007/978-3-030-24289-3_34

The high-quality ITS can be considered an important supporter for the manufacturing movement toward the fourth stage of industrialization [3, 4]. We, therefore, propose in this work the application of data-driven modeling through the machine learning approach. Our modeling process is based on the classification and regression algorithm to learn anomaly events from product ordering stream. The learned model is designed to be an intelligent part of the supply chain management module for monitoring unusual events.

After presenting literature review in Sect. 2, we explain our modeling method in Sect. 3. The model evaluation results are illustrated in Sect. 4. We conclude our work in Sect. 5.

2 Literature Review

In logistics and supply chain management, an accurate forecasting of customers' order is significant for not only a cost-effective manufacturing planning, but also a timely material and product distribution [5] to fulfill the demand of customers. The needs for an accurate forecasting technique can be found in so many literature across a variety of health-related domains ranging from drinking water distribution network [6, 7], to electricity and home energy demands [8–10], outpatient space in the hospital [11], amount of food donations [12], and retail pharmacies [13].

Forecasting has long been an important tool in the business domain to project customers' demand trends. Retail industry is the business section that has heavily applied forecasting for efficient business planning and managing. Computational forecasting method has been used to predict the fashion demand [14], to project the number of tourists [15], to estimate the growth in on-line retailing [16], to identify an optimal retail location [17], to plan replenishment in the discount retail chain [18], to approximately quantify the need for high-end luxury products [19], and to estimate the demand for retailing through automated vending system [20].

Business processes have indeed been strongly linked to industrial movements since the first industrial revolution with mass mechanization to the fourth one with full digitization through the cyber-physical systems. In the current movement of the Industry 4.0, numerous machine learning techniques and soft computing approaches have been extensively applied in many smart manufacturing industries. Intelligent analysis has been applied within a number of supply chain management processes [21–26].

Machine learning has the ability to learn from sales data, and then report in an automatic manner about consumer behavior and preferences. Various machine learning techniques have been applied for such tasks. These techniques include clustering [27, 28], artificial neural network [29], fuzzy models [30], support vector machine [31], and many others [32, 33].

Several recent studies have reported that advanced machine learning techniques such as support vector machine, genetic algorithm, artificial neural network, and deep learning outperform traditional statistical-based forecasting. We also apply machine learning technique using the classification and regression tree algorithm to learn anomaly events from the historical product delivery data. Details of our methodology are explained in the following section.

3 Modeling Method for Anomaly Detection

3.1 Product Order Data Characteristics

The focus of this work is to develop a model to detect anomaly customer order events aiming to support smart supply chain management system, especially in product delivery planning. Our model building method is data-driven in the sense that the historical data are used in the training process of the automatic model creation step. The product order data used in our work are public-domain contributed by researchers from Brazil [34].

The original dataset contains 60 records of the daily delivery parcel service company in Brazil. Each record contains information related to the product distribution, as summarized and shown in Table 1. Pair of attributes showing very strong correlation (that is, correlation > ±0.70) are highlighted with bold red font as shown in Table 2.

Table 1. Data attribute characteristics.

Name	Meaning	Type
A1	Banking orders (1)	Integer
A2	Banking orders (2)	Integer
A3	Banking orders (3)	Integer
A4	Day of the week (Monday to Friday)	Category
A5	Fiscal sector orders	Real
A6	Non-urgent orders	Real
A7	Order type A	Real
A8	Order type B	Real
A9	Order type C	Real
A10	Orders from the traffic controller sector	Integer
A11	Total orders	Real
A12	Urgent orders	Real
A13	Week of the month	Category

3.2 Modeling Process

The purpose of this work is to derive anomaly events from customer orders. But the original dataset contains only 60 records and such a dataset is too small to capture anomaly events. We thus over-sampling the dataset to contain 100,000 records and make a series of steps as shown in Fig. 1.

The anomaly detection modeling process starts from computing anomaly index value, which is a measure of dissimilarity of a data record as compared to other data records in the same group [35]. All data records are then ranked based on this index

Table 2. Correlation among data attributes.

	A1	A2	A3	A4	A5	A6	A7	A8	A9	A10	A11	A12
A2	0.26											
A3	0.22	-0.11										
A4	-0.05	-0.58	-0.01									
A5	0.004	-0.06	0.30	-0.13								
A6	0.73	0.79	0.13	-0.42	-0.06							
A7	0.68	0.29	0.23	-0.07	0.07	0.56						
A8	0.59	0.71	0.07	-0.38	-0.12	0.83	0.44					
A9	0.33	0.72	0.03	-0.45	0.01	0.75	0.22	0.52				
A10	-0.16	0.24	0.23	-0.34	0.20	0.25	-0.15	0.13	0.44			
A11	0.63	0.80	0.10	-0.44	-0.05	0.94	0.56	0.90	0.81	0.25		
A12	0.23	0.66	0.03	-0.52	-0.01	0.57	0.41	0.51	0.77	0.24	0.73	
A13	0.39	0.15	-0.16	-0.21	0.001	0.24	0.25	0.31	-0.04	-0.19	0.21	0.12

value from the highest to the lowest. Data record with the highest anomaly index value reflect the unusualness of that record. We set the minimum threshold of anomaly index as 2.0. Data records having anomaly index lower than this threshold are considered normal cases. Otherwise, the data will be labeled as anomaly events.

After identifying anomaly data records (steps 1–3), we select normal cases from the least anomalous group of with the same amount as the abnormal cases (step 4). The purpose of this step is to generate a training set with balancing proportion between the two groups of data (normal cases and anomalous cases). The data set is then used to train the classification and regression learning algorithm [36] to build the tree model called classification and regression tree, or CART, in step 5.

The CART model is finally assessed its classifying performance on separating normal customer orders from the abnormal ones. On evaluating model performance (step 6), we use the out-of-sample method, that is, the hold-out test data (around 30% of the 100,000 data records) are unseen by the tree-learning algorithm. The final product of the proposed methodology is the CART model that has the capability of automatic differentiating normal orders from the anomalous ones.

4   Model Creation and Evaluation Results

4.1   Anomaly Detection Model

After computing anomaly index of each data record in step 1, we found that there are 1,142 records showing the anomaly index values higher than 2.0. We then select other 1,142 data records from the group of normal data that have the lowest anomaly index value. The justification of this selection is for creating a balance data set having the same amount of normal and abnormal cases. Moreover, the selection of data group having lowest anomaly index is for the high contrast to the anomaly cases. We investigate characteristics of both normal (illustrated in Fig. 2) and anomalous cases (Fig. 3) with the web graph tool to explore the dominant attributes.

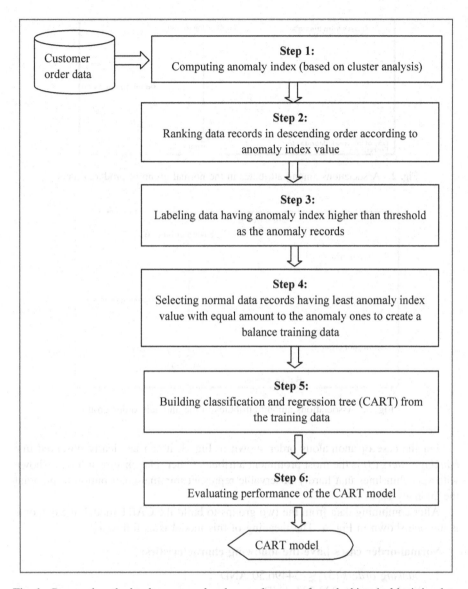

Fig. 1. Proposed method to learn normal and anomaly events from the historical logistics data.

The thickness of lines in the web graph represents the weight of association that has been counted from number of data records supporting that relationship. The thick line shows strong association, while the thin line illustrates less significant relationship. It can be seen from the web graph in Fig. 2 that for the group of normal product order, the most outstanding attribute related to normal order is *week of the month*. The other three attributes expecting useful for identifying the normal orders are *orders from the traffic controller sector, day of the week*, and *banking orders (3)*. These three attributes are, however, less significant than the *week of the month* attribute.

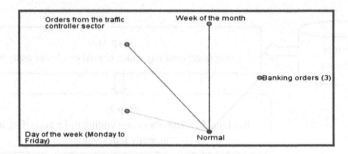

Fig. 2. Associations among attributes in the normal group of product orders.

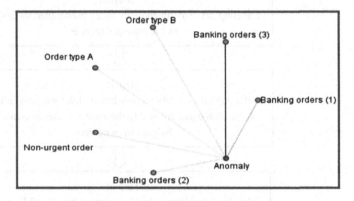

Fig. 3. Associations among attributes in the anomaly order group.

For the case of anomalous order shown in Fig. 3, it can be clearly observed that *banking orders (3)* is the most prominent attribute. Other relationships in Fig. 3 shown with very thin lines that hardly observable represent minimal contribution to pinpoint the anomaly cases.

After combining data from the two groups to build the CART model, the outcome is the one shown in Fig. 4. The meaning of this model is as follows:

Normal-order cases have the following characteristics:

1: *banking orders (3)* ≤ 34496.50 AND
   total orders ≤ 333.334 AND
   orders from the traffic controller sector > 26033.50

Anomaly-order cases have the following characteristics:

1: *banking orders (3)* ≤ 34496.50 AND
   total orders ≤ 333.334 AND
   orders from the traffic controller sector ≤ 26033.50
2: *banking orders (3)* ≤ 34496.50 AND
   total orders > 333.334
3: *banking orders (3)* > 34496.50

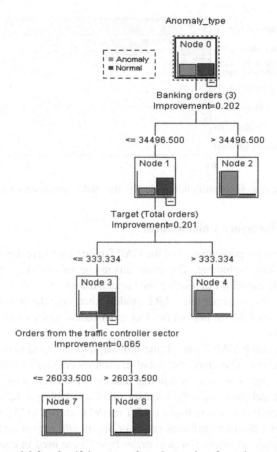

Fig. 4. A CART model for classifying normal product orders from the anomaly ones system.

The CART model captures *banking orders (3)*, *total orders*, and *orders from the traffic controller sector* as the three most discriminative attributes to differentiate normal orders from the abnormal ones. Importance of other attributes can be seen from Fig. 5.

On the full scale of 1.0 to reflect the highest importance on predicting the target outcome of normal/anomaly order, the attribute *banking orders (3)* is the most prominent one with the importance value of 0.44. The attribute *total orders* comes in second with the importance value of 0.38. The attribute *orders from the traffic controller sector* is the third one with 0.08 importance. The attributes *banking orders (1)*, *order type A*, *urgent order*, and *non-urgent order* have equal importance value of 0.01.

The final step is the accuracy evaluation of the CART model to differentiate anomaly orders from the normal ones. We perform the hold-out method by splitting data into a training data set (containing 1,566 records) and a test data set (with the remaining 718 records). The CART model can classify correctly 696 records (out of the 718 records). This comprises of the 96.94% of the accuracy rate, and the error rate is as low as 3.06%. We consider it a very satisfied model for detecting anomaly events.

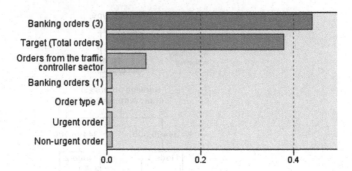

Fig. 5. Importance analysis of attributes to identify the total orders as either normal or anomaly.

4.2   Model Performance Enhancement

To further improve the performance of the CART model, we investigate the possibility of applying boosting technique. The main advantage of boosting is that instead of generating a single model for predicting the target attribute, we rather use ten models to predict the target. We generate ten CART models, then vote the outcome of the target attribute as either anomaly or normal product order based on the majority voting of the ten CART models.

On generating each CART model, the training data are randomly chosen to comprise of 1,566 records. Therefore, the detail in each model can be different depending on the random samples used as a training dataset. Moreover, from all available 13 predictors, the model may use only a subset of all available predictors. The top-five frequently used attributes on building a CART model is shown in Fig. 6. It can be seen from the figure that the five attributes (*week of the month, urgent order, total orders, orders from the traffic controller sector, order type C*) are used in every of the CART ensemble.

The performances of all ten models are also summarized in Table 3. The predictive accuracy of a single model is varied from 77.50% to 98.50%. However, to use boosting technique on predicting the anomaly/normal product order, all models are used as an ensemble. The final predicting outcome is obtained through the voting scheme. Therefore, the performance of the ensemble is much better than a single model. The ensemble quality in terms of the accuracy from voting scheme is displayed in Fig. 7.

The accuracy rate shown in Fig. 7 has been evaluated from the training dataset. To fairly compare predictive performance of the ensemble model based on boosting technique against a single CART model, we apply a separate test set. The test set is applied to both the ensemble model and the single CART model scheme. We found that on testing with the out-of-sample data, the ensemble based on boosting technique yields the accuracy rate as high as 98.89%, which is almost two percents better that a single CART model.

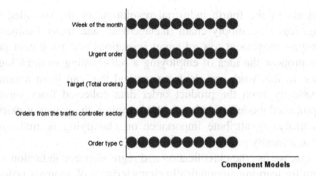

Fig. 6. Frequently used attributes for predicting anomaly/normal product order of the CART ensemble built from ten models.

Table 3. Performances of the ten CART models.

Model	Number of predictors	Model size (#nodes)	Accuracy (%)
1	12	7	98.30
2	13	11	96.70
3	13	15	92.40
4	12	15	94.30
5	12	9	94.10
6	13	13	95.70
7	13	19	77.50
8	12	15	90.90
9	11	11	98.50
10	12	11	85.40

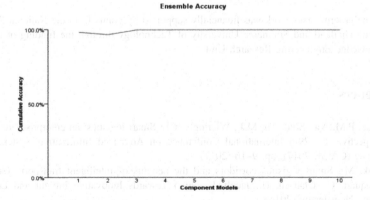

Fig. 7. Ensemble accuracy from a combination of CART models.

5 Conclusion

In the current era of the fourth industrial revolution, or the so-called Industry 4.0, manufacturing, logistics, supply chain management, and many business sectors are facing challenging movement toward smart operations and intelligent production. In this work, we propose the idea of employing a self-learning methodology to support smart logistics. In this work, we devise a method that can learn anomaly detection model automatically from the product order data collected from various customer groups. The proposed model induction method employs the power of machine learning technique on analyzing attribute importance on classifying normal customer order events from the anomaly cases.

In our design, we use the classification and regression tree induction technique as a main algorithm for learning automatically characteristics of anomaly orders that can be differentiated from the normal orders. The selection of tree formalism is due to the fact that the tree structure can facilitate reasoning on tracing back the pre-condition leading to the predicted outcome. On the data preparation step, we use anomaly index computed from the cluster analysis to justify whether the data record is normal or abnormal cases. The anomalous records are extracted and incorporated with the same amount of normal records to train the tree induction model. The evaluation result of normal/anomaly event detection of the tree model shows the accuracy rate as high as 96.94%. This result reveals that our proposed method yield an accurate discriminative model that is appropriate for embedded in the smart logistics and supply chain management system.

On evaluating performance of the tree model, we also apply the ensemble method by using a boosting technique to build ten models. Then applying all ten models to predict the outcome of the target attribute. All ten predicting results from the ensemble are combined based on the voting scheme. We found from the experimental result that the ensemble of tree models can improve predicting accuracy from 96.94% to 98.89%. The ensemble is thus a promising technique to build a tree model to detect anomaly event. We thus plan to further investigate other ensemble schemes on this particular domain.

Acknowledgment. This work was financially supported by grants from the National Research Council of Thailand and Suranaree University of Technology through the funding of the Data and Knowledge Engineering Research Unit.

References

1. Singh, P.M., van Sinderen, M.J., Wieringa, R.J.: Smart logistics: an enterprise architecture perspective. In: 29th International Conference on Advanced Information Systems Engineering (CAiSE 2017), pp. 9–16 (2017)
2. Oonk, M.: Smart logistics corridors and the benefits of intelligent transport system. In: Blanquart, C., Clausen, U., Jacob, B. (eds.) Towards Innovative Freight and Logistics. Wiley, New Jersey (2016)

3. Stock, T., Seliger, G.: Opportunities of sustainable manufacturing in industry 4.0. Proc. CIRP **40**, 536–541 (2016)
4. Delfmann, W., ten Hompel, M., Kersten, W., Schmidt, T., Stolzle, W.: Logistics as a science – central research questions in the era of the fourth industrial revolution. Logist. Res. **11**, 1–13 (2017)
5. Syntetos, A.A., Babai, Z., Boylan, J.E., Kolassa, S., Nikolopoulos, K.: Supply chain forecasting: theory, practice, their gap and the future. Eur. J. Oper. Res. **252**(1), 1–26 (2016)
6. Rangel, H.R., Puig, V., Farias, R.L., Flores, J.J.: Short-term demand forecast using a bank of neural network models trained using genetic algorithms for the optimal management of drinking water networks. J. Hydroinform. **19**(1), 1–16 (2017)
7. Lopez Farias, R., Puig, V., Rodriguez Rangel, H., Flores, J.: Multi-model prediction for demand forecast in water distribution networks. Energies **11**(3), 660 (2018). 1–12
8. AL-Musaylh, M.S., Deo, R.C., Li, Y., Adamowski, J.F.: Two-phase particle swarm optimized-support vector regression hybrid model integrated with improved empirical mode decomposition with adaptive noise for multiple-horizon electricity demand forecasting. Appl. Energy **2017**, 422–439 (2018)
9. Koolen, D., Sadat-Razavi, N., Ketter, W.: Machine learning for identifying demand patterns of home energy management systems with dynamic electricity pricing. Appl. Sci. **7**(11), 1160 (2017)
10. Wang, Y., Chen, Q., Gan, D., Yang, J., Kirschen, D.S., Kang, C.: Deep learning-based socio-demographic information identification from smart meter data. IEEE Trans. Smart Grid (2018). https://doi.org/10.1109/tsg.2018.2805723
11. Jiang, S., Chin, K.S., Wang, L., Qu, G., Tsui, K.L.: Modified genetic algorithm-based feature selection combined with pre-trained deep neural network for demand forecasting in outpatient department. Expert Syst. Appl. **82**, 216–230 (2017)
12. Pugh, N., Davis, L.B.: Forecast and analysis of food donations using support vector regression. In: 2017 IEEE International Conference on Big Data (Big Data), pp. 3261–3267 (2017)
13. Papanagnou, C.I., Matthews-Amune, O.: Coping with demand volatility in retail pharmacies with the aid of big data exploration. Comput. Oper. Res. **98**, 343–354 (2018)
14. Ren, S., Chan, H.L., Ram, P.: A comparative study on fashion demand forecasting models with multiple sources of uncertainty. Ann. Oper. Res. **257**(1–2), 335–355 (2017)
15. Chang, Y.W., Tsai, C.Y.: Apply deep learning neural network to forecast number of tourists. In: 31st International Conference on Advanced Information Networking and Applications Workshops (WAINA), pp. 259–264 (2017)
16. Qin, Z., Bowman, J., Bewli, J.: A Bayesian framework for large-scale geo-demand estimation in on-line retailing. Ann. Oper. Res. **263**(1–2), 231–245 (2018)
17. Fisher, M., Glaeser, C.K., Su, X.: Optimal retail location: empirical methodology and application to practice. SSRN Electron. J. (2016). https://papers.ssrn.com/sol3/papers.cfm?abstract_id=2842064
18. Akyuz, A.O., Uysal, M., Bulbul, B.A., Uysal, M.O.: Ensemble approach for time series analysis in demand forecasting: Ensemble learning. In: 2017 IEEE International Conference on INnovations in Intelligent SysTems and Applications (INISTA), pp. 7–12 (2017)
19. Qu, T., Zhang, J.H., Chan, F.T.S., Srivastava, R.S., Tiwari, M.K., Park, W.Y.: Demand prediction and price optimization for semi-luxury supermarket segment. Comput. Ind. Eng. **113**, 91–102 (2017)
20. Semenov, V.P., Chernokulsky, V.V., Razmochaeva, N.V.: Research of artificial intelligence in the retail management problems. In: 2017 IEEE II International Conference on Control in Technical Systems (CTS), pp. 333–336 (2017)

21. Aqil, D.S.M., Ali, S.M., Burney, S.: A survey of soft computing applications for decision making in supply chain management. In: 2017 IEEE 3rd International Conference on Engineering Technologies and Social Sciences (ICETSS), pp. 1–6 (2017)
22. Martínez-López, F.J., Casillas, J.: Artificial intelligence-based systems applied in industrial marketing: an historical overview, current and future insights. Ind. Mark. Manage. **42**(4), 489–495 (2013)
23. Milgrom, P., Tadelis, S.: How artificial intelligence and machine learning can impact market design. National Bureau of Economic Research, Cambridge, MA, w24282 (2018)
24. Simchi-Levi, D.: The new frontier of price optimization. MIT Sloan Manag. Rev. **59**(1), 21–26 (2017)
25. Simchi-Levi, D., Wu, M.X.: Powering retailers' digitization through analytics and automation. Int. J. Prod. Res. **56**(1–2), 809–816 (2018)
26. Syam, N., Sharma, A.: Waiting for a sales renaissance in the fourth industrial revolution: machine learning and artificial intelligence in sales research and practice. Ind. Mark. Manag. **69**, 135–146 (2018)
27. Chen, I.F., Lu, C.J.: Sales forecasting by combining clustering and machine-learning techniques for computer retailing. Neural Comput. Appl. **28**(9), 2633–2647 (2017)
28. Murray, P.W., Agard, B., Barajas, M.A.: Forecasting supply chain demand by clustering customers. IFAC-PapersOnLine **48**(3), 1834–1839 (2015)
29. Shakya, S., Kern, M., Owusu, G., Chin, C.M.: Neural network demand models and evolutionary optimisers for dynamic pricing. Knowl.-Based Syst. **29**, 44–53 (2012)
30. Efendigil, T., Önüt, S., Kahraman, C.: A decision support system for demand forecasting with artificial neural networks and neuro-fuzzy models: a comparative analysis. Expert Syst. Appl. **36**(3), 6697–6707 (2009)
31. Carbonneau, R., Laframboise, K., Vahidov, R.: Application of machine learning techniques for supply chain demand forecasting. Eur. J. Oper. Res. **184**(3), 1140–1154 (2008)
32. Feng, Q., Shanthikumar, J.G.: How research in production and operations management may evolve in the era of big data. Prod. Oper. Manag. **27**(9), 1670–1684 (2018)
33. Böse, J.H., et al.: Probabilistic demand forecasting at scale. VLDB Endow. **10**(12), 1694–1705 (2017)
34. Pinto Ferreira, R., Martiniano, A., Ferreira, A., Ferreira, A., Jose Sassi, R.: Study on daily demand forecasting orders using artificial neural network. IEEE Latin Am. Trans. **14**(3), 1519–1525 (2016)
35. McCormick, K., Abbott, D., Brown, M.S., Khabaza, T., Mutchler, S.R.: IBM SPSS Modeler Cookbook. Packt Publishing, Birmingham (2013)
36. Breiman, L., Friedman, J.H., Olshen, R.A., Stone, C.J.: Classification and Regression Tree. Wadsworth & Brooks/Cole. Advanced Books & Software (1984)

Educational Data Mining: A Profile Analysis of Brazilian Students

Edna Dias Canedo[1]([⊠]) [iD], Heloise Acco Tives Leão[2] [iD],
Rhandy Rafhael de Carvalho[1], Ruyther Parente da Costa[1] [iD],
Giovanni Almeida Santos[1] [iD], and Marcio Vinicius Okimoto[1]

[1] University of Brasília (UnB), Brasília, DF 70910-900, Brazil
{ednacanedo,giovannix}@unb.br, rhandyrafhael@gmail.com, ruyther@me.com,
marciobtos@gmail.com
[2] Lutheran University Center of Palmas (CEULP), Palmas, TO, Brazil
heloise.acco@gmail.com

Abstract. This paper presents an analysis of data referring to the profile of Brazilian students in the year 2016, according to the Higher Education Census. The information provided by this census is used to carry out various analyses related to the current situation of Brazilian education, as well as the profile of students and institutions. In this work, we analyze the modality of courses offered by educational institutions, investigating the profile and the quantitative of students who have scholarship, and how they enter the courses. We also investigate the distribution of students according to the informed skin color/race. The method used to conduct this research involved the application of the steps proposed by the CRISP-DM Reference Model and the use of the Apriori association algorithm to identify and analyze the data set. The results show that 30% of students choose not to report their skin color; Of those who reported, 37.4% are white and 6% are black. Approximately 82% of the students entered higher education through the traditional method (entrance examination), and 82.3% of the male and 77.2% of the female opted for face-to-face courses.

Keywords: Educational Data Mining · Apriori algorithm ·
CRISP-DM · Brazilian students profile

1 Introduction

Several areas of knowledge generate data at an impressive pace. The large increase in data storage and collection has created a demand for techniques capable of extracting potentially useful information from the mass of data. Historically, the notion of mining databases to find useful data patterns has received many names, such as Knowledge Discovery in Databases (KDD), Knowledge Extraction, Data Harvesting, among others. Despite the different names, and in some cases different approaches, these terms have as main objective the extraction of knowledge from databases. Data mining is the non-trivial process of

© Springer Nature Switzerland AG 2019
S. Misra et al. (Eds.): ICCSA 2019, LNCS 11619, pp. 473–488, 2019.
https://doi.org/10.1007/978-3-030-24289-3_35

identifying valid, potentially useful and understandable patterns in the mass of data, with a strong emphasis on working with large amounts of real data [20].

Data mining techniques are increasingly gaining significance in the education sector. As in many other sectors, higher education is discovering the potential impact of these techniques on the learning process and outcomes to move towards a university of the new era, providing educational policymakers with data-based models essential for supporting goals to enhance the efficiency and quality of teaching and learning [2].

Educational data mining (EDM) and Learning Analytics (LA) are two specific areas that are used to represent the use and the application of data mining in higher education and other educational settings. EDM can be defined as the application of traditional data mining techniques to the analysis of educational data, aiming at solving problems in the educational context [6]. Some applications of EDM include the development of e-learning systems [22], distance education, pedagogical support [15], educational data collection [10], student and teacher performance forecasts, evaluation of the quantity needed for the distribution of teachers versus number of schools, among others [9,18]. EDM techniques can reveal useful information to educators and government bodies to help them design or modify the curriculum structure of courses, schools and/or universities. They can help to identify at-risk students, identifying priority teaching and learning needs for different groups of students and teachers (teacher training), increasing the passing rates in schools and undergraduate courses, effectively evaluating institutional and teacher performance, maximizing the resources of schools and/or universities, and optimizing and renewing the curricular programs of the courses.

LA is a closely related endeavor, with somewhat more emphasis on simultaneously investigating automatically collected data along with human observation of the teaching and learning context. Overall, cyberlearning emphasizes the integration of learning sciences theories with these techniques in order to improve the design of learning systems and to better understand how people learn within them. The use of EDM and LA in the educational context has the potential to shape the existing models of teaching and learning by providing new solutions to the interaction problem. EDM and LA are used to offer more personalized, adaptive, and interactive educational environments to enhance learning outcomes, teaching and learning effectiveness, and optimizing institutional proficiency, as well as mapping both professor and student performance [25].

This paper investigates the profile of Brazilian students related to the teaching modality (face-to-face or distance learning) and the study period they chose to attend when they entered higher education. It also analyzes the profile of the students as to skin color, type of university entrance, and if they have a scholarship. To conduct this study, we defined the following research questions (RQ):

RQ.1: What is the profile of Brazilian higher education students related to the different teaching modalities offered (face-to-face or distance learning)?

RQ.2: What is the profile of Brazilian higher education students related to the existence of a scholarship?

RQ.3: What is the form of admission of students to educational institutions?

RQ.4: What is the distribution of Brazilian students according to skin color/race and gender?

This paper is organized as follows. Section 2 presents the state of the art related to educational data mining, as well as mining techniques. In addition, related works to this paper are presented. Section 3 details the method adopted to develop this work. Section 4 presents the results of the CRISP-DM phases. The conclusions and future work are presented in Sect. 5.

2   Educational Data Mining

Educational systems are increasingly engineered to capture and store data on users' interactions with a system. These data can be analyzed using statistical, machine learning, and data mining techniques. The development of computational tools for data analysis, standardization of data logging formats, and increased computation/processing power is enabling learning scientists to investigate research questions using this data. Educational Data Mining (EDM), and the application of Data Mining techniques in data from online education platforms or environments. EDM has emerged as a research area in recent years by researchers in several areas of knowledge seeking to analyze large volumes of data in order to solve educational research issues [30]. Overall, EDM draws on traditional statistical techniques and shares further challenges with other analytic uses of research data, such as: 1. Combining needed data from different systems, which can be difficult. 2. Achieving construct validity and interpretability of results. 3. Understanding consequential validity and use of results to drive decisions. 4. Deciding whether use of data to drive high-stakes and/or low-stakes decisions is warranted. 5. Establishing safeguards for privacy and ethics of data use [27].

EDM and the research area whose main focus is the development of methods to explore databases collected in educational environments, allowing a standard in the approach of educational data mining. Thus, it is possible to more effectively and adequately understand information about teachers, schools, management and students. It allows understanding how learners learn, the context in which learning occurs, how teachers are motivated and/or followed, and other factors that influence teaching learning. The EDM process converts raw data from educational systems into useful information that can be used by developers, teachers, educational researchers, etc. This process does not differ much from other areas of application to that of data mining because it is based on the same steps of the data mining process in general [30]. The educational data mining process comprises the following steps [26], [17]: **1. Preprocessing**: The data obtained with the educational environment must first be pre-processed to transform it into a format suitable for mining. Some of the main tasks of preprocessing are: cleaning, selection of attributes, transformation attributes, data integration, and so on; **2. Data Mining (Extracting Patterns)**: It is the central step that identifies the whole process. During this stage, data mining techniques are applied to previously pre-processed data; **3. Post processing**: It is the final step in which the results obtained or model are interpreted and used to make decisions about the educational environment.

Data generated by students and teachers in e-learning environments can provide rapid and important insights into the performance, motivation and level of participation of students and teachers in a particular subject or course. These understandings may suggest significant changes and interventions in methodology or even individual contact with students and teachers who are unmotivated or have low interaction with the school and/or academic community [33]. Furthermore, the evaluation and monitoring practices of students learning is considered as an essential aspect in higher education. Performance monitoring includes assessments and evaluation processes, which play a vital role in providing valuable information that help students, instructor, administrators, and policy makers in higher education institutions to make decisions. The changing factors in contemporary education has led to the use of various data mining techniques to monitor student performance which offers various investigation methods to analyze and discover hidden information in educational systems. The data extracted by such systems continuously comprise the score for certain learning goals so to generate grades and profile learner [2].

2.1   Mining Techniques

According to Mobasher et al. [24], there is no consensus in the literature regarding the ideal data mining technique for each application, not even the criteria to be used for the evaluation of the different data mining techniques. Among the techniques considered efficient in the literature for data mining, are the rules of association that seek to find links between attributes, i.e., based on the assumption that the presence of an attribute in an event implies the presence of another attribute in the same event [29]. The employment of mining with rules of association is appropriate to analyze educational data where it is intended to identify patterns of the learning process and to improve the academic performance of students or teachers in different courses and or school levels, whether in primary, secondary or higher education [24].

In the paper presented by Abu-Oda and Alaa [1], different data mining approaches are applied in order to examine and predict student drop-outs through their university programs. In this study is analyzed 1290 records of students of the course of computer science, between 2005 and 2011. The data collected included a school history, the syllabus of the subjects taught in the first two years of the course, the average student's school, and whether or not the student graduated from the chosen course upon admission to the University. To classify and predict the data of students who dropped out of the course, different classifiers were used in the data set, including Decision Tree (DT) and Bayesian networks. In the paper presented by Baker [7], we identify the application of data association rules to improve the quality of managerial decisions to provide a quality education, aiming to analyze the data and discover factors that affect the results to increase the chances of success for students and teachers.

2.2 Association Algorithms

Among the association algorithms, the algorithm Apriori, is the algorithm most used to discover rules of association, according to Literature [5]. The Apriori algorithm performs several analyzes on the transaction database, and is able to work with a large number of attributes, resulting in several combinatorial alternatives between them, from successive searches throughout the database and achieving optimum performance in terms of processing [5]. When it is desired to show the frequency and identification of patterns in a data set, the Apriori algorithm is widely used since it presents the frequency of a certain set of selected data. During its application the attributes are tested several times in search of expanded rules which represent patterns of its population [16]. This algorithm works in two steps: in the first step the main frequent item is determined; in the second step the general rule that presents the characteristics of the data set is extracted. The algorithm uses a "bottom up" approach, where frequent subsets are extended once, which is called candidate generation. Each candidate set is tested multiple times until no expanded rule is found [16].

In the use of the algorithm Apriori, the measures that influence the discovery of the rules are: 1. Support that is the percentage of cases where it contains both A and B; 2. Trust that is percentage of cases containing A that also contains B; and 3. Trust is the confidence rate with the percentage of cases containing B [19].

2.3 Related Works

Alom and Courtney [3] made an assessment of the role of student gender on successive rates of educational completion in Australia from primary school Year 1 through to successful completion of high school, and, thereafter, enrolment in university. The results suggested that gender played an important role, especially in some states, and that, in general, enrolment numbers in university in 2016 appeared to be on par with those completing Year 12 in 2015.

The work presented by Fernandes et al. [13] presents an analysis of the academic performance of public school students at the federal district. The authors use federal district education system databases to understand student profiles and their learning styles, in an effort to develop educational policies that improve academic performance and reduce failure rates at the end of each school year. Fonseca and Namen [14] identify factors that relate the profiles and their influences - positive and negative - in students' learning of the mathematics discipline. The authors apply Knowledge Discovery in Databases (KDD) in order to identify the factors that relate the profile of the teachers who teach the Mathematics discipline to the proficiency obtained by their students.

Ashish et al. [12] perform a systematic review of literature from 1983 to 2016 on the clustering algorithm and its applicability and usability in the context of educational data mining. Future insights are outlined based on the revised literature, and the possibilities for further research have been identified. The work presents that the main advantage of the clustering algorithm application to the data analysis is that it provides a relatively unambiguous learning style scheme to the students, considering a certain number of variables, such as the time spent in completing the learning tasks, group learning, student behavior in the classroom and student motivation for learning.

Asif et al. [4] use data mining methods to study the performance of undergraduate students, focusing on two aspects of their performance. First, predict the academic level of students at the end of a four-year study program. Second, they study typical progressions and combine them with predicted outcomes. Two major groups of students were identified: low performing students and high performing students. The results indicate that by focusing on a small number of courses that are particularly good or bad performance indicators, it is possible to provide timely alerts and support for underachieving students, as well as advice and opportunities for high performance students.

Amirah et al. [28] perform a systematic review of the literature in order to identify the most appropriate methods to predict the performance of students using data mining techniques in educational institutions in Malaysia. Furthermore, they investigate the factors that affect student outcomes in specific courses within the context of Malaysia. The authors propose a model to improve students' performance. The main contribution of the work is to demonstrate how the prediction algorithm can be used to identify the most important attributes in the data of the students to improve their use and success in a more efficient way, using educational data mining techniques, allowing benefits and impacts for students, educators and academic institutions. In the paper presented by [32], analytical approaches to learning, educational data mining and human computer interaction are synthesized to explore the development of more usable forecast models and representations of forecast models using data from a solution environment of collaborative geometry problems: virtual math teams.

3   Method

According to data mining techniques [16, 21, 23] and educational data mining [7, 24], the Apriori algorithm was chosen to support the task of finding association rules in the context of this work and the reference model CRISP-DM [8] to perform the data mining steps, perform tests to evaluate the results found, present results and analyzes, as well as make suggestions based on the conclusions obtained, of possible solutions to implement improvements in the object analyzed with the objective of increasing the satisfaction of teachers, students and the community of the educational system of the analyzed region.

The CRISP-DM reference model defines a set of sequential steps to guide data mining and allows the mining process to be fast, reliable, and with greater managerial control [11]. CRISP-DM involves six phases: domain understanding, data comprehension, data preparation, modeling, evaluation and implementation [19]. The adoption of these phases helps in defining the flows to be used to execute the mining project. Each phase is structured into several activities, which run cyclically to meet the objectives of data mining [19]. CRISP-DM is a complete and documented methodology. All phases are organized, structured and defined, so the project is easily understood and reviewed [8]. For this study, all CRISP-DM phases were used, except for the implantation phase, which will be performed in our future work.

4 Analysis of Results

Due to the breadth of the analyzed database (11,449.222 lines) and the difficulty in manipulating the data due to its size, the student data file was divided according to the gender of the participants (male - 44.3% of data and female - 55.6% of data). From the analysis of the 99 attributes in the microdata base, it was possible to identify the relevant attributes to answer the Research Questions delimited in this work. The selected dataset is displayed in Table 1. It was used the R-Studio data mining tool [31], which has packages and tools to perform most of the mining steps.

The application of the Apriori algorithm in the national database, containing the records from all Brazil, used the default parameters of the algorithm, e.g., Support in 10% and Trust in 90%. With this application, a set of 272 rules was generated for the data set of the female students and 262 rules for the data set of the male students. Figure 1 presents the rules obtained for the profile of female students in relation to the chosen teaching modality. According to the results, it is possible to conclude that the female students who choose the type of face-to-face teaching were not admitted in higher education through the ENEM and also do not have student funding. Furthermore, the predominant academic degree of this group of students is baccalaureate, the study shift is nocturnal and the administrative category of the place of study is in For-Profit Private Institution. Regarding students who choose distance education, one can only verify that the highest incidence of cases is related to students who were not admitted in higher education through ENEM and that the administrative category of the place of study is Institution of Private for-profit education.

In relation to the profile of male students according to the chosen teaching modality, it was observed that the set of generated rules is very similar to the rules generated for female students, using the same variables, being the similar result for the two groups evaluated. The profile of female students considering the existence of student financing to pay for their studies in higher education, presents the main rules obtained: according to the results presented in Fig. 2 it is possible to identify students who do not have a scholarship to assist in the financing of their studies, declare themselves predominantly as being of white color or race, or have not made the declaration for this variable. Furthermore, the teaching modality is predominantly presential model. Students who do not have student funding have a high incidence of study at night, although some study in the morning. In relation to students who have a scholarship to assist

Table 1. Description of attributes analyzed

Variable name	Description	Description of categories
CATEGORY	Administrative category code	1. Federal Public 2. Public State 3. Municipal Public 4. Private for profit 5. Private non-profit 7. Special
SHIFT	Course shift code to which the student is linked	1. Morning 2. Evening 3. Nightly 4. Integral 5. Distance Education (EaD) (.) Not applicable
GRADE	Code of the academic degree conferred to the graduate by the course	1. Bachelor degree 2. Graduation 3. Technological (.) Not applicable
MODALITY	Course modality code	1. Presential 2. Distance Education (EaD)
COLOR_RACE	Skin Color/Race code	1. White 2. Black 3. Brown 4. Yellow 5. Indigenous 6. Not declared 0. Not declared
ENEM	Informs if the student has enrolled in the course by ENEM	0. No 1. Yes
FINANCING	Informs if the student uses student financing	0. No 1. Yes

in the financing of their studies, most preferred not to declare their color/race, besides the teaching modality being the face-to-face model. Students with student funding also have a high incidence of study at night.

Regarding the profile of male students, considering the existence of funding for higher education studies, as shown in Fig. 3, the following results were obtained: it is possible to identify students who do not have a scholarship to help finance their studies, did not enter higher education through ENEM. These students opted for private non-profit and for-profit institutions, with study hours at night and by the academic degree of baccalaureate and modality of teaching both face-to-face and distance learning. Regarding students who have scholarships to help fund their studies, students declare themselves predominantly as

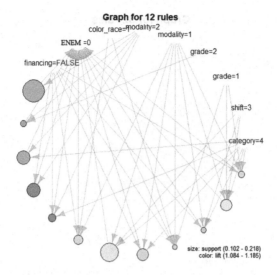

Fig. 1. Evaluation of the profile of female students in relation to the teaching modality.

being of the brown color/race, in addition to the main teaching modality being the face-to-face model and the academic degree being baccalaureate. For those students with student financing, a high incidence of study was observed at night.

Figure 4 presents the main rules obtained for the profile of female students in relation to entering higher education through ENEM. The results show that students who entered through the ENEM or through another form of access have an almost identical profile. These students chose mainly the night shift for study, with little incidence in the rules for the morning study period, the teaching modality is baccalaureate and these students mostly chose not to declare their color/race.

With regard to the male students on the form of entrance into higher education through the ENEM, the Fig. 5 presents the main rules obtained. With the analysis of the result, it is noticed that the identified students declared themselves predominantly as being of the color/race white or brown, are attending the academic degree of baccalaureate, study predominantly in private non-profit and for-profit educational institutions and do not have student financing. Regarding to students who have entered higher education without the ENEM, such as the college entrance examination, their main characteristics are of color/white race and they are studying the academic bachelor degree in the night shift.

With the application of mining classifier algorithms, from the use of the R-Studio tool [31], it was possible to obtain an overview regarding the students' choices according to their gender. Regarding the administrative category chosen by the students, as can be seen in Fig. 6, it is possible to identify that 45% chose private for-profit institutions, 32% study in non-profit private institutions. Approximately 15% chose to study in federal public institutions and 7% in state public institutions. The high choice of private institutions is mainly due to the

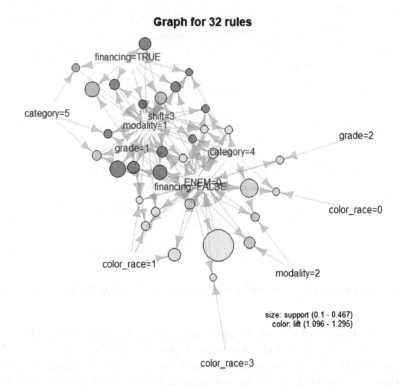

Fig. 2. Evaluation of the profile of female students in relation to the existence of student financing.

greater number of places offered by these institutions. In the classification by gender, a slight predominance by male (15.6%) in federal public institutions is observed when compared to the number of female (12.4%). This predominance is reversed in private for-profit institutions with the distribution of vacancies for male (43.5%) and for female (47.0%).

Regarding the distribution of students by color/race, as shown in Fig. 7, an interesting fact that can be verified is that almost 30% of the students chose not to declare their color/race. Among students who declare their breeding it is noticed that most are of the white color/race (about 37.4%), less than 1% declared themselves indigenous and only about 6% declared themselves black. The variation in all color/race classes between male and female is less than 1%.

Regarding the method of enrollment in higher education, as shown in Fig. 8, the most prevalent was the traditional methods (tests and college entrance examination), being still the most common for students, being around 82%. Only 18% of the students chose to enter higher education through ENEM.

Figure 9 presents the distribution of students according to the existence of student financing. 51.1% of male students and 51.3% of female students declare they do not have student funding, 27.7% of male students and 30.6% of female students declare they do not have student funding and 21.2% of male and 18.2% of female chose not to declare this characteristic.

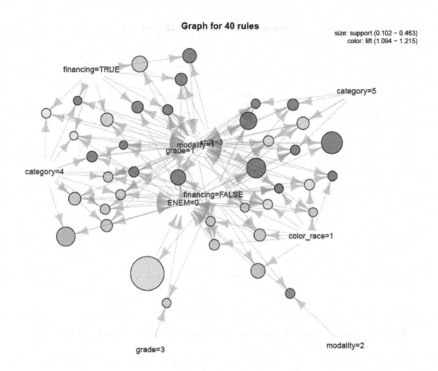

Fig. 3. Evaluation of the profile of male students in relation to the existence of student financing.

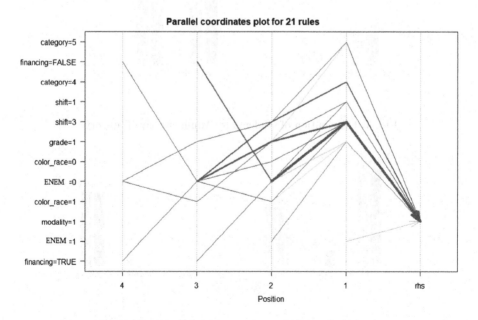

Fig. 4. Profile evaluation of female students who have joined ENEM.

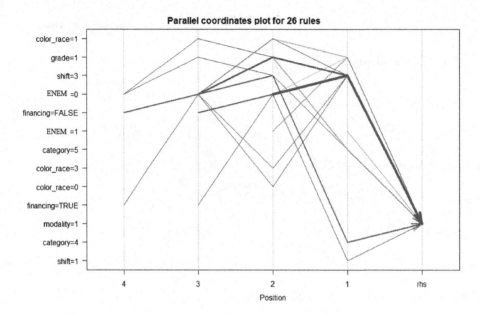

Fig. 5. Profile evaluation of male students who have joined the ENEM.

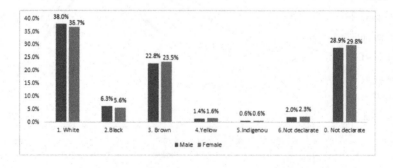

Fig. 6. Distribution of students by Administrative Category.

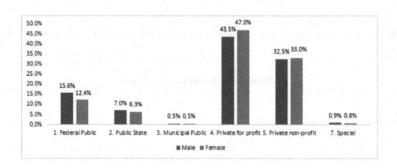

Fig. 7. Distribution of students by color/race.

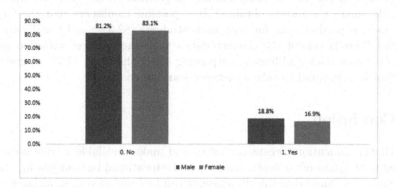

Fig. 8. Distribution of students by the admission method in higher education.

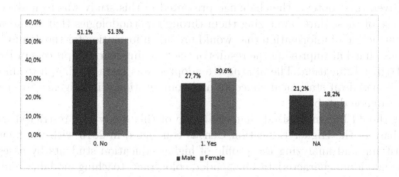

Fig. 9. Distribution of students through the existence of student financing.

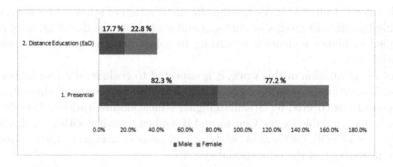

Fig. 10. Distribution of students by Teaching Modality.

The last characteristic analyzed was in relation to the teaching modality. Figure 10 shows the results obtained. It is possible to observe that the face-to-face model is predominant for both male students (82.3%) and female students (77.2%). This is one of the characteristics with the greatest variation in the choice between male and female, surpassing 5% of the total. 17.7% of male and 22.8% of female opted to take a distance learning course.

5   Conclusion

The Higher Education Census organizes and makes available a wide data base related to the data of students, teachers and educational institutions for studies and diagnoses. Analyzing this database, it can be concluded that, although they are an important source of information, they are often not fully exploited due to the inherent difficulties of the large amount of data involved, which is beyond the human capacity to interpret, being necessary the use of suitable tools for its manipulation and analysis.

Given this context, the challenge presented in this study was to make effective use of these data, analyzing them through methodologies that would allow the extraction of information that would provide information for the definition of actions aimed at improving the results of the teaching-learning process of Brazilian Higher Education. The alternative adopted was Data Mining, a technology that is based on statistical concepts and computational intelligence to analyze large volume databases.

It should be emphasized that the scope of this study was restricted to the database of the Higher Education Census conducted in 2016 with the focus on identifying and analyzing the profile of higher education students by assessing their individual characteristics by gender, color/race, teaching modality and student financing.

The results obtained from the data mining made possible the profile description of the Brazilian higher education student in relation to the different types of teaching offered (face-to-face or distance education), allowing to identify that more than 80% of Brazilian students chose modality of face-to-face teaching. Furthermore, it allowed investigating the distribution of scholarships for student funding by different groups of students and evaluating the distribution of places occupied in higher education according to color/race and gender informed by the students.

As a continuation of this work, it is expected to evaluate data on higher education institutions, available courses, the profile of teachers and characteristics of the locations covered by Brazilian higher education institutions. This data set is also made available by the Census and if studied together with the other information can identify patterns of behavior and propose actions to further assist in the improvement of the educational system.

Acknowledgment. This research work has the support of the Research Support Foundation of the Federal District (FAPDF).

References

1. Abu-Oda, G.S., El-Halees, A.M.: Data mining in higher education: university student dropout case study. Int. J. Data Min. Knowl. Manage. Process **5**(1), 15 (2015)
2. Aldowah, H., Al-Samarraie, H., Fauzy, W.M.: Educational data mining and learning analytics for 21st century higher education: a review and synthesis. Telematics Inform. **37**, 13–49 (2019)
3. Alom, B., Courtney, M.: Educational data mining: a case study perspectives from primary to university education in australia. Int. J. Inf. Technol. Comput. Sci. (IJITCS) **10**(2), 1–9 (2018)
4. Asif, R., Merceron, A., Ali, S.A., Haider, N.G.: Analyzing undergraduate students' performance using educational data mining. Comput. Educ. **113**, 177–194 (2017). https://doi.org/10.1016/j.compedu.2017.05.007
5. Awan, S., Dadan, R.: Graduate rate analysis of student using data mining and algorithm apriori. Int. J. Soft Comput. **12**(5), 287–293 (2017)
6. Baker, R., et al.: Data mining for education. Int. Encycl. Educ. **7**(3), 112–118 (2010)
7. Baker, R.S., Inventado, P.S.: Educational data mining and learning analytics. In: Larusson, J.A., White, B. (eds.) Learn. Anal., pp. 61–75. Springer, New York (2014). https://doi.org/10.1007/978-1-4614-3305-7_4
8. Barclay, C., Dennis, A., Shepherd, J.: Application of the crisp-dm model in predicting high school students' examination (CSEC/CXC) performance. In: Knowledge Discovery Process and Methods to Enhance Organizational Performance, p. 279 (2015)
9. Canedo, E.D., Santos, G.A., de Freitas, S.A.A.: Analysis of the teaching-learning methodology adopted in the introduction to computer science classes. In: 2017 IEEE Frontiers in Education Conference (FIE), pp. 1–8. IEEE (2017)
10. Chakraborty, B., Chakma, K., Mukherjee, A.: A density-based clustering algorithm and experiments on student dataset with noises using rough set theory. In: 2016 IEEE International Conference on Engineering and Technology (ICETECH), pp. 431–436. IEEE (2016)
11. Chapman, P., et al.: CRISP-DM 1.0 step-by-step data mining guide. CRISP DM consortium (updated 2010) (1999) (2000)
12. Dutt, A., Ismail, M.A., Herawan, T.: A systematic review on educational data mining. IEEE Access **5**, 15991–16005 (2017)
13. Fernandes, E., Holanda, M., Victorino, M., Borges, V., Carvalho, R., Van Erven, G.: Educational data mining: predictive analysis of academic performance of public school students in the capital of brazil. J. Bus. Res. (2018). Elsevier
14. Fonseca, S.O.D., Namen, A.A.: Data mining on INEP databases: an initial analysis aiming to improve Brazilian educational system. Educação em Revista **32**(1), 133–157 (2016)
15. Hung, J.L., Crooks, S.M.: Examining online learning patterns with data mining techniques in peer-moderated and teacher-moderated courses. J. Educ. Comput. Res. **40**(2), 183–210 (2009)
16. Jang, S., Park, K., Kim, Y., Cho, H., Yoon, T.: Comparison of H5N1, H5N8, and H3N2 using decision tree and apriori algorithm. J. Biosci. Med. **3**(06), 49 (2015)
17. Jha, J., Ragha, L.: Educational data mining using improved apriori algorithm. Int. J. Inf. Comput. Technol. **3**(5), 411–418 (2013)
18. Kabra, R., Bichkar, R.: Performance prediction of engineering students using decision trees. Int. J. Comput. Appl. **36**(11), 8–12 (2011)

19. Kalgotra, P., Sharda, R.: Progression analysis of signals: extending CRISP-DM to stream analytics. In: 2016 IEEE International Conference on Big Data (Big Data), pp. 2880–2885. IEEE (2016)

20. Kavitha, G., Raj, L.: Educational data mining and learning analytics - educational assistance for teaching and learning. CoRR abs/1706.03327 (2017)

21. woo Kim, C., Ahn, S.H., Yoon, T.: Comparison of flavivirus using datamining-apriori, k-means, and decision tree algorithm. In: 2017 19th International Conference on Advanced Communication Technology (ICACT), pp. 454–457. IEEE (2017)

22. Lara, J.A., Lizcano, D., Martínez, M.A., Pazos, J., Riera, T.: A system for knowledge discovery in e-learning environments within the european higher education area-application to student data from open university of madrid, udima. Comput. Educ. 72, 23–36 (2014)

23. Luna, J.M., Padillo, F., Pechenizkiy, M., Ventura, S.: Apriori versions based on mapreduce for mining frequent patterns on big data. IEEE Trans. Cybern. 99, 1–15 (2017)

24. Mobasher, G., Shawish, A., Ibrahim, O.: Educational data mining rule based recommender systems. In: CSEDU (1), pp. 292–299 (2017)

25. Paiva, R., Bittencourt, I.I., Lemos, W., Vinicius, A., Dermeval, D.: Visualizing learning analytics and educational data mining outputs. In: Penstein Rosé, C., Martínez-Maldonado, R., Hoppe, H.U., Luckin, R., Mavrikis, M., Porayska-Pomsta, K., McLaren, B., du Boulay, B. (eds.) AIED 2018. LNCS (LNAI), vol. 10948, pp. 251–256. Springer, Cham (2018). https://doi.org/10.1007/978-3-319-93846-2_46

26. Papamitsiou, Z., Economides, A.A.: Learning analytics and educational data mining in practice: a systematic literature review of empirical evidence. J. Educ. Technol. Soc. 17(4), 49–64 (2014)

27. Ray, S., Saeed, M.: Applications of educational data mining and learning analytics tools in handling big data in higher education. In: Alani, M.M., Tawfik, H., Saeed, M., Anya, O. (eds.) Applications of Big Data Analytics, pp. 135–160. Springer, Cham (2018). https://doi.org/10.1007/978-3-319-76472-6_7

28. Shahiri, A.M., Husain, W., et al.: A review on predicting student's performance using data mining techniques. Procedia Comput. Sci. 72, 414–422 (2015)

29. da Silva, L.A., Peres, S.M., Boscarioli, C.: Introdução à mineração de dados: com aplicações em R. Elsevier Brasil (2017)

30. Silva, R., Ramos, J.L.C., Rodrigues, R., Gomes, A.S., Fonseca, A.: Mineração de dados educacionais na análise das interações dos alunos em um ambiente virtual de aprendizagem. In: Brazilian Symposium on Computers in Education (Simpósio Brasileiro de Informática na Educação-SBIE), vol. 26, p. 1197 (2015)

31. Studio, R.: RStudio: integrated development environment for R, p. 74. RStudio Inc., Boston (2012)

32. Xing, W., Guo, R., Petakovic, E., Goggins, S.: Participation-based student final performance prediction model through interpretable genetic programming: integrating learning analytics, educational data mining and theory. Comput. Hum. Behav. 47, 168–181 (2015)

33. Yukselturk, E., Ozekes, S., Türel, Y.K.: Predicting dropout student: an application of data mining methods in an online education program. Eur J. Open Distance E-learn. 17(1), 118–133 (2014)

The Pollicina Project: A Social Learning Management System to Create Personalized Cultural Itineraries

Silvia Calegari(✉), Paolo Avogadro, Floriana Meluso, and Matteo Dominoni

University of Milano-Bicocca, DISCo, Viale Sarca 336 Building 14,
20126 Milano, Italy
{silvia.calegari,paolo.avogadro,matteo.dominoni}@unimib.it,
f.meluso1@campus.unimib.it
http://www.idea.disco.unimib.it/
https://www.progettopollicina.eu/

Abstract. The Pollicina project is aimed at defining a social learning management system, called Educational Social Network (EduSN), that follows the principles of the flipped learning paradigm. Students are involved to create thematic cultural paths on the territory through the cultural institutions that joined the project (such as: museums, churches, archaeological sites, etc.). With this new tool it is possible to obtain an active participation in the cultural life: students will approach the historical and cultural issues through a direct involvement in enjoyable activities, sharing experiences, ideas, multimedia material and social feedback. This paper presents the "ArtTour" service dedicated to the definition of the cultural paths.

Keywords: Learning technologies · Flipped learning ·
Art and teaching · Cultural itineraries

1 Introduction

In the last decade the educational landscape has been undergoing an important change due mainly to the use of the social media that have transformed the way on how students interact among each other. Social media technology is moving rapidly in the educational context as it enables students to create and share information, ideas, experiences through virtual learning communities [13]. As reported by Ram and Sinha, in fact: "The current generations' exposure towards technical advancements, availability of mobile computing power and ubiquitousness of internet has impacted the way in which learners chose to learn" [14]. There is a strong intersection between the educational social media technology and the flipped learning paradigm since the first one allows to improve the students' learning by offering advantages over traditional educational schemas [7,9]. In fact, the flipped learning is considered an emerging model to support education where lessons, that traditionally happen within the classroom, take also

S. Misra et al. (Eds.): ICCSA 2019, LNCS 11619, pp. 489–503, 2019.
https://doi.org/10.1007/978-3-030-24289-3_36

place out-of-the-school *any time* and *any where*: the activity in the classroom is based on organizing a peer approach where students report their own learning experiences and teachers participate as moderators [8,11]. In this respect, collective knowledge is produced and shared for later use in a new peer-to-peer activity by encouraging critical thinking, student collaboration, and the support of different student learning styles and capabilities [6,17]. Other minor objectives of the adoption of the flipped methodology are the decrease class absenteeism, a positive impact on students' grades, and an improvement of the relationships among students [5,16], so that students become active participants rather than passive listeners. In addition, the role of the teacher assumes more importance as he/she acts not only as a moderator of the learning activities but his/her presence goes beyond the classroom, even if virtually, because of any prescribed homework could benefit from enriched content and assistance/feedback [13].

This paper presents the Pollicina project [4] that is a collaborative coordinated social learning environment which allows to bring the students closer to cultural heritages (museums, churches, archaeological sites, etc.) by creating knowledge itineraries linking several cultural institutions distributed in the territory. This project follows the principles of the flipped learning paradigm where the use of the social media technology supports the learning practices in order to allow the students to approach the historical and cultural topics through a direct involvement in activities such as comments, experiences, and ideas. Collaborative teaching among groups of peers induces a synergy for the active production of the paths where students can also enrich the heterogeneous material (e.g., paintings, archaeological finds, statues, etc.) provided by the cultural heritage institutions that joined the project. Teachers define the topics of the itinerary and supervise, with experts of cultural institutions, the work of the students thus establishing a novel form of social learning dedicated to the art topic. The objective is to get the students closer to the cultural heritage of the territory by defining personalized itineraries according to several factors ranging from a formal approach (i.e., the educational knowledge of cultural objects) to an informal approach (i.e., any perspectives associated with their personal experiences, emotions, soft skills, etc.). The output consists of personalized cultural itineraries that allow the students to focus their visit only on a portion of cultural objects provided by the cultural institutions namely the ones chosen for the specific thematic of the cultural path. This novel approach to the cultural visit is becoming more and more important for museums and cultural institutions that intend to collect individuals' personal perspectives to complement and augment the *official cultural paths* provided by the cultural institutions [1,12].

This paper is organized as follows. Section 2 gives an overview of the Pollicina project, Sect. 3 presents the *ArtTour* service dedicated to the building of the cultural paths, and Sect. 4 proposes some first user experiences evaluations of the *ArtTour* service. Finally, in Sect. 5 the conclusions are stated.

2   The Pollicina Project

Pollicina is a cultural navigator based on the flipped learning paradigm [4], it is developed under the Regional Operational Program of the European Fund

Fig. 1. Three logical dimensions of the EduSN platform: *Territory*, *Scholastic Environment*, and *User Experience*.

for Regional Development 2014–2020 (POR FESR 2014–2020) of the Regione Lombardia in Italy (the project has a time-line of two years and now we are at the end of the second year). The main goal of this project is to provide a collaborative tool which allows the students to create cultural paths connecting artworks belonging to different cultural institutions distributed in the territory, following a theme provided by the teacher. According to the flipped learning paradigm, learning is enriched and becomes more effective if the students become the builders of their own instruction under the guidance of a coach (which is usually the teacher or a group of experts), who gives them sources of information, monitors their collaboration and validates their results. In this respect, cooperative learning is fundamental to obtain various forms of proficiency (cognitive, relational, expressive, etc.) through discussions and comparisons within an active process of knowledge building. To achieve these educational objectives, different methodological and technological approaches have to been adopted.

EduSN, Pollicina's platform, combines standard aspects of an e-learning environment with social features such as networking, collaboration and knowledge sharing capabilities, as well as interactive tools that enable users to share ideas and contents. EduSN is a Social Learning Management System dedicated to the building of cultural itineraries and it is developed as a SaaS (software as a service) for enabling groups of students to elaborate the cultural homework anywhere and anytime. In detail, EduSN addresses (according to the Italian academic institutions): LEVEL 1) primary school students (6–10 years), LEVEL 2) secondary school students of first-degree (11–13 years), and LEVEL 3) secondary school students of second-degree (14–19 years).

Although the educative paradigm of flipped learning is gaining momentum, there are still few tools which actively help the teachers to prepare the setting for the novel kind of lessons involved. The cultural lessons in fact need to be re-designed in order to allow the students to re-create the cultural knowledge by accessing to fundamental units of knowledge. These knowledge units need to be prepared according to the skills and capabilities of the students. The role of the students, on the other hand, is to find the correlations which are at the core of the understanding process. The cultural path creation within the EduSN platform is structured in three fundamental dimensions as shown in Fig. 1:

– Territory: it contains the *Data Filling* service [3] dedicated to the digitalization of the materials provided by the cultural institutions which are partners of the project. These artworks need to be catalogued and inserted in EduSN in order to be available at the time of the cultural paths creation according to the ad-hoc data representation defined for the project. This service is propaedeutic for the definition of the personalized itineraries because it is aimed at defining the knowledge that will be stored in the repository. In detail, the job consists in filling a form for each cultural object by following several collaborative phases of the defined workflow for establishing a high quality level of the material enriched by students. During this workflow the students have both the role of content creators and of reviewers. Once a form passes a first peer review process, it is then checked by the teachers, who can reject the job, asking for modifications, or bring it to the final level where the expert of the museum decides whether further modifications are needed or the quality is above a previously defined threshold.

– Scholastic Environment: it contains the *ArtTour* and *Game* services. The former revolves around the creation of customized cultural paths by accessing to the pool of artworks stored in the EduSN's repository and it is the core service explained in this paper (see Sect. 3), the latter is dedicated to the definition of the cultural itineraries by adopting pleasant learning activities for the younger students (i.e., like puzzle, quiz, word and image association, etc.).

– User Experience: the very last phase consists in the actual realization of the visits according to the defined cultural paths. During this phase the students visit on site, and are able to access live the artworks which form part of the cultural paths with the help of a dedicated App. The students are allowed to get more information on the artworks and to access to augmented reality services through their mobile devices. The App connected with the augmented reality allows to form a social network revolving around the artworks and the ideas which connect these artworks. In this respect, this dimension contains the *Visit* service for the storage of the cultural itineraries and the associations of the related student's experience gathered during the visit, and the *Magazine* service for collecting the most interesting cultural itineraries.

Currently the project involves 12 heterogeneous schools of all educational levels (i.e., starting from the primary school level up to secondary schools), for a total of about 900 users and 26 cultural institutions of the Regione Lombardia. Approximately 300 secondary school students are involved in "alternanza scuola lavoro" activities (i.e., an Italian teaching method created in collaboration between schools and companies to offer students skills that can be used in the job market), including aspects of user centred design. With the new scholastic year, we are planning to increase the audience of users (both schools and cultural institutions), and to complete the development of the whole EduSN's features.

3   The ArtTour Service

In the last years, it has become more and more important for the cultural institutions to propose initiatives to improve the experience of visitors with the support of technology. For several years the PATCH workshop [1] has gathered researchers and practitioners to sensitize them in regards of innovative activities that allow to personalize and deliver context-aware cultural heritage experiences with the help of new technologies. The ArtTour service is the Pollicina's core activity and it is dedicated to the definition of the customized cultural itineraries thanks to the collaboration of the students. Given a topic by the teacher, the students propose an itinerary after several phases: selection/filter of the cultural object, storytelling of the cultural objects selected, and the definition of the related cultural path according to the belongingness to specific cultural heritage institutions by the use of indoor/outdoor maps for creating the related logistic paths. The cultural institutions are distributed in the territory and each path correlates heterogeneous cultural objects located within different sites by giving the opportunity to discover new semantic links. Another important feature is that the paths are not proposed by the cultural experts of the museums but they are created in a bottom-up modality. The students, organized in groups, collaborate by sharing information and ideas in order to produce cultural paths under the supervision of the teacher. A path becomes the starting point of a visit focused only on the portion of the cultural material related to the theme, this allows to stimulate the student's interest by avoiding dispersion related with loosely connected material which could become a boring activity. The use of technology (i.e., smartphones, tablets, etc.) could also improve the experience of the visit by allowing the students to enrich the knowledge of each cultural heritage object with emoticons, comments, photos, vocal reactions, etc.

In the following we introduce the phases of the ArtTour service.

3.1   Phase 1: Settings of the Cultural Path

In the first phase, a teacher defines the thematic of the cultural path and the groups of students that will have to create it. In detail, the thematic is composed by three fields: (1) title, (2) textual description, and (3) a list of concepts that identify the topics of the thematic where to each concept is possible to associate a colour. The thematic can be selected as public (i.e., made available to the Pollicina's users as a starting track for creating paths on a similar content) or private (i.e., made available only for the teacher who created it). A teacher assigns the thematic to a group of students, it is important to notice that, in Pollicina, the members of a group can belong to different classes or schools, thus extending the class concept. Another important step of the process regards the attribution of roles to the students who can have different responsibilities during a task in order to acquire learning awareness and improve their self-esteem. In practice, the teacher has to choose a student supervisor who acts as the first moderator during all the learning activities performed by peers. This role can be changed in any moment by the teacher. At the end, the teacher establishes the time-line of the learning activities in order to constrain the work within a given temporal range (in order to avoid dispersion, and to help the students to focus on their tasks).

3.2   Phase 2: Development of the Cultural Path

Once the thematic has been defined, the students can analyze and study the arguments starting from the concepts defined in the previous phase by the teacher. In detail, the conceptual map is built on the thematic, where the *title* is the central node, and the *list of concepts* are its children nodes. At this point, the students can develop the conceptual map by adding new nodes, each one establishing a subtopic of the thematic itself. In this respect a conceptual map is a visual organizer of knowledge that can enrich students' understanding of new concepts. During the definition of the conceptual map, a student can interact with each node by assigning a his/her social preference regarding the pertinence of such node to the theme and she/he can access to the whole set of cultural objects associated with the selected node. In detail, the creation of the conceptual map is a collaborative process among all the students of a group, based in their interaction via a social wall developed for this purpose in the EduSN platform. A student can in any moment select the two modalities of work changing from the conceptual map to the social wall (and vice-versa). In fact, each concept defined in Phase 1 creates automatically a virtual and collaborative work space within the social wall where students can create a post-it. Each post-it generates subtopics (associated with a given concept) which, on the conceptual map, appear as children nodes. A post-it is defined by a title (mandatory), a description (mandatory) where the students have to motivate the insertion of such post-it, an image, and a list of artworks selected by the Pollicina's repository. The students can choose the relevant cultural materials with the help of a search engine (presented in [15]) that enables innovative soft-clustering aimed at discovering artworks with similarities in respect to the ones of the selected subtopic. As a future activity we will also define a recommender system dedicated to discover semantic similarity for multimedia materials associated with the same cultural itinerary included in the path [2].

Figure 2 shows an example of a conceptual map defined by students and a teacher with the supervision of a cultural expert related to the topic of the urban change over time in particular referred to the city of Milan in Italy. The central node (containing the title) is *Milan: yesterday and today*, while the list of four concepts defined in Phase 1 includes: *means of transportation, Routes of Communication, Common Spaces*, and *Architecture*. Figure 3 shows a portion of the social wall related to the first phases of the student's and it contains several post-its for the *Architecture* and *Common Spaces* concepts. The students can specify social preferences by clicking on like/dislike functionalities with the peculiarity that such social selection has to be motivated with a comment, this feature was decided in order to foster a higher level of responsibility for the students during this learning activity. It is possible to associate, artworks with a post-it: a student performs a query by using the search engine and from the set of the ranked artworks, he/she can drag on the post-it the selected material (e.g. the *Il ponte di Porta Ticinese, Dintorni di Milano*, etc. pictured within Fig. 3).

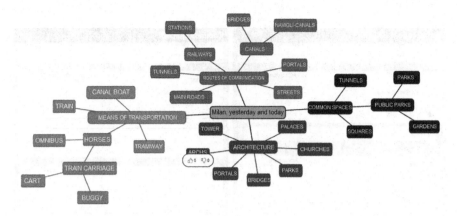

Fig. 2. Conceptual map of the thematic *Milan: yesterday and today* defined with the support of the cultural expert.

3.3   Phase 3: Choice of the Cultural Heritage Objects

This phase is aimed at the selection of the artworks that will be inserted in the path. The student supervisor, after the analysis of the social wall and of the conceptual map, identifies the arguments of interest for the peers (i.e., list of post-its from the social wall of Phase 2) and divides logically the students within groups. Each group is later expected to deepen the subtopic of the selected post-it. Figure 4 shows the selection of the post-it *Navigli-Canals* and the related set of artworks (i.e., *Il Naviglio di Porta Romana lungo la via Francesco Sforza, Il Naviglio presso San Marco*, etc.). In this phase, a student can personalize the path not only by selecting the artworks (by clicking on the green button at the top right corner of the image of the artwork) but he/she can also customize the specific artwork. For example, Fig. 5 shows the form containing the information of the artwork called *Il Naviglio di Porta Romana lungo la via Francesco Sforza*. A student, by clicking on the *Add content* button can add new multimedia material (i.e., images, video, text) he/she has previously collected, for example from the Web. This feature allows to enrich the information content of the EduSN's repository. In addition, it is listed all the information related to the selected artwork and a student can personalize the content information visible during the on site visit. For example, in Fig. 5 he/she can select the field *Description about the cultural heritage*, and at the time of the visit this field will be visible.

3.4   Phase 4: Planning of the Cultural Path in the Territory

When the path with all the artworks is defined, the students have to edit the narrative text correlated to the path. They can access to a concurrent and collaborative editor for sharing ideas and content and the visual map they produced. Figure 6 shows the visual map on the thematic proposed in this paper. In detail, a visual map graphically represents the nodes (post-it) and the selected artworks. In this way, the students have a visual correlation between the artworks and

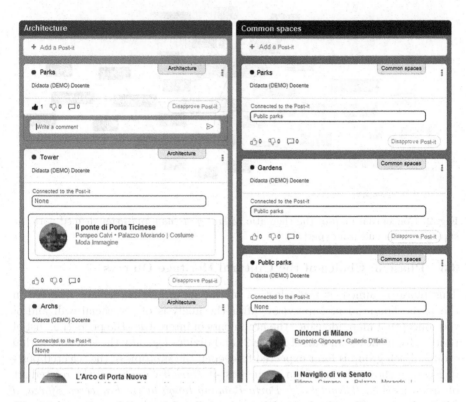

Fig. 3. A portion of the social wall constructed by students and experts about the thematic *Milan: yesterday and today.*

Fig. 4. Selection of the artworks that have to be included in the path related to the thematic *Milan: yesterday and today.*

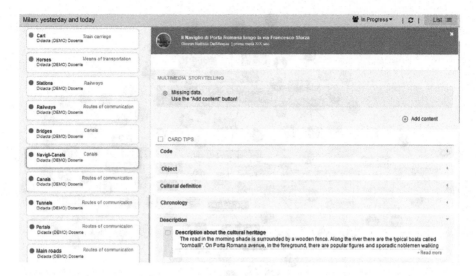

Fig. 5. Detailed vision of the artwork entitled *Il Naviglio di Porta Romana lungo la via Francesco Sforza.*

the corresponding subtopic. Each final artwork is classified according to cultural institutions of belongingness. The platform provides the geographical location of each cultural institution in order to facilitate and organize the visits in the territory: it is possible to establish the order of the visits to the cultural institutions according to several features like for example, number of artworks for cultural institutions, geographical distance among the selected cultural institutions, etc. (see Fig. 7 (left) and (right) where three museums with label A, B, and C have been selected for the visit).

4   User Centered Design Evaluations

Pollicina aims at becoming a valuable new tool in the landscape of flipped learning. For this reason its main users, students and teachers, are at the center of the project and their feedback allows to improve the platform every day. In order to accomplish this result we proposed a poll with a series of questions. A subset of 194 students who participated to the project within the "alternanza scuola lavoro" activity, answered to the questions of our survey. Also 8 teachers provided their point of view by answering to the questions of our survey, nonetheless the results for the teachers and the students have been considered separately since their roles are quite distinct. The survey has been designed in order to obtain information about three fundamental aspects of the interaction between the users and the platform:

– the quality of the platform
– the usability of the platform
– the overall satisfaction achieved after the usage

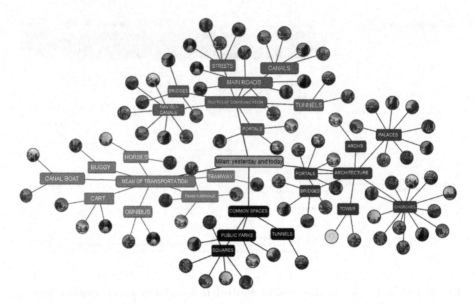

Fig. 6. Visual map of the selected artworks for the path about the thematic *Milan: yesterday and today.*

Each of the interviewed subjects was given a series of questions, for which he/she could answer with a number in the range from 1 to 5, where the lower values were associated with negative feelings in relation to Pollicina (e.g. bad quality, low usability, and low satisfaction), while the higher values were positive (e.g. high quality, high usability, and high satisfaction). The results have further been split between males (53 individuals) and females (149 individuals) in order

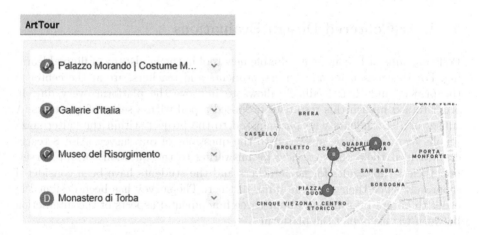

Fig. 7. (Left) List of cultural institutions, (Right) Geographical map.

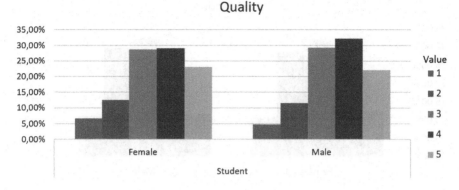

Fig. 8. The *quality* of the platform.

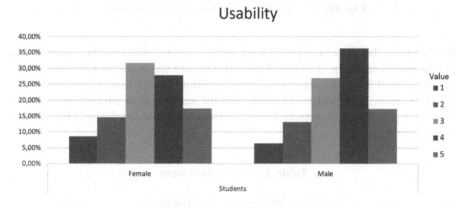

Fig. 9. The *usability* of the platform.

to understand if there are significant differences between the approaches of the two genders (this might lead to specialized interfaces in the future).

For each analyzed aspect it has been calculated the fraction of answers for each particular value (dividing the raw number by the total number of answers). It should be noted that, within this part of the survey, the users had to choose one and only one value for all of the questions. In the Figs. 8, 9 and 10 we show the students' answers for each aspect. The *quality* of the platform refers to how the users perceive the platform as a tool and if it allows to reach the learning goals. *Usability* aims at understanding if the interface was clear and intuitive. In practice we wanted to see if the students and the teachers were able to correctly use the tools they had, if they were helped by the platform, and if they enjoyed the experience. The *satisfaction* is related with the overall point of view of the users, which takes into account both if the interaction with the platform was easy and intuitive, and the fact that the learning goals had been reached. It is possible to observe that, in all of the graphs the distributions are skewed towards high values. This is particularly true in the case of the male audience, for which

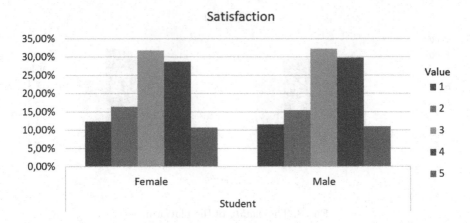

Fig. 10. The overall *satisfaction* of the experience.

the mode of the distributions is 4 for both *usability* and *quality*, while it is 3 for the *satisfaction*. In the case of female students the mode is 4 for the *quality* indicator, and 3 for the other two. The distributions are in any case skewed to the right, showing a positive attitude also for females. It is interesting to notice that for all the three aspects male users return better feedback than their female counterparts.

Table 1. Weighted averages.

	Students		Teachers	
	Females	Males	Females	Males
Quality	3.49	3.55	3.03	3.75
Usability	3.31	3.45	3.17	3.33
Satisfaction	3.09	3.13	3.25	4.25

Although the *quality* values are sufficient in both cases, the opinions of female and male teachers are rather different. In the case of *usability*, the teachers had more difficulty than the students. A possible explanation of this result might be linked to the fact that the younger generations are digital native and for such reason they have an easier interaction with information technologies. Finally, the results of the teachers who participated to the poll show a higher level of *satisfaction* than the students (Table 1).

We also asked which were the most important services among those proposed by the platform. In this part of the survey the users (both the students and teachers) were asked to choose one or more services. Figure 11 shows the amount of preferences associated with each functionality. It is possible to notice that the Conceptual Map has been particularly appreciated, probably because it allows to connect the artworks and the concepts with a visual network.

Most important functionalities

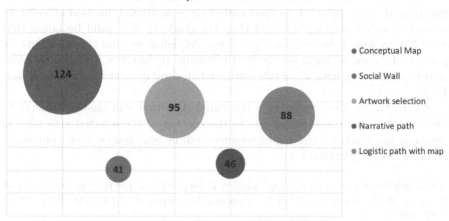

Fig. 11. Most important functionalities according to all the users.

A further request was to choose among possible extensions of the platform (allowing for multiple selections), with the following results: Improved functionalities for artwork search (89), Collaboration functionalities like chats (71), a system where to save the single artwork forms (88), and a personal note area (81). The most striking result involves the low preferences associated with collaboration extensions, probably due to the fact that nowadays there are already many communication tools and, the students might not feel the need for further niche communication systems.

5   Conclusions and Future Work

The goal of the Pollicina project is to develop a collaborative social suite called Educational Social Network (EduSN), that follows the principles of the flipped learning paradigm. Students are involved to create thematic cultural paths by using the artworks provided by the cultural institutions that joined Pollicina project. With this new learning tool we aim at improving the participation in the cultural life: users will approach the historical and cultural issues through a direct involvement in pleasant activities sharing comments, experiences, ideas, social feedback. This paper presented the ArtTour service dedicated to the definition of the cultural paths. This service is structured in 4 phases: "Setting of the Cultural Path", for the definition of the thematic; "Development of the Cultural Path", which allows groups of peers to work together to define the conceptual map about the thematic; "Choice of the Cultural Path", where students can learn the knowledge of the selected artworks and enrich the content by uploading new multimedia materials; and "Cultural Path in the Territory", enabling students and teachers to create a storytelling of the path and decide which cultural institutions to visit.

The survey that we proposed showed a general satisfaction level for Pollicina. In particular the teachers appreciated the educational function of Pollicina returning higher *satisfaction* level than the students. It should be noted that EduSN's version of the present paper is not yet definitive, and the criticisms are going to be used to improve the final platform. In future works, we are planning to expand the network of scholastic and cultural institutions trough all over Italy.

Currently we are developing a dedicated App that will enable students to perform their visits and access live to the content of the selected artworks. In addition, the students' visiting experiences will be enriched by their comments, social feedback, pictures, etc.

Acknowledgments. The Pollicina project is supported by the Regional Operational Program of the European Fund for Regional Development 2014–2020 (POR FESR 2014–2020).

References

1. Ardissono, L., Gena, C., Kuflik, T.: Umap 2017 patch 2017: personalized access to cultural heritage organizers' welcome. In: Adjunct Publication of the 25th Conference on User Modeling, Adaptation and Personalization, UMAP 2017, pp. 317–319. ACM, New York (2017). http://doi.acm.org/10.1145/3099023.3099085
2. Baker, K., Verstockt, S.: Cultural heritage routing: a recreational navigation-based approach in exploring cultural heritage. J. Comput. Cult. Herit. **10**(4), 20:1–24:20 (2017). http://doi.acm.org/10.1145/3040200
3. Calegari, S., Dominoni, M.: The pollicina project: a collaborative and educational social suite to build cultural itineraries. In: Luigini, A. (ed.) EARTH 2018. AISC, vol. 919, pp. 225–234. Springer, Cham (2019). https://doi.org/10.1007/978-3-030-12240-9_24
4. Calegari, S., Meluso, F., Avogadro, P., Dominoni, M.: A navigator for sharing cultural heritages in an educational context: the Pollicina project. In: 7th International Conference. The Future of Education, Edited by Pixel, pp. 16–20 (2017). ISBN: 978-88-6292-868-7
5. Chan, Y.C., Lo, C.K., Hew, K.F.: An exploratory study of using the next generation science standards (NGSS) to flip hong kong secondary school science education. In: Proceedings of the 2Nd International Conference on E-Society, E-Education and E-Technology, ICSET 2018, pp. 10–15. ACM, New York (2018). http://doi.acm.org/10.1145/3268808.3268817
6. Chen, M.H., Chao, Y.C.J., Hung, H.T.: Learning in a flipped English classroom from university students' perspectives. In: Proceedings of the 6th International Conference on Information and Education Technology, ICIET 2018, pp. 33–37. ACM, New York (2018). http://doi.acm.org/10.1145/3178158.3178171
7. Chun, B.A., Heo, H.J.: The effect of flipped learning on academic performance as an innovative method for overcoming ebbinghaus' forgetting curve. In: Proceedings of the 6th International Conference on Information and Education Technology, ICIET 2018, pp. 56–60. ACM, New York (2018). http://doi.acm.org/10.1145/3178158.3178206

8. Fidalgo-Blanco, A., Sein-Echaluce, M.L., García-Peñalvo, F.J.: APFT: active peer-based flip teaching. In: Proceedings of the 5th International Conference on Technological Ecosystems for Enhancing Multiculturality, TEEM 2017, pp. 83:1–83:7. ACM, New York (2017). http://doi.acm.org/10.1145/3144826.3145433

9. Fidalgo-Blanco, Á., Sein-Echaluce, M.L., García-Peñalvo, F.J.: MAIN: method for applying innovation in education. In: García-Peñalvo [10], pp. 806–813. https://doi.org/10.1145/3284179.3284313

10. García-Peñalvo, F.J. (ed.): Proceedings of the Sixth International Conference on Technological Ecosystems for Enhancing Multiculturality, Salamanca, Spain, 24–26 October 2018, ACM (2018). https://doi.org/10.1145/3284179

11. Heines, J.M., Popyack, J.L., Morrison, B., Lockwood, K., Baldwin, D.: Panel on flipped classrooms. In: Proceedings of the 46th ACM Technical Symposium on Computer Science Education, SIGCSE 2015, pp. 174–175. ACM, New York (2015). http://doi.acm.org/10.1145/2676723.2677328

12. Lin, Y., Bai, X., Ye, Y., Real, W.: Constructing narratives using fast feedback. In: iConference 2012, Toronto, Ontario, Canada, 7–10 February 2012, pp. 486–487 (2012). https://doi.org/10.1145/2132176.2132258

13. Oliveira, L.: Flipping the classroom with multimedia resources to regulate learning pace: a case study. In: García-Peñalvo [10], pp. 708–715. https://doi.org/10.1145/3284179.3284311

14. Ram, M.P., Sinha, A.: An implementation framework for flipped classrooms in higher education. In: Proceedings of the Special Collection on eGovernment Innovations in India, ICEGOV 2017, pp. 18–26. ACM, New York (2017). http://doi.acm.org/10.1145/3055219.3055224

15. Re Depaolini, M., Ciucci, D., Calegari, S., Dominoni, M.: External indices for rough clustering. In: Nguyen, H.S., Ha, Q.-T., Li, T., Przybyła-Kasperek, M. (eds.) IJCRS 2018. LNCS (LNAI), vol. 11103, pp. 378–391. Springer, Cham (2018). https://doi.org/10.1007/978-3-319-99368-3_29

16. Santos, A.P., et al.: Development of flipped classroom model to improve the students' performance. In: García-Peñalvo [10], pp. 703–707. https://doi.org/10.1145/3284179.3284298

17. Szafir, D., Mutlu, B.: Artful: adaptive review technology for flipped learning. In: Proceedings of the SIGCHI Conference on Human Factors in Computing Systems, CHI 2013, ACM, New York (2013)

Use of AHP and Promethee for Research Project Portfolio Selection

Heloise Acco Tives Leão[1]([⊠])(iD), Edna Dias Canedo[2](iD),
Pedro Henrique Teixeira Costa[2], Márcio Vinicius Okimoto[2],
and Giovanni Almeida Santos[2](iD)

[1] Department of Computer Science, Lutheran University Center of Palmas
(CEULP), P.O. Box 85, Palmas, TO, Brazil
heloise.acco@gmail.com, marciobtos@gmail.com, giovannix@unb.br
[2] Department of Computer Science, University of Brasília (UnB), P.O. Box 4466,
Brasília, DF 70910-900, Brazil
ednacanedo@unb.br, phtcosta@gmail.com

Abstract. Multiple Criteria Decision Analysis (MCDA) methods are increasingly used in complex decision problems that involves several decision parameters, often faced by the decision makers involved in the planning process. The need to rank projects submitted to research scholarship programs in higher education institutions is a common practice that can be supported by the application of the AHP and Promethee II methods. This work applies the use of these methods in the selection of research scholarship projects, based on a case study, carried out with data from the Call for Proposals of the Institutional Program for Scientific Initiation (ProIC/PIBIC) - 2017/2018 of the University of Brasília (UnB). The methodology involved the construction of the model with multiple criteria in order to facilitate the decision making with the formalization and definition of the decision alternatives for the ranking of the projects submitted by the teachers. The results showed a classification adhering to the items considered relevant by the Institution in the classification of projects. Although the constructed model has been applied in the context of a single institution, it can be used by other institutions of higher education, since the ranking criteria defined by the Bodies of Fomentation are similar.

Keywords: Analytic Hierarchy Process · Promethee II ·
Multiple Criteria Decision Analysis · Ranking project

1 Introduction

Decision makers, whether they are individuals or committees, have difficulty processing and systematically evaluating relevant information. This assessment process involves confronting trade-offs between the alternatives under consideration. Each decision maker will need to prioritize what matters most. If more than one individual is involved, the priorities of involved decision makers can, and

© Springer Nature Switzerland AG 2019
S. Misra et al. (Eds.): ICCSA 2019, LNCS 11619, pp. 504–517, 2019.
https://doi.org/10.1007/978-3-030-24289-3_37

frequently do, conflict, increasing the difficulty and complexity of the decision-making process. Despite this complexity, decisions are made: even sticking with status quo is itself a decision. Relying on informal processes or judgments can lead to sub-optimal decisions. Without a formal process to evaluate alternatives and priorities, there may be inconsistency, variability, or a lack of predictability on a particular factor's or criterion's importance in the decision. The decision makers' credibility and potentially legitimacy may come into question, and this is especially true for accountability on a decision made by a university if there is a lack of transparency about how a decision was made [23].

The decision-making process can be improved by working with decision makers and stakeholders providing support and structure to the process. Using structured, explicit approaches to decisions involving multiple criteria can improve the quality of decision making and a set of techniques, known under the collective heading multiple criteria decision analysis (MCDA), are useful for this purpose. This set of techniques provides clarity on which criteria are relevant, the importance attached to each, and how to use this information in a framework for assessing the available alternatives. By doing so, they can help increase the consistency, transparency, and legitimacy of decisions [23].

Each year, the University of Brasília (UnB) publishes three notices exclusively for the selection of undergraduate students to participate in research projects, such as: Program of Scientific Initiation (PIBIC), Program of Scientific Initiation in Technological Development and Innovation (PIBITI) and Program of Scientific Initiation in Affirmative Actions (PIBIC-AF), the latter aimed at students who are beneficiaries of social inclusion policies. The selection of projects and scholarship holders is currently performed by the sum of the scores obtained in the criteria defined in the selection document. In these criteria there is a maximum score to be accepted, but there is no weight assignment to the criteria.

The use of Multiple Criteria Decision Analysis (MCDA) is an efficient and effective tool for integrating stakeholders' values and preferences into multi-criteria scenarios and provides support for the complex decision-making process [11]. In the definition of rankings and assistance in the selection of candidates, the use of MCDA is frequent, since it can help in the structuring of the problem, in the evaluation of the candidates and in the selection itself, guaranteeing the consideration of all the criteria established by those involved in the decision [17].

This paper will present the literature review on the use of MCDA methods to classify projects, research grants or the like, as well as the results of the study of the application of the AHP and PROMETHEE II methods in a real scenario.

This paper is organized as follows. Section 2 presents the state of the art related to decision-making process. Section 3 presents the research methodology adopted to develop this work. In the Sect. 4, the results and discussion are detailed. The conclusions and future work are presented in Sect. 5.

2   Background

The decision-making process has undergone changes over the last decades. The criteria definition is a phase of great importance in the decision-making process, since it is through the defined criteria that the decision-making model will be created, thus allowing the establishment of preferential relations between existing alternatives [3]. With this, it is perceived that the quality of the construction of this model is fundamental for the quality of the support to the decision, as well as to provide greater effectiveness to the decision making process and greater chance of reaching the defined objectives.

Multiple Criteria Decision Analysis (MCDA) has been an area of rapid growth in operations research and management science during the last decades [8]. It is noticed that the MCDA methods aim to improve the degree of conformity and coherence between the evolution of a decision-making process, the value systems and the objectives involved in this process [9].

To achieve these objectives, concepts, tools and procedures must be defined. Trying to help open the way between ambiguities, uncertainties, and the abundance of bifurcations in the decision-making process. Multicriteria Decision Analysis is organized into three main phases [2] (Fig. 1):

1. Identification and structuring of the problem: before the analysis begins, stakeholders, including facilitators and technical analysts, need to develop a common understanding of the problem, the decisions that must be made, and the criteria by which those decisions will be judged and evaluated.
2. Construction and use of the model: formal models are developed so that the alternative policies or actions under analysis can be compared systematically and transparently.
3. Development of action plans: the analysis does not "solve" the decision problem. This requires the implementation of results, this means transforming the analysis made into specific action plans. With this, the use of MCDA processes must support the implementation and use of the method.

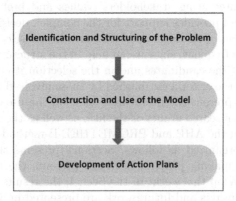

Fig. 1. Phases of Multicriteria Decision Analysis

In the specific case of the ranking and selection of projects, the main objective is to select a set of projects from all available projects considering only their individual characteristics and the constraints imposed by the system [14]. Considering this restriction, it was identified from the analysis of the case studies that the use of MCDA with the classification (ranking) methods AHP [16], is used to support the solution of similar problems in the literature.

2.1 Analytic Hierarchy Process

The Analytic Hierarchy Process (AHP), was developed by [20] drawing on mathematics and psychology [9]. This method has been extensively studied and refined, with the aim of providing a means to represent hierarchically the elements involved in a process of choice [11]. Because of its simplicity, ease of use, and great flexibility, the AHP has been studied extensively and used in nearly all applications related to MCDA since its development. The integrated AHP can result in a more realistic and promising decision than a stand alone AHP. There is no doubt that AHP is one of the most popular MCDA approaches [15,20].

Basically, the AHP method consists of a structured technique to assist in making complex decisions. Instead of prescribing an optimal decision, it provides mechanisms for decision-makers to find a solution that fits their needs and helps them understand the problem. This is possible, since with the use of the method, a comprehensive and rational structure is provided to define and organize a problem and from there represent and quantify its elements, relate these elements to the general objectives and evaluate the proposed solutions [25].

It also characterizes the method of organizing decision variables into successive levels of importance, examining the interrelationship between the parties and simplifying the decision-making process. For its correct application to be performed, the AHP encompasses 5 main steps, as presented by [11,20] and [6]. These steps are (Fig. 2):

1. Define the problem and determine the type of knowledge sought.
2. Structure the decision making hierarchy and from this define the objectives through a perspective in levels. In this hierarchy the main objective is presented with criteria and subcriteria and lower levels represent the alternatives list.
3. Construct a set of comparison matrices with each pair, where each element of a higher level is used to compare the elements of the level immediately below it.
4. The hierarchical synthesis is then presented, after repeated execution of the steps until all pairwise comparisons are made.
5. Together with the presentation of the ranking resulting from the implementation of the AHP method must be provided the consistency index and the consistency rate of the application of the method.

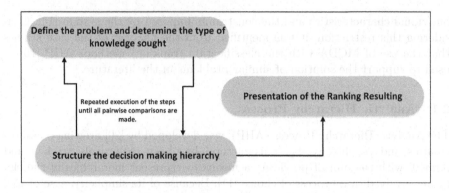

Fig. 2. Steps of Analytic Hierarchy Process

2.2 Promethee

In the 1980s, Brans and Vincke [4] presented the PROMETHEE (Preference Ranking Method for Enrichment Evaluation) methods, with the proposal to build and exploit a relationship of over-classification of values [4], clearly understood by decision-makers, adding simplicity and stability to the methods previously used [1].

Initially, were presented the methods PROMETHEE I, which provides a partial ranking of actions, and PROMETHEE II, which results in a complete classification performed through the pairwise comparison of alternatives [4]. From this, some variations of the PROMETHEE methods have been proposed to be used in different circumstances and to solve problems of ordering and application in systems hierarchy of water supply and sewage projects [5] and selection of projects from the strategic planning of a Brazilian electric sector company [14]. Among the variations of PROMETHEE, can be mentioned the PROMETHEE-III, IV, V and VI [5].

PROMETHEE II has proven to be efficient when it comes to project ranking, since it deals with the complete classification of many alternatives from the best to the worst in terms of conflicting criteria [22], calculating the positive and negative flows of preferences for each alternative. The positive flow happens when one alternative is exercising dominance in the others and the negative flow, when an alternative is dominated by the others [21].

In order to be correctly implemented, the execution of 4 steps of the method is indicated, consisting of [4]:

1. Define the preference function, which shows the preference of the decision maker for an alternative "a" to another alternative "b" in relation to a criterion;
2. Calculate the preference index, used to quantitatively compare alternatives in pairs, taking all the criteria into consideration comprehensively;
3. Construct an overcoming valued graph, where the inflows and outflows are determined by preference indexes; and
4. Present the alternatives of classification according to the result generated.

As can be seen, the central idea of PROMETHEE is the pairwise comparison of alternatives with the criteria first, one by one, then comprehensively [21], providing a deep insight into the alternatives since it takes into account the preferences and priorities of the decision maker [24].

2.3 Related Works

Haddad et al. [12] proposed an expert system to select a most suitable discrete MCDA method using an approach that analyses problem characteristics, MCDA methods characteristics, risk and uncertainty in inputs and applies sensitivity analysis to the inputs for a decisional problem. The approach provided decision makers with a suggested candidate method that delivers a robust outcome. Two MCDA methods are compared and one is recommended by calculating the minimum percentage change in criteria weights and performance measures required to alter the ranking of any two alternatives. A MCDA method was recommended based on a best compromise in minimum percentage change required in inputs to alter the ranking of alternatives.

Strategies of ranking and prioritization of projects directly influence the performance of organizations and the cost-benefit relationship of project development. The work carried out by [7] reports that due to the scarcity of funding and appropriate technologies, the ranking and selection projects of a portfolio can become a problem of the decision making process.

In this context, the work presented by [7] applies a project prioritization mechanism within a broad set of proposals, in order to identify the projects that best satisfy a set of criteria defined by decision makers. In order to carry out this rankings, MCDA techniques are applied, such as the AHP, which has been shown to be able to assist in the prioritization of projects by companies and institutions in different fields of activity.

MCDA methods are also applied in the prioritization of new Information and Communication Technology (ICT) projects. The work developed by [19] presents the application of a multicriteria analysis method and business process modeling using Business Process Modeling Notation (BPMN). In this work, the ICT department of an educational institution was used as the case study. In order to carry out the desired process, it was initially modeled the prioritization scheme of new projects of the department, to perform the survey of criteria, attribution of weights and values, divided between two evaluations: management and ICT.

The implementation of the PROMETHEE method proposed by [19] provided a general ranking of the evaluated projects, which were separated into two rankings with the management and ICT assessments in order to compare. The analysis of the obtained results allowed to conclude the validity of the MCDA methods to help in the selection and management of projects portfolio.

Morton et al. [18] present a formal model of the use of MCDA methods to guide selection of a subset of available projects, in order to maximize the resulting portfolio performance against multiple criteria. Criteria should be defined in order to meet the availability of existing resources, as well as to meet the constraints listed by decision makers.

3   Research Methodology

The choice of the appropriate MCDA method to deal with the problem proposed in this work was based on a review of the literature on the subject. From the search term repeated in the search bases it was possible to identify, filter and select articles to compose the systematic review. The digital search libraries of the literature review were: DBLP; ACM; Scopus; IEEExplorer.

After a complete reading of the articles selected during the search process, it was possible to describe the literature review and define the methods to be used in the case study the AHP and PROMETHEE II due to several studies reporting case studies with the respective methods. With the implementation of the methods and results obtained, these were compared and discussed in order to form a proposal for the standardization of the ranking of projects and research grants at the University of Brasília (UnB).

According to the standard defined by Belton [2] to guide the phases of MCDA problems, this work, in the case study, carried out in the identification and structuring stage of the problem the tasks of: mapping the existing scenario, project objectives delimitation, stakeholder's determination, analysis of possible alternatives, uncertainty survey, external environment assessment, definition of restrictions and criteria to be used.

To support the definition of the criteria to be used in this case study was applied in the data from the call results of the Institutional Program for Scientific Initiation ProIC/PIBIC - 2017/2018 of the University of Brasília [13], with the support of WEKA software [13], the use of the AttributeSelection algorithm. This algorithm, that uses CfsSubsetEval for attribute evaluation and BestFirst for search, brought the indication of the most relevant criteria to be used in the case study.

From this it was possible to construct the model with multiple criteria, in order to facilitate the decision making with the formalization and definition of decision alternatives for the problem in question – Scientific Initiation Projects Selection at University of Brasília (UnB).

The application of the chosen methods and comparison of the results is presented in the Results and Discussion Section, where a proposal is made of a method that provides conditions to rank in a reliable and structured way, in order to improve the quality of the selection process of the program, a set of research projects among all the enrolled projects taking into account the restrictions and criteria of each notice and forming a solution that can be replicated over time, thus maintaining consistency and standard in the evaluations carried out.

3.1   Identification and Structuring of the Problem

Currently, the project selection form for the Scientific Initiation Program (PIBIC) of the University of Brasília (UnB) is carried out in the conventional way, in which the completed forms are evaluated through a web system, that is, document conferencing. This information is collected through a file extractor that includes this information.

After extraction, the information is sorted and classified manually beginning with the restrictions set forth in the notice and in the sequence the grades counting process is performed for the projects, teachers and students participating in the program selection process. Among the stakeholders involved in the implementation of this case study are:

– Directorate of Scientific Initiation of the Deanery of Research and Postgraduate Studies (DIRIC) that is responsible for formulating and managing (executing, coordinating and evaluating) the policy and scientific initiation program of UnB;
– Undergraduate students enrolled in any Institution of Higher Education;
– The faculty members of the University of Brasilia, in actual exercise and the retirees or visitors of UnB.

It was identified as an external environment and complementary to the application of the model, the research promotion institutions that sponsor the projects of Scientific Initiation and the impact, be it positive or negative, of the academic and practical application of the selected projects.

As alternatives in the process of ranking and selection of projects, all the projects that have been submitted to the notice are in a single file in spreadsheet format, with the information and the items foreseen for the classification of the projects and their teachers (mentors) and students to perform the analysis.

During the analysis of the selection process and execution of research projects by PIBIC of the UnB, several uncertainties were mapped, being the most relevant:

– Lack of financial support from research promotion institutions, which may make it unfeasible to launch calls for projects selection;
– Change in current legislation, which may bring legal and/or financial uncertainty to projects in progress;
– Specificities or not clarification of the details of the projects selection process of the UnB, which can lead to the selection of projects with merit inferior to those not selected.

According to the articles selected in the literature review, the definition of the criteria is a phase of great importance in the decision making process. Thus, in this case study, the selection process and classification of project applications was made based on the understanding of the attributes contained in the official announcement of the Institutional Program of Scientific Initiation (ProIC/PIBIC) - 2017/2018 of UnB, being:

- For the Mentor profile: total point limit - 60 points
  - Guidance experience completed: Co-guidance; Master; Doctorate.
  - Scientific, technological and/or artistic-cultural production: Articles; Book chapters; Patents; Books.
- For the scientific merit of the proposal: total point limit-40 points
  - Summary of teacher research project;
  - Student Work Plan;
  - Technical and economic feasibility (only when there is restriction).

With the application of the data mining algorithm, the criteria related to the Guidance note, Publication note, Project note, and Work Plan note were selected, and it was not necessary to include sub-criteria such as guideline sharing, master's and doctorate. The weights of the criteria followed the standard already defined in the edict. A restriction was added for project classification, which is the minimum grade that should be achieved in the criteria related to the Project note and note of the Work Plan. These two criteria must achieve at least 50% of the total possible grade in the assessment. The summary of the definition of criteria and weights used is presented in the Table 1. From the definition of the criteria, restrictions and weights for each criterion it was possible to start the construction of the proposed model.

Table 1. List of weights, elimination criteria and weights assigned to the criteria.

Index	Criteria	Original weight	Minimum grade	Criteria weight
0	Orientation Grade	4,0	0,0	4,0
1	Publication Grade	2,0	0,0	2,0
2	Project Grade	1,5	5,0	1,5
3	Work Plan Grade	2,5	5,0	2,5

3.2 Construction of the Proposed Model

The project was developed in the Java language [10] and consists of 6 modules, totaling 3,300 lines of code. To support the data load, a parser has been implemented to read the data from the worksheet and load the modeled entities that represent the domain of the problem, for example: project, student and supervisor. From this, a filter was performed through the application of the constraints defined in the project, being: minimum grade of 3 attributes (student performance index (IRA), project note, and work plan note) and technical feasibility. It is important to note that if any of the constraints are not satisfied, the project is immediately disqualified.

In order to carry out the case study, a filter was applied to the data coming from the notice of PIBIC - 2017/2018 of UnB, selecting only projects related to the area of exact sciences, resulting a set of 409 projects to be used in the application test of implemented algorithms. In assessing the steps required to apply the AHP method, it is seen that steps 1. Define the problem and determine the type of knowledge sought and 2. Structure the hierarchy of decision making, which in this case consisted of the definition of the weights presented in the Table 1, were executed.

For each defined criterion the alternatives preference matrix within the same criterion was calculated. This calculation is done by comparing the division of the weight of a given criterion by the weight of each of the other existing criteria. It is important to note in this case that a value can only be included in the matrix when it is greater than zero. With this, each alternative can be compared with all the others. Figure 3 presents the creation of the matrix of preferences between the criteria.

Building a set of matching matrices was necessary to convert the list of projects into a list of alternatives. From this, the execution of the method can be performed by repeating step 3 until a comparison of all the criteria and alternatives is performed, calculating the consistency index and the consistency ratio, as presented in Fig. 3. The result of the application of the AHP method will be presented in the Results section, along with the comparison of the result of the application of the PROMETHEE II method.

For the creation of the application model of the PROMETHEE II method, it was identified that step 1. Definition of the preference function, which presents the preference of the decision maker for an alternative "a" with respect to another alternative "b" in relation to a criterion and 2. Calculate the preference index, used to quantitatively compare alternatives in pairs, taking all the criteria into consideration comprehensively, were performed respectively.

In the execution of step 3. To determine the output and input flows by means of relevant preference indexes, three functions were tested in each criterion: usual, linear and Gaussian. For the linear function, the indifference and preference thresholds were defined for each criterion. Orientation Grade: 5 and 20; Publication Grade: 3 and 9; Project Grade: 3 and 8; Work Plan Grade: 5 and 12.

Step 4 of PROMETHEE II, which consists of presenting the classification alternatives according to the generated result, as well as the result of applying the AHP method will be presented in the next section.

4   Results and Discussion

The first 20 results of the application of the AHP and PROMETHEE II methods in their variations are presented in Table 2. In the analysis of this result must be considered the descending order of classification from the final grade attribute that contains the official data obtained for the projects of the notice of the Institutional Program of Scientific Initiation (ProIC/PIBIC) - 2017/2018 of UnB. In the Table 2 Rank Promethee USUAL = USUAL; Rank Promethee LINEAR = LINEAR; Rank Promethee GAUSSIAN = GAUSSIAN.

In what concerns the selection of projects, it is necessary to respect the quantity of vacancies for paid or voluntary projects existing at UnB, according

Table 2. Implementation results and case study tests.

Project	Final grade	Rank AHP	USUAL	LINEAR	GAUSSIANO
28768	100	1	1	1	1
28474	100	2	2	2	2
28480	100	3	3	3	3
28448	91	4	25	4	14
28499	91	5	26	5	15
28376	90	7	7	6	4
28511	90	8	8	7	5
28513	90	9	9	8	6
28157	88	11	11	10	10
28400	88	12	12	11	11
28401	88	13	13	12	12
28463	88	14	14	13	13
28225	88	15	4	14	7
28226	88	16	5	15	8
28227	88	17	6	16	9
28530	86	6	79	9	62
28399	86	19	46	18	23
28497	86	22	27	19	16
28299	85	18	59	17	48
28321	85	20	30	22	18
28321	85	20	30	22	18

to the rule that the first classified can be described as "Remunerated Approved"; then inserted the "Volunteer Approvals". The other projects not disqualified by the restrictions imposed, will be ordered in a "Paid Waiting List" and ending with the "Waiting List of Volunteers".

```
INFO   AhpExecutor:23 - Criterion: Orientation Grade
INFO   AhpExecutor:23 - Criterion: Publication Grade
INFO   AhpExecutor:23 - Criterion: Project Grade
INFO   AhpExecutor:23 - Criterion: Work Plan Grade
INFO   AhpExecutor:25 - Criteria judgement:
1,0000 2,0000 2,6667 1,6000
0,5000 1,0000 1,3333 0,8000
0,3750 0,7500 1,0000 0,6000
0,6250 1,2500 1,6667 1,0000
```

Fig. 3. Result of the first matrix coupled with the application test using AHP.

It can be seen from the analysis of the results contained in the Table 2, that the application of the methods only follows the same pattern for the first 3 projects and that the rankings generated by the application of the PROMETHEE II method using the usual and Gaussian functions generated a less consistent classification and because of this they were not used in the deepening of this case study.

The rankings generated by the application of the AHP and PROMETHEE II methods using the linear function presented a higher consistency index and were therefore analyzed in a higher level of detail to compose the proposed method that will provide conditions to reliably rank and structure project classifications and research grants from UnB.

The proposal made from the results generated in this case study, consists in the use of the PROMETHEE II method using the linear function, since it presented greater efficiency in the classification of the projects and the resulting ordering was considered consistent and coherent with the existing values in the analyzed attributes.

It is worth mentioning that the implementation of the application with the use of the AHP and PROMETHEE II methods used the adjusted criteria for some items that in the notice had a maximum scoring limit, focusing on the application of the methods in the attributes of "Orientation Grade", "Work Plan Grade", the "Grade Publication" and the "Grade Project", with weights defined to indicate the importance and relevance to each item.

5 Conclusion

The application of MCDA methods for ranking projects and research grants from teaching institutions proved to be satisfactory for the case study developed. It can be noticed that the results of the application of the AHP and PROMETHEE II methods in the data coming from the UnB's Scientific Initiation Program (ProIC/PIBIC) - 2017/2018, resulted in a different classification from that obtained officially for the same data.

This difference is explained by the intrinsic characteristics of the applied methods that differ from the simple sum and rank currently used in the evaluated institution. The comparison between the AHP and PROMETHEE II results showed that according to the existing criteria, the AHP and PROMETHEE II method using the linear function are the most suitable for project classification.

It is expected that the proposal made in this work can be used and provide conditions to reliably and structuredly rank project data in order to improve the quality of the program selection process used by UnB.

The application developed will be delivered to the unit responsible for the projects selection of the UnB, where the rankings can be tested from the perspective proposed in this study and a commission can validate and homologate the results obtained. It can then be integrated with existing systems in order to optimize their execution.

The criteria suggested as relevant to the process may be adequate according to similar needs, considering the constraints and particularities of each case.

With this, the steps followed in this project can be replicated and created standards of evaluation and selection of research projects with greater coherence, being possible the use of the application by any Institution that wishes to evaluate its projects.

Acknowledgments. This research work has the support of the Research Support Foundation of the Federal District (FAPDF).

References

1. de Araújo, A.G., de Almeida, A.T.: Apoio à decisão na seleção de investimentos em petróleo e gás: uma aplicação utilizando o método PROMETHEE. In: Gest. Prod. 2009, vol. 16, no. 4, pp. 534–543 (2009)
2. Belton, V., Stewart, T.: Multiple Criteria Decision Analysis: An Integrated Approach. Springer, Dordrecht (2002). https://doi.org/10.1007/978-1-4615-1495-4
3. Bouyssou, D.: Building Criteria: A Prerequisite For MCDA. Universite de Paris Dauphine Place du Marechal De Lattre de Tassigny, LAMSADE (1990)
4. Brans, J.P., Vincke, P.H.: A preference ranking organization method, the PROMETHEE method for MCDM. Manage. Sci. **31**, 647–656 (1985)
5. Campos, V.R.: Modelo de apoio à decisão multicritério para priorização de projetos em saneamento (2011). http://www.teses.usp.br/teses/disponiveis/18/18157/tde-08022012-104925/pt-br.php
6. Carladous, S., Tacnet, J.M., Dezert, J., Han, D., Batton-Hubert, M.: Evaluation of efficiency of torrential protective structures with new BF-TOPSIS methods. In: 2016 19th International Conference on Information Fusion (FUSION), pp. 2267–2274, July 2016
7. Chatterjee, K., Hossain, S.A., Kar, S.: Prioritization of project proposals in portfolio management using fuzzy AHP. OPSEARCH **55**(2), 478–501 (2018)
8. Chen, L., Xu, Z.: A new prioritized multi-criteria outranking method: the prioritized PROMETHEE. J. Intell. Fuzzy Syst. **29**(5), 2099–2110 (2015). https://doi.org/10.3233/IFS-151686
9. e Costa, C.B., Vincke, P.: Multiple criteria decision aid: an overview. In: Bana e Costa, C.A. (ed.) Readings in Multiple Criteria Decision Aid, pp. 3–14. Springer, Heidelberg (1990). https://doi.org/10.1007/978-3-642-75935-2_1
10. Deitel, P., Deitel, H.: Java How to Program. Prentice Hall Press, Upper Saddle River (2011)
11. Elmokrini, A., Benabbou, L., Berrado, A.: Multi-criteria distribution network selection. In: 2015 10th International Conference on Intelligent Systems: Theories and Applications (SITA), pp. 1–6 (2015). https://doi.org/10.1109/SITA.2015.7358393
12. Haddad, M., Sanders, D., Bausch, N., Tewkesbury, G., Gegov, A., Hassan, M.: Learning to make intelligent decisions using an expert system for the intelligent selection of either PROMETHEE II or the analytical hierarchy process. In: Arai, K., Kapoor, S., Bhatia, R. (eds.) IntelliSys 2018. AISC, vol. 868, pp. 1303–1316. Springer, Cham (2019). https://doi.org/10.1007/978-3-030-01054-6_91
13. Hall, M., Frank, E., Holmes, G., Pfahringer, B., Reutemann, P., Witten, I.H.: The weka data mining software: an update. ACM SIGKDD Explor. Newslett. **11**(1), 10–18 (2009)
14. López, H.M.L., de Almeida, A.T.: Utilizando PROMETHEE V para seleção de portfólio de projetos de uma empresa de energia elétrica. Production **24**(3), 559–571 (2014)

15. Ho, W., Ma, X.: The state-of-the-art integrations and applications of the analytic hierarchy process. Eur. J. Oper. Res. **267**(2), 399–414 (2018)
16. Karasakal, E., Aker, P.: A multicriteria sorting approach based on data envelopment analysis for R&D project selection problems. In: Omega, December 2017, vol. 73, pp. 79–92 (2017)
17. Tavakkoli-Moghaddam, R., Sotoudeh-Anvari, A., Siadat, A.: A multi-criteria group decision-making approach for facility location selection using PROMETHEE under a fuzzy environment. In: Kamiński, B., Kersten, G.E., Szapiro, T. (eds.) GDN 2015. LNBIP, vol. 218, pp. 145–156. Springer, Cham (2015). https://doi.org/10.1007/978-3-319-19515-5_12
18. Morton, A., Keisler, J.M., Salo, A.: Multicriteria portfolio decision analysis for project selection. In: Greco, S., Ehrgott, M., Figueira, J. (eds.) Multiple Criteria Decision Analysis, pp. 1269–1298. Springer, New York (2016). https://doi.org/10.1007/978-1-4939-3094-4_28
19. Mussa, M., Cordeiro, R., Freitas, R., Hora, H., Silva, S.: Priorização de projetos de ti através da modelagem do processo e utilização do método promethee. Revista de Gestão dos Países de Língua Portuguesa **17**(1), 56–75 (2018)
20. Saaty, T.: The Analytic Hierarchy Process: Planning, Priority Setting, Resource Allocation. Advanced book program, McGraw-Hill (1980). https://books.google.com.br/books?id=Xxi7AAAAIAAJ
21. da Silva, A.M., de Melo, R.M.: Uma abordagem multicritério para a seleção de serviços de consultoria e certificação de sistemas de gestão da qualidade. In: Gest. Prod., 28 September 2017 (2017)
22. Soylu, B.: Integrating prometheeii with the tchebycheff function for multi criteria decision making. Int. J. Inf. Technol. Decis. Making **9**(4), 525–545 (2010)
23. Thokala, P., et al.: Multiple criteria decision analysis for health care decision making—an introduction: report 1 of the ispor mcda emerging good practices task force. Value Health **19**(1), 1–13 (2016). https://doi.org/10.1016/j.jval.2015.12.003, http://www.sciencedirect.com/science/article/pii/S1098301515051359
24. Toinard, C., Ravier, T., Céerin, C., Ngoko, Y.: The promethee method for cloud brokering with trust and assurance criteria. In: 2015 IEEE International Parallel and Distributed Processing Symposium Workshop (2015)
25. Wang, C., Zhou, F., Vergeest, J.: Multi-objective optimization for the functional configuration design of mobile devices using analytic hierarchy process. In: 2009 Second International Symposium on Intelligent Information Technology and Security Informatics, pp. 137–142 (2009). https://doi.org/10.1109/IITSI.2009.37

A Two-Phase Bug Localization Approach Based on Multi-layer Perceptrons and Distributional Features

Damiano Distante⬤ and Stefano Faralli(✉)⬤

University of Rome Unitelma Sapienza, Rome, Italy
{damiano.distante,stefano.faralli}@unitelmasapienza.it

Abstract. Bug localization is a challenging and time-consuming task of the process of bug fixing and, more in general, of software maintenance. Several approaches have been proposed in the literature which support developers in this task by identifying source code files in which the bug is likely to be located. However, the research on this topic never stopped, looking for new methods providing better accuracy and/or better efficiency. In this paper, we propose a two-phase bug localization approach which leverages multi-layer neural networks and distributional features. First phase locations are obtained thanks to a neural network trained on word embeddings representations of fixed bug reports. The second phase refines bug locations taking into account the number of times source code files co-occur in fixed bug locations. To evaluate the approach, we conducted a large-scale experiment on five open source projects, namely *Mozilla*, *Eclipse*, *Dolphin*, *httpd*, and *gcc*. Results show that, thanks to pre-trained word embeddings, we were able to implement a scalable approach with a training running time of few hours on large datasets. Performances are comparable to other existing deep learning approaches.

Keywords: Software maintenance · Bug localization ·
Machine learning · Word embeddings · Multilayer perceptron networks

1 Introduction

A software bug is a defect or mistake in the code of a computer program or system that may cause it to produce an unintended and unexpected behavior.

To inform developers of the presence of bugs, users describe the observed erroneous behaviors in the form of bug reports collected by issue trackers such as Bugzilla[1].

After a bug is reported, its life-cycle [7] towards resolution is started[2]. Such life-cycle usually includes a first phase of bug triage in which the bug is verified

---

[1] https://www.bugzilla.org.
[2] https://www.bugzilla.org/docs/4.2/en/html/lifecycle.html.

© Springer Nature Switzerland AG 2019
S. Misra et al. (Eds.): ICCSA 2019, LNCS 11619, pp. 518–532, 2019.
https://doi.org/10.1007/978-3-030-24289-3_38

to be actually present, its severity is assessed, and a level of priority is assigned. Next, the bug is assigned to a developer that will first try to localize it in the source code and then find a way to solve it. A patch fixing the bug is then provided and, once it is verified to actually work, it is later introduced in the system so to remove the bug from next releases of the software.

Bug localization is the task aimed at identifying the portion of the source code of a software system causing its to expose an erroneous behavior. This code portion may actually be spread over several source code files and, depending on the size and complexity of the software system, the task of bug localization may be very challenging and time-consuming.

In order to support developers in accomplishing this task, different approaches have been proposed in the literature (see Sect. 5) which adopt a variety of source code analysis and data mining techniques. However, the research on this topic never stopped, looking for both more scalable and more effective approaches [15].

In this work, we propose a two-phase bug localization approach based on multi-layer perceptrons and distributional features that has proved to effectively address the scalability issue.

In particular, in the first phase we leverage pre-trained compact vectors (also known as word embeddings) to represent bug reports. In the second phase we exploit observed distributional features to possibly improve the localization results provided by the neural network.

To evaluate our approach, we first tested it on a dataset including more than 300,000 bugs of 5 open source projects (namely, *Mozilla*, *Eclipse*, *Dolphin*, *httpd*, and *gcc*) and then answered the following research questions:

- **RQ1:** *To what extent are word embeddings based bug reports representations informative enough to train multi-layer perceptron networks to perform bug localization?*
- **RQ2:** *To what extent is it possible to improve the performance of the above classifiers by introducing observed distributional features.*

The paper is organized as follows. In Sect. 2 we formally introduce the task of bug localization. In Sect. 3 we describe the proposed two-phase approach in detail. In Sect. 4 we estimate the performances of the system and discuss our findings. The current state of the is briefly described in Sect. 5. Finally in Sect. 6 we report conclusive remarks and announce future work.

2   Problem Statement

The task of automatic bug localization consists in predicting the source code files in which the fault in the code causing the erroneous behavior of the system is located.

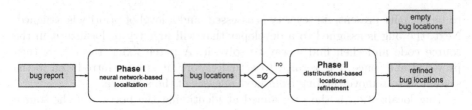

Fig. 1. Workflow of the two-phase approach.

More formally, let:

- ID_{new} be the ID of a new reported bug for a given system;
- $file_r$ be one of the source code files of the system;
- $Loc(ID_x)$ be the function that maps each bug ID_x into a vector such that $Loc(ID_x)_r$ is 1 if $file_r$ is involved into the fix of the bug ID_x;

then, the task of bug localization is defined as the prediction of the values of the function $Loc(ID_{new})$ for any arbitrary new reported bug.

We explain our approach for automatic bug localization in detail in next Sect. 3.

3   Approach

Our approach for bug localization is composed of two phases (see Fig. 1). In Phase 1, we predict the location of a newly reported bug ID_{new} using a localization function $Loc(ID_x)$ learned on top of *summaries* of past resolved bugs via Multi-Layer Perceptron (MLP) networks. The *summary* (or short description) of a bug is a short sentence provided by the bug reporter at reporting time which succinctly describes what the bug is about (e.g., *"Problem in user interface refresh"*). In Phase 2, we complement locations obtained in Phase 1 (particularly for bugs for which $Loc(ID_x)$ produced an empty result) by using distributional features.

3.1   Phase 1: Multi-layer Perceptron Network

To predict locations of a newly reported bug ID_{new} reported at time t_{new}, we propose a supervised approach (see Fig. 2) where:

1. we collect the set of resolved bugs RB, with a resolution time in between the two timestamps $(t_{new} - \Delta, t_{new})$, for which we could find one or more commits in the git repository of the project applied to fix the bug. In order to identify such commits, we search for a reference to the bug ID_x in the commit notes using a specific search pattern (regular expression) for each project.
2. for each collected bug $ID_x \in RB$ we compute a word embeddings vector as follows:

$$W(S(ID_x)) = \frac{\sum_{i=0}^{|S(ID_x)|} \boldsymbol{we}(word_i(S(ID_x)))}{|S(ID_x)|}$$

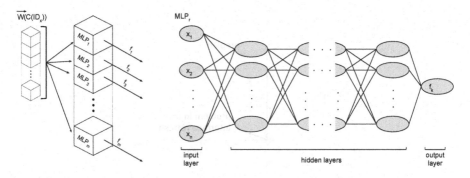

Fig. 2. Representation of the stack of Multi-Layer Perceptron networks used in Phase 1 of our approach to predict the location of fresh new reported bugs.

where: (i) $|S(ID_x)|$ is the number of words forming the *summary* of the reported bug (e.g., for a provided *summary* of the kind "Problem in user interface refresh" we count 5 words); (ii) $word_i$ is the function that returns the i-th word of a provided text (e.g., $word_4$("Problem in user interface refresh") returns "interface"); (iii) *we* is a function that retrieves a pre-trained word embedding vector for a given word from a given repository. Hence, we construct a vector representation of the text of the *summary* as the average of the vector representations of each word forming the text. In Fig. 3 we show an example (in two dimensions) where the word embedding vector for the *summary* "problem in user interface refresh" is obtained as the average vector of the component words "problem", "in", "user", "interface" and "refresh".

3. we define a localization function $Loc(ID_x)_r$, which for a given bug $ID_x \in RB$ and for a given file $file_r$ of the project returns:

$$Loc(ID_x)_r = \begin{cases} 1, & \text{if } file_r \text{ was modified to fix bug } ID_x \\ 0, & \text{otherwise} \end{cases}$$

in other words the function $Loc(ID_x)_r$ determines if a $file_r$ has been involved in a commit for the resolution of the bug ID_x;

4. as represented in Fig. 2, for each file f_r we train a multi-layer perceptron network MLP_r to predict if a file f_r is involved in the fix of a bug:

$$Loc(ID_{new})_r = MLP_r(W(ID_{new})).$$

Each MLP_r is trained on the feature vectors $W(ID_x)$ and on the target binary values of $Loc(ID_x)_r$ for the bugs $ID_x \in RB$ using a standard back propagation algorithm to determine networks weights and biases. The predicted localization of a bug ID_{new} will be the set $L(ID_{new}) = \{f_r : MLP_r(W(ID_{new})) = 1\}$.

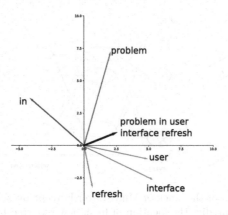

Fig. 3. Artificial example of creation of the word embeddings for a *summary* "problem in user interface refresh". The resulting vector is the average vector of the bidimensional word embedding vectors for the words "problem", "in", "user", "interface" and "refresh".

3.2   Phase 2: Distributional-Based Localization

To address the presence of empty predictions for a new reported bug ID_{new} (which affects the recall performances of the Phase 1 approach) we propose the following strategy:

Step. 1 we compute $W(S(ID_{new}))$ as described in Sect. 3.1 step 2;

Step. 2 for each candidate file f_i involved in a commit which fixes a bug $ID_t \in RB$, we define $BL_{f_i} = \{ID_t : Loc(ID_t)_i = 1\}$ and create the following average vector representation:

$$W(f_i) = \frac{\sum\limits_{ID_t \in BL_{f_i}} W(C(ID_t))}{|BL_{f_i}|};$$

Step. 3 we remove from the set of candidates those files f_i such that $|BL_{f_i}|$ is less then a parameter threshold $FreqTH$;

Step. 4 we then assign to the remaining candidate locations f_i the cosine similarity with the vector $W(S(ID_{new}))$ as follows:

$$score(ID_{new})_{f_i} = \frac{W(S(ID_{new})) \cdot W(f_i)}{||W(S(ID_{new}))|| \cdot ||W(f_i)||};$$

Step. 5 we remove from the set of candidate locations those files f_i such that $score(ID_{new})_{f_i}$ is less then a parameter $SimTH$ threshold;

Step. 6 we finally create $L(ID_{new})$ as the set of top K scored candidate files.

4 Experiments

To evaluate the effectiveness of the proposed approach we designed two experiments. The experiments (see Sects. 4.3 and 4.4) were devoted to estimate the performances of each phase, namely the MLP based approach (described in Sect. 3.1) and the distributional based one (described in Sect. 3.2). The following two paragraphs describe the dataset and the measures involved in the two experiments.

Table 1. Selected timestamps

T	Training set starts	Training set ends and test set starts	Test set ends
1	28 October 2001	30 May 2003	27 July 2003
2	17 June 2003	15 January 2005	14 March 2005
3	2 February 2005	4 September 2006	1 November 2006
4	21 September 2006	22 April 2008	19 June 2008
5	10 May 2008	9 December 2009	5 February 2010
6	27 December 2009	29 July 2011	25 September 2011
7	16 August 2011	16 March 2013	13 May 2013
8	3 April 2013	3 November 2014	30 December 2014

4.1 Dataset

Our dataset includes more than 300,000 fixed bugs across 5 open source software systems (namely, *Mozilla, Eclipse, Dolphin, httpd,* and *gcc*) covering a period of 13 years between 28 October 2001 and 30 December 2014.

To recreate a realistic scenario, we split the 13 years into eight time windows from which we collected the fixed bug reports for both training and test (see Table 1). We empirically experimented better results with windows of about 19 and 2 months for training and test, respectively.

We extracted bug reports of fixed bugs from the *Bugzilla issue tracker* of each of the open source projects. For each fixed bug we harvested from the corresponding project version control system (a git repository) the list of source code files involved in the fix.

In Table 2, for each of the systems and time windows, we report the number of bugs and fixed files observed, with averages and standard deviations.

For the implementation of the step 2 of Phase 1 approach (see Sect. 3.1) we adopt *Glove* as a set of pre-trained word embedding vector collection [9]. *Glove* is a general model for distributed word representation. Training is performed on aggregated global word-word co-occurrence statistics from a corpus.

We used pre-trained vectors of length 300 from the collection "glove.6B" trained on a corpus made with the combination of "Wikipedia 2014" and "Gigaword 5" and covering 400K uncased words[3,4].

---

[3] https://nlp.stanford.edu/projects/glove/.

[4] https://catalog.ldc.upenn.edu/LDC2011T07.

Table 2. Dataset descriptive statistics

	T	#bugs total	train	test	files total	avg	std		T	#bugs total	train	test	files total	avg	std
mozilla.core	1	3,659	3,218	441	6,459	6.12	16.98	mozilla.firefox	1	96	31	65	48	3.55	2.39
	2	2,258	1,816	442	6,130	7.57	40.41		2	149	107	42	245	2.94	6.06
	3	3,600	3,144	456	7,699	5.55	28.34		3	1,120	899	221	1538	3.22	10.94
	4	4,517	4,168	349	16,756	7.45	101.8		4	1,148	997	151	1,458	3.06	5.89
	5	7,109	6,481	628	16,716	6.47	23.89		5	1,650	1,587	63	1,805	3.53	5.85
	6	11,623	9,923	1,700	27,054	7.11	40.76		6	2,019	1,761	258	2,994	4.26	11.23
	7	17,493	15,074	2,419	43,207	8.55	57.73		7	2,750	2,431	319	6,093	5.59	33.87
	8	21,725	19,680	2,045	54,293	8.95	45.63		8	5,687	5,247	440	8,816	4.98	10.57
eclipse.platform	1	483	29	454	1,620	146	357.92	gcc	1	—	—	—	—	—	—
	2	1,265	432	833	102	1.16	1.10		2	2,283	1,896	387	9,380	9.13	108.37
	3	1,793	1,224	569	4,294	8.84	134.71		3	2,818	2,505	313	4,347	7.10	17.85
	4	1,279	453	826	3,619	17.26	214.35		4	2,420	2,136	284	7,344	12.47	171.78
	5	993	669	324	4,588	13.14	162.27		5	2,316	1,958	358	11,907	833.81	1650.43
	6	681	526	155	3,989	47.33	369.53		6	2,987	2,657	330	11,770	34.63	344.22
	7	253	111	142	310	4.16	11.69		7	2,459	2,078	381	10,184	18.69	254.24
	8	220	72	148	370	7.75	24.39		8	2,228	1,765	463	7,294	11.46	154.37
dolphin	1	—	—	—	—	—	—	httpd	1	—	—	—	—	—	—
	2	—	—	—	—	—	—		2	357	324	33	296	2.01	2.26
	3	—	—	—	—	—	—		3	155	145	10	157	1.76	1.40
	4	130	69	61	67	2.32	1.99		4	213	172	41	413	3.64	16.74
	5	246	155	91	109	2.22	2.03		5	132	110	22	147	2.23	2.76
	6	193	135	58	127	2.51	2.32		6	200	161	39	237	2.49	2.84
	7	249	228	21	159	2.97	3.16		7	190	175	15	214	2.50	3.08
	8	170	163	7	127	2.14	1.66		8	122	112	10	134	2.25	2.60

We release the datasets under a Creative Commons Attribution 4.0 International (CC BY 4.0) license at the following link: https://sites.google.com/unitelmasapienza.it/buglocalization.

4.2 Measures

To evaluate our two phase approach for each time window T, we identify the training set RB (see Sect. 3) as the set of bugs resolved during the observation time window and $Test(T)$ as the test set. For each $ID_n \in Test(T)$, let $A(ID_n)$ be the set of actual locations for the bug ID_n and $L(ID_n)$ the set of predicted locations; we compute true positives (TP), false positives (FP), false negatives (FN) and true negatives (TN) as follows:

$$TP_n = |L(ID_n) \cap A(ID_n)|;$$
$$FP_n = |L(ID_n)/A(ID_n)|;$$
$$FN_n = |A(ID_n)/L(ID_n)|;$$

$$TN(ID_n) = |\bigcup_{ID_i \in RB} A(ID_i)| - FN_n - TP_n - FP_n.$$

Then, we aggregate the above values as $TP(T)$, $TN(T)$, $FP(T)$ and $FN(T)$ summing the $TP(ID_n)$, $TN(ID_n)$, $FP(ID_n)$ and $FN(ID_n)$ respectively of each bug with $ID_n \in Test(T)$.

We then compute standard precision, recall and F_1 as follows:

$$P = \frac{TP(T)}{TP(T)+FP(T)};$$

$$R = \frac{TP(T)}{TP(T)+FN(T)};$$

$$F_1 = 2 * \frac{(P(T)*R(T))}{P(T)+R(T)}.$$

To better estimate the performances we do report the following measures:

- FullyCovered (FC), the ratio of bugs for which the system provides a full correct location:

$$FC = \frac{|ID_n \in Test(T) : A(ID_n) = L(ID_n)|}{|Test(t)|}$$

- FullyUncovered (FU), the ratio of bugs for which the system provide an empty set of files:

$$FU = \frac{|ID_n \in Test(T) : L(ID_n) = \emptyset|}{|Test(T)|}$$

- PartiallyCovered (PC), the ratio of bugs for which the system provide at least a file (wrong or correct):

$$PC = \frac{|ID_n \in Test(T) : |L(ID_n)| > 0|}{|Test(T)|}$$

Finally, we additionally defined $R'(T)$ as the recall estimated by counting true positives and false negatives only when at least an answer (correct or wrong) is provided by our system.

4.3   Evaluation of Phase 1

To evaluate the Phase 1 approach described in Sect. 3.1 we empirically defined the layout of MLP networks by setting different values for the number and sizes of the hidden layers. Best performing networks consists of four hidden layers with 250, 160, 80 and 40 perceptrons respectively. We fixed an upper bound to the number of iterations equals to 500, and applied standard scaling to input vectors.[5]

In Table 3 we report for each dataset portion and for each time window T the resulting performance of bug localization. We noticed that:

- the average F_1 range from .51($\pm$.04) to .78($\pm$.11) for *gcc* and *eclipse.platform* respectively;

---

[5] For the implementation of the MLP network we used scikit-learn 0.19.2.

Table 3. Phase 1 Localization performances. Accuracies are around 0.99; Random performances are all under .001; Conf is the 0.95 confidence interval.

	mozilla.core							mozilla.firefox							eclipse.platform						
T	F_1	P	R	FC	PC	FU	R'	F_1	P	R	FC	PC	FU	R'	F_1	P	R	FC	PC	FU	R'
1	.63	.98	.46	.35	.68	.32	.58	.59	.52	.69	.60	1.0	.00	.68	.66	.66	.66	.66	1.0	.00	.66
2	.58	.98	.40	.37	.71	.28	.64	.87	1.0	.80	.75	.75	.25	1.0	.94	.98	.91	.91	.96	.03	.93
3	.49	.97	.33	.29	.58	.41	.55	.77	.98	.63	.50	.76	.23	.72	.70	.85	.59	.57	.80	.19	.74
4	.67	.95	.52	.41	.79	.20	.61	.60	.99	.43	.46	.76	.23	.47	.57	.89	.42	.69	.79	.20	.84
5	.62	.94	.46	.28	.73	.26	.53	.58	.93	.42	.35	.66	.33	.62	.63	.72	.56	.47	.80	.20	.62
6	.61	.92	.45	.32	.77	.22	.49	.58	.98	.41	.29	.74	.25	.48	.91	.95	.87	.78	.95	.04	.88
7	.50	.89	.34	.31	.79	.20	.38	.52	.87	.37	.28	.70	.29	.42	.86	1.0	.75	.57	.57	.42	1.0
8	.64	.89	.50	.29	.74	.25	.55	.49	.93	.33	.40	.76	.23	.42	1.0	1.0	1.0	1.0	1.0	.00	1.0
Avg	.59	.94	.43	.33	.72	.27	.54	.62	.9	.51	.45	.77	.23	.60	.78	.88	.72	.70	.86	.13	.83
Conf	.04	.02	.05	.03	.05	.05	.05	.09	.11	.12	.11	.07	.07	.14	.11	.09	.14	.12	.10	.10	.10

	dolphin							httpd							gcc						
T	F_1	P	R	FC	PC	FU	R'	F_1	P	R	FC	PC	FU	R'	F_1	P	R	FC	PC	FU	R'
1	—	—	—	—	—	—	—	—	—	—	—	—	—	—	—	—	—	—	—	—	—
2	—	—	—	—	—	—	—	.67	1.0	.50	.37	.62	.37	.72	.71	.91	.58	.24	.99	.04	.58
3	—	—	—	—	—	—	—	1.0	1.0	1.0	1.0	1.0	.00	1.0	.75	.95	.61	.24	.98	.01	.61
4	.84	.88	.79	.72	.86	.13	.88	.87	1.0	.77	.70	.77	.22	.95	.11	.99	.05	.19	.95	.04	.06
5	.87	.90	.83	.79	.96	.03	.86	.69	1.0	.53	.70	.70	.30	1.0	.56	.48	.65	.26	.99	.04	.65
6	.32	1.0	.19	.33	.50	.50	.66	.16	.67	.09	.23	.35	.64	.16	.26	.70	.16	.27	.98	.01	.15
7	.76	.93	.64	.53	.69	.31	.77	.25	1.0	.14	.20	.20	.80	1.0	.93	.99	.88	.13	.99	.04	.88
8	.80	1.0	.66	.60	.60	.40	1.0	1.0	1.0	1.0	1.0	1.0	.00	1.0	.25	.95	.14	.25	.99	.04	.14
Avg	.72	.94	.62	.59	.72	.27	.83	.66	.95	.57	.60	.66	.33	.83	.51	.85	.43	.22	.98	.03	.44
Conf	.19	.05	.22	.16	.16	.17	.11	.25	.09	.27	.25	.22	.22	.23	.23	.14	.23	.03	.01	.01	.23

- the average ratio of FullyCoverd (FC) (see Sect. 4.2) is in the range .22($\pm$.03) to .77($\pm$.07) for *gcc* and *mozilla.firefox* respectively;
- the average ratio of PartiallyCoverd (PC) (see Sect. 4.2) is in the range .66($\pm$.22) to .98($\pm$.01) for *httpd* and *gcc* respectively.

In general the reported estimations enable us to deduce that the proposed system performs better when location consists in average of a fewer number of files per bug, and when there is a number of observed files in the training set which is large enough to cover the localization of unobserved bug (recall) but small enough to simplify the classification task (precision).

Finally, the R' measure (see Sect. 4.2) and the average ratio of bugs PC (for which at least a correct or wrong answer is provided) suggest the investigation of a second phase approach to complement the predicted partial localization.

4.4 Evaluation of Phase 2

In this section we estimate the performances of the proposed second phase approach (see Sect. 3.2) to refine the localization results provided by the MLP-based approach (see Sect. 3.1). Since the proposed methodology includes three parameters namely $FreqTH$, $SimTH$ and K (steps 3, 5 and 6 Sect. 3.1) we performed the parameter estimation on the *mozilla.core* dataset. First we tuned the $SimTH$ threshold and found the highest improvements of F_1,P,R for

Table 4. Phase 2 parameter tuning performances. We report the results of the comparison of best performance against MLP for some meaningful values of $SimTH$, when varying the two parameters $FreqTH$ and K in the set $\{1,2,3,4,5,6,7,8,9,10\}$. Conf is the 0.95 confidence interval.

mozilla.core

T	SimTH = 0.8			SimTH = 0.9			SimTH = 0.925			SimTH = 0.950			SimTH = 0.975		
	F_1	P	R	F_1	P	R	F_1	P	R	F_1	P	R	F_1	P	R
1	−.008	−.055	.020	.001	−.003	.019	.006	.000	.017	.008	.000	.017	.008	.000	.016
2	−.004	−.043	.022	.003	−.011	.020	.006	−.001	.014	.003	−.002	.010	.002	−.002	.010
3	−.007	−.117	.035	.011	−.024	.034	.016	−.003	.035	.025	−.001	.029	.026	−.001	.028
4	−.014	−.062	.024	.004	−.017	.030	.012	−.004	.030	.015	−.002	.026	.015	−.002	.026
5	−.005	−.034	.013	−.001	−.005	.008	−.000	−.002	.007	.000	−.000	.005	.000	.000	.004
6	−.009	−.043	.007	−.002	−.011	.007	−.001	−.004	.006	−.000	−.001	.005	.000	−.000	.005
7	−.005	−.033	.005	−.001	−.014	.005	−.001	−.007	.003	−.000	−.002	.002	.000	−.001	.003
8	−.006	−.037	.008	−.001	−.017	.010	.001	−.008	.010	.002	−.003	.009	.003	−.001	.009
Avg	−.007	−.053	.017	.002	−.013	.017	.005	−.004	.015	.007	−.001	.013	.007	−.001	.013
Conf	.003	.023	.009	.004	.006	.009	.005	.002	.010	.008	.001	.008	.008	.001	.008

Table 5. Phase 2 localization performances $K = 10$, $FreqTH = 2$, $SimTH = 0.95$.

T	mozilla core			firefox			eclipse platform			dolphin			httpd			gcc		
	F_1	P	R	F_1	P	R	F_1	P	R	F_1	P	R	F_1	P	R	F_1	P	R
1	.64	.98	.47	.59	.53	.69	.66	.66	.66	—	—	—	—	—	—	—	—	—
2	.58	.98	.41	.81	.85	.77	.94	.98	.91	—	—	—	.67	1.0	.50	.71	.91	.58
3	.51	.97	.35	.77	.98	.63	.70	.85	.59	—	—	—	1.0	1.0	1.0	.75	.95	.62
4	.67	.93	.54	.61	.99	.44	.57	.89	.42	.84	.89	.80	.87	1.0	.77	.13	.99	.07
5	.62	.94	.46	.64	.92	.49	.63	.72	.56	.87	.90	.84	.69	1.0	.54	.56	.49	.65
6	.61	.92	.45	.60	.97	.43	.91	.95	.88	.32	1.0	.19	.20	.71	.11	.26	.70	.16
7	.50	.89	.34	.53	.84	.38	.89	1.0	.80	.76	.93	.64	.25	1.0	.14	.93	.99	.88
8	.65	.89	.51	.49	.89	.34	1.0	1.0	1.0	.80	1.00	.66	1.0	1.0	1.0	.25	.95	.14
Avg	.60	.94	.44	.63	.87	.52	.79	.88	.73	.72	.94	.63	.67	.96	.58	.51	.85	.44
Conf	.05	.03	.06	.09	.12	.13	.14	.11	.17	.28	.07	.32	.31	.10	.34	.28	.17	.29

$SimTH \in \{0.950, 0.975\}$ see Table 4. Second we tuned $FreqTH$ and K and found the highest performances for $FreqTH = 2$ and $K = 10$ across the majority of time windows T. In Fig. 4 we report the diagrams of F_1, P and R for $T = 8$.

In Table 5 we report for each dataset portion and for each time window T the resulting performances after the second phase classification rearrangement. We observed that, across the datasets, the F_1 improvement is limited to a +1% and it is due to the increment of the recall performances.

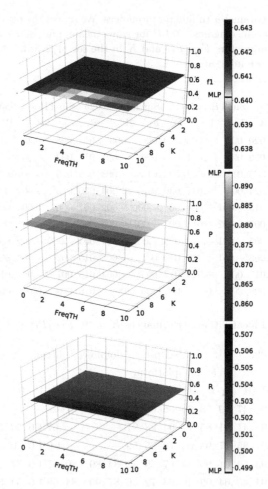

Fig. 4. From top to bottom F_1, P and R of Phase 2 approach with "mozilla.core", $T = 8$ $SimTH = 0.975$, valuing the two parameters $FreqTH$ and K in the set $\{1, 2, 3, 4, 5, 6, 7, 8, 9, 10\}$.

4.5   Discussion

Our initial research questions (see Sect. 1) aimed at investigating the ability of bug reports, combined with observed distributional features, to be enough informative to learn models to predict the localization of fresh newly reported bugs.

To answer both questions, we proposed a two-phase approach (see Sect. 3) where, in contrast with existing deep-learning techniques and to cope with the scalability issue, bug reports are encoded with pre-trained vectors (i.e., Glove word embeddings).

From the results of our experiments (see Sect. 4) we can deduce the following:

RQ1: Bug report *summaries* are written in natural language, with different styles and can be from truly informative to ambiguous and of scarce textual content. In other words, in our experiments, due to the nature of bug report *summaries* and their arbitrary, we observed a wide variety of cases where our approach, is able to correctly predict the expected bug location (see the values of the FullyCoverd (FC) measure in Table 3) but also a wide range of cases where the system is not able to provide any answer (FullyUncovered (FU)). Moreover, the adoption of pre-trained word embeddings vectors enables the design of standard MLP networks which, in contrast to deep learning techniques, are able to benefit from both the availability of a compact input representation and the ability of applying standard back-propagation optimization algorithms. Overall, thanks to pre-trained word embeddings, we were able to implement scalable neural network classifiers with a training running time of few hours for our largest dataset (i.e., *mozilla.core*) on a single quad-core machine with 16 GB of RAM.

We also experimented to train our MLP networks with a combination of input vectors built on bug report *summaries* and bug report *descriptions*.[6] and observed a not significant improvement in recall but a substantial drop in precision.

RQ2: The simple distributional-based technique adopted for the second phase localization refinement is not able to significantly improve the results for the different datasets.

5   Related Work

Due to the high effort that localizing bugs in the source code of a software system usually requires, many approaches have been devised to support developers in this task and to automatize it.

Recently, as surveyed in [15], the state of the art approaches were based on a variety of information retrieval techniques devoted to localize a bug considering a bug report as a query and by "retrieving" the most relevant source files.

---

[6] also known as the comment at bug reporting time.

Latent Dirichlet Allocation-based document model [13] are used in [6,8,10] among others, to leverage topic models and to rank relevant source files.

In [1,2,11,16] among others, the most relevant source files are identified comparing the similarity between bug reports and between source files. Instead in [12] among others, the authors also combine information extracted from version history services.

To reduce the number of false positives in [3] relevant source file are provided only if "enough" evidence is provided by bug reports and version histories.

In [14] the authors localize bugs by leveraging domain knowledge through functional decomposition of source code files into methods, API descriptions of library components used in the code, the bug-fixing history, and the code change history.

Deep learning approaches have been recently investigated.

In [5], the authors propose a framework called Defect Prediction via Convolutional Neural Network (DP-CNN). Deep learning is applied to programs' Abstract Syntax Trees (ASTs) to encode source code tokens as numerical vectors trough word embedding. Then, the vectors are used to train a Convolutional Neural Network to automatically learn semantic and structural features of programs.

In [4] the authors presented a similar combination of deep learning and informational retrieval techniques. Revised Vector Space Model (rVSM) [3] are used to collect features for the textual similarity between bug reports and source files; instead, deep neural networks (DNN) are used to learn how to relate words in bug reports to code tokens and words in source files.

6   Conclusion and Future Work

We presented a two-phase bug localization approach based on multi-layer perceptrons networks and distributional features.

Phase 1 of our approach (see Sect. 3.1) uses MLP networks to learn a model from pre-trained word embedding representations of bug report *summaries* and predict bug locations. We observed in our experiment (see Sect. 4.3) that Phase 1 is a scalable method to compute partial, but precise, bug locations.

Phase 2 of our approach (see Sect. 3.2) uses distributional features to complement partial bug locations provided by Phase 1. Unfortunately, in our experiment (see Sect. 4.4) we did not observe a significant performance improvement.

Overall, we believe that Phase 1 methodology partial solutions can help the execution of more comprehensive approaches (such as those mentioned in Sect. 5), hence, coping with their scalability issues.

We are working on improving Phase 2 of our approach by investigating scalable solutions, such as those proposed in [5].

References

1. Davies, S., Roper, M., Wood, M.: Using bug report similarity to enhance bug localisation. In: 2012 19th Working Conference on Reverse Engineering, pp. 125–134, October 2012. https://doi.org/10.1109/WCRE.2012.22
2. Dilshener, T., Wermelinger, M., Yu, Y.: Locating bugs without looking back. In: Proceedings of the 13th International Conference on Mining Software Repositories, MSR 2016, pp. 286–290. ACM, New York (2016)
3. Kim, D., Tao, Y., Kim, S., Zeller, A.: Where should we fix this bug? a two-phase recommendation model. IEEE Trans. Software Eng. **39**(11), 1597–1610 (2013). https://doi.org/10.1109/TSE.2013.24
4. Lam, A.N., Nguyen, A.T., Nguyen, H.A., Nguyen, T.N.: Bug localization with combination of deep learning and information retrieval. In: 2017 IEEE/ACM 25th International Conference on Program Comprehension (ICPC), pp. 218–229, May 2017. https://doi.org/10.1109/ICPC.2017.24
5. Li, J., He, P., Zhu, J., Lyu, M.R.: Software defect prediction via convolutional neural network. In: 2017 IEEE International Conference on Software Quality, Reliability and Security (QRS), pp. 318–328, July 2017. https://doi.org/10.1109/QRS.2017.42
6. Lukins, S.K., Kraft, N.A., Etzkorn, L.H.: Bug localization using latent dirichlet allocation. Inf. Softw. Technol. **52**(9), 972–990 (2010). https://doi.org/10.1016/j.infsof.2010.04.002, http://www.sciencedirect.com/science/article/pii/S0950584910000650
7. Murphy-Hill, E., Zimmermann, T., Bird, C., Nagappan, N.: The design of bug fixes. In: 2013 35th International Conference on Software Engineering (ICSE), pp. 332–341, May 2013. https://doi.org/10.1109/ICSE.2013.6606579
8. Nguyen, A.T., Nguyen, T.T., Al-Kofahi, J., Nguyen, H.V., Nguyen, T.N.: A topic-based approach for narrowing the search space of buggy files from a bug report. In: 2011 26th IEEE/ACM International Conference on Automated Software Engineering (ASE 2011), pp. 263–272, November 2011. https://doi.org/10.1109/ASE.2011.6100062
9. Pennington, J., Socher, R., Manning, C.D.: Glove: global vectors for word representation. In: EMNLP, vol. 14, pp. 1532–1543 (2014)
10. Rao, S., Kak, A.: Retrieval from software libraries for bug localization: a comparative study of generic and composite text models. In: Proceedings of the 8th Working Conference on Mining Software Repositories, MSR 2011, pp. 43–52. ACM, New York (2011). https://doi.org/10.1145/1985441.1985451, https://doi.org/10.1145/1985441.1985451
11. Wang, S., Lo, D., Lawall, J.: Compositional vector space models for improved bug localization. In: 2014 IEEE International Conference on Software Maintenance and Evolution, pp. 171–180, September 2014. https://doi.org/10.1109/ICSME.2014.39
12. Wang, S., Lo, D.: Version history, similar report, and structure: putting them together for improved bug localization. In: Proceedings of the 22nd International Conference on Program Comprehension, ICPC 2014, pp. 53–63. ACM, New York (2014). https://doi.org/10.1145/2597008.2597148
13. Wei, X., Croft, W.B.: Lda-based document models for ad-hoc retrieval. In: Proceedings of the 29th Annual International ACM SIGIR Conference on Research and Development in Information Retrieval, SIGIR 2006, pp. 178–185. ACM, New York (2006). https://doi.org/10.1145/1148170.1148204

14. Ye, X., Bunescu, R., Liu, C.: Learning to rank relevant files for bug reports using domain knowledge. In: Proceedings of the 22nd ACM SIGSOFT International Symposium on Foundations of Software Engineering, FSE 2014, pp. 689–699. ACM, New York (2014). https://doi.org/10.1145/2635868.2635874
15. Zhang, T., Jiang, H., Luo, X., Chan, A.T.: A literature review of research in bug resolution: tasks, challenges and future directions. Comput. J. **59**(5), 741–773 (2016). https://doi.org/10.1093/comjnl/bxv114
16. Zhou, J., Zhang, H., Lo, D.: Where should the bugs be fixed? more accurate information retrieval-based bug localization based on bug reports. In: 2012 34th International Conference on Software Engineering (ICSE), pp. 14–24, June 2012. https://doi.org/10.1109/ICSE.2012.6227210

Development of a Technological Platform for Knowledge Discovery

Nadezhda Yarushkina⬛, Aleksey Filippov(✉)⬛, and Vadim Moshkin⬛

Ulyanovsk State Technical University, Severny Venets Str., 32,
432027 Ulyanovsk, Russian Federation
{jng,al.filippov}@ulstu.ru, postforvadim@ya.ru
http://www.ulstu.ru/

Abstract. The paper considers the architecture of the technological platform designed for construction of the knowledge base (KB) by integrating a set of logical rules with fuzzy ontologies. The KB represents the storage of knowledge and contexts of different problem areas (PrA). The PrA ontology context is a specific state of the KB content that an expert can choose from a set of available states. The state is a result of either versioning or constructing the KB content from different points of views. Also, the paper describes the application of the KB in the inference of expert recommendations on solving the problem situations that occurred in the process of local area network functioning.

Keywords: Knowledge base · Ontology · Context · Problem area ·
Fuzzy ontology · Inference

1 Introduction

Modern organizations have a large amount of accumulated knowledge presented in the form of various corporate knowledge bases. Tools for creating wiki-resources are usually used for the organization of corporate knowledge bases. Technologies for creating wiki-resources are user-oriented and make it easy to create corporate knowledge bases of any complexity. Technologies for creating wiki-resources do not have a convenient way of querying knowledge for third-party software systems. Technologies for creating wiki-resources cannot discover new knowledge based on existing ones [1–4]. Thus, the development of a technological platform (TP) is necessary to solve the following tasks:

- the TP should not require additional skills and knowledge from the user;
- the TP should provide the programmer the familiar and easy to use data access mechanism;
- the TP should provide an inference mechanism to implement knowledge discovery (KD) functionality;

The study was supported by the Ministry of Science and Higher Education of the Russian Federation in framework of projects 2.4760.2017/8.9 and 2.1182.2017/4.6.

© Springer Nature Switzerland AG 2019
S. Misra et al. (Eds.): ICCSA 2019, LNCS 11619, pp. 533–544, 2019.
https://doi.org/10.1007/978-3-030-24289-3_39

– the TP should provide functions to the automation of the process of obtaining essential knowledge about problem area (PrA) in the internal knowledge base (KB).

At the moment, a lot of researchers use the ontological approach for the organization of the knowledge bases of expert and intelligent systems: Bobillo, Straccia [5,6], Gao, Liu [7], Bianchini [8], Guarino [9], Guizzardi [10], Falbo [11], Stumme [12], Gruber [13], Medche [14]. Ontology is a model for representing knowledge of the PrA. Graph-oriented database management system (Graph DBMS) Neo4j [15] was chosen to store the description of the PrA in the form of an applied ontology since the ontology is a graph. In this case, it is only necessary to limit the set of nodes and graph relations into which ontologies on OWL will be translated.

The inference is the process of reasoning from the premises to the conclusion. Reasoners [16,17] are used to implementing the function of inference and form logical consequences from many statements, facts, and axioms. Currently, the Semantic Web Rule Language (SWRL) is used to record logical rules for reasoners [18]. However, Neo4j does not assume the possibility of using default reasoners. Thus, there is a need to develop a mechanism for inference based on the content of a KB [5,6].

For successful translation, the wiki-resource into KB entities is required to assign the wiki-resource elements to TBox (structure) and ABox (content) of ontology [19].

2 The Model of the Fuzzy Domain KB Content with Contexts Support

Contexts of the KB represent the parts of ontology in space and time. Each space context is associated with a value from 0 to 1 defining the expert level of expertise in the part of the PrA. Time contexts allow using versioning of the PrA ontology and give an opportunity to monitor the dynamics of the ontology development. The fuzzy nature of the KB appears in the process of integration of contexts of the domain ontology.

The problem of developing the model of fuzzy domain KB with support of logical rules for inference is coming up. One of the KB main objectives is providing the mechanism for adapting the TP [20,21] to the concrete PrA with the use of methods of ontological analysis and data engineering.

Let the following definition represents the model of the KB content:

$$O = \langle T, C^{T_i}, I^{T_i}, P^{T_i}, S^{T_i}, F^{T_i}, R^{T_i} \rangle, i = \overline{1, t}, \tag{1}$$

where t is a number of the KB contexts,
$T = \{T_1, T_2, \ldots, T_t\}$ is a set of KB contexts,
$C^{T_i} = \{C_1^{T_i}, C_2^{T_i}, \ldots, C_n^{T_i}\}$ is a set of KB classes within the i-th context,
$I^{T_i} = \{I_1^{T_i}, I_2^{T_i}, \ldots, I_n^{T_i}\}$ is a set of KB objects within the i-th context,
$P^{T_i} = \{P_1^{T_i}, P_2^{T_i}, \ldots, P_n^{T_i}\}$ is a set of KB classes properties within the i-th context,

$S^{T_i} = \{S_1^{T_i}, S_2^{T_i}, \ldots, S_n^{T_i}\}$ is a set of KB objects states within the i-th context,
$F^{T_i} = \{F_1^{T_i}, F_2^{T_i}, \ldots, F_n^{T_i}\}$ is a set of the logical rules fixed in the KB within the i-th context, logical rules are used to implement the functions of inference by the content of KB,
R^{T_i} is a set of KB relations within the i-th context defined as:

$$R^{T_i} = \{R_C^{T_i}, R_I^{T_i}, R_P^{T_i}, R_S^{T_i}, R_F^{T_i}\},$$

where $R_C^{T_i}$ is a set of relations defining hierarchy of KB classes within the i-th context,
$R_I^{T_i}$ is a set of relations defining the "class-object" KB tie within the i-th context,
$R_P^{T_i}$ is a set of relations defining the "class-class property" KB tie within the i-th context,
$R_S^{T_i}$ is a set of relations defining the "object-object state" KB tie within the i-th context,
$R_F^{T_i}$ is a set of relations generated on the basis of logical KB rules in the context of the i-th context.

Figure 1 shows an example of the translation of the OWL representation of the ontology of family relations into the entities of the KB.

As seen in Fig. 1:

– OWL class "Person" was translated into the KB class with the same name;
– OWL individuals "Alex", "Helen", "Kate" and "17" was translated into the KB objects with same names;
– KB objects "Alex", "Helen" and "Kate" are objects of KB class "Person";
– KB object "17" is the object of built-in KB class "Integer";
– OWL data property "hasAge" was translated into the KB property with the same name;
– OWL object properties "hasFather" and "hasSister" was translated into the KB properties with the same names;
– OWL data property assertion "Helen hasAge 17" was translated into the KB state with the same name, the range of this state is "Helen", the domain of this state is "17";
– OWL object property assertion "Helen hasFather Alex" was translated into the KB state with the same name, the range of this state is "Helen", the domain of this state is "Alex";
– OWL object property assertion "Helen hasSister Kate" was translated into the KB state with the same name, the range of this state is "Helen", the domain of this state is "Kate".

2.1   The Inference on the Contents of KB

Formally the logical rule of the KB is:

$$F^{T_i} = \langle A^{Tree}, A^{SWRL}, A^{Cypher} \rangle,$$

where T_i is a i-th context of the KB,

A^{Tree} is a tree-like representation of the logical rule F^{T_i},

A^{SWRL} is a SWRL representation of the logical rule F^{T_i},

A^{Cypher} is a Cypher representation of the logical rule F^{T_i}.

A tree-like representation A^{Tree} of the logical rule F^{T_i} is:

$$A^{Tree} = \langle Ant, Cons \rangle,$$

where $Ant = Ant_1 \Theta Ant_2 \Theta \ldots \Theta Ant_n$ is a antecedent (condition) of the logical rule F^{T_i};

$\Theta \in \{AND, OR\}$ is a set of permissible logical operations between antecedent atoms;

$Cons$ is a consequent (consequence) of the logical rule F^{T_i}.

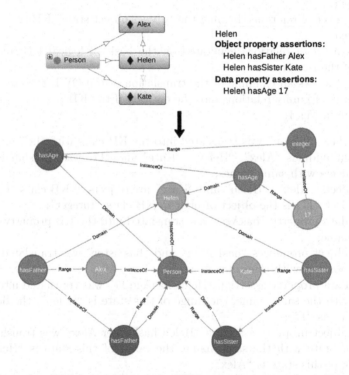

Fig. 1. Example of the translation of the OWL representation of ontology of family relations into the content of the KB.

The rules in the SWRL language are translated into their tree-like representations when imported into the KB of logical rules. The presence of a tree-like representation of a logical rule allows forming both an SWRL-representation of a logical rule and a Cypher-representation based on it.

For example, consider the process of translating the following SWRL rules into a tree-like representation (Fig. 2):

```
hasFather(?a,?b) => hasChild(?b,?a)
hasSister(?c,?a) & hasFather(?c,?b) => hasChild(?b,?a)
```

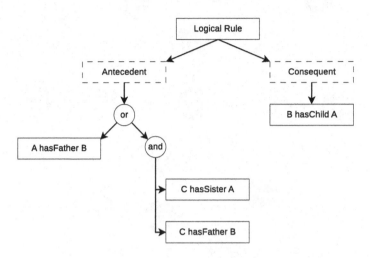

Fig. 2. Example of the tree-like representation of the logical rule.

The tree-like representation of the logical rule that presented in Fig. 2 is translated into the following Cypher representation:

```
MATCH (s1:Statement{name: "hasChild", lr: true})
MATCH (r1a)<-[:Domain]-(:Statement{name:"hasFather"})-
[:Range]->(r1b)
MERGE (r1b)-[:Domain]->(s1)
MERGE (r1a)-[:Range]->(s1)
MATCH (s1:Statement{name: "hasChild", lr: true})
MATCH (r2c)<-[:Domain]-(:Statement{name:"hasSister"})-
[:Range]->(r2a)
MATCH (r2c)<-[:Domain]-(:Statement{name:"hasFather"})-
[:Range]->(r2b)
MERGE (r2b)-[:Domain]->(s1)
MERGE (r2a)-[:Range]->(s1)
```

Relations of a particular type are formed by using the constructed Cypher queries to represent the logical rule between entities of the KB. Figure 3 shows the content of KB after executing the Cypher queries that were built for the tree-like representation of logical rule shown in Fig. 2. These relations correspond to the antecedent atoms of the logical rule. Formed relationships provide the inference from the contents of the KB.

As shown in Fig. 3, after the execution of the Cypher query from the Cypher representation of the logical rule (Fig. 2) the KB property with name "hasChild"

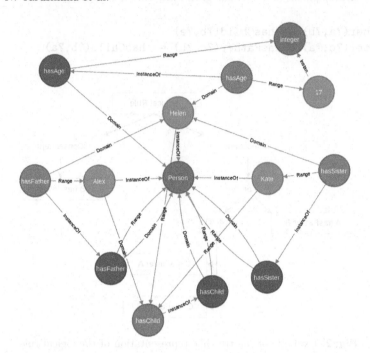

Fig. 3. The result of executing Cypher queries for the logical rule.

and the KB state with name "hasChild" were created. The range of created KB state "hasChild" is "Alex", the domains are "Helen" and "Kate".

3   Extracting Knowledge from Wiki-Resources

Let us represent the wiki-resource content by the following definition:

$$WIKI = \langle C, P, R \rangle, \tag{2}$$

where $C = \{C_1, C_2, \ldots, C_n\}$ is a set of wiki-resource categories,
$P = \{P_1, P_2, \ldots, P_i, \ldots, P_n\}$ is a set of wiki-resource pages defined as:

$$P_i = \langle N, I \rangle,$$

where N is a name of the i-th wiki-resource page P_i,
I is a infobox of the i-th wiki-resource page P_i defined as:

$$I = \{(K_1, V_1), (K_2, V_2), \ldots, (K_i, V_i), \ldots, (K_n, V_n)\},$$

where K_i is the i-th property of the infobox I of the wiki-resource page P_i,

V_i is a value of the i-th property K_i of the infobox I of the wiki-resource page P_i,

R is a set of relations between wiki-resource entities:

$$R = \{R_C, R_P, R_{CP}\},$$

where R_C is a set of relations defining a hierarchy of wiki-resource categories,
  R_P is a set of relations defining the "page-page" tie (hyperlinks),
  R_{CP} is a set of relations defining the "category-page" tie.
  The following function is used to translate the wiki-resource content into KB content:

$$\phi\,(WIKI): \{C^{WIKI}, P^{WIKI}, R^{WIKI}\} \rightarrow \{C^O, I^O, P^O, S^O, R^O\}^{T_i},$$

where $\{C^{WIKI}, P^{WIKI}, R^{WIKI}\}$ is a set of wiki-resource entities (Eq. 2),
  $\{C^O, I^O, P^O, S^O, R^O\}^{T_i}$ is a set of KB entities within the context T_i (Eq. 1).
  Table 1 contains the result of mapping the wiki-resource entities to the KB entities [22].

Table 1. The correspondence between the wiki-resource entities and the entities of KB

The entities of knowledge base	The entities of wiki-resource
Class	Category
Subclass	Subcategory
Object	Page
Class properties	The infobox elements (properties)
Object states	The infobox elements (values)
Relations	Hyperlinks

Thus, it becomes possible to extract knowledge from the structure of wiki-resource and present the extracted knowledge as content of KB.

4   The Architecture of the Technological Platform

Figure 4 shows that the TP consists of the following subsystems:

1. Ontology storage:
   - Neo4j;
   - KB content management module;
   - module for import of fuzzy ontologies with a set of SWRL rules.
2. Inference subsystem:
   - inference module.
3. Subsystem for interaction with users:
   - screen forms generation module.
4. Subsystem for importing data from wiki-resources:
   - module for importing data from wiki-resources.

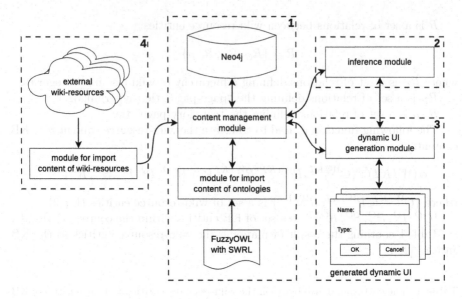

Fig. 4. Knowledge base architecture.

The dynamic graphical user interface (GUI) mechanism is used to simplify the work with KB of untrained users and control of user input [23,24].

Need to map the KB entities to the GUI elements to build a GUI based on the contents of the KB. Formally, the GUI model can be represented as follows:

$$UI = \langle L, C, I, P, S \rangle, \tag{3}$$

where $L = \{L_1, L_2, \ldots, L_n\}$ is a set of graphical GUI components (for example, ListBox, TextBox, ComboBox, etc.),

$C = \{C_1, C_2, \ldots, C_n\}$ is a set of KB classes,

$I = \{I_1, I_2, \ldots, I_n\}$ is a set of KB objects,

$P = \{P_1, P_2, \ldots, P_n\}$ is a set of KB properties,

$S = \{S_1, S_2, \ldots, S_n\}$ is a set of KB states.

The following function is used to build a GUI based on the content of KB:

$$\phi(O) : \{C^O, I^O, P^O, S^O, F^O, R^O\}^{T_i} \rightarrow \{L^{UI}, C^{UI}, I^{UI}, P^{UI}, S^{UI}\},$$

where $\{C^O, I^O, P^O, S^O, F^O, R^O\}^{T_i}$ is a set of KB entities represented by definition (1) within the i-th context;

$\{L^{UI}, C^{UI}, I^{UI}, P^{UI}, S^{UI}\}$ is a set of GUI entities represented by the definition (3).

Thus, the contents of the KB are mapped to a set of GUI components. This mapping makes it easier to work with KB for a user who does not have skills in ontological analysis and knowledge engineering. It also allows you to monitor the logical integrity of the user input, which leads to a reduction in the number of potential input errors.

5   Experiments

A set of experiments on constructing the ontology of the PrA of the local area network (LAN) state estimation in the process of simulated traffic increase was carried out. The ontology was constructed with the use of the TP. The TP also gives the ability of the inference of expert recommendations on solving the problem situations that occurred in the process of LAN functioning.

The following actions were taken:

1. The group of experts developed FuzzyOWL-ontology and the set of SWRL rules. Ontology and the set of SWRL rules were developed with the use of tools of the TP. Each expert worked with his ontology context. Weight was appropriated to each context. The weight of the expert is defined in the subareas of the PrA. The weight of the expert expressed in value from [0,1].
2. Thirty problem situations of decrease of the LAN performance were simulated on the tested LAN. Technical characteristics of the tested LAN outlined in the table of the results of the experiments. The reasons for the problem situation occurred should be detected.
3. The equipment performances in each simulated situation and the characteristics of the network were put into the KB. The LAN architecture also was put into the KB. The platform inference subsystem performed the output of one or several recommendations for the LAN state correction.
4. A group of expert estimated the correctness of the obtained recommendations. These experts were not involved in the KB development process.

The developed ontology of the LAN state analysis has a hierarchical organization. The developed ontology includes 81 classes, 104 properties, about 200 ontology instances and the set of SWRL-rules.

Table 2 contains the LAN architecture. Also, that table contains some modeled problems in the process of artificial traffic increase in a network. Recommendations on solving the problems generated by the platform tools in the process of inference are presented in Table 2.

Lan architecture is Star network, the number of workstations is 14, the server OS is Windows Server 2008 R2, the network switch is D-Link DGS-3420-28SC, 20 ports, the switch RAM is 2 Mb, the operating mode – 100 Mb/s Full Duplex, the media access control method is CSMA/CD, QoS is on, patch cable type is UTP, the category is 5E, port RJ-45.

5.1   Comparison of the Inference by Fuzzy and Crisp Ontologies

A set of experiments was carried in the TP to compare the interaction of ontological analysis and inference mechanisms by fuzzy and crisp ontologies. The possible problem situations occurred in LAN functioning in the process of traffic increase were simulated.

The LAN of IT-department of Ulyanovsk State Technical University was chosen as an object for the experiments. The comparative analysis of the inference methodologies in the process of modeling problem situations in the LAN functioning is shown on Fig. 5.

Table 2. The modeled processes of artificial traffic increase in a network

Modeled problems	The recommendations
The fast increase of the background load, increase of the user software reaction time	The reason is the overload of the communication channel. It requires network architecture changes. The number of stations in the overloaded domains should be reduced. The stations that create the most significant load should be connected to the switch ports
Half Duplex mode is enabled, the background load increase	The reason is the mismatch between the characteristics of a network switch and the traffic volume. It requires replacement of a switch or change of its settings
Damage of one network patch cable; increase of collision number	The reason is the problem with connection patch cables. The reason is the wrong organization of ground of the computers connected in the local network
Defects of switch ports, increase of CRC errors number, the background load increase	The reason is the problem of the network switch ports or the patch cable damage leading to a problem host
Defects of an Ethernet adapter, the rapid increase of some local and remote collisions	The reason is the problem in the Ethernet adapter settings of the domain server. The user should check the Ethernet adapter and the correctness of its settings

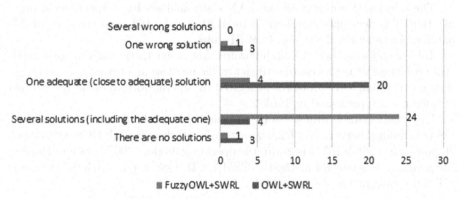

Fig. 5. The results of 30 experiments to the comparison of the inference by fuzzy and crisp ontologies.

The results of experiments show that fuzzy ontology based on FuzzyOWL format showed a more wide range of variants. The variants are sorted by the degree of relevance of recommendations. The risks of loss of possible variants of the logical inference block are significantly reduced.

6 Conclusion

Development of a technological platform for KD is necessary for automation of the process of obtaining essential knowledge about PrA in the internal KB. TP should not require users to have additional skills in knowledge engineering and ontological analysis. TP should provide inference functions.

Contexts of the KB represent the ontology content in space and time. Space contexts allow solving the problem of the expert level of competence in the specific part of the PrA. Each context is associated with a value from 0 to 1 defining the expert level of competence in the part of the PrA.

Time contexts allow using versioning of the PrA ontology. Time contexts give an opportunity to monitor the dynamics of the ontology development and to return to the defined state of the ontology.

The integration of the inference mechanism and the fuzzy ontology in the context of the KB provide a TP of expert decision support for specialists of different organizations. The contents of the KB are mapped to a set of GUI components. Dynamically generated GUI makes it easier to work with KB for a user who does not have skills in ontological analysis and knowledge engineering. It also allows you to monitor the logical integrity of the user input, which leads to a reduction in the number of potential input errors.

Fuzzy ontology based on FuzzyOWL format showed a more wide range of variants. The variants are sorted by the degree of relevance of recommendations. The risks of loss of possible variants of the logical inference block are significantly reduced.

References

1. Rubiolo, M., Caliusco, M.L., Stegmayer, G., Coronel, M., Gareli Fabrizi, M.: Knowledge discovery through ontology matching: an approach based on an artificial neural network model. Inf. Sci. **194**, 107–119 (2012)
2. Renu, R.S., Mocko, G., Koneru, A.: Use of big data and knowledge discovery to create data backbones for decision support systems. Procedia Comput. Sci. **20**, 446–453 (2013)
3. Ltifi, H., Kolski, C., Ben Ayed, M., Alimi, A.M.: A human-centred design approach for developing dynamic decision support system based on knowledge discovery in databases. J. Decis. Syst. **22**, 69–96 (2013)
4. Rajpathak, D., Chougule, R., Bandyopadhyay, P.: A domain-specific decision support system for knowledge discovery using association and text mining. Knowl. Inf. Syst. **31**, 405–432 (2012)
5. Bobillo, F., Straccia, U.: FuzzyDL: an expressive fuzzy description logic reasoner. In: Proceedings of the 17th IEEE International Conference on Fuzzy Systems (FUZZ-IEEE 2008), pp. 923–930 (2008)
6. Bobillo, F., Straccia, U.: Representing fuzzy ontologies in OWL 2. In: Proceedings of the 19th IEEE International Conference on Fuzzy Systems (FUZZ-IEEE 2010), pp. 2695–2700 (2010)
7. Gao, M., Liu, C.: Extending OWL by fuzzy description logic. In: Proceedings of the 17th IEEE International Conference on Tools with Artificial Intelligence (ICTAI 2005), pp. 562–567 (2005)

8. Bianchini, D., De Antonellis, V., Pernici, B., Plebani, P.: Ontology-based methodology for E-service discovery. Inf. Syst. **31**, 361–380 (2005)
9. Guarino, N., Musen, M.A.: Ten years of applied ontology. Appl. Ontol. **10**, 169–170 (2015)
10. Guizzardi, G., Guarino, N., Almeida, J.P.A.: Ontological considerations about the representation of events and endurants in business models. In: La Rosa, M., Loos, P., Pastor, O. (eds.) BPM 2016. LNCS, vol. 9850, pp. 20–36. Springer, Cham (2016). https://doi.org/10.1007/978-3-319-45348-4_2
11. Falbo, R.A., Quirino, G.K., Nardi, J.C., Barcellos, M.P., Guizzardi, G., Guarino, N.: An ontology pattern language for service modeling. In: Proceedings of the 31st Annual ACM Symposium on Applied Computing, pp. 321–326 (2016)
12. Hotho, A., Staab, S., Stumme, G.: Ontologies improve text document clustering data mining. In: ICDM 2003, pp. 541–544 (2003)
13. Gruber, T.: Ontology. http://tomgruber.org/writing/ontology-in-encyclopedia-of-dbs.pdf. Accessed 14 Jan 2019
14. Medche, A., Staab, S.: Ontology learning for the Semantic Web. https://www.csee.umbc.edu/courses/771/papers/ieeeIntelligentSystems/ontologyLearning.pdf. Accessed 14 Jan 2019
15. Neo4j: Official site. https://neo4j.com/product. Accessed 14 Jan 2019
16. Dentler, K., Cornet, R., ten Teije, A., de Keizer, N.: Comparison of reasoners for large ontologies in the OWL 2 EL profile. Seman. Web **2**, 71–87 (2011)
17. Pellet Framework Available. https://github.com/stardog-union/pellet. Accessed 14 Jan 2019
18. SWRL: A semantic web rule language combining OWL and RuleML. https://www.w3.org/Submission/SWRL. Accessed 14 Jan 2019
19. Suchanek, F.M., Kasneci, G., Weikum, G.: YAGO: a core of semantic knowledge unifying WordNet and Wikipedia. In: Proceedings of the 16th International Conference on World Wide Web, pp. 697–706 (2007)
20. Yarushkina, N., Filippov, A., Moshkin, V.: Development of the unified technological platform for constructing the domain knowledge base through the context analysis. In: Kravets, A., Shcherbakov, M., Kultsova, M., Groumpos, P. (eds.) CIT&DS 2017. Communications in Computer and Information Science, vol. 754, pp. 62–72. Springer, Cham (2017). https://doi.org/10.1007/978-3-319-65551-2_5
21. Yarushkina, N.G., Filippov, A.A., Moshkin, V.S., Filippova, L.I.: Application of the fuzzy knowledge base in the construction of expert systems. Inf. Technol. Ind. **6**, 32–37 (2018)
22. Shestakov, V.K.: Development and maintenance of information systems based on ontology and Wiki-technology, Electronic Libraries: Advanced Methods and Technologies, Digital Collections, pp. 299–306 (2011). (in Russian)
23. Hattori, S., Takama, Y.: Recommender system employing personal-value-based user model. J. Adv. Comput. Intell. Intell. Inform. (JACIII) **18**, 157–165 (2014)
24. Ruy, F.B., Reginato, C.C., Santos, V.A., Falbo, R.A., Guizzardi, G.: Ontology engineering by combining ontology patterns. In: Johannesson, P., Lee, M.L., Liddle, S.W., Opdahl, A.L., López, Ó.P. (eds.) ER 2015. LNCS, vol. 9381, pp. 173–186. Springer, Cham (2015). https://doi.org/10.1007/978-3-319-25264-3_13

Integration of Fuzzy OWL Ontologies and Fuzzy Time Series in the Determination of Faulty Technical Units

Nadezhda Yarushkina(ID), Ilya Andreev(ID), Vadim Moshkin(✉)(ID), and Irina Moshkina(ID)

Ulyanovsk State Technical University, Severny Venets Street, 32, 432027 Ulyanovsk, Russian Federation
{jng, v.moshkin, i.timina}@ulstu.ru, ares-ilya@ya.ru

Abstract. The method of constructing fuzzy ontologies was investigated in the framework of this work. An ontological model for assessing the state of helicopter units has been developed. The article provides a formal description of fuzzy ontologies and features of the representation of elements of fuzzy axioms in FuzzyOWL notation. According to the proposed approach, the summarizing of the state of a complex technical system is carried out by means of an inference based on a fuzzy ontology. Objects, properties and axioms of fuzzy ontology determine the parameters of the membership functions and linguistic variables of the objects of analysis in the form of time series. A software product was developed to implement the proposed approach. As part of this work, experiments were conducted to search for anomalous situations and search for possible faulty helicopter units using the developed approach to the integration of fuzzy time series and fuzzy ontology. For the first time, the results of the inference of knowledge based on the integration of fuzzy time series and fuzzy ontologies in the tasks of analyzing the diagnosis of complex technical systems were obtained. The proposed approach of hybridization of fuzzy time series and fuzzy ontologies made it possible to reliably recognize anomalous situations with a certain degree of truth, and to find possible faulty aggregates corresponding to each anomalous situation.

Keywords: Fuzzy time series · Fuzzy ontology · Fuzzy OWL · Summary

1 Introduction

The uncertainty of data and information incompleteness is an inalienable part of any complex technical system, in which the functioning quality of processes depends on a person. In the analysis, modeling, and design of such systems, a large distribution was obtained by expert systems that use experience and knowledge of the expert.

Expert assessment is the some qualitative aspect's linguistic form of the system element being evaluated or even of the system itself.

© Springer Nature Switzerland AG 2019
S. Misra et al. (Eds.): ICCSA 2019, LNCS 11619, pp. 545–555, 2019.
https://doi.org/10.1007/978-3-030-24289-3_40

Currently, the inference methodology of expert assessments based on the subject ontologies that play the role of a knowledge base in decision support systems (DSS) is used in various subject areas, including in the field of situational control in the energy sector [1], designing complex diagnostic systems [2], etc. Also, ontologies have been used as a knowledge base of intelligent risk prevention systems in the context of heterogeneous information for the complex technical systems critical infrastructure design phase [3].

Despite the application breadth, the classical languages of ontology and semantic networks, which are usually used to summarize and characterize the features of a subject domain, cannot be used to solve uncertainties and inaccuracies in the knowledge inherent in most real world applications in this area.

Fuzzy set theory, as well as fuzzy logic, is formalism suitable for processing incomplete knowledge, therefore ontologies based on such logic are adequate means of formalization.

One of the most effective solutions for representing a knowledge base in the context of accounting for fuzziness and uncertainty in human reasoning and evaluations in the DSS is a representation in the form of fuzzy ontologies. For example, fuzzy ontologies are used in such systems as disease diagnosis systems [4], fuzzy search engines [5], knowledge systems based on group decision making about the importance of data [6], etc. In most cases, such systems operate with facts objects or terms that are described in natural language and contain the features of the considered domain.

Fuzzy time series (FTS) is a way to obtain expert assessments that satisfy the conditions for completeness, consistency, and adequacy [7].

One of the main areas of application for FTS is process diagnostics. Diagnosis is the process by which a search for problems in the system occurs: defects, anomalies, faults, or lack thereof. When solving problems of diagnostics of complex technical systems, the state of which is determined by the data set in the form of FTS, it is advisable to apply methods for comparing the dynamics of processes with the expected or required dynamics.

Therefore an urgent task requiring a systemic solution is the interpretation of the results of the analysis in the form of expert assessments. To summarize the results obtained in the analysis of FTS, a system of rules is usually applied, which are stored in the knowledge base of the expert system. The knowledge base for solving this problem is ontologies and similar graph forms of knowledge representation and storage, which allow to take into account the semantic features of the object of the specified subject area, and not only their inference [8, 9].

Interpretation of the extracted comparisons in the form of expert assessments, the values of which are presented in the form of semantic units that correspond to certain classes of fuzzy ontology, taking into account the deviations between the current and the required FTS, can be obtained by solving the problem of integrating FTS and fuzzy ontology. Thus, the purpose of this work is the development of algorithms and models for the integration of fuzzy ontologies and FTS in the tasks of diagnosing complex technical systems.

2   Fuzzy Time Series and Fuzzy Ontology Model

The models and algorithms for analyzing and forecasting the FTS are described in detail in [10, 11]. At present, the basic notation of the fuzzy ontology representation is the FuzzyOWL standard [12–14]. Formally FuzzyOWL-ontology is:

$$I = (If, Cf, Pf, Af, Df, Qf, Lf, Modf),$$

where

- *If* is an Individual that simply represents an individual of the vocabulary;
- *Cf* is a Concept that represents a fuzzy concept of the vocabulary:

$$C_f = \left\{ C_f^A, C_f^C \right\},$$

where C_f^A are Abstract Concepts, C_f^C - Concrete Concepts;

- *Pf is* Property that represents a fuzzy role:

$$P_f = \left\{ P_f^A, P_f^C \right\},$$

where P_f^A are Object Properties, P_f^C are Datatype Properties;

- *Df* is Axiom that represents the axioms:

$$D_f = \left\{ A_f^{ABox}, A_f^{TBox}, A_f^{RBox} \right\},$$

where A_f^{ABox} is the Abox that contains role assertions between individuals and membership assertions, A_f^{TBox} is the Tbox that contains assertions about concepts such as subsumption and equivalence, A_f^{RBox} is the RBox that contains assertions about roles and role hierarchies. Some of the axioms are subclasses of FuzzyAxiom, which indicates that the axiom is not either true or false, but that it is true to some extent.

- *Of* is Degree that represents a degree which can be added to an instance of FuzzyAxiom:

$$Of = \left\{ LD_f, MD_f, ND_f, Var_f \right\},$$

where LD_f are Linguistic Degrees, MD_f are Modifier Degrees, ND_f are Numeric Degrees, Var_f are Variables.

- *Lf* is Fuzzy Logic represents different families of fuzzy operators that can be used to give different semantics to the logic.

$$L_f = \left\{ L_f^{Luk}, L_f^{Zad}, L_f^{Goed}, L_f^{Prod} \right\},$$

where L_f^{Luk} is the fuzzy operators logic of Lukasiewicz, L_f^{Zad} is the fuzzy operators logic of Zadeh, L_f^{Goed} is the fuzzy operators logic of Goedel, L_f^{Prod} is the fuzzy operators of product logic;

- *Modf* is Fuzzy Modifier that represents a fuzzy modifier, which can be used to modify the membership function of a fuzzy concept or a fuzzy role. Current sub-classes are Linear Fuzzy Modifier and Triangular Fuzzy Modifier.

Table 1 shows the elements of fuzzy axioms FuzzyOWL, as well as their possible representation.

Table 1. Elements of fuzzy axioms in FuzzyOWL

№	Element	Possible values	Representation in FuzzyOWL
1	LD_f – Linguistic Degrees	«high», «above average», «low»	`<AnnotationAssertion>` `<AnnotationProperty` `IRI="#fuzzyLabel"/>` `<IRI>#HighLoad</IRI>` `<Literal` `datatypeIRI="&rdf;PlainLiteral">fuzz` `yOwl2 fuzzyType="datatype";` `Datatype type="rightshoulder";` `a="15.0";` `b="30.0";/fuzzyOwl2</Literal>` `</AnnotationAssertion>`
2	MD_f – Modifier Degrees	«very», «not very»	`type="modified" modifier="very"`
3	ND_f – Numeric Degrees	$0 \leq ND \leq 1$	`Degree Value=0,6`
4	Var_f – Variables	a, b,c, k1, k2	`b="30.0";`
5	L_f – Fuzzy Logic	Zadeh, Lukasiewicz Goedel and Product	`hasSemantics="Zadeh"`
6	*Modf* – Fuzzy Modifier	Linear, Triangular	`<Datatype type="triangular" a="32.0"` `b="41.0" c="50.0" />`

3 Subject Area

Consider the use of the integration approach of FTS and fuzzy ontologies in solving the problem of diagnosing the state of a helicopter. Diagnostics of a helicopter consists in checking its units in order to establish their exploitation and the possibility of using the helicopter.

The result of the diagnosis will be assessment values of physical quantities key indicators. The main goal is to assess the danger of values. To solve this problem, it is necessary to construct models of the behavior of the selected nodes and make conclusions about the health of the nodes by using the models. Models are built at expert base of assessment about the conduct of a particular component.

Table 2 show the parameters of the membership functions used for construct the FTS (Table 2).

Table 2. Parameters of the membership function

Physical parameter	Range boundaries	Very little	Little	Good	Big	Very big
Exhaust gases temperature, °C	0–1000	a < 100 b = 200 c = 200,5	a = 100 b = 275 c = 350,5	a = 350 b = 560 c = 600,5	a = 600 b = 700 c = 720,5	a = 720 b = 800 c > 1000
Engine oil temperature, °C	0–150	a < 0 b = 5 c = 10,5	a = 10 b = 15 c = 20,5	a = 20 b = 30 c = 60,5	a = 80 b = 100 c = 120,5	a = 120 b = 135 c > 150
Engine oil pressure, kgf/cm²	0–20	a < 0 b = 1 c = 2,05	a = 2,0 b = 3,5 c = 5,05	a = 5,00 b = 8 c = 10,5	a = 10 b = 12 c = 15,5	a = 15,2 b = 17,5 c > 20
Main gearbox oil temperature, °C	0–100	a < 0 b = 5 c = 10,5	a = 10 b = 15 c = 20,5	a = 20 b = 35 c = 50,5	a = 50 b = 70 c = 80,5	a = 80 b = 90 c > 100
Main gearbox oil pressure, kgf/cm²	0–8	a < 0 b = 1 c = 2,05	a = 2,0 b = 2,5 c = 3,5	a = 3,45 b = 4 c = 4,55	a = 4,50 b = 5 c = 7,55	a = 7,5 b = 7,8 c > 8

Thus 5 fuzzy labels are defined for each physical quantity. The task of analyzing technical time series is reduced to the task of searching for anomalous situations in TS of main gearbox and engine propulsion system physical quantities indicators. The analysis is a sequence of the following steps:

1. Formation of FTS on the basis of the received information on the values of key physical quantities after the end of helicopter flight.
2. Search known abnormal situations in the resulting FTS.
3. Determination of the correct operation of the nodes. Work is incorrect if at least one abnormal situation.

The fuzzy ontology was developed for experiments. The developed FuzzyOWL ontology has a hierarchical structure and includes 55 classes, eight object properties, 40 data types.

Table 3 contains objects properties of the used in the work (OP - oil pressure, EGT - exhaust gas temperature, OT - oil temperature, PP - power plant).

Table 3. Property of objects

Property	Domain	Range
has OP main gearbox	main gearbox	OP main gearbox
has OP left engine	PP gearbox	OP PP gearbox
has OP right engine	PP gearbox	OP PP gearbox
has EGT left engine x	PP gearbox	EGT PP gearbox
has EGT right engine	PP gearbox	EGT PP gearbox
has OT main gearbox	main gearbox	OT main gearbox
has OT left engine	PP gearbox	OT PP gearbox
has OT right engine	PP gearbox	OT PP gearbox

Property declaration example for « hasOPMainGearbox»

```
<SubObjectPropertyOf>
  <ObjectProperty IRI="# hasOPMainGearbox"/>
  <ObjectProperty IRI="owl:topObjectProperty"/>
</SubObjectPropertyOf>
<ObjectPropertyDomain>
  <ObjectProperty IRI="# hasOPMainGearbox"/>
  <Class IRI="#MainGearbox"/>
</ObjectPropertyDomain>
<ObjectPropertyRange>
  <ObjectProperty IRI="# hasOPMainGearbox"/>
  <Class IRI="#OTMainGearbox"/>
</ObjectPropertyRange>
```

In addition, 40 data types were allocated: 5 fuzzy labels for 8 variants of relationships. The data type parameters correspond to the parameters of the membership function. The type of membership function in all data types was chosen triangular.

Example of declaring a data type in FuzzyOWL notation:

```
<AnnotationAssertion>
  <AnnotationProperty IRI="#fuzzyLabel"/>
  <IRI>#BigOPMainGearbox </IRI>
  <Literal datatypeIRI="&rdf;PlainLiteral">
    <fuzzyOwl2 fuzzyType="datatype">
      <Datatype type="triangular" a="4.50" b="5" c="7.5" />
    </fuzzyOwl2>
  </Literal>
</AnnotationAssertion>
```

As an object of experiments, time series for the diagnostics of helicopter units and the fuzzy ontology of the helicopter units design were investigated. In the course of these experiments, the fuzzy time series and fuzzy ontologies integration algorithms were used.

4   FTS and Fuzzy Ontology Integration System

A software system was developed to solve the problems of forming the inference of the recommendation based on the integration of fuzzy time series and fuzzy ontologies. The software system is written in C# on the .NET 4.5 platform. The system development was carried out in the Microsoft Visual Studio 2015 environment. SQLite was used as the DBMS. The exchange protocol is a function call to the SQLite library. This method simplifies the program and shortens the response time. To store the database (definitions, tables, indexes, and the data itself), a single standard file is used on the computer on which the program runs.

The expert develops a fuzzy ontology of the domain with the help of the ontology editor Protégé. To check the adequacy and consistency of the ontology, the built-in Reasoner HermiT or FACT++ is used. The scheme of the used software package is presented in Fig. 1.

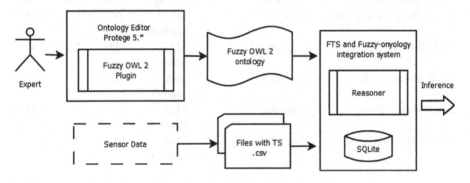

Fig. 1. FTS and fuzzy-ontology integration system.

The user has the opportunity to conduct research using the developed integration system. A prerequisite for obtaining an inference is to combine a time series with annotation properties. The result of the study is the resulting list of abnormal situations and possible faulty helicopter units.

5   Experiments

Diagnostics of a helicopter consists in checking its units in order to establish their serviceability and the possibility of operating the whole helicopter. The result of the diagnosis will be an assessment of the values of key physical quantities. The main goal is to assess the danger of values. To check the adequacy of the algorithm for integrating fuzzy time series and fuzzy ontology based on FuzzyOWL, as well as the correctness of the software that implements this algorithm, a series of experiments were conducted in which possible problem situations were performed. As part of the experiment, the following actions were carried out:

1. The expert has developed a fuzzy ontology according to the FuzzyOWL standard. To build a fuzzy ontology, the Protégé [16] editor with the connected FuzzyOWL Plugin [17] was used.
2. FuzzyOWL fuzzy ontology data types contain parameters of membership functions.
3. FuzzyOWL fuzzy ontology data types contain a binding to a specific class of ontology (Table 4).

Table 4. Data type descriptions

Datatype	Type of membership function	Specific class	a	b	c
VeryLittleEGTLeftEngine	Triangular	PP engine	100	200	200,5
Little EGTLeftEngine	Triangular	PP engine	200	275	350,5
GoodEGTLeftEngine	Triangular	PP engine	350	560	600,5
Big EGTLeftEngine	Triangular	PP engine	600	700	720,5
VeryBigEGTLeftEngine	Triangular	PP engine	720	800	1000
VeryLittleOPMainGearbox	Triangular	Main gearbox	0	1	2,05
LittleOPMainGearbox	Triangular	Main gearbox	2,0	2,5	3,5
GoodOPMainGearbox	Triangular	Main gearbox	3,45	4	4,55
BigOPMainGearbox	Triangular	Main gearbox	4,5	5	7,55
VeryBigOPMainGearbox	Triangular	Main gearbox	7,5	7,8	8

The task of the experiments is to search for possible faulty helicopter units. The analysis represents the sequence of the following steps.:

(1) the formation of TS on the basis of the obtained information on the values of key physical quantities after running the machine;
(2) search for defective helicopter units in the received TS;
(3) determination of defective helicopter units.

A helicopter unit will be considered faulty if at least one abnormal situation is detected for a physical quantity associated with a specific ontology class corresponding to the faulty unit.

The effectiveness of the diagnostic algorithm of technical systems can be evaluated when solving the problem of modeling the behavior of helicopter units. The system should correctly identify possible faulty helicopter units. To confirm the efficiency, it is necessary to analyze the data characterizing the machines, both without defects and with possible defects, and then analyze the information about the faulty units obtained by the system and received from an expert.

For the experiment, data were obtained on the run of the three machines, and data was generated that simulates certain abnormal situations. Description of the time series is given in Table 5.

Table 5. Description of time series

Series number	Airplane number	Period	TvG1	TvG2	Pm1	Pm2	Pmp	Tm1	Tm2	Tmp
1	210111	15.09.2050	739,59	258,85	2,3	0,8	0	58,1	59,2	29,3
2	210111	16.09.2050	757,29	256,93	2,4	0,8	0	57,1	59	29,3
3	210111	30.09.2050	503	227,78	7,4	0,8	1,8	47,5	51,3	29
4	210111	12.04.2052	536,85	520,93	7,6	6,6	4	53,9	56,5	35
5	240111	11.09.2054	176,43	178	0,8	0,8	0	42,5	46	31,3
6	240111	12.09.2054	176,57	178	0,8	0,8	0	42,5	46	31,3
7	240111	13.11.2046	483	448,85	6,4	5,6	3,4	49,5	51,9	23,5
8	240111	11.08.2047	479,13	0	6,4	5,4	3,3	51,6	55,1	29
9	250111	22.01.2046	189,72	206,22	0,8	1	1,6	52,5	55,5	24,5
10	250111	23.01.2046	193,3	209,22	0,8	1	1,6	52,5	55,5	24,5

The following designations are used: TVG1 - left engine exhaust temperature, TVG2 - right engine exhaust temperature, Pm1 - left engine oil pressure, Pm2 - right engine oil pressure, Tm1 - left engine oil temperature, Tm2 - right oil temperature engine, Pmp - oil pressure of the main gearbox, Tmp - oil temperature of the main gearbox.

Experiments were conducted with ten-time series. The results of experiments are shown in Table 6.

Table 6. Experiment results

Period	TvG1	TvG2	Pm1	Pm2	Pmp	Tm1	Tm2	Tmp	Faulty part
15.09.2050	739,59	258,85	2,3	0,8	0	58,1	59,2	29,3	#EnginePowerPlant
16.09.2050	757,29	256,93	2,4	0,8	0	57,1	59	29,3	#EnginePowerPlant
30.09.2050	503	227,78	7,4	0,8	1,8	47,5	51,3	29	#EnginePowerPlant
12.04.2052	536,85	520,93	7,6	6,6	4	53,9	56,5	35	No broken parts
11.09.2054	176,43	178	0,8	0,8	0	42,5	46	31,3	#MainGearbox
12.09.2054	176,57	178	0,8	0,8	0	42,5	46	31,3	#MainGearbox
13.11.2046	483	448,85	6,4	5,6	3,4	49,5	51,9	23,5	No broken parts
11.08.2047	479,13	0	6,4	5,4	3,3	51,6	55,1	29	#MainGearbox
22.01.2046	189,72	206,22	0,8	1	1,6	52,5	55,5	24,5	#EnginePowerPlant
23.01.2046	193,3	209,22	0,8	1	1,6	52,5	55,5	24,5	#MainGearbox

The result of the experiment is the construction of a fuzzy time series fuzzy ontology allowed us to conclude that the helicopter unit was malfunctioning when analyzing the precise values of the aggregates.

6 Conclusion

In this work, it was investigated by the method of constructing fuzzy ontologies and ontological model state helicopter units has been developed. In the process of integrating fuzzy time series and fuzzy ontology, the method integrating TS and ontology was implemented, and a software product was developed that ensures the implementation of this method.

Also, experiments were conducted to search for anomalous situations and search for possible faulty units using the developed approach to the integration of fuzzy time series and fuzzy ontology.

According to the results of the experiments, we can conclude that the proposed approach of hybridization of FTS and fuzzy ontologies allows one to reliably recognize anomalous situations with a degree of truth, and to find possible faulty units corresponding to each abnormal situation. The work is relevant, since the phenomenon of uncertainty, expressed in terms and concepts, is quite common in human knowledge.

Acknowledgments. The study was supported by:

- The Ministry of Education and Science of the Russian Federation in the framework of the projects No. 2.1182.2017/4.6 and 2.1182.2017;
- The Russian Foundation for Basic Research (Grants No. 19-07-00999 and 18-37-00450, 18-47-732007).

References

1. Massel, L.V., Vorozhtsova, T.N., Pjatkova, N.I.: Ontology engineering to support strategic decision-making in the energy sector. Ontology Designing **7**(1), 66–76 (2017). https://doi.org/10.18287/2223-9537-2017-7-1-66-76
2. Grischenko, M.A., Dorodnykh, N.O., Korshunov, S.A., Yurin, A.Y.: Ontology-based development of diagnostic intelligent systems. Ontology Designing **8**(2), 265–284 (2018). https://doi.org/10.18287/2223-9537-2018-8-2-265-284. (in Russian)
3. Kovalev, S.M., Kolodenkova, A.E.: Knowledge base design for the intelligent system for control and preventions of risk situations in the design stage of complex technical systems. Ontology Designing **7**(4), 398–409 (2017). https://doi.org/10.18287/2223-9537-2017-7-4-398-409. (in Russian)
4. Torshizi, A.D., Zarandi, M.H.F., Torshizi, G.D., Eghbali, K.: A hybrid fuzzy-ontology based intelligent system to determine level of severity and treatment recommendation for Benign Prostatic Hyperplasia. Comput. Methods Programs Biomed. **113**(1), 301–313 (2014)
5. Lai, L.F., Wu, C., Lin, P., Huang, L.: Developing a fuzzy search engine based on fuzzy ontology and semantic search. In: 2011 IEEE International Conference on Fuzzy Systems (FUZZ-IEEE 2011), pp. 2684–2689 (2011)

6. Morente-Molinera, J.A., Pérez, I.J., Ureña, M.R., Herrera-Viedma, E.: Creating knowledge databases for storing and sharing people knowledge automatically using group decision making and fuzzy ontologies. Inf. Sci. **328**, 418–434 (2016)
7. Yarushkina, N.G., Afanasyeva, T.V., Perfilyeva, I.G.: Intellectual Analysis of Time Series: Textbook. UlSTU, Ulyanovsk (2010). (in Russian)
8. Natalya, F.N., Deborah, L.M.: Ontology development 101: a guide to creating your first ontology. Stanford Knowledge Systems Laboratory Technical report KSL-01-05 and Stanford Medical Informatics Technical Report SMI-2001-0880, March 2001
9. Yarushkina, N.G., Filippov, A.A., Moshkin, V.S., Filippova, L.I.: Application of the fuzzy knowledge base in the construction of expert systems. IT Ind. **6**(2), 31–36 (2018)
10. Afanaseva, T.V., Namestnikov, A.M., Perfilyeva, I.G., Romanov, A.A., Yarushkina, N.G.: Time Series Forecasting: Fuzzy Models. UlSTU, Ulyanovsk (2014). (in Russian)
11. Romanov, A.A., Egov, E.N., Moshkina, I.A., Dyakov, I.F.: Extraction and Forecasting of the International Scientific and Practical Conference "Fzz 2018", Russia, Ulyanovsk, 23–25 October 2018, pp. 50–55 (2018)
12. Bobillo, F., Straccia, U.: Fuzzy ontology representation using OWL 2. Int. J. Approximate Reasoning **52**, 1073–1094 (2011)
13. Lee, C.S., Jian, Z.W., Huang, L.K.: A fuzzy ontology. IEEE Trans. Syst. Man Cybern. Part B **5**, 859–880 (2005)
14. Straccia, U.: Towards a fuzzy description: logic for the semantic web. In: 2nd European Semantic Web Conference, pp. 167–181 (2005)
15. Yarushkina, N.G., Filippov, A.A., Moshkin, V.S.: Development of a knowledge base based on context analysis of external information resources. In: Proceedings of the International Conference Information Technology and Nanotechnology, DS-ITNT 2018. Session Data Science, Samara, Russia, 24–27 April 2018, pp. 328–337 (2018)
16. Protégé: Ontology editor. https://protege.stanford.edu
17. Fuzzy Ontology Representation using OWL 2. http://www.umbertostraccia.it/cs/software/FuzzyOWL/index.html

Usage of Multiple RTL Features
for Earthquakes Prediction

P. Proskura[1]([✉]), A. Zaytsev[2], I. Braslavsky[1], E. Egorov[2], and E. Burnaev[2]

[1] Institute of Information Transmission Problems Russian Academy of Science,
Moscow, Russia
polina.231.11@gmail.com
[2] Skolkovo Institute of Science and Technology, Moscow, Russia
{a.zaytsev,e.egorov,e.burnaev}@skoltech.ru

Abstract. We construct a classification model, that predicts if an earthquake with the magnitude above a threshold will take place at a given location in a time range 30–180 days from now. A common approach is to use expert-generated features like Region-Time-Length (RTL) features as an input to the model. The proposed approach aggregates of multiple generated RTL features to take into account effects at various scales and to improve the quality of a machine learning model. For our data on Japan earthquakes 1992–2005 and predictions at locations given in this database, the best model provides precision as high as 0.95 and recall as high as 0.98.

Keywords: Machine learning · RTL features · Earthquakes prediction

1 Introduction

Physical modeling now fails to provide an accurate earthquake predictions because of the complex nonlinear behavior of seismicity. Instead researches adopt data-based approaches and construct machine learning or statistics-inspired models based on past data on earthquakes [3].

There are a number of problem statements related to earthquake predictions: consider a target region and predict place and time of the next earthquake, split the region into a grid and predict earthquake at the each of them, consider each earthquake as a separate event with given location and time and predict the value of this magnitude [3]. In this paper, we consider the third problem statement and construct a model that predicts if the magnitude exceeds a given threshold for an earthquake at a given location and time.

A starting point of a model for earthquake prediction is an empirical relationship or a physical modeling that provide a representation of reality. Often this representation is not good enough, and one adopts a machine learning approach on top of the physics-driven description.

Supported by Skoltech.

S. Misra et al. (Eds.): ICCSA 2019, LNCS 11619, pp. 556–565, 2019.
https://doi.org/10.1007/978-3-030-24289-3_41

For the problem of the prediction of earthquakes scientists consider several empirical statistical relationships e.g. Gutenberg–Richter law and Omori–Utsu (O–U) law. Gutenberg–Richter law [11] expresses the relationship between the magnitude and total number of earthquakes in the following way:

$$\log N = a - bM, \tag{1}$$

where N is the number of events with the magnitude greater than M, a and b (commonly referred to as the **b-value**) are coefficients fitted using given data. Omori–Utsu (O–U) law [18] represents the decay of aftershock activity with time

$$\dot{N}(t) = \frac{C_1}{(C_2 + t)^p}, \tag{2}$$

where t is time, N is a number of earthquakes, C_1, C_2 and decay exponent p (commonly referred to as the **p-value**) are coefficients fitted using given data. Both these models provide high-level description on number of earthquakes in the target region, moreover, Omori–Utsu law provides a connection between past and future seismologic activity in a region. Another physics-inspired features are RTL features [17] that provide an aggregation of past seismic activity into a single feature by weighting of past earthquakes that occur near the point, where we want to predict an earthquake. RTL features also have a number of hyperparameters to be fitted using collected data.

On top of these features we can construct a machine learning model [2, 4, 15, 16]. An example of such a work [4] considered the prediction of earthquakes as a binary classification problem. Authors generated 51 meaningful seismic features calculated for a dataset at hand based on well-known seismic heuristics such as "Standard Deviation of b-value" or "Time (T) of n events". As models they used various ensemble methods such as Random Forest, Rotation Forest and RotBoost.

In this paper we consider a different problem statement: we want to predict earthquakes at distant time interval. As input features we use normalized RTL features with different parameters and at different time scales. We examine a number of machine learning techniques to make use of generated features.

During evaluation of the models and model construction we take into account peculiarities of the problem: imbalance of classes (there are only a few large earthquakes in the dataset) [5, 6]; data are time-series based; there are no external features for these data, and we need to generate features from the data on past earthquakes.

2   Problem Statement

In the given dataset each earthquake has 4 parameters: location (x, y), time t and magnitude M. We define that the earthquake takes place $c(x, y, t) = 1$ at some location (x, y, t) if there is at least one earthquake of magnitude $M_e \geq M_c$ with coordinates (x_e, y_e, t_e) satisfying the following constraints:

$$||(x, y) - (x_e, y_e)||_2 \leq R_c, \quad \delta_c < t_e - t < T_c. \tag{3}$$

Otherwise we define that $c(x, y, t) = 0$

Our goal is to construct a model that predicts if there is an earthquake in a time cylinder $[T + T_{min}, T + T_{max}]$ using information about all earthquakes up to time T.

We aggregate information about earthquakes up to time T in a vector of features of fixed length $\mathbf{x}$. In particular we generate RTL features using procedure described in Subsect. 4.1. Figure 1 demonstrates used space-time cylinder used for generation of input features and the target interval for prediction.

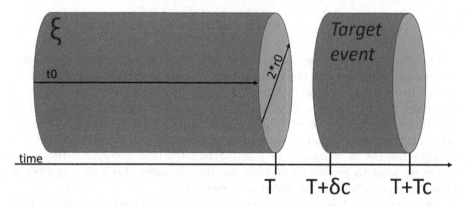

Fig. 1. Space-time cylinder used for generation of RTL features and interval considered for prediction

After these procedure for all earthquakes in a database we have a pair $(\mathbf{x}_i, c_i)$ with c_i defined by (3) with the magnitude threshold $M_c = 5$. All these pairs form a sample $D = \{(\mathbf{x}_i, c_i)\}_{i=1}^{n}$ of size n. Our goal is to create a model $\hat{c}(x, y, t)$ that resembles true relationship $c(x, y, t)$.

3   Data

We study the prediction of strong earthquakes in the middle-term horizon. Strong earthquake is an earthquake with the magnitude higher than $M_c = 5$. Predictions of earthquakes are related with the difficulties:

- The sample is unbalanced. In Japan, from 1990 to 2016, there were $247, 204$ earthquakes. Consider a distribution by the magnitudes which is shown in Fig. 2. The most part of classifiers and their metrics are common with balanced samples, where the amount of target class is approximately the half of the total. Thus in our case, the tuning of classifier and choice of metrics are needed to make them more sensitive to the target class.
- The dataset is nonhomogeneous as the network of seismic stations changes with time. So, the process of features generation is harder, because every couple measurements are needed to be evaluate for approximate equality.

– There is a lag in time between available and desired prediction interval, because exact point is unavailable according to our measurements.

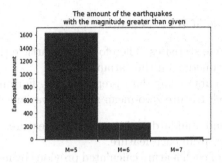

Fig. 2. Histogram of magnitudes: earthquakes with greater magnitude consist a small part of the sample, as the total sample size is about 300000 and there are only about 2000 with a magnitude greater or equal to 5 among them.

4   Methods

4.1   RTL Features

As inputs for Machine Learning model we use RTL features. The basic assumption of the **Region-Time-Length (RTL)** algorithm [17] is that the influence weight of each prior event on the main event under investigation may be quantified in the form of a weight. Weights become larger when an earthquake is larger in magnitude or is closer to the investigated place or time. Thus, **RTL** characterizes the level of seismicity at the point of space in the certain time.

The **RTL** takes into account weighted quantities associated with three parameters (time, place and magnitude) of earthquakes. A **RTL** parameter is defined as the product of the following three functions:

$$\mathsf{RTL}(x, y, t, M) = \mathsf{R}(x, y, t, M) \cdot \mathsf{T}(x, y, t, M) \cdot \mathsf{L}(x, y, t, M),$$

where $\mathsf{R}(x, y, t, M)$ is an epicentral distance, $\mathsf{T}(x, y, t, M)$ is a time distance and $\mathsf{L}(x, y, t, M)$ is a rupture length. They depend on the size of the space-time cylinder $\mathcal{E}_{r_0, t_0}$, defined by radius r_0 and time length t_0.

$$\mathsf{R}(x, y, t, M) = \sum_{e_i \in \mathcal{E}} \exp\left(-\frac{r_i}{r_0}\right),$$

$$\mathsf{T}(x, y, t, M) = \sum_{e_i \in \mathcal{E}} \exp\left(-\frac{t - t_i}{t_0}\right),$$

$$\mathsf{L}(x, y, t, M) = \sum_{e_i \in \mathcal{E}} \left(\frac{l_i}{r_i}\right).$$

where e_i is full description of an earthquake (x_i, y_i, t_i, M_i), l_i is an empirical relationship specific for Japan $\log l_i = 0.5M_i - 1.8$, $r_i = \sqrt{(x - x_i)^2 + (y - y_i)^2}$. We use only earthquakes with magnitude at least $M_i \geq M_0 = 5$.

4.2 Normalization of RTL Features

RTL is a very unstable statistics. Therefore in the article [13] authors proposed to normalize the parameters on the variances.

Normalization occurs during data preprocessing. For our case we transform the data to make each feature zero-mean and unit-variance [1]:

– Calculate mean and standard variance for each feature.
– Subtract the mean from each feature.
– Divide the values of each feature calculated previous by its standard deviation.

Also subtracting the moving average instead of mean. It helps to take into account time trend.

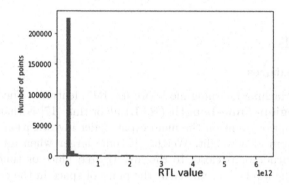

Fig. 3. Histogram of RTL values for each point. Small values prevail.

The negative **RTL** means a lower seismicity compared to the background rate around the investigated place, and the positive **RTL** represents a higher seismicity compared to the background Fig. 3. We are interested in both types of anomalies.

4.3 Classifiers

As classifiers we used the following machine learning methods:

– **Major RTL** is the method which estimates the threshold for RTL features. We evaluate our model to count optimal threshold from the train sample. If the value less than that threshold than the label is 0, 1 otherwise. Using the estimated threshold we label new data points.

- **Logistic regression** is a statistical model used to predict the probability of occurrence of an event. The model is the following:

$$Pr(c = 1|\mathbf{x}) = f(\boldsymbol{theta}^T\mathbf{x} + b),$$

where $f(z) = \frac{1}{1+e^{-z}}$ is a logistic function, and $\boldsymbol{theta}$ and b are the parameters of the model estimated from data [9].
- **Random Forest** is an ensemble classifier that is developed on the basis of majority voting of decision trees. Various number of decision trees are generated over bootstrap samples of the training dataset. The final decision is based on aggregation of the predictions obtained by all the decision trees. Thus, a Random Forest allows to find complicated relationships in the data, but at the same time more resistant to retraining [12].
- **AdaBoost** is another method that combines classifiers into ensembles. The key feature of this is that it introduces weights for all objects. At each iteration, the weights of each incorrectly classified object increase, so a new classifier ensemble focuses attention on these objects. AdaBoost is sensitive to noise and rejects in data. However, it is less prone to overfitting compared with other algorithms of machine learning [8].
- **Gradient Boosting** is an ensemble method that builds an ensemble of trees one-by-one, then the predictions of the individual trees are summed. The next decision tree tries to cover the discrepancy between the target function $f(x)$ and the current ensemble prediction by reconstructing the residual. Thus, an iteration process is constructed, in each iteration of which the loss function is minimized by gradient descent [10]. Another nice feature of Gradient Boosting is ability to treat imbalanced-classification problems after simple modifications [14].

4.4 Resampling Techniques

The problem at hand is imbalanced: number of objects with big enough earthquakes is significantly higher, than number of objects with relatively small earthquakes with magnitude smaller than 5. So, it is natural to apply machine learning heuristics that can deal with the problem. Here we consider two simple, yet efficient techniques for resampling: we modify our initial training sample to make more emphasis on minor class objects:

- Oversampling—increase weights of minor class objects in a random way
- Undersampling—drop some major class objects to balance number of instances of each class in a training sample.

5 Results

Selection of used metrics is motivate by imbalanced of the problem at hand. In addition to common Precision, Recall and ROC AUC we look at F1-score and PR AUC. See definitions of the metrics in Appendix A.

5.1   Models for RTl Features Generated with a Single Pair of Hyperparameters (r_0, T_0)

We use the following grid for **RTL** parameters:

$$r_0 = [10, 25, 50, 100], \quad t_0 = [30, 90, 180, 365].$$

The grid to find the best way to predict earthquakes was multidimensional and included (r_0, t_0) array, different values of adjusted magnitude, number of test samples and different classifiers.

Results of the grid with the best test size and best $t0$ for every $r0$ are given in Table 1. The best result is for Gradient Boosting [7], for the greater size of cylinder and for the smaller gap between time of measurements and the target event. Gradient Boosting works better than Logistic Regression because of non-linear behaviour of dependence of the magnitude of earthquakes on RTL features. Both these approaches work better than Major RTL because of difficulties of the RTL model, so more sophisticated machine learning approaches work better than simple threshold rule for the problem of earthquakes prediction.

Table 1. Results for different values of hyperparameters for generation of RTL features: the better results are for bigger size of cylinder

r0	best t0	Algorithm	Precision	Recall	F1	ROC AUC	PR AUC
10	180	Logistic Regression	0.54	0.36	0.43	0.64	0.53
		Random Forest	0.62	0.51	0.56	0.76	0.69
		AdaBoost	0.63	0.50	0.56	0.77	0.83
		Gradient Boosting	0.62	0.52	0.56	0.80	0.69
		Major_RTL	0.57	0.47	0.47	0.52	0.77
25	90	Logistic Regression	0.72	0.58	0.64	0.70	0.44
		Random Forest	0.79	0.51	0.62	0.74	0.68
		AdaBoost	0.75	0.67	0.71	0.77	0.53
		Gradient Boosting	0.82	0.6	0.69	0.79	0.77
		Major_RTL	0.67	0.52	0.62	0.70	0.60
50	180	Logistic Regression	0.91	0.84	0.88	0.83	0.67
		Random Forest	0.91	0.84	0.87	0.80	0.70
		AdaBoost	0.83	0.96	0.89	0.81	0.74
		Gradient Boosting	0.89	0.92	0.91	0.87	0.73
		Major_RTL	0.60	0.74	0.74	0.80	0.71
100	180	Logistic Regression	0.94	0.94	0.94	0.80	**0.94**
		Random Forest	**0.97**	0.90	0.94	0.89	0.90
		AdaBoost	0.96	0.96	0.96	0.92	0.90
		Gradient Boosting	0.95	**0.98**	**0.97**	**0.93**	**0.94**
		Major_RTL	0.90	0.86	0.89	0.83	0.89

5.2   Aggregation of a Number of RTL Features

In this section we used 16 calculated RTL features as inputs for a machine learning models. Quality of obtained models are available in Table 2. The improvement compared to the single best RTL feature with $M_c = 50, R_c = 50, \delta_c = 10, T_c = 180$ is insignificant. We conclude, that we can't get more information going this way.

Table 2. Result for usage of multiple RTL features with different hyperparameters for generation

Algorithm	Precision	Recall	F1	ROC AUC	PR AUC
Gradient Boosting (best single RTL)	0.97	0.96	0.96	0.95	0.94
Major_RTL	0.90	0.85	0.89	0.82	0.89
Logistic Regression	0.94	0.95	0.94	0.81	0.94
Random Forest	0.97	0.90	0.94	0.89	0.90
AdaBoost	0.97	0.96	0.97	0.92	0.90
Gradient Boosting	0.95	0.98	0.97	0.93	0.93

5.3   Usage of Resampling Techniques

There are a number of resampling techniques that can deal with imbalanced classification problems [5,6]. Here we consider oversampling, undersampling and balanced approaches. The results are in Table 3. For each approach we used machine learning algorithm that provided the best overall performance. We see that both undersampling and oversampling improve the quality of models.

Table 3. Model quality for application of imbalanced classification approaches. In these experiments we used a training sample of smaller size

Approach	Algorithm	Precision	Recall	F1
Initial	Gradient Boosting	0.84	0.59	0.59
Oversampling	Random Forest	0.94	0.99	0.97
Undersampling	Random Forest	0.96	0.87	0.91

6   Conclusion

We considered the problem of middle term earthquakes prediction. Usage of Machine learning provide an improvement compared to the state-of-the-art major_RTL method.

In particular the model based on Gradient Boosting with RTL features as inputs provide the best performance. However, for many cases RTL features generated using one set of hyperparameters one suitable RTL feature is not worse than a set of them generated using a set of hyperparameters. Another heuristic that improves quality of the earthquake prediction models is resampling to deal with imbalance of a given data.

Acknowledgements. The research was partially supported by the Russian Foundation for Basic Research grant 16-29-09649 ofi m.

A   Quality Metrics for Classification Problem

Introduce necessary definitions: Classification problem can be formulated as whether this object belongs to the target class or not.

- True Positive—if the object belongs to the target class and we predict that it belongs.
- True Negative—if the object doesn't belong to the target class and we predict that it doesn't.
- False Positive—if the object doesn't belong to the target class but we predict that it does.
- False Negative—if the object belongs to the target class but we predict that it doesn't.

The **precision** score quantifies the ability of a classifier to not label a negative example as positive. The is the probability that a positive prediction made by the classifier is positive. The score is in the range $[0, 1]$ with 0 is the worst, and 1 is perfect. The precision score can be defined as:

$$\textbf{Precision} = \frac{TruePositive}{TruePositive + FalsePositive}$$

The **recall** score quantifies the ability of the classifier to find all the positive samples. It defines what part of positive samples have been chosen by classifier as positive. The score is in the range $[0, 1]$ with 0 is the worst, and 1 is perfect.

$$\textbf{Recall} = \frac{TruePositive}{TruePositive + FalseNegative}$$

The **F1-score** is a single metric that combines both precision and recall via their harmonic mean. It measures the test accuracy and reaches its best value at 1 (perfect precision and recall) and worst at 0.

$$\textbf{F1} = 2\frac{PrecisionRecall}{Precision + Recall}$$

ROC AUC score counts the curve area under the Roc_curve. Roc_curve is the plot True Positive rate from the False Positive rate, which defines as

$$TruePositiveRate = \frac{TruePositive}{TruePositive + FalseNegative}$$

$$FalsePositiveRate = \frac{FalsePositive}{FalsePositive + TrueNegative}$$

ROC AUC score measures the quality of binary classifier. The best value is 1, value 0.5 is equal to random classification.

PR AUC score counts the curve area under the Precision_Recall_curve: Precision from Recall. Precision-Recall is a useful measure of success of prediction when the classes are very imbalanced. The perfect classifier curve ends in $(1.0, 1.0)$ and has area under it that equals 1.

References

1. Aksoy, S., Haralick, R.M.: Feature normalization and likelihood-based similarity measures for image retrieval. Pattern Recogn. Lett. **22**(5), 563–582 (2001)
2. Asencio-Cortés, G., Martínez-Álvarez, F., Morales-Esteban, A., Reyes, J.: A sensitivity study of seismicity indicators in supervised learning to improve earthquake prediction. Knowl.-Based Syst. **101**, 15–30 (2016)
3. Asim, K.M., Awais, M., Martínez-Álvarez, F., Iqbal, T.: Seismic activity prediction using computational intelligence techniques in northern Pakistan. Acta Geophys. **65**(5), 919–930 (2017)
4. Asim, K., Martínez-Álvarez, F., Basit, A., Iqbal, T.: Earthquake magnitude prediction in Hindukush region using machine learning techniques. Nat. Hazards **85**(1), 471–486 (2017)
5. Burnaev, E., Erofeev, P., Papanov, A.: Influence of resampling on accuracy of imbalanced classification. In: Eighth International Conference on Machine Vision (ICMV 2015), vol. 9875, p. 987521. International Society for Optics and Photonics (2015)
6. Burnaev, E., Erofeev, P., Smolyakov, D.: Model selection for anomaly detection. In: Eighth International Conference on Machine Vision (ICMV 2015), vol. 9875, p. 987525. International Society for Optics and Photonics (2015)
7. Chen, T., Guestrin, C.: XGBoost: a scalable tree boosting system. In: Proceedings of the 22nd ACM SIGKDD International Conference on Knowledge Discovery and Data Mining, pp. 785–794. ACM (2016)
8. Freund, Y., Schapire, R.: A short introduction to boosting. J. Jpn. Soc. Artif. Intell. **14**, 771–780 (1999)
9. Friedman, J., Hastie, T., Tibshirani, R., et al.: Additive logistic regression: a statistical view of boosting (with discussion and a rejoinder by the authors). Ann. Stat. **28**(2), 337–407 (2000)
10. Friedman, J.H.: Greedy function approximation: a gradient boosting machine. Ann. Stat. **29**, 1189–1232 (2001)
11. Gutenberg, B., Richter, C.: Seismicity of the Earth and associated phenomena (1951)
12. Ho, T.K.: Random decision forests. In: Proceedings of 3rd International Conference on Document Analysis and Recognition, vol. 1, pp. 278–282. IEEE (1995)
13. Huang, Q.: Seismicity pattern changes prior to large earthquakes-an approach of the RTL algorithm. Terr. Atmos. Oceanic Sci. **15**(3), 469–492 (2004)
14. Kozlovskaia, N., Zaytsev, A.: Deep ensembles for imbalanced classification. In: 16th IEEE International Conference on Machine Learning and Applications (ICMLA), pp. 908–913. IEEE (2017)
15. Panakkat, A., Adeli, H.: Neural network models for earthquake magnitude prediction using multiple seismicity indicators. Int. J. Neural Syst. **17**(01), 13–33 (2007)
16. Rouet-Leduc, B., Hulbert, C., Lubbers, N., Barros, K., Humphreys, C.J., Johnson, P.A.: Machine learning predicts laboratory earthquakes. Geophys. Res. Lett. **44**(18), 9276–9282 (2017)
17. Sobolev, G., Tyupkin, Y.: Low-seismicity precursors of large earthquakes in Kamchatka. Volcanol. Seismol. **18**, 433–446 (1997)
18. Utsu, T., Ogata, Y., et al.: The centenary of the Omori formula for a decay law of aftershock activity. J. Phys. Earth **43**(1), 1–33 (1995)

Privacy vs. Utility: An Enhanced K-coRated

Ze Xiang[1], Ghada El-Haddad[2(✉)], and Esma Aïmeur[2]

[1] Beihang University, Beijing Shi, China
seanxiangze@buaa.edu.cn
[2] Department of Computer Science and Operations Research,
University of Montreal, Montreal, Canada
{elhaddag, aimeur}@iro.umontreal.ca

Abstract. In recommender systems, collaborative filtering (CF) techniques are becoming increasingly popular with the evolution of the Internet. Such techniques are based on filtering or evaluating items through the opinions of online consumers. They use patterns learned from their behavior or preferences to make recommendation. In this context, it is of great importance to protect users' privacy when there is a need to publish data for a specific purpose which conduct to the usefulness of collaborative recommender systems. However, too much protection to individual privacy will lead to the loss of data utility. How to balance between privacy and utility is challenging. In this paper, we propose a privacy-preserving method based on k-means and k-coRating privacy-preserving model. First, we evaluate the k-coRated model by privacy and utility. Then, according to the drawbacks of it, we introduce our solutions to address the problem. Finally, we make a comparison between our model and k-coRated model in different aspects. As a result, our model outperforms k-coRated model with respect to utility as well as privacy.

Keywords: Privacy · Utility · Balance · K-coRated · Recommendation system · K-means

1 Introduction

In 2006, Netflix held a competition to award $1 million to the best winner who could improve the performance of its recommendation system[1]. In 2007, two researchers from The University of Texas claimed that they were able to re-identify users in the published data with film ratings on the Internet Movie Database. They proposed an attack model [1] based on the assumption of the knowledge gained by attackers. By comparing the auxiliary information gained by attackers and published data, the model could either re-identify a user or tell that he is not in the data released.

On December 28, 2009, a news report[2] announced that Netflix was sued for the privacy breach. On March 2010, Netflix decided [2] to cancel the pursue a second Prize

---

[1] Netflix. 2006. Netflix Prize. Retrieved December 17, 2018 from https://www.netflixprize.com/.
[2] Netflix Sued for Largest Voluntary Privacy Breach To Date. Retrieved December 17, 2018 from https://privacylaw.proskauer.com/2009/12/articles/invasion-of-privacy/.

© Springer Nature Switzerland AG 2019
S. Misra et al. (Eds.): ICCSA 2019, LNCS 11619, pp. 566–578, 2019.
https://doi.org/10.1007/978-3-030-24289-3_42

competition being previously announced in the same year and to respond to a lawsuit and Federal Trade Commission privacy concerns.

Although the event of Netflix privacy disclosure has passed for many years, privacy-preserving receives much attention recently as data mining technology is booming. Indeed, privacy is getting much attention in the literature [3–5]. Many models are proposed to define privacy awareness and how to protect people from the aspect of cyber-security.

However, nowadays as a significant change in business domains, it is unavoidable for organizations and companies to cooperate. On the one hand, they have to share their data to get their targeted result; on the other hand, they are afraid of invading users' privacy when sharing data. Therefore, filling methods to evaluate the performance of balancing privacy and utility become a challenge [6].

Data publication usually involves two main issues. One is to protect users' privacy. The other is to ensure the utility of data. Because when the publisher tries to anonymize user record, it must lead to data modification, which will further lead to a decrease in data utility. It is a trade off between individual privacy and data utility.

Nowadays, there is a large stream of literature on privacy, scientific studies have widely addressed privacy models [7–9]. They tried to classify attributes of user record into sensitive data (such as disease and salary), non-sensitive data and quasi-identifiers (such as zip code, age, and gender). Based on that, they proposed methods to protect sensitive data and quasi-identifiers in order to make people indistinguishable. However, such classification is heuristic and varies from person to person because people have different definitions of privacy. Additionally, prior studies proposed privacy protection models based on encryption [10–12], but generally, it is impractical considering the computational time.

As for data utility, as per our knowledge, there is no universal standard to evaluate the utility of data since it depends on the scenario adopted and the methods applied. In the same context, previous works have proposed a data utility model in the scenario of fog computing environments [13]. However, it just gives an abstract definition of utility and is not effective in practice. In another study, the authors proposed an anonymization method to improve data utility for classification [14], but for utility assessment, they evaluate it based on the performance of classification, which does not apply to other scenarios.

When considering both privacy and utility, the compromise between them is problematic. In previous studies [15], the authors specified that there is no trade off actually if assuming that attackers and scientists have the same background in knowledge and technology, while other works [16–18] tried to reach a balance in specific fields.

In the field of the recommendation system, the data of users involves their history of purchases, personal preferences and browsing records, which can be sensitive sometimes. Therefore, publishers like Netflix should give the same emphasis to user privacy as data utility when they try to release the data. On the one hand, they must anonymize users' information, on the other hand, they must ensure data utility. Since there is no universal standard for utility, we propose two aspects to increase utility empirically and based on those we propose a creative method to enhance a privacy-preserving model named k-coRated.

In Sect. 2, we briefly introduce some related work about privacy, utility and the balance between them. In Sect. 3, we introduce the k-coRated model and highlight its advantages and disadvantages, and based on that; we propose our method to solve the problem. In the same section, we simulate a cyber-attack model to evaluate our model and make a comparison between it and the k-coRated model. We present the results with the experiments in Sect. 4. Finally, we conclude this paper in the last section and discuss future work.

2 Background and Related Work

As the technology of data mining is booming and collecting people's data is increasing, there are rising concerns over people's privacy. Preserving confidential data of users while producing accurate predictions is one of the extremely important directions of the researches about recommendation systems [19]. However, how to define privacy and where is the boundary of privacy remain questionable. Several kinds of research have been done attempting to define what privacy is and to provide methods to protect it. For example, K-Anonymity [20] proposed an innovative model explaining privacy by the difficulty to distinguish someone from others. Based on K-Anonymity, L-Diversity [21] and T-Closeness [22] offered stronger protection considering the diversity and distribution of attributes of people. They try to define and extend privacy in different aspects, but there is no universal formalized definition of privacy until the appearance of differential privacy [23], which offers a theoretical framework to protect privacy in statistical databases.

While literature has widely explored privacy protection from malicious cyber-attack, privacy concerns within the publication of data are receiving more and more attention. It is necessary to protect users' privacy while ensuring the utility of data. Brickell and Shmatikov [15] stated that there could be no tradeoff between privacy and utility if we assume that attackers and scientists have the same level of knowledge.

However, Li and Li [17] pointed out that they have got the wrong way and offered a new perspective on data publishing. Most work relates utility to data modification. Chen et al. [24] proposed a novel way to evaluate utility based on the framework of differential privacy. Johnson et al. [16] proposed to trade off utility and privacy on full data. Rastogi et al. [18] discussed the boundary between privacy and utility. Based on prior knowledge of attackers, they were able to analyze when it is possible to design an algorithm to ensure privacy and utility.

Encryption/decryption is another technique for privacy preserving. This kind of technique is applied in distributed computing scenario with a very time-consuming. It consists by encrypting original data before being used. Although such method can ensure recommendation accuracy however there are some limitations regarding to its application. It is unpractical to encrypt/decrypt large datasets and many data mining computations cannot be achieved by encryption/decryption. As a result, the scopes of its usage are restricted.

Zhang et al. [6, 8] proposed a privacy preserving model inspired from k-anonymity technique named k-coRated in order to provide privacy to the data of the movie recommendation system. The authors proposed this model with k-coRating to retain data privacy of rating-style datasets by replacing some null ratings with "well-predicted" scores and enhance the data utility measured by prediction accuracy. However, they omitted to balance privacy with utility. In the following section, we discuss their work in detail and propose our enhanced method.

3   Methodology

In this section, we show our methodology step by step. First, in Subsect. 3.1, we introduce the k-coRated method. Second, in Subsect. 3.2, we discuss its drawback with respect to utility and propose our method based on the hybrid of k-means. In the remaining subsections, we give a more detailed discussion about our method.

3.1   Introduction to K-coRated

The k-coRated model defined user's privacy from the items they rated. It only cares whether a user has rated an item or not. The model is suitable for ratings with a small scale, like the 5-star rating system. However, with large scale rating system, it is not that effective regarding privacy protection. Below we show the definition of k-coRated privacy and related concepts.

Definition 3.1. For any user $u \in U$ and any item $i \in I$, $R_{u,\,i}$ is the rating of user u to item i, we define that

$$u[i] = \begin{cases} 0, & R_{u,i} = NULL \\ 1, & otherwise \end{cases} \tag{1}$$

Definition 3.2 (coRated Equivalence). Any two users $u, v \in U$ are of coRated Equivalence if for all $i \in I$, $u[i] = v[i]$.

Definition 3.3 (k-coRated Privacy). A rating matrix satisfies k-coRated privacy if each user $u \in U$ has at least k-1 coRated Equivalence users.

In the work of k-coRated model [20], the authors proved that to make a rating matrix satisfy k-coRated privacy is NP-hard problem and proposed a heuristic algorithm to do it; we summarize the process to two steps. First, they start to group the users by a specific criterion. Second, they fill the original rating matrix with a predicted rating to make it satisfy k-coRated privacy. Although they claimed that it could provide a considerable degree of privacy protection to the users in the data published, they omitted to weigh the balance between user privacy and data utility.

In this paper, we implemented their proposed algorithm and found that after processing by the k-coRated method, the original rating matrix of MovieLens 100 k dataset, which has 80,000 ratings at first, had about 370,000 ratings after anonymization. Thus, the number of ratings that it added to the matrix is so large.

However, as per our knowledge, there is no universal standard to evaluate utility, because it depends on the scenario to which data is going to be applied. Even in the field of the recommendation system, it is still hard to define utility for the fact that it is uncertain that what property of rating leads to a better recommendation.

3.2   Utility Concern and Solutions

Since it is impossible to evaluate utility absolutely, we propose a method with comparably better utility. In the best case, we wish to realize our objective without any modification to data. For that reason, we choose the method of anonymizing data by adding noise and getting less modification. Consequently, if it is unavoidable to make some changes to data, we hope it as little as possible.

Furthermore, the reason why we bypass modification to data is that original data is the best because people in their daily life generate it and the numbers that we add to the matrix are fake. However, if what we add to the original matrix equals what will happen or happened in the real world, then the utility of data should remain the same. So, a better prediction will also result in better utility.

Less Modification: We hope to reach k-coRated privacy with the least modification to data. First, we adopt k-means to improve clustering of users hoping that users in the same cluster have already co-rated most items. Then we propose a new way to do the modification, called Delete Little to Add Less (L2L).

Better Prediction: User-based Collaborative Filtering (CF) methods are typically used in the field of recommendation system and proved to have better results than item-based CF methods. In order to predict the preference of a user u to item i, denoting as $P_{u,i}$, user-based CF methods would like to refer to the preferences of K-nearest neighbors (k-NN) [25] of u, denoting as $N N_u$. In our work, we adopt the formula below to make the prediction.

$$P_{u,i} = \bar{u} + \frac{\sum v \in N N u \, \text{sim}(u,v) * Rv, \text{i}}{\sum v \in N N u \, \text{sim}(u,v)} \tag{2}$$

$\bar{u}$ is the average rating of user u, $\text{sim}(u,v)$ is the degree of similarity between user u and user v.

3.3   Less Modifications: K-Means

Since we only care about whether a user has rated an item or not, before we apply k-means to our scenario, we should do some normalization.

Definition 3.4 (Normalized Rating Matrix). A rating matrix R is normalized if $R_{u,i}$ satisfy the following equation.

$$R[u,i] = \begin{cases} 1, & \text{User } u \text{ has rated item } i \\ 0, & otherwise \end{cases} \tag{3}$$

Since the performance of k-means largely depends on the selection of initial centers, a selection, closer to the real final center, can provide better clusters. In order to get a better basis for measuring the initial set of centers, we conclude two properties of an initial and right set of center heuristically that help to determine a way to find initial centers.

Distance: the initial centers should be distant enough to each other and not located in the same cluster.

Density: the initial center must have many other points around it.

Below, we give the mathematical definitions of density and distance based on the Euclidean distance between users. To balance between distance and density, we propose a weight function between the normalized results of distance and density. Based on those definitions, we design Algorithm 1, as shown in Table 1, to find better initial centers.

Definition 3.5 (dis). for any user u and $v \in U$,

$$dis(u, v) = \sqrt{\sum_i (u[i] - v[i])^2} \tag{4}$$

Definition 3.6 (density). for any user $u \in U$,

$$Density(u) = \frac{1}{\sum_{v \in U} dis(u, v)} \tag{5}$$

Definition 3.7 (distance). for any user $u \in U$,

$$Distance(u) = \sum_{v \in Centers} dis(u, v) \tag{6}$$

Definition 3.8 (weight). For any user $u \in U$,

$$weight(u) = \alpha * \widehat{distance}(u) + (1 - \alpha) * \widehat{density}(u) \tag{7}$$

where $* \widehat{distance}(u)$ and $\widehat{density}(u)$ are the normalized results between [0,1].

3.4 Less Modification: L2L

L2L is inspired by the scenario that in a cluster of users, some items are rated by most of the users while a few people rate some items. To those rated by few, it is better to delete them. Figure 1 shows the process of L2L and makes a comparison between it and k-coRated method.

In Fig. 1, the illustrated Table 1 is the original matrix. Four users have rated items from 1 to 5, in order to make them k-coRated following the old method, we add predicted ratings to fill the null blank and get the illustrated Table 2. However, some items are rated by only a few users, like item 1 and item 5 in the illustrated Table 1. Based on our approach, we delete those rated by few users; thus in Fig. 1, we delete the ratings of ($User_1$, $Item_1$), ($User_2$, $Item_1$) and ($User_3$, $Item_5$), then we add predicted ratings to ($User_2$, $Item_4$) and ($User_3$, $Item_2$).

However, how to decide which part to be deleted? Which items are the part that rated by few?

Table 1. Algorithm 1: DD-based initial centers

Input:
k, the number of initial centers
R, normalized rating matrix
Output:
k initial centers
1: Initialize centers=[]
2: Compute density for every user in R
3: Set the user with max density as the first center
4: **while** len(centers)! $= k$ **do**
5:    Compute weight for every user in R except those in centers
6:    Add a user with max weight to centers
7: **end while**
8: **return** centers

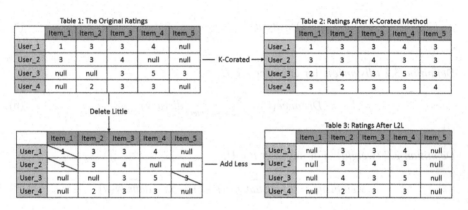

Fig. 1. Process of L2L

Definition 3.9. Below, we define what is the centroid of a cluster C, denoting as $ctr(C)$. For each item $i \in I$,

$$ctr(C)[i] = \frac{\sum_{u \in U} u[i]}{|C|} \qquad (8)$$

Based on $ctr(C)$, we propose that for any item i, if $ctr(C)[i] \leq \beta$, then i belongs to the part to be deleted. β is a hyperparameter, which is given by the user of the algorithm based on different scenarios.

3.5 Better Prediction

We base our prediction on Eq. 2. A Better prediction comes from a better definition of similarity between two users. Meanwhile, a better set of nearest neighbors will also result in better prediction.

We make a comparison between the currently popular definitions of similarity, including cosine-based, correlation-based, distance-based, Jaccard-based, and trust-based and pick the best among them. Moreover, we choose the top N similar users of user u as $N N_u$.

4   Experiments and Results

In this section, we evaluate our model regarding privacy and utility and compare it with [8]. In order to evaluate privacy, we introduce an attack model first. Considering that there is no universal standard evaluation of utility, we build our assessment by comparing the number of ratings in the matrix and evaluating the performance of data regarding collaborative filtering.

4.1   Experiment Design

Our experiments are performed using MovieLens 100k dataset, which consists of 100,000 ratings from 943 users on 1682 items. Our algorithms are implemented in python on a machine with an Intel Core i7-8700 CPU 3.20 GHz, 32 GB RAM running Windows10 64-bit operation system.

4.2   Privacy

Narayanan and Shmatikov proposed the attack model [1]. In this model (NS attack model), they assume that attackers have gained auxiliary information of users, denoted as Aux. They suppose that Aux contains m pieces of information, and n of them are correct considering that attackers may not have the right source of information. Every user has a piece of record in the database, denoted as Rec. The model defines a function called $Score$, which takes Rec of a user and Aux that attackers have gained as parameters and output a number as an indicator of the extent to which the user may be the target user of Aux.

$$Score(Rec, Aux) = \sum_{i \in supp(Aux)} wt(i) * Sim(Rec_i, Aux_i) \qquad (9)$$

For all the users in the published data, it gets a list of scores by applying Score to every Rec of users. Max_1, Max_2, and σ denote the highest score, second highest score, and the standard deviation of scores, respectively. If $\frac{Max_1 - Max_2}{\sigma} < \phi$, where ϕ is a fixed parameter called eccentricity, then there is no match for Aux, otherwise the record with the highest score is of the target user. The value of $\frac{Max_1 - Max_2}{\sigma}$ indicates how much the best-match record outperforms others and ϕ is a threshold. Therefore, the model not only requires that the target user record is the one with the highest score, but also that it must outstand other records. The Algorithm 2, shown in Table 1, explains the NS attack model step by step.

We simulated the NS attack by assuming that attackers gained 8 and 16 pieces of information in total, respectively. Figure 2 compares the performance of privacy between our method and k-coRated method. The y-axis indicates the probability to be re-identified for users in the data, and the x-axis indicates the information gained by attackers. From both two sub-figures, we can see that although there is little difference between our method and k-coRated method when attackers gain few pieces of information, our method outperforms k-coRated method almost two times regarding the possibility to be re-identified as attackers know more.

Table 2. Algorithm 2: scoreboard-RH [1]

Input:
    Aux, the auxiliary information gained by attackers
    D, the rating dataset φ, eccentricity
Output:
    the match record or empty set
1: For each record *Rec* ∈ *D*, compute *Score(Rec, Aux)*
2: Compute $Max_1 = Max_1(S)$, $Max_2 = Max_2(S)$, $\sigma = std(S)$,
   where $S = (Score(Rec,Aux), Rec) \in D$
3: **If** $\frac{Max_1 - Max_2}{\sigma} < \phi$, **then**
4:   **return** an empty set
5: **else**
6:   **return** the match record with the highest
7: **endif**

4.3   Utility: Number of Ratings

We compare the number of ratings in the matrix, which reflects the modification to the data. In order to make the two methods comparable, we make them have the same number of clusters. Figure 3 shows the results of two methods when clustering users into 10, 20 and 30 groups. From Fig. 3, we can determine that after being processed by our method, the number of ratings in the matrix stays around 260,000 while after being processed by the k-coRated method, it increased from about 400,000 to 600,000 as the number of user clusters increases. **Therefore, our method significantly reduces data modification and provides better data utility**.

4.4   Utility: Performance of CF

Since our data is about the recommendation system and collaborative filtering is commonly used in the field, so we decided to test the utility of the data based on the performance of collaborative filtering. We implement different prediction strategy proposed by [8] and use RMSE to evaluate the performance of CF. Below, we explain what RMSE is.

Given the N actual/predicted pairs $(R_{u,\ i},\ P_{u,\ i})$, the *RMSE* of the N pairs is computed as follows:

$$RMSE = \sqrt{\frac{\sum(Ru, i - Pu, i)^2}{N}} \tag{10}$$

Figure 4 shows the performance of our method compared to the k-coRated method. In each case, we use the same definitions of similarity according to Eq. 2 to make the prediction, and we choose the nearest neighbors from the top 5 to 100 most similar users.

From Fig. 4a, the best *RMSE* is about 0.98 when adopting correlation-based similarity definition and choosing nearest neighbors from top 80, while from Fig. 4b, the best *RMSE* is about 0.94 when adopting correlation-based similarity definition and choosing nearest neighbors from the top 40. **Therefore, our method increases the utility of data considering the performance of CF.**

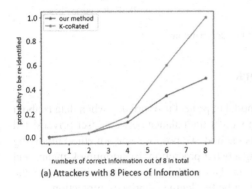 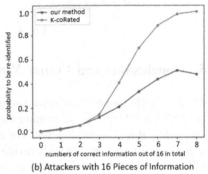

(a) Attackers with 8 Pieces of Information   (b) Attackers with 16 Pieces of Information

Fig. 2. Privacy comparison

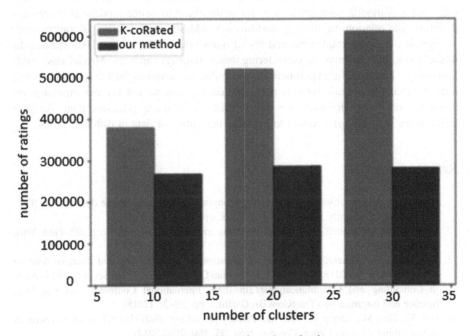

Fig. 3. Comparison of number of ratings

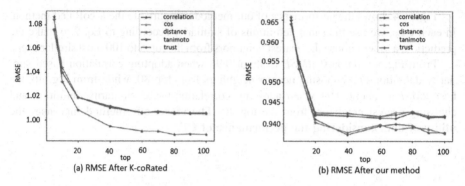

Fig. 4. Utility comparison

5 Conclusions and Future Work

Zhang et al. [8] proposed an innovative model to protect user privacy when data is about to be released. However, they omitted to weight the balance between user privacy and data utility. Based on the drawbacks of its method, we propose a new method involving less modification to the data and providing a better prediction. By adopting k-means and L2L, we achieve a significant reduction in data modification. Meanwhile, under the evaluation of NS attack, we even provide a better degree of privacy protection.

However, since there is no universal standard to evaluate utility, it is hard to judge whether the utility of our method is acceptable or not. Even though, it is intuitively right that less modification leads to better utility, how to define modification remains doubtful. The relationship among modification, addition, and deletion is complicated.

Besides, we only implement and tested our work on MovieLens 100k dataset. In future work, we believe in considering other datasets such as MovieLens 10M, Epinions or Netflix. The experiment on those datasets requires further considerations. Indeed, since MovieLens 100k is not a big dataset, we do not lay our emphasis on computational time. However, we will consider it in more extensive data. Another future work is to design a model to evaluate the utility of data in different fields.

References

1. Narayanan, A., Shmatikov, V.: Robust de-anonymization of large sparse datasets. In: IEEE Symposium on Security and Privacy, SP 2008, pp. 111–125 (2008)
2. Lohr, S.: Netflix cancels contest after concerns are raised about privacy, p. B3. New York Times (2010)
3. El Haddad, G., Aïmeur, E., Hage, H.: Understanding trust, privacy and financial fears in online payment. In: 2018 17th IEEE International Conference on Trust, Security and Privacy in Computing and Communications/12th IEEE International Conference on Big Data Science and Engineering (TrustCom/BigDataSE), pp. 28–36 (2018)
4. Gai, K., Qiu, M., Xiong, Z., Liu, M.: Privacy-preserving multi-channel communication in edge-of-things. Future Gener. Comput. Syst. **85**, 190–200 (2018)

5. Barth, S., de Jong, M.: The privacy paradox–investigating discrepancies between expressed privacy concerns and actual online behavior–a systematic literature review. Telemat. Inform. **34**, 1038–1058 (2017)
6. Zhang, F., Lee, V.E., Jin, R.: k-CoRating: filling up data to obtain privacy and utility. In: AAAI, pp. 320–328 (2014)
7. Ye, Y., Wang, L., Han, J., Qiu, S., Luo, F.: An anonymization method combining anatomy and permutation for protecting privacy in microdata with multiple sensitive attributes. In: 2017 International Conference on Machine Learning and Cybernetics (ICMLC), pp. 404–411 (2017)
8. Zhang, F., Lee, V.E., Jin, R., Garg, S., Choo, K.-K.R., Maasberg, M., et al.: Privacy-aware smart city: a case study in collaborative filtering recommender systems. J. Parallel Distrib. Comput. **127**, 145–159 (2018)
9. Zhang, Q., Liu, H., Wu, Y., Lin, C., Lin, G.: Grey maximum distance to average vector based on quasi identifier attribute. In 2017 International Conference on Grey Systems and Intelligent Services (GSIS), p. 119 (2017)
10. Bos, J.W., Castryck, W., Iliashenko, I., Vercauteren, F.: Privacy-friendly forecasting for the smart grid using homomorphic encryption and the group method of data handling. In: International Conference on Cryptology in Africa, pp. 184–201 (2017)
11. Wu, L., Chen, B., Zeadally, S., He, D.: An efficient and secure searchable public key encryption scheme with privacy protection for cloud storage. Soft Comput. **22**, 1–12 (2018)
12. Raisaro, J.L., Choi, G., Pradervand, S., Colsenet, R., Jacquemont, N., Rosat, N., et al.: Protecting privacy and security of genomic data in I2B2 with homomorphic encryption and differential privacy. IEEE/ACM Trans. Comput. Biol. Bioinf. **15**, 1413–1426 (2018)
13. Cappiello, C., Plebani, P., Vitali, M.: A data utility model for data-intensive applications in fog computing environments. In: Mahmood, Z. (ed.) Fog Computing, pp. 183–202. Springer, Cham (2018). https://doi.org/10.1007/978-3-319-94890-4_9
14. Han, J., Yu, J., Lu, J., Peng, H., Wu, J.: An anonymization method to improve data utility for classification. In: International Symposium on Cyberspace Safety and Security, pp. 57–71 (2017)
15. Brickell, J., Shmatikov, V.: The cost of privacy: destruction of data-mining utility in anonymized data publishing. In: Proceedings of the 14th ACM SIGKDD International Conference on Knowledge Discovery and Data Mining, pp. 70–78 (2008)
16. Johnson, M.P., Zhao, L., Chakraborty, S.: Achieving Pareto-optimal MI-based privacy-utility tradeoffs under full data. IEEE J. Sel. Top. Signal Process. **12**, 1093–1105 (2018)
17. Li, T., Li, N.: On the tradeoff between privacy and utility in data publishing. In: Proceedings of the 15th ACM SIGKDD International Conference on Knowledge Discovery and Data Mining, pp. 517–526 (2009)
18. Rastogi, V., Suciu, D., Hong, S.: The boundary between privacy and utility in data publishing. In: Proceedings of the 33rd International Conference on Very Large Data Bases, pp. 531–542 (2007)
19. Batmaz, Z., Kaleli, C.: Methods of privacy preserving in collaborative filtering. In: 2017 International Conference on Computer Science and Engineering (UBMK), pp. 261–266 (2017)
20. Sweeney, L.: k-anonymity: a model for protecting privacy. Int. J. Uncertainty Fuzziness Knowl.-Based Syst. **10**, 557–570 (2002)
21. Machanavajjhala, A., Gehrke, J., Kifer, D.: ℓ-density: privacy beyond k-anonymity. In: Proceedings of the International Conference on Data Engineering (ICDE 2006), Atlanta, Georgia (2006)

22. Li, N., Li, T., Venkatasubramanian, S.: t-closeness: privacy beyond k-anonymity and l-diversity. In: IEEE 23rd International Conference on Data Engineering, ICDE 2007, pp. 106–115 (2007)
23. Dwork, C.: Differential privacy: a survey of results. In: International Conference on Theory and Applications of Models of Computation, pp. 1–19 (2008)
24. Chen, K.-C., Yu, C.-M., Tai, B.-C., Li, S.-C., Tsou, Y.-T., Huang, Y., et al.: Data-driven approach for evaluating risk of disclosure and utility in differentially private data release. In: 2017 IEEE 31st International Conference on Advanced Information Networking and Applications (AINA), pp. 1130–1137 (2017)
25. Keller, J.M., Gray, M.R., Givens, J.A.: A fuzzy k-nearest neighbor algorithm. IEEE Trans. Syst. Man Cybern. 580–585 (1985)

Polarity Classification of Tweets Considering the Poster's Emotional Change by a Combination of Naive Bayes and LSTM

Kiichi Tago[1]([⊠])[iD], Kosuke Takagi[1], and Qun Jin[2][iD]

[1] Graduate School of Human Sciences, Waseda University, Tokorozawa, Japan
{kiichi.tg,10yentini}@ruri.waseda.jp
[2] Faculty of Human Sciences, Waseda University, Tokorozawa, Japan
jin@waseda.jp

Abstract. Twitter, as a popular social networking service, is used all over the world, with which users post tweets for various purposes. When users post tweets, an emotion may be behind the messages. As the emotion changes over time, we should better consider their emotional changes and states when analyzing the tweets. In this study, we improve polarity classification by considering the poster's emotional state. Firstly, we analyze the sentence structure of a tweet and calculate emotion scores for each category by Naive Bayes. Then, the poster's emotion state is estimated by the emotion scores, and a prediction model of emotional state is created by Long Short Term Memory (LSTM). Based on the predicted emotional state, weights are added to the scores. Finally, polarity classification is performed based on the weighted emotion scores for each category. In our experiments, our approach showed better accuracy than other related studies.

Keywords: Twitter · Polarity classification · Naive Bayes · Deep learning

1 Introduction

On Twitter, users can post tweets in real time, and many users express their opinions and feelings when interacting with other users. There are many studies that investigate the emotions in tweets.

Our emotions change over time. We can regard them as a series of flows. For example, if something happy happens, we will feel better for a certain period. Conversely, if something unpleasant happens, our feelings get worse and the remarks will be negative. It means that the emotional state of a poster may change at a different time. Therefore, we should consider the poster's emotional state behind the posted tweets when analyzing them.

© Springer Nature Switzerland AG 2019
S. Misra et al. (Eds.): ICCSA 2019, LNCS 11619, pp. 579–588, 2019.
https://doi.org/10.1007/978-3-030-24289-3_43

Until now, many studies have focused on the emotional tweets themselves, and few studies take into account the emotional state of the posters. The accuracy of polarity classification has been improved by machine learning. However, how to estimate the emotional state behind the tweets is not well discussed. Hulliyah et al. [7] surveyed emotion recognition methods for sentiment analysis, but the emotional state was not considered.

In this study, we propose a polarity classification approach that takes into account the poster's emotional state. In our approach, emotion classification by Naive Bayes is combined with Long Short Term Memory (LSTM). LSTM is a kind of deep learning, and it can create a time series model. We estimate the emotional state from emotion scores obtained by Naive Bayes, and predict the poster's emotional change with LSTM. By using predicted emotions for weighting scores, we can classify tweets based on not only emotional words but also the poster's emotion changes. By this mean, our approach is more user-centric.

The rest of this paper is organized as follows. In Sect. 2, we overview related research on emotion analysis and polarity classification on Twitter. In Sect. 3, we describe and explain our proposed approach. We show our experiments and discuss the results in Sect. 4. Finally, a summary of this study and future works are described in Sect. 5.

2   Related Work

2.1   Emotion Analysis for Social Media

A user's emotional state changes along the time axis. A tweet is a text posted by a human user, and emotion may be behind the tweet. As Braunstein et al. [2] suggested, a human mind should be considered not only from the explicit aspect but also the implicit aspect. In addition, to analyze and classify tweets more accurately, it would be necessary to analyze both the tweets and their posters.

Beasley and Mason [1] investigated the relationship between emotional expression in social media and subjective emotion using questionnaires. Kramer [8] analyzed Facebook posts and revealed differences between an emotion trend of holidays and that of weekdays. Nguyen et al. [9] created a model to predict emotion changes in a group based on machine learnings. Fujita et al. [4] investigated whether emotional tweets affect others' posts. They revealed that positive tweets affect others while negative tweets are hard to spread.

2.2   Emotion Detection and Classification

Polarity analysis is a typical theme of natural language processing, and recently machine learning such as deep learning is used. In order to take into account the appearance order and context of sentences, Recurrent Neural Network (RNN) and LSTM are applied. Vateekul and Koomsubha [14] performed emotion classification for Thai tweets data using LSTM. In their experiments, LSTM showed higher accuracy in emotion classification than SVM and Naive Bayes. Su et al. [11] showed that word2vec and LSTM can be combined to improve the emotion classification. Maulidiah and Sarno [3] showed that their approach can classify tweets with an accuracy of 74% by weighting emoticons.

In order to evaluate emotion, multiple datasets are prepared [10,15]. As a typical dataset, there is Sentiment140 [5]. This dataset is used to classify positive and negative. Uysal and Murphey [13] used multiple datasets including Sentiment140 and verified the classification accuracy by the characteristic selection of words. Huang et al. [6] proposed an emotion evaluation model using random forest and clarified emotional tendency by places. They also used Sentiment140 to evaluate their model.

2.3 Position of This Study

When analyzing tweets, the emotional state of the poster was rarely taken into account. Beasley [1] evaluated the relationship between the emotional state of the user and emotional tweets. Their results showed that there was no significant correlation. However, there is a gap between subjective emotion and objective emotion. Therefore, even though the poster him/herself is not aware, potential emotions may appear in the tweets.

In this paper, we propose a polarity classification approach considering the emotional state in chronological order. Naive Bayes, which is a statistical method, is adopted for calculating emotion scores. Moreover, we adopt LSTM, which is mainly used for time series analysis. Using LSTM, we consider the poster's emotional state as time series data and predict the emotional state.

3   Polarity Classification Considering Emotional States

The overview of our approach is shown in Fig. 1. Firstly, tweets posted by a user are collected. Secondly, dependency analysis is performed on the relationships between words. Thirdly, a score for a positive and negative category is calculated by Naive Bayes. Thereafter, emotional states are estimated by LSTM, and category scores are weighted based on the estimated state. Finally, using the weighted category scores, the polarity of tweets is judged.

3.1   Dependency Analysis

Dependency analysis is a method to analyze the structure of a sentence. The words such as "very" and "little" have a function to change the meanings of related words. By understanding the relationship between words, we can evaluate the polarity more effectively. Dependency analysis is used to adjust the category score attached by Naive Bayes.

To perform dependency analysis, various tools such as Cabocha and MST-Parser are provided. In this study, we use Syntaxnet[1]. This is the neural network framework released by Google in 2016.

---

[1] https://github.com/tensorflow/models/tree/master/research/syntaxnet.

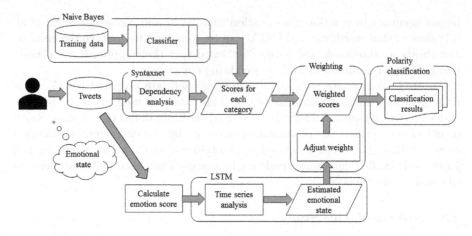

Fig. 1. Our proposed approach

3.2 Calculating Category Scores by Naive Bayes

After performing dependency analysis, positive and negative emotion category scores are calculated by Naive Bayes. Naive Bayes is a kind of supervised learning and classifies tweets based on the probability that a word appears in each category. Based on the probability, the score for each category is calculated for the word. In this method, it is assumed that words appear independently.

3.3 Estimating Emotional State by LSTM

Using Naive Bayes, the scores of positive category and negative category for tweets are calculated separately. Based on the method proposed in our previous study [12], the total score is calculated for each category. The total positive score of the tweet ($TPST$) can be expressed in Eq. (1).

$$TPST = \sum_{i=1}^{n} PES_i \tag{1}$$

where n represents the number of words in the tweet. PES_i represents the positive emotion score of a word. The positive emotion score is calculated by Naive Bayes based on the probability that a word appears in the positive category.

The total negative score of the tweet ($TNST$) can be calculated in Eq. (2).

$$TNST = \sum_{i=1}^{n} NES_i \tag{2}$$

where n represents the number of words in the tweet. NES_i represents the negative emotion score of a word. The negative emotion score is calculated by Naive Bayes in the same way as the positive score.

Estimation of emotional state is carried out by time series analysis. Nguyen et al. [9] defined the ratio of positive tweet count as an emotion tendency, and we referred to their approach. As a poster's emotional state, we use the positive emotion ratio to measure the emotional state (EST) for a tweet. EST is defined as follows:

$$EST = \frac{TPST}{TPST + TNST} \tag{3}$$

where $TPST$ is the score of the positive category of the tweet, and $TNST$ is the score of the negative category. The range of EST is from 0 to 1. Since EST represents the ratio of positive emotion ratio, it can be regarded as a positive tendency if it is larger than 0.5, and negative if it is smaller than 0.5.

3.4   Weighting Category Score Based on Predicted EST

To predict EST, LSTM, which is a kind of deep learning, is used. LSTM is an extension of RNN. It is composed of a cell, an input gate, an output gate, and a forget gate. By using the forget gate, LSTM can store not only short-term but also long-term memory. Therefore, the time series can be predicted more accurately.

We estimate EST by creating a time series model for each poster. If the poster is in a state of pleasure, it has a high likelihood to post a positive tweet next time. Based on the predicted EST ($PEST$), $TPST$ and $TNST$ are weighted. The detail will be described in Sect. 4.3.

3.5   Polarity Classification Based on Weighted Category Scores

Based on weighted category scores, the tweet is classified. The tweet has a weighted score for each category: $TPST$ and $TNST$. If $TPST$ is higher than $TNST$, the tweet is regarded as positive. Otherwise, the tweet is regarded as negative.

4   Experiments and Discussion

4.1   Dataset and Preparation

We used the Sentiment140 dataset collected by Go et al. [5]. This dataset is used for polarity analysis and consists of positive 800,000 tweets and negative 800,000 tweets. We randomly selected 100,000 tweets (positive 50,000 tweets and negative 50,000 tweets) as training data. As described in [5], tweets of each category were collected based on emoticons. They collected not only tweets but also usernames and tweet dates as well.

In this experiment, we arranged users in descending order by the number of tweets and selected users with more tweets. We excluded accounts for advertisements and users who posted only positive or negative tweets.

As a result, three users, "mcraddictal", "SallytheShizzle" and "VioletsCRUK", were selected. "mcraddictal" has 66 positive tweets and 209 negative tweets. "SallytheShizzle" has 97 positive tweets and 182 negative tweets. "VioletsCRUK" has 217 positive tweets and 61 negative tweets.

4.2 Dependency Analysis and Category Scoring by Naive Bayes

To analyze the structure of sentences, we used Syntaxnet. After dependency analysis, we calculated category scores for a tweet by Naive Bayes. As described above, we trained Naive Bayes with 100,000 tweets.

Based on the relation of the words obtained by dependency analysis, we adjusted to the score of the related word. For example, the tweet "I'm very happy" is emphasized by the meaning of "very", and "It's little better" is weakened by the meaning of "little". In addition, the tweet "I'm not happy" is reversed the meaning of "I'm happy". Therefore, referred to our previous study [12], we set weighted magnification as 1.5 times for "very" and 76 synonyms, 0.5 times for "little" and 96 synonyms, and -1 times for "not" and nine synonyms. Based on the result of the dependency analysis, we weighted scores of related words. The total score of the categories for a tweet is calculated and expressed as $TPST$ and $TNST$.

4.3 Estimating Emotional States and Weighting Scores

After calculating the score for each category, a user's emotional state was estimated. We calculated EST for each tweet. We used EST to measure emotional states, and modeled them with LSTM. For each user, we used their first 200 tweets as training data, and the rest as test data. We ran LSTM on Python and set hyper-parameters as follows:

- Hidden layer: 5
- Epoch: 100
- Timewindow: 3

Vateekul et al. [14] investigated the hyper-parameters of LSTM for polarity classification in Thai language. Their result showed that classification accuracy was the best when the hidden layer parameter was set to five. Refer to their study, we also set the hidden layer parameter as five. Using the created model, we estimated $PEST$ for each user.

If a certain period of time has passed since the last tweet, it is considered that the influence on the next tweet would be small. Therefore, we did not weight tweets which passed for a certain period from the previous tweet. To decided the time period, we referred to Fujita's study [4]. They studied the influence of users' emotional tweet in chronological order, and they collected users who tweeted more than 10 times in a day. In this study, we set the time period as 146 min, which is the average interval of one tweet.

We examined the following four experiments to weight scores.

- Experiment 0: Baseline (Dependency analysis and Naive Bayes)
  Emotional state prediction is not used. Polarity classification is carried out using the score obtained by Naive Bayes classification after dependency analysis. In this experiment, we directly use $TPST$ and $TNST$ in Eqs. (1) and (2) as polarity scores (PS).
- Experiment 1: We adjust PS as follows.

$$PS = \begin{cases} (1 + \frac{PEST-0.5}{0.5})TPST & (PEST \geq 0.5) \\ (1 + \frac{0.5-PEST}{0.5})TNST & (PEST < 0.5) \end{cases} \quad (4)$$

If $PEST$ is larger than or equal to 0.5, the weight is set based on $TPST$, and when $PEST$ approaches 1, the weight approaches doubles. Conversely, if it is smaller than 0.5, the weight is set according to $TNST$, and when $PEST$ approaches 0, the weight becomes 2 times.
- Experiment 2: We adjust PS using $TPST$ only as follows.

$$PS = \begin{cases} (2PEST)TPST & (PEST \geq 0.5) \\ (PEST + 0.5)TPST & (PEST < 0.5) \end{cases} \quad (5)$$

If $PEST$ approaches 0.5 to 1, the weight approaches doubles. Conversely, if it approaches 0, the weight becomes half.
- Experiment 3: Firstly we change the range of $PEST$ from -1 to 1, and we adjust the weight of PS using $TPST$ and $TNST$ as follows.

$$PS = \begin{cases} (1 + PEST)TPST & (PEST \geq 0) \\ (1 - PEST)TNST & (PEST < 0) \end{cases} \quad (6)$$

If $PEST$ is larger than or equal to 0, the weight is set according to $TPST$, and when $PEST$ approaches 1, the weight becomes doubles. Conversely, when $PEST$ is smaller than 0, the weight is set according to $TNST$, and when $PEST$ approaches -1, the weight becomes 2 times.

4.4   Results and Discussions

The classification accuracies are shown in Table 1, and $PEST$ is shown in Fig. 2. The accuracy of Experiment 3 was better than the baseline and Uysal's study [13]. Uysal trained classifiers using the Sentiment140 and investigated the appropriate word feature. Our training dataset is also based on Sentiment 140. The classifier is expected to have similar accuracy. From the result, our approach is of higher accuracy than Uysal's study, which implies that it is effective to consider emotional states for polarity analysis.

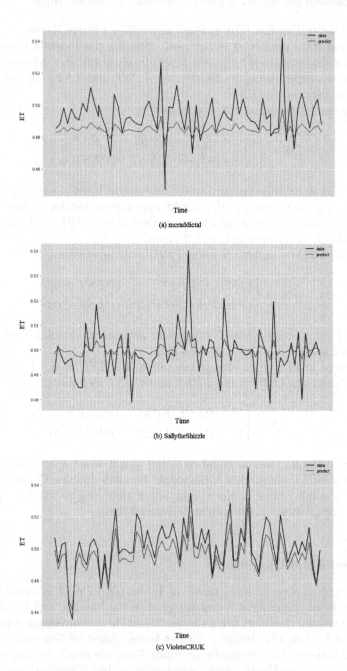

Fig. 2. Predicted emotion states for three users

Table 1. Classification accuracy (%)

	Positive	Negative	Total
Uysal [13]	-	-	71.5
Experiment 0: Baseline	75.9	75.1	75.5
Experiment 1	81.0	56.4	62.8
Experiment 2	75.9	75.2	75.5
Experiment 3	74.1	78.8	**77.6**
Vateekul [14] *	-	-	75.3

* This study classified polarity tweets using LSTM with a different dataset they collected themselves.

In Experiment 1, the accuracy for negative category declined. In Experiment 2, the total accuracy was the same as the baseline. Experiment 3 got the best result, which shows that by adjusting the emotion scores it becomes an optimization problem, and there is a possibility that classification accuracy can be improved.

Through the experiments, we found some improvements could be made. The first is that we should get all the tweets of a poster. In this study, we created the model using tweets explicitly positive and negative only. When $TPST$ and $TNST$ are almost the same, it can be regarded as a neutral tweet. How to detect neutral tweets should be considered. With the same reason, we should use all the tweets to estimate emotional states.

5 Conclusion

In this paper, we proposed an improved approach to take into account emotional states of human users in polarity analysis. Firstly, we performed the dependency analysis and analyzed the relationships between words. Next, a Naive Bayes classifier was trained, and the score for each category was calculated in consideration of the result of dependency analysis. A user's emotional state was estimated from the calculated scores and a time series model was created by LSTM. Finally, the category scores were weighted based on the predicted emotional states and classification was performed. As a result, our method showed better classification accuracy than the baseline and other related study.

For our future work, we will create the time series model using all tweet, not limited to explicitly positive or negative, including neutral tweets. Moreover, we will further investigate the hyper-parameters setting of LSTM and adjust the weights for polarity scores.

References

1. Beasley, A., Mason, W.: Emotional states vs. emotional words in social media. In: Proceedings of ACM Web Science Conference, WebSci 2015, pp. 1–10. ACM, New York, NY, USA (2015)
2. Braunstein, L.M., Gross, J.J., Ochsner, K.N.: Explicit and implicit emotion regulation: a multi-level framework. Soc. Cogn. Affect. Neurosci. **12**(10), 1545–1557 (2017)
3. Elfajr, N.M., Sarno, R.: Sentiment analysis using weighted emoticons and sentiwordnet for Indonesian language. In: Proceedings of 2018 International Seminar on Application for Technology of Information and Communication, pp. 234–238 (2018)
4. Fujita, M., Watanabe, J., Kawamoto, K., Akitomi, T., Ara, K.: A method for analyzing influence of emotions of posts in SNS conversations. In: Proceedings of International Conference on Social Intelligence and Technology, pp. 20–27, May 2013
5. Go, A., Bhayani, R., Huang, L.: Twitter sentiment classification using distant supervision. CS224N Project report, pp. 1–6, Stanford (2009)
6. Huang, A., Ebert, D., Rider, P.: You are what you tweet: a new hybrid model for sentiment analysis. In: Perner, P. (ed.) MLDM 2017. LNCS (LNAI), vol. 10358, pp. 403–416. Springer, Cham (2017). https://doi.org/10.1007/978-3-319-62416-7_29
7. Hulliyah, K., Bakar, N.S.A.A., Ismail, A.R.: Emotion recognition and brain mapping for sentiment analysis: a review. In: Proceedings of 2017 Second International Conference on Informatics and Computing (ICIC2017), pp. 1–5, November 2017
8. Kramer, A.D.: An unobtrusive behavioral model of "gross national happiness". In: Proceedings of SIGCHI Conference on Human Factors in Computing Systems, CHI 2010, pp. 287–290. ACM, New York, NY, USA (2010)
9. Nguyen, L.T., Wu, P., Chan, W., Peng, W., Zhang, Y.: Predicting collective sentiment dynamics from time-series social media. In: Proceedings of First International Workshop on Issues of Sentiment Discovery and Opinion Mining, pp. 1–8. ACM, New York, NY, USA (2012)
10. Saif, H., Fernandez, M., He, Y., Alani, H.: Evaluation datasets for twitter sentiment analysis: a survey and a new dataset, the STS-gold. In: Proceedings of 1st International Workshop on Emotion and Sentiment in Social and Expressive Media: Approaches and Perspectives from AI (ESSEM2013), pp. 9–21 (2013)
11. Su, M., Wu, C., Huang, K., Hong, Q.: LSTM-based text emotion recognition using semantic and emotional word vectors. In: Proceedings of First Asian Conference on Affective Computing and Intelligent Interaction (ACII Asia), pp. 1–6, May 2018
12. Tago, K., Takagi, K., Kasuya, S., Jin, Q.: Analyzing influence of emotional tweets on user relationships using naive bayes and dependency parsing. World Wide Web **22**, 1263–1278 (2018)
13. Uysal, A.K., Murphey, Y.L.: Sentiment classification: feature selection based approaches versus deep learning. In: Proceedings of IEEE International Conference on Computer and Information Technology (CIT2017), pp. 23–30, August 2017
14. Vateekul, P., Koomsubha, T.: A study of sentiment analysis using deep learning techniques on Thai twitter data. In: Proceedings of 13th International Joint Conference on Computer Science and Software Engineering (JCSSE2016), pp. 1–6, July 2016
15. Wagh, R., Punde, P.: Survey on sentiment analysis using twitter dataset. In: Proceedings of 2018 Second International Conference on Electronics, Communication and Aerospace Technology (ICECA2018), pp. 208–211, March 2018

Investigating Cyclic Visit Pattern of Mobility Through Analysis of Geopositioning Data

Ha Yoon Song[✉] and Suchan Hong

Department of Computer Engineering, Hongik University, Seoul, Republic of Korea
hayoon@hongik.ac.kr, suchanhong@naver.com

Abstract. Intuitions guide us that there are cyclic patterns for a person to visit a location, and there is a tendency of multiple cycles in visiting patterns. Nowadays, it is possible for a person to collect personal mobility data due to the help of smartphones and other portable devices. These devices collects raw geolocation (or geopositioning) data and the set of geolocation data can be analyzed in various ways. Based on location clusters distilled from raw geolocation data, we can establish mobility model of a person and investigate cyclic patterns of a person to visit location clusters. Based on the aggregate personal mobility models collected over several years, we calculated and analyzed the cluster revisiting time and visualized it as a graph. Regarding geolocation data for location clusters as set of time sequence, number of visiting cluster is measured in a unit of minutes. The number of visits from whole data is normalized in every 15 min. For various geolocation data set of a volunteer, cyclic patterns of a visit are examined in terms of autocorrelation, autocovariance and intervisiting time.

Keywords: Mobility pattern analysis · Mobility modeling ·
Temporal mobility · Cyclic mobility pattern · Recurrent location visit

1 Introduction

Recently IoT and smart city are emerging with 4IR, commonly known as 4th Industrial Revolution. This also requires a model of human mobility based on individual geolocation information. The effort to create profit by applying the model of human mobility pattern to various industrial environments has been diversified, and basic research on this has become important. Human mobility pattern model become available thanks to smart and IoT devices which can collects large amount of geolocation data. This sort of research will be a help to Location Based Services (LBS).

This work was supported by the National Research Foundation of Korea (NRF) grant funded by the Korea government (MEST) (NRF-2019R1F1A1056123).

S. Misra et al. (Eds.): ICCSA 2019, LNCS 11619, pp. 589–602, 2019.
https://doi.org/10.1007/978-3-030-24289-3_44

We can understand the relation between individual location and cluster based on human mobility information model. People are staying in one place or move to another place in a time sequence. We used human geolocation data to analyze revisiting time to the location. In other words, it would be valuable to figure out cyclic visit pattern to a location cluster latent in human mobility model. Objects other than human also have their own mobility pattern. Therefore, we can also examine object mobility pattern. However our research is based on human mobility data since human is one of the most active mobile object.

In this paper, we use two things to conduct time analysis to mobility pattern: (1) geolocation information collected over a period of time. (2) Individual integrated mobility model by using collected geolocation information. The geolocation information is composed of <date, time, UNIX time, latitude and longitude>, and the information of individual integrated mobility model is composed of <cluster number, latitude of cluster center, longitude of cluster center, and cluster radius>. The time analysis on mobility pattern is based on internal cluster data among all geolocation data. A volunteer provided sets of raw geopositioning data, and named the data set as CDY. The volunteer had collected geolocation data by smartphone with an app named Sports Tracker [1] and GPS receiver manufactured by Garmin [2].

The paper is comprised of the following parts. Section 2 introduces existing studies using geolocation data, and Sect. 3 introduces a method of predicting mobility patterns by time series analysis. In Sect. 4, we describe the experimental results on the mobility pattern prediction method. In Sect. 5, we conclude the paper with a summary.

2   Existing Research

There has been research based on geolocation data in many ways. Creating individual mobility model with geopositioning data is one of the base of our research by use of clustering with Expectation Maximization algorithm [3,4]. The EM (expectation maximization) algorithm is a clustering algorithm first proposed by Hartley in 1958 [5] and systematized by Dempster in 1977 [6], and is an algorithm that creates an optimized model through the iterative refinement process after generating the initial model. The expectation maximization algorithm is an algorithm for finding parameters with maximum likelihood and maximum a posteriori through iterative refinement process. Log-likelihood function is used to evaluate the suitability of the model when finding parameter. In the expectation stage, when $\theta^{(t)}$ is given, we define the expectation value Q of the likelihood when a new θ is used. In the maximization step, a new parameter $\theta^{(t+1)}$ that maximizes Q is calculated. The EM algorithm is used as follows. The initial value of the parameter θ is arbitrary set. It stops when $\theta^{(t)}$ is sufficiently converged to some value. When converged, the probability of moving among the generated clusters is generated in a form of Markov chains. A Study on generating group mobility model based on individual mobility model exists [7].

In order to generate a collective mobility model, the distance between the clusters must be obtained. Here, Haversine formula [8] is necessary to find the distance on earth, which is the distance between two points on a sphere given their longitudes and latitudes. The following shows the details of Haversine formula.

$$latitude = (latitude_2 - latitude_1) \times \pi/180$$
$$longitude = (longitude_2 - longitude_1) \times \pi/180$$
$$latitude_1 = latitude_1 \times \pi/180$$
$$latitude_2 = latitude_2 \times \pi/180$$
$$a = sin(latitude/2)^2 + cos(latitude_1) \times cos(latitude_2) \times sin(longitude/2)^2$$
$$c = 2 \times atan2(\sqrt{a}, \sqrt{(1-a)})$$

then the distance between to geopositioning locations is

d = R × c where R is earth's radius (mean radius = 6,371 km).

Compare the distance and the radius between the centers of the clusters in the two individual mobility models, respectively. If the distance of the cluster center is less than the sum of the radii of the two clusters, a macro and a micro cluster are created. When clustering, the micro cluster collects all location information that is common to both clusters. The macro cluster collects and clusters all location information contained in at least one of two clusters. Based on EM algorithm and Haversine formula, meaningful location clusters were distilled from raw geopositioning data as shown in [4]. The location clusters identified will be the basis for the following chapter.

A method to capture the relation between a human mobility and the social context by data analysis [9] exists but not that much related to our research. There also has been study on extracting human mobility patterns from GPS data. They identified the relation between human mobility data and sociological aspects of human movements.

The other research is regarding a template that decompose seasonal trend for long time series. A method to decompose complex long time series into seasonality, trend, and remainder components. It enables time series irregularity detection and forecasting [10].

Although there have been many studies, to our knowledge, no research has been done on cyclic pattern of object mobility. Our research attempts to find relationship between object mobility over time domain.

3 Temporal Analysis on Mobility Pattern

In this study, we try to analyze the correlation by using temporal data in order to identify cyclic movement patterns through the location data. We try to identify the relationship between time and place based on the characteristics of staying in one place (location cluster) or moving to another place over time. One of the key point is to find out the meaningful sets of duration of cycle in mobility pattern.

3.1 Considerations

In order to determine if there is a correlation between time and place, it is necessary to determine whether there is a certain rule for the time range in the cluster. Therefore, we extracted the clusters with the individual integrated mobility models and confirmed the time of visiting the two most notable clusters. In this aspect, autocorrelation and autocovariance analysis were used to confirm the positional correlation over time. Autocorrelation, $R(t, \tau)$, measures the correlation coefficient with the intervisit time variable (τ) in the same time series. t stands for arbitrary time in the time series. The formula is as follows:

$$R(t, \tau) = E[X(t) \times X(t + \tau)]$$

Autocovariance, $C_X(t, \tau)$, is also a measure of the covariance with the time variable (τ) in the same time series. The formula is as follows.

$$C_X(t, \tau) = Cov[X(t), X(t + \tau)], \text{ or } C_X(t, \tau) = R_X(t, \tau) - \mu_t \mu_{t+\tau}$$

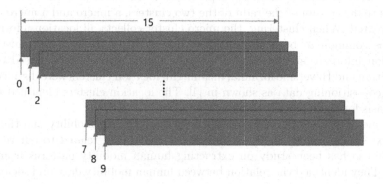

Fig. 1. Concept of time slice

3.2 Timing Analysis Based on Time Slice Window

Use of constant time array is required to obtain autocorrelation and autocovariance. The unit of time slice in our research is in 15 min. In other words, we regarded the data as meaningful in case that people stayed for more than 15 min. Figure 1 shows the concept of time slices.

The window slides over time and the range of time is 15 min. For the first step, our initial interest is the geolocation data for a specific clusters inside a time slice. Over the whole time domain, for every time slices, we calculated autocorrelation and autocovariance by using $E[X(t)]$ and $E[X(t + \tau)]$ as shown in Fig. 2.

We used mobility data from May 2013 to November 2017. Due to large amount of data and computation to calculate correlation and covariance, we used parallel programming technique, as known as GPGPU programming to save computation time. The experiments were done on the PC with Intel i7 CPU with 16 GB RAM and nVidia 980Ti GPU.

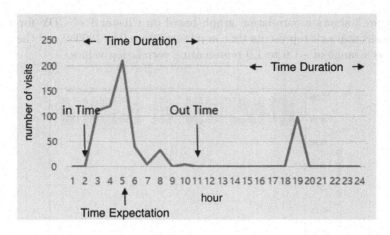

Fig. 2. In time, out time, time expectation with respect to time and number of visit

Table 1. Correlation coefficient

Range of correlation coefficient	Meaning
$-1.0 \leq r \leq -0.7$	very strong negative $(-)$ correlation
$-0.7 < r \leq -0.3$	strong negative $(-)$ correlation
$-0.3 < r \leq -0.1$	weak negative $(-)$ correlation
$-0.1 < r \leq 0.1$	no correlation
$0.1 < r \leq 0.3$	weak positive $(+)$ correlation
$0.3 < r \leq 0.7$	strong positive $(+)$ correlation
$0.7 < r \leq 1.0$	very strong positive $(+)$ correlation

4 Analyzed Results

4.1 Analyzed Results of Cyclic Revisit Time to Location Clusters

Firstly, we analyzed the correlation coefficient values to see whether they are meaningful according to the revisit time. Meaning of the value of correlation coefficient can be represented as shown in the following Table 1.

Each results can be represented in a graphical form and each graphs were drawn for two cases: (1) very strong negative $(-)$ correlation and (2) very strong positive $(+)$ correlation.

Figure 3 through Fig. 16 graphically represent the time which has very strong positive or negative correlation as represented in Table 1. Figures 3, 7, 9, 11, 13 and 15 are related with Cluster 1. Figures 4, 8, 10, 12, 14 and 16 are related with Cluster 2.

The difference between Cluster 1 and Cluster 2 must be compared for further analysis.

Figure 3 shows a correlation graph based on Cluster 1 of CDY for week 1. The horizontal axis represents time in minutes from 0 to 100080 and the vertical axis has a range of −1.0 to 1.0 representing correlation values.

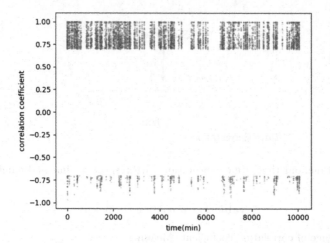

Fig. 3. Correlation graph for Cluster 1 for CDY data of the 1st week

Figure 4 shows a correlation graph based on Cluster 2 of CDY for week 1. Comparing with Fig. 3, correlation pattern is not overlapped and correlation pattern shows sparse frequency than that of Cluster 1. In other words, correlation in cluster 2 is less clear than that of cluster 1. In addition, it is possible to verify that the strong negative correlation coefficient is empty in 10000 to 10080 min of Fig. 4, whereas strong positive correlation coefficient is imprinted. This can be interpreted that Fig. 4 from 10000 to 10080 min have a high correlation.

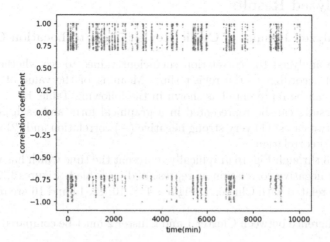

Fig. 4. Correlation graph for Cluster 2 for CDY data of the 1st week

Figure 5 shows a correlation graph based on Cluster 2 of CDY for week 2. All the data were sliced into 10080 min to calculate the correlation coefficient. Here in week 2, very strong positive correlation only shows in 0 to 9000 min. From the result, we can say that probability of revisiting Cluster 2 is high, whereas it is low from 9000 to 10080 min.

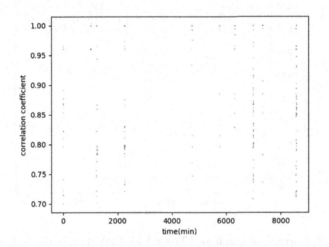

Fig. 5. Correlation graph for Cluster 2 for CDY data of the 2nd week

Figure 6 shows a correlation graph based on Cluster 2 of CDY for week 4. In contrast to Fig. 5, it shows many blanks. Few of very strong positive correlation can be found in 0 to 100 min, 7000 to 7500 min, and around 10000 min. These time domain doesn't have negative correlations which is closed to −1 value. Therefore, it is highly likely to revisit on 0 to minutes, 7000 to 7500 min, and 10000 min on week 4.

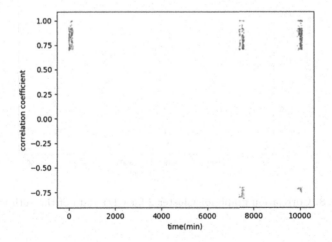

Fig. 6. Correlation graph for Cluster 2 for CDY data of the 4th week

Figures 7 and 8 shows a correlation graph based on Cluster 1 and Cluster 2 of CDY for week 10. By comparison, Cluster 1 shows revisiting time without distinguished intervisit time interval.

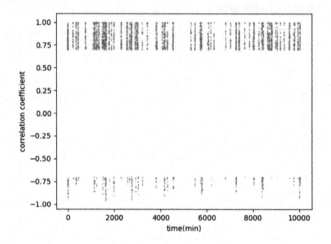

Fig. 7. Correlation graph for Cluster 1 for CDY data of the 10th week

Figure 8, shows similar pattern with Fig. 7. But it shows clear distinct pattern which is divided into 8 parts. Here, it can be said that revisit cycle is around 1 day or 1,440 min.

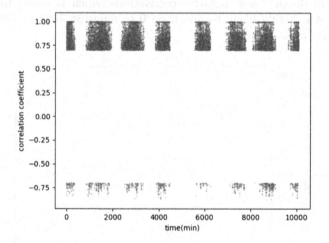

Fig. 8. Correlation graph for Cluster 2 for CDY data of the 10th week

Figures 9 and 10 shows a correlation graph based on Cluster 1 and Cluster 2 of CDY for week 11. Both graphs shows empty space from 7800 and 9300 min. From this result, we can see CDY didn't visit Cluster 1 nor Cluster 2 on 6th day of week 11.

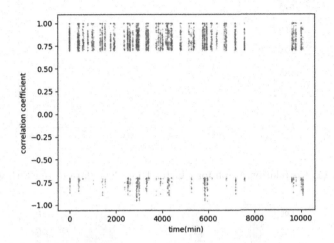

Fig. 9. Correlation graph for Cluster 1 for CDY data of the 11th week

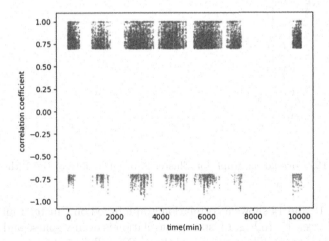

Fig. 10. Correlation graph for Cluster 2 for CDY data of the 11th week

Figures 11 and 12 shows a correlation graph based on Cluster 1 and Cluster 2 of CDY for week 12. Both graphs shows similar pattern where 3500 min to 6000 min is empty. But Cluster 2 shows additional empty space around 2000 min, around 8000 min, and around 9000 min. Here, we can see neither of clusters were visited from 3500 min to 6000 min. And Cluster 2 was not visited around 2000 min, 8000 min and 9000 min additionally.

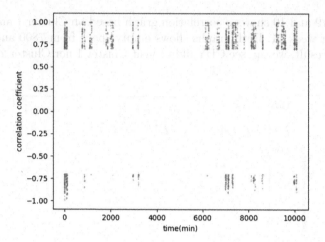

Fig. 11. Correlation graph for Cluster 1 for CDY data of the 12th week

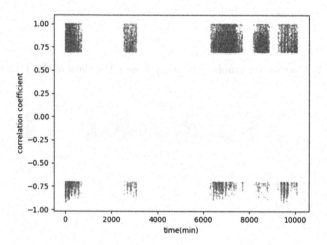

Fig. 12. Correlation graph for Cluster 2 for CDY data of the 12th week

Figures 13 and 14 shows a correlation graph based on Cluster 1 and Cluster 2 of CDY for week 17. In Fig. 13, strong correlation is evenly sparse and it does not have specific pattern. This can be said that CDY will visited Cluster 1 regardless of time in week 17.

Figure 14 differs from Fig. 13. It is divided into six zones in total, with a distinguished strong correlation pattern. Here, CDY is highly likely to visit Cluster 2 in dense zone and not visit in empty zone. There's no empty space between day 2 to day 3 and day 6 to day 7. Here, we can see CDY is mostly likely to stay in Cluster 2. There's some strong positive domain without strong negative correlation. This can be said that it's highly likely to revisit.

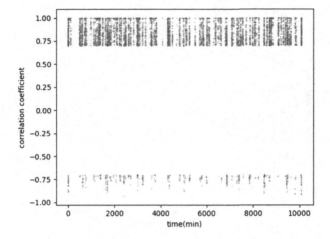

Fig. 13. Correlation graph for Cluster 1 for CDY data of the 17th week

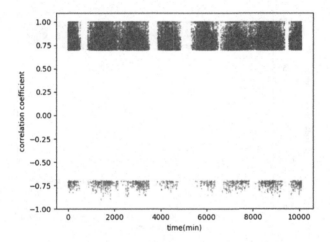

Fig. 14. Correlation graph for Cluster 2 for CDY data of the 17th week

Figures 15 and 16 shows a correlation graph based on Cluster 1 and Cluster 2 of CDY for week 21. Unlike most graphs in other weeks, strong positive correlation can be found in both Figs. 15 and 16. When comparing with week 17, Fig. 15 shows a similar pattern to Fig. 13. But Fig. 16 shows more dense correlation pattern than Fig. 14 without any empty space. As a result, we can see it's highly likely to visit steadily in week 21. We can conclude that CDY is more likely to visit rather than not visit.

In most of the figures, it is notable that the similar amount of time interval for both highly positive correlations and highly negative correlations. It can be concluded that the negative correlation and the positive correlation shows similar pattern. However, in each of the figures, it is highly dense where the correlation

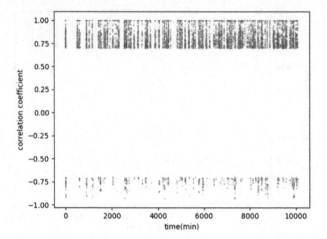

Fig. 15. Correlation graph for Cluster 1 for CDY data of the 21st week

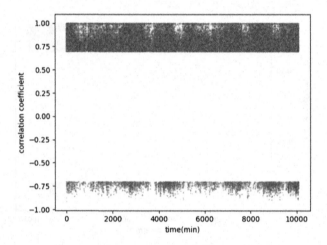

Fig. 16. Correlation graph for Cluster 2 for CDY data of the 21st week

is larger than 0.7 and less than or equal to 1.0, but values close to −1.0 is really sparse, where correlation values are less than −0.7 and greater than −1.0. It can be concluded that positive (+) correlation appears more frequently than negative (−) correlation. Then, it can be judged that the time with positive correlation usually exists strongly and more meaningful than negative correlation. This trend became clear and clear as we proceeded our analysis with wider range of time domain.

Table 2 shows the top 25 results with strong correlation coefficients. Cluster 1 and Cluster 2 are compared with each other and the top 25 are represented in the table. The column cluster 1 and cluster 2 shows the number of visits to the corresponding cluster. Each column has intervisit time τ in the next column. In Cluster 1, the intervisit time τ is in the top 25 from 1 min to 21 min and

Table 2. Top 25 categories with strong correlation coefficients

Rank	Cluster 1	τ (min)	Cluster 2	τ (min)
1	10,332	1	2,196	1
2	3,724	2	961	1,719
3	2,060	3	830	2
4	1,077	4	635	3,301
5	943	9	634	1,328
6	918	11	573	3
7	903	10	477	25
8	879	5	477	15
9	874	8	473	40
10	832	7	466	4
11	824	6	463	47
12	771	12	461	65
13	747	14	460	43
14	736	13	444	63
15	698	15	438	86
16	601	16	434	337
17	578	17	434	45
18	566	20	430	49
19	538	19	428	39
20	530	18	424	58
21	518	10,070	423	117
22	499	21	423	24
23	488	10,078	415	70
24	486	10,077	411	37
25	486	10,069	410	67

includes 10,069 min, 10,070 min, 10,077 min, and 10,078 min. For these 25 cases, the volunteer is more likely to stay after a visit. For Cluster 2, we can see that the intervisit time τ is bigger than that of Cluster 1. For example, Cluster 2 can be interpreted as having many visits after 1,719 min, and having visited again after 3,301 min. As a result, Cluster 2 has clearer revisit times than Cluster 1.

5   Conclusion

In this paper, a temporal analysis of mobility data is presented to determine what form the mobility pattern is in the object mobility model, especially cyclic patterns latent in mobility model. Raw geopositioning data sets were collected by a volunteer. The concept of time slice window is incorporated. The auto-correlation and autocovariance were calculated by time slice over the collected geopositioning data. The figures showing the graph of the correlation coefficient over time were presented as correlation coefficient between 0.7 and 1.0 which is strong positive, and as correlation coefficient between -0.7 and -1.0 which is strong negative. A strong positive correlation coefficient was found and a strong negative correlation coefficient was simultaneously found as shown in the figures, and the intervisit time can be identified representing cyclic mobility patterns. Through the analysis, we found out the frequency of cyclic revisit for each notable location cluster and also identified the intervisit time to location clusters with high correlations. This sort of cyclic pattern analysis must be useful tool to design various Location Based Service (LBS). For the future research, we need to investigate more persons' mobility data and geolocation data collected by other objects such as Internet of Things (IoT) devices with the same analysis method. There's a other location data collecting app named Swarm [11], which is developed by Foursquare group [12]. This could be used in future research too. Even though we guess the personal mobility pattern shows similar cyclic pattern, however, it may differ from person to person. For the mobility of IoT objects, no results were reported while it must be great interest of related researchers.

References

1. Pheasant, D., Larue, M.: Active sports tracker and method. U.S. Patent Application No 11/609,634 (2006)
2. Garmin. Garmin gpsmap 62s (2015). https://buy.garmin.com/en-US/US/on-the-trail/discontinued/gpsmap-62s/prod63801.html
3. Kim, H., Song, H.Y.: Daily life mobility of a student: from position data to human mobility model through expectation maximization clustering. In: Kim, T., et al. (eds.) MulGraB 2011. CCIS, vol. 263, pp. 88–97. Springer, Heidelberg (2011). https://doi.org/10.1007/978-3-642-27186-1_11
4. Song, H.Y.: Probabilistic space-time analysis of human mobility patterns. WSEAS Trans. Comput. **15**, 222–238 (2016)
5. Hartley, H.: Maximum likelihood estimation from incomplete data. Biometrics **14**, 174–194 (1958)
6. Rubin, D.B., Dempster, A.P., Laird, N.M.: Maximum likelihood from incomplete data via the EM algorithm. J. R. Stat. Soc. **39**(01), 1–38 (1977)
7. Song, H.Y., Kim, D.: A method for group mobility model construction. In: Multimedia, Computer Graphics and Broadcasting, Korean Institute of Information Scientists and Engineers (2015)
8. Robusto, C.: The cosine-haversine formula. Am. Math. Mon. **64**(1), 38–40 (1957)
9. Gaito, S., Zignani, M.: Extracting human mobility patterns from GPS-based traces. In: IFIP Wireless Days (2010)
10. Song, X., Wen, Q., Gao, J.: RobustSTL: a robust seasonal-trend decomposition algorithm for long time series. In: IFIP Wireless Days (2018)
11. Sahin, E.: Swarm robotics: from sources of inspiration to domains of application. In: International Workshop on Swarm Robotics (2004)
12. Wiese, J., Lindqvist, J., Cranshaw, J.: I'm the mayor of my house: examining why people use foursquare-a social driven (2012)

Finding the Best Location for Logistics Hub Based on Actual Parcel Delivery Data

Ha Yoon Song[✉] and Insoo Han

Hongik University, Mapo-gu, Seoul, Republic of Korea
hayoon@hongik.ac.kr, haninsoo9989@gmail.com

Abstract. So many national and international packets are traveling around in this time. The parcel delivery service is a major part of nationwide logistics. It is reported that wrong routes for logistic causes economical disadvantage both in time and in cost. It is possible to collect actual delivery data from logistics company or Internet of Things devices. Based on actual route of packet delivery, we collected 100,000 delivery data over Republic of Korea and analyzed for optimal hub candidate locations in terms of minimum distance and minimum time. From the raw delivery data set, actual delivery paths were calculated in terms of big data analytics Using Longest Common Route Subsequence algorithm, the most common paths can be identified. From the economic aspect, regarding minimum distance and time, optimal hub location candidates were voted and identified. With several hub locations, optimal distance and time can be calculated from the location of optimal hub candidates.

Keywords: Parcel service · Optimum logistics hub location ·
Longest Common Route Subsequence algorithm · Big data analytics

1 Introduction

Parcel delivery service is one of major axis in national or international economy. Investigating lots of delivery route shows that improper routes of parcel delivery rises costs extra distance and time for parcel delivery and causes economical disadvantage of nations. The hub and spoke method of parcel delivery is commonly used in most of nations [1,2]. It does mean, the location of hub is one of the critical parameter for economical parcel delivery [3]. In this paper, we tried to determine an optimum location of logistics hub based on actual delivery data. From the parcel delivery company, we collected 100,000 delivery data including source and destination, actual routs of delivery, current location hub and others. The data is collected in Republic of Korea and only public data was utilized. The area size of Republic of Korea is 1,002,000 ha and 5,100,0000 population

This work was supported by the National Research Foundation of Korea (NRF) grant funded by the Korea government (MEST) (NRF-2019R1F1A1056123).

© Springer Nature Switzerland AG 2019
S. Misra et al. (Eds.): ICCSA 2019, LNCS 11619, pp. 603–615, 2019.
https://doi.org/10.1007/978-3-030-24289-3_45

which leads to high density population. The major purpose of this research is to avoid inefficient delivery cost by selecting a good hub location with minimum distance and minimum time for delivery. Very few research dealt with this topic. For example, Yunhe Ma of Beijing Jiaotong University showed an mathematical approach over virtual data set in order to figure out best hub locations [4]. Other researches done at National Taiwan University by Yon-Chun Chou analyzed hub transshipment across flexible time periods in order to decrease workload and sojourn time [5].

This paper is structured as follows. Section 2 discuss about the process outline of this research including algorithm we used. Section 3 visualizes results on actual maps, according to the process shown in Sect. 2. Section 4 shows logistics hub candidates based on the previous analysis results, as well as benefits in terms of time and distance. We will conclude this paper in Sect. 4 with future direction of further research.

2   Process Outline

We collected 100,000 raw data of parcel delivery. Then the actual route of parcel delivery will be collected. Based on the Longest Common Route Subsequence (LCRS) algorithm, we will deduce the most populated locations of parcel delivery. Among the most populated locations, several locations can be identified by voting mechanism. Then the most populated locations be reduced to candidates of optimal logistics hub. From the concepts of Longest Common Sequence (LCS) by Bergroth [6] and Sebastian [7], LCRS algorithm were developed for this research.

2.1   Source Data Set

Table 1 shows sample data of parcel delivery route. Pathnum stand for parcel identifier, category stands for parcel contents category. The column p_order

Table 1. Sample source data

Pathnum	Category	p_order	Name	Time	lat	lng
620703310075	Digital	0	start point	201901171735	35.1002578	129.0264814
620703310075	Digital	1	waypoint1	201901180244	36.2518725	127.6236381
620703310075	Digital	2	waypoint2	201901181056	38.2070148	128.5918489
620703310075	Digital	3	waypoint3	201901181346	38.1673391	128.516669
620703310075	Digital	4	end point	201901181648	38.3801292	128.4674385
...	...	...	...	...	...	...
620703311442	Apparel	0	start point	201901170745	35.1002578	129.0264814
620703311442	Apparel	1	waypoint1	201901180218	36.2518725	127.6236381
620703311442	Apparel	2	waypoint2	201901180823	35.1761938	129.0797244
620703311442	Apparel	3	waypoint3	201901180838	35.1088179	129.0101733
620703311442	Apparel	4	end point	201901181044	35.1088179	129.01017335

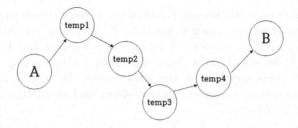

Fig. 1. Example of route with subsequences

stands for specific route point, such that 0 for starting point, 1 for waypoint 1, 2 for waypoint 2, 3 for waypoint 3 and 4 for destination of parcel routes. If p_order contains 4, it does mean the parcel has been delivered. The column name represents actual location name. Time is for time at the location. Latitude is abbreviated as lat and longitude is abbreviated as lng. By preprocessing of 100,000 parcel deliver route data, 20,000 data is found valid for this research.

2.2   Route Data Set

One whole parcel delivery route tends to be divided into several sub routes as shown in Fig. 1. Table 2 shows sample route data. The column pnum shows the

Table 2. Sample route data

Pathnum	pnum	Type	s_address	e_address	Duration	dist	num	Route
620703310576	1	2	start point	waypoint1	1:40	14 km	0	start point
620703310576	1	2	start point	waypoint1	1:40	14 km	1	temp1
620703310576	1	2	start point	waypoint1	1:40	14 km	2	temp2
...	...	...	...	...	...	...	...	...
620703310576	1	2	start point	waypoint1	1:40	14 km	30	temp30
620703310576	2	2	waypoint1	waypoint2	2:38	23 km	0	temp31
620703310576	2	2	waypoint1	waypoint2	2:38	23 km	1	temp32
620703310576	2	2	waypoint1	waypoint2	2:38	23 km	2	temp33
620703310576	2	2	waypoint1	waypoint2	2:38	23 km	3	temp34
...	...	...	...	...	...	...	...	...
620703310576	2	2	waypoint1	waypoint2	2:38	23 km	28	temp59
620703310576	3	2	waypoint2	waypoint3	1:20	12 km	0	temp60
...	...	...	...	...	...	...	...	...
620703310576	3	2	waypoint2	waypoint3	1:20	12 km	14	temp73
620703310576	4	2	waypoint3	end point	0:48	8 km	0	temp74
...	...	...	...	...	...	...	...	...
620703310576	4	2	waypoint3	end point	0:48	8 km	6	temp80
620703310576	5	1	start point	end point	5:10	48 km	0	start point
620703310576	5	1	start point	end point	5:10	48 km	1	temp1
...	...	...	...	...	...	...	...	...
620703310576	5	1	start point	end point	5:10	48 km	23	end

sequence number of each subroute. For example, pnum 1 stands that the parcel is on the subroute from start point to waypoint 1, and pnum 3 stands at the parcel is on the subroute from waypoint 2 to waypoint 3 and so on. The exceptional pnum 5 stands for direct route from start point to end point, which is type 1. Once there exists waypoint in the whole route, the type is 2. The column num stands for subroute number. Routs column includes actual address of the corresponding location.

Algorithm 1. Longest Common Route Subsequence Algorithm

Input: route sequence for pathnum A and pathnum B
Output: A Set of Longest common Route subsequence, A Set of position
PreProcessing(*Path*) {
  1: dp[len(A)][len(B)] // two dimentional array to check if two route sequence are identical
  2: lcrs[len(A)][len(B)] // two dimentional array for common route subsequence
  3: **for** (p=0; p < len(A); p++) **do** // len(A) = length of array A
  4:    **for** (q=0; q < len(B); q++) **do**
  5:       **if** A[p]=B[q] **then**
  6:          dp[p+1][q+1] = dp[p][q]+1
  7:          **if** A[p] != Null **then**
  8:             lcrs[p+1][q+1] = lcrs[p][q]+A[p]
  9:          **end if**
 10:       **else**
 11:          dp[p+1][q+1] = maximum of $dp[p][q+1]$ and $dp[p+1][q]$
 12:          lcrs[p+1][q+1] = lcs[p][q+1] or lcrs[p+1][q]
 13:       **end if**
 14:    **end for**
 15: **end for**
 16: **return** [lcrs]
 17: }

2.3   Longest Common Route Subsequence

We developed LCRS algorithm as shown in Algorithm 1. The result of LCRS algorithm on the route data set is shown in Table 3. The time complexity of algorithm is $O(n^2)$ for the number of data, n. The column type is the same to that of Table 2. The column index stands for the sequence index of common subsequence between pathnum_A and pathnum_B. For example, for two parcels with pathnum_A and pathnum_B, index of 11 stands for 11 common location in the longest common route subsequence between pathnum_A and pathnum_B.

Table 3. Sample LCRS data

pathnum_A	pathnum_B	Type	Index	Route
620703310576	620703310580	1	1	48 Gumdannam-ro, Hanam-si
620703310576	620703310580	1	2	Geomdan Mountain Road
620703310576	620703310580	1	3	Dong Seoul Tolgate
620703310576	620703310580	1	4	Deokgye Temple Street
...	...	...	...	...
620703310576	620703310580	1	11	92 Deokgye-ro, Yangsan-si
620703310576	620703310580	2	1	48 Gumdannam-ro, Hanam-si
620703310576	620703310580	2	2	Geomdan Mountain Road
...	...	...	...	...
620703310576	620703310580	2	5	Central Road

2.4 Voting for Optimal Hub Location

The voting is done by the count of location visit for parcel delivery. Table 4 shows sample voting results. The columns voting_range_start and voting_range_end stands for range of parcel identification number for voting. Table 4 shows that 100,000 parcels in a range of [620703310000, 620703410000] were searched for voting. As we stated already, 20,000 data out of 100,000 were utilized in our whole process. The column location means actual location in a path. The column counts the number of votes, i.e. higher count stands for higher population of parcel in the corresponding location. Algorithm 2 is an algorithm for this voting mechanism. It works on SQL of LCRS database and results in voting count of locations.

Table 4. Sample voting data

voting_range_start	voting_range_start	Location	Count
620703310000	620703410000	Gyeongbu Expressway	86434
620703310000	620703410000	Yeongdong Expressway	57717
620703310000	620703410000	Gunjin 2-gil	53415
...	...	...	...
620703310000	620703410000	Jamsil Station	11

Algorithm 2. Voting

Input: A Set of Longest common Route subsequence
Output: A Set of Voting
PreProcessing(*voting*) {
1: inputDB.execute("SELECT route FROM position")
2: // inputDB is database of input data
3: route = inputDB.fetchall() // route is route data array of input data
4: **for** (i=0; i < len(*route*); i++) **do** // len(*A*) = length of array A
5:     outputDB.execute("SELECT count FROM position WHERE route = 'route[i]'") // outputDB is database of output data
6:     routeCount = outputDB.fetchall()
7:     **if** routeCount == 0 **then**
8:         values = [(route[i], 1)]
9:         outputDB.execute("INSERT INTO position values (?,?)", values)
10:        outputDB.commit()
11:    **else**
12:        outputDB.execute("UPDATE position SET count = 'count' WHERE route = 'route[i]'")
13:        outputDB.fetchall()
14:    **end if**
15: **end for**
16: **return** [Voting]
17: }

---

3   Experimental Results

In this section, as we defined process outline in Sect. 2, we will provide results in a visual manner for each process steps. For the visualization, only part of data is utilized in order to have more clear figures.

3.1   Visualization of Source Data

Figure 2 shows mapping of raw parcel route data, and it is easy to figure out highly populated routes. There is one central location of highest population and there is actually a logistics hub named Okcheon hub. In case that there is another hub, the total costs for logistics could be decreased. Our purpose is to find location candidate for another hub as we will discuss in later subsections.

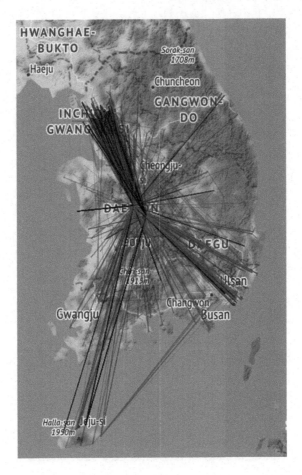

Fig. 2. Map with source data

3.2   Visualization of Route Data

Table 1 shows the density of route population with 10% of source data. The darker area shows the higher population of parcel route. The darkest area shown in the center of Fig. 3 locates Okcheon hub. Another darkest area in upper left corner locates capital city of Republic of Korea, Seoul. Lower right area with higher population locates Busan.

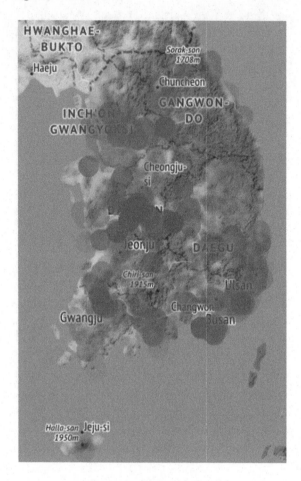

Fig. 3. Map with route data

3.3   Experimental Results About LCRS Data

Figure 4 shows the result of LCRS algorithm with 10% of raw source data. With LCRS algorithm, highly populated areas are clearly identified. With these result, we can identify highly crowded routes.

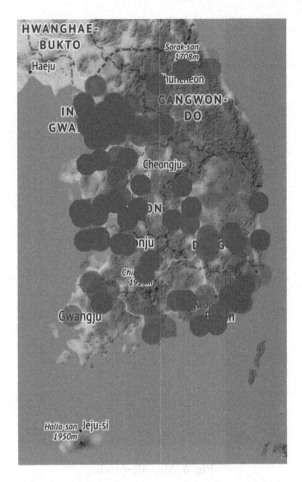

Fig. 4. Map of results from LCRS

3.4   Voting Results About LCRS Data

Figure 5 show the result of voting from the result of LCRS algorithm. By increasing of radius of candidate area, we identified notable locations more clearly. The most crowded route is Gyeongbu expressway from Busan to Okcheon hub. Three most populated locations are Seoul, Busan and Okcheon hub.

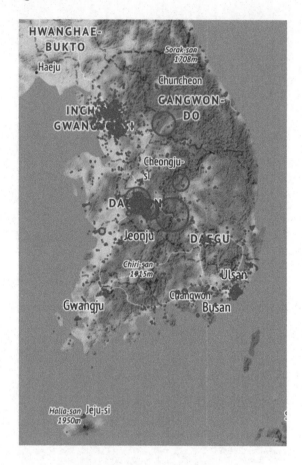

Fig. 5. Map after voting

3.5   Candidate Location for Logistic Hub

However, from the results shown in Fig. 5, there are another candidate area as shown in Fig. 6 where area A stands for 'Okcheon', B stands for 'Geumsan', C stands for 'Boeun', and D stands for 'Moongyeong'.

Fig. 6. Map with candidate locations for logistic hub

4   Conclusions and Future Research

$$actual\_distance = \sum Distance(start, Hub) + Distance(Hub, end) \quad (1)$$

$$candidate\_distance = \sum Distance(start, candidate) + Distance(candidate, end) \quad (2)$$

$$actual\_time = \sum Time(start, Hub) + Time(Hub, end) \quad (3)$$

$$candidate\_time = \sum Time(start, candidate) + Time(candidate, end) \quad (4)$$

After these analysis by proposed process, the best hub candidates can be
determined by calculating economical benefits from the distance and time perspective of each hub candidate [8]. actual_distance (Eq. 1) is expression to calculate actual delivery distance with current Okcheon hub. actual_time (Eq. 2)
is expression to calculate actual delivery time with current Okcheon hub. can-
didate_distance (Eq. 3) is expression to calculate actual delivery distance with
new candidate hubs. candidate_time (Eq. 4) is expression to calculate actual
delivery time with new candidate hubs. Based on the equations, Algorithm 3
shows the process of benefit calculation for candidate hubs. Candidate hub is
one of Boeun, Moongyeong, and Geumsan. Hub stands for current existing hub,
Okcheon. Table 5 shows calculated values for economic benefits with every hubs.
Distances is presented in kilometers and time is presented in minutes. As a result,
once we place hub at Geumsan we can have reduced total distance of 50,000 km
and reduced time of 20,600 min total 20,000 parcels delivered.

Table 5. Benefits on transportation distance with hub candidates

Hub candidate	Actual distance	Candidate distance	Distance benefit	Actual time	Candidate time	Time benefit
Okcheon	137.78	-	-	110.19	-	-
Boeun	-	141.76	−3.98	-	113.44	−3.25
Moongyeong	-	146.01	−8.23	-	121.40	−11.21
Geumsan	-	135.28	2.5	-	109.16	1.03

Algorithm 3. Bebefit Calculation

Input: A Set of origin source data
Output: A Set of distance and time data about candidate hub
PreProcessing(*conclusions*) {
1: **for** (i=0; i < len(*InputDataSet*); i++) **do** // len(A) = length of array A
2:     **if** name == 'Okcheon' **then**
3:         name = 'candidate hub address'
4:         inputDB.execute("select   Distinct(pathnum)   from   position   where
    name='Okcheon'") // inputDB = input database
5:         SelectedPathnum = inputDB.fetchall()
6:         USE route crawling program Where pathnum = Selected Pathnum That
    Used 2nd process
7:     **end if**
8: **end for**
9: **return** [Conclusions]
10: }

It is reported that the biggest parcel courier handles 1,000,000,000 parcel
delivery for one year. Considering this huge number of delivery, the national

economy can have big benefit with the construction of new hub. Of course, another considerations must be done from the aspect of new construction.

In addition, we can have more detailed result with our method once we can obtain the whole data owned by logistics companies. Even though the parcel delivery system is applied in Republic of Korea, the similar methods can be applied to other countries. Another point of future research is application of parallel computing techniques such as GPGPU, since we spend much of time to finish every process step with 100,000 raw data. It is desirable to reduce computation time in order to repeat our process for new data set or for data sets of other nations.

References

1. Deltas, G., Desmet, K., Facchini, G.: Hub-and-spoke free trade areas: theory and evidence from Israel. Can. J. Econ. **45**, 942–977 (2012)
2. Andriamananjara, S., Das, G.G.: Hub-and-spokes free-trade-agreements in the presence of technology spillovers: an application to the western hemisphere. USITC Office of Economics Working Paper No. 2004-09-A, 13 September 2004
3. Wonnacott, R.J., Kowalczyk, C.: Hubs and spokes, and free trade in the Americas. National Bureau of Economic Research 1050 Massachusetts Avenue Cambridge, MA 02138, October 1992
4. Pang, J., Ma, Y., Wang, X.: Research on hub location and routing distribution for hub-and-spoke logistics network. In: 6th International Conference on Machinery, Materials, Environment, Biotechnology and Computer, January 2016
5. Chen, H.-M., Chou, Y.-C., Chen, Y.-H.: Pickup and delivery routing with hub transshipment across flexible time periods for improving dual objectives on workload and waiting time. Transp. Res. Part E Logist. Transp. Rev. **61**, 98–114 (2014)
6. Hakonen, H., Bergroth, L., Raita, T.: A survey of longest common subsequence algorithm. In: Seventh International Symposium on String Processing and Information Retrieval, SPIRE 2000. IEEE, 06 August 2002
7. Deorowicz, S.: Quadratic-time algorithm for a string constrained LCS problem. Inf. Process. Lett. **112**(11), 423–426 (2012)
8. Kim, N.-S., Lee, E.-J.: Development of public transport competitiveness indicator using web maps comparison of travel time and distance between public transportation and passenger cars. Korean Soc. Transp. **73**, 536–566 (2015)

Ensuring the Consistency Between User Requirements and Graphical User Interfaces: A Behavior-Based Automated Approach

Thiago Rocha Silva[1]([⊠]) [iD], Marco Winckler[2] [iD],
and Hallvard Trætteberg[1]

[1] Department of Computer Science, Norwegian University of Science
and Technology (NTNU), Trondheim, Norway
{thiago.silva,hal}@ntnu.no
[2] SPARKS-I3S, Université Nice Sophia Antipolis (Polytech),
Sophia Antipolis, France
winckler@unice.fr

Abstract. Ensuring the consistency between Graphical User Interfaces (GUIs) and user requirements is a critical aspect of the design process since it is through the GUIs that users perceive the system and experience the available features in order to achieve their goals. This paper presents an approach based on Behavior-Driven Development (BDD) which employs an ontology in order to provide automated assessment for web GUIs. The approach has been evaluated by exploiting user requirements described by a group of experts in the flight tickets e-commerce domain. Such requirements gave rise to a set of User Stories that have been used to automatically assess the GUIs of an existing web system for booking business trips. The results have shown our approach was able to identify different types of inconsistencies in the set of GUIs analyzed, allowing to build an effective correspondence between user requirements and their representation on the GUI.

Keywords: Behavior-Driven Development (BDD) · User Stories ·
Graphical User Interfaces · User Requirements Assessment

1 Introduction

In most of existing computing systems, Graphical User Interfaces (GUIs) are the part of the system that mediates the interaction between the user and the system's core functions. A GUI can be decomposed in two parts: (*i*) the presentation, that describes how graphical elements are organized to visually inform the functions/services available; and (*ii*) the interactive behavior, that processes user's actions transforming them into requests to core functions, and ultimately providing feedback about the current state of the system. In the users' point of view, if some feature/core function is not available through the GUI, this feature does not exist at all. Being the main bridge between the system and the end user, GUIs are a crucial artifact to be assessed against user requirements. As Hellmann [1] pointed out, the simplest way to perform GUI testing is with manual testing, wherein a human tester interacts with an application to verify that its responses are correct. A human

© Springer Nature Switzerland AG 2019
S. Misra et al. (Eds.): ICCSA 2019, LNCS 11619, pp. 616–632, 2019.
https://doi.org/10.1007/978-3-030-24289-3_46

tester can easily interact with an application and recognize when an error occurs, but manual testing is very slow and error-prone. If testing should be done frequently, then manually testing a GUI quickly becomes unfeasible.

Automated tools exist to simplify and automate this process. Most GUI testing tools work on the capture/replay paradigm [2–5]. In this paradigm, testing tools monitor the set of interactions between a human tester and the system and record these steps so that they can be replayed later as automated tests. However, capture/replay tools (CRTs) do not tend to record tests in a human-readable manner, meaning that it is much more difficult to modify an existing test than to record a new one [6]. Other tools are designed to make direct calls to the system using the native support for automation of each user interface environment. When testing user interfaces presented by means of a web browser, for example, how these direct calls are made, and the features they support depends on the target browser. Such approaches tend to be much more flexible to implement automated testing for GUIs, and tests specified by them tend to be easier to maintain, but they carry the same problem of low human-readability.

The low human-readability of tests is part of a wide problem related to the communication gap between domain experts and developers, which is a long-time issue in software engineering and one of the main reasons for project failure. Misunderstandings about the user requirements and their design on user interfaces are a frequent source of modeling issues and final products which not meet the expected system behavior. Motivated by such a gap, some approaches and tools have emerged to raise the abstraction level of requirements and test specifications. Behavior-Driven Development (BDD) [7] is one of these approaches which has stood out in the software engineering community as an effective means to provide automated acceptance testing by specifying natural language user requirements and their tests in a single textual artifact. BDD benefits from a requirements specification based on User Stories [8] which are easily understandable for both technical and non-technical stakeholders.

A common drawback of these approaches is that the set of behaviors specified for requirements and tests are not directly executable, i.e., a developer will be required to implement the code for such behaviors in order to run them on GUIs. This motivated us to investigate the use of a predefined set of interactive behaviors on GUIs which could be implemented once and then reused to allow automated tests without the intervention of a developer. This paper presents an approach based on BDD and User Stories to support the specification and the automated assessment of user requirements on web GUIs of interactive systems. The set of user-system interactive behaviors is provided by means of an ontology [9, 10]. The following sections present the foundations of this work, the proposed approach with its technical implementation, and the results we got when using the approach to assess the GUIs of a web system to book business trips.

2 Foundations

2.1 Behavior-Driven Development

Behavior-Driven Development (BDD) is a specialization of Test-Driven Development (TDD) [11], and is intended to make the practice of writing automated testing more accessible and intuitive to newcomers and experts alike. It shifts the vocabulary from being test-based to behavior-based. It positions itself as a development paradigm, emphasizing communication and automation as equal goals. In BDD, the behaviors represent both the requirements specification and the test cases.

BDD drives development teams to a requirements specification based on User Stories in an understandable natural language format. This format allows specifying executable requirements by means of a Domain-Specific Language (DSL) provided by Gherkin[1]. Gherkin is a DSL that lets users and developers describe software behavior without detailing how that behavior is implemented. Gherkin serves two purposes: documentation and automated tests. By using this language, requirements specifications can be used to implement automated tests, conducting to living documentation and making easier for clients and other stakeholders to set their final acceptance tests.

User Stories were firstly proposed by Cohn [8] and provide in the same artifact a narrative, briefly describing a feature in the business point of view, and a set of scenarios to give details about business rules and to be used as acceptance criteria, giving concrete examples about what should be tested to consider a given feature as done. Cohn and North [8, 12] propose a useful template for that:

```
Title (one line describing the story)
Narrative: As a [role], I want [feature], So that [benefit]
Scenario 1: Title
Given [context], When [event], Then [outcome]
```

This structure is largely used in Behavior-Driven Development (BDD) and has been named by North [12] as "BDD story". According to this template, a User Story is described with a *title*, a *narrative* and a set of *scenarios* representing acceptance criteria. The title provides a general description of the story, referring to a feature this story represents. The *narrative* describes the referred feature in terms of the role that will benefit from the feature, the feature itself, and the benefit it will bring to the business. The acceptance criteria are defined through a set of *scenarios*, each one with a *title* and three main clauses: "*Given*" to provide the context in which the scenario will be actioned, "*When*" to describe events that will trigger the scenario and "*Then*" to present outcomes that might be checked to verify the proper behavior of the system. Each one of these clauses can include an "*And*" statement to provide multiple contexts, events and/or outcomes. Each statement in this representation is called a *step*.

2.2 Ontological Support for GUI Automated Testing

Our approach is based on previous works which explore an ontology to describe common behaviors with a standard vocabulary for writing User Stories [9, 10]. The main benefit of this strategy is that User Stories using this common vocabulary can support specification and execution of automated test scenarios on GUIs. The ontology covers concepts related to presentation and behavior of interactive components used in web and mobile applications. It also models concepts describing the structure of User Stories, tasks, scenarios, and GUIs.

---

[1] https://cucumber.io/docs/gherkin/.

The dialog part of a GUI, as illustrated by Fig. 1, is described using the ontology by means of concepts borrowed from abstract state machines. The User Story *scenario* meant to be run in a given GUI is represented as a *transition*. *States* are used to represent the original and resulting GUIs after a transition occur (states A and B in Fig. 1). Scenarios in the transition state always have at least one or more *conditions* (represented in scenarios by the *"Given"* clause), one or more *events* (represented in scenarios by the *"When"* clause), and one or more *actions* (represented in scenarios by the *"Then"* clause). The presentation part of a GUI is described in the ontology through *interaction elements* which represent an abstraction of the different widgets commonly used in web and mobile user interfaces.

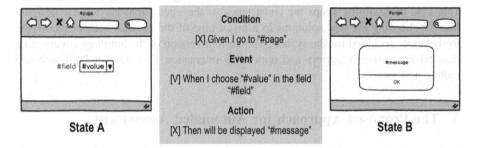

Fig. 1. Representation of a User Story scenario using the state machine concepts.

The common behaviors in the ontology describe textually how users could interact with the system whilst manipulating graphical elements of the user interface. An example of behavior specification is illustrated by Fig. 2. The specification of behaviors encompasses when the interaction can be performed (using *"Given"*, *"When"* and/or *"Then"* clauses), and which graphical elements (i.e. *CheckBoxes, TextFields, Buttons*, etc.) can be affected. Altogether, behaviors and interaction elements are used to implement the test of expected system behavior. In the example of Fig. 2, the behavior *"I choose '<value>' referring to '<field>'"* has two parameters: *"<value>"* and *"<field>"*. The first parameter is associated to data, whilst the second parameter refers to the interaction elements supported by this behavior: *Radio Button, CheckBox, Calendar* and *Link*.

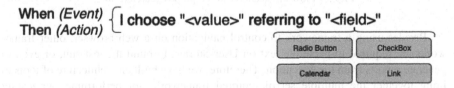

Fig. 2. Structure of a behavior as specified in the ontology.

The ontological model describes only behaviors that report steps performing actions directly on the user interface through interaction elements. This is a powerful resource because it allows keeping the ontological model domain-free, which means it is not subject to particular business characteristics in the User Stories, promoting the reuse of steps in multiple scenarios. Thus, steps can be easily reused to build different behaviors for different scenarios in different business domains.

When representing the various interaction elements that can attend a given behavior, the ontology also allows extending multiple design solutions for the UI while still keeping the consistency of the interaction. For example, even if a *Dropdown List* has been chosen to attend, for example, a behavior *setInTheField* in the first version of a prototype, an *Auto Complete* field could be chosen to attend this behavior on a next version, once both UI elements share the same ontological property for this behavior. This kind of flexibility keeps the consistency of the interaction, leaving the designer free for choosing the best solutions in a given time of the project, without modifying the behavior specified for the system. The current version of the ontology covers more than 60 interactive behaviors and almost 40 interaction elements for both web and mobile user interfaces.

3   The Proposed Approach for Automated Assessment

GUIs are fully functional versions of a user interface implemented in a given programming language for a given platform. The assessment of a GUI is made by dynamically running tests on its presentation layer with the aid of external testing frameworks. Such frameworks are able to simulate a user interacting with a GUI by running the set of scenarios described in the User Stories. Our premise for assessing such GUIs is thus the availability of an external testing framework able to run tests on a given environment. Despite the support ontology supports a specification for both web and mobile environments, so far, our approach only implements tests with Selenium Web-Driver for running directly on a web browser. For assessing GUIs implemented for other environments, our approach would require integration with other testing frameworks.

Fig. 3. Flow of execution in the proposed architecture.

Besides using a framework to control navigation on a web browser, other frameworks are required to parse the text on User Stories, to build the test suit, or even to generate reports from the execution. Therefore, we have built an architecture of tools to bring together the multiple set of required frameworks for performing our testing approach on GUIs. The integrated tools architecture we propose for testing GUIs is essentially based on Demoisele Behave, JBehave, Selenium WebDriver, JUnit and Maven. We use Selenium WebDriver to run navigational behaviors, and JBehave and

Demoiselle Behave to parse the scenario script. Test results provided by the JUnit API indicate visually which tests are passed and which ones failed and why. Execution reports of User Stories, scenarios and steps can also be obtained by using the JBehave API.

Such an architecture allows users to automate testing on web user interfaces by following our behavior-based approach. The architecture has three main modules: *Core*, *Parser*, and *Runner*. The *Core* is responsible for the main interfaces of the framework by orchestrating the information among the other modules. The *Parser* is responsible for the abstraction of the component that will transform the story into Java code to send to the *Runner* through standard or project-specific sentences. The *Runner* is responsible for the abstraction of the component that will perform navigation on the user interface, such as Selenium WebDriver or even JUnit directly. The framework identifies stories written in TXT to be sent to the *Parser* module and later to the *Runner*, which is responsible for interacting with a web browser using the Selenium WebDriver. To run tests in such an architecture, story files are charged as inputs for the parser, that translates the natural language behaviors into Java methods, and then selects a runner to perform the navigational commands on a given targeted web browser. This flow of execution is illustrated in Fig. 3.

3.1 Implementation

We have structured packages and classes in different layers to implement our architectural approach. Pre-defined behaviors charged from the ontology are implemented in a class called *CommonSteps*. New extended behaviors, that are not initially covered by the ontology, can be implemented in the *MySteps* class. These new behaviors will then be parsed to Java methods as illustrated in Fig. 4. So, steps in User Stories are mapped to either *CommonSteps* or *MySteps* behaviors in order to be run.

Fig. 4. Parsing a step from a TXT file to a Java method.

The Presentation Layer includes the *MyPages* class which implements the link between abstract UI components defined in the ontology and the concrete UI components instantiated on the interface under testing. This link is crucial to allow the Selenium WebDriver and other external testing frameworks to automatically run scenarios in the right components on the UI. To link these components, the *MyPages* class identifies a screen map ("*@ScreenMap*") which address the web page location, and several element maps ("*@ElementMap*") which link the various abstract UI elements in the User Stories with their concrete UI siblings on the user interface. This link is made by manually associating the name of each abstract UI element with their concrete locators (such as IDs, XPaths, or any other web element identifier). This is illustrated by Fig. 5.

Finally, the *MyTest* class is a JUnit class in charge of triggering the tests, pointing which scenarios should be executed at a time. These three basic classes (*MySteps*, *MyPages* and *MyTest*) can also be modeled with different names into packages "*steps*", "*pages*" and "*tests*", in order to separate concerns and implements different classes for different pages or features.

```
@ScreenMap(name = "Flight Search", location = "https://www.aa.com/homePage.do?locale=en_US")
public class MyPages {

    @ElementMap(name = "Round trip", locatorType = ElementLocatorType.XPath, locator = "//*[@id='journeyTypeRT']")
    private Radio RoundTrip;

    @ElementMap(name = "One-way", locatorType = ElementLocatorType.XPath, locator = "//*[@id='journeyTypeOW']")
    private Radio OneWay;

    @ElementMap(name = "Departure Date", locatorType = ElementLocatorType.XPath, locator = "id('depDate')")
    private TextField DepartureDate;
```

Fig. 5. *MyPage* Java class.

The structure of the Java project is presented in Fig. 6. Notice that the three aforementioned classes are packed in the package "*java*" and the User Stories in the package "*resources*". On the right side of the figure, the structure of the *MyTest* class is presented highlighting the addition of the new extended behaviors in the *MySteps* class, and all the stories in the "*/stories*" folder being triggered by a JUnit test method.

```
                                            MyTest.java ⊠
                                          1  package fr.irit.ics.test;
                                          2
▼ src/test/java                           3⊕ import org.junit.Test;□
  ▼ fr.irit.ics.test                      6
    ▶ MyPages.java                         7  public class MyTest {
    ▶ MySteps.java                         8
    ▶ MyTest.java                          9      private BehaveContext eng = BehaveContext.getInstance();
                                          10
▼ src/test/resources                      11⊕     public MyTest() {
  ▼ stories                               12          eng.addSteps(new MySteps());
      example.story                       13      }
                                          14
                                          15⊕     @Test
                                          16      public void testAllStories() throws Throwable {
                                          17          eng.run("/stories");
                                          18      }
                                          19
                                          20  }
                                          21
```

Fig. 6. Package tree (on the left) and *MyTest* class (on the right).

A resource that facilitates the written of User Stories is the immediate feedback concerning the existence of behaviors in the ontology to address the step that is being written. Figure 7 illustrates this resource. Notice that all the steps in the scenario have been recognized, i.e. there are equivalent behaviors in the ontology to address them, except the step *"When I set the date '12/20/2017' in the field 'Return'"* that has been underlined to alert that such a step is not recognized by the ontology (actually the right step in this case is generic: *"... I set '<value>' in the field '<element>'"*, like has been used in the following line). When clicking on the alert icon, a message to say that "no step is matching" will be shown. Additional feedback is also given recognizing in the step the mention to values and interactive elements when they are surrounded by quotation marks.

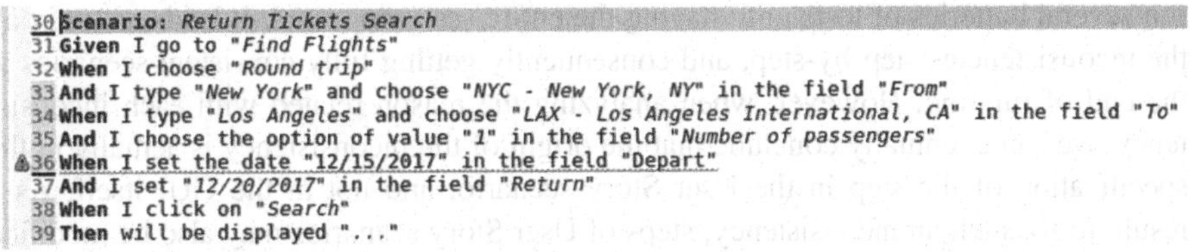

```
30 Scenario: Return Tickets Search
31 Given I go to "Find Flights"
32 When I choose "Round trip"
33 And I type "New York" and choose "NYC - New York, NY" in the field "From"
34 When I type "Los Angeles" and choose "LAX - Los Angeles International, CA" in the field "To"
35 And I choose the option of value "1" in the field "Number of passengers"
⚠36 When I set the date "12/15/2017" in the field "Depart"
37 And I set "12/20/2017" in the field "Return"
38 When I click on "Search"
39 Then will be displayed "..."
```

Fig. 7. Writing a User Story and getting instant feedback of unknown steps.

The testing results are presented through the classical JUnit green/red bar within the Eclipse IDE. By the end of the tests, a JBehave detailed report is automatically generated in the project folder. Additionally, for each error found, screenshots are taken and stored to allow a better analyze of the results afterwards. Examples of these features are presented in Fig. 8.

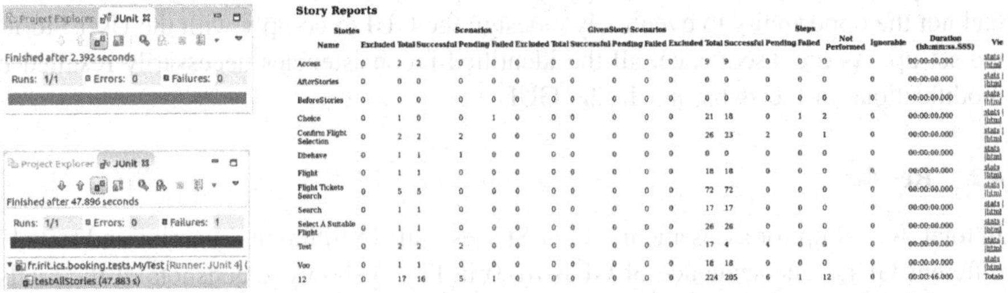

Fig. 8. JUnit green/red bar at the left, and JBehave detailed report at the right. (Color figure online)

4 Case Study

To evaluate our approach, we have conducted a case study with an existing web system for booking business trips. In a previous study [13], domain experts were invited to produce some User Stories to describe a feature they considered important to that system. In the present study, the User Stories produced by the participants were refined to get a representative set of user requirements to be assessed on the GUIs of the existing system. Thus, the main goal was investigating which types of inconsistencies our approach would be able to identify when assessing the GUIs.

4.1 Methodology

With the aim of simulating a software testing lifecycle, we first set up an initial version of User Stories and their respective acceptance criteria for assessment. After that, we manually located the identifiers of each interaction element on the considered GUIs to assign them to the "*MyPage*" class. Finally, we automatically ran the scenarios on the GUIs. The implemented strategy for running tests parses each step of the scenario at a time, so if an error is found out, the test stops until the error is fixed. That requires to run several batteries of tests until having the entire scenario tested. It leads us to fix all the inconsistencies step-by-step, and consequently getting fully consistent scenarios at the end of running. However, when analyzing the reason related with each inconsistency, we can eventually conclude that the origin of the inconsistency is actually in the specification of the step in the User Story scenario, and not in the GUI itself. As a result, to fix such an inconsistency, steps of User Story scenarios may also be modified along the battery of tests to comply with a consistent specification of the user requirements. An immediate consequence of this fact is that the steps used to test a given version of a GUI can be different than that ones used to test another GUI previously. It means that regression tests are crucial to ensure that a given modification in the set of User Stories scenarios did not break some previous test on other GUIs and made some of them (that so far was consistent with the requirements) inconsistent again.

For the purpose of this study, we assumed that the released version of the existing booking system (and of course its GUIs) represents the unequivocal statement of the user requirements, once, for the purpose of this study, we cannot modify it. As such, we had not the opportunity to eventually redesign the GUI to comply with the User Stories we set up. As a consequence, all the identified inconsistencies necessarily resulted in modifications in the steps, not in the GUI.

4.2   Results

In total, we set up for assessment 3 User Stories with 15 different scenarios and tested 7 different GUIs. The sequence of GUIs (*a–f*) in Fig. 9 shows screenshots of the GUIs. The GUI *(a)* represents the interface for searching flights based on a round trip (and *(b)* based on a one-way/multidestination trip). The GUI *(c)* presents the next GUI in sequence, showing the list of flights matching a selection criterion. When the user selects one of the available flights, then the system turns out to the state shown in *(d)*. The user, at this state, can confirm his/her selection or change the fare profile of his/her flight. The GUI *(e)* finally shows the interface to confirm a flight selection. The user can accept the general terms and conditions and confirm the booking or withdraw the trip. In the latter case, the system asks the user to confirm the choice *(f)*. If the user does not confirm the withdrawing or opt to confirm the trip at the first stage, then the system shows a message confirming the booking.

To discuss the results that we got when testing the system, we present in Table 1 results of several batteries of tests in each GUI to perform the set of scenarios considered for the User Stories. We present sequentially each step of the target scenario and the errors that have been found throughout the batteries. Notice that successfully-run, repeated steps in sequential scenarios were omitted and some entire scenarios have been reused to reach a given state for the system before the test begins.

The first battery of tests has identified an error at the step 10 in the first scenario. The actual message displayed by the system was different, so the step was updated. Following this, when running the second scenario, the second battery of tests identified a problem with the identification/location of the field *"Departure Time Frame"*. The same occurred with the field *"Arrival Time Frame"* (third battery). In the fourth battery, the test identified the absence of the field *"Number of Passengers"*, which was

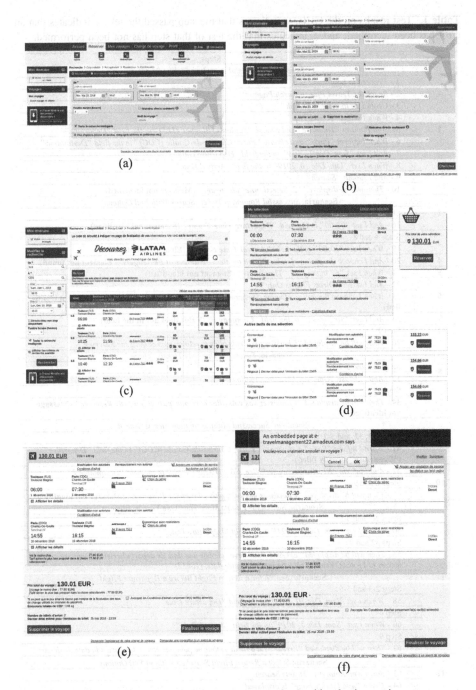

Fig. 9. GUIs of the existing web system for booking business trips.

Table 1. Test results on the GUIs. ✓ indicates that the step passed the test, ✗ indicates that an error has been identified, and ▲ indicates that the test of that step has not been performed.

Battery	Steps
	Scenario: *Successful Roundtrip Tickets Search*
	✓ 1 - *Proceed to Login*
	✓ 2 - *Reach the Travel Planet Search Page*
	✓ 3 - *Given I go to "Flight Search"*
	✓ 4 - *When I select "Round Trip"*
1	✓ 5 - *And I inform "Toulouse" and choose "Toulouse, Blagnac (TLS)" in the field "Departure"*
	✓ 6 - *When I inform "Paris" and choose "Paris, Charles-de-Gaulle (CDG)" in the field "Destination"*
	✓ 7 - *And I set "Sam, Déc 1, 2019" in the field "Departure Date"*
	✓ 8 - *When I set "Lun, Déc 10, 2019" in the field "Arrival Date"*
	✓ 9 - *And I submit "Search"*
	✗ 10 - *Then will be displayed "**2. Sélectionner un voyage**"* **(Message not identified)**
	Scenario: *Successful Roundtrip Tickets Search With Full Options*
2	✓ Steps 2-3 and 5-7
	✗ 16 - *And I set "08:00" in the field "**Departure Time Frame**"* **(Element not identified)**
3	✓ Steps 4 and 8
	✗ 19 - *When I set "10:00" in the field "**Arrival Time Frame**"* **(Element not identified)**
4	✗ 20 - *And I choose the option of value "2" in the field "**Number of Passengers**"* **(Element not found)**
5	✗ 21 - *When I set "6" in the field "**Timeframe**"* **(Element not identified)**
6	✓ 22 - *And I select "Direct Flights Only"*
	✗ 23 - *When I choose the option of value "Economique" in the field "**Flight Class**"* **(Element not identified)**
7	✗ 24 - *And I set "Air France" in the field "**Company 1**"* **(Value does not fit the field)**
	✓ Step 9
	✓ 26 - *Then will be displayed "Choisissez vos vols aller et retour, puis cliquez sur Réserver."*
	Scenario: *Successful One-way Tickets Search*
8	✓ Steps 2-3 and 5-7
	✓ 32 - *And I choose "One-way / Multidestination"*
	✓ Step 9
	✗ 34 - *Then will be displayed "**Choisissez vos vols aller et retour, puis cliquez sur Réserver.**"* **(Message not identified)**
	Scenario: *Successful Multidestination Tickets Search*
9	✓ Steps 2-3, 32, and 5-7
	✗ 41 - *When I inform "Paris" and choose "Paris, Charles-de-Gaulle (CDG)" in the field "**Departure**"* **("Departure" already filled)**
	✓ 42 - *And I inform "Nice" and choose "Nice, Côte D'Azur (NCE)" in the field "Destination 2"*
10	✓ Steps 8 and 9
	✗ 45 - *Then will be displayed "**Choisissez vos vols, puis cliquez sur Réserver.**"* **(Message not identified)**
	Scenario: *Search for Flights More Than One Year in Advance*
	✓ Steps 2-3 and 5-6
	✓ 50 - *When I set "Dim, Déc 1, 2021" in the field "Departure Date"*
	✓ Steps 32 and 9
	✓ 53 - *Then will be displayed "Erreur : Vous devez choisir une date de départ ultérieure comprise entre 4 heures et 11 mois. Veuillez sélectionner une autre date. (10032)"*
11	**Scenario:** *Search for a Return Flight Before a Departure Flight*
	✓ Steps 2-3 and 5-6
	✓ 58 - *When I set "Lun, Déc 10, 2019" in the field "Departure Date"*
	✓ Step 4
	✓ 60 - *When I set "Sam, Déc 1, 2019" in the field "Arrival Date"*
	✓ Step 9
	✓ 62 - *Then will be displayed "Erreur : La date de retour ne peut pas être antérieure à la date de départ."*
	Scenario: *Select a Return Flight Searched Without Full Options*
12	✓ 63 - *Successful Roundtrip Tickets Search*
	✓ 64 - *Given "Availability Page" is displayed*
	✓ 65 - *When I click on "No Bag" referring to "Air France 7519"*
	✗ 66 - *And I click on "**No Bag**" referring to "Air France 7522"* **("No Bag" already filled)**
	✓ 67 - *When I click on "Book"*
	✓ 68 - *Then will be displayed "J'accepte les Conditions d'achat concernant le(s) tarif(s) aérien(s)."*
	Scenario: *Select a Return Flight Searched With Full Options*
	✓ 69 - *Successful Roundtrip Tickets Search With Full Options*

(continued)

Table 1. (*continued*)

	✓	Step 64
	✓	71 - *When I click on "Air France 7519" referring to "No Bag"*
	✓	72 - *And I click on "Air France 7522" referring to "No Bag"*
13	✓	Steps 67-68
		Scenario: *Select a One-way Flight*
	✓	75 - *Successful One-way Tickets Search*
	✓	Steps 64, 71 and 67-68
		Scenario: *Select a Multidestination Flight*
	✓	80 - *Successful Multidestination Tickets Search*
	✓	Steps 64 and 71
	✕	83 - *And I click on "Air France 7700" referring to "No Bag"* (**Element "Air France 7700" not found**)
14	✓	Steps 67-68
		Scenario: *Confirm a Flight Selection*
	✓	86 - *Select a Return Flight Searched Without Full Options*
	✓	87 - *Given "Confirmation Page" is displayed*
	✓	88 - *When I choose "I accept the General Terms and Conditions."*
	⚠	89 - *And I click on "Finalize the trip"* (**Pending**)
	⚠	90 - *Then will be displayed "Votre voyage a été confirmé!"* (**Pending**)
		Scenario: *Confirm a Flight Selection (Full Version)*
	✓	91 - *Select a Return Flight Searched With Full Options*
	⚠	Steps 87-90 (**Pending**)
		Scenario: *Confirm a Flight Selection for a One-Way Trip*
15	✓	96 - *Select a One-way Flight*
	⚠	Steps 87-90 (**Pending**)
		Scenario: *Confirm a Flight Selection for a Multidestination Trip*
	✓	101 - *Select a Multidestination Flight*
	⚠	Steps 87-90 (**Pending**)
		Scenario: *Decline a Flight Selection*
	✓	Step 96 and 87
	✓	108 - *When I click on "Decline the trip"*
	✓	109 - *Then will be displayed "Voulez-vous vraiment annuler ce voyage ?" in the dialog box*
	✓	110 - *When I confirm the dialog box*
	✓	111 - *Then will be displayed "Votre voyage a été annulé."*

not implemented on the interface. In fifth and sixth batteries, the fields *"Timeframe"* and *"Flight Class"* were not located as well, due to the same reason of the fields *"Departure Time Frame"* and *"Arrival Time Frame"*. We noticed that these four fields are *Selects* (*Combo Boxes*), so, for some unknown reason, the implementation of such fields on the GUI does not allow to identify them either using IDs or XPaths. As during this study, we had no access to the source code of the application to implement some correction and run the test again, we decided to cut the respective steps off the scenario.

In the seventh battery, the test identified an error with the length of the field *"Company 1"*. The *Text Field* implemented on the GUI supports only two characters, so the value "Air France" does not fit. In fact, the user must inform a two-character internal code for the company he/she wants to select. In this case, the appropriate code for "Air France" is "AF", so the value in the step was updated to this value. In the eight battery of tests, all the steps for the second scenario succeeded running, and the third scenario started to run. An error was identified just in the last step due to conflicting messages.

In the ninth battery running the fourth scenario, the step 41 failed once the field *"Departure"* had already been field before with *"Toulouse, Blagnac (TLS)"* as the first departure of a multidestination trip. The field had to be renamed to correctly identify the second departure field. It was named as *"Departure 2"*. The same solution was applied to the second instances of *"Destination"* (that was renamed to *"Destination 2"*), and *"Departure Date"* (that was renamed to *"Departure Date 2"*). In the tenth battery of tests, an error was identified just at the last step (45) once more due to conflicting messages. Finally, the eleventh battery got all the scenarios passed, which validated a User Story named *"Flight Ticket Search"*.

In the twelfth battery of tests, an error was found at the step 66 for the seventh scenario. The field *"No Bag"* has already been filled by the previous step (65), so the test fails. Besides that, the flight Air France 7522 was not available for booking anymore, so we changed for the flight Air France 7518. At the end, the solution was to give different names for each field referencing each mentioned flight. So, both steps were rewritten to *"When I click on '<flight>' referring to 'No Bag'"* in order to use unique identifiers for the flights.

The thirteenth battery of tests run successfully the eighth and ninth scenarios but stopped with an error at the step 83 of the tenth scenario. For multidestination trips, the GUI contains an additional step before reaching the second flight leg. The user must select the first flight leg, put the flight in a basket, and only then select the flight for the second flight leg. For the fourteenth battery of tests, we updated the respective scenario to add this additional step. That got all the scenarios passed, which validated a User Story named *"Select a Suitable Flight"*. In the fifteenth and last battery of tests, we got all the remaining scenarios for a User Story named *"Confirm Flight Selection"* passed. Nonetheless, we intentionally did not conclude the four first scenarios once they would effectively register a fake business trip in the system, so they were set as pending.

4.3   Discussion and Limitations

By summarizing the results presented above, below we can categorize the types of inconsistencies found by our testing approach when assessing the GUIs as follows:

- Message not identified
- Element or value not found
- Inexistent elements
- Values that do not fit the field
- Fields already filled in
- Element not identified

As presented above, we identified 6 different types in the tested scenarios. *"Elements not identified"* was the most frequent type and refers to elements that do not carry a unique and single identifier (or carry a dynamic generated one) and/or cannot be reached by using their XPaths. When observing the unsuccessful tries to find the fields *"Departure Time Frame"* and *"Arrival Time Frame"*, for example, we remarked that it is a recurrent problem when automating testing on GUIs. Some web frameworks for developing the presentation layer dynamically generates different identifiers each time the GUI is charged, which makes very hard the work of previously identifying them to implement the test. Besides that, some developers skip informing unique identifiers for the fields. XPath identifiers help in most cases, but there still are some situations where the identification of locators gets very compromised.

Constant changing, or conflicting messages is another frequent issue (type of inconsistency *"message not identified"*). Messages sometimes change in the GUI and the requirements specification is not updated accordingly. As a consequence, the message specified in the step to be verified in the user interface is not found on the screen. Not identifying elements or values due to dynamic data behavior is also an issue. The type of inconsistency *"element or value not found"* refers to fields or values that are expected to be shown on the user interface (and are able to be identified by the locators there) but, due the dynamic data behavior in the system, are not shown up. An example from the case study is a flight, which was mentioned to be verified as an example of data value in the step and was not identified in the list of resultant flights because it was not available for booking anymore. There is also the case of elements that are really inexistent on the user interface (type of inconsistency *"inexistent elements"*). These elements are mentioned in the step as part of the requirements specification, but simply have not been implemented in the GUI.

Fields that were already filled in when a given step tries to reach them are also a source of inconsistencies (type of inconsistency *"fields already filled in"*). As happened in the case study when testing the fields *"Departure"* and *"Destination"* for a multidestination trip, due to the second flight leg, the elements were referenced with the same name more than once. When the test tried to fill in the same field a second time for the second flight leg, the inconsistency has shown up. In this case, both the step and the mapping of interaction elements on the user interface must be updated to reference unequivocally different elements for each desired interaction.

The last type of inconsistency identified refers to values mentioned in the step that do not fit the field they were designed to fill in (type of inconsistency *"values that do not fit the field"*). During the case study, the field *"Company 1"* was expected to receive the value "Air France" as described in the step, but the concrete field *"Company 1"* on the GUI had been modeled to support only two characters. This type of inconsistency can also be extended to other incompatibilities between the type of data expected and what the field actually supports. Examples include strings to be filled in number-only fields, unformatted numbers to be filled in date-time fields, and so on.

By analyzing the variety of inconsistency problems that have been identified in this case study, we can remark that some types of inconsistencies have shown to be more critical than others. While simple inconsistencies like messages and elements not found (or even inexistent) are easy to solve, some other inconsistencies can reveal crucial problems of modeling or important incompatibilities between the requirements specification and its design in GUIs. Fields already filled-in, for example, denotes inconsistencies that expose important design errors.

It is also worth mentioning that our approach implements a strategy of co-execution to assess user requirements and GUIs. Unlike static approaches, which benefit from an instantaneous consistency checking to analyze several hundreds of source files at the same time; co-execution approaches benefit from allowing running models simultaneously with visual feedback at real-time about the correspondence of entities that are being assessed in each model. Co-execution approaches usually have the drawback of demanding a high investment to prepare and adapt the artifacts for testing. In our approach however, such an investment is restricted to the mapping of widgets on the respective GUIs under testing. As the great benefit of co-execution on GUIs is providing visual feedback during the execution simulating a real user interacting with interaction elements at real-time, this process can end up being very slow with the growing number of user interfaces and scenarios to be tested. As far as the simulation of real user actions is not a concern, such a drawback can be reduced by using GUI-less browser implementations such as HtmlUnit, which benefits from high-level manipulation of web pages without the need of actually running the browser and co-executing the simulated user actions. Like static approaches, this strategy is suitable for environments demanding high-availability and continuous testing.

As a threat to validity, we report that both the conduction of the study and the interpretation and analysis of the results have been initially made by the authors. So, to mitigate a bias in the interpretation of such results, they were cross-checked by independent reviewers.

5 Conclusion

The approach we present in this paper has the main advantage of ensuring a reliable automated acceptance testing of user requirements. Due to its flexible architecture, the approach also succeeds to provide automated testing for GUIs developed under whatever technology for designing the presentation layer of web pages. For other environments, it would be enough to use external testing frameworks adapted to running tests on such environments. The gain in terms of reuse, maintenance, and coverage that can be obtained with the approach is another crucial advantage to highlight. Except for the initial manual assignment of interaction element identifiers on the considered GUIs to the "*MyPage*" class, the approach runs in a fully automated process. When compared with manual assessment, our automated approach benefits from high-availability of tests with a high human-readability. The automation also helps to cover a larger set of scenarios that could hardly and costly be covered by manual inspections.

This approach has also been extended and adapted to assess early user interface design artifacts [14–18]. As an integrated approach, User Stories can also be assigned to automatically assess task models and GUI prototypes in different levels of abstraction, ensuring a consistent verification, validation, and testing (VV&T) approach for interactive systems with immediate feedback about the consistency of artifacts and user requirements since the early stages of development.

Next steps on this research include evaluating the impact of maintaining and successively evolving GUIs throughout a real software development process where issues related to scalability should be addressed. Concerning the tools, they are not yet freely available for download and general use since the interface for testing is still running on console mode. When evolving it in the future, a technological transfer to the industry could be envisioned. Concerning the features, in addition to the current resource of providing immediate feedback for the recognized steps, it is also envisioned the development of an Eclipse plugin to suggest and autocomplete steps of the User Stories scenarios based on the interactive behaviors of the ontology.

References

1. Hellmann, T.D.: Automated GUI Testing for Agile Development Environments. University of Calgary (2015)
2. Chen, W., Tsai, T., Chao, H.: Integration of specification-based and CR-based approaches for GUI testing. In: 19th International Conference on Advanced Information Networking and Applications (2005). https://doi.org/10.1109/AINA.2005.223
3. Bowen, J., Reeves, S.: UI-driven test-first development of interactive systems. In: Engineering Interactive Computing Systems, pp. 165–174 (2011). https://doi.org/10.1145/1996461.1996515
4. Holmes, A., Kellogg, M.: Automating functional tests using selenium. In: AGILE 2006 (2006). https://doi.org/10.1109/AGILE.2006.19
5. Meszaros, G.: Agile regression testing using record & playback. In: Object-Oriented Programming, Systems, Languages, and Applications (2003). https://doi.org/10.1145/949344.949442
6. Andersson, J., Geoff, B.: The video store revisited yet again: adventures in GUI acceptance testing. In: Extreme Programming and Agile Processes in Software Engineering (2004). https://doi.org/10.1007/978-3-540-24853-8_1
7. Chelimsky, D., Astels, D., Helmkamp, B., North, D., Dennis, Z., Hellesoy, A.: The RSpec Book: Behaviour Driven Development with RSpec, Cucumber, and Friends. Pragmatic Bookshelf (2010)
8. Cohn, M.: User Stories Applied for Agile Software Development. Addison-Wesley (2004)
9. Silva, T.R., Hak, J.-L., Winckler, M.: A behavior-based ontology for supporting automated assessment of interactive systems. In: Proceedings of the 11th IEEE International Conference on Semantic Computing (ICSC 2017), pp. 250–257 (2017). https://doi.org/10.1109/ICSC.2017.73
10. Silva, T.R., Hak, J.-L., Winckler, M.: A formal ontology for describing interactive behaviors and supporting automated testing on user interfaces. Int. J. Semant. Comput. 11(04), 513–539 (2017). https://doi.org/10.1142/S1793351X17400219
11. Beck, K.: Test Driven Development: By Example, 1st edn. Addison-Wesley Professional (2002)
12. North, D.: What's in a Story? (2019). https://dannorth.net/whats-in-a-story/. Accessed 01 Jan 2019
13. Silva, T.R., Winckler, M., Bach, C.: Evaluating the usage of predefined interactive behaviors for writing user stories: an empirical study with potential product owners. Cogn. Technol. Work 1–21 (2019, in press). https://doi.org/10.1007/s10111-019-00566-3
14. Silva, T.R., Winckler, M.A.A.: Towards automated requirements checking throughout development processes of interactive systems. In: 2nd Workshop on Continuous Requirements Engineering (CRE), REFSQ 2016, pp. 1–2 (2016)
15. Silva, T.R.: Definition of a behavior-driven model for requirements specification and testing of interactive systems. In: Proceedings of the 24th International Requirements Engineering Conference (RE 2016), pp. 444–449 (2016). https://doi.org/10.1109/RE.2016.12
16. Silva, T.R., Hak, J.-L., Winckler, M.: Testing prototypes and final user interfaces through an ontological perspective for behavior-driven development. In: Bogdan, C., Gulliksen, J., Sauer, S., Forbrig, P., Winckler, M., Johnson, C., Palanque, P., Bernhaupt, R., Kis, F. (eds.) HCSE/HESSD -2016. LNCS, vol. 9856, pp. 86–107. Springer, Cham (2016). https://doi.org/10.1007/978-3-319-44902-9_7

17. Silva, T.R., Hak, J.-L., Winckler, M.: An approach for multi-artifact testing through an ontological perspective for behavior-driven development. Complex Syst. Inform. Model. Q. **7**, 81–107 (2016). https://doi.org/10.7250/csimq.2016-7.05
18. Silva, T.R., Winckler, M.: A scenario-based approach for checking consistency in user interface design artifacts. In: Proceedings of the 16th Brazilian Symposium on Human Factors in Computing Systems (IHC 2017), vol. 1, pp. 21–30 (2017). https://doi.org/10.1145/3160504.3160506

Applying a Multilayer Perceptron for Traffic Flow Prediction to Empower a Smart Ecosystem

Yan Mendes Ferreira[1]([✉]), Lucas Rodrigues Frank[1], Eduardo Pagani Julio[1],
Francisco Henrique C. Ferreira[1], Bruno José Dembogurski[2],
and Edelberto Franco Silva[1]

[1] Federal University of Juiz de Fora, Juiz de Fora, Brazil
{yanmendes,lucasrodrigues,eduardo.pagani,francisco.henrique,
edelberto}@ice.ufjf.br
[2] Federal Rural University of Rio de Janeiro, Rio de Janeiro, Brazil
brunodembogurski@ufrrj.br

Abstract. A direct impact of population density is more cities suffering from constant traffic jams. Thinking this way, Intelligent Transportation Systems, a key area in smart cities, uses computational intelligence techniques and analyses to aid in traffic dimensioning solutions. In this context, accurate traffic prediction models are vital to creating a more autonomous and intelligent environment. With an increase in projects for intelligent cities, research in the area of computational intelligence becomes a necessity, since its models can address complex real-world problems, which are usually difficult for conventional methods. In this work, an application is introduced applying machine learning to empower a smart ecosystem. To validate it, an extensive evaluation was performed, comparing it with the state-of-the-art and, also, verifying the impact of parameter variation and activation functions on the model of traffic flow prediction. All evaluations were done using real data traffic of two very distinct scenarios. Firstly, a free traffic flow scenario was evaluated in a benchmark dataset. Then, both models were evaluated in a complex traffic scenario where traffic flow is not continuous nor large. In both scenarios, the presented application, called SmartTraffic, outperforms the current state-of-the-art, with a performance gain of over 100% when compared in the first scenario and an improvement of approximately 31%, on average, in the second one.

Keywords: Smart cities · Machine learning · Traffic flow prediction · Intelligent Transportation Systems · Smart Campus

1 Introduction

New concepts and solutions where smart objects and smart applications play an important role have emerged in the last few years, such as smart cities [2].

© Springer Nature Switzerland AG 2019
S. Misra et al. (Eds.): ICCSA 2019, LNCS 11619, pp. 633–648, 2019.
https://doi.org/10.1007/978-3-030-24289-3_47

The concept of intelligent cities addresses the use of intelligent technologies to solve the challenges of urban practices such as socio-environmental, economic and cultural activities. In this paper, we focus on traffic management, a segment of Intelligent Transportation Systems (ITS) [6,8,12] that tackles traffic dimensioning and orientation.

ITS aim to better the use of urban space and time, enhancing also the people quality of life by helping people to move around more easily, safely and economically, in a more environmentally friendly manner [5].

As part of these initiatives, accurate traffic prediction models are vital for creating an autonomous and intelligent environment [8]. Although these models are mostly used for whole cities, the concept can be also applied to other smaller but complex environments, like an university campus [2,16].

The SmartCampus[1] project is an effort to create a smart environment in an university campus. To make this possible, many initiatives are being proposed to promote the integration between existing campus' services and the development of new ones. A better comprehension of vehicle traffic in the campus, combined with validating an accurate prediction model can provide information for future applications and supporting decision making.

The university campus interconnects two key neighborhoods of our city and allows free citizen and vehicle traffic through its entrances. Thus, traffic volume is not limited to its students, professors and staff, but also by those who use the campus as a place to practice leisure or exercising activities and those who just pass by. The heterogeneous characteristics of the drivers and their behavior profiles (academic, leisure or passerby) make the prediction task harder since the traffic volume vary throughout the day. This variance is intrinsically linked to the drivers' profile and their schedules - e.g. beginning of academic activities and morning commuters going to work. All data is captured by a security solution recently acquired by the University that is presented in Sect. 3.

The main contribution of this work is a study on predictive techniques in the context of traffic volume estimation, culminating in an application - Smart Traffic -.

The secondary contributions derived from SmartTraffic are threefold: (i) a comparison of the performance of two distinct approaches of traffic volume estimation, adopting the best-performing one; (ii) evaluation of the performance of two activation functions in the opted model and (iii) a review of these models' parameters and their effect in the prediction accuracy. All these are done utilizing two distinct datasets, as discussed in Sect. 4. The evaluations are done using real data traffic in two very distinct scenarios: (i) a free traffic flow scenario and (ii) a complex scenario without large nor continuous traffic flow.

The rest of this paper is organized as follows. Initially, the related work in Sect. 2 is discussed. Section 3 presents this work architectural proposal and describes its workflow. Moreover, in Sect. 4, the experimental results are presented. Finally, Sect. 5 summarizes the paper and outlines future research directions.

---

[1] https://www.campusinteligente.ufjf.br/.

2   Related Work

In this section, ITS related papers will be discussed, focusing on traffic prediction. For this reason, each one will be discussed separately and then a comparison will be made between this works proposal and the ones in the literature.

The work [8], mentioned from now on by Huang *et al.*, poses as one of the state-of-the-art solutions for traffic flow prediction. The authors propose a Deep Learning Architecture which is achieved by training a Deep Belief Network (DBN) - that can be seen as a stack of Restricted Boltzmann Machines (RBMs) -. The RBM is an unsupervised pattern learning Artificial Neural Network (ANN) that learns through a greedy layerwise training. To fine tune the model's parameters, a supervised regression layer is added on top of the DBN. Using the premise that traffic is a correlated network, the idea of multi-task regression was exploited in the supervised learning process.

The authors implement different traffic flow forecast approaches and compare to their own architecture, outperforming all the others. Despite utilizing a sigmoid regression layer, the authors point the possibility of replacing it by other regression algorithms such as Support Vector Regression (SVR).

In [13], the authors also applied a deep learning strategy and reinforced the use of historical data to predict traffic flow. Its model is based on Stacked Autoencoders (SAE): A deep neural network that aims to reproduce the input layer into the output layer by adjusting the synapses weights. They train the network in a greedy fashion. The unsupervised learning algorithm parameters are then fine-tuned with a sigmoid regression layer.

The model presented in [7] propose the use of the Gated Recurrent Units (GRU). That is a modification of the Long Short Term Memory (LSTM) neural network, whose main characteristic is the storage of information. Thus, allowing the consideration of previous entries when processing new data, enabling it to work with time series.

While the LSTM has been used as a predictive model for traffic flow in previous works such as [15,18], GRU has not been used for this purpose until then. These two models are evaluated, comparing the results with an AutoRegressive Integrated Moving Average (ARIMA) model, concluding that both models outperformed the ARIMA model, and that in 84% of the tests the model GRU outperformed the LSTM.

It is valid to mention that the authors do not assess the scalability of the proposed model and all tests are conducted utilizing a very small amount of data (4 weeks). Since the work proposed in this paper aims to empower a smart ecosystem, scalability is key, therefore this solution was not implemented and evaluated.

The previously mentioned papers evaluate their architectures with free-flowing highways, which is a less challenging task. Differently, [4] propose an architecture composed by a spin-off implementation of a SVR, suited for online applications called On-line SVR (Ol-SVR) [14]. The authors propose an architecture that works both in typical and atypical scenarios (e.g. vehicular crashes, work zone, holidays, etc). They compare their approach with other solutions from the literature, showing that their proposal present a solid option for both scenarios, even though it was outperformed in some cases.

All mentioned papers utilize the dataset PeMS - introduced in the Sect. 4.1 - to evaluate their proposal. The first three utilize data collected on highways, both recent and historical - *i.e.* traffic volume of past weeks on the same weekday -, while the latter utilizes both typical and atypical traffic scenarios for their evaluation, but only recent data is inputted in the prediction process. The approaches found in the literature are summarized on Table 1 and compared to the one presented in this paper.

Table 1. Related work comparison.

Work	Architecture	Historical	Atypical traffic
[8]	DBN + SVR	X	
[13]	SAE + SR	X	
[7]	GRU	X	
[14]	Ol-SVR		X
SmartTraffic	MLP	X	X

3 Proposal

As anticipated in Sect. 1, the SmartCampus project is an effort to promote a more intelligent and autonomous university campus. To achieve that, a series of smaller initiatives are being proposed and implemented as services and applications that will be available in an integrated API.

SmartTraffic is one of these initiatives' pilot, whose main objective is to provide live traffic volume estimation, serving as a support for future applications - *e.g.* estimating parking spots availability - and supporting the administration in the decision-making process, such as estimating traffic volume in a public event on the campus.

The data source that made this initiative possible comes from the security software, Sentry[2]. It is responsible for registering all vehicles license plates that pass through its cameras. It is worth mentioning that, among other transformations, the plates are hashed to preserve anonymity. It's important to reinforce that the hardware and software used could be replaced by a non-professional camera and open-source software - *e.g. OpenCV Library*.

Figure 1 synthesizes the proposal. The SmartCampus project provides encapsulated services as endpoints of an API and the workflow adopted in the implementation of SmartTraffic application is presented. Foremost, it exposes the utilized predictor and then discuss the steps in this pipeline in the following subsections.

---

[2] https://www.sentry.com.br/.

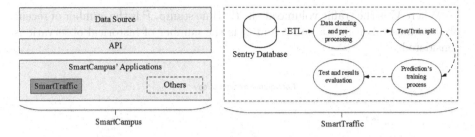

Fig. 1. SmartCampus project global view and SmartTraffic's pipeline.

3.1 Model Specification

Time series models are well-known problem solvers for traffic flow prediction. From simpler and traditional models, as the ARIMA [19], to more complex and non-linear [9], the time series approach is well-taken in the literature. Opposed to that, another noteworthy line of research utilize data-driven algorithms such as ANNs [11] or Local Weighted Learning [17] to solve traffic flow prediction problems.

This work proposal, SmartTraffic, is composed of a triple-layered Multilayer Perceptron (MLP) ANN. The usage of an MLP is justified based on the success of forecasting cyclic scenarios as seen in the work of [3].

The MLP is an ANN where all neurons in a layer are connected to all other neurons in adjacent layers. It contains an input layer, a number of hidden layers - three in this particular architecture - and an output layer. Since the result is a one dimension answer, the traffic flow forecast, the output layer contains only one neuron. The model is described in Eq. 1.

$$f(t+1) = \sum_{i=2}^{4} W_i \cdot g(W_{i-1}^T \cdot x_{i-1} + b_{i-1}) + b_i \qquad (1)$$

Where: W_i and W_{i-1} is the set of weights of the ith and $i-1^{th}$ layer, respectively. b_i and b_{i-1} are the bias added to the $i+1^{th}$ and i^{th} layer, respectively. Furthermore, $g(x)$ is the activation function and, finally, x_{i-1} is the set of neurons of the $i-1^{th}$ layer.

The input layer fed to the network, defined in Eq. 2, are past observations, *i.e.* the traffic volume. Moreover, since a cyclic pattern was observed - as seen in Fig. 2 -, the model does not use only recent observations but also historic observations, *i.e.* the traffic volume of the same weekday and time of day in previous weeks. The use of historical data shows an improvement in results as seen in the work of [1, 8, 13].

$$x_1 = \{\#V_t,\ \#V_{t-1},\ ...,\ \#V_{t-P}\} \cup$$
$$\{\#V_{t+1-(1\ week)},\ \#V_{t+1-(2\ weeks)},\ ...,\ \#V_{t+1-(Q\ weeks)}\} \qquad (2)$$

Where V_t is the traffic volume at the tth time stamp, P is the number of recent observations taken into account and Q is the number of historical observations considered.

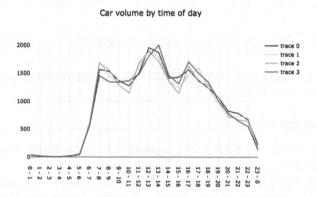

Fig. 2. Traffic volume of every wednesday in the month of september of 2017 in our university, where x-axis is the hours of a day and y-axis the car volume for four different traces.

The network learns through backpropagation [20]. In this paper, two distinct neuron activation functions are evaluated: logistic function (Logi), defined in Eq. 3, and REctified Linear Unit (ReLU), defined in Eq. 4. Those were chosen due to their popularity in the literature and their very different behaviour. The solver for the weight optimization process of choice was the stochastic gradient descent [10].

$$g(x) = \frac{1}{1 + e^{-x}} \qquad (3) \qquad\qquad g(x) = max(0, x) \qquad (4)$$

In order to guarantee reproducibility and to compare this works proposal with [8], the *scikit-learn*[3] implementations of the MLP regressor, RBM and SVR was chosen.

3.2 Data Cleaning and Pre-processing

During peaks in traffic, the software would register multiple entries for a single vehicle since it would move slow enough for the system to trigger another snapshot. All observations of the same vehicle within a 1-minute range were removed and only the first was maintained.

Some entries would not have a license plate linked to it. Since the provided dataset only had raw data and no study of the vehicle detection software was conducted, we could deal with this limitation in two different ways. It could be

---

[3] http://scikit-learn.org/.

a fault in the image processing algorithm but it was indeed a vehicle and should be kept as a valid information or it was a capture of something other than a vehicle - e.g. bike or pedestrian - and should be removed. The latter was the chosen option.

The time of day is crucial in the evaluation process. It was observed that between 20:00 and 07:00 - as seen in Fig. 2 - the volume of cars was much lower than the rest of the day. For this reason, the dataset was split in two and two predictors were trained, one for each time period. Since traffic is practically non-existent between 20:00 and 07:00 and both predictors' accuracy was very high ($\simeq$98%), only the evaluation of the dataset between 07:00 and 20:00 is shown in this work.

Another partition in the data is relative to weekdays and weekends. The traffic on weekends is mainly from people utilizing the campus as a leisure space and a very different traffic behavior was observed. The same strategy was applied here - splitting the datasets -. Due to space restrictions, we show the results of weekday's predictions only.

After splitting these sets, the traffic volume was aggregated in a time window and normalized. The normalization is applied to both datasets whereas the others processes are applied only to the university dataset.

3.3 Test/Train Split

For both scenarios a train-test split of 2/3 and 1/3, respectively, was conducted. It is noteworthy that in Huang et al. [8] original paper, the authors used 10 months of the dataset to train their model and only 2 months to test it. Even though the test set represents 17% of the dataset size, the experiments presented here utilize 33% to minimize overfitting effects and, therefore, there is a marginal difference between the results obtained in this work and [8].

3.4 Test and Evaluation Results

Along with P and Q introduced in Sect. 3.1, the number of neurons N in the hidden layer compose the parameters of the proposed architecture. The same parameters are used by Huang et al. [8]. However, N represents the number of components in the DBN's stack.

Even though it is possible to fine tune these parameters utilizing optimization approaches like a genetic algorithm or grid search, due to the large search spaces, random search offered a better solution since its more computationally efficient.

After performing initial tests to evaluate the model performance with different parameterizations, the following ranges were chosen: P ranging from 10 to 15 with a gap of 1, Q ranging from 0 to 5 and N ranging from 80 to 120 with 10 as a gap.

Even though there is no correlation between the number of neurons in the hidden layers and the number of components in the RBM, after the initial tests, the same range was positively evaluated for both parameters. Moreover, Huang et al. [8] achieved their best results utilizing a similar number of components.

Since the synapses weights' initial values are directly related to the prediction's performance, the best option was to randomly attribute them. We utilized cross-validation to assess our results. More precisely, we applied K-fold with $K = 3$ and five repetitions.

4   Evaluation

In this section, the model previously presented is validated and compared with the results presented in [8] in two distinct scenarios: initially, with the PeMS benchmark dataset, in Sect. 4.1 and then, in Sect. 4.2, a scenario where traffic is not continuous nor large.

It is valid to mention that this work focus on comparing the results with Huang et al. [8] approach since it was the technique that obtained the best results in the literature, considering the state-of-the-art review done during this work.

Moreover, a parametrization analysis of both models is assessed in order to further increase this monograph contribution for the PeMS scenario. The same analysis for the University scenario is not shown due to the results' similarity and, therefore, lack of relevance. Since different activation functions are also being evaluated, all parametrization analysis will be based on the results generated by best performing function.

We evaluate the models' performance in both scenarios using the Mean Absolute Percentage Error (MAPE) metric. It is defined in Eq. 5.

$$MAPE = \frac{1}{n} \sum_{t=1}^{n} \left| \frac{\hat{y}_t - y_t}{\hat{y}_t} \right| \quad (5) \qquad R^2 = 1 - \frac{\sum_{t=1}^{n}(y(t) - \hat{y_1}(t))^2}{\sum_{t=1}^{n}(y(t) - \hat{y_2}(t))^2} \quad (6)$$

For the second scenario, an adaptation of the Coefficient of Determination metric was also used, denoted by R^2, to assess the improvement of the Smart-Traffic model over Huang et al. [8] proposals.

To do this, the area between the curves produced by the models' prediction - $\hat{y_1}(t)$ and $\hat{y_2}(t)$ - and the true function - $y(t)$ - is compared. It is defined in Eq. 6. The greater the value of R^2, the greater the improvement of one model over the other.

Finally, the performance the proposed model in both scenarios is evaluated utilizing two different activation functions, as described in Sect. 3.1, comparing the results obtained.

All tests were run in a machine which has the following configuration: Intel Core i7-3770 CPU @ 3.40 GHz × 8 processor, 8 GB of RAM and on a 64-bit Ubuntu 16.04 operational system. The programming language of choice was Python 3.5.2.

4.1   PeMS

Scenario Description. The PeMS[4] is a well known benchmark dataset for traffic-related problems. It consists of an open repository of data collected by a network of sensors. Its sensors are spread across the state of California that register traffic-related information such as vehicle volume in a highway.

In order to reproduce the test scenario from [8], a dataset with the same characteristics used by them was extracted, *i.e.* 12 months from the fifty most busy roads in the year of 2011.

Results. Initially, statistical analysis is conducted to assess the impact of each variable in each models' performance, *i.e.* a two-factor (NN or RBM) and (i) six treatments for P (10, 11, 12, 13, 14, 15), (ii) Q (0, 1, 2, 3, 4, 5) and (iii) five treatments N (80, 90, 100, 110, 120). All analysis were done with the aid of the IBM SPSS tool[5] and all tests were done using a significance level of 5%.

Since the experimental sample is over 30 elements (180 to be more precise), a Kolmogorov-Smirnov (KS) normality test was conducted. Since neither of the factors presented a normal distribution, a homoscedasticity test is not needed.

Next, the following hypothesis are formulated for each individual treatment and a non-parametric Kruskal-Wallis (KW) test is conducted. This is the appropriate choice considering there are three or more treatments. The results of the KW test are shown in Table 2.

- **HP0**: Increasing the parameter P value does not substantially influantiates neither models' prediction, *i.e* $\mu_{P=10} = \mu_{P=11} = \mu_{P=12} = \mu_{P=13} = \mu_{P=14} = \mu_{P=15}$
  HP1: Increasing the parameter P value substantially influences both models' prediction, *i.e* at least one of the equities does not hold
- **HQ0**: Increasing the parameter Q value does not substantially influantiates neither models' prediction, *i.e* $\mu_{Q=0} = \mu_{Q=1} = \mu_{Q=2} = \mu_{Q=3} = \mu_{Q=4} = \mu_{Q=5}$
  HQ1: Increasing the parameter Q value substantially influences both models' prediction, *i.e* at least one of the equities does not hold
- **HN0**: Increasing the parameter N value does not substantially influantiates neither models' prediction, *i.e* $\mu_{N=80} = \mu_{N=90} = \mu_{N=100} = \mu_{N=110} = \mu_{N=120}$
  HN1: Increasing the parameter N value substantially influences both models' prediction, *i.e* at least one of the equities does not hold

Given the test results in Table 2, the null hypothesis HP0 and HN0 are accepted. In other words, at a confidence level of 95%, increasing the value of the parameter P and N does not substantially influence neither models' prediction. Hence, the means for different values for P and N are statistically equivalents. A graphical interpretation of this results can be seen in the boxplots in Figs. 3 and 4.

---

[4] http://pems.dot.ca.gov.
[5] https://www.ibm.com/analytics/spss-statistics-software.

Table 2. KW's test results for each factor and treatment with a 5% significance level.

	Huang et al.	SmartTraffic
P p-value	0.203	0.818
Q p-value	0.000	0.000
N p-value	0.799	0.143

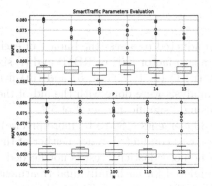

Fig. 3. Proposed model's performance in relation to the parameters P and N for the PeMS dataset.

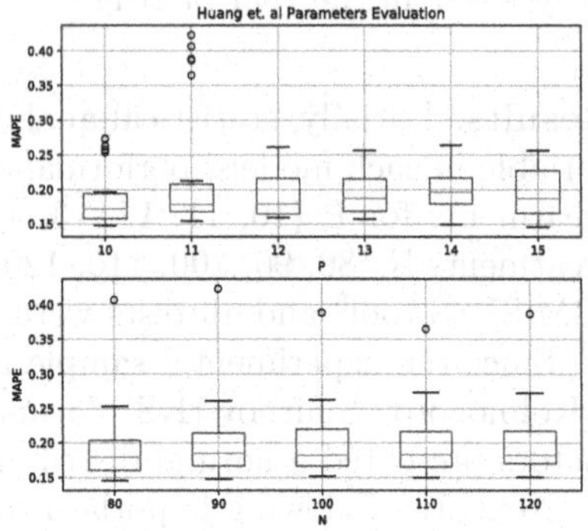

Fig. 4. Huang *et al.* [8]'s performance in relation to the parameters P and N for the PeMS dataset.

Moreover, the alternative hypothesis HQ1 is accepted. That is, at a confidence level of 95%, increasing the value of the parameter Q substantially influences both models' prediction. Therefore, at least one of the equities does not hold. To assess which, a pairwise test using the non-parametric Mann-Whitney (MW) test is performed. This is summarized in Table 3. The numbers above the main diagonal represent the p-value for the pair utilizing Huang et al. [8] means while the numbers below represent the SmartTraffic approach.

Besides two particular cases (NN $Q = 1, Q = 4$ and $Q = 2$ and $Q = 5$), the alternate hypothesis holds true in the pairwise comparison, *i.e.* increasing the parameter Q - use of historical data -, significantly changes the prediction process since means for different values for Q are statistically distinct.

Table 3. Pairwise MW test for variable Q.

Q value	0	1	2	3	4	5
0		.000	.000	.000	.000	.000
1	.000		.000	.000	.000	.000
2	.000	.000		.000	.000	.000
3	.000	.002	.000		.019	.000
4	.000	.790	.001	.009		.005
5	.000	.007	.095	.000	.028	

Considering the test results and statistical analysis, there is strong evidence that the usage of historical data strongly influences the prediction process in a positive manner as observed in both Boxplots Figs. 5 and 6.

The usage of historical data, $i.e.$ $Q > 0$, improves both models' performances, ratifying the evidences pointed by [1,8,13]. The model proposed by Huang et al. [8] shows, on average, a steady improvement the more historical data it uses. As for the model proposed in this monograph, the usage of historical data is crucial in the prediction process, but it does not seem to take as much advantage of it as the previously mentioned models does. All these considerations are drawn from Figs. 5 and 6.

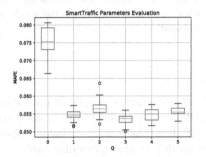

Fig. 5. Proposed model's performance in relation to the parameter Q for the PeMS dataset.

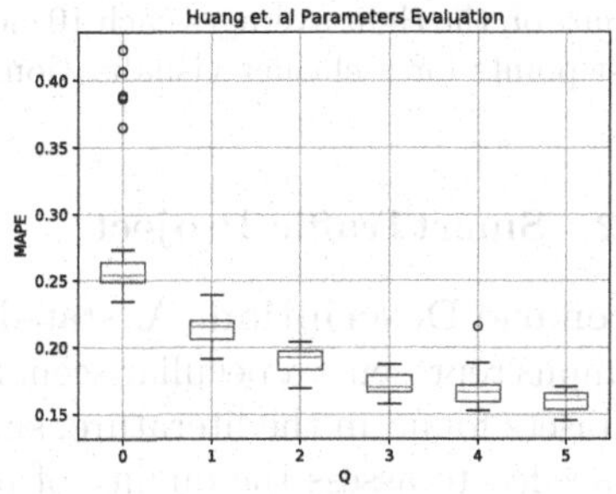

Fig. 6. Huang *et al.* [8]'s performance in relation to the parameter Q for the PeMS dataset.

The MAPE metric evaluation, presented in Fig. 7, shows that the SmartTraffic consistently outperforms Huang *et al.*'s approach. This can be verified by the best performing model, which had the following configuration: $P = 11$, $Q = 3$, $N = 120$ and it scored a 5.00% average MAPE and its best performance resulted in a MAPE of 4.68%. A plot of said model is shown in Fig. 8.

In comparison, the Huang *et al.* approach obtained an average MAPE of 14.68% and its best performance resulted in a 9.93% MAPE. Even though there are implementation and parametrization differences, the results obtained on the same dataset are comparable by, approximately, 1% for the best model.

The superiority of the ReLU (Eq. 4) over the Logistic function (Eq. 3) is incontestable for this scenario, since it outperforms the latter in every test run, as seen in Fig. 7.

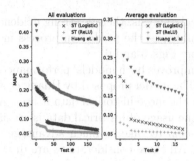
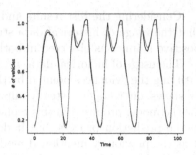

Fig. 7. All configuration evaluations for both models on the left chart. The chart on the right averages each 10 closest points for a cleaner visualization.

Fig. 8. Prediction curve of the Smart-Traffic. The black line represents the true value and the red one the model's forecast.

4.2 SmartTraffic Project

Scenario Description. As stated throughout the paper, this specific university campus represents a peculiar scenario. Its traffic does not reflect most benchmark datasets found in the literature, such as PeMS. For that reason, an investigation is needed to assess the quality of prediction models in this particular case.

An overview image of the university's campus is presented in Fig. 9. There are three capture points, the northern and southern gate, represented by the numbers 1 and 2, respectively, and one in the road that leads to another major nucleus in the university campus, represented by the number 3. The traffic direction in the highlighted ring is one-way and flows counter-clockwise and the only entrances and exits are the cited gates. From now on the capture points will be referred by their numbers on the map.

Due to hardware problems, 2 was nonoperative during a considerable period of time that overlaps with the data this project had access to. Thus, these were discarded and all tests were performed using data from points 1 and 3.

The data captured was processed to fit the project needs and it correlates timestamps to how many vehicles passed through at that time. Even though this is a configurable parameter in the service, in the conducted experiments those values were grouped in chunks of 5 min, since it is the most used time window by related works.

Even though it is a major converging point for traffic in the city, the traffic volume is not big nor stable during the day. The raw dataset contains 249,142 entries, but it has many gaps between timestamps, mainly between midnight and 6am, where traffic usually is inexistent.

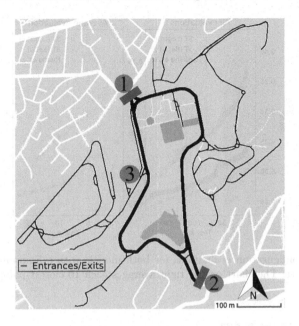

Fig. 9. Data collection points.

Results. Regarding the data, due to zeros computed, a smoothing utilizing the additive, *i.e.* add-1 estimation, also called *Laplace smoothing*, was performed. It is described in Eq. 7, where, k equals 1, $c(w_i)$ represents how many times the $i - est$ element of the array appears on the data and V is the size of the set.

$$P_{Add-k}(\omega_i|\omega i - 1) = \frac{c(\omega_{i-1}, \omega_i) + k}{c(\omega_{i-1}) + kV} \tag{7}$$

After, a symmetric behavior is performed when forecasting, utilizing $P = 5$-minute recent time frames to forecast the aggregate traffic in the next 5 min.

SmartTraffic outperforms Huang *et al.* by a satisfactory margin as seen in Fig. 10, even though the results were not as good as the free-flowing scenario.

The proposed application obtained an average MAPE of 14.22% and the best performance was 13.36% in its best model configuration, which was: $P = 11$, $Q = 5$ and $N = 110$. Huang's approach obtained its best performance for the following configuration: $P = 13$, $Q = 5$ and $N = 100$, scoring an average MAPE of 18.74% and a best performance of 18.47%.

For all tests ran, the R^2 metric was computed with models that had the same parameter configuration, comparing both their performances'. A boxplot of this metric is plotted in Fig. 11, which reinforces the proposed model superiority over the state-of-the-art, specially with the ReLU (Eq. 4) activation function.

The distribution for all evaluations shows that, on average, SmartTraffic is approximately 31% better than Huang *et al.*, considering the same parameter configuration. It is also possible to see that 50% of these evaluations are between

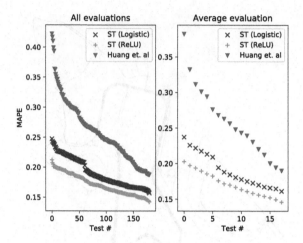

Fig. 10. All configuration evaluations for both models with a 5-minute time window on the left chart. The chart on the right averages each 10 closest points for a cleaner visualization.

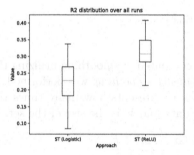

Fig. 11. R^2 metric boxplot for the university dataset over all runs with models that had the same parameter configuration.

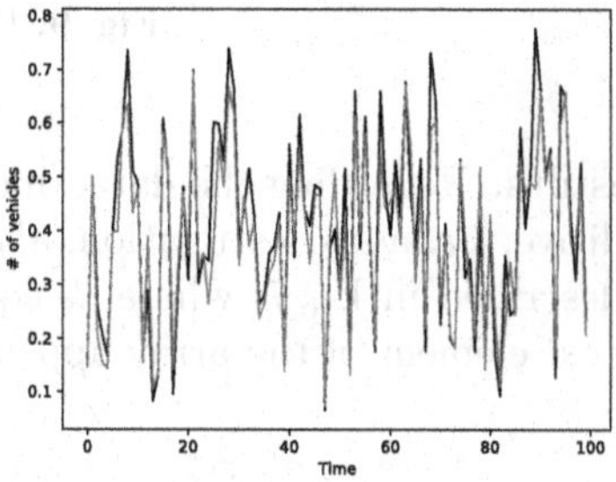

Fig. 12. Prediction curve for Smart-Traffic. The black line represents the real value and the red one the model's forecast.

28% and 34%, *i.e.* half of all SmartTraffic tests are better in this percentage range. Finally, it is possible to see that 25% of these values are between 35% and 40%.

This analysis reinforces the superiority of the ReLU (Eq. 4) over the logistic (Eq. 3) activation function, specially because the second quartile of the results achieved by the ReLU network begins after the third quartile of the logistic one's ends.

However, the major performance difference between the scenarios is due to the traffic volume. The traffic volume perceived in the PeMS dataset are in the order of hundreds of thousands, when in our scenario it doesn't sum up to more than a few dozen cars during peak hours in a five minutes time window. Even though it is attenuated by the normalization process, it is more penalizing than when dealing with large numbers.

On top of that, at both entrances, there are several traffic-controlling tools: roundabout, traffic lights, bumpers and narrower lanes. Because of that, the traffic doesn't flow continuously in the capture points, making the observations a non-stationary time series with high peaks and low valleys as seen in Fig. 12. Thus, we hypothesize that this is the main reason behind the drop in precision when compared to the other scenario.

5 Conclusion

This paper presented the SmartTraffic, one of the pilot initiatives of the Smart-Campus project, an effort to support traffic-related applications in order to create a more intelligent and autonomous campus. Moreover, it presents an extensive evaluation of different state-of-the-art solutions using real data traffic in two very distinct scenarios: (i) a free traffic flow scenario and (ii) a complex scenario without large nor continuous traffic flow.

Also, the results of the statistical analysis conducted ratified the evidences pointed by [1,8,13] that the usage of historical data helps the prediction accuracy, guiding future efforts. Finally, a comparison between two activation functions is done.

As for future work, the experiments will be re-run enabling more points of data collection. Another possible investigation is the effect of splitting the raw data into even more datasets with more similar characteristics, e.g. months, since a significant improvement was observed when splitting the data in day/night cycles. Finally, conducting a study to cluster users with similar profiles would enlighten the visualization of the relationship between user profiles and traffic flow, allowing the prediction of traffic based on users' profile.

References

1. Abadi, A., Rajabioun, T., Ioannou, P.A.: Traffic flow prediction for road transportation networks with limited traffic data. IEEE Trans. Intell. Transp. Syst. **16**(2), 653–662 (2015)
2. Abuarqoub, A., et al.: A survey on internet of thing enabled smart campus applications. In: Proceedings of the International Conference on Future Networks and Distributed Systems, p. 38. ACM (2017)
3. Campos, L.: Modelo Estocástico Periódico baseado em Redes Neurais. Ph.D. thesis, Tese de Doutorado, Pontifícia Universidade Católica do Rio de Janeiro (PUC-Rio) (2010)
4. Castro-Neto, M., Jeong, Y.S., Jeong, M.K., Han, L.D.: Online-SVR for short-term traffic flow prediction under typical and atypical traffic conditions. Expert Syst. Appl. **36**(3), 6164–6173 (2009)
5. Coni, M., Garau, C., Pinna, F.: How has Cagliari changed its citizens in smart citizens? Exploring the influence of ITS technology on urban social interactions. In: Gervasi, O., et al. (eds.) ICCSA 2018. LNCS, vol. 10962, pp. 573–588. Springer, Cham (2018). https://doi.org/10.1007/978-3-319-95168-3_39

6. Dalal, K., Dahiya, P.: State-of-the-art in vanets: the core of intelligent transportation system. IUP J. Electr. Electron. Eng. **10**(1), 27 (2017)
7. Fu, R., Zhang, Z., Li, L.: Using LSTM and GRU neural network methods for traffic flow prediction. In: 2016 31st Youth Academic Annual Conference of Chinese Association of Automation (YAC), pp. 324–328, November 2016. https://doi.org/10.1109/YAC.2016.7804912
8. Huang, W., Song, G., Hong, H., Xie, K.: Deep architecture for traffic flow prediction: deep belief networks with multitask learning. IEEE Trans. Intell. Transp. Syst. **15**(5), 2191–2201 (2014)
9. Ishak, S., Al-Deek, H.: Performance evaluation of short-term time-series traffic prediction model. J. Transp. Eng. **128**(6), 490–498 (2002)
10. Kingma, D.P., Ba, J.: Adam: a method for stochastic optimization. arXiv preprint arXiv:1412.6980 (2014)
11. Kumar, K., Parida, M., Katiyar, V.: Short term traffic flow prediction for a non urban highway using artificial neural network. Procedia-Soc. Behav. Sci. **104**, 755–764 (2013)
12. Loce, R.P., Bala, R., Trivedi, M.: Computer Vision and Imaging in Intelligent Transportation Systems. Wiley, Hoboken (2017)
13. Lv, Y., Duan, Y., Kang, W., Li, Z., Wang, F.Y.: Traffic flow prediction with big data: a deep learning approach. IEEE Trans. Intell. Transp. Syst. **16**(2), 865–873 (2015)
14. Ma, J., Theiler, J., Perkins, S.: Accurate on-line support vector regression. Neural Comput. **15**(11), 2683–2703 (2003)
15. Ma, X., Tao, Z., Wang, Y., Yu, H., Wang, Y.: Long short-term memory neural network for traffic speed prediction using remote microwave sensor data. Transp. Res. Part C Emerg. Technol. **54**, 187–197 (2015)
16. Nati, M., Gluhak, A., Abangar, H., Headley, W.: Smartcampus: a user-centric testbed for internet of things experimentation. In: 2013 16th International Symposium on Wireless Personal Multimedia Communications (WPMC), pp. 1–6, June 2013
17. Shuai, M., Xie, K., Pu, W., Song, G., Ma, X.: An online approach based on locally weighted learning for short-term traffic flow prediction. In: Proceedings of the 16th ACM SIGSPATIAL International Conference on Advances in Geographic Information Systems, p. 45. ACM (2008)
18. Tian, Y., Pan, L.: Predicting short-term traffic flow by long short-term memory recurrent neural network. In: 2015 IEEE International Conference on Smart City/SocialCom/SustainCom (SmartCity), pp. 153–158. IEEE (2015)
19. Van Der Voort, M., Dougherty, M., Watson, S.: Combining Kohonen maps with arima time series models to forecast traffic flow. Transp. Res. Part C Emerg. Technol. **4**(5), 307–318 (1996)
20. Werbos, P.J.: Backpropagation through time: what it does and how to do it. Proc. IEEE **78**(10), 1550–1560 (1990)

An Approach for Improving Automatic Mouth Emotion Recognition

Giulio Biondi[1,2] 🆔, Valentina Franzoni[2,3](✉) 🆔, Osvaldo Gervasi[2](✉) 🆔,
and Damiano Perri[2] 🆔

[1] Department of Mathematics and Computer Science,
University of Florence, Florence, Italy
[2] Department of Mathematics and Computer Science,
University of Perugia, Perugia, Italy
osvaldo.gervasi@unipg.it, osvaldo.gervasi@mail.com
[3] Department of Computer, Sapienza University of Rome, Control,
and Management Engineering "Antonio Ruberti", Rome, Italy
franzoni@dis.uniroma1.it

Abstract. The study proposes and tests a technique for automated emotion recognition through mouth detection via Convolutional Neural Networks (CNN), meant to be applied for supporting people with health disorders with communication skills issues (e.g. muscle wasting, stroke, autism, or, more simply, pain) in order to recognize emotions and generate real-time feedback, or data feeding supporting systems. The software system starts the computation identifying if a face is present on the acquired image, then it looks for the mouth location and extracts the corresponding features. Both tasks are carried out using Haar Feature-based Classifiers, which guarantee fast execution and promising performance. If our previous works focused on visual micro-expressions for personalized training on a single user, this strategy aims to train the system also on generalized faces data sets.

1 Introduction

In this work, we present a system for mouth-based visual emotion recognition. Our purpose is to lay the basis for a health-care system for people who suffer from severe disease, e.g., strokes, or conditions such as autism, who may benefit from automated support of emotion recognition. Such systems can detect basic emotions from smartphone or computer camera devices, to produce feedback, either text, audio or visual for other humans, or a digital output to support other connected services. Connecting such an architecture to appropriate services could help users to convey their or others' emotions more effectively, providing augmented emotional stimuli, e.g., in case of users affected from a pathology which involve social relationship abilities, or when users experiment difficulties in recognizing emotions expressed by others. The system could also call a human assistant, e.g., for hospitalized patients feeling intense pain. In this paper, we focus on the mouth expression in correctly determining the emotion

© Springer Nature Switzerland AG 2019
S. Misra et al. (Eds.): ICCSA 2019, LNCS 11619, pp. 649–664, 2019.
https://doi.org/10.1007/978-3-030-24289-3_48

expressed by a subject. A crucial step is the selection of a reference model which classifies emotions, e.g., Ekman, [54] Plutchik, and Lovheim [15]. We selected a basic subset of the Ekmann emotions: *Joy* and *Disgust*, together with the *Neutral* condition (i.e., no emotion expressed). Joy is among the simplest emotions to recognize through face expression, thus an ideal candidate for results comparisons concerning the state-of-the-art. Disgust, instead, is present in much fewer instances in available data sets, because it is more difficult to stimulate, and it is a less ideal but more interesting example of computation. We include the neutral state as a control state for recognition results on both emotions.

2   Problem Description and Proposed Solution

Our study exploits the high precision of CNN processing to process mouth images to recognize emotional states. On one hand, we expect the system's capability to exploit best on the single user with personalized training; on the other hand, in this work we also test the technique on generic faces data sets, in order to find solutions to the following research questions:

- *With which precision it is possible to recognize facial emotions solely from the mouth?*
- *Is the proposed technique capable of recognizing emotions if trained on a generalized set of facial images?*

In a user-centered implementation, the user trains the network on her/his facial expressions and the software supports personalized emotional feedback for each particular user: personal traits, such as scars or flaws, or individual variations in emotional feeling and expression, help the training to precise recognition. Then, we train the software also to recognize different users. In order to obtain optimized results, the ambient light setting needs a proper setup:

- **Robustness**: The algorithm must be able to operate even in the presence of low-quality data (e.g., low resolution, bad light conditions);
- **Scalability**: The user position should not be necessarily fixed in front of the camera, in order to avoid constraining the person. Therefore, the software should be able to recognize the user despite her/his position.
- **Luminosity**: an important problem is precisely that of the variation of light. In computer vision ([1]), the variation of the lens involves an alteration of the information ([41]. No complete control of the detected information is achieved: the system will be able to withstand variations in brightness without compromising the original information.

The proposed solution has been implemented in C++ and OpenCV graphics libraries; hence, it is compatible with all operating systems, with high reliability and constant support from the community.

3   State of the Art

Deep Learning and Image Classification

The recent scientific focus on Deep Learning towards the end of the XX century has contributed to the rebirth of significant interest in neural networks. The real impact of Deep Learning began in the context of speech recognition around the year 2010, when two Microsoft Research employees, Lil Deng and Geoenix Hinton, realized that using large amounts of data for training a deep neural network resulted in lowering error rates far below the state of the art [20]. Discoveries in the field of hardware have certainly contributed to the rise of interest in Deep Learning. In particular, the ever-powerful GPUs seem to be able to perform the countless mathematical calculations of matrices and vectors in Deep Learning [11–13]. Actual GPUs allow reducing workout times from the weeks to a day. Recently, deep learning has been used for several types of research aiming at the classification of images and learning, trying to solve the limitations of machine learning, which reside in overfitting and domain dependence, with image adaptation, kernel randomization [14] and transfer learning [21]. Commitment has been dedicated by researchers to exploit domain dependence as a feature, where personalized classification can quickly exploit a particular user or entity, especially for smart-home systems [35] and microblog sentiment tagging [37]. Alternative approaches consider evolutionary algorithms, [27,58,59] random walks on semantic networks of images [25,26,60] and max-product neural networks.

History and Description of Neural Networks

Convolutional Neural Networks are among the most used methods for affective image classification [2,22] thanks to their flexibility for transfer learning, and easy tools available on the Web [34]. An artificial Neural Network (NN), composed of artificial neurons 1, or nodes, can be used for solving artificial intelligence (AI) problems. NNs are biologically inspired, where a neural network is a network or circuit of neurons in the brain. The connections of the biological neuron are modeled as weights: a positive weight reflects an excitatory connection, while negative values mean inhibitory connections. In 1983 Geoff Hinton, now an emeritus professor at University of Toronto, co-invented Boltzmann machines, [45] one of the first types of neural networks to use statistical probabilities, then updating the strength of the connections within a neural network with backpropagation. [46] In the late-1970s and early-1980s, Hinton began working with neural networks when they were deeply unfashionable, because most computer scientists believed the technique was a dead end, while a better approach to Artificial Intelligence (AI) could be to explicitly encode human expertise in rules sets. Today we know that deep neural networks using backpropagation underpin most advances in AI, from Facebook friends automatic tagging, to the voice recognition capabilities of Amazon Alexa and Google Home, to its translation capability from previously difficult languages, such as Mandarin. LeCun, then,

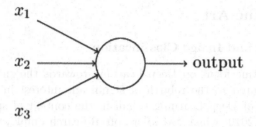

Fig. 1. A simple example of a 3-input perceptron

was a post-doc with Hinton's supervision, developing Convolutional Neural Networks as an improvement of the work on backpropagation. Bengio, who worked with LeCun on computer vision at Bell Labs, applied neural networks to natural language processing, leading to enormous advances in computer translation. Recently, he also built a model to allow neural networks to create novel and realistic images. In March 2019, Hinton, LeCun and Bengio received together the Turing Award, considered the Nobel prize for computing, for their advances in Artificial Intelligence with Deep Learning. [47] As we can see in Fig. 1, a single perceptron (i.e., the NN atom) takes several binary inputs, $x_1, x_2, \ldots, x_n$ and produces a single binary output. Weights $w_1, w_2, \ldots, w_n$ can be introduced to express the importance of the respective inputs to the output. The neuron's output, 0 or 1, is determined whether the weighted sum $\sum_j w_j x_j$ is less/greater than a threshold parameter value of the network:

$$
output = \begin{cases} 0 & if \sum_j w_j x_j \\ 1 & if \sum_j w_j x_j \end{cases} \tag{1}
$$

By varying the weights and threshold, we can get different models of decision-making, thus different devices device capable to make decisions by weighting up evidence. A real NN will have several perceptrons in each column, and several cascade columns, where each columns is called a *layer*. A several-layers NN of perceptrons can engage sophisticated decision-making, adding variations to the comparison to the threshold. Several types of layers can be adapted to different calculation aims.

Convolutional Neural Networks

A Convolutional Neural Network (CNN) is a class of deep neural networks, most commonly applied to analyzing visual content, with excellent results on image recognition, segmentation, detection and retrieval. [10,44] The key enabling factors behind such relevant results were principally techniques to scale up the networks to millions of parameters, where labeled data sets are needed to support the learning process. CNNs are able, under such conditions, to learn powerful and interpretative image features. Convolutional layers apply an operation of convolution to the input, which emulates the response of an individual neuron to visual stimuli, processes data only for its receptive field. A set of kernels (i.e., learning parameters), with a small receptive field, extend through the full depth of the input volume. A forward pass convolutes each filter across width and height of the volume in input, calculating the dot product between the filter entries and the input, thus producing a 2-dimensional activation map. The network results to learn filters activating when some specific type of feature is detected in a particular position of the input. Although fully connected neural networks can be used to learn features as well as classify data, a relevant amount of neurons is necessary due to the large input sizes of images, where compression is not always a good idea because any pixel may be relevant. E.g., a fully connected layer for an image of size 100×100 will have 10000 weights for each neuron. The operation of convolution offers a great solution to the problem, so tat the network can be deeper with fewer parameters. E.g., tiling regions of size 5×5, regardless of image size, having the same shared weights, require just 25 kernels. The problem of exploding gradients in traditional NNs with many layers is solved using backpropagation. Convolutional networks may also include local or global pooling layers, to reduce data dimension using a combination of the outputs of neuron clusters obtaining one neuron in the following layer.

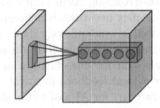

Fig. 2. A single CNN layer

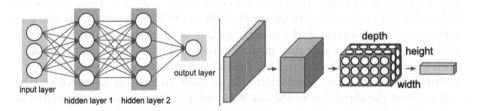

Fig. 3. Left: A regular 3-layer Neural Network. Right: A Convolutional Network arranges its neurons in three dimensions (width, height, depth). The input layer holds the image.

The neurons in a layer will be connected to a small region of the previous layer, as illustrated in Fig. 2, instead of all of the neurons, as happens in the fully-connected layer, which connects all the neurons in one layer to every neuron in another layer. A simple CNN is a sequence of layers, each of which transforms one volume of activations to another through a differentiable function. Typically, three types of layers are used: Convolutional Layer, Pooling Layer, and Fully-Connected Layer, which are then stacked together to form a full CNN architecture (see Fig. 3). In this way, CNN transforms the original image layer by layer from the original pixel values to the final class scores. Note that some layers contain parameters, and others do not. [43] In particular, the convolutional and the fully-connected layers perform transformations as a function of both the activations in the input volume, both the the weights and biases of the neurons (i.e. the parameters). On the other hand, the pooling and *RELU* layers, which apply an element-wise activation function, such as the $max(0, x)$, will implement a fixed function.

Artificial Intelligence Assisting Health Care

For computerized health care assisting, multidisciplinary studies in Artificial Intelligence, Augmented Reality and Robotics stressed out the importance of computer science for automatizing real-life tasks for assistive and learning objects, [56] such as detecting words from labial movements (i.e. automated lip detection) [29], Virtual reality for prosthetic training [24] or neural telerehabilitation of patients with stroke [6], vocal interfaces for robotics applications [30]. As an application of complex networks, it is possible to predict bacteria diffusion patterns, [36,61] as well as epidemiology data [23], having a viral spread. To be mentioned, huge advances are happening on medical image recognition and multi-stage feature selection for classification of cancer data [32], and of text corpora for medical or patient feedback in social networks. One of the most promising advances of recent years for AI-assisted health care is the opportunity to have light-implementation Mobile Apps, that can be quickly developed to be used in a friendly manner [5], to assist and support disabled users for communication and learning tasks. Such applications can be run directly on personal smartphones or wearable devices, for health monitoring and prognosis [8] as well as for interactive support for people with disabilities or conditions that can influence communication and learning, such as autism spectrum disorders [7]. Using cloud services or networks in the Internet of Things (IoT), makes possible both to connect such devices to high capability servers, both to collect data in a distributed collaborative perspective [19], in order to feed big knowledge-bases, and increase the capability of the single object, i.e. of its owner, as a member of a vast interactive collective dynamic knowledge (i.e. a Big Data) network.

Affective Computing and Emotion Recognition

Multidisciplinary approaches recently stressed out the importance of recognizing and extracting affective and mental states, in particular emotions, for communication, understanding, and supporting humans in any task with automated detectors and artificial assistants having machine emotional intelligence [3]. In real-life problems, individuals transform overwhelming amounts of heterogeneous data in a manageable and personalized subset of classified items. The process of recognition of moods and sentiments is mostly complex. Recent research underlines that primary emotional states such as happiness, sadness, anger, disgust, or neutral state [38] can be recognized based on text, [31] physiological clues such as heart rate, skin conductance and face expression, differently from sentiment, moods and affect, which are more complex states and can be better managed with a multidimensional approach [15,39]. Since Rosalind Picard defined the challenges for Affective Computing in 2003 [4], numerous advances have been made in the task of emotion recognition, such as defining collective influence of emotions expressed online [9], stating that emotional expressiveness is the crucial fuel that sustains communities; studying cultural aspects of emotions in art [16] and its variations; create emotionally engaging experiences in games [33], where affective changes are crucial to the conscious experience of the world around us. Some of the more ethical and critical challenges defined by Rosalind Picard, however, remain open. For example, many of the modalities for emotion recognition (e.g., blood chemistry, brain activity, neurotransmitters) are not readily available, commercial tools are limited [18], data sets for training are not general [17] and people's emotion is so idiosyncratic and variable, that there is difficult to recognize an individual's emotional states from available data [4]. Moreover, the challenge to use Affective Computing to help people, e.g., with self-aid tools is not widely faced in research, preferring applications to marketing [55].

4   The Proposed Emotion Recognition Engine

We based our Emotion Recognition Engine on popular open-source libraries: the image processing features are provided by OpenCV [48], version 3.1.0. First, the software recognizes the presence of a face in the image; when a face is found, the algorithm looks for the mouth location and extracts the corresponding subframe. [28] Both tasks are carried out using Haar Feature-based Classifiers [49], which guarantee fast execution and promising performance. A face detection pre-trained classifier is integrated into OpenCV; the mouth classifier, instead, is the one used in [50]. During the training phase, samples of the subject are captured from the camera at regular intervals (or fed from disk) and used to produce a set of mouth snapshots. Such snapshots will form, after shuffling, the training, validation, and test set, with the first two used to train the networks with the Deep Learning framework Caffe [34]. The remaining images are subsequently used to test the performances of the networks. The system has been designed to perform both offline and online recognition, i.e. recognize emotions from a series of pre-stored images or directly from a video feed.

4.1   The Structure of the EmEx2 CNN

In order to have a direct approach to the world of conundrum neural networks, the EmEx [42] approach, which we used in part of our tests, focuses on detecting user-centered emotions from the mouth. Network layers are set up to extract the specific information of the image data, accurately setting the parameters to have a valid recognition. In our CNN, training data are labeled with emotions, and the results of the layer computation are evaluated in terms of accuracy and loss. The neural network architecture is based on the popular *LeNet-5*, [62], consisting of several layers connected. The main level is for the *data set* and the corresponding tags. The second layer is the *convoluted layer*, where the convolution operations are performed on the input images, extracting features about each frame in each class. Then, a *pooling layer* is used to reduce the parameter magnitude, reducing in width and height, the volume of previously created data, with a time gain in computation. For scaling, a max function of a variable set is used. Different convolutional and pooling layers follow. An *inner product layer innerProduct* groups the information in a single numeric value, to be processed again in the following phases. The system is now capable of returning a vector representation of neurons, and it will no longer be possible to apply unambiguous layers. Another layer of innerProduct is then applied to put the layers in sequence. Thus, the last one will have an output parameter that equal to the number of classes needed for the classification. The K final values will be the parameters of a probability function that allows the final classification. In the training phase, the network ends with an *Accuracy layer* for network accuracy calculation, and with a *Loss layer* for the calculation of the error function needed for a correct and useful training phase. In the classification phase, instead, a *SoftMax layer* is the final layer to classify new images, which are not included in the data set (i.e., the test set images in our experiments). This layer calculates the likelihood of the most appropriate class in the grading phase, and therefore, its output represents the final solution.

4.2   The Structure of the AlexNet CNN

AlexNet [10], the second network that we used in our experiments, is a network presented as a winner of the 2012 ImageNet Large-Scale Visual Recognition Challenge (ILSVRC), on the ImageNet [52] data set, which includes ≈1.2 million pictures representing 1000 different objects in over 22000 categories. [53] Feed-forward networks could offer the power needed for such a huge data set, requiring much preprocessing work. Using still modern techniques, such as data augmentation and dropout, AlexaNet exploited the benefits of CNN and backed them up with record-breaking performance in the competition. The AlexaNet CNN is used in several applications; it consists of five convolutional layers, followed by three fully connected layers. Also, three max-pooling layers are inserted after, respectively, the first, second, and fifth convolutional layer, while the first two fully-connected layers are followed by a dropout layer, to avoid overfitting.

5   Image Collection and Training Phase

The first data set is a generalized faces data set, including faces from different ethnicity, gender, age: the *10k US Adult Faces database* [57] from the Maryland Laboratory of Brain and Cognition of the USA National Institute of Mental

Health, which includes 637 faces images labeled with *Neutral* state and 1511 with *Joy* emotion.

For the experiments regarding a single user, we collected images for *Joy*, *Disgust*, and *Neutral*. During the training phase, the subject was presented with a list of videos and pictures, selected to elicit a particular emotion in the audience. In particular, a set of 62 short videos was used to elicit *Joy*, whereas 140 images were selected for *Disgust*. The participants were asked to sit, one by one, and watch the videos/images, while their reactions were recorded by the camera. Later, samples were extracted from the sections of the videos, which showed an evident reaction to the stimuli, at a rate of three frames per second. For the *Neutral* state, the test subject's expression was recorded watching relaxing images, where no particular emotion was elicited. As a basic rule, we decided that no media could be watched more than once, as the reaction would not be spontaneous anymore in case of multiple views. The collected samples were then shuffled, to equitably distribute frames belonging to the same sequences between training set, validation set, and test set.

6   Experiments Design and Results

Three experiments were performed for this work, using the previously described two networks, i.e., AlexNet and Emex. In the first experiment, the networks were trained and tested on the data set composed of samples that we collected from our test subjects; in the second experiment, the same test was repeated on the *10k US Adult Faces* database. Finally, a cross-domain experiment was conducted, testing the networks trained on 10k US Adult Faces database sample to recognize emotions in our single-users data sets.

6.1   Single-User Test

The first test was conducted on the samples collected from each test subjects, in order to see how the networks perform training and testing on the same user in different conditions, e.g., before and after a degenerative pathology, which may prevent the patient from expressing his own emotions and related needs in words. Results, shown in Table 1, show that both networks easily overfit. During the training phase, a perfect accuracy (i.e., 1) was achieved after a few iterations: 50 for the EmEx network, and 150 for the Alexnet network. Further iterations were not necessary, because both networks showed a constant behavior, correctly classifying all the test images. The different training time to obtain the best performances is due to the much higher complexity of the AlexNet network with respect to EmEx, [40, 42] in terms of the number of parameters to be optimized. AlexNet was originally designed for a much more complex problem, as stated in Sect. 4.2, i.e., the identification of objects belonging to an extremely high number of classes. It is worth noticing that, although our task was quicker to tackle, inter-class differences may be less evident for our task than for the original ImageNet data. Therefore, our problem is more difficult to solve. Furthermore, the number of training samples used in our experiment was purposefully small, to assess performances in a context where high computing capabilities and data sets are not available, e.g., where the user can train emotional expressions on a mobile environment or a common desktop/laptop, with a relatively small number of images. Moreover, if such images are shot through a video, they will have less intra-dataset differences.

Table 1. Results of tests using both test networks on the single-user data set

Network	Training steps	Accuracy	Micro-Averaged F1
AlexNet	50	0.5437	0.5437
AlexNet	100	0.5340	0.5340
AlexNet	150	1	1
AlexNet	200	0.6484	0.6484
EmEx	50	1	1
EmEx	100	1	1
EmEx	150	1	1
EmEx	200	1	1

6.2 Multiple-Users Test

The second test was performed on the *10k US Adult Faces database* [57], including multiple-users images. This test includes only *Joy* and *Neutral*, due to the lack of enough training samples for *Disgust*. For both classes, 444 samples were included in the training set, for a total of 888 images, while the validation test set comprised 56 images per class. All the images that were left out, i.e., 814 for joy and 56 for neutral, were used to calculate the metrics. The settings used for the network training, which differ from the original ones, are:

- Train batch size: 10
- Test batch size: 16
- Test iterations: 7
- Test interval: 50
- Maximum number of iterations: 1000
- Random state seed: 1234

The ADAM [51] optimizer was used on both networks. *AlexNet* achieved a maximum training accuracy of ≈0.84 after 400 iterations, while *EmEx* peaked at a higher ≈0.91 score after 800 iterations. However, as shown in the results, AlexNet holds a better generalization ability, thanks to its complexity, achieving both higher accuracy and F1 scores with respect to the EmEx network. Complete results are reported in Table 2 and Fig. 4.

Table 2. Results of tests using the two networks on the 10k US Adult Faces database images. Best figures for AlexNet in bold; for EmEx in italic bold

Steps	AlexNet		EmEx	
	Accuracy	F1	Accuracy	F1
100	0.0644	0.0000	0.8264	0.8993
200	0.0644	0.0000	0.8161	0.8922
300	0.8713	0.9272	0.7621	0.8549
400	0.8506	0.9140	0.7816	0.8684
500	0.8172	0.8923	0.7575	0.8517
600	0.8897	0.9385	0.7540	0.8491
700	**0.8966**	**0.9426**	0.8276	0.8992
800	0.7770	0.8651	*0.8517*	*0.9145*
900	0.8207	0.8949	0.8115	0.8886
1000	0.6931	0.8044	0.7701	0.8603

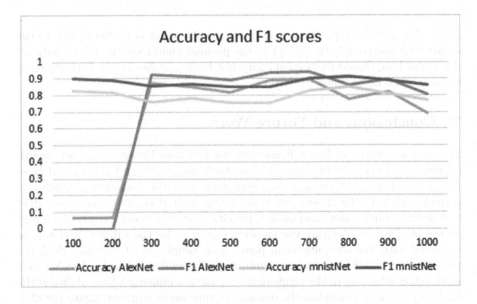

Fig. 4. Recognition performance of the two networks on the test samples

6.3 Cross Test

Both the AlexNet and EmEx networks trained on the 10k US Adult Faces database were tested on the data set created for the Single-user test in Sect. 6.1; results are reported in Table 3. Interestingly, the EmEx network performed consistingly better than AlexNet, showing a better generalization capability in a completely different environment from the one it was trained for, e.g., with

Table 3. Results of tests using the two networks trained on the 10k US Adult Faces database on the Single-user data set. Best figures for AlexNet in bold, for EmEx in italic bold

Steps	AlexNet		EmEx	
	Accuracy	F1	Accuracy	F1
100	0.5054	0	0.6344	0.6793
200	0.7098	0.5846	0.4301	0.4647
300	0.6237	0.3860	0.8065	0.7568
400	0.6990	0.5625	0.8602	0.8354
500	0.5484	0.2500	*0.8925*	*0.8781*
600	0.6667	0.4918	0.8495	0.8205
700	0.6667	0.4918	0.8280	0.7895
800	0.6129	0.3571	0.8172	0.7733
900	**0.7204**	**0.6061**	0.8172	0.7733
1000	0.5699	0.2308	0.8172	0.7733

respect to light, user position, and image quality. This is probably due to the ability of AlexNet to better adapt to the peculiar characteristics of the data set it is trained on, thanks to its complexity, but having problems in a fairly different settings when no samples are given.

7   Conclusions and Future Work

In this work, we described a framework for Emotion Recognition from mouth expressions. Experiments, conducted on both single-user and generalized faces data sets, show good recognition performances of the framework, which can correctly identify the chosen emotions, using limited computational resources and doing it both online and offline. Results show that mouth expressions play an essential role in defining the emotion conveyed by the subject, and can be exploited with low computational power and complexity of systems. Both the tested networks achieved high recognition performances, with the AlexNet network better adapting to the single data set, and a seemingly better ability of the EmEx network to generalize the domain. Future works will investigate the ability of the framework in recognizing more emotions, and include the publication of our single-users image collection.

References

1. Cootes, T.F., Taylor, C.J., Cooper, D.H., Graham, J.: Active shape models-their training and application. Comput. Vis. Image Underst. **61**(1), 38–59 (1995)
2. Stiefelhagen, R., Yang, J., Waibel, A.: A model-based gaze tracking system. Int. J. Artif. Intell. Tools **6**(2), 193–209 (1997)

3. Picard, R.W., Vyzas, E., Healey, J.: Toward machine emotional intelligence: analysis of affective physiological state. IEEE Trans. Pattern Anal. Mach. Intell. **23**(10), 1175–1191 (2001)
4. Picard, R.W.: Affective computing: challenges. Int. J. Hum. Comput. Stud. **59**(1–2), 55–64 (2003). https://doi.org/10.1016/S1071-5819(03)00052-1
5. Franzoni, V., Gervasi, O.: Guidelines for web usability and accessibility on the Nintendo Wii. In: Gavrilova, M.L., Tan, C.J.K. (eds.) Transactions on Computational Science VI. LNCS, vol. 5730, pp. 19–40. Springer, Heidelberg (2009). https://doi.org/10.1007/978-3-642-10649-1_2
6. Gervasi, O., Magni, R., Zampolini, M.: Nu!RehaVR: virtual reality in neuro telerehabilitation of patients with traumatic brain injury and stroke. Virtual Reality **14**(2), 131–141 (2010). https://doi.org/10.1007/s10055-009-0149-7
7. Hayes, G.R., Hirano, S., Marcu, G., Monibi, M., Nguyen, D.H., Yeganyan, M.: Interactive visual supports for children with autism. Pers. Ubiquitous Comput. **14**(7), 663–680 (2010). https://doi.org/10.1007/s00779-010-0294-8
8. Pantelopoulos, A., Bourbakis, N.G.: A survey on wearable sensor-based systems for health monitoring and prognosis. IEEE Trans. Syst. Man Cybern. C: Appl. Rev. **40**(1), 1–12 (2010). art. no. 5306098
9. Chmiel, A., et al.: Collective emotions online and their influence on community life. PLoS ONE **6**(7), 1–8 (2011). https://doi.org/10.1371/journal.pone.0022207. art. no. e22207
10. Krizhevsky, A., Sutskever, I., Hinton, G.: ImageNet classification with deep convolutional neural networks. In: 25th International Conference on Advance in Neural Information Processing System, pp. 1106–1114 (2012)
11. Gervasi, O., Russo, D., Vella, F.: The AES implantation based on OpenCL for multi/many core architecture. In: 2010 International Conference on Computational Science and its Applications, pp. 129–134, Fukuoka, ICCSA 2010, Washington, DC, USA. IEEE Computer Society (2010). https://doi.org/10.1109/ICCSA.2010.44
12. Vella, F., Neri, I., Gervasi, O., Tasso, S.: A simulation framework for scheduling performance evaluation on CPU-GPU heterogeneous system. In: Murgante, B., Gervasi, O., Misra, S., Nedjah, N., Rocha, A.M.A.C., Taniar, D., Apduhan, B.O. (eds.) ICCSA 2012. LNCS, vol. 7336, pp. 457–469. Springer, Heidelberg (2012). https://doi.org/10.1007/978-3-642-31128-4_34
13. Mariotti, M., Gervasi, O., Vella, F., Cuzzocrea, A., Costantini, A.: Strategies and systems towards grids and clouds integration: a DBMS-based solution. Future Gener. Comput. Syst. **88**, 718–729 (2018). https://doi.org/10.1016/j.future.2017.02.047
14. Neumann, M., Patricia, N., Garnett, R., Kersting, K.: Efficient graph Kernels by randomization. In: Flach, P.A., De Bie, T., Cristianini, N. (eds.) ECML PKDD 2012. LNCS (LNAI), vol. 7523, pp. 378–393. Springer, Heidelberg (2012). https://doi.org/10.1007/978-3-642-33460-3_30
15. Franzoni, V., Poggioni, V., Zollo, F.: Automated classification of book blurbs according to the emotional tags of the social network Zazie. In: CEUR Workshop Proceedings, vol. 1096, pp. 83–94 (2013). https://doi.org/10.13140/RG.2.1.3194.7689
16. Bertola, F., Patti, V.: Emotional responses to artworks in online collections. In: UMAP Workshops Proceedings, vol. 997 (2013)
17. Saif, H., Fernandez, M., He, Y., Alani, H.: Evaluation datasets for twitter sentiment analysis a survey and a new dataset, the STS-Gold. In: CEUR Workshop Proceedings, vol. 1096, pp. 9–21 (2013)

18. Cieliebak, M., Dürr, O., Uzdilli, F.: Potential and limitations of commercial sentiment detection tools. In: CEUR Workshop Proceedings, vol. 1096, pp. 47–58 (2013)

19. Tasso, S., Pallottelli, S., Rui, M., Laganá, A.: Learning objects efficient handling in a federation of science distributed repositories. In: Murgante, B., et al. (eds.) ICCSA 2014. LNCS, vol. 8579, pp. 615–626. Springer, Cham (2014). https://doi.org/10.1007/978-3-319-09144-0_42

20. LeCun, Y., Bengio, Y., Hinton, G.: Deep learning, Nature Publishing Group, a division of Macmillan Publishers Limited. All Rights Reserved, vol. 521, pp. 436–444 (2015). https://doi.org/10.1038/nature14539, ISBN: 0028-0836, 7553

21. Patel, V.M., Gopalan, R., Li, R., Chellappa, R.: Visual domain adaptation: a survey of recent advances. IEEE Signal Process. Mag. $32(3)$, 53–69 (2015). art. no. 7078994,

22. Peng, K.-C., Chen, T., Sadovnik, A., Gallagher, A.: A mixed bag of emotions: model, predict, and transfer emotion distributions. In: Proceedings of the IEEE Computer Society Conference on Computer Vision and Pattern Recognition, pp. 860–868, 07-12-June-2015, art. no. 7298687

23. Voirin, N., Payet, C., Barrat, A., Cattuto, C., Khanafer, N., Regis, C., Kim, B.-A., Comte, B., Casalegno, J.-S., Lina, B., Vanhems, P.: Combining high-resolution contact data with virological data to investigate influenza transmission in a tertiary care hospital. Infect. Control Hosp. Epidemiol. $36(3)$, 254–260 (2015)

24. Phelan, I., Arden, M., Garcia, C., Roast, C.: Exploring virtual reality and prosthetic training. In: 2015 IEEE Virtual Reality Conference, VR 2015 - Proceedings, pp. 353–354 (2015), art. no. 7223441

25. Franzoni, V., Milani, A., Pallottelli, S., Leung, C.H.C., Li, Y.: Context-based image semantic similarity. In: 12th International Conference on Fuzzy Systems and Knowledge Discovery, FSKD 2015, pp. 1280–1284 (2015), art. no. 7382127

26. Pallottelli S., Franzoni V., Milani A.: Multi-path traces in semantic graphs for latent knowledge elicitation. In: Proceedings - International Conference on Natural Computation, pp. 281–288, January 2016. https://doi.org/10.1109/ICNC.2015.7378004

27. Franzoni V., Milani A.: Semantic context extraction from collaborative networks. In: Proceedings of the 2015 IEEE 19th International Conference on Computer Supported Cooperative Work in Design, CSCWD 2015, pp. 131–136 (2015). https://doi.org/10.1109/CSCWD.2015.7230946

28. Lewis, T.W., Powers, D.M.W.: Lip contour detection techniques based on front view of face. J. Global Res. Comput. Sci. vol. 2, no. 5, pp. 43–46 (2011). ISSN: 2229-371X

29. Gervasi, O., Magni, R., Ferri, M.: A method for predicting words by interpreting labial movements. In: Gervasi, O., et al. (eds.) ICCSA 2016. LNCS, vol. 9787, pp. 450–464. Springer, Cham (2016). https://doi.org/10.1007/978-3-319-42108-7_34

30. Bastianelli, E., Nardi, D., Aiello, L.C., Giacomelli, F., Manes, N.: Speaky for robots: the development of vocal interfaces for robotic applications. Appl. Intell. $44(1)$, 43–66 (2016). https://doi.org/10.1007/s10489-015-0695-5

31. Biondi, G., Franzoni, V., Li, Y., Milani, A.: Web-based similarity for emotion recognition in web objects. In: Proceedings of the 9th International Conference on Utility and Cloud Computing, UCC 2016, pp. 327–332, Shanghai, China, 6–9 December 2016

32. Alkuhlani, A., Nassef, M., Farag, I.: Multistage feature selection approach for high-dimensional cancer data. Soft Comput. $21(22)$, 6895–6906 (2017)

33. Canossa, A., Badler, J., El-Nasr, M.S., Anderson, E.: Eliciting emotions in design of games - a theory driven approach. In: CEUR Workshop Proceedings vol. 1680, pp. 34–40 (2016)
34. Caffe Framework: Github. https://github.com/BVLC/caffe. Accessed 12 Sept 2018
35. Lou, Y., Wu, W., Vatavu, R.-D., Tsai, W.T.: Personalized gesture interactions for cyber-physical smart-home environments. Sci. China Inf. Sci. **60**(7), 072104 (2017). https://doi.org/10.1007/s11432-015-1014-7
36. Franzoni, V., Chiancone, A., Milani, A.: A multistrain bacterial diffusion model for link prediction. Int. J. Pattern Recognit. Artif. Intell. **31**(11), 1759024 (2017). https://doi.org/10.1142/S0218001417590248
37. Cui, W., Du, Y., Shen, Z., Zhou, Y., Li, J.: Personalized microblog recommendation using sentimental features. In: 2017 IEEE International Conference on Big Data and Smart Computing, BigComp 2017, pp. 455–456 (2017). https://doi.org/10.1109/BIGCOMP.2017.7881756. art. no. 7881756
38. Angelov, P., et al.: Cybernetics of the mind learning individuals perceptions autonomously. IEEE Syst., Man, Cybern. Mag. **3**(2), 6–17 (2017). https://doi.org/10.1109/MSMC.2017.2664478
39. Franzoni, V., Milani, A., Vallverdu, J.: Emotional affordances in human-machine interactive planning and negotiation. In: Proceedings of WI 2017, Workshop on Affective Computing and Emotion Recognition (ACER), pp. 924–930 (2017). https://doi.org/10.1145/3106426.3109421
40. Riganelli, M., Franzoni, V., Gervasi, O., Tasso, S.: EmEx, a Tool for automated emotive face recognition using convolutional neural networks. In: Gervasi, O., et al. (eds.) ICCSA 2017. LNCS, vol. 10406, pp. 692–704. Springer, Cham (2017). https://doi.org/10.1007/978-3-319-62398-6_49
41. Franzoni, V.: Autonomous hexapod robot with artificial vision and remote control by Myo-electric gestures. In: Cyber-Physical Systems for Next-Generation Networks, pp. 143–162 (2018). https://doi.org/10.4018/978-1-5225-5510-0.ch007
42. Gervasi, O., Franzoni, V., Riganelli, A., Tasso, S.: Automating facial emotion recognition. Web Intell. **17**(1), 17–27 (2019). https://doi.org/10.3233/WEB-190397
43. Mezzetti, G.: Design and experimentation of target-driven visual navigation in simulated and real environment via deep reinforcement learning architecture for robotics applications, Master Laurea Thesis, University of Perugia (2019)
44. Farabet, C., Couprie, C., Najman, L., LeCun, Y.: Learning hierarchical features for scene labeling. IEEE Trans. Pattern Anal. Mach. Intell. **35**(8), 1915–1929 (2013)
45. Fahlman, S.E., Geoffrey, E.H., Terrence, J.S.: Massively parallel architectures for AI: NETL, Thistle, and Boltzmann machines. In: National Conference on Artificial Intelligence, AAAI (1983)
46. Plaut, D.C., Nowlan, S.J., Hinton, G.E.: Experiments on learning by back propagation. Technical report CMU-CS-86-126, Computer Science Department, Carnegie-Mellon University, Pittsburgh, PA (1986)
47. LeCun, Y., Bengio, Y., Hinton, G.: Deep learning. Nature **521**(7553), 436 (2015)
48. Bradski, G.: The OpenCV Library. Dr. Dobb's J. Soft. Tools **25**, 120–125 (2000)
49. Viola, P., Jones, M.: Rapid object detection using a boosted cascade of simple features (2005)
50. Castrillón Santana, M., Déniz Suárez, O., Hernández Sosa, D., Lorenzo Navarro, J.: Using incremental principal component analysis to learn a gender classifier automatically. In: 1st Spanish Workshop on Biometrics, Girona, Spain (2007)
51. Kingma, D. P., Ba, J.: Adam: a method for stochastic optimization (2014)

52. Deng, J., Dong, W., Socher, R., Li, L.-J., Kai, L., Li, F.-F.: ImageNet: a large-scale hierarchical image database. In: 2009 IEEE Conference on Computer Vision and Pattern Recognition (2009)

53. AlexNet Caffe Implementation. https://github.com/weiliu89/caffe/tree/ssd/models/bvlc_alexnet. Accessed 2019

54. Ekman, P.: An argument for basic emotions. Cogn. Emot. (1992). https://doi.org/10.1080/02699939208411068

55. Franzoni, V., Milani, A.: Emotion recognition for self-aid in addiction treatment, psychotherapy, and nonviolent communication. In: Misra, S. et al. (eds.) ICCSA 2019. LNCS, vol. 11620, pp. 391–404 (2019)

56. Franzoni, V., Milani, A., Nardi, D., Vallverdú, J.: Emotional machines: the next revolution. Web Intell. **17**(1), 1–7 (2019)

57. Bainbridge, W.A., Isola, P., Oliva, A.: The intrinsic memorability of face images. J. Exp. Psychol. Gen. **142**(4), 1323–1334 (2013)

58. Milani, A., Poggioni, V.: Planning in reactive environments. Comput. Intell. **23**(4), 439–463 (2007). https://doi.org/10.1111/j.1467-8640.2007.00315.x

59. Baioletti, M., Milani, A., Poggioni, V., Rossi, F.: Experimental evaluation of pheromone models in ACOPlan. Ann. Math. Artif. Intell. **62**(43528), 187–217 (2011). https://doi.org/10.1007/s10472-011-9265-7

60. Ukey, N., Niyogi, R., Singh, K., Milani, A., Poggioni, V.: A bidirectional heuristic search for web service composition with costs. Int. J. Web Grid Serv. **6**(2), 160–175 (2010). https://doi.org/10.1504/IJWGS.2010.033790

61. Chiancone, A., Franzoni, V., Niyogi, R., Milani, A.: Improving link ranking quality by Quasi-common neighbourhood. In: Proceedings of 15th ICCSA 2015, pp. 21–26 (2015). https://doi.org/10.1109/ICCSA.2015.19

62. Lecun, Y., Bottou, L., Bengio, Y., Haffner, P.: Gradient-based learning applied to document recognition. Proc. IEEE **86**(11), 2278–2324 (1998). https://doi.org/10.1109/5.726791

Towards a Learning-Based Performance Modeling for Accelerating Deep Neural Networks

Damiano Perri[1]📧, Paolo Sylos Labini[2], Osvaldo Gervasi[1(✉)]📧,
Sergio Tasso[1]📧, and Flavio Vella[2]📧

[1] Department of Mathematics and Computer Science,
University of Perugia, Perugia, Italy
osvaldo.gervasi@unipg.it, osvaldo.gervasi@gmail.com
[2] Lab for Advanced Computing and Systems,
Free University of Bozen-Bolzano, Bolzano, Italy

Abstract. Emerging applications such as Deep Learning are often data-driven, thus traditional approaches based on auto-tuners are not performance effective across the wide range of inputs used in practice. In the present paper, we start an investigation of predictive models based on machine learning techniques in order to optimize Convolution Neural Networks (CNNs). As a use-case, we focus on the ARM Compute Library which provides three different implementations of the convolution operator at different numeric precision. Starting from a collation of benchmarks, we build and validate models learned by Decision Tree and naive Bayesian classifier. Preliminary experiments on Midgard-based ARM Mali GPU show that our predictive model outperforms all the convolution operators manually selected by the library.

1 Introduction

With the advent of big-data and data-driven applications such as deep learning, convolutional neural network for image classification and graph analytics among the others, the traditional library design looses performance portability mainly due to the unpredictable size and structure of the data. Specific algorithms and implementations are mostly designed by taking into account specific characteristics of the input or the targeting architecture. Autotuners partially mitigate this problem by adapting the implementation to the underline architecture, for example by selecting the best Local Work Size on OpenCL compliant GPUs [14]. Vendors libraries (e.g., Nvidia CuBLAS) still apply manual heuristics in order to select at runtime highly-optimized code for specific inputs. Convolution, the most crucial and computationally expensive part of both the training and inference step in CNNs, represents a notable example where it is quite hard to determine the best implementation for a given input [11]. The choice among direct, Image-to-column, FFT-based or Winograd-based algorithms may vary even in the same CNN, since different layers requires convolution operators to act on different input sizes.

ⓒ Springer Nature Switzerland AG 2019
S. Misra et al. (Eds.): ICCSA 2019, LNCS 11619, pp. 665–676, 2019.
https://doi.org/10.1007/978-3-030-24289-3_49

The aim of this work is to study a model-driven approach in order to improve the performance of the ARM Compute library by predicting the best convolution methods for a given convolution layers. Therefore, the model must be able to discriminate the architecture, numerical precision and input size.

The contributions of this preliminary work is twofold:

- we describe a methodology to generate the dataset used to build a predictive model.
- we evaluate a machine-learning based model on a convolutional neural networks on ARM GPUs

The rest of paper is organized as follows. Section 2 provides a brief description of related works. The background is given in Sect. 3. The main contribution of the work is reported on Sect. 4 (Methodology) and Sect. 5 (Experiments). Section 6 concludes the paper by underlining the lesson learned and the possibilities for future works.

2   Related Work

The size of the input matrices and kernels has been carefully analyzed as a function of different systems (server CPU, server GPU, mobile phone) by M. Cho and D. Brand in [2]. The authors carried out a systematic comparison between the main convolution methods (Winograd, image to column and Generic Matrix Multiplication and Fast Fourier Transform). The effects of multiple input channels have been studied by A. Vasudevan et al. in [20], who carried out a systematic analysis of the performances of the Image to Column and GEMM method varying the input channels and kernel sizes (e.g: 3×3 and 5×5), benchmarking the performances on various architectures (Intel Core i5-4570 and ARM Cortex-A57) on different neural networks (VGG-16, GoogleNet, AlexNet). The effects on performances of varying the accuracy has been studied by Vella et al. [12]. As reported, a reduction of the accuracy by 7% increases three times the performances on a Firefly board. Input aware techniques [6] are recently used to address the problem of performance portability on different applications [4,10]. Other seminal works successfully investigated predictive models for the performance modeling [17] for accelerating linear algebra routines [3] or improving the scheduling of processes on hybrid systems [19]. Their results inspired us to adopt a Machine Learning approach to find optimal implementations of the convolution operation and provided several insights for our experimental setup.

3   Background

Convolutional Neural Networks (CNNs) are a class of deep, feed-forward artificial neural networks that are often used to recognize objects in images. CNNs are composed by a set of layers linked by consecutive convolution operations. In image classification tasks, each layer is organized as a multi-channel, two-dimensional collections of neurons. Layers, along with the convolution operators acting on them, are characterized by several parameters such as width, height, depth, filter dimension, pad and stride. The last layer (output layer) is reduced to a single vector of probability scores, so that a CNN transforms the original pixel values of an input image to the final class scores. The shape of such layers is usually fixed beforehand, while the kernel coefficient of their convolution operators are tuned through training.

Convolution. A great number of standard signal-processing operations are described by linear and time invariant operators. Their action on a function f can be implemented through convolution with a filter (or kernel) k, indicated with the $*$ operator and defined as:

$$(f * k)(t) = \int f(\tau)k(t - \tau)d\tau \tag{1}$$

Often, convolution is applied to discrete, finite signals, such as digital images. For computing a convolution in the notable case of 2-dimensional, single channel digital images, a variation of Eq. (1) is employed:

$$(f * k)(x, y) = \sum_{i=0}^{M} \sum_{j=0}^{N} f(i, j)k(x - i, y - j) \tag{2}$$

Thus, convolution changes the value (color, transparency, etc.) of a pixel to a weighted sum of all other pixels. These weights are the entries of the kernel matrix k, translated so that its center lies on the target pixel. Usually, the kernel matrix is null everywhere but a small region around its center, so that the value of a point after a convolution depends only on its close neighbours. The size of the non-zero part of the kernel may be arbitrary, but a 3×3 matrix if often used in image processing applications.

Convolution is thus a general purpose filter effect for images. Varying the convolution kernel, we may obtain a variety of effects, such as enhancing the edges, increasing the contrast, dilating or eroding the area occupied by the objects in the picture, and so on.

Performing a "direct convolution" and computing directly Eq. (2) can be unnecessarily costly, so other indirect methods are often preferred. The following sections reports a brief overview of some of these methods.

Coppersmith Winograd. In 1969, Strassen developed a matrix multiplication algorithm with complexity $O(n^{2.81})$, outperforming the standard $O(n^3)$ algorithm through the use of a number of intermediate products and additions. Subsequently, in 1986, he developed the "laser method", which further reduced the complexity to $O(n^{2.48})$. The following year, Coppersmith and Winograd developed a faster, now popular algorithm with complexity equal to $O(n^{2.375477})$. Although this algorithm comes with a lower asymptotic cost than its predecessors, a large multiplicative constant in the omega notation makes it truly efficient only when the matrices have particularly large dimensions. Since it is possible to recast Eq. (2) as a product of matrices, a Winograd-based convolution is possible, and actually very efficient and numerically stable, especially for small 3×3 kernels.

Fast Fourier Transform. Since Fourier functions are the eigenfunctions of the convolution operator, convolution is easily performed in the Fourier domain as a multiplication between the function and the kernel coefficients. The Fast Fourier Transform (FFT) is a computationally fast way of obtaining the Fourier coefficients of a signal. A convolution through FFT can be very efficient when it involves large filters, since the cost of applying the filter in the Fourier domain is small compared to that of transforming the two signals. Unfortunately, as already noted, most modern applications use very small filters that can easily run on highly parallel system, making FFT-based convolution less convenient. Combined with an inherently weak numerical precision, this makes it hard for the FFT procedure to compete with some other methods. For comparison, we report here results extracted from the work of Andrew Lavin and Scott Gray on the comparison between FFT-based and Winograd-based convolution methods. In November 2015, they tested the two algorithms by running them on nVidia Maxwell architecture, specifically using a Titan X graphics card.

Using 32 bit floating point and a 3×3 filter, Winograd performed better: it achieved an error rate of $1.53 * 10^{-5}$, against the $4.01 * 10^{-5}$ of the FFT. Interestingly, when using 16 bit floating point, the two techniques obtained the same level of precision, but in both cases the Winograd speed performances were better by a factor of 2.44.

Image to Column and GEMM. GEneral Matrix to Matrix Multiplication (GEMM) indicates the standard low-level routine for performing matrix-matrix multiplications. Its implementations are usually extremely optimized for speed and can benefit from special floating point hardware. Since images and kernels are represented in memory as five-dimensional arrays (colored RGB), it is necessary to reshape them into 2D matrices in order to perform GEMM. To this end, a color channel is first selected, and then the an *Image to column* procedure is applied. Image-to-column rearranges discrete image blocks into columns, and then dispose the concatenated columns in a new matrix. The order of the columns in the new matrix is determined by traversing the original image in a column-wise manner. This operation has the considerable disadvantage of increasing the occupied memory, since the pixels of the image are replicated for the generation of the new matrix. Once the matrix associated with the image is obtained, the same procedure is applied to the kernel array, and a new matrix is then generated to be used for multiplication. Since GEMM is highly optimized, it can allow better performance than direct convolution. As can be understood, the occupation of memory increases as a result of the generation of several new matrices: with a $n*n$ kernel matrix, for example, a column matrix which is k^2 times larger than the original image is generated.

Yet, in most situations this consistent memory cost comes with a yet more consistent speedup, so that the *image to column and GEMM* approach is employed by a number of Deep Neural Network (DNN) frameworks that target GPUs such as Caffe, Theano and Torch.

3.1 Supervised Classifiers

In the present work we evaluate two of the simplest supervised machine learning methods used for classification and regression, the Decision Tree (DT) [13], and naive Bayesian classifier (nBC) [16]. These straightforward, white-box models greatly simplify this preliminary study and allow us to concentrate on the feasibility of the proposed task.

In the future, we plan to investigate the relation between the characteristics of the input and the parallel implementation of convolution operator provided by the ARM Compute Library through the use of more sophisticated classifiers.

Decision Tree. A *decision tree* is an abstract structure similar to a flow chart graph. In such a tree, nodes identifies decision points, or tests, whit arcs representing outcomes of such test. When the task is classification, leafs are interpreted as class labels, so that traversing the tree from the root to a leaf determines a solution of the decision problem. When creating a decision tree for a particular classification problem, one aims to minimize the overall depth while maximizing accuracy, so that the average classification instance is solved traversing the smallest possible number of decision nodes. We employed standard ML tools like pruning and used metrics such as the Gini index to reduce complexity and limit overfitting in our DTs.

Naive Bayesian Classifier. A Bayesian network is described by a direct acyclic graph, with nodes representing random variables and arcs representing dependencies. Linked nodes shares a direct dependency, while unconnected ones are implied to be conditionally independent. In such networks, nodes have a probability distribution that can be assumed or calculated from their neighbours'. This makes it very easy to ask and answer queries about the probability of a variable given some evidence on the others. In a naive Bayes classifier, all class labels are considered conditionally independent from each other, and depends only on a single input parent node. Despite their extreme simplification, these classifiers have demonstrated exceptionally capable in a variety of real classification tasks. The distributions and the dependency structure of a Bayesian network can be constructed ad-hoc from previous knowledge of the system or learned from a dataset, and a variety of algorithms exists for training naive Bayes classifiers. Our choices in this regard are described in the next section along with the employed methodology.

4 Methodology and Framework Description

The proposed methodology can be logically divided in three steps: the *dataset generation*, where we studied the performances of three convolution implementations on a variety of CNN layer shapes, recording the most successful in each instance; the *training*, where we used the dataset to train our classifiers at coupling a layer shape with the optimal convolution implementation for that layer; and finally the *model validation*, were we investigated the performance of our model-driven convolution against the optimal and standard approaches.

In what follows, we describe these steps and provide some information on the details of our implementation. The code is available git on https://github.com/DamianoP/AdaptiveMethods.

Dataset. In the first part, we evaluated the performance of the direct, Winograd-based and GEMM-based implementations of the convolution operator. We generated the dataset by collecting the outcome of more than 4000 experiments on artificial CNN layer architectures, stored the performances of each implementation on each layer and identified the fastest in view of the training step.

Each convolution layer, as mentioned in Sect. 3, is completely described by five parameters. Three regards the input image: its width W, its height H, its number of channels C_IN. Two characterize the kernel: its side length $KERNEL\_SIZE$, and the number of output channels C_OUT. We generate the layers varying each parameter separately. Specifically, the parameter W and H can take the values 7, 128 or 256. The parameter C_IN ranges between 3 and 2048 with a multiplicative factor of 32. 384 and 768 were also added to these values. The parameter KERNEL_SIZE ranges between 1 and 11 with an increment factor of 1. The parameter C_OUT ranges between 8 and 1024 with a multiplicative factor of 2, 384 and 768 were also added to these values. The stride and padding parameters are set to 1.

Our python script `tool-prepare-dataset` generates a dataset of performances by executing NNTest over several artificial CNN shapes. The dataset is stored in a `.csv` as list of tuples, each containing the feature set of the layer a label with the fastest implementation. An example is reported in Fig. 1.

```
1  ,W,H,C_IN,KERNEL_SIZE,C_OUT (filters count),STRIDE,PAD,,Layer name
2  ,7,7,256,1,256,1,1,,Test 1
3  ,7,7,256,1,512,1,1,,Test 2
4  ,7,7,256,1,1024,1,1,,Test 3
5  ,7,7,256,3,256,1,1,,Test 4
6  ,7,7,256,3,512,1,1,,Test 5
7  ........................
8  ,X1,X2,X3,X4,X5,X6,X7,,Test N
```

Fig. 1. Example of tensor shapes.

After generation, each input shape was used to evaluate the three implementations provided by the ARM Compute Library and by CK NNTest: direct convolution, winograd, Image to column and GEMM. This step returns two different files as output. The first one is used by existing ML framework (.arff file) like Weka [9] and Scikit-learn [15]. The second one represent the dataset. Each row is a pair (tensor, label). Specifically the label is an ordered list of pairs (algorithm name, execution time).

Training. In this phase, we trained the Bayesian and the decision tree classifiers on the dataset. The training, in our case carried through the Scikit-Learn python library, aimed to predict performances of convolution implementation based on the feature set of a layer.

In our code, the pyhton script modelGenerator.py, takes an .arff dataset file as input and outputs a .joblib file that contains the trained model. Based on the information contained in the .arff and .csv file from the dataset generation phase, we derived the optimal classifier parameter to be used in the next phase for the model evaluation.

Model Evaluation. Finally, we evaluate the quality of the model in terms of accuracy and performance. We test our classifiers on two real-world CNNs: Inception v3 [18], composed by 66 convolution layers, and MobileNets, composed by 15 convolution layers.

In our code, for each network we initialize a new classifier, loading in memory the data of the previously trained .joblib model. Our script scans the .csv layers list and follows this procedure:

- The classifier predicts the fastest algorithm for the current layer.
- The script retrieves the optimal implementation using the ranking file, for comparison with the classifier's choice.
- The script stores the calculation times of the three implementation, and the classifier prediction.

Finally, a summary is generated, storing the calculation time of the entire network. The results are plotted in a figure such as Fig. 3a, the details of which will be explained in the next section.

5 Preliminary Results

Before discussing preliminary results, we describe the hardware/software infrastructure used for the experiment below.

5.1 Experimental Setup

The hardware setup used for the tests is an ARM Soc with an ARM Mali-T860 equipped with 4 Mali core able to operate at 2 GHz of frequency and 4 GB of DDR3.

We used the ARM Compute Library, an open-source collection of low-level routines optimized for ARM CPU and GPU architectures targeted at image processing, computer vision, and machine learning. It provides basic arithmetic, mathematical, and binary operators and CNN building blocks. As for convolution, it is implemented in three different ways: image to column and GEMM, direct convolution and Winograd. All those methods can be selected at run-time. Depending on the ARM architecture, numeric precision and specific input each methods can exhibit different performance [12,22].

For benchmarks of each convolution implementation and for the generation of the datasets we used the NNTest library [8,12], an open-source library for collaboratively validating, benchmarking and optimizing neural net operators across platforms, frameworks and datasets.

Concerning the model generation frameworks, we use Weka and Scikit-learn. They provide several classification, regression and clustering algorithms. This was used for the training, the tuning and the validation of predictive models.

5.2   Results

In the present section we evaluate the performance of the predictive models trained by a DT and nBC against the implementations of the convolution operator provided by the ARM Compute Library. We analyze the accuracy of the classifiers as well as the execution time of the ARM Compute Library by using predictive models. In Fig. 2b and Fig. 3b, we show the inference phase by using "Inception v3" CNN.

On top of each picture we indicate the classifiers used for training the predictive model, the numerical precision, the convolution neural network and the related number of layers. In each figures, the Y axis represents the execution time needed to perform the convolution operator over of all the layers (microseconds). The columns denote the execution time of each different implementation of convolution:

- image to column and GEMM method;
- direct convolution method;
- Winograd method;
- method predicted by the model;
- the possible best algorithm oracle (the oracle gives information about the best algorithm. The best algorithm is selected by choosing the one with the minimum execution time between Winograd, Image to column and GEMM, Direct Convolution for the layer currently analyzed.)

Table 1. Classifier: naive Bayes classifier

	Accuracy	vs IMG to column and GEMM	vs Direct convolution	vs Winograd
MobileNets	93.33%	0.99X	3.02X	winograd failed
Inception v3	81.82%	1.14X	2.48X	winograd failed

Table 2. Classifier: decision tree

	Accuracy	vs IMG to column and GEMM	vs Direct convolution	vs Winograd
MobileNets	100.00%	1.00X	3.04X	winograd failed
Inception v3	96.97%	1.15X	2.51X	winograd failed

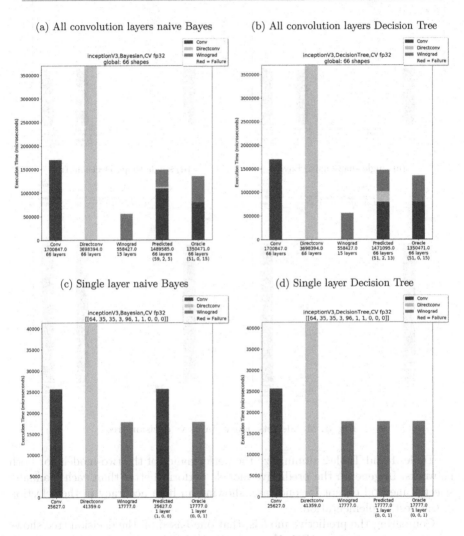

(a) All convolution layers naive Bayes　　　(b) All convolution layers Decision Tree

(c) Single layer naive Bayes　　　(d) Single layer Decision Tree

Fig. 2. Inception V3: naive Bayes vs decision tree

Below each column we report the total time in microseconds and the number of layers correctly completed. In addition, the columns related to the predictive model and the oracle report a triple representing the times *image to column and GEMM*, *direct convolution* and *Winograd* have been selected by that method.

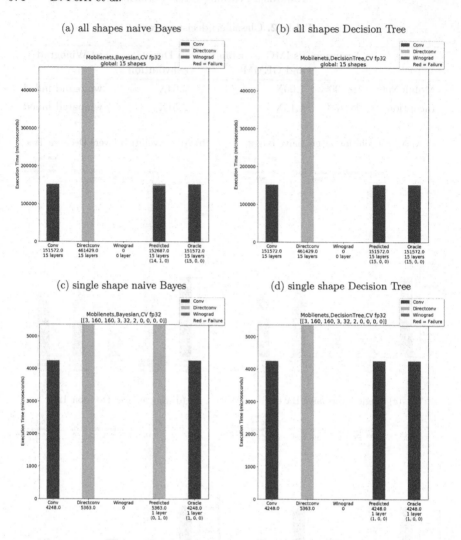

Fig. 3. MobileNets: naive Bayes vs decision tree

Tables 1 and Table 2 summarize the performance of the two models for both networks. In general, the predictive models perform better than each manually selected method except for one case, showing an high accuracy in the selection of the best implementation.

Comparing the predictive models, that one based on the decision tree shows a better accuracy than nBC. However the overall computation times are still comparable.

The results for InceptionV3 are detailed in Fig. 2a. In the two top images the performance over the whole network are shown. The performances of the models learned from both classifiers are slightly worse than the optimal ones. However, the library that uses the model driven approach achieves an improvement over the handed-selected methods.

In the bottom images, a specific layer has been considered. In this example, the model based on the Bayesian approach erroneously selected a GEMM convolution instead of Winograd. Contrarily, the decision tree make the right prediction.

The same analysis is reported for MobileNets in Fig. 3a. For this network, the optimal convolution implementation was always GEMM. In general, the model learned by the decision tree shows better performance than the model based on naive Bayes classifier and the statically selected methods.

6   Conclusions and Future Work

We investigate the opportunity of using learned models to accelerate convolution operator in the case of a library that exhibits multiple implementations. We evaluate our predictive models on two different CNN, InsectionV3 and MobileNet (inference phase) on a low-power consumption ARM GPU.

Our approach outperforms the ARM Compute Library with speed-ups up to $3x$. Future developments are going to focus on the improvement of the predictive models with more sophisticated and tunable classifiers. Also, since the dataset generation is the most expensive part of the proposed methodology, we are going to investigate solutions based on reinforcement learning. We will also explore predictive models for accelerating irregular application like graph analytics [1, 21], for selecting the best parallel strategy on GPU [7] or optimizing communication on distributed systems [5].

Acknowledgments. We thank *Dividiti Inc.* for the huge support on CK and NNTest and for providing hardware resources.

References

1. Bernaschi, M., Bisson, M., Mastrostefano, E., Vella, F.: Multilevel parallelism for the exploration of large-scale graphs. IEEE Trans. Multi-scale Comput. Syst. **4**(3), 204–216 (2018)
2. Cho, M., Brand, D.: MEC: memory-efficient convolution for deep neural network. CoRR, abs/1706.06873 (2017)
3. Cianfriglia, M., Vella, F., Nugteren, C., Lokhmotov, A., Fursin, G.: A model-driven approach for a new generation of adaptive libraries. arXiv preprint arXiv:1806.07060 (2018)
4. Cosenza, B., Durillo, J.J., Ermon, S., Juurlink, B.: Autotuning stencil computations with structural ordinal regression learning. In: 2017 IEEE International Parallel and Distributed Processing Symposium (IPDPS), pp. 287–296. IEEE (2017)
5. Di Girolamo, S., Vella, F., Hoefler, T.: Transparent caching for RMA systems. In: 2017 IEEE International Parallel and Distributed Processing Symposium (IPDPS), pp. 1018–1027. IEEE (2017)
6. Falch, T.L., Elster, A.C.: Machine learning based auto-tuning for enhanced OpenCL performance portability. In: 2015 IEEE International Parallel and Distributed Processing Symposium Workshop (IPDPSW), pp. 1231–1240. IEEE (2015)

7. Formisano, A., Gentilini, R., Vella, F.: Accelerating energy games solvers on modern architectures. In: Proceedings of the Seventh Workshop on Irregular Applications: Architectures and Algorithms, p. 12. ACM (2017)
8. Fursin, G., Temam, O.: Collective optimization: a practical collaborative approach. ACM Trans. Archit. Code Optim. (TACO) **7**(4), 20 (2010)
9. Hall, M., Frank, E., Holmes, G., Pfahringer, B., Reutemann, P., Witten, I.H.: The weka data mining software: an update. ACM SIGKDD Explor. Newslett. **11**(1), 10–18 (2009)
10. Hou, K., Feng, W.-c., Che, S.: Auto-tuning strategies for parallelizing sparse matrix-vector (SPMV) multiplication on multi-and many-core processors. In: 2017 IEEE International Parallel and Distributed Processing Symposium Workshops (IPDPSW), pp. 713–722. IEEE (2017)
11. Krizhevsky, A., Sutskever, I., Hinton, G.E.: Imagenet classification with deep convolutional neural networks. Adv. Neural Inf. Process. Syst. **25**, 1097–1105 (2012)
12. Lokhmotov, A., Chunosov, N., Vella, F., Fursin, G.: Multi-objective autotuning of mobilenets across the full software/hardware stack. In: Proceedings of the 1st on Reproducible Quality-Efficient Systems Tournament on Co-designing Pareto-efficient Deep Learning, p. 6. ACM (2018)
13. Maron, M.E.: Automatic indexing: an experimental inquiry. J. ACM (JACM) **8**(3), 404–417 (1961)
14. Nugteren, C., Codreanu, V.: CLTune: a generic auto-tuner for OpenCL kernels. In: 2015 IEEE 9th International Symposium on Embedded Multicore/Many-core Systems-on-Chip (MCSoC), pp. 195–202 (2015)
15. Pedregosa, F., et al.: Scikit-learn: machine learning in python. J. Mach. Learn. Res. **12**, 2825–2830 (2011)
16. Safavian, S.R., Landgrebe, D.: A survey of decision tree classifier methodology. IEEE Trans. Syst. Man Cybern. **21**(3), 660–674 (1991)
17. Singer, B., Veloso, M.: Learning to predict performance from formula modeling and training data. In: ICML, pp. 887–894 (2000)
18. Szegedy, C., Vanhoucke, V., Ioffe, S., Shlens, J., Wojna, Z.: Rethinking the inception architecture for computer vision. In: Proceedings of the IEEE Conference on Computer Vision and Pattern Recognition, pp. 2818–2826 (2016)
19. Tasso, S., Gervasi, O., Vella, F., Cuzzocrea, A.: A simulation framework for efficient resource management on hybrid systems. In: 2015 IEEE 18th International Conference on Computational Science and Engineering, pp. 216–223. IEEE (2015)
20. Vasudevan, A., Anderson, A., Gregg, D.: Parallel multi channel convolution using general matrix multiplication. CoRR, abs/1704.04428 (2017)
21. Vella, F., Bernaschi, M., Carbone, G.: Dynamic merging of frontiers for accelerating the evaluation of betweenness centrality. J. Exp. Algorithmics (JEA) **23**, 1–4 (2018)
22. Zheng, L., Chen, T.: Optimizing deep learning workloads on arm GPU with TVM. In: Proceedings of the 1st on Reproducible Quality-Efficient Systems Tournament on Co-Designing Pareto-Efficient Deep Learning, p. 3. ACM (2018)

Equid—A Static Analysis Framework for Industrial Applications

Maxim Menshikov[✉]

Saint Petersburg State University, 7–9, Universitetskaya nab.,
St. Petersburg 199034, Russian Federation
info@menshikov.org

Abstract. The rise of the software engineering industry sparkled the research on static analyzers in both academia and industry. Academic tools historically have an exhaustive feature set but don't easily apply to industrial applications, and industrial verifiers are still very limited. The Equid project, which loosely stands for "Engine for performing queries on unified intermediate representations of program and domain models" is an attempt to fill the gap between theory and practice by building a language-agnostic analyzer in close contact with development and security community. In this introductory paper we set project goals, reveal motivation and describe code processing stages, such as preprocessing, translation to project's own intermediate codes, virtual machine execution, constraint solving, all done to make static and interactive contract violation checks easier, more precise yet informative. The project is compared to other analyzers. We believe that such a framework can draw attention to industrial uses clearly missed by verification communities and help shape a vision of universal static analyzer architectures.

Keywords: Static analysis framework · Virtual machine ·
Intermediate representation · Type system · Multi Solver ·
Generalized Syntax Tree · Language-agnostic analysis

1 Introduction

Developing large software packages comprising numerous tools, especially when depending on specialized hardware, is hard. A number of bugs can occur at different abstraction layers—operating system core, shell, network setup, userland or even hardware levels. Searching for an error in such an environment is tedious, and static analyzer's abilities in this field are limited by the authors' vision. In many situations, built-in universal detectors are not enough to detect and fix the issue. Moreover, extinguishing the error fire is pointless if the analysis is not integrated into the development environment. Inability to find a satisfying utility becomes a major reason behind stopping using verification at all [9]. Academic tools aren't easy to use and thus are hard to enforce at a corporate level. With rich software "forward"- and reverse engineering experience, we aim to fill this

© Springer Nature Switzerland AG 2019
S. Misra et al. (Eds.): ICCSA 2019, LNCS 11619, pp. 677–692, 2019.
https://doi.org/10.1007/978-3-030-24289-3_50

gap by making our own framework designed for industrial applications. This paper is the first attempt to present our perception of static analysis field.

Project's goal. Make a static analyzer which would fit industrial applications, be universal and customizable to a reasonable extent. Support C and RuC [24] languages.

Paper's goal. Introduce an analyzer framework and its internals to a wider audience, describe the approaches to memory modeling and code execution. We understand that it is impossible to cover all aspects of the tool within a single paper well enough, nevertheless, having a starting point for consequent papers is highly desirable.

Motivation. Authors are not aware of the tools doing precise yet refinable analysis and integrating properly to the development of industrial applications: the tools are usually black boxes. The RuC (a safer alternative to C) support suggested by A.N. Terekhov required a tunable verifier to suit current and future language features.

Novelty. The project is an example of unique architecture for performing various kinds of analyses based on virtual machine framework. The focus on memory operation precision through the type system. The Multi Solver, combining SMT and Abstract Interpretation results. RuC support.

The paper is organized as follows. An architecture for multi-language support and flow- and context-sensitive analyses is outlined in Sects. 3 and 4, the solver and type system design is explained in Sect. 5. The common infrastructure is shown in Sect. 6. The whole solution is evaluated in Sect. 7.

1.1 Industrial Applications

In the quest for supporting industrial applications, the development is based upon the following observations:

- Industrial tools are usually large and debugged to some extent, the occurrence of memory corruption and other undesired events is unlikely. That makes the extensive state space exploration redundant. Of course, some critical components might need it.
- Static analysis tools in the best case must be *supplementary to the programming process*: it is hard to prove *all* the algorithms automatically, so the developer should help the tool. As large code bases tend to suffer from ownership problems (nobody besides the author can understand what is going on inside, sometimes even he can not), the contracts are a natural extension to the documentation.
- Contracts—not only functional but also memory access, etc—are usually enough to find the majority of observable bugs.

- There are cases when state space exploration on demand is required. The trivial example is using buggy third-party modules, which are for some reason mandatory (e.g. platform drivers). We won't cover queries in this paper as this is definitely worth an additional investigation.
- The static analyzer has to support "night analysis", load distribution and must be easily invokable.

This leads to a conclusion that a good tool is not necessarily able to prove all the properties, but should rather help the developer write a readable, better documented, more reviewable code. However, it doesn't mean the support of state-of-art techniques is omitted, we are all hands for it and develop them, but it might be impractical to focus on it before getting more feedback from current users.

2 Operation Schema and Classes of Detectable Errors

The project is schematically depicted in Fig. 1 (explanation follows). It is aimed at finding a few specific error classes:

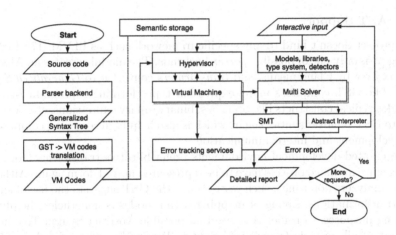

Fig. 1. Full analyzer's operation flowchart

1. **Contract violations.** This is done on the basis of the model checker generating SMT formulas out of the virtual machine operational codes.
   Advantages of the analyzer in this area: the arbitrary level of memory abstraction precision (through the use of CPU/Compiler/type abstractions).
2. **Memory safety errors.** This class of errors is detected by a combination of the model checker and abstract interpreter.
   Advantages: controllable memory abstraction level. Precision is modifiable.
3. **Always reachable/unreachable paths.** Such error conditions are detected by using a model checker.
4. **AST errors, e.g. duplicate operands.** This is detected on the Generalized Syntax Tree (GST) level. Advantages: GST detectors may get insight from other levels.

The project uses a notion of a Semantic Storage. This entity is responsible for saving, retrieving and grouping of Resources, Fragments, Expressions, Virtual Machine codes and other artifacts of the analysis process, saved in an internal format and augmented with key-value metadata. It is essentially a MongoDB database running the background. The use of the database is not mandatory as long as the artifacts may fit into the RAM, large projects may get a substantial stability improvement using it. The aim is to cover it extensively in a separate paper, but parts of it are mentioned in [19].

The other benefit of the analyzer is that it brings lingual agnosticism: analysis is the same for any language and adding a new one is not time-consuming. All kinds of analysis are glued up through common communication means. Objects have properties, such as name, invocation context, GST/SMT mapping, etc, which are saved to a semantic data storage and are accessible at an arbitrary time by developed detectors, which in general work on the top of Virtual Machine operational codes.

3   Processing Architecture

3.1   AST Support

The project doesn't bind to any specific framework such as LLVM [17]. Instead, Clang [2] is only one of possible *parser* backends. The module creates an Abstract Syntax Tree by Clang means, and *transformers* convert it to *Generalized Syntax Tree*. The GST comprises many expression types forming a program *basis*—it includes typical constructs like branches, binary/unary expressions, etc. A transition to GST removes syntax sugar, which is also helpful in removing complexities of development and intercommunication.

Integrated development environments prefer bijective transformers for refactoring since modified objects have to be represented in AST form again. Although static analyzers don't have such restriction—the GST suggests the use of surjective transformations, saving of mapping within nodes is nonetheless helpful for printing purposes. Consider A a set of all possible Abstract Syntax Tree nodes, G a set of all possible Generalized Syntax Tree nodes. Then $f : A \rightarrow G$ is a transformer from AST to GST.

From a technical standpoint, the A is heavily bound to parser's implementation. The GST and transformation schema impose a few implicit restrictions on input parsers. They are enforced within Roslyn and are feasible for Clang.

1. All AST nodes must be inherited from the same base class or be distinguishable anyhow. As Clang declaration and statement nodes are distinct, an additional wrapper around A is formed.
2. Each AST node must have a parent and explicit children.

3.2   Languages

The analyzer supports two languages: C and RuC. LLVM/Clang provides support for C, and the transformation between LLVM/Clang and GST is currently mostly 1-1. The second language, besides obvious Unicode keywords (which are easily removable), supports syntax sugar for threads. The initial support is added via decomposition to functions invokable in place.

The design of the GST generally supports C#, so the applicability to object-oriented programming languages is trivial, although such use requires a mangling of method names and injection of metadata to GST. Functional programming languages require GST improvements. However, due to the industrial use background, the project focuses its efforts on C-like languages.

Another important role of GST is to mine useful persistent relations between program statements. Consider $X = (x_1, x_2, ..., x_n)$ an ordered set of same-level statements, where $x_i \in X$ $(i = 1...n)$ is a single statement. If there exists some property separating a set to two distinct (possibly, empty) ordered sets, it is possible to find a separator $F(X) = \{(x_1, x_2, .., x_{n_1}), (x_{n_1+1}, ..., x_n)\}$, where x_{n_1} is a separator statement. At the end of this operation, we get two ordered sets X_1, X_2. If there are multiple properties, the rule is to separate sets sequentially.

A one-pass analysis might employ a conservative sequential algorithm. Consider $X_1, X_2, ..., X_m$ ordered sets produced on previous stages (in a degenerate case, X_1 might be the only set, and it might be empty). Then each new statement forms a single-element set X', which is either appended to X_m in case there is no separator for (X_m, X'), or renamed to a set X_{m+1} used in next iterations.

These sets are called *fragments* in the analyzer. Fragments are a convenient way to group statements by various signs, e.g. the convention is that any structural statements (branches, loops) reside in isolated fragments by default, each *locking* call such as **spin_lock** immediately changes the intercommunication environment. Lockset-like analyses are exceptionally trivial because of that. Also, fragments may have designated **goto** labels, a single parent and a number of children. The next fragment in execution order, as well as sibling, can be calculated in a runtime. The GST augmented with such information is called *extended*, and it provides a number of advantages to the traditional AST approach: the Lockset-like analysis, the simplification of processing.

The expressions in Fragments are additionally simplified by means of the analyzer. While this may be considered bad practice since every real-world compiler optimizes and reorders instruction set itself, relying on the other entity like LLVM is even more dangerous because it still suggests one specific untraceable behavior. The manual simplification of Fragments gives a possibility to at least add meta information that expression is potentially dangerous.

4   Virtual Machine Framework for Flow and Context Sensitivity

The Virtual Machine framework is *by the very nature of it* a symbolic execution engine yet in a traditional, not program analysis sense. It keeps a track of entry point sets, executes Virtual Machine codes and maintains the resource aggregation. All the *actual* analysis is outsourced to the Solver framework, meaning that Virtual Machines do no more than just a provision of flow- and context-sensitivity. In this section, we define high-level means used to make it so.

4.1   Virtual Machine Language

Extended GST is not a convenient form for a flow-sensitive analysis, although it can be used to find simple mistakes. Understanding a real execution order in presence of syntax sugar (e.g. **goto, break**) requires a different representation.

LLVM IR and similar intermediate codes resembling machine execution is the usual solution for this issue. During the early evaluation the following problems were observed for an environment without intermediate code between LLVM → SMT/other verification means:

1. Loading/storing various analyzer-specific globals is impossible without making an IR augmented with some other kind of instructions, or introducing phantom variables.
2. Using third-party project limits parsing to what it supports. Interpreted languages have a good chance of being easier convertible to less hardware-like IR.
3. It doesn't give a chance to introduce custom types not mimicking hardware types.

Project's IR is free of these problems and is bound to flat GST expressions (their grammar is not enforced by IR). IR reveals expression's key properties, i.e. what does the expression actually mean to the analyzer. Part of possible operation code kinds are listed in Table 1 (actually, more kinds are supported). The IR is also bound to semantic storage behind: every referenced resource has ID [19], making it possible to save or unload them dynamically, reducing the memory footprint. This allows using a distributed technology stack and simplifies the process for all consequent analyses.

4.2   Hypervisor and Virtual Machines

A hypervisor is on the top of hierarchy [19], it manages virtual machines running the programs in VM language. When a flow-sensitive analysis is requested, the Hypervisor inserts function summaries (generated using Craig interpolation [18]) or annotations instead of *invoke* calls. In context-sensitive case, a sequence of *enter/exit* operations with function body unrolled to some extent is constituted instead of *invoke*. While simplified extended GST mostly deals with constant values and references, the result of a function call is saved to a designated *Variable* set by *enter* command. By enumerating functions during the execution and flexibility, the Virtual Machine-based framework is fairly effective in achieving flow and context sensitivity.

5   Solver Architecture

The solver's architecture is a core of the whole analyzer. The key to effective operation lies in combining the abstract type system with the results of multiple fairly different solvers.

Table 1. Virtual Machine language operational codes

Command	Description	Example
declare	Fetch a resource from semantic storage and add it to the current visibility area	*declare resource*
assign	Assign a value to a variable	*assign x = y*
branch end branch	Add a condition for next operational codes before enclosing *end branch*	*branch x > 5 assign z = 5 end branch*
check	A condition which is determined to be always false. The body is never processed	*assign x = 0 check x > 0*
constraint	A condition which is determined to be always true. The body is always processed	*assign x = 0 constraint x = 0*
invoke	Invoke a function with a given set of parameters and save the result to a variable	*invoke res = f with arguments (x, y)*
system	Invoke an internal command. Similar to *invoke*, except that internal functions are called by name, not by resource handle	*system assert with arguments (x > 0)*
enter exit	Start a new visibility block, setting where to save results. This function is heavily used for inlining. Must be finished with *exit*	*enter store result \to z*

5.1 Type System

Literals and variables have straight-forward types. Unary expressions mostly resemble the type of their subexpression: parentheses, increments. **Dereference** and **address-of** expressions change inner type indirection level. Ternary operations in C require second and third operands to be of the same type (but it is not a strict requirement in other languages). The hardest are binary expressions which have a very detailed description in C standard [1].

The GST contains a type field in each node whenever it is applicable. In other cases, a static analyzer may deduce the type from expression's semantic meaning (defined by the target language) and subexpression types.

The other problem is that machine representation for unambiguous types can be different (mostly varying by endianness in the real world), and compiler chooses the most adequate representation for ambiguous types, e.g. plain **int** might be signed or unsigned, 2^n bit long. The CPU choice might limit the integer to 32 bit or any other target architecture register size. Any analyzer which tends to be type-precise, not necessarily supporting type reinterpretations, has to take this into account. For Equid, a variety of low-level types was created, as

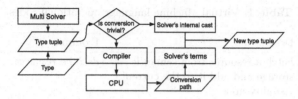

Fig. 2. Type conversions in the presence of cheap and expensive methods

well as their symbolic and numerical conversions to and from the *widest* types, all glued together via CPU and Compiler classes for various vendors/versions. Precise conversions are costly, so each solver might employ a different cheap schema for trivial cases, e.g. CPU endianness means not much for properly coded applications. Those which don't obey the compatibility rules might enable costly abstraction and decrease the efficiency of the whole analysis process.

The schema of type conversions is provided in Fig. 2. Mentioned *tuples* are introduced in consequent paragraphs.

5.2 SMT Solver Backend

Theorem solver supporting major SMT features is essential to an analyzer: it is used for contract violation checks. The project turns the whole function(s) to a set of *assert* clauses and checks the negation of the *goal*.

The reason for choosing CVC4 [6] as the main solver is that it is robust and provides a well-defined native C++ interface. The latter is notable since intensive input/output operations may have an impact on performance. The number of theories supported by CVC4 is impressive [4]. The infrastructure is not limited to this solver, however, major efforts are put into separating CVC4 responsibilities from the rest of the analyzer. They include:

- Effective assignment *access path* generation must be done in target solver's framework. Access path in terms of our project is a variable with a collection of transformations, required to actually assign a value to that variable. To understand why is it important, consider the following example. $array[x] = y$ in terms of imperative languages is only suitable for initialization, the real assignment is slightly different: $array = old\_array\ WITH\ [x] := y$. In more complex left expressions, e.g. $array[x].member1[y][z].member2$, the need for access path is more obvious.
- The generic type system doesn't depend on the solver, but cheap casts must reuse as many solver's abilities as possible—they include truncation/widening of bit vectors, built-in casts operation. Also, as there is no direct mapping between C types and CVC4 types, so they are passed inside the analyzer in tuples (t_s, t), where $t_s \in T_s$ is a solver's type and $t \in T$ is a real type. This way the cast operation can always perform the conversion from (T_s, T) to (T_s, T'), choosing the most appropriate T'_s.
- Predicate system is implemented entirely in solver's terms mainly because not all solvers actually need predicates.

5.3 Abstract Interpreter

Built-in abstract interpreter augments the SMT formula of the main solver with the knowledge retrieved in the form of abstract domains—interval or polyhedral (still in development). At one hand, it interprets the Virtual Machine codes, produces an over-approximation of the semantics. This over-approximation is passed to the Model Checker, causing it to reduce the state space for SMT [11], which results in improved precision. On the other hand, a secondary solver like this is capable of detecting errors on its own, especially when combined with a described type system and symbolic/numeric domains developed for these purposes. A trivial abstract interpreter is also used for pointer analysis. The abstract interpreter is actively participating in CEGAR [10]-like analysis. In our tests, it doesn't have any significant influence on analysis time.

5.4 The Multi Solver

The power of both solvers is combined in one Multi Solver (MS). The main idea is that SMT solver and Abstract Interpreter collect their own data sets and save it to MS context, which is extremely volatile because of its flow/context-sensitive nature. The processing is as follows (Fig. 3):

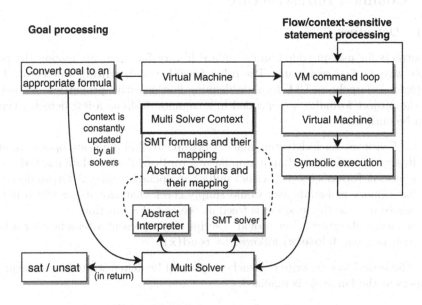

Fig. 3. Multi Solver operation scheme

1. Each virtual machine creates a context based on rules provided by Hypervisor.
2. VM codes are processed by VM itself.
3. VM codes are passed to Multi Solver:

(a) *Branches, loops*: MS processes such commands by wrapping the inner commands into blocks, excluding them if they are unreachable. At the end of branch/loop processing, MS wraps inner commands to the conditions more correct from **else if** point of view.

(b) Other commands are passed to SMT/AI solvers. The SMT solver produces SMT formulas for each program statement and AI solver generates abstract domains. This information is saved to the SMT/AI context both of which are parts of MS context.

4. Goals are passed to Multi Solver:

(a) The MS chooses the most convenient interpretation of formulas for the specific case. There are cases when unaltered abstraction is superior (e.g. when analyzed program state space is reasonably small), in other cases, like when the loop is potentially boundless or at least not proven to be different, the overapproximation replaces it.

(b) The sat/unsat result is provided.

Our implementation may also refine the abstraction, but this part is not ready for presentation. We found the described algorithm effective in real-world applications.

6   Common Infrastructure

6.1   Detectors

Contracts for user-provided and standard library functions are among the possible ways to find real issues. The other feasible way is writing a detector. The detector is largely an LTL formula defining flow-sensitive properties. Although in the project formulas are encoded in a common fashion, a few detector types can be outlined:

1. GST visitors. Such detectors make it possible to find duplicate operands, etc.
2. Resource/variable markup manipulators. **malloc** allocates data marked up as *allocated*, **fopen**'s result is either null or an opened handle. A trivial detector for memory or handle leak would simply check that any object which is not passed outside the function is freed at the end of a function.
3. Sequence observers. User-provided script might present a template for a bad sequence, e.g. **fclose(x)** followed by **read(x)**.

The actual way to write out such scripts will be demonstrated in consequent papers as the language is finalized.

6.2   Standard Library

A standard library for C and RuC is physically located in separate header files, which are preloaded to a semantic context on each analyzer's start. We have a prototype recompiling annotations to C code with over sixfold faster load, thanks to missing parser invocation. The processing of library functions is a

MapReduce-like approach [21], in a sense that they are by default tagged as *non-existent* and are replaced with real implementation if the user overrides it.

Annotations are provided in ACSL form[1]. The project features an ANTLR [23]-based parser transforming the input to GST, therefore all solver/virtual machine APIs can take advantage of the ACSL just like the annotations are simply statements inside the code. The assert clauses are directly mapped to *assert* VM commands and preconditions/postconditions turn to check/constraint/nop commands based on the context: obvious omissions are made for start entry points, a currently verified function, etc. The contracts overall provide an extremely fast initial bug search.

7   Evaluation

In this section, we check the resulting framework synthetically and practically.

7.1   Syntax Construct Support

The syntax support requires teamwork of many modules, and the following syntax constructions (beyond simple ones) work in the project:

1. The GST natively supports real functions and generally promotes their native invocation. Self-modifying code is strongly prohibited, and call indirection works only within visibility range, which might be set in globals, within a single function or within investigated call chain. Thus, the analyzer is not applicable for the cases with many accessors. There is a workaround for the problem—a declarative pointer analysis, in which pointer targets are set within ACSL comments.
2. Branches and loops are processed within the bounded model checking framework, and when this is not enough to prove properties—abstract interpreter provides a safe abstraction of them. Still, it is not precise and we aim at the unbounded processing.
3. Array support involves a kind of shape analysis with array summaries. This ensures the precision in the most common cases (e.g. sequential array reads) but is extremely overapproximating in random access tests and large objects. The abstraction might turn to a more precise one in case the object is reasonably small (the actual size is configurable).
4. Unions are not supported properly. The support is generally provided (on the basis of memory abstraction), but no major efforts had been put into making it work properly.
5. The **goto** instruction is very widespread in C programs for safer resource deallocation in error cases. It is supported by Fragments and transparently propagated to all layers. Jumps (e.g. **setjmp**) are supported, but their use is discouraged because they break the fragment model.

---

[1] https://github.com/maximmenshikov/acsl-grammar.

7.2   Common Errors and Contract Violations

Significant efforts were put into testing software on real many-purpose industrial projects. Our example included a 500 KLOC operating system management application.

For the project, domain-specific rules were added in the form of ACSL function models. The following modifications were required:

1. It was determined that in such specific use cases it is required to add a *declarative* pointer analysis. The core of the application is considered stable, however, a number of ways to perform indirect function call complicate analysis. Declarative pointer analysis is based on the notion of function aliases, e.g. */feature/x/enable* tree-like name instead of cryptic internal names. After such a modification analyzer was able to find common contract violations.
2. The tested project also had weaknesses undetected by any other analyzer (e.g. uninitialized structure members) due to cryptic module structure. With the verifier aware of it, all weaknesses were detected. While the efforts for supporting such project were significant (a few days to support the whole project), most of the modifications were needed due to the immaturity of the analyzer.

Of course, numerous errors were found in the analyzer during the evaluation. The project suffered from all sorts of null pointer dereferences and other unpredicted situations, which is not uncommon [7]. For example, the project was not expecting nested functions to appear that often and therefore lacked an entry point selection for that case.

7.3   Toyota ITC Benchmarks

In the author's master thesis, the analyzer was tested against a supported subset of Toyota ITC benchmarks. The actual versions at the moment of writing were **Clang 3.9, Frama-C Silicon, cppcheck 1.76**—for this test, we reused the results from [20]. The *w_Defects* part was analyzed and compared to other analyzers. A solid percentage of detections was achieved—like 90% of bugs in supported categories (Table 2). For all such cases, the project acts similarly to Frama-C, sometimes worse, sometimes a bit better.

However, the test doesn't include inter-procedural analysis and many other aspects, so the evaluation is incomplete. A bigger evaluation is scheduled after planned functionality improvements.

Table 2. Error detection count with Toyota ITC benchmarks

Test	Equid	Frama-C	Clang	cppcheck	Total
bit_shift	17	17	14	11	17
buffer_overrun_dynamic	30	32	1	2	32
buffer_underrun_dynamic	35	39	2	3	39
data_lost	19	3	—	—	19
data_overflow	25	16	—	9	25
data_underflow	12	8	—	5	12
littlemem_st	11	11	—	—	11
null_pointer	15	16	13	12	17
overrun_st	47	54	2	21	54
ptr_subtraction	2	1	—	—	2
underrun_st	13	13	2	5	13
uninit_pointer	10	16	11	5	16
zero_division	16	16	13	8	16

7.4 Querying Code

One of the project's ongoing development processes is deep querying of software properties. The querying language is not yet ready for public presentation, therefore it is a subject for disclosing in consequent papers. By and large, the language is an LTL which augments Virtual Machine codes, which are later proven by Multi Solver.

The author managed to apply it to a limited scope of a large 3rd party Linux kernel driver (500+ KLOC) and find reasons for errors in it. It required some efforts to build proper models—but no automatic search tools were able to catch most of the problems in such a badly structured code. It can be considered a success.

7.5 The Computational Cost of the Approach

At this early stage, we were unable to properly verify how the approach compares with other analyzers in terms of computational cost, yet we *estimated* if the costs are at least sane. Yet in our preliminary estimations, the time to analyze files is comparable with Frama-C [16].

Looking through the process, there are a few basic steps. *Source to GST transformation* doesn't add up significantly because it is almost stateless (*Resources* are the part of GST, but there are relatively little of them compared to expressions). *GST to VM code* mapping is not cheap, although it is hard to find an analyzer which doesn't do this in any form (GCC/LLVM [17] IR, CIL [22]). So, this can be considered as not harmful. The algorithm doesn't overestimate SMT and tries to reuse as many computations as possible. Thus the cost of the whole solution solely depends on the abstraction, which can be refined.

The RAM/ROM usage may go higher when using distributed technology stack [19]. This is expected and therefore not harmful.

8 Related Work

There is no deficiency in this research area.

The CPAChecker [8] platform is by far the closest project ideologically. It aims to make the analysis configurable just as our project does, additionally, it provides interfaces to SMT solvers, interpolation, octagon and BDD libraries. CPAChecker only supports C. It uses CIL [22] language as an intermediate representation. Frama-C [16] is great regarding precision and informativeness [20], and it is full of plugins. Also, our project uses the same format for annotations—ACSL. SPIN [14] is specifically bound to checking models in the specific format. We prefer a smaller and more readable format for industrial applications which won't result in writing a completely separate model, but it is impossible to underestimate the contribution of this model checker to a verification field.

Svace [15] is an effort of the Institute of System Programming to make a universal static analyzer for C/C++/Java/C#. A lightweight analysis is started for each language, the main part generates a call graph and then a set of checkers test routines against known problems. We find the analyzer polished, with incremental analysis and a web interface for results. The project is battle-tested in Android and Tizen operating systems. Borealis [5] is one of the examples with similar technical means—it features a Model Checking combined with Abstract Interpretation, just like Equid. However, it is based upon LLVM IR, which is closer to metal than our language. Absence of GST limits input languages yet simplifies the initial development. The goal of our project is a bit shifted towards industrial applications.

The intermediate representations have gone a long way. The most famous IR is LLVM [17], which is essentially an assembler-like language. SAIL [12] is providing a good IR-to-source mapping and is used for almost the same purposes as our language—reducing the need to reason about complex expressions. The good point about it is an integration with GCC which results in low overhead. REIL [13] is more focused on disassembling input files. Frama-C [16] and CPA Checker [8] use modified CIL (C intermediate language). Even judging by its name, it is limited to C language. Roslyn [3] (.NET Compiler Platform) shares ideas of GST (in a sense that common syntax nodes can be used for both C# and Visual Basic.NET), and the Common Intermediate Language is a distant analog for Virtual Machine Language, although not made specifically for static analysis purposes. Overall, no project specifically aims at using separate semantic storage, additionally simplifying the use of distributed technology stack.

9 Future Work

Although the first results are promising, there is still a lot of work to do. The author is looking towards improving abstract interpreter. More advanced domains are in progress, a stricter abstraction refinement for type system is also being developed. The solver system requires a more complex pointer analysis than implemented at the moment of writing. Further augmenting the Virtual

Machine language with environment/resource model data is a way forward to the whole proving process.

Another part to care about is threading support. It is important as is for all languages, but is essential [25] for covering a complete set of RuC functionality. It was done in the first version—a race condition finder but was largely forgotten in the new version. In the end, the analyzer needs countless improvements on library annotations, the full project runs, etc.

10   Conclusion

The paper introduced Equid, a static analyzer for industrial applications. Main algorithms used in the analyzer are presented. The parsing approach is based on the notion of Generalized Syntax Tree, which is a unification of C/RuC abstract syntax trees. The Hypervisor/Virtual Machine framework for flow- and context sensitivity is presented. We describe our solution for verifying function contracts, a part of Multi Solver combining Abstract Interpretation and Model Checking to one cooperating framework. The analyzer was successfully tested in the telecommunications industry and compared to the known tools, with reasonable success in supported categories. As there are not many frameworks for industrial purposes, we believe that bringing a configurable solution benefits the community and might draw attention to the functionality required for the industry.

References

1. C11 Standard ISO/IEC 9899:2011. https://www.iso.org/standard/57853.html
2. Clang: a C language family frontend for LLVM. http://clang.llvm.org
3. Roslyn -.NET Compiler Platform. https://github.com/dotnet/roslyn
4. SMT-COMP 2018 Results. http://smtcomp.sourceforge.net/2018/results-summary.shtml
5. Akhin, M., Belyaev, M., Itsykson, V.: Borealis bounded model checker: the coming of age story. In: Mazzara, M., Meyer, B. (eds.) Present and Ulterior Software Engineering, pp. 119–137. Springer, Cham (2017). https://doi.org/10.1007/978-3-319-67425-4_8
6. Barrett, C., et al.: CVC4. In: Gopalakrishnan, G., Qadeer, S. (eds.) CAV 2011. LNCS, vol. 6806, pp. 171–177. Springer, Heidelberg (2011). https://doi.org/10.1007/978-3-642-22110-1_14
7. Bessey, A., et al.: A few billion lines of code later: using static analysis to find bugs in the real world. Commun. ACM **53**(2), 66–75 (2010)
8. Beyer, D., Keremoglu, M.E.: CPACHECKER: a tool for configurable software verification. In: Gopalakrishnan, G., Qadeer, S. (eds.) CAV 2011. LNCS, vol. 6806, pp. 184–190. Springer, Heidelberg (2011). https://doi.org/10.1007/978-3-642-22110-1_16
9. Christakis, M., Bird, C.: What developers want and need from program analysis: an empirical study. In: 31st IEEE/ACM International Conference on Automated Software Engineering (ASE), pp. 332–343. IEEE (2016)

10. Clarke, E., Grumberg, O., Jha, S., Lu, Y., Veith, H.: Counterexample-guided abstraction refinement. In: Emerson, E.A., Sistla, A.P. (eds.) CAV 2000. LNCS, vol. 1855, pp. 154–169. Springer, Heidelberg (2000). https://doi.org/10.1007/10722167_15
11. Cousot, P., Cousot, R.: Refining model checking by abstract interpretation. Autom. Soft. Eng. 6(1), 69–95 (1999). https://doi.org/10.1023/A:1008649901864
12. Dillig, I., Dillig, T., Aiken, A.: SAIL: static analysis intermediate language with a two-level representation. Technical report. Stanford University (2009)
13. Dullien, T., Porst, S.: REIL : a platform-independent intermediate representation of disassembled code for static code analysis (2009)
14. Holzmann, G.J.: The model checker SPIN. IEEE Trans. Softw. Eng. 23(5), 279–295 (1997)
15. Ivannikov, V., Belevantsev, A., Borodin, A., Ignatiev, V., Zhurikhin, D., Avetisyan, A.: Static analyzer Svace for finding defects in a source program code. Program Comput. Soft. 40(5), 265–275 (2014). https://doi.org/10.1134/S0361768814050041
16. Kirchner, F., Kosmatov, N., Prevosto, V., Signoles, J., Yakobowski, B.: Frama-C: a software analysis perspective. Form. Asp. Comp. 27(3), 573–609 (2015). https://doi.org/10.1007/s00165-014-0326-7
17. Lattner, C., Adve, V.: LLVM: a compilation framework for lifelong program analysis & transformation. In: Proceedings of the International Symposium on Code Generation and Optimization: Feedback-Directed and Runtime Optimization, p. 75c. IEEE Computer Society (2004)
18. McMillan, K.: Applications of craig interpolation to model checking. In: Marcinkowski, J., Tarlecki, A. (eds.) CSL 2004. LNCS, vol. 3210, pp. 22–23. Springer, Heidelberg (2004). https://doi.org/10.1007/978-3-540-30124-0_3
19. Menshchikov, M.: Scalable semantic virtual machine framework for language-agnostic static analysis. In: Distributed Computing and Grid-technologies in Science and Education, pp. 213–217 (2018)
20. Menshchikov, M., Lepikhin, T.: 5W+1H static analysis report quality measure. In: Itsykson, V., Scedrov, A., Zakharov, V. (eds.) TMPA 2017. CCIS, vol. 779, pp. 114–126. Springer, Cham (2018). https://doi.org/10.1007/978-3-319-71734-0_10
21. Menshchikov, M.A., Lepikhin, T.A.: Applying MapReduce to static analysis. Control Proc. Stab. 4(1), 433–444 (2017)
22. Necula, G.C., McPeak, S., Rahul, S.P., Weimer, W.: CIL: intermediate language and tools for analysis and transformation of C programs. In: Horspool, R.N. (ed.) CC 2002. LNCS, vol. 2304, pp. 213–228. Springer, Heidelberg (2002). https://doi.org/10.1007/3-540-45937-5_16
23. Parr, T.: The definitive ANTLR 4 reference. Pragmatic Bookshelf (2013)
24. Terekhov, A.N.: Programming and compiler techniques educational tool. Comput. Tools Educ. 1, 36–47 (2016)
25. Terekhov, A.N., Golovan, A.A., Terekhov, M.A.: Parallel programs in RuC project. Comput. Tools Educ. 2, 25–30 (2018)

Metalanguage and Knowledgebase for Kazakh Morphology

Gaziza Yelibayeva$^{(\boxtimes)}$, Assel Mukanova, Altynbek Sharipbay,
Altanbek Zulkhazhav, Banu Yergesh, and Gulmira Bekmanova

L.N. Gumilyov Eurasian National University, Astana, Kazakhstan
gaziza_y@mail.ru, asiserikovna@gmail.com,
sharalt@mail.ru, altinbekpin@gmail.com,
b.yergesh@gmail.com, gulmira-r@yandex.kz

Abstract. Currently, the volume of various information resources in the Turkic languages is increasing. Processing of such resources requires thesauri and corpora created using a single metalanguage (tagging language) and the knowledge base of subject areas. This article proposes a meta-language of the morphological concepts of the Turkic languages on the example of the Kazakh language, which was used to create the knowledge base of the morphology of the Kazakh language in the Protégé environment. The results of the work were used to develop software applications for semantic search and knowledge extraction, as well as an assessment of knowledge applications on the morphology of the Kazakh language in the e-learning system.

Keywords: Kazakh language · Knowledge representation ·
Knowledge extraction · Metalanguage · Morphological rules · Ontology ·
Protégé

1 Introduction

To process natural languages, it is necessary to create a tagging system. The existing metalanguages mainly contain the concepts of the Roman-Germanic and the Slavic language groups. These metalanguages are not suitable for the description of the Turkic languages, which have many concepts different from the mentioned language groups. Therefore, the creation of the UniTurk meta-language for tagging up texts of the Turkic languages, including the Kazakh language, is an urgent task. Such a metalanguage will allow to unify tagging, facilitate their understanding and use common software, and conduct various studies on linguistic-statistical comparative analysis among the Turkic languages [1–3].

The metalanguage is needed to create a common resource with which all the developers of the Turkic electronic corpora could work. Such a resource could serve as a reference system for both developers and users of the Turkic electronic corpora. The most appropriate components of such a resource that meet the required conditions are ontological models of the grammar of the Turkic languages.

It is known that ontologies are used as data sources for many natural language processing applications, they allow to process complex and diverse information in a

S. Misra et al. (Eds.): ICCSA 2019, LNCS 11619, pp. 693–706, 2019.
https://doi.org/10.1007/978-3-030-24289-3_51

more efficient way. When managing knowledge of subject areas, ontological models are applied at the structuring stage and are considered as special knowledge bases. An ontology can act as a knowledge base framework, that is, can create a framework used to describe key concepts related to a specific subject area, and can formally be represented as the following triple [4, 5]:

$$O = <X, R, F>$$ (1)

where X is a finite set of concepts (terms) of the domain, which is represented by the ontology O; R is a finite set of relationships between the concepts (terms) of a given domain; F is a finite set of interpretation functions defined on concepts or relations of ontology O. The role of the interpretation function can be played by a verbal explanation of a term (annotation), a formula for calculating the meaning of a term, an algorithmic description, and also a definition in the form of a logical formula.

Ontological modeling of the morphological concepts of the Kazakh language was done in the Protégé environment, which allows simplifying the process of creating, downloading, changing and transforming the knowledge base, and to provide it for general use for joint viewing and editing [6, 7].

2 Related Works

The metalanguage is designed for tagging up the texts of natural languages and by using its means, it is possible to express all that is expressible by means of the object language and to designate all signs, expressions of the object language, which have names. In the metalanguage, one can express the properties of the object language expression and the relations between them. Here one can formulate definitions, notation, rules of formation and transformation for the objective language expressions [8].

There are well-known tagging systems, such as Penn Treebank [9] and CLAWS tagging system [10], which is used for tagging the British Corpus [9], and the tagging system of the Brownian Corpus in the US National Corpus [11, 12]. The tagging systems are described in more details in [13, 14]. All these systems are mainly used for tagging the English language.

Currently there are more than ten electronic corpora for Turkic languages: the Kazakh language corpus [15–17]; the Tatar language corpus "Tugan tel" [18, 19], the Turkish language corpus [20]; the Crimean Tatar language corpus [21], Chuvash language [22], etc. One of the main components of these corpora is the system of morphological, syntactic and semantic tagging. Morphological tagging systems vary in some corpora.

There are various domain models based on ontology. For example, [23] considers the ontological model of hotel services in order to compare actual reviews with automatically generated ones. Some works [24, 25] present formal models for nouns in the Kazakh language and the use of semantic graphs to describe ontological models. The articles [26, 27] compare the ontological models on the example of the nouns in the Kazakh language with the other Turkic (Kyrgyz and Uzbek) languages, and [28] compares adjectives in the Kazakh and the Turkish languages.

3   Metalanguage for Kazakh Morphology

Table 1 presents the UniTurk tags on the example of the morphology concepts description for the Kazakh language. The first column of the table contains tag designations, the second - designations of the concepts as names in English, the third – tag names in Kazakh.

Table 1.   Tags of the concepts of the Kazakh language morphology.

Tag	Name_English	Name_Kazakh
N	Noun	Зат есім
ANIM	Animate Noun	Жанды зат есім
INAM	Inanimate Noun	Жансыз зат есім
CMMN	Common Noun	Жалпы зат есім
PRPR	Proper Noun	Жалқы зат есім
CNCR	Concrete Noun	Деректі зат есім
ABST	Abstract Noun	Дерексіз зат есім
CASES_category	Cases	Септік жалғауы
NOM	Nominative case	Атау септік
GEN	Genitive case	Ілік септік
DIR	Direction- dative case	Барыс септік
ACC	Accusative case	Табыс септік
LOC	Locative case	Жатыс септік
ABL	Ablative case	Шығыс септік
INST	Instrumental case	Көмектес септік
NUMBER_category	Plural endings	Көптік жалғауы
SG	Singular	Жекеше
PL	Plural	Көпше
PERSON_category	Personal ending	Жіктік жалғауы
P1SG1	1 personal singular	1 жақ жекеше
P2SG1	2 personal singular	2 жақ жекеше (анайы)
P2SG.P1	2 personal singular formal	2 жақ жекеше (сыпайы)
P3SG	3 personal singular	3 жақ жекеше
P1PL1	1 personal plural	1 жақ көпше
P2PL1	2 personal plural	2 жақ көпше (анайы)
P2PL.P1	2 personal plural formal	2 жақ көпше (сыпайы)
P3PL	3 personal plural	3 жақ көпше
POSS_category	Possessive ending	Тәуелдік жалғауы
POSS.1SG	1 possessive singular	1 жақ жекеше

(*continued*)

Table 1. (*continued*)

Tag	Name_English	Name_Kazakh
POSS.2SG	2 possessive singular	2 жақ жекеше (анайы)
POSS.2SG.P	2 possessive singular formal	2 жақ жекеше (сыпайы)
POSS.3SG	3 possessive singular	3 жақ жекеше
POSS.1PL	1 possesive plural	1 жақ көпше
POSS.2PL	2 possesive plural	2 жақ көпше (анайы)
POSS.2PL.P	2 possesive plural formal	2 жақ көпше (сыпайы)
POSS.3PL	3 possesive plural	3 жақ көпше
Suffixes	Suffixes	Жұрнақ
WF	Word-formative	Сөз тудырушы жұрнақтар
NNWF	Suffixes that form the noun from nouns	Зат есімнен зат есім тудыратын жұрнақтар
VNWF	Suffixes that form the noun from verbs	Етістіктерден зат есім тудыратын жұрнақтар
AdjNWF	Suffixes that form the noun from adjectives	Сын есімнен зат есім тудыратын жұрнақтар
NumNWF	Suffixes that form the noun from numerals	Сан есімнен зат есім тудыратын жұрнақтар
WC	Word inflection	Сөз түрлендіруші жұрнақтар
NWC	Suffixes that change the meaning of nouns	Зат есімнің рең мәнін тудыратын жұрнақтары
HIP	Hipocoristic	Еркелету
DIM	Diminutive	Кішірейту
SIM	Similative	Келемеждеу, мысқылдау
HON	Honorific	Сыйлау, құрметтеу, үлкен тұту
PEJ	Pejorative	Менсінбеу, кемсіту
V	Verb	Етістік
Adj	Adjective	Сын есім
Num	Numeral	Сан есім
Pron	Pronoun	Есімдік
Adv	Adverb	Үстеу
FW	Function words	Шылау
Intrj	Interjection	Одағай
IW	Imitative words	Еліктеу сөздер

The text part consists not only of the name of the concepts, but also the definitions, questions, and examples in Kazakh language. As a result of the study, a tagging system for morphological concepts of the Kazakh language was obtained (Fig. 1).

Tag	Name_English	Name_Kazakh	definition	questions	example
N	Noun	Зат есім	заттың, құбылыстын, оқиғаның атын білдіреді	кім? не?	
CASES category	Case ending	Септік жалғауы	сөйлемдегі сөздерді бір-бірімен жалғасытырып, септестіріп тұратын қосымшалар		
NOM	Nominative case	Атау септік		кім? не?	бала
GEN	Genitive case	Ілік септік		кімнің? ненің?	баланың
DIR	Direction- dative	Барыс септік		кімге? неге?	балаға
ACC	Accusative(initial)	Табыс септік		кімді? нені?	баланы
LOC	Locative case	Жатыс		кімде? неде?	балада
ABL	Ablative case	Шығыс		кімнен?	баладан
INST	Instrumental case	Көмектес		кіммен? немен?	баламен
NUMBER category	Plural endings	Көптік жалғауы	нәрсенің көптігін білдіретін		
SG	Singular	жекеше		кім? не?	бала
PL	Plural	көпше		кімдер? нелер?	балалар
PERSON category	Personal ending	Жіктік жалғауы			
P1SG1	1 personal singular	1 жақ			Мен баламын
P2SG1	2 personal singular	2 жақ			Сен баласын
P2SG.P1	2 personal singular	2 жақ			Сіз баласыз
P3SG	3 personal singular	3 жақ			Ол бала
P1PL1	1 personal plural	1 жақ көпше			Біз баламыз
P2PL1	2 personal plural	2 жақ көпше			Сендер баласындар
P2PL.P1	2 personal plural formal	2 жақ көпше сыпайы			Сіздер баласыздар
P3PL	3 personal plural	3 жақ көпше			Олар балалар
POSS category	Possesive ending	Тәуелдік жалғауы	үш жақтың біріне белгілі бір заттың меншікті екенін білдіретін	кімім? нем? кімін? нең?	

Fig. 1. Fragment of a tagging system for morphological concepts of the Kazakh language.

4   Knowledgebase for Kazakh Morphology

4.1   Architecture

Morphology is a section of grammar, the main objects of which are words of the natural languages, their significant parts, and morphological features. The tasks of morphology, therefore, include the definition of a word as a special language object and a description of its internal structure [29]. According to this definition, the following concepts should be covered in the knowledge base architecture: *word, morpheme, parts of speech* and *morphological category*.

Word

A word is the central unit of a language.

Morpheme

In words, the minimum significant distinguished parts are morphemes. The main morpheme is the root, which bears the main meaning of the word, and the other morphemes are called affixes (suffix and ending).

1. Morpheme
   1.1 Root
   1.2 Affix
       1.2.1 Suffix
       1.2.2 Ending

Parts of Speech

Parts of speech are classes into which words are distributed according to their grammatical properties. There are nine parts of speech in the Kazakh language:

1. Noun
2. Adjective
3. Numeral
4. Pronoun
5. Verb
6. Adverb
7. Conjunction
8. Interjection
9. Imitative words

All parts of speech have certain properties, and all these properties are implemented in ontology.

Morphological Category

The morphological category is the affixal variations of words, which is an expression of the grammatical category of this word pattern. In the Kazakh language, there are different morphological categories, for example, for a noun (case category, number, person and possessiveness), adjective (degree of comparison) and verb (mood category, time, person, type, voice), etc.

1. The category of CASE
   1.1. Genitive case
   1.2. Direction-dative case
   1.3. Accusative case
   1.4. Ablative case
   1.5. Locative case
   1.6. Instrumental case
2. The category of NUMBER
3. The category of PERSON
4. The category of POSSESSIVE
5. Degrees of Comparison
6. The category of MOOD

7. The category of TENSE
8. The category of VOICE

All the above-mentioned concepts of the morphology of the Kazakh language were included into the applied ontology.

4.2 Implementation

Applied ontology "The morphology of the Kazakh language" consists of separate individuals, properties and classes, as well as interpretation functions defined on the ontology concepts or relations.

In this section, the ontology "Morphology of the Kazakh language" was implemented in accordance with the architecture in the Protégé environment. This environment is used to represent knowledge in the form of classes, individuals belonging to classes, and properties between them. All classes of morphological concepts of the Kazakh language are displayed in Fig. 2.

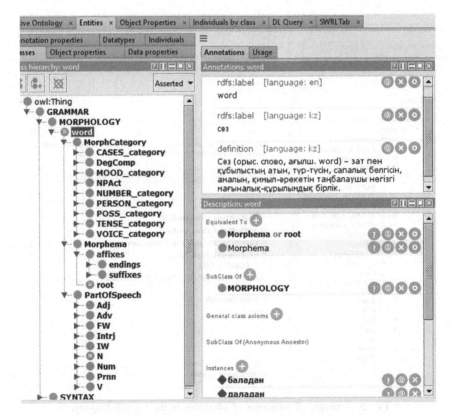

Fig. 2. Ontology "Morphology of the Kazakh language".

After the classes were created, the fields – properties – were written in them. Properties of objects define some relationship between two objects (classes, individuals). For example, the concept "Adj" (adjective) is characterized by the following properties (Fig. 3): the type can be either "qualitative adjective" (Qual) or "relative adjective" (Rel), in which the meanings of adjectives change. Therefore, we introduce the property "hasSemanticType" (has a semantic meaning), and describe it by an existential constraint (or limitation by a quantifier of existence):

$$\exists R.(A \cup B) \tag{2}$$

where $R = hasSemanticType$, $A = Qual$, $B = Rel$.

It can also specify that the adjective has the category of comparison degree:

$$\exists R.A \tag{3}$$

where $R = hasMorphCategory$, $A = DegComp$.

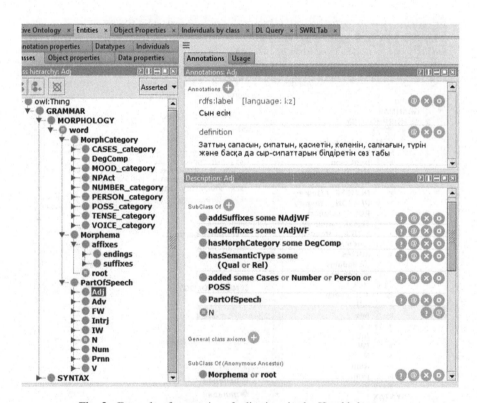

Fig. 3. Example of properties of adjectives in the Kazakh language.

The Fig. 4 shows some properties of nouns in the Kazakh language, which are defined by the following formulae:

$$\exists addSuffixes.(NNWF) \tag{4}$$

$$\exists addSuffixes.(VNWF) \tag{5}$$

$$\exists addSuffixes.(WC) \tag{6}$$

$$\exists added.(Number \cup POSS \cup Person \cup Cases) \tag{7}$$

$$\exists hasSemanticType.(ABST \cup CNCR) \tag{8}$$

$$\exists hasSemanticType.(ANIM \cup INAM) \tag{9}$$

$$\exists hasSemanticType.(CMMN \cup PRPR) \tag{10}$$

$$\exists hasMorphCategory.(CASES\_category \cup NUMBER\_category \\ \cup PERSON\_category \cup POSS\_category) \tag{11}$$

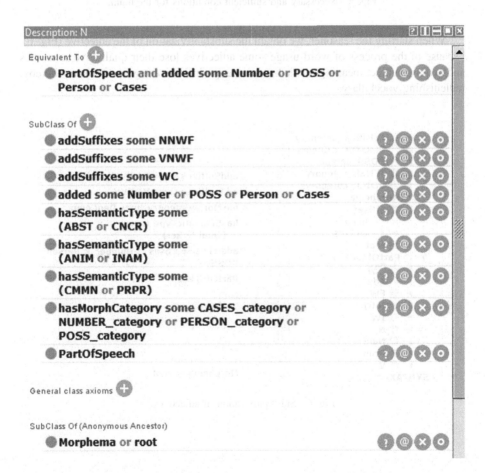

Fig. 4. Example of the properties of nouns in the Kazakh language.

There is also the considered concept of substantivization, which is a transition of other parts of speech (adjectives, verbs, participles, numerals) to the category of nouns, due to their ability to directly indicate the subject (which means it will answer the question "who?" or "what?"). For the noun, the necessary condition is to add to it the ending (Number, POSS, Person, Cases). In order to get the substantivization of other parts of speech into a noun, we will convert the necessary conditions into necessary and sufficient conditions (Fig. 5).

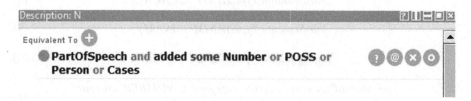

Fig. 5. Necessary and sufficient conditions for the noun.

When starting the reasoner, we obtain the substantivization of the adjective (Fig. 6), because in the process of word usage some adjectives lose their qualitative semantics and acquire subject meaning, i.e. substantivate, go into the category of nouns, thereby, replenishing vocabulary.

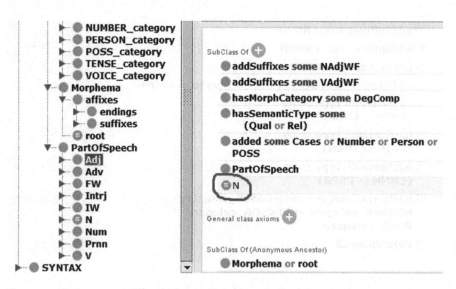

Fig. 6. Substantivization of adjectives.

For the morphological category NAbl (noun in the ablative case) there are necessary and sufficient conditions:

$$NAbl \equiv \exists hasRoot(root \cap (\forall hasPOS(N)) \cap \exists hasEnding(AblEnd)) \quad (12)$$

This allows defining the word "даладан - from outside", which is an individual of the concept "word" in the category NAbl. The Fig. 7 presents the description of the category NAbl and its implementation after launching the reasoner.

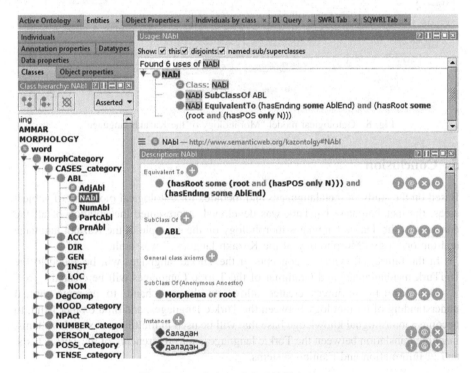

Fig. 7. Description of the NAbl category.

Thus, the created ontological model "Morphology of the Kazakh language" (Fig. 8) includes all the concepts and relations between them that are associated with the morphological features of the Kazakh language [30–32].

To formalize the morphological rules of natural languages, it is also possible to use alternative models, such as formal grammars, and languages of functional, logical, and production programming, and others.

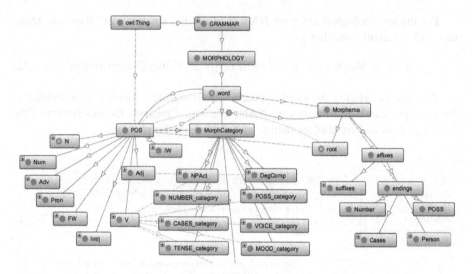

Fig. 8. Ontological model "Morphology of the Kazakh language".

5 Conclusion

Based on the study of metalanguages and methods for ontological modeling of subject areas, the metalanguage UniTurk was developed, it presented the notation of all the concepts of the Turkic languages morphology on the example of the Kazakh language and the ontology "Morphology of the Kazakh language" was built.

In the future, all syntactic concepts of the Turkic languages will be added to the UniTurk metalanguage and Grammar of the Turkic Languages will be created.

The linguistic resources created allow, on the one hand, to promote mutual understanding of terminology between the Turkic languages, and on the other hand, to become a multilingual knowledge base that will be used in multilingual search systems, machine translation between the Turkic languages, auto-referencing of the Turkic texts, and in information and training systems.

Acknowledgments. The work was supported by the grant financing for scientific and technical programs and projects by the Ministry of Science and Education of the Republic of Kazakhstan (Grant No. AP05132249, 2018–2020).

References

1. Bekmanova, G., et al.: A uniform morphological analyzer for the Kazakh and Turkish languages. In: Proceedings of the Sixth International Conference on Analysis of Images, Social Networks and Texts, Moscow, Russia, pp. 20–30 (2017)
2. Zhetkenbay, L., Sharipbay, A.A., Bekmanova, G.T., Kazhymukhan, D., Kamanur, U.: Comparison of the morphological rules of the Kazakh and Turkish languages. J. Math. Mech. Comput. Sci. **100**(4), 42–51 (2018)

3. Sharipbaev, A.A., Bekmanova, G.T., Buribayeva, A.K., Yergesh, B.Zh., Mukanova, A.S., Kaliyev, A.K.: Semantic neural network model of morphological rules of the agglutinative languages. In: Proceedings of the 6th International Conference on Soft Computing and Intelligent Systems, The 13th International Symposium on Advanced Intelligent Systems, Kobe, Japan, pp. 1094–1099 (2012)
4. Tsukanova N.I.: Ontological model for knowledge representation and organization, Moscow (2015)
5. Smekhun Y.A.: Ontologies in the knowledge based systems: possibilities of their application. Int. Res. J. https://doi.org/10.18454/IRJ.2016.47.086. Accessed 25 Feb 2019
6. Protégé. http://protege.stanford.edu. Accessed 10 Mar 2019
7. Gruber, T.R.: Toward principles for the design of ontologies used for knowledge sharing. Int. J. Hum Comput Stud. 43(5–6), 907–928 (1995)
8. Zalevskaya A.A.: Introduction to Psycholinguistics: A Textbook. Moscow (2000)
9. Marcus, M.P., Santorini, B., Marcinkiewicz, M.A.: Building a large annotated corpus of English: the Penn Treebank. Comput. Ling. pp. 313–330 (1993)
10. Garside, R.: The CLAWS word-tagging System. In: Garside, R., Leech, G., Sampson, G. (eds.) The Computational Analysis of English: A Corpus-based Approach. Longman, London (1987)
11. The Open American National Corpus. http://www.anc.org. Accessed 10 Dec 2018
12. Ide, N.: The American national corpus: then, now, and tomorrow. In: Selected Proceedings of the 2008 HCSNet Workshop on Designing the Australian National Corpus: Mustering Languages, Cascadilla Proceedings Project, Sommerville, MA (2008)
13. Jurafsky, D., Martin, J.H.: Speech and Language Processing: An Introduction to Natural Language Processing. Computational Linguistics and Speech Recognition. 2nd edn. Prentice-Hall (2009)
14. Indurkhya, N., Damerau, F.J.: Handbook of Natural Language Processing. 2nd edn. Chapman & Hall/CRC (2010)
15. Kazakh Language Corpus. http://kazcorpus.kz/. Accessed 10 Dec 2018
16. Makhambetov, O., Makazhanov, A., Yessenbayev, Zh., Matkarimov, B., Sabyrgaliyev, I., Sharafudinov, A.:. Assembling the Kazakh language corpus. In: Proceedings of the 2013 Conference on Empirical Methods in Natural Language Processing, pp. 1022–1031 (2013)
17. Madiyeva, G.B., Umatova, ZhM: About Almaty Corpus of the Kazakh language KazNU messenger. "Pholology" Series 5(157), 99–103 (2015)
18. Tatar National corpus "Tugan tel". http://tugantel.tatar. Accessed 10 Dec 2018
19. Galieva, A., Khakimov, B., Gatiatullin A.: On the way to the relevant grammatical tagset for the tatar national corpus. In: 8th International Conference on Corpus Linguistics, Málaga, Spain, pp. 121–129 (2016)
20. Turkish National Corpus (TNC). http://www.tnc.org.tr/. Accessed 10 Dec 2018
21. Kubedinova, L., Gatiatullin, A.: Morphological tagging of crimean tatar electronic corpus. In: Proceedings of the international conference "Turkic languages processing", Kazan, Tatarstan, pp. 331–337 (2015)
22. Zheltov, P.: Morphological annotation system for the national corpus of the chuvash language. In: Proceedings of the international conference "Turkic languages processing", Kazan, Tatarstan, pp. 328–331 (2015)
23. Bekmanova, G., Sharipbay, A., Omarbekova, A., Yelibayeva G., Yergesh B.: Adequate assessment of the customers' actual reviews through comparing them with the fake ones. In: Proceedings of 2017 International Conference on Engineering & Technology (ICET 2017), Antalya, Turkey (2017). ISBN: 978-1-5386-1949-0

24. Yergesh, B., Mukanova, A., Sharipbay, A., Bekmanova, G., Razakhova, B.: Semantic hyper-graph based representation of nouns in the Kazakh language. Computacion y Sistemas 18(3), 627–635 (2014)
25. Mukanova, A., Yergesh, B., Bekmanova, G., Razakhova, B., Sharipbay, A.: Formal models of nouns in the Kazakh language. Leonardo Electron. J. Practices Technol. 13(25), 264–273 (2014)
26. Aripov, M., Sharipbay, A., Abdurakhmonova, N., Razakhova B.: Ontology of grammar rules as example of noun of Uzbek and Kazakh languages. In: Abstract of the VI International Conference "Modern Problems of Applied Mathematics and Information Technology - Al-Khorezmiy 2018", pp. 37–38, Tashkent, Uzbekistan (2018)
27. Sharipbay, A., Yergesh, B., Yelibayeva, G., Israilova, N., Bakasova, P., Zhetkenbay L.: Ontological models matching of nouns of Kazakh and Kyrgyz languages. In: Proceedings of the International Conference on Computer Processing of Turkic Languages, Tashkent, Uzbekistan, pp. 182–188 (2018)
28. Zhetkenbay, L., Sharipbay, A., Bekmanova, G., Kamanur, U.: Ontological modeling of morphological rules for the adjectives in Kazakh and Turkish languages. J. Theor. Appl. Inf. Technol. 91(2), 257–263 (2016)
29. Momynova, B.K., Satkenova, ZhB: Morphology of the Kazakh language: a teaching aid. Almaty, Kazakhstan (2014)
30. Yskakov, A.: Modern Kazakh Language, 2 edn. Almaty, Kazakhstan (1991)
31. The Kazakh grammar. Phonetics, word formation, morphology, syntax. Astana, Kazakhstan (2002)
32. Institute of State language development: The Kazakh Language (Short grammar reference book). Almaty, Kazakhstan (2010)

A Bayesian Information Criterion for Unsupervised Learning Based on an Objective Prior

Ildar Baimuratov[1] , Yulia Shichkina[2(✉)] , Elena Stankova[3] ,
Nataly Zhukova[1,4] , and Nguyen Than[1]

[1] ITMO University, St. Petersburg, Russia
baimuratov.i@gmail.com, nazhukova@mail.ru
[2] St. Petersburg State Electrotechnical University, St. Petersburg, Russia
strange.y@mail.ru
[3] St. Petersburg State University, St. Petersburg, Russia
[4] St. Petersburg Institute for Informatics and Automation of the Russian
Academy of Sciences, St. Petersburg, Russia

Abstract. Data processing techniques, such as mathematical formulas, statistical methods and machine learning algorithms, require a set of tools for evaluating knowledge extracted from data. In unsupervised learning it is impossible to use referential or predictive estimation. Therefore, the only reliable way to evaluate results of unsupervised learning is information estimation. Unfortunately, information estimation suffer from underfitting and overfitting. We propose a new method for evaluating unsupervised learning results, which is based on the Bayesian criterion for optimal decision and an objective prior probability distribution of partitions. We illustrate the proposed method application on Fisher's iris data set by comparing original label distribution with results of clustering with different numbers of clusters. We show the method prevents underfitting and overfitting and verify it by comparing the recommended value with posterior distribution.

Keywords: Unsupervised learning · Information estimation ·
Bayesian criterion · Objective prior

1 Introduction

Data processing techniques, such as mathematical formulas, statistical methods and machine learning algorithms, require a set of tools for evaluating knowledge extracted from data. There are several ways to perform such estimation. Based on the research presented in [1], we consider the following estimation methods: referential, predictive and informational.

In unsupervised learning it is impossible to use referential or predictive estimation. Referential methods require some reference model which is believed to

ⓒ Springer Nature Switzerland AG 2019
S. Misra et al. (Eds.): ICCSA 2019, LNCS 11619, pp. 707–716, 2019.
https://doi.org/10.1007/978-3-030-24289-3_52

represent our best guess about the knowledge hidden in data. Predictive methods also have limitation as they require some outer evaluation of predictions. Therefore, the only reliable way to estimate results of unsupervised learning is information estimation.

1.1   Information Measures Underfitting/Overfitting

Unfortunately, information estimation, like many other methods for solving optimization problems, suffer from overfitting. Overfitting is a situation where a model corresponds not only to the relations between variables, but also to random noise in data [2]. A model incompleteness can be caused either by a bias—an error that occurs since the model used is not able to describe the dependencies in the data or by a variance—an error that occurs due to increased sensitivity to noise. Bias and variance, in turn, are related to model complexity—a quantity derived from the type of the model, the amount of input data and the number of parameters. A model that is too simple has high bias and vice versa—a model that is too complex has high variance.

Let us show that informational measures suffer from overfitting. In order to do it consider the Fisher's iris data set [3] and estimate mutual information of two random variables A and B [4], where A is the real class of an instance and B is some unique identifier, with respect to the original probability distribution of instances. This data set contains $N = 150$ instances of $A = 3$ different classes, therefore, $P(n) = \frac{1}{150}$, $P(a) = \frac{1}{3}$ and $P(b) = \frac{1}{150}$. Mutual information $MI(Y, X)$ of two discrete random variables is determined by the formula

$$MI(Y, X) = \sum_x \sum_y P(x, y) \log \frac{P(x, y)}{P(x)P(y)}. \tag{1}$$

Therefore, $MI(A, N) \approx 1,58$ and $MI(B, N) \approx 7,23$.

One can use mutual information to compare a result of classification with a reference model or to estimate the amount of knowledge gained after data processing. We are interested in unsupervised learning, therefore, in the second case. For estimating the amount of extracted knowledge mutual information is used in some algorithms for constructing decision trees. In such algorithms, preference is given to attributes with the highest mutual information. Therefore, for a decision tree of the mentioned data set one should choose the attribute B as the first node, but the resulting model, consisting of 150 classes, would be too complicated. Therefore, it is an example of overfitting.

There are various ways of avoiding overfitting:

- Cross-validation,
- Regularization,
- Prior probabilities,
- Bayes factor et al. [1].

One of the typical methods for solving the problem described above is the regularization of mutual information $MI(X, Y)$ using the entropy $H(X)$. The ratio

$$IGR(X, Y) = \frac{MI(X, Y)}{H(Y)} \tag{2}$$

is called the information gain ratio [9].

However, there are cases, where IGR is not applicable. One case is where Y is completely determined by X, i.e. there is a function $f : X \to Y$. In this case $H(Y|X) = 0$. Then, as

$$MI(Y|X) = H(Y) - H(Y|X) \tag{3}$$

it holds that,

$$H(Y|X) = 0 \Rightarrow MI(Y, X) = H(Y) \tag{4}$$

therefore,

$$H(X|Y) = 0 \Rightarrow IGR(X, Y) = 1 \tag{5}$$

Thus, if there is a function $f : X \to Y$, IGR is useless. Classification task is indeed a search of a function for assigning labels to data, therefore, IGR is useless for estimating classification in unsupervised learning. The example described above is an example of classification.

1.2 Objective Priors

In this paper we suggest to consider objective priors for preventing overfitting/underfitting. A prior probability distribution of a random variable is a distribution that characterizes its value before obtaining experimental data. There is informative and uninformative, or objective, prior distributions. An uninformative, or objective, distribution expresses vague or general information about a variable and has the following advantages:

- invariance with respect to parameters structure;
- inverse dependence on model complexity;
- independence from subjective assumptions.

Nowadays, applications of objective priors in regression and classification tasks are actively researched [5–8].

An example of objective prior usage is adjusted mutual information [10]. The idea of adjusted mutual information is to adjust mutual information of two random variables with joint probability distribution of their partitions. Suppose there are N points, two partitions U and V, and the number of points $a_i = |U_i|$ for $U_i \subseteq U, i = 1...R$ and $b_j = |V_j|$ for $V_j \in V, j = 1...C$, then the total number of ways to distribute the set N over the two partitions U and V is Ω

$$\Omega = \frac{(N!)^2}{\prod_i a_i! \prod_j b_j!} \tag{6}$$

Every two joint partitions U and V can be represented as a contingency table M

$$M = [n_{ij}]_{j=1...C}^{i=1...R} \tag{7}$$

Suppose there is some contingency table M, then there are w different ways to distribute points so that this M is obtained

$$w = \frac{N!}{\prod_i \prod_j n_{ij}!} \tag{8}$$

Thus, the probability $P(M|a,b)$ for some M with respect to the set $\mathcal{M}$ of all possible contingency tables is determined by the formula

$$P(M|a,b) = \frac{w}{W} \tag{9}$$

Mutual information $MI(M)$ of the contingency table M is determined by the formula

$$MI(M) = \sum_i \sum_j \frac{n_{ij}}{N} \log \frac{N \dot{n}_{ij}}{a_i b_j} \tag{10}$$

then the average mutual information of all possible joint partitions of random variables X and Y is defined as the expectation of mutual information $E(MI(M)|a,b)$

$$E(MI(X,Y)) = E(MI(M)|a,b) = \sum_{M \in \mathcal{M}} MI(M) P(M|a,b) \tag{11}$$

Finally, adjusted mutual information $AMI(X,Y)$ is defined as follows

$$AMI(X,Y) = \frac{MI(X,Y) - E(MI(X,Y))}{max(H(X), H(Y)) - E(MI(X,Y))} \tag{12}$$

Thus, hypergeometric distribution of two joint partitions is used in adjusted mutual information as an objective prior. The most natural way to use adjusted mutual information is to estimate clustering result. But again it estimates similarity of a resulting partition to a reference partition, while we are interested in a method for estimating knowledge gain.

2   A Bayesian Information Criterion Based on an Objective Prior

In this paper we propose a new method for information estimation, intended to estimate knowledge, gained in result of data processing, that is useful in unsupervised learning. The method is applicable to functionally dependent random variables and based on the Bayes criterion for optimal decision and an objective prior probability distribution of partitions.

2.1 Basic Definitions

Suppose there is a function $f : X \to Y$, then for every $y_i \in Y$ there is an inverse image $X_i \subseteq X$

$$X_i = \{x : f(x) = y_i\} \tag{13}$$

We consider partition $part(X) = X_1 \cup ... \cup X_k$ as a resulting model of X, knowledge gain of which we are going to evaluate. A structure of a partition is described by a number of subsets k and a partition $\bar{n}$ of a number $n = |X|$, such that $n_i = |X_i|$ and $n_1 + ... + n_k = n$.

We use relative entropy, or Kullback—Leibler divergence [11], for basic information gain estimation

$$D_{KL}(X||Y) = \sum_i P(x_i) \log \frac{P(x_i)}{Q(x_i)} \tag{14}$$

Considering $P(x_i) = \frac{|X_i|}{|X|}$ and $Q(x_i) = \frac{1}{|X|}$, we get

$$D_{KL}(part(X)||X) = \sum_i \frac{|X_i|}{|X|} \log |X_i| \tag{15}$$

But we propose to adjust relative entropy with an objective prior to prevent overfitting/underfitting.

2.2 The Bayesian Criterion for Optimal Decision

Preventing overfitting/underfitting means to find an optimal structure of a model. In decision theory various criteria are used to find the optimal choice. Given a set of all possible actions A, a set of states of nature Θ, its probability distribution $P(\theta)$ and a utility function $U(a, \theta)$ for an action $a \in A$ and a state of nature $\theta \in \Theta$, consider the Bayes criterion for choosing an optimal action a^* [12]

$$a_b^* = \operatorname*{argmax}_i \sum_j P(\theta_j) U(a_i, \theta_j) \tag{16}$$

Given a set X, we consider the set of all possible functions X^X on X, which forms the set of all possible partitions $Part(X)$ of X. Every partition $part(X) \in Part(X)$ has a certain structure $k_i, \bar{n}_j$. Assuming $A = \{k\}$, $\Theta = \{\bar{n}\}$ and $U(a_i, \theta_j) = D_{KL}(part_{ij}(X)||X)$, we get expected relative entropy $E(D_{KL}(part_k(X)||X))$, ED_{KL} for short, of a partition $part_k(X)$ for given number of subsets k

$$E(D_{KL}(part_k(X)||X)) = \sum_j P(\bar{n}_j) D_{KL}(part_{kj}(X)||X) \tag{17}$$

and the Bayesian criterion for optimal number of subsets k_b^*

$$k_b^* = \operatorname*{argmax}_i \sum_j P(\bar{n}_j) D_{KL}(part_{ij}(X)||X) \tag{18}$$

It only requires to define the probability distribution $P(\bar{n})$.

2.3   The Objective Prior Distribution of Number Partitions

Let us define the objective prior distribution $P(\bar{n})$ for Bayes criterion of optimal number of subsets k_b^*. Given a set X, we denote a set of all possible functions on X as $F = X^X$ and a set of functions that result in some number partition $\bar{n}_i$ as $F_i \subseteq F$. Let $|X| = n$ and m is a number of elements of $\bar{n}$ with a given value v, such that $v_1 + \dots + v_m = k$, then

$$P(\bar{n}_i) = \frac{|F_i|}{|F|} \tag{19}$$

where $|F| = n^n$ and

$$|F_i| = \frac{n!}{n_1!\dots n_k!} \frac{n!}{k!(n-k)!} \frac{k!}{v_1!\dots v_m!} \tag{20}$$

Objective prior $P(\bar{n}_i)$ and, therefore, the criterion k_b^* is defined for every set X.

2.4   Other Criteria

There are other criteria in decision theory. If probability distribution $P(\theta)$ is unknown, one can assume states of nature Θ to be equiprobable

$$a_l^* = \operatorname*{argmax}_i \sum_j \frac{1}{|\Theta|} U(a_i, \theta_j) \tag{21}$$

or minimize possible loss

$$a_w^* = \operatorname*{argmax}_i \min_j U(a_i, \theta_j) \tag{22}$$

Laplace and Wald criteria respectively.

Performing analogous substitutions, we get Laplace criterion for optimal number of subsets k_l^*

$$k_l^* = \operatorname*{argmax}_i \sum_j \frac{1}{|\{\bar{n}\}|} D_{KL}(part_{ij}(X)||X) \tag{23}$$

and Wald criterion for k_w^*

$$k_w^* = \operatorname*{argmax}_i \min_j D_{KL}(part_{ij}(X)||X) \tag{24}$$

However, the last criterion does not help with underfitting, as for any n it holds that $k_w^* = 1$, because

$$\min D_{KL}(part_1(X)||X) = \max D_{KL}(part(X)||X) = 1 \tag{25}$$

while Laplace criterion k_l^* may be used, if probability $P(\bar{n})$ is too complex to calculate.

3   Evaluating Unsupervised Learning Results

Consider the Fisher's iris data set, mentioned above, to demonstrate the proposed method. We compare the original labels distribution with $k = 3$ with more or less numbers of classes, $k = 2$ and $k = 4$ respectively. We use k-means clustering algorithm for $k = 2, 4$ to compare expected relative entropy of particular partitions. The results are given in the Table 1. As we can see, partitioning a set of 150 objects yields more expected relative entropy for $k = 4$ than for $k = 3$ and $k = 2$.

Table 1. Results of comparing

k	$\bar{n}$	D_{KL}	P	PD_{KL}	ED_{KL}
2	53, 97	0.85	1.20e-281	1.02e-281	5.30e-278
3	50, 50, 50	0.78	4.32e-252	3.37e-252	6.13e-250
4	50, 40, 28, 32	0.72	5.38e-233	3.87e-233	1.15e-229

However, this function has a global maximum, i.e. there is k_b^* such that for $k' > k_b^*$ expected relative entropy decreases. To show that, let us consider another experiment. The idea is to simulate numerous results of various unsupervised classification and clustering instances to get posterior distribution and calculate expected relative entropy for every possible k. Thus, we will get a posterior number of subsets k_p^* with the maximum expected relative entropy and compare it with k_b^*.

Due to complexity issues we consider $n = 75$. The plot of expected relative entropy for $k = 1, ..., 75$ is given at the Fig. 1. As we see, $max(ED_{KL}) = 1.20e - 02$ for $k_b^* = 47$.

To simulate posterior k_b^* distribution, we considered various clustering methods that do not require k as an input parameter, such as hierarchical clustering [13], affinity propagation [14], mean shift [15] and DBSCAN [16], but it turned out that their results have subjective bias, caused by hyperparameter values, set by a user, or by an algorithm logic itself, which may differ from objective dependencies beneath data. Therefore, we suggest to assign labels randomly, assuming that for large number of samples s the distribution would be similar to real results.

The result of the experiment is given at the Fig. 2. As we can see, k_p^* comes near to k_b^* and equals to it nearly after 1000 samples. Thus, we demonstrated that prior criterion k_b^* has global maximum and correlates with posterior distribution.

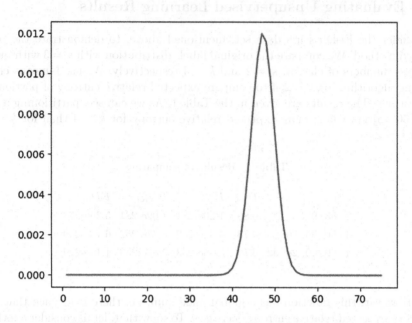

Fig. 1. Expected entropy for $n = 75$ and $k = 1, ..., 75$

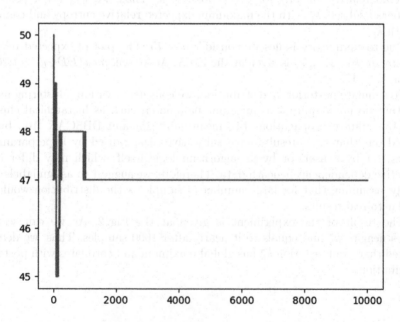

Fig. 2. k_p^* for $n = 75$ and $s = 1, ..., 10000$

4   Conclusion

Summing up, we suggested that information estimation is the only reliable way to evaluate results of unsupervised learning and demonstrated that information measures, like mutual information, suffer from underfitting and overfitting. We considered objective priors as a method for preventing underfitting/overfitting, since they have particular advantages, and proposed a new method for evaluating partition of a set, considered as unsupervised classification or clustering result. It includes, on the one hand, the Bayesian criterion for optimal decision, considering number of subsets as set of actions, corresponding number partitions as states of nature and relative entropy as utility function, and, on the other hand, the objective prior probability distribution of number partitions with respect to a number of all set partitions. We illustrated the resulting criterion application on Fisher's iris data set by comparing original label distribution with results of clustering with different numbers of clusters and demonstrated that the criterion has a global maximum and correlates with posterior distribution for large numbers.

Acknowledgments. The research was funded by RFBR and CITMA according to the research project №18-57-34001 and was funded by RFBR according to the research project №19-07-00784

References

1. Piironen, J., Vehtari, A.: Comparison of Bayesian predictive methods for model selection. Stat. Comput. **27**(3), 711–735 (2017). https://doi.org/10.1007/s11222-016-9649-y
2. Lever, J., Krzywinski, M., Altman, N.: Points of significance: model selection and overfitting. Nat. Methods **13**(9), 703–704 (2016)
3. Fisher, R.A.: The use of multiple measurements in taxonomic problems. Ann. Eugen. **7**(2), 179–188 (1936)
4. Cover, T.M., Thomas, J.A.: Elements of Information Theory. Wiley, New York (1991)
5. Simpson, D., Rue, H., Riebler, A., Martins, T.G., Sørbye, S.H.: Penalising model component complexity: a principled, practical approach to constructing priors. Stat. Sci. **32**(1), 1–28 (2017)
6. Mattingly, H.H., Transtrum, M.K., Abbott, M.C., Machta, B.B.: Maximizing the information learned from finite data selects a simple model. Proc. Nat. Acad. Sci. U.S.A. **115**(8), 1760–1765 (2018)
7. Palmieri, F.A.N., Ciuonzo, D.: Objective priors from maximum entropy in data classification. Inf. Fusion **14**(2), 186–198 (2013)
8. Sørbye, S.H., Rue, H.: Penalised complexity priors for stationary autoregressive processes. J. Time Ser. Anal. **38**(6), 923–935 (2017)
9. Quinlan, J.R.: Induction of decision trees. Mach. learn. **1**(1), 81–106 (1986)
10. Vinh, N.X., Epps, J., Bailey, J.: Information theoretic measures for clusterings comparison: variants, properties, normalization and correction for chance. J. Mach. Learn. Res. **11**, 2837–2854 (2010)
11. Kullback, S., Leibler, R.A.: On information and sufficiency. Ann. Math. Stat. **22**(1), 79–86 (1951)

12. Berger, J.O.: Statistical Decision Theory and Bayesian Analysis. Springer Series in Statistics, 2nd edn. Springer, New York (1985). https://doi.org/10.1007/978-1-4757-4286-2
13. Ward Jr., J.H.: Hierarchical grouping to optimize an objective function. J. Am. Stat. Assoc. **58**(301), 236–244 (1963)
14. Frey, B.J., Dueck, D.: Clustering by passing messages between data points. Science **315**(5814), 972–976 (2007)
15. Comaniciu, D., Meer, P.: Mean shift: a robust approach toward feature space analysis. IEEE Trans. Pattern Anal. Mach. Intell. **24**(5), 603–619 (2002)
16. Ester, M., Kriegel, H.P., Sander, J., Xu, X.: A density-based algorithm for discovering clusters in large spatial databases with noise. In: Proceedings of the 2nd International Conference on Knowledge Discovery and Data Mining, pp. 226–231, Portland (1996)

Methods for Analyzing Polarity of the Kazakh Texts Related to the Terrorist Threats

Gulmira Bekmanova[✉], Gaziza Yelibayeva, Saltanat Aubakirova,
Nurgul Dyussupova, Altynbek Sharipbay, and Rozamgul Nyazova

L.N. Gumilyov Eurasian National University, Astana, Kazakhstan
gulmira-r@yandex.kz, gaziza_y@mail.ru,
saltanat759@mail.ru, sharalt@mail.ru,
nurgulya_1991@bk.ru, rozamgul@list.ru

Abstract. In this work we described the rule-based method, using dictionary for sentiment analysis of texts in the Kazakh language related to the terrorist threats. It provides an overview of the methods for analyzing polarity, parser, which analyzes the pages on the content of keywords from the database, morphological, syntactic and sentiment analysis of the texts in the Kazakh language.

Keywords: Sentiment analysis · Kazakh language · Classification ·
Production rules · Rule-based method · Morphological rules · Syntax rules ·
Forbidden content · Parser

1 Introduction

Sentiment analysis or opinion mining in natural languages is one of the fast growing natural language processing technologies. Sentiment analysis, also called opinion analysis, is a field of research that analyzes people's opinions, suggestions, assessments, attitudes and emotions in relation to such subjects as products, services, organizations, individuals, problems, events, topics and their attributes [1].

Many resources and systems have been developed for sentiment analysis of texts by now for English [1, 2]. A number of researches are conducting on sentiment analysis for Russian [3, 4], Turkish [5–7], Spanish [8], Arabic [9, 10] and other languages [8]. One approach was proposed for Spanish language to the subjectivity detection on Twitter micro texts that explores the uses of the structured information of the social network framework. For Arabic, there is a semantic approach to discover user attitudes and business insights from Arabic social media by building an Arabic Sentiment Ontology that contains groups of words which express different sentiments in different dialects [13]. Currently, there are emerging semantic models that recognize emotions and words and their expressions in different languages.

The work [11], which presents SEMO, a semantic model for recognizing emotions, which allows users to identify and quantify the emotional load associated with basic emotions hidden in short, emotionally saturated sentences (for example, news headlines, tweets, signatures). The idea, assessing semantic similarity of concepts by considering the occurrences and coincidences of the terms describing them on the pages

© Springer Nature Switzerland AG 2019
S. Misra et al. (Eds.): ICCSA 2019, LNCS 11619, pp. 717–730, 2019.
https://doi.org/10.1007/978-3-030-24289-3_53

indexed by the search system, can be directly extended to emotions and words expressing them in different languages.

Here are some works on the analysis of attitudes for dual languages, Kazakh and Russian [12, 13]. The work [12] describes modern approaches for solving the problem of analyzing the opinions of news articles in the Kazakh and Russian languages using deep recurrent neural networks. Thus, studies show that good results can be achieved even without knowing the linguistic features of a particular language. It also proposes a model of deep neural network, which uses two-lingual embedding of words, to solve effectively the problem of mood classification for a given pair of languages. They apply this approach to two corpora of two different language pairs: English-Russian and Russian-Kazakh. It shows how to train a classifier in one language and predict it in another one. This approach ensures an accuracy of 73% for English and 74% for Russian languages. There are methods, proposed to analyze the mood of the texts in Kazakh, such as a baseline method, which reaches an accuracy of 60% and a method for studying bilingual embedding from a large unlabeled corpus using bilingual word pairs [13]. The analysis of the mood of the texts written in Kazakh is not sufficiently studied. The studies were conducted in [14–16], for the Kazakh language.

Computers are beginning to acquire the ability to recognize emotions. In 1995, Picard [17] reported on the key issues of "affective computing", calculations that are associated with emotions, arise from them or affect them. Since then, many studies have been conducted. Many studies are related to the recognition of emotions from texts. The work [18] proposes an approach for recognizing emotions using network similarities. It also proposes a model for ranking emotions, based on semantic indicators of proximity, for example, Confidence, PMI, PMING.

There are many mobile devices such as smartphones, tablets, cameras and PCs in the world today. In addition, many applications for audio, video, chatting are being introduced day by day. Accordingly, the amount of text, audio and video information is increased. Therefore, the task of extracting emotions from textual, graphic, audio and video information becomes an important task.

Emotions are extracted not only from texts, but also from audio and video content [19, 20], from images [21]. Such applications can be used as marketing in social media, brand positioning, elections and financial forecasting.

The term "threat" usually refers to a specific unlawful act with the intent of one person to harm another one, which is expressed orally, in written or in another way. We will consider only written threats, which we will call prohibited content. In [22, 23], sentiment analysis is used to detect some prohibited content on the Internet. The determination of prohibited content by means of sentiment analysis is a new direction and works, that the authors of this article consider as useful for the further research, were published in the last ten years. The next article discusses the use of data mining techniques to detect prohibited terrorist activities on the network (Mahesh, Mahesh, Vinayababu 2010) [22]. The work [23] describes a system that detects forbidden statements with an accuracy of more than 80%, using natural language processing techniques and machine learning.

This work can be considered as an introduction and an attempt to apply the linguistic approach to identify texts containing prohibited content of a terrorist nature, which is written in the Kazakh language with keywords in English and Russian languages. For this reason, this article describes the rule-based methods used in the analysis of feelings, and the approaches used to determine moods through the formalization of morphological and syntactic rules.

2 Method for Analyzing Text Polarity

There are three main methods for determining the text polarity:

1. Analysis of a text using vector analysis methods (often using n-gram models), comparing a text with the previously marked reference corpus on the chosen proximity measure and classifying (classification) it as negative or positive based on the result of the comparison.

2. Search for emotive vocabulary (lexical polarity) in the text according to pre-compiled polarity dictionaries (lists of patterns) using linguistic analysis. Based on the found emotive vocabulary, the text can be evaluated on a scale, which reflects the number of negative and positive vocabulary. This method can use both lists of patterns that are inserted into regular expressions, and rules for combining polarity vocabulary within a sentence.

3. Mixed method (combination of the first and the second approaches).

The analysis of the text polarity, which we are implementing now, consists of several stages (Fig. 1).

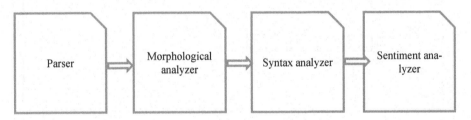

Fig. 1. Stages of the text polarity analysis

At the first stage, the processing of web pages is carried out by the special parser, which analyzes the pages for the content of keywords from the database (in our case, keywords of forbidden content).

At the second stage, the text of selected web pages is processed by a morphological analyzer to determine the parts of speech and the characteristics of each parts of speech.

At the third stage, a simplified syntax analyzer works: words and phrases are combined into polarity chains; the subject, predicate, and object are identified in the sentence.

At the fourth stage, a simplified sentiment analyzer works, it determines the polarity of the text.

3 Parser and Database

Parser is software for collecting and converting textual data into a structured format. The processing of web pages is carried out by the special parser, which analyzes the pages to determine if they contain the key words from the knowledge base (in our case, keywords of forbidden content). The operation of the parser is simple, and its effectiveness depends entirely on the knowledge base. The interface of the parser is shown in Fig. 2.

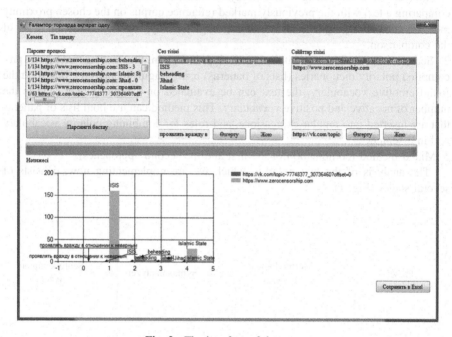

Fig. 2. The interface of the parser

WordNet [24] was used as a prototype of the database structure for the parser, SENTIWORDNET [25] was used at the stage of sentiment analysis. The database was filled completely symmetrically in three languages: Kazakh, English and Russian. This is because, historically, Kazakhstanis often use a mixed language, for example, they speak Kazakh, using terms or stable expressions from Russian and/or English.

WordNet is a large lexical database of the English language. Nouns, verbs, adjectives and adverbs are grouped into sets of cognitive synonyms (synsets), each of them expresses a distinct concept. Synsets are interlinked by means of conceptual-semantic and lexical relations. The resulting network of meaningfully related words and concepts can be navigated with the browser. WordNet is also freely and publicly available for download. WordNet's structure makes useful tool for computational linguistics and natural language processing. WordNet superficially resembles a thesaurus, in that it groups words together based on their meanings. However, there are some important distinctions. First, WordNet interlinks not just word forms—strings of letters—but specific senses of words. As a result, words that are found in close proximity to one another in the network are semantically disambiguated. Second, WordNet labels the semantic relations among words, whereas the groupings of words in a thesaurus does not follow any explicit pattern other than meaning similarity [24].

The work [25] presented SENTI WORDNET 3.0, an enhanced lexical resource explicitly devised for supporting sentiment classification and opinion mining applications (Table 1).

Table 1. Fragment of the table in the WordNet format

Noun	Adjective	Verb	Definition	Hyperonym	Hyponym	Holonim	...
Wahhabism			Religious - political trend in Sunni Islam, the middle of the XVIII century. It is based on the teachings of Muhammad al-Wahhab, Salafis	Islam, a radical religious and political movement		Islam	
Gazavat			War for faith is one of the jihad aspects	Holy War, Islam		Islam	
Jihad			The struggle for faith is used by the organizers of the terrorist activities for involving Muslims in it	Holy War, Islam		Islam	
Islamism			World outlook and practical activities of fanatical adherents of Islam, whose faith its institutions (dogmas) in culture, in public, political and economic life, applying extreme measures to achieve goals	Islam, a radical religious and political movement		Islam	
Pan-Islamism			Religious and political current in Islam, preaching the idea of the unity of Muslims around the world and the need for their unity in a single Muslim state. Often it is used as a cover for policy intervention in the affairs of other states and support for various extremist and terrorist structures	Islam, religious and political ideology		Islam	
Religious extremism			Intolerance towards people who have other religions, accompanied by calls for committing or committing antisocial, often unlawful, including violent, acts against citizens	Islam, a radical religious and political movement		Extremism	

(continued)

Table 1. (*continued*)

Noun	Adjective	Verb	Definition	Hyperonym	Hyponym	Holonim	...
Salafism			A direction in Islam that unites Muslim religious figures who, at different periods of the history of Islam, made calls to orient themselves toward the way of life and faith of the early Muslim community, to righteous ancestors (as-salaf as-salihun). Salafia means "understanding of religion in the form in which it was understood by the prophet and his companions"	Islam, a radical religious and political movement		Tawhid (monotheism)	
...							

Social networks "Vkontakte" and "Facebook", and selected foreign Internet resources distributing terrorist content were selected for the research and replenishment of the database. To begin with, we directly reviewed the individual profiles of social network users, mentioning prohibited words from the list provided by the US Department of National Security in 2011, which is used to analyze networks for prohibited content [26].

4 Morphological Analysis

The Kazakh language is a typical Turkic language, retaining most of the features common to this group and possessing a number of typical Kypchak features. The structural-typological characteristic of the Kazakh language is mainly related to its membership in agglutinative languages. As a rule, a description of the agglutinative type applies a features set, which takes into account not only phonetic, but also morphological and syntactic features. The order of the endings in the Kazakh language is strictly defined. For example, for nouns, first the plural endings are added to the base of the word, then the possessive endings (meaning the object belongs to a person), then the case endings and then the conjugation form endings (added only to animate nouns). In general, it can be said that the Kazakh language is a well formalized language. We have developed a rule-based morphological analyzer, which is described in [27–29].

5 Syntax Analyzer

Visual analysis of prohibited content shows that it consists of only simple sentences, that is, they do not have complex compound sentences. It follows that to build a syntax analyzer of prohibited content, it is sufficient to formalize and implement the syntax rules for simple sentences in the Kazakh language, that is, to build a simplified parser.

There are 20 types of simple sentences in the Kazakh language. The formalization of the syntax rules of simple sentences and the construction of the corresponding syntactic analyzer are given in [30]. Some examples of simple sentences containing forbidden fragments are provided below.

A simple sentence consisting of the subject will be represented as:

$$SS\,(Q(Q1(S))M(M1(N\,Adj\,Pron\,Adv))) \tag{1}$$

Where SS – simple sentence

Q – structure

Q1– structure with the first index

S – Subject

M – semantics

M1 – semantics with the first index

N – Noun

Adj – Adjective

Pron – Pronoun

Adv – Adverb

Example: Bomb. Explosion.

A simple sentence consisting of the subject and the predicate will be presented as:

$$SS(Q(Q2(S\,P))M(M2(MS\,(N\,Adv\,Num)MP\,(N\,V\,Adj\,Adv\,Num))))) \tag{2}$$

Where SS – simple sentence

Q – structure

Q2 – structure with the second index

S – Subject

P – Predicate

M – semantics

M2 – semantics with the second index

MS – semantics of subject

N – Noun

Adv – Adverb

Num – Numeral

MP – semantics of predicate

N – Noun

V – Verb

Adj – Adjective

Adv – Adverb

Num – Numeral

Example: The bomb exploded. The explosion occurred. Set fire. The explosion is terrible. The building was crushed. Four blew up. Infidels died.

A simple sentence consisting of the subject, the complement and the predicate will be presented as:

$$SS(Q(Q3(S\,O\,P))M(M3(MS\,(N\,Pron\,Num\,Adj)\,MA\,(N\,Pron\,Num\,Adj)\,MP\,(N\,V))))$$

$$(3)$$

Where SS – simple sentence
Q – structure
Q3 – structure with the third index
S – Subject
O – Object
P – Predicate
M – semantics
M3 – semantics with the third index
MS – semantics of subject
N – Noun
Pron – Pronoun
Num – Numeral
Adj – Adjective
MA – semantics of object
N – Noun
Pron – Pronoun
Num – Numeral
Adj – Adjective
MP – semantics of predicate
N – Noun
V – Verb

Example: Terrorists crashed the city. Five soldiers got killed.

The complete list of formal syntactic rules for simple sentences is as follows:

SS (Q(Q1(S)) M(M1(N Adj Pron Adv)))

SS(Q(Q2(S P)) M(M2(MS (N Adv Num)MP (N V Adj Adv Num)))))

SS(Q(Q$_3$(S O P)) M(M$_3$(M$_S$ (N Pron Num Adj) M$_A$(N Pron Num Adj) M$_P$ (N V)))).

SS(Q(Q$_4$(S C P)) M(M$_4$(M$_S$ (N Pron Num Adj) M$_C$(N Adv Num Adj) M$_P$ (V)))).

SS(Q(Q$_5$(S A C P)) M(M$_5$(M$_S$ (N Pron Num Adj) M$_A$(N Adj Num Pron) M$_C$ (N Adv) M$_P$(V)))).

SS(Q(Q$_6$(S A C P)) M(M$_6$(M$_S$ (N Pron Num Adj) M$_C$(N Adv Pron) M$_A$ (N Pron Adj Num) M$_P$(V)))).

SS(Q(Q$_7$(S D A P)) M(M$_7$(M$_S$ (N Pron Adj Num) M$_D$(Adv Pron Num Adv) M$_A$ (N Adj Num) M$_P$(V)))).

SS(Q(Q$_8$(A D S P)) M(M$_8$(M$_A$ (N Pron Adj Num) M$_D$(Adj Adv Num) M$_S$ (N Num Adj) M$_P$(V)))).

$SS(Q(Q_9(A\ C\ S\ P))\ M(M_9(M_A\ (N\ Pron\ Adj\ Num)\ M_C(Adv\ Num)\ M_S\ (N\ Pron\ Adj\ Num)\ M_P(V))))$.

$SS(Q(Q_{10}(A\ S\ C\ P))\ M(M_{10}(M_A\ (N\ Pron\ Adj\ Num)\ M_S(N\ Pron\ Num\ Adv\ Adj)\ M_C\ (Adv\ Num)\ M_P(V))))$.

$SS(Q(Q_{11}(C\ S\ A\ P))\ M(M_{11}(M_C\ (N\ Num\ Adv)\ M_S(N\ Pron\ Num\ Adv\ Adj)\ M_A\ (Adv\ Num)\ M_P(V))))$.

$SS(Q(Q_{12}(D\ S\ A\ P))\ M(M_{12}(M_D\ (Adj\ Num\ Adv\ Pron)\ M_S(N\ Adj)\ M_A\ (N\ Adj\ Adv\ Num)\ M_P(V))))$.

$SS(Q(Q_{13}(D\ S\ C\ P))\ M(M_{13}(M_D\ (Adj\ Num\ Adv\ Pron)\ M_S(N\ Adj)\ M_C\ (N\ Adj\ Adv\ Num)\ M_P(V))))$.

$SS(Q(Q_{14}(S\ C\ D\ A\ P))\ M(M_{14}(M_S\ (N\ Pron\ Adj\ Num)\ M_C(N\ Adv)\ M_D\ (N\ Adj\ Adv\ Num)\ M_A\ (N\ Adj\ Num)\ M_P(V))))$.

$SS(Q(Q_{15}(S\ D\ A\ C\ P))\ M(M_{15}(M_S\ (N\ Pron\ Adj\ Num)\ M_D(Adj\ Adv\ Num)\ M_A\ (N\ Adj\ Num)\ M_C\ (N\ Adv\ Adj)\ M_P(V))))$.

$SS(Q(Q_{16}(C\ S\ D\ A\ P))\ M(M_{16}(M_C\ (N\ Adv\ Num)\ M_S(N\ Pron\ Num\ Adj)\ M_D(Num\ Adj)\ M_A(N\ Num\ Adj)\ M_P(V))))$.

$SS(Q(Q_{17}(C\ A\ D\ S\ P))\ M(M_{17}(M_C\ (N\ Adv\ Num)\ M_A(N\ Pron\ Num\ Adj)\ M_D(Num\ Adj)\ M_S(N\ Pron\ Num\ Adj)\ M_P(V))))$.

$SS(Q(Q_{18}(D\ S\ C\ A\ P))\ M(M_{18}(M_D\ (Adj\ Adv\ Num)\ M_S(N\ Pron\ Num\ Adj)\ M_C(Adv\ N)\ M_A(N\ Pron\ Num\ Adj)\ M_P(V))))$.

$SS(Q(Q_{19}(D\ S\ A\ C\ P))\ M(M_{19}(M_D\ (Adj\ Adv\ Num)\ M_S(N\ Pron\ Num\ Adj)\ M_A(N\ Pron\ Num\ Adj)\ M_C(Adv\ N)\ M_P(V))))$.

$SS(Q(Q_{20}(D\ A\ S\ C\ P))\ M(M_{20}(M_D\ (Adj\ Adv\ Num)\ M_A(N\ Pron\ Num\ Adj)\ M_S(N\ Pron\ Num\ Adj)\ M_C(Adv\ N)\ M_P(V))))$.

The input of the syntactic analyzer is the text containing elements of forbidden content with morphological tags.

At this stage, the initial syntax analysis is performed: words and phrases are combined into polarity chains, the subject, predicate and object are distinguished in the sentence. The result of the syntactic analyzer will be the text containing forbidden content marked by morphological and syntactic tags.

6 Sentiment Analysis

At this stage, the polarity object is highlighted. It is set by the user or determined automatically: in each sentence, a so-called named entity is searched, for example, a proper name, animate real, etc. For a given object, the polarity of the text is calculated [14–16, 31]. To work at the sentiment analysis stage, a database of words and phrases that are emotional in color and refer to prohibited content (hereinafter - the prohibited fragment) is used. In our case, we use database tables that have a SENTI WORDNET database structure (Table 2).

Table 2. Fragment of the table in the SENTI WORDNET format

#POS	PosScore	NegScore	Terms	Gloss
n	0	0,5	Ваххабизм#1 Уаннабизм#1 Вахабизм#1 Уанабизм#1 (Wahhabism)	XVIII ғасырдың ортасында Мұхаммад әл- Ваххаб оқытуларының негізінде пайда болған сүнниттік исламның радикалды-саяси ағын, салафиттер (a Sunni Islamic doctrine and radical-political movement founded by Muhammad al-Wahhab in the XVIII century, Salafi)
n	0	0,875	Газават#1 Жиһад#1 кәпірлерге_қарсы_соғыс#1 Аллаһтың_жолында_күресу#1 (Gazawat, war against infidels, war in God's path)	«Дін үшін соғыс», джихадтың бір бөлігі (War for religion, a part of jihad)
n	0	0,875	Джихад#1 аль_Жиһад#1 Жиһад#1 Жиһат#1 исламдық_джихад#1 (jihad, al-jihad, Islamic jihad)	Дін үшін соғыс, мұсылмандарды еліктіру үшін қолданылатын түсінік (war for religion, a concept is used to attract muslims)
n	0	0,5	Исламизм#1 (Islamism)	Исламның бірбеткей, ессіз ұстанушыларының көзқарастары мен тәжірибелік іс-әрекеттері, оның (ислам) белгілерінің бастылығын уағыздап жүрулері қоғамда, саясатта және экономикалық өмір қырларында, мақсаттарына жету үшін шекті іс-әрекеттерді орындау (views and practical actions of one-sided and unconscious Islam followers, preaching the unity of its signs, executing ultimate actions to meet their goals in society, politics and economic life)
n	0	0,5	Панисламизм#1 (Panislamism)	XIX ғасырдың соңында пайда болған, мұсылман реформаторы Джемал ад-Дина ал-Афгани (1839–1897) есімімен байланысты идеология және қозғалыс; жер бетіндегі барлық мұсылманқауымынын бірлігі концепциясы мен олардын біртұтас ислам мемлекетіне бірігу қажеттілігіне негізделген діни-саяси идеология және тәжирибе. Көбінесе әртүрлі террористік және экстремистік топтарды ақшалай қолдау үшін "жаппа" ретінде қолданылады (ideology and movement related the name of Islamic reformer Jemal al-Dina al-Afgani (1839–1897) formed in the XIX century; religious-political ideology and practice which is based in the idea of necessity of association for all Islamic communities in the world; mostly used in different terrorist and extremism groups as "cover" to get financial support)
n	0	0,875	Діни экстремизм#1 (religious extremism)	Басқа дінді ұстайтын адардармен есептеспеушілік, қоғамға қарсы,

(continued)

Table 2. *(continued)*

#POS	PosScore	NegScore	Terms	Gloss
				құқыққа қарсы, зорлықтық іс-әрекеттерді жасауға үндеумен қатар жүреді. діттеген саяси мақсаттарына қол жеткізу үшін, дінді қалқан ете отырып әрекет етуші, дінге ешқандай қатысы жоқ іс-қимыл. Басқаша атағанда - терроризм (лаңкестік). Мұндай әрекеттер көбіне мемлекеттің құрамын күшпен өзгертуге немесе үкіметті басып алуға бағытталады. Қауіпті жағдайға айналған осындай әрекеттерді іске асыру, көбіне қарулы топтар құрып, өзара өшіктіру әдістерін қолдану арқылы дін және ұлттық қайшылықтарды қоздырумен, сондай-ақ адам құқын жаппай бұзумен қатар жүреді. (ignoring other religion followers, goes together with a call to do violent actions against society, rights; actions which are not related to religion but using it as a "cover". In other words, it is terrorism. Usually, these actions are targeted to change a state composition or take it over by force; goes together with actions for creating armed groups, unleashing religious and national contradictions, violating human rights)
n	0	0,5	Сәләфия#1 салафия#1 (salafia)	Ислам дінінің негізі боп табылатын Құран мен Сүннетті «әс-сәләф әс-салихун», яғни Мұхаммед пайғамбардың (салл Аллаһу ғалейһи уә сәлләм) сахабалары, олардың ізбасарлары мен Ислам үмметінің имамдары қалай түсінсе солай түсіну дегенді білдіред (means to understand Quran and Sunni, which are the basis of the Islam religion, as companions of the prophet Muhammad and followers and Islam community (ummah) understand)
...				

7   Evaluation of Results

Currently, methods for objective testing of textual markup systems have not yet been developed. Therefore, the testing method currently used by us is based on periodic subjective evaluations of small text collections by an expert [32].

8   Conclusion

In this paper, we have developed a method for analyzing the polarity of the Kazakh texts related to terrorist threats. The database for the parser and sentiment analysis was developed. The syntax rules of simple sentences in the Kazakh language, which are sufficient for the presentation of texts related to terrorist threats, have been formalized. The stages of morphological, syntactic and sentiment analysis of texts in the Kazakh language are described.

The development of this work and the replenishment of the database and knowledge base of the prohibited content will allow detecting sites leading to terrorist propaganda. Currently, the database contains 1200 entries, which allowed us to detect more than 50 similar sites. Content analysis of sites allowed expanding the database with new keywords. Previously obtained results of determining the polarity of texts made it possible to automatically determine the list of sites that have extremely negative content. We hope that this work will be developed by virtue of its practical significance for society.

References

1. Liu, B.: Sentiment Analysis and Opinion Mining. Morgan & Claypool Publishers (2012)
2. Pang, B., Lee, L.: Opinion mining and sentiment analysis. Foundations and Trends® in Information Retrieval. Now Publishers (2008)
3. Loukachevitch, N.V., Chetviorkin, I.I.: Evaluating Sentiment Analysis Systems in Russian. Artif. Intell. Decis. Making **1**, 25–33 (2014). (In Russian)
4. Chetvirokin, I., Loukachevitch, N.: Sentiment analysis track at ROMIP 2012. In: Proceedings of International Conference Dialog-2013, vol. 2, pp. 40–50 (2013)
5. Akba, F., Uçan, A., Sezer, E.A., Sever, H.: Assessment of feature selection metrics for sentiment analyses: Turkish movie reviews. In: Proceedings of the 8th European Conference on Data Mining, pp. 180–184 (2014)
6. Yıldırım, E., Çetin, F., Eryiğit, G., Temel, T.: The impact of NLP on Turkish sentiment analysis. In: Proceedings of the TURKLANG 2014 International Conference on Turkic Language Processing, Istanbul (2014)
7. Eryiğit, G., Çetin, F., Yanık, M., Temel, T., Çiçekli, I.: TURKSENT: a sentiment annotation tool for social media. In: Proceedings of the 7th Linguistic Annotation Workshop & Interoperability with Discourse, ACL 2013, Sofia, Bulgaria (2013)
8. Sixto, J., Almeida, A., López-de-Ipiña, D.: An approach to subjectivity detection on twitter using the structured information. In: Nguyen, N.-T., Manolopoulos, Y., Iliadis, L., Trawiński, B. (eds.) ICCCI 2016. LNCS (LNAI), vol. 9875, pp. 121–130. Springer, Cham (2016). https://doi.org/10.1007/978-3-319-45243-2_11

9. Mohammad, S., Salameh, M., Kiritchenko, S.: Sentiment lexicons for Arabic social media. In: Proceedings of the 10th Edition of the Language Resources and Evaluation Conference, Portorož (Slovenia) (2016)
10. Samir, T., Abdul-Nabi, I.: Semantic sentiment analysis in Arabic social media. J. King Saud Univ. Comput. Inf. Sci. **29**(2), 229–233 (2016)
11. Franzoni, V., Milani, A., Biondi, G: SEMO: a semantic model for emotion recognition in web objects. In: Proceedings IEEE/WIC/ACM International Conference on Web Intelligence, WI (2017)
12. Sakenovich, N.S., Zharmagambetov, A.S.: On one approach of solving sentiment analysis task for Kazakh and Russian languages using deep learning. In: Nguyen, N.-T., Manolopoulos, Y., Iliadis, L., Trawiński, B. (eds.) ICCCI 2016. LNCS (LNAI), vol. 9876, pp. 537–545. Springer, Cham (2016). https://doi.org/10.1007/978-3-319-45246-3_51
13. Abdullin, Y.B., Ivanov, V.V.: Deep learning model for bilingual sentiment classification of short texts. Sci. Tech. J. Inf. Technol. Mech. Opt. **17**(1), 129–136 (2017)
14. Yergesh, B., Bekmanova, G., Sharipbay, A.: Sentiment analysis of Kazakh text and their polarity. In: Web Intelligence (2019)
15. Yergesh, B., Bekmanova, G., Sharipbay, A.: Sentiment analysis on the hotel reviews in the Kazakh language. In: 2nd International Conference on Computer Science and Engineering, UBMK (2017)
16. Yergesh, B., Bekmanova, G., Sharipbay, A., Yergesh, M.: Ontology-based sentiment analysis of Kazakh sentences. In: Gervasi, O., Murgante, B., Misra, S., Borruso, G., Torre, C.M., Rocha, A.M.A.C., Taniar, D., Apduhan, B.O., Stankova, E., Cuzzocrea, A. (eds.) ICCSA 2017. LNCS, vol. 10406, pp. 669–677. Springer, Cham (2017). https://doi.org/10.1007/978-3-319-62398-6_47
17. Picard, R.W.: Affective Computing. MIT Media Laboratory Perceptual Computing Section Technical Report No. 321. Media Lab. Massachusetts Institute of Technology, Cambridge University (1995)
18. Biondi, G., Franzoni, V., Li, Y., Milani, A.: Web-based similarity for emotion recognition in web objects. In: Proceedings - 9th IEEE/ACM International Conference on Utility and Cloud Computing, UCC 2016, pp. 327–332 (2016)
19. Poria, S., Chaturvedi, I., Cambria, E., Hussain, A.: Convolutional MKL based multimodal emotion recognition and sentiment analysis. In: Proceedings - IEEE International Conference on Data Mining, ICDM, Art. no. 7837868, pp. 439–448 (2017)
20. Arunnehru, J., Kalaiselvi Geetha, M.: Automatic human emotion recognition in surveillance video. Stud. Comput. Intell. **660**, 321–342 (2017)
21. Jiang, R., Ho, A.T.S., Cheheb, I., Al-Maadeed, N., Al-Maadeed, S., Bouridane, A.: Emotion recognition from scrambled facial images via many graph embedding. Pattern Recogn. **67**, 245–251 (2017)
22. Mahesh, S., Mahesh, T.R.: Vinayababu, M: Using data mining techniques for detecting terror-related activities on the WEB. J. Theor. Appl. Inf. Technol. **16**(2), 99–104 (2010)
23. De Smedt, T., De Pauw, G., Van Ostaeyen, P.: Automatic Detection of Online Jihadist Hate Speech: CLiPS Technical Report Series (2018)
24. https://wordnet.princeton.edu/
25. Esuli A., Baccianella S., Sebastiani F.: SentiWordNet 3.0: an enhanced lexical resource for sentiment analysis and opinion mining. In: Proceedings of the International Conference on Language Resources and Evaluation, Valletta, Malta (2010)
26. Analyst's Desktop Binder, U.S. Department of Homeland Security [Электронный ресурс]. https://epic.org/foia/epic-v-dhs-media-monitoring/Analyst-Desktop-Binder-REDACTED.pdf

27. Sharipbayev, A., Bekmanova, G., Buribayeva, A., Mukanova, A., Kaliyev, A.: Semantic neural network model of morphological rules of the agglutinative languages. In: The 6th International Conference on Soft Computing and Intelligent Systems. The 13th International Symposium on Advanced Intelligent Systems, Kobe, Japan, pp. 1094–1099 (2012)

28. Yergesh, B., Mukanova, A., Sharipbay, A., Bekmanova, G., Razakhova, B.: Semantic hyper-graph based representation of nouns in the Kazakh language. Computacion y Sistemas **18**(3), 627–635 (2014)

29. Zhetkenbay, L., Sharipbay, A., Bekmanova, G., Kamanur, U.: Ontological modeling of morphological rules for the adjectives in Kazakh and Turkish languages. J. Theor. Appl. Inf. Technol. **91**, 257–263 (2016)

30. Razakhova, B.Sh., Sharipbaev, A.A.: Formalization of syntactic rules of the Kazakh language Вестник. Special issue.- Astana: L.N. Gumilyov ENU, pp. 42–50 (2012)

31. Yergesh, B., Sharipbay, A., Bekmanova, G., Lipnitskii, S.: Sentiment analysis of Kazakh phrases based on morphological rules. Theor. Appl. Sci. Tech. J. **2**(38), 39–42 (2016). Kyrgyz State Technical University named after I. Razzakov

32. Pazelskaya, A., Solovyev, A.: A method of sentiment analysis in Russian texts. In: Dialog (2011)

Evaluation of Bio-Inspired Algorithms in Cluster-Based Kriging Optimization

Carlos Yasojima[✉], Tamara Ramos, Tiago Araujo,
Bianchi Meiguins, Nelson Neto, and Jefferson Morais

Postgraduate Program of Computer Science, Federal University of Pará,
Belém, Pará, Brazil
takeshiyasojima@gmail.com, tamarasabrininew@gmail.com,
{tiagoaraujo,nelsonneto,jmorais}@ufpa.br

Abstract. Kriging is one of the most used spatial estimation methods in real-world applications. In kriging estimation, some parameters must be estimated in order to reach a good accuracy in the interpolation process, however, this step is still a challenge. Various optimization methods have been tested to find good parameters to this process, however, in recent years, many authors are using bio-inspired techniques and reaching good results in estimating these parameters. This paper presents a comparison between well-known bio-inspired techniques such as Genetic Algorithms, Differential Evolution and Particle Swarm Optimization in the estimation of the essential kriging parameters: nugget, sill, range, angle, and factor. We also proposed an improved cluster-based kriging method to perform the tests. The results shows that the algorithms have a similar accuracy in estimating these parameters, and the number of clusters have a high impact on the results.

Keywords: Bio-inspired algorithms · Artificial Intelligence · Geostatistic · Kriging

1 Introduction

Kriging is a geostatistical interpolation technique that predicts the value of observations in unknown locations based on previously collected data. The kriging error or interpolation error is minimized by studying and modeling the spatial distribution of points already obtained. This spatial distribution or spatial variation is expressed in the form of an experimental variogram [1].

The experimental variogram can be considered as a graphical representation of the data distribution and also expresses the data variance with the increment of the sampling distance. The variogram is the basis for the application of the kriging method. Thus, the kriging process is defined in three main steps. First, the experimental variogram is calculated. Then, the theoretical variogram is modeled to represent the experimental variogram. Finally, the value of a given point is predicted using the built theoretical model.

© Springer Nature Switzerland AG 2019
S. Misra et al. (Eds.): ICCSA 2019, LNCS 11619, pp. 731–744, 2019.
https://doi.org/10.1007/978-3-030-24289-3_54

The theoretical variogram can be modeled, for example, by estimating some parameters: nugget, sill, range, factor, and angle in anisotropy problems, where the spatial behavior is different in distinct directions.

Artificial Intelligence Techniques have been used with kriging technique to produce better results as shown in [2–10], whereas it is still a challenge to determine what method is better structured for a database.

As stated in [7] and applied in [8], bio-inspired algorithms, in general, are suited to help define the theoretical variogram parameters. Furthermore, these types of algorithms do not require a single initial value as input, but rather an interval. In [3], the authors achieved good results adopting Genetic algorithm technique.

Various researches have been implementing bio-inspired algorithms to optimize these parameters, such as Genetic Algorithms (GA) [6, 8, 9], Differential Evolution (DE) [10, 11] and more recently PSO [12]. However, it is important to compare the behavior of these algorithms when applied to the same problem and study their effectiveness in optimizing variogram parameters.

In order to evaluate these algorithms, it is important to select the method to evaluate the goodness of each solution. In [8], it is shown that the interpolation cost function, which we use as the fitness function to evaluate the set of parameters, generally yield better results at the expense of computational cost. Well-known cost functions, such as Weighted Least Squares, Maximum Likelihood and variations were not considered in this paper.

To apply state-of-art kriging methodologies, we use Cluster-Kriging method proposed in [13]. In this method, the spatial data are divided into different sub-groups, where each data is interpolated using only data from same group. A limitation of Abedini methodology is a single variogram for all groups, we propose the estimation and optimization of different parameters to each group. Some problems of this improvement are solved using K-Nearest Neighbour method and data preprocessing as shown in the next section.

In this context, the purpose of this paper is to evaluate well-known bio-inspired techniques such as Genetic Algorithms, Differential Evolution and Particle Swarm Optimization in the estimation of the essential kriging parameters. We also proposed an improved cluster-based kriging method to perform the tests. The results show that the algorithms have a similar performance, but the clustering algorithm and the number of clusters might have a high impact on the kriging results.

This paper is organized as follows. Section 2 consists of the theoretical background involving important concepts for the understanding of this paper. In Sect. 3, the steps of the proposed method are detailed. Section 4 presents the databases used in this work besides the results of the experiments performed. Finally, Sect. 5 presents final considerations.

2 Background

This section presents a brief explanation of the main concepts discussed in this paper.

2.1 Kriging

Let Z be a set of measurements of a target variable denoted as $\{z(s_1), z(s_2), \ldots, z(s_N)\}$, where $s_i = (x_i, y_i)$ is a data point in a spatial database; x_i and y_i are its coordinates (primary locations); and N is the number of observations.

Values of the target variable at some new location s_0 can be calculated using a spatial prediction model. The standard version of kriging is called ordinary kriging (OK), where the predictions are based on the model:

$$\hat{z}_{OK}(s_0) = \sum_{i=1}^{n} w_i(s_0).z(s_i) = \lambda_0^T \cdot \mathbf{z} \tag{1}$$

where λ_0 is a vector of kriging weights (w_i), and z is the vector of N observations at primary locations.

So, to estimate the weights, we calculate the semivariances $\gamma(h)$ based on the differences between the neighboring values:

$$\gamma(h) = \frac{1}{2} E[(z(s_i) - z(s_i + h))^2] \tag{2}$$

where $z(s_i)$ is the observation of the target variable at some point location, and $z(s_i + h)$ is the observation of the neighbour at a distance $s_i + h$.

Suppose that there are N point observations, this yields $Nx(N-2)/2$ pairs for which a semivariance can be calculated. If we plot all semivariances versus their separation distances a variogram cloud is produced. For an easier visualization of this variogram cloud, the values are commonly averaged for a standard distance called "lag". If we display such averaged data, then we get the standard experimental variogram, which can be seen in Fig. 1.

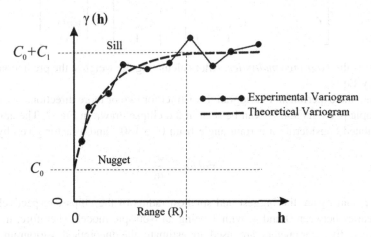

Fig. 1. Kriging variogram and parameters.

Once we calculate the experimental variogram, we can fit it using a theoretical model, such as linear, spherical, exponential, gaussian, among others. The variograms are commonly fitted using a cost function (e.g. weighted least squares [15]). Hence, the main objective is to minimize this cost function. The theoretical model used in this work is the exponential one, given by

$$C(h) = \begin{pmatrix} C_0 + C_1 & |h| = 0 \\ C_1 \cdot [e^{-(\frac{h}{R})}] & |h| > 0 \end{pmatrix} \tag{3}$$

where R is the practical range, which is the coordinate where the model starts to flatten out.

C_0 is the "nugget effect" that is attributed to measurements errors or spatial sources of variation at distances smaller than the sampling interval. $C_0 + C_1$ is the sill, which is the value that the model attains at the practical range. These parameters, also called coefficients, determine the theoretical variogram as illustrated in Fig. 1.

Once we have estimated the theoretical model, we can use it to derive semivariances at all locations and solve the kriging weights. The ordinary kriging (OK) weights are solved multiplying the covariances:

$$\lambda_0 = \mathbf{C}^{-1} \cdot \mathbf{c_0}; \quad C(|h| = 0) = C_0 + C_1 \tag{4}$$

where C is the covariance matrix derived for $N \times N$ observations and c_0 is the vector of covariances at a new location. Note that the C is in fact a $(N+1) \times (N+1)$ matrix if it is used to derive kriging weights, since one extra row and column are used to ensure that the sum of weights is equal to one:

$$\begin{bmatrix} C_{(s_1,s_1)} & \cdots & C_{(s_N,s_1)} & 1 \\ \vdots & \ddots & \vdots & \vdots \\ C_{(s_N,s_1)} & \cdots & C_{(s_N,s_N)} & 1 \\ 1 & \cdots & 1 & 0 \end{bmatrix}^{-1} \begin{bmatrix} C_{(s_0,s_1)} \\ \vdots \\ C_{(s_0,s_N)} \\ 1 \end{bmatrix} = \begin{bmatrix} w_1(s_0) \\ \vdots \\ w_N(s_0) \\ \varphi \end{bmatrix} \tag{5}$$

where φ is the *Lagrange multiplier*. After calculating the weights, the prediction is then given by Eq. 1.

When the experimental variogram is distinct for two or more directions, we have an anisotropic phenomenon, as can be seen in the ellipse drawn in Fig. 2. The anisotropy is calculated considering a certain angle from 0 to 180°, and a factor given by

$$Factor = \frac{a_2}{a_1} \tag{6}$$

where a_1 and a_2 are the biggest and smallest radius of the ellipse, respectively. This factor varies between 0 and 1, with 1 being an isotropic model. Therefore, in case of anisotropy, five parameters are used to estimate the theoretical variogram model: nugget, sill, range, angle, and the anisotropy factor.

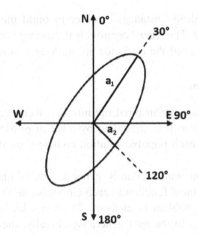

Fig. 2. Example of anisotropy and its parameters.

2.2   KNN

K-Nearest Neighbor (KNN) [14] is a supervised machine learning algorithm used for both classification and regression problems. It is a non-parametric approach that uses training data directly for classification. More specifically, the KNN algorithm classifies a new point based on the training set points that are close to it.

Given a training data set $\{(s_1, q_1), \ldots, (s_N, q_N)\}$, with N points, each point (s, q) consists of a vector $s \in R^L$ and a label $q \in \{1, \ldots Q\}$. Let $s_0 = (p_1, \ldots p_L)$ be a new point not yet classified (i.e. without label). In order to classify this new point, the KNN algorithm calculates the distance between s_0 and the other points in the training set using a measure of similarity. The K nearest points (i.e. with smaller distances) in relation to s_0 are then stored. In the sequel, it is verified which is the most frequent label among the K neighbors, and this elected label q is associated with the new point.

A well-known measure of similarity and also used in this work is the Euclidean Distance, which is defined by

$$d(\mathbf{s}, \hat{\mathbf{s}}) = \sqrt{\sum\nolimits_{i=1}^{L} (p_i - \hat{p}_i)^2} \qquad (7)$$

where p_i and $\hat{p}_i$ are elements of vectors $\mathbf{s}$ and $\hat{\mathbf{s}}$, respectively.

2.3   K-Means

K-means [14] is one of the simplest unsupervised learning algorithms that solve the clustering problem. This clustering algorithm partitions the database into U clusters, where the value of U is provided by the user.

The k-means algorithm starts by initializing a set of U centroids, one for each cluster. A widely used initialization method is the random selection among the points in the database. Each point is then associated with the nearest centroid based on a measure of similarity (e.g. Euclidean Distance) in order to build the groups. After that, the centroids are recalculated. The "new" centroid is the average of the "old" cluster points. This process is repeated until the centroids are no longer modified.

2.4 Genetic Algorithm

Genetic algorithm [15] is a bio-inspired optimization technique that uses natural evolution theory as inspiration. It is structured by a set of possible solutions. This set is called "population" and each possible solution contain a set of parameters, which we call a "chromosome".

Initially, a population with randomly generated individuals/chromosomes is created. Then, we apply a fitness function to each chromosome to evaluate its goodness or how well it solved the problem in analysis. Then, a selection operator chooses the individuals who will pass to the next generation. Finally, the crossover and mutation operators are applied to the individuals chosen by the selection operator. The algorithm runs until a stopping criterion is fulfilled, such as the number of generations.

We used the R package "ga" [16] when performing tests.

2.5 Differential Evolution

The Differential Evolution algorithm is an optimization technique similar to genetic algorithms in its structure. Similar operators like crossover, mutation and selection are used, however this algorithm focus on the mutation operation to generate the population of individuals/chromossomes. In other words, the DE perturbs the population with of randomly selected chromosomes by using their components to construct trial vectors. The recombination (crossover) operator efficiently shuffles information about successful combinations, enabling the search for a better solution space [17].

We used the R package "DEOptim" [18] when performing tests.

2.6 Particle Swarm Optimization

The PSO uses similar structure from DE and GA algorithms to evaluate each individual (also called particles), however, instead of using crossover, mutation, and selection methods, new solutions are created by "moving" the particle around the search space based on two factors: a) The best fitness achieved by the particle so far b) The best fitness achieved by any particle in the neighborhood [19].

The structure of a particle consists of four parameters, current location (identical to the GA chromosome), current velocity, best local fitness and best global fitness. For every iteration, each particle is updated with a new location based on the other 3 parameters. Nowadays PSO has been successfully applied to various real world problems and it represents current state of art nature inspired algorithm [19].

2.7 Cost Function and Evaluation Metric

The cost function used as the fitness function of all algorithms were the interpolation error cost function [8]. We obtain the error by applying the Kriging at each data point

(Leave-one-out Cross Validation) of the Train database using the parameters of the solution, and calculating the Mean Squared Error after all points have been tested.

To evaluate and compare the algorithms, we applied the 10-fold cross validation, where 10 iterations of tests are performed with 90% train data and 10% test data. Every version of the test database is different from each other. After all iterations, we calculate the mean of the MSE (Mean Squared Error) of each.

3 Methodology

The main objective of this research is to study the behavior and results of the three bio-inspired algorithms, Genetic Algorithm, Differential Evolution, and Particle Swarm Optimization in the optimization of the Kriging parameters: Nugget, Sill, Range, Factor, and Angle.

In order to test the algorithms, we propose the application of Abedini's Cluster Kriging methodology but improving the technique by applying a solution to allocate unknown points to the clusters obtained by the K-means clustering technique. In this scenario, we first apply a preprocessing step using standardization algorithms and treatment of outliers, after that the K-means is used to find k groups of the data, in this clustering step, the KNN method is used to improve the clustering groups. For each k group of data, the bio-inspired algorithms are used to find parameters of the Kriging method. Lastly, the unknown points are allocated to the previously determined clusters using also the KNN method, these points are then interpolated using the kriging parameters and data of that given cluster.

To analyze the results, we applied the 10-fold cross-validation method. In each of the 10 iterations of this method, the data is split into 90% train data, where we apply k-means and the optimization methods (GA, DE, and PSO), and 10% test data (Each iteration has different test data), where we classify using the KNN method into the clusters to apply the kriging method. Summarizing, at each n-fold, we have these steps:

1. Preprocess Data;
2. Partition data into 90% train and 10% test;
3. Split train data into k clusters;
4. Select kriging parameters for each cluster individually via bio-inspired techniques;
5. Allocate each data from test database to a cluster via KNN method;
6. Apply kriging to each data from test database with their respective cluster and parameters;
7. Calculate Mean Squared Error.

The complete flow chart can be seen in the Fig. 3.

3.1 Data Preprocessing

In the data preprocessing step, the spatial information x and y, and the target variable, in this case zinc, were normalized between 0 and 1. This was important to ensure that every variable has the same weight in the clustering process and to avoid cluster overlapping. In the sequel, we used the Z-score test with 99% confidence to remove outliers.

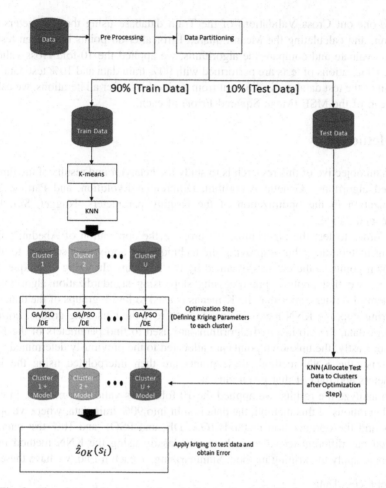

Fig. 3. Flowchart of the proposed method to evaluate the bio-inspired algorithms.

3.2 Data Clustering

After we preprocess the data and partition the data, the train database is split into k clusters using spatial information x and y, and the target variable. As shown in [13], the clustering process often results into overlapped clusters. These overlapping cause problems when allocating unknown (new) data into clusters. To minimize this, all data were previously normalized between 0 and 1, then, each point were classified again into one of the groups found by K-means. This process ensured that all groups were not overlapped. In the following figures we illustrate this scenario, where in Fig. 4(a), especially when the number of clusters are bigger than 4, we do not see a spatial uniformity as observed in Fig. 4(b) where the normalization and KNN was applied. The black circle highlighted in Fig. 4(a), demonstrate an overlapped clusters.

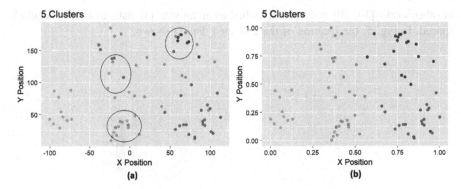

Fig. 4. K-means results (a) Without normalization, (b) With normalization step.

3.3 Optimization Phase

For each cluster obtained by the K-means technique, we apply an optimization technique to find optimal parameters, nugget, sill, range, factor and angle of the Kriging phase. The accuracy of the interpolation are directly correlated to how good these parameters are.

Each bio-inspired algorithm was evaluated based on the best set of parameters found. These parameters are tested when interpolating the test database and the accuracy and error is calculated.

3.4 Classification and Kriging

After we obtain the clusters and their respective kriging parameters, each data of the test database is allocated to a cluster based on KNN method. The KNN method receive the spatial location of the new or unknown point (x and y) and set its cluster based on the nearest neighbors, the most common cluster label found in these neighbors is set to the new point.

In the kriging (interpolation) phase, this new point only takes account the data from its cluster allocated in the previous step, and consequently the parameters found by the optimization techniques for that group.

4   Tests and Results

In this section, we discuss configuration of the tests and show the results.

4.1   Database (Study Area)

The database selected in this research represents the mountainous region of Wolfcamp Aquifer in West Texas/New Mexico. The area has been studied because of its potential site for nuclear-waste disposal. In the wolfcamp aquifer, 85 measurements were collected along this region, each representing piezometric wells. This study area has used in other works [13, 20] and been classified as an anisotropic data area and irregularly spaced. In Fig. 5, the location of the collected data is shown.

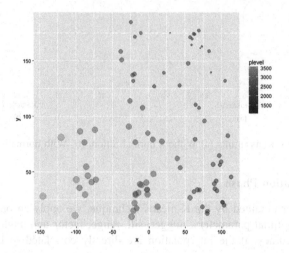

Fig. 5. Wolfcamp aquifer study area, color and size of points indicates the value of target variable. (Color figure online)

4.2   Experiments

In order to evaluate and compare the results for the three bio-inspired algorithms, a manual tuning was performed. The population size and number of iterations values were the same for all algorithms, and other specific parameters of each algorithm were tested manually. The best parameters found for each algorithm are shown in Table 1.

The chromosome (GA and DE) and particle (PSO) had the following configuration:

- Nugget;
- Sill;
- Range;
- Factor;
- Angle;

Some parameters of the experimental variogram were fixed for tests simplicity, such as number of lags, model type and nugget effect with values 10, Exponential and 0 respectively.

The range of each parameter to be optimized were defined as shown in Table 2.

Table 1. Bio-inspired techniques parameters used in tests.

Algorithm	Parameter	Value
GA	Population size	100
	Iterations	10
	Crossover probability	0.8
	Mutation probability	0.1
	Elitism	5% of population
	Selection method	Roulette
	Crossover method	Deep [21] real coded
	Mutation method	Deep [22] real coded
DE	Population size	100
	Iterations	10
	Crossover probability	0.6
	Differential weight	0.2
	Method	de/rand/1/bin
PSO	Particles	100
	Iterations	10
	Social constant	2
	Cognitive constant	2
	Inertia range	0.4 to 0.8

Table 2. Lower and Upper bounds of variables.

Bound	Nugget	Range	Sill	Angle	Factor
Lower bound	0	0	0	0	0
Upper bound	0	Max distance between 2 points	Variance of target variable * 5	180	1

Table 3. MSE results for each bio-inspired algorithm for 2 to 5 clusters (test data).

Algorithm		2 Clusters	3 Clusters	4 Clusters	5 Clusters
GA	Mean	0.091	0.062	0.114	0.138
	Stand. Dev.	0.074	0.066	0.107	0.123
DE	Mean	0.082	0.086	0.099	0.178
	Stand. Dev.	0.063	0.078	0.109	0.209
PSO	Mean	0.093	0.073	0.098	0.132
	Stand. Dev.	0.081	0.059	0.097	0.116

As stated earlier, we used the 10-fold cross validation method. Consequently, 10 tests were ran for each number of clusters for each algorithm. The results can be seen in Table 3.

The best overall result for all algorithms were achieved using 3 clusters with GA. With 5 clusters the algorithms achieved the highest MSE of all configurations. The GA algorithm performed the best with 3 clusters, where the DE algorithm found the best results with 2 clusters, with 4 or 5 clusters the PSO algorithm performed the best.

We can infer that a high number of clusters does not imply a better accuracy of the method, since the worst result is obtained using 5 clusters for all tested algorithms. Therefore, a step for choosing the best number of groups could be interesting for the methodology. Some indicators of clustering goodness, such as Silhouette or Dunn, could be applied to further study this behavior.

Analyzing the boxplot in Fig. 6, we can interpret that the error is sensible to the clustering process, where some occurrences as the outliers found with 3, 4 and 5 clusters have high impact in the Kriging interpolation process.

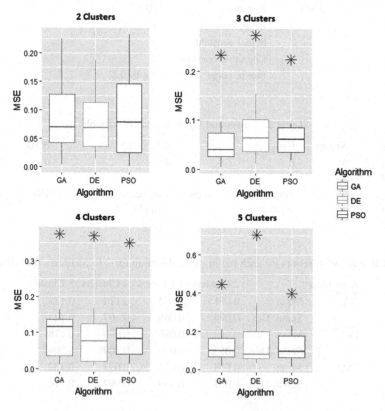

Fig. 6. Boxplot of the obtained results for each algorithm and cluster from 2 to 5.

5 Conclusions

The results obtained with the proposed methodology using data clustering, evolutionary techniques demonstrated a similar behavior in all algorithms (GA, DE and PSO). Some issues and improvements that must be highlighted:

- Computational cost is big with bio-inspired techniques and interpolation cost function when optimizing kriging parameters.
- The algorithms can probably achieve even better results with more generations and bigger population.
- A big standard deviation infer that the kriging process is sensitive to the cluster obtained in the K-means process.

According to our findings, we conclude that the bio-inspired algorithms have similar behavior when estimating parameters for this study case and parameters. Nevertheless, it is obvious that further research is needed. Future works include evaluating other clustering algorithms and evaluating them with some indicators, adding figures of metric and kriging maps to measure the quality of the formed groups. Evaluate others bio-inspired optimization methods is another important issue to be addressed, considering the use of information visualization techniques to analyze the evolutionary behavior and convergence curve.

References

1. Hengl, T.: A Practical Guide to Geostatistical Mapping. 52 edn. (2009)
2. Tugrul, B., Polat, H.: Privacy-preserving kriging interpolation on distributed data. In: Murgante, B., et al. (eds.) ICCSA 2014. LNCS, vol. 8584, pp. 695–708. Springer, Cham (2014). https://doi.org/10.1007/978-3-319-09153-2_52
3. Schernthanner, H., Steppan, S., Kuntzsch, C., Borg, E., Asche, H.: Automated web-based geoprocessing of rental prices. In: Gervasi, O., et al. (eds.) ICCSA 2017. LNCS, vol. 10407, pp. 512–524. Springer, Cham (2017). https://doi.org/10.1007/978-3-319-62401-3_37
4. Ocal, D., Kentel, E.: A GIS tool to estimate flow at ungaged basins using the map correlation method. In: Gervasi, O., et al. (eds.) ICCSA 2017. LNCS, vol. 10407, pp. 377–391. Springer, Cham (2017). https://doi.org/10.1007/978-3-319-62401-3_28
5. Wei, Z., Liu, Z., Chen, Q.: Ga-based kriging for isoline drawing. In: 2010 International Conference on Environmental Science and Information Application Technology (ESIAT), vol. 2, pp. 170–173. IEEE (2010)
6. Xialin, Z., Zhengping, W., Zhanglin, L., Chonglong, W.: An intelligent improvement on the reliability of ordinary kriging estimates by a GA. In: 2010 Second WRI Global Congress on Intelligent Systems (GCIS), vol. 2, pp. 61–64. IEEE (2010)
7. Gonçalves, I., Kumaira, S., Guadagnin, F.: A machine learning approach to the potential-field method for implicit modeling of geological structures. Comput. Geosci. **103**, 173–182 (2017)
8. Li, Z., Zhang, X., Clarke, K., Liu, G., Zhu, R.: An automatic variogram modeling method with high reliability fitness and estimates. Comput. Geosci. **120**, 48–59 (2018)

9. Abedini, M.J., Nasseri, M., Burn, D.H.: The use of a genetic algorithm-based search strategy in geostatistics: application to a set of anisotropic piezometric head data. Comput. Geosci. **41**, 136–146 (2012)
10. Rat Atalay, F., Ertunç, G.: Metaheuristic kriging: a new spatial estimation method. Hacet. J. Math. Stat. **46**(3), 483–492 (2017)
11. Shang, X., Ma, P., Yang, M.: An improved kriging model based on differential evolution. In: Proceedings of The 9th EUROSIM Congress on Modelling and Simulation, EUROSIM 2016, no. 142, pp. 356–361 (2018)
12. Wang, Z., Chang, Z., Luo, Q., Hua, S., Zhao, H., Kang, Y.: Optimization of riveting parameters using kriging and particle swarm optimization to improve deformation homogeneity in aircraft assembly. Adv. Mech. Eng. **9**(8), 1687814017719003 (2017)
13. Abedini, M.J., Nasseri, M., Ansari, A.: Cluster-based ordinary kriging of piezometric head in West Texas/New Mexico-testing of hypothesis. J. Hydrol. **351**(3–4), 360–367 (2008)
14. Witten, I.H., Frank, E., Hall, M.A., Pal, C.J.: Data Mining: Practical Machine Learning Tools and Techniques. Morgan Kaufmann, Burlington (2016)
15. Goldberg, D.E., Holland, J.H.: Genetic algorithms and machine learning. Mach. Learn. **3**(2), 95–99 (1988)
16. Scrucca, L.: GA: a package for genetic algorithms in R. J. Stat. Softw. **53**(4), 1–37 (2013)
17. Karaboğa, D., Ökdem, S.: A simple and global optimization algorithm for engineering problems: differential evolution algorithm. Turk. J. Electr. Eng. Comput. Sci. **12**(1), 53–60 (2004)
18. Mullen, K.M., Ardia, D., Gil, D.L., Windover, D., Cline, J.: DEoptim: an R package for global optimization by differential evolution. J. Stat. Softw. **40**, 1–26 (2009)
19. Mishra, K.K., Tiwari, S., Misra, A.K.: A bio inspired algorithm for solving optimization problems. In: 2011 2nd International Conference on Computer and Communication Technology, pp. 653–659 (2011)
20. Cressie, N.: Fitting variogram models by weighted least squares. J. Int. Assoc. Math. Geol. **17**(5), 563–586 (1985)
21. Deep, K., Thakur, M.: A new crossover operator for real coded genetic algorithms. Appl. Math. Comput. **188**(1), 895–911 (2007)
22. Deep, K., Thakur, M.: A new mutation operator for real coded genetic algorithms. Appl. Math. Comput. **193**(1), 211–230 (2007)

Matching Ontologies with Word2Vec-Based Neural Network

Nikolay Teslya[✉] and Sergey Savosin

SPIIRAS, 14th line, 39, 199178 St. Petersburg, Russia
{teslya,SVSavosin}@iias.spb.su

Abstract. To date, knowledge engineering researchers have proposed a large number of ontology matching methods. In this paper, to solve the ontology mapping problem, it is proposed to use a vector language model based on the Word2Vec statistical model set. The vector model is implemented using a neural network based on the TensorFlow framework. The peculiarity of the method is the use of the baseline pre-trained Wor2Vec model based on texts from the English Wikipedia and Google News, which is consistently extended on the basis of relationships specific to the ontologies being matched. This approach allows the use of semantics of the language bypassing situations in which, due to the form of a word or a specific term, it is impossible to find a correspondence of ontology concepts.

Keywords: Ontology matching · Neural network · Word2Vec · Ontology

1 Introduction

To date, knowledge engineering researchers have proposed a large number of ontology matching methods. A large review of the methods was carried out in the book by Shvaiko and Euzenat "Ontology matching" [4]. In the classification of comparison methods proposed by them, two independent hierarchies are distinguished, the difference between which consists in considering the subject of comparison and the source of data based on the analysis of context (semantic and syntactic) and content (terminological, structural, extensional and semantic). The method proposed in this paper relates to syntactic methods for the investigation of ontology entities and according to another hierarchy, to the synthesis of semantic methods of context analysis with terminological methods of content analysis.

In the category of contextual matching methods, the main role is the analysis of the meanings of the terms used to label the ontology entities and the connections between them. The analysis is carried out using the top-level ontologies,

Funding: The reported study was funded by RFBR, project numbers 17-07-00327, 17-07-00328.

S. Misra et al. (Eds.): ICCSA 2019, LNCS 11619, pp. 745–756, 2019.
https://doi.org/10.1007/978-3-030-24289-3_55

linked data, dictionaries and thesauri. Methods of processing natural language are also used to bring the used forms of words to normal vocabulary forms, allowing to simplify the interaction with thesauri and dictionaries.

The extension of the considered methods is the use of background sources of knowledge, which include any information about the ontology and its individual concepts. There are several categories of sources of background knowledge - explicit (those that do not require additional processing of information used) and implicit (requiring additional processing to extract knowledge). Examples of explicit sources are Linked Data [7]; domain-specific ontologies [1]; common-purpose ontologies; classifiers; dictionaries and thesauri (WordNet [9]); lexical databases (WordNet, DANTE). Examples of implicit sources include ontology design patterns and ontology matching patterns [6, 15, 16, 20].

Also there exists a scheme of the method based on the use of the problem area upper ontology as a source of background knowledge for ontology matching [18, 20]. The method includes two steps: (1) anchoring the source and target concepts of the matched ontologies to the background knowledge ontology; (2) defining if the relationship between the source and target concepts exists by searching for a similar relationship in the background knowledge ontology. Paper [21] extends the results of previous works of the authors, considering the use of several ontologies as sources of background knowledge.

Background knowledge can also be used to train the neural network used in the ontology matching. Such networks most often refer to the type of classifying networks, as in the study of ontology concepts, it is necessary to cross-define the degree of proximity of the concepts of matched ontologies. For example, in [13], a neural network is proposed for ontology matching that expands the ability to represent and display complex relationships in a neural network for identical elements searching (Identical Elements Neural Network). The network can learn the high-level properties of concepts in various tasks and use them to find a correspondence between tasks. This allows to train the network to find correspondence for specific concepts between different problem areas.

The transformation of the task of mapping ontology concept instances into the problem of binary classification and its solution using machine learning methods is proposed in [14]. To reach this goal, a similarity vector was developed, independent of the presence of coinciding properties in the instances of concepts. The training of neural network to classify pairs of concepts for the sets of matches and mismatches is carried out based on this vector. To improve performance, it is suggested to use information about already existing alignments. As a classification mechanism, a random decision tree was chosen to construct weak classifiers, which are combined using the AdaBoost algorithm.

In this paper, it is proposed to use the neural network based on the TensorFlow framework implementing the Word2Vec model for comparing ontology concepts. Previously, this model was used in similar tasks, in particular, to build a common taxonomy of several [18, 21], for research ontologies in different languages [5]. The original is the additional training of a pre-trained model to take into account the peculiarities of the semantic links between the names of concepts in specific ontologies in order to more accurately match the semantics of the ontology problem domain.

The paper is structured as follows. Section 2 briefly describes Word2Vec model and how it can be used for ontology matching. Section 3 provides structure of neural network to implement Word2Vec model in terms of neural networks. In Sect. 4 the ontology matching method based on the Word2Vec neural network is described. Section 5 provides implementation of proposed method and Sect. 6 describes some experiment results.

2 Word2Vec Model

As a source of background knowledge for ontologies matching, it is proposed to use the vector word space, reflecting the semantics of the problem domain. This approach is part of the natural language processing associated with distributional semantics.

The main idea of distributional semantics is the mapping of each word of text to a contextual vector of large dimension, the components of which are represented by real number. A set of vectors forms a vector space of words in which semantically close words will be located closer than words not related by semantics (see Fig. 1).

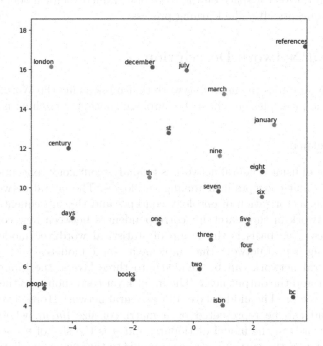

Fig. 1. Example of vector space

One of the main groups of models used to implement the vector representation of words is Word2Vec [10–12]. Its use allows both to predict a word depending on a context (continuous bag-of-words architecture), and to predict a context by a word (skip-gram architecture) using single vector model. Moreover, the word order in the context is not an important parameter (due to the so-called "bag of words" principle).

The vector space of words is represented by a matrix whose dimensions are determined by a dictionary size (the number of words that can be recognized) and the dimension of the vector. The greater the dimension of the vector used to display the word, the more accurately the semantic meanings of the words can be separated. To determine the parameters of the vector, training based on the analysis of the context of the word is used. For this, latent semantic analysis is used. [2,8], softmax using the Huffman tree (to reduce calculation) or the inverse problem of maximizing the objective likelihood function, minimizing log-likelihood of samples. During the training, the semantic proximity between words is calculated on the basis of their positions in the text and/or ontology graph and an assessment is made of the hidden factors that make up the components of word vector. In this case, semantically close words in the vector space will be located side by side, which allows the use of the vector space of words when comparing ontologies to define semantically close ontology concepts. The task of the neural network in this case is to find the closest concepts of compared ontologies in the vector space on the basis of a trained vector model of names of ontologies concepts after the learning process.

3   Neural Network Description

This section describes the neural network that implements the Word2Vec model and the basic principles on which the ontology concepts matching is built.

3.1   Structure

The purpose of using a neural network is to analyze ontology concepts and cross-search for similar concepts in matching ontologies. The neural network work is based on the vectorization of ontology concepts and the subsequent training of a neural network in the search for correspondences between new concepts and familiar ones. The basis is the group of statistical word2vec models and the corresponding neural network that implements these models.

The neural network can be divided into three layers: the input layer, the hidden layer and the output layer. The input layer corresponds to the dimension of the word vector. The hidden layer of the neural network stores a vector model of titles, and can be represented by a matrix of size $[m, n]$, where m is the number of words in the model dictionary, and n is the size of the word vector. The dimension of the output layer corresponds to the size of the dictionary. The neurons of the output layer contain the sigmoid activation function [3], which activates neurons depending on the value of the vector in hidden layer. Neurons with the maximum value of the activation function will contain the names of the concepts that are as close as possible to the name of the ontology concept, which is input to the neural network. The result of the neural network are the values of similarity coefficients for each of the elements of the output layer.

3.2   Learning

Learning for a hidden layer of a neural network requires processing of a large corpora of natural language texts. Examples of such cases are encyclopedias articles, electronic libraries, and news or messages archives. An obvious advantage of this approach is control over the learning process, which consists in using only domain-specific texts. However, the learning process takes a significant amount of time (from 12 h when using one device with CPU and without graphics accelerators) or requires significant computational resources (with graphics accelerators, or parallelization of computations on several devices).

The learning process can be skipped when using a previously trained vector word model containing the semantics of the problem areas of the ontologies under consideration. Such a model will contain a large number of words, but due to the dimension of the vector space it will require very large volume and RAM size. The model used can be further trained on the context of ontology concepts (neighboring concepts, relationships between concepts, characteristics of concepts), so that it most fully reflects the semantics for a specific ontology. During training, the presence of ontology terms in the vector model is checked. If the word vector is present in the vector model, then for neighboring concepts and ontology properties, the elements of the corresponding vectors are adjusted to bring them together in vector space. Adjustment is carried out by the backward propagation method by calculating the difference between the expected output of the neural network and the real output, and applying the difference to the vectors of the hidden layer inside the neural network. In the case of the absence of a vector in the vocabulary, it is added to the model along with the corresponding output neuron, after which the elements are calculated for the new vector also on the basis of the back propagation of the error. The use of a pre-trained vector word model is necessary in order to exclude a situation in which there is no vector representation of the concept label from the compared ontology. If the label of the concept is not in the model, then it will be ignored, since the capabilities of the neural network are limited to the names included in the dictionary. One of the possible solutions to this problem is the stemming (search for the basis of the word) and lemmatization (bringing the word form to the normal (vocabulary) form) of words, followed by the search for the corresponding forms in the vector model. The trained vector model of words can also be saved for future use in order to reduce the learning time of the neural network for the ontology studied.

4   Ontology Matching Model

The general scheme of the developed method is based on expanding the ontology matching process developed by the project team earlier by adding background knowledge hidden in the vector space of words. The input method accepts the ontologies O_1 and O_2 in the OWL format and returns the result of the comparison in the form of an alignment matrix for ontology concepts A as well as its visualization in the form of a bipartite graph. The basic scheme of the method is based on the use of entities labels and the context of the concepts of these ontologies.

The work of the method can be divided into three stages (see Fig. 2). The first stage is related to the processing of initial ontologies, during which the abstract and operational contexts are identified, as well as the problem area of each ontology is extracted. At the second stage, the mapping of processed ontologies based on methods using matching patterns and concept contexts takes place. To improve the quality of comparison methods different sources of background knowledge are used. The work of the matching methods at the second stage is performed in parallel and independently with the formation of intermediate matrices of ontology concepts. At the third stage of work, the composition of intermediate correspondence matrices is carried out with the formation of the final matrix, which is the final result of the work of the developed ontology matching method.

Consider in detail each of the stages. The first stage is the processing of the initial ontologies. During the processing, abstract and operational contexts are allocated for each ontology $F(O_i) = (AK_i, OK_i)$, reflecting the structure and instances of ontology concepts, respectively. The abstract context is

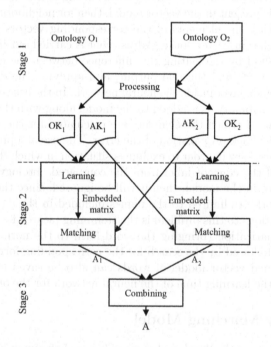

Fig. 2. The scheme of ontology matching method

represented using the object network of constraints [17], which allows to store more information about the structure of concepts and the ontology itself, which is subsequently used in the search for matching concepts. The operational context includes instances of ontology concepts, taking into account the values of their properties, the type and nature of links. For the pair of ontologies, the problem area is determined by the operational context using topic modeling methods [19]. Since these methods are used primarily to build topic models of texts, ontologies need to be converted into a textual representation, for which information from the operational context is used. The texts in this case are all the labels of the concepts of ontologies and the text parameters of the entity instances, collected in the so-called "bag of words".

The second stage is the comparison. Due to the fact that the proposed method implies cross-matching of ontologies, at the second stage two sub-stages can be distinguished, associated with the matching of each ontologies.

When searching for correspondence between concepts, the matching ontologies O_1 and O_2 are transmitted in the processed format of abstract and operational contexts to the neural network. From each ontology, the string characteristics of the concepts are retrieved - the labels of the concepts, their properties, relationships. A pre-trained vector word model is loaded into the hidden layer of the neural network. Then the neural network is additionally trained using first O_1 ontology concepts to recognize their belonging to a given ontology. The training based on the fact that for each ontology concept its semantic proximity with neighboring concepts and links with them is checked. If the value of the output neurons does not correspond to the context of the concept, the corresponding vectors are recalculated. Upon completion of the learning process, concepts from the O_2 ontology are fed to the input of the neural network and are checked to which concepts from the O_1 ontology they most fully correspond (the value of the activation function is checked, which lies in the range $[0, 1]$, where 0 is the lack of correspondence, 1 is full compliance). The maximum value of the activation function and its corresponding concepts are recorded in the intermediate matrix of ontology correspondence A_1. After checking all the concepts from the ontology O_2 in a similar way, the ontologies are replaced - the network is retrained to recognize the concepts from the ontology O_2 and checks the consistency of the concepts from the ontology O_1.

At the third stage, the intermediate comparison results are combined in the final alignment matrix by calculating the average value of each coefficient $A = 1/2A_1 + 1/2A_2$. The choice of simple arithmetic average is due to the equivalence of matching procedures.

5   Ontology Matching Model Implementation

To implement the Word2Vec model in the neural network, the TensorFlow library was used. The training was based on English Wikipedia texts (dump from 2017, 4 billion words with a vector space dimension of 300 - the size of the trained model is about 8 GB), which were pre-processed to eliminate service words, unions and words that are not part of the problem area. The last is required in order to reduce the dimension of the embedding matrix during training and use. Also used pre-trained model on the news texts from Google News. The size of the pre-trained model dictionary is about 3 million words and phrases, and the vector space dimension is 300 components (the file size of the trained model requires about 3 GB of HDD space to store).

Python v3.7 was chosen as the main programming language for the development of the prototype. The main advantage of using it for the presented task is the availability of powerful modules for processing science data with large data arrays, such as numpy, scikit, etc. which have a simple interface and C kernel implementation, as well as the TensorFlow library for configuring and evaluation a neural network.

Ontologies in OWL are loaded and processed using the owlready2 library. This library allows to convert ontology classes into Python objects of the and vice versa, which greatly simplifies their processing.

For the convenience of displaying the found matches, visualization based on a weighted bipartite graph was used. The vertices of the graph are the concepts of ontologies, arcs are correspondence between concepts and the weights of the arcs are the coefficient of conformity of the concepts. The networkx library was used for visualization.

The software architecture of the ontology matching module is presented in the Fig. 3.

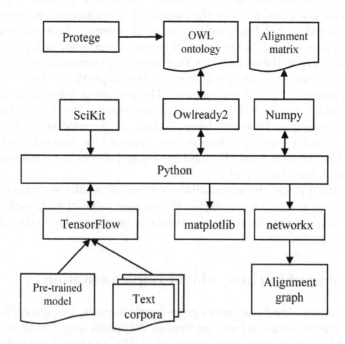

Fig. 3. Software architecture of ontology matching module

6   Evaluation

To test the proposed approach, a set of data used in the competition on ontology comparison - OAEI was used. Each year, several data tracks are formed from various problem areas in which developers offer their methods for comparison and determine the best estimated precision, recall and F-Measure. The proposed approach was tested on the Conference track data set of 2018.

Conference track contains 16 ontologies united by the domain of conference organization. These ontologies are developed to be suitable for ontology matching task because of their heterogeneous character of origin (see Fig. 4).

Ontologies have been based upon three types of underlying resources:

- actual conference and its web pages,
- actual software tool for conference organization support,
- experience of people with personal participation in organization of actual conference.

Fig. 4. An example of an ontology from the conference suite

Fig. 5. The result of comparing two ontologies

Table 1. Evaluation metrics

Metric	Proposed approach	ALOD2Vec	StringEquiv	AML
Precision	0.79	0.71	0.8	0.84
Recall	0.65	0.5	0.43	0.66
F1-measure	0.36	0.59	0.56	0.74

All experiments were performed on a test bench with the following configuration: CPU Intel(R)Core(TM)i7-4770K 3.1 GHz, RAM 16G, and GPU NVidia(R)GeForce 770. The matching of ontologies was carried out in pairs, $C_m^2 = 120$ matching procedures were made. Figure 5 presents examples of matching results for the random ontologies from the set.

According to the results of the proposed method tests, the accuracy of the work was evaluated. Traditionally, ontology comparison problems were estimated by parameters precision (the fraction of retrieved documents that are relevant to the query), recall (percent of all relevant documents that is returned by the search) and F-measure. The results are presented in Table 1 with comparison of other approaches from *ra1-M3* evaluation modality that is ontologies that can be downloaded and compared by using both classes and properties [22].

Low F-measure can be explained by the number of all ontology concepts exceeds the number of coinciding ones. In addition, the proposed method requires additional configuration in the part of the neural network learning process for ontology concepts to account for more background knowledge sources.

7   Conclusion

The results of the work show that the use of background knowledge, enclosed in the semantics of the problem area, really allows to process for the ontology matching task. The use of a neural network that implements the model of the vector space of words allowed to partially extract the background knowledge and utilize it to analyze the names of ontology concepts. The results obtained can be improved by analyzing the structure of the ontology: characteristics of concepts, instances, domains of characteristics, analysis of types of links.

As directions for further work, we can highlight the study of existing pre-trained models and different implementations of word vector space on their completeness and accuracy of semantic separation, which is important when comparing ontologies from similar problem areas. Another focus is the creation of corpuses of texts and the training of models for frequent problem areas. The main goal in this case is to reduce the dimension of the embedding matrix, by eliminating concepts that are not correspond to used problem area without losing the semantic connectedness of the remaining concepts. In addition, reducing the size of buildings for training will speed up the learning process.

References

1. Chaves, M.S., de Freitas, L.A., Vieira, R.: Hontology: a multilingual ontology for the accommodation sector in the tourism industry. In: Filipe, J., Dietz, J.L.G. (eds.) KEOD, pp. 149–154. SciTePress (2012). http://dblp.uni-trier.de/db/conf/ic3k/keod2012.html#ChavesFV12
2. Deerwester, S., Dumais, S.T., Furnas, G.W., Landauer, T.K., Harshman, R.: Indexing by latent semantic analysis. J. Am. Soc. Inform. Sci. **41**(6), 391–407 (1990)
3. Elfwing, S., Uchibe, E., Doya, K.: Sigmoid-weighted linear units for neural network function approximation in reinforcement learning. Neural Netw. **107**, 3–11 (2018). https://doi.org/10.1016/j.neunet.2017.12.012
4. Euzenat, J., Shvaiko, P.: Ontology Matching. Springer, Heidelberg (2013). https://doi.org/10.1007/978-3-642-38721-0
5. Gromann, D., Declerck, T.: Comparing pretrained multilingual word embeddings on an ontology alignment task. In: Proceedings of the 11th International Conference on Language Resources and Evaluation, pp. 230–236 (2018)
6. Hamdi, F., Reynaud, C., Safar, B.: Pattern-based mapping refinement. In: Cimiano, P., Pinto, H.S. (eds.) EKAW 2010. LNCS (LNAI), vol. 6317, pp. 1–15. Springer, Heidelberg (2010). https://doi.org/10.1007/978-3-642-16438-5_1
7. Hecht, T., Buche, P., Dibie, J., Ibanescu, L., dos Santos, C.T.: Ontology alignment using web linked ontologies as background knowledge. In: Guillet, F., Pinaud, B., Venturini, G. (eds.) Advances in Knowledge Discovery and Management. SCI, vol. 665, pp. 207–227. Springer, Cham (2017). https://doi.org/10.1007/978-3-319-45763-5_11

8. Landauer, T.K., Foltz, P.W., Laham, D.: An introduction to latent semantic analysis. Discourse Process. **25**(2–3), 259–284 (1998). https://doi.org/10.1080/01638539809545028

9. Lin, F., Sandkuhl, K.: A survey of exploiting WordNet in ontology matching. In: Bramer, M. (ed.) IFIP AI 2008. ITIFIP, vol. 276, pp. 341–350. Springer, Boston, MA (2008). https://doi.org/10.1007/978-0-387-09695-7_33

10. Mikolov, T., Chen, K., Corrado, G., Dean, J.: Efficient estimation of word representations in vector space, pp. 1–12, January 2013. http://arxiv.org/abs/1301.3781

11. Mikolov, T., Sutskever, I., Chen, K., Corrado, G., Dean, J.: Distributed representations of words and phrases and their compositionality, pp. 319–333, October 2013

12. Onal, K.D., et al.: Neural information retrieval: at the end of the early years. Inform. Retrieval J. **21**(2–3), 111–182 (2018). https://doi.org/10.1007/s10791-017-9321-y

13. Peng, Y., Munro, P., Mao, M.: Ontology mapping neural network: an approach to learning and inferring correspondences among ontologies. In: CEUR Workshop Proceedings, vol. 658, pp. 65–68 (2010)

14. Rong, S., Niu, X., Xiang, E.W., Wang, H., Yang, Q., Yu, Y.: A machine learning approach for instance matching based on similarity metrics. In: Cudré-Mauroux, P., et al. (eds.) ISWC 2012. LNCS, vol. 7649, pp. 460–475. Springer, Heidelberg (2012). https://doi.org/10.1007/978-3-642-35176-1_29

15. Scharffe, F., Euzenat, J., Fensel, D.: Towards design patterns for ontology alignment. In: Proceedings of the 2008 ACM Symposium on Applied Computing - SAC 2008, p. 2321. ACM Press, New York (2008). https://doi.org/10.1145/1363686.1364236

16. Scharffe, F., Zamazal, O., Fensel, D.: Ontology alignment design patterns. Knowl. Inform. Syst. **4**(1), 1–28 (2014). https://doi.org/10.1007/s10115-013-0633-y

17. Smirnov, A., Levashova, T., Kashevnik, A.: Ontology-based resource interoperability in socio-cyber-physical systems collaboration scenario. Inform. Technol. Ind. **6**(2), 19–24 (2018)

18. St. Chifu, E., Letia, I.A.: A neural model for unsupervised taxonomy enrichment. In: Proceedings of the 10th International Conference on Information Integration and Web-based Applications and Services, iiWAS 2008, pp. 264–270 (2008). https://doi.org/10.1145/1497308.1497358

19. Steyvers, M., Griffiths, T.: Probabilistic topic models. Handb. Latent Semant. Anal. **427**(7), 424–440 (2007)

20. Svab-Zamazal, O., Svatek, V.: Towards ontology matching via pattern-based detection of semantic structures in owl ontologies. In: Proceedings of the Znalosti Czecho-Slovak Knowledge Technology conference (2009)

21. Wohlgenannt, G., Minic, F.: Using Word2Vec to build a simple ontology learning system. In: CEUR Workshop Proceedings, vol. 1690, pp. 2–5 (2016)

22. Zamazal, O., Cheatham, M., Jana, V.: Results of evaluation for the conference track within OAEI 2018 (2018). http://oaei.ontologymatching.org/2018/results/conference/index.html#ra1-M3. Accessed 5 May 2019

Improving the Performance of an Integer Linear Programming Community Detection Algorithm Through Clique Filtering

Luiz Henrique Nogueira Lorena[1], Marcos Gonçalves Quiles[1(✉)], and Luiz Antonio Nogueira Lorena[2]

[1] Institute of Science and Technology, Federal University of São Paulo (UNIFESP), São José dos Campos, SP, Brazil
luiz.lorena@hotmail.com, quiles@unifesp.br
[2] National Institute for Space Research (INPE), São José dos Campos, SP, Brazil
lorena@lac.inpe.br

Abstract. Different fields of science use network representation as a framework to model their systems. The analysis of network structure can give us essential information about the system. However, the size of such a network can limit the applicability of some fundamental techniques like mathematical programming. Thus, here we propose a novel network size reduction technique based on a clique filtering approach. Our goal is twofold: (1) reduce the network size and speed up the community detection process, and (2) preserve the modularity of the original partition in the context of the exact model. Conducted experiments show the feasibility and correctness of the proposed technique.

Keywords: Community detection · Integer linear programming · Preprocessing technique

1 Introduction

Network representation is being used to model systems in different fields of science, like computer science, physics, chemistry, biology, and sociology [2,13, 18]. The goal is to uncover meaningful information about the system by analyzing the structure and dynamic of the network.

One particular network structure, relevant in different contexts of science, is the community or modular structure. A community can be defined as a group of nodes densely connected. Finding the communities of a network is an actively studied problem, and several techniques have been proposed in the literature, from heuristic to exact methods [5,6].

A great number of techniques are based on the optimization of a quality function. Newman's modularity [12] is the most popular quality function used

© Springer Nature Switzerland AG 2019
S. Misra et al. (Eds.): ICCSA 2019, LNCS 11619, pp. 757–769, 2019.
https://doi.org/10.1007/978-3-030-24289-3_56

to estimate the goodness of a partition obtained by a community detection technique. High values of modularity indicate good partitions. Hence, modularity-based techniques try to obtain partitions that maximize such quality function.

This work focus on solving the community detection problem via the modularity-based Linear Programming (ILP) formulation proposed by Argawal et al. [1]. This approach, however, may create models that are large and time-consuming to solve. The size of the models may restrict the use of such technique. Hence, here we are interested in strategies that can reduce such computational burden.

Recent research aims to reduce the number of edges and/or nodes of a network while maintaining some of its structural properties. Such properties may include shortest paths and connectivity, cuts, source-to-sink flow, spectral properties and modularity [3,4,7,8,10,17,20]. The work of Arenas et al. [3] is particularly interesting in the context of modularity maximization. It shows that some peripheral cliques can be filtered from the network, creating a smaller network representation. By using this reduced network, they achieved a speedup in their community detection heuristic while preserving the quality of the obtained solutions.

Arenas et al. [3] technique, however, is limited to cliques composed by two or three nodes. Hence, here, we waive this restriction by proposing a technique capable of filtering larger cliques. Our goal is to speed up the community detection process and to preserve the quality of the obtained solutions, in the context of the exact model.

The computational experiments shows that, by reducing the size of the network, we are able to obtain ILP models that have a reduced number of variables and constraints. Such models require less memory and computation time to solve.

This work is organized as follows. First, community detection via ILP is presented in Sect. 2, highlighting its properties and limitations. In Sect. 3 the clique filtering approach proposed by Arenas et al. [3] is presented, and a relevant property discovered in their work is discussed. Section 4 introduces the new clique filtering algorithm. The computational experiments are reported in Sect. 5. Finally, conclusions are discussed in Sect. 6, along with future work directions.

2   Modularity Maximization via ILP

The following notation will be used throughout this paper. A network is represented by an undirected weighted graph $G = (V, E)$, consisting of $n = |V|$ nodes and $m = |E|$ edges. The edge weights are stored in an adjacency matrix A composed by $|V| \times |V|$ elements.

Newman [14] proposed modularity as a measure to evaluate the quality of a partition obtained by a community detection method. It takes values in the interval $[-\frac{1}{2}, 1]$. High values of modularity indicate good partitions. To calculate modularity, we assume $\mathcal{P} = \{C_1, C_2, \dots, C_p\}$ as the partition obtained by a community detection method. $\mathcal{P}$ represents a collection of p disjoint subsets of nodes C (communities). In the context of G it is defined as follows

$$Q(\mathcal{P}) = \frac{1}{2s} \sum_{i=1}^{n} \sum_{j=1}^{n} \left(A_{ij} - \frac{s_i s_j}{2s} \right) \delta_{ij} \tag{1}$$

where
$$x_{ij} = \begin{cases} 1 & \text{if } i \text{ and } j \text{ are in the same community} \\ 0 & \text{otherwise} \end{cases}$$

and A_{ij} is the weight of the edge $\{i,j\}$. Expressions s_i and s_j represents the strength of node i and j, respectively. The strength of a node is the sum of the edge weights incident to it, and it is calculated as $s_i = \sum_{j=1}^{n} A_{ij}$. Finally, s represents the sum of all edge weights in A, and it is calculated as $s = \frac{1}{2} \sum_{i=1}^{n} \sum_{j=1}^{n} A_{ij}$.

Modularity maximization can be formulated as an ILP by following the steps provided by Agarwal et al. [1]. The objective function is derived from modularity formula presented in Eq. 1. Binary variables x_{ij} are introduced, assuming a value equal to 1 if i and j belong to the same community and 0 otherwise.

$$\frac{1}{2s} \sum_{i=1}^{n} \sum_{j=1}^{n} \left(A_{ij} - \frac{s_i s_j}{2s} \right) x_{ij}$$

The expression inside the parentheses is the modularity matrix M_{ij} defined by Newman et al. [15]. Consequently, the objective function can be simplified to

$$\frac{1}{2s} \sum_{i=1}^{n} \sum_{j=1}^{n} M_{ij} x_{ij}$$

Variables x_{ii} can be replaced by a constant in the objective function, since $x_{ii} = 1$ for all nodes i:

$$C = \frac{1}{2s} \sum_{i=1}^{n} M_{ii}$$

Since $x_{ij} = x_{ji}$ for all nodes i and j, variables x_{ij} where $i > j$ can be removed from the model by doubling the objective function. Hence, the following ILP model is obtained:

$$Maximize \ \frac{1}{s} \sum_{i=1}^{n-1} \sum_{j=i+1}^{n} M_{ij} x_{ij} + C$$

$$subject \ to$$
$$x_{ij} + x_{jk} - x_{ik} \geq 0, \quad M_{ij} \geq 0 \vee M_{jk} \geq 0 \tag{2}$$
$$x_{ij} - x_{jk} + x_{ik} \geq 0, \quad M_{ij} \geq 0 \vee M_{ik} \geq 0 \tag{3}$$
$$-x_{ij} + x_{jk} + x_{ik} \geq 0, \quad M_{jk} \geq 0 \vee M_{ik} \geq 0 \tag{4}$$
$$x_{ij} \in \{0,1\}, \quad i,j \in [1..n]$$

where
$$x_{ij} = \begin{cases} 0 & \text{if } i \text{ and } j \text{ are in the same community} \\ 1 & \text{otherwise.} \end{cases}$$

The transitivity constraints (2–4) assures that: if node i is in the same community as j, and j and k are in the same community, then i must be in the same community as k.

The original model by Agarwal et al. [1] has $O(n^2)$ variables and $O(n^3)$ transitivity constraints, and tends to grow fast as the size of the network increases. A recent work by Miyauchi et al. [11] showed that some of the transitivity constraints are redundant and can be eliminated during model construction. They provided conditional clauses that check for redundant constraints and prevent its creation. We use such strategy here to extend original ILP model. This explains the conditional $M_{ij} \geq 0 \vee M_{jk} \geq 0$ introduced in constraint (2). If the conditional is not respected the constraint is not inserted in the model.

The major drawback of the ILP approach is the size of its model. It is heavily affected by the number of nodes of the network being modeled. Consequently, any technique that could reduce the number of nodes in the network while maintaining some of its structural properties would be of great value. In the next section, a technique with such capabilities is discussed. This technique was used as the base to create the new filtering algorithm proposed in this work.

3   Clique Filtering

Some basic concepts are important in the context of the topic discussed in this section. A clique is a subset of V, such that every two distinct nodes are adjacent. A node whose removal disconnects a connected graph is called an articulation point.

In this work we focus on a particular type of clique, denoted here as K_s, where $s = |V_s|$ represents the number of elements in the clique. This clique is peripheral and have one specific node, denoted here as v^*, that is an articulation point. Figure 1 show examples of cliques K_2 and K_3.

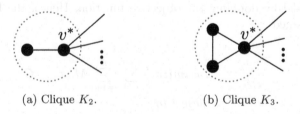

(a) Clique K_2.   (b) Clique K_3.

Fig. 1. Type of cliques filtered by Arenas et al. [3].

Arenas et al. [3] proposed a filtering technique for reducing the size of a network while preserving modularity. It is able to filter cliques K_2 and K_3 (Fig. 1) by collapsing such structures into a smaller network representation.

Their experimental results shows that their technique can reduce the size of networks, speed up the community detection heuristic and preserve the quality of the obtained solution.

In [3] a relevant property of modularity is used to reduce the size of the network: nodes forming a community in the optimal partition can be represented by a unique node in the reduced network. The basic idea is that each node and edge removed during the filtering process contributed to the original graph modularity value. Hence, to preserve this value, such contribution needs to be taken into account while calculating the reduced graph modularity. Figure 2 shows how this property can be used to create a smaller network representation.

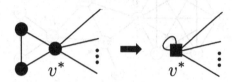

Fig. 2. Reducing a network size by collapsing nodes and edges.

In Fig. 2, node v^* will store in the weight of its self-loop the info about the filtering process that will be relevant for the modularity computation. The self-loop weight will accumulate the weight of the collapsed edges that were incident to v^*. The remaining $s - 1$ clique nodes and respective edges are collapsed into a smaller network representation.

The following section presents the algorithm to identify and filter larger cliques K_s. The strategy to reduce the size of the network presented in this section will be employed to create a smaller network representation.

4   Clique Filter (CF) Algorithm

The proposed filter is based on the identification of cliques K_s (Fig. 3). Cliques K_2 are easily identified by the degree of the node incident to the articulation point v^*. However, to identify cliques with $s \geq 3$ we follow a different approach based on the local clustering coefficient of a node.

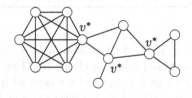

Fig. 3. Example with three cliques K_s.

The local clustering coefficient (LCC) [19] of a node quantifies how close its neighbors are to being a complete graph (clique). This measure assumes its maximum value (1.0) when every neighbor of i is connected (clique), and its minimum (0.0) when there are no connections between the neighbors of i.

By using the LCC, we can observe in Fig. 4 that cliques with $s \geq 3$ are composed by $s - 1$ nodes with LCC equal to 1.0. The only node with a different LCC is the articulation point v^*. This property was used as a starting point to create the new clique filtering algorithm.

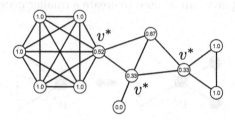

Fig. 4. Identifying larger cliques K_s.

Algorithm 1 presents the proposed clique filtering algorithm (CF). The objective is to receive a network as input G and output a reduced network representation G'. The algorithm is composed of four steps. Figure 5 depicts the behavior of each step of Algorithm 1 on a sample network. In the first step of the algorithm all nodes of G are assigned to its own group (Fig. 5a). The group ownership will guide the construction of the reduced network in the final step of the algorithm.

Algorithm 1. Clique Filter (CF).

---

input : A weighted graph $G = (V, E)$
output: A weighted graph $G' = (V', E')$

1 Assign each node of G to its own group
2 Calculate the LCC of each node in G
3 For all nodes in G, check if it has degree 1 or all its neighbors except one has LCC equal to 1.0. If so, assign the node and its neighbors to the same group of the articulation point v^*
4 Create a smaller network representation G' based on the group ownership of G

In the second step, the LCC of the nodes in G is calculated (Fig. 5b). Step three test if each node in G belongs to a clique K_s (Fig. 5c). Nodes with degree one are participants of cliques K_2 and nodes where all its neighbors except one has LCC equal to 1.0 are participant of a larger clique K_s. Such nodes and all its neighbors are assigned to the group of the articulation point (v^*) of K_s.

Finally, at step 4, the strategy discussed in Sect. 3 is used to create a reduced network representation G' (Fig. 5d). Nodes that belongs to the same group in G are collapsed into a single node in G', the edges connecting nodes in the same group are collapsed into a self-loop whose weight will be the sum of the weight of the collapsed edges. Groups composed by individual nodes in G remains unchanged, preserving their structural properties in the reduced network G'.

The worst-case time complexity for Algorithm 1 is $O(m^{\frac{3}{2}})$. The local clustering coefficient algorithm used on step 2 is the dominant factor of this time complexity. The remaining steps have linear time complexity.

The reduced network representation obtained by CF algorithm can be used directly in the ILP formulation described in Sect. 2. In the following section, the experimental results show how the reduced network can benefit the exact model.

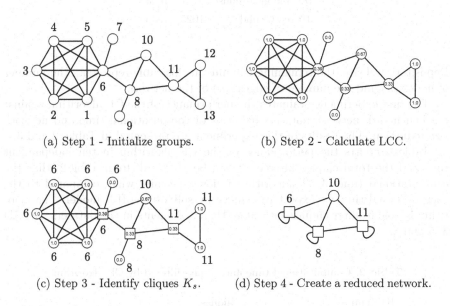

(a) Step 1 - Initialize groups.   (b) Step 2 - Calculate LCC.

(c) Step 3 - Identify cliques K_s.   (d) Step 4 - Create a reduced network.

Fig. 5. Example illustrating each step of Algorithm 1.

5 Experimental Results

In this section, experiments were conducted in order to verify the validity of the CF algorithm. The experiments and algorithms were coded in C++14 and executed on a computer with the following configuration: Intel Core i7-6770HQ (3,5 GHz) with 32 GB RAM running Windows 10 64-Bit. The commercial solver IBM ILOG CPLEX [9] 12.7.1 was used to solve the ILP models.

Table 1 presents the datasets used in this work. Only the giant components of the networks were used in the experiments. All datasets were downloaded from the Network Repository website [16]. Each dataset received a unique id (first column). The second column presents the dataset name in the Network

Table 1. Benchmark datasets used in the experiments.

ID	Dataset	n	m
1	lemis	77	254
2	GD00-A	83	125
3	ca-sandi-auths	86	124
4	rt-retweet	96	177
5	netscience	379	914
6	bio-DM-LC	483	997
7	power-494-bus	494	586
8	bio-diseasome	516	1188
9	bio-grid-mouse	791	1098
10	ca-CSphd	1025	1043

Repository website, the remaining columns in this table represents the number of nodes (n) and the number of edges (m) of the network.

The first experiment evaluates the performance of the CF algorithm against the benchmark network datasets in terms of computational time and network size reduction. The results of this experiment are presented in Tables 2 and 3.

Table 2 reports the performance of the CF algorithm in ten independent runs and the total cliques filtered. It can be observed, from Table 2, that the computational time of CF algorithm is low, specially when compared to the computational time we expect to achieve by solving the ILP model. The algorithm is able to filter cliques with more than 3 elements in the datasets with ID 3, 5 and 8.

Table 2. Computational time and cliques filtered by CF algorithm.

ID	Time	Cliques
1	4.8×10^{-5} (1.3×10^{-6})	$K_2(17)$ $K_3(1)$
2	3.9×10^{-5} (4.7×10^{-7})	$K_2(19)$
3	4.2×10^{-5} (1.7×10^{-6})	$K_2(24)$ $K_3(5)$ $K_4(1)$
4	4.1×10^{-5} (1.8×10^{-6})	$K_2(53)$
5	6.5×10^{-5} (9.9×10^{-7})	$K_2(27)$ $K_3(16)$ $K_4(6)$ $K_5(4)$
6	5.8×10^{-5} (2.5×10^{-6})	$K_2(143)$
7	5.3×10^{-5} (1.6×10^{-6})	$K_2(146)$ $K_3(2)$
8	8.2×10^{-5} (1.4×10^{-6})	$K_2(90)$ $K_3(25)$ $K_4(8)$ $K_5(4)$ $K_6(2)$
9	6.8×10^{-5} (1.4×10^{-6})	$K_2(409)$ $K_3(1)$
10	1.2×10^{-4} (4.1×10^{-6})	$K_2(693)$

Table 3. Size of the original and reduced network.

ID	G		G'		%Reduction	
	n	m	n'	m'	%n	%m
1	77	254	58	242	24.68	4.72
2	83	125	64	118	22.89	5.60
3	86	124	57	98	43.02	20.97
4	96	177	43	95	55.21	46.33
5	379	914	286	803	24.54	12.14
6	483	997	340	935	29.61	6.22
7	494	586	344	544	30.36	7.17
8	516	1188	326	992	36.82	16.50
9	791	1098	380	843	51.96	23.22
10	1025	1043	332	588	67.61	43.62

Table 3 presents a comparison between the original (G) and filtered network (G') regarding its size. The percentage of network size reduction is presented in column *%Reduction*. It can be observed, from Table 3, that there is a reduction in the number of nodes in G' that goes from 22.89% up to 67.61%. The reduction in the number of edges goes from 4.72% up to 46.33%.

The next experiment was conducted to test the main hypothesis of this work, which states that the ILP technique can obtain a performance improvement and retain its quality by using the smaller network obtained by the CF algorithm. The results of this experiment are presented in Tables 4 and 5.

Table 4. Optimal solution and size of the original and filtered network ILP models.

ID	Q	#Variables		#Constraints	
		G	G'	G	G'
1	0.56000	2926	**1653**	34685	**23110**
2	0.53091	3403	**2016**	18434	**11581**
3	0.73683	3655	**1176**	20369	**7085**
4	0.67966	4560	**903**	21511	**4954**
5	0.84858	71631	**40755**	682739	**428071**
6	0.77869	116403	**57630**	946606	**566353**
7	0.85999	121771	**58996**	575323	**295959**
8	0.83199	132870	**52975**	1211786	**578838**
9	0.80101	312445	**72010**	1716725	**510436**
10	0.92558	524800	**54946**	2128786	**230136**

Table 5. Computational time and memory consumption of the original and filtered network ILP models.

ID	Time		Memory		%Reduction	
	G	G'	G	G'	%Time	%Memory
1	0.61	**0.42**	23.44	**15.88**	31.15	32.24
2	2.23	**1.46**	13.72	**8.90**	34.53	35.11
3	0.41	**0.15**	14.59	**6.18**	63.41	57.68
4	0.64	**0.18**	16.54	**4.42**	71.88	73.28
5	43.40	**20.67**	415.71	**269.53**	52.37	35.16
6	5315.57	**1692.86**	636.14	**361.01**	68.15	43.25
7	90419.51	**17586.84**	392.28	**199.97**	80.55	49.02
8	22966.99	**3046.39**	761.88	**364.17**	86.74	52.20
9	26551.02	**390.40**	1139.08	**341.81**	98.53	69.99
10	2512.05	**86.39**	1522.37	**169.82**	96.56	88.85

Table 4 presents the modularity (Q) and the size of the ILP models of the original (G) and reduced network (G'). It can be observed, from Table 4, that the modularity of the obtained solutions is preserved for both ILP models. However, the ILP models created for the reduced networks (G') are smaller in terms of the number of variables and constraints.

Table 5 reports the computational time and the memory consumption of the ILP models of the original (G) and reduced network (G'). It can be observed that the size reduction granted an improvement in performance of the ILP technique. There is a considerable percentage of reduction in terms of computational time and memory consumption. The percentage of reduction in time ranged from 31.15% up to 98.53%. For the datasets 6, 7, 8 and 9 it was possible to reduce the computational time from hours to minutes. For dataset 7, it was required one day to solve the ILP model for G, whereas the G' ILP model was solved in approximately five hours. The percentage of reduction in memory consumption was above 32.24% for all datasets. It achieved its highest value of 88.85% for the dataset 10, reducing the memory consumption from 1.5 GB to 169 MB.

Finally, Fig. 6 presents a comparison between the partitions obtained for the dataset with ID 5 (netscience). Figure 6a shows the partition obtained by solving the ILP model based on the original network (G), cliques filtered by the CF algorithm are highlighted in black. Figure 6b presents the partition obtained in the context of the reduced network (G'), the black color highlight nodes that received the cliques collapsed by the filtering algorithm. It can be observed that the groups obtained for the original network are preserved.

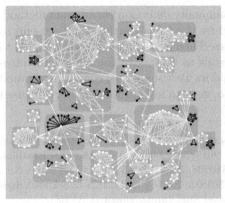 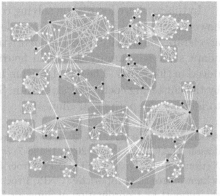

(a) Original network optimal solution.   (b) Filtered network optimal solution.

Fig. 6. Comparing the optimal solution obtained for the original and filtered network of the dataset with ID 5.

6 Conclusions

Finding communities in networks is an actively studied topic, and several techniques were proposed in the literature. Modularity maximization via ILP is an interesting approach to obtain exact solutions for this problem. However, this technique is heavily affected by the size of the network because the resulting ILP models tends to grow fast as the number of nodes in the network increases.

Hence, this work proposed an algorithm, denoted here as CF, capable of reducing the size of the network by filtering peripheral cliques. The aim is to reduce the size of the network so it increases the performance of the ILP technique and the quality of its solution. The algorithm is based on the work by Arenas et al. [3], which showed that some peripheral cliques can be filtered from the graph, creating a smaller network representation without losing information relevant in the context of community detection. Their technique, however, is limited to cliques composed of two or three nodes.

The CF algorithm extends [3] work, by providing an approach to identify larger peripheral cliques via the local clustering coefficient of their members. The worst-case time complexity for CF is dominated by the local clustering coefficient calculus, however, the computational effort is relatively small when compared with computational time required to solve the ILP model based on the reduced network obtained as an output from the CF algorithm.

The proposed algorithm was validated in benchmark network datasets used in scientific literature. The experimental results shows that CF was capable of reducing the size of all the networks in a small computational time. The reduction in network size granted a considerable improvement in the performance of the ILP technique in terms of computational time and memory consumption. The quality of the solution obtained, measured via modularity, was preserved as well.

In this work we focused on solving community detection via an exact method, however, the gain in reduction provided by the CF algorithm can be useful to accelerate community detection heuristics. Therefore, as future work, we plan to adapt some community detection heuristics to work with the reductions introduced in this paper. The CF algorithm has its worst-case time complexity limited by the clustering coefficient algorithm. So, we plan to improve the algorithm used to identify the peripheral cliques.

Acknowledgment. M.G.Q. acknowledges the support by São Paulo Research Foundation (FAPESP, Proc. 2011/18496-7 & 2015/50122-0) and by the the the Brazilian National Research Council (CNPq Proc. 310908/2015-9 & 434886/2018-1). L.A.N.L. acknowledges the support by (CNPq Proc. 301836/2014-0) and L.H.N.L. acknowledges the support by Coordination of Superior Level Staff Improvement (CAPES).

References

1. Agarwal, G., Kempe, D.: Modularity-maximizing graph communities via mathematical programming. Eur. Phys. J. B **66**(3), 409–418 (2008)
2. Albert, R., Barabási, A.L.: Statistical mechanics of complex networks. Rev. Modern Phys. **74**(1), 47 (2002). https://doi.org/10.1103/RevModPhys.74.47
3. Arenas, A., Duch, J., Fernández, A., Gómez, S.: Size reduction of complex networks preserving modularity. New J. Phys. **9**(6), 176 (2007). https://doi.org/10.1088/1367-2630/9/6/176
4. Bonchi, F., Morales, G.D.F., Gionis, A., Ukkonen, A.: Activity preserving graph simplification. Data Min. Knowl. Discov. **27**(3), 321–343 (2013)
5. Fortunato, S.: Community detection in graphs. Phys. Rep. **486**(3–5), 75–174 (2010)
6. Fortunato, S., Hric, D.: Community detection in networks: a user guide. Phys. Rep. **659**, 1–44 (2016)
7. Gemmetto, V., Cardillo, A., Garlaschelli, D.: Irreducible network backbones: unbiased graph filtering via maximum entropy. arXiv preprint arXiv:1706.00230 (2017)
8. Gionis, A., Rozenshtein, P., Tatti, N., Terzi, E.: Community-aware network sparsification. In: Proceedings of the 2017 SIAM International Conference on Data Mining, pp. 426–434. SIAM (2017)
9. IBM: IBM ILOG CPLEX 12.7.1 (1987–2017)
10. Kim, J.R., Kim, J., Kwon, Y.K., Lee, H.Y., Heslop-Harrison, P., Cho, K.H.: Reduction of complex signaling networks to a representative kernel. Sci. Signal. **4**(175), ra35–ra35 (2011)
11. Miyauchi, A., Sukegawa, N.: Redundant constraints in the standard formulation for the clique partitioning problem. Optim. Lett. **9**(1), 199–207 (2015)
12. Newman, M.E.J., Girvan, M.: Finding and evaluating community structure in networks. Phys. Rev. E **69**, 026113 (2004). https://doi.org/10.1103/PhysRevE.69.026113
13. Newman, M.E.: The structure and function of complex networks. SIAM Rev. **45**(2), 167–256 (2003). https://doi.org/10.1137/S003614450342480
14. Newman, M.E.: Analysis of weighted networks. Phys. Rev. E **70**(5), 056131 (2004)
15. Newman, M.E.: Modularity and community structure in networks. Proc. Natl. Acad. Sci. **103**(23), 8577–8582 (2006). https://doi.org/10.1073/pnas.0601602103

16. Rossi, R.A., Ahmed, N.K.: The network data repository with interactive graph analytics and visualization. In: Proceedings of the Twenty-Ninth AAAI Conference on Artificial Intelligence (2015). http://networkrepository.com
17. Stanley, N., Kwitt, R., Niethammer, M., Mucha, P.J.: Compressing networks with super nodes. CoRR abs/1706.04110 (2017). http://arxiv.org/abs/1706.04110
18. Strogatz, S.H.: Exploring complex networks. Nature **410**(6825), 268–276 (2001). https://doi.org/10.1038/35065725
19. Watts, D.J., Strogatz, S.H.: Collective dynamics of 'small-world' networks. Nature **393**(6684), 440–442 (1998). https://doi.org/10.1038/30918
20. Xiao, Y., MacArthur, B.D., Wang, H., Xiong, M., Wang, W.: Network quotients: structural skeletons of complex systems. Phys. Rev. E **78**(4), 046102 (2008)

Dealing with Uncertainty in Software Architecture on the Internet-of-Things with Digital Twins

Flavio Oquendo(✉)

IRISA – UMR CNRS 6074, University Bretagne Sud, Vannes, France
flavio.oquendo@irisa.fr

Abstract. When architecting Software-intensive Systems-of-Systems (SoS) on the Internet-of-Things (IoT), architects face two sorts of uncertainties. First, they have only limited knowledge about the operational environment where the SoS will actually be deployed. Second, the constituent systems which will compose the SoS might not be known a priori (at design-time) or their availability (at run-time) is affected by dynamic factors, due to the openness of the IoT. The consequent research question is thereby how to deal with uncertainty in the design of an SoS architecture on the IoT. To tackle this challenging issue, this paper addresses the notion of uncertainty due to partial information in SoS and proposes an enhanced SoS Architecture Description language (SosADL) for expressing SoS architectures on the IoT under uncertainty. The core SosADL is extended with concurrent constraints and the concept of digital twins coupling the physical and virtual worlds. This novel approach is supported by an integrated toolset, the SosADL Studio. Validation results demonstrate its effectiveness in an SoS architecture for platooning of self-driving vehicles.

Keywords: Architectural design uncertainty ·
Software architecture description · Systems-of-Systems (SoS) · Digital twins ·
Internet-of-Things (IoT)

1 Introduction

Uncertainty [29] is an intrinsic characteristic of complex systems, may it be human, natural, or engineered systems [33]. Indeed, complex systems are by essence unpredictable, thereby raising different types of uncertainties. This is particularly the case in the design of engineered systems, where uncertainty has been a major complicating factor.

Uncertainty may be classified as aleatory or epistemic. Aleatory uncertainty (a.k.a. as stochastic or objective uncertainty) results from uncontrollable phenomena that are uncertain by nature. Uncertainty is due to the inherent randomness of these phenomena. It is irreducible, and is generally expressed, in probability theory, by random variables or stochastic processes. Epistemic uncertainty (a.k.a. systematic or subjective uncertainty) results from the lack of knowledge about identified phenomena. Uncertainty is due to partial information. It is reducible, i.e. can be reduced by acquiring more refined data about the phenomenon.

© Springer Nature Switzerland AG 2019
S. Misra et al. (Eds.): ICCSA 2019, LNCS 11619, pp. 770–786, 2019.
https://doi.org/10.1007/978-3-030-24289-3_57

In the last three decades, research on design under uncertainty has received increasing attention, especially in Systems Engineering [1], and in recent years in Software Engineering [35]. Both types of uncertainty have been addressed, in particular aleatory uncertainty has been extensively studied.

Regarding Software Engineering, uncertainty is mainly associated to the design of software-intensive systems, and more recently of Software-intensive Systems-of-Systems (SoS) [15, 23] on the Internet-of-Things (IoT) [32]. Indeed, due to the open and very dynamic nature of the IoT, when architecturally designing an SoS on the IoT, an architect does not know which will be the actual IoT systems that will become constituents of the SoS, these being predominantly discovered at run-time. Thereby, the architecture description needs to deal with the uncertainty of the presence or absence of the required constituent systems. Furthermore, even for those that are present, their inherent independence magnifies uncertainty.

Moreover, the correct SoS architecture on the IoT depends not only on the constituent IoT systems but also, largely, on the operational environment where the SoS is deployed. Actually, an operational environment enabled by the IoT, where an SoS will perform at run-time, is inherently incompletely known at design-time [12], thereby information available at design-time is only partial.

The challenge, in the description of an SoS architecture on the IoT, is to be able to handle the uncertainty raised by partial information on the constituent systems which will concretely operate in the SoS at run-time as well as on the characteristics of the concrete operational environment where the SoS will actually operate.

Therefore, from the perspective of the software architecture, the key research question is how to deal with uncertainty in the description of an SoS architecture on the IoT.

This is particularly a hard question to answer because IoT is an open-world, thereby it is not feasible to exhaustively anticipate and resolve all possible situations that an SoS will face. These open environments expose the SoS to a myriad of cases that are impossible to predict.

To address this challenging issue, this paper examines the notion of uncertainty in SoS and presents the features that we have added to SosADL, a novel formal SoS Architecture Description Language (ADL), to be able to deal with uncertainty in the architectural design of SoSs on the IoT, enabling the description of SoS architectures that operate with only partially known IoT constituent systems in partially known environments on the IoT. In particular, in the released *SosADL for IoT under Uncertainty*, we leveraged the notion of digital twin [9] (replica of the physical counterpart of an IoT system or "thing" on the IoT) as the core architectural concept for representing SoS architectures on the IoT at design-time, and self-managing the SoS architectures once deployed on the IoT at run-time. In our approach, digital twins of "things" on the IoT coordinate their operation with other digital twins on the IoT in a shared operational environment based on the expression and enforcement of concurrent constraints.

This paper relies on previous publications on SosADL, which presented its concepts and notation [19] and its underlain formal theory [20]. It builds on the approach for copying with uncertainty in SoSs [26], on the mechanisms for raising emergent behaviors [22, 24], and on principles for self-organization [25].

This paper adds to these, the presentation of the SosADL enhancements bringing contributions beyond the state-of-the-art for dealing with uncertainty when architecting SoSs on the IoT, resulting in the novel *SosADL for IoT under Uncertainty*.

The remainder of this paper is organized as follows. Section 2 introduces a motivating case study for dealing with uncertainty in SoS on the IoT. Section 3 presents the enhancements to SosADL that enables the handling of uncertainty on the IoT. Section 4 demonstrates how the enhanced SosADL can be applied for describing SoS architectures on the IoT under uncertainty. In Sect. 5 we briefly present the implementation of SosADL Studio, now supporting uncertainty. In Sect. 6, we position our proposal for dealing with uncertainty in SoS architectural design with related work. To conclude, we summarize in Sect. 7 the main contributions of this paper and outline future work.

2   Motivating Case Study for Dealing with Uncertainty in SoS

For motivating the problematics of architectural design under uncertainty of SoSs on the IoT, let us introduce hereafter an excerpt of a pilot study [21] we have carried out to concretely present the issues of uncertainty and set the basis for the presentation of *SosADL for IoT under Uncertainty*.

We will focus on the Platooning SoS, part of emergency response, and its intended emergent behavior to create and maintain platoons of self-driving vehicles through self-organization under uncertainty in the framework of the IoT for Vehicles, a.k.a. Internet-of-Vehicles (IoV) [32]. Platooning is the process of automated vehicles (in this case self-driving vehicles) autonomously forming road convoys.

2.1   Essentials for Architecting Platoons of Self-Driving Vehicles on the IoT

The constituent systems of the Platooning SoS are self-driving vehicles, which embody radars (in particular lidars, light detection and ranging), sensors, driverless steering, and Vehicular Ad-hoc Networks (VANETs), depicted in Fig. 1 (left). Using these devices, the self-driving vehicle can sense information from the physical operational environment and from other vehicles, process this information, communicate it to other vehicles through VANETs as well as feed it to drivers (if any).

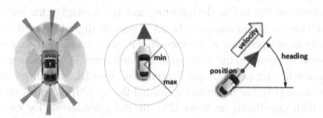

Fig. 1. Automated vehicles: (left) radars/lidars, sensors and VANETs; (middle) min safe separation and max perception range; (right) velocity in terms of speed and heading

As also depicted in Fig. 1 (middle), there are two critical zones around a vehicle: the minimal safe separation from vehicles in front or behind it and in general for any kind of obstacle (the min safe distance) and the maximal separation (the max perception range of the radars/sensors and of VANETs enabling to communicate with other vehicles in front or behind it).

As again depicted in Fig. 1 (right), each vehicle is equipped with GPS for positioning and with controls for heading and speed to determine and steer its velocity. These data may be transmitted via VANETs to the neighboring vehicles. In addition to real time position in terms of GPS coordinates, a connected vehicle may also share the GPS coordinate of its destination.

When platooning, a group of vehicles can safely travel closely together like in a convoy [13], as shown in Fig. 2.

Fig. 2. Vehicles in a platoon: virtual leader and followers

More precisely, platooning is the process of vehicles autonomously following a leader to form a road convoy. It requires that each vehicle in the platoon control its velocity and the relative distance to the vehicle in front of it, and possibly also to the one behind of it. This is performed by interacting through radars/sensors as well as coordinating through VANETs.

2.2 Uncertainty in the Self-Driving Vehicle Platooning SoS

Let us now address an uncertainty that must be dealt with in Platooning SoSs, i.e. uncertainty due to imprecision (a form of partial information): on-board sensors in a vehicle have limited sensing capability and range, thereby providing imprecise measures. Also, environmental noise can alter the precision of the sensed information. Also, in VANETs, communication delay may affect the accuracy of the transmitted information.

It means that an SoS architect, while designing an SoS architecture for platooning needs to take into account that the sensed distance from a self-driving vehicle to the platoonmate in front of it is approximate. The SoS architect also needs to take into account that the min safe separation distance and the max perception range (shown in Fig. 1) may vary according to road surface and weather conditions (therefore they are uncertain). Moreover, the min safe separation distance varies with the speed. For instance, a vehicle needs ca. 14 m to fully stop (avoiding collision with the vehicle in front of it) if its speed is of 50 km/h once brakes are pressed down in dry weather on a well-maintained road pavement. It is of ca. 38 m if the speed is of 80 km/h and is of ca. 75 m if the speed is of 110 km/h and so on.

Indeed, for guaranteeing collision avoidance in the platoon, i.e. no collision at any time, the platoonmates must follow each other in a distance that is safe for braking to avoid the vehicle that is driving in front of it (considering the different uncertainties in sensed or received information). Moreover, in platooning, the distance between a platoonmate and the vehicle in front of it must be sufficient to discourage interference from other vehicles, i.e. avoiding to have other vehicles (not participating in the platoon) entering in-between two platoonmates causing the undesired split of the platoon.

The architecture of the Platooning SoS needs thereby to specify how different self-driving vehicles (unknown at design-time) will form platoons (different platoons may be formed), while coping with these different uncertainties, in particular related to the distance of neighboring self-driving vehicles. The platoon must make coordinated movements correctly and safely, being guaranteed collision free.

3 Extending SosADL for IoT Under Uncertainty

Over the years, many ADLs have been conceived for precisely describing software architectures where every aspect is known at design-time regarding both its constituents and the operational environment. As studied in [14], no current ADL is able to handle the uncertainty required for describing SoS architectures.

To fill this gap, we extended SosADL with new conceptual abstractions and constructs for describing SoS architectures on the IoT while dealing with uncertainty, resulting in the novel *SosADL for IoT under Uncertainty*.

3.1 Enhancing SosADL with Digital Twins for Architecting SoS on the IoT

To fill the identified gap, the first question to investigate is: what are the architectural abstractions suitable for architecting SoS on the IoT?

Conceptually, the IoT is essentially the Internet of "things" which exist in the physical world and are represented in the virtual world. A "thing" is formed of devices (sensors and actuators) which interact with the physical world through sensing and actuating as well as of a controller for managing its own behavior based on its devices, including networking devices (which may be for connecting to wireless or wired networks, mobile ad hoc or fixed, local or global). In fine, a "thing" or IoT system provides the basic functionalities or services of the IoT.

There are different notions and reference architectures for designing and implementing software-intensive systems or SoSs on the IoT. Among these, we adopted the notion of digital twin [9], which fits well the needs for coupling the physical and virtual worlds in terms of "things" or IoT systems, as required in SoSs on the IoT.

In fact, the notion of "twin" has been applied since the seventies by the NASA in the Apollo Program, which replicated the spacecrafts in order to solve technical problems during their mission. Recently, the technological progress has made possible the creation of an evolved "twin" notion, i.e. the "digital twin" (sometimes also called digital shadow). A digital twin provides a digital replica (in the Edge, Fog, or the Cloud) of its physical counterpart which is virtually indistinguishable from its physical twin (in the sense that it dynamically replicates the behavior and properties of the physical twin as well as enriches the replica with additional information about the physical counterpart). The digital twin is indeed the dynamic digital representation of its physical counterpart. It can thereby be used to represent the physical counterpart during the design and operation of the SoS architecture on the IoT. In the virtual world, the digital twin represents the physical twin, which resides in the physical world. The digital twin is thereby a relevant architectural abstraction that is virtually indistinguishable from its physical counterpart.

The conceptual model of a digital twin contains three main parts: (i) physical twin in the real world; (ii) digital twin in the virtual world; and (iii) the connections of input data and output command that ties the digital and real counterparts together.

In general, the digital twin monitors the physical twin through data provided by sensors as well as information coming from human domain experts to maintain a utility replica of the physical entity. It acts back on the physical twin through actuators.

Digital twins have mostly been applied in the context of Industrial IoT [7]. In particular, in Industry 4.0, digital twins generally support simulation of the behaviors of their physical twins, in real-time, and sometimes are supported by augmented reality.

Also note that digital twin is a notion that has variation in terms of meaning and scope, which often depend of their purpose.

In SosADL for IoT, we apply the notion of digital twin as a concept for the architectural design of an SoS as well as a concept to dynamically reconfigure the architecture during the operation of the SoS.

Architecturally speaking, in SosADL for IoT, a digital twin is a digital replica of a real-world "thing" on the IoT aiming to provide a dynamic virtual representation of its physical counterpart. The concept of digital twin thereby drives the design of SoS architectures on the IoT by coordinating the digital twins of their constituent systems.

In the SoS architecture description, what are represented are therefore digital twins. In an SoS architecture description with SosADL for IoT:

- digital twins of IoT constituent systems are SoS architectural elements defined by intention (declaratively in terms of abstract systems) and instantiated at run-time (concretized);
- digital mediators are connectors of SoS architectural elements in the virtual world, defined by intention (declaratively in terms of abstract mediators) and created at run-time (concretized by the SoS) to achieve a goal, part of an encompassing mission (note that their architectural role is to mediate the interaction of digital twins of IoT constituent systems for creating emergent behavior);
- digital coalitions are SoS architectural compositions in the virtual world of mediated digital twins of IoT constituent systems, defined by intention (declaratively in terms of possible systems and mediators as well as the policies for their on-the-fly compositions) and evolutionarily formed at run-time (concretized) to achieve an SoS mission in an operational environment.

Coming back to our motivating case study, the SoS architecture description on the IoT of Vehicles (IoV) will specify how an SoS architecture is able to create, on the fly, and maintain emergent behaviors from elementary connected vehicles (represented by their digital twins), where the actual vehicles are not known at design time.

The connected vehicles (which are mobile "things" on the IoT) are represented and managed in the virtual world while casually connected with the real world. Through digital coalitions, mediations among "things" are architected to produce emergent behaviors, as it is the case in platooning of self-driving vehicles.

In this way, the proposed digital twin notion supported by SosADL for IoT provides the basis to formally architect evolutionary SoS on the IoT. In particular, it supports reasoning of platooning properties in the virtual world and its control-command in the real world through the IoV.

3.2   Handling Uncertainty for Architecting SoS on the IoT

Now, the second question to investigate is: which theory is suitable for addressing the needs for dealing with uncertainty in IoT-enabled operational environments.

There are in fact several theories for handling uncertainty. Regarding the design of systems, the main ones are the theories of probability (associated to statistics and usually applied to address aleatory uncertainty), of possibility (related to fuzziness and usually applied to address epistemic uncertainty), and the interval mathematics (associated to imprecision, and that can also be applied to address epistemic uncertainty) [1]. As the research issue we are addressing in this work is essentially the one of imprecision due to uncertainty in the physical measures of the physical environment where the constituents of an SoS are operating, the theory that suits is the one of intervals.

There are in fact different interval mathematics [11]. The underlying principle of the interval theories is that of enclosing uncertain measured values in intervals. In our approach, we express intervals through constraints, e.g. to express the distance for the braking of a self-driving vehicle. Thereby, if the speed of a self-driving vehicle is 50 km/h, knowing that 14 m are needed to fully stop it (avoiding collision with the vehicle in front of it) in case of dry weather on a well-maintained road pavement, we represent the uncertainty related to road surface conditions by the constraint: "the min safe distance is between 12 m (in excellent-maintained road surfaces) and 18 m (in poorly-maintained road surfaces)". As weather also influences the min safe distance, if raining it becomes "between 14 m and 22 m" (ranging from excellent-maintained road surfaces to poorly-maintained ones).

More precisely, our approach to deal with uncertainty in SoS architecture description on the IoT is grounded on the constraint interpretation of intervals based on process algebra, the π-Calculus [16], and concurrent constraints [17].

Therefore, for dealing with uncertainty in SoS architectural design and especially in the description of designed SoS architectures on the IoT, SosADL was enhanced to enable the representation of partial information as well as to enable to reasoning on partial information to affect the emergent behavior of SoSs. By the decentralized nature of SoSs, these representation and reasoning mechanisms are expressed from the viewpoint of each digital twin of an IoT constituent system and of the digital mediators enabling their interactions (thereby influencing individual behaviors as well as the raising of emergent behaviors).

Based on the representation of uncertainty in terms of constraints, the subsequent question now is how these constraints can be manipulated by the concurrent IoT constituent systems of an SoS on the IoT.

Our approach to solve this question is two-fold: first, we extended the formal foundation of the core SosADL which is grounded on the π-Calculus [16] with concurrent constraints for representing and reasoning about partial information; second, we integrated three sorts of architectural abstractions to SosADL for IoT, i.e. digital twins, digital mediators, and digital coalitions, which manipulate concurrent constraints.

The novel π-Calculus for SoS [20], which extends the original π-Calculus with concurrent constraints, generalizes the π-Calculus with the notion of computing based on partial information.

In the π-Calculus for SoS, a behavior (of a digital twin of an IoT constituent system or of a digital mediator) is described by the actions that it can carry out as well as the constraints that it enforces or copes with. Two constructs have been added to SosADL to manipulate constraints: one is the *tell* construct which enables a digital entity to add a constraint to its operational environment in the virtual world, and the other is the *ask* construct which enables a digital entity to query if a constraint can be inferred from its operational environment in the virtual world. Other constructs have been extended to handle concurrent constraints, in particular the *compose* construct was enhanced to deal with concurrent composition of behaviors and constraints, and the *connection* construct to restrict the interface that a behavior can use to interact with others while enforcing constraints. The *untell* construct is also provided for removing a constraint from the digital environment.

Intuitively speaking, based on π-Calculus for SoS, a digital entity can *tell* to the digital environment about the pieces of information that it knows, while maintaining private information internally. A digital entity can also *ask* information from the digital environment that influences its own behavior or even *untell* previously told constraints.

4   Describing SoS Architecture for IoT Under Uncertainty

To demonstrate how *SosADL for IoT under Uncertainty* can be applied to architecturally describe SoS architectures on the IoT under uncertainty, we will present hereafter the architecture description of the Platooning SoS of self-driving vehicles introduced in the motivating case-study.

4.1   Emergent Behavior for the Platooning SoS of Self-Driving Vehicles

Fundamentally, in a Platooning SoS of self-driving vehicles, the emergent behavior of platooning results from three micro-scale behaviors of platoonmates (vehicles that are members of a platoon), as shown in Fig. 3, which together enforce the constraints that are required for enabling platoons (see [25] for details of self-organizing SoSs).

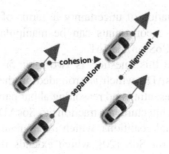

Fig. 3. Cohesion, separation, and alignment behaviors

The micro-scale behaviors for guaranteeing platooning are:

- *Cohesion behavior*: every platoonmate must steer to follow the platoonmate just in front of it (if any) while not losing the near platoonmate behind it (if any), thereby maintaining liaison;
- *Separation behavior*: every platoonmate must steer to avoid the near platoonmate in front of it, thereby avoiding rear collision;
- *Alignment behavior*: every platoonmate must steer to move towards the platoonmate in front of it, or towards the destination if no near platoonmate is in front of it while attempting to match velocity (heading and speed) with nearby platoonmates.

These micro-scale behaviors (cohesion, separation, and alignment), combined together determine the acceleration vector that drives a platoonmate. From the point of view of a vehicle, each micro-scale behavior engenders an independent request for a steering maneuver to be carried out by the self-driving vehicle.

Note that these micro-scale behaviors governing cohesion, separation, and alignment, constrained by the relative positions of nearby platoonmates, were demonstrated sufficient to guarantee the formation of platoons [31].

4.2 SoS Architecture Description with Uncertainty for UGV-Based Platooning

Now that we have introduced the three micro-scale behaviors providing the necessary and sufficient conditions to create and maintain the emergent behavior of vehicle platooning, let us demonstrate how to apply *SosADL for IoT under Uncertainty* to describe the SoS architecture of vehicle platooning under uncertainty using digital twins as well as explain the operational semantics of the resulting SoS architecture during the formation and maintenance of platoons. Recall that each self-driving vehicle has its own autopilot and may drive in autonomous mode to a destination.

We will first focus on the digital mediators enforcing the micro-scale behaviors required for creating and maintaining platoons (we will not present the interface of the digital twins of the IoT constituent systems of the platooning SoS, i.e. the self-driving vehicles, due to page limit). Then, we will describe the abstract architecture of the SoS on the IoT as a whole in terms of a digital coalition for achieving the macro-scale platooning behavior.

Let us now declare, in *SosADL for IoT under Uncertainty*, the digital mediator *Platooning* which will make possible the emergence of the platooning macro-scale behavior of the SoS of self-driving vehicles.

As shown in Listing 1, *Platooning* is described as a digital mediator abstraction: we declare the duties of the mediated self-driving vehicle in terms of position and command and the mediation among self-driving vehicles participating in the platoon as the steering behavior. By creating concretions, a digital mediator will be synthesized for each digital twin of a self-driving vehicle that participates in the fleet.

By the application of the three micro-scale behaviors, i.e. separation, alignment, and cohesion, commanding the digitally mediated vehicle, every self-driving vehicle in the platoon, will stepwise behave to align and get closer to neighboring self-driving vehicles, while avoiding collision.

```
//use user-defined library for route information
with RouteInformation
//declaring the platoon mediating behavior
digital mediator Platooning(max:Distance,min:Distance) is {
  //determining the position of the mediated vehicle
  duty position is{
    //inputting vehicle's latitude and longitude
    connection coordinate is in{Coordinate}
    //inputting vehicle's direction with heading angle
    connection heading is in{Heading}
    //inputting vehicle's velocity
    connection speed is in{Speed}}
  duty command is{
    //commanding for steering the mediated vehicle
    connection drive_ctrl is out{[heading:Heading,speed=Speed]}}
  abstraction separation(…) is {…}
  abstraction alignment(…) is {…}
  abstraction cohesion(…) is {…}
  behavior steering(…) is {…}
}
```

Listing 1. Digital mediator declaration in SosADL for IoT under Uncertainty

Note that a platoon may increase of size by having vehicles (which are not in the platoon) maneuvering to join the platoon or decrease of size by having vehicles in the platoon maneuvering to leave it.

Let us now describe the digital mediating behavior in Listing 2. Once the steering behavior receives the position of the mediated self-driving vehicle (firstly getting its coordinate, and secondly its heading), the *tell* construct asserts the received position into its local environment, enabling sharing with other digitally mediated self-driving vehicles. Next, the *ask* construct is used to ask for the positions of platoonmates that are in the perception range of the digitally mediated self-driving vehicle. With the result of the query stored, the digital mediator first checks if there is any. If not, i.e. if no other self-driving vehicle is in the neighborhood of the digitally mediated self-driving vehicle, the mediated self-driving vehicle continues to drive in the same direction, moving forward. If there are self-driving vehicles in the neighborhood of the digitally mediated self-driving vehicle, the platooning mediator behavior looks for the nearest platoonmate. It then checks whether the distance to the mediated self-driving vehicle is less than the minimum separation value (*min*, passed in parameter). If it is the case, the steering behavior applies the separation micro-scale behavior. If it is not, the steering behavior commands the digitally mediated self-driving vehicle applying the alignment micro-scale behavior and then the cohesion micro-scale behavior based on the positions of the neighboring platoonmates.

Let us now describe the SoS architecture for forming the platooning in Listing 3. It is described by declaring first, the digital twins of SoS constituent systems (they are the digital entities of the IoT constituent systems that can participate in the SoS), second, the digital mediators (they are created and managed for coordinating the constituent systems via their digital twins), and third, the digital coalitions that can be formed to achieve the SoS emergent behavior of vehicle platooning.

```
behavior steering() is {
 repeat {
  //get the coordinate of the mediated self-driving vehicle
  via position::coordinate receive vehicle_coordinate
  //get the heading of the mediated self-driving vehicle
  via position::heading receive vehicle_heading
  //get the speed of the mediated self-driving vehicle
  via position::speed receive vehicle_speed
  //tell the position to other digital mediators
  tell vehicle is [coordinate=vehicle_coordinate,
   heading=vehicle_heading,speed=vehicle_speed]
  //ask if any vehicle is in the neighborhood
  value neighbors is ask vehicle suchthat {
   //in the radar range of the self-driving vehicle, i.e. < max
   vehicle::coordinate::distance(vehicle_coordinate)<max}
  //if there are vehicles in the radar range
  if (neighbors::notEmpty()) then {
   //identify nearest neighbor in front
   value front_mate is neighbors::nearest_in_front()
   //identify nearest neighbor in back
   value back_mate is neighbors::nearest_in_back()
   //if too close in front, i.e. < min separation
   if (vehicle_coordinate::distance(front_mate::coordinate)<min)
    then //separate to avoid collition
     separation(vehicle,front_mate)
    else {//align by velocity matching
     alignment(vehicle,front_mate,back_mate)
     //maintain nearest mates in range
     cohesion(vehicle,front_mate,back_mate)}
  }
 }
}
```

Listing 2. Platoon mediating behavior in SosADL for IoT under Uncertainty

The SoS architecture description, shown in Listing 3, comprises the declaration of a sequence of digital twins of IoT constituent systems complying with the system abstraction of self-driving vehicle and a sequence of digital mediators conforming with the mediator abstraction of *Platooning* (as declared in Listing 1).

Based on the digital twins of these systems and mediator abstractions, the digital coalition for creating emergent behavior is declared, named as *platoon*, as shown in Listing 3. In particular, the digital coalition of self-driving vehicles is described as a sequence of digital twins of self-driving vehicles where each digital twin has an associated steering digital mediator created in the digital coalition, with the specified perception range distance (*max*) and minimum separation distance (*min*) as parameters. The emergent behavior of the digital coalition, i.e. *platoon*, is produced by the macro-scale behavior created by supervenience from the mediating behaviors, which apply the micro-scale behaviors according to each situation.

It is indeed by the application of the mediating behaviors, commanding the digitally mediated self-driving vehicles by applying the defined micro-scale behaviors, that every self-driving vehicle in the fleet, will stepwise behave to align and get closer to neighboring vehicles, while avoiding collision. At the macro-scale level, the fleet of self-driving vehicles will progressively form and maintain the platoon.

It is worth noting that the platoon which is formed is the result of the application of the micro-scale behaviors to each self-driving vehicle in the platoon via its digital twin.

```
//use the IoV system abstraction and Platooning mediator abstraction
  with SelfDrivingVehicle,Platooning
  architecture PlatooningSoS(max:Distance,min:Distance) is {
  coalition platoon is compose{
   fleet is sequence{SelfDrivingVehicle()}
   platooning is sequence{Platooning(max,min)}
  } binding {
     forall {vehicle in fleet suchthat
       exists{one steer in platooning suchthat
         unify one{steer::position} to one{vehicle::position}
         unify one{steer::command} to one{vehicle::command}}}}
  }
```

Listing 3. SoS architecture description for platooning in SosADL for IoT under Uncertainty

Each self-driving vehicle is not aware of the rest of the platoon, except for its own neighbors, generally composed of the platoonmates in front of and behind itself. For instance, the self-driving vehicle in the platoon is not aware of the size of the platoon, i.e. of how many members has a platoon.

Besides, it is worth pointing out that it is the locality of the rules that ensures the scalability of the emergent behavior of platoon in terms of digitally mediated twins.

5 Implementation of SosADL Studio for IoT with Uncertainty

The complexity inherent to SoS architectures on the IoT under uncertainty calls for the automated support of SoS architectural design by software tools. Indeed, for supporting the architecture-centric formal development of SoSs using *SosADL for IoT under Uncertainty*, we have developed an SoS Architecture Development Environment, named SosADL Studio [27].

This toolset is constructed as plugins in Eclipse. It provides a model-driven architecture development environment where the SosADL meta-model is defined in EMF/Ecore (http://eclipse.org/modeling/emf/), with the textual concrete syntax expressed in Xtext (http://eclipse.org/Xtext/), the graphical concrete syntax developed in Sirius (http://eclipse.org/sirius/), and the type checker implemented in Xtend (http://www.eclipse.org/xtend/), after having being proved using the Coq proof assistant (http://coq.inria.fr/) [28].

The type-checked architecture is then converted in terms of input-output Symbolic Transition Systems to feed UPPAAL (http://www.uppaal.org/) for model checking.

At that point, the SoS architecture is guaranteed well-formed (through the type checker) and well-behaved (through the model checker).

To support uncertainty in SoS architecture descriptions by the resolution of concurrent constraints of the checked SoS architecture, a constraint solving mechanism was implemented on top of the Kodkod Solver (http://alloy.mit.edu/kodkod/). It is used to solve the system of architectural constraints formulated in the architectural model at run-time (based on *tell, ask, untell* constructs) and to "find" (i.e. dynamically create) mediated structures that satisfy these constraints. It operates thereby as an architectural model finder, enabling to discover SoS concrete architectures which comply with the given SoS abstract architecture and operational environment, based on Propositional Satisfiability Theory (SAT) [10]. The concretization of the SoS architecture is incremental and based on the discover of digital twins on the IoT. Each time a digital twin of a constituent system become known by the SoS, a better SAT solution may be computed, reconfiguring the digital coalition of the SoS. Kodkod Solver indeed support model finding in partially defined models, which can be incrementally instantiated.

The remaining issue is thereby to guarantee that the architected emergent behaviors are able to be produced and to guarantee that they will behave correctly under uncertainty, as required.

To provide this guarantee, SosADL Studio supports simulation of SoS architectures. It takes as input the SoS architecture description in terms of digital twins, its operational environment (via concrete specifications of environmental gates given how constituent systems sense local environments), and produces different simulation models in Discrete Event System Specification (DEVS, http://www.ms4systems.com/).

For supporting verification of the emergent behaviors of SoS architectures under uncertainty, we have conceived a novel logic, named DynBLTL [30], for expressing properties of SoS architectures under a multivalued logic and verifying these properties with statistical model checking using PLASMA (http://project.inria.fr/plasma-lab/) [4].

Through the different features of the SosADL Studio, an SoS architect is able to guarantee different SoS architectural properties on the IoT in the presence of uncertainty, in particular enforcing safety [28].

6 Related Work

Uncertainty is a topic of research in different disciplines, including social sciences, natural sciences, and engineering [33]. In engineering, uncertainty is intrinsically related to design, termed "design under uncertainty". The notion of uncertainty has not, however, the same meaning in these different disciplines, encompassing, as a matter of fact, a multiplicity of concepts.

Recently, uncertainty has been the subject of research in software-intensive systems engineering [6]. In particular, [35] proposes a taxonomy of uncertainty for dynamically self-adaptive software-intensive systems, focusing on cyber-physical systems and their operation in unpredictable physical environments.

Since the rise of IoT, the nature of SoS has evolved, and uncertainty has become a critical issue, increasingly been cited in SoS roadmaps for the coming years, e.g. the European Roadmap for SoS Engineering [5], which expresses the needs for constructing Cyber-Physical SoSs on the IoT. Notably, the INCOSE Systems Engineering Vision for 2025 [12] highlights the need to cope with uncertainty at analysis, architectural design, and operation of SoSs.

More recently, the OMG (an industrial standard organization) has highlighted the importance of dealing with uncertainty during the lifecycle of a software-intensive system or SoS, and launched an initiative for supporting uncertainty modeling in its model engineering standards [18].

Over the years, in Software Engineering, various techniques were studied for documenting, specifying, and managing uncertainty in software-intensive systems [6, 8].

More particularly in software-intensive systems or SoS, uncertainty has been predominantly studied in requirements engineering. In particular, the RELAX requirements specification language [34] was defined to express requirements under uncertainty based on fuzzy branching temporal logic. RELAX supports the explicit specification of environmental uncertainty in requirements statements. FLAGS [2] extended KAOS [3] using possibility theory to mitigate the uncertainty of the goals. RELAX and FLAGS do not address architectural design, but are able to express requirements under uncertainty that are relevant to be used for architectural design.

While uncertainty is inherent to SoS [15] and has been addressed in requirements engineering, the study of uncertainty in SoS architecture is still highly unexplored [14].

Indeed, if the importance of dealing with uncertainty when designing software-intensive systems and SoS architectures is widely recognized, only a dearth of techniques having been proposed for handling uncertainty in software architecture description [26]. Notably, none has proposed a formal Architecture Description Language (ADL) enabling to deal with uncertainty in SoS architecture description [14].

Actually, many researches were conducted to address the issue of formally describing the architecture of single software-intensive systems. However, no existing ADL is able to describe even single systems architecture under uncertainty, being limited by their formal foundations which require complete information at design-time.

The significant difference of the formal basis of ADLs for single systems and the π-Calculus for SoS underlying *SosADL for IoT under Uncertainty* is the treatment of partial information (i.e. each SoS constituent has incomplete information on the state of the operational environment). While in single systems, all components have access to complete information, in SoS, all constituents have access to imperfect information by nature. In SoSs, partial information contributes to systematic uncertainty.

In summary, based on the study of the state-of-the-art, *SosADL for IoT under Uncertainty* is positioned as a pioneering ADL, being the first formal ADL enabling the expression of systematic uncertainty in SoS architecture description relying on concurrent constraints and constraint solving mechanisms, being specialized for IoT relying on digital twins and digital mediators and coalitions.

7   Conclusion and Future Work

In this paper we have raised the issue of uncertainty in the architectural design of SoSs, and identified the major sources of uncertainty for architecting SoSs on the IoT. In particular, we faced up the research challenge of how to deal with uncertainty in the design of an SoS architecture on the IoT. To solve this issue, this paper proposed enhancements to SosADL. On the one hand, the underlying theory of SosADL was enhanced with concurrent constraints for expressing uncertainty due to imprecision (partial knowledge) and on the other hand, novel architectural abstractions were integrated into SosADL for treating the duality of "things" on the IoT, through the notion of digital twin, synchronously coupled with its physical counterpart, and their coordination using digital mediators, for forming digital coalitions to produce the required SoS emergent behaviors.

Using the enhanced SosADL presented in this paper, *SosADL on the IoT under Uncertainty*, SoS architectures on the IoT are abstractly described by declaring the constraints which must be satisfied when the concrete architecture is synthesized in a specific operational environment where "things" are IoT systems communicating via the IoT. The behavior of digital twins of constituent systems as well as the behavior of digital mediators are specified by handling constraints representing and reasoning about partial information.

SosADL and more recently this enhanced SosADL have been applied in several case studies and pilots where the suitability of SosADL and the supporting toolchain has been validated, including SoS architecture descriptions under uncertainty on the IoT.

On-going and future work is mainly related with the application of *SosADL for IoT under Uncertainty* in industrial-scale projects. They include in particular joint work with SEGULA for applying the extended SosADL to architect SoSs in the domain of the Industrial IoT. Description of SoS architectures on the IoT under uncertainty, and their validation and verification using the SosADL toolchain, are main threads of these pilot projects.

References

1. Ayyub, B., Klir, G.: Uncertainty Modeling and Analysis in Engineering and the Sciences. Chapman & Hall, Boca Raton (2006)
2. Baresi, L., Pasquale, L., Spoletini, P.: Fuzzy goals for requirements-driven adaptation. In: 18th IEEE RE, Sydney, Australia, September 2010
3. Cailliau, A., van Lamsweerde, A.: Handling knowledge uncertainty in risk-based requirements engineering. In: 23rd RE, Ottawa, Canada (2015)
4. Cavalcante, E., Quilbeuf, J., Traonouez, L.-M., Oquendo, F., Batista, T., Legay, A.: Statistical model checking of dynamic software architectures. In: Tekinerdogan, B., Zdun, U., Babar, A. (eds.) ECSA 2016. LNCS, vol. 9839, pp. 185–200. Springer, Cham (2016). https://doi.org/10.1007/978-3-319-48992-6_14
5. CPSoS: European Research and Innovation Agenda on Cyber-Physical Systems-of-Systems 2016–2025 (2016). http://www.cpsos.eu/roadmap/

6. Esfahani, N., Malek, S.: Uncertainty in self-adaptive software systems. In: de Lemos, R., Giese, H., Müller, H.A., Shaw, M. (eds.) Software Engineering for Self-Adaptive Systems II. LNCS, vol. 7475, pp. 214–238. Springer, Heidelberg (2013). https://doi.org/10.1007/978-3-642-35813-5_9

7. Tao, F., Zhang, M., Nee, A.Y.C.: Digital Twin Driven Smart Manufacturing. Academic Press, Cambridge (2019)

8. Garlan, D.: Software engineering in an uncertain world. In: ACM Future of Software Engineering Research, Santa Fe, NM, USA, November 2010

9. Grieves, M.: Virtually Perfect: Driving Innovative and Lean Products through Product Lifecycle Management. Space Coast Press, Cocoa Beach (2011)

10. Guessi, M., Oquendo, F., Nakagawa, E.Y.: Checking the architectural feasibility of systems-of-systems using formal descriptions. In: 11th IEEE SoSE, Kongsberg, Norway (2016)

11. Hubbard, D.W.: How to Measure Anything, 3rd edn. Wiley, Hoboken (2014)

12. INCOSE: SE Vision 2025 (2014). www.incose.org/AboutSE/sevision

13. Jia, D., Lu, K., Wang, J., Zhang, X., Shen, X.: A survey on platoon-based vehicular cyber-physical systems. IEEE Commun. Surv. Tutor. 18(1), 263–284 (2016)

14. Klein, J., van Vliet, H.: A systematic review of system-of-systems architecture research. In: 9th ACM QoSA, Vancouver, Canada, June 2013

15. Maier, M.W.: Architecting principles for systems-of-systems. Syst. Eng. J. 1(4), 267–284 (1998)

16. Milner, R.: Communicating and Mobile Systems: The π-Calculus. Cambridge Press, Cambridge (1999)

17. Olarte, C., Rueda, C., Valencia, F.D.: Models and emerging trends of concurrent constraint programming. Int. J. Constraints 18, 535–578 (2013)

18. OMG: Precise Semantics for Uncertainty Modeling, Request For Proposal, OMG Document ad/2017-12-01, December 2017

19. Oquendo, F.: Formally describing the software architecture of systems-of-systems with SosADL. In: 11th IEEE SoSE, Kongsberg, Norway, June 2016

20. Oquendo, F.: The π-calculus for SoS: novel π-calculus for the formal modeling of software-intensive systems-of-systems. In: Communicating Process Architectures (CPA), vol. 69 (2016)

21. Oquendo, F.: Case study on formally describing the architecture of a software-intensive system-of-systems with SosADL. In: 15th IEEE SMC, Budapest, Hungary, October 2016

22. Oquendo, F.: Formally describing the architectural behavior of software-intensive systems-of-systems with SosADL. In: 21st IEEE ICECCS, Dubai, UAE, November 2016

23. Oquendo, F.: Software architecture challenges and emerging research in software-intensive systems-of-systems. In: Tekinerdogan, B., Zdun, U., Babar, A. (eds.) ECSA 2016. LNCS, vol. 9839, pp. 3–21. Springer, Cham (2016). https://doi.org/10.1007/978-3-319-48992-6_1

24. Oquendo, F.: Architecturally describing the emergent behavior of software-intensive system-of-systems with SosADL. In: 12th IEEE SoSE, Waikoloa, Hawaii, USA, June 2017

25. Oquendo, F.: Formally describing self-organizing architectures for systems-of-systems on the internet-of-things. In: Cuesta, C.E., Garlan, D., Pérez, J. (eds.) ECSA 2018. LNCS, vol. 11048, pp. 20–36. Springer, Cham (2018). https://doi.org/10.1007/978-3-030-00761-4_2

26. Oquendo, F.: Coping with uncertainty in systems-of-systems architecture modeling. In: 14th IEEE SoSE, Anchorage, Alaska, USA, May 2019

27. Oquendo, F., Buisson, J., Leroux, E., Moguérou, G., Quilbeuf, J.: The SosADL architect studio. In: SiSoS 2016, Copenhagen, DK. ACM, November 2016

28. Oquendo, F., Buisson, J., Leroux, E., Moguérou, G.: A formal approach for architecting software-intensive systems-of-systems with guarantees. In: 13th IEEE SoSE, Paris, France, June 2018

29. Oxford Dict. https://en.oxforddictionaries.com/definition/uncertainty
30. Quilbeuf, J., Cavalcante, E., Traonouez, L.-M., Oquendo, F., Batista, T., Legay, A.: A logic for the statistical model checking of dynamic software architectures. In: Margaria, T., Steffen, B. (eds.) ISoLA 2016. LNCS, vol. 9952, pp. 806–820. Springer, Cham (2016). https://doi.org/10.1007/978-3-319-47166-2_56
31. Reynolds, C.W.: Flocks, herds, and schools: a distributed behavioral model, in computer graphics. In: 14th SIGGRAPH, Anaheim, USA (1987)
32. Roca, D., Nemirovsky, D., Nemirovsky, M., Milito, R., Valero, M.: Emergent behaviors in the internet-of-things: the ultimate ultra-large-scale system. In: IEEE Micro, vol. 36, no. 6, November–December 2016
33. Thunnissen, D.P.: Uncertainty classification for the design and development of complex systems. In: 3rd Predictive Methods Conference (PMC), Newport Beach, CA, USA, June 2003
34. Whittle, J., Sawyer, P., Bencomo, N., Cheng, B.H.C., Bruel, J.-M.: RELAX: a language to address uncertainty in self-adaptive systems requirement. Requir. Eng. J. 15(2), 177–196 (2010)
35. Zhang, M., Selic, B., Ali, S., Yue, T., Okariz, O., Norgren, R.: Understanding uncertainty in cyber-physical systems: a conceptual model. In: Wąsowski, A., Lönn, H. (eds.) ECMFA 2016. LNCS, vol. 9764, pp. 247–264. Springer, Cham (2016). https://doi.org/10.1007/978-3-319-42061-5_16

A Big-Data-Analytics System
for Supporting Decision Making Processes
in Complex Smart-City Applications

Alfredo Cuzzocrea$^{(\boxtimes)}$, Massimiliano Nolich, and Walter Ukovich

DIA Department, University of Trieste, Trieste, Italy
{alfredo.cuzzocrea,mnolich,walter.ukovich}@dia.units.it

Abstract. Water is a fundamental element for the life of the ecosystem and of the human beings. Seas and oceans consist in the vastest available space on the planet. Water management is thus a critical issue in the context of smart-city applications, which maybe addressed via consolidated big data analytics methodologies. In addition to this, monitoring the quality of the water in order to decide current and future policy for having a high-quality ecosystem is today possible using connected and distributed devices. In such context, the relevant amount of data that can be acquired can be classified in order to create a big-data analytics-based Decision Support System (DSS) that represents a useful tool towards multiple purposes ranging from environmental monitoring and spatial planning to leisure activities, fishing and bathing. In this paper we propose a general design of a DSS for water quality management and we present several use cases that show how the system can be helpful to face operational, tactical and strategical decisions.

Keywords: Big data analytics · Smart city applications ·
Decision support systems · Water management

1 Introduction

Water is a fundamental element for the life of the ecosystem and of the human beings, thus becoming a global issue. Share water and identify it as a precious good it is unavoidable for all humankind. As the World Water Council [7] remembers "Together we make water a global priority", and this goal can be achieved by mobilizing actions on critical water issues at all levels and focusing on the political dimension of water security, adaptation and sustainability. Sharing water is non-questionable, but it is how to share the information related to it, because they are strictly connected to environment's and at the end to our health. The scientific knowledge tells us that water is the most widespread substance in our Planet. Water covers about the 71% of the Earth surface, the total amount of water resources is approximately of 1,386 million cubic kilometers, with more than 1,338 million cubic kilometers covered by Oceans, Seas, & Bays. A reliable

© Springer Nature Switzerland AG 2019
S. Misra et al. (Eds.): ICCSA 2019, LNCS 11619, pp. 787–802, 2019.
https://doi.org/10.1007/978-3-030-24289-3_58

evaluation of the global water resources was collected by Soviet scientists and presented by Igor Shiklomanov in a summarizing table called "Water reserves on the earth" [21], that follows, proposed in graphical version [1]. These are accurate but only approximate estimations, since water is a substance in continuous dynamism and in permanent motion. Increase and enhance the knowledge of this substance, which has a special role with respect to the others, is an arduous but essential mission, due to water vital influence on the natural environment.

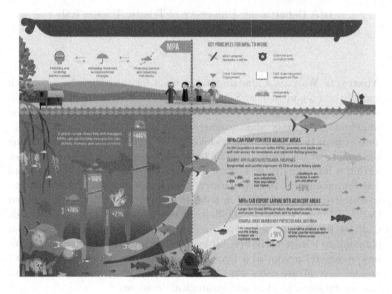

Fig. 1. Sea environment to be monitored

The World Meteorological Organization (WMO) [6], in order to satisfy the need of knowledge and consciousness relating to the water resources, proposes the "The Guide to Hydrological Practices" [5,9], that is almost the major output of the activities of the WMO Commission for Hydrology (CHy); the first edition of the Guide to Hydrometeorological Practices was published in 1965. This is just an example of document edited on the purpose to offer methodical guidelines to brave the challenge of the water issue. Another example is the one presented in the framework of the International Hydrological Programme [22] that focuses on the freshwater aspects proposing, at the same time, some basics consideration regarding water resources in general, some of them touched upon also in this article. A lot of conferences and activities in general focused in the water issue are promoted by many local and international, governmental and non-governmental organizations. Some of which have made a significant breakthrough in convincing humankind to tackle climate change as the agreement on the climate of Paris in 2015 promoted by Jen Schwartz. This put in evidence how the interconnection offered by the new devices and instruments of communication can sensitize and improve knowledge, transposing a local problem into a global issue, where every person, with regard to his skills and social role, can intervene. The question needs to be faced from all possible points of view, and the progress towards better water quality must be shared in a constructively competitive research race. The quality of the water can be monitored, in order to decide current and future policy for having a high-quality ecosystem, by using connected and distributed devices. Nowadays we have an enormous quantity of studies but also new technologies, that can make a further leap forward towards future actions to be taken. Due to the modern technology, for example, it is possible to compare a very extended amount of data, as NASA exalt "Big Data Helps Scientists Dig Deeper", with the phenomenon known as "big data", computers crunch vast quantities of information to identify useful patterns [1]. Another emerging use of the relevant amount of data that can be acquired, is to classify them in order to create a Decision Support System (DSS), which represent a useful tool towards multiple purposes.

In this paper, we will focus on purposes that range from environmental monitoring and spatial planning to leisure activities, fishing and bathing, like in so-called Marine Protected Areas (MPA) (Fig. 1). In particular, we propose a methodology to manage water quality that can be helpful to face operational, tactical and strategic decisions, putting in evidence the ones strictly related to surface water quality. In doing this, we recognize water management as a critical issue in the context of smart-city applications (e.g., [15,28,31]), which maybe addressed via consolidated big data analytics methodologies (e.g., [18,24,29]). We present a general architecture for a big-data analytics-based Decision Support System for surface water monitoring. Surface water are those that collect on the surface of the earth; waterways, lakes, wetlands, seas and oceans constitute surface water. The main goal of the proposed DSS is allowing to collaborate and reuse data inputs according to different business models, sharing and improving the data needed for different decision makers insisting on the same surface water facility. The main characteristic is the fusion of different data sources in order to enhance both the temporal sampling and the spatial sampling.

The rest of the paper is structured as follows. In Sect. 2 a literature review on existent decision support systems for water management is presented. Then, Sect. 3 introduces the Environmental parameters typically used to define water quality and the related KPI used to measure it. Section 4 describes the general architecture of the proposed DSS. Section 5 describes actors, business cases and related KPI, and Sect. 6 presents some preliminary experimental results. Finally, Sect. 7 outlines conclusion and future developments.

2   Literature Review

Decision Support System has been widely studied and applied in different field, as for example in logistics [16], mobility [13,17], security [14,19], comfort [20,26], etc. In the management of water and ecosystems, the concept of sustainability nowadays often named as a goal for businesses, nonprofit organizations and governments. Sustainability is the need of a constant and preferably growing wellbeing and the prospect of leaving future generations with a quality of life that is not inferior to the current one. From this type of approach arises the development of the Triple Bottom Line (TBL) framework that involves three macro spheres of influence: social, environmental and financial [25]. This approach can be developed in different specific contexts and integrated in a Decision Support System. An example of the integration between biological information and modelling with the TBL approach will be briefly exposed in section V, in relation to the increasing complexity of fishery management [2]. Increasing the possibility of investigation increases also the complexity of the model used to understand a specific problem. The U.S. Geological Survey National Water Quality Assessment Program [3] uses the calibrated SPAtially Referenced Regression On Watershed attributes (SPARROW) models to investigate in stream-water quality in relation to human activities and natural processes [4]. The high level of experience necessary for its use has meant that this model could only be accessed through a DSS that simplified the processing and re-presented in tools that were easier to interpret [11]. Different approaches and methods of investigation are useful to describe the condition of the water and the environment in general. The tools for measuring, collecting and processing data improve in precision, quantity and quality, as the parameters of investigation. What is fundamentally essential to be more efficient and effective in terms of time and resources, and also up with the times and consistent with the efforts made is to be, as much as possible, collaborative.

3   Environmental Water Quality Parameters

To cope with quality of surface water, a wide set of parameters can be observed to evaluate the state of the water. In literature, the water pollutants can be classified into broad categories [10]. In Table 1 we have extended the broad categories of [10] to include also visual pollution and other perception based parameters. The resultant broad categories are marked in Table 1 with a letter for practical identification in the following:

The parameters introduced in Table 1 are variables that can be measured. Such measures can represent directly a Key Performance Indicator (KPI) to evaluate the quality of water or they can be combined to obtain more complex KPI. For example, in literature [10] several sets of KPI are defined to monitor the water quality, as for example:

- water stress index;
- total faecal coliforms;
- days of operation at required standards;
- repair times for high priority inoperative lines;
- percentage of total suspended solids;
- amount of potentially dangerous organisms (i.e., e. coli, naked amoebae, etc.);
- compliance in quality when compared to legal standards;
- dissolved air floatation performance;
- total cost of operations;
- metrics that measure specific systems and support vital to consistent operations.

Table 1. Water pollutant categories

	Categories	Parameters (some examples)	General use
A	Basic variables	Water temperature, pH, salinity, dissolved oxygen, and discharge	Used for a general characterization of water quality.
B	Organic pollution indicators	Dissolved oxygen, Biochemical Oxygen Demand (BOD), Chemical Oxygen Demand (COD), ammonium	
C	Organic micropollutants	Such as pesticides and the numerous chemical substances used in industrial processes. PCB, HCH, PAH	
D	Specific major ions	Chloride, sulphate, sodium, potassium, calcium and magnesium. As essential factors in determining the suitability of water for most uses (eg. public water supply, livestock watering and crop irrigation)	
E	Microbiological indicator organism	Total coliforms, fecal coliforms and fecal streptococci bacteria	
F	Biological indicators of the environmental state of the ecosystem	Phytoplankton, zooplankton, zoobenthos, fish, macrophytes and birds and animals related to surface waters	
G	Suspended particulate matter	Suspended solids, turbidity and organic matter (TOC, BOD and COD)	
H	Metals	Cadmium, mercury, copper, zinc	
I	Indicators of eutrophication	Nutrients (eg. nitrogen and phosphorus), and various biological effect variables (eg. chlorophyll a, Secchi disc transparency, phytoplankton, zoobenthos)	
J	Indicators of acidification	pH, alkalinity, conductivity, sulphate, nitrate, aluminium, phytoplankton	
K	Indicators of radioactivity	Total alpha and beta activity, 137Cs, 90Sr	
L	Visual pollution	Tarry residues, glass, plastic, rubber	
M	Perception based parameters	Color, turbidity, smell	

In general, KPI are not static and unchanging. Moreover, they strictly depend on the business context that they are applied.

4   DSS Architecture

The aim of this work is to propose a Collaborative DSS capable of aggregate and integrate different data sources regarding the measurement of the parameters affecting water quality (see Table 1) in order to produce added value in different application scenarios. The proposed Collaborative DSS can improve data to generate new information for a specific application domain using the related scientific knowledge.

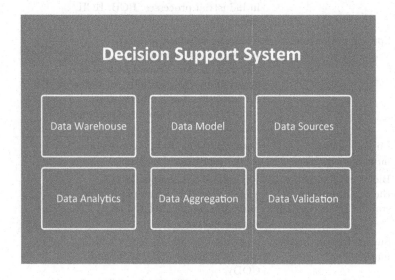

Fig. 2. DSS main features

The main objectives of the proposed Collaborative DSS are depicted in Fig. 2 and are described as follows:

1. Share information regarding data quality already acquire from public authorities;
2. Share information regarding specific measurement campaign in specific region;
3. Aggregate information around different data sources;
4. Provide evaluation and KPI for different specific application sectors;
5. Stimulate the citizen to evaluate the state of surface water and signal problems to the authorities by using the DSS.

The structure of the proposed Collaborative DSS, suited for managing the environmental quality of both salt and fresh water, is the following. The system consists of a platform with which you can interact both via web pages and via smartphone Apps. Every user has to register to the Collaborative DSS giving his/her references. After the registration, typical power usage of the system can be guaranteed via log in. According to user liability assigned during the registration phase, the information he/she sends will have a different degree of reliability. The DSS can manage data coming from institutional bodies and individual citizens, from research areas and from economic bodies (for example, aquaculture companies) or even data from the marinas or managing institution, tour operators or from the tourists themselves. The collected data is geo-referenced. Some of the collected data are already certified if acquired from certified entities, some other are not certified if collected by causal users. Those data is managed by the Collaborative DSS taking into account the different degrees of reliability. Each user can send its own data to the Collaborative DSS: measurements made with expensive professional tools or with portable instruments or subjective perception and visual information related to the quality of the water. The Collaborative DSS can be tailored to different applicative scenarios. For each scenario, the platform provides an indication of the water status in the area of interest. The output of the Collaborative DSS aim at reducing the workload of the decision makers by providing a semaphore indicating the status of the water in the given scenario. The semaphore will be green if the quality in high, it is yellow if the quality is medium and it is red if the water quality is not acceptable. The best practices, derived from experts knowledge in the specific field, will drive the choice of the best decision-making policies to be realized.

5 Business Cases

5.1 Stakeholders Involved

For the Collaborative DSS a wide set of stakeholders can be outlined. We propose to consider the following categories of actors, that can include all the possible involved stakeholders:

1. Citizen: people that interact with surface water;
2. Active citizen: citizen that actively produces data to update data relative the region he/she is moving;
3. Private Company: private firm that operates near/on surface water, for example fishing company, maritime transport company, etc.;
4. Public Company: private firm that operates near/on surface water, for example environmental research company, wastewater management company, etc.;
5. Public Authority: police, territorial entity, etc.

5.2 Business Models

The actors introduced above can operate in different operative scenarios. In the following we define three business cases that point out that the same water parameter can have different evaluation in different scenarios. The business cases considered in the following are Bathing, Fishing and Aquaculture, and Protected Natural Area. In Fig. 3 is represented the interconnection among the measured parameters (Table 1) and the applicative business cases considered. Note that in Fig. 3 the same parameter can be involved in different business cases with different evaluation criteria. The aim of Fig. 3 to show how the interconnection at different granularity levels can identify and characterize the specific business case.

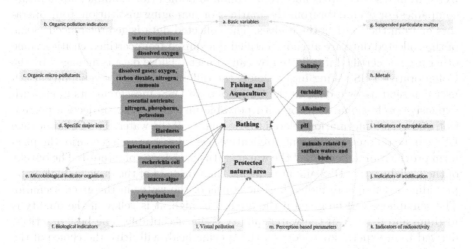

Fig. 3. Mind map of parameters for different business cases

Business Case 1: Bathing. In this case (see Fig. 4), we consider the typical behaviour of a tourist that during summer would like to have a bath at the sea/lake/river and he/she guesses about the status of the water of the region they are attending. The most observed parameters that prove the quality of bathing water are the presence of enterococci and escherichia coli, or the presence of cyanobacteria or microalgae but also other parameter could be taken into account. As European Commission directives remembers the waters are classified according to their level of quality: poor, sufficient, good or excellent. We knows, for example, that the activities to guarantee that the citizens are adequately informed are yet supervised.

Especially during the summer seasons warnings of danger to bathing are easily identifiable and they are managed by authorities. One of the possible way to extend the capability to prevent water quality contamination is enlarging the area of observation. The covered area can be improved by collecting different sources. The tourists can become a citizen science providing, for example, himself/herself with simple measuring instruments or engaging monitoring instruments to pleasure crafts. This kind of measure have to be evaluated by the proposed Collaborative DSS to appropriately enforce the knowledge of the surface water quality.

Relevant parameters to evaluate the water quality for bathing can be derived according to the Bathing Water Directive [8] and considering other relevant

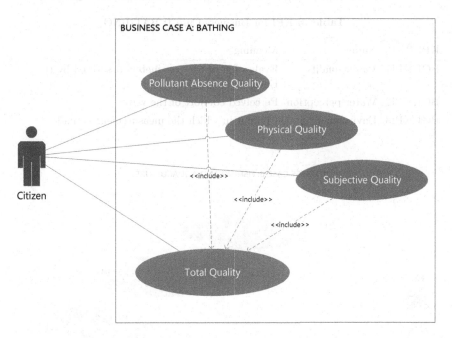

Fig. 4. Business Case 1 use case

Table 2. Water parameters for Business Case 1: BATHING

Categories	Parameters BC1
A	Temperature
A	Salinity
G M	Turbidity
E	Intestinal enterococci
E	Escherichia coli
F	Macro-algae
F I J	Phytoplankton
L	Tarry residues, glass, plastic, rubber
M	Color, smell

human perception as shown in Table 2. Note that in Table 2 we have introduced some parameters belonging to visual pollution an perception based parameters.

Business Case 2: Fishing and Aquaculture. This business case (see Fig. 5) is considered due to the importance of the aquatic environment for fishing and aquaculture. The water quality requirements have different range for different fish species and this aspect has a strong impact on the fish under culture [27] (Table 3).

Table 3. KPI for Business Case 1: BATHING

KPI BC1	Name	Meaning
BC1_KPI1	Water quality	Evaluation of the parameters described by the European legislation
BC1_KPI2	Water perception	Perceived comfort of the water
BC1_KPI3	Environment	Context in which the measurement is made

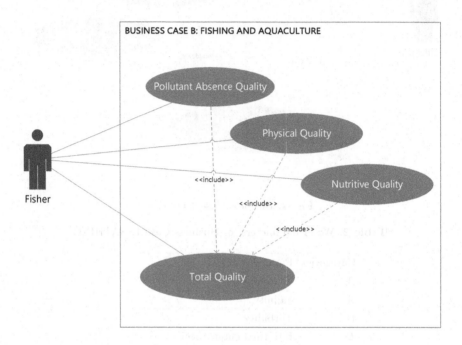

Fig. 5. Business Case 2 use case

In Table 4 relevant parameters to evaluate the water quality in case of Fishing and Aquaculture are presented. It is worth to note that, analyzing Table 4, the parameters considered are related to presence of pollutants and the nutritional characteristics of the water and that visual and perceptional parameters are not considered.

Starting from the measured parameters of Table 4 we propose the relevant KPI for the Fishing and Aquaculture business case. In Table 5 we propose to consider water quality, nutritional proprieties and abundance of fish KPI.

Business Case 3: Protected Natural Areas. With the term protected natural area (see Fig. 6) we include all those natural areas characterized by heterogeneous landscapes and of particular importance regarding wildlife, flora and fauna, including anything that makes them of special environmental interest. Due to their beauty and uniqueness the tourism is promoted but always in respect to the preservation of the environment. Protected natural areas can be designed

Table 4. KPI for Business Case 2: FISHING and AQUACULTURE

Categories	Parameters BC2
A	Temperature
A J	pH
A	Salinity
G M	Turbidity
A B	Dissolved oxygen
B	Other dissolved gasses: carbon dioxide, nitrogen, ammonia
J	Alkalinity
I	Essential nutrients: Nitrogen, Phosphorus, Potassium

Table 5. KPI for Business Case 2: FISHING and AQUACULTURE

KPI BC2	Name	Meaning
BC2_KPI1	Water quality	Presence pollutants in the water
BC2_KPI2	Nutritional properties	Presence of nutrients
BC2_KPI3	Abundance of fish	Presence of organisms influencing fish life

by public institutions or private individuals, such as charitable or research institutions. Coastal protected areas are constantly monitored in regards of water quality to be sure that the eligible standard values of quality are not exceeded, then compromising the status of all the investigated area. Those values can be shared to all the people interested in, because it is usually an information of public domain. Conversely, the measures analyzed and elaborated from researchers can be shared with the legal entity responsible of the protected area and, after validation, shared in the appropriate form to all the people interested in the results. At the same time a tourist can stumble upon some evident anomaly in the water surface quality, for example an oil stain, and alert immediately the authority sending some simple kind of messages to the Collaborative DSS. When the tourist identifies some generic anomalous event, the Collaborative DSS decides on the status of the water and what kind of action has to be taken. The warning can be of different kinds and starts from different users with different reliability. For this reason, in a such delicate context, the communication interface of the Collaborative DSS has to be adequate for different users. This permits to weight at the same time the warning and the information in relation to their origin. In such context the measures taken by researchers, with a high level of reliability, can effectively turn from local into global consistency and collaborate to the aim of the global environment issue.

In Table 6 relevant parameters to evaluate the water quality in case of Protected natural area are proposed. Note analyzing Table 6 that visual pollution and perception based parameters are considered relevant to define the KPI for this business case.

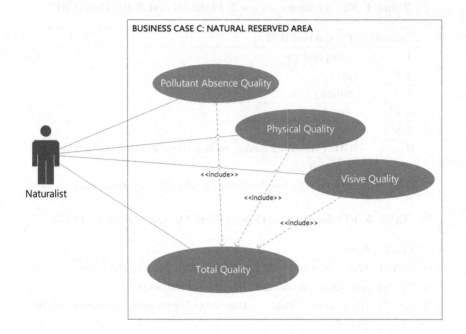

Fig. 6. Business Case 3 use case

Table 6. Water parameters for Business Case 3: PROTECTED NATURAL AREA

Categories	Parameters BC3
A B	Dissolved oxygen
F I J	Phytoplankton
G M	Turbidity
F	Birds and animals related to surface waters
L	Tarry residues, glass, plastic, rubber
M	Color, smell

Table 7. KPI for Business Case 3: PROTECTED NATURAL AREA

KPI BC3	Name	Meaning
BC3_KPI1	Water quality	Presence pollutants in the water
BC3_KPI2	Water affinity	Congruence with the environmental attitude of the neighborhood
BC3_KPI3	Flora and fauna	Well-being and biodiversity of the environment

Starting from the parameters listed in Table 6 we have defined relevant KPI for the protected area business case. In Table 7 we propose to consider water quality, water affinity and flora and fauna KPI.

6   Preliminary Experimental Results

The proposed system has been tested by feeding in information from different data sources. Business Cases presented in Sect. 5 have been considered. In the preliminary experimental results presented in this Section, the Gulf of Trieste region of the Adriatic Sea in Italy has been analyzed.

More precisely, in Fig. 7 an example of quality evaluation of the water for bathing is reported.

Figure 8 shows an example of aquaculture water quality evaluation is presented. In this example, some artificial problematic values of pH of the water has been added, in order to show that the proposed DSS generates warning in case of water parameters out of ranges.

Finally, Fig. 9 illustrates the water quality analysis of reserved areas.

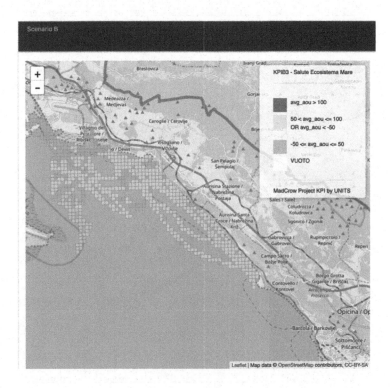

Fig. 7. Business Case 1: experimental results

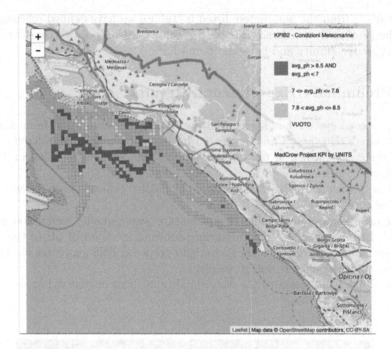

Fig. 8. Business Case 2: experimental results

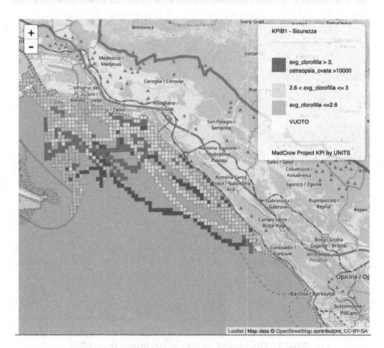

Fig. 9. Business Case 3: experimental results

7 Conclusions and Future Work

In this paper we have analyzes the potentiality of a Collaborative DSS approach in order to face the problem of the reuse of water quality data in different applications. DSS input variables have been collected into broad categories to simplify their interpretation. Starting from the parameters belonging to such broad categories we have outlined three relevant business cases and related KPI that reuse and reinterpret the meaning of the common parameters adapting them to the specific application. Note that the same parameter can affect mere than one KPI and can be interpret in different way in different business cases. Future work will be conducted for implementing this approach using real data collecting from public institution and voluntary measurement from citizen scientist. Also, performance issues in the context of the underlying big data processing layer will be considered (e.g., [12,23,30]).

References

1. https://earthobservatory.nasa.gov/Features/LandsatBigData/
2. https://www.ncbi.nlm.nih.gov/pmc/articles/PMC4422616/
3. https://water.usgs.gov/nawqa/
4. https://water.usgs.gov/nawqa/sparrow/
5. Guide to hydrological practise, management of water resources and application of hydrological practise: World Meteorological Organizaion (Weather-Climate-Water), WMO-No. 168, 6th edn. (2009)
6. World Meteorological Organization
7. World Water Council
8. Directive 2006/7/EEC of the European parliament and of the council of 15 February 2006 concerning the management of bathing water quality and repealing directive 76/160/EEC. Official J. Eur. Union (2006)
9. Guide to hydrological practise, hydrology - from measurement to hydrological information: World Meteorological Organizaion (Weather-Climate-Water), WMO-No. 168, 6th edn. (2008)
10. Surface water quality monitoring: European Environment Agency (2008)
11. Booth, N.L., Everman, E.J., Kuo, I.-L., Sprague, L., Murphy, L.: A web-based decision support system for assessing regional water-quality conditions and management actions. J. Am. Water Res. Assoc. (2011)
12. Braun, P., Cameron, J.J., Cuzzocrea, A., Jiang, F., Leung, C.K.-S.: Effectively and efficiently mining frequent patterns from dense graph streams on disk. In: 18th International Conference in Knowledge Based and Intelligent Information and Engineering Systems, KES 2014, Gdynia, Poland, 15–17 September 2014, pp. 338–347 (2014)
13. Clemente, M., Fanti, M.P., Iacobellis, G., Nolich, M., Ukovich, W.: A decision support system for user-based vehicle relocation in car sharing systems. IEEE Trans. Syst. Man Cybern. Syst. 48(8), 1283–1296 (2018)
14. Cuzzocrea, A., Nolich, M., Ukovich, W.: An innovative architecture for supporting cyber-physical security systems. In: Gervasi, O., et al. (eds.) ICCSA 2018. LNCS, vol. 10964, pp. 658–667. Springer, Cham (2018). https://doi.org/10.1007/978-3-319-95174-4_50

15. Elshenawy, M., Abdulhai, B., El-Darieby, M.: Towards a service-oriented cyber-physical systems of systems for smart city mobility applications. Future Gener. Comp. Syst. **79**, 575–587 (2018)

16. Fanti, M.P., Iacobellis, G., Nolich, M., Rusich, A., Ukovich, W.: A decision support system for cooperative logistics. IEEE Trans. Autom. Sci. Eng. **14**(2), 732–744 (2017)

17. Fanti, M.P., Nolich, M., Roccotelli, M., Ukovich, W.: Virtual sensors for electromobility. In: 2018 5th International Conference on Control, Decision and Information Technologies, CoDIT 2018, pp. 635–640 (2018)

18. Li, K.-C., Jiang, H., Yang, L.T., Cuzzocrea, A. (eds.): Big Data - Algorithms, Analytics, and Applications. Chapman and Hall/CRC (2015)

19. Menegatti, E., Cavasin, M., Pagello, E., Mumolo, E., Nolich, M.: Combining audio and video surveillance with a mobile robot. Int. J. Artif. Intell. Tools **16**(2), 377–398 (2007)

20. Nolich, M., Spoladore, D., Carciotti, S., Buqi, R., Sacco, M.: Cabin as a home: a novel comfort optimization framework for IoT equipped smart environments and applications on cruise ships. Sensors **19**(5) (2019)

21. Shiklomanov, I.: World fresh water resources. In: Gleick, P.H. (ed.) Water in Crisis: A Guide to the World's Fresh Water Resources (1993)

22. Shiklomanov, I.A.: World water resources, a new appraisial and assessment for the 21st century. In: International Hydrological Programme (1998)

23. Silva, B.N., Khan, M., Han, K.: Big data analytics embedded smart city architecture for performance enhancement through real-time data processing and decision-making. Wireless Commun. Mob. Comput. **2017** (2017)

24. Silva, B.N., et al.: Urban planning and smart city decision management empowered by real-time data processing using big data analytics. Sensors **18**(9), 2994 (2018)

25. Slaper, T.F., Hall, T.J.: The triple bottom line: what is it and how does it work? Indiana Bus. Rev. (2011)

26. Spoladore, D., Arlati, S., Carciotti, S., Nolich, M., Sacco, M.: RoomFort: an ontology-based comfort management application for hotels. Electronics **7**(12) (2018)

27. Towers, L.: How to achieve good water quality management in aquaculture. The Fish Site (2015)

28. Wang, T., Liang, Y., Jia, W., Arif, M., Liu, A., Xie, M.: Coupling resource management based on fog computing in smart city systems. J. Netw. Comput. Appl. **135**, 11–19 (2019)

29. Wu, Z., Yin, W., Cao, J., Xu, G., Cuzzocrea, A.: Community detection in multi-relational social networks. In: Lin, X., Manolopoulos, Y., Srivastava, D., Huang, G. (eds.) WISE 2013. LNCS, vol. 8181, pp. 43–56. Springer, Heidelberg (2013). https://doi.org/10.1007/978-3-642-41154-0_4

30. Yang, C.-T., Liu, J.-C., Hsu, C.-H., Chou, W.-L.: On improvement of cloud virtual machine availability with virtualization fault tolerance mechanism. J. Supercomputing **69**(3), 1103–1122 (2014)

31. Zhu, N., Zhao, H.: IoT applications in the ecological industry chain from information security and smart city perspectives. Comput. Electr. Eng. **65**, 34–43 (2018)

Binomial Characterization
of Cryptographic Sequences

Sara D. Cardell[1($\boxtimes$)] and Amparo Fúster-Sabater[2]

[1] Instituto de Matemática, Estatística e Computação Científica, UNICAMP,
R. Sérgio Buarque de Holanda, 651, Campinas, SP 13083-859, Brazil
sdcardell@ime.unicamp.br
[2] Instituto de Tecnologías Físicas y de la Información,
C.S.I.C., Serrano 144, 28006 Madrid, Spain
amparo@iec.csic.es

Abstract. The generalized self-shrinking generator is a sequence generator that produces binary sequences with good cryptographic properties. On the other hand, the binomial sequences are a well-defined class of sequences that can be obtained considering infinite successions of binomial coefficients modulo 2. In this work, we see that the generalized sequences can be computed as a finite binary sum of binomial sequences. Moreover, the cryptographic parameters of the generalized sequences can be studied in terms of the binomial sequences.

Keywords: Generalized generator · Binomial sequence ·
Binomial characterization · Decimation · Cryptography

1 Introduction

Protection of confidential information uses an encryption function called *cipher* to convert the original message or *plaintext* into the ciphered message or *ciphertext*. In symmetric cryptography, there is a single piece of secret information called *key* that is shared by both communicating parties.

Inside the symmetric cryptography, stream ciphers are the simplest and fastest among all the encryption procedures so they are in widespread use and can be found in different technological applications e.g. the encryption system E0 in Bluetooth network specifications [6], the SNOW 3G Generator [12] in wireless communication of high-speed data with 4G/LTE (Long-Term Evolution) technology or the algorithm RC4 in Microsoft Word and Excel spreadsheet [17]. The conjunction of simplicity and speed in a single process preserves the leading part of the stream ciphers in any cryptographic application.

The main concern in stream cipher design is to generate from a short and truly random key a long and pseudorandom sequence called *keystream* sequence. For encryption, the sender performs the bitwise XOR (exclusive-OR) operation among the bits of the plaintext and the keystream sequence. The result is the ciphertext that is sent to the receiver. For decryption, the receiver generates the

© Springer Nature Switzerland AG 2019
S. Misra et al. (Eds.): ICCSA 2019, LNCS 11619, pp. 803–816, 2019.
https://doi.org/10.1007/978-3-030-24289-3_59

same keystream sequence, performs the same bitwise XOR operation between the received ciphertext and the keystream sequence and recovers the original message. Recall that both encryption and decryption procedures use the same XOR logic operation, that is a simple and balanced operation.

Most keystream generators are based on maximal-length Linear Feedback Shift Registers (LFSRs) [10] whose output sequences, the so-called PN-sequences, are combined in a nonlinear way to produce pseudorandom sequences for cryptographic application. Nonlinear filters, combinational generators, clock-controlled generators or irregularly decimated generators are some of the most popular keystream generators. See [9,15,16] for a comprehensive introduction to this topic.

Inside the family of irregularly decimated generators, we can enumerate: (a) the *shrinking generator* [5] that involves two LFSRs, (b) the *self-shrinking generator* [14] involving only one LFSR and (c) the most representative element of this family, the *generalized self-shrinking generator* or family of generators [11], that includes the self-shrinking generator as one of its members. Irregularly decimated generators produce sequences that exhibit good cryptographic properties: long periods, excellent run distribution and self-correlation, balancedness [7], simplicity of implementation, etc. The underlying idea of this type of generators is the irregular decimation of a PN-sequence according to the bits of another. The decimation result is a sequence that will be used as keystream sequence in the encryption/decryption procedure. This work focuses on the generalized self-shrinking generators and their output sequences the so-called *generalized self-shrunken sequences* (GSS sequences) or simply generalized sequences.

On the other hand, the binomial sequences are a family of binary sequences whose terms are binomial numbers reduced modulo 2. More precisely, the binomial sequences correspond to the diagonals of the Sierpinski's triangle modulo 2. In this way, the binomial sequences exhibit many attractive properties that can be very useful in the analysis and generation of keystream sequences. In this work, it is shown the close relationship between generalized sequences and the class of binomial sequences, in the sense that these binomial sequences can be used to analyse the cryptographic properties of those generalized sequences.

The work is organized as follows. Fundamental and basic concepts used throughout the work are introduced in Sect. 2. Next in Sect. 3, the characteristics of the binomial sequences are discussed in detail. The representation and computation of generalized sequences in terms of binomial sequences is the subject of Sect. 4. Finally, conclusions in Sect. 5 end the paper.

2   Preliminaries

In this section, we present some basic concepts about sequences that we need to know before introducing the main results.

2.1   Binary Sequences

Let $\mathbb{F}_2$ be the Galois field of two elements. We say $\{a_n\} = \{a_0, a_1, a_2 \ldots\}$ is a binary sequence if its terms $a_n \in \mathbb{F}_2$, for $n = 0, 1, 2, \ldots$. The sequence $\{a_n\}$ is periodic if and only if there exists an integer T such that $a_{n+T} = a_n$, for all $n \geq 0$.

Let r be a positive integer, and let $d_1, d_2, d_3, \ldots, d_r$ be constant coefficients with $d_i \in \mathbb{F}_2$. A binary sequence $\{a_n\}$ satisfying the relationship

$$a_{n+r} = d_r a_n + d_{r-1} a_{n+1} + \cdots + d_3 a_{n+r-3} + d_2 a_{n+r-2} + d_1 a_{n+r-1}, \quad n \geq 0, \quad (1)$$

is called a (r-th order) linear recurring sequence in $\mathbb{F}_2$. The terms $\{a_0, a_1, \ldots, a_{r-1}\}$ are referred to as the initial values (or initial state) and determine the rest of the sequence uniquely. A relation of the form given by the Eq. (1) is called a (r-th order) linear recurrence relationship.

The monic polynomial

$$p(x) = d_r + d_{r-1}x + \cdots + d_3 x^{r-3} + d_2 x^{r-2} + d_1 x^{r-1} + x^r \in \mathbb{F}_2[x]$$

is called the characteristic polynomial of the linear recurring sequence and $\{a_n\}$ is said to be generated by $p(x)$.

The generation of linear recurring sequences can be implemented on Linear Feedback Shift Registers (LFSRs) [10]. These structures handle information in the form of binary elements and they are based on shifts and linear feedback. In fact, a LFSR is an electronic device with r memory cells (stages), shift to the adjacent stage and linear feedback to the empty stage. If the characteristic polynomial of the linear recurring sequence is primitive [10], then the LFSR is said to be maximal-length and its output sequence has period $T = 2^r - 1$. Such an output sequence is called PN-sequence (pseudonoise sequence).

Linear complexity, LC, is a much used metric of the security of a keystream sequence [16]. Roughly speaking, LC measures the amount of sequence bits needed to reconstruct the rest of the sequence. In a more precise way, LC of a sequence $\{a_n\}$ is defined as the length of the shortest LFSR that generates such a sequence or, equivalently, as the lowest order linear recurrence relationship that generates such a sequence. In cryptographic terms, LC must be as large as possible; the recommended value is approximately half the sequence period, $LC \simeq T/2$.

2.2   The Family of Generalized Sequences

The more representative element in the class of irregularly decimated generators is the generalized self-shrinking generator (or simply generalized generator) [11], a particularization of the shrinking generator [3,5] that includes the sequences generated by: the self-shrinking generator [1,14], the modified self-shrinking generator [2,13] and the t-modified self-shrinking generator [4]. The family of generalized sequences is described as follows:

Definition 1. *Let* $\{a_n\}$ *($n = 0, 1, 2, \ldots$) be a PN-sequence generated by a maximal-length LFSR with an L-degree characteristic polynomial. Let p be an integer and* $\{v_n\}$ *($n = 0, 1, 2, \ldots$) be an p-position left shifted version of* $\{a_n\}$ *with ($p = 0, 1, 2, \ldots, 2^L - 2$). The decimation rule is very simple:*

1. *If* $a_n = 1$, *then* v_n *is output.*
2. *If* $a_n = 0$, *then* v_n *is discarded and there is no output bit.*

Thus, for each p an output sequence $\{s_0\, s_1\, s_2 \ldots\}$ *denoted by* $\{S(p)_n\}$ *($n \geq 0$) is generated. Such a sequence is called the generalized self-shrunken sequence (GSS-sequence) (or simply generalized sequence) associated with the shift p.*

Recall that $\{a_n\}$ remains fixed while $\{v_n\}$ is the sliding sequence or left-shifted version of $\{a_n\}$. When p ranges in the interval $p \in [0, 1, 2, \ldots, 2^L - 2]$, then the family of $2^L - 1$ generalized sequences is obtained. For each possible sequence $\{v_n\}$ and after the application of the decimation rule, a new generalized sequence is generated. The GSS-sequence family includes the $2^L - 1$ generalized self-shrunken sequences plus the identically null sequence. Some important facts extracted from [8,11] are enumerated:

1. This family always includes [8] the sequence $\{111111\ldots\}$ for $p = 0$ and the sequences $\{101010\ldots\}$ and $\{010101\ldots\}$ for $p = q, q+1$, respectively, where q is an integer corresponding to the power $\alpha^q \in \mathbb{F}_{2^L}$ satisfying $\alpha^{q+1} = \alpha^q + 1$.
2. All the sequences in this family are balanced except for sequences $\{0000\ldots\}$ and $\{1111\ldots\}$, [11, Theorem 1].
3. By construction, the family of generalized self-shrinking sequences consists of 2^L sequences of 2^{L-1} bits each of them [11, Section I]. Consequently, the period of each one of these sequences is a factor of 2^{L-1}.
4. The family of generalized self-shrinking sequences has structure of Abelian group whose group operation is the bit-wise addition mod 2, the neutral element is the sequence $\{0000\ldots\}$ and the inverse element of each sequence is the own sequence, [11, Theorem 2].
5. The self-shrinking sequence is a member of the GSS-sequence family [11, Section I] with shift $p = 2^{L-1}$.

Example 1. For an LFSR with characteristic polynomial $p(x) = 1 + x + x^4$ and initial state $\{1\ 1\ 1\ 1\}$, we get the generalized sequences (GSS-sequences) shown in Table 1. The bits in bold in the different sequences $\{v_n\}$ are the digits of the corresponding GSS-sequences associated to their corresponding p. The PN-sequence $\{a_n\}$ with period $T = 2^4 - 1$ is written at the bottom of the table. Note that the sequences corresponding to $p = 2, 8$ are the same but starting at different terms. The same holds for the sequences corresponding to $p = 1, 5, 6, 14$ and $p = 3, 4, 10, 13$. In brief, inside the family of generalized sequences there are shifted versions of the same sequence.

Next a new class of binary sequences that allow one to analyze the GSS-sequences are introduced.

Table 1. GSS-sequences for $p(x) = 1 + x + x^4$

p	$\{v_n\}$ sequences	GSS-sequence
0	111100010011010	11111111
1	111000100110101	11100100
2	110001001101011	11000011
3	100010011010111	10001101
4	000100110101111	00011011
5	001001101011110	00100111
6	010011010111100	01001110
7	100110101111000	10010110
8	001101011110001	00111100
9	011010111100010	01101001
10	110101111000100	11011000
11	101011110001001	10101010
12	010111100010011	01010101
13	101111000100110	10110001
14	011110001001101	01110010
	111100010011010	

Table 2. Binomial coefficients, binomial sequences, periods and complexities

Binomial coeff.	Binomial sequences	Period	Linear complexity
$\binom{n}{0}$	1 1 1 1 1 1 1 1	$T_0 = 1$	$LC_0 = 1$
$\binom{n}{1}$	0 1 0 1 0 1 0 1	$T_1 = 2$	$LC_1 = 2$
$\binom{n}{2}$	0 0 1 1 0 0 1 1	$T_2 = 4$	$LC_2 = 3$
$\binom{n}{3}$	0 0 0 1 0 0 0 1	$T_3 = 4$	$LC_3 = 4$
$\binom{n}{4}$	0 0 0 0 1 1 1 1	$T_4 = 8$	$LC_4 = 5$
$\binom{n}{5}$	0 0 0 0 0 1 0 1	$T_5 = 8$	$LC_5 = 6$
$\binom{n}{6}$	0 0 0 0 0 0 1 1	$T_6 = 8$	$LC_6 = 7$
$\binom{n}{7}$	0 0 0 0 0 0 0 1	$T_7 = 8$	$LC_7 = 8$

3 Binomial Sequences

The binomial coefficient $\binom{n}{i}$ is the coefficient of the power x^i in the polynomial expansion of $(1 + x)^n$. For every positive integer n, it is a well-known fact that $\binom{n}{0} = 1$ and $\binom{n}{i} = 0$ for $i > n$. Moreover, it is worth noticing that if we arrange these binomial coefficients into rows for successive values of $n = 0, 1, 2, \ldots$, then the generated structure is the Pascal's triangle (see Fig. 1a). The most-left diagonal is the identically 1 sequence, the next diagonal is the sequence of natural numbers $\{1, 2, 3, \ldots\}$, the next one is the sequence of triangular num-

(a) Binomial coefficients arranged
as the Pascal's triangle

(b) Sierpinski's triangle

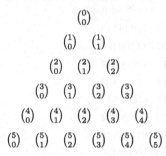

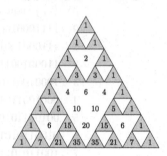

Fig. 1. Pascal's and Sierpinski's triangles

bers $\{1, 3, 6, 10, \ldots\}$, etc. Other interesting sequences (tetrahedral numbers, pentatope numbers, hexagonal numbers, Fibonacci sequence, etc.) can be found over the diagonals of this triangle. On the other hand, if we color the odd numbers of the Pascal's triangle and shade the other ones, we can find the Sierpinski's triangle (see Fig. 1b).

The binomial coefficients reduced modulo 2 allow us to introduce the concept of binomial sequence.

Definition 2. *Given a fixed integer $k \geq 0$, the sequence $\{b_n^k\}_{n \geq 0}$ given by:*

$$b_n^k = \begin{cases} 0 & \text{if } n < k \\ \binom{n}{k} \bmod 2 & \text{if } n \geq k \end{cases}$$

*is known as the **binary k-th binomial sequence**.*

Table 2 shows the binomial sequences and the values of their periods and linear complexities, denoted by T_k and LC_k, respectively, for the first binomial coefficients $\binom{n}{k}$, $k = 0, 1, \ldots, 7$. In Appendix A, one can find the first 32 binomial sequences. Moreover, we can see the pattern and repetitive structure of such sequences.

Recall that the successive binomial sequences correspond to the successive diagonals of the Sierpinski's triangle (see Fig. 1b) reduced modulo 2.

Next, the relation between binomial sequences and every binary sequence with period a power of 2 appears in the following result.

Theorem 1. *Let $\{z_n\}$ be a binary sequence with period $T = 2^L$, L being a positive integer. Then, every binary sequence $\{z_n\}$ can be written as a linear combination of binomial sequences.*

Proof. Since the period of $\{z_n\}$ is a power of 2, then the next equation holds:

$$(E^{2^L} + 1)z_n = (E + 1)^{2^L} z_n = 0,$$

Table 3. GSS-sequences for $p(x) = 1 + x + x^4$

p	α^p	$\{S(p)\}$	p	α^p	$\{S(p)\}$
0	1	1 1 1 1 1 1 1 1	8	$\alpha^8 = 1 + \alpha^2$	0 0 1 1 1 1 0 0
1	α	1 1 1 0 0 1 0 0	9	$\alpha^9 = \alpha + \alpha^3$	0 1 1 0 1 0 0 1
2	α^2	1 1 0 0 0 0 1 1	10	$\alpha^{10} = 1 + \alpha + \alpha^2$	1 1 0 1 1 0 0 0
3	α^3	1 0 0 0 1 1 0 1	11	$\alpha^{11} = \alpha + \alpha^2 + \alpha^3$	1 0 1 0 1 0 1 0
4	$\alpha^4 = 1 + \alpha$	0 0 0 1 1 0 1 1	12	$\alpha^{12} = 1 + \alpha + \alpha^2 + \alpha^3$	0 1 0 1 0 1 0 1
5	$\alpha^5 = \alpha + \alpha^2$	0 0 1 0 0 1 1 1	13	$\alpha^{13} = 1 + \alpha^2 + \alpha^3$	1 0 1 1 0 0 0 1
6	$\alpha^6 = \alpha^2 + \alpha^3$	0 1 0 0 1 1 1 0	14	$\alpha^{14} = 1 + \alpha^3$	0 1 1 1 0 0 1 0
7	$\alpha^7 = 1 + \alpha + \alpha^3$	1 0 0 1 0 1 1 0			

where E is the shifting operator that acts on the terms of a sequence $\{a_n\}$, that is: $E^k a_n = a_{n+k}$ for all integer $k \geq 0$.

The characteristic polynomial of the previous equation is $(x + 1)^m$ with $m = 2^L$, that is $x = 1$ is the unique root of the polynomial $(x + 1)$ but with multiplicity m. Therefore, the binary solutions of this equation are given [9] by the expression:

$$z_n = c_0 \binom{n}{0} + c_1 \binom{n}{1} + \cdots + c_{T-1} \binom{n}{T-1} \quad \text{for } n \geq 0, \tag{2}$$

where the coefficients $c_i \in \mathbb{F}_2$ and $\binom{n}{i}$ are binomial coefficients reduced modulo 2. When n takes successive values $n = 0, 1, 2, \ldots$, then each binomial coefficient modulo 2 defines a different binomial sequence. Thus, the sequence $\{z_n\}$ is just the bit-wise XOR of such binomial sequences weighted by binary coefficients c_i.

Different choices of c_i will produce different sequences $\{z_n\}$ with distinct characteristics and properties, but all of them with period 2^l, $0 \leq l \leq L$.

Since the generalized sequences have periods that are powers of 2, then the previous theorem can be directly applied to the GSS-sequence family. In this way, every generalized sequence can be written as a linear combination of binomial sequences as shown in the Eq. (2).

4   Binomial Characterization of Generalized Sequences

According to Theorem 1, a binary sequence of period power of 2 is the bit-wise XOR of binomial sequences. Therefore, we introduce the following definition.

Definition 3. *The set of binomial sequences necessary to obtain a binary sequence of period power of 2 is called the **binomial characterization** of such a sequence.*

In this section, we analyze the binomial characterization of the different sequences in the class of GSS-sequences. Let $\mathbb{F}_{2^L}$ be an additive group, then we can construct the group isomorphism:

$$\phi : (\mathbb{F}_{2^L}, +) \longrightarrow (\mathcal{S}, +)$$
$$\alpha^p \longrightarrow \{S(p)\}, \tag{3}$$

which defines a relationship between α^p (α being a root of $p(x)$, the LFSR characteristic polynomial) and the generalized sequence $\{S(p)\}$ (see Table 3 for the isomorphism (3) corresponding to the polynomial $p(x) = 1 + x + x^4$).

Now, we are going to write the most simple sequences of the generalized sequence family in terms of their binomial characterizations. In fact, we have seen in Subsect. 2.2 that there exists an integer $q \in \{0, 1, \ldots, 2^{L-2}\}$ such that $\alpha^{q+1} = 1 + \alpha^q$. The generalized sequences corresponding to α^q and α^{q+1} are $\{1\,0\,1\,0\,1\,0\,1\,0\ldots\}$ and $\{0\,1\,0\,1\,0\,1\,0\,1\ldots\}$ and their binomial characterizations are $\binom{n}{0} + \binom{n}{1}$ and $\binom{n}{1}$, respectively. In the same way, for α^0 its corresponding generalized sequence is $\{1\,1\,1\,1\,1\,1\,1\,1\ldots\}$ with binomial characterization $\binom{n}{0}$. Coming back to Example 1, we have now that $q = 11$ and consequently

$$\phi(\alpha^{11}) = \{S(11)\} = \{1\,0\,1\,0\,1\,0\,1\,0\ldots\} = \binom{n}{0} + \binom{n}{1}$$

$$\phi(\alpha^{12}) = \{S(12)\} = \{0\,1\,0\,1\,0\,1\,0\,1\ldots\} = \binom{n}{1}$$

$$\phi(\alpha^0) = \{S(0)\} = \{1\,1\,1\,1\,1\,1\,1\,1\ldots\} = \binom{n}{0}$$

These three basic binomial characterizations allow us to determine the binomial representation for the rest of generalized sequences.

4.1 Partition of the Generalized Sequences

In this section we study the additive subgroups of $(\mathbb{F}_{2^L}, +)$, which will help us to divide the set of generalized sequences associated to a given polynomial into separated groups.

Let us start considering the additive subgroup of $\mathbb{F}_{2^L}$ of order 4 given by:

$$S_4 = \{0, 1, \alpha^q, \alpha^{q+1}\}.$$

If we denote the zero sequence by $\mathbf{0}$, the corresponding sequences through the isomorphism defined in Eq. (3) are:

$$\phi(S_4) = \left\{ \mathbf{0}, \binom{n}{0}, \binom{n}{1}, \binom{n}{0} + \binom{n}{1} \right\}$$

Consider now every subgroup of order 8 that contains S_4. They are of the form

$$\{0, 1, \alpha^q, \alpha^{q+1}, \alpha^{q_1}, \alpha^{q_2}, \alpha^{q_3}, \alpha^{q_4}\},$$

Table 4. Binomial characterization of the GSS-sequences $\{S(p)\}$ of Example 1

p	$\{S(p)\}$	Binomial characterization
0	1 1 1 1 1 1 1 1	$\binom{n}{0}$
1	1 1 1 0 0 1 0 0	$\binom{n}{0} + \binom{n}{3} + \binom{n}{4} + \binom{n}{5}$
2	1 1 0 0 0 0 1 1	$\binom{n}{0} + \binom{n}{2} + \binom{n}{4}$
3	1 0 0 0 1 1 0 1	$\binom{n}{0} + \binom{n}{1} + \binom{n}{2} + \binom{n}{3} + \binom{n}{5}$
4	0 0 0 1 1 0 1 1	$\binom{n}{3} + \binom{n}{4} + \binom{n}{5}$
5	0 0 1 0 0 1 1 1	$\binom{n}{2} + \binom{n}{3} + \binom{n}{5}$
6	0 1 0 0 1 1 1 0	$\binom{n}{1} + \binom{n}{3} + \binom{n}{4} + \binom{n}{5}$
7	1 0 0 1 0 1 1 0	$\binom{n}{0} + \binom{n}{1} + \binom{n}{2} + \binom{n}{4}$
8	0 0 1 1 1 1 0 0	$\binom{n}{2} + \binom{n}{4}$
9	0 1 1 0 1 0 0 1	$\binom{n}{1} + \binom{n}{2} + \binom{n}{4}$
10	1 1 0 1 1 0 0 0	$\binom{n}{0} + \binom{n}{2} + \binom{n}{3} + \binom{n}{5}$
11	1 0 1 0 1 0 1 0	$\binom{n}{0} + \binom{n}{1}$
12	0 1 0 1 0 1 0 1	$\binom{n}{1}$
13	1 0 1 1 0 0 0 1	$\binom{n}{0} + \binom{n}{1} + \binom{n}{3} + \binom{n}{4} + \binom{n}{5}$
14	0 1 1 1 0 0 1 0	$\binom{n}{1} + \binom{n}{2} + \binom{n}{3} + \binom{n}{5}$

such that,

$$\alpha^{q_1} + \alpha^{q_2} = 1,$$
$$\alpha^{q_1} + \alpha^{q_3} = \alpha^{q},$$
$$\alpha^{q_1} + \alpha^{q_4} = \alpha^{q+1}.$$

Clearly, the binomial characterization of the corresponding sequences will have a common part $\Delta = \sum_{i=2}^{2^{L-1}-(L-2)} a_i \binom{n}{i}$, with $a_i \in \mathbb{F}_2$ and they will have the form:

$$\left\{0, \binom{n}{0}, \binom{n}{1}, \binom{n}{0} + \binom{n}{1}, \Delta, \Delta + \binom{n}{0}, \Delta + \binom{n}{1}, \Delta + \binom{n}{0} + \binom{n}{1}\right\}$$

Example 2. Consider again the Example 1. In Table 4, we can see the binomial characterization of each GSS-sequence produced by $p(x) = 1 + x + x^4$. For instance, consider the four sequences:

$$\left\{\binom{n}{4} + \binom{n}{2}, \binom{n}{4} + \binom{n}{2} + \binom{n}{0}, \binom{n}{4} + \binom{n}{2} + \binom{n}{1}, \binom{n}{4} + \binom{n}{2} + \binom{n}{0} + \binom{n}{1}\right\}$$

Their common part is $\Delta = \binom{n}{4} + \binom{n}{2}$ and they correspond to $\alpha^8, \alpha^2, \alpha^9$ and α^7, respectively. In this case, $q = 11$ and the corresponding additive subgroup is:

$$\left\{0, 1, \alpha^{11}, \alpha^{12}, \alpha^8, \alpha^2, \alpha^9, \alpha^7\right\}$$

As a consequence of what we have seen before, we can divide the set of GSS-sequences into sets of four elements each of them sharing the same common part. Therefore, given a primitive polynomial of degree L, we can generate 2^L GSS-sequences that can be divided into 2^{L-2} groups (including the trivial group $\{\mathbf{0}, \binom{n}{0}, \binom{n}{1}, \binom{n}{0} + \binom{n}{1}\}$).

In addition, it is possible to determine the linear complexity and period of the different generalized sequences in terms of their binomial characterizations.

The linear complexity of a generalized sequence is given by the expression:

$$LC = k + 1,$$

where k is the greatest integer of the sequence $\binom{n}{k}$ in the binomial characterization of the generalized sequence.

The period of a generalized sequence is the period of the binomial sequence $\binom{n}{k}$ where k is the greatest integer in the binomial characterization of the generalized sequence. In Example 1, for sequences in green we have $LC = 5$ and $T = 8$.

For the class of generalized sequences associated to a characteristic polynomial $p(x)$, it can be checked that there are $L - 2$ different linear complexities LC_i among the generalized sequences of the same family (apart from the trivial ones $0, 1, 2$) satisfying:

$$LC_1 > LC_2 > \cdots > LC_{L-3} > LC_{L-2},$$

with $LC_i > 2^{L-2}$ [11]. Indeed, there are $2^{L-(i+2)}$ groups (containing four sequences each of them) with linear complexity LC_i. Let us consider the primitive polynomial $p(x) = 1 + x + x^6$ of degree 6. Such a polynomial generates 64 GSS-sequences divided into 16 groups of 4 sequences each group:

▷ 8 groups with $LC_1 = 28$
▷ 4 groups with $LC_2 = 27$
▷ 2 groups with $LC_3 = 26$
▷ 1 group with $LC_4 = 25$
▷ The group $\{\mathbf{0}, \binom{n}{0}, \binom{n}{1}, \binom{n}{0} + \binom{n}{1}\}$

4.2   Obtaining Generalized Sequences from Different Groups

It is obvious that if we have a generalized sequence, then we can obtain the other 3 sequences in the same group XOR-ing it with the sequences $\binom{n}{0}$, $\binom{n}{1}$ and $\binom{n}{0} + \binom{n}{1}$, respectively. However, can we obtain a generalized sequence from sequences contained in other groups? Due to the additive group structure, the answer is yes.

Consider the 64 generalized sequences generated with $p(x) = 1 + x + x^6$, see Appendix B. Four different linear complexities LC_i, $i = 1, 2, 3, 4$, appear:

$$LC_1 = 28, \quad LC_2 = 27, \quad LC_3 = 26 \quad \text{and} \quad LC_4 = 25.$$

Table 5. Binomial sequences $\binom{n}{LC_i-1}$ in the previous groups

	$\binom{n}{27}$	$\binom{n}{26}$	$\binom{n}{25}$	$\binom{n}{24}$		$\binom{n}{27}$	$\binom{n}{26}$	$\binom{n}{25}$	$\binom{n}{24}$
A_1	✔	✔	✔	✔	B_1	✔	✔		
A_2	✔			✔	B_2	✔			
A_3	✔	✔		✔	B_3	✔			✔
A_4	✔		✔	✔	B_4	✔	✔	✔	
A_5	✔		✔		C_1		✔		
A_6	✔	✔			C_2		✔	✔	
A_7	✔				D_1				✔
A_8	✔	✔	✔						

These sequences can be divided into 16 groups of 4 sequences each of them distributed as follows:

$$A_j = \{\text{Subgroup of sequences with } LC = 28\}, \text{ for } j = 1, 2, \ldots, 8$$
$$B_j = \{\text{Subgroup of sequences with } LC = 27\}, \text{ for } j = 1, 2, \ldots, 4$$
$$C_j = \{\text{Subgroup of sequences with } LC = 26\}, \text{ for } j = 1, 2$$
$$D_j = \{\text{Subgroup of sequences with } LC = 25\}, \text{ for } j = 1$$

plus the four trivial sequences.

Each term $\binom{n}{LC_i-1}$, $i = 1, 2, 3, 4$, appears in the binomial characterization of 8 subgroups, see Table 5. It is possible to check that for every value of LC_i, $i = 1, 2, 3, 4$, there exists a group, whose binomial characterization contains exclusively one of the terms $\binom{n}{LC_i-1}$. In our case, these groups are A_7, B_2, C_1 and D_1. Therefore, if we have four sequences, each of them in one of the previous groups, then we can generate the other 64 generalized sequences.

In general, for a primitive polynomial of degree L, we have 2^L sequences divided into 2^{L-2} groups and $L - 2$ different linear complexities LC_i, $i = 1, 2, \ldots, L - 2$. Each term $\binom{n}{LC_i-1}$ appears 2^{L-3} times in the binomial characterizations of the generalized sequences. As we observed before, there are $L - 2$ groups that contain exclusively one element $\binom{n}{LC_i-1}$, $i = 1, 2, \ldots, L - 2$. This means that we only need $L - 2$ sequences of the family to generate the other 2^L generalized sequences.

5   Conclusions

The binary sequences considered in this work, the so-called generalized sequences, exhibit good cryptographic properties such as long periods and large linear complexities. This makes this sequences suitable for stream cipher applications. On the other hand, the binomial sequences are basic structures able to construct all the binary sequences whose periods are powers of 2; consequently, they are able to construct all the generalized sequences. In addition, the cryptographic parameters of these sequences can be determined via the binomial sequences.

At the same time, the family of generalized sequences can be analyzed and partitioned in terms of its binomial characterization. Moreover, the binomial sequences allow one to generate the whole generalized family from a minimum number of its elements.

Acknowledgements. Research partially supported by Ministerio de Economía, Industria y Competitividad, Agencia Estatal de Investigación, and Fondo Europeo de Desarrollo Regional (FEDER, UE) under project COPCIS (TIN2017-84844-C2-1-R) and by Comunidad de Madrid (Spain) under project CYNAMON (P2018/TCS-4566), also co-funded by European Union FEDER funds. The first author was supported by CAPES (Brazil).

Appendix A

$$
\begin{array}{|cc|cc|cc|cc|cccccccc|cccccccc|cccccccc|l}
\hline
1&1&1&1&1&1&1&1&1&1&1&1&1&1&1&1&1&1&1&1&1&1&1&1&1&1&1&1&1&1&1&1 & \binom{n}{0}\\
0&1&0&1&0&1&0&1&0&1&0&1&0&1&0&1&0&1&0&1&0&1&0&1&0&1&0&1&0&1&0&1 & \binom{n}{1}\\
0&0&1&1&0&0&1&1&0&0&1&1&0&0&1&1&0&0&1&1&0&0&1&1&0&0&1&1&0&0&1&1 & \binom{n}{2}\\
0&0&0&1&0&0&0&1&0&0&0&1&0&0&0&1&0&0&0&1&0&0&0&1&0&0&0&1&0&0&0&1 & \binom{n}{3}\\
\hline
0&0&0&0&1&1&1&1&0&0&0&0&1&1&1&1&0&0&0&0&1&1&1&1&0&0&0&0&1&1&1&1 & \binom{n}{4}\\
0&0&0&0&0&1&0&1&0&0&0&0&0&1&0&1&0&0&0&0&0&1&0&1&0&0&0&0&0&1&0&1 & \binom{n}{5}\\
0&0&0&0&0&0&1&1&0&0&0&0&0&0&1&1&0&0&0&0&0&0&1&1&0&0&0&0&0&0&1&1 & \binom{n}{6}\\
0&0&0&0&0&0&0&1&0&0&0&0&0&0&0&1&0&0&0&0&0&0&0&1&0&0&0&0&0&0&0&1 & \binom{n}{7}\\
\hline
0&0&0&0&0&0&0&0&1&1&1&1&1&1&1&1&0&0&0&0&0&0&0&0&1&1&1&1&1&1&1&1 & \binom{n}{8}\\
0&0&0&0&0&0&0&0&0&1&0&1&0&1&0&1&0&0&0&0&0&0&0&0&0&1&0&1&0&1&0&1 & \binom{n}{9}\\
0&0&0&0&0&0&0&0&0&0&1&1&0&0&1&1&0&0&0&0&0&0&0&0&1&1&0&0&1&1&0&0 & \binom{n}{10}\\
0&0&0&0&0&0&0&0&0&0&0&1&0&1&0&1&0&0&0&0&0&0&0&0&0&0&0&1&0&1&0&1 & \binom{n}{11}\\
0&0&0&0&0&0&0&0&0&0&0&0&1&1&1&1&0&0&0&0&0&0&0&0&0&0&0&0&1&1&1&1 & \binom{n}{12}\\
0&0&0&0&0&0&0&0&0&0&0&0&0&1&0&1&0&0&0&0&0&0&0&0&0&0&0&0&0&1&0&1 & \binom{n}{13}\\
0&0&0&0&0&0&0&0&0&0&0&0&0&0&1&1&0&0&0&0&0&0&0&0&0&0&0&0&0&0&1&1 & \binom{n}{14}\\
0&0&0&0&0&0&0&0&0&0&0&0&0&0&0&1&0&0&0&0&0&0&0&0&0&0&0&0&0&0&0&1 & \binom{n}{15}\\
\hline
0&0&0&0&0&0&0&0&0&0&0&0&0&0&0&0&1&1&1&1&1&1&1&1&1&1&1&1&1&1&1&1 & \binom{n}{16}\\
0&0&0&0&0&0&0&0&0&0&0&0&0&0&0&0&0&1&0&1&0&1&0&1&0&1&0&1&0&1&0&1 & \binom{n}{17}\\
0&0&0&0&0&0&0&0&0&0&0&0&0&0&0&0&0&0&1&1&0&0&1&1&0&0&1&1&0&0&1&1 & \binom{n}{18}\\
0&0&0&0&0&0&0&0&0&0&0&0&0&0&0&0&0&0&0&1&0&0&0&1&0&0&0&1&0&0&0&1 & \binom{n}{19}\\
0&0&0&0&0&0&0&0&0&0&0&0&0&0&0&0&0&0&0&0&1&1&1&1&0&0&0&0&1&1&1&1 & \binom{n}{20}\\
0&0&0&0&0&0&0&0&0&0&0&0&0&0&0&0&0&0&0&0&0&1&0&1&0&0&0&0&0&1&0&1 & \binom{n}{21}\\
0&0&0&0&0&0&0&0&0&0&0&0&0&0&0&0&0&0&0&0&0&0&1&1&0&0&0&0&0&0&1&1 & \binom{n}{22}\\
0&0&0&0&0&0&0&0&0&0&0&0&0&0&0&0&0&0&0&0&0&0&0&1&0&0&0&0&0&0&0&1 & \binom{n}{23}\\
\hline
0&0&0&0&0&0&0&0&0&0&0&0&0&0&0&0&0&0&0&0&0&0&0&0&1&1&1&1&1&1&1&1 & \binom{n}{24}\\
0&0&0&0&0&0&0&0&0&0&0&0&0&0&0&0&0&0&0&0&0&0&0&0&0&1&0&1&0&1&0&1 & \binom{n}{25}\\
0&0&0&0&0&0&0&0&0&0&0&0&0&0&0&0&0&0&0&0&0&0&0&0&0&0&1&1&0&0&1&1 & \binom{n}{26}\\
0&0&0&0&0&0&0&0&0&0&0&0&0&0&0&0&0&0&0&0&0&0&0&0&0&0&0&1&0&0&0&1 & \binom{n}{27}\\
0&0&0&0&0&0&0&0&0&0&0&0&0&0&0&0&0&0&0&0&0&0&0&0&0&0&0&0&1&1&1&1 & \binom{n}{28}\\
0&0&0&0&0&0&0&0&0&0&0&0&0&0&0&0&0&0&0&0&0&0&0&0&0&0&0&0&0&1&0&1 & \binom{n}{29}\\
0&0&0&0&0&0&0&0&0&0&0&0&0&0&0&0&0&0&0&0&0&0&0&0&0&0&0&0&0&0&1&1 & \binom{n}{30}\\
0&0&0&0&0&0&0&0&0&0&0&0&0&0&0&0&0&0&0&0&0&0&0&0&0&0&0&0&0&0&0&1 & \binom{n}{31}\\
\hline
\end{array}
$$

Appendix B

GSS-sequences for $p(x) = 1 + x + x^6$

$O = \{\binom{n}{0}, \binom{n}{1}, \binom{n}{0} + \binom{n}{1}\}$

$A_1 = \{\binom{n}{0}, \binom{n}{1}, \binom{n}{0} + \binom{n}{1}\} + \binom{n}{5} + \binom{n}{6} + \binom{n}{8} + \binom{n}{11} + \binom{n}{12} + \binom{n}{13} + \binom{n}{15} + \binom{n}{18} + \binom{n}{20} + \binom{n}{24} + \binom{n}{25} + \binom{n}{26} + \binom{n}{27}$

$A_2 = \{\binom{n}{0}, \binom{n}{1}, \binom{n}{0} + \binom{n}{1}\} + \binom{n}{4} + \binom{n}{5} + \binom{n}{6} + \binom{n}{9} + \binom{n}{11} + \binom{n}{12} + \binom{n}{13} + \binom{n}{15} + \binom{n}{17} + \binom{n}{19} + \binom{n}{22} + \binom{n}{24} + \binom{n}{27}$

$B_1 = \{\binom{n}{0}, \binom{n}{1}, \binom{n}{0} + \binom{n}{1}\} + \binom{n}{4} + \binom{n}{8} + \binom{n}{9} + \binom{n}{17} + \binom{n}{18} + \binom{n}{19} + \binom{n}{20} + \binom{n}{22} + \binom{n}{25} + \binom{n}{26}$

$A_3 = \{\binom{n}{0}, \binom{n}{1}, \binom{n}{0} + \binom{n}{1}\} + \binom{n}{3} + \binom{n}{5} + \binom{n}{6} + \binom{n}{7} + \binom{n}{8} + \binom{n}{9} + \binom{n}{10} + \binom{n}{14} + \binom{n}{15} + \binom{n}{16} + \binom{n}{17} + \binom{n}{18} + \binom{n}{24} + \binom{n}{26} + \binom{n}{27}$

$C_1 = \{\binom{n}{0}, \binom{n}{1}, \binom{n}{0} + \binom{n}{1}\} + \binom{n}{3} + \binom{n}{7} + \binom{n}{9} + \binom{n}{10} + \binom{n}{11} + \binom{n}{12} + \binom{n}{13} + \binom{n}{14} + \binom{n}{16} + \binom{n}{17} + \binom{n}{20} + \binom{n}{25}$

$B_2 = \{\binom{n}{0}, \binom{n}{1}, \binom{n}{0} + \binom{n}{1}\} + \binom{n}{3} + \binom{n}{4} + \binom{n}{7} + \binom{n}{8} + \binom{n}{10} + \binom{n}{11} + \binom{n}{12} + \binom{n}{13} + \binom{n}{14} + \binom{n}{16} + \binom{n}{18} + \binom{n}{19} + \binom{n}{22} + \binom{n}{26}$

$A_4 = \{\binom{n}{0}, \binom{n}{1}, \binom{n}{0} + \binom{n}{1}\} + \binom{n}{3} + \binom{n}{4} + \binom{n}{5} + \binom{n}{6} + \binom{n}{7} + \binom{n}{10} + \binom{n}{14} + \binom{n}{15} + \binom{n}{16} + \binom{n}{19} + \binom{n}{20} + \binom{n}{22} + \binom{n}{24} + \binom{n}{25} + \binom{n}{27}$

$A_5 = \{\binom{n}{0}, \binom{n}{1}, \binom{n}{0} + \binom{n}{1}\} + \binom{n}{2} + \binom{n}{3} + \binom{n}{4} + \binom{n}{5} + \binom{n}{7} + \binom{n}{8} + \binom{n}{12} + \binom{n}{14} + \binom{n}{15} + \binom{n}{19} + \binom{n}{20} + \binom{n}{25} + \binom{n}{27}$

$B_3 = \{\binom{n}{0}, \binom{n}{1}, \binom{n}{0} + \binom{n}{1}\} + \binom{n}{2} + \binom{n}{3} + \binom{n}{4} + \binom{n}{6} + \binom{n}{7} + \binom{n}{11} + \binom{n}{13} + \binom{n}{14} + \binom{n}{18} + \binom{n}{19} + \binom{n}{24} + \binom{n}{26}$

$C_2 = \{\binom{n}{0}, \binom{n}{1}, \binom{n}{0} + \binom{n}{1}\} + \binom{n}{2} + \binom{n}{3} + \binom{n}{6} + \binom{n}{7} + \binom{n}{9} + \binom{n}{11} + \binom{n}{13} + \binom{n}{14} + \binom{n}{17} + \binom{n}{20} + \binom{n}{22} + \binom{n}{24} + \binom{n}{25}$

$A_6 = \{\binom{n}{0}, \binom{n}{1}, \binom{n}{0} + \binom{n}{1}\} + \binom{n}{2} + \binom{n}{3} + \binom{n}{5} + \binom{n}{7} + \binom{n}{9} + \binom{n}{12} + \binom{n}{14} + \binom{n}{15} + \binom{n}{17} + \binom{n}{18} + \binom{n}{22} + \binom{n}{26} + \binom{n}{27}$

$B_4 = \{\binom{n}{0}, \binom{n}{1}, \binom{n}{0} + \binom{n}{1}\} + \binom{n}{2} + \binom{n}{4} + \binom{n}{6} + \binom{n}{9} + \binom{n}{10} + \binom{n}{12} + \binom{n}{16} + \binom{n}{17} + \binom{n}{18} + \binom{n}{19} + \binom{n}{20} + \binom{n}{26} + \binom{n}{27}$

$A_7 = \{\binom{n}{0}, \binom{n}{1}, \binom{n}{0} + \binom{n}{1}\} + \binom{n}{2} + \binom{n}{4} + \binom{n}{5} + \binom{n}{8} + \binom{n}{9} + \binom{n}{10} + \binom{n}{11} + \binom{n}{13} + \binom{n}{15} + \binom{n}{16} + \binom{n}{17} + \binom{n}{19} + \binom{n}{24}$

$A_8 = \{\binom{n}{0}, \binom{n}{1}, \binom{n}{0} + \binom{n}{1}\} + \binom{n}{2} + \binom{n}{5} + \binom{n}{10} + \binom{n}{11} + \binom{n}{13} + \binom{n}{15} + \binom{n}{16} + \binom{n}{18} + \binom{n}{20} + \binom{n}{22} + \binom{n}{26} + \binom{n}{27}$

$D_1 = \{\binom{n}{0}, \binom{n}{1}, \binom{n}{0} + \binom{n}{1}\} + \binom{n}{2} + \binom{n}{6} + \binom{n}{8} + \binom{n}{10} + \binom{n}{12} + \binom{n}{16} + \binom{n}{22} + \binom{n}{24}$

References

1. Cardell, S.D., Fúster-Sabater, A.: Linear models for the self-shrinking generator based on CA. J. Cell. Automata **11**(2–3), 195–211 (2016)
2. Cardell, S.D., Fúster-Sabater, A.: Recovering the MSS-sequence via CA. Procedia Comput. Sci. **80**, 599–606 (2016)
3. Cardell, S.D., Fúster-Sabater, A.: Modelling the shrinking generator in terms of linear CA. Adv. Math. Commun. **10**(4), 797–809 (2016)
4. Cardell, S.D., Fúster-Sabater, A.: The t-modified self-shrinking generator? In: Shi, Y., et al. (eds.) ICCS 2018. LNCS, vol. 10860, pp. 653–663. Springer, Cham (2018). https://doi.org/10.1007/978-3-319-93698-7_50
5. Coppersmith, D., Krawczyk, H., Mansour, Y.: The shrinking generator. In: Stinson, D.R. (ed.) CRYPTO 1993. LNCS, vol. 773, pp. 22–39. Springer, Heidelberg (1994). https://doi.org/10.1007/3-540-48329-2_3
6. Fluhrer, S., Lucks, S.: Analysis of the E_0 encryption system. In: Vaudenay, S., Youssef, A.M. (eds.) SAC 2001. LNCS, vol. 2259, pp. 38–48. Springer, Heidelberg (2001). https://doi.org/10.1007/3-540-45537-X_3
7. Fúster-Sabater, A., García-Mochales, P.: A simple computational model for acceptance/rejection of binary sequence generators. Appl. Math. Model. **31**(8), 1548–1558 (2007)
8. Fúster-Sabater, A., Caballero-Gil, P.: Chaotic modelling of the generalized self-shrinking generator. Appl. Soft Comput. **11**(2), 1876–1880 (2011)
9. Fúster-Sabater, A.: Generation of cryptographic sequences by means of difference equations. Appl. Math. Inf. Sci. **8**(2), 1–10 (2014)
10. Golomb, S.W.: Shift Register-Sequences. Aegean Park Press, Laguna Hill (1982)
11. Hu, Y., Xiao, G.: Generalized self-shrinking generator. IEEE Trans. Inf. Theor. **50**(4), 714–719 (2004)
12. Jenkins, C., Schulte, M., Glossner, J.: Instructions and hardware designs for accelerating SNOW 3G on a software-defined radio platform. Analog Integr. Circ. Sig. Process. **69**(2–3), 207–218 (2011)
13. Kanso, A.: Modified self-shrinking generator. Comput. Electr. Eng. **36**(1), 993–1001 (2010)
14. Meier, W., Staffelbach, O.: The self-shrinking generator. In: De Santis, A. (ed.) EUROCRYPT 1994. LNCS, vol. 950, pp. 205–214. Springer, Heidelberg (1995). https://doi.org/10.1007/BFb0053436
15. Menezes, A.J., et al.: Handbook of Applied Cryptography. CRC Press, New York (1997)
16. Paar, C., Pelzl, J.: Understanding Cryptography. Springer, Heidelberg (2010). https://doi.org/10.1007/978-3-642-04101-3
17. Paul, G., Maitra, S.: RC4 Stream Cipher and its Variants. CRC Press, Taylor and Francis Group, Boca Raton (2012)

Supply Chain Simulation in a Big Data Context: Risks and Uncertainty Analysis

António A. C. Vieira$^{(\boxtimes)}$ (iD), Luís M. S. Dias (iD), Maribel Y. Santos (iD),
Guilherme A. B. Pereira (iD), and José A. Oliveira (iD)

ALGORITMI Research Centre, University of Minho, Braga, Portugal
{antonio.vieira,lsd,gui,zan}@dps.uminho.pt,
maribel@dsi.uminho.pt

Abstract. Due to their complex and dynamic nature, Supply Chains are prone to risks that may occur at any time and place. To tackle this problem, simulation can be used. However, such models should use Big Data technologies, in order to provide the level of data and detail contained in the data sources associated to the business processes. In this regard, this paper considered a real case of an automotive electronics Supply chain. Hence, the purpose of this paper is to propose a simulation tool, which uses real industrial data, provided by a Big Data Warehouse, and use such decision-support artifact to test different types of risks. More concretely, risks in the supply and demand end of the network are analyzed. The presented results also demonstrate the possible benefits that can be achieved by using simulation in the analysis of risks in a Supply Chain.

Keywords: Simulation · Supply chain · Big data · Risk management

1 Introduction

Supply Chains (SC) operate under 2 dimensions: uncertainty and complexity [1]. This nature has been further enhanced by currently adopted industrial practices (e.g., just-in-time, shorter product life cycle). On one hand, this makes modern SC leaner costlier, greener, with fewer buffers and stored materials; on the other hand, this also exposes organizations to disruptions when certain events occur [2]. These events result in unanticipated and unpredictable consequences, which affect the performance of individual entities of a SC and other entities with relationships with the affected one, possibly including several SC [3]. As Sodhi et al. [4] assert, consequences can come in revenue, reputation and other types of losses. In fact, several examples exist in literature which report on such cases, e.g. [1, 3, 5–7]. The impact of such events may be enormously negative in several ways. Thus, companies require tools to allow them to mitigate such consequences. Despite this, few companies have succeeded in taking actions to smooth these negative impacts [2, 3, 8].

The aforementioned events are characterized by being very rare, unpredictable and of great impact on the performance of the SC [3]. Due to these characteristics, organizations struggle to deal with them, as decision-makers lack information about the SC network and environment, hence being unable to predict where, when and how much impact can a given event deliver. The uncertainty surrounding the possible outcomes of

© Springer Nature Switzerland AG 2019
S. Misra et al. (Eds.): ICCSA 2019, LNCS 11619, pp. 817–829, 2019.
https://doi.org/10.1007/978-3-030-24289-3_60

the aforementioned events, portrays an exposure to what literature refers to as risks [9]. Thus, risks can be interpreted as events that may occur at any part of the SC (uncertainty), causing negative impact on it, in many possible ways.

Ho et al. [5] argued that these risks can be classified in different ways, including: internal or external; operational or disruption; and others. The authors also provided their own framework for classifications of SC risks, included:

- Manufacturing or internal risks: occur within a plant;
- Supply: occur in the supplier's side of the SC;
- Demand: occur in the customer's side of the SC;
- External: events very rare with severe consequences to SC, generally consisting in risks of natural order (e.g., weather-related or earthquakes) or man-made (e.g., wars, terrorist attacks, political-related), which have origin outside the SC.

Following the author's risks classification, this paper proposes a SC simulation model, developed in SIMIO [10], which assesses the impact of supply and demand risks in a SC of the automotive industry, by using real industrial data form a plant of the Bosch organization. The data is originated from several data sources and a Big Data Warehouse (BDW) was implemented to store, integrate and provide such data to the simulation model. Thus, the presented SC simulation model uses Big Data to test the system's performance under supply and demand risks.

The research that was conducted to develop the BDW has already been published [11], as well as a prototype of the simulation model [12]. This previously presented model did not use real industrial data, but rather used the typically available approach in simulation, consisting in using random distributions, to validate the data model, i.e., the variables selected for the project. Having validated such data model, the next step in the project was to complement the simulation model, so that it is capable of using data provided by the BDW and assess certain types of risks.

This paper is organized as follows. Next section analyzes related works in literature. Section 3 provides a characterization of the SC under study. Section 4 briefly describes the development approach that was followed, focusing on the data modeling in a Big Data context and in the data-driven simulation approach. Section 5 presents the obtained results by using the simulation model to test the performance of the SC under supply and demand risks. Finally, conclusions and future research directions are provided in the last section.

2 Related Work

The literature of SC simulation studies is vast. However, to the best of the authors' knowledge, it can be argued that such solutions, in what regards the use of Big Data technologies, are limited. This is corroborated by several studies [13–15]. With the lack of such studies, this section focuses on reviewing the SC studies that applied simulation using some type of external data storage (e.g. relational databases) that provides data to the proposed simulation model.

Cheng et al. [16] used GBSE (General Business Simulation Environment) to propose a simulation model to help making tactical level decisions in a SC. Their simulation model offered 2D visualization and a direct connection to an external database. The authors tested the response of holding cost, transportation cost and order delivery time to different forecast accuracy levels, production strategies (namely, make-to-order, make-to-stock and postponement) and special transportation costs.

Fornasiero et al. [17] and Macchion et al. [18] proposed a SIMIO simulation model, which assessed the impact of orders size in the SC performance. In [17], Fornasiero et al. based their experiments on order size, lead time variation and supplier scrap rate to achieve findings regarding the impact on the delivery time to customer, customer order quality and inventory costs. Later, Macchion et al. [18] assessed the impact of order size, inventory management policy, supplier's lead time and quality on inventory level and order lead time. Fornasiero et al. [17] applied their model to a fashion industry comprised by 60 suppliers and 1 manufacturer, whilst Macchion et al. [18] applied it to a SC of the footwear industry comprised by 4 suppliers, 1 warehouse, 1 manufacturer, 1 distributor and 2 customers. In both studies, the authors reported that their simulation models are able to retrieve data from the ERP system.

Sahoo and Mani [19] presented a simulation model in ExtendSim to model a SC of the biomass industry. The modelled SC comprised producer and farmer of biomass and suppliers which transported the raw materials to the plant, which could store them or process them for later bioenergy production, in order to deliver heat and electricity to customers. The simulation model used a direct connection to a database, which, among other operational data, stored weather data for long time periods. This data was used by the authors to test the exposure of the SC to KPIs (Key Performance Indicators) such as: quantity produced, inventory levels, transportation quantity, transportation costs and handling cost. Lastly, Ponte et al. [20] evaluated the impact that inventory management and different forecast methods have on the demand variation propagation upstream the SC.

3 Supply Chain Characterization

This project is being developed at a plant of the Bosch Group, which concerns with producing automotive electronic components. This section first briefly describes the SC at hand, to give a perspective of the scale and complexity of the network in analysis. Figure 1 shows the countries and the number of suppliers per country, which supply materials to the plant.

The numbers in each country represent the number of suppliers from that country. The lines placed between these countries and the plant represent the number of material shipments; the width is proportional to the number of shipments. Finally, the color scale of each country is associated to the number of different types of materials that suppliers from that country provide to the plant. According with the considered data, around 7 000 different types of materials are actively being supplied by roughly 500 different suppliers, located in more than 30 countries. Moreover, as the figure shows, Germany, Netherlands, Switzerland, Spain, China, Taiwan and Malasya are the countries that supply more types of materials. Also suggested by Fig. 1, the plant received materials from more than 400 suppliers, especially from Europe and Asia, with Germany (209 suppliers) and Netherlands (10 suppliers) having more suppliers and shipments from Europe, and Malasya (16 suppliers), Taiwan (13 suppliers), China (12 suppliers), Hong Kong (11 suppliers) and Singapore (7 suppliers) having more shipments from Asia. All these suppliers shipped more than 200 000 deliveries, during the last year. Figure 2 illustrates a summary of the main material and information flows of this SC system.

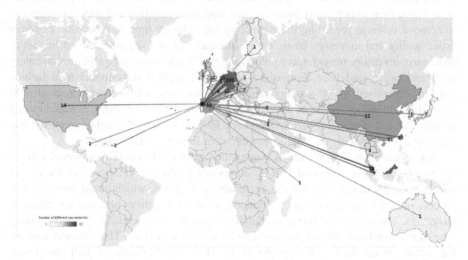

Fig. 1. Geographic location, number of suppliers, different raw materials provided and number of shipments per suppliers.

As the below figure depicts, to comply with final customers' orders, the plant places orders to its suppliers, which later culminate in arrivals. Most of these arrivals occur within the scheduled date. However, some suppliers provide the orders before the scheduled data. In these situations, these materials are stored in a special warehouse until the scheduled date is met. This way, the plant is not responsible for storage costs of these materials. On the other hand, supplier deliveries may be delayed, potentially resulting in orders arriving after the scheduled data. Whilst the previous situation (materials arriving before the scheduled date) may originate high warehousing costs, this last situation may originate material shortages, which can jeopardize the production and hence customers' orders. To bypass this, special freights are scheduled, which are usually faster but also have considerably higher associated costs.

When materials arrive to the plant, the contents are examined to assess their quality and if the order requirements were met. Afterwards, the materials are put in the respective storage unit, e.g. boxes or pallets, in the respective quantities, to be stored in the warehouse. The warehouse is divided in 2 main locations, both storing raw materials, but storage location 1 is being used for electronic components, while the other for bulkier materials. In its turn, each storage location is divided in multiple bins, wherein each one stores a type of material and a storage unit (e.g., box), at the same time. When materials are sent to the warehouse, they are always allocated to an empty storage bin.

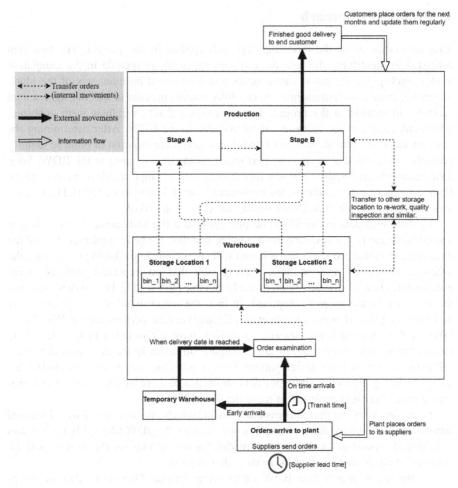

Fig. 2. Summary of material and information flows of the SC system.

The production is divided in 2 main areas: Stage A, where the main electronic components are produced; and Stage B, where the finished goods are produced, using electronic raw materials stored in the warehouse (form either storage location) and also other components produced in Stage A. Finally, when production in Stage B finishes, materials are ready to be delivered to final customers.

Figure 2 also shows that besides the main movements, others exist, which represent movements for quality inspection, re-works and other similar activities required to ensure the quality of the final product. It is important to consider these movements, as they represent materials temporarily not available to be transferred to production. As can be observed, these movements are represented with bidirectional arrows, as the materials are later transferred back to another bin of the warehouse, or back to the production, depending on the situation. The movements depicted in Fig. 2 represent the main ones that occur in the plant. However, there are many others, most of them used for quality inspection, re-work and similar tasks.

4 Proposed Approach

This section describes the modeling approach applied in this project. The first step consisted in identifying the relevant business processes to include in the simulation model. Such processes entail data sources which are used by managers of the plant. Therefore, those data sources must be carefully studied in order to identify the relevant variables to include in the project. In fact, roughly 2 000 variables were analyzed, which culminated in the inclusion of around 200 in the BDW. After determining the relevant variables, further interviews and data analysis are required in order to identify possible treatments that have to be performed on the data to store in the BDW. Such data treatments are required, for several reasons, such as empty fields or wrong values. Having defined such treatments, the traditional Extract-Transform-Load (ETL) process was conducted, which ended with storing the data in the BDW.

To store such data in the BDW, despite being in a Big Data context, data schemas should be defined, as it revealed the following benefits: (1) better understanding of the data, organizational processes and relevant KPIs to include in the BDW; (2) ensures the inclusion of the all relevant data, making sure that no important attributes were excluded; (3) helps in the definition of the Hive tables to use [11]. Due to these reasons, the next step in the project comprised, in fact, the dimensional model, proposed by Kimball (see [21]). However, Costa et al. [22] analyzed the performance of Hive-based DWs in Big Data environments (i.e., a BDW), having concluded that, in Big Data environments, fully denormalized tables outperform tables in the dimensional format, following the star schema design pattern. Furthermore, the authors also concluded that adequate data partitioning strategies data showed a clear reduction in the query execution time. This was analyzed in more detail in [23].

Therefore, after the multidimensional model, which provided the above discussed benefits, the tables were denormalized, hence creating the BDW tables. Figure 3 shows a simplified version of the dimensional model that was defined for this project, and the consequent BDW tables which were thereafter created.

As the figure shows, five BDW tables were defined. One stores data of orders placed to suppliers and the posterior receipts (OrdersSentAndReceived). The remaining four represent movements that occur within the plant. With these tables, the simulation model was connected to the Big Data cluster to retrieve the data. Afterwards, the model was adapted to reflect this stored data.

The model runs in a built-in 3D environment with only one physical object, which sets the location of the plant. Thus, entities travel without any links (since there are no physical objects), with their movements being specified by processes which model the behavior of the entities, according with the data in the BDW. Due to this data-driven approach, the simulation model is able to automatically adapt to data changes in the BDW. Figure 4 shows an example of such processes, which models the lead time of the suppliers, and the posterior material shipment to the plant. In its turn, Fig. 5 illustrates the simulation model reproducing the historical data stored in the BDW.

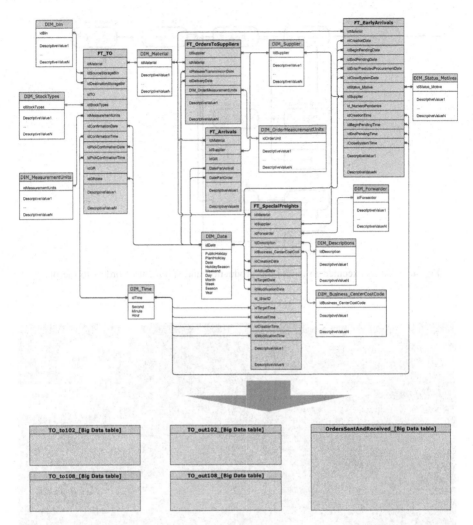

Fig. 3. Traditional dimensional model (top part of the figure) and created BDW tables (bottom part of the figure).

The figure shows yellow circles, which represent orders in production in the respective geographic supplier location; the location of these entities represents the exact location of the supplier, as stored in the BDW, however, as a supplier may have multiple orders at the same time, a small deviation in the location of each order is applied, so that it is possible to see all entities. Finally, the number presented above each yellow entity represents the number of days remaining for the order to be shipped to the plant. This number decreases as the simulation clock advances in time. When it is time to ship the order, the symbol of the orders change to the respective transport type and their speed is also adjusted to the transportation lead time represented in the BDW.

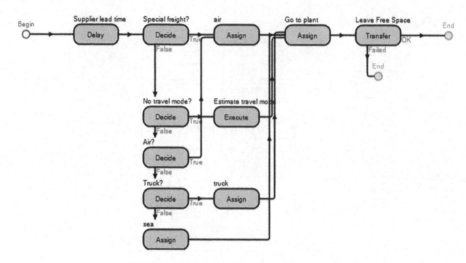

Fig. 4. Process executed to model the production and shipment of orders to the plant.

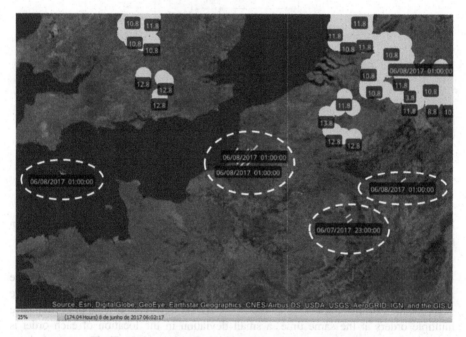

Fig. 5. Orders being sent to the plant. (Color figure online)

Figure 5 shows some of these entities highlighted. The date time values below each entity represent the instant when those deliveries were shipped to the plant. When orders arrive to the plant, they are stocked, so that they can be managed by the plant's internal material movements.

5 Supply Chain Simulation in a Big Data Context

This section comprises both supply and demand risks, each one analyzed in one of the two following subsections. Hence, the experiments conducted in this section consist in using the simulation model to reproduce the historical data stored in the BDW, while also incorporating risks, through the utilization of random distributions. Thus, these experiments must consider a given number of replications, which will use different random seeds, thus attenuating the differences provided by such distributions. In this regard, 10 replications were executed for these scenarios.

5.1 Supply Risks

In this experiment, a variable lead time was applied to all orders placed to suppliers, by considering a triangular distribution with minimum of 0 days (no delay), mode of 2 days and maximum of 5 days. This way, all orders will either arrive at the date specified in the BDW, or later, allowing the impact of such delay to be analyzed. The opposite to this would be to analyze the orders that arrive before the schedule date. However, as explained in Sect. 3, these cases do not have a significant impact on the plant, as the plant does not incur in excessive warehousing costs of storing these materials in the dedicated warehouse for early arrivals. Figure 6 shows the number of arrivals per day, illustrated with a greed-red color scale for supplier delays of 0 to 5 days, respectively.

The below figure shows that the number of orders that arrived on-time is minimum and that the orders that arrive with 2 days of delay were the most common case, which is in accordance to the distribution used to set the supplier's delay time. To analyze the impact that such delays could have on the performance of the plant, Fig. 7 shows the

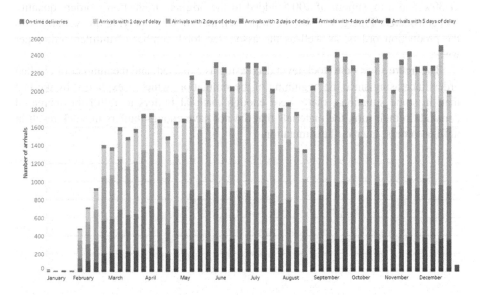

Fig. 6. Number of arrivals per week and the respective arrival delay time

total special freights costs and the total number of unfilled orders that these delays originated. As can be seen, the maximum number of unfilled orders per week was 350, which totalized more than 60 000 000 € with special freights during the year.

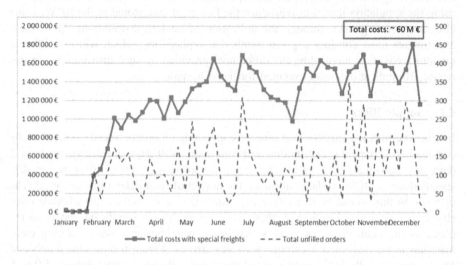

Fig. 7. Total special freights costs and number of unfilled orders per week due to the supplier's delay time.

5.2 Demand Risks

To analyze this type of risks, a triangular distribution with a minimum of 0%, a mode of 30% and a maximum of 100% added to the original production's orders quantity was considered. Figure 8 shows the impact on the stock by applying this variability to the production orders, as well as the associated total number of unfilled orders per week.

The figure shows the stock level decreasing as expected, and the number of unfilled orders increasing since the beginning of the simulation, which is explained by the fact that, in some situations, there were enough material buffers to fulfill the increased demand. In their turn, the materials that did not have enough buffers in stock result in unfilled orders, later in the simulation.

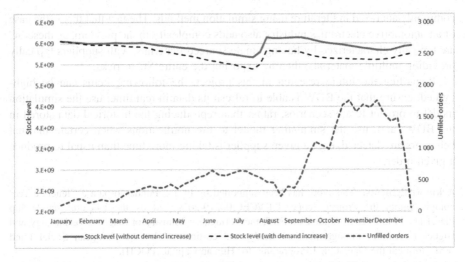

Fig. 8. Stock level and total number of unfilled orders per week for (1) normal demand and (2) increased demand scenarios.

6 Conclusions

The main contributions from this paper derives from the presented simulation model, which is able to reproduce the historical Big Data stored in the BDW. In fact, while some studies exist which reported the use of data storage and analysis with simulation, no study was found coupling the benefits of Big Data technologies with the latter. The simulation model also allows certain types of variability (e.g., delays and quantity required by production) to be considered. This way, apart from reproducing the historical data from the BDW, the simulation model also incorporates disruption scenarios.

The solution's animation feature and its integration with a Google Maps view should also be stressed because, from the analyzed literature, the lack of studies investing in animation features of their SC systems was noteworthy. Thus, the simulation runs on a 3D world map view, which enriches its visualization, with all the associated benefits.

While out of the scope of this paper, other features of the presented solution can also be emphasized, such as its ability to automatically retrieve data from the BDW and adapt to changes or new data, hence matching the main characteristics of a real-time simulation. In fact, none of the suppliers' locations, as well as the entities' movements, were manually modelled, since the model is able to automatically adjust its elements to the data it gets from the BDW; i.e., the model is drawn by the data and not by the users. In addition, the user may fire disruptive events at any given time, duration and location (e.g., disrupt suppliers in a geographic location) and use the simulation model to assess its impact in the performance of the plant.

Lastly, regarding the area of applicability, this paper targeted a SC larger (in number of suppliers from different countries and number of materials) than the most commonly analyzed in literature using simulation methods. The fact that this is the case of an automotive electronics industry also adds complexity to the problem, as these SC are typically characterized by having single sourced materials, with suppliers typically providing multiple materials, thereby exposing the entire SC to risks.

Regarding the future research in this project, the following items can be highlighted: ensure that the BDW is able to refresh its data in real time; use the simulation model to project future scenarios, rather than reproducing the historical data stored in the BDW; and, use the simulating model to fire notifications when certain unusual behaviors are detected, e.g., a given supplier is taking more time than usual to produce a given order.

Acknowledgments. This work has been supported by FCT – Fundação para a Ciência e Tecnologia within the Project Scope: UID/CEC/00319/2019 and by the Doctoral scholarship PDE/BDE/114566/2016 funded by FCT, the Portuguese Ministry of Science, Technology and Higher Education, through national funds, and co-financed by the European Social Fund (ESF) through the Operational Programme for Human Capital (POCH).

References

1. Colicchia, C., Strozzi, F.: Supply chain risk management: a new methodology for a systematic literature review. Supply Chain Manag. **17**(4), 403–418 (2012)
2. Ghadge, A., Dani, S., Kalawsky, R.: Supply chain risk management: present and future scope. Int. J. Logist. Manag. **23**(3), 313–339 (2012)
3. Fahimnia, B., Tang, C.S., Davarzani, H., Sarkis, J.: Quantitative models for managing supply chain risks: a review. Eur. J. Oper. Res. **247**(1), 1–15 (2015)
4. Sodhi, M.S., Son, B.-G., Tang, C.S.: Researchers' perspectives on supply chain risk management. Prod. Oper. Manag. **21**(1), 1–13 (2012)
5. Ho, W., Zheng, T., Yildiz, H., Talluri, S.: Supply chain risk management: a literature review. Int. J. Prod. Res. **53**(16), 5031–5069 (2015)
6. Sáenz, M.J., Revilla, E.: Creating more resilient supply chains. MIT Sloan Manag. Rev. **55**(4), 22–24 (2014)
7. Rao, S., Goldsby, T.J.: Supply chain risks: a review and typology. Int. J. Logistics Manag. **20**(1), 97–123 (2009)
8. Fan, Y., Stevenson, M.: A review of supply chain risk management: definition, theory, and research agenda. Int. J. Phys. Distrib. Logist. Manag. **48**(3), 205–230 (2018)
9. Kilubi, I.: The strategies of supply chain risk management – a synthesis and classification. Int. J. Logist. Res. Appl. **19**(6), 604–629 (2016)
10. Dias, L.M.S., Vieira, A.A.C., Pereira, G.A.B., Oliveira, J.A.: Discrete simulation software ranking-a top list of the worldwide most popular and used tools. In: Proceedings - Winter Simulation Conference (2017)
11. Vieira, A.A., Pedro, L., Santos, M.Y., Fernandes, J.M., Dias, L.M.: Data requirements elicitation in big data warehousing. In: European, Mediterranean and Middle Eastern Conference on Information Systems (EMCIS) (2018)
12. Vieira, A.A., Dias, L.M., Santos, M.Y., Pereira, G.A., Oliveira, J.A.: Simulation of an automotive supply chain in Simio: data model validation. In: European Modeling and Simulation Symposium (EMSS) - Part of International Multidisciplinary Modeling & Simulation Multiconference (I3 M) (2018)

13. Tiwari, S., Wee, H.M., Daryanto, Y.: Big data analytics in supply chain management between 2010 and 2016: insights to industries. Comput. Ind. Eng. **115**, 319–330 (2018)
14. Zhong, R.Y., Newman, S.T., Huang, G.Q., Lan, S.: Big data for supply chain management in the service and manufacturing sectors: challenges, opportunities, and future perspectives. Comput. Ind. Eng. **101**, 572–591 (2016)
15. Vieira, A.A., Dias, L.M., Santos, M.Y., Pereira, G.A., Oliveira, J.A.: Setting an industry 4.0 research and development agenda for simulation – a literature review. Int. J. Simul. Model. **17**(3), 377–390 (2018)
16. Cheng, F., Lee, Y.M., Ding, H.W., Wang, W., Stephens, S.: Simulating order fulfillment and supply planning for a vertically aligned industry solution business. In: Proceedings of the 40th Conference on Winter Simulation, pp. 2609–2615 (2008)
17. Fornasiero, R., Macchion, L., Vinelli, A.: Supply chain configuration towards customization: a comparison between small and large series production. IFAC-PapersOnLine **28**(3), 1428–1433 (2015)
18. Macchion, L., Fornasiero, R., Vinelli, A.: Supply chain configurations: a model to evaluate performance in customised productions. Int. J. Prod. Res. **55**(5), 1386–1399 (2017)
19. Sahoo, K., Mani, S.: GIS based discrete event modeling and simulation of biomass supply chain. In: Proceedings - Winter Simulation Conference, vol. 2016-February, pp. 967–978 (2016)
20. Ponte, B., Sierra, E., de la Fuente, D., Lozano, J.: Exploring the interaction of inventory policies across the supply chain: an agent-based approach. Comput. Oper. Res. **78**, 335–348 (2017)
21. Kimball, R., Ross, M.: The Data Warehouse Toolkit: The Complete Guide to Dimensional Modeling. Wiley (2011)
22. Costa, E., Costa, C., Santos, M.Y.: Efficient big data modelling and organization for Hadoop hive-based data warehouses. In: Themistocleous, M., Morabito, V. (eds.) EMCIS 2017. LNBIP, vol. 299, pp. 3–16. Springer, Cham (2017). https://doi.org/10.1007/978-3-319-65930-5_1
23. Costa, E., Costa, C., Santos, M.Y.: Evaluating partitioning and bucketing strategies for Hive-based Big Data Warehousing systems. J. Big Data **6**(1), 34 (2019)

Text Classification for Italian Proficiency Evaluation

Alfredo Milani[1] , Stefania Spina[2], Valentino Santucci[2], Luisa Piersanti[1],
Marco Simonetti[3], and Giulio Biondi[4(✉)]

[1] Department of Mathematics and Computer Science, University of Perugia,
Perugia, Italy
milani@unipg.it, luisa.piersanti@studenti.unipg.it
[2] University for Foreigners of Perugia, Perugia, Italy
{stefania.spina,valentino.santucci}@unistrapg.it
[3] Liceo Artistico "G. Marconi", Foligno, Italy
[4] Department of Mathematics and Computer Science, University of Florence,
Florence, Italy
giulio.biondi@unifi.it

Abstract. NLP technologies and components have an increasing diffusion in mass analysis of text based dialogues, such as classifiers for sentiment polarity, trends clustering of online messages and hate speech detection. In this work we present the design and the implementation an automatic classification tool for the evaluation of the complexity of Italian texts as understood by a speaker of Italian as a second language. The classification is done within the Common European Framework of Reference for Languages (CEFR) which aims at classifying speakers language proficiency. Results of preliminary experiments on a data set of real texts, annotated by experts and used in actual CEFR exam sessions, show a strong ability of the proposed system to label texts with the correct language proficiency class and a great potential for its integration in learning tools, such systems supporting examiners in tests design and automatic evaluation of writing abilities.

Keywords: Learning systems · Language proficiency classifier ·
Text classifier · PoS

1 Introduction

The recent increasing diffusion of NLP components for texts classification, such as those applied for the detection of sentiment polarity [4,13], trends and hate speech detection [25] in online communication, is due to the maturity of service technologies, such as text parsing, filtering [20], PoS tagging and the availability of powerful machine learning tools, efficiently integrated in programming environment or libraries [6,22]. Moreover, a vast amount of data is available on the web to be exploited by automated tools, either in structured [5] or semi-unstructured [14] form for language-related purposes, e.g. determining objects'

S. Misra et al. (Eds.): ICCSA 2019, LNCS 11619, pp. 830–841, 2019.
https://doi.org/10.1007/978-3-030-24289-3_61

similarity [12]. While most applications mentioned above work at a somewhat "gross grain" level of linguistic analysis (e.g. polarity, hate speech etc.) not many applications are available for more refined classification of text. Moreover, due to the relevant populations movements in late year and the consequent educational actions for integration of newcomers, there is a great interest in Europe for teaching second language and for all the related supporting learning technologies [11]. Languages teaching is an area in which being able to rank [8] a text, with respect to the language skills and ability required for writing/reading it, is a crucial task in order to meet the teaching goals. During teaching a too easy or too difficult text can prove useless or impossible to understand for the learners; on the other hand, the appropriate classification of a text is essential in assessing or certifying language proficiency. The Common European Framework of Reference for Languages (CEFR) [1] is a standard aiming at classifying speakers language proficiency and it is typically used for assessing second language learners (L2). The CEFR certification consists in six classes of increasing difficult A1, A2, B1, B2, C1, C2, the same letter pairs corresponding to three level of proficiency *beginner*, *intermediate* and *advanced*. The proficiency in a language typically depends on elements such as the use of a basic or advanced vocabulary of term, the complexity of the syntactic structure, the use of idiomatic phrases, the use of synonyms and conceptually close words [15] to avoid repetitions, and so forth. While it is easy for an experienced examiner to assess the level of proficiency necessary for understanding a given text, it is not easy to provide a deterministic procedure for assessing a text, because the relative weight of the linguistic elements is varying depending on the context [3,16,24]. The general approach proposed in this paper is to extract from the text the linguistic features upon which the proficiency class is believed to depend, and instead of directly encoding a classification procedure, we are using the examiners experience, embedded in the labeling of pre-classified exams texts, to train different types of classifiers. In Sect. 2 the general architecture of the system is introduced while, in the next section, the process of extracting the linguistic features relevant for proficiency classification is presented. The classifiers used in the implementation are briefly recalled in Sect. 4. The data set used in the experiments and results obtained are then presented and discussed. Conclusions are finally drawn in Sect. 6.

2   A Text Proficiency Classification Architecture

The workflow of the classification process can be divided into four phases, namely *data set transformation and cleaning, extraction of basic linguistic structures, extraction of more complex linguistic features* and *classifier training*.

2.1   Data Set Transformation and Cleaning

In the first phase, the appropriate features for the experiments are extracted from the corpus of annotated texts provided by the *Centro Valutazione Certificazioni Linguistiche of University for Foreigners of Perugia* used to test the

text comprehension skill of L2 Italian speakers. In the corpus, each text is annotated with its corresponding CEFR level i.e. A1, A2, B1, B2, C1, C2. For the
preliminary experiments, texts of levels B2 and C2 have been used. Some basic
pre-processing have been performed, in order to overcome some problems of the
TINT software [23], which was used in the subsequent phases.

2.2 Extraction of Basic Linguistic Structures

In this phase, the previously mentioned software Tint is used to elaborate the
records. Tint is a natural language processing (NLP) pipeline, developed on the
basis of Stanford CoreNLP [21] and specifically adapted to Italian language.
Tint offers basic NLP features [23], such as tokenization, sentence splitting and
lemmatization, as well as advanced ones with, among others, PoS tagging and
dependency parsing. The outputs of this phase are single tokens, sentences and
dependency trees information; all of these structure are used for the extraction
and computation of appropriate linguistic features [17,19,29] (Table 1).

Table 1. Sample PoS tagging output

Word	PoS TAG	Description
John	SP	Proper noun
is	VA	Auxiliary verb
preparing	V	Verb
the	RB	Determinative article
exam	S	Common noun
of	E	Preposition
Computational	SP	Proper noun
Linguistics	SP	Proper noun
.	FS	Sentence boundary punctuation

2.3 Classifier Training

The architecture is parametric with respect to three different types of classifiers, namely Decision Trees, Random Forests and Support Vector Machines
(SVM). Their performance have experimentally analyzed and compared. In the
implementation we have used the classifiers' versions available in the Python
scikit-learn open-source package, which offers a variety of tools for classification,
regression and clustering tasks.

3   Linguistic Features Extraction

In order to perform the classification task, it is necessary to build a training set containing the linguistic features of the original corpus which are relevant for assessing language proficiency in the language. The choice has been inspired by the work done for the READ-IT project [10], an SVM classifier aimed at assessing the readability of text in Italian language for people with scarce ability in reading and writing or mild intellectual disability. The features, we have focused on, can be grouped in four main areas:

- Raw text features
- Lexical features
- Morpho-syntactic features
- Syntactic Features

Raw text features express simple quantitative characteristics, such as the mean word length and sentence length of the text. Lexical features look at the relative frequency of words, regardless of their syntactic role and dependencies. For this purpose, three collections [9] are considered: fundamental (F), high usage (HU) and high availability (HA) words. The internal distributions, i.e. the percentage of lemmas belonging to each of the three corpora w.r.t. to the whole text, are calculated, as well as the lemmas within the first 100 tokens in the text and the percentage of basic lemmas in the text. Morphological and syntactic features are also taken into account: lexical density, Part of Speech tags distribution, distribution of verbal moods. Finally, other features which are clues of text complexity are extracted from the dependency parse-tree, such as the maximum depth among all the parse trees, and the number and the depth of subordinate phrases.

4   Classifiers for Text Features

In this section, the classifiers used in the experiments are briefly recalled. Three popular classifying algorithms were considered [26], i.e. Decision Trees, Random Forests and Support Vector Machines. During the training phase, the Nested Cross Validation procedure has been chosen [27,28].

4.1   Nested Cross Validation

Nested Cross Validation is used to tune the hyper-parameters of the classifiers and fit a model using different splits, to avoid information used for perfor-mance tests leak into the hyper-parameters optimization process; such proce-dure reduces over-fitting problems, since different data is used for the two tasks. Therefore, Nested Cross Validation takes into account Cross Validation tech-nique and the Hyper-parameters optimization. Cross Validation is one of the *Resampling Techniques* that repeatedly trains a new model, each time with a different part of the training set in order to encounter each record at least once

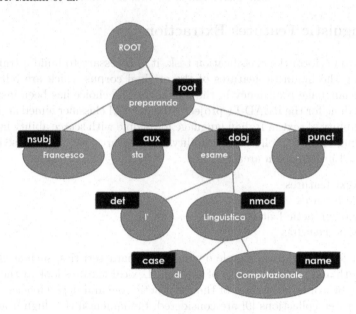

Fig. 1. The dependency parsing tree for a sample sentence.

in the training set. Resampling is an expensive method but luckily, nowadays we are able to perform it with little effort in resources and time. Stratified K-Fold Cross Validation in particular, splits initially the whole data set in two parts: training set and test set. The training set has to be fitted; for k times, it is split into k equal parts where k-1 pieces represent the training subset and only one subset is the validation set. Because it is stratified, each set has almost an equal distribution of records of each class as the entire data set. At each iteration the validation set is different. The model is fitted in the training part and then, it is tested on the validation set. The result obtained, i.e. a measure of accuracy, will be averaged with the other results returned by the other cross validation rounds. At the end of the process, the model is fitted on the training part and it is ready to make the final evaluation: making predictions on the test set (Figs. 1 and 2).

Hyper-parameters are that kind of parameters of a learning function that need to be set before the learning process begins. On the contrary, parameters are learnt during the learning process. Hyper-parameters optimization is a problem concerned with finding the optimal sequence of hyper-parameters of a learning algorithm in order to obtain the optimal classification model with the best scoring function value: in this project, `f1 macro` has been chosen as scoring function. There are various hyper-parameters optimization techniques; in this work, Grid Search is employed. For each hyper-parameter, i.e. the number of estimators in a random forest, a vector containing the candidate values it can take is created. Then, the Cartesian Product between the candidate values of all the parameters to be optimized is computed and all the combination of

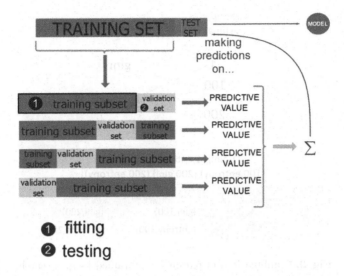

① fitting
② testing

Fig. 2. Phases of cross validation.

parameters in the product, i.e. in the grid, are tested [2]. For each parameter of the learning function, only one of the values inside the corresponding vector will be chosen and assigned to it.

In order to assess the quality of a certain sequence of hyper-parameters in the whole data set, cross validation is executed for each sequence of hyper-parameters. It is clear that setting many values for the hyper-parameters means a critical increase in the complexity of the problem. Nested Cross Validation is more advanced than the classical CV: in fact at each round of the outer cross validation, a Grid Search CV is executed on the training subset. Grid Search CV is essentially the research of the best configuration of the model's hyper parameters, through an internal Cross Validation. For each possible hyper parameters configuration, an internal cross validation is executed on the training subset. The configuration with the lowest test error will be chosen for that outer Cross Validation round and it will make predictions on the test part of the current outer cross validation round (Fig. 3).

4.2 Decision Trees

Decision Trees are data structures characterized by a single root node, internal nodes and leaves nodes. For each node n, except the root, it is defined a unique parent node p [7]. Leaves nodes have no descendants, while internal nodes have both ancestors and descendants. The structure of a Decision Tree embeds a set of rules. For each node, we evaluate a decision; basing on the outcome, one of the edges that start from that node will be followed and a new decision node evaluated. This procedure is iterated until is reached a leaf node. In other words, a path, that begins from the root and ends in a leaf, represents a series

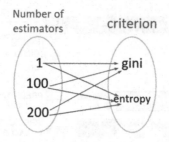

{(1,gini),(1,entropy),(100,gini),
(100,entropy),(200,gini),(200,entropy)}

Criterion / no. estimators	100	200
gini	{gini,100}	{gini,200}
entropy	{entropy,100}	{entropy,200}

Fig. 3. Combinations of parameters obtained by grid search.

of evaluations and decisions where the leaf represents the final classification decision, i.e. the label to assign to the data item under evaluation. There is a unique path from any node to the root. In a leaf node, there is a class label and the subset of instances that belongs to that class and that respect the rules imposed in the path followed in order to reach the leaf. The label assigned to the leaf is the one related to the maximum number of instances there. The best case is when the leaves have only records of one class with Gini impurity almost equal to 0. At the beginning, when the decision tree still needs to be built, we have a set of data items, i.e. a set of vectors feature values, represented by X and the corresponding class labels y, where each vector is assigned a class label. To build the decision tree, there are many techniques. For instance, at each step we could choose a rule of splitting. The vectors that follow it, will be grouped together with their classes in a node. The others will be grouped in another node. This procedure is called recursive binary splitting because it incrementally grows the decision tree by making two child nodes for each parent node. It is furthermore, a greedy procedure because at each time, for each possible splitting rule, the best split with minimal Gini impurity is chosen [18] (Fig. 4).

4.3 Random Forests

As stated before, one of the disadvantages of decision trees is their inclination to overfit the data, especially when a tree becomes very depth. Random Forests avoid the problem following the Bagging Algorithm [4]. The idea of the algorithm is to split the training set T of size n in m training sets Ti of the same dimension n'; there could be some elements repeated in the various subsets, that's why it is called "random sample with replacement" [7,18]. Then, m Decision Tree models are fitted with the m samples created before. In classification problems, each

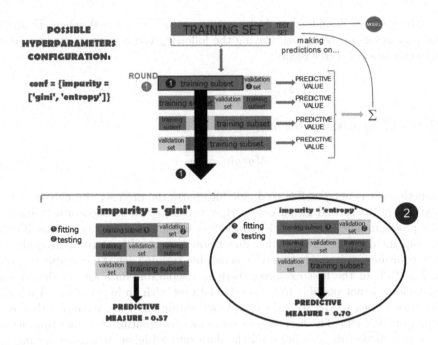

Fig. 4. Nested cross validation.

model will predict a class and the final result will be the one which received the greatest number of votes. The advantage of this method is:

- averaging the results of many trees instead of one, will make the results less sensible to noises.
- training m models with different parts of the training set will make them more independent from each other.

It is suggested to fit at least a few hundred of decision trees. In order to improve the quality of predictions, it is applied not only Bagging Algorithm on the data but also on the features. Feature Bagging at each split makes a "bag" of m features, where usually $m = \sqrt{p}$ p, from a total of p predictors. In the current split, only one of the m predictors contained in that bag will be chosen as node-splitting rule.

4.4 SVM

Support-Vector Machine is a classifier whose goal is to find the optimal hyper-plane that maximizes the margin [18]; for instance, in a binary classification problem, an hyper-plane is the boundary that divides the instances of a class from the other. The optimal hyper-plane is the one that maximizes the separation between the two classes. Hyper-planes are multi-dimensional objects.

The decision boundary could be written as $\vec{w} \cdot \vec{x} + b = 0$, where $\vec{w}$ and b are parameters of the model. Having the following constraints we could predict the class label of a test record:

$$f(x_i) = \begin{cases} 1, & \text{if } \vec{w} \cdot \vec{x} + b \geq 1 \\ -1, & \text{if } \vec{w} \cdot \vec{x} + b \leq 1 \end{cases}$$

The goal is to maximize the margin:

$$Margin = \frac{2}{\|\vec{w}\|^2}$$

Sometimes it is not possible to divide into parts the data set through an hyper plane as in the second graph below. However, there's a solution or a "trick" to this problem. The "kernel trick" consists in using a kernel function that allows to map the data set into a higher dimensional space without computing all the new coordinates, in order to have a separable training set. An example is given in Fig. 2.13. In the first example, there is a separable data set. In the second example, it is not possible to divide the data set with an hyper-plane. Applying the kernel trick to the second example we obtain the third example, that is a separable problem. The kernel function in fact, calculating the inner product of each pair of vectors, can bring all the data into a higher dimension, saving up in terms of computational resources. RBF (Radial Basis Function) kernel is one of the most popular.

5   Experiments Design and Results

For the experiments, a Nested Cross Validation procedure has been employed [28]. Nested Cross Validation is used to tune the hyper-parameters of the classifiers and fit a model using different splits, to avoid information used for performance tests leak into the hyper-parameters optimization process; such procedure reduces over-fitting problems, since different data is used for the two tasks. The number of inner and outer stratification was set to 5; in the inner loop, a Grid Search was executed to tune the parameter, using *f1 macro* as the scoring function. In addition, for the decision tree and random Forest classifiers, the maximum depth was set to $\log_2 |features|$ to avoid over-fitting. After tuning the hyper-parameters and creating the model, tests were performed on the test set. The chosen metrics were *accuracy, macro-averaged f1 score, macro-averaged*

Table 2. Classification results

Classifier	Accuracy	F1-score macro	Precision macro	Recall macro
Decision Tree 2C	0,9292	0,9281	0,9265	0,9303
Random Forest 2C	0,9292	0,9278	0,9278	0,9278
SVM 2C	0,9336	0,9318	0,9355	0,9291

precision and *macro-averaged recall*; results are shown in Table 2. Results are very promising, as for each metric a score higher than 0.9 is achieved, In particular, the best overall classifier is SVM, with Decision Trees and Random Forest delivering slightly lower and comparable performance.

6 Conclusions

In this work we have introduced a model for classifying Italian texts according to the CEFR classification system for second language learners used in language teaching and certification. The proposed architecture relies on linguistics features extractions, which make use of corpora of terms of increasing complexity level and morpho-syntactic features measuring the complexity of dependency parse tree. The tree types of experimented classifiers, decision tree, random forest and SVM, all show outstanding precision performance greater than 90% on Italian texts actually used in official CEFR certification exams. The proposed methodology has a great potential of being extended to other languages, with quite straightforward adaptations. The preliminary experiments have been held on texts belonging to two well separated classes B2 and C2, therefore more systematic further experiments, using texts ranging over all the six CEFR classes, are planned as a future development. A great potential for massive language education is also represented by the integration of the classification module in exam design application supporting examiner or automatic language proficiency examination systems.

References

1. Council of Europe Language Policy Portal. https://www.coe.int/en/web/language-policy/home
2. What is underfitting and overfitting and how to deal with it. https://medium.com/greyatom/what-is-underfitting-and-overfitting-in-machine-learning-and-how-to-deal-with-it-6803a989c76
3. Bachman, L., Palmer, A.: Language Assessment in Practice. Oxford University Press, Oxford (2010)
4. Biondi, G., Franzoni, V., Li, Y., Milani, A.: Web-based similarity for emotion recognition in web objects. In: Proceedings of the 9th International Conference on Utility and Cloud Computing, UCC 2016, pp. 327–332. ACM, New York (2016). https://doi.org/10.1145/2996890.3007883, http://doi.acm.org/10.1145/2996890.3007883
5. Bizer, C., Heath, T., Berners-Lee, T.: Linked data: the story so far. In: Sheth, A. (ed.) Semantic Services, Interoperability and Web Applications: Emerging Concepts, pp. 205–227. IGI Global, Hershey (2011). https://doi.org/10.4018/978-1-60960-593-3.ch008
6. Bojanowski, P., Grave, E., Joulin, A., Mikolov, T.: Enriching word vectors with subword information. arXiv preprint arXiv:1607.04606 (2016)
7. Breiman, L., Friedman, J., Stone, C.J., Olshen, R.A.: Classification and Regression Trees. The Wadsworth and Brooks-Cole Statistics-Probability Series. Taylor & Francis, Abingdon (1984)

8. Chiancone, A., Franzoni, V., Niyogi, R., Milani, A.: Improving link ranking quality by quasi-common neighbourhood, pp. 21–26. IEEE Press (2015). https://doi.org/10.1109/ICCSA.2015.19

9. De Mauro, T., Chiari, I.: Il Nuovo Vocabolario di Base della Lingua Italiana (forthcoming)

10. Dell'Orletta, F., Montemagni, S., Venturi, G.: Read-it: Assessing readability of Italian texts with a view to text simplification. In: Proceedings of the Second Workshop on Speech and Language Processing for Assistive Technologies, pp. 73–83. Association for Computational Linguistics, Edinburgh, July 2011

11. European Commission/EACEA/Eurydice: Key Data on Teaching Languages at School in Europe. Eurydice European Unit, Brussels. Technical report (2017)

12. Franzoni, V., Leung, C.H.C., Li, Y., Mengoni, P., Milani, A.: Set similarity measures for images based on collective knowledge. In: Gervasi, O., et al. (eds.) ICCSA 2015. LNCS, vol. 9155, pp. 408–417. Springer, Cham (2015). https://doi.org/10.1007/978-3-319-21404-7_30

13. Franzoni, V., Li, Y., Mengoni, P.: A path-based model for emotion abstraction on Facebook using sentiment analysis and taxonomy knowledge, pp. 947–952. IEEE Press (2017). https://doi.org/10.1145/3106426.3109420

14. Franzoni, V., Mencacci, M., Mengoni, P., Milani, A.: Heuristics for semantic path search in Wikipedia. In: Murgante, B., et al. (eds.) ICCSA 2014, Part VI. LNCS, vol. 8584, pp. 327–340. Springer, Cham (2014). https://doi.org/10.1007/978-3-319-09153-2_25

15. Franzoni, V., Milani, A.: PMING distance: a collaborative semantic proximity measure, vol. 2, pp. 442–449. IEEE Press (2012) .https://doi.org/10.1109/WI-IAT.2012.226

16. Franzoni, V., Milani, A., Pallottelli, S., Leung, C., Li, Y.: Context-based image semantic similarity, pp. 1280–1284. IEEE Press (2016). https://doi.org/10.1109/FSKD.2015.7382127

17. Graesser, A., McNamara, D., Louwerse, M., Cai, Z.: Coh-metrix: analysis of text on cohesion and language. Behav. Res. Methods Instrum. Comput. **36**, 193–202 (2004)

18. James, G., Witten, D., Hastie, T., Tibshirani, R.: An Introduction to Statistical Learning: With Applications in R. Springer Texts in Statistics. Springer, New York (2014). https://doi.org/10.1007/978-1-4614-7138-7

19. Kincaid, P., Fishburne, R.P., Rogers R.L.: Derivation of new readability formulas for navy enlisted personnel. Research Branch Report, pp. 8–75. Chief of Naval Training, Millington (1975)

20. Leung, C.H.C., Li, Y., Milani, A., Franzoni, V.: Collective evolutionary concept distance based query expansion for effective web document retrieval. In: Murgante, B., et al. (eds.) ICCSA 2013, Part IV. LNCS, vol. 7974, pp. 657–672. Springer, Heidelberg (2013). https://doi.org/10.1007/978-3-642-39649-6_47

21. Manning, C.D., Surdeanu, M., Bauer, J., Finkel, J., Bethard, S.J., McClosky, D.: The Stanford CoreNLP natural language processing toolkit. In: Association for Computational Linguistics (ACL) System Demonstrations, pp. 55–60 (2014)

22. Mikolov, T., Sutskever, I., Chen, K., Corrado, G.S., Dean, J.: Distributed representations of words and phrases and their compositionality. In: Burges, C.J.C., Bottou, L., Welling, M., Ghahramani, Z., Weinberger, K.Q. (eds.) Advances in Neural Information Processing Systems, vol. 26, pp. 3111–3119. Curran Associates, Inc. (2013)

23. Palmero Aprosio, A., Moretti, G.: Italy goes to Stanford: a collection of CoreNLP modules for Italian. arXiv e-prints, September 2016

24. Purpura, J.: Cognition and language assessment. In: The Companion to Language Assessment, vol. III, pp. 1453–1476 (2014)
25. Santucci, V., Spina, S., Milani, A., Biondi, G., Bari, G.D.: Detecting hate speech for Italian language in social media (2018)
26. Shalev-Shwartz, S., Ben-David, S.: Understanding Machine Learning: From Theory to Algorithms. Cambridge University Press, Cambridge (2014)
27. Varma, S., Simon, R.: Bias in error estimation when using cross-validation for-model selection. BMC Bioinformatics **7**(1), 91 (2006). https://doi.org/10.1186/1471-2105-7-91
28. Wainer, J., Cawley, G.C.: Nested cross-validation when selecting classifiers is overzealous for most practical applications. CoRR abs/1809.09446 (2018)
29. Xiaobin, C., Meurers, D.: Ctap: a web-based tool supporting automatic complexity analysis. Research Branch Report, pp. 8–75. Chief of Naval Training, Millington (1975)

Author Index

Printed in the United States
By Bookmasters